The Complete
City Maps
of
Michigan

Dave Daenzer

CitMap,
Traverse City, Michigan

Additional copies of this book may be ordered by sending
$19.95 plus $3.50 for shipping and handling to
CitMap, 8951 Trezwood Tr., Traverse City, MI. 49684

Photographs: Bob Brodbeck - Detroit skyline and downtown Traverse City
Maps provided by - Bondata
Library of Congress Catalog Card Number: 90-84569
ISBN: 1-56464-899-0

Printed in the United States of America

Contents

Dear Traveler:

This book of maps represents many months of research, meticulous planning, and design... to produce a product that helps you find your way easier and more efficiently.

We use only the best and most reliable sources to confirm map details. However, even with the best of efforts, errors can occur so we cannot guarantee absolute accuracy for each map. Please let us know of any corrections or comments you may have.

In the interest of saving time and conserving energy, may this guide prove itself worthy of the investment.

Drive carefully.

Sincerely,

Dave Daenzer

Dave Daenzer, Publisher
CitMap
8951 Trezwood Tr.
Traverse City, Michigan 49684

UPPER MICHIGAN

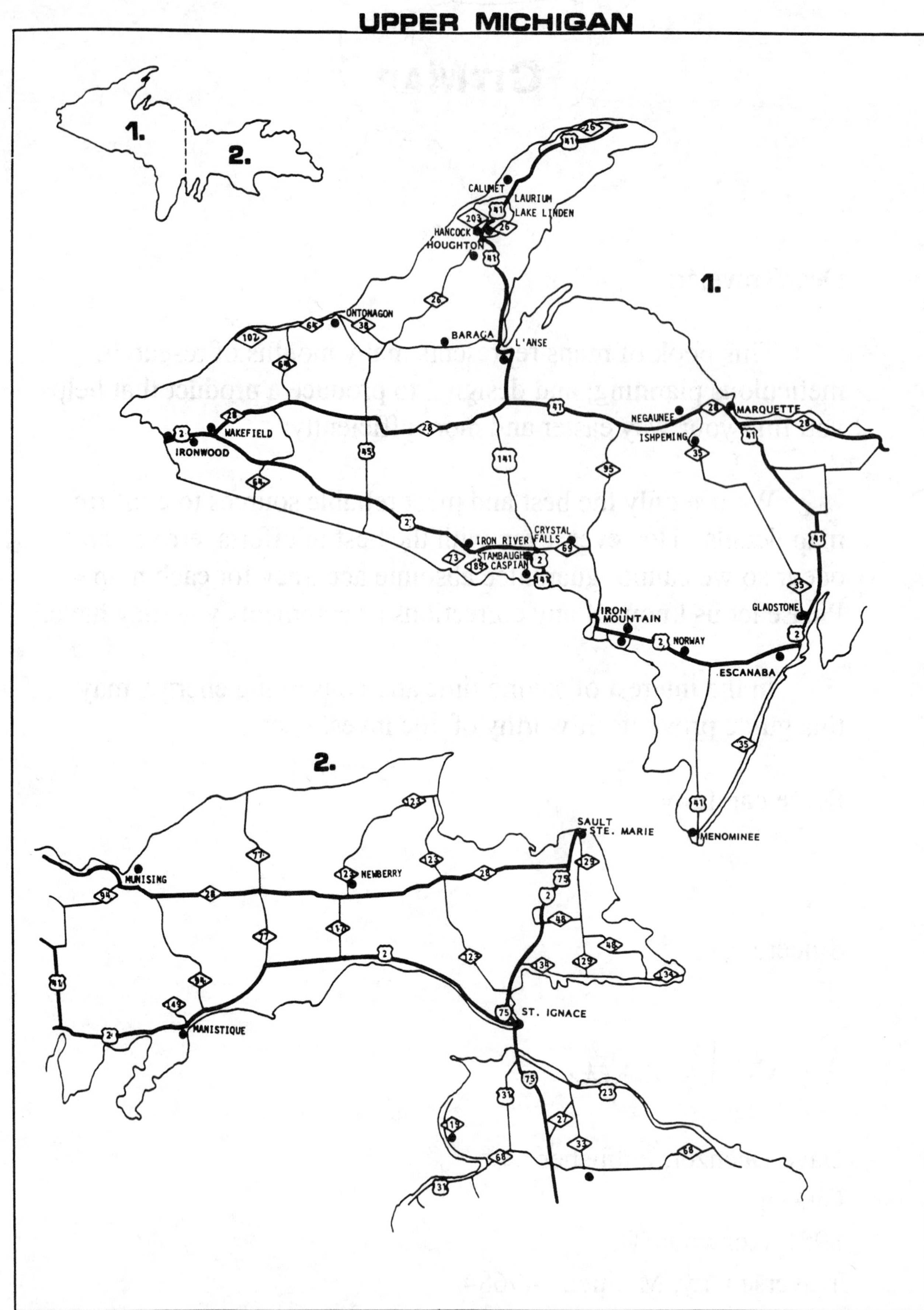

MICHIGAN

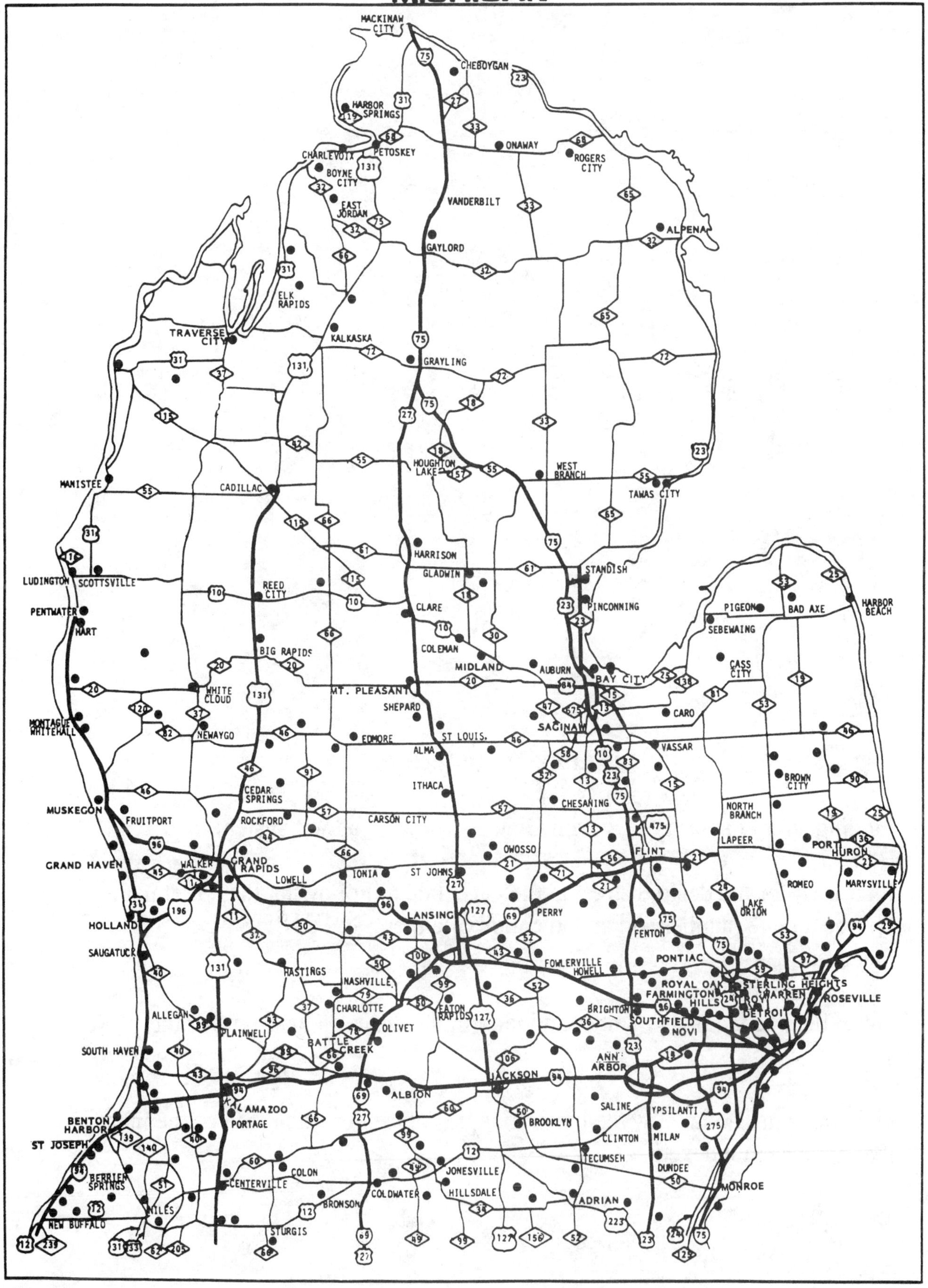

MACKINAW CITY
CHEBOYGAN
HARBOR SPRINGS
PETOSKEY
ONAWAY
CHARLEVOIX
ROGERS CITY
BOYNE CITY
EAST JORDAN
VANDERBILT
ALPENA
GAYLORD
ELK RAPIDS
TRAVERSE CITY
KALKASKA
GRAYLING
HOUGHTON LAKE
WEST BRANCH
MANISTEE
CADILLAC
TAWAS CITY
HARRISON
GLADWIN
STANDISH
LUDINGTON
SCOTTSVILLE
REED CITY
CLARE
PINCONNING
PIGEON
BAD AXE
HARBOR BEACH
PENTWATER
HART
SEBEWAING
COLEMAN
MIDLAND
BIG RAPIDS
CASS CITY
AUBURN
BAY CITY
WHITE CLOUD
MT. PLEASANT
SHEPARD
CARO
MONTAGUE
WHITEHALL
NEWAYGO
SAGINAW
EDMORE
ST LOUIS
ALMA
VASSAR
BROWN CITY
ITHACA
CEDAR SPRINGS
MUSKEGON
FRUITPORT
ROCKFORD
CHESANING
NORTH BRANCH
CARSON CITY
LAPEER
OWOSSO
FLINT
PORT HURON
GRAND HAVEN
WALKER
GRAND RAPIDS
LOWELL
IONIA
ST JOHNS
ROMEO
MARYSVILLE
PERRY
LAKE ORION
HOLLAND
LANSING
FENTON
SAUGATUCK
HASTINGS
FOWLERVILLE
HOWELL
PONTIAC
NASHVILLE
ROYAL OAK
STERLING HEIGHTS
FARMINGTON HILLS
TROY
WARREN
ROSEVILLE
CHARLOTTE
EATON RAPIDS
BRIGHTON
DETROIT
ALLEGAN
OLIVET
SOUTHFIELD
NOVI
PLAINWELL
BATTLE CREEK
SOUTH HAVEN
ANN ARBOR
JACKSON
KALAMAZOO
ALBION
BENTON HARBOR
PORTAGE
SALINE
YPSILANTI
BROOKLYN
ST JOSEPH
CLINTON
MILAN
TECUMSEH
BERRIEN SPRINGS
COLON
JONESVILLE
DUNDEE
CENTERVILLE
MONROE
COLDWATER
HILLSDALE
ADRIAN
NILES
BRONSON
NEW BUFFALO
STURGIS

....	CITY BOUNDARY
———	MAJOR ROADS Includes State Hwys, US Hwys, Interstates and Major Thorofares
———	CITY STREETS
———	*WATER FEATURES*
++++++++	RAILROADS
N	NORTH DIRECTIONAL ARROW
NE NW SE SW	QUADRANT LABELS
▲	QUADRANT DIVIDER
	POPULATIONS TOTALS FROM THE 1990 CENSUS

Index Instructions

Finding street names is easy with CitMap's new Quadrant system.

First look for the desired street in the City Index. Following the street name will be a plate number and an indication of either a NW, NE, SW, or SE Quadrant.

Go to the needed plate number and look in the desired Quadrant for the street.

Quadrants are defined by the black triangles placed on each side of the maps that have been indexed.

Example:	City	Street	Plate #	Quadrant
	Ann Arbor	Pittsfield Blvd.	6	SW

MICHIGAN CITY INDEX

MICHIGAN CITY INDEX

MICHIGAN CITY INDEX

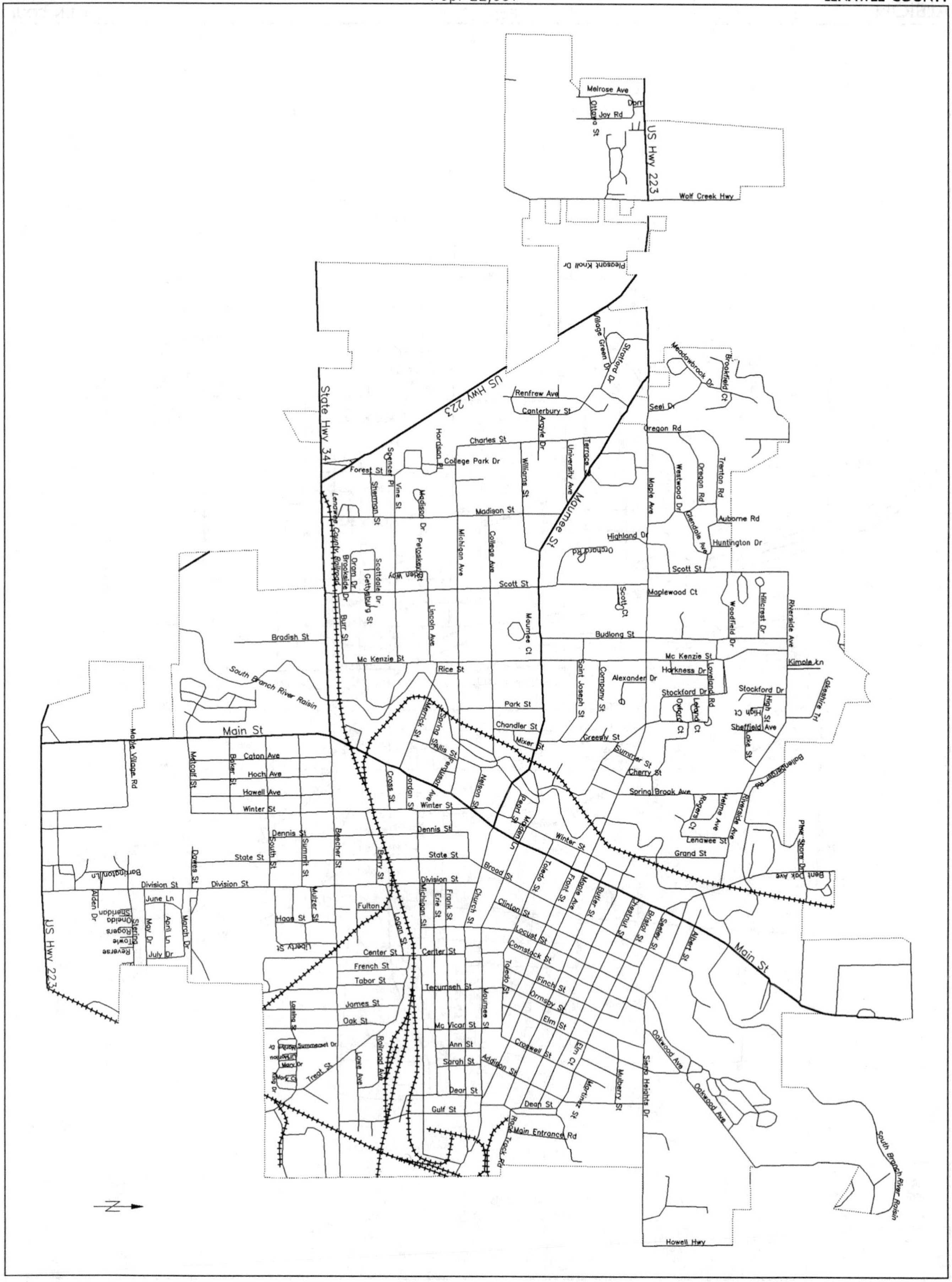

ADRAIN

Pop. 22,097

LENAWEE COUNTY

Melrose Ave
Dorn
Joy Rd
Ottawa St
US Hwy 223
Wolf Creek Hwy
Pleasant Knoll Dr
Village Green Dr
Stratford Dr
Meadowbrook Dr
Brookfield Ct
Renfrew Ave
Canterbury St
Seal Dr
Oregon Rd
State Hwy 34
Charles St
Hardison Pl
Spencer Pl
College Park Dr
Forest St
Argyle Dr
Terrace
University Ave
Williams St
Westwood Dr
Oregon Rd
Trenton Rd
Sherman St
Vine St
Madison Dr
Maple Ave
Maumee St
Glendale Ave
Auborne Rd
Madison St
Highland Dr
Huntington Dr
Orchard Rd
Lenawee County Railroad
Oram Dr
Brookside Dr
Scottdale Dr
Gettysburg St
Petoskey St
Glen Way
Michigan Ave
College Ave
Scott St
Maplewood Ct
Scott Ct
Hillcrest Dr
Woodfield Dr
Riverside Ave
Burr St
Lincoln Ave
Maumee Ct
Bradish St
Budlong St
Mc Kenzie St
Rice St
Saint Joseph St
Company St
Alexander Dr
Harkness Dr
Loveland Rd
Kimole Ln
South Branch River Raisin
Stockford Dr
Oxford Ct
Leland Ct
High St
High Ct
Lakeshire Trl
Park St
Sheffield Ave
Merrick St
Spring St
Chandler St
Greeley St
Lake St
Main St
Allis St
Mixer St
Summer St
Ballenberger Rd
Maple Village Rd
Metcalf St
Caton Ave
Baker St
Hoch Ave
Cross St
Ferguson
Cherry St
Howell Ave
Jordan St
Nelson St
Spring Brook Ave
Winter St
Peal St
Rogers Ct
Helme Ave
Riverside Ave
Dennis St
Dennis St
Madden St
Pine Shore Dr
Lenawee St
State St
State St
Winter St
Grand St
Barrington Ln
Dawes St
South St
Summit St
Beecher St
Berry St
Broad St
Toledo St
Front St
Maple Ave
Butler St
Chestnut St
Bristol St
Bent Oak Ave
Division St
Division St
Division St
Church St
June Ln
Mulzer St
Fulton
Michigan St
Erie St
Frank St
Clinton St
Seeley St
Albert St
Alden Dr
Sheridan
Oneida
Rogers
Towle
Sterling
May Dr
April Ln
March Dr
Haas St
Logan St
Locust St
Reverse
July Dr
Liberty St
Center St
Center St
Comstock St
Main St
French St
Tabor St
Tecumseh St
Finch St
James St
Toledo St
Ormsby St
Maumee St
Oak St
Mc Vicar St
Elm St
Lasing St
Summerset Dr
Mary Dr
King Dr
Railroad Ave
Ann St
Crosswell St
Oakwood Ave
Treat St
Lowe Ave
Sarah St
Addison St
Elm Ct
Mulberry St
Siena Heights Dr
Oakwood Ave
Dear St
Martinez St
Gulf St
Dean St
Main Entrance Rd
Rock Track Rd
South Branch River Raisin
Howell Hwy
US Hwy 223

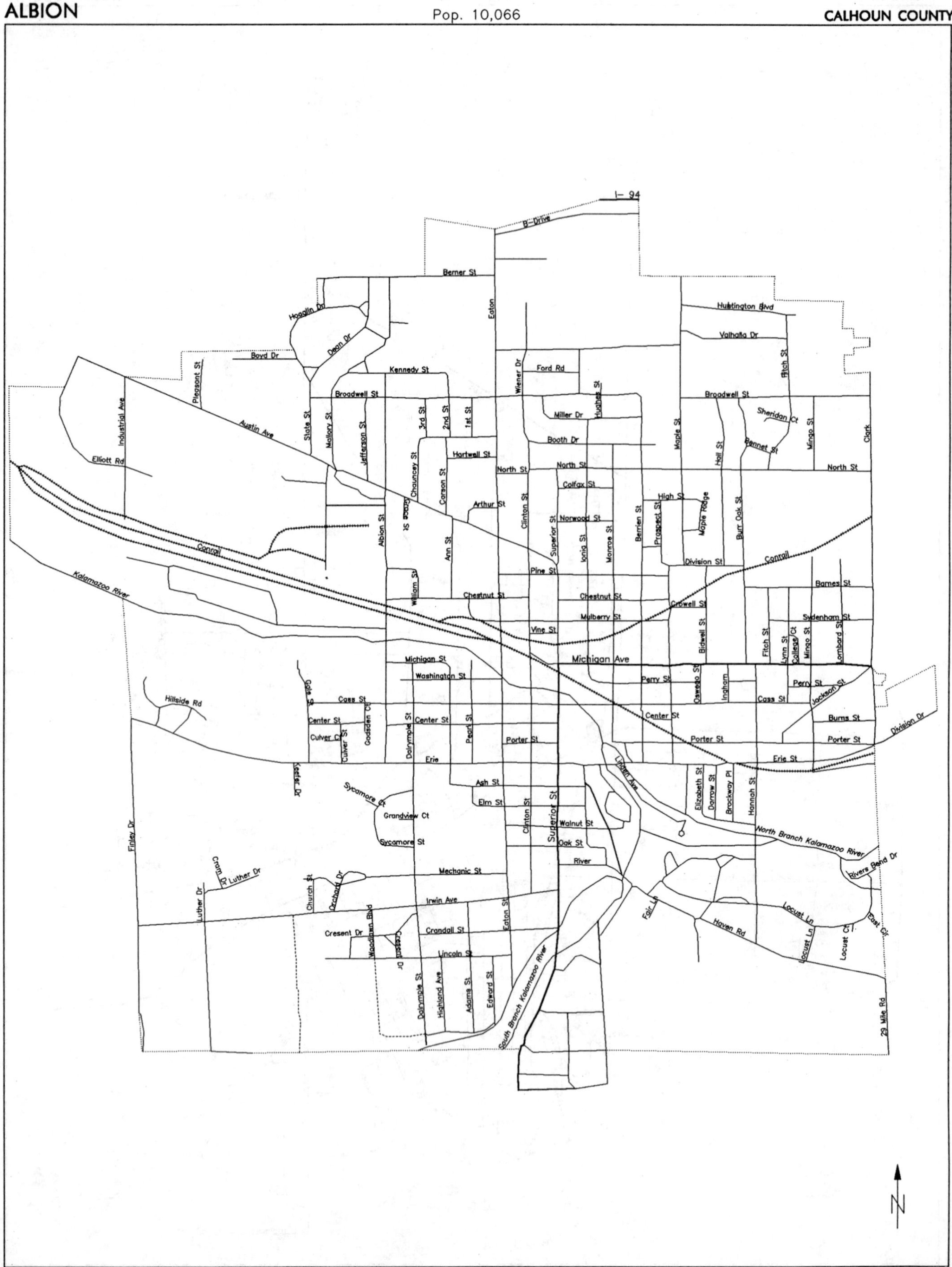
I- 94
B-Drive
Berner St
Eaton
Hoaglin Dr
Dean Dr
Boyd Dr
Kennedy St
Broadwell St
Ford Rd
Wiener Dr
Huntington Blvd
Valhalla Dr
Fitch St
Pleasant St
Industrial Ave
Austin Ave
State St
Mallory St
Jefferson St
Chauncey St
3rd St
2nd St
1st St
Miller Dr
Hughes St
Booth Dr
Maple St
Hall St
Sheridan Ct
Bennet St
Mingo St
Clark
North St
Elliott Rd
Hartwell St
Carson St
Grace St
Colfax St
High St
Prospect St
Maple Ridge
Burr Oak St
Arthur St
Clinton St
Norwood St
Berrien St
Superior St
Ionia St
Monroe St
Albion St
Ann St
Division St
Conrail
Kalamazoo River
William St
Pine St
Barnes St
Chestnut St
Crowell St
Mulberry St
Sydenham St
Vine St
Bidwell St
Lynn St
College Ct
Lombard St
Michigan St
Michigan Ave
Washington St
Perry St
Oswego St
Ingham
Hillside Rd
Gale St
Cass St
Jackson St
Center St
Burns St
Culver Ct
Culver St
Godsden Ct
Dalrymple St
Pearl St
Porter St
Division Dr
Erie
Erie St
Linden Ave
Keefer Dr
Sycamore Ct
Ash St
Elm St
Elizabeth St
Darrow St
Brockway Pl
Hannah St
Grandview Ct
Sycamore St
Walnut St
Oak St
North Branch Kalamazoo River
Finley Dr
River
Cram Dr
Luther Dr
Mechanic St
Rivers Bend Dr
Church St
Orchard Dr
Irwin Ave
Fair Ln
Locust Ln
East Ct
Woodlawn Blvd
Crandall St
Eaton St
Haven Rd
Cresent Dr
Lincoln St
Locust Ct
Highland Ave
Adams St
Edward St
South Branch Kalamazoo River
29 Mile Rd
N

Mill St
Lee St
Cherry Road
St Clair Blvd
Washington St
Sunset St
Blauvelt Ave
Maple Ave
Dixie Blvd
Cole Blvd
Golfview Ave
Golfview Ave
Cemetery Dr
Fruit St
Smith St
Orchard St
Mill St
Michigan St
St Clair River Dr
Green St
Orchard St
Fruit St
Summer St
Howard St
Columbia St
Scout Dr
Clay St
Pleasant Road
Clay St
State St
Clinton St
Market St
St Clair Blvd
Washington St
Liberty St
Sheldon Ave
Edward St
Fossett St
Henrietta Ave
Robbins Dr
Townsend Cres
Worfolk Dr
Pointe Trembie Rd (M~29)
Townsend Cres
Michigan St
St Clair Dr
Eckfield Dr
Island Ct
Kenyon Road
Batteaux Canal
Ruskin Ave
Townsend Dr
Willard Ave
Helen
Conley Ave
Edgewater Ave
Lathrop Ave
Michigan St
Virginia Lane
Marine City Drain
St Hwy 29
Locust Lane
Sherwood Lane
Virginia Ave
North Ave
Center
Colonial Lane
Algona Lane
Parkway Dr
Kendall
Algona Ct
North Ave
Park Dr
Dixie Blvd
Roselawn Ave
Channel Side Dr
Venetian Way
Lochaven Dr
Interlochen Dr
Delta Dr
N

Pop. 4,547

Goodrich St
Goodwin St
Sherman St
Sherman St
Sunset Dr
Sherman Ct
Vernon St
Academy St
Russell St
Robinson St
Hudson St
Arnold St
Tamarack St
Elm St
Lake Dr
Lincoln St
Brookside Dr
Thomas St
Tannery Creek
Knapp St
Circle Dr
Ely St
Arbor St
Julia St
James St
Russell St
Adams St
Delano St
Davis St
Terrace St
Douglas St
Park Dr
Park Drive Ct
Jenner Dr
Linn St
Maple St
Grove St
Crescent St
Pine St
Hastings St
Jackson St
Linn St
Cherry St
Lane St
Trowbridge St
Cutler St
Monroe St
Kalamazoo River
Kalamazoo River
Glass St
Allett St
Hubbard St
Chestnut St
North St
Ammerman St
Walcott St
Riverside Dr
Riverview Park Dr
Babylon Road
118th Ave
Hickory Ave
Cypress St
River St
Locust St
State St
Marshall St
Old Plank Road
Cook St
Race St
Della Ct
Cora St
Ida St
Jenny St
Wayne St
4th St
Kalamazoo St
5th St
Mill Road
Park Ave
Hill St
Catherine Ct
Division St
Herkimer St
6th St
Oak Ct
Bond St
Weeks St
Charles St
Green St
Main St
Glenn St
Front St
Bridge Road
Rossman Creek
Pleasant St
Swan Ave
Allegan Ave
Streeter St
Chichester St
Eastern Ave
Padgham Dr
Grand St
Lowe St
Eastern Ave
Hooker Road
Airport Dr
Ridge Ct
13th Ave
Padgham Field Municipal Airpor
29th St
Rossman Creek

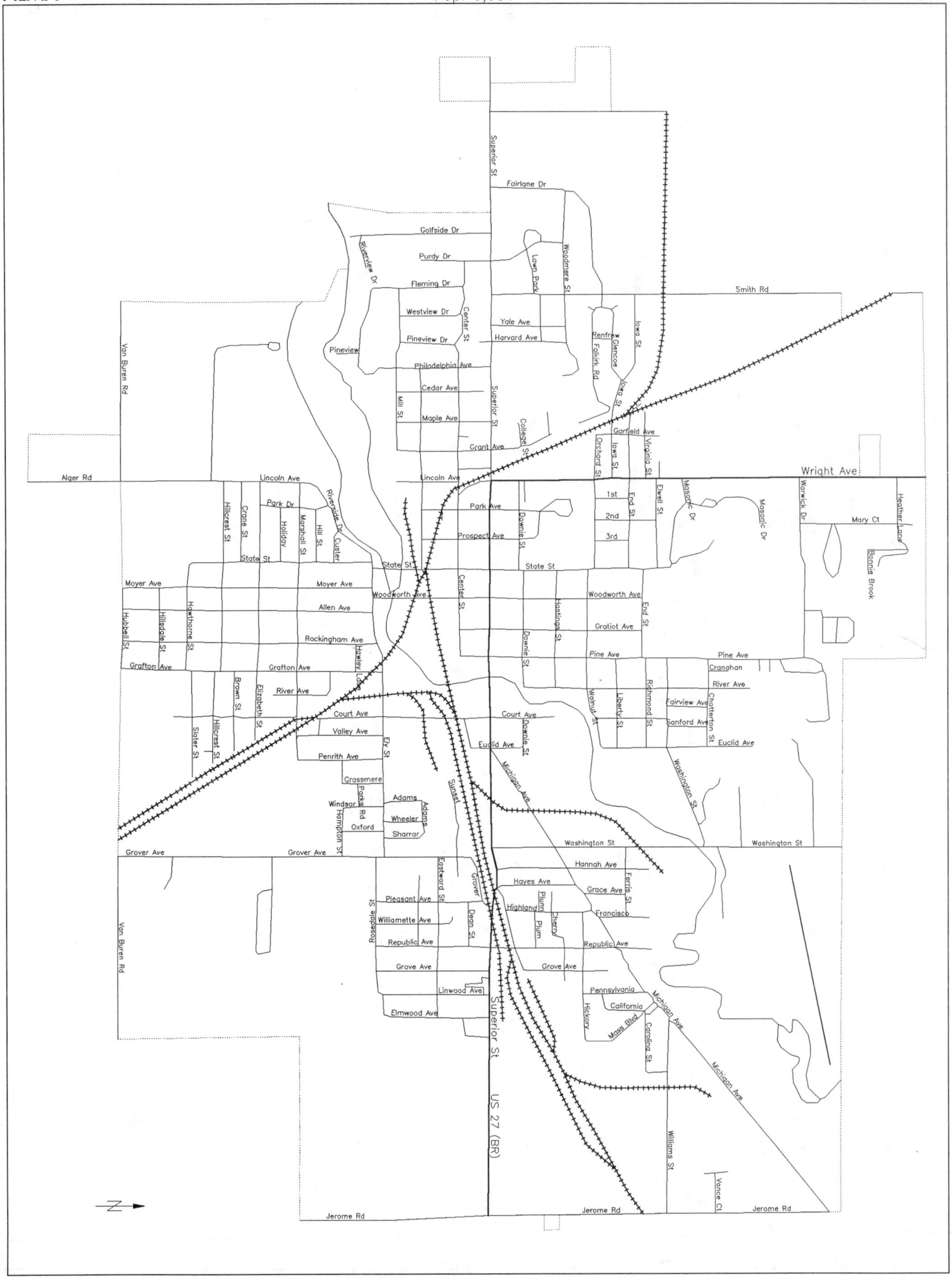
Superior St
Fairlane Dr
Golfside Dr
Riverview Dr
Purdy Dr
Lawn Park
Woodmere St
Fleming Dr
Smith Rd
Westview Dr
Center St
Yale Ave
Harvard Ave
Renfrew
Glencoe
Iowa St
Falkirk Rd
Pineview
Pineview Dr
Philadelphia Ave
Van Buren Rd
Cedar Ave
Mill St
Maple Ave
College St
Grant Ave
Garfield Ave
Orchard St
Virginia St
Alger Rd
Lincoln Ave
Wright Ave
Warwick Dr
Heather Lane
1st
2nd
3rd
End St
Elwell St
Masonic Dr
Mary Ct
Park Dr
Park Ave
Prospect Ave
Downie St
Hillcrest St
Crane St
Holiday
Marshall St
Hill St
Riverside Dr
Custer
State St
Bonnie Brook
Moyer Ave
Woodworth Ave
Allen Ave
Hubbell St
Hillsdale St
Hawthorne St
Hastings St
Gratiot Ave
Rockingham Ave
Hawley Lane
Grafton Ave
Pine Ave
Cranahan
River Ave
Brown St
Elizabeth St
Walnut St
Liberty St
Richmond St
Fairview Ave
Chatterton St
Court Ave
Sanford Ave
Valley Ave
Slater St
Euclid Ave
Ely St
Penrith Ave
Washington St
Michigan Ave
Grassmere
Sunset
Windsor
Parks Rd
Adams
Hampton St
Wheeler
Oxford
Sharrar
Grover Ave
Hannah Ave
Eastward St
Grover
Hayes Ave
Ferris St
Grace Ave
Pleasant Ave
Highland
Plum
Cherry
Francisco
Rosedale St
Williamette Ave
Dean St
Republic Ave
Grove Ave
Linwood Ave
Pennsylvania
California
Elmwood Ave
Hickory
Mass Blvd
Carolina St
US 27 (BR)
Williams St
Vance Ct
Jerome Rd

Tubspring Road
Howland Road
Huntington
Fenwick
Dorset
Aberdeen
Canterbury
Oak
Amherst
Suffield
Avon
Elmdale
Viewfield
Wakefield
Thornbury
Van Dyke
North St
Maple
Church St
Johnson
Stream
Centennial
Washington
School
Day
Mari Lane
Almont St
Juliet
Currier Ave
Hamilton
Black Ct
St Clair St
Spring St
Heim Dr
Hansberger
Mill St
Cherry
Branch
Stone
Bates Al
Teeds
Water
Westwinds
Westwinds
North Branch Clinton River
Kidder Road
Allison Dr
Kay Ct
Bernice
June
Cheryl
McIntosh Dr
McIntosh Dr
Spy Ct
Dawn
Stream
Main
N

ALPENA

Pop. 11,354

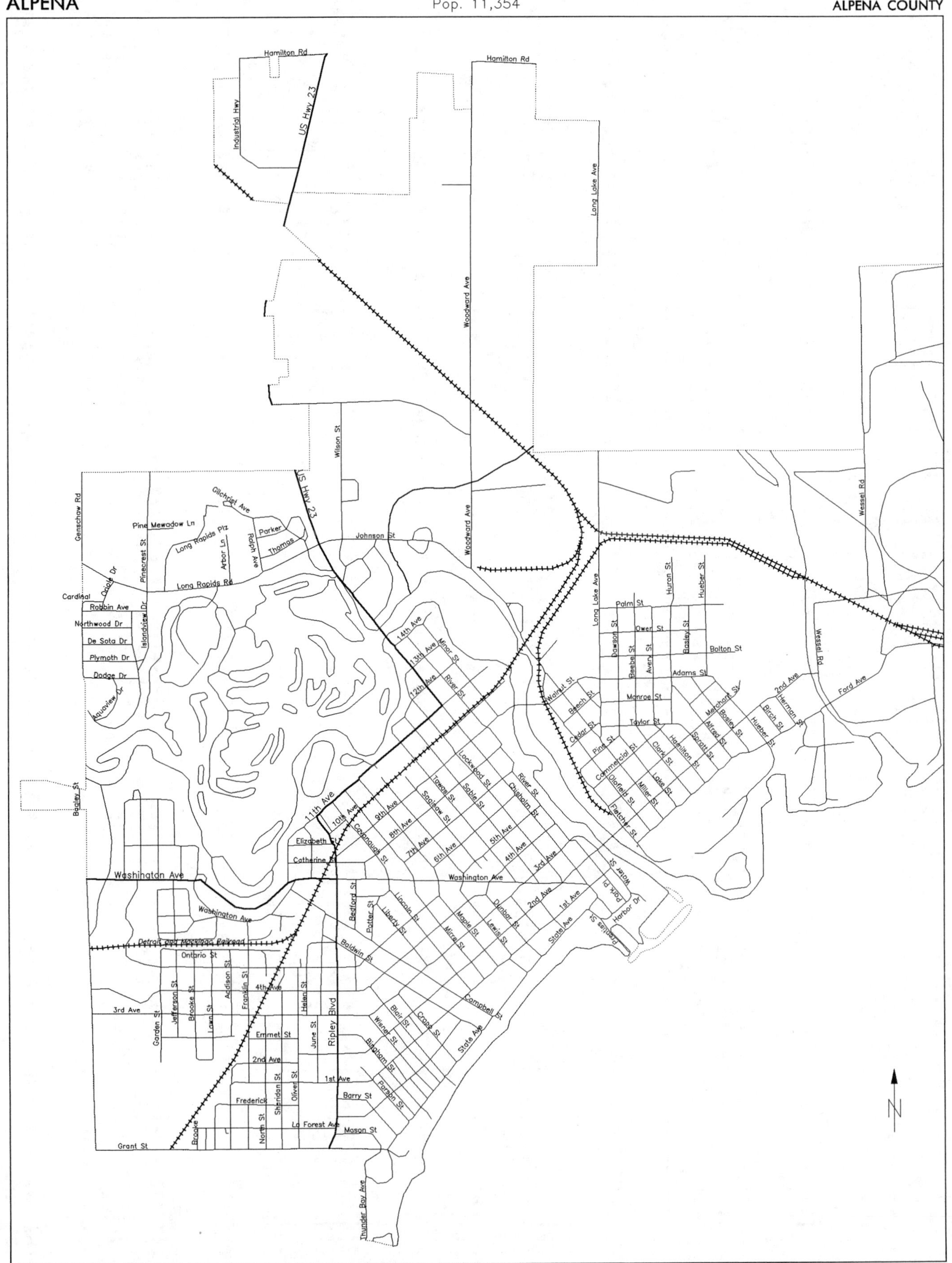

1st St	1	SE
1st St	4	NE
2nd St	1	SE
2nd St	4	NE
3rd St	1	SE
3rd St	4	NE
4th Ave	2	SW
4th Ave	5	NW
4th St	1	SE
4th St	4	NE
5th Ave	2	SW
5th Ave	5	NW
5th St	1	SE
5th St	4	NE
6th St	4	NE
7th St	1	SE
7th St	4	SE
8th St	1	SE
9th St	1	SE
Abbott Ave	1	SW
Aberdeen Dr	5	NE
Adams St	5	NW
Adare Cir	5	NE
Adare Ct	5	NE
Adare Rd	5	NE
Adare St	5	NE
Adrienne Dr	4	NW
Agin Ct	4	NE
Alexandria	1	NE
Algonac St	4	NE
Alhambra Dr	4	NE
Alice St	1	SE
Allen Dr	1	SE
Allison Dr	1	SW
Alpine St	5	SW
Alton Ct	3	NW
Amesbury Dr	4	NE
Amherst Ave	2	SW
Anderson Ave	5	NE
Anderson Ct	5	NE
Andover Rd	3	SW
Andrea Ct	1	SW
Ann Arbor	4	SE
Ann St	1	SE
Ann St	2	SW
Antietam Dr	3	NW
Apple St	2	SW
Appleway	5	NE
Applewood Ct	1	NE
Arbana Dr	1	SE
Arbor St	5	NW
Arbor View Blvd	1	SE
Arbordale Dr	4	NE
Arch St	5	NW
Archwood Dr	1	SW
Ardenne Dr		KY
Ardenne Dr	3	NW
Ardmoor Dr	4	NE
Arella Blvd	4	NE
Argo Dr	2	SW
Argonne Dr	2	NE
Argyle Cres	1	SE
Arlene St	1	SE
Arlington Blvd	5	NE
Arrowwood Trl	2	NW
Ascot Rd	4	NE
Ashley St	2	SW
Ashley St	5	NW
Astor Ave	5	NW
Atterberry Ct	4	NW
Atterberry Dr	4	NW
Au Sable Pl	5	NE
Audubon Dr	4	NE
Aurora St	2	NE
Austin Ave	5	NE
Avalon Pl	5	NE
Avon Rd	5	NE
Avondale Ave	4	NE
Awixa Rd	5	NE
Baits Dr	2	SW
Baldwin Ave	5	NW
Baldwin Pl	5	NW
Balmoral Ct	1	NE
Barber Ave	1	SW
Barber St	1	SW
Barclay Ct	3	SW
Bardstown Trl	3	SW
Barnard Rd	4	NE
Barrington Pl	4	NE
Barrister Rd	3	SW
Barton Dr	2	NW
Barton Shore Dr	1	NE
Barton Shore Dr	2	NW
Bates Dr	2	SE
Bateson Ct	2	NW
Bath St	1	SE
Baxter Rd	2	SE
Baxter Rd	3	SW
Baylis Dr	5	SE
Beacon Field	5	SE
Beacon Hill Ln	5	SE
Beakes	2	SW
Beal Ave	2	NE
Bedford Rd	5	NE
Beechwood Dr	1	SE
Belfield Cir	5	NE
Belgrade Notch	1	NW
Bellwood Ave	6	SW
Belmar Pl	4	NE
Belmont Rd	5	NE
Belvidere St	6	SW
Bemidji Ct	1	SE
Bemidji Dr	1	SE
Bending Rd	1	SE
Benjamin St	5	NW
Bens St	4	NW
Berkley Ave	4	NE
Berkshire Rd	5	NE

Bernice Ave	1	SW
Birch Hollow Dr	5	SE
Bird Rd	1	NE
Bird Road	1	NE
Birk Ave	4	NE
Bishop St	2	SE
Blain Ct	5	SE
Blake Way	6	NW
Blakely Ct	5	NW
Blaney Dr	4	NE
Blueberry Ln	1	NW
Bluett Dr	2	NE
Bluett Dr	3	NW
Boardwalk Dr	5	SW
Bolgos Cir	3	NW
Bombridge Ct	5	SW
Bonisteel Blvd	2	SE
Bowen St	2	SW
Braeburn Cir	5	SE
Braeburn Ct	5	SE
Braeside Pl	4	NE
Brampton Ct	4	NE
Brandywine Dr	6	SW
Braun Ct	2	SW
Breckenridge Dr	4	NW
Brede Pl	2	NW
Bredefield St	2	NW
Brentwood Ct	5	SW
Brentwood Dr	5	SW
Briarcliff St	2	NE
Briarwood Cir	4	SE
Briarwood Cir	5	SW
Brierwood Ct	1	SE
Brierwood St	1	SE
Bristol Ct	6	NW
Broadview Ln	2	NE
Broadway	2	SW
Brock Ct	5	NW
Brockman Blvd	5	NW
Brook Ridge Ct	2	SW
Brookfield Dr	4	SE
Brooklyn Ave	5	NW
Brooks Rd	1	SE
Brookside Dr	2	NW
Brookside St	2	NW
Brookwood Pl	5	NW
Brown St	5	NW
Bruce St	1	SE
Bucholz Ct	1	SE
Buckingham Ct	5	NE
Buckingham Rd	5	NE
Buena Vista	1	SE
Bunker Hill Dr	2	NE
Burbank Dr	3	NW
Burgundy Rd	3	SW
Burlingame Ct	5	SE
Burlington Ct	2	NE
Burlington St	2	NE
Burlington	5	SW
Burns Ct	3	SW
Burr Oak Dr	4	NW
Burson Pl	5	NE
Burton Rd	6	SW
Burwood Ave	1	SW
Burwood Ave	4	NW
Bury Ct	2	NE
Butternut	5	SE
Bydding Rd	1	SE
Calumet Ave	5	SE
Calvin St	1	SW
Cambridge Ct	5	NW
Cambridge Rd	5	NW
Camelot Rd	5	NE
Canal St	2	SW
Candlewick Dr	5	SE
Canterbury St	5	SE
Canterbury St	6	SW
Carbeck Dr	1	SW
Cardinal Ave	5	SE
Carey St	2	SW
Carhart Rd	5	NE
Carl Ct	3	NW
Carmel Ln	5	SE
Carol Dr	4	NW
Carolina Ave	1	SW
Carolina Ave	4	NW
Carolyn St	6	SW
Cascade Dr	5	SE
Catalina Ave	4	NE
Catalpa Cir	5	SE
Catherine St	2	SW
Cayuga Pl	5	NE
Cedar Bend Dr	2	SW
Center Dr	1	SW
Central St	1	SW
Chalmers Dr	6	NW
Champagne Dr	5	SE
Chandler Rd	2	SW
Chapel Ct	4	NE
Chapin St	1	SE
Charing Cross	6	SW
Charles St	2	SW
Charlton Ave	1	SW
Charter Pl	3	SW
Chatham Way	3	SW
Chaucer Ct	4	NE
Chaucer Dr	4	NE
Chelsea Cir	5	SE
Cherokee Dr	5	NE
Cherry St	1	SE
Cherry Stone Ct	3	SW
Cherry Tree	6	SW
Cherry Tree Ln	6	SW
Chesterfield Dr	5	SE
Chestnut Rd	5	NE
Church St	2	SW
Church St	5	NW
Churchill Dr	4	NE

Circle Dr	1	SW
City Dr	1	SW
Clague Ave	4	NE
Clair Cir	1	SE
Clarendon Dr	1	SW
Cloverdale Rd	2	NW
Coler Rd	5	NW
Colgate Cir	1	SE
Collingwood	1	SW
Colony Ct	5	SE
Colony Rd	5	SE
Columbia Ave	5	SE
Commerce Dr	4	NW
Commonwealth	3	NW
Concord Rd	2	SE
Concord Rd	5	NE
Cooley Ave	1	SE
Copley Ave	5	NE
Corey St	2	SW
Cornwell Pl	2	SW
Coronada Dr	4	NE
Covington Dr	4	NE
Cram Cir	2	SE
Cram Pl	2	SE
Cranbrook Rd	5	SE
Crawford Ln	3	SW
Creal Cres	1	SE
Creal Ct	1	SE
Creek Dr	6	SW
Cressfield Ln	1	SE
Crest Ave	1	SE
Crest Ave	4	NE
Crestland Dr	5	NW
Crosby Cres	4	NE
Cross St	5	NW
Culver St	1	SE
Cumberland	5	SE
Danbury Ln	1	NW
Daniel St	1	SE
Darrow St	6	SW
Dartmoor Rd	4	NE
David Ct	2	NW
Davis Ave	4	NE
Davis Ave	5	NW
Day St	5	NE
Dean Rd	3	SW
Delafield Dr	2	NW
Delaware Dr	4	NE
Delta Dr	1	SW
Delwood Dr	1	SW
Depot St	2	SW
Detroit St	2	SW
Devolson Ave	5	NE
Devonshire Rd	5	NE
Dewey St	5	NW
Dexter Ann	1	SW
Dexter Ann	1	SW
Dexter Ave	1	SE
Dhu Varren Rd	2	NW
Dhu Varren	2	NW
Dicken Dr	4	NW
Dines Ct	3	SW
Division St	2	SW
Division St	5	NW
Dobson Pl	3	SW
Dogwood Ct	4	NE
Dolph Dr	1	SW
Donegal Ct	6	SW
Dorchester Rd	5	SE
Dorset Rd	5	NE
Doty Ave	1	SE
Dover Ct	4	NE
Dover Pl	5	NE
Dowing Ct	5	SE
Down Up Cir	1	NE
Drappatz	5	NE
Duane Ct	1	SW
Duffield	2	SE
Duncan St	1	SW
Dundee Dr	4	SE
Dunmore Rd	4	NE
Dunnington Dr	4	NW
Dupont Cir	1	SW
Durango Dr	4	NW
Dwight St	5	SE
Earhart Rd	3	SW
Earhart Rd	6	NW
Earhart Road	3	SW
Eastover Pl	5	NE
Easy St	5	SE
Eber White Blvd	1	SE
Eber White Blvd	4	NE
Eddy St	5	SE
Eden Ct	5	SE
Edgewood Ave	4	NE
Edgewood Dr	6	SW
Edgewood Pl	4	NE
Edinborough Rd	6	NW
Edmund Pl	1	SE
Edwards St	2	SW
Eisenhower	4	SE
Eisenhower	5	SE
Elder Blvd	4	NE
Eli Dr	6	SW
Elizabeth Ave	5	NE
Elizabeth St	2	SW
Ell Pl	6	SW
Ellsworth Rd	5	SE
Ellsworth Rd	6	SW
Ellsworth Road	6	SW
Elm St	2	SW
Elm St	5	NW
Elmcrest Dr	1	SE
Elmwood Ave	6	SW
Elmwood Dr	6	NW
Ember Way	5	SE
Emerald Ave	5	SE
Englave Dr	1	NE

Englewood Ct	5	SE
Esch Ave	5	SW
Esch Ct	5	SW
Essex Rd	5	SE
Eton Ct	4	NW
Evelyn Ct	4	NE
Evergreen Dr	1	SW
Evergreen Pl	2	SE
Exmoor Rd	5	NE
Exmoor Rd	6	NW
Fair Oaks Pkwy	5	NE
Fair St	1	SW
Fairlane Dr	5	NE
Fairmount Dr	3	SW
Fairview Ave	1	SW
Farmbrook Ct	5	SE
Faust Ct	5	SE
Faye Dr	1	SW
Federal Blvd	4	NE
Felch St	1	SE
Felch St	2	SW
Fenwick Ct	5	SW
Fenwood Dr	5	NE
Ferdon Rd	5	NE
Ferndale Pl	5	NW
Fernwood Ave	6	SW
Fernwood St	6	SW
Ferry St	1	SW
Fieldcrest Dr	4	NE
Fieldcrest Dr	5	SW
Fletcher St	2	SW
Folkstone Ct	3	SW
Forest Ave	2	SW
Forest Ave	5	NW
Forest Ct	5	NW
Forest St	5	NW
Foss Ct	1	NW
Foss St	1	NW
Foster Road	1	NW
Fountain St	1	SE
Fox Hunt Dr	3	SW
Foxcroft Rd	5	NE
Franklin Blvd	4	NE
Franklin Ct	1	NW
Franklin St	1	SW
Frederick Dr	3	SW
Frieze Ave	5	NE
Fuller St	2	SW
Fulmer Ct	1	SW
Fulmer St	1	SW
Gallway Ct	6	SW
Garden Cir	1	SE
Garden Cir	4	NW
Garden Homes	1	SW
Garden Homes	1	SW
Gardner Ave	5	NW
Geddes Ave	2	SW
Geddes Ave	5	NE
Geddes Heights	2	SE
Geddes Rd	2	SE
Geddes Rd	3	SW
Geddes Rd	6	NW
Geddes Road	3	SW
Geddes Road	6	NW
Geneva Rd	4	NW
Georgetown	3	NW
Gettysburg Rd	3	NW
Gilbert Ct	2	SW
Gladstone Ave	5	SE
Glastonbury Rd	4	NE
Glazier Way	2	SE
Glazier Way	3	SW
Glen Ave	2	SW
Glen Leven Rd	4	NE
Glenbridge Ct	5	SW
Glenbrook Ct	4	SE
Glendale Cir	1	SE
Glendale Dr	1	SE
Glendale St	1	SE
Glendaloch Cir	5	NE
Glendaloch Rd	5	NE
Glenwood Rd	5	NE
Glenwood Rd	6	NW
Glenwood St	1	SW
Gloucester Way	6	SW
Golden Ave	5	NW
Golfview Lane	5	NW
Golfview Ln	5	NW
Gott St	1	SE
Grace St	1	SE
Gralake Ave	1	SW
Granada Ave	4	NE
Grandview Dr	1	SE
Granger Ave	5	NW
Green Brier	3	SW
Green Hills Dr	3	SW
Green Rd	3	SW
Green Road	3	NW
Greenbrier	3	SW
Greene St	5	NW
Greenview Dr	4	NE
Greenwood Ave	5	NW
Gross Rd	6	SW
Haisley Dr	1	SW
Hall Ave	5	NE
Hamilton Pl	2	SW
Hampshire Rd	5	SE
Hampstead	1	NE
Hampton Ct	4	NE
Hanover Ct	4	NE
Hanover Rd	4	NE
Hansen Dr	4	NW
Harbal Dr	2	SW
Harbrooke Ave	1	SE
Harding Rd	5	NE
Hardyke Ct	5	SE
Harpst St	5	NW
Hartford St	4	NE

Harvard Pl	2	SE
Harvard Pl	5	NE
Hasper Dr	1	SW
Hatcher Cres	1	SW
Hatcher St	1	SE
Haven	5	NE
Haverhill Dr	2	NE
Hawthorn Rd	5	NE
Hayes Ct	5	SW
Hayward St	2	SE
Hazelwood St	1	SW
Heather Way	5	NE
Heatheridge St	5	NE
Heatherway	5	NE
Helen St	1	SW
Hemlock Ct	5	SE
Hemlock Dr	5	SE
Henry St	1	SW
Henry St	5	NW
Herbert St	2	SE
Hermina Ct	1	SE
Hermitage Rd	5	NE
Hewett Dr	4	NE
Hiawatha Pl	2	NW
Hickory Ave	4	NW
Hickory Rd	5	NE
Hidden Valley	5	SW
High Orchard Dr	3	SW
High St	2	SW
Highlake Ave	1	SW
Highland Ln	2	SE
Highland Rd	2	SE
Highland Rd	5	NE
Hikone Rd	5	SE
Hill St	5	NW
Hillcrest Dr	1	SE
Hilldale Dr	2	NW
Hillridge Blvd	1	SE
Hillside Ct	5	NE
Hilltop Dr	1	SW
Hilton Blvd	5	SW
Hiscock St	1	SE
Hiscock St	2	SW
Hockey Ln	1	SE
Hogback Road	6	NW
Hollywood Dr	1	SW
Holyoke Ln	1	NE
Homestead	5	SE
Hoover Ave	4	NE
Hoover Ave	5	NW
Horman Ct	5	NW
Hospital Dr	2	SW
Howley Ct	2	SW
Hubbard Rd	2	SE
Hubbard St	2	SE
Hubbard St	3	SW
Hunting Valley	5	NE
Huntington Ct	5	NE
Huntington Dr	2	SE
Huntington Dr	5	NE
Huntington Pl	5	NE
Huron Pkwy	2	SE
Huron Pkwy	3	SW
Huron Pkwy	6	NW
Huron River Dr	1	NE
Huron River Dr	2	NW
Huron River Dr	5	NE
Huron River Dr	6	NW
Huron St	1	SE
Huron St	2	SW
Huronview Blvd	1	SE
Huronview Blvd	2	NW
Hutchins Ave	4	NE
I- 94		
I- 94	1	SW
I- 94	4	NW
I- 94	5	SW
I- 94	6	SW
Independence	5	SE
Indian River Dr	2	SE
Indianola Dr	2	SW
Industrial Hwy	5	SW
Ingalls St	2	SW
Ironwood Dr	1	SW
Iroquois Ave	5	NW
Island Dr	2	SW
Island Drive Ct	2	SW
Ivydale	4	NE
Ivywood Dr	4	NE
Jackson Ave	1	SW
Jackson Pl	1	SW
Jackson Rd	1	SW
Jackson Road	1	SW
James St	5	NE
Jay Lee Ct	5	SE
Jeanne Ave	6	NW
Jefferson Ct	4	NE
Jefferson St	2	SW
Jefferson St	4	NE
Jefferson St	5	NW
Jewett Ave	5	NW
John St	5	NW
Jonathan Ct	5	SE
Jones Dr	2	SW
Jorn Ct	5	NW
Joseph St	5	SE
Judson Ct	5	NW
Kay Pkwy	4	NE
Kearney Rd	5	NE
Keech Ave	4	NE
Keech Ave	5	NW
Kellogg St	2	SW
Kelly Green Rd	1	SW
Kenilworth Dr	5	NE
Kensington Dr	5	SW
Kent St	4	NW
Kenwood Ave	1	SE
Keppler Ct	1	SE

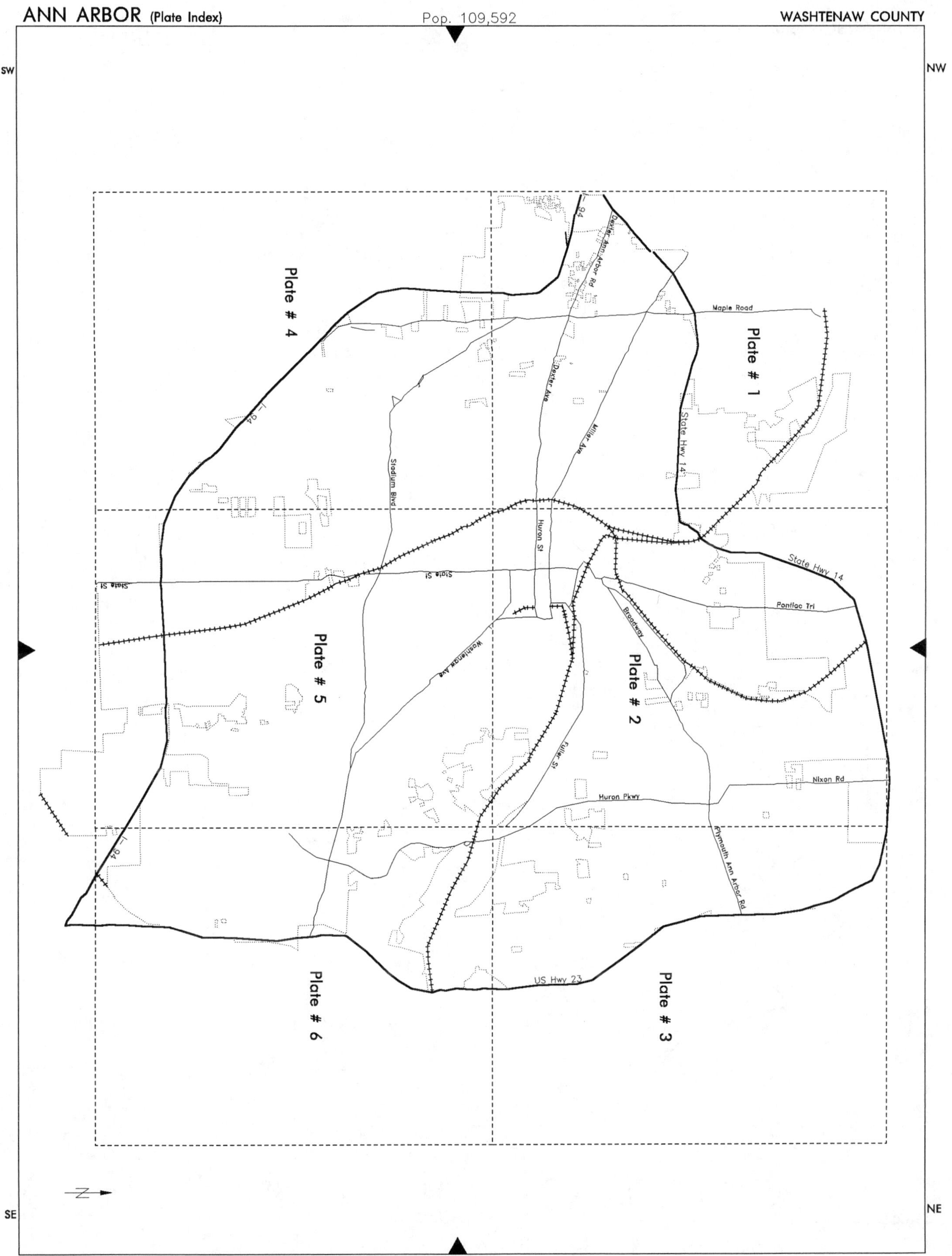
SW
NW
SE
NE
Plate # 1
Plate # 2
Plate # 3
Plate # 4
Plate # 5
Plate # 6
Maple Road
Dexter Ann Arbor Rd
Dexter Ave
Miller Ave
State Hwy 14
Stadium Blvd
Huron St
State St
Pontiac Trl
Broadway
Washtenaw Ave
Fuller St
Nixon Rd
Huron Pkwy
Plymouth Ann Arbor Rd
US Hwy 23
I-94

NW NE

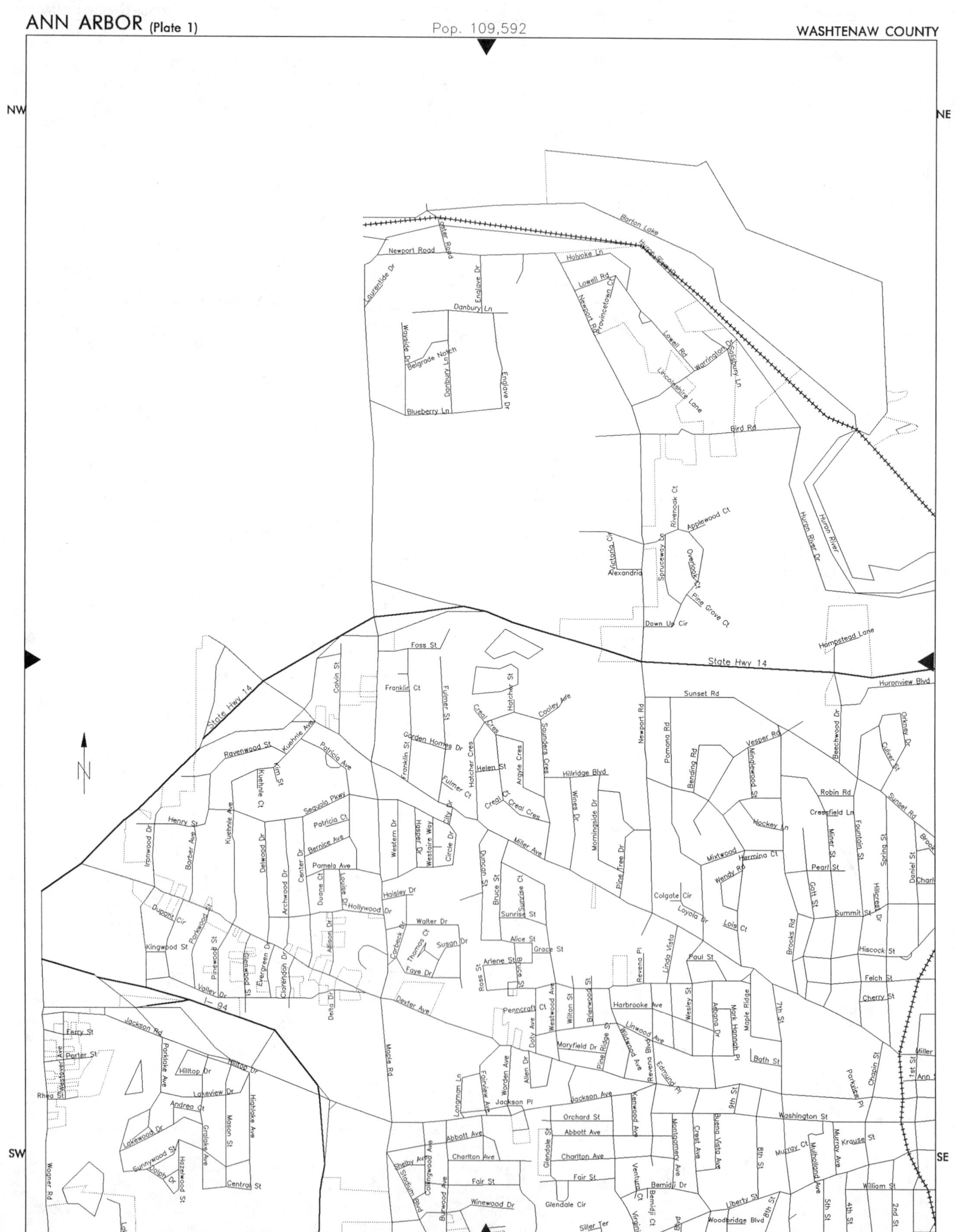
Barton Lake
Huron River Dr
Newport Road
Foster Road
Holyoke Ln
Laurentide Dr
Englave Dr
Danbury Ln
Lowell Rd
Newport Rd
Provincetown Ct
Wayside Dr
Belgrade Notch
Warrington Dr
Salisbury Ln
Lincolnshire Lane
Blueberry Ln
Bird Rd
Rivenoak Ct
Applewood Ct
Victoria Cir
Spruceway Ln
Overlook Ct
Alexandria
Huron River
Pine Grove Ct
Down Up Cir
Hampstead Lane
Foss St
State Hwy 14
Huronview Blvd
Calvin St
Franklin Ct
Fulmer St
Hatcher St
Cooley Ave
Sunset Rd
Creal Cres
Saunders Cres
Newport Rd
Pomona Rd
Beechwood Dr
Orkney Dr
Culver St
Garden Homes Dr
Vesper Rd
Ravenwood St
Kuehnle Ave
Patricia Ave
Franklin St
Hatcher Cres
Helen St
Argyle Cres
Hillridge Blvd
Bending Rd
Mandlewood St
Kuehnle Ct
Kim St
Fulmer Ct
Robin Rd
Sequoia Pkwy
Creal Ct
Wines Dr
Cresfield Ln
Sunset Rd
Henry St
Patricia Ct
Western Dr
Hasper Dr
Westaire Way
City Dr
Morningside Dr
Hockey Ln
Ironwood Dr
Barber Ave
Kuehnle Ave
Delwood Dr
Bernice Ave
Circle Dr
Miller Ave
Minter St
Fountain St
Spring St
Daniel St
Pamela Ave
Pine Tree Dr
Mixtwood
Hermina Ct
Wendy Rd
Pearl St
Archwood Dr
Center Dr
Duane Ct
Louise Dr
Haisley Dr
Duncan St
Bruce St
Sunrise Ct
Colgate Cir
Gott St
Hillcrest Dr
Dupont Cir
Parkwood St
Hollywood Dr
Sunrise St
Loyola Dr
Summit St
Walter Dr
Lois Ct
Brooks Rd
Kingwood St
Pinewood St
Glenwood St
Evergreen Dr
Clarendon Dr
Allison Dr
Carbeck Dr
Thomas Ct
Susan Dr
Alice St
Grace St
Revena Pl
Linda Vista
Paul St
Hiscock St
Arlene St
Faye Dr
Ross St
Bruce St
Felch St
Valley Dr
I-94
Delta Dr
Dexter Ave
Penncraft Ct
Westwood Ave
Wilton St
Briarwood St
Harbrooke Ave
Wesley St
Arbana Dr
Mark Hannah Pl
Maple Ridge
7th St
Cherry St
Jackson Rd
Ferry St
Doty Ave
Linwood Ave
Miller
Porter St
Parklake Ave
Maple Rd
Maryfield Dr
Pine Ridge St
Bath St
Westover Ave
Hilltop Dr
Allen Dr
Revena Blvd
Edmund Pl
Chapin St
1st St
Ann
Rhea St
Lakeview Dr
Highlake Ave
Longman Ln
Fairview Ave
Worden Ave
Jackson Pl
Jackson Ave
Kenwood Ave
9th St
Parkview Pl
Andrea Ct
Mason St
Orchard St
Washington St
Abbott Ave
Glendale St
Montgomery Ave
Crest Ave
Buena Vista Ave
Krause St
Lakewood Dr
Gralake Ave
Murray Ct
Mulholland Ave
Murray Ave
Sunnywood St
Charlton Ave
8th St
Wagner Rd
Dolph Dr
Hazelwood St
Shelby Ave
Collingwood Ave
Stadium Blvd
Fair St
Ventura Ct
Bemidji Dr
William St
Central St
Burwood Ave
Winewood Dr
Glendale Cir
Virginia
Bemidji Ct
Liberty St
8th St
5th St
4th St
2nd St
Siller Ter
Woodbridge Blvd

SW SE

NW
NE
SW
SE
US Hwy 23
State Hwy 14
Dhu Varren Road
Dhu Varren Rd
Plymouth Ann Arbor Rd
Huron River Dr
Huron River
Huron Pkwy
Nixon Road
Barton Dr
Skydale Dr
Larkspur St
Manor Dr
Brookside Dr
Hilldale Dr
Northside Ave
Wickfield Ct
Arrowwood Trl
Pontiac Trl
Bateson Ct
Placid Way
Tuebingen Pkwy
Lakehurst Ln
Traver Blvd
Lancashire
Meade Ct
Haverhill Dr
Lexington Dr
Bunker Hill Dr
Antietam Dr
Bluett Dr
Renfrew St
Prairie St
Sandalwood Cir
Burlington Ct
Burlington St
Briarcliff St
Windwood Dr
Whisperwood
Long Shore Dr
Chandler Rd
Hiawatha Pl
Barton Dr
David Ct
Traver Rd
Traver Ct
Amherst Ave
Taylor St
Peach St
Indianola Dr
Ottawa St
Argo Dr
Pear St
Willow Ln
Upland Dr
Shirley Ln
Lake Lila Ln
Village Green Rd
Bishop St
Mc Intyre Dr
Broadview Ln
Herbal Dr
Cram Pl
Hubbard St
Hubbard Rd
Gilbert Ct
Hayward St
Plymouth Ann Arbor Rd
Jones Dr
Broadway
Cedar Bend Dr
Kellogg St
Wright St
Bowen St
Main St
Herbert St
Bates Dr
Murfin Ave
Bonisteel Blvd
Beal Ave
Glazier Way
Brook Ridge Ct
Charles St
Howley Ct
Maiden Ln
Nielsen Ct
Island Dr
Maiden Lane Ct
Wall St
Canal St
Summit St
Depot St
Felch St
Beakes
Detroit St
Elizabeth St
Nyc Railroad
Medical Center Dr
Kingsley St
Cornwell Pl
Braun Ct
Lawrence St
Thayer St
Ingalls St
Catherine St
Miller Ave
Ann St
Huron St
Simpson Dr
Hospital Dr
Washington St
Park Ter
Washtenaw Ave
Washington Heights
Nichols Dr
Fuller St
Lakehaven Dr
5th Ave
Liberty St
Fletcher St
Observatory St
Ashley St
4th Ave
Thompson St
Division St
University Ave
William St
Maynard St
Hamilton Pl
Jefferson St
Packard St
Wilmot Ct
Elm St
Walnut
Linden
Geddes Ave
Geddes Heights Dr
Church
Ridgeway
Highland Ln
Concord Rd
Highland Rd
Lafayette Rd
Regent Dr
Evergreen Pl
Orchard Hills Dr
Rock Creek Dr
Huntington Dr
Huntington Ct
Pine View Ct
Rumsey

NW
NE
SW
SE
US Hwy 23
Whisperwood Dr
Green Rd
Burbank Dr
Richmond Ct
Rumsey Dr
Lexington Dr
Carl Ct
Bolgos Cir
Alton Ct
Antietam Dr
Trenton Ct
Yellowstone Dr
Georgetown Blvd
Yorktown Dr
Commonwealth Dr
Ardenne Dr
Plymouth Ann Arbor Rd
Baxter Rd
Frederick Dr
Middleton Dr
Dean Rd
Hubbard St
Chatham Way
Crawford Ln
Mac Gregor Ln
Natalie Ln
Larchmont Dr
Sulgrave Pl
Vintage Valley Rd
Burgundy Rd
Folkstone Ct
Kipling Dr
Paisley Ct
Bardstown Trl
Andover Rd
Pepper Pike
Wynnstone Dr
Dobson Pl
Wolverhampton
Windemere Ct
Windemere Dr
Sturbridge Ct
Charter Pl
Marlborough Dr
Earhart Rd
Dines Ct
Glazier Way
Stenton Ct
Trenton Dr
Waldenwood Dr
Riddeline Road
Wellington Cross
Cherry Stone Ct
Barclay Ct
Watershed Dr
Ridgmarr Sq
Green Hills Dr
Peninsula Ct
Watersedge Dr
Skynob Dr
Pemberton Dr
Burns Ct
Fox Hunt Dr
Huron Pkwy
Windy Crest Dr
Sumac Lane
High Orchard Dr
Geddes Road
Pine Brae
N

NW
NE
SW
SE
I-94
Liberty Road
Liberty St
Stadium Blvd
Scio Church Rd
Main St
Ann Arbor Saline Rd
Eisenhower Pkwy
Northbrook Dr
Delaware Dr
Weldon Blvd
Pauline Blvd
Seventh St
Briarwood Cir
Rolling Meadows Dr
Oakbrook Dr
Waymarket Rd

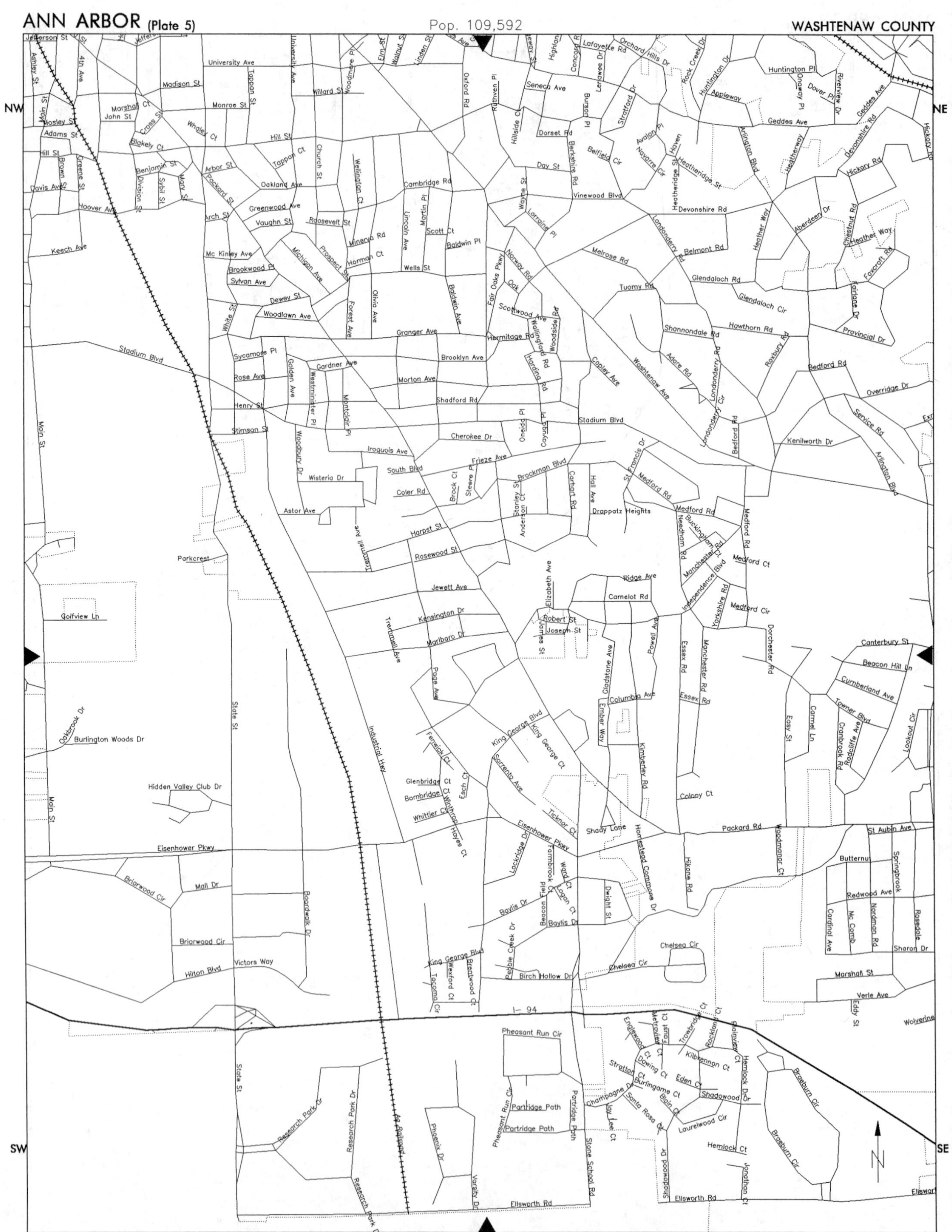
NW
NE
SW
SE
Jefferson St
Ashley St
4th Ave
University Ave
Tappan St
Madison St
Monroe St
Willard St
Main St
Mosley St
Adams St
Hill St
Brown
Greene St
Davis Ave
Hoover Ave
Keech Ave
Marshall Ct
John St
Cross St
Whaley Ct
Blakely Ct
Benjamin St
Division St
Sybil St
Mary St
Arbor St
Packard St
Oakland Ave
Greenwood Ave
Vaughn St
Arch St
Roosevelt St
Tappan Ct
Church St
Wellington Ct
Cambridge Rd
Martin Pl
Lincoln Ave
Scott Ct
Baldwin Pl
Minerva Rd
Horman Ct
Wells St
Mc Kinley Ave
Brookwood Pl
Sylvan Ave
Michigan Ave
Prospect St
Dewey St
Woodlawn Ave
White St
Forest Ave
Olivia Ave
Baldwin Ave
Granger Ave
Oxford Rd
Ruthven Pl
Seneca Ave
Hillside Ct
Dorset Rd
Day St
Wayne St
Lorraine Pl
Burson Pl
Berkshire Rd
Belfield Cir
Vinewood Blvd
Lafayette Rd
Orchard Hills Dr
Stratford Dr
Avalon Pl
Navarre Cir
Haven
Heatheridge St
Devonshire Rd
Londonderry Rd
Huntington Dr
Rock Creek Dr
Appleway
Huntington Pl
Onaway Pl
Dover Pl
Riverview Dr
Geddes Ave
Arlington Blvd
Heatherway
Heather Way
Aberdeen Dr
Chestnut Rd
Devonshire Rd
Hickory Rd
Foxcroft Rd
Fairlane Dr
Provincial Dr
Belmont Rd
Glendaloch Rd
Glendaloch Cir
Melrose Rd
Tuomy Rd
Fair Oaks Pkwy
Norway Rd
Oak
Scottwood Ave
Woodside Rd
Wallingford Rd
Hermitage Rd
Harding Rd
Shannondale Rd
Hawthorn Rd
Roxbury Rd
Adare Rd
Washtenaw Ave
Copley Ave
Stadium Blvd
Sycamore Pl
Rose Ave
Henry St
Stimson St
Golden Ave
Westminster Pl
Gardner Ave
Montclair Pl
Brooklyn Ave
Morton Ave
Shadford Rd
Cherokee Dr
Oneida Pl
Iroquois Ave
Woodbury Dr
South Blvd
Wisteria Dr
Coler Rd
Astor Ave
Brock Ct
Steere Pl
Frieze Ave
Brockman Blvd
Stanley St
Anderson Ct
Carhart Rd
Hall Ave
Drappatz Heights
St Francis Dr
Medford Rd
Needham Rd
Buckingham Ct
Manchester Rd
Independence Blvd
Medford Ct
Bedford Rd
Londonderry Cir
Kenilworth Dr
Service Rd
Overridge Dr
Bedford Rd
Harpst St
Rosewood St
Parkcrest
Jewett Ave
Elizabeth Ave
Ridge Ave
Camelot Rd
Yorkshire Rd
Medford Cir
Kensington Dr
Marlboro Dr
Robert St
Joseph St
James St
Powell Ave
Golfview Ln
Page Ave
Gladstone Ave
Columbia Ave
Ember Way
Essex Rd
Manchester Rd
Dorchester Rd
Canterbury St
Beacon Hill Ln
Cumberland Ave
Towner Blvd
Cranbrook Rd
Radcliffe Ave
Lookout Cir
Carmel Ln
Easy St
Oakbrook Dr
Burlington Woods Dr
State St
Industrial Hwy
King George Blvd
King George Ct
Sorrento Ave
Fenwick Ct
Glenbridge Ct
Bombridge Ct
Whittier Ct
Hayes Ct
Winthrop
Esch Ct
Kimberley Rd
Colony Ct
Hidden Valley Club Dr
Ticknor Ct
Shady Lane
Packard Rd
Woodmanor Ct
St Aubin Ave
Eisenhower Pkwy
Lockridge Dr
Tarnbrook Ct
Homestead Commons Dr
Hikone Rd
Butternut
Springbrook
Redwood Ave
Mall Dr
Briarwood Cir
Boardwalk Dr
Ward Ct
Logan Ct
Dwight St
Baylis Dr
Beacon Field
Cardinal Ave
Mc Comb
Nordman Rd
Rosedale
Sharon Dr
Briarwood Cir
Victors Way
Hilton Blvd
Pebble Creek Dr
King George Blvd
Wexford Ct
Brentwood Ct
Tacoma Cir
Birch Hollow Dr
Chelsea Cir
Marshall St
Verle Ave
Eddy St
Wolverine
I- 94
Pheasant Run Cir
Englewood Ct
Metroview Ct
Faust Ct
Trowbridge
Rockland Ct
Pontiac Ct
Dowing Ct
Kilbrennan Ct
Stratton Ct
Burlingame Ct
Eden Ct
Blain Ct
Shadowood Ct
Hemlock Dr
Braeburn Cir
Champagne Dr
Santa Rosa Dr
Laurelwood Cir
Hemlock Ct
Jonathan Ct
Jay Lee Ct
Partridge Path
Partridge Path
Pheasant Run Cir
Research Park Dr
Research Park Dr
Phoenix Dr
Varsity Dr
Stone School Rd
Shadowood Dr
Ellsworth Rd
Ellsworth

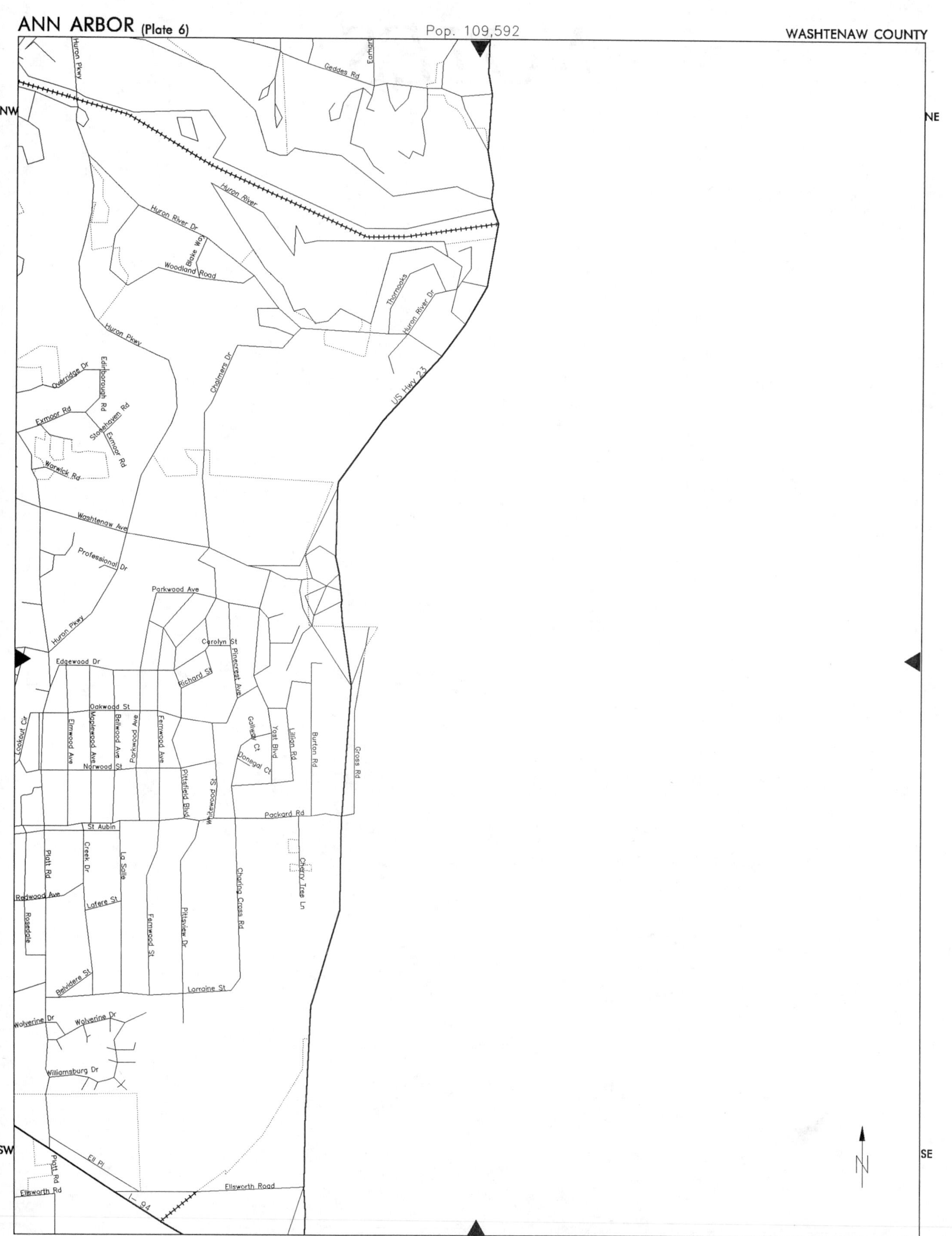
NW
NE
SW
SE
Huron Pkwy
Geddes Rd
Earhart
Huron River
Huron River Dr
Blake Way
Woodland Road
Thornoaks
Huron River Dr
Huron Pkwy
Chalmers Dr
US Hwy 23
Overridge Dr
Edinborough Rd
Exmoor Rd
Stonehaven Rd
Exmoor Rd
Warwick Rd
Washtenaw Ave
Professional Dr
Parkwood Ave
Huron Pkwy
Carolyn St
Pinecrest Ave
Richard St
Edgewood Dr
Oakwood St
Lookout Cir
Elmwood Ave
Maplewood Ave
Bellwood Ave
Parkwood Ave
Fernwood Ave
Norwood St
Galloway Ct
Yost Blvd
Lillian Rd
Burton Rd
Gross Rd
Donegal Ct
Pittsfield Blvd
Whitewood St
Packard Rd
St Aubin
Platt Rd
Creek Dr
La Salle
Cherry Tree Ln
Charing Cross Rd
Redwood Ave
Lafere St
Rosedale
Fernwood St
Pittsview Dr
Belvidere St
Lorraine St
Wolverine Dr
Wolverine Dr
Williamsburg Dr
Platt Rd
Elli Pl
Ellsworth Rd
Ellsworth Road
I-94
N

NOTES

Armada Center Road
Branch Coon Creek
Burk
Spencer St
Prospect St
Barrows
Fulton
1st
Fair
Main St
Simons St
Teitz
Main St
Main St
Crull St
Branch Coon Creek
Torrey
Georgian Ct
Hollweg St
Franklin Lane
Provincial Ct
Church
Floral
Morrison
Colonial
Lathrop
Lathrop
Depot
Grand Trunk Western Railroad
N

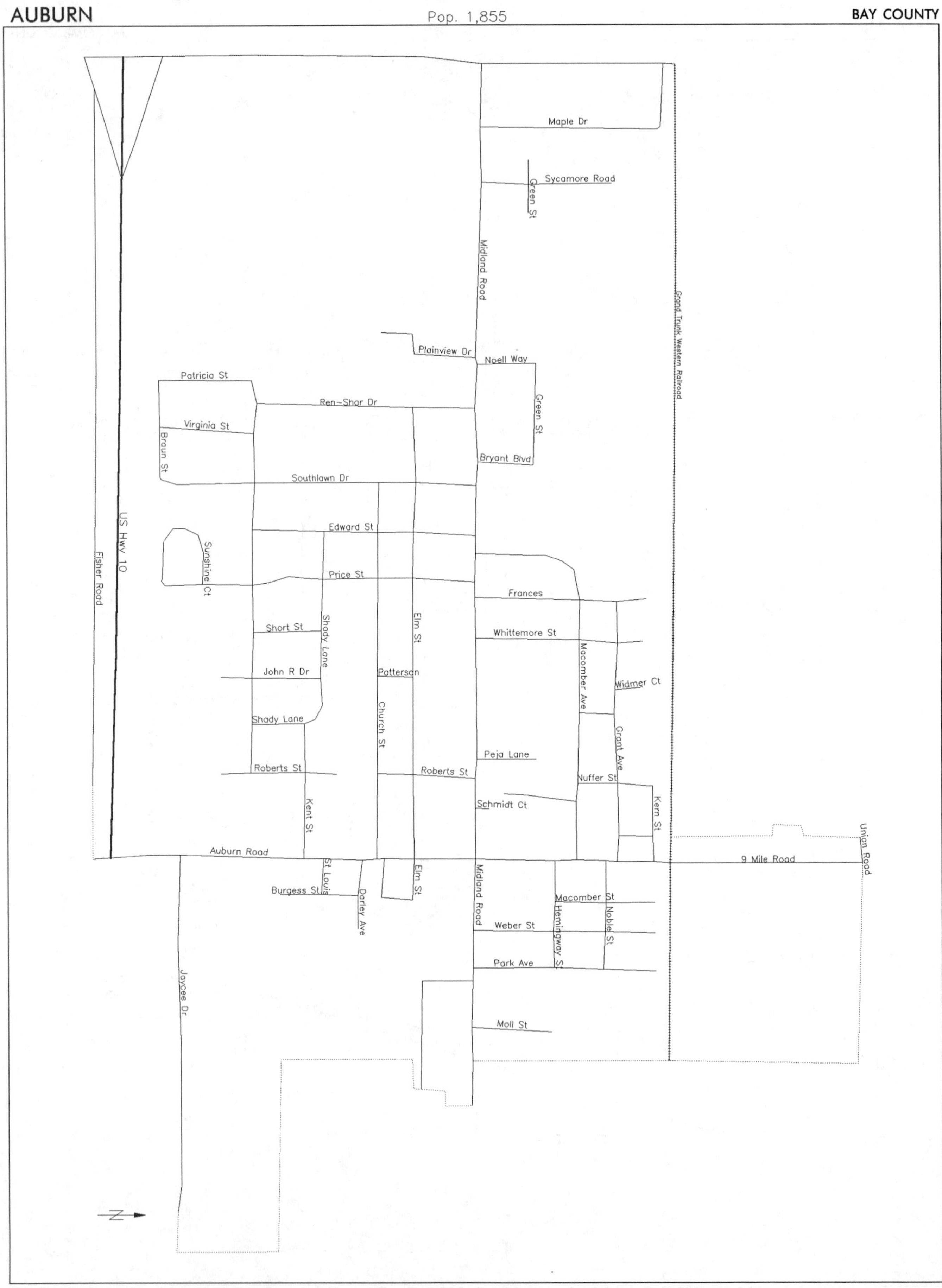
Maple Dr
Sycamore Road
Green St
Midland Road
Grand Trunk Western Railroad
Plainview Dr
Noell Way
Patricia St
Ren-Shar Dr
Virginia St
Green St
Braun St
Bryant Blvd
Southlawn Dr
US Hwy 10
Edward St
Sunshine Ct
Fisher Road
Price St
Frances
Short St
Shady Lane
Elm St
Whittemore St
John R Dr
Patterson
Macomber Ave
Widmer Ct
Shady Lane
Church St
Grant Ave
Peja Lane
Roberts St
Roberts St
Nuffer St
Kent St
Schmidt Ct
Kern St
Union Road
Auburn Road
9 Mile Road
St Louis
Elm St
Midland Road
Burgess St
Darley Ave
Macomber St
Hemingway St
Noble St
Weber St
Park Ave
Jaycee Dr
Moll St
N

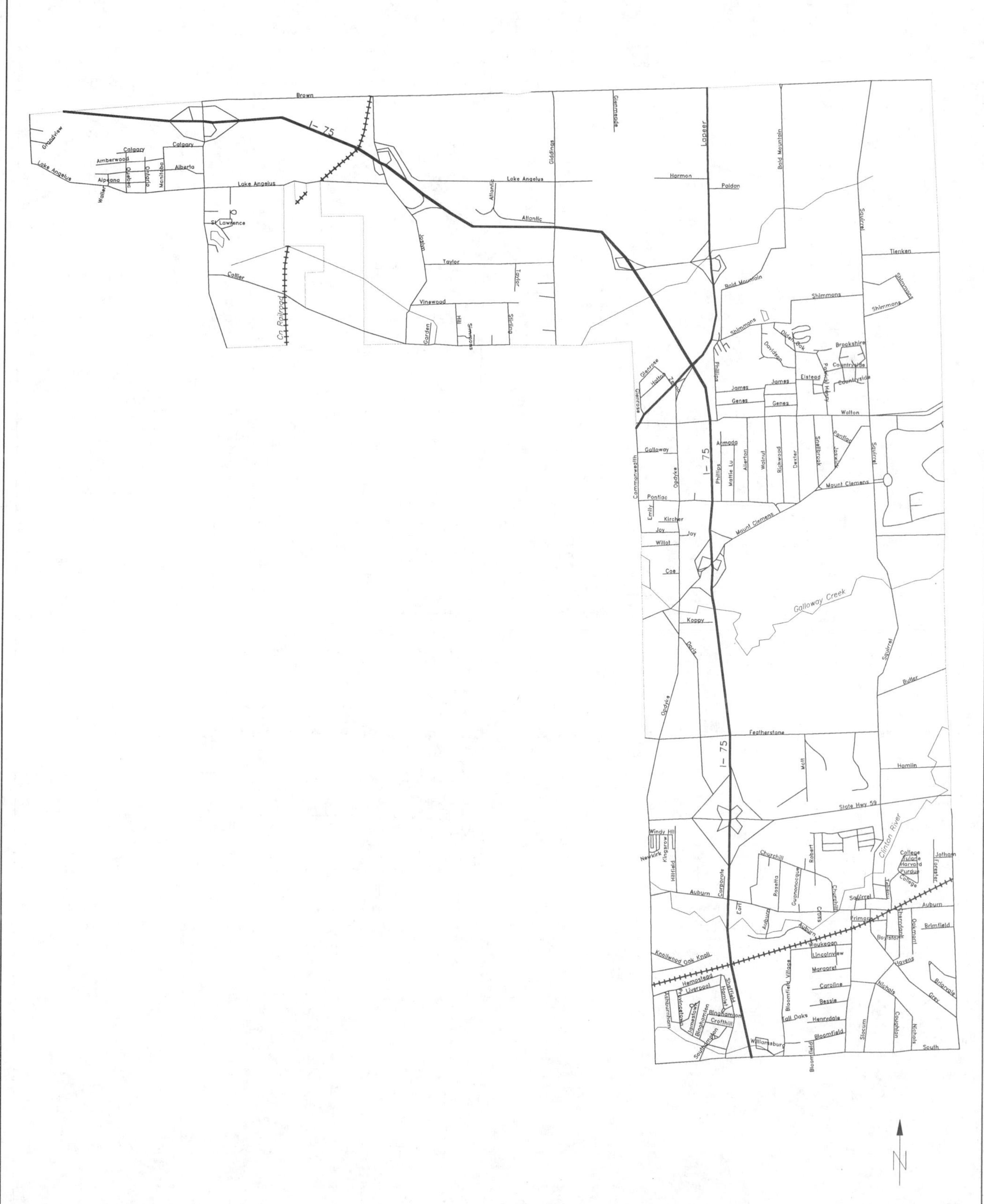
Brown
I- 75
Grandview
Calgary
Amberwood
Alberta
Manitoba
Lake Angelus
Alpena
Walter
St Lawrence
Collier
Cn Railroad
Giddings
Atlantic
Joslyn
Taylor
Vinewood
Garden
Hill
Simmons
Stirling
Lapeer
Harmon
Paldan
Bald Mountain
Squirrel
Tienken
Shimmons
Brookshire
Countryside
Phillips
James
Genes
Elstead
Walton
Armada
Mattie Lu
Allerton
Walnut
Richwood
Dexter
Pontiac
Galloway
Commonwealth
Opdyke
Emily
Kircher
Joy
Willot
Coe
Mount Clemens
Galloway Creek
Kappy
Doris
Butler
Featherstone
Mott
Hamlin
State Hwy 59
Clinton River
Windy Hill
Newkirk
Kingsrow
Hillfield
Auburn
Corporate
Earl
Churchill
Rosetta
Robert
College
Tulane
Harvard
Purdue
Jotham
Forestec
Primary
Oakmont
Brimfield
Knollwood
Oak Knoll
Waukegan
Lincolnview
Margaret
Caroline
Bessie
Henrydale
Bloomfield
Bloomfield Village
Hempstead
Liverpool
Binghamton
Crofthill
Southampton
Tall Oaks
Williamsburg
Slocum
Coughton
Nichols
Grey
South
Briarvale
Havens
N

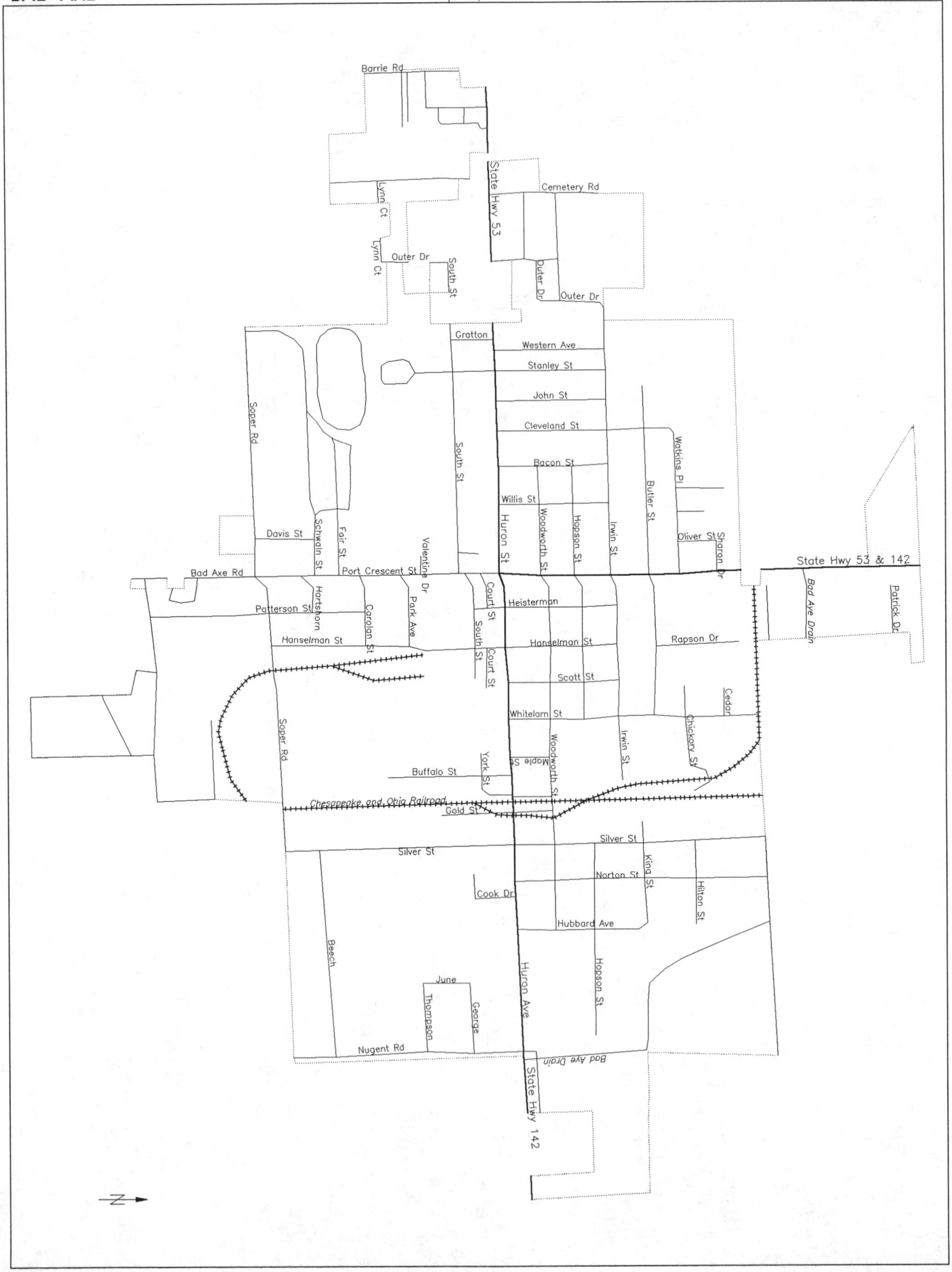

Barrie Rd
State Hwy 53
Cemetery Rd
Lynn Ct
Lynn Ct
Outer Dr
South St
Outer Dr
Outer Dr
Gratton
Western Ave
Stanley St
John St
Cleveland St
Soper Rd
South St
Watkins Pl
Bacon St
Willis St
Butler St
Davis St
Schwalm St
Fair St
Valentine Dr
Huron St
Woodworth St
Hopson St
Irwin St
Oliver St
Sharon Dr
State Hwy 53 & 142
Bad Axe Rd
Port Crescent St
Court St
Heisterman
Bad Axe Drain
Patrick Dr
Patterson St
Hartshorn
Carolan St
Park Ave
South St
Hanselman St
Hanselman St
Rapson Dr
Court St
Scott St
Cedar
Whitelam St
Soper Rd
Woodworth St
Irwin St
Chickory St
Maple St
York St
Buffalo St
Chesapeake and Ohio Railroad
Gold St
Silver St
Silver St
Norton St
King St
Cook Dr
Hilton St
Hubbard Ave
Beech
Hopson St
June
Thompson
George
Huron Ave
Nugent Rd
Bad Axe Drain
State Hwy 142
N

BANGOR

Pop. 1,922

Greenhouse Rd
Center St
Hastings Ct
Hastings St
Kalamazoo St
Chesapeake and Ohio Railway
North St
High St
2nd St
1st St
South Branch Black River
Bangor St
3rd St
Main St
Black River Rd
State Hwy 43
Funk St
Cemetery Rd
Center St
Washington St
Lafler St
Monroe St
Morrison Ave
Exchange St
Pine St
Cherry St
Joy St
Division Ave
Alexander Ave
Randolph St
Park Rd
Union St
Union St
Walnut St
Charles St
Lincoln Ave
Cass St
Cass St
State Hwy 43
Apple Blossom Dr
Douglass St
Douglass St
Prospect Ct
Park Rd
Morrison Ave
Clark St
Walnut St
Maple St
Chase St
Oliver St
Arlington St
Center Ct
David Walton Dr
Ollie Hosier Dr
Chesapeake and Ohio Railway
Cedar Drain
N

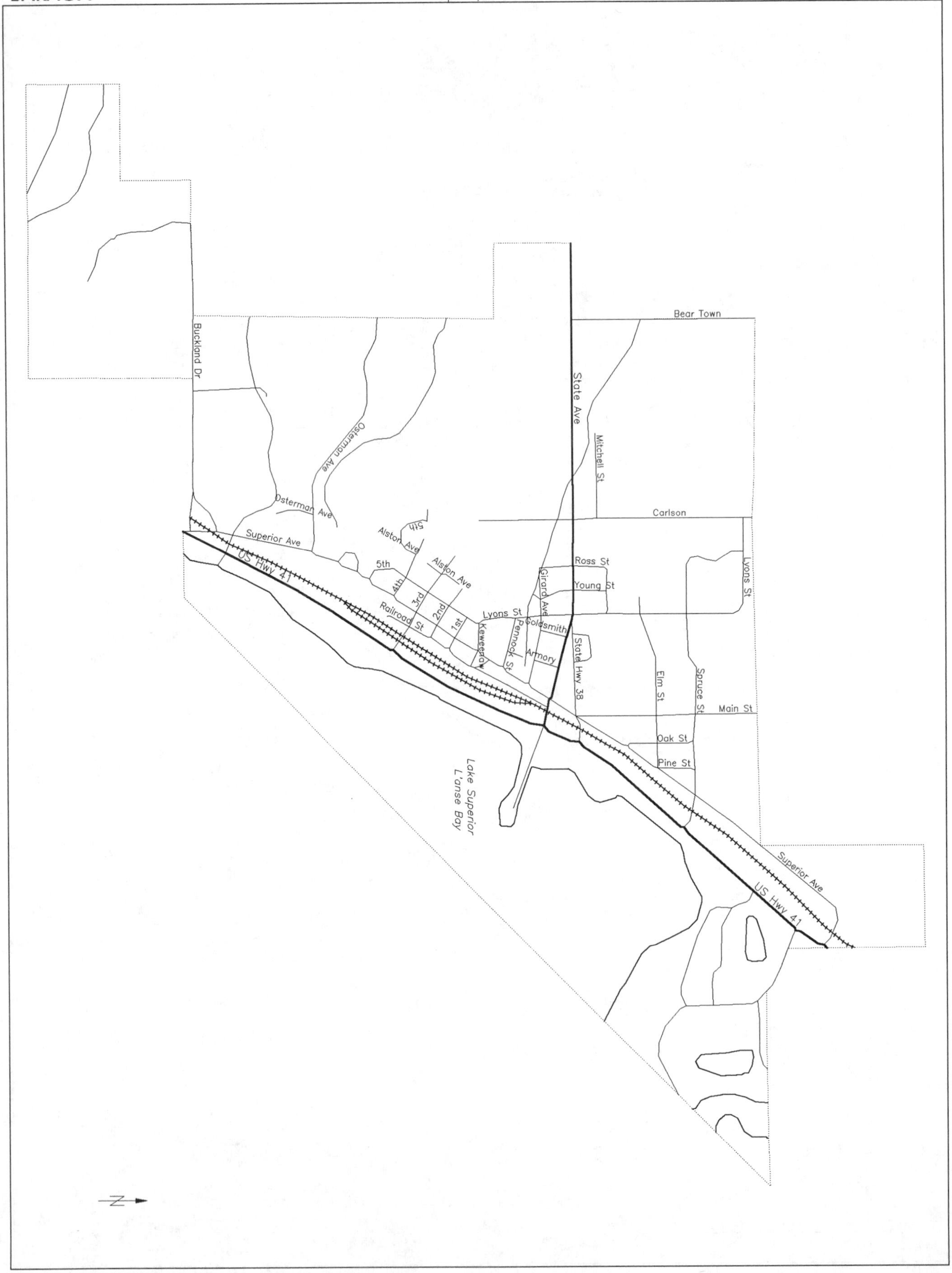

Bear Town
Buckland Dr
State Ave
Mitchell St
Osterman Ave
Osterman Ave
Carlson
Superior Ave
Alston Ave
5th
5th
Alston Ave
4th
3rd
2nd
1st
Ross St
Young St
Girard Ave
Lyons St
Lyons St
Goldsmith
Railroad St
Keweenaw
Pennock St
Armory
State Hwy 38
Elm St
Spruce St
Main St
Oak St
Pine St
US Hwy 41
Lake Superior
L'anse Bay
Superior Ave
US Hwy 41
N

NOTES

Plate # 1
Plate # 2
Plate # 3
Plate # 4
Plate # 5
Springfield city
Dickman Rd
Bedford Rd
Michigan Ave
Helmer Rd
Capital Ave
Columbia Ave
I– 194
I– 94
Goguac Lake
State Hwy 66

N

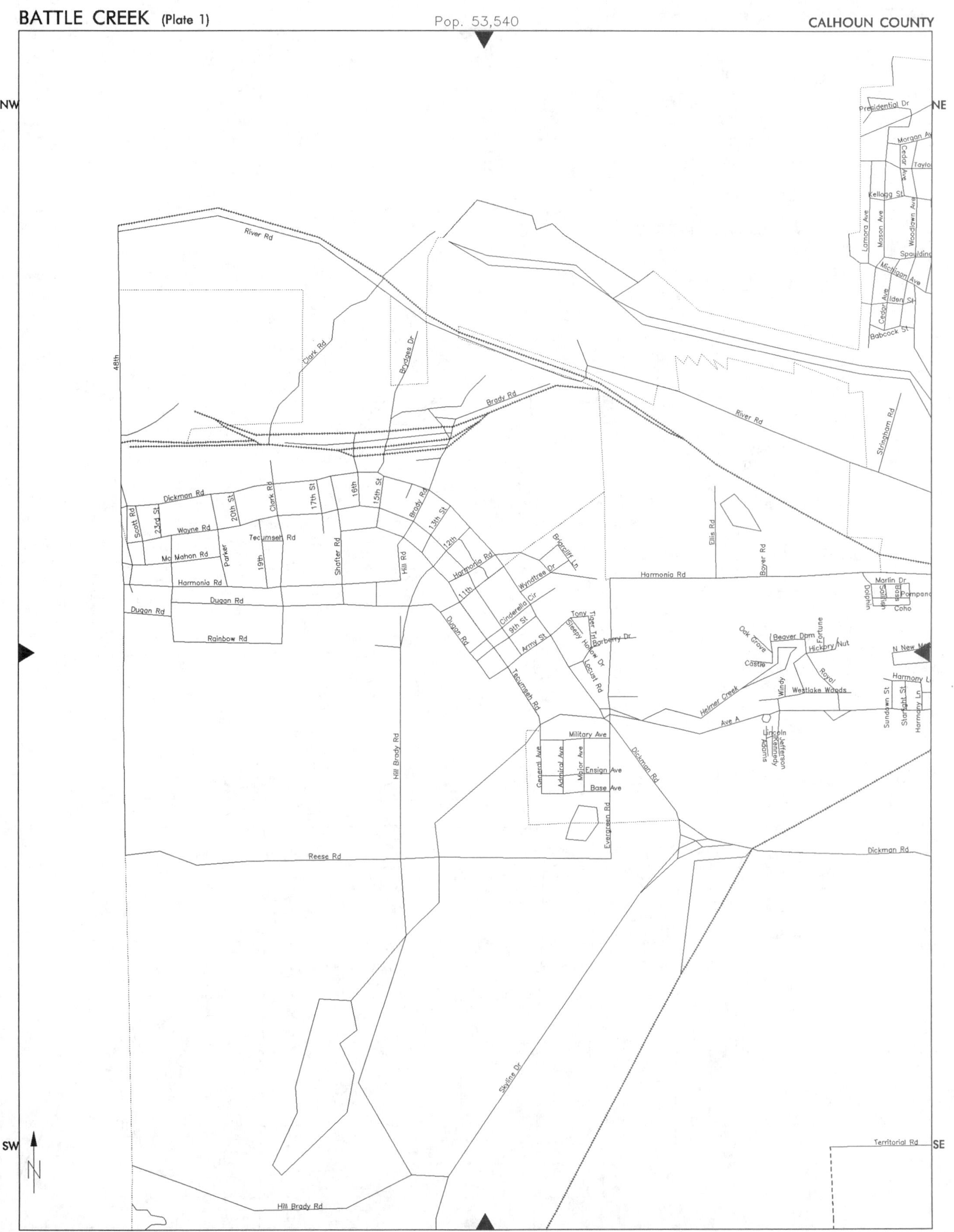
NW
NE
SW
SE
River Rd
48th
Clark Rd
Bridges Dr
Brady Rd
Dickman Rd
Scott Rd
23rd St
Wayne Rd
20th St
Clark Rd
17th St
16th
15th St
Brady Rd
13th St
12th
Tecumseh Rd
Mc Mahon Rd
Parker
19th
Shafter Rd
Hill Rd
Harmonia Rd
Harmonia Rd
11th
Briarcliff Ln.
Wyndtree Dr
Cinderella Cir
9th St
Army St
Dugan Rd
Dugan Rd
Dugan Rd
Rainbow Rd
Tecumseh Rd
Tony Tiger Trl
Sleepy Hollow Dr
Barberry Dr
Locust Rd
Military Ave
General Ave
Admiral Ave
Major Ave
Ensign Ave
Base Ave
Evergreen Rd
Dickman Rd
Hill Brady Rd
Reese Rd
Skyline Dr
Hill Brady Rd
Ellis Rd
Boyer Rd
Harmonia Rd
River Rd
Stringham Rd
Presidential Dr
Morgan Ave
Cedar Ave
Kellogg St
Lamora Ave
Mason Ave
Woodlawn Ave
Michigan Ave
Cedar Ave
Iden St
Babcock St
Marlin Dr
Dolphin
Salmon
Bass
Pompano
Coho
Oak Grove
Beaver Dam
Fortune
Hickory Nut
Castle
Royal
Windy
Westlake Woods
Helmer Creek
Ave A
Lincoln
Kennedy
Adams
Jefferson
N New
Harmony
Sundown St
Starlight St
Harmony Ln
Dickman Rd
Territorial Rd
N

Springfield city
Kalamazoo River
Conrail Railroad
NW
NE
SW
SE

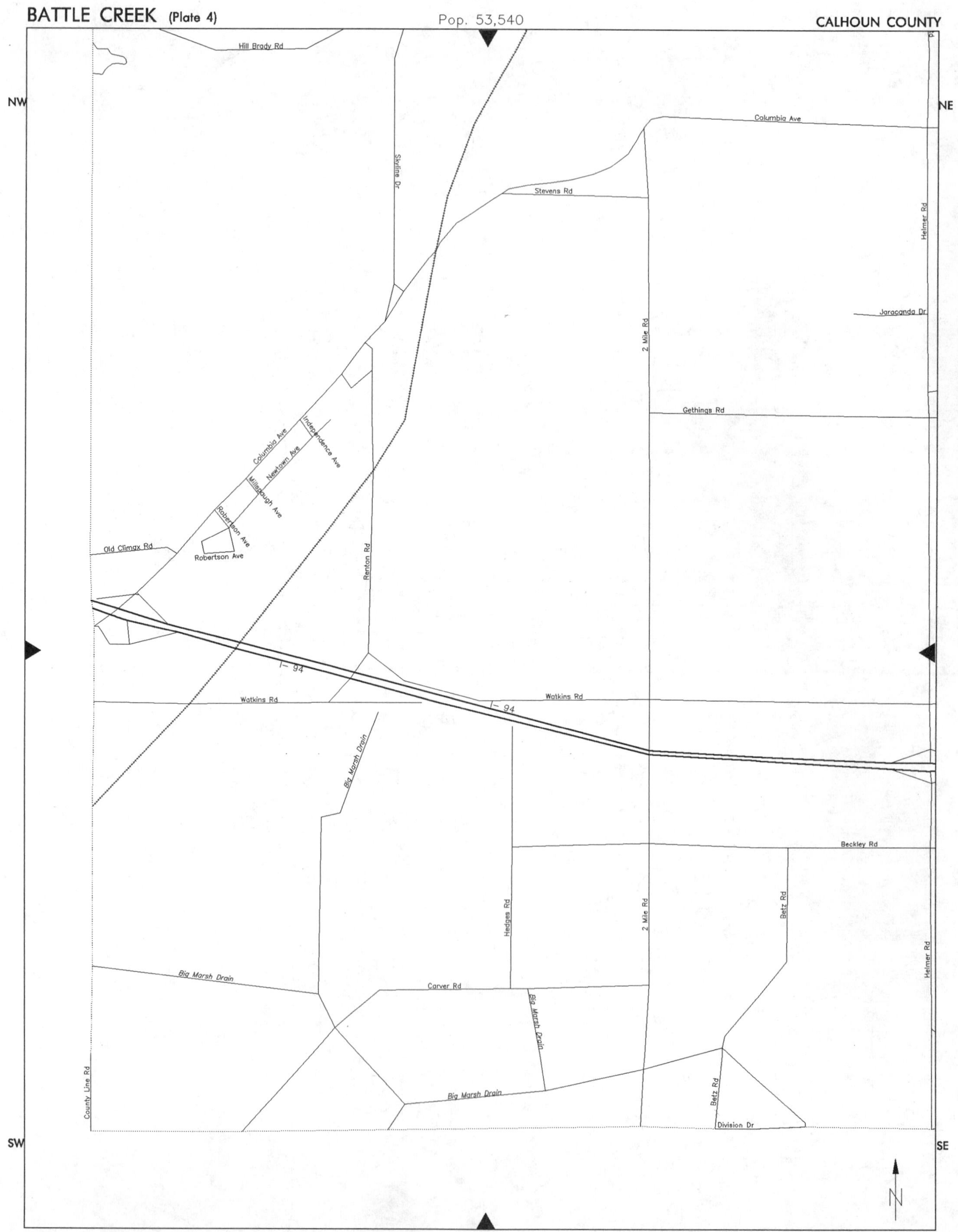
NW
NE
SW
SE
Hill Brady Rd
Columbia Ave
Skyline Dr
Stevens Rd
Helmer Rd
Jaracanda Dr
2 Mile Rd
Gethings Rd
Columbia Ave
Independence Ave
Newtown Ave
Millspaugh Ave
Robertson Ave
Old Climax Rd
Robertson Ave
Renton Rd
I- 94
Watkins Rd
Watkins Rd
I- 94
Big Marsh Drain
Beckley Rd
Hedges Rd
2 Mile Rd
Betz Rd
Helmer Rd
Big Marsh Drain
Carver Rd
Big Marsh Drain
County Line Rd
Big Marsh Drain
Betz Rd
Division Dr
N

NW
NE
SW
SE
N
Goguac Lake
Columbia Ave
Helmer Rd
Jaracanda Dr
Private Rd
Country Club Dr
Minges Channel
Bay Point Dr
Bayshore Dr
Lynwood Dr
Minges Brook
Buckley Ln
Pheasant Run Rd
Harvest Ln
Watkins Rd
I- 94
Nichols Rd
Beckley Rd
Minges Rd
Hickory St
Wealthy Ave
Fairway Dr
Fuller Dr
Hamilton Ln
Langley Rd
Beckwith Rd
Rebecca Rd
Christy Rd
Mason Rd
Knapp Rd
Summit Dr
Timothy Ln
Wildrose Ln
Sonoma Rd
Perry Rd
Tiffany
3 1/2 Mile Rd
5 Mile Rd
6 Mile Rd
State Hwy 66
I- 194
Heather Hills Dr
Greentree
Rambling
Oakbrook
Glen Cross Rd
Brickyard Creek
Minges Creek Pl
Lois Dr
Brookfield Dr
Brookfield Ct
Riverside Dr
Shortridge Dr
Birch Hill Dr
Edgebrook Dr
Minges Cir
Wah Wah Tay See Way
Beachfield Dr
Briar Hill Dr
Country Club Ter
Morningside Dr
Meadow Dr
Dover Dale
Chapel Hill Dr
Enlow Ct
Sheffield Rd
Treehaven Ln
Golden Ave
York Ave
Keystone Dr
Hayman Ave
Weeks Ave
Woods Rd
Jean Ln
Darragh Dr
Griffin Ct
Foster Dr
Columbia Ave
Lakeview Ave
Harold St
John R St
Grand Blvd Ct
Marine Dr
Leitch Ct
Highland Ave
Wentworth Ave
Iroquois Ave
Surby Ave
Latimer Ln
Waupakisco Beach
Wa Wee Nork Dr
Kelwood Ln
Sunnyside Dr
Hazelwood Ct
Wheaton Ave
Peets Cove
Pepperidge Ln
Charles E Pl
Orchard Ln
Sherman Dr
Lakeshore Dr
Blackhawk Dr
Birch Ln
Sherwood Dr
Loyd Dr
Brunswick Dr
Buick St
Alco Ave
Apperson Rd
Orleans
Westover
Devoll Ct
Arbor St
Woodrow Ave
Lillie St
Breezy Bluff
Lakewood Dr
Woodland Dr
George Pl
Lakeside Dr
Jennings Rd
Cascade Dr
Rich Ln
Shadywood Ln
Stafford Ave
Capital Ave
Leland Dr
Brewer Dr
Martha Dr
Winston Dr
Eastfield Dr
Southfield Dr
Westfield Dr
Edgehill Rd
Westway Pl
Frances Dr
Eastway Dr
Hills Dr
Oakland Pl
Williams Dr
Christopher Ln
Moorland Dr
Valleyview Rd
Minges Forest Ln
Hillbrook Dr
Oakside Dr
Parkway Dr
Hamilton Ln
Reyn Cr
Hamilton Ln
Dunham Dr
Adams Rd
Columbine Ln
Woodbine Ln
Thornapple Dr
Birchwood Ln
Watkins Ln

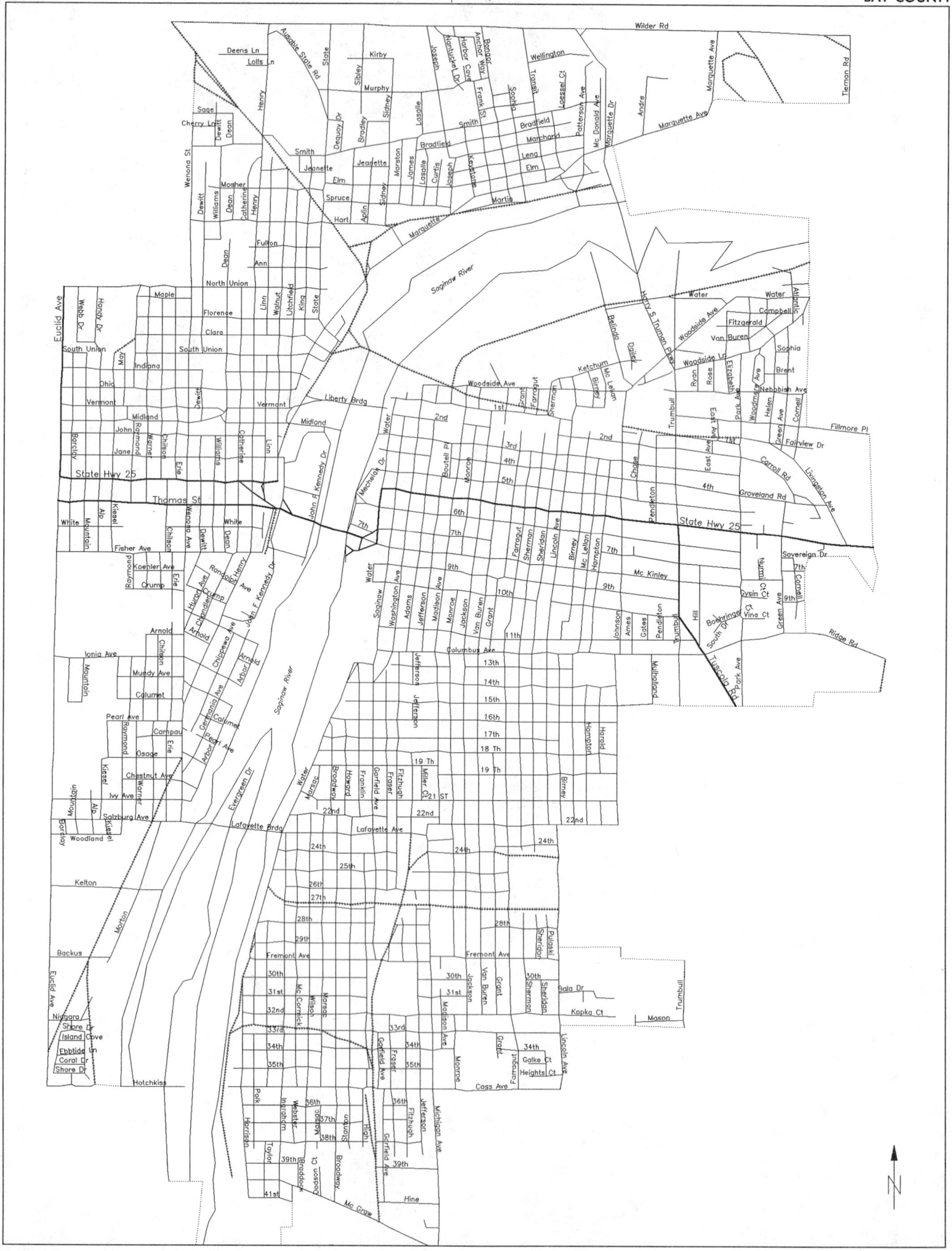

BAY CITY

Pop. 38,936

BAY COUNTY

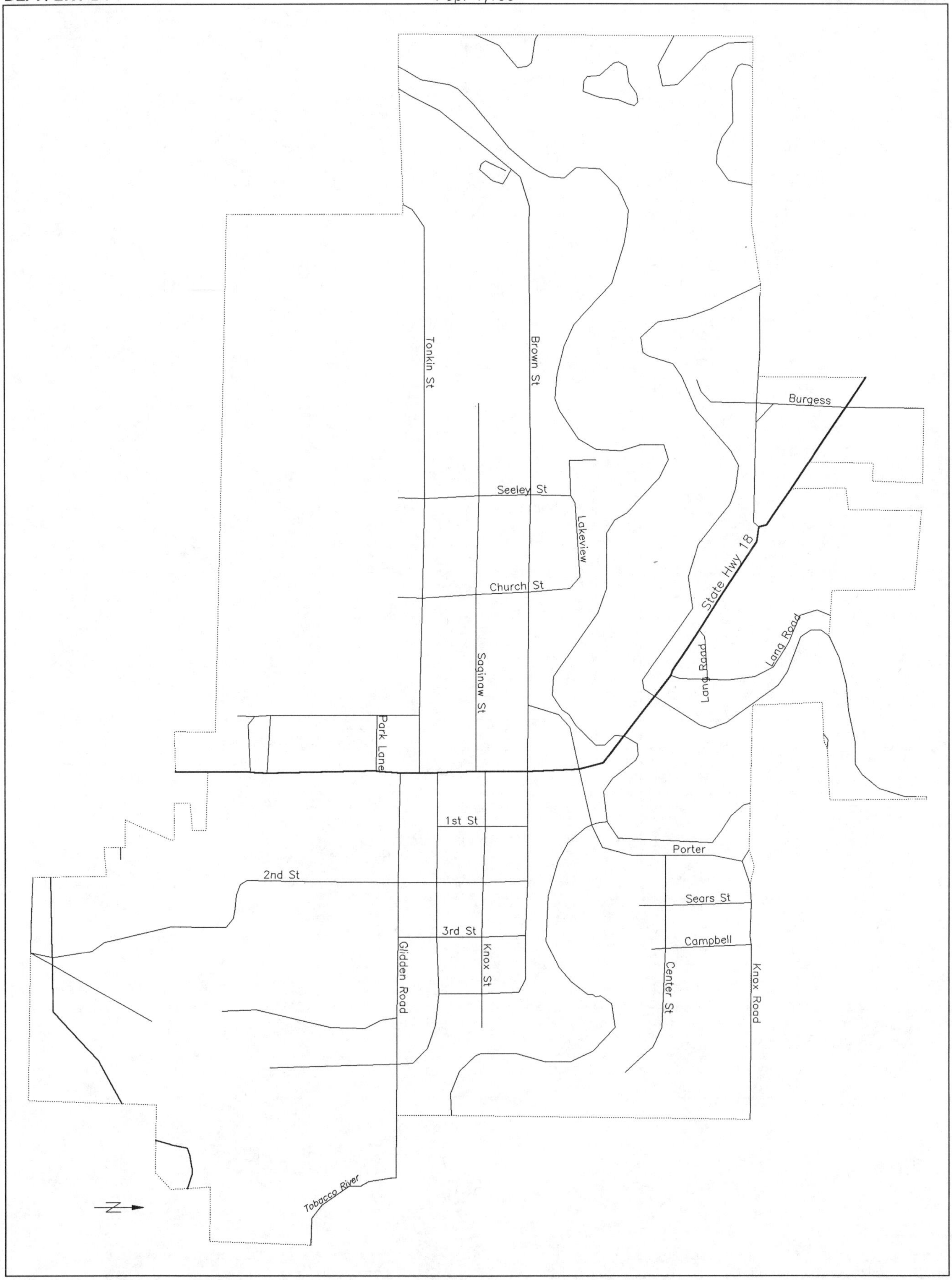

Tonkin St
Brown St
Burgess
Seeley St
Lakeview
Church St
State Hwy 18
Lang Road
Lang Road
Saginaw St
Park Lane
1st St
Porter
2nd St
Sears St
3rd St
Campbell
Glidden Road
Knox St
Center St
Knox Road
Tobacco River
N

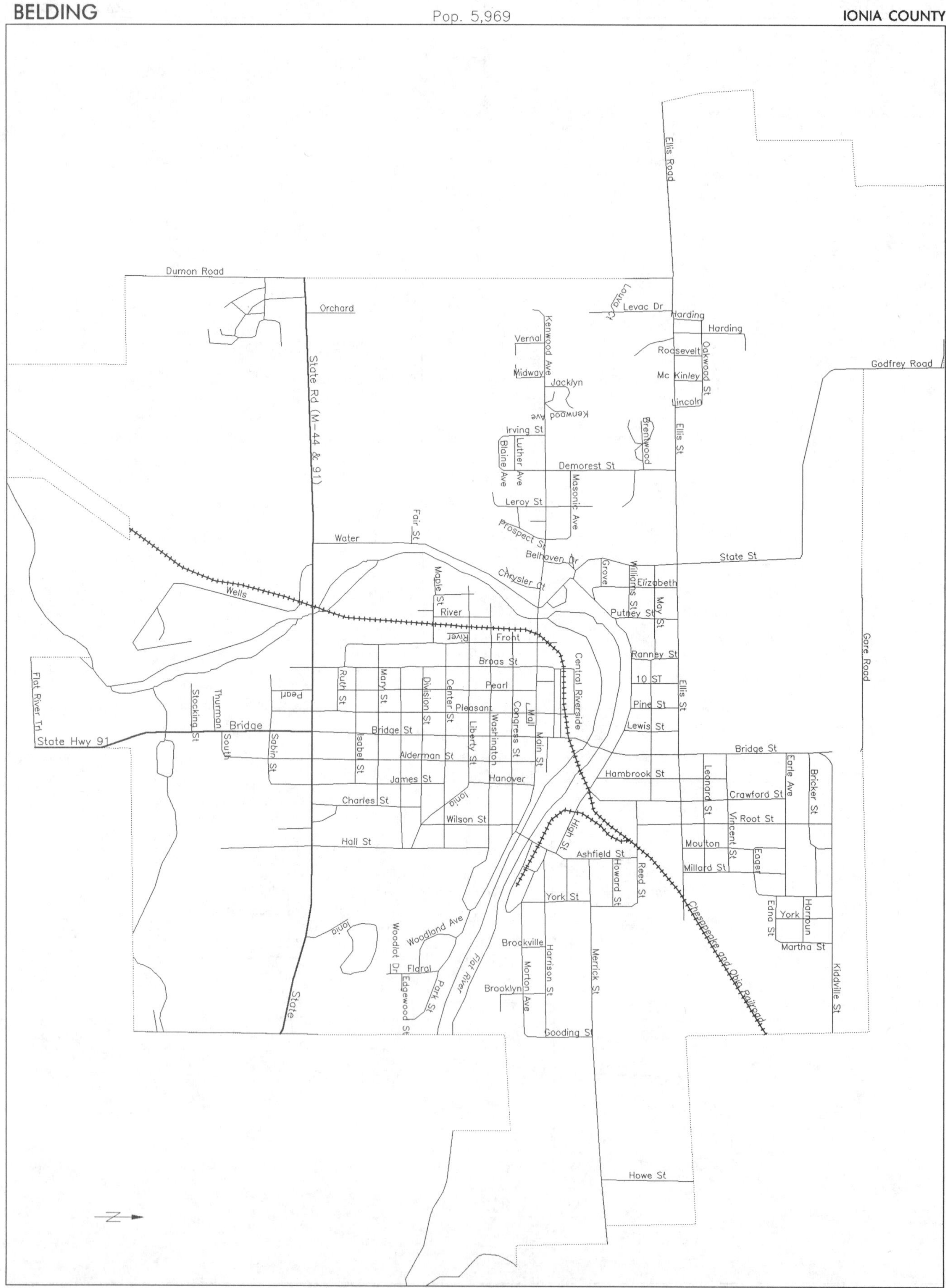
Dumon Road
Orchard
State Rd (M-44 & 91)
Ellis Road
Levac Dr
Harding
Harding
Roosevelt
Oakwood St
Mc Kinley
Lincoln
Godfrey Road
Vernal
Kenwood Ave
Midway
Jacklyn
Kenwood Ave
Irving St
Blaine Ave
Luther Ave
Brentwood
Ellis St
Demorest St
Masonic Ave
Leroy St
Prospect St
Water
Fair St
Belhaven Dr
Chrysler Ct
Grove
Williams St
Elizabeth
State St
Wells
Maple St
River
River
Front
Putney St
May St
Gore Road
Broas St
Ranney St
Central Riverside
10 ST
Pearl
Pearl
Ruth St
Mary St
Division St
Center St
Pleasant
Congress St
Mall
Pine St
Flat River Trl
Stocking St
Thurman
Bridge
Sabin St
Bridge St
Washington
Main St
Lewis St
State Hwy 91
South
Isabel St
Alderman St
Liberty St
Bridge St
Hambrook St
Leonard St
Earle Ave
Bricker St
James St
Hanover
Charles St
Ionia
Crawford St
Wilson St
High St
Vincent St
Root St
Hall St
Moulton
Ashfield St
Eager
Millard St
Howard St
Reed St
York St
Edna St
York
Harroun
Woodlot Dr
Woodland Ave
Ionia
Brookville
Harrison St
Martha St
Floral
Edgewood St
Park St
Flat River
Morton Ave
Merrick St
Chesapeake and Ohio Railroad
Brooklyn
Kiddville St
State
Gooding St
Howe St

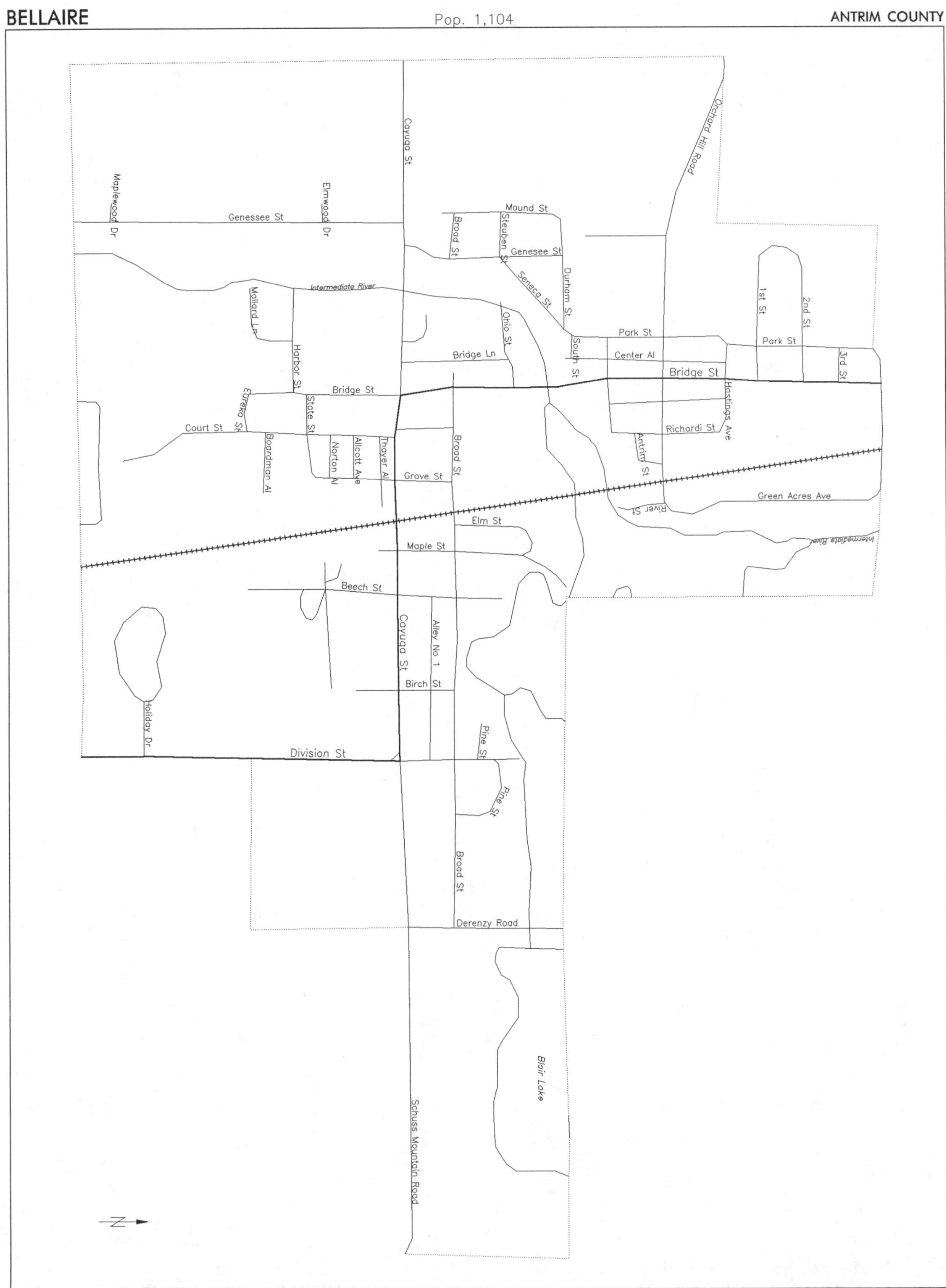
Cayuga St
Orchard Hill Road
Maplewood Dr
Elmwood Dr
Genessee St
Mound St
Broad St
Steuben St
Genesee St
Seneca St
Durham St
Intermediate River
Mallard Ln
Ohio St
Harbor St
Bridge Ln
South St
Park St
Center Al
1st St
2nd St
Park St
3rd St
Bridge St
Hastings Ave
Eureka St
Bridge St
State St
Court St
Boardman Al
Norton Al
Allcott Ave
Thayer Al
Grove St
Richardi St
Antrim St
River St
Green Acres Ave
Elm St
Maple St
Intermediate River
Beech St
Cayuga St
Alley No 1
Birch St
Holiday Dr
Division St
Pine St
Pine St
Broad St
Derenzy Road
Blair Lake
Schuss Mountain Road
N

Belleville Road
5th St
Liberty St
High St
Roys St
4th St
Main St
Charles St
3rd St
Church St
Brain St
2nd St
1st St
Edison Ave
High St
Columbia Ave
Wabash Ave
Henry St
Davis St
and W. Railroad
Liberty St
Potter Dr
Harley St
Potter Dr
Biggs Ave
Wexford Ave
Huron River Dr
Biggs Ave
Edgemont Ave
Greylock St
Bedell St
Clarence St
Roland St
Angola St
Madelon St
Robbe St
Savage St
Sheldon Road
Sumpter Road
Owen Road
Carmell
Belle Villa Blvd
Carmell
Anaheim
Spencer St
Hubbard Drain
Estrada Dr
Menlo Park Dr
Santa Clara
Menlo Park Dr
San Carlos
Hull Road
N

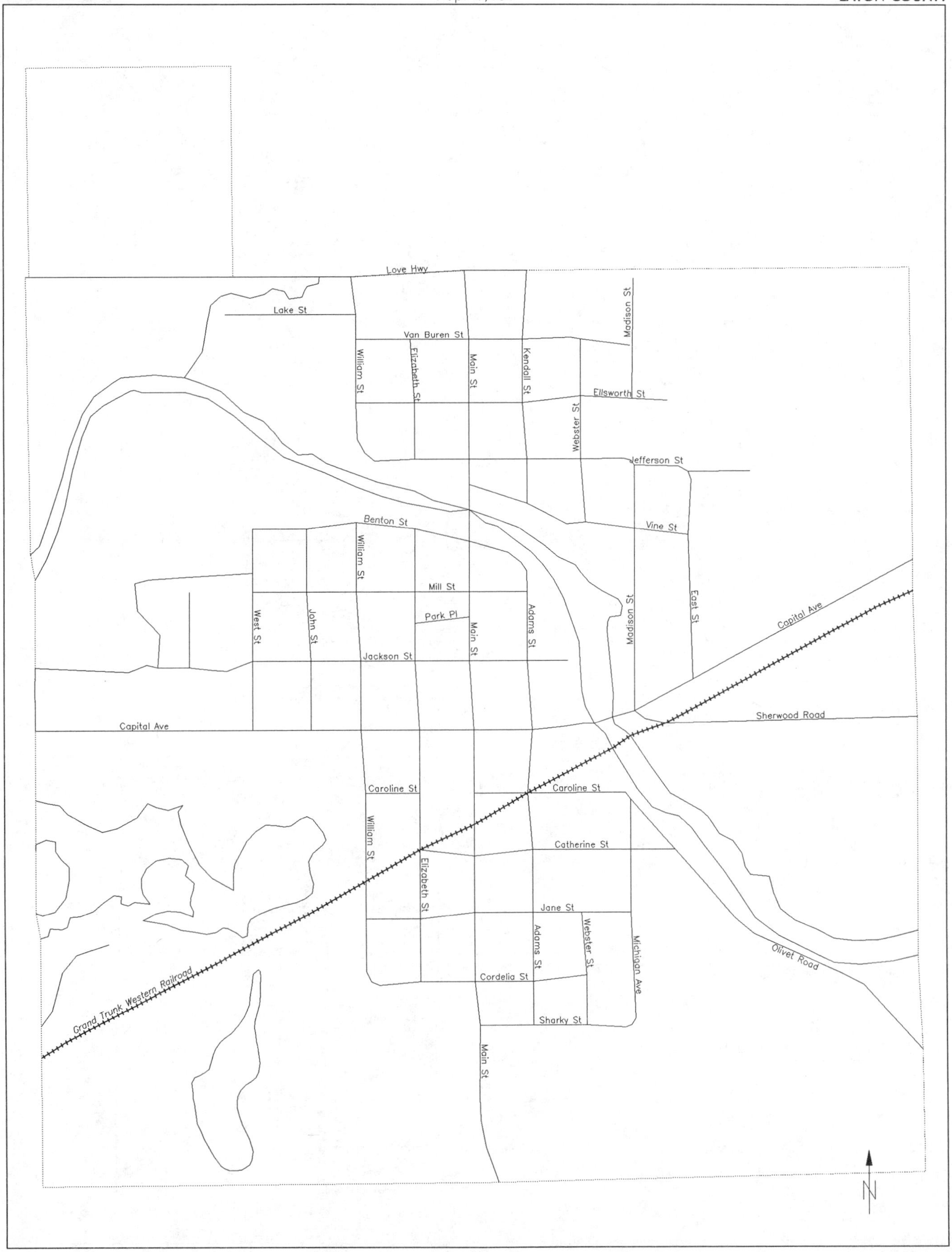

Love Hwy
Lake St
Van Buren St
Madison St
William St
Elizabeth St
Main St
Kendall St
Ellsworth St
Webster St
Jefferson St
Benton St
Vine St
William St
Mill St
Park Pl
West St
John St
Main St
Adams St
Madison St
East St
Jackson St
Capital Ave
Capital Ave
Sherwood Road
Caroline St
Caroline St
William St
Catherine St
Elizabeth St
Jane St
Adams St
Webster St
Michigan Ave
Cordelia St
Sharky St
Olivet Road
Grand Trunk Western Railroad
Main St
N

BENTON HARBOR

Pop. 12,818

BERRIEN COUNTY

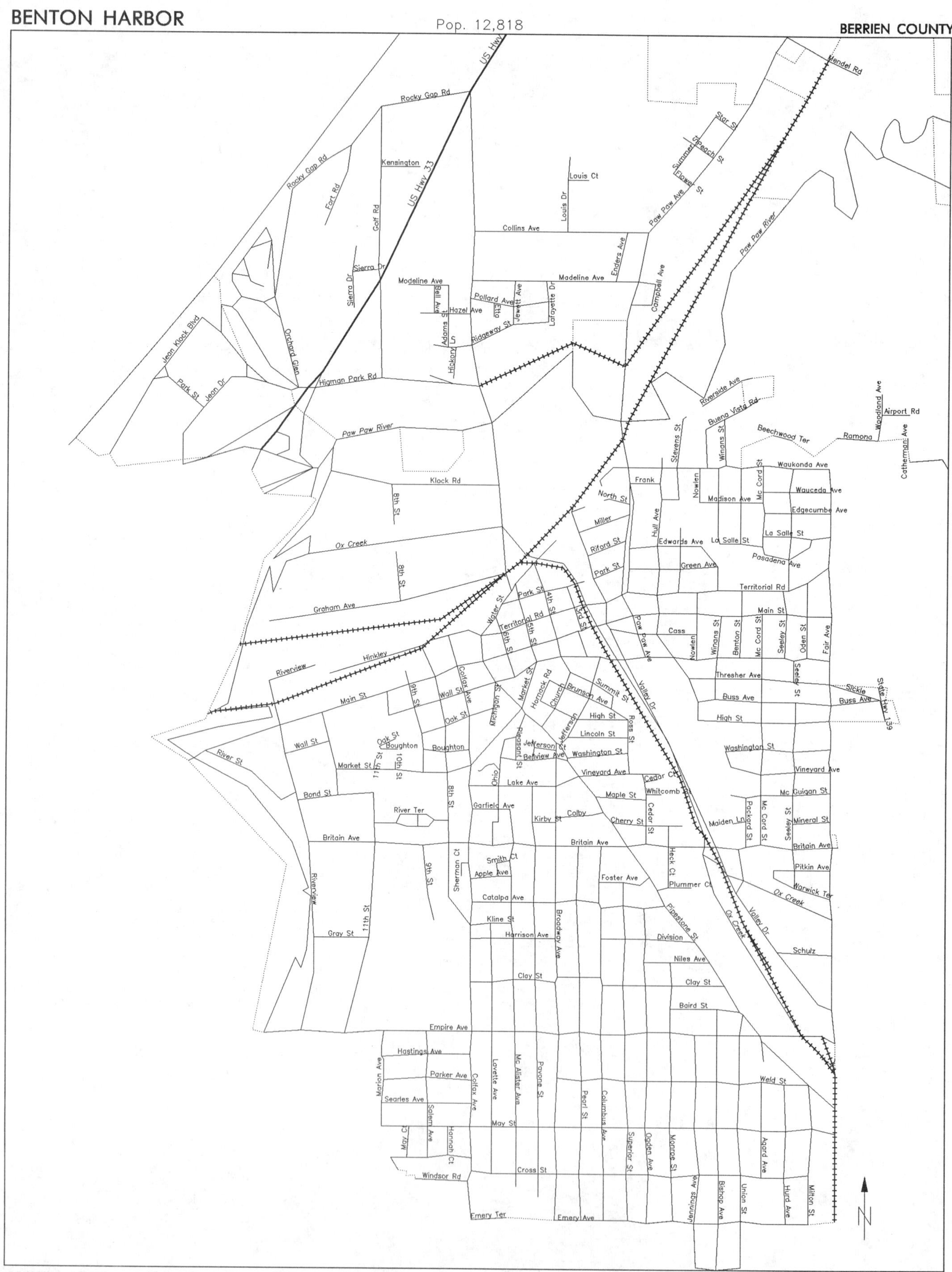

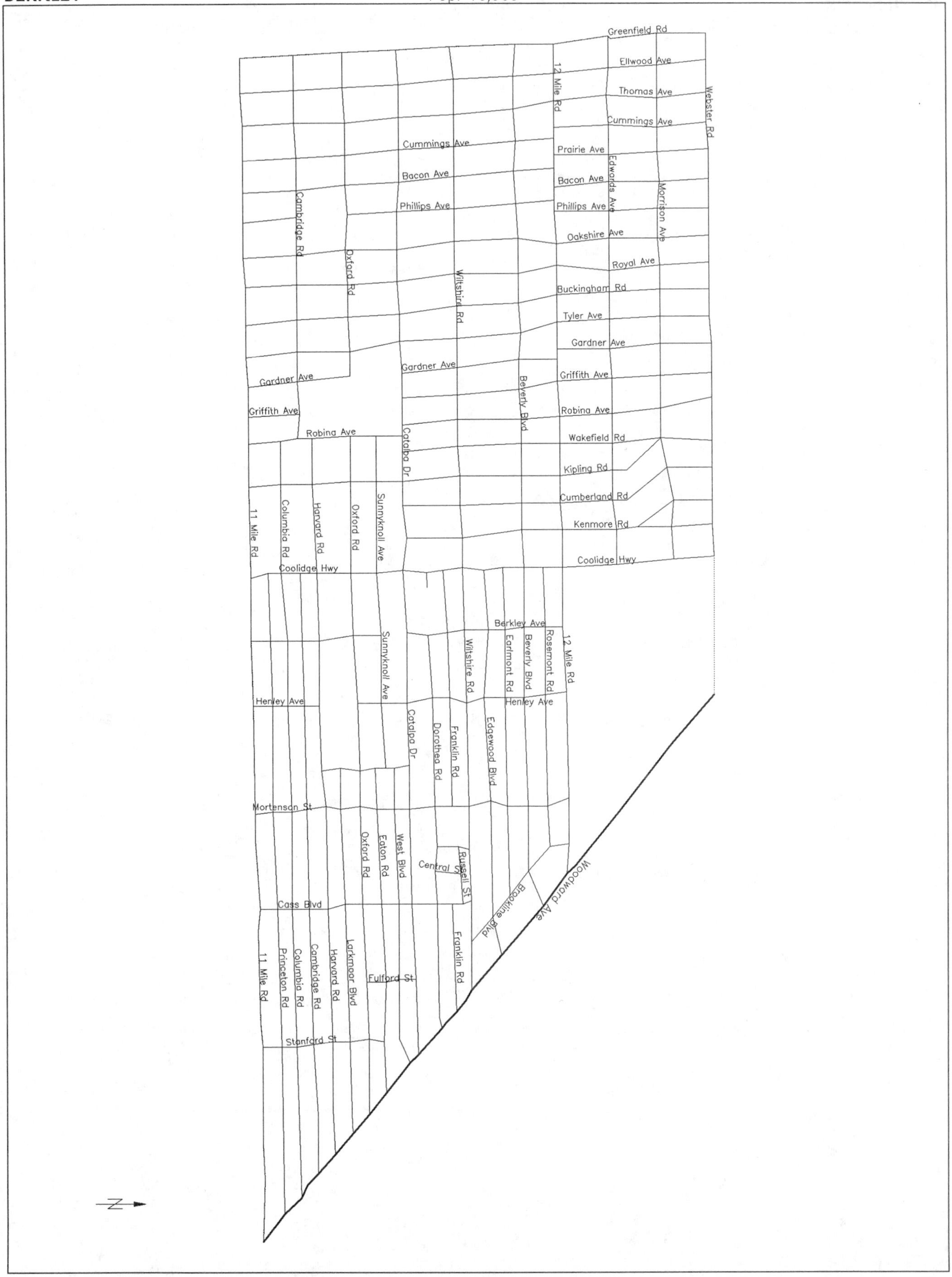
Greenfield Rd
Ellwood Ave
Thomas Ave
Cummings Ave
Webster Rd
12 Mile Rd
Cummings Ave
Prairie Ave
Bacon Ave
Bacon Ave
Edwards Ave
Morrison Ave
Phillips Ave
Phillips Ave
Oakshire Ave
Cambridge Rd
Oxford Rd
Royal Ave
Wiltshire Rd
Buckingham Rd
Tyler Ave
Gardner Ave
Gardner Ave
Gardner Ave
Griffith Ave
Griffith Ave
Beverly Blvd
Robina Ave
Robina Ave
Wakefield Rd
Catalpa Dr
Kipling Rd
Cumberland Rd
Kenmore Rd
11 Mile Rd
Columbia Rd
Harvard Rd
Oxford Rd
Sunnyknoll Ave
Coolidge Hwy
Coolidge Hwy
Berkley Ave
Sunnyknoll Ave
Wiltshire Rd
Earlmont Rd
Beverly Blvd
Rosemont Rd
12 Mile Rd
Henley Ave
Henley Ave
Catalpa Dr
Dorothea Rd
Franklin Rd
Edgewood Blvd
Mortenson St
Oxford Rd
Eaton Rd
West Blvd
Central St
Russell St
Woodward Ave
Brookline Blvd
Cass Blvd
11 Mile Rd
Princeton Rd
Columbia Rd
Cambridge Rd
Harvard Rd
Larkmoor Blvd
Fulford St
Franklin Rd
Stanford St
N

BERRIEN SPRINGS

Pop. 1,927

Highland Dr
Parn Dr
Washington
St. Joseph River
George Ave
Main St
Mechanic St
Washington
US Hwy 33
Kephart Ln
Shaker Farm Rd
Hamilton St
US Hwy 33
Union St
River Dr
Bluff St
Madison St
Broadway
Mars St
West
Ferry St
Island Park
Pardee Island
Sylester Ave
Union St
Pitt St
Mars St
Harrison St
Julius St
Murdock St
Mechanic St
Main St
Rose Hill Road
Cass St
Shawnee Road
Michigan Ave
Main St
Park St
Park Ave
Terre Coupe Road
Tudor Road
Fisher Ct
Lake Chapin
Lake St
N

US Hwy 2
Marshalk Road
Old County Road
Hill Ave
Glyuna St
Woolsey St
Hadley St
Ester Ave
Porter St
Barber St
Yale Ave
Spring St
Johnson Road
Eli Ave
Hillcrest Ave
Massie Ave
3rd Ave
2nd Ave
1st Ave
Spur St
State St
Longyear St
Galena St
Lead St
Iron St
Fairview St
Hillcrest Ave
Silver St
Gold St
Cinnabar St
Hematite St
Spring St
Granite
4th Ave
Mine St
Mine St
Colby Road
Moore St
Moore St
Carlson St
Alquist St
Langford St
St John S Road
Colby St
Sophie St
Sophie St
Case St
Case St
Tilden Road
Josephine St
Louis St
A ST
Sellar St
Longyear St
Clayberg St
Beecher St
Beecher St
Peck St
Osmose Road
Sartoris Road
Howell St
Sellar St
Rose St
Gold St
East St
Tamarack Ave
Re Road
Tilden Road
Sartoris Road
Sellar St
Chicago and Northwestern RR
Hemlock Ave
Silver St
Spruce Ave
Pine Ave
Balsam Ave
Cinnabar St
Cedar Ave
Palms Road
Lead St
Koski Road

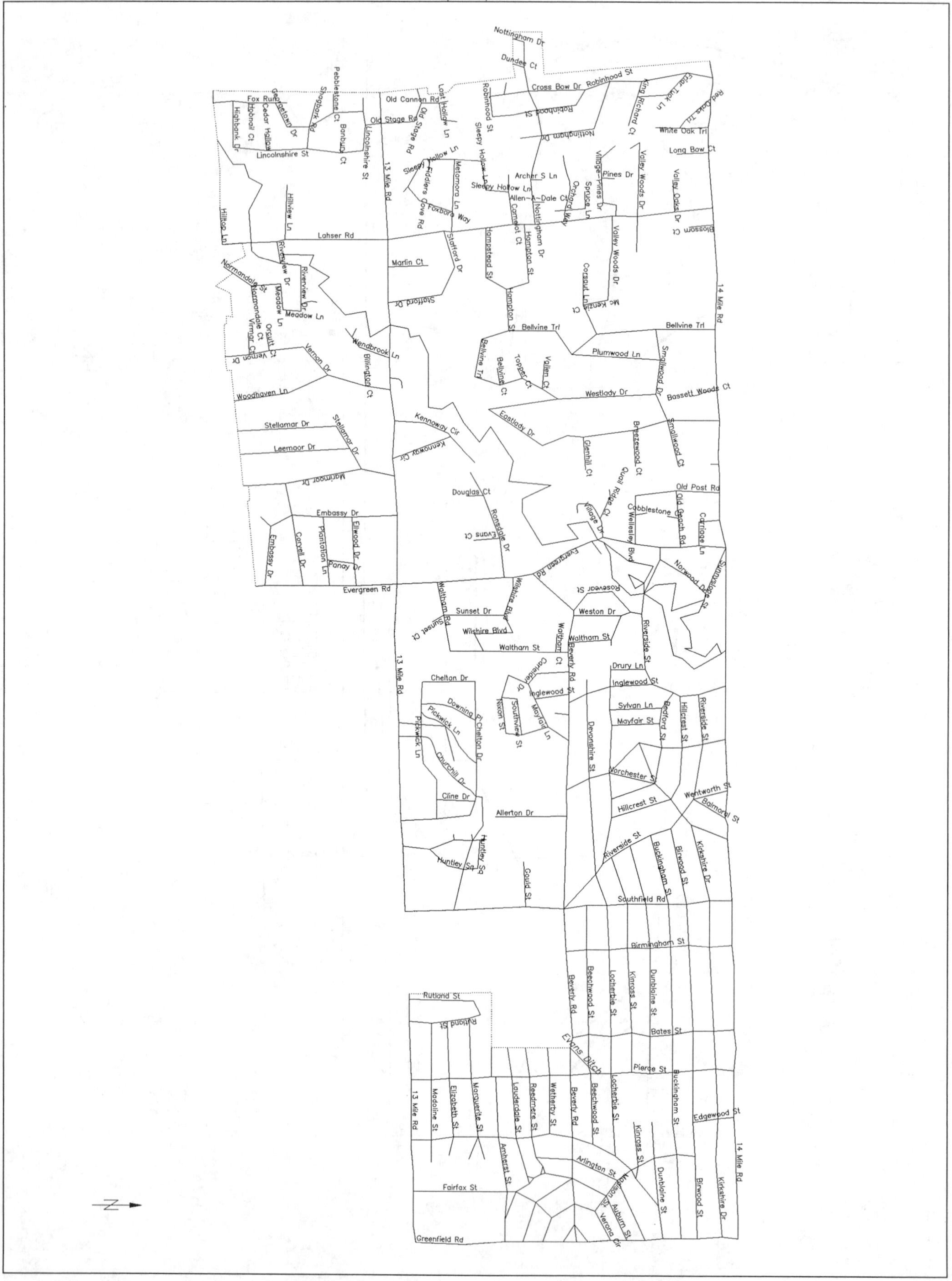

Nottingham Dr
Dundee Ct
Cross Bow Dr
Robinhood St
King Richard Ct
Friar Tuck Ln
Red Oaks Trl
White Oak Trl
Long Bow Ct
Valley Woods Dr
Valley Oaks Dr
Blossom Ct
Fox Run
Georgetown Dr
Cedar Hollow
Hobnail Ct
Highbank Dr
Pebblestone Ct
Shagbark Rd
Banbury Ct
Lincolnshire St
Lincolnshire Ct
Old Cannon Rd
Old Stage Rd
Lost Hollow Ln
Robinhood St
Sleepy Hollow St
Sleepy Hollow Ln
Fiddlers Cove Rd
Metamora Ln
Foxboro Way
Archer S Ln
Allen-A-Dale Ct
Camelot Ct
Nottingham Dr
Hampton St
Orchard Way
Spruce Ln
Village Pines Dr
Pines Dr
Hilltop Ln
Hillview Ln
Lahser Rd
13 Mile Rd
14 Mile Rd
Marlin Ct
Stafford Dr
Homestead St
Corsaut Ln
Mc Kenzie Ct
Normandale St
Riverview Dr
Meadow Ln
Orchard Ct
Virmar Ct
Vernon Dr
Wendbrook Ln
Billington Ct
Bellvine Trl
Plumwood Ln
Smallwood Dr
Bassett Woods Ct
Topper Ct
Vallen Ct
Westlady Dr
Eastlady Dr
Woodhaven Ln
Stellamar Dr
Leemoor Dr
Marimoor Dr
Kennoway Cir
Breezewood Ct
Glenhill Ct
Smallwood Ct
Quail Ridge Ct
Old Post Rd
Old Coach Rd
Carriage Ln
Cobblestone Ct
Wellesley Blvd
Village Dr
Douglas Ct
Ronsdale Dr
Evans Ct
Embassy Dr
Carvell Dr
Plantation Ln
Ellwood Dr
Ponay Dr
Evergreen Rd
Norwood Dr
Sunnyslope Ct
Rosevear St
Weston Dr
Riverside St
Waltham Rd
Sunset Dr
Sunset Ct
Wilshire Blvd
Waltham St
Waltham Ct
Beverly Rd
Drury Ln
Inglewood St
Corlette Ct
Chelton Dr
Downing Pl
Pickwick Ln
Churchill Dr
Nixon St
Southview St
Mayland Ln
Devonshire St
Sylvan Ln
Mayfair St
Bedford St
Hillcrest St
Dorchester St
Wentworth St
Balmoral St
Cline Dr
Allerton Dr
Huntley Sq
Gould St
Buckingham St
Birwood St
Kirkshire Dr
Southfield Rd
Birmingham St
Beechwood St
Locherbie St
Kinross St
Dunblaine St
Bates St
Rutland St
Evans Ditch
Pierce St
Edgewood St
Madoline St
Elizabeth St
Marguerite St
Lauderdale St
Reedmere St
Wetherby St
Amherst St
Arlington St
Auburn St
Verona Cir
Fairfax St
Greenfield Rd
N

BIG RAPIDS

Pop. 12,603

MECOSTA COUNTY

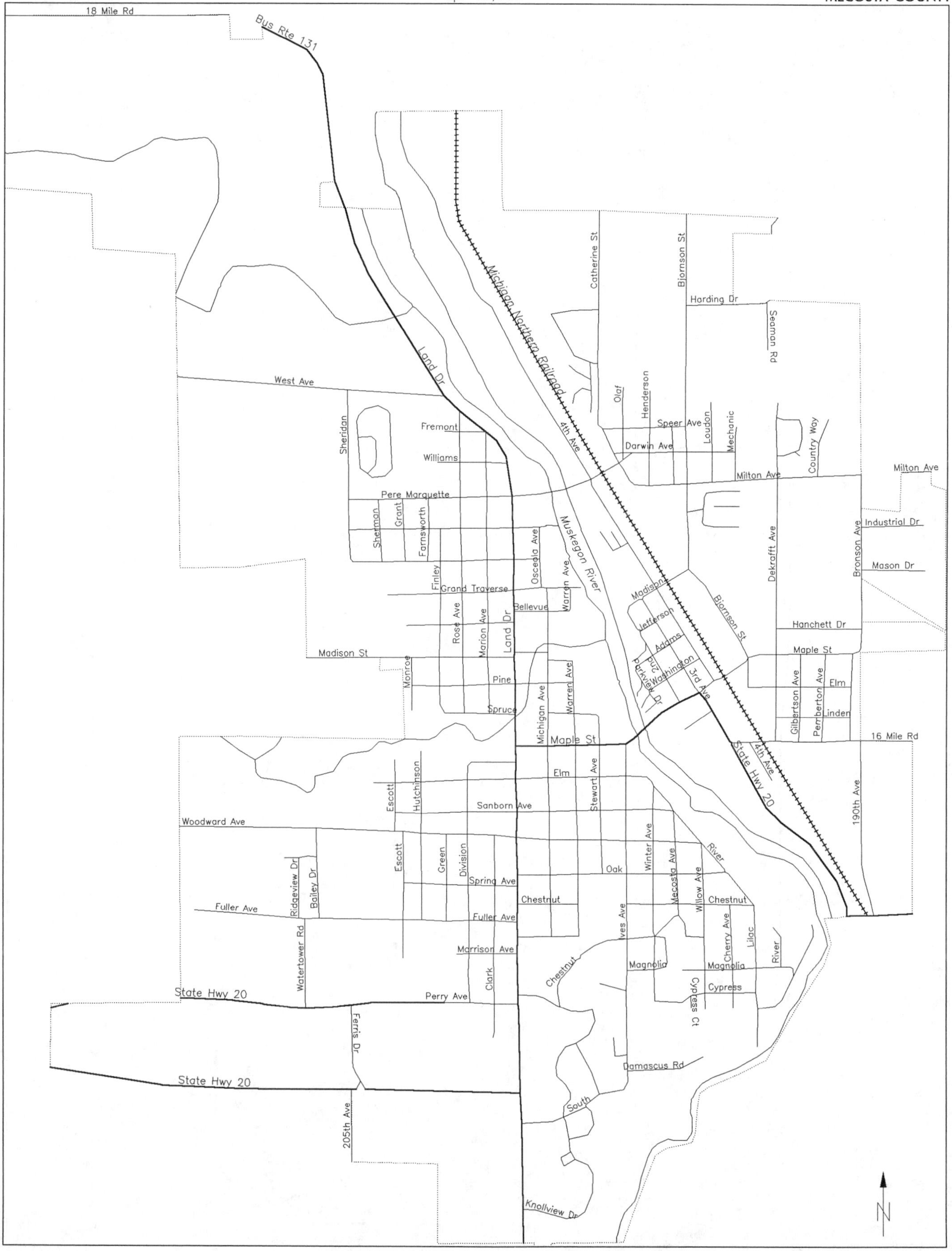

18 Mile Rd
Bus Rte 131
Michigan Northern Railroad
Catherine St
Bjornson St
Harding Dr
Seaman Rd
Land Dr
West Ave
Olaf
Henderson
Speer Ave
Loudon
Mechanic
Country Way
4th Ave
Fremont
Sheridan
Williams
Darwin Ave
Milton Ave
Milton Ave
Pere Marquette
Sherman
Grant
Farnsworth
Osceola Ave
Muskegon River
Dekrafft Ave
Bronson Ave
Industrial Dr
Mason Dr
Finley
Grand Traverse
Warren Ave
Madison
Bjornson St
Bellevue
Rose Ave
Marion Ave
Land Dr
Jefferson
Hanchett Dr
Madison St
Adams
Maple St
Monroe
Parkview Dr
2nd
Washington
3rd Ave
Pine
Warren Ave
Gilbertson Ave
Pemberton Ave
Elm
Spruce
Michigan Ave
Linden
Maple St
16 Mile Rd
4th Ave
State Hwy 20
Elm
Escott
Hutchinson
Stewart Ave
190th Ave
Sanborn Ave
Woodward Ave
Winter Ave
River
Escott
Green
Division
Ridgeview Dr
Bailey Dr
Oak
Mecosta Ave
Willow Ave
Spring Ave
Chestnut
Chestnut
Fuller Ave
Fuller Ave
Ives Ave
Cherry Ave
Lilac
Watertower Rd
Morrison Ave
Magnolia
Magnolia
River
Chestnut
Clark
Cypress Ct
Cypress
State Hwy 20
Perry Ave
Ferris Dr
Damascus Rd
State Hwy 20
South
205th Ave
Knollview Dr
N

BINGHAM FARMS

Pop. 1,001

OAKLAND COUNTY

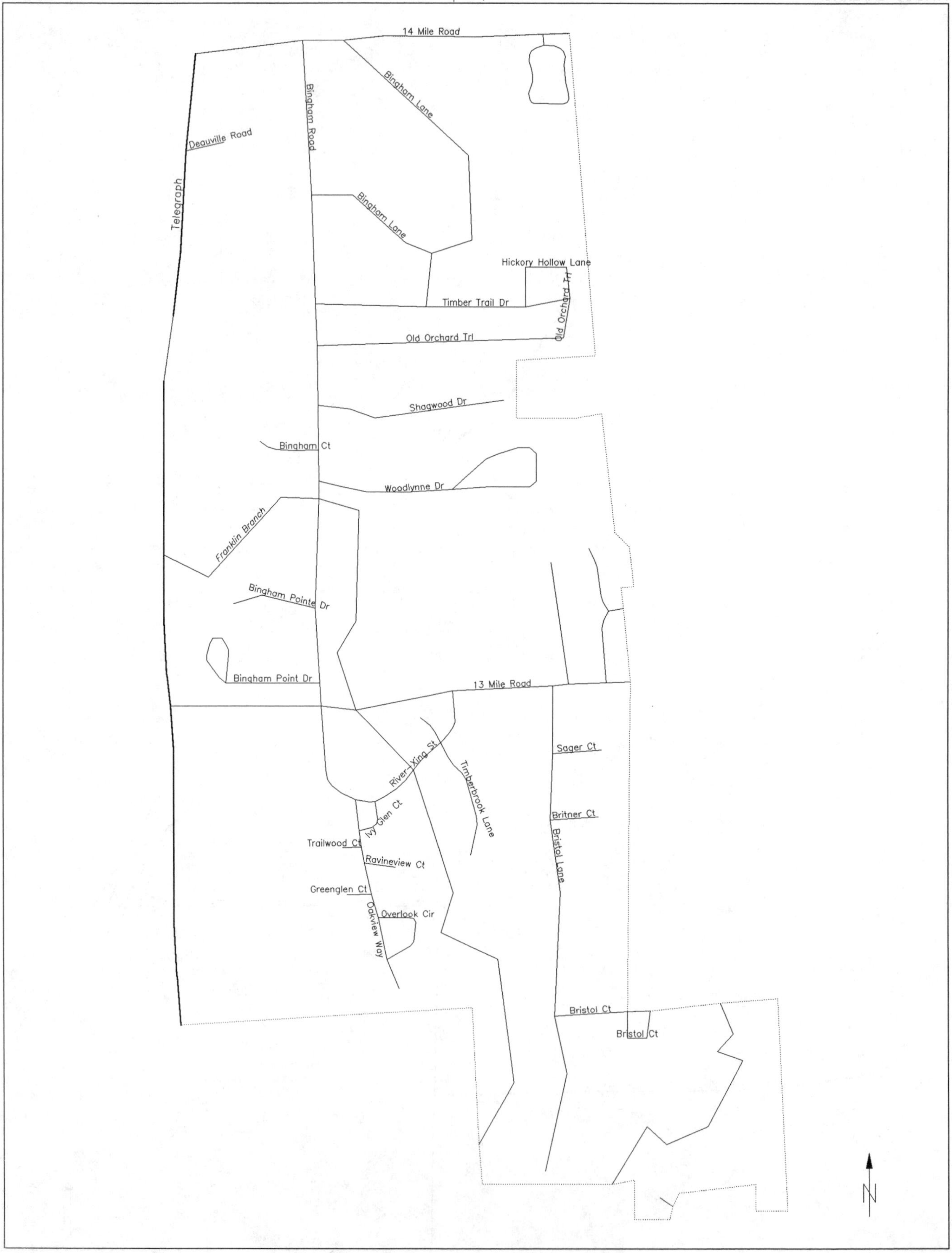
14 Mile Road
Bingham Lane
Bingham Road
Deauville Road
Telegraph
Bingham Lane
Hickory Hollow Lane
Old Orchard Trl
Timber Trail Dr
Old Orchard Trl
Shagwood Dr
Bingham Ct
Woodlynne Dr
Franklin Branch
Bingham Pointe Dr
Bingham Point Dr
13 Mile Road
Sager Ct
River Xing St
Timberbrook Lane
Ivy Glen Ct
Trailwood Ct
Ravineview Ct
Britner Ct
Bristol Lane
Greenglen Ct
Overlook Cir
Oakview Way
Bristol Ct
Bristol Ct
N

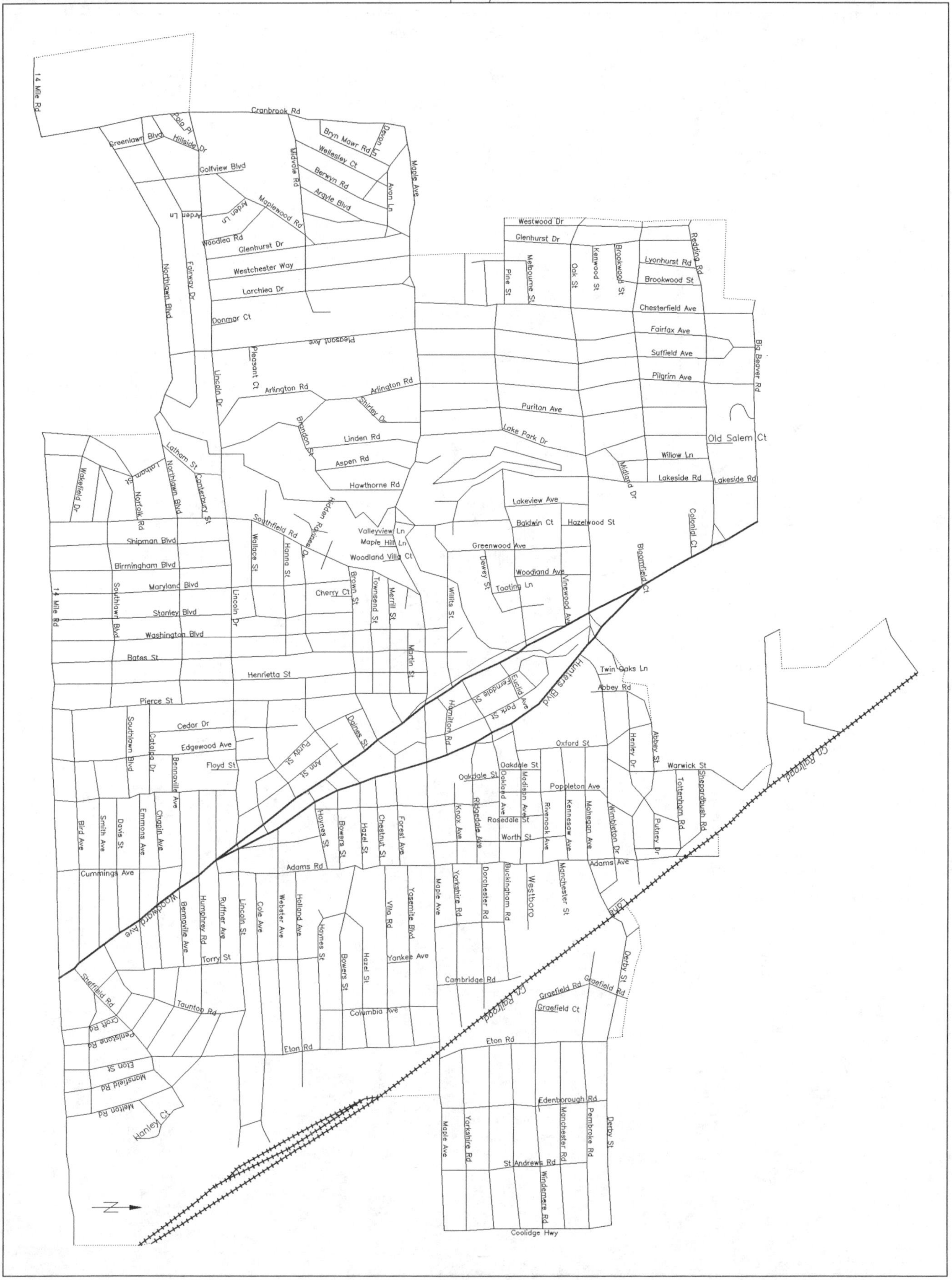

14 Mile Rd
Cranbrook Rd
Polo Pl
Greenlawn Blvd
Hillside Dr
Bryn Mawr Rd
Devon Ln
Wellesley Ct
Berwyn Rd
Argyle Blvd
Midvale Rd
Avon Ln
Maple Ave
Golfview Blvd
Arden Ln
Maplewood Rd
Woodlea Rd
Glenhurst Dr
Westchester Way
Larchlea Dr
Northlawn Blvd
Fairway Dr
Donmar Ct
Pleasant Ave
Pleasant Ct
Lincoln Dr
Arlington Rd
Shirley Dr
Brandon St
Linden Rd
Aspen Rd
Hawthorne Rd
Westwood Dr
Glenhurst Dr
Melbourne St
Pine St
Oak St
Kenwood St
Brookwood St
Redding Rd
Lyonhurst Rd
Brookwood St
Chesterfield Ave
Fairfax Ave
Suffield Ave
Pilgrim Ave
Big Beaver Rd
Puritan Ave
Lake Park Dr
Old Salem Ct
Willow Ln
Midland Dr
Lakeside Rd
Lakeside Rd
Lakeview Ave
Baldwin Ct
Hazelwood St
Colonial Ct
Bloomfield Ct
Greenwood Ave
Dewey St
Woodland Ave
Tooting Ln
Vinewood Ave
Wakefield Dr
Lathrop Rd
Latham St
Northlawn Blvd
Canterbury St
Norfolk Rd
Southfield Rd
Hidden Rd
Ravines Dr
Valleyview Ln
Maple Hill Ln
Woodland Villa Ct
Shipman Blvd
Birmingham Blvd
Maryland Blvd
Stanley Blvd
Washington Blvd
Bates St
14 Mile Rd
Southlawn Blvd
Lincoln Dr
Wallace St
Hanna St
Brown St
Cherry Ct
Townsend St
Merrill St
Willits St
Martin St
Henrietta St
Pierce St
Twin Oaks Ln
Abbey Rd
Ferndale St
Euclid Ave
Park St
Hunter Blvd
Hamilton Rd
Southlawn Blvd
Catalpa Dr
Cedar Dr
Edgewood Ave
Floyd St
Bennaville Ave
Purdy St
Ann St
Daines St
Oxford St
Henley Dr
Abbey St
Warwick St
Oakdale St
Oakdale St
Oakland Ave
Madison Ave
Poppleton Ave
Tottenham Rd
Shepardbush Rd
Bird Ave
Smith Ave
Davis St
Emmons Ave
Chapin Ave
Haynes St
Bowers St
Hazel St
Chestnut St
Forest Ave
Knox Ave
Ridgedale Ave
Rosedale St
Worth St
Rivenoak Ave
Kennesaw Ave
Mohegan Ave
Wimbleton Dr
Putney Dr
GT Railroad
Cummings Ave
Adams Rd
Adams Ave
Woodward Ave
Bennaville Ave
Humphrey Rd
Ruffner Ave
Lincoln St
Cole Ave
Webster Ave
Holland Ave
Haynes St
Villa Rd
Yosemite Blvd
Maple Ave
Yorkshire Rd
Dorchester Rd
Buckingham Rd
Westboro
Manchester St
Torry St
Bowers St
Hazel St
Yankee Ave
Derby St
Cambridge Rd
Grefield Rd
Grefield Rd
Grefield Ct
GT Railroad
Sheffield Rd
Taunton Rd
Croft Rd
Penistone Rd
Columbia Ave
Eton Rd
Eton Rd
Eton St
Mansfield Rd
Melton Rd
Hanley Ct
Edenborough Rd
Maple Ave
Yorkshire Rd
Manchester Rd
Pembroke Rd
Derby St
St Andrews Rd
Windemere Rd
Coolidge Hwy

North St
East St
South St
West St
Blissfield Hwy
River Raisin
Quick St
Beagle St
Brenot Dr
Monroe St
Maple St
Adrian St
Worth St
Franklin St
Church St
Carpenter Ave
River St
River Raisin
High St
Main St
River Dr
Sunset Dr
Haas Dr
Victory St
Woodmont St
Fairhaven Dr
Pershing St
Grant St
Lane St
Sherman St
Cross St
Railroad St
Case St
Union St
Giles St
Hazzard Ct
Joy St
Joy St
Joy St
Kingsberry Ct
Cantebury Dr
Monroe St
Pearl St
Lane St
Cherry St
Wilber St
Jefferson St
White St
Cherry St
King St
Gasner St
Depot St
Russel St
Cole St
Walnut St
Veterans Ave
Sugar St
Parkwood Ave
Jipson St
N

Hickory Glen Ln
Wishbone St
Wishbone St
Hunters Pond
Hunters Crag
Kingsley Trl
Hunt Club Dr
Hunt Club Dr
Eastways Rd
Parkman St
Randall Ln
Woodwind Dr
Chestnut Cir
Chestnut Dr
Monorwood Dr
Renton Ct
Woodward
Balfour Dr
Whitehall St
Pine Ridge
Pine Ridge
Opdyke Rd
Kensington Rd
Long Lake Rd
Hidden Valley St
Valley Rd
Rathmore Rd
Valley Rd
Valley Rd
Rathmore Rd
Scenic Oaks Dr
Tiverton Rd
Huntingwood Ln
Stonycroft St
Hillwood Dr
Tiverton Rd
Hammond Ct
Rathmore Rd
Longwood Dr
Randolph Ct
Long Lake Rd
Long Lake Rd
High Oak St
Concord Rd
Surria Ct
Barbour Ter
Long Lake Rd
Orchard Ridge Rd
Epping Ln
Vaughn Rd
Barbour Ln
Barden Rd
Barden Ct
Vaughan-Ridge Rd
Bloomfield Hills Pkwy
Kensington Rd
Conge St
Oaknob Rd
Pembroke Dr
Denbar Rd
Guilford Rd
Barden Rd
Guilford Rd
Guilford Rd
Trowbridge Rd
Burnham Rd
Whysaw Ln
Stratford Ln
Stratford Pl
Stratford Ln
Stratford Ln
Orchard Ridge Rd
Country Club Dr
Barden Rd
Keswick Rd
Barden Rd
Eton Cross Rd
Burnham Rd
Kingsbrook Ln
Canterbury Rd
Valley Way
Tamarack Way
Ridgewood Rd
Vaughn Rd
Faculty Way
Faculty Way
Cranbrook Lake
Cranbrook Rd
Brady Ln
Kingsley Manor Dr
Barbara Ln
Windemere
Canterbury Cres
Hillcrest Dr
Orchard Ridge Rd
Academy Way
Edgemere St
Lone Pine Hill Rd
Linda Ln
Linda Knoll St
Warrington St
Willow Glen
Charing Cross Ct
Lahser Rd
Lonepine Rd
Lonepine Rd
Thetford Ln
Bennington Dr
Bennington Dr
Rudgate Rd
Lone Pine Ct
Martell Rd
Goodhue Rd
Cedar Rd
Goodhue Rd
Goodhue Rd
Cranbrook Rd
Cranbrook Ct
Kennebec Ct
Woods Hole Way
Martell Rd
Dunston Rd
Endicott Lake
Lakewood St
Chesterfield Rd
Falmouth Dr
Rudgate Rd
Marblehead Dr
Sebago Ln
Joyce Ct
Haverhill Dr
Woodridge Rd
Doningham Ln
Lowell Ct
Woodberry Dr
Hilltop Ct
Endicott St
Endicott St
Yarboro Dr
Haverhill Dr
Harlan Dr
Dunston Ct
Dunston Rd
Cabot Pl
Merrimac Ct
Nantucket Dr
Martell Rd
Quarton Ln
Orchard Ln
N

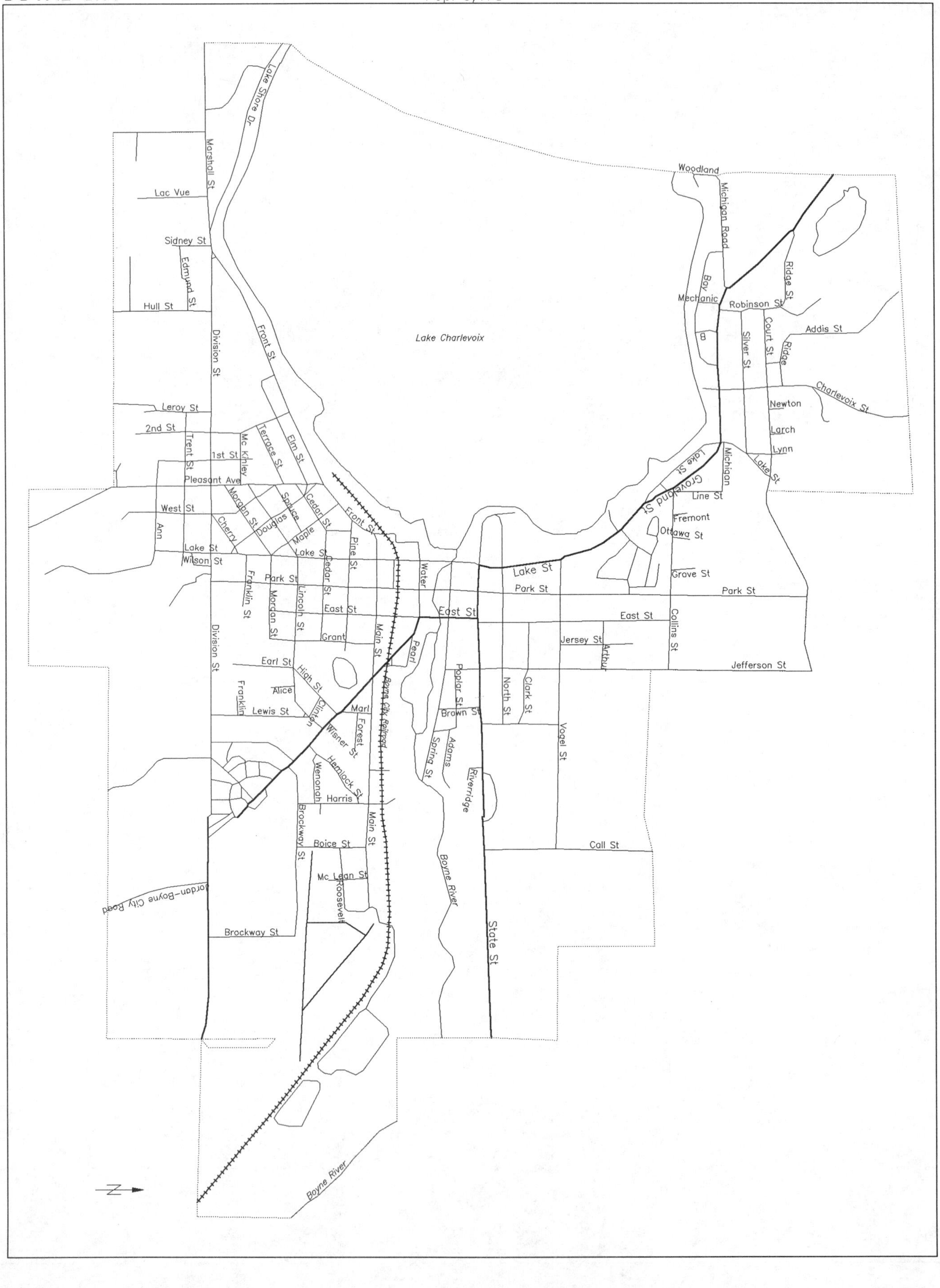
Lake Charlevoix
Lake Shore Dr
Marshall St
Lac Vue
Sidney St
Edmund St
Hull St
Division St
Front St
Leroy St
2nd St
Trent St
1st St
Mc Kinley
Terrace St
Elm St
Pleasant Ave
West St
Morgan St
Spruce
Cedar St
Douglas
Cherry
Maple
Front St
Ann
Lake St
Wilson St
Lake St
Pine St
Cedar St
Water
Park St
Franklin St
Morgan St
Lincoln St
East St
Grant
Main St
Pearl
East St
Earl St
High St
Alice
Franklin
Lewis St
Clinton
Marl
Wisner St
Forest
Boyne City Railroad
Hemlock St
Wenonah
Harris
Brockway St
Boice St
Main St
Mc Lean St
Roosevelt
Jordan-Boyne City Road
Brockway St
Poplar St
Brown St
Spring St
Adams
Riverridge
Boyne River
State St
North St
Clark St
Vogel St
Call St
Lake St
Park St
East St
Jersey St
Arthur
Jefferson St
Collins St
Park St
Grove St
Ottawa St
Fremont
Line St
Groveland St
Lake St
Michigan
Woodland
Michigan Road
Bay
Mechanic
Robinson St
Ridge St
Silver St
Court St
Ridge
Addis St
Charlevoix St
Newton
Larch
Lynn
Lake St
Boyne River
N

BRECKENRIDGE Pop. 1,301 **GRATIOT COUNTY**

Olive Road
Eaton St
Mc Clelland Road
Elm St
Wisner Road
Pine St
Summit St
Maple St
Sexton St
Eastman St
Spruce St
Wright St
Main St
Chesapeake and Ohio Railroad
Saginaw St (M-46)
Saginaw St
Pine St
Chestnut St
Chestnut St
2nd St
3rd St
4th St
5th St
6th St
7th St
Cedar Ct
Cedar St
Birch St
8th St
1st St
N

Circle Dr
Circle Dr
Dunewood Dr
Big Beech Trl
Kevin Dr
Hillside Ct
Evergreen Dr
Bridgman Park Road
Circle Hill Dr
Butternut St
Basswood St
Hazel St
Beechnut St
Circle Hill Dr
Hillside Ct
Thompson Ct
Karen Ct
Ridge Rd
Dunewood Dr
Red Arrow Hwy
Rambo Road
I–94
Vista Dr
Donna Dr
Floral
Floral
Baldwin Road
Chesapeake and Ohio Railroad
Toth St
Oak St
Vine St
Pine St
Vineyard Ave
Maplewood Ave
Wilton St
Cherry St
Maple St
Legion St
Post St
Orchard St
Park St
Millard Ave
Mathieu St
Elm St
Oak St
Vine St
Church St
Church St
Clark St
Papalardo St
Pearl Ave
Lake St
Tower St
School St
Vine St
Gast Road
N

BRIGHTON

Pop. 5,686

LIVINGSTON COUNTY

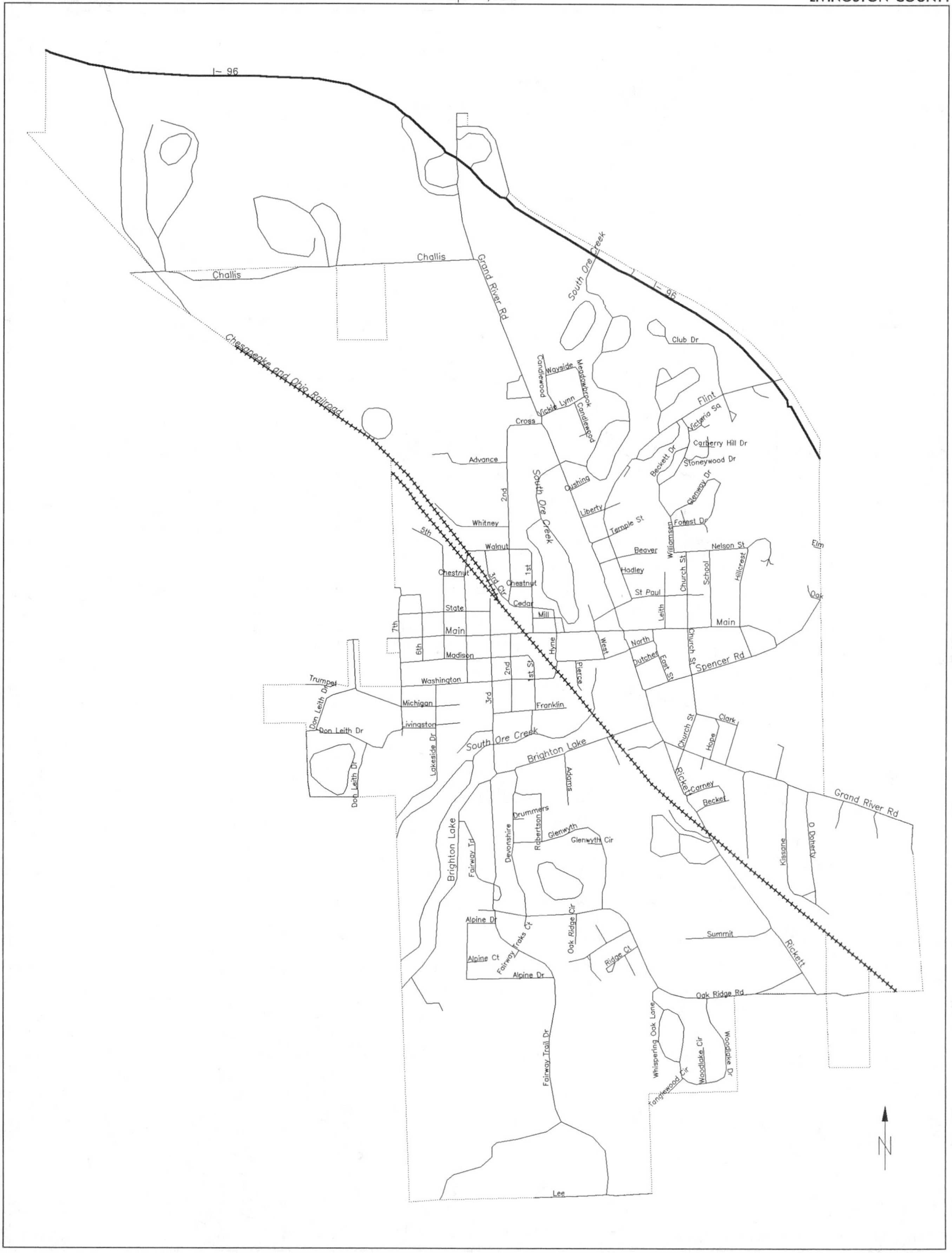

BRONSON

Pop. 2,342

BRANCH COUNTY

BROOKLYN

Pop. 1,027

JACKSON COUNTY

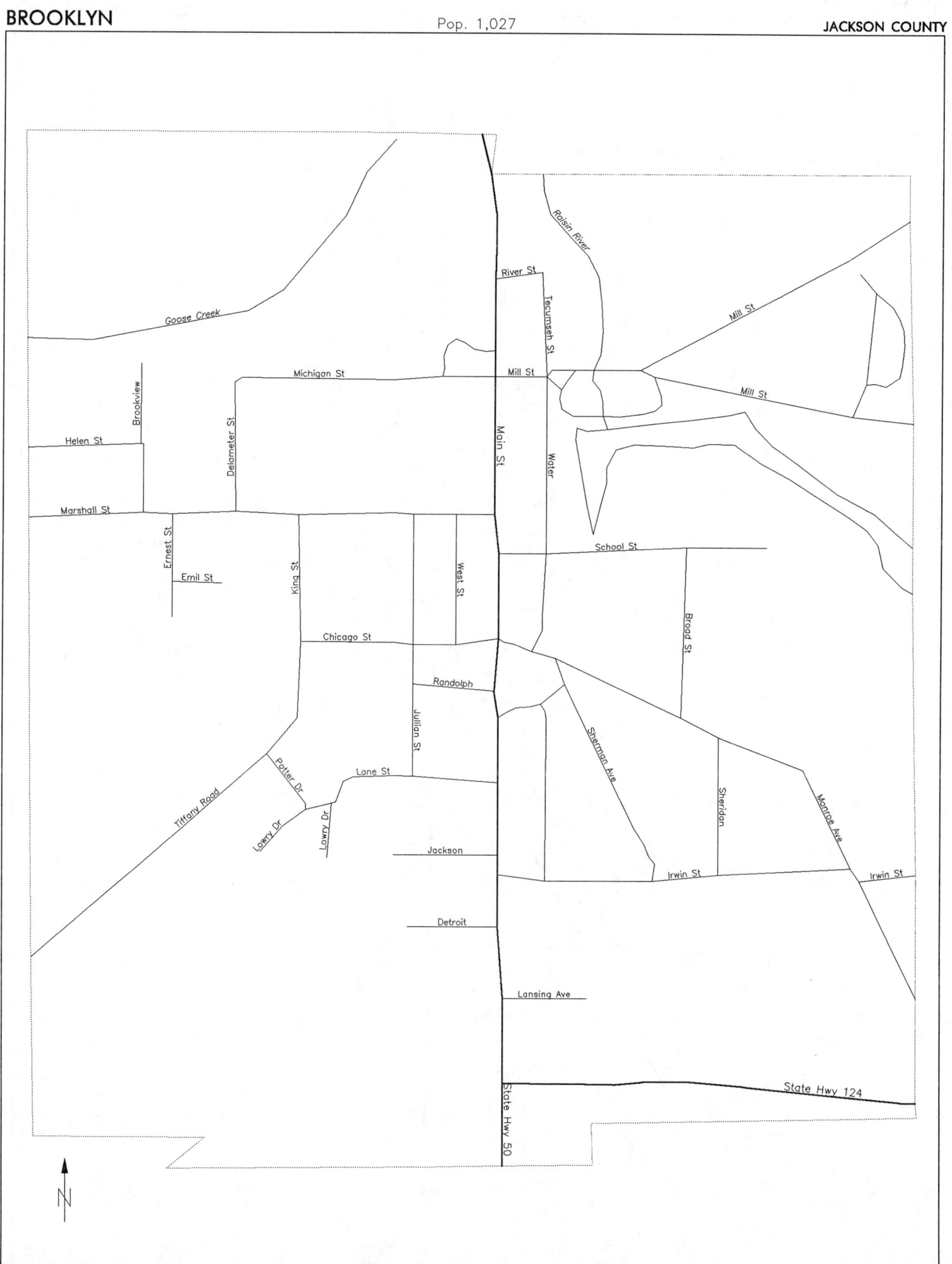

Cade Road
Cade Road
Belview Road
Main St
Vine
Thelman
George St
2nd St
Reed St
Grant
Wood
Lincoln St
Lincoln Road
Welles St
Maple
Vine
4th St
Walter St
Maple St
2nd St
3rd St
1st
Main St
Ruby Road
Maple Valley Road
Lapeer and Sanilac Drain

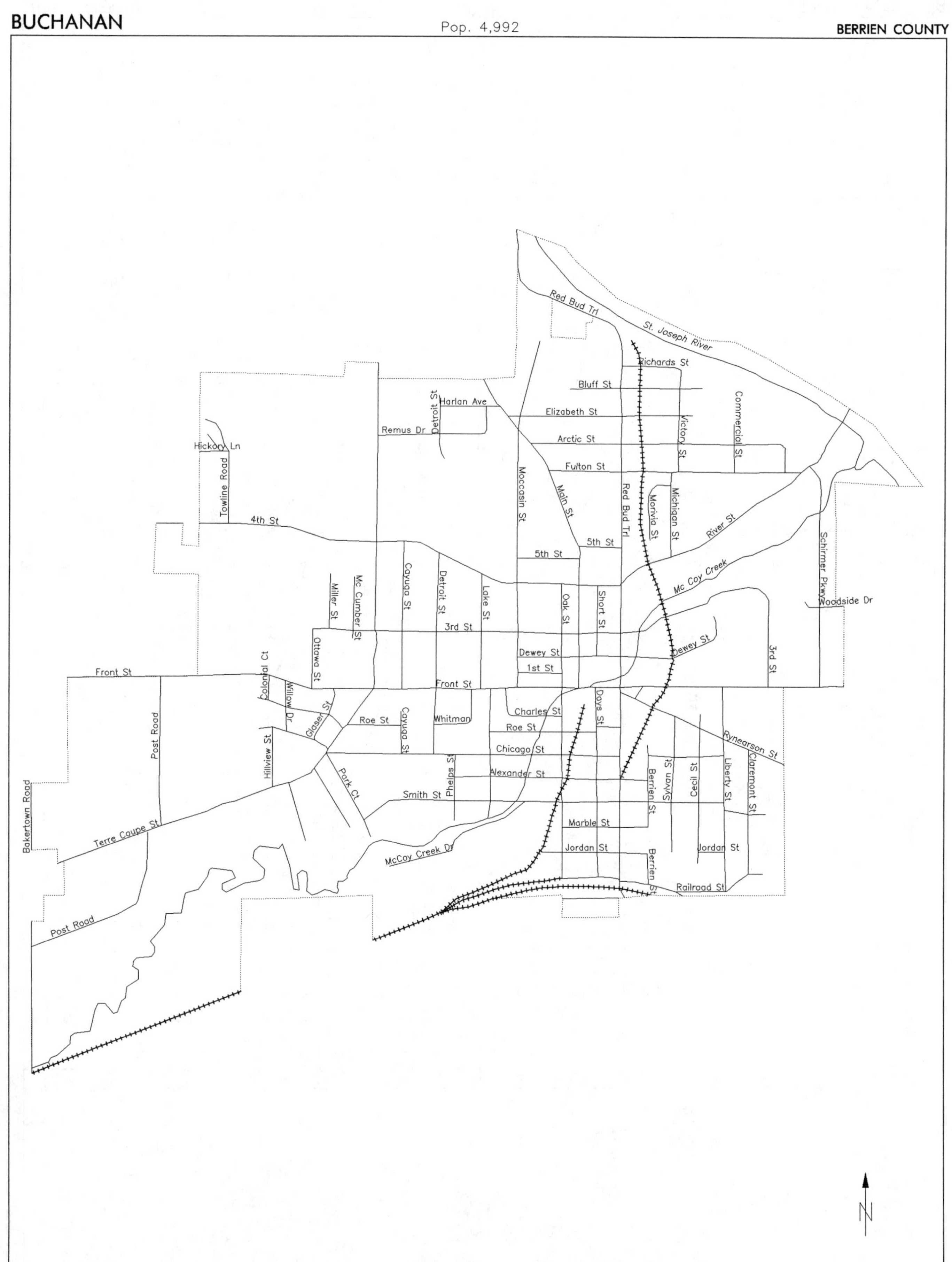
Red Bud Trl
St. Joseph River
Richards St
Bluff St
Harlan Ave
Detroit St
Elizabeth St
Remus Dr
Arctic St
Victory St
Commercial St
Hickory Ln
Fulton St
Towline Road
Moccasin St
Main St
Red Bud Trl
Morivia St
Michigan St
4th St
River St
5th St
5th St
Schirmer Pkwy
Mc Coy Creek
Woodside Dr
Mc Cumber St
Cayuga St
Detroit St
Lake St
Oak St
Short St
Miller St
3rd St
Ottawa St
Dewey St
Dewey St
3rd St
Colonial Ct
1st St
Front St
Front St
Willow Dr
Charles St
Days St
Glaser St
Roe St
Cayuga St
Whitman
Roe St
Post Road
Hillview St
Chicago St
Rynearson St
Claremont St
Phelps St
Alexander St
Sylvan St
Cecil St
Liberty St
Park Ct
Smith St
Berrien St
Bakertown Road
Terre Coupe St
Marble St
Jordan St
Jordan St
McCoy Creek Dr
Berrien St
Railroad St
Post Road
N

I- 475
Bristol Rd
Saginaw Rd
Dort Hwy
Plate # 2
Center Rd
Plate # 1
Atherton Rd
Davison Rd
Genesee Rd
Maple Ave
Bristol Rd
Potter Rd
Potter Blvd
Lapeer Rd
Belsay Rd
Belsay Rd
I- 69
Vassar Rd
Vassar Rd
N

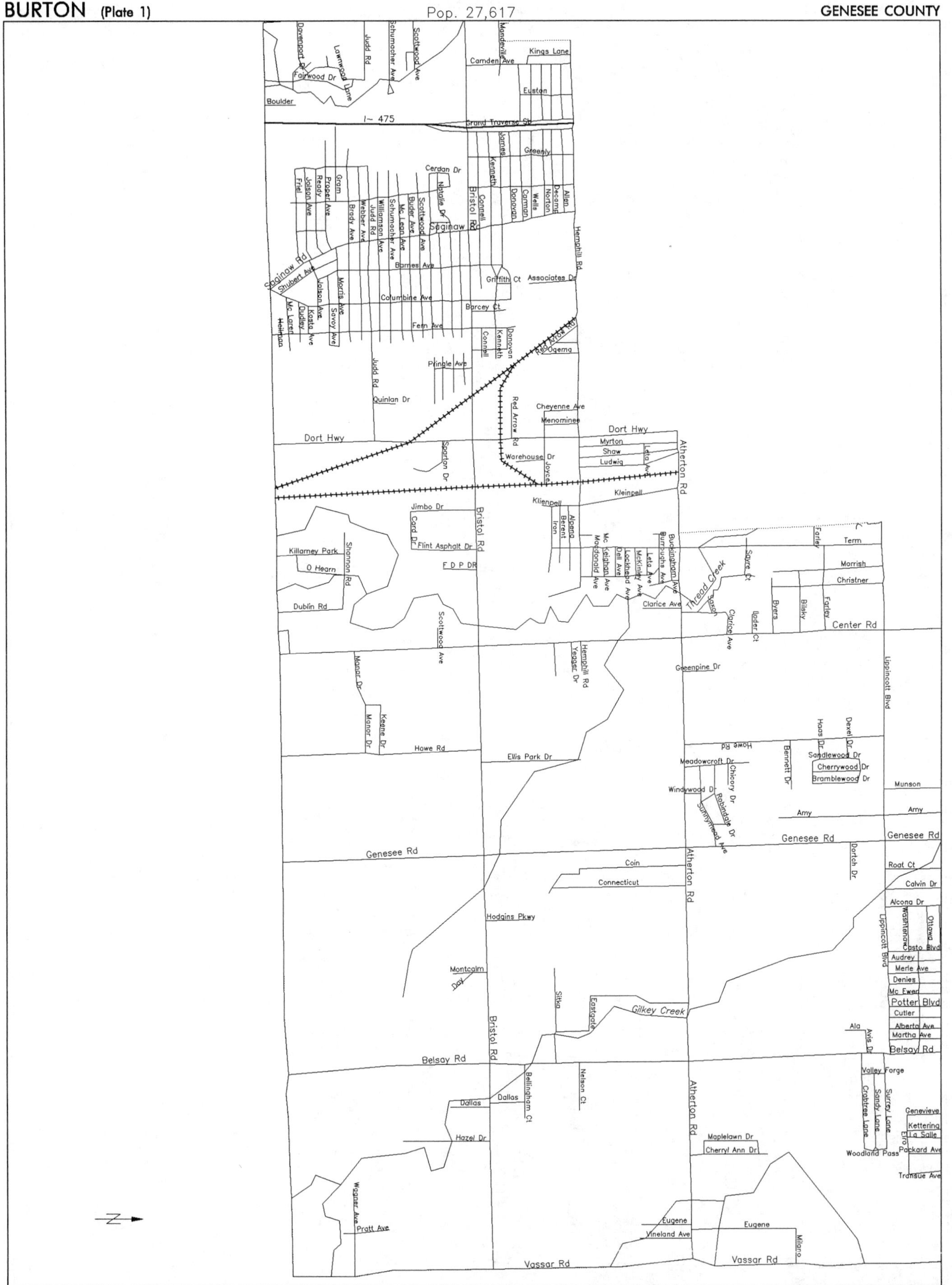
I-475
Grand Traverse St
Dort Hwy
Saginaw Rd
Bristol Rd
Hemphill Rd
Atherton Rd
Center Rd
Howe Rd
Genesee Rd
Belsay Rd
Vassar Rd
Lippincott Blvd
Potter Blvd
Thread Creek
Gilkey Creek
Red Arrow Rd
Judd Rd
Scottwood Ave
Columbine Ave
Barnes Ave
Fern Ave
Kings Lane
Camden Ave
Euston
Boulder
Fairwood Dr
Connecticut
Coin
Hodgins Pkwy
Maplelawn Dr
Cherryl Ann Dr
Eugene
Vineland Ave
Pratt Ave
Hazel Dr
Dallas
Ellis Park Dr
Genesee Rd
Amy
Munson
Clarice Ave
Kleinpell
Jimbo Dr
Flint Asphalt Dr
Killarney Park
O Hearn
Dublin Rd
Shannon Rd

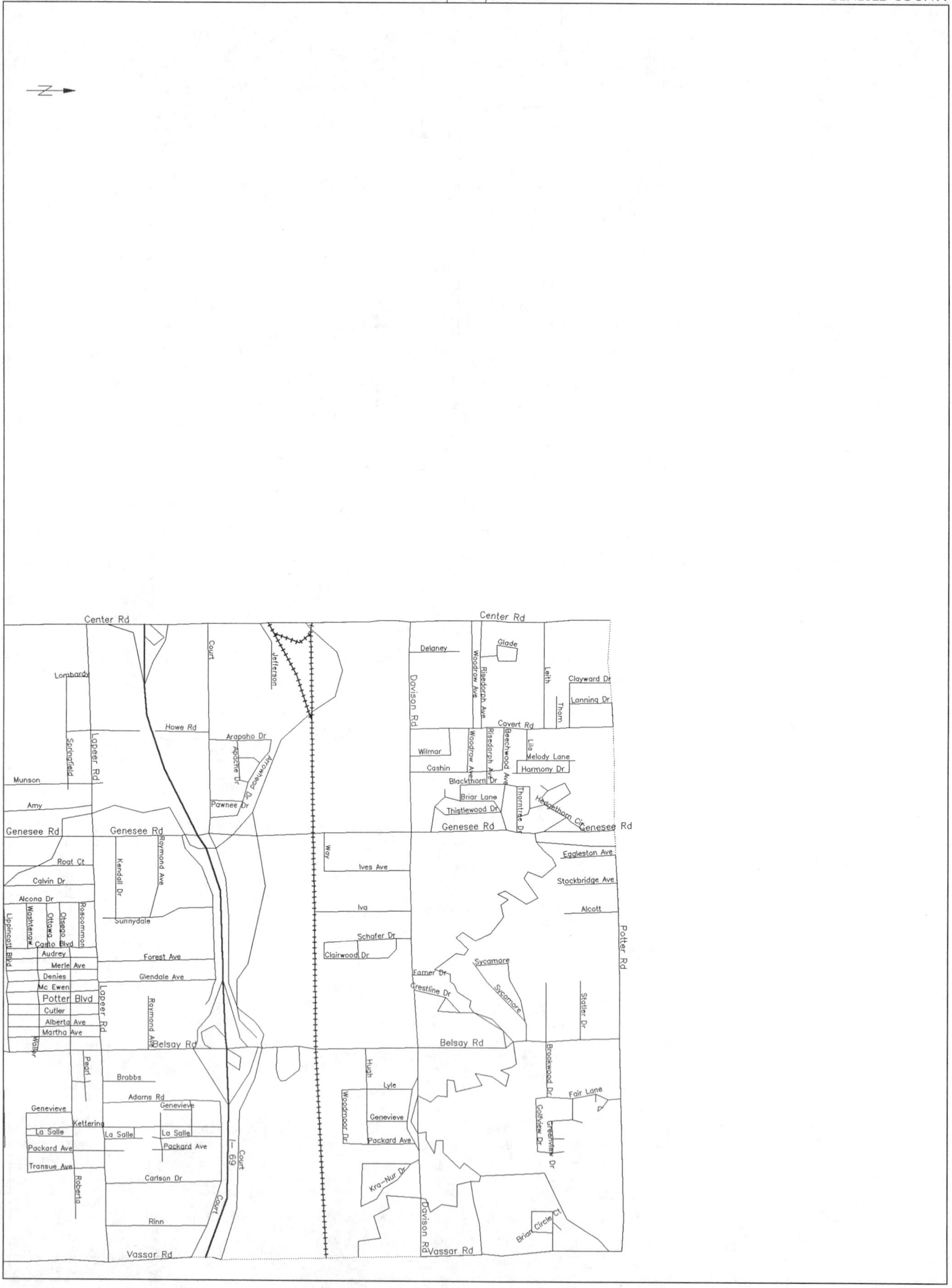
Center Rd
Center Rd
Lombardy
Munson
Amy
Springfield
Lapeer Rd
Howe Rd
Court
Jefferson
Arapaho Dr
Apache Dr
Arrowhead Dr
Pawnee Dr
Delaney
Glade
Woodrow Ave
Risedorph Ave
Leith
Clayward Dr
Lanning Dr
Thorn
Davison Rd
Covert Rd
Wilmar
Cashin
Beechwood Ave
Lila
Melody Lane
Harmony Dr
Blackthorn Dr
Briar Lane
Thistlewood Dr
Thorntree Dr
Hedgethorn Cir
Genesee Rd
Genesee Rd
Genesee Rd
Genesee Rd
Root Ct
Calvin Dr
Alcona Dr
Kendall Dr
Raymond Ave
Lippincott Blvd
Washtenaw
Ottawa
Otsego
Roscommon
Casto Blvd
Sunnydale
Way
Ives Ave
Eggleston Ave
Stockbridge Ave
Iva
Alcott
Schafer Dr
Clairwood Dr
Audrey
Merle Ave
Denies
Mc Ewen
Potter Blvd
Cutler
Alberta Ave
Martha Ave
Forest Ave
Glendale Ave
Farmer Dr
Crestline Dr
Sycamore
Sycamore
Potter Rd
Statler Dr
Walter
Belsay Rd
Belsay Rd
Pearl
Brabbs
Adams Rd
Genevieve
Genevieve
Kettering
La Salle
La Salle
La Salle
Packard Ave
Packard Ave
Transue Ave
Roberta
Carlson Dr
Rinn
I-69
Court
Court
Hugh
Lyle
Woodmoor Dr
Genevieve
Packard Ave
Kra-Nur Dr
Brookwood Dr
Fair Lane
Golfview Dr
Greenview Dr
Briar Circle Ct
Vassar Rd
Vassar Rd

Lake Cadillac
State Hwy 55
State Hwy 115
Lake Mitchell Dr
North Blvd
Sunnyside Dr
Division St
Mitchell St
Clam River
Ann Arbor Railroad
Seneca Pl
Leeson Ave
13th St
8th Ave
7th Ave
6th Ave
5th Ave
3rd Ave
Plett Rd
Crosby Rd
43 1/2 ROAD
Lansing
Pearl St
Lake St

Pop. 1,583

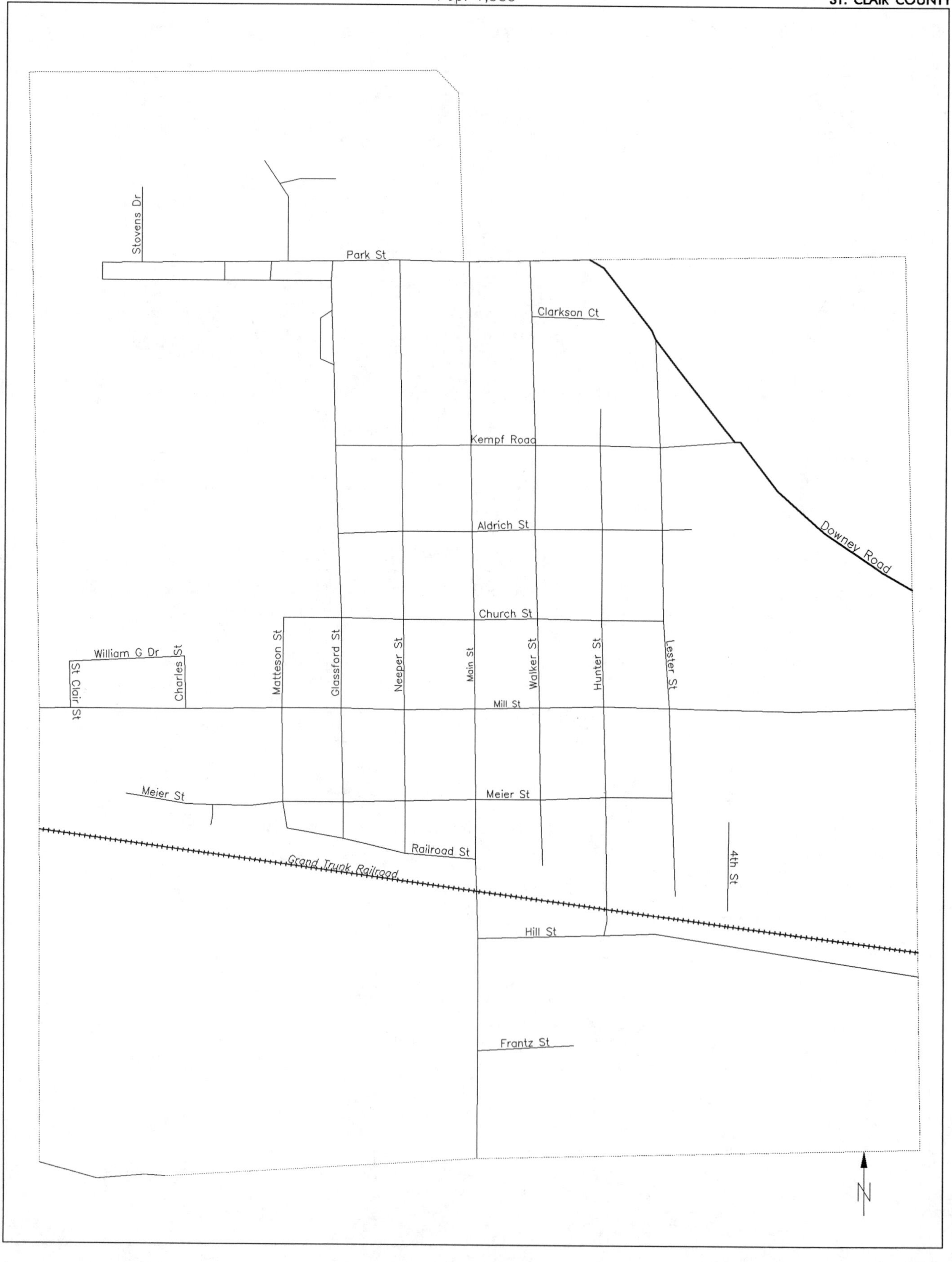

Stovens Dr
Park St
Clarkson Ct
Kempf Road
Aldrich St
Downey Road
Church St
William G Dr
St Clair St
Charles St
Matteson St
Glassford St
Neeper St
Main St
Walker St
Hunter St
Lester St
Mill St
Meier St
Meier St
Railroad St
Grand Trunk Railroad
4th St
Hill St
Frantz St
N

Maxwell Road
Stream
Horan St
Crane St
Matthews St
Pine St
Ash Ave
Ash Ave
Porter St
Mill St
Hand St
Meigs St
Stream
Beaver St
Monroe Ave
Monroe Ave
Jones Road
Spicer St
Kent St
Kent St
Kent St
Center St
Center St
Ann St
Harris St
Stream
Ford St
Stream
Maxwell Road
Jones Road
N

Pop. 4,054

Luder Rd
View Dr
Mary Jane Ct
View Dr
Cleaver Rd
Rodd Dr
Northwood Dr
Northwood Dr
Faust Dr
Pamela Dr
Eddy Dr
Eddy Dr
Knollwood Dr
Turner Dr
Collingwood Dr
Collingwood Dr
Tower St
Gilford St
State Hwy 81
Quinn Ave
Allen St
Sherman St
Parkway Dr
Almer St
Palmer St
Fremont St
Pearl St
Sheridan
Bush St
Millwood Ave
Grant St
Burnside St
Court St
Sherman St
Bush St
Lincoln St
Burnside St
Court St
Meek St
Lincoln
Ward
Gibbs St
Frank St
Atwood St
Kinyon St
Gardner Ave
Bates
Hamilton St
Adams St
Joy
Montague Ave
Alexander St
Butler St
Monroe St
Ellis St
Meadow Dr
Hooper St
Rustic Ct
Congress St
Hamilton
Norman St
Madison St
Almer St
Wells St
M.C. Railroad
Gamble St
Green St
Congress St
State St
Columbia St
Park Dr
Westchester Dr
Appletree Lane
Van Geisen Rd
1st St
2nd St
3rd St
State Hwy 81
N

CARSON CITY

Pop. 1,158

MONTCALM COUNTY

Garfield St
Division St
Olive St
William St
Mercantile St
Grove St
Linden St
Pine
Carson St
West St
Sherman St
Main St
Main St
7th St
Elm St
West St
Elizabeth St
William St
Abbott St
Miner St
Mercantile St
Division St
1st St
2nd St
3rd St
4th St
5th St
Maple St
6th St
Gratiot St
Walnut St
Walnut St
6th St
N

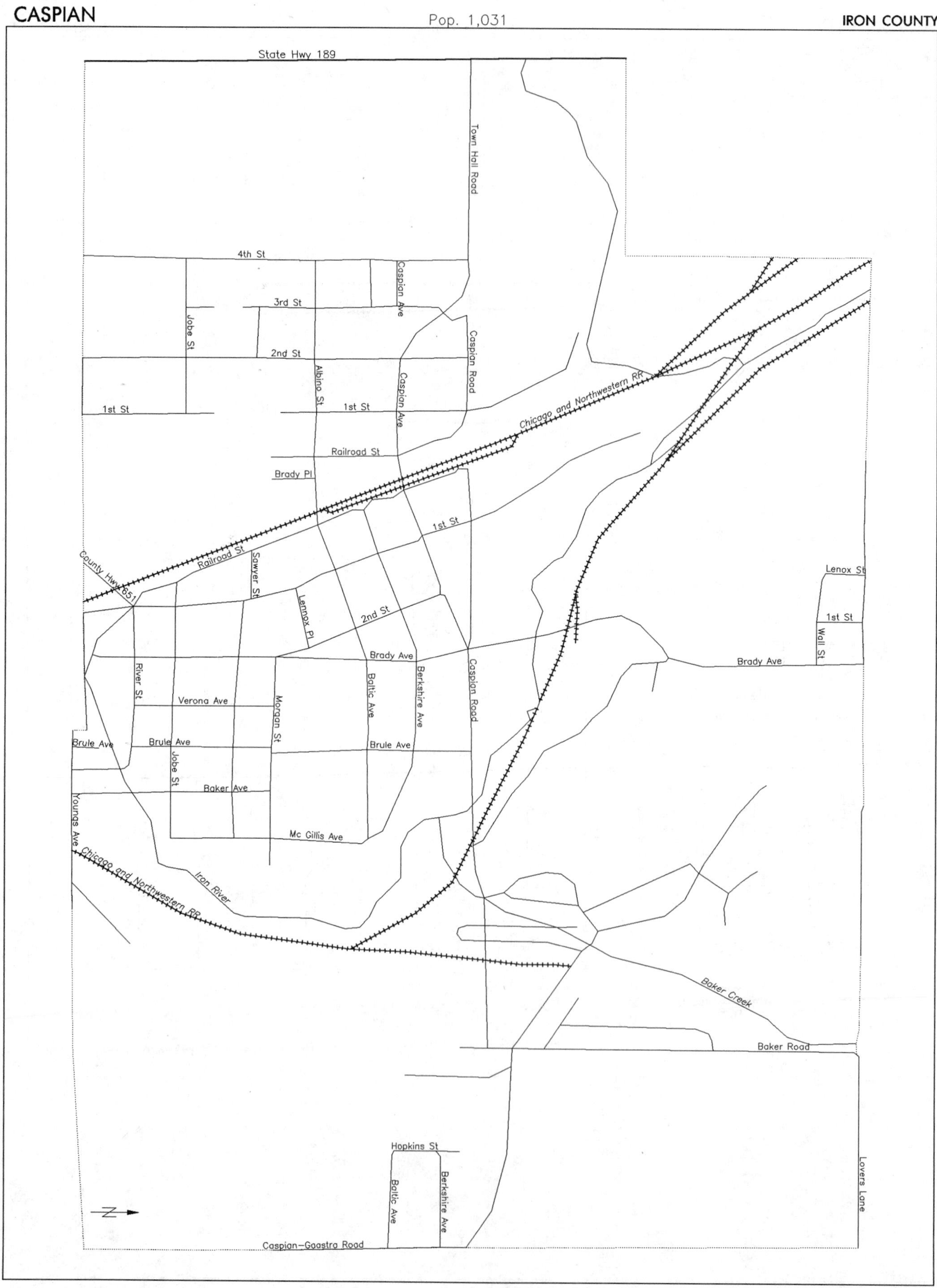
State Hwy 189
Town Hall Road
4th St
3rd St
2nd St
1st St
Jobe St
Caspian Ave
Caspian Road
Albino St
Railroad St
Brady Pl
Chicago and Northwestern RR
County Hwy 651
Railroad St
Sawyer St
Lennox Pl
2nd St
Brady Ave
River St
Verona Ave
Morgan St
Baltic Ave
Berkshire Ave
Brule Ave
Jobe St
Baker Ave
Mc Gillis Ave
Youngs Ave
Iron River
Lenox St
Wall St
Baker Creek
Baker Road
Hopkins St
Lovers Lane
Caspian–Gaastra Road

Bulen Dr
Spruce
Chestnut Blvd
Beechwood Dr
Spruce
Hospital Dr
Crestwood Dr
Crestwood Cir
Seeger St
Ale
Brenda Dr
Hillcrest Dr
Virginia St
Huron
Dale
Huron St
Kennebec Dr
Rose
Seed
Hospital Dr
Huron St
Huron St
Hill
Scotty Mc Cullough Dr
Nestle St
Church St
Weaver St
Downing St
Main
Main
(M-81)
Grand Trunk Railroad
Pine St
Center Drain
Comment Dr
Brooker
West St
Leach St
Seeger
Oak
Maple St
Sherman
Ale
Woodland
Elclare
Herron
Houghton St
3rd St
4th St
Garfield St
Garfield St
6th St
M ST
7th St
Doerr Road
Schell St
Industrial
Park St
Division
N

CASSOPOLIS

Pop. 1,822

St Hwy 62
Fairgrounds Ln
Hilton St
Rowland St
O Keefe St
Horne Rd
Broadway
1st St
Graham St
Graham St
Rowland St
Pearl St
Center St
Cemetery
Disbrow St
1st St
2nd St
Grand Trunk Western Railroad
Follett Dr
York St
York St
Darwin St
Fulton St
East St
Michigan Ave
Lakeview Ct
State St
State St
Irving St
Spencer Rd
Jefferson St
Depot St
Water St
Sherman St
South St
Stone Lake
Sherman Ln
Harding St
Railroad St
Robinhood Ct
Johnson St
Maple St
Maple St
Park Shore Dr
Sherman Ln
Reed St
Grand Trunk Western Railroad
O Keefe St
Hilltop Ln
Hilltop Ln
St Hwy 60
N

18 Mile Road
Linda St
Fredrick St
Carol St
Susan St
Allan St
Allan St
Sarah St
Main St
Michigan Northern Railroad
Cedar Creek
Pine St
7th St
Johnston
Robinson
Oak St
5th St
Maple St
Elm St
2nd St
Main St
1st St
Grant St
Park St
Cherry St
Ash St
Ash St
Beech St
Beech St
Church St
Denton St
7th St
Muskegon St
3rd St
Cedar St
8th St
6th St
5th St
Spring St
Linda St
Ronald St
Marie
Ann St
Jeffrey St
4th St
Pear St
Main St
South
South
West St
7th St
Northland Dr.
White Creek Ave
16 Mile Road

Pop. 9,026

I- 696
11 Mile Rd
Potomac Ave
Menge Ave
McKinley Ave
Potomac Ct
Sylvan Ave
Bernice Ave
Virginia Park Ave
Arsenal Ave
Lillian Ave
Sunburst Ave
Van Dyke Rd
Liberal St
Lawrence
Pc Railroad
Busch Ave
Helen Ave
Dale Ave
Evelyn Ave
Sylvan Ave
Central Ave
Gronow Ave
Harding Ave
Engleman Ave
Engleman Rd
Paul G Hazen Dr
Weigand St
Weingartz St
Braun Ave
Ritter St
Comfort St
Warren Blvd
Jenerous St
Liberal St
Alex St
10 Mile Rd
Dewey St
Godin St
Landau St
Wyland St
Konczal St
Wermuth St
Conner St
Wainwright St
Pershing Rd
Coolidge
Colin Kelly St
Sherwood Ave
Rosemary Ct
Edward St
Mac Arthur Ave
Theisen St
Weil St
Weil St
Decatur Ave
Decatur Ave
Victory St
Henry St
Laura Ct
Rinke Ave
Kaltz Ave
State Park St
State Park St
Sterling St
Sterling St
Sterling St
Superior Ave
Mac Arthur Ave
Standard Ave
Lorraine Ave
Stephens Rd
Wood St
N

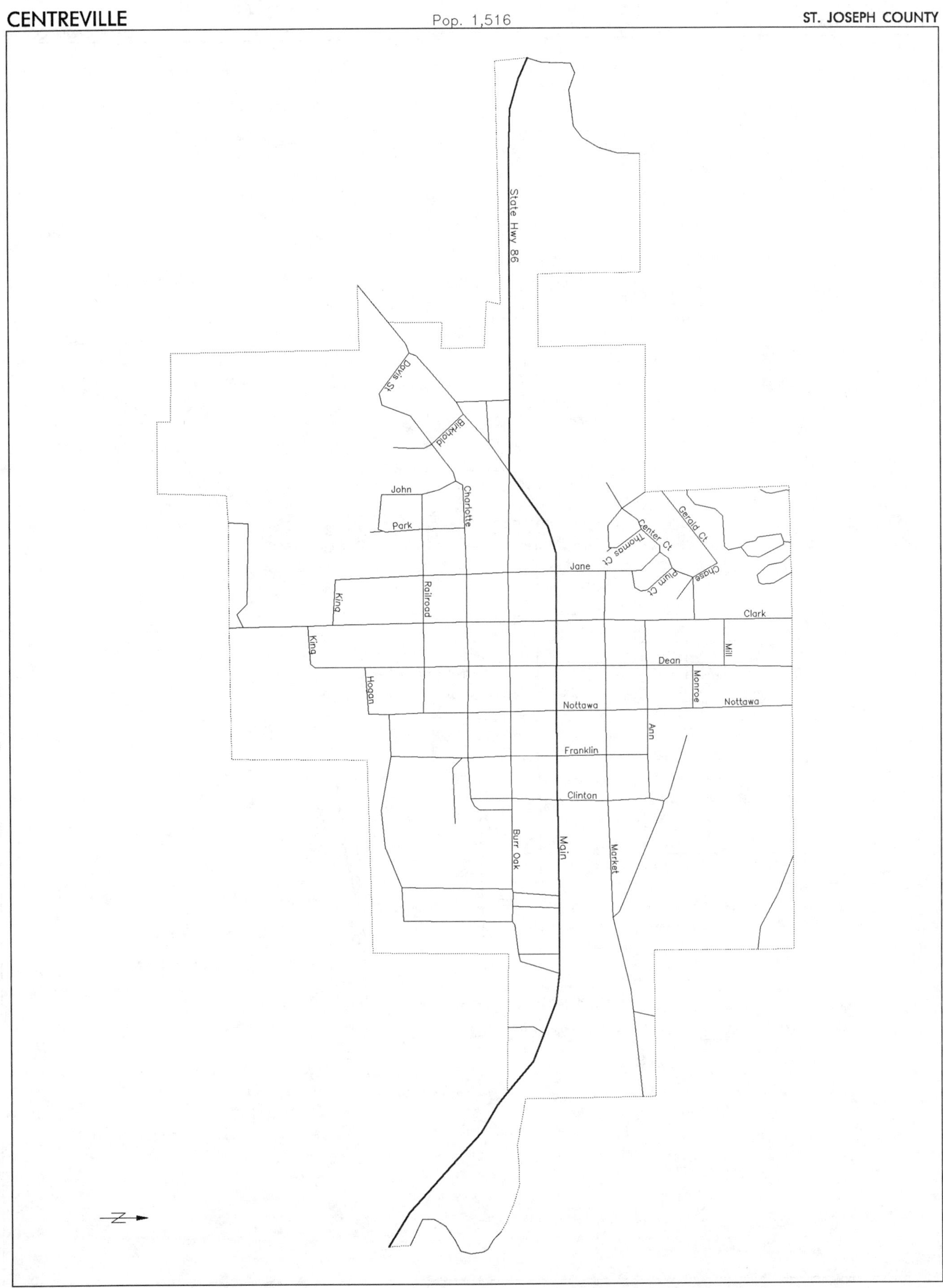
State Hwy 86
Davis St
Birkhold
John
Park
Charlotte
Jane
Thomas Ct
Center Ct
Gerald Ct
Plum Ct
Chase
King
Railroad
Clark
King
Mill
Dean
Hogan
Monroe
Nottawa
Nottawa
Ann
Franklin
Clinton
Burr Oak
Main
Market
N

Mount Mc Sauba Rd
Ance Rd
Taylor Rd
Mercer Blvd
Division St
Michigan Ave
Crouter
Meech St
Oak
Central
Prospect St
Burns St
Nettleton
Lewis
Nicholsie
Ainslie
Elm St
Cherry St
Dixon Ave
Chicago Ave
Chesapeake and Ohio Railroad
Pine River Lane
Park Ave
Clinton St
Mason
Antrim St
Newman St
Hurlbut Ave
Upright Ave
Lincoln Ave
Garfield Ave
Lake St
Sherman St
State
Bridge St
Belvedere Ave
Stockman
Alice
Ferry Ave
Robinson
Wood
Green
Norwood Rd
Charlo
Beacon
Grant
Carpenter Ave
May St
Meadowlane
Eaton Ave
Hampton
Terrace
St Johns Rd
Municipal Airport
State Hwy 66
Stover Rd
Old Norwood Rd
Marion Center Rd
Stover Creek
N

CHARLOTTE

Pop. 8,083

EATON COUNTY

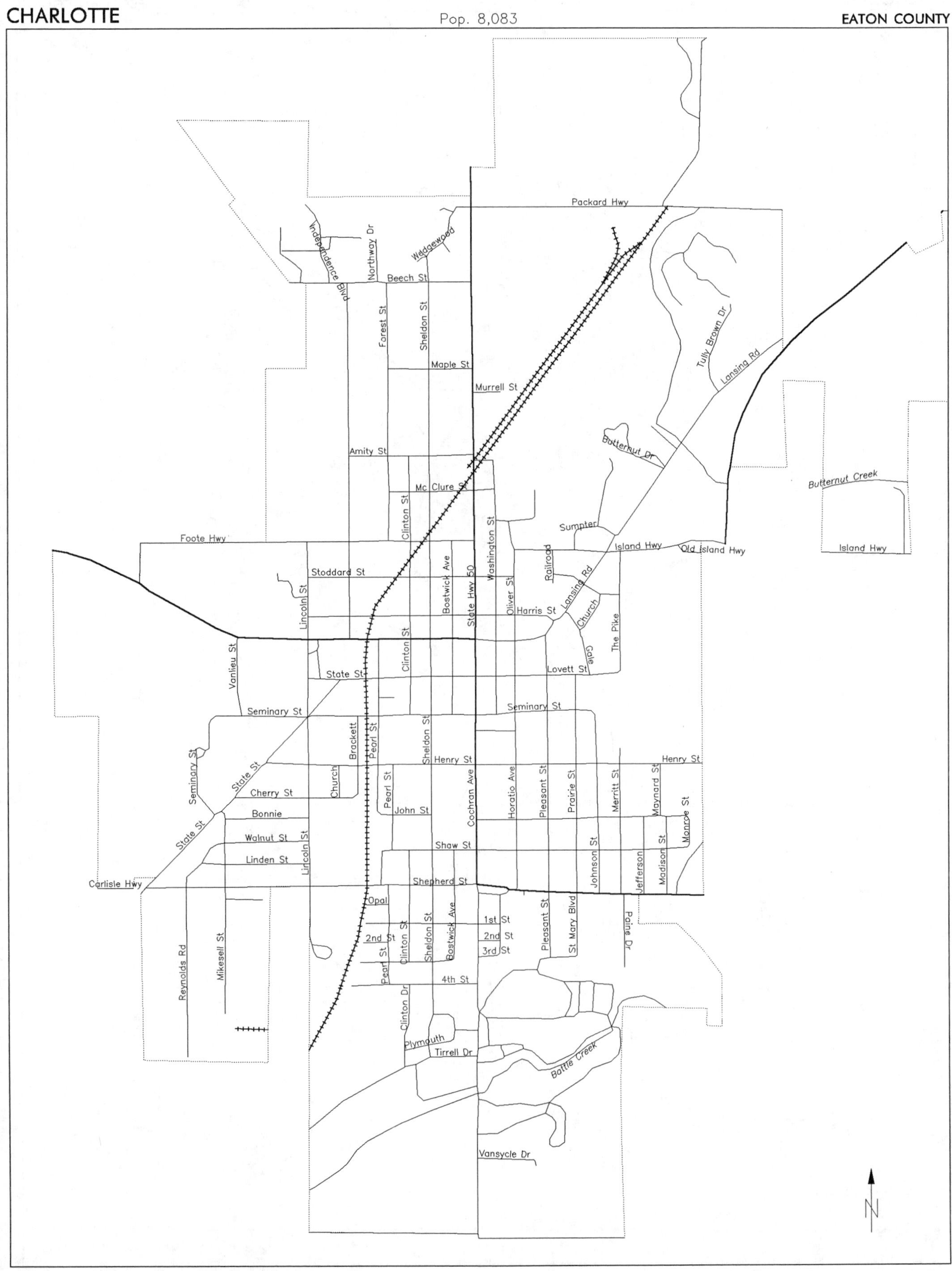

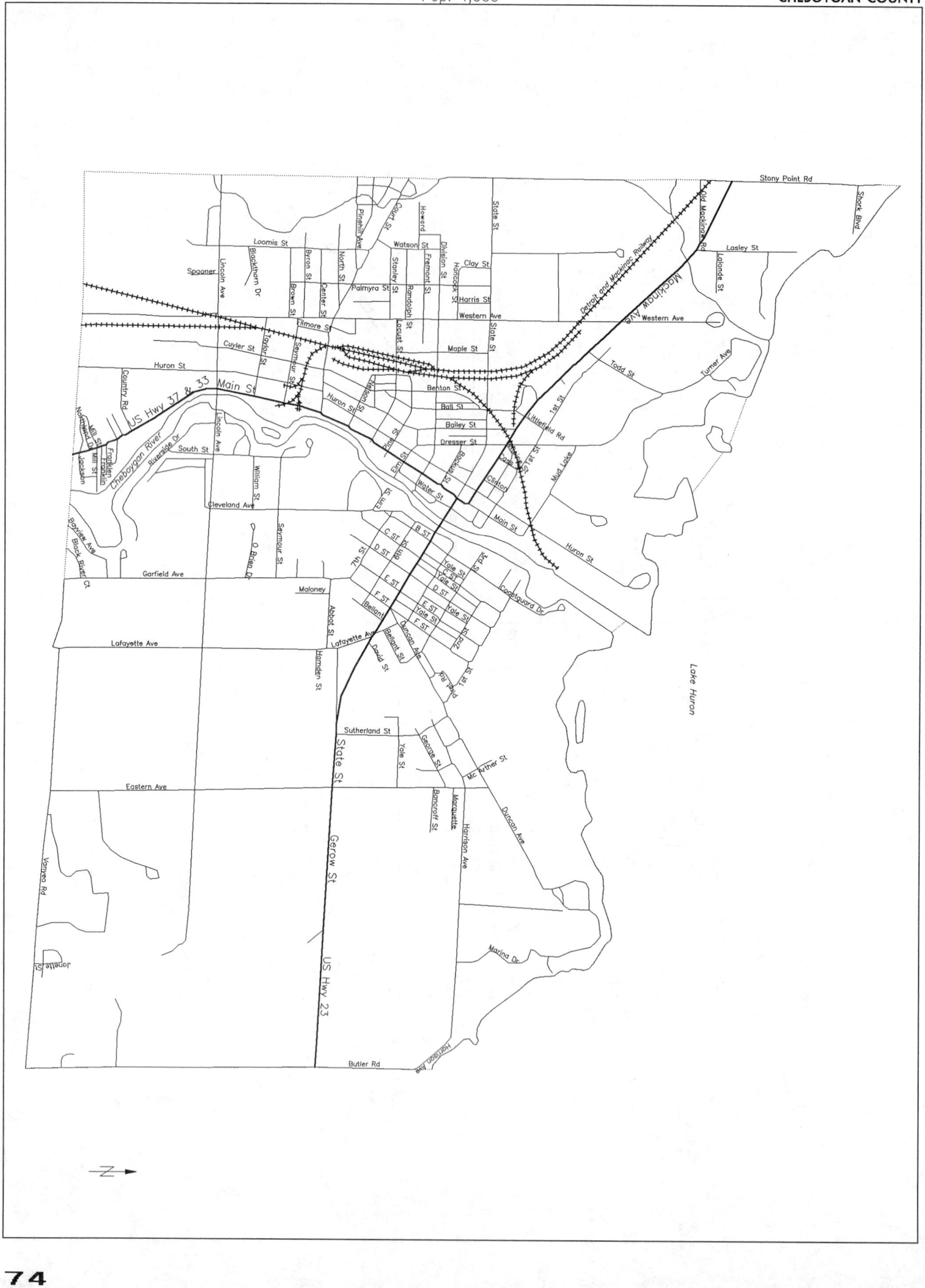

Stony Point Rd
Shark Blvd
Lasley St
Lalonde St
Old Mackinaw Rd
Mackinaw Ave
Detroit and Mackinac Railway
Western Ave
Turner Ave
Todd St
1st St
Littlefield Rd
Mud Lake
State St
Howard
Court St
Pinehill Ave
Loomis St
Watson St
Division St
Clay St
Hancock St
Harris St
Western Ave
Spooner
Lincoln Ave
Blackthorn Dr
Byron St
North St
Stanley St
Fremont St
Palmyra St
Randolph St
Brown St
Center St
Filmore St
Locust St
Maple St
Cuyler St
Taylor St
Seymour St
Huron St
Main St
US Hwy 27 & 33
Country Rd
Benton St
Nelson St
Huron St
Ball St
Bailey St
Dresser St
Pine St
Elm St
Backus St
Clinton
Water St
Main St
Huron St
Northland Dr
Mill St
Mill St
Franklin
Franklin
Jackson
Cheboygan River
Riverside Dr
South St
William St
Cleveland Ave
Bayview Ave
Black River Ct
O Brian Dr
Seymour St
Garfield Ave
Maloney
B ST
C ST
D ST
E ST
F ST
7th St
6th St
Yale St
Pt Dr
Coastguard Dr
Bellant
Abbot St
Lafayette Ave
Lafayette Ave
Hamden St
David St
Bellant St
Duncan Ave
2nd St
1st St
Pitkin Rd
Lake Huron
Sutherland St
State St
Yale St
George St
Mc Arthur St
Eastern Ave
Bancroft St
Marquette
Harrison Ave
Duncan Ave
Gerow St
Vanyea Rd
Marina Dr
Janette St
US Hwy 23
Butler Rd
Harrison Ave

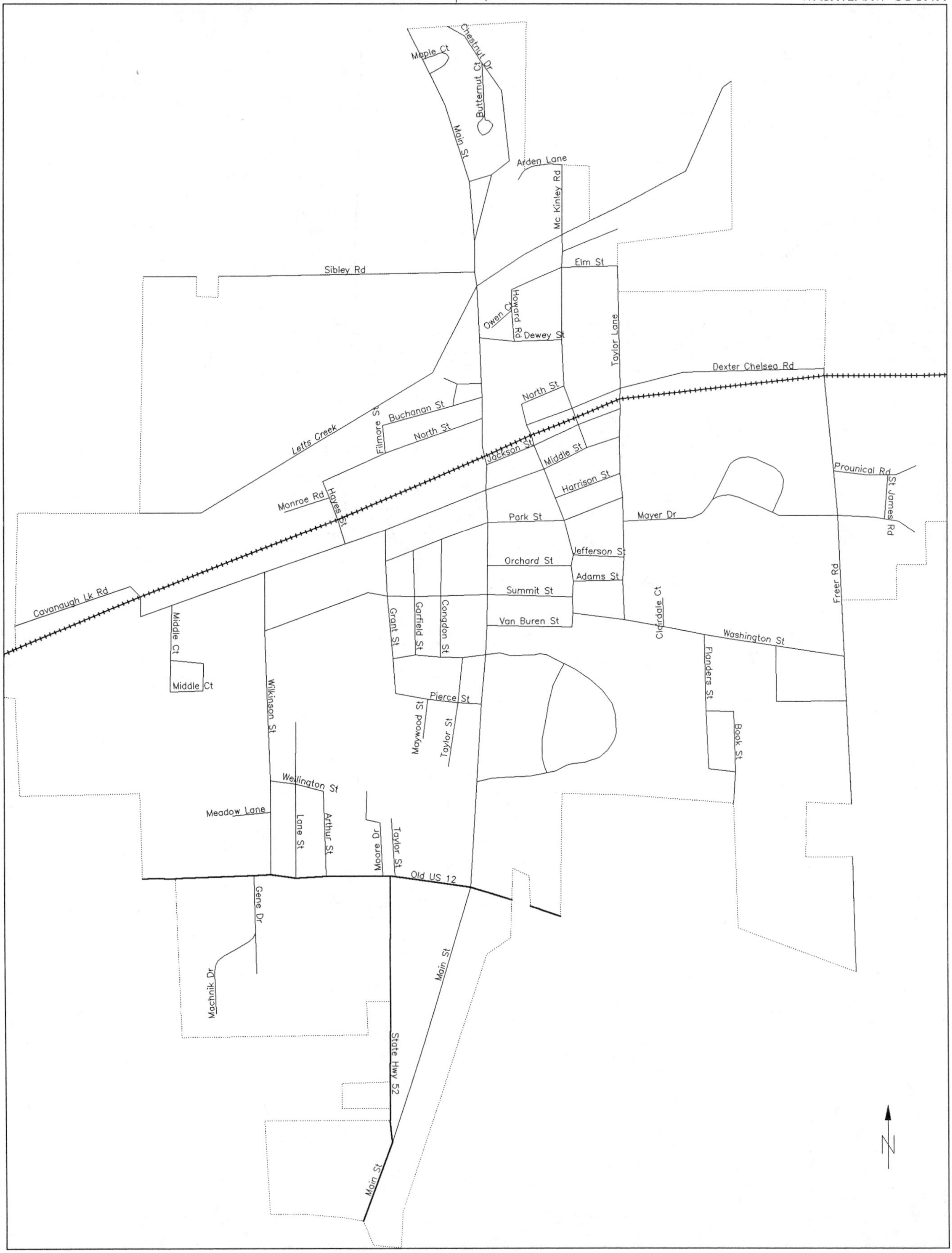

CHELSEA

Pop. 3,772

WASHTENAW COUNTY

Chestnut Dr
Maple Ct
Butternut Ct
Main St
Arden Lane
Mc Kinley Rd
Sibley Rd
Elm St
Owen Ct
Howard Rd
Dewey St
Taylor Lane
Dexter Chelsea Rd
North St
Buchanan St
Filmore St
North St
Letts Creek
Jackson St
Middle St
Harrison St
Monroe Rd
Hayes St
Prounical Rd
St James Rd
Park St
Mayer Dr
Jefferson St
Orchard St
Adams St
Summit St
Cavanaugh Lk Rd
Middle Ct
Grant St
Garfield St
Congdon St
Van Buren St
Claridale Ct
Washington St
Freer Rd
Middle Ct
Flanders St
Wilkinson St
Pierce St
Maywood St
Taylor St
Book St
Wellington St
Meadow Lane
Lane St
Arthur St
Moore Dr
Taylor St
Old US 12
Gene Dr
Machnik Dr
Main St
State Hwy 52
Main St
N

Chesaning Airport
Brady St
4th St
4th St
Pearl St
Pine St
3rd St
3rd St
Firwood St
Bentley St
1st St
Jilmar St
Lockwood
1st St
1st St
Pine St
Lansing St
Thayer St
Liberty St
Lockwood St
Charles St
Wood St
Wood St
Pearl St
Clark St
Clark St
Owosso St
Clark St
Line St
Line St
Line St
Leonard St
Mason St
Oak Grove Dr
Brady St
Chapman St
Chapman St
Lincoln St
Line St
Front St
Pearl St
Shiawassee River
Pine St
Brady St
Mason St
Canal St
Shiawassee River
Commercial St
Canal St
Washington St
Main St
Main St
Main St
State Hwy 57
Center St
Andress St
Andress St
Hampton St
Abingdon St
Sunnyside St
Gasper St
Sunflower St
Neitling St
Julia St
Julia St
Willis St
Liberty St
Volkmer St

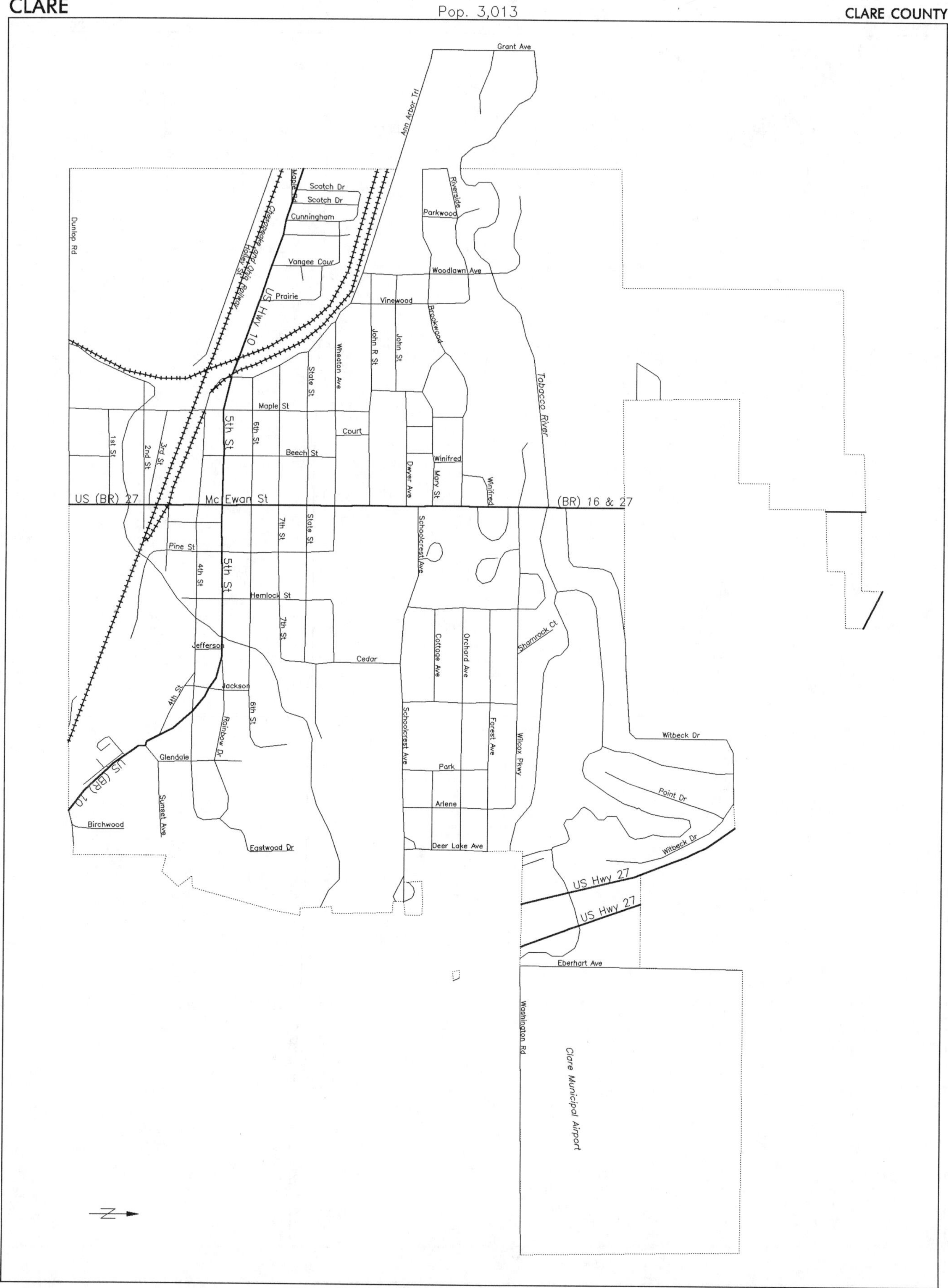
Grant Ave
Ann Arbor Trl
Scotch Dr
Scotch Dr
Cunningham
Vangee Cour
Prairie
Maple Rd
Chesapeake and Ohio Railway
Holley St
US Hwy 10
Dunlop Rd
Riverside
Parkwood
Woodlawn Ave
Vinewood
Brookwood
John R St
John St
Wheaton Ave
State St
Tobacco River
Maple St
1st St
2nd St
3rd St
5th St
6th St
Court
Beech St
Winifred
Dwyer Ave
Mary St
Winifred
US (BR) 27
Mc Ewan St
(BR) 16 & 27
7th St
State St
Schoolcrest Ave
Pine St
4th St
5th St
Hemlock St
7th St
Shamrock Ct
Jefferson
Cedar
Cottage Ave
Orchard Ave
Jackson
4th St
6th St
Rainbow Dr
Schoolcrest Ave
Forest Ave
Wilcox Pkwy
Witbeck Dr
Glendale
US (BR) 10
Park
Point Dr
Birchwood
Sunset Ave
Arlene
Eastwood Dr
Deer Lake Ave
Witbeck Dr
US Hwy 27
US Hwy 27
Eberhart Ave
Washington Rd
Clare Municipal Airport

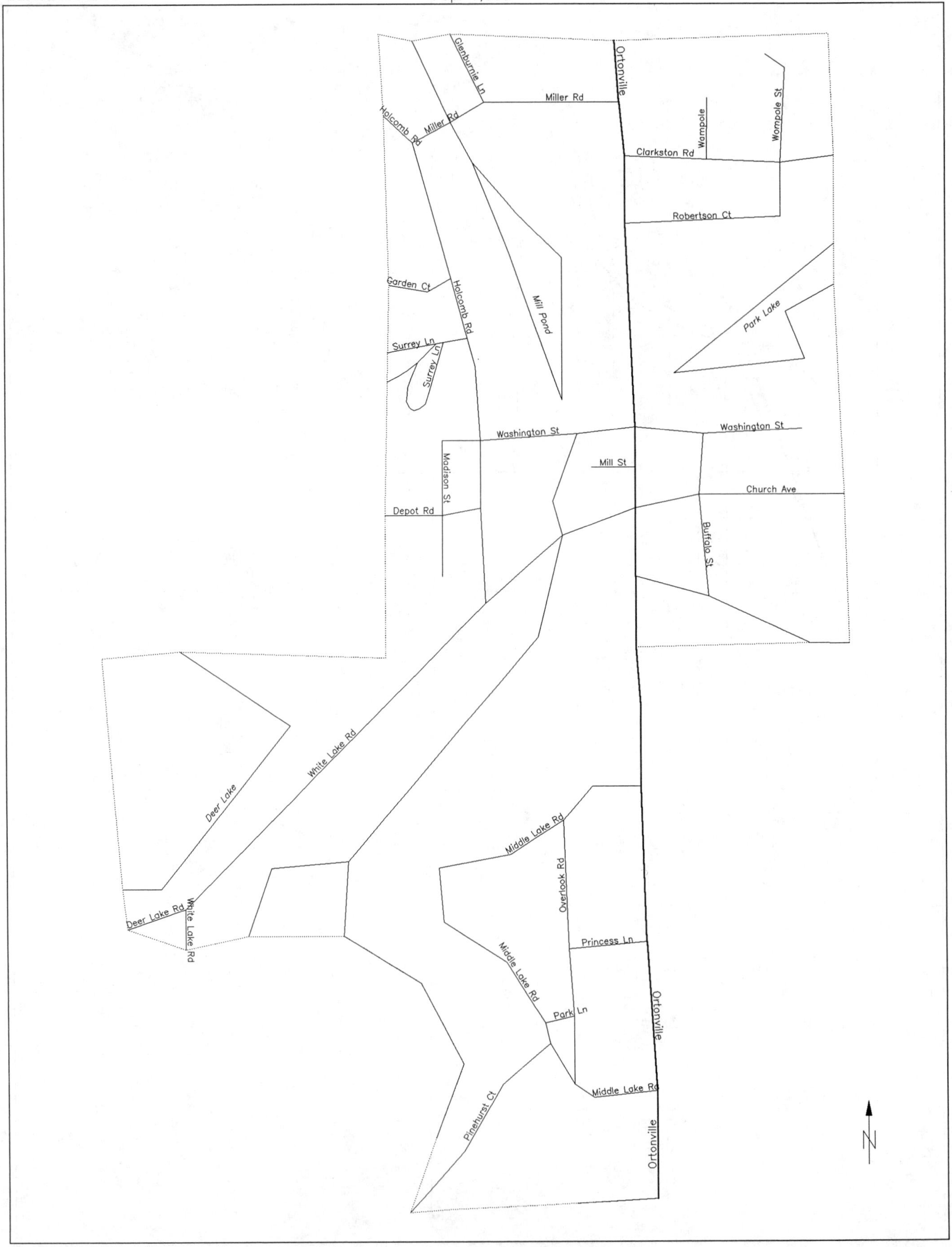

Glenburnie Ln
Ortonville
Miller Rd
Holcomb Rd
Miller Rd
Wampole
Wompole St
Clarkston Rd
Robertson Ct
Mill Pond
Park Lake
Garden Ct
Holcomb Rd
Surrey Ln
Surrey Ln
Washington St
Washington St
Madison St
Mill St
Church Ave
Depot Rd
Buffalo St
White Lake Rd
Deer Lake
Middle Lake Rd
Overlook Rd
Deer Lake Rd
White Lake Rd
Princess Ln
Middle Lake Rd
Park Ln
Ortonville
Pinehurst Ct
Middle Lake Rd
Ortonville
N

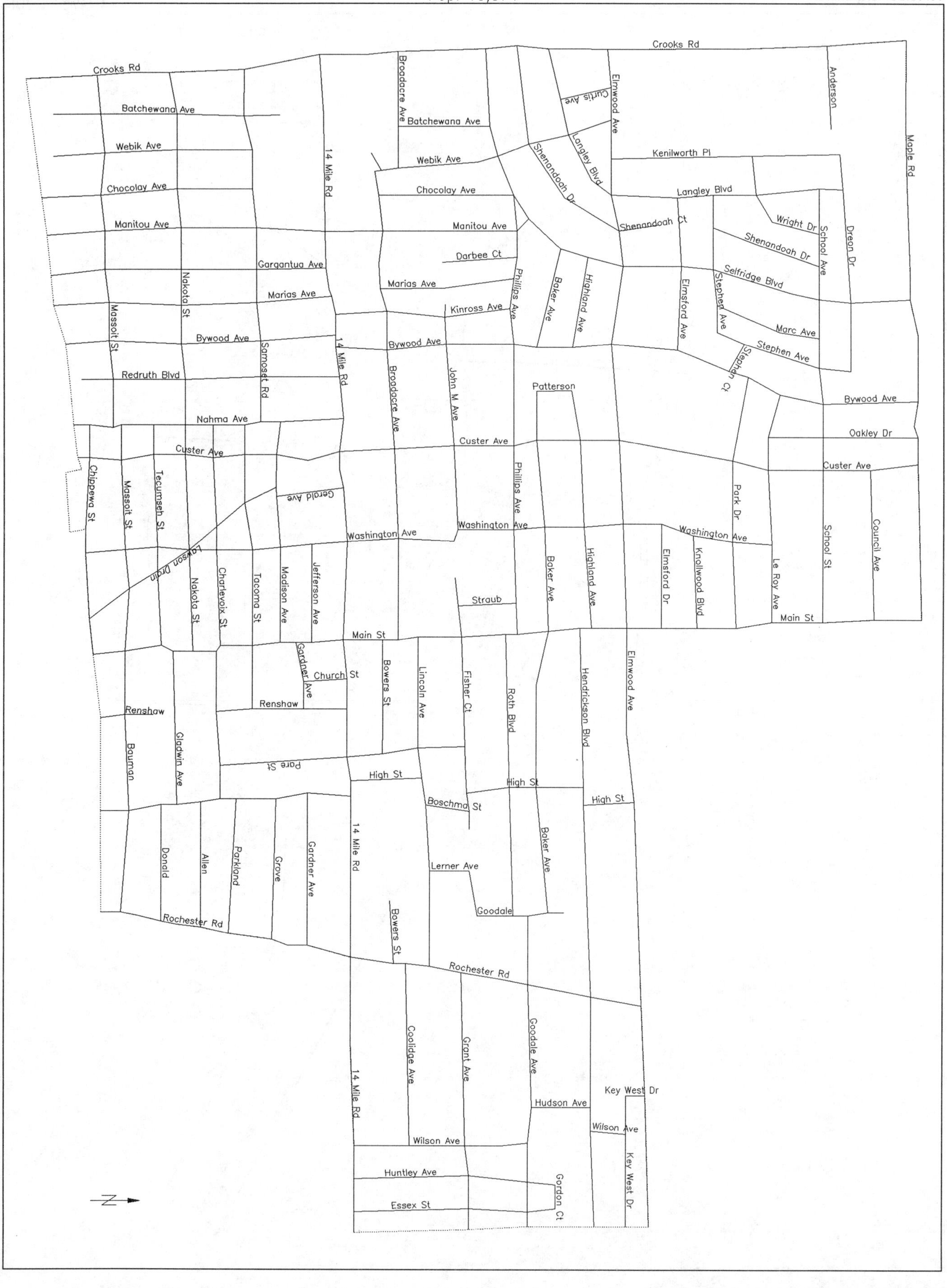

Crooks Rd
Batchewana Ave
Webik Ave
Chocolay Ave
Manitou Ave
Gargantua Ave
Marias Ave
Bywood Ave
Redruth Blvd
Nahma Ave
Custer Ave
Massoit St
Nakota St
Samoset Rd
14 Mile Rd
Broadacre Ave
Darbee Ct
Kinross Ave
John M Ave
Phillips Ave
Baker Ave
Highland Ave
Shenandoah Dr
Langley Blvd
Curtis Ave
Elmwood Ave
Kenilworth Pl
Shenandoah Ct
Elmsford Ave
Stephen Ave
Selfridge Blvd
Wright Dr
School Ave
Dreon Dr
Marc Ave
Stephen Ct
Anderson
Maple Rd
Patterson
Oakley Dr
Chippewa St
Tecumseh St
Gerald Ave
Washington Ave
Lawson Drain
Charlevoix St
Tacoma St
Madison Ave
Jefferson Ave
Straub
Elmsford Dr
Knollwood Blvd
Park Dr
Le Roy Ave
School St
Council Ave
Main St
Gardner Ave
Church St
Bowers St
Lincoln Ave
Fisher Ct
Roth Blvd
Hendrickson Blvd
Renshaw
Bauman
Gladwin Ave
Pare St
High St
Boschma St
Lerner Ave
Goodale
Donald
Allen
Parkland
Grove
Gardner Ave
Rochester Rd
Coolidge Ave
Grant Ave
Goodale Ave
Hudson Ave
Key West Dr
Wilson Ave
Huntley Ave
Essex St
Gordon Ct
N

Little Acorn
Edward J
Cherokee
Oak Tree Dr
Jackson St
Un 7th
Wolverine Cir
Loomis St
Marion St
Nellie Ct
Kathy Dr
Michigan Ave
Coman St
Burton St
Clinton St
Donna Dr
Litchfield St
Edger St
Currier St
Kehoe Road
US Hwy 12
Church St
Franklin St
Raisin River
River St
Clark St
Sunset Dr
Locust St
Tyrrell St
Stream
Gibson Road
Colebrook Dr
Bartlett
Sunset Dr
Conrail Railroad
Tecumseh Clinton Hwy
N

Goddard Dr
Tacoma St
Pine Run
Pine St
Vienna St
Lincoln St
Old St
Allen Dr
Jefferson St
New St
Hughes St
Johnson St
Young St
Palmer St
Darrow St
Campbell St
Curry St
Alexander St
State St
State St
Railway St
Smith St
Pine St
Center St
Young St
Griffes St
Bluff St
Tuscola Road
Mill St
Mill St
Clay St
Eureka Park View
Johnson St
Beech St
Poplar St
Rogers Lodge Road
Upland Dr
Maple St
Cherry St
Oak St
Vienna Road
Park St
Poplar St
Sheldon Ave
Clarion St
Pine Run Creek
Fuller Blvd
Fuller Road
Elm St
Poplar St
N

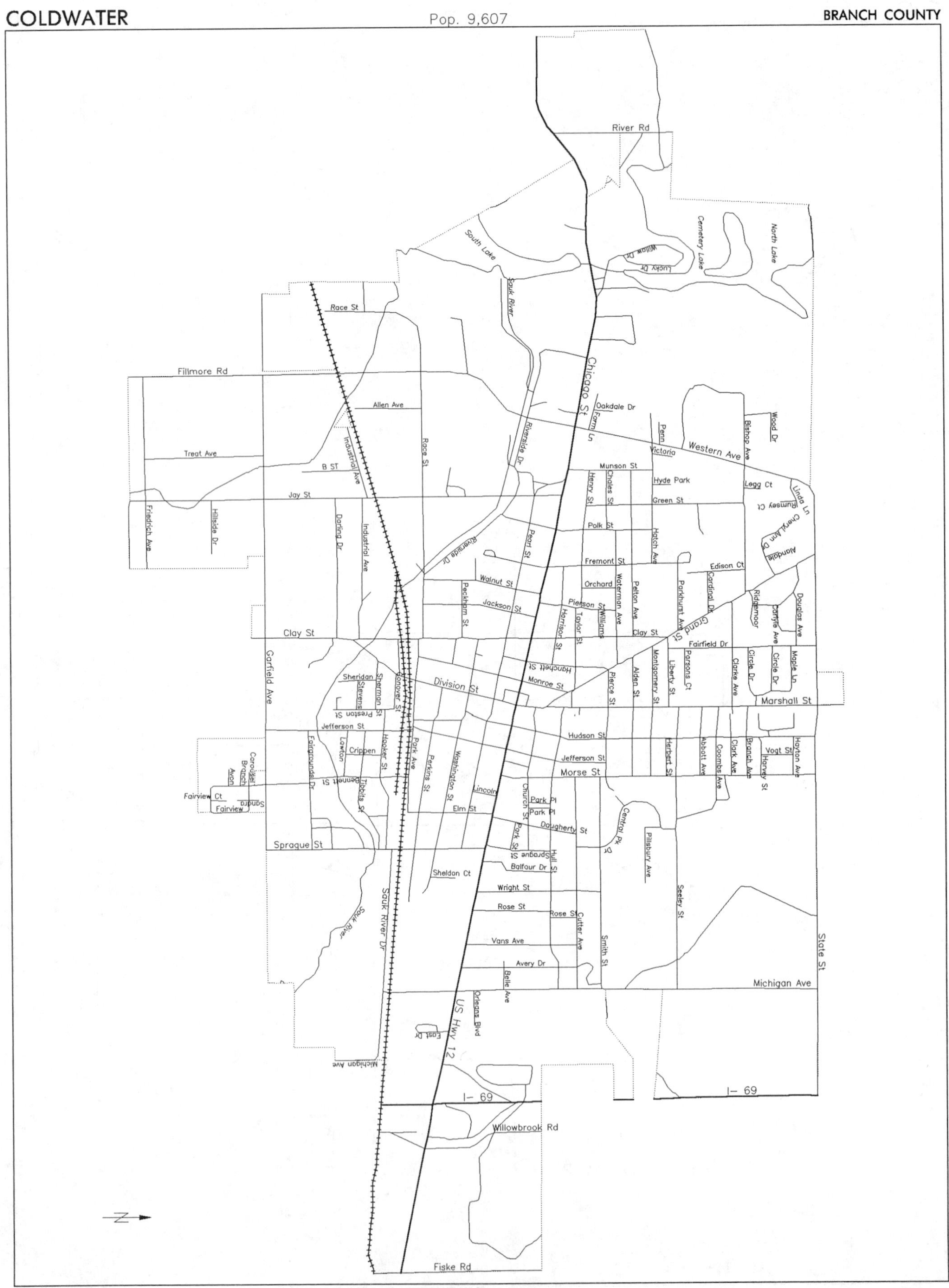
River Rd
South Lake
Cemetery Lake
North Lake
Willow Dr
Lucky Dr
Sauk River
Race St
Fillmore Rd
Chicago St
Allen Ave
Oakdale Dr
Farm Ln
Wood Dr
Bishop Ave
Penn
Western Ave
Victoria
Treat Ave
B ST
Industrial Ave
Race St
Riverside Dr
Munson St
Henry St
Chales St
Hyde Park
Legg Ct
Linda Ln
Rumsey Ct
Jay St
Green St
Cheryl Ann Dr
Friedrich Ave
Hillside Dr
Darling Dr
Industrial Ave
Riverside Dr
Pearl St
Polk St
Alandale
Fremont St
Hatch Ave
Edison Ct
Walnut St
Orchard
Cardinal Dr
Ridgemoor
Peckham St
Jackson St
Pierson St
Harrison St
Taylor St
Williams
Waterman Ave
Pelton Ave
Parkhurst Ave
Grand St
Carlyle Ave
Douglas Ave
Clay St
Clay St
Fairfield Dr
Garfield Ave
Hanchett St
Montgomery Ave
Liberty St
Parsons Ct
Clarke Ave
Circle Dr
Circle Dr
Maple Ln
Sheridan
Stevens
Sherman St
Hanover St
Division St
Monroe St
Pierce St
Alden St
Marshall St
Preston St
Jefferson St
Hudson St
Fairgrounds Dr
Lawton
Crippen
Hooker St
Park Ave
Perkins St
Washington St
Jefferson St
Herbert St
Abbott Ave
Coombs Ave
Clark Ave
Branch Ave
Harvey St
Vogt St
Hayton Ave
Carousel
Branch
Avon
Bennett St
Tibbits St
Morse St
Fairview Ct
Fairview
Sandra
Lincoln
Church St
Park Pl
Park Pl
Elm St
Dougherty St
Central Pk Dr
Pillsbury Ave
Sprague St
Park St
Sprague St
Hull St
Balfour Dr
Sheldon Ct
Wright St
Seeley St
Sauk River Dr
Sauk River
Rose St
Rose St
Cutter Ave
Vans Ave
Smith St
State St
Avery Dr
Belle Ave
Michigan Ave
Orleans Blvd
US Hwy 12
East Dr
Michigan Ave
I- 69
I- 69
Willowbrook Rd
Fiske Rd

Mill St
Murphy St
Murphy St
6th St
Floyd St
Center St
Elizabeth St
Fraser St
Simons St
Sheler St
Moore Lane Rd
Mill St
Railway St
Mary St
8th St
7th St
Jefferson St
Hamilton
Monroe
Graham St
6th St
5th St
Adams St
3rd St
Jefferson St
2nd St
4th St
Washington St
Jefferson Rd
A ST
Webster St
2nd St
Adams St
Barbour St
A ST
Chesapeake and Ohio Railroad
Jackson St
Webster St
1st St
Washington St
Marsh St
Railway St
5th St
2nd St
1st St
Miller St
Dickenson Rd
Railway St
4th St
Pere Marquette Rd
Coleman Rd
N

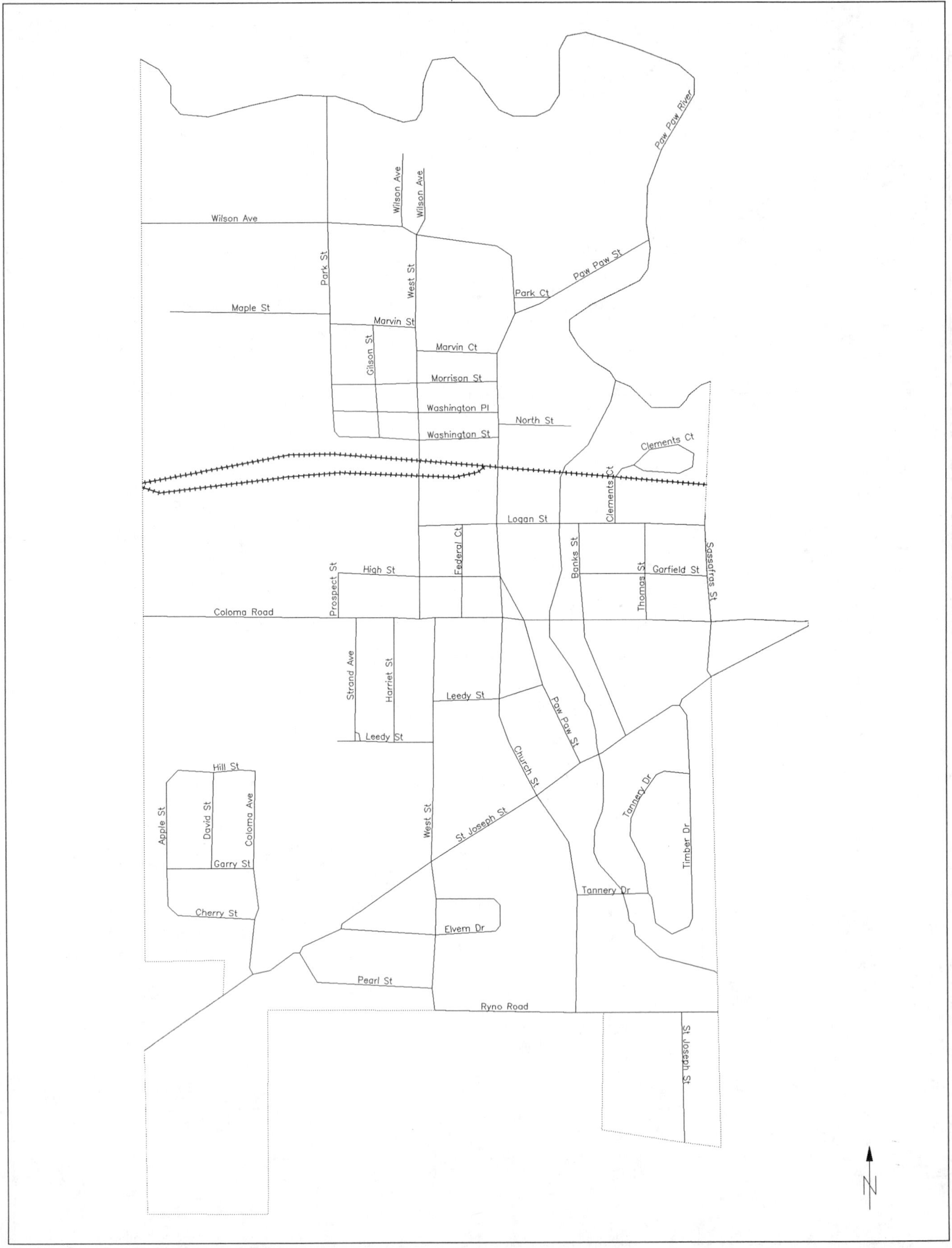

Paw Paw River
Wilson Ave
Wilson Ave
Wilson Ave
Park St
West St
Paw Paw St
Park Ct
Maple St
Marvin St
Gilson St
Marvin Ct
Morrison St
Washington Pl
North St
Washington St
Clements Ct
Clements Ct
Logan St
Federal Ct
Banks St
Prospect St
High St
Thomas St
Garfield St
Sassafras St
Coloma Road
Strand Ave
Harriet St
Leedy St
Paw Paw St
Leedy St
Church St
Hill St
Tannery Dr
Apple St
David St
Coloma Ave
West St
St Joseph St
Timber Dr
Garry St
Tannery Dr
Cherry St
Elvern Dr
Pearl St
Ryno Road
St Joseph St
N

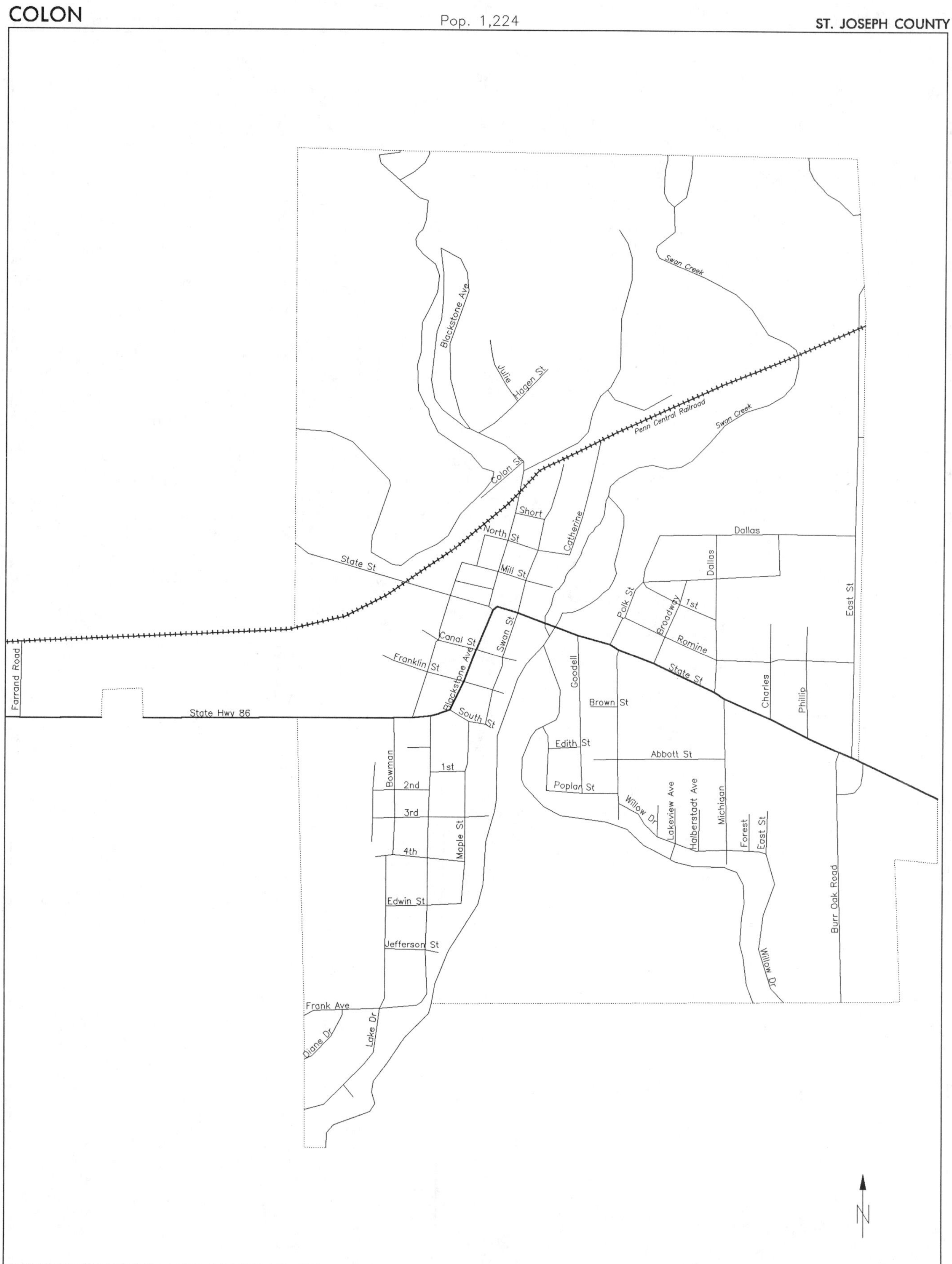
Blackstone Ave
Julie
Hagen St
Swan Creek
Penn Central Railroad
Swan Creek
Colon St
Short
Catherine
North St
Mill St
State St
Dallas
Dallas
Polk St
Broadway
1st
Romine
East St
Canal St
Swan St
Franklin St
Blackstone Ave
Goodell
State St
Brown St
Charles
Phillip
Farrand Road
State Hwy 86
South St
Edith St
Abbott St
1st
Bowman
2nd
Poplar St
3rd
Willow Dr
Lakeview Ave
Halberstadt Ave
Michigan
Forest
East St
Maple St
4th
Edwin St
Burr Oak Road
Jefferson St
Willow Dr
Frank Ave
Diane Dr
Lake Dr
N

CONSTANTINE

Pop. 2,032

ST. JOSEPH COUNTY

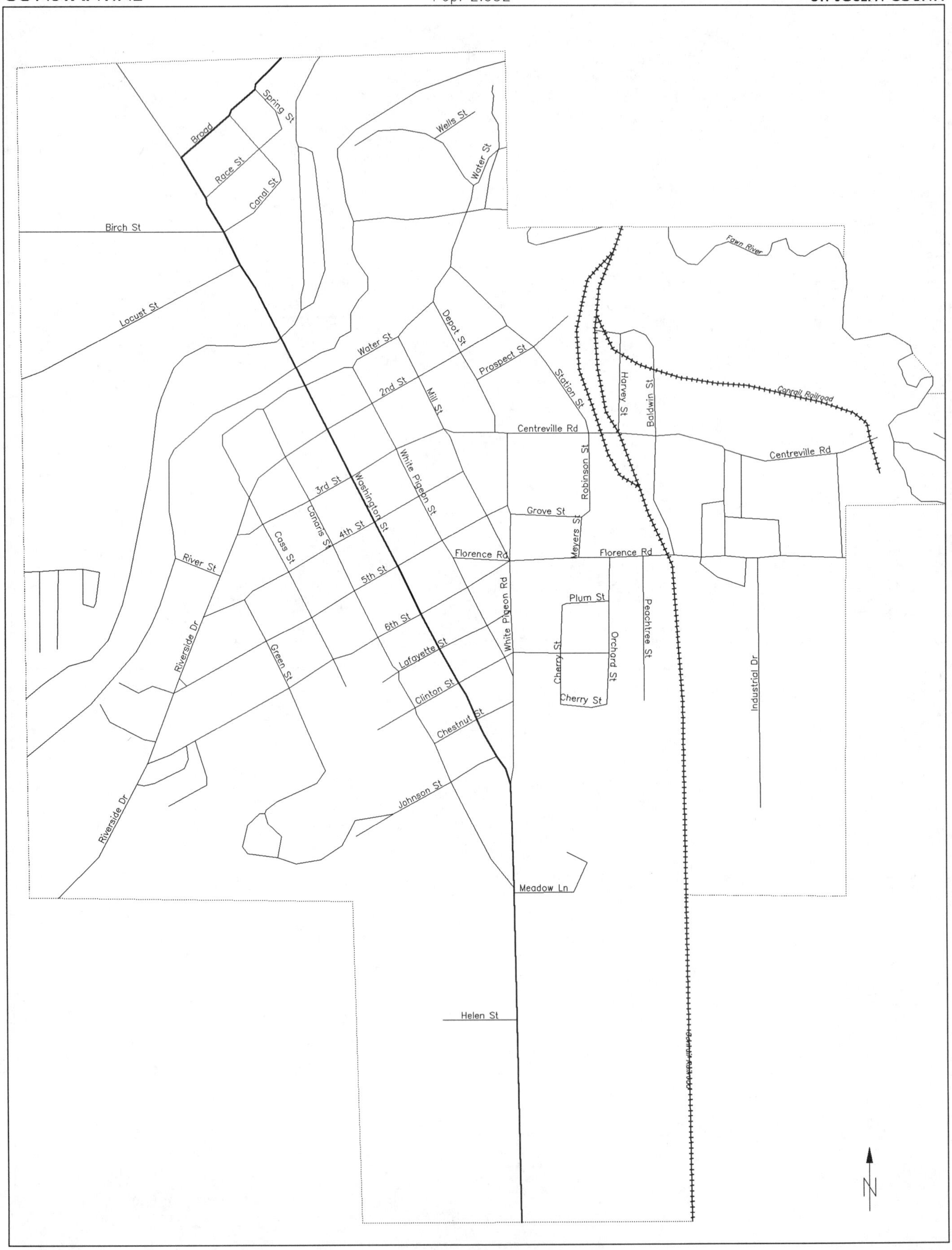

Broad
Spring St
Race St
Canal St
Wells St
Water St
Birch St
Locust St
Fawn River
Depot St
Water St
Prospect St
Station St
Harvey St
Baldwin St
Conrail Railroad
2nd St
Mill St
Centreville Rd
Centreville Rd
Robinson St
White Pigeon St
3rd St
Washington St
Canaris St
4th St
Cass St
Grove St
Meyers St
Florence Rd
Florence Rd
River St
5th St
White Pigeon Rd
Plum St
Peachtree St
Orchard St
Cherry St
Cherry St
6th St
Lafayette St
Green St
Riverside Dr
Clinton St
Chestnut St
Industrial Dr
Johnson St
Riverside Dr
Meadow Ln
Helen St
N

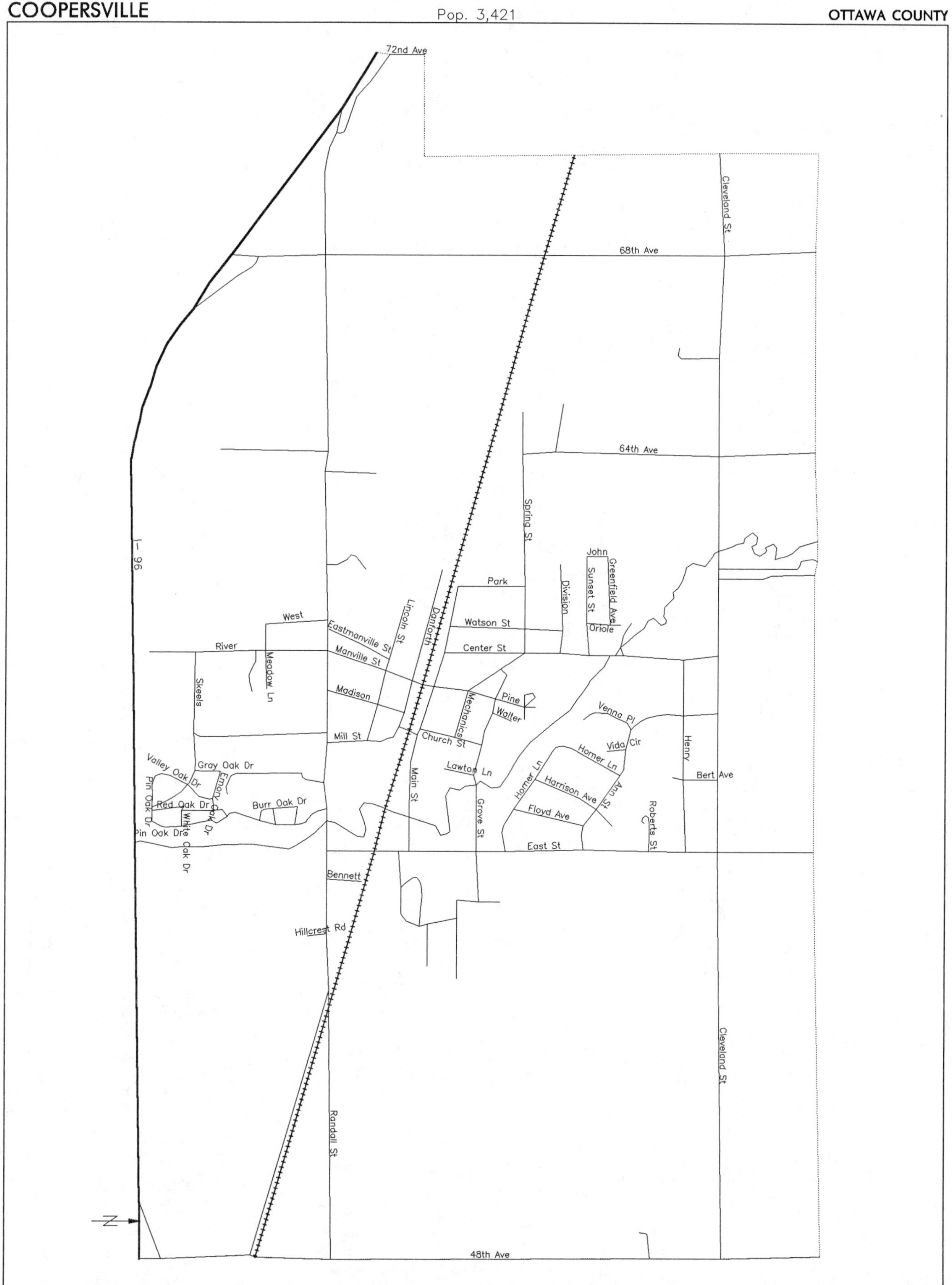
72nd Ave
68th Ave
64th Ave
Cleveland St
Spring St
I-96
John
Greenfield Ave
Sunset St
Division
Park
Watson St
Orlole
Center St
West
Eastmanville St
Lincoln St
Danforth
River
Manville St
Meadow Ln
Skeels
Madison
Pine
Mechanics
Walter
Venna Pl
Mill St
Church St
Vida Cir
Henry
Homer Ln
Valley Oak Dr
Gray Oak Dr
Emory Oak Dr
Lawton Ln
Bert Ave
Pin Oak Dr
Red Oak Dr
Burr Oak Dr
Main St
Grove St
Harrison Ave
Ann St
White Oak Dr
Floyd Ave
Roberts St
East St
Bennett
Hillcrest Rd
Randall St
48th Ave

Corunna Ave (M-71)
Corunna Ave
Ridgeview
Ridgeview
Cornell Road
Crestview Dr
Knoll St
Crestview Dr
Hasting St
Cherry St
Pine St
State Hwy 21
Norton St
Norton St
Margaret St
Mizner St
Backus St
Ferry St
Oak St
Sleeseman Dr
Cary St
Mill St
Woodworth St
Shiwassee St
Shiawassee St
Lyman St
Mack St
St Mary St
Brady St
Brady St
State St
McDonnell St
King St
Walnut St
Comstock St
Mc Neil St
Williams St
Oliver St
King St
Kingsley St
Mc Arthur St
Parklane St
3 Oaks Dr
Mc Neil St
Parmenter Road
Louise St

CROSWELL

Pop. 2,174

SANILAC COUNTY

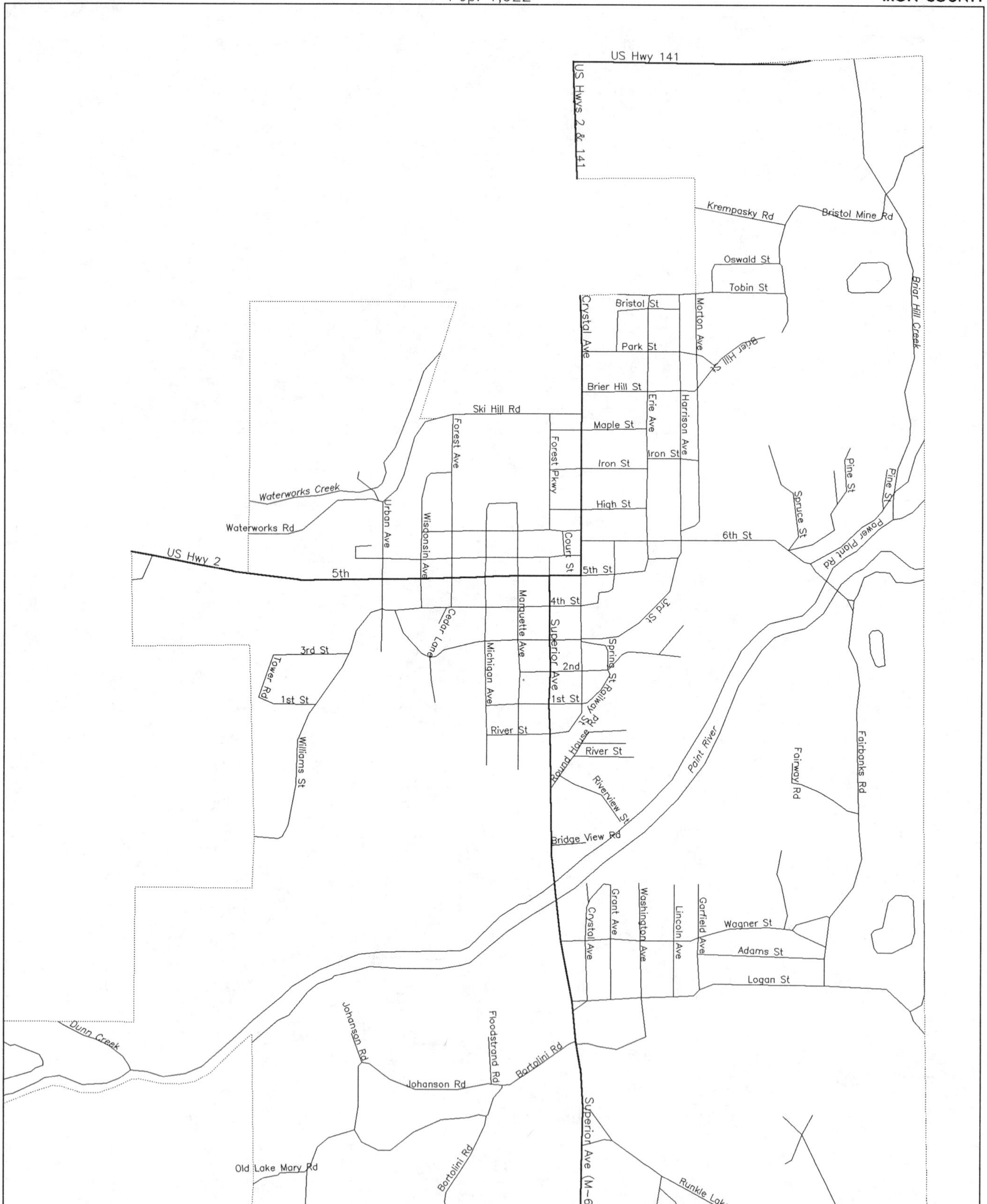

US Hwy 141
US Hwys 2 & 141
Krempasky Rd
Bristol Mine Rd
Oswald St
Tobin St
Briar Hill Creek
Bristol St
Crystal Ave
Morton Ave
Park St
Brier Hill St
Brier Hill St
Erie Ave
Harrison Ave
Ski Hill Rd
Maple St
Forest Ave
Forest Pkwy
Iron St
Iron St
Waterworks Creek
High St
Pine St
Pine St
Spruce St
Waterworks Rd
Urban Ave
Wisconsin Ave
Court St
6th St
Power Plant Rd
US Hwy 2
5th
5th St
4th St
3rd St
Cedar Lane
Marquette Ave
Superior Ave
3rd St
Michigan Ave
Spring St
2nd
Tower Rd
1st St
1st St
Railway St
River St
Round House Rd
River St
Williams St
Point River
Fairway Rd
Fairbanks Rd
Riverview St
Bridge View Rd
Grant Ave
Washington Ave
Lincoln Ave
Garfield Ave
Crystal Ave
Wagner St
Adams St
Logan St
Dunn Creek
Johanson Rd
Floodstrand Rd
Bortolini Rd
Johanson Rd
Superior Ave (M-69)
Old Lake Mary Rd
Bortolini Rd
Runkle Lake Rd
N

DAVISON

Pop. 5,693

GENESEE COUNTY

Street	Map	Quadrant
Abbott Ln	3	NE
Abington Ln	3	SE
Academy St	2	SE
Adams Ln	3	NE
Akron St	4	NE
Alber Ave	1	SW
Alexandrine St	2	NE
Alice St	2	SE
Amazon St	4	NE
American Rd	3	NE
Amherst Ln	3	NE
Andover Rd	3	NE
Antony Ave	1	SW
Appoline Ave	1	SE
Argyle Ave	1	SW
Argyle Ave	4	NW
Arlington St	2	NE
Arthur Ave	1	SW
Ash St	3	SW
Ashby Ln	3	NE
Auburn St	2	NW
Audette St	2	SE
Audette St	3	SW
Audrey St	2	SE
Automobile Culb	3	NW
Automoble Club	3	NW
Avondale Ave	2	SW
Bailey St	2	SW
Banner St	2	SW
Barbie Ave	1	SW
Barclay Ct	3	NE
Barclay Ct	4	NW
Barclay St	4	NW
Barington Ct	2	NE
Barrie Ave	1	SW
Beaver St	2	NE
Beech St	2	SE
Beech St	3	SW
Beechmont St	2	SW
Beechtree Dr	3	NW
Belmont St	2	NE
Bennett St	2	SE
Bennington Ln	3	NE
Berkley St	2	NW
Berkshire St	4	SE
Bertram St	1	SE
Berwick Ln	3	SE
Bingham St	1	SW
Bingham St	4	NW
Birch St	2	SW
Birchcrest St	3	SE
Blair Ln	3	SE
Bland St	4	SE
Blesser Ave	1	SW
Boldt St	2	SW
Boone Ln	3	NE
Boston St	2	SW
Bradford Ln	3	NE
Brady Rd	2	NE
Brady St	2	NE
Brady St	3	SW
Brainard St	2	NE
Brandt Ave	1	SE
Brentwood St	2	NE
Brewster Rd	3	NE
Brookline Ln	3	NE
Brookwood Ln	4	SW
Bryan St	4	NW
Buckingham St	2	NW
Burger St	2	NE
Burley St	4	SE
Burlwood Dr	3	NW
Burns St	2	SW
Butler Rd	4	SW
Byfield Ln	3	SE
Byrd St	3	SW
Calhoun Ave	1	SW
Calhoun Ave	4	NW
Calhoun St	1	SW
Calhoun St	4	NW
Calvin St	2	SW
Cambridge Ave	2	SW
Cambridge Dr	2	SW
Cambridge St	2	SW
Campbell St	2	SE
Canterbury St	4	SE
Carlton Ln	3	NE
Carlysle Ave	2	SW
Carlysle Ave	3	SW
Carlysle Ct	3	SW
Carlysle St	3	SW
Cass St	2	SE
Castle Ave	1	SE
Century Dr	4	NW
Charles St	4	NW
Chase St	1	SW
Chase St	4	NW
Cherry Hill Ct	2	NE
Cherry Hill Rd	2	NW
Cherry St	2	SW
Chestnut St	3	SW
Chicago St	2	SW
Chovin St	3	NE
Christine Ct	3	SW
Claremont St	2	NW
Cleveland St	2	SE
Clinton Ln	3	NE
Clinton River	3	NW
Cobb St	2	NE
Coburn St	2	NW
Coleman Ave	1	SW
Colony Ln	4	SW
Colson Ave	3	NE
Colson Ave	4	NW
Columbia St	2	SE
Commerce Dr	3	NE
Commerce Dr	4	SW
Cooke St	2	SW
Cornell St	2	SW
Coulter Ave	1	SE
Covington Ct	3	NW
Crandell St	3	SW
Crescent Ct	2	SW
Crescent St	2	NW
Crestview St	2	SW
Croissant St	3	SW
Cromwell St	2	NE
Culver St	3	SW
Curtis Ave	3	NE
Dacosta St	2	NE
Dale Pl	4	NE
Dallas St	3	SW
Danvers	3	NE
Danvers Ln	3	NE
Danvers St	3	NE
Dartmouth Ave	2	SW
Dartmouth Ave	3	SW
Dearborn Rd	3	SE
Dearborn Rd	4	SE
Decatur St	2	SE
Denwood St	2	NW
Detroit St	3	SW
Devonshire St	2	NE
Diversey Ave	1	SW
Dix Ave	4	SE
Donald Ave	1	SW
Donaldson St	2	SE
Donaldson St	3	SW
Dover Ln	3	NE
Doxtator St	2	NW
Drexel St	2	NW
Driscoll Ave	3	NE
Dudley St	2	SE
Dunning St	2	SW
Eagle St	4	NE
Eastham Rd	3	SE
Edgerton Ln	3	NE
Edgewood St	3	SW
Edison St	2	SE
Edna St	2	SE
Edsel St	4	NE
Edward St	2	NW
Edward T Arcy	2	SE
Elizabeth St	2	NE
Ellar St	4	NW
Elm St	2	SE
Elm St	3	SW
Elmdale St	2	SE
Elmwood Ct	2	NW
Elmwood St	2	NW
Emanon Ave	1	SE
Emerson St	2	SW
Enfield Ln	3	NE
Esper Blvd	1	SE
Essex St	4	SE
Eugene Ave	4	NE
Evergreen Rd	3	NW
Executive Plaza	3	NE
Fairlane Dr	3	NW
Fairlane Woods	3	NW
Fairmont Ct	2	NW
Fairmont St	2	SW
Fairway Ct	2	SW
Fairway Dr	2	SW
Falcon St	2	NE
Fern St	3	SE
Ferney Ave	4	NE
Firestone St	3	NE
Ford Rd	1	SE
Ford Rd	2	NE
Ford Rd	3	NW
Ford Rd	4	NW
Fordson Dr	2	NW
Fort Dearborn	2	NE
Francis St	2	SE
Franklin St	2	NW
Freda Ave	1	SE
Frederick St	4	SE
Gabriel Richard	3	NW
Garden Ct	2	SW
Garrison Pl	2	SE
Garrison St	2	SE
Gary Ave	1	SE
Geneva St	2	SW
Gertrude St	2	SE
Glover St	3	SW
Golfcrest Ct	2	NE
Golfcrest Dr	2	NE
Golfview Dr	2	NE
Gould Ave	1	SW
Graham Ave	1	SE
Greenfield Rd	1	SW
Greenfield Rd	3	NE
Greenfield Rd	4	SW
Gregory St	2	SE
Grindley Park	2	SE
Gulley Pl	2	NW
Gulley Rd	2	SW
Haggerty Ave	1	SW
Haigh St	2	SE
Hamilton St	2	SE
Hampshire Ct	2	NE
Hampton Ct	2	NW
Harding St	2	SE
Hartwell Ave	1	SE
Hartwell Ave	4	NW
Harvard St	2	SW
Hawthorne St	2	NE
Heinze St	2	NE
Helen Ave	3	NE
Hemlock Ave	1	SW
Henn Ave	1	SW
Henson Ave	1	SW
Heritage Pkwy	2	SW
Hickory St	2	SW
Highland St	2	SW
Highview St	2	NW
Hillcrest Dr	2	SW
Hipp St	3	SW
Hollander St	2	NW
Holly Ave	4	NE
Hollywood St	3	SW
Homeplace St	2	SW
Homer St	2	SE
Horger St	1	SW
Horger St	4	NW
Houston St	3	SW
Howard St	2	SE
Howe St	2	NE
Hubbard Dr	3	NW
Hubbard Dr	4	NW
Hubbard St	2	SE
Hubbell St	2	NE
Hudson St	2	NW
Huron St	3	SW
I- 94	4	NW
Ina St	2	NE
Indiana Ave	1	SE
Industrial Ave	4	SE
Industrial St	4	SE
Iris Ave	4	NE
Jackson St	3	SW
Jefferson St	2	SE
Jerome St	3	NE
John Montieth	3	NW
Jonathon Ave	1	SE
Jonathon St	1	SE
Jonathon St	4	NW
Kandt St	2	SW
Katherine St	2	SE
Kean St	2	SW
Kendal Ave	1	SW
Kendal Ave	4	NW
Kenilworth Ave	1	SW
Kenilworth Ave	4	NW
Kenilworth St	4	NW
Kensington St	2	NE
Kentucky Ave	1	SE
Kimberley Ln	4	SW
Kingsbury St	2	NW
Kingsley Ave	1	SE
Knollwood Dr	3	SE
Knollwood Dr	4	SW
Korte Ave	3	NE
Lafayette St	2	NW
Lane Ct	2	NE
Lane Ct	3	NW
Lanson Ct	4	NW
Lanson St	4	NW
Lapeer St	4	NE
Lapham St	4	NW
Law St	2	NE
Lawrence Ave	2	NW
Lawrence St	2	NE
Leland Ct	2	SW
Lemington Ct	3	NW
Leonard St	4	NW
Liberty Ave	4	NE
Liberty Ct	4	NE
Lincoln St	2	SE
Linden Ave	3	SE
Linden St	3	SW
Lindenwood Dr	3	SE
Lindenwood Dr	4	SW
Lithgow Ave	4	NW
Littlefield Ave	1	SE
Lloyd Ct	2	SW
Locust St	2	SE
Lodge Ln	2	NW
Lois Ave	4	NW
Lone Oak Dr	3	NW
Long St	2	NE
Longmeadow	3	NE
Lonyo St	1	SE
Lowrey St	4	NE
Madison St	2	SW
Manor Ave	1	SE
Maple St	1	SW
Maple St	4	NW
Marie St	4	NE
Marion St	2	NW
Marlboro St	2	NE
Marshall St	2	NW
Martha St	2	NE
Marvin Ave	4	NE
Mason St	2	SE
May St	2	SE
Mayburn St	2	NW
Mayfair St	3	SW
Mc Kinley Ave	2	SE
Mc Millan St	2	NE
Mead Ave	1	SW
Mead Ave	3	NE
Meadowlane Rd	2	NE
Melborn St	2	NW
Mercantile Dr	4	NW
Mercier Ave	4	NE
Mercury Dr	3	NE
Meridan St	2	SW
Merrick St	2	SE
Michels St	4	NW
Michigan Ave	2	NE
Michigan Ave	3	NW
Michigan Ave	4	NW
Middlebury Ct	3	NE
Middlebury Dr	3	NE
Middlebury Dr	4	NW
Middlebury St	3	NE
Middlebury St	4	NW
Middlepoint Ave	1	SE
Middlesex Ave	1	SW
Middlesex Ave	4	NW
Middlesex St	4	NW
Mildred St	2	NW
Military St	2	SE
Miller Rd	1	SE
Miller Rd	4	NE
Millrace Ct	3	NW
Mohawk St	2	NW
Monroe St	2	SE
Morley Ct	2	NE
Morley St	2	NE
Morningside	4	SE
Moross Ave	1	SW
Moross St	1	SW
Morross Ave	1	SE
Morross Ct	1	SW
Morross St	1	SE
Morrow Cir	1	SE
Murray St	2	NE
Myrtle Ave	2	NW
Nash St	2	NE
Neckel Ave	1	SW
Neckel Ave	4	NW
Neckel St	4	NW
New York St	2	SW
Newman St	2	SE
Newman St	3	NW
Newton St	2	NW
Nightingale St	2	NW
Nona St	2	SE
Normandale St	3	NE
Normile Ave	1	SE
Northampton St	3	SW
Northeast Dr	1	SE
Northwood Dr	3	NW
Notre Dame St	2	SW
Nottingham Ct	3	NW
Nowlin Ct	3	SW
Nowlin St	2	SE
Nowlin St	3	SW
Oak St	2	NW
Oakman Blvd	1	SE
Oakman Blvd	4	NW
Oakwood Blvd	2	SE
Oakwood Blvd	3	SW
Olmstead St	2	SE
Omar Ave	4	NE
Opal Dr	3	NE
Orchard Ave	1	SW
Orchard St	4	NW
Osborn St	4	NW
Outer Dr	2	SE
Outer Dr	3	SW
Outer Drive Ct	2	NE
Oxford St	2	SW
Palmer Ave	3	NE
Pardee Rd	2	SE
Park Lane Blvd	3	NE
Park St	2	SE
Parker St	2	SE
Parkside Ct	2	NE
Patton Ave	1	SE
Paul Ave	1	SW
Payne Ave	1	SW
Payne Ct	3	NE
Pelham Rd	3	SW
Pembrooke Ct	3	NW
Penn St	2	SW
Penn St	3	SW
Pine St	3	SW
Pinehurst Ave	1	SE
Point St	2	SW
Polk St	2	SE
Porath Ave	4	NE
Porath Ct	4	NE
Porter St	2	SE
Princeton Ave	2	SW
Prospect St	3	NE
Prospect St	4	NW
Queen St	2	SE
Rainbow Dr	3	SE
Raymond Ct	3	SW
Raymond St	3	SW
Reginald St	2	NE
Reuter Ave	1	SE
Reuter St	1	SE
Reuter St	4	NW
Rex St	2	NW
Richmond Ave	2	NW
Ridgemont Ct	2	NW
River Ln	2	NE
Riverdale Dr	2	SW
Riverside Dr	4	SE
Robert St	4	NE
Robertson Ave	4	NW
Robin St	2	NW
Robindale Ct	2	NW
Robindale St	2	NW
Rockford St	2	NW
Roemer St	4	NW
Roosevelt St	2	SE
Rosalie Ave	3	NE
Rosevere St	2	NW
Ross St	2	SW
Rotunda Dr	2	SE
Rotunda Dr	3	SW
Rotunda Dr	4	NW
Roulo St	4	NE
Rowe St	2	NW
Royalvale Ln	3	NW
Ruby Ave	3	NE
Ruby Ave	4	NW
Russell St	2	NE
Salina St	4	SE
Saulino Ct	4	NE
Schaefer Hwy	1	SW
Schaefer Hwy	4	SW
Schlaff St	4	NW
Scott St	2	SW
Seymour St	3	NE
Seymour St	4	NW
Shaddick Ave	1	SE
Shady Hollow	2	NE
Sheridan St	2	NW
Sherwood St	3	SE
Silvery Ln	2	NW
Smith St	3	SW
Snow Ct	3	SE
Snow Rd	2	SE
Snow Rd	3	SW
Southern St	4	NE
Southfield Frwy	3	NW
Southfield Frwy	3	SE
Southfield Rd	3	SE
Springwells Blvd	4	SW
St Stephens St	4	NE
Steadman Ave	1	SW
Steadman Ave	3	NE
Stecker St	4	NE
Stephens St	2	SE
Sterling St	2	NW
Stuart Ln	3	SE
Summer St	2	SE
Sussex St	2	NE
Sylvan St	2	NE
Syracuse St	2	SW
Tannahill St	2	NE
Telegraph Rd	2	NW
Tenny St	2	SE
Ternes Ave	1	SW
Ternes St	1	SW
Ternes St	4	NW
Texas St	3	SW
Thayer Ave	1	SE
Theisen Ave	1	SE
Thomas Pl	2	SW
Tillman St	2	SE
Timber Ridge Dr	3	NW
Timberlane Ct	3	NW
Tireman Ave	1	SW
Town Center Dr	3	NW
Trenton Ter	2	NW
Trowbridge Ave	2	SW
Tuxedo Ave	4	SE
US 39	3	SE
Union St	2	SW
Valleyview Dr	3	NW
Vassar St	2	SE
Venice St	3	SW
Vernon St	2	NW
Vernor Hwy	4	SE
Village Rd	2	SE
Village Rd	3	SW
Vivian St	2	SW
Wagner Ct	2	NE
Walnut St	3	SE
Walwit St	3	NE
Ward St	2	NW
Warren Ave	1	SW
Warwick Ct	2	SW
Washington St	2	SE
Watsonia St	2	NE
Waverly St	2	NW
Waynewood Ct	3	SW
Weddel St	3	SW
Welch St	4	NE
Wellesley St	4	NW
Wellington St	2	NE
Wessex Ct	3	NW
West Cir	2	NE
West Ln	2	NE
West Ln	3	NW
Westland Ave	3	NE
Westlawn St	4	SE
Westminster Ct	3	SW
Westwood St	2	SW
Whitlock Ave	1	SE
Whitmore St	2	SE
Whittier Pl	2	SW
Whitting Ave	4	SE
Wildbranch Dr	3	NW
Wildwood St	2	NE
William St	2	SE
Williamsburg Dr	4	SW
Williamson Ave	1	SW
Williamson Ave	4	NW
Williamson Ct	1	SW
Williamson St	4	NW
Willow St	3	SW
Willoway St	2	NE
Wilson Ave	2	NW
Winchester Dr	2	SW
Windham Ln	3	NE
Winona St	2	NW
Wiscasset Rd	3	SE
Wisconsin Ave	1	SE
Woodbury Ln	3	NE
Woodcrest Dr	2	NE
Woodcroft Dr	2	SW
Woodland Dr	3	SE
Woodside Dr	3	SW
Woodworth St	3	NE
Woodworth St	4	NW
Wren Ave	4	NE
Wyoming Ave	1	SE
Wyoming Ave	4	NE
Yale St	2	SW
Yinger Ave	1	SW
York St	2	NE
Yorkshire Ct	3	NW
Ziegler St	3	SW

NOTES

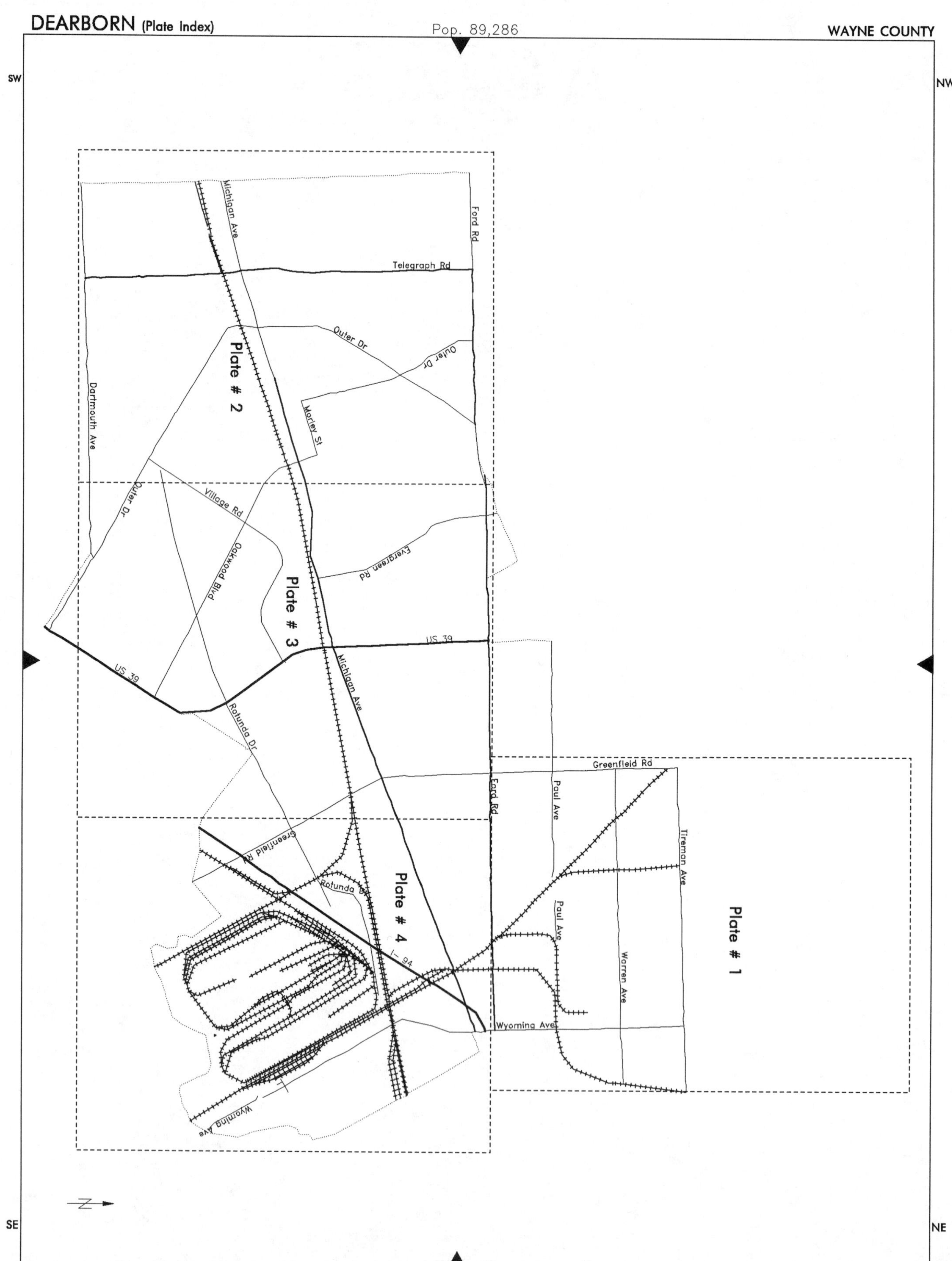
SW
NW
SE
NE
Michigan Ave
Ford Rd
Telegraph Rd
Outer Dr
Plate # 2
Dartmouth Ave
Morley St
Village Rd
Oakwood Blvd
Evergreen Rd
Plate # 3
US 39
Rotunda Dr
Greenfield Rd
Paul Ave
Tireman Ave
Plate # 4
Warren Ave
Plate # 1
I- 94
Wyoming Ave

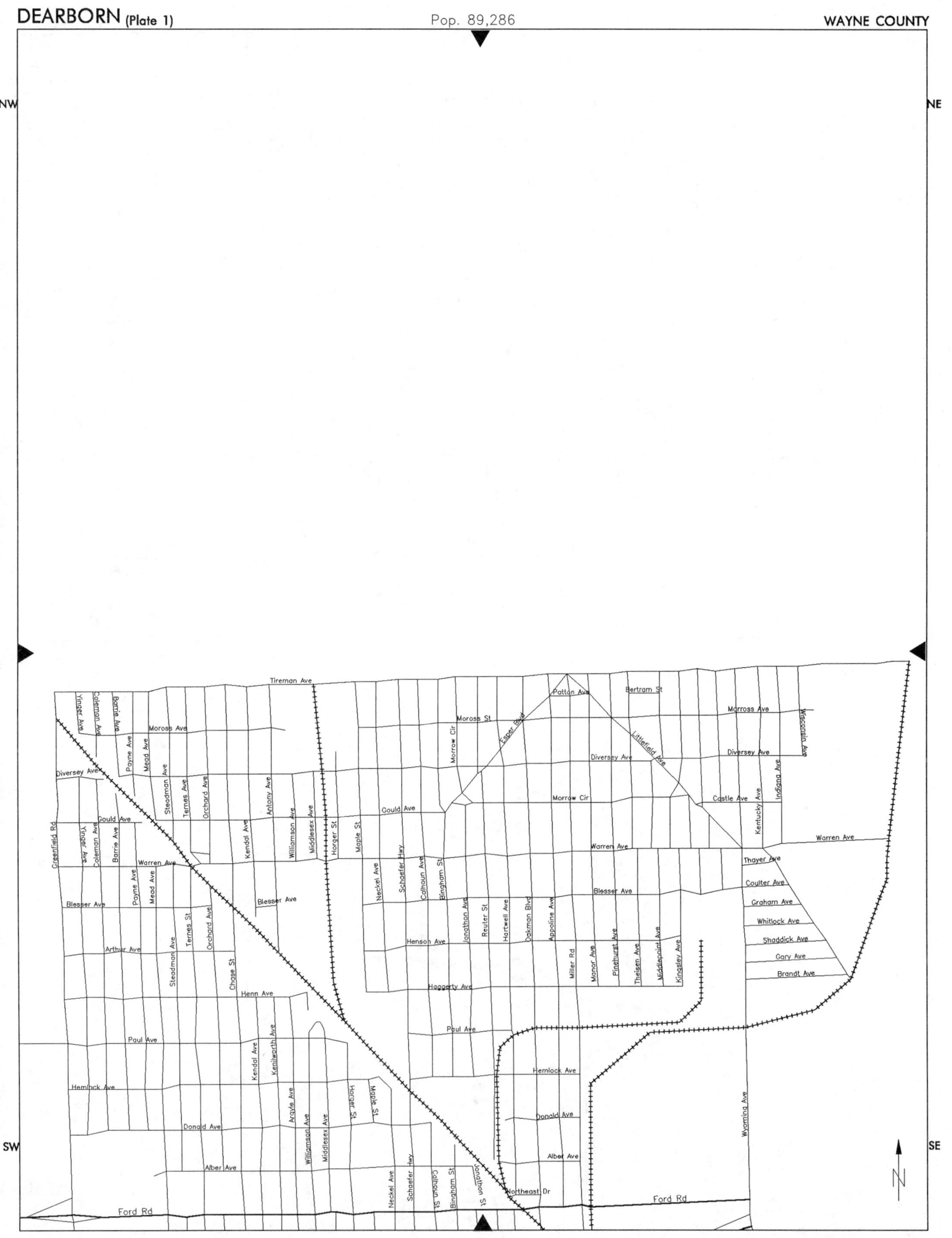
NW
NE
SW
SE
Tireman Ave
Yinger Ave
Coleman Ave
Barrie Ave
Moross Ave
Payne Ave
Mead Ave
Diversey Ave
Steadman Ave
Ternes Ave
Orchard Ave
Antony Ave
Williamson Ave
Middlesex Ave
Gould Ave
Greenfield Rd
Kendal Ave
Horger St
Maple St
Warren Ave
Blesser Ave
Arthur Ave
Chase St
Henn Ave
Paul Ave
Kenilworth Ave
Hemlock Ave
Argyle Ave
Donald Ave
Alber Ave
Ford Rd
Moross St
Morrow Cir
Esper Blvd
Patton Ave
Bertram St
Littlefield Ave
Neckel Ave
Schaefer Hwy
Calhoun Ave
Bingham St
Jonathon Ave
Reuter St
Hartwell Ave
Oakman Blvd
Appoline Ave
Miller Rd
Manor Ave
Pinehurst Ave
Theisen Ave
Middlepoint Ave
Kingsley Ave
Henson Ave
Haggerty Ave
Calhoun St
Jonathon St
Northeast Dr
Morross Ave
Wisconsin Ave
Castle Ave
Kentucky Ave
Indiana Ave
Thayer Ave
Coulter Ave
Graham Ave
Whitlock Ave
Shaddick Ave
Gary Ave
Brandt Ave
Wyoming Ave
N

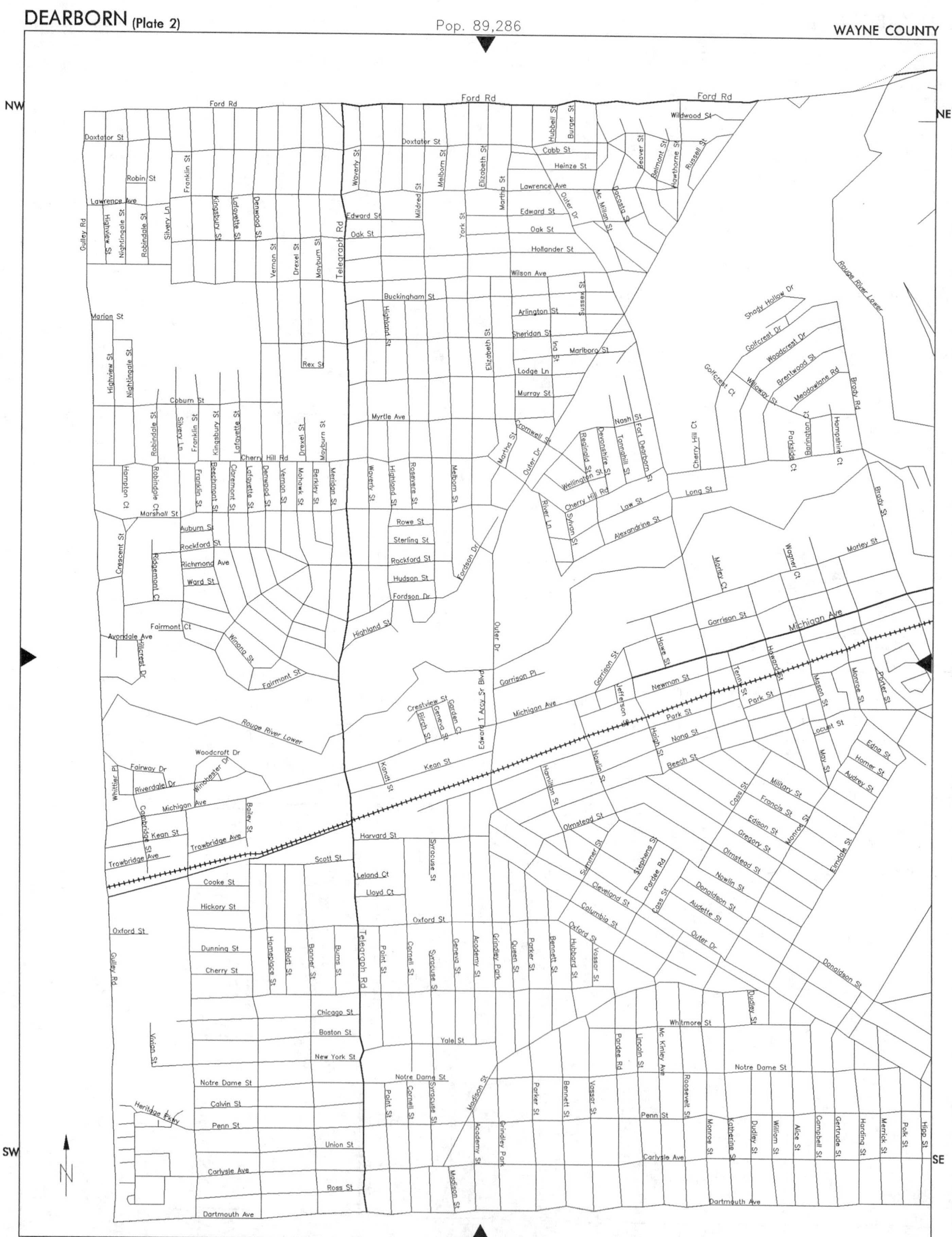
NW
NE
SW
SE
N
Ford Rd
Wildwood St
Doxtator St
Cobb St
Heinze St
Hubbell St
Burger St
Beaver St
Belmont St
Hawthorne St
Russell St
Robin St
Lawrence Ave
Gulley Rd
Highview St
Nightingale St
Robindale St
Silvery Ln
Franklin St
Kingsbury St
Lafayette St
Denwood St
Vernon St
Drexel St
Mayburn St
Telegraph Rd
Waverly St
Mildred St
Melborn St
Elizabeth St
Martha St
York St
Outer Dr
Mc Millan St
Dacosta St
Edward St
Oak St
Hollander St
Wilson Ave
Buckingham St
Highland St
Arlington St
Sussex St
Sheridan St
Marlboro St
Ina St
Lodge Ln
Murray St
Marion St
Rex St
Coburn St
Myrtle Ave
Cromwell St
Nash St
Fort Dearborn St
Tonnahill St
Devonshire St
Reginald St
Wellington St
Cherry Hill Rd
Cherry Hill Ct
Long St
Law St
Alexandrine St
River Ln
Sylvan St
Rouge River Lower
Shady Hollow Dr
Golfcrest Dr
Woodcrest Dr
Golfcrest Ct
Brentwood St
Willoway St
Meadowlane Rd
Brady Rd
Brady St
Parkside Ct
Hampshire Ct
Hampton Ct
Robindale Ct
Beechmont St
Claremont St
Mohawk St
Berkley St
Meridan St
Roseyera St
Marshall St
Crescent St
Auburn St
Rockford St
Richmond Ave
Ward St
Ridgemont Ct
Rowe St
Sterling St
Hudson St
Fordson Dr
Fairmont Ct
Avondale Ave
Hillcrest Dr
Winona St
Fairmont St
Morley St
Morley Ct
Wagner Ct
Garrison St
Michigan Ave
Howe St
Howard St
Garrison Pl
Edward T Accy Sr Blvd
Jefferson St
Newman St
Tenny St
Park St
Mason St
Monroe St
Porter St
Crestview St
Garden Ct
Geneva St
Birch St
Locust St
Nona St
Haigh St
Edna St
Homer St
Audrey St
Kean St
Kandt St
Beech St
Nowlin St
Hamilton St
May St
Military St
Cass St
Francis St
Edison St
Gregory St
Olmstead St
Monroe St
Elmdale St
Woodcroft Dr
Fairway Dr
Whittier Pl
Riverdale Dr
Winchester Dr
Cambridge St
Bailey St
Trowbridge Ave
Harvard St
Scott St
Syracuse St
Summer St
Stephens St
Pardee Rd
Cleveland St
Columbia St
Donaldson St
Audette St
Leland Ct
Lloyd Ct
Cooke St
Hickory St
Oxford St
Dunning St
Cherry St
Homeplace St
Boldt St
Banner St
Burns St
Point St
Cornell St
Academy St
Grindley Park
Queen St
Parker St
Bennett St
Hubbard St
Vassar St
Dudley St
Chicago St
Boston St
New York St
Yale St
Whitmore St
Lincoln St
Mc Kinley Ave
Notre Dame St
Vivian St
Heritage Pkwy
Calvin St
Penn St
Madison St
Roosevelt St
Union St
Carlysle Ave
Ross St
Dartmouth Ave
Katherine St
William St
Alice St
Campbell St
Gertrude St
Harding St
Merrick St
Polk St
Hipp St

NW
NE
SW
SE
Ford Rd
Automobile Culb Dr
Executive Plaza Dr
Nottingham Ct
Wessex Ct
Fairlane Woods Dr
Royalvale Ln
Pembrooke Ct
Lemington Ct
Timberlane Ct
Yorkshire Ct
Southfield Frwy
US 39
Park Lane Blvd
Mercury Dr
Greenfield Rd
Mead Ave
Steadman Ave
Ternes St
Payne Ct
Colson Ave
Normandale St
Hubbard Dr
Beechtree Dr
Gabriel Richard St
Timber Ridge Dr
Lone Oak Dr
Evergreen Rd
American Rd
Jerome St
Korte Ave
Westland Ave
Rosalie Ave
Helen Ave
Palmer Ave
Curtis Ave
Walwit St
Firestone St
Chovin St
Barclay Ct
Opal Dr
Prospect St
Town Center Dr
Burlwood Dr
Rouge River
Fairlane Dr
Michigan Ave
Enfield Ln
Dover Ln
Carlton Ln
Bennington Ln
Abbott Ln
Commerce Dr
Bradford Ln
Ashby Ln
Longmeadow Rd
Brewster Rd
Adams Ln
Middlebury Ct
Woodbury Ln
Danvers
Clinton Ln
Middlebury Dr
Amherst Ln
Woodland Dr
Windham Ln
Abington Ln
Byfield Ln
Dearborn Rd
Knollwood Dr
Stuart Ln
Brookwo
Blair Ct
Lindenwood Dr
Colony
Kimberle
Village Rd
Rotunda Dr
Oakwood Blvd
Ash St
Pelham Rd
Woodside Dr
Detroit St
Texas St
Byrd St
Edgewood St
Snow Rd
Houston St
Snow Ct
Culver St
Hollywood St
Glover St
Crandell St
Venice St
Sherwood St
Birchcrest St
Linden St
Walnut St
Southfield Rd
Donaldson St
Audette St
Nowlin Ct
Westminster Ct
Outer Dr
Hipp St
Huron St
Mayfair St
Carlysle St
Dallas St
Northampton St
Raymond Ct
Chestnut St
Smith St
Raymond St
Willow St
Weddel St
Jackson St
Ziegler St
Dartmouth Ave
N

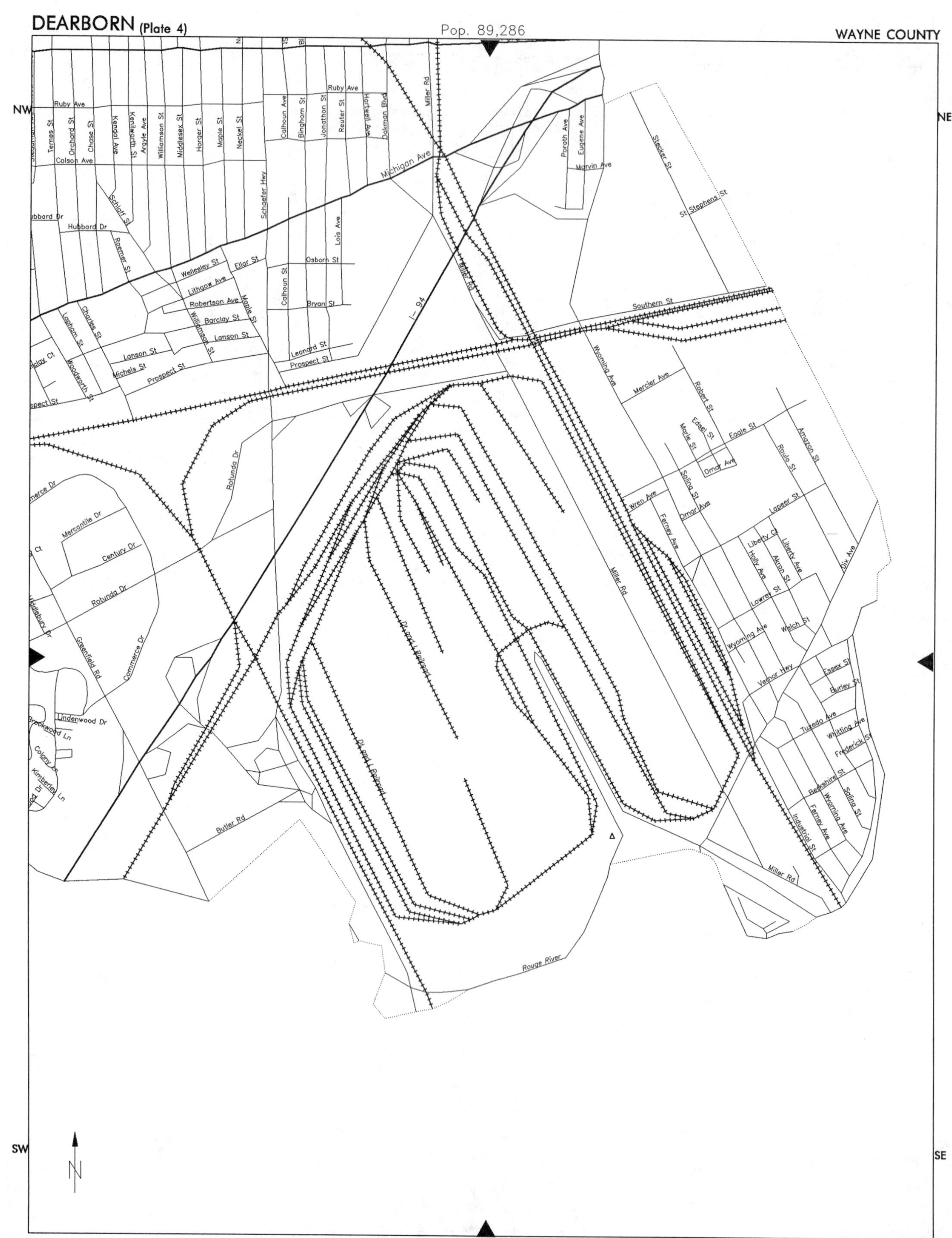
NW
NE
SW
SE
N
Ruby Ave
Temes St
Orchard St
Chase St
Colson Ave
Kendal Ave
Kenilworth St
Argyle Ave
Williamson St
Middlesex St
Horger St
Maple St
Neckel St
Calhoun Ave
Bingham St
Jonathon St
Reuter St
Hartwell Ave
Oakman Blvd
Miller Rd
Michigan Ave
Porath Ave
Eugene Ave
Marvin Ave
Stecker St
St Stephens St
Hubbard Dr
Schlaff St
Roemer St
Schaefer Hwy
Lois Ave
Osborn St
Wellesley St
Ellar St
Lithgow Ave
Robertson Ave
Barclay St
Lanson St
Calhoun St
Bryan St
Southern St
I-94
Lapham St
Charles St
Woodworth St
Michels St
Prospect St
Leonard St
Wyoming Ave
Mercier Ave
Robert St
Edsel St
Marie St
Eagle St
Amazon St
Roulo St
Omar Ave
Salina St
Wren Ave
Ferney Ave
Lapeer St
Rotunda Dr
Mercantile Dr
Century Dr
Liberty Ct
Liberty Ave
Holly Ave
Akron St
Lowrey St
Welch St
Dix Ave
Greenfield Rd
Commerce Dr
DL and I Railroad
Vernor Hwy
Essex St
Burley St
Tuxedo Ave
Whiting Ave
Frederick St
Lindenwood Dr
Brookwood Ln
Colony Ct
Kimberley Ln
Butler Rd
Berkshire St
Industrial St
Rouge River

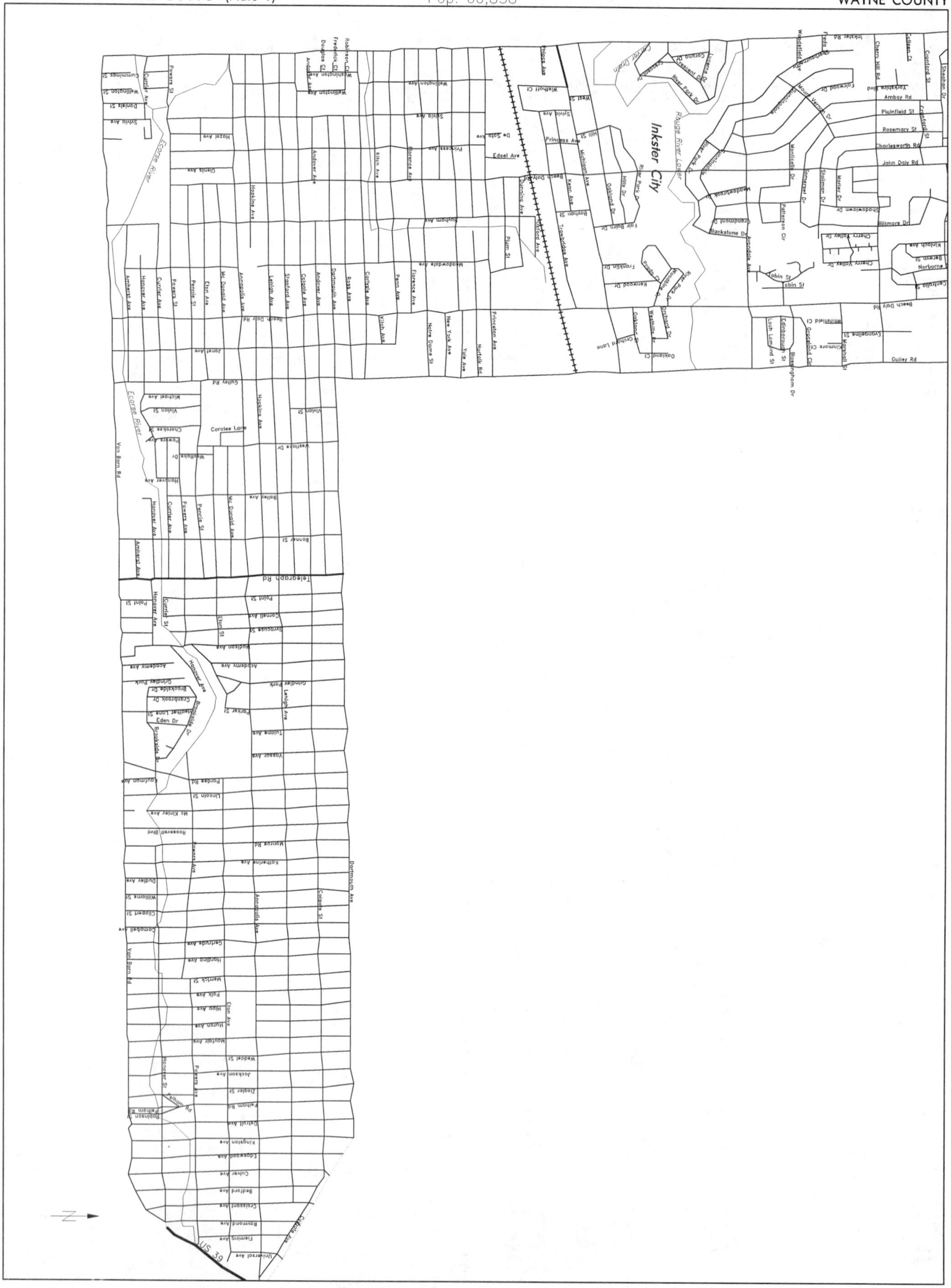

Inkster City

Telegraph Rd

US 39

DEARBORN HEIGHTS (Plate 2) Pop. 60,838 WAYNE COUNTY

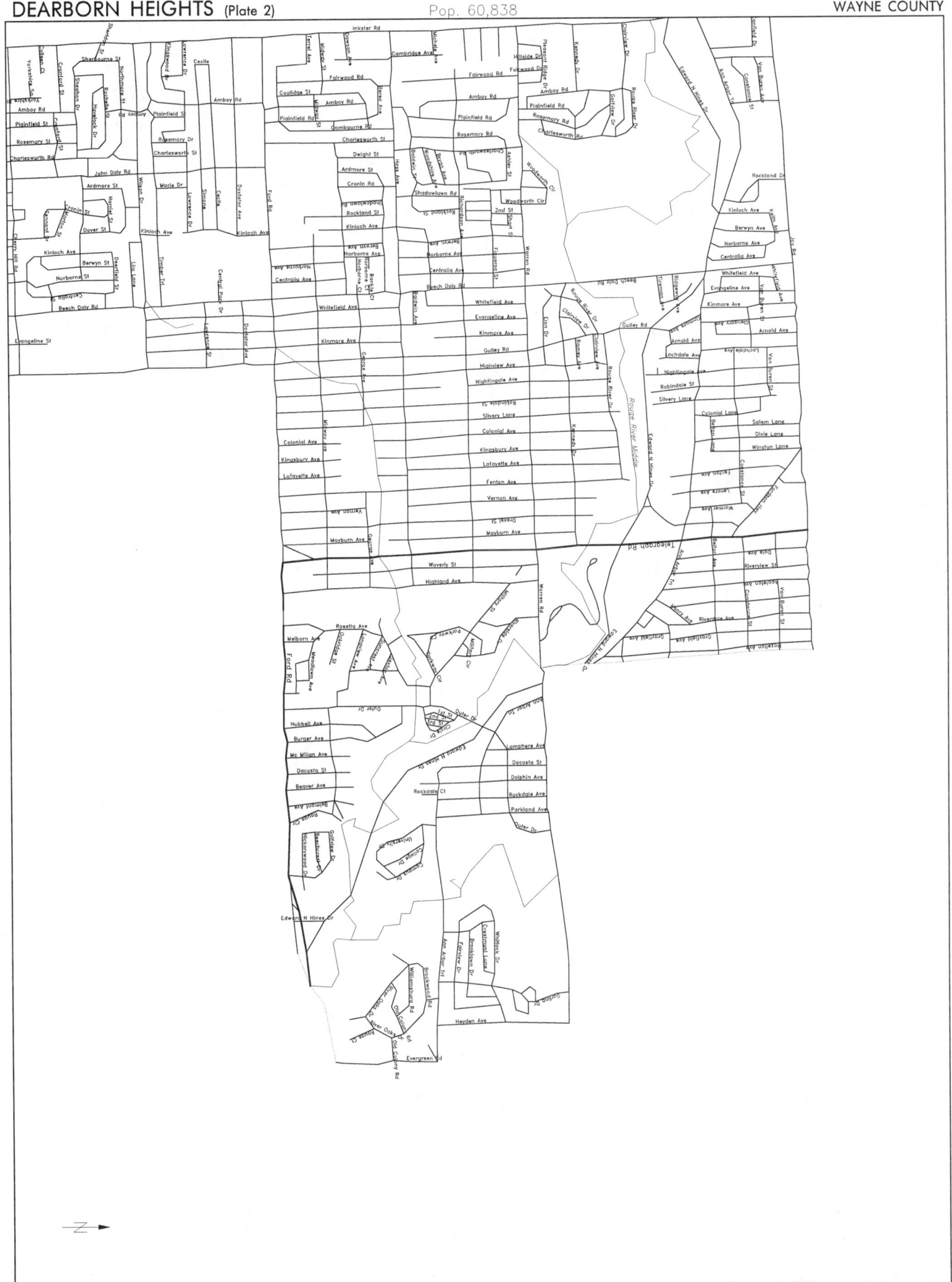

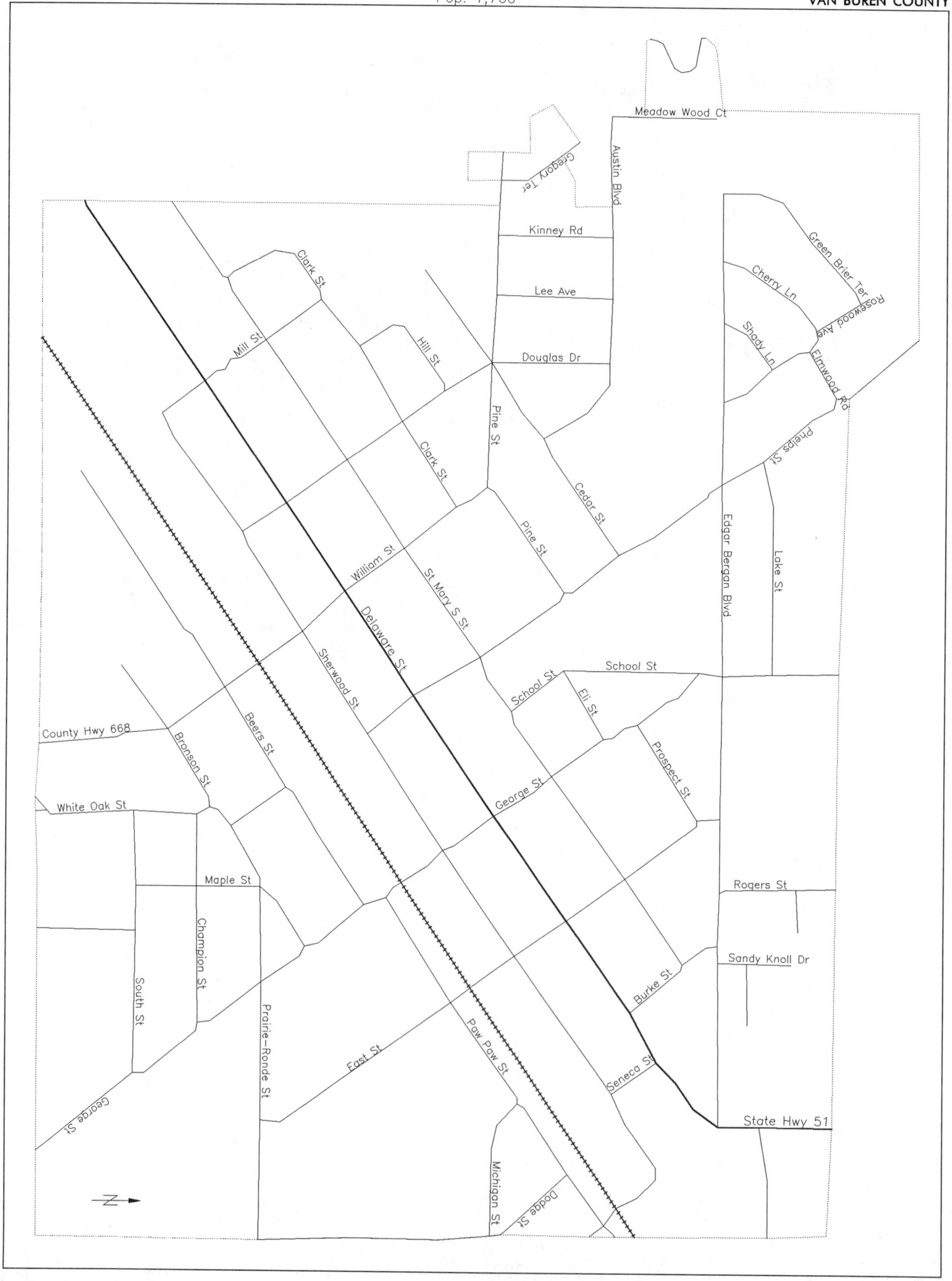

Meadow Wood Ct
Gregory Ter
Austin Blvd
Kinney Rd
Lee Ave
Clark St
Mill St
Hill St
Douglas Dr
Green Brier Ter
Cherry Ln
Rosewood Ave
Shady Ln
Elmwood Rd
Pine St
Clark St
Cedar St
Phelps St
Edgar Bergan Blvd
Lake St
William St
Pine St
St Mary S St
Delaware St
Sherwood St
School St
School St
Eli St
County Hwy 668
Bronson St
Beers St
Prospect St
George St
White Oak St
Maple St
Rogers St
Champion St
Sandy Knoll Dr
South St
Burke St
Prairie-Ronde St
East St
Paw Paw St
Seneca St
George St
State Hwy 51
Michigan St
Dodge St
N

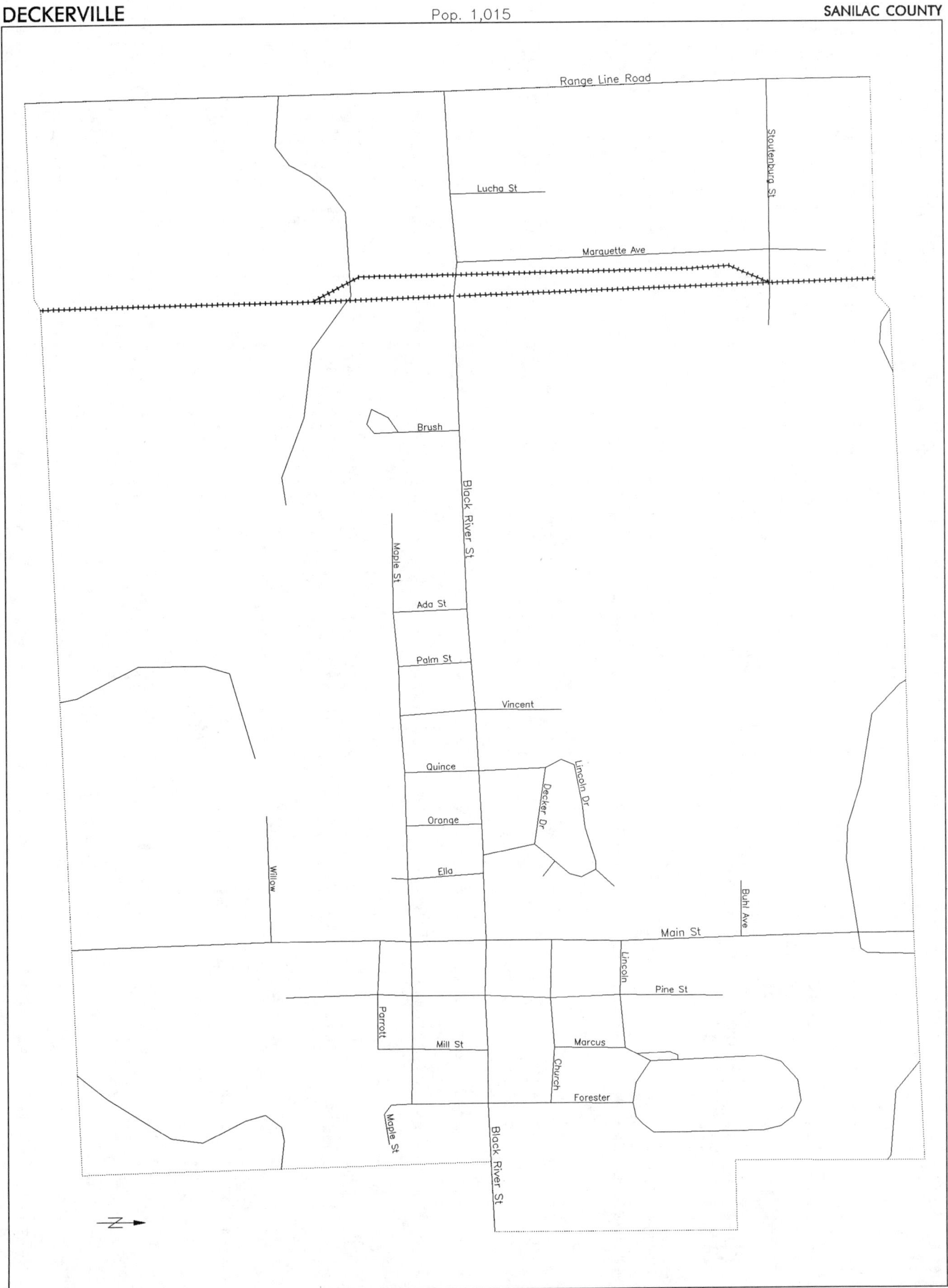
Range Line Road
Stoutenburg St
Lucha St
Marquette Ave
Brush
Black River St
Maple St
Ada St
Palm St
Vincent
Quince
Lincoln Dr
Decker Dr
Orange
Ella
Willow
Buhl Ave
Main St
Lincoln
Pine St
Parrott
Mill St
Marcus
Church
Forester
Maple St
Black River St

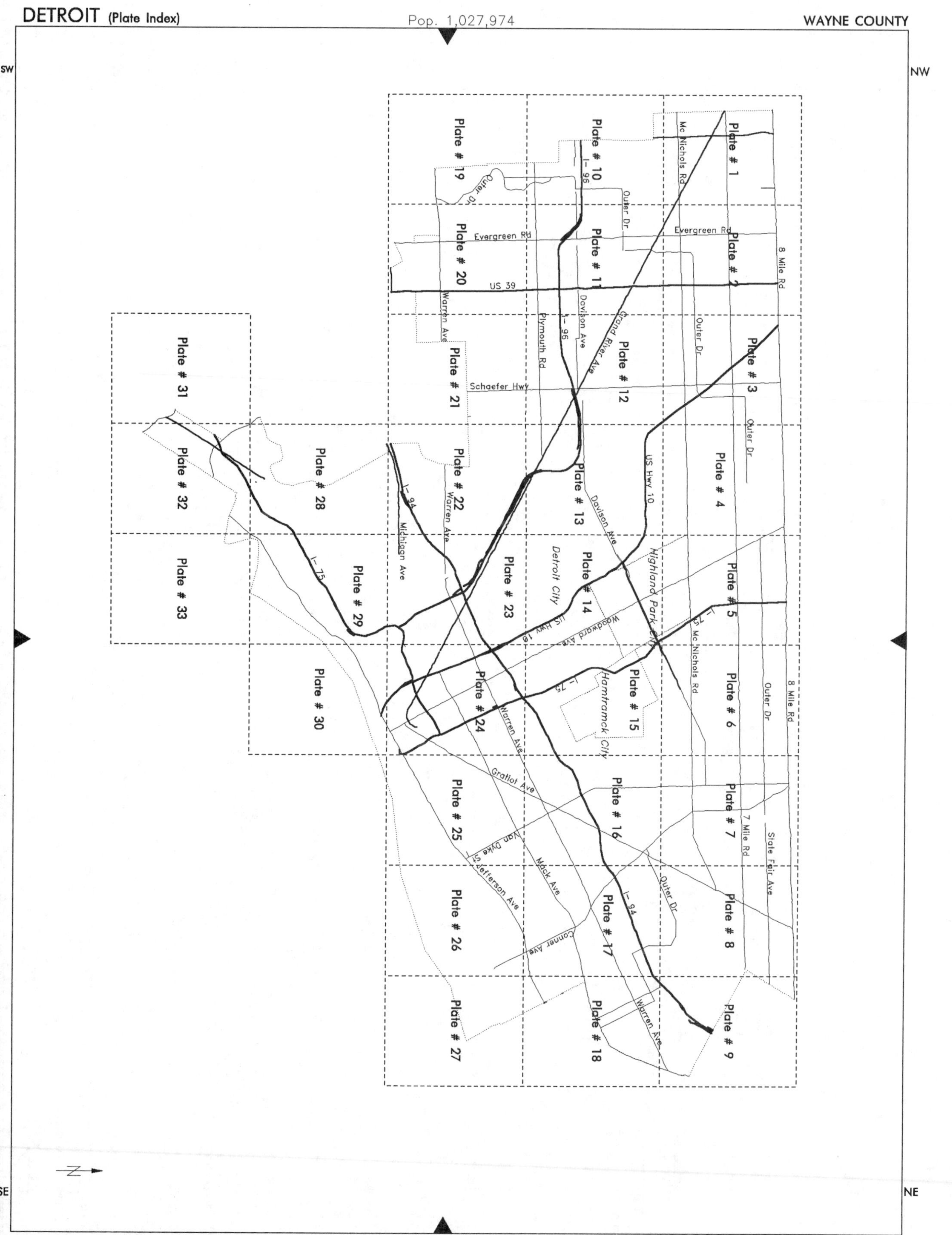
SW
NW
SE
NE
Plate # 1
Plate # 2
Plate # 3
Plate # 4
Plate # 5
Plate # 6
Plate # 7
Plate # 8
Plate # 9
Plate # 10
Plate # 11
Plate # 12
Plate # 13
Plate # 14
Plate # 15
Plate # 16
Plate # 17
Plate # 18
Plate # 19
Plate # 20
Plate # 21
Plate # 22
Plate # 23
Plate # 24
Plate # 25
Plate # 26
Plate # 27
Plate # 28
Plate # 29
Plate # 30
Plate # 31
Plate # 32
Plate # 33
Mc Nichols Rd
Outer Dr
Evergreen Rd
8 Mile Rd
US 39
I- 96
Davison Ave
Grand River Ave
Plymouth Rd
Warren Ave
Schaefer Hwy
US Hwy 10
I- 94
Michigan Ave
I- 75
Detroit City
Highland Park City
Woodward Ave
US Hwy 16
Hamtramck City
Gratiot Ave
Van Dyke
E Jefferson Ave
Mack Ave
Conner Ave
7 Mile Rd
State Fair Ave

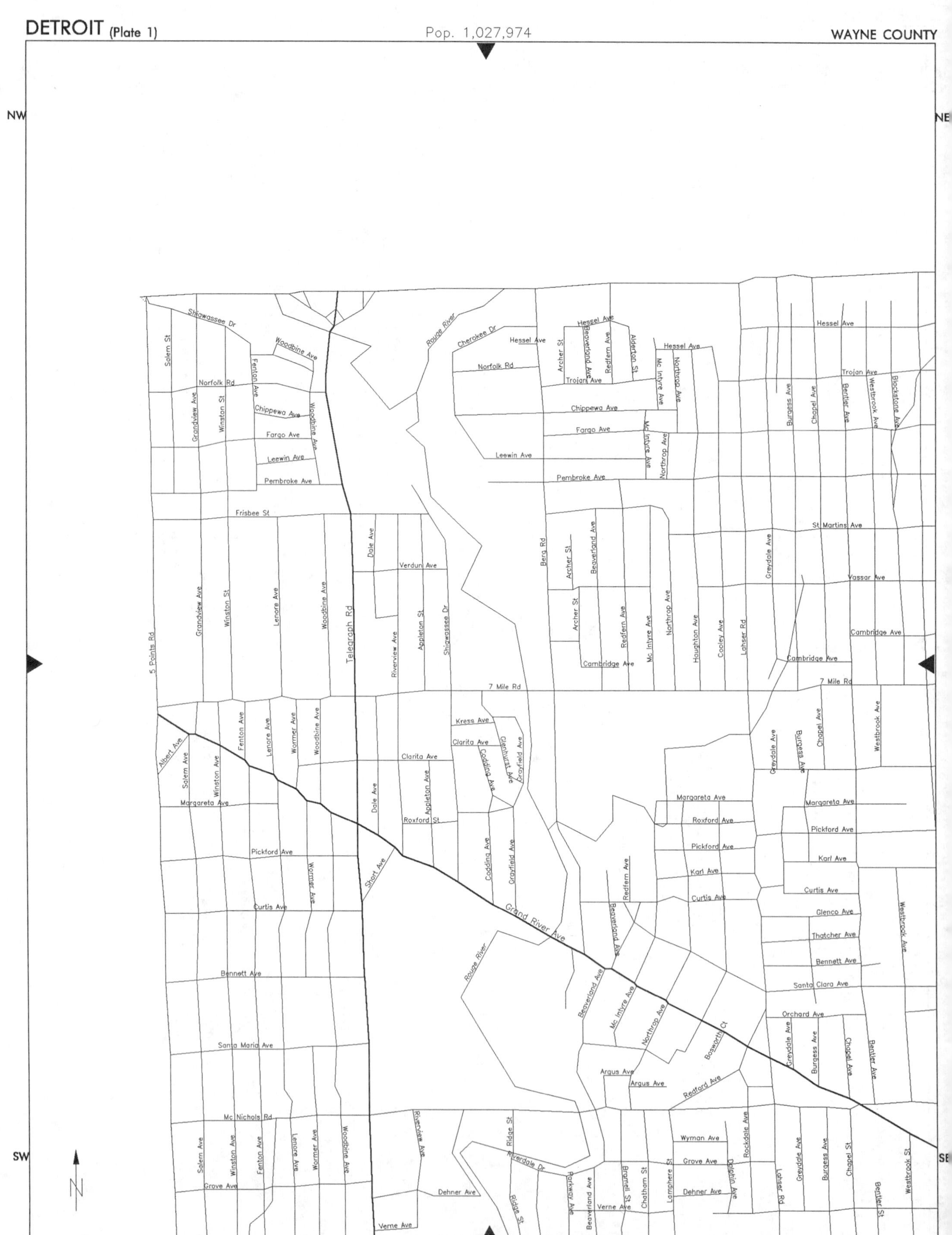
NW
NE
SW
SE
Shiawassee Dr
Woodbine Ave
Rouge River
Cherokee Dr
Hessel Ave
Trojan Ave
Norfolk Rd
Chippewa Ave
Fargo Ave
Leewin Ave
Pembroke Ave
Frisbee St
St Martins Ave
Verdun Ave
Vassar Ave
Cambridge Ave
7 Mile Rd
Kress Ave
Clarita Ave
Margareta Ave
Roxford St
Roxford Ave
Pickford Ave
Karl Ave
Curtis Ave
Glenco Ave
Thatcher Ave
Bennett Ave
Santa Clara Ave
Santa Maria Ave
Orchard Ave
Grand River Ave
Argus Ave
Redford Ave
Bosworth Ct
Mc Nichols Rd
Wyman Ave
Grove Ave
Dehner Ave
Verne Ave
Riverdale Dr
5 Points Rd
Telegraph Rd
Berg Rd
Lahser Rd
Greydale Ave
Burgess Ave
Chapel Ave
Bentler Ave
Westbrook Ave
Blackstone Ave
Houghton Ave
Cooley Ave
Northrop Ave
Mc Intyre Ave
Redfern Ave
Beaverland Ave
Archer St
Alderton St
Salem St
Salem Ave
Grandview Ave
Winston St
Winston Ave
Fenton Ave
Lenore Ave
Wormer Ave
Woodbine Ave
Dale Ave
Riverview Ave
Appleton St
Appleton Ave
Shiawassee Dr
Glenhurst Ave
Grayfield Ave
Codding Ave
Albert Ave
Short Ave
Ridge St
Parkway Ave
Brunell St
Chatham St
Lamphere St
Dolphin Ave
Rockdale Ave
Chapel St
Bentler St
Westbrook St

DETROIT (Plate 2) Pop. 1,027,974 WAYNE COUNTY

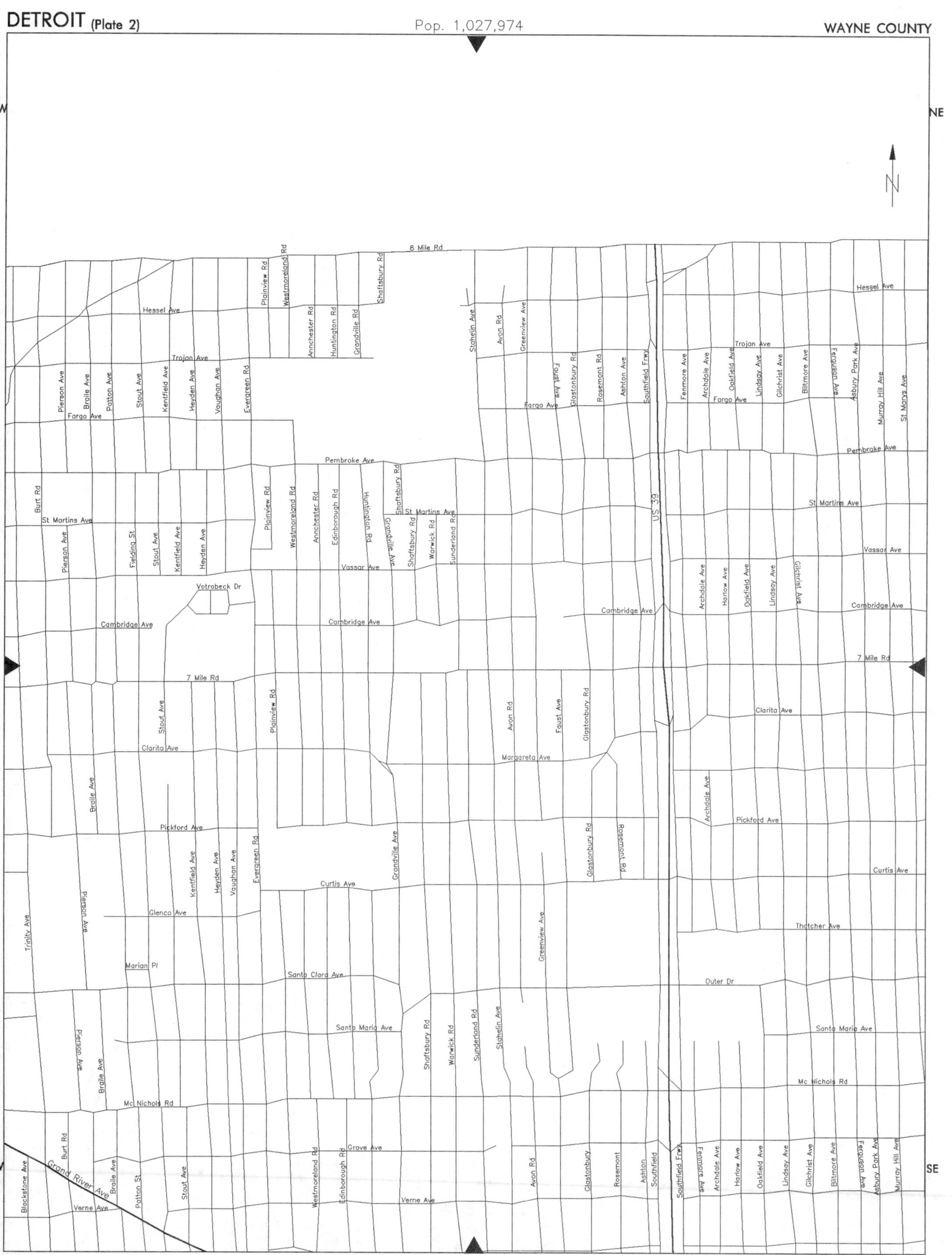

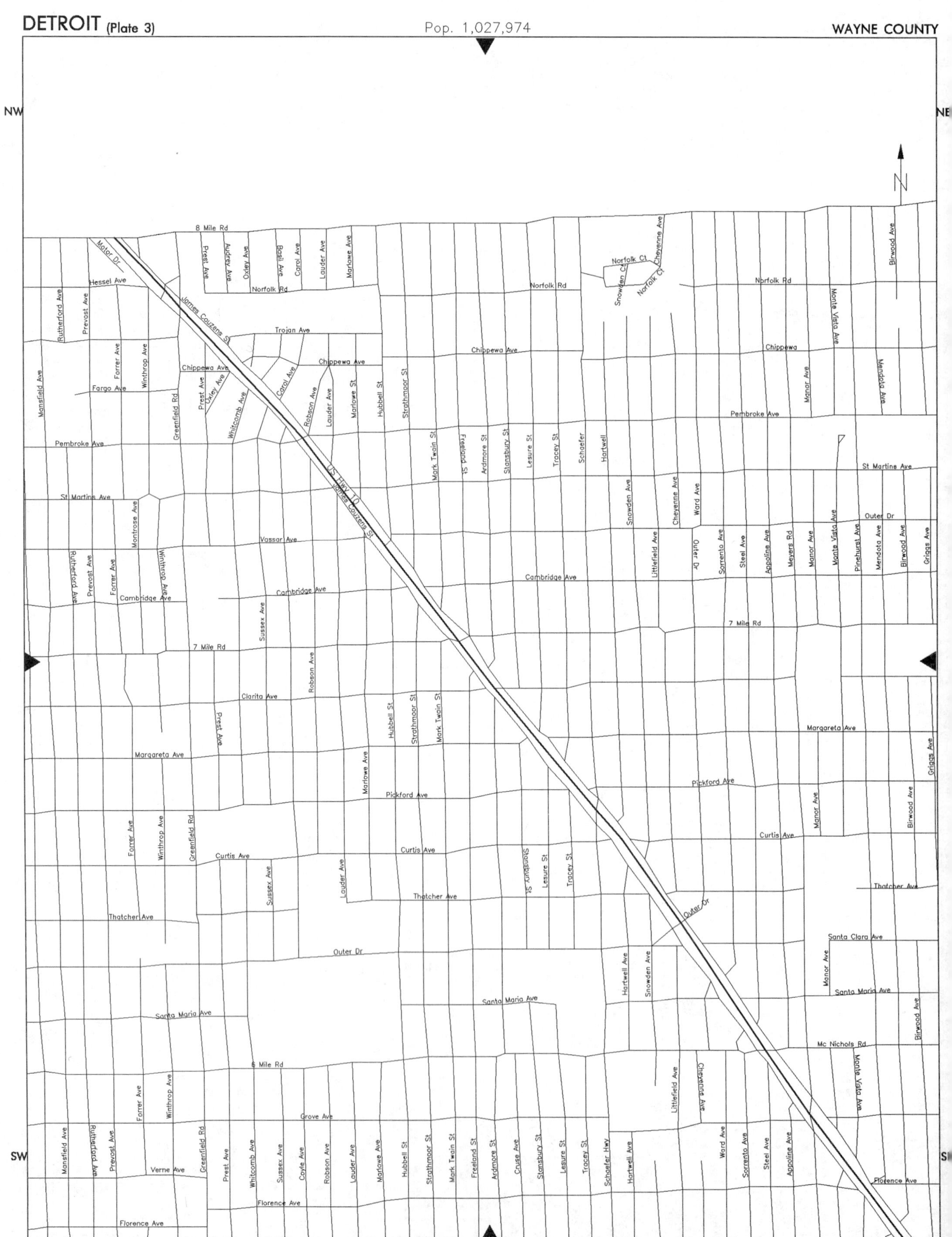
NW
NE
SW
SE
N
8 Mile Rd
7 Mile Rd
6 Mile Rd
US Hwy 10
James Couzens St
Motor Dr
Hessel Ave
Norfolk Rd
Trojan Ave
Chippewa Ave
Fargo Ave
Pembroke Ave
St Martins Ave
Vassar Ave
Cambridge Ave
Clarita Ave
Margareta Ave
Pickford Ave
Curtis Ave
Thatcher Ave
Outer Dr
Santa Clara Ave
Santa Maria Ave
Mc Nichols Rd
Grove Ave
Verne Ave
Florence Ave
Mansfield Ave
Rutherford Ave
Prevost Ave
Forrer Ave
Winthrop Ave
Montrose Ave
Greenfield Rd
Prest Ave
Whitcomb Ave
Sussex Ave
Coyle Ave
Robson Ave
Lauder Ave
Marlowe Ave
Hubbell St
Strathmoor St
Mark Twain St
Freeland St
Ardmore St
Cruse Ave
Stansbury St
Lesure St
Tracey St
Schaefer
Schaefer Hwy
Hartwell
Hartwell Ave
Snowden Ave
Littlefield Ave
Cheyenne Ave
Ward Ave
Sorrento Ave
Steel Ave
Appoline Ave
Meyers Rd
Manor Ave
Monte Vista Ave
Pinehurst Ave
Mendota Ave
Birwood Ave
Griggs Ave
Audrey Ave
Oxley Ave
Basil Ave
Carol Ave
Norfolk Ct
Snowden Ct
Chippewa

8 Mile Rd
Woodstock Dr
Norfolk Rd
Chippewa Ave
Pembroke Ave
St Martins Ave
Cranbrook Dr
Kingswood St
Outer Dr
Cambridge Ave
7 Mile Rd
Clarita Ave
Margareta Ave
Pickford Ave
Curtis Ave
London Ave
Thatcher Ave
Santa Clara Ave
Santa Maria Ave
Mc Nichols Rd
Grove Ave
Mary Grove Dr
Florence Ave
Puritan Ave
Strathcona Dr
Argyle Cres
Lowell St
Suffolk Dr
Woodston Dr
Lucerne St
Gloucester Dr
Sherbourne St
Canterbury St
Shrewsbury St
Roslyn Rd
Stratford St
Renfrew Rd
Berkeley St
Pontchartrain St
Hamilton Ave
Fairway Dr
Parkside Ave
Warrington St
Oak Dr
Birchcrest Dr
Fairfield Ave
Muirland Ave
Wildemere Ave
Belden St
Quincy St
Griggs Ave
Ilene Ave
Washburn Ave
Wyoming Ave
Kentucky Ave
Indiana Ave
Wisconsin Ave
Ohio Ave
Cherrylawn Ave
Northlawn Ave
Roselawn Ave
Greenlawn Ave
Woodingham Dr
Santa Barbara Ave
San Juan Dr
Prairie Ave
Monica Ave
Santa Rosa Dr
Stoepel Ave
Livernois Ave
Pennington Ave
Gardendale St
Piccadilly St
Sheffield St
Wakefield St
Renfrew St
Briarcliff St
Lichfield Rd
Turner Ave
Tuller Ave
Lilac Ave
Petoskey Ave
Lawton Ave
Princeton Ave
Linwood Ave
Normandy Ave
La Salle Ave
Baylis Ave
Inverness Ave
Log Cabin Ave
NW
NE
SE
N

NW
NE
SW
SE
8 Mile Rd
Kenneth St
Alameda St
Colton St
Winchester Ave
Fayette St
Gary St
Charleston St
Danbury Ave
Exeter St
Derby St
John R Rd
Coventry Ave
Keating Ave
Andover Ave
Irvington Ave
Yacama Ave
Omira Ave
Pointer St
Lumpkin St
Remington Ave
Cameron Ave
Hawthorne Ave
Cardoni Ave
Russell Ave
Hanna Ave
Hull Ave
Greeley Ave
Ripelle St
Orleans St
Marx Ave
Dequindre Ave
St Aubin St
Conant Ave
State Fair Ave
Adeline St
Fernhill St
Lantz Ave
Annin St
Carmel St
Penrose St
Balmoral St
Larchwood St
7 Mile Rd
Ralston St
Strathcona Dr
Woodward Ave
Afton St
Wellesley Dr
Burlington Dr
Lincolnshire Dr
Hershey St
Havana St
Carman St
Blake St
Emery Ave
Brentwood St
Hollywood Ave
Robinwood St
Robinwood Ave
Goldengate Ave
Hildale Ave
Grixdale Ave
Greendale St
Margaret St
Margaret Ave
Savannah St
Erle St
Nevada Ave
Montana St
Minnesota Ave
Worcester Pl
Longwood Pl
Longwood Ave
Cedarhurst Pl
Parkhurst Pl
Dakota Ave
Arizona St
Edgevale Ave
Brush St
Wanda Ave
Oakland Ave
Madeira Ave
Stender Ave
Merrill Plaisance St
Hamilton Ave
Whitmore Dr
Manderson Rd
Alwyne Lane
Pontchartrain St
Covington Dr
Merton Rd
Mc Nichols Rd
Hill Ave
North Ave
Grove Ave
Brighton St
Portage St
Geneva Ave
Florence Ave
Louise Ave
Eason Ave
Puritan Ave
Moss Ave
12th Ave
Joslyn St
2nd Ave
3rd Ave
Stevens Ave
Candler Ave
Ferris Ave
Midland Ave
Bartlett St
Victor St
Modern Ave
I-75

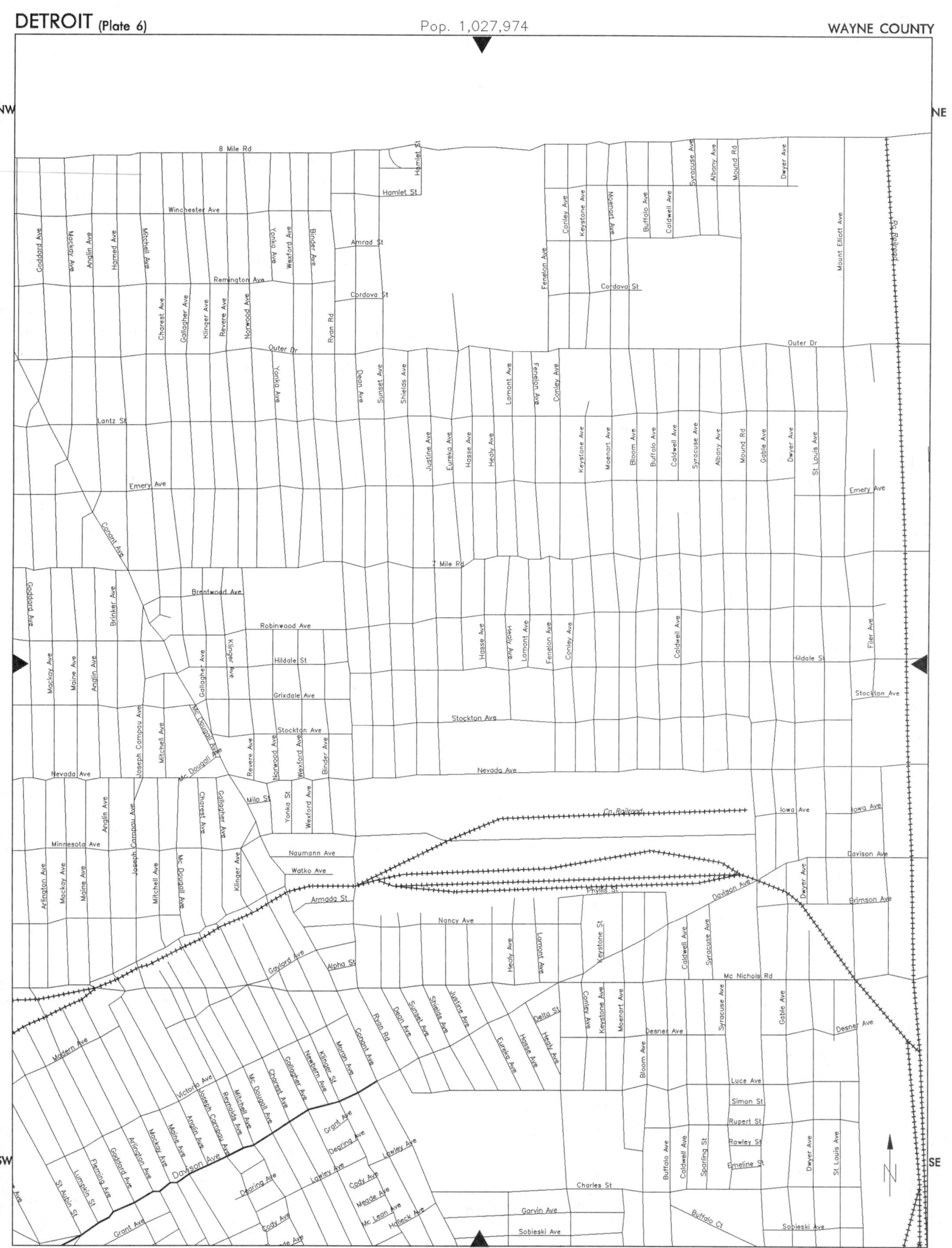
NW
NE
SW
SE
8 Mile Rd
Hamlet St
Winchester Ave
Goddard Ave
Mackay Ave
Anglin Ave
Harned Ave
Mitchell Ave
Yonka Ave
Wexford Ave
Binder Ave
Amrad St
Remington Ave
Cordova St
Charest Ave
Gallagher Ave
Klinger Ave
Revere Ave
Norwood Ave
Ryan Rd
Outer Dr
Conley Ave
Keystone Ave
Moenart Ave
Buffalo Ave
Caldwell Ave
Syracuse Ave
Albany Ave
Mound Rd
Dwyer Ave
Fenelon Ave
Mount Elliott Ave
Rr Railroad
Lantz St
Dean Ave
Sunset Ave
Shields Ave
Lamont Ave
Justine Ave
Eureka Ave
Hasse Ave
Healy Ave
Bloom Ave
Gable Ave
St Louis Ave
Emery Ave
Conant Ave
7 Mile Rd
Brentwood Ave
Brinker Ave
Robinwood Ave
Hildale St
Maine Ave
Filer Ave
Grixdale Ave
Stockton Ave
Joseph Campau Ave
Mc Dougall Ave
Nevada Ave
Milo St
Iowa Ave
Cn Railroad
Minnesota Ave
Naumann Ave
Watko Ave
Davison Ave
Arlington Ave
Armada St
Phyllis St
Brimson Ave
Nancy Ave
Gaylord Ave
Alpha St
Mc Nichols Rd
Modern Ave
Moran Ave
Newbern Ave
Klinger St
Delta St
Desner Ave
Victoria Ave
Reynolds Ave
Luce Ave
Simon St
Rupert St
Grant Ave
Deering Ave
Rowley St
Lawley Ave
Sparling St
Emeline St
Fleming Ave
Lumpkin St
St Aubin St
Cody Ave
Meade Ave
Charles St
Mc Lean Ave
Halleck Ave
Garvin Ave
Buffalo Ct
Sobieski Ave
N

DETROIT (Plate 7)

Pop. 1,027,974

WAYNE COUNTY

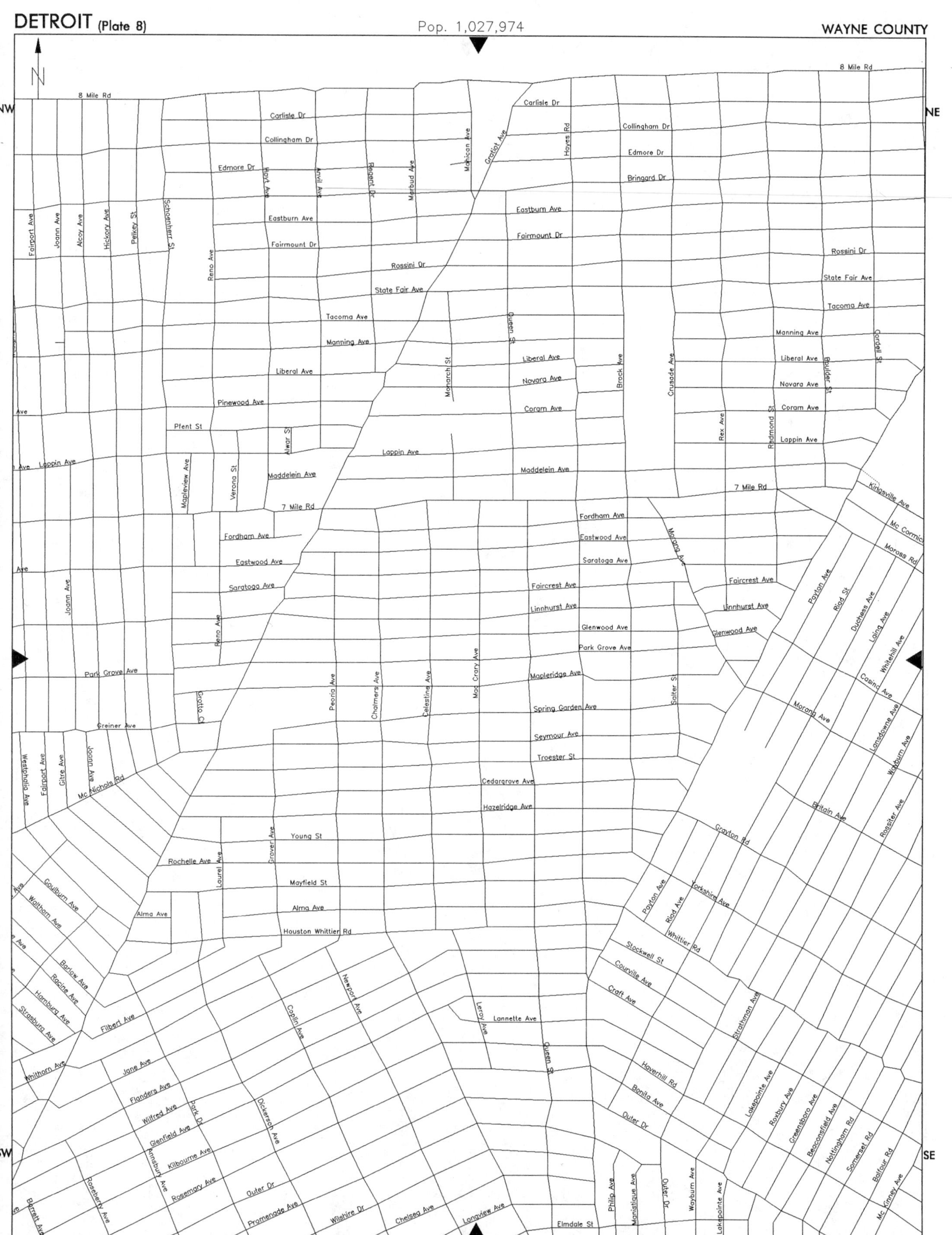
N
NW
NE
SW
SE
8 Mile Rd
8 Mile Rd
Carlisle Dr
Carlisle Dr
Collingham Dr
Collingham Dr
Edmore Dr
Edmore Dr
Bringard Dr
Hoyt Ave
Anvil Ave
Regent Dr
Marbud Ave
Mohican Ave
Gratiot Ave
Hayes Rd
Eastburn Ave
Eastburn Ave
Fairmount Dr
Fairmount Dr
Fairport Ave
Joann Ave
Alcoy Ave
Hickory Ave
Pelkey St
Schoenherr St
Reno Ave
Rossini Dr
Rossini Dr
State Fair Ave
State Fair Ave
Tacoma Ave
Tacoma Ave
Manning Ave
Manning Ave
Queen St
Liberal Ave
Liberal Ave
Liberal Ave
Novara Ave
Novara Ave
Monarch St
Brock Ave
Crusade Ave
Boulder St
Cordell St
Pinewood Ave
Coram Ave
Coram Ave
Pfent St
Alwar St
Rex Ave
Redmond St
Lappin Ave
Lappin Ave
Lappin Ave
Mapleview Ave
Verona St
Maddelein Ave
Maddelein Ave
7 Mile Rd
7 Mile Rd
Kingsville Ave
Mc Cormick
Moross Rd
Fordham Ave
Fordham Ave
Eastwood Ave
Eastwood Ave
Morang Ave
Saratoga Ave
Saratoga Ave
Faircrest Ave
Faircrest Ave
Payton Ave
Riad St
Duchess Ave
Laing Ave
Whitehill Ave
Linnhurst Ave
Linnhurst Ave
Glenwood Ave
Glenwood Ave
Park Grove Ave
Park Grove Ave
Casino Ave
Mapleridge Ave
Peoria Ave
Chalmers Ave
Celestine Ave
Mac Crary Ave
Salter St
Spring Garden Ave
Morang Ave
Lansdowne Ave
Grotto Ct
Seymour Ave
Greiner Ave
Troester St
Westphalia Ave
Fairport Ave
Gitre Ave
Joann Ave
Mc Nichols Rd
Cedargrove Ave
Hazelridge Ave
Wayburn Ave
Britain Ave
Rossiter Ave
Young St
Grayton Rd
Rochelle Ave
Laurel Ave
Grover Ave
Mayfield St
Payton Ave
Yorkshire Ave
Goulburn Ave
Waltham Ave
Alma Ave
Alma Ave
Riad Ave
Houston Whittier Rd
Whittier Rd
Stockwell St
Courville Ave
Craft Ave
Barlow Ave
Racine Ave
Hamburg Ave
Strasburg Ave
Newport Ave
Caplin Ave
Leroy Ave
Lannette Ave
Strathman Ave
Filbert Ave
Queen St
Whithorn Ave
Jane Ave
Haverhill Rd
Flanders Ave
Bonita Ave
Lakepointe Ave
Wilfred Ave
Park Dr
Dickerson Ave
Roxbury Ave
Outer Dr
Greensboro Ave
Glenfield Ave
Beaconsfield Ave
Kilbourne Ave
Nottingham Rd
Amsbury Ave
Somerset Rd
Rosemary Ave
Rosberry Ave
Outer Dr
Balfour Rd
Philip Ave
Manistique Ave
Outer Dr
Wayburn Ave
Lakepointe Ave
Mc Kinney Ave
Barrett Ave
Promenade Ave
Wilshire Dr
Chelsea Ave
Longview Ave
Elmdale St

NW
NE
SW
SE
8 Mile Rd
Carlisle Dr
Collingham Dr
Edmore Dr
Shakespeare St
Cushing St
Bringard Dr
Eastburn Ave
Fairmount Dr
Rossini Dr
Kelly Rd
State Fair Ave
Manning Ave
Kingsville Ave
Mc Cormick St
Moross Rd
Whitehill Ave
Lansdowne Ave
Wayburn Ave
Rossiter Ave
Beaconsfield Ave
Nottingham Rd
Somerset Rd
Balfour Rd
Mc Kinney Ave
Worden St
Peerless Ave
Marne Ave
Duprey Ave
Lanark Ave
Sanilac Ave
Camley Ave
Roxbury Ave
Lakepointe Ave
Alstead St
Rockcastle St
Edgefield St
Tyrone Ave
Cheshire St
Chester Ave
Malling St
Berden St
Canyon Ave
Meuse Ave
Merlin Ave
Britain Ave
Harvard Rd
Boleyn St
Grayton Rd
Yorkshire Ave
Bishop Ave
Kensington Rd
Everts Ave
Whittier Rd
Courville Ave
Bedford Rd
Devonshire Rd
I-94
Minerva St
Linville Ave
Chandler Park Dr
Hillcrest Ave
Lannoo St
Mack Ave
Radnor Ave
Farmbrook Ave
Lodewyck Ave
Marseilles Ave
University Pl
Bluehill Ave
Cadieux Ave
Oldtown St
Southampton St
Frankfort Ave
Gateshead St
Ashley Ave
Lafontaine St
Anatole St
Opal St
Warren Ave
Harper Ave
Audubon Ave
Whittier Rd
Kensington Rd
Yorkshire Ave
Bishop Ave
Grayton Rd
Harvard Rd
Guilford Ave
Woodhall St
Neff Rd
Hereford Ave
N

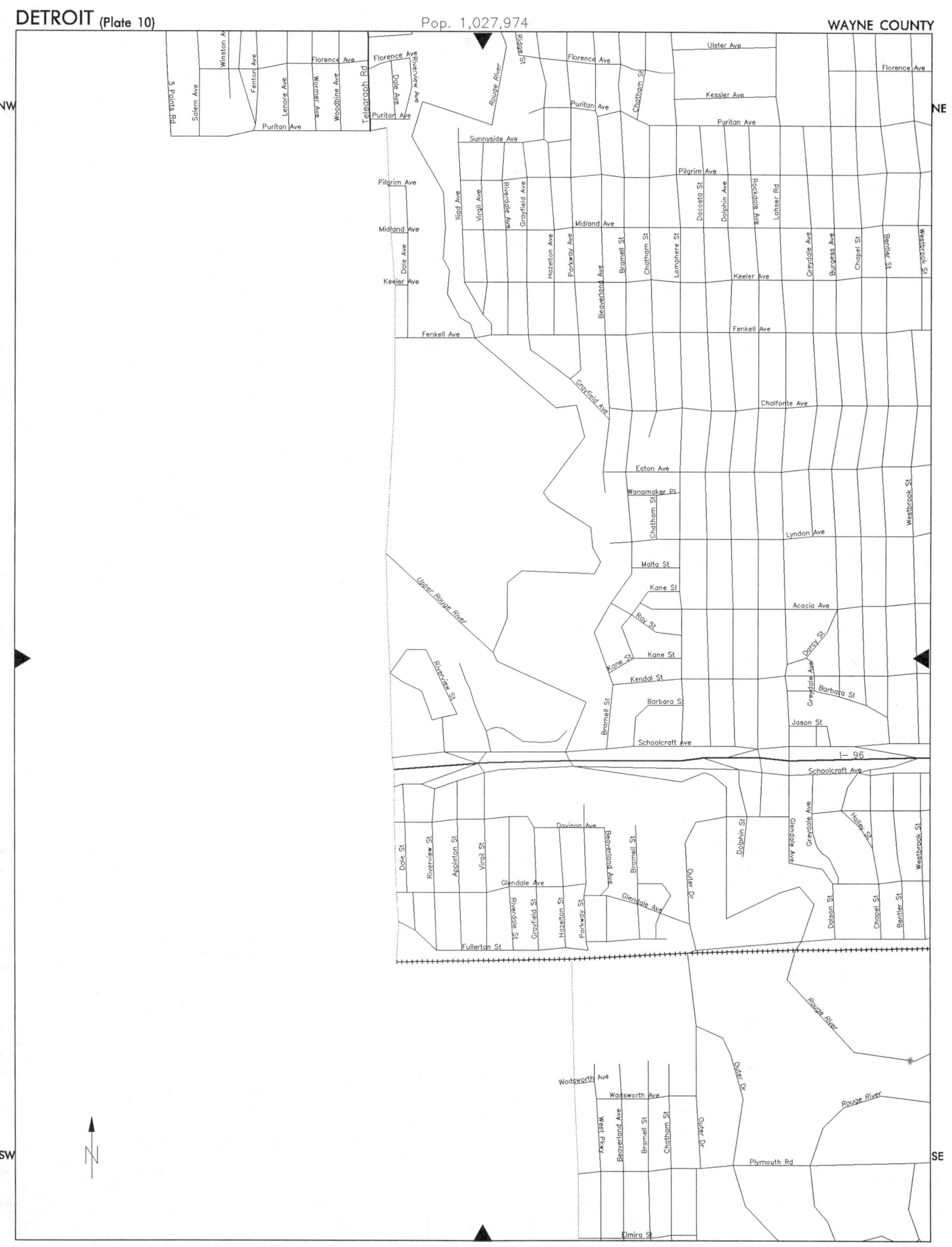
NW
NE
SW
SE
N
5 Points Rd
Salem Ave
Winston Ave
Fenton Ave
Lenore Ave
Wormer Ave
Woodbine Ave
Telegraph Rd
Florence Ave
Riverview Ave
Dale Ave
Puritan Ave
Rouge River
Ridge St
Chatham St
Ulster Ave
Kessler Ave
Sunnyside Ave
Pilgrim Ave
Midland Ave
Keeler Ave
Fenkell Ave
Iliad Ave
Virgil Ave
Riverdale Ave
Grayfield Ave
Hazelton Ave
Parkway Ave
Beaverland Ave
Bramell St
Lamphere St
Dacosta St
Dolphin Ave
Rockdale Ave
Lahser Rd
Greydale Ave
Burgess Ave
Chapel St
Bentler St
Westbrook St
Chalfonte Ave
Eaton Ave
Wanamaker Pl
Lyndon Ave
Malta St
Kane St
Acacia Ave
Ray St
Darcy St
Kendal St
Barbara St
Jason St
Upper Rouge River
Riverview St
Schoolcraft Ave
I- 96
Davison Ave
Dale St
Riverview St
Appleton St
Virgil St
Glendale Ave
Riverdale St
Grayfield St
Hazelton St
Parkway St
Outer Dr
Dolphin St
Hailey St
Dolson St
Fullerton St
Wadsworth Ave
West Pkwy
Plymouth Rd
Elmira St

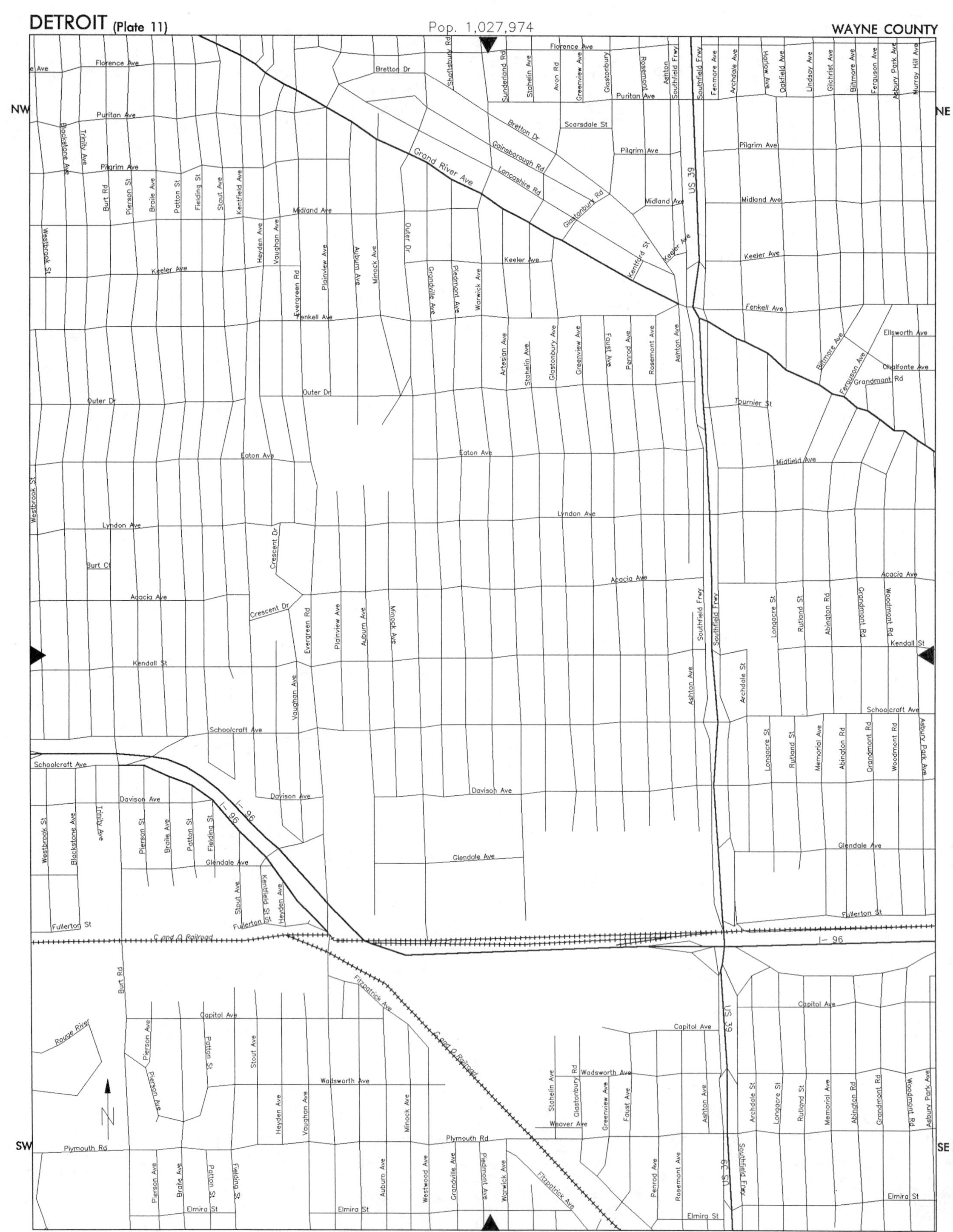
NW
NE
SW
SE
Grand River Ave
Southfield Frwy
US 39
I- 96
C and O Railroad
Fitzpatrick Ave
Rouge River
Plymouth Rd
Schoolcraft Ave
Outer Dr
Fenkell Ave
Davison Ave
Lyndon Ave
Eaton Ave
Keeler Ave
Midland Ave
Puritan Ave
Florence Ave
Pilgrim Ave
Acacia Ave
Kendall St
Glendale Ave
Fullerton St
Capitol Ave
Wadsworth Ave
Elmira St

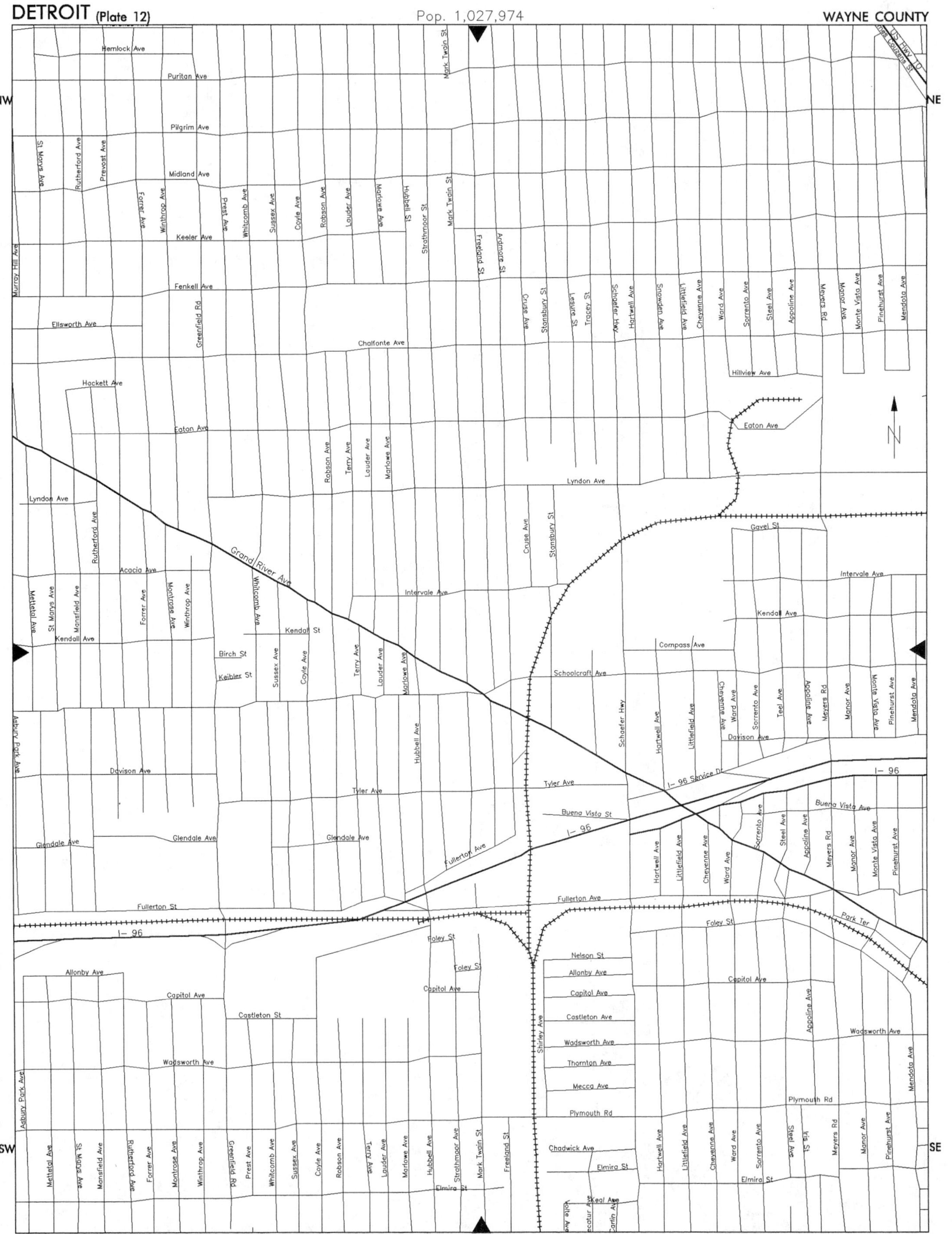
NW
NE
SW
SE
N
Hemlock Ave
Puritan Ave
Mark Twain St
US Hwy 10
Pilgrim Ave
St Marys Ave
Rutherford Ave
Prevost Ave
Midland Ave
Forrer Ave
Winthrop Ave
Prest Ave
Whitcomb Ave
Sussex Ave
Coyle Ave
Robson Ave
Lauder Ave
Marlowe Ave
Hubbell St
Strathmoor St
Keeler Ave
Freeland St
Ardmore St
Murray Hill Ave
Fenkell Ave
Greenfield Rd
Cruse Ave
Stansbury St
Lesure St
Tracey St
Schaefer Hwy
Hartwell Ave
Snowden Ave
Littlefield Ave
Cheyenne Ave
Ward Ave
Sorrento Ave
Steel Ave
Appoline Ave
Meyers Rd
Manor Ave
Monte Vista Ave
Pinehurst Ave
Mendota Ave
Ellsworth Ave
Chalfonte Ave
Hillview Ave
Hackett Ave
Eaton Ave
Terry Ave
Lyndon Ave
Grand River Ave
Gavel St
Acacia Ave
Mettetal Ave
Mansfield Ave
Montrose Ave
Intervale Ave
Kendall Ave
Kendall St
Birch St
Keibler St
Compass Ave
Schoolcraft Ave
Teel Ave
Asbury Park Ave
Hubbell Ave
Davison Ave
I- 96 Service Dr
I- 96
Tyler Ave
Buena Vista St
Buena Vista Ave
Glendale Ave
Fullerton Ave
Fullerton St
Park Ter
Foley St
Allonby Ave
Nelson St
Capitol Ave
Castleton St
Castleton Ave
Shirley Ave
Wadsworth Ave
Thornton Ave
Mecca Ave
Plymouth Rd
Chadwick Ave
Elmira St
Iris St
Strathmoor Ave
Mark Twain St
Freeland St
Keal Ave
Carlin Ave

DETROIT (Plate 13) Pop. 1,027,974 WAYNE COUNTY

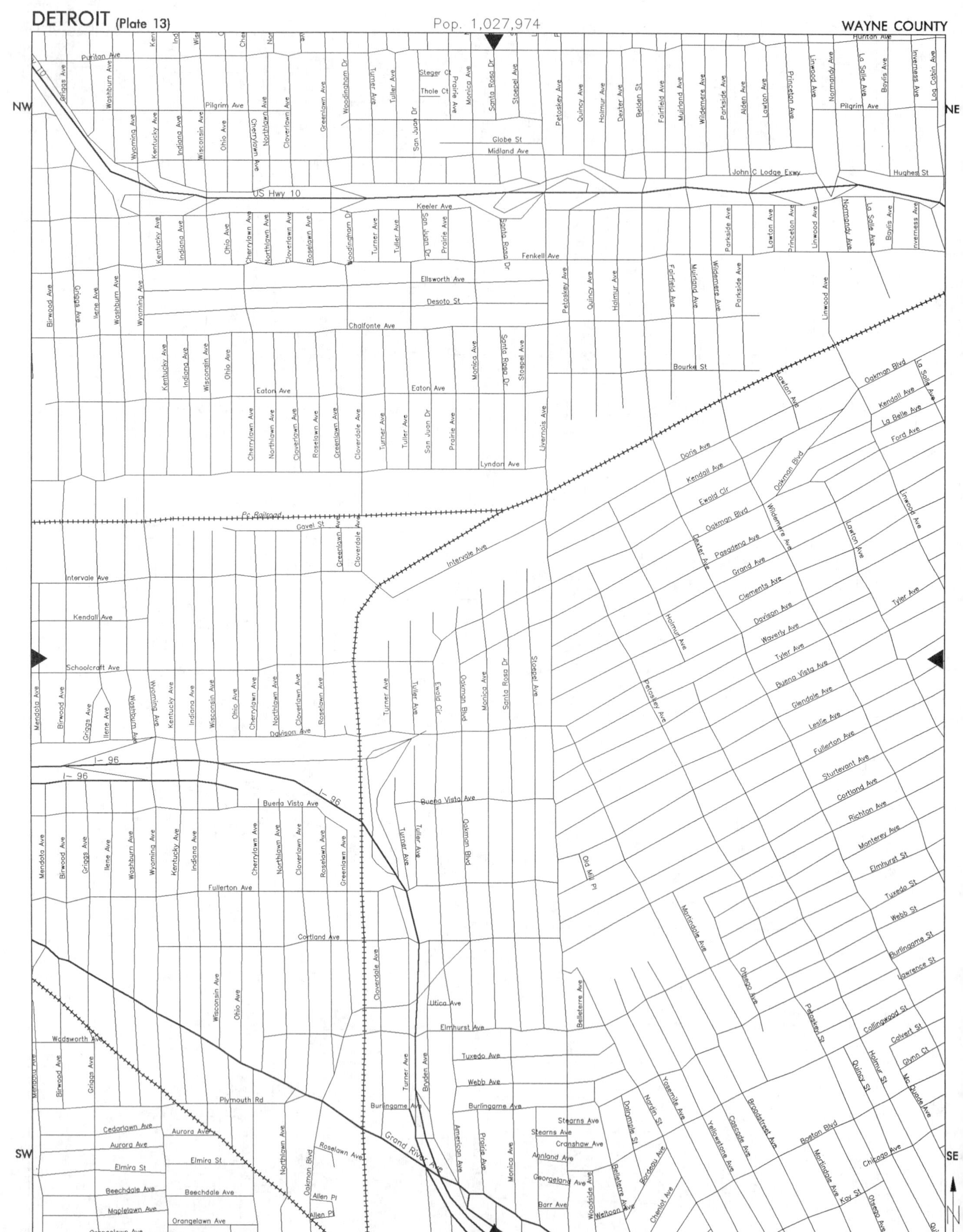

Highland Park City
Detroit City
NW
NE
SW
SE
N
John C Lodge Fwy
US Hwy 10
Davison Frwy
Rosa Parks Blvd
Woodward Ave
Oakland Ave
Linwood Ave
Joy Rd

NW
NE
SW
SE
N
Hamtramck City
I-75
I-94
Chrysler Exwy
Grant Ave
Dearing Ave
Lawley Ave
Cody Ave
Meade Ave
Mc Lean Ave
Halleck Ave
Burnside Ave
Mc Pherson Ave
Carpenter Ave
Dequindre Ave
St Aubin St
Goddard Ave
Arlington Ave
Macklay Ave
Moine Ave
Sobieski Ave
Fredro Ave
Bristow Ave
Caely Ave
Commor Ave
Eldridge Ave
Talbot Ave
Casmere Ave
Harold Ave
Prescott Ave
Ellery St
Bloom Ave
Buffalo Ct
Gable Ave
Dwyer Ave
St Louis Ave
Mound Rd
Caniff Ave
Mount Elliott Ct
Lynch Rd
Neibel Ave
Botsford Ave
Zinow Ave
Pulaski Ave
Whalen Ave
Burger Ave
Holmes Ave
Fleming Ave
Lumpkin St
Joseph Campau Ave
Mitchell Ave
Mc Dougall Ave
Charest Ave
Gallagher Ave
Sobieski Ave
Klinger Ave
Moran Ave
Conant Ave
Alpena Ave
Selfridge St
Oklahoma St
Nagel St
Falcon Ave
Whitfield Ave
Buffalo Ave
Yemans Ave
Evaline Ave
Edwin Ave
Norwalk Ave
Doremus Ave
Comstock Ave
Brockton Ave
Huber Ave
Hedge Ave
Marcus Ave
Domine St
Holbrook Ave
Atlas St
Rosedale Ct
Grand Haven Ave
Dyar Ave
Sidman Ave
Trowbridge Ave
Belmont Ave
Russell St
Lynn St
Poland Ave
Latham Ave
Lehmann Ave
Hanley Ave
Jacob Ave
Roosevelt Ave
Goodson Ave
Florian Ave
Bernard Ave
Brombach Ave
Vincent Ave
Christopher Ave
Dodge St
Georgia Ave
Richardson St
Newhall St
Oliver Ave
Dorothy Ave
Heintz St
Miller Rd
Selkirk St
Farr St
Cymbal St
Benham St
Varney St
Ackley St
Le Grand St
Strong St
Boston Blvd
Oakland Ave
Arden Park St
Westminster Ave
Kenilworth Ave
Leicester Ct
Owen Ave
Josephine Ave
Holbrook Ave
King St
Alger St
Hague Ave
Cardoni Ave
Hindle St
Delmar St
Cameron St
Goodwin St
Greeley St
Gillett St
Dallas St
Alger Ave
Hague Ave
Wellington Ave
Philadelphia Ave
Euclid Ave
Hewitt Ave
Faber Ave
Danforth Ave
Andrus Ave
Grayling Ave
Alice Ave
Denton Ave
Berres St
Dan Ave
Rockwood Ave
Manhattan Ave
Butler Ave
Caia St
Klinger St
Winkelman St
Dwyer Ave
Klein St
Mount Elliott Ave
Hague St
Wellington St
Philadelphia St
Euclid St
Forsyce St
Morrow St
Marston Ave
Chrysler Dr
Rioplle St
Hartwick St
Clay Ave
John R St
Kingsley Ct
Melbourne Ave
Mount Vernon Ave
Marston Ave
Chandler Ave
Brush St
Beaubien St
Smith Ave
Bethune Ave
Custer Ave
Horton Ave
Grand Blvd
Milwaukee Ave
Baltimore Ave
Woodward Ave
2nd Blvd
St Antoine St
Melrose St
Cameron St
Oakland Ave
Hastings St
Piquette Ave
Russell St
Widman Pl
St Aubin Blvd
Ripelle St
Harper Ave
Medbury Ave
Grand Blvd
Elmwood St
Palmer Ave
Ferry Ave
Kirby Ave
Frederick Ave
Grandy St
Hendrie Ave
Mc Dougall Ave
Joseph Campau Ave
Mitchell Ave
Chene St
Dubois St
St Aubin St
Roby St

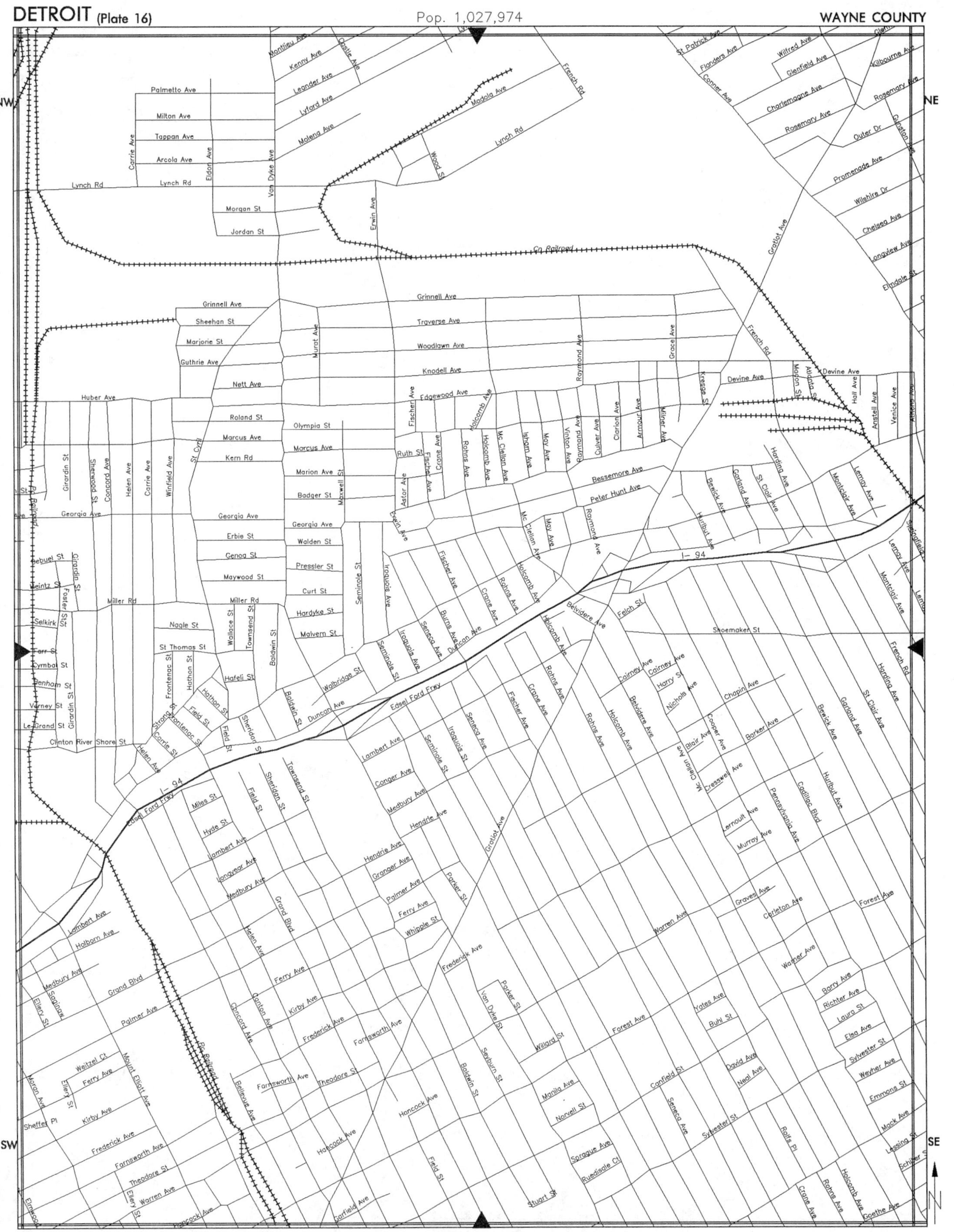

DETROIT (Plate 17)

Pop. 1,027,974

WAYNE COUNTY

NW
NE
SW
SE
I-94
Linville Ave
Chandler Park Dr
Southampton St
Berkshire Rd
Chatsworth Rd
Frankfort Ave
Warren Ave
Cadieux Ave
New York Ave
Cornwall Ave
Ontario Ave
Sioux St
Munich Ave
Cincinnati Ave
Waveney Ave
Detroit Ave
Minneapolis Ave
Neff Rd
Woodhall Ave
Guilford Ave
Bluehill Ave
Pomona Ave
Bremen St
Muncey Ave
Windsor Ave
Hereford Ave
University Pl
Marseilles Ave
Lodewyck Ave
Farmbrook Ave
Radnor Ave
Mack Ave
Harvard Rd
Gravier Ave
Denver Ave
Neveux Ave
Grayton Rd
Bishop Ave
Yorkshire Ave
Kensington Rd
Outer Dr
Audubon Ave
Wallingford Ave
Rosewood St
Munich Ave
Waveney Ave
Bremen St
Devonshire Rd
Bedford Rd
3 Mile Dr St
Brunswick St
Courville St
Haverhill Rd
Buckingham Rd
Berkshire Rd
Chatsworth Rd
Balfour Rd
Somerset Rd
Nottingham Rd
Beaconsfield Ave
Barham Ave
Lakepointe Ave
Maryland Ave
Wayburn Ave
Lozier St
Alter Rd
Ashland Ave
Charlevoix Ave
Vernor Hwy
Kercheval Ave
Brooks St
Alter Rd
Ashland Ave
Hampton St
Philip Ave
Marlborough St
Chalmers Ave
Lakewood St
Newport Ave
Jefferson Ave
Fairfax Ave
Manistique Ave
Philip Ave
Marlborough St
Chalmers Ave
Lakewood St
Newport Ave
Eastlawn St
Piper Blvd
Coplin Ave
Freud St

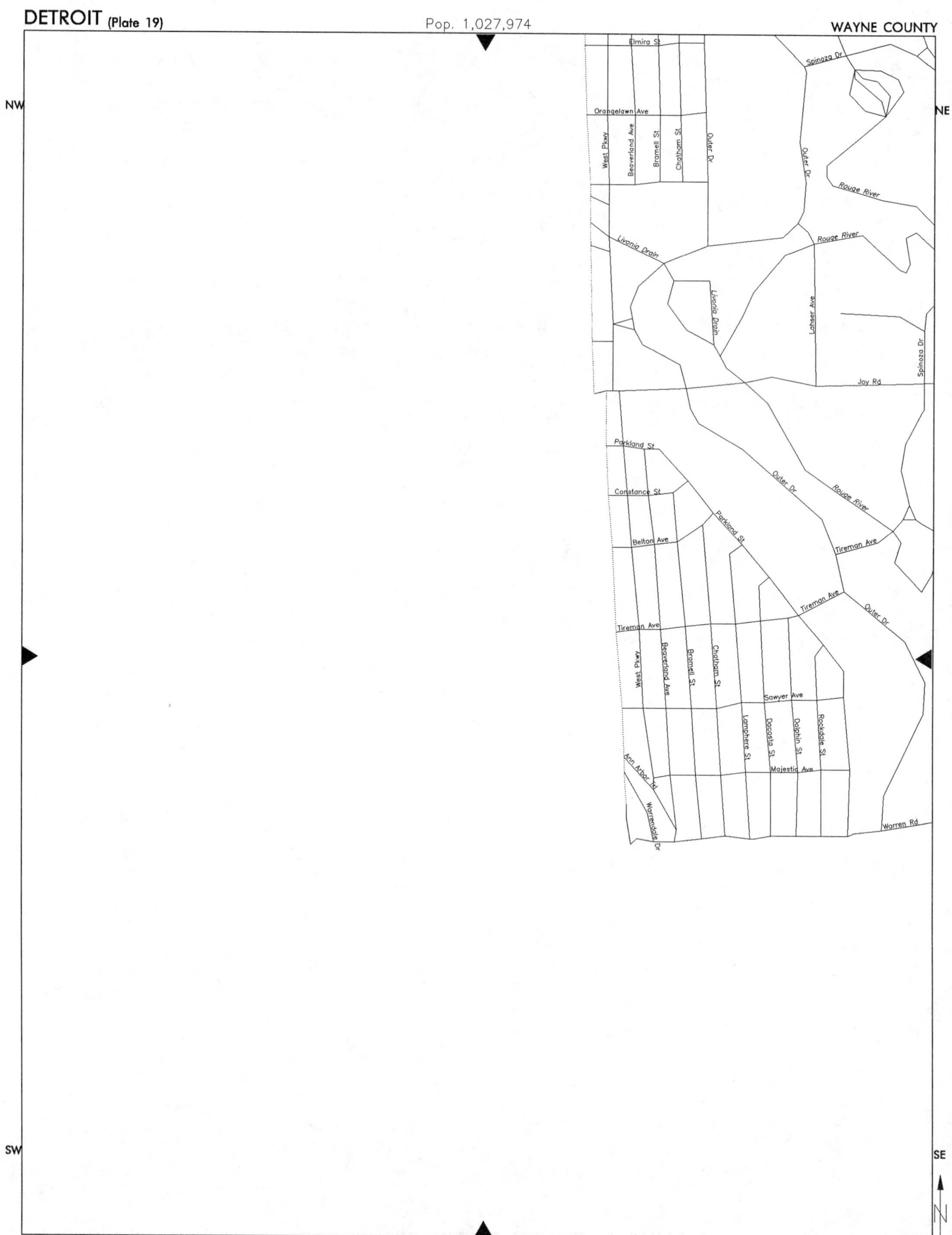
NW
NE
SW
SE
N
Elmira St
Spinoza Dr
Orangelawn Ave
West Pkwy
Beaverland Ave
Bramell St
Chatham St
Outer Dr
Rouge River
Livonia Drain
Lahser Ave
Spinoza Dr
Joy Rd
Parkland St
Constance St
Belton Ave
Tireman Ave
Sawyer Ave
Lamphere St
Dacosta St
Dolphin St
Rockdale St
Majestic Ave
Ann Arbor Trl
Warrendale Dr
Warren Rd

NW
NE
SW
SE
N
Heyden Ct
Orangelawn Ave
Chicago Ave
Westfield Ave
Cathedral Ave
Dover Ave
Joy Rd
Van Buren Ave
Constance St
Belton Ave
Tireman Ave
Sawyer Ave
Warren Ave
Warren Rd
Whitlock Ave
Paul Ave
Dayton Ave
Kirkwood Ave
Ford Rd
Spinoza Dr
Trinity Ave
Burt Rd
Pierson St
Braile Ave
Patton St
Fielding St
Stout Ave
Heyden Ave
Vaughan Ave
Evergreen Rd
Plainview Ave
Auburn Ave
Minock Ave
Westwood Ave
Grandville Ave
Piedmont Ave
Warwick Ave
Artesian Ave
Stahelin Ave
Brace Ave
Greenview Ave
Faust Ave
Penrod Ave
Rosemont Ave
Ashton Ave
Weaver Ave
Fitzpatrick Ave
Fitzpatrick Ct
Southfield Frwy
US 39
Archdale St
Longacre St
Rutland St
Memorial Ave
Abington Rd
Grandmont Rd
Woodmont Rd
Ellis Ave
Claybum Ave
Majestic
Longacre Ave
Archdale Ave

DETROIT (Plate 21)

Pop. 1,027,974

WAYNE COUNTY

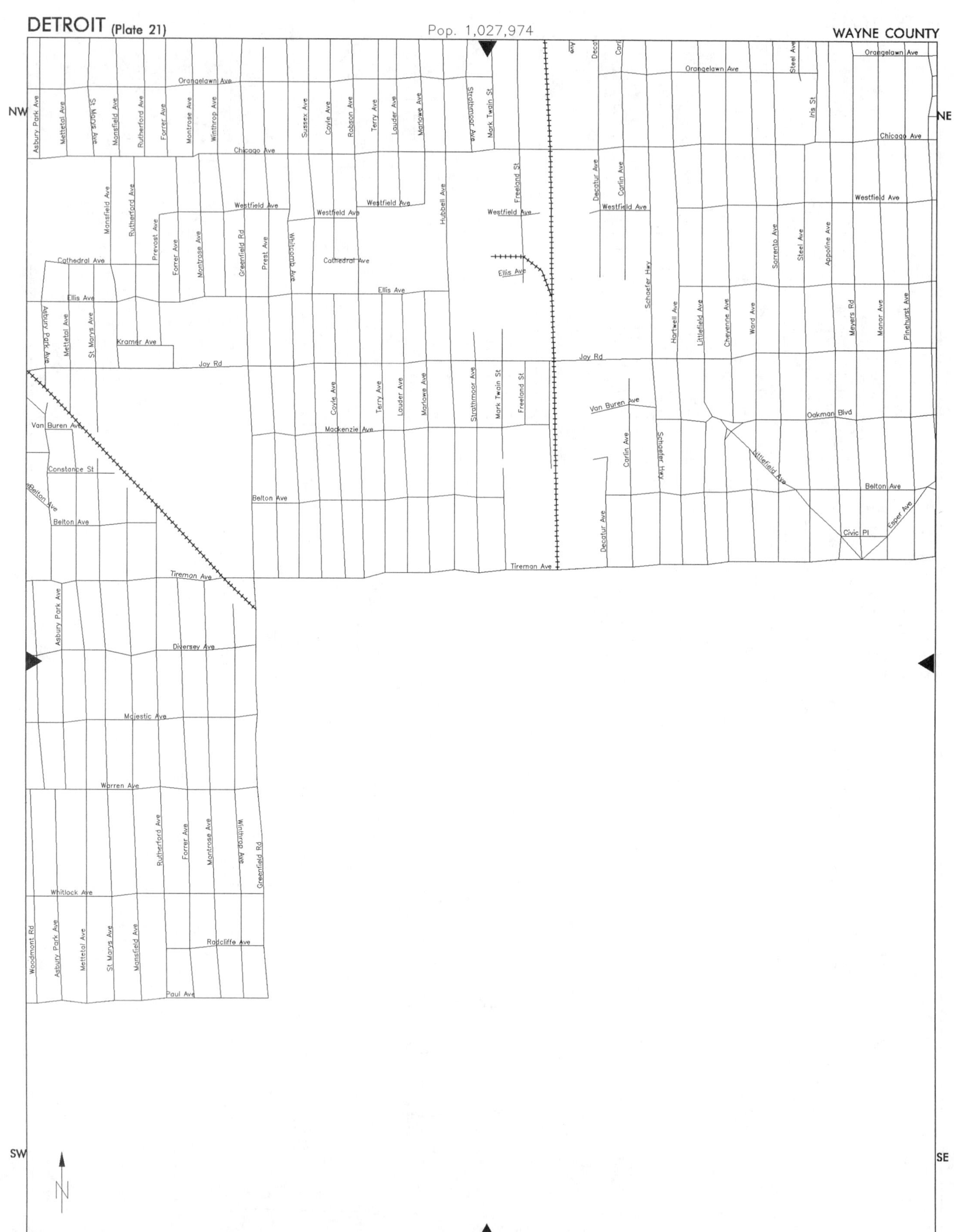

Pop. 1,027,974

WAYNE COUNTY

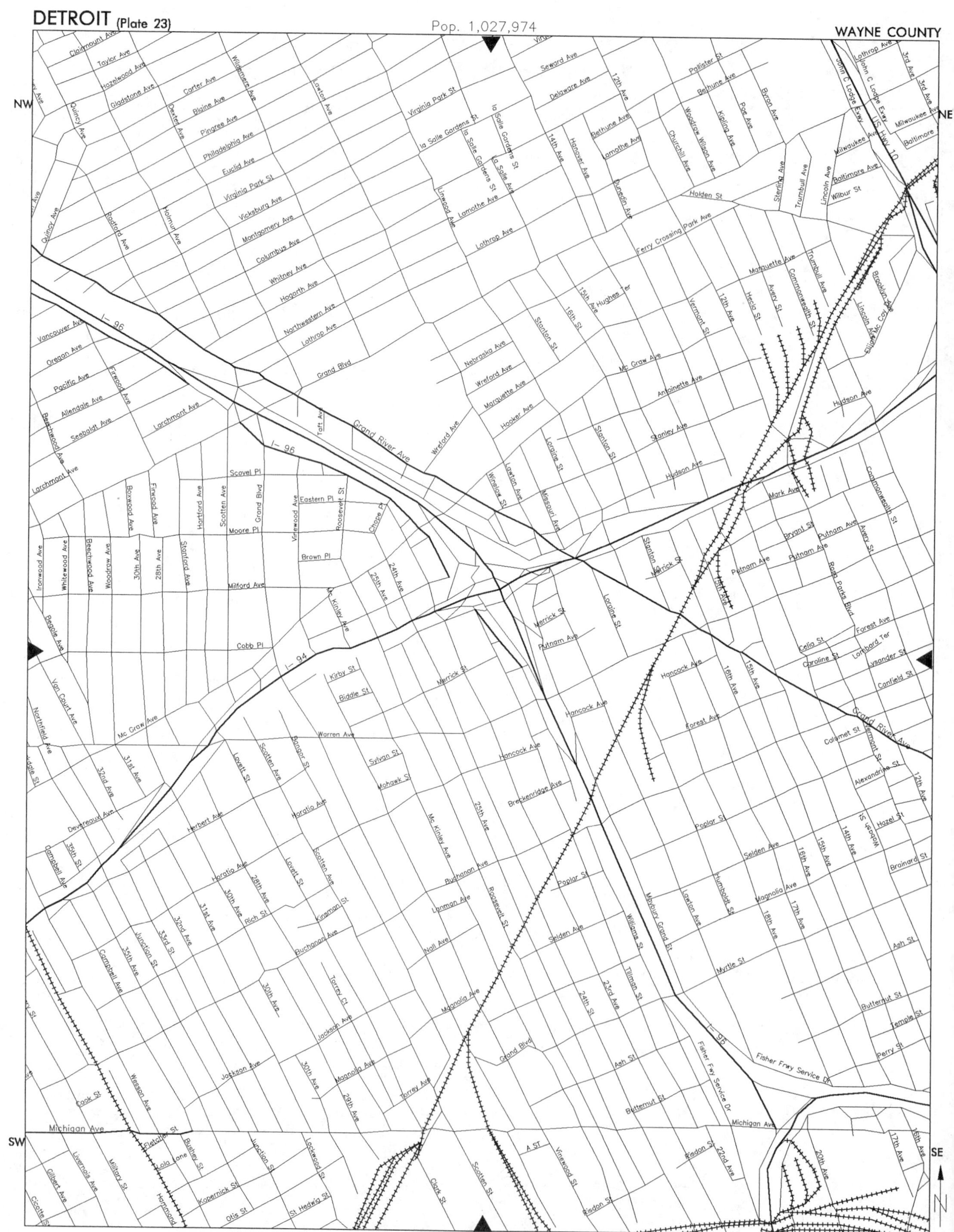

DETROIT (Plate 24) Pop. 1,027,974 WAYNE COUNTY

NW
NE
SW
SE
N
Detroit River
Grand Blvd
Gratiot Ave
Jefferson Ave
Vernor Hwy
Mack Ave
Kercheval Ave
St Paul Ave
Lafayette St
Larned St
Congress St
Atwater St
Woodbridge St
Franklin St
Chene St
Joseph Campau Ave
Mc Dougall Ave
St Aubin St
Dubois St
Orleans St
Rivard St
Riopelle St
Bellevue Ave
Meldrum St
Beaufait Ave
Canton Ave
Helen Ave
Concord Ave
Field St
Townsend St
Baldwin St
Seyburn St
Van Dyke St
Parker St
Maxwell Ave
Seminole St
Goethe Ave
Charlevoix Ave
Canfield St
Canfield Ave
Sylvester St
Stuart St
Pulford St
Zender Pl
Preston St
Benson Ave
Hunt St
Elba St
Heidelberg St
Ludden St
Arndt St
Hendricks St
Moran St
Burlage Pl
Willis Ave
Superior St
Fremont Pl
Alexandrine St
Leland St
Illinois St
St Joseph St
Mitchell Ave
Grandy St
Hale St
Scott St
Pierce St
Erskine St
Watson St
Wilkins St
Brewster St
Alfred St
Division St
Warren Ave
Platt St
Hancock Ave
Aaron St
Forest Ave
Garfield Ave
Gaistor St
Mc Dougall Ave
Thompson Ct
Ellery Pl
Ellery St
Heck Pl
Mount Elliott Ave
Miller Ct
Prince Hall Dr
Elmwood St
Antietam Ave
Hyde Park Dr
Bryanston Crescent St
Chene Ct
Robert Bradby
Chateaufort Pl
Cherboneau Pl
Thornhill Pl
Pembridge Pl
Bloomsbury Pl
Trevor Pl
Macomb St
Wood Cir
St Maron St
Monroe St
Leib St
Fort St
Jefferson Ct
Iron St
Wight St
Adair St
Walker St
Du Charme Pl
Navarre Pl
Bartle Ave
Beals St
Iroquois St
Burns Ave
Fischer Ave
Durand St
Shipherd Rd
Coe Ave
Shipherd Ct
Van Dyke Pl
Agnes Ave
Mathews Ave
Donald Pl
Tregaway Pl
Kolb St
Crane Ave
Louis Ave
Vernor Hwy
Lokman St
Brinket
Belvidere Ave
Riverside St
Casino Way
Central Way
Muse St

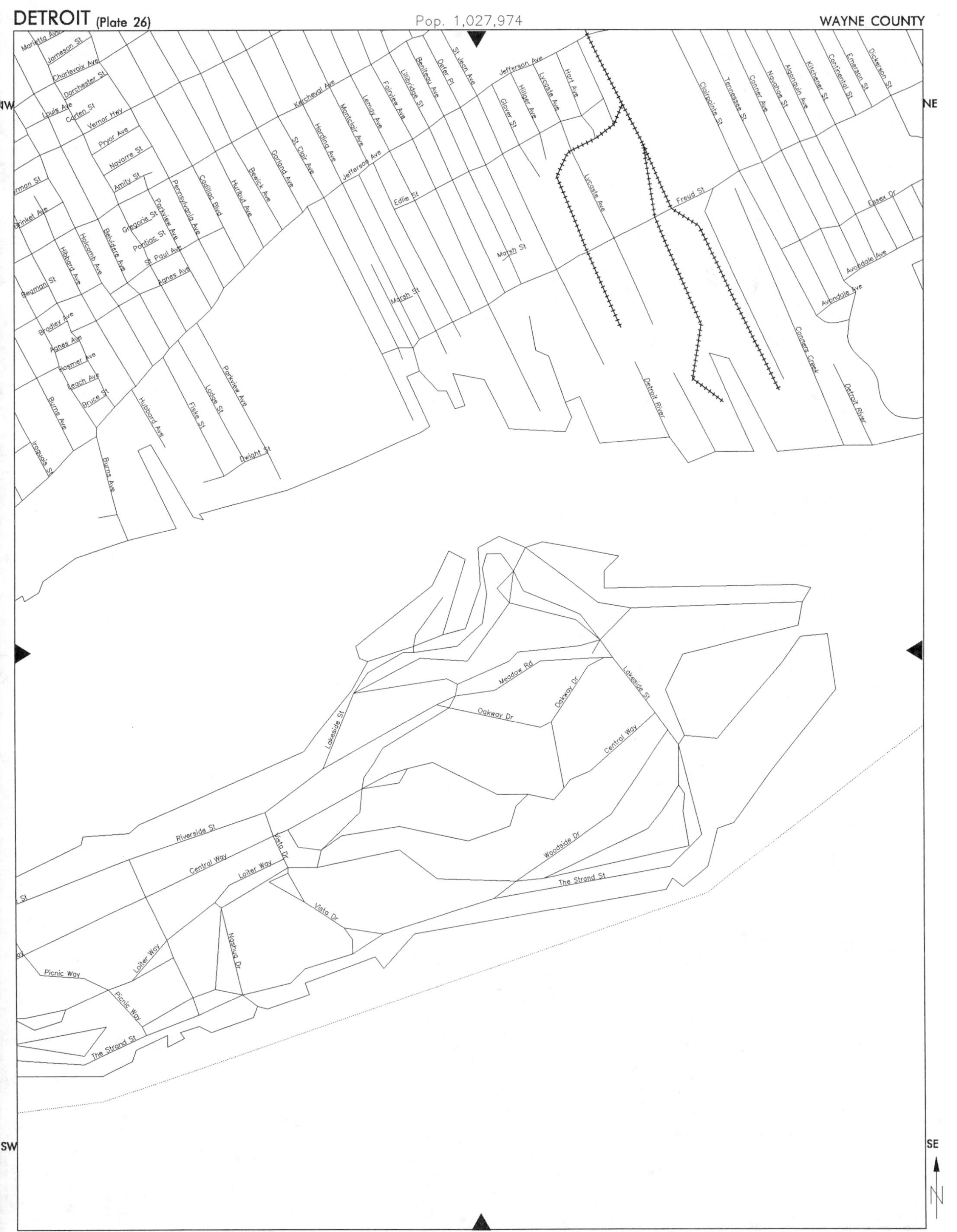
Jefferson Ave
Kercheval Ave
Lakeside St
Meadow Rd
Oakway Dr
Central Way
Riverside St
Vista Dr
Loiter Way
Woodside Dr
The Strand St
Picnic Way
Nashua Dr
Detroit River
Conners Creek
Freud St
Marsh St
Dwight St
Lodge St
Fiske St
Parkview Ave
Hubbard Ave
Burns Ave
Iroquois St
Avondale Ave
Essex Dr
Clairpointe St
Tennessee St
Conner Ave
Navahoe St
Algonquin Ave
Kitchener St
Continental St
Emerson St
Dickerson St
Lycaste Ave
Hart Ave
Hillger Ave
Glover St
St Jean Ave
Defer Pl
Beniteau Ave
Lillibridge St
Fairview Ave
Lemay Ave
Montclair Ave
Harding Ave
St Clair Ave
Garland Ave
Beaconsfield Ave
Hurlbut Ave
Cadillac Blvd
Pennsylvania Ave
Parkview Ave
Edlie St
Marietta Ave
Jameson St
Charlevoix Ave
Dorchester St
Louis Ave
Carten St
Vernor Hwy
Pryor Ave
Navarre St
Amity St
Gregorie St
Pontiac St
St Paul Ave
Agnes Ave
Belvidere Ave
Holcomb Ave
Hibbard Ave
Beaman St
Bradley Ave
Hosmer Ave
Leach Ave
Bruce St
NW
NE
SW
SE
N

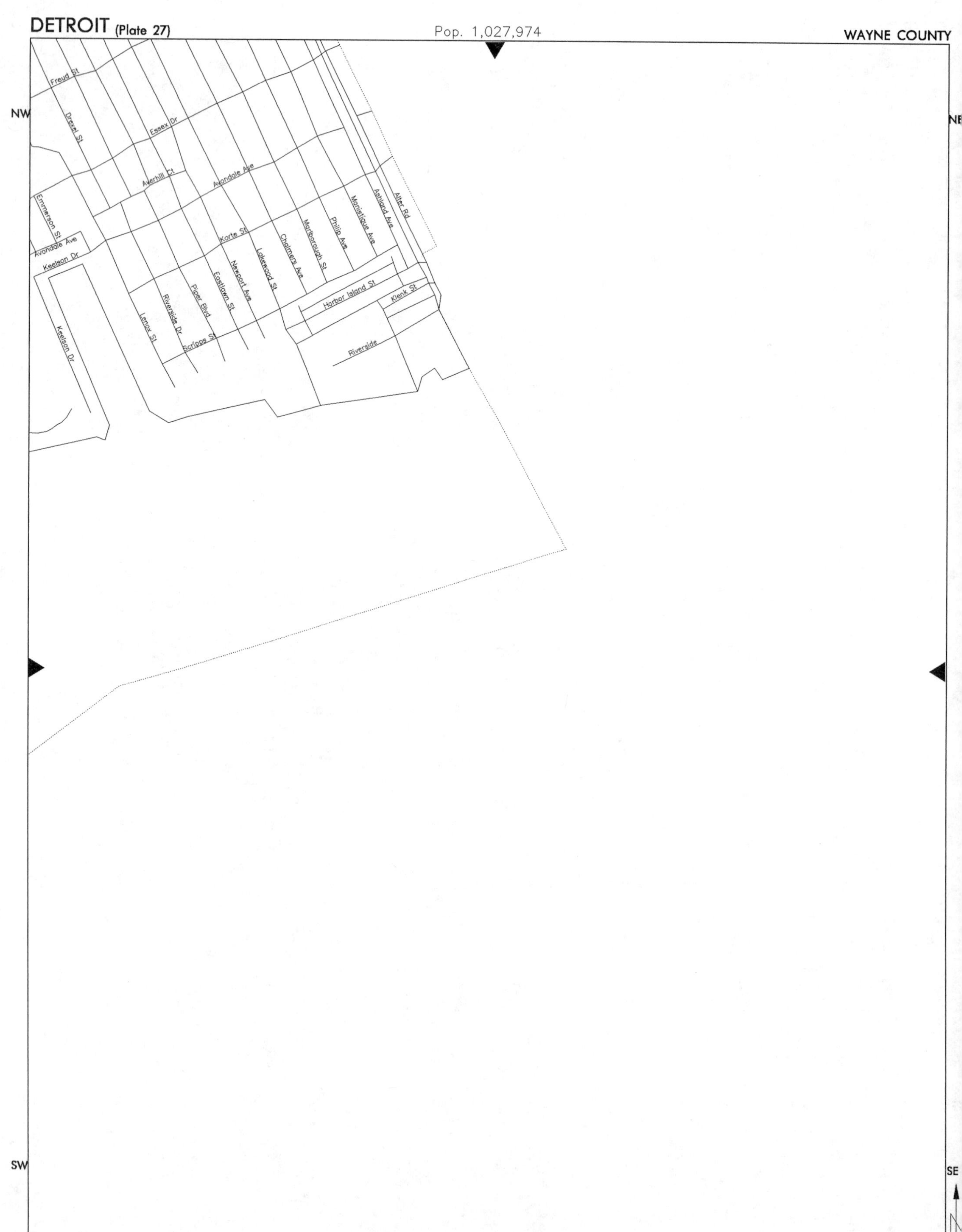
NW
NE
SW
SE
Freud St
Drexel St
Essex Dr
Averhill Ct
Avondale Ave
Emmerson St
Avondale Ave
Keelson Dr
Keelson Dr
Korte St
Ashland Ave
Alter Rd
Manistique Ave
Philip Ave
Marlborough St
Chalmers Ave
Lakewood St
Newport Ave
Eastlawn St
Piper Blvd
Riverside Dr
Lenox St
Scripps St
Harbor Island St
Klenk St
Riverside

Michigan Ave
Western Ave
Arnold Ave
Lawndale Ave
Trenton Ave
Cabot St
St John Ave
Baubee Ave
St Stephens Ave
Ternes Ave
Lumley Ave
Springwells Ave
Casper Ave
Parkwood Ave
Waldo Ave
Edward Ave
Bulwer Ave
Clippert Ave
Mercier Ave
Bruckner Ave
Martin St
Central Ave
Clayton Ave
John Kronk St
Lonyo Ave
Western St
Dix Ave
Woodmere St
Belle St
Springwells St
Pitt St
Green St
Hanaugh St
Stair St
Pearl St
Wendell St
Casper St
Carson St
Norman St
Inglis St
Whittaker St
Senator St
Navy St
Ferris St
Lawndale St
Oakdale St
Sharon St
Cahalan St
Lane St
Gartner St
Evans St
Vernor Hwy
Mullane St
Mandale St
Logan St
Elsmere St
Avis St
Longworth St
Falcon St
Horner St
Rathbone St
Chamberlain St
Lafayette Ave
Olivet St
Witt St
Fulton St
Fort St
Baby Creek
Dieterl St
I-75
Powell St
Rouge River
Ormond St
Rouge St
Dearborn St
Kaier St
Stone St
Sire St
Cobalt St
Fortune St
Harbaugh St
South St
Gerisch
Heidt St
Luther St
Dix Ave
Fordson St
Denmark St
Miller Rd
Flora St
Barron St
Graham St
Melville St
Lyon St
Colonial Ave
Sanders St
Mellon St
Ormond St
Oakwood Blvd
Crown St
Dupont St
Dey St
Keller St
Thaddeus St
Major St
Fordale St
Bayside St
Dumfries St
Waring St
Stoker St
Forman St
Gates St
Leigh St
Copland St
W
NE
SW
SE
N

NW
NE
SW
SE
N
St Hedwig St
Konkel St
Otis St
Military St
Livernois Ave
Gilbert Ave
Clippert Ave
Cicotte St
Deming St
Brandon St
Toledo St
Ruskin St
Standish St
Randall St
21st St
20th St
Grand Blvd
25th Ave
Vinewood St
Vernor Hwy
Mc Gregor St
Merritt St
Plumer St
Midway St
Federal St
Hammond St
Wolff St
Palms St
Clarkdale St
Bagley St
Lambie Pl
24th St
Shady Lane
Page St
Hubbard St
Ida St
Porter St
Clark Ct
Fairbanks St
Toledo St
Mc Millan St
Uthes St
Ferdinand St
Mc Kinstry St
Clark St
Lansing St
Morrell St
Manson St
Romeyn St
Mc Millan St
Newberry St
Bivouac St
Baker St
Eldred St
Christiancy St
Rogers St
Porter St
Howard St
Amherst St
Dix Ave
Vernor Hwy
Stratton St
Desmond St
Cadet St
Dragoon St
Senator St
Navy St
Gartner St
Goldsmith St
Caspian St
Regular St
Military St
Cartridge St
Army St
Bostwick St
Rademacher St
Cahalan St
Lane St
Logan St
Chatfield St
Rowan St
Lisbon St
Beard St
Army St
Lexington St
Lafayette Ave
Lawrence St
Caspian St
Crawford St
Musket St
Lafayette Ave
Wheelock St
Solvay St
Central Ave
Fisher Fwy Service Dr
I-75
Fisher Fwy
23rd St
24th St
Fort St
Grand Blvd
Vinewood St
Swain St
Scotten St
Pelham St
Clark St
Mc Kinstry
Ferdinand St
Morrell St
Anthon St
Fort St
Gaynor Ct
Lauderdale St
Summit St
Jefferson Ave
Hussar St
Driggs St
Harvey St
Reeder St
Jefferson Ave
Reissman St
Olivet St
Gilman St
Harrington St
Post St
Rankin St
Wabash Railroad
Crawford St
Livernois Ave
Dragoon St
Military St
Reid St
Holly St
Jefferson Ave
Waterman St
Rademacher St
Reid St
End St
Schroeder St
Harrington St
Bacon St
Green St
Cottrell St
Solvay St
Crossley St
Erie St
Melville St
South St
Yale St
Dill Pl
Sanders St
Anderson St
DI and J Railroad
Vanderbilt St
Thaddeus St
Burdeno St
Jefferson Ave
Medina St
Barnes St
End St
Rouge River
Jefferson Ave

Labrosse St
Porter St
Abbott St
Howard St
Lafayette Ave
10th Ave
Trumbull St
Brooklyn St
6th Ave
3rd Ave
2nd Blvd
US Hwy 10
Jefferson Ave
Bagley St
14th St
Wabash St
Vermont St
18th Ave
17th Ave
16th Ave
Wabash Pl
14th St
Lafferty
Vermont St
Cromwell St
Sampson St
Howard St
Lafayette Blvd
15th St
Fort St
Jefferson Ave
20th St
21st St
Trover St
St Anne St
Ambassador Bridge St
NE
SE

NW
SW
Dumfries Rd
Francis Ave
Gleason St
Waring St
Dartmouth St
Greyfriars St
Peters St
Outer Dr
Fort St
Edsel St
Le Blanc St
Electric St
Liddesdale St
N

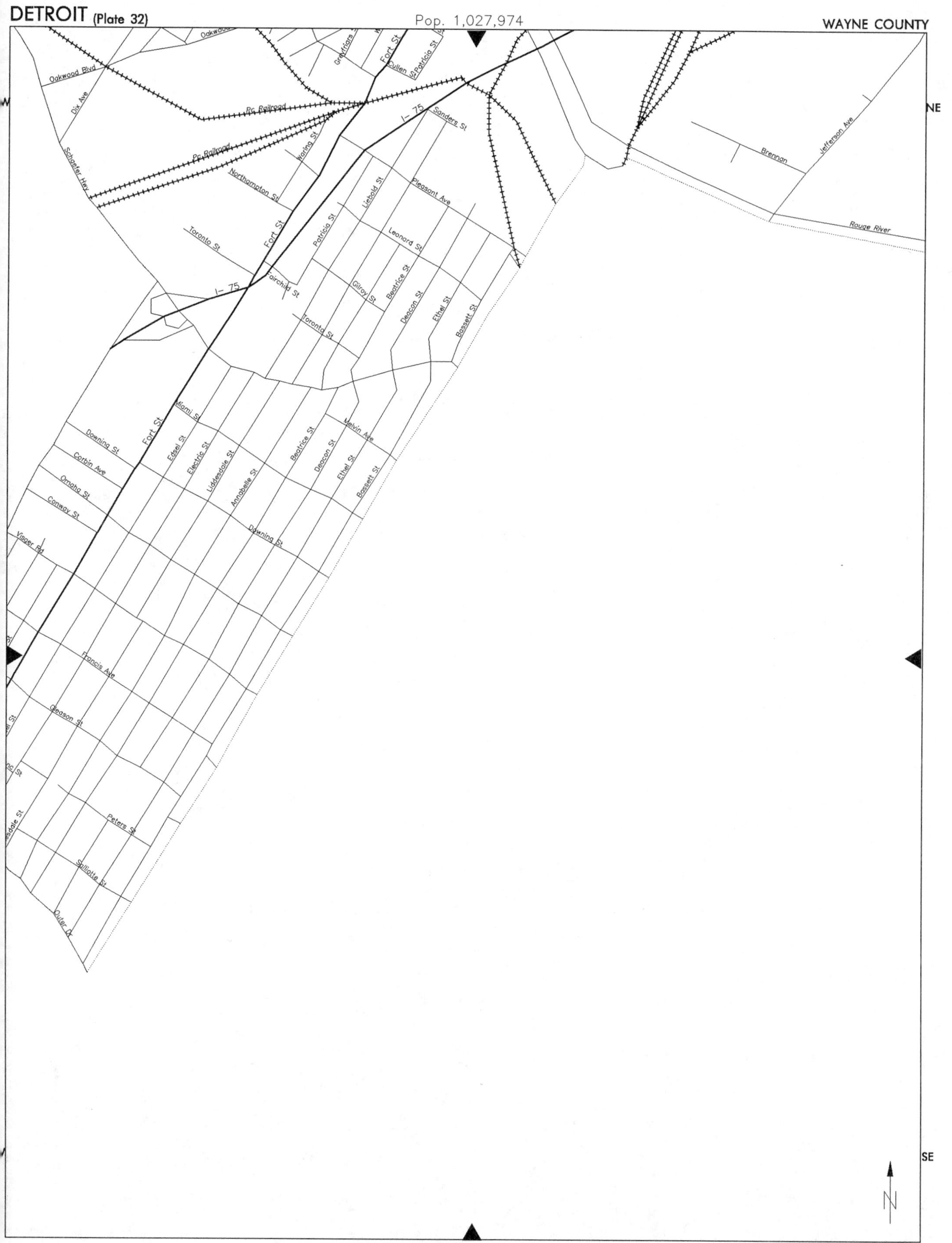
Oakwood Blvd
Dix Ave
Schaefer Hwy
Rc Railroad
Northampton St
Waring St
Fort St
I- 75
Sanders St
Liebold St
Pleasant Ave
Patricia St
Leonard St
Toronto St
Fairchild St
Gilroy St
Beatrice St
Deacon St
Ethel St
Bassett St
Miami St
Melvin Ave
Downing St
Corbin Ave
Omaha St
Conway St
Edsel St
Electric St
Liddesdale St
Annabelle St
Visger Rd
Francis Ave
Gleason St
Peters St
Spilliotte St
Outer Dr
Brennan
Jefferson Ave
Rouge River
NE
SE
N

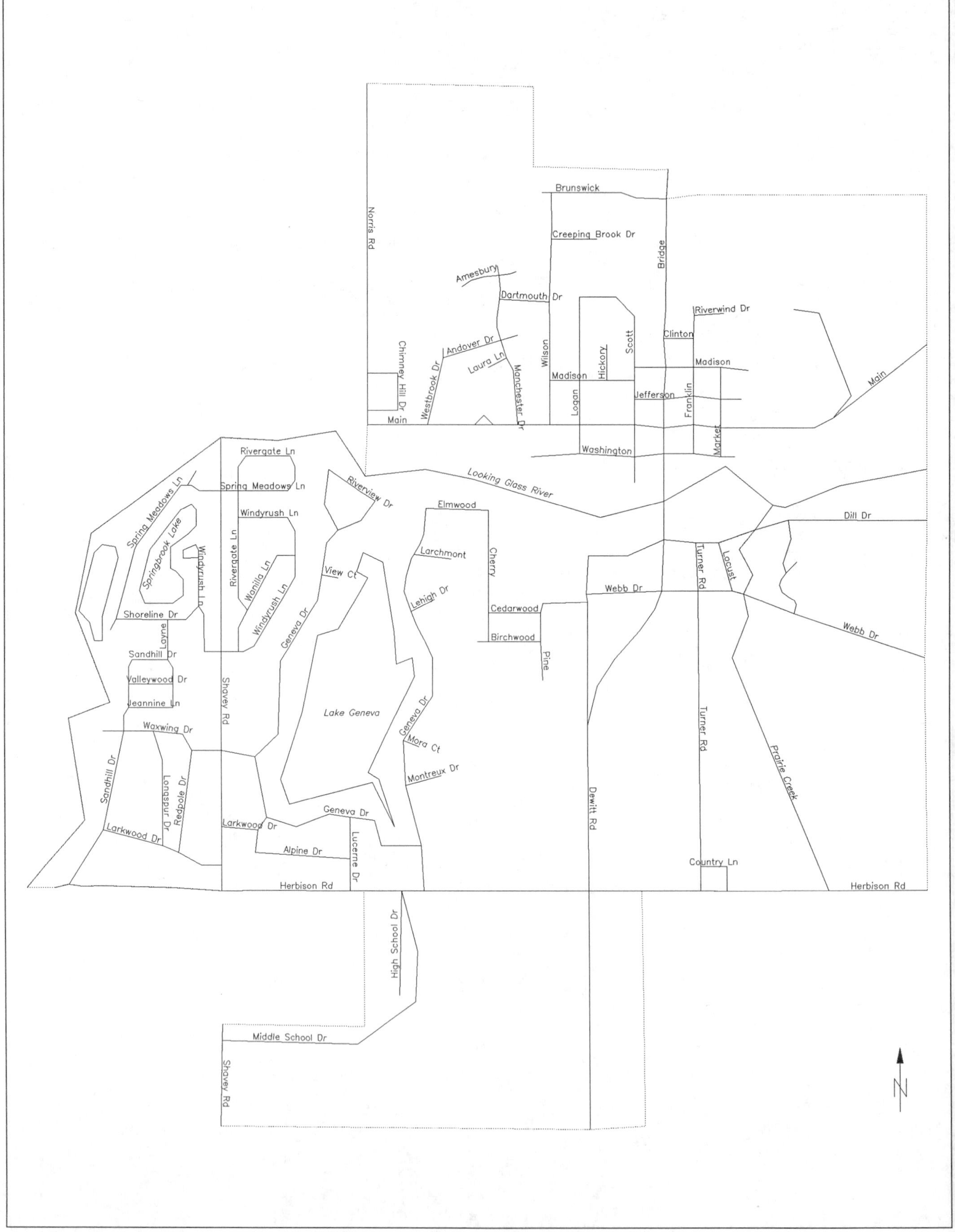

Brunswick
Creeping Brook Dr
Norris Rd
Bridge
Amesbury
Dartmouth Dr
Riverwind Dr
Clinton
Andover Dr
Chimney Hill Dr
Laura Ln
Wilson
Hickory
Scott
Madison
Madison
Westbrook Dr
Manchester Dr
Logan
Jefferson
Franklin
Main
Main
Market
Washington
Rivergate Ln
Looking Glass River
Spring Meadows Ln
Spring Meadows Ln
Riverview Dr
Elmwood
Dill Dr
Windyrush Ln
Springbrook Lake
Windyrush Ln
Riverqate Ln
Wanilla Ln
Windyrush Ln
Larchmont
Cherry
View Ct
Turner Rd
Locust
Lehigh Dr
Webb Dr
Shoreline Dr
Geneva Dr
Cedarwood
Webb Dr
Layne
Birchwood
Sandhill Dr
Pine
Valleywood Dr
Shavey Rd
Jeannine Ln
Lake Geneva
Geneva Dr
Turner Rd
Waxwing Dr
Mora Ct
Prairie Creek
Sandhill Dr
Longspur Dr
Redpole Dr
Montreux Dr
Dewitt Rd
Geneva Dr
Larkwood Dr
Larkwood Dr
Lucerne Dr
Alpine Dr
Country Ln
Herbison Rd
Herbison Rd
High School Dr
Middle School Dr
Shavey Rd
N

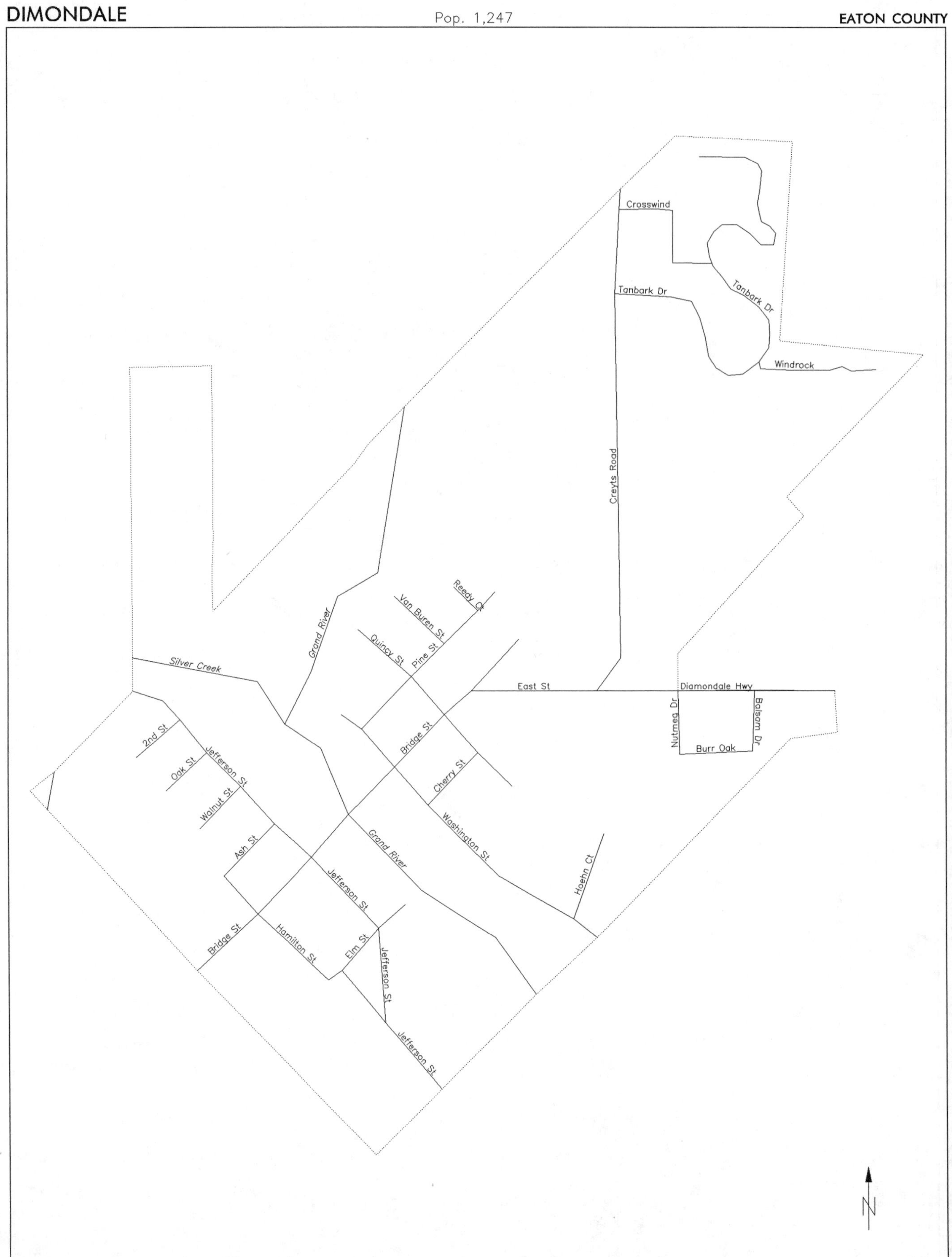
Crosswind
Tanbark Dr
Tanbark Dr
Windrock
Creyts Road
Reedy Ct
Van Buren St
Quincy St
Pine St
Grand River
Silver Creek
East St
Diamondale Hwy
Nutmeg Dr
Balsam Dr
Burr Oak
2nd St
Oak St
Jefferson St
Walnut St
Bridge St
Cherry St
Washington St
Ash St
Grand River
Hoehn Ct
Jefferson St
Bridge St
Hamilton St
Elm St
Jefferson St
Jefferson St
N

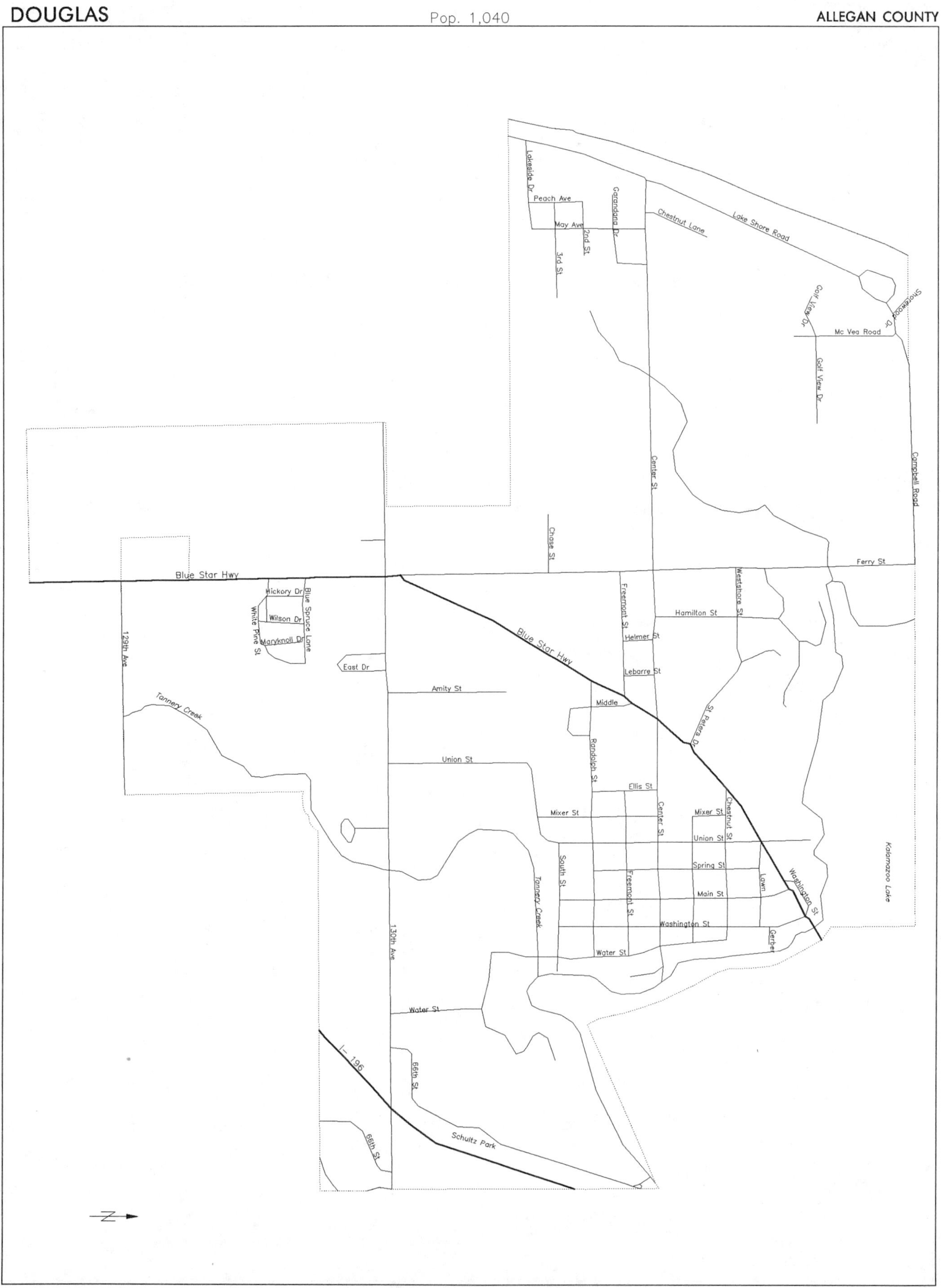

Lakeside Dr
Peach Ave
May Ave
2nd St
3rd St
Garandana Dr
Chestnut Lane
Lake Shore Road
Golf View Dr
Shorewood Dr
Mc Vea Road
Campbell Road
Center St
Chase St
Ferry St
Blue Star Hwy
Hickory Dr
Blue Spruce Lane
White Pine St
Wilson Dr
Maryknoll Dr
129th Ave
East Dr
Tannery Creek
Westshore St
Fremont St
Hamilton St
Helmer St
Lebarre St
Amity St
Middle
St Peters Dr
Randolph St
Union St
Ellis St
Mixer St
Chestnut St
South St
Spring St
Lawn
Main St
Washington St
Gerber
Water St
Kalamazoo Lake
130th Ave
I- 196
66th St
Schultz Park
N

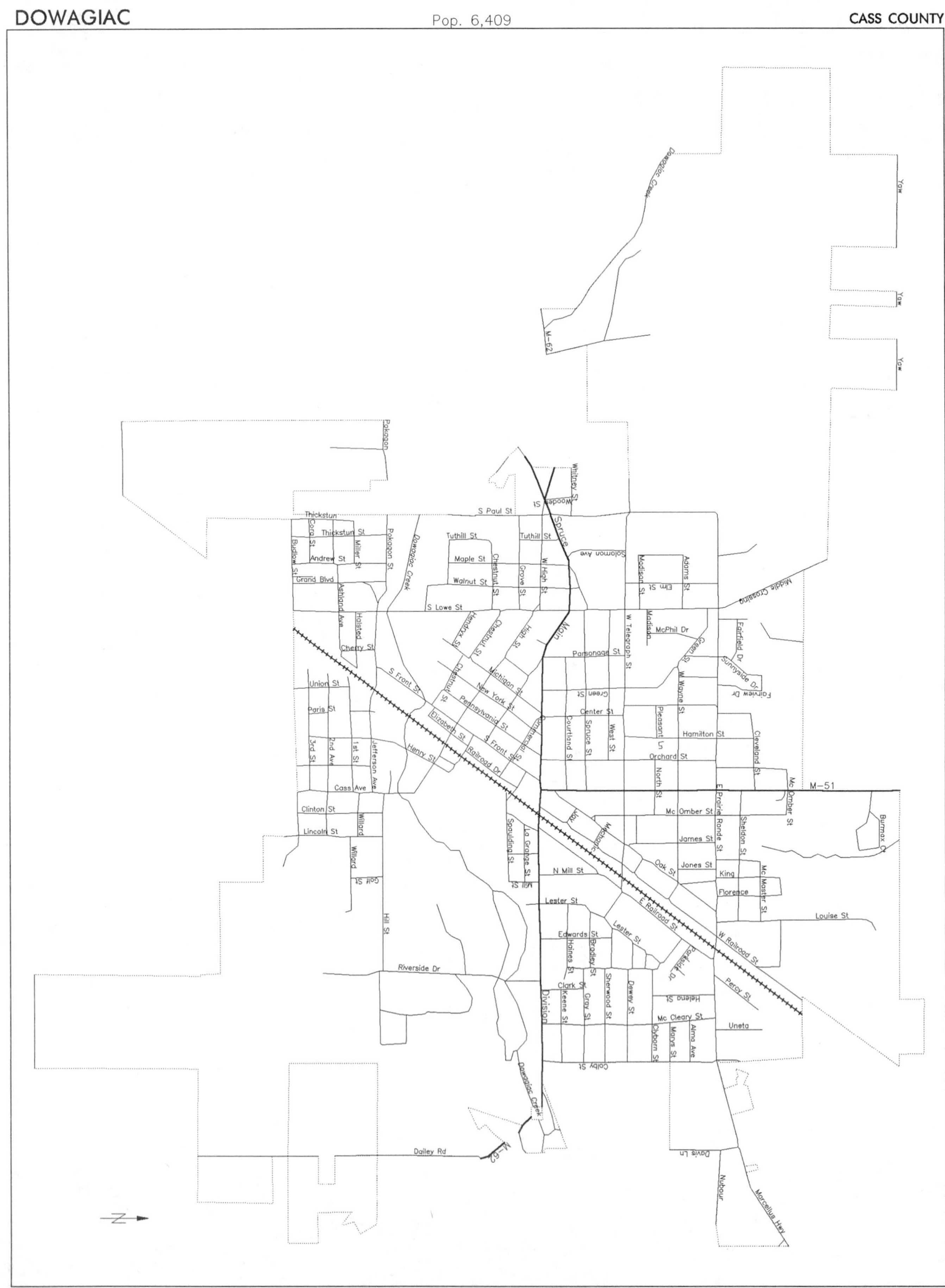
Dowagiac Creek
Yaw
M-62
Pokagon
Whitney St
Woodes St
S Paul St
Thickstun
Thickstun St
Tuthill St
Spruce
Solomon Ave
Maple St
Walnut St
S Lowe St
Grand Blvd
Andrew St
Miller St
Pokagon St
Madison St
Adams St
Elm St
Middle Crossing
Main
McPhil Dr
Parsonage St
W Telegraph St
Fairfield Dr
Sunnyside Dr
Fairview Dr
Green St
W Wayne St
Union St
Paris St
S Front St
New York St
Michigan St
Pennsylvania St
Elizabeth St
Railroad Dr
Henry St
Commercial
Center St
Courtland St
Spruce St
West St
Pleasant Ln
Hamilton St
Orchard St
Cleveland St
North St
Cass Ave
Jefferson Ave
M-51
Mc Omber St
Mc Omber St
E Prairie Ronde St
Sheldon St
Burmax Ct
Clinton St
Lincoln St
Willard
Spaulding St
La Grange St
James St
Jones St
Oak St
N Mill St
King
Florence
Mc Master St
Golf St
Mill St
Lester St
E Railroad St
W Railroad St
Louise St
Hill St
Edwards St
Haines St
Bradley St
Lester St
Parkside Dr
Riverside Dr
Clark St
Keene St
Gray St
Sherwood St
Dewey St
Helena St
Percy St
Division
Mc Cleary St
Uneta
Clyborn St
Marys St
Alma Ave
Colby St
Dailey Rd
Davis Ln
Nubour
Marcellus Hwy
N

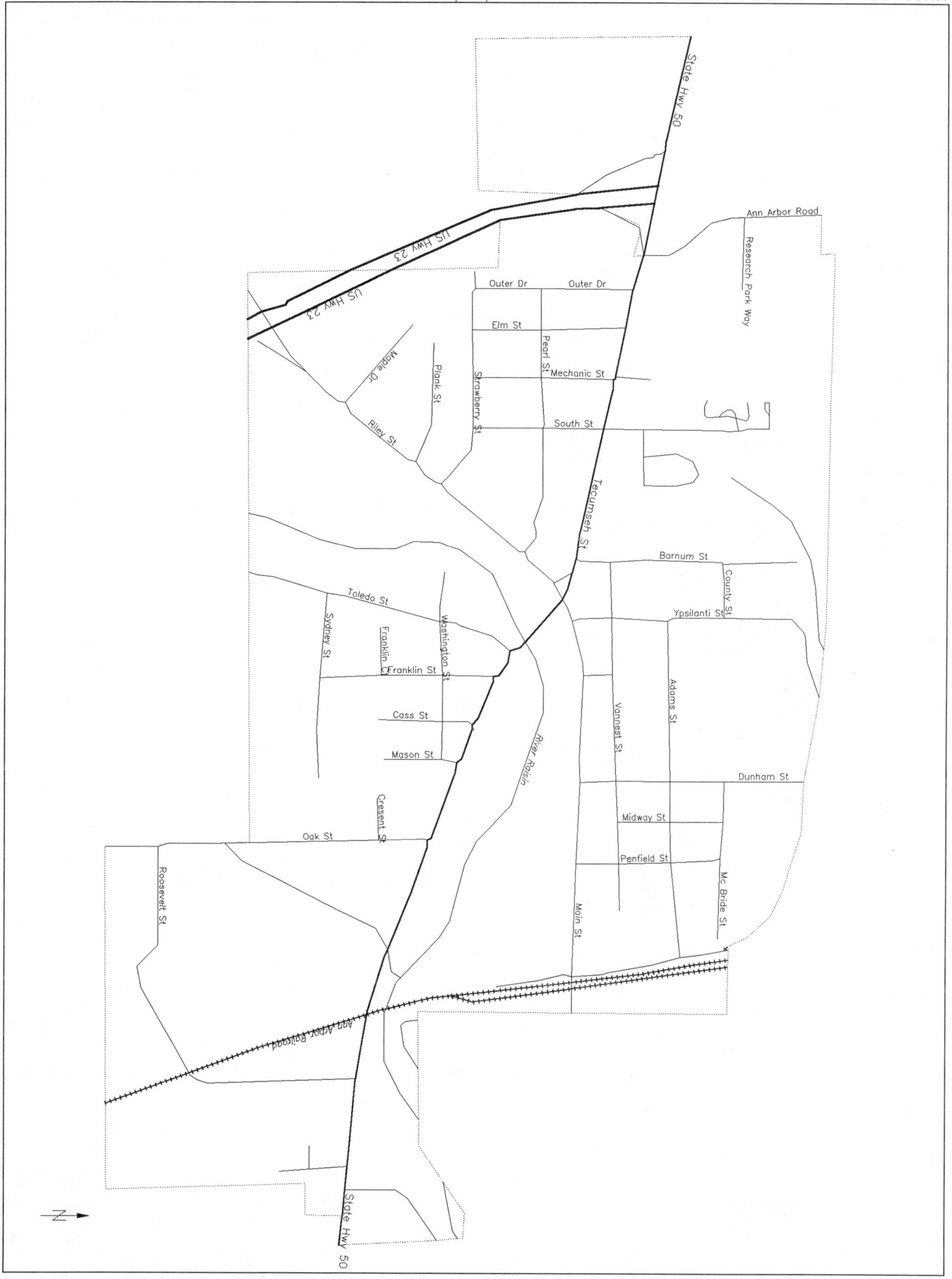

State Hwy 50
US Hwy 23
US Hwy 23
Ann Arbor Road
Research Park Way
Outer Dr
Outer Dr
Elm St
Pearl St
Maple Dr
Plank St
Strawberry St
Mechanic St
South St
Riley St
Tecumseh St
Barnum St
County St
Toledo St
Ypsilanti St
Sydney St
Franklin Ct
Washington St
Franklin St
Adams St
Vannest St
Cass St
Mason St
River Raisin
Dunham St
Cresent St
Midway St
Oak St
Penfield St
Roosevelt St
Mc Bride St
Main St
Ann Arbor Railroad
State Hwy 50

Lansing Rd
Oak St
Monroe Rd
Centenial Ct
Canterbury Ln
Summit St
Stuart St
Cambridge Dr
Monroe St
Clare St
Mason St
Lincoln St
Lenawee St
Wayne St
Saginaw St
Mackinaw St
Harvard Dr
Princeton Dr
Oakland St
Spring St
Montcalm St
Livingston
Dartmouth Dr
Yale Dr
Olivet St
Marquette St
Elm St
Kent St
Pine St
Sycamore St
Huron St
Hampton Rd
Gratiot St
Mercer St
Obert St
Wickshire Ln
Shiawassee St
Tuscola St
Vanderbilt Dr
Genesee St
Fitch St
Courtland St
Brookfield St
Clinton St
Maryette St
Brand St
Main St
Hale St
Atwater St
Cook St
Fitzgerald St
Division St
Campbell St
Brown St
Mc Bride St
Ann Arbor St
Russel St
Holmes St
Vinewood St
Perry St
Gomas Ct
Maple St
Lovejoy St
John St
Manfred Rd
Fauble St
Naldrette St
Threemile Creek
N

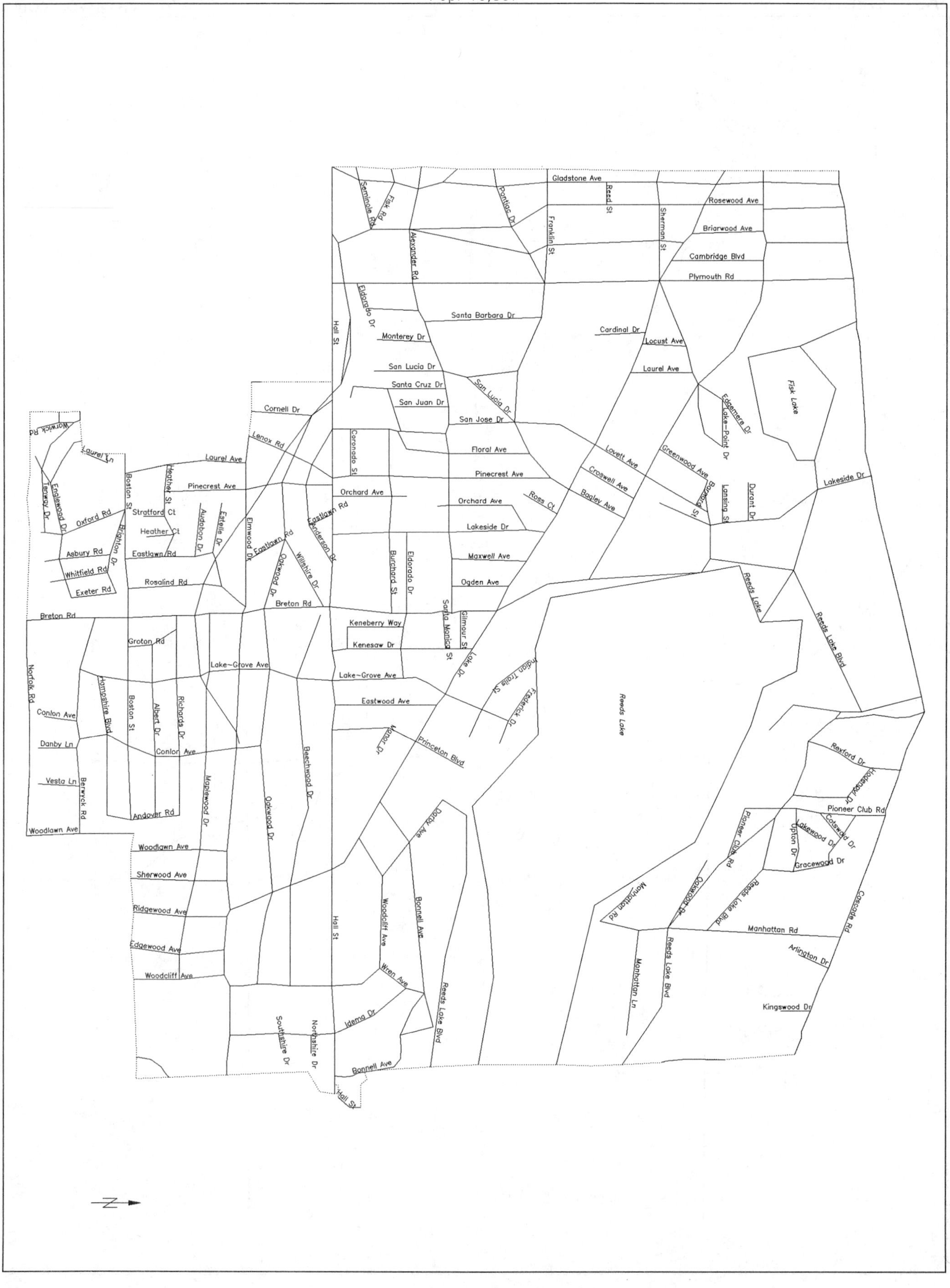

Gladstone Ave
Reed St
Rosewood Ave
Briarwood Ave
Cambridge Blvd
Plymouth Rd
Sherman St
Franklin St
Pontiac Dr
Seminole Rd
Fisk Rd
Alexander Rd
Eldorado Dr
Hall St
Santa Barbara Dr
Monterey Dr
San Lucia Dr
Santa Cruz Dr
San Juan Dr
San Jose Dr
Cardinal Dr
Locust Ave
Laurel Ave
Fisk Lake
Edgemere Dr
Lake-Point Dr
Lovett Ave
Greenwood Ave
Croswell Ave
Bagley Ave
Ross Ct
Lansing St
Durant Dr
Lakeside Dr
Cornell Dr
Lenox Rd
Coronado St
Floral Ave
Pinecrest Ave
Orchard Ave
Lakeside Dr
Maxwell Ave
Ogden Ave
Warwick Rd
Laurel Ln
Laurel Ave
Pinecrest Ave
Heather St
Boston St
Endewood Dr
Oxford Rd
Stratford Ct
Heather Ct
Audubon Dr
Estelle Dr
Elmwood Dr
Eastlawn Rd
Oakwood Dr
Wilshire Dr
Anderson Dr
Burchard St
Eldorado Dr
Brighton Dr
Asbury Rd
Whitfield Rd
Exeter Rd
Eastlawn Rd
Rosalind Rd
Breton Rd
Breton Rd
Santa Monica St
Gilmour St
Reeds Lake
Reeds Lake Blvd
Keneberry Way
Kenesaw Dr
Lake-Grove Ave
Lake-Grove Ave
Groton Rd
Norfolk Rd
Hampshire Blvd
Boston St
Albert Dr
Richards Dr
Conlon Ave
Danby Ln
Vesta Ln
Berwick Rd
Woodlawn Ave
Andover Rd
Conlon Ave
Eastwood Ave
Indian Trails St
Frederick Dr
Lake Dr
Manor Dr
Princeton Blvd
Reeds Lake
Maplewood Dr
Oakwood Dr
Beechwood Dr
Derby Ave
Woodlawn Ave
Sherwood Ave
Ridgewood Ave
Edgewood Ave
Woodcliff Ave
Hall St
Woodcliff Ave
Bonnell Ave
Wren Ave
Reeds Lake Blvd
Idema Dr
Southshire Dr
Northshire Dr
Bonnell Ave
Hall St
Rexford Dr
Hodenpyl Dr
Pioneer Club Rd
Pioneer Club Rd
Upton Dr
Lakewood Dr
Cotswold Dr
Gracewood Dr
Manhattan Rd
Oakwood Dr
Reeds Lake Blvd
Manhattan Rd
Cascade Rd
Arlington Dr
Manhattan Ln
Reeds Lake Blvd
Kingswood Dr
N

EAST JORDAN

Pop. 2,240

CHARLEVOIX COUNTY

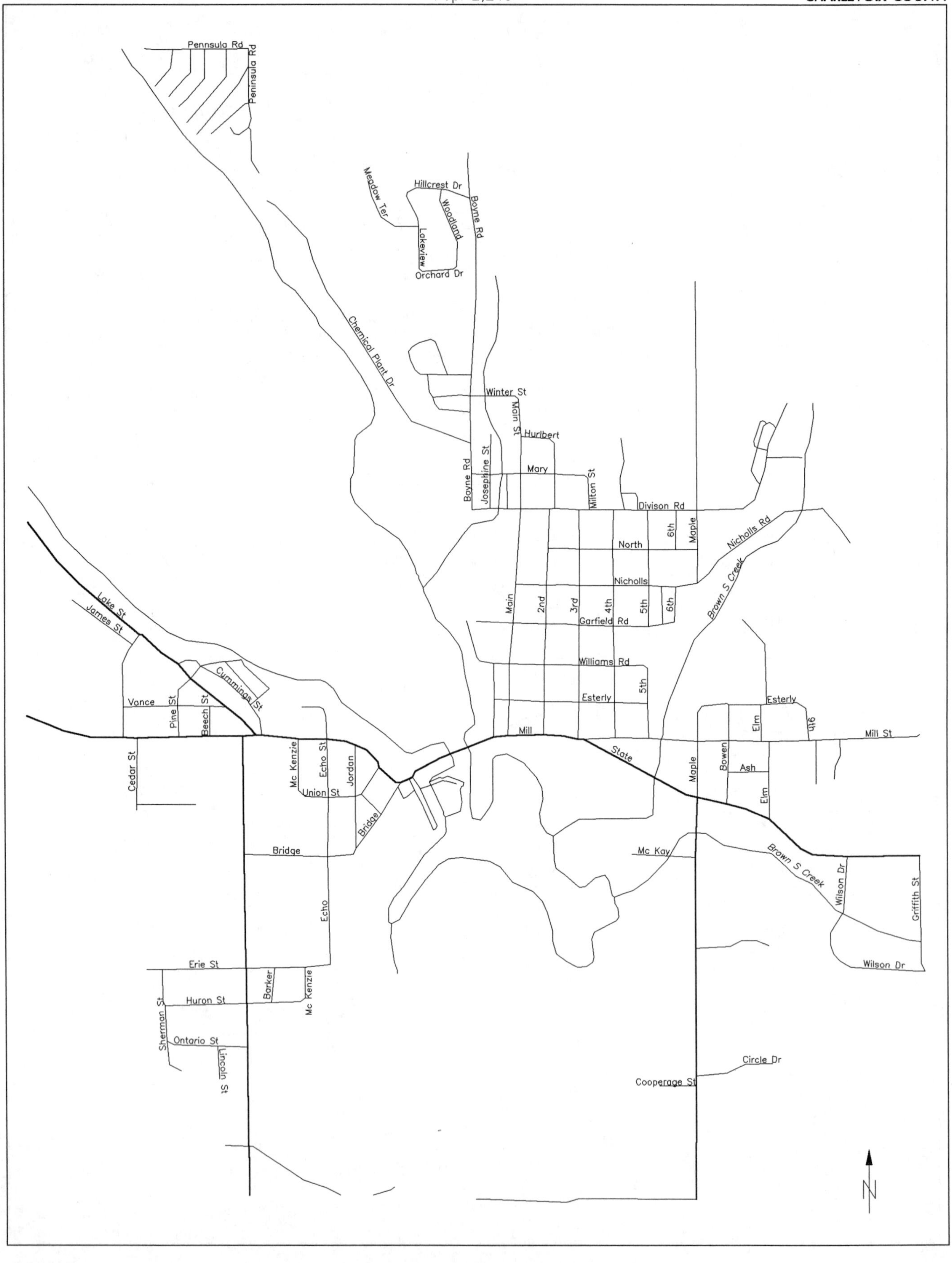
Pennsula Rd
Peninsula Rd
Meadow Ter
Hillcrest Dr
Woodland
Boyne Rd
Lakeview
Orchard Dr
Chemical Plant Dr
Winter St
Main St
Hurlbert
Boyne Rd
Josephine St
Mary
Milton St
Divison Rd
6th
Maple
North
Nicholls Rd
Nicholls
Brown S Creek
Main
2nd
3rd
4th
5th
6th
Garfield Rd
Lake St
James St
Williams Rd
Cummings St
Vance
Pine St
Beech St
Esterly
5th
Esterly
Elm
6th
Mill
Mill St
Cedar St
Mc Kenzie
Echo St
Jordan
Union St
State
Maple
Bowen
Ash
Elm
Bridge
Bridge
Mc Kay
Brown S Creek
Wilson Dr
Griffith St
Echo
Wilson Dr
Erie St
Barker
Mc Kenzie
Huron St
Sherman St
Ontario St
Lincoln St
Circle Dr
Cooperage St
N

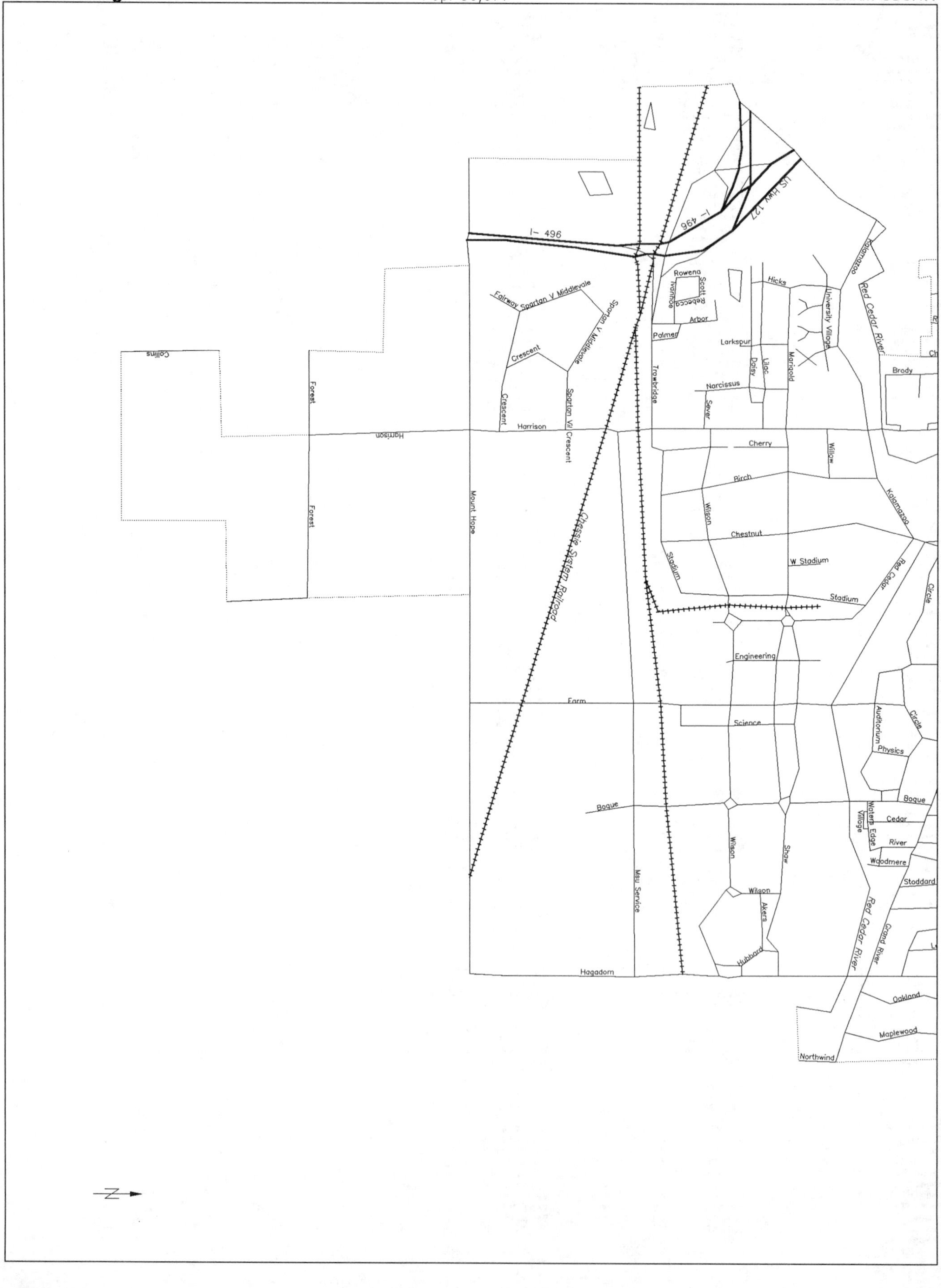

I- 496
US Hwy 127
Rowena
Scott
Ivanhoe
Rebecca
Arbor
Palmer
Hicks
University Village
Red Cedar River
Kalamazoo
Fairway
Spartan V Middlevale
Crescent
Larkspur
Daisy
Lilac
Marigold
Trowbridge
Narcissus
Sever
Brody
Collins
Forest
Harrison
Spartan Vil Crescent
Cherry
Willow
Birch
Wilson
Chestnut
Mount Hope
Chessie System Railroad
Stadium
W Stadium
Red Cedar
Circle
Engineering
Farm
Science
Auditorium
Physics
Bogue
Waters Edge
Village
Cedar
River
Woodmere
Shaw
Stoddard
Msu Service
Akers
Hubbard
Grand River
Hagadorn
Oakland
Maplewood
Northwind

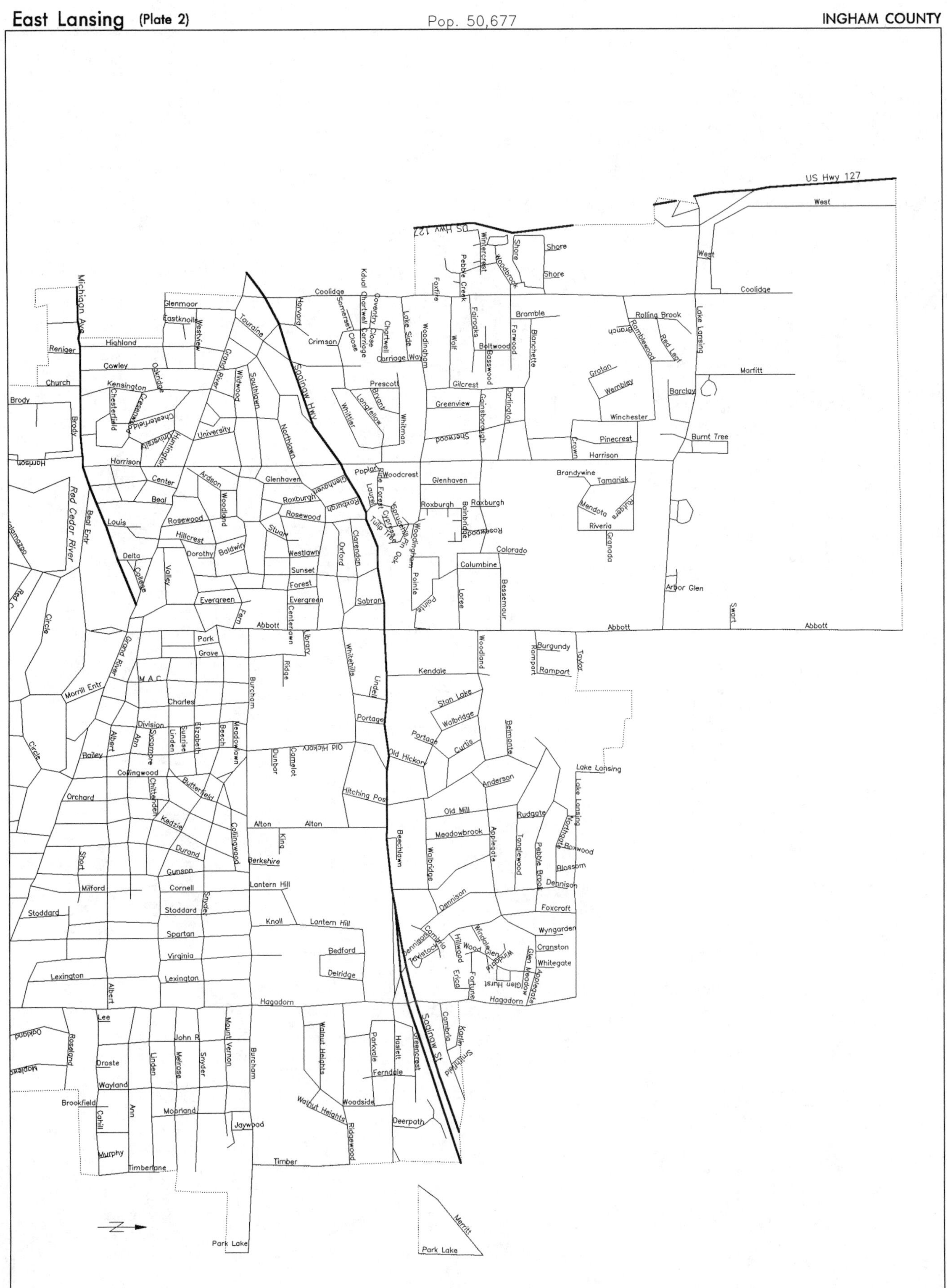

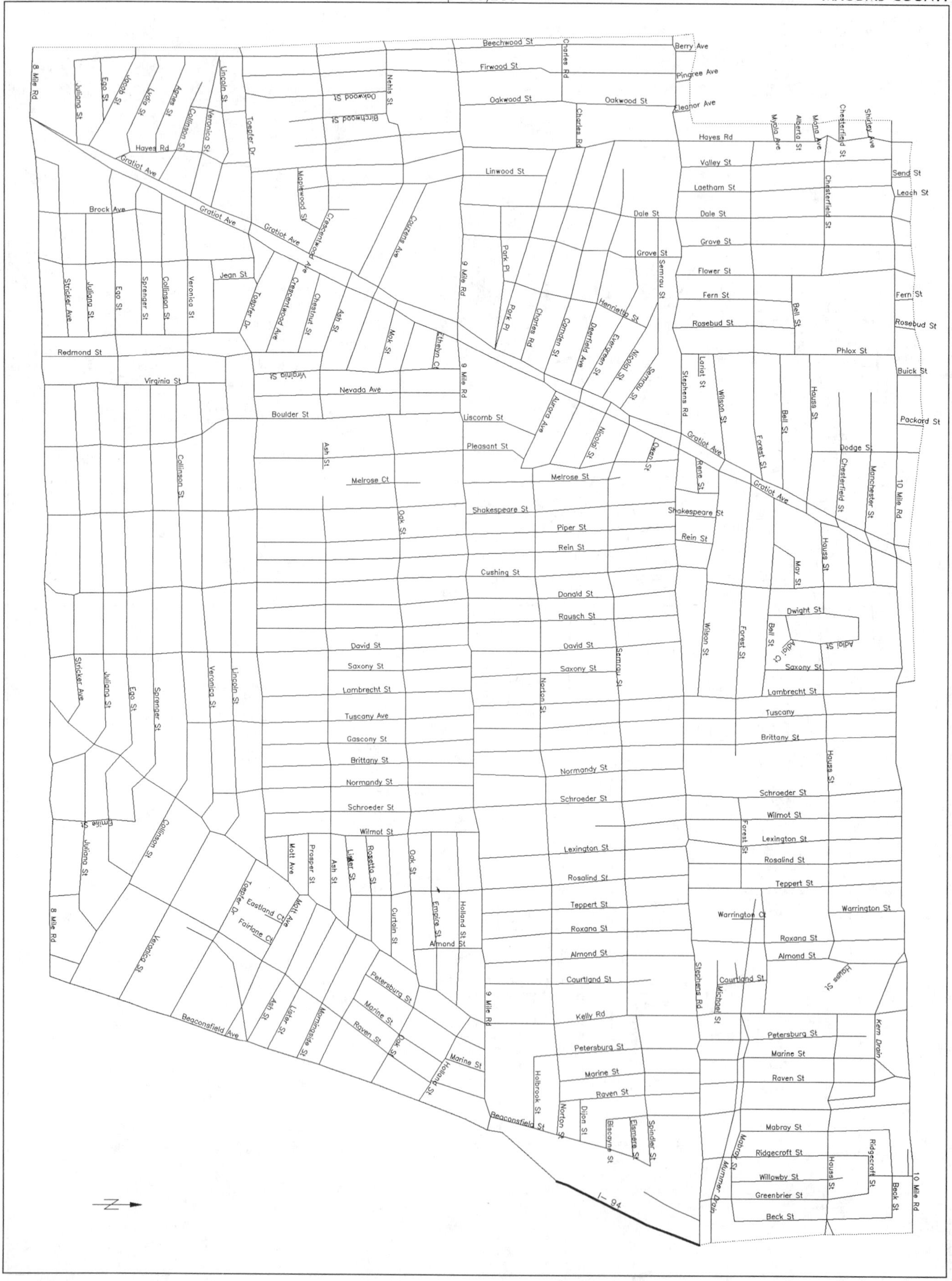

EAST POINT

Pop. 35,283

MACOMB COUNTY

River St
Genesee St
Bridge St
Mercer St
Huron St
Pine St
Ogeman St
Provost St
Wilkinson St
Loske St
Church St
Sawyer St
Washington St
Franklin St
Jefferson St
Newman St
Bay St
Main St
Tawas St
Smith St
Lincoln St
Westover St
State St
Wadsworth St
Alice
Adams St
Evans St
Grant St
Emery St
Oakes St
US Hwy 23
TAWAS BAY
Court Dr
Tawas Beach and Point Rd
Lincoln St
De Roisia Trl
Rainbow Dr
Maple Dr
Tawas Lake Rd
Court St
Colony Rd
Royal Rd
Geller Ct
Park St
Warren Ave
Wood Ave
Tawas Lake
Tawas Lake Rd
South St
Center Woods Dr
Clifford St
Lakewood Dr
Smith St
Wadsworth Rd
Woodlawn Ave
Bennington St
Fox Ave
Badger Ave
Old Airport Rd
Green Rd
Owosso Dr
Lakewood Dr
Airport Dr
Park Dr
Schill Rd
N

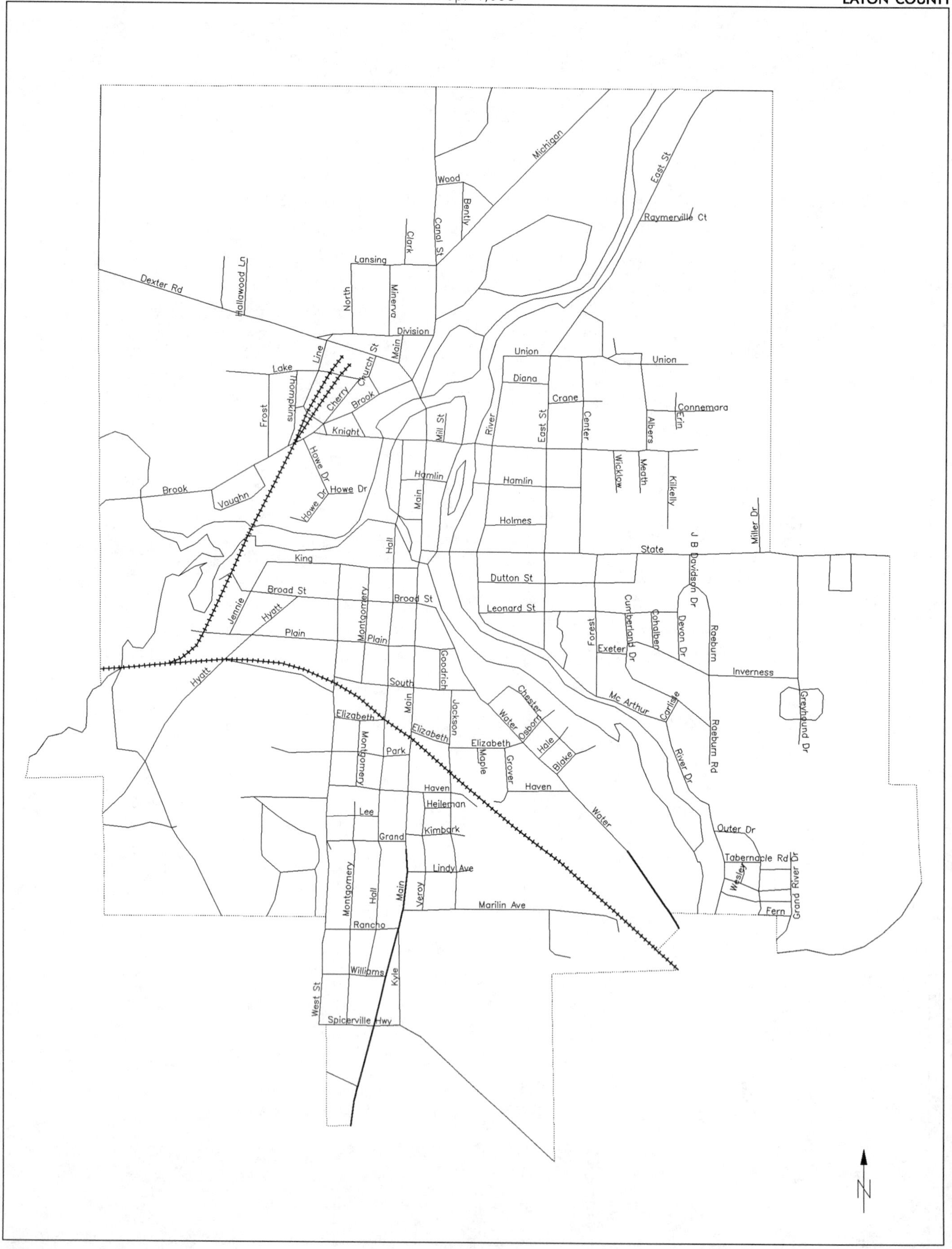

EATON RAPIDS

Pop. 4,695

EATON COUNTY

Visger Road
19th St
18th St
17th St
16th St
15th St
14th St
13th St
12th St
11th St
10th St
9th St
8th St
Francis Ave
Hyacinth Ave
Oliver Ct
Salliotte Ave
16th St
Outer Dr
13th St
Agnes St
7th St
Auburn Ave
Rockwood Ave
Glenwood Ave
Ruth Ave
Alexander Ave
Rockwood Ave
Glenwood Ave
Ironton Ave
Virginia Ct
Bell Ave
Union Ave
Ridge Ave
Knox Ave
Elton Ave
High St
Tecumseh Ave
Fink Road
Charlotte Ave
Jefferson Ave
Florence St
Joseph Ave
Alexis Ave
Charlotte Ave
Drennan St
Salliotte Ave
Sunnyside Ave
Alexis Ave
Eliza St
Josephine Ave
Cherrygrove St
Broadway Ave
Josephine Ave
Woodward Ave
Woodward Ave
Westfield Ave
Outer Dr
Pc Railroad
Dt and I Railroad
Westfield Ave
Ecorse River
Pepper Road
Cicotte St
10th St
9th St
8th St
7th St
Cicotte St
5th St
Beach St
Beach St
Labadie Ct
Labadie St
Bondie St
Cicotte St
Reno St
Labadie St
6th St
3rd St
2nd St
Bonzano St
Goodell Ave
Applegrove St
Pitt St
Monroe Ave
Alexander Ct
Benson Ave
Cicotte St
Southfield Road
9th St
8th St
White Ave
1st St
Labadie St
Webster St
Bourassa St
7th St
6th St
5th St
4th St
Suburban Ave
White St
Le Blanc St
Jefferson Ave
Mill St
Ecorse River
N

EDMORE

Pop. 1,126

1st
North St
2nd St
3rd St
4th St
5th St
Neff Road
Railroad St
Home St
Baldwin St
Norway
Home St
Main St
Juniper St
Main St
Lewis St
Sheldon
Gilson St
Industrial Park Dr
Pine St
Pine St
Maple
Moore St
Brown St
2nd St
3rd St
4th St
Forest St
1st
Camp St
3rd St
Crescent Dr
Greenfield
1st
5th St
Johnson St
Charlotte St
Brown St
Center St
Gatehouse Dr
N

Pleasant Lake
Edgewater Dr
Washington Blvd
Lake Ct
Cass St
Cemetery Road
St Hwy 62 (M-62)
Hamilton St
Jefferson St
East St
US Hwy 12
Claire St
Stuart St
Circle Dr
Taylor St
1st St
Lake St
Main St
Main St
Main St
Grand Trunk Western Railroad
Church St
Gateway Road
Barber St
Maple St
Davis St
Wilkinson
Center St
Elkhart Road
Ewing Ct
Meadowview Dr
M-62
Section Road
N

Pop. 1,626

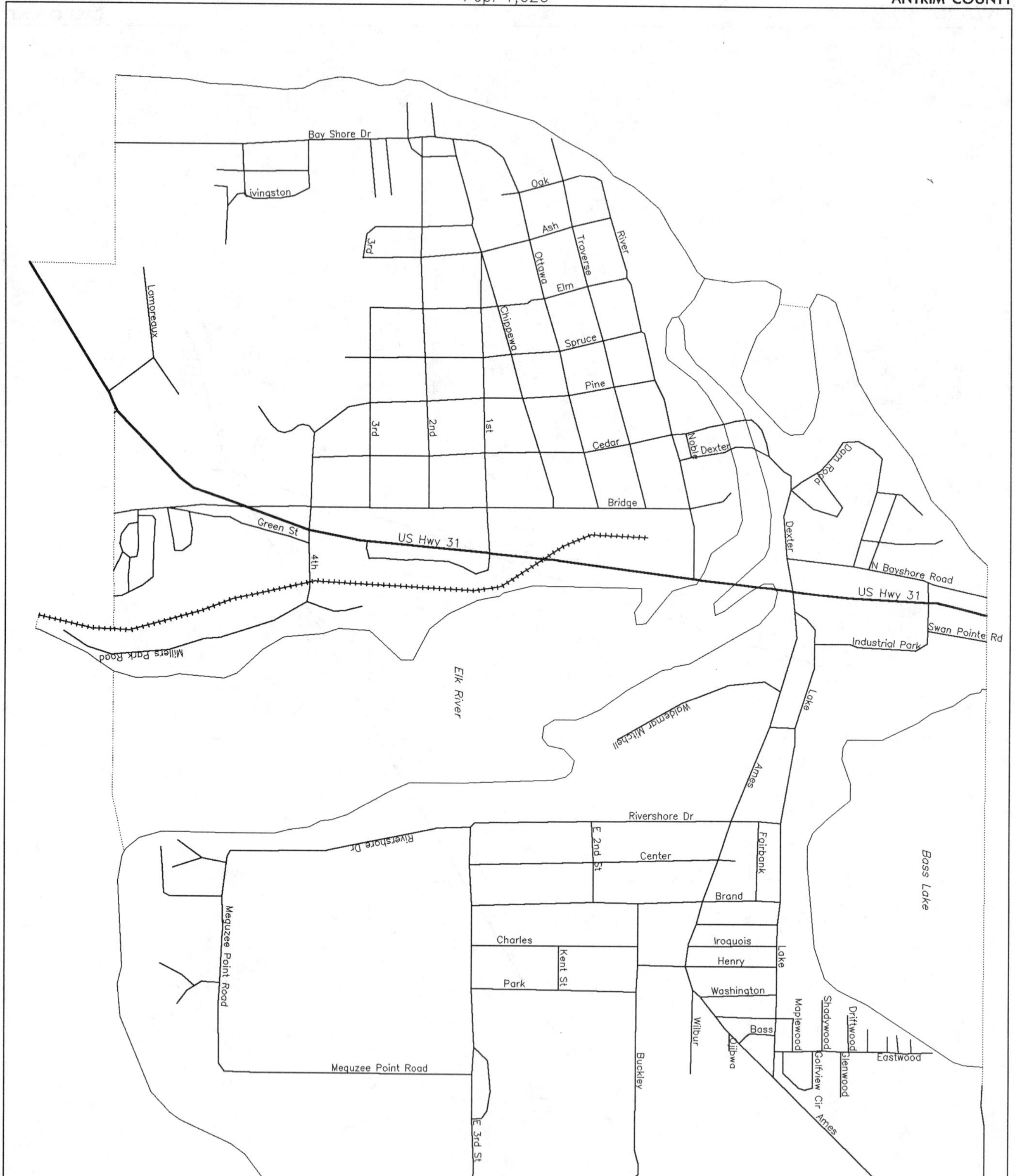
Bay Shore Dr
Livingston
Oak
Ash
Traverse
River
Ottawa
3rd
Elm
Lamoreaux
Chippewa
Spruce
Pine
3rd
2nd
1st
Noble
Dexter
Cedar
Darn Road
Bridge
Green St
US Hwy 31
4th
Dexter
N Bayshore Road
US Hwy 31
Swan Pointe Rd
Industrial Park
Millers Park Road
Elk River
Lake
Waldemar Mitchell
Ames
Riversphore Dr
Rivershore Dr
E 2nd St
Fairbank
Center
Bass Lake
Brand
Mequzee Point Road
Charles
Kent St
Iroquois
Henry
Lake
Park
Washington
Maplewood
Shadywood
Driftwood
Wilbur
Bass
Ojibwa
Eastwood
Glenwood
Golfview Cir
Mequzee Point Road
Buckley
Ames
E 3rd St
Cairn Hwy
Green Acres Lane
N

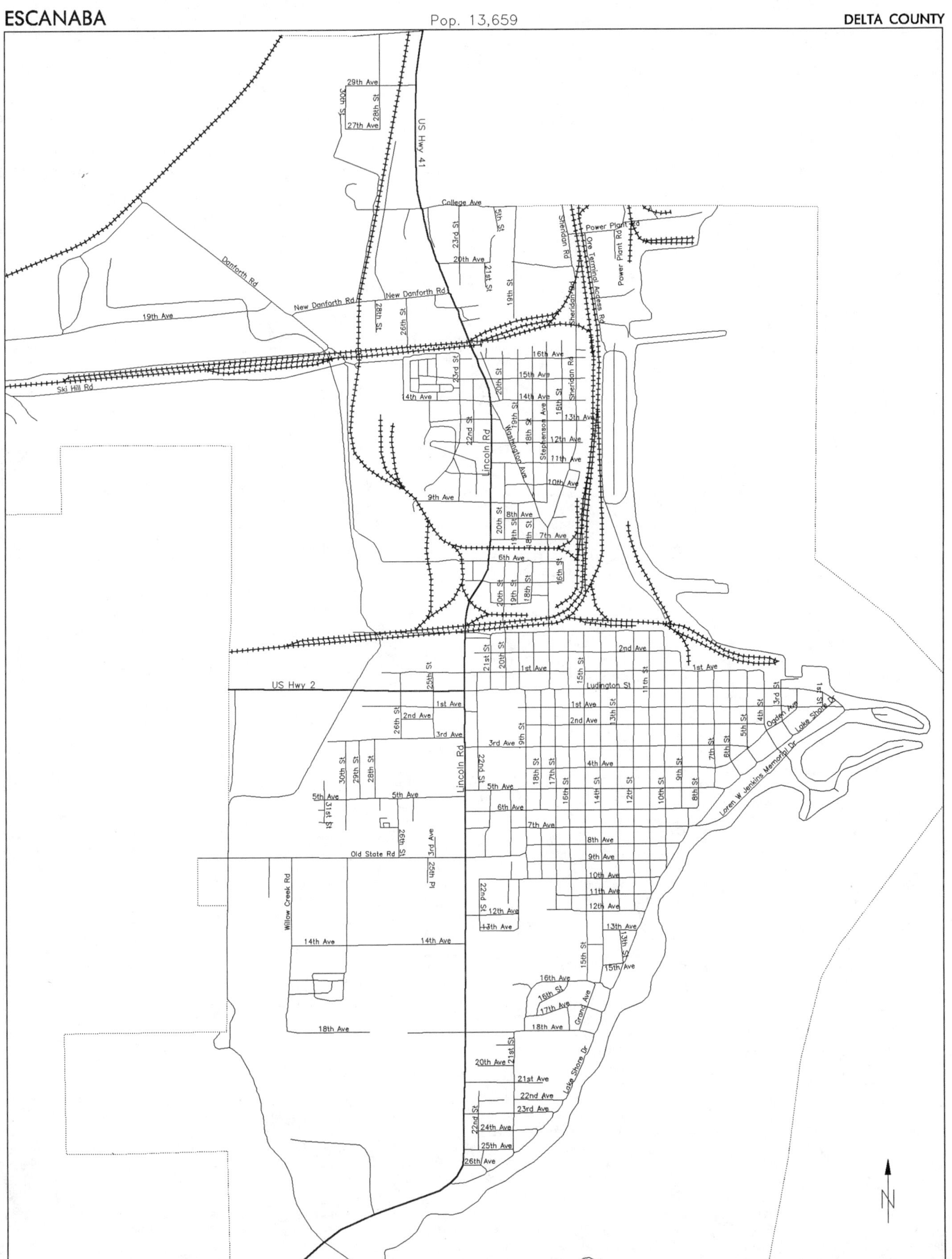
US Hwy 41
US Hwy 2
Lincoln Rd
College Ave
Danforth Rd
New Danforth Rd
19th Ave
Ski Hill Rd
Sheridan Rd
Power Plant Rd
Ore Terminal Access Rd
Washington Ave
Stephenson Ave
Ludington St
Ogden Ave
Lake Shore Dr
Loren W Jenkins Memorial Dr
Old State Rd
Willow Creek Rd
Grand Ave
14th Ave
18th Ave
N

ESSEXVILLE

Pop. 4,088

Saginaw River
Pine St
Saginaw River
Jarman St
Elm St
Maple St
Main St
Lynn St
Prairie St
Prairie St
Prairie St
James St
Brentwood Pl
Smith St
Langstaff St
Dunbar St
Ames St
Elm St
Maple St
Woodside Ave
Mercer St
Ward St
Cotter St
Lynn St
Essex St
Franklin Ct
Sharlear Dr
Orchard Ct
Scheurmann St
Mc Donnell St
Burns St
Hudson St
Oak St
Elm St
Ash St
Maple St
Parker St
Sharlear Dr
Oakland Ct
Pitre Ct
Ivy Ct
Sharlear Dr
3rd St
Garside Dr
Borton Ave
Cornell St
Caroline St
Rust St
Edgewood Dr
Virginia Dr
Meadow Dr
Villaire St
Oakland Dr
Eda St
Valerie Ct
Deary St
Burns St
Hart St
Sharpe St
Main St
Birney St
Pine St
Thompson St
Thompson Ave
Hall St
Marshall St
Plummer Ave
Sovey Ct
Nebobish Ave
N

Ingersoll Road
US Hwy 10
Chase Road
Chesapeake and Ohio Railway
Lucas Road
95th Ave
5th St
Fair St
Recreation Ave
7 Mile Road
5th St
7th St
1st St
Washington St
90th Ave
Cedar St
10th St
Products Ave
4th St
Cherry St
12th St
Oak St
Hemlock St
9th St
Hemlock St
11th St
Pine St
Railroad Ave
6th St
5th St
3rd St
2nd St
Main St
River St
River St
8th St
Park St

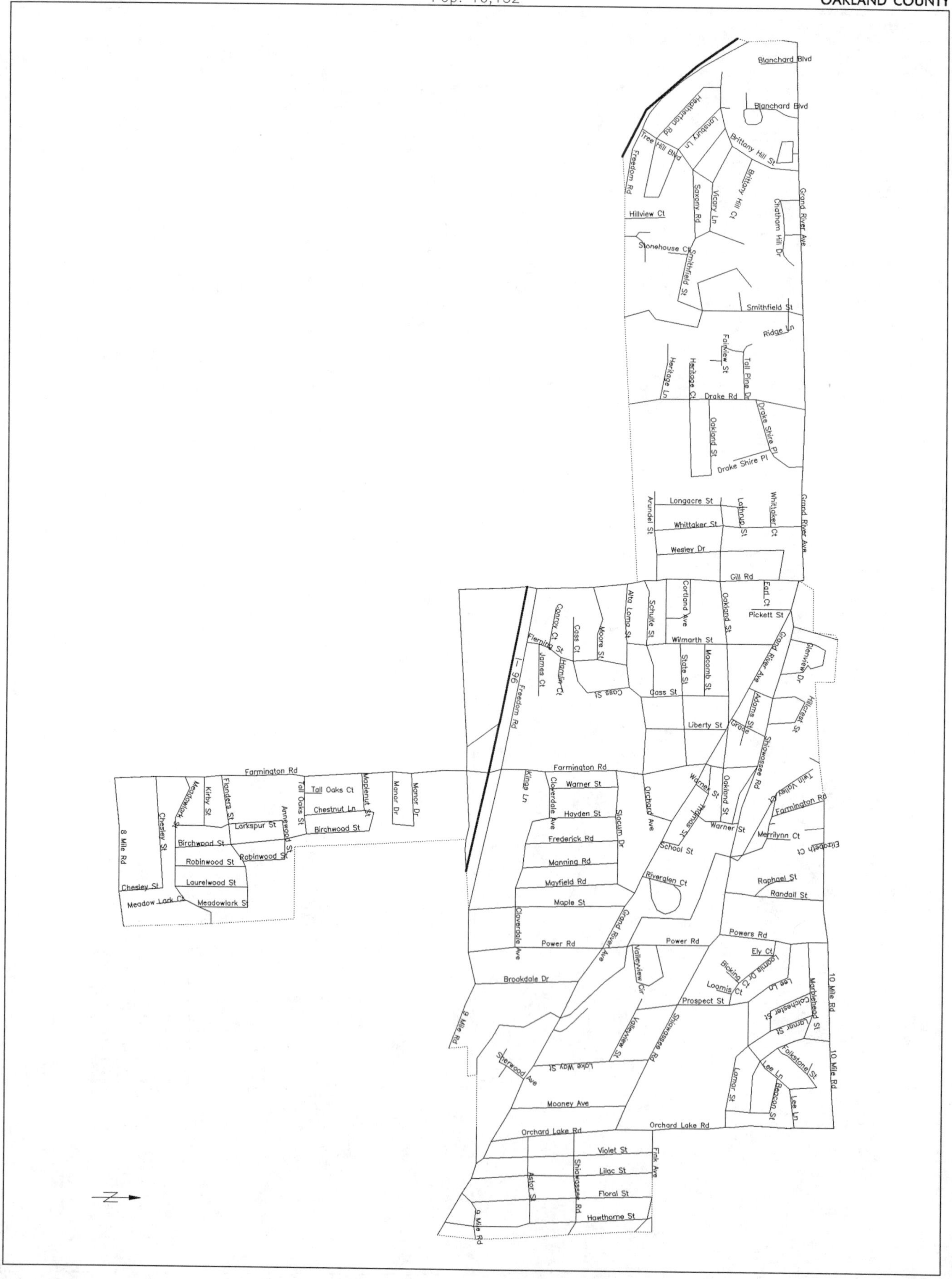
Blanchard Blvd
Blanchard Blvd
Heatherton Rd
Lansbury Ln
Tree Hill Blvd
Brittany Hill St
Freedom Rd
Brittany Hill Ct
Saxony Rd
Vicary Ln
Chatham Hill Dr
Grand River Ave
Hillview Ct
Stonehouse Ct
Smithfield St
Smithfield St
Ridge Ln
Fairview St
Tall Pine Dr
Heritage Ln
Heritage Ct
Drake Rd
Oakland St
Drake Shire Pl
Drake Shire Pl
Arundel St
Longacre St
Lathrup St
Whittaker Ct
Grand River Ave
Whittaker St
Wesley Dr
Gill Rd
Alta Loma St
Schulte St
Cortland Ave
Oakland St
Earl Ct
Pickett St
Conroy Ct
Cass Ct
Moore St
Fleming St
James Ct
Hamlin Ct
Wilmarth St
State St
Macomb St
Grand River Ave
Glenview Dr
I-96
Freedom Rd
Cass St
Cass St
Adams St
Hillcrest St
Liberty St
Grace
Shiawassee Rd
Farmington Rd
Farmington Rd
Meadowlark Rd
Kirby St
Flanders St
Tall Oaks St
Tall Oaks Ct
Maplenut St
Manor Dr
Manor Dr
Kings Ln
Warner St
Cloverdale Ave
Orchard Ave
Warner St
Oakland St
Twin Valley Ct
Farmington Rd
Chestnut Ln
Hayden St
Slocum Dr
Thomas St
Warner St
8 Mile Rd
Chesley St
Larkspur St
Annewood St
Birchwood St
Merrilynn Ct
Elizabeth Ct
Birchwood St
Frederick Rd
School St
Robinwood St
Robinwood St
Manning Rd
Riverglen Ct
Raphael St
Chesley St
Laurelwood St
Mayfield Rd
Randall St
Meadow Lark Ct
Meadowlark St
Maple St
Cloverdale Ave
Grand River Ave
Powers Rd
Power Rd
Power Rd
Ely Ct
Valleyview Cir
Bicking Ct
Loomis Dr Ct
Lee Ln
Brookdale Dr
Loomis Ct
Marblehead St
10 Mile Rd
Prospect St
Colchester St
9 Mile Rd
Valleyview St
Shiawassee Rd
Lamar St
Sherwood Ave
Lake Way St
Folkstone St
Lee Ln
10 Mile Rd
Lamar St
Beacon St
Lee Ln
Mooney Ave
Orchard Lake Rd
Orchard Lake Rd
Violet St
Fink Ave
Lilac St
Astor St
Shiawassee Rd
Floral St
Hawthorne St
9 Mile Rd
N

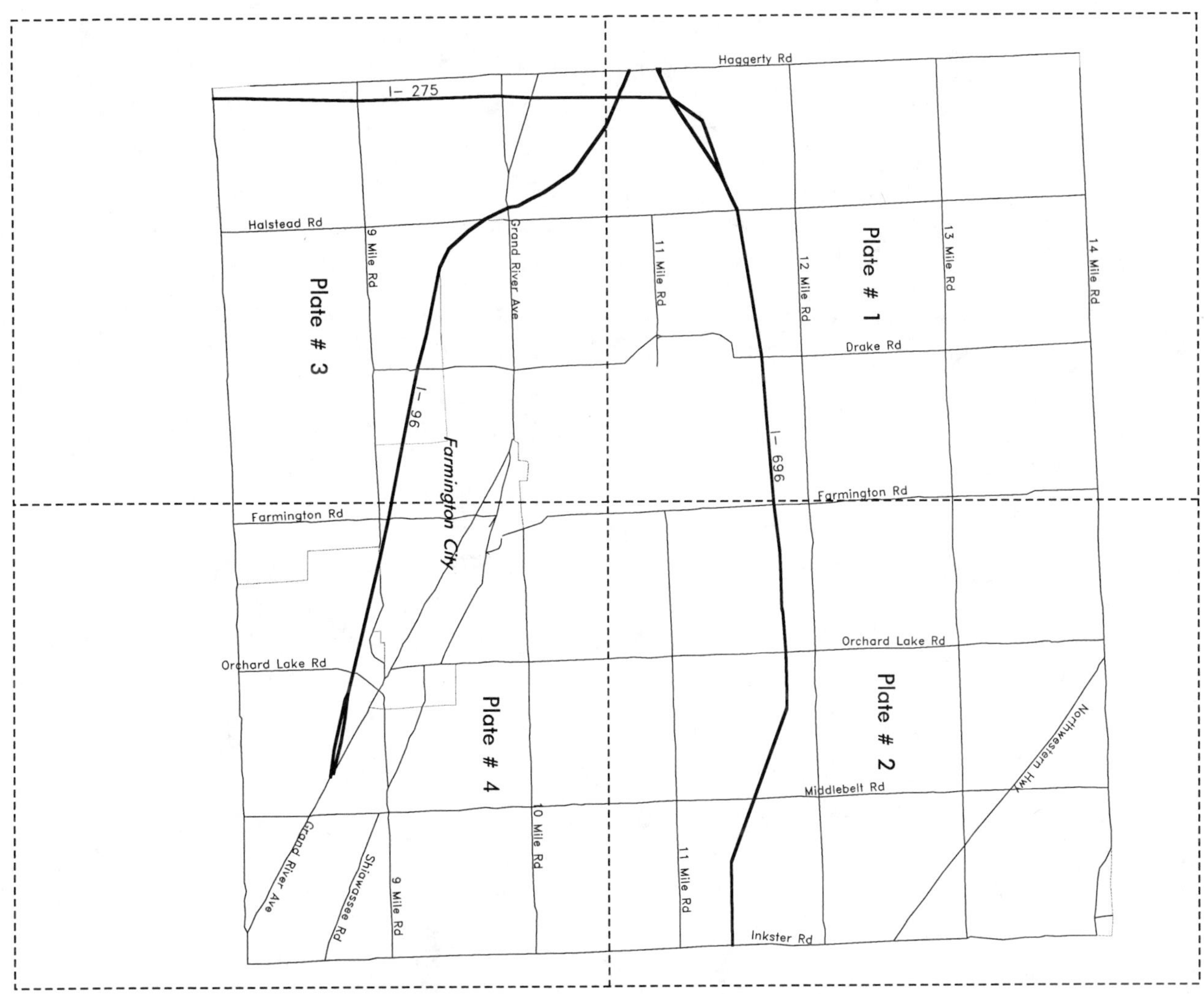
Haggerty Rd
I- 275
Halstead Rd
9 Mile Rd
Grand River Ave
11 Mile Rd
12 Mile Rd
13 Mile Rd
14 Mile Rd
Plate # 1
Plate # 3
Drake Rd
I- 96
Farmington City
I- 696
Farmington Rd
Farmington Rd
Orchard Lake Rd
Orchard Lake Rd
Plate # 4
Plate # 2
Northwestern Hwy
Middlebelt Rd
10 Mile Rd
11 Mile Rd
9 Mile Rd
Shiawassee Rd
Grand River Ave
Inkster Rd

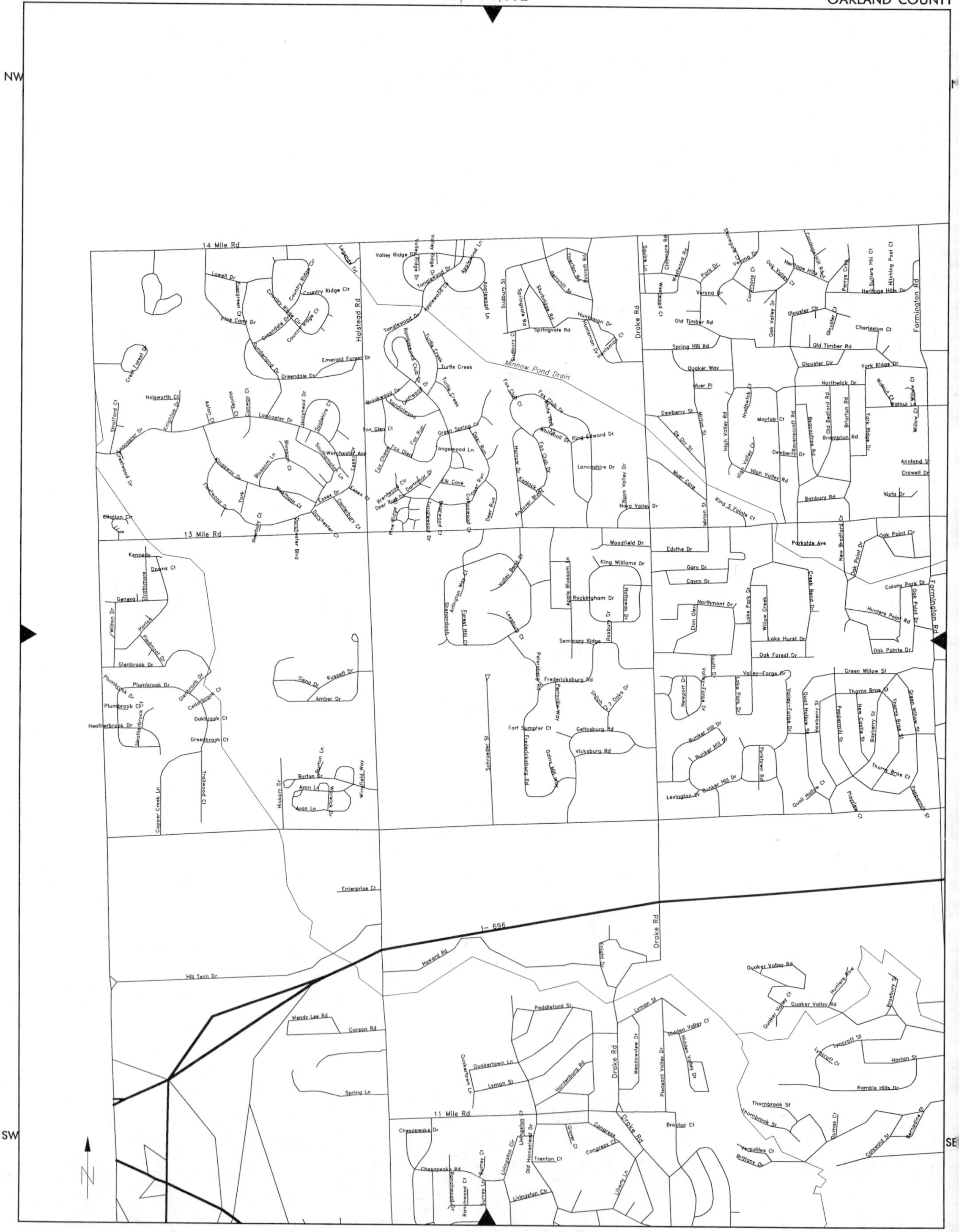

FARMINGTON HILLS (Plate 1)

Pop. 74,652

OAKLAND COUNTY

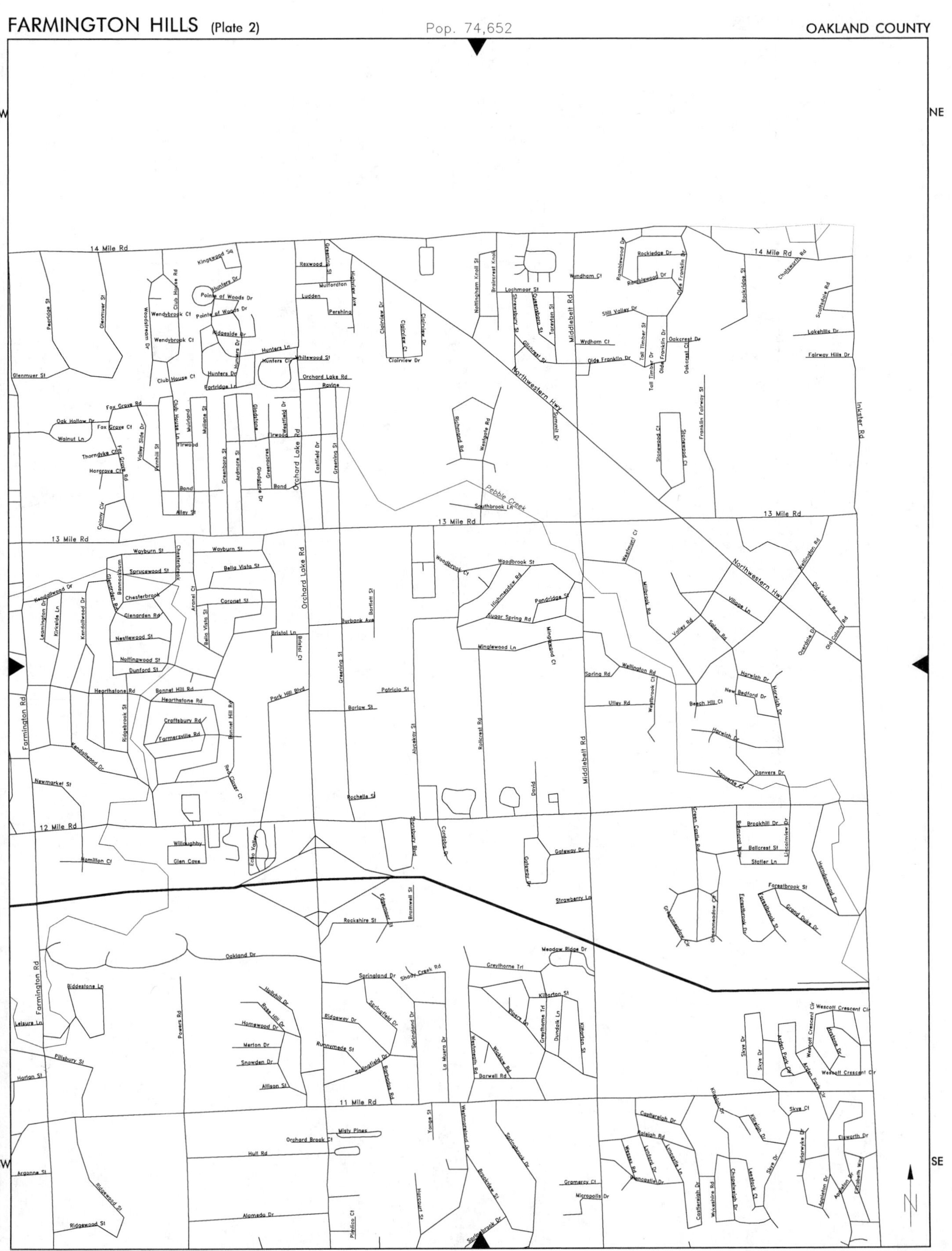
NW
NE
SW
SE
14 Mile Rd
13 Mile Rd
12 Mile Rd
11 Mile Rd
Orchard Lake Rd
Middlebelt Rd
Farmington Rd
Inkster Rd
Northwestern Hwy
Pebble Creek
Oakland Dr
Powers Rd
Glenmuer St
Pearlidge St
Kingswood Sq
Club House Rd
Club House Ct
Club House Ln
Pointe of Woods Dr
Wendybrook Ct
Hunters Ln
Hunters Dr
Whitewood St
Orchard Lake Rd
Ravine
Rexwood
Ludden
Pershing
Clairview Dr
Clairview Ct
Lochmoor St
Wyndham Ct
Rockledge Dr
Olde Franklin Dr
Tall Timber Dr
Oakcrest Dr
Fairway Hills Dr
Lakehills Dr
Scottsdale Rd
Chatsworth Rd
Rockridge St
Franklin Fairway St
Stonewood Ct
Richmond Rd
Westgate Rd
Southbrook Ln
Fox Grove Rd
Oak Hollow Dr
Walnut Ln
Valley Side Dr
Firwood
Muirland
Mulliane St
Gladstone
Greenacres
Eastfield Dr
Greening St
Bond
Alley St
Colony Cir
Wayburn St
Bella Vista St
Coronet St
Sprucewood St
Chesterbrook
Glengarden Rd
Nestlewood St
Nottingwood St
Dunford St
Hearthstone Rd
Bonnet Hill Rd
Craftsbury Rd
Farmersville Rd
Kendallwood Dr
Newmarket St
Bristol Ln
Park Hill Blvd
Burbank Ave
Bartlett St
Patricia St
Barlow St
Rochelle St
Woodbrook St
Woodbrook Ct
Highmeadow Rd
Pondridge St
Sugar Spring Rd
Minglewood Ln
Minglewood Ct
Rollcrest Rd
David
Wellington Rd
Westmont Ct
Spring Rd
Utley Rd
Westbrook Ct
Valley Rd
Village Ln
Salem Rd
Old Colony Rd
Harwich Dr
New Bedford Dr
Beech Hill Ct
Danvers Dr
Willoughby
Glen Cove
Hamilton Ct
Gateway Dr
Strawberry Ln
Brookhill Dr
Bellcrest St
Statler Ln
Forestbrook St
Grand Duke Dr
Rockshire St
Bromwell St
Springland Dr
Shady Creek Rd
Greythorne Trl
Meadow Ridge Dr
Biddestone Ln
Leisure Ln
Hollyhill Dr
Rose Hill Dr
Homewood Dr
Merton Dr
Snowden Dr
Allison St
Pillsbury St
Horton St
Ridgeway Dr
Runnymede St
Springfield Dr
La Muera Dr
Dundalk Ln
Killarton St
Barwell Rd
Skye Dr
Skye Ct
Wescott Crescent Cir
Wescott Crescent Ct
Arden Park Dr
Castlereigh Dr
Raleigh Rd
Lancastle Dr
Wykeshire Rd
Elsworth Dr
Appleton Dr
Misty Pines
Orchard Brook Ct
Hull Rd
Alameda Dr
Argonne St
Ridgewood St
Gramercy Ct
Micropolis Dr
Pimlico Ct
Yonge St
Springbrook Dr
N

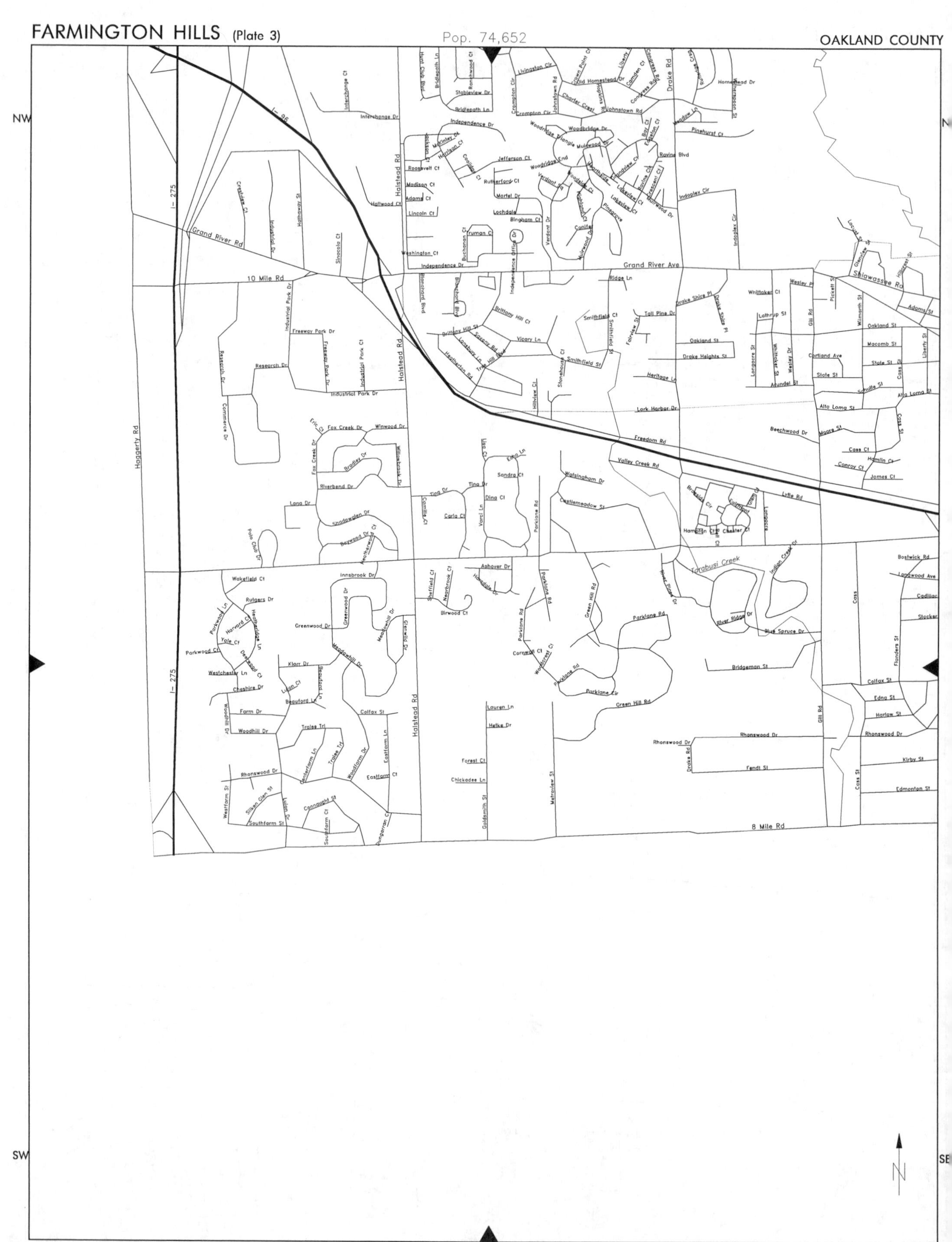
NW
SW
SE
Grand River Ave
10 Mile Rd
8 Mile Rd
Halstead Rd
Haggerty Rd
Drake Rd
I-275
I-96
Tarabusi Creek
Freedom Rd
N

FARMINGTON HILLS (Plate 4)

Pop. 74,652

OAKLAND COUNTY

FENNVILLE

Pop. 1,023

ALLEGAN COUNTY

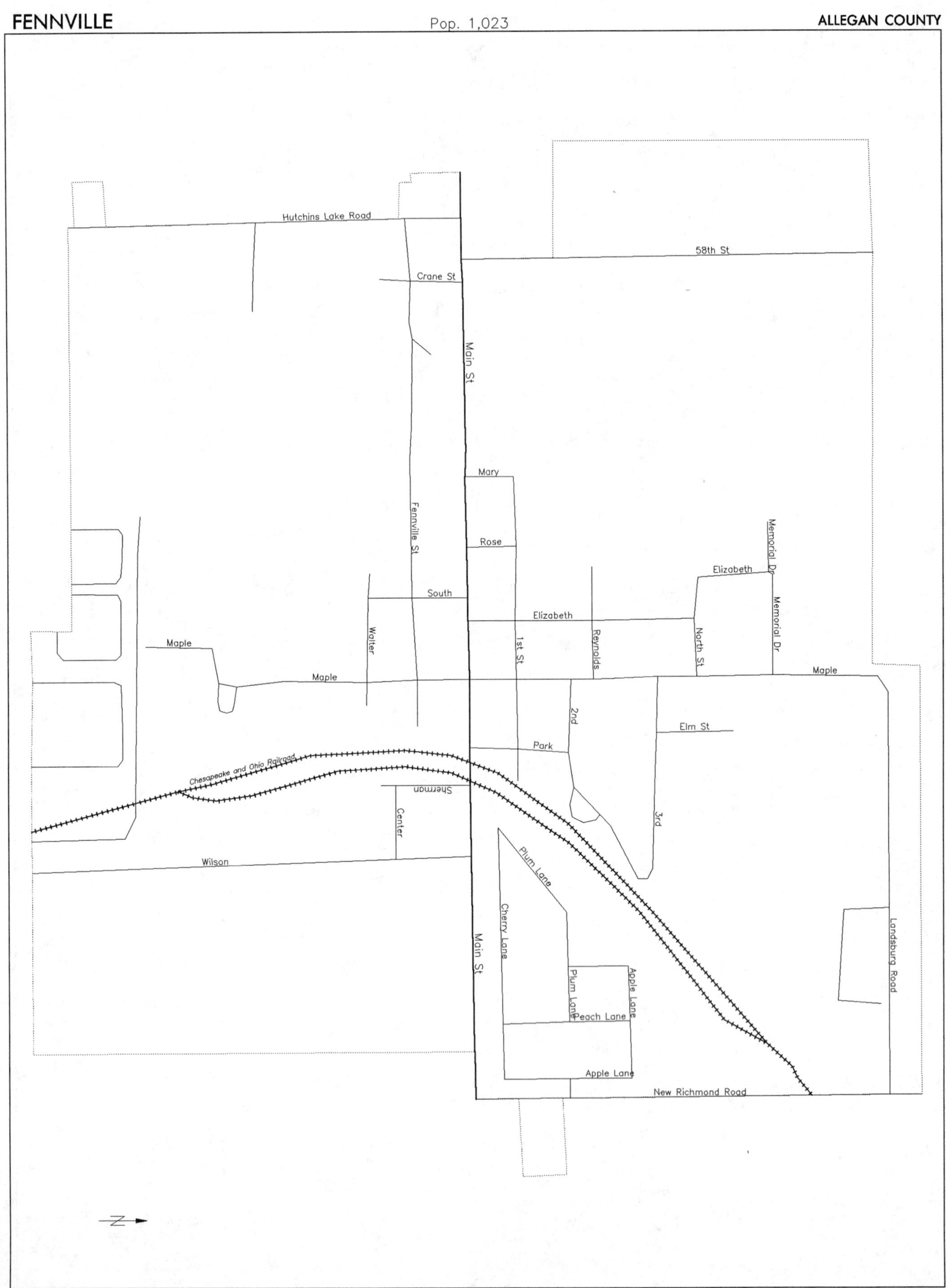

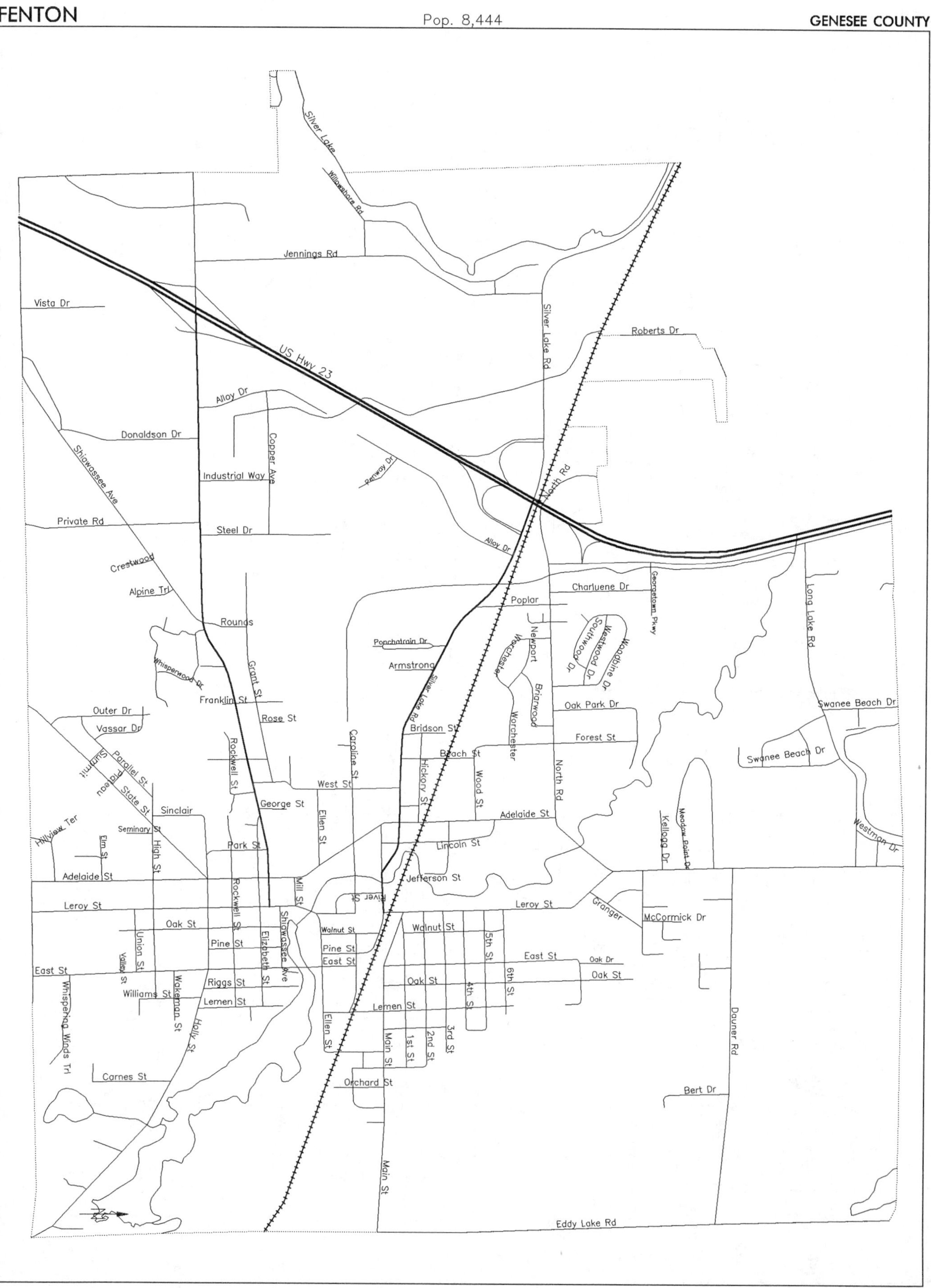
Silver Lake
Willowshore Rd
Jennings Rd
Vista Dr
Roberts Dr
Silver Lake Rd
US Hwy 23
Alloy Dr
Donaldson Dr
Copper Ave
Industrial Way
Shiawassee Ave
Penway Dr
North Rd
Private Rd
Steel Dr
Alloy Dr
Crestwood
Alpine Trl
Charluene Dr
Georgetown Pkwy
Long Lake Rd
Poplar
Rounds
Ponchatrain Dr
Newport
Southwood Dr
Westwood Dr
Woodbine Dr
Armstrong
Worchester
Whisperwood Dr
Silver Lake Rd
Briarwood
Grant St
Franklin St
Oak Park Dr
Swanee Beach Dr
Outer Dr
Rose St
Vassar Dr
Bridson St
Worchester
Forest St
Caroline St
Beach St
Swanee Beach Dr
Summit
Parallel St
Rockwell St
Hickory St
Wood St
North Rd
Old Orchard
State St
West St
Sinclair
George St
Adelaide St
Hillview Ter
Seminary St
Ellen St
Meadow Point Dr
Kellogg Dr
Westman Dr
Elm St
High St
Park St
Lincoln St
Adelaide St
Mill St
Jefferson St
River St
Leroy St
Leroy St
Granger
Oak St
Rockwell St
Shiawassee Ave
McCormick Dr
Union St
Walnut St
Walnut St
Pine St
Elizabeth St
Pine St
5th St
East St
Oak Dr
East St
Valley St
East St
Oak St
Williams St
Riggs St
Oak St
6th St
Wakeman St
Lemen St
4th St
Whispering Winds Trl
Holly St
Lemen St
Dauner Rd
Ellen St
Main St
1st St
2nd St
3rd St
Carnes St
Orchard St
Bert Dr
Main St
Eddy Lake Rd

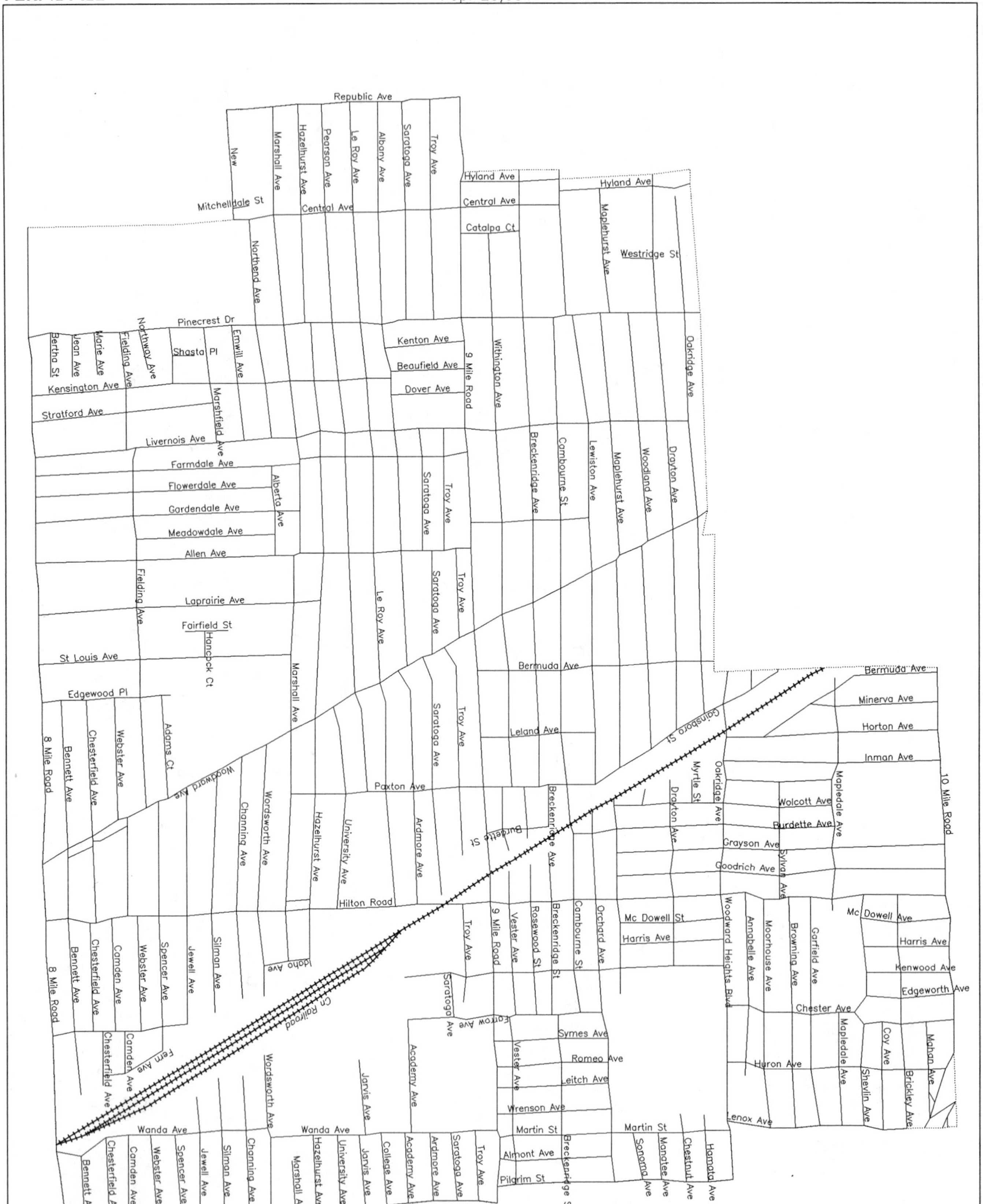

Republic Ave
New
Marshall Ave
Hazelhurst Ave
Pearson Ave
Le Roy Ave
Albany Ave
Saratoga Ave
Troy Ave
Mitchelldale St
Central Ave
Hyland Ave
Central Ave
Catalpa Ct
Hyland Ave
Maplehurst Ave
Westridge St
Northend Ave
Pinecrest Dr
Bertha St
Jean Ave
Marie Ave
Fielding Ave
Northway Ave
Shasta Pl
Emwill Ave
Kenton Ave
Beaufield Ave
Dover Ave
9 Mile Road
Withington Ave
Oakridge Ave
Kensington Ave
Stratford Ave
Marshfield Ave
Livernois Ave
Farmdale Ave
Flowerdale Ave
Gardendale Ave
Meadowdale Ave
Allen Ave
Alberta Ave
Saratoga Ave
Troy Ave
Breckenridge Ave
Cambourne St
Lewiston Ave
Maplehurst Ave
Woodland Ave
Drayton Ave
Fielding Ave
Lapraire Ave
Fairfield St
Hancock Ct
Le Roy Ave
Saratoga Ave
Troy Ave
St Louis Ave
Bermuda Ave
Bermuda Ave
Edgewood Pl
Marshall Ave
Minerva Ave
Horton Ave
Inman Ave
8 Mile Road
Bennett Ave
Chesterfield Ave
Webster Ave
Adams Ct
Woodward Ave
Saratoga Ave
Troy Ave
Leland Ave
Gainsboro St
Paxton Ave
Channing Ave
Wordsworth Ave
Hazelhurst Ave
University Ave
Ardmore Ave
Burdette St
Breckenridge Ave
Drayton Ave
Myrtle St
Oakridge Ave
Wolcott Ave
Burdette Ave
Mapledale Ave
10 Mile Road
Grayson Ave
Goodrich Ave
Sylvan Ave
Hilton Road
Bennett Ave
Chesterfield Ave
Camden Ave
Webster Ave
Spencer Ave
Jewell Ave
Silman Ave
Idaho Ave
Cn Railroad
Troy Ave
9 Mile Road
Vester Ave
Rosewood St
Breckenridge St
Cambourne St
Orchard Ave
Mc Dowell St
Harris Ave
Woodward Heights Blvd
Annabelle Ave
Moorhouse Ave
Browning Ave
Garfield Ave
Mc Dowell Ave
Harris Ave
Kenwood Ave
Edgeworth Ave
8 Mile Road
Saratoga Ave
Farrow Ave
Chester Ave
Chesterfield Ave
Camden Ave
Fern Ave
Symes Ave
Romeo Ave
Leitch Ave
Wordsworth Ave
Academy Ave
Jarvis Ave
Vester Ave
Mapledale Ave
Coy Ave
Mahan Ave
Huron Ave
Shevlin Ave
Brickley Ave
Wrenson Ave
Lenox Ave
Wanda Ave
Wanda Ave
Martin St
Martin St
Bennett Ave
Chesterfield Ave
Camden Ave
Webster Ave
Spencer Ave
Jewell Ave
Silman Ave
Channing Ave
Marshall Ave
Hazelhurst Ave
University Ave
Jarvis Ave
College Ave
Academy Ave
Ardmore Ave
Saratoga Ave
Troy Ave
Almont Ave
Pilgrim St
Breckenridge St
Sonoma Ave
Manatee Ave
Chestnut Ave
Hamata Ave
End St
N

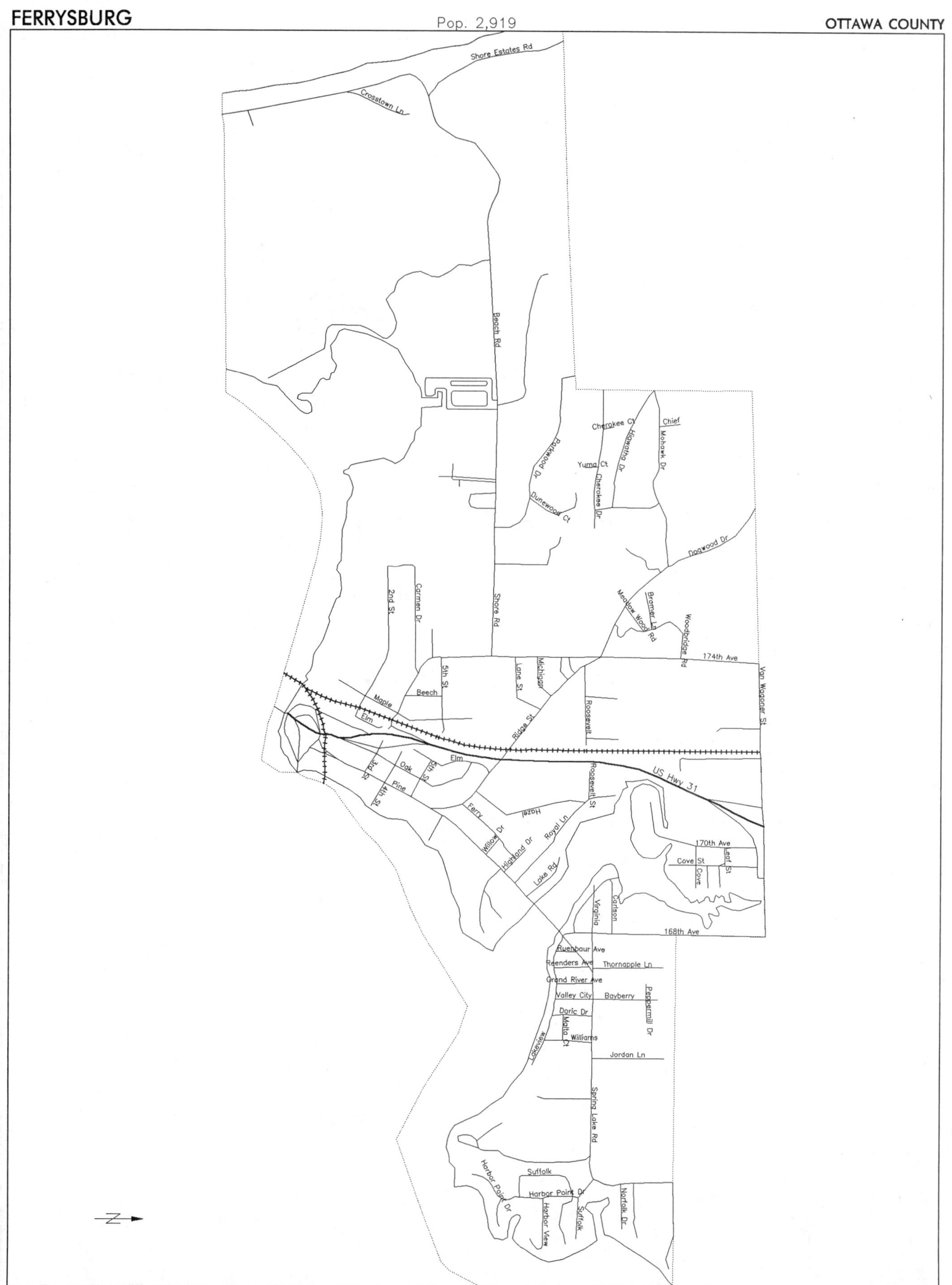
Shore Estates Rd
Crosstown Ln
Beach Rd
Shore Rd
Cherokee Ct
Chief
Hiawatha Dr
Mohawk Dr
Parkwood Dr
Yuma Ct
Cherokee Dr
Dunewood Ct
Dogwood Dr
Meadow Wood Rd
Bramer Ln
Woodbridge Rd
174th Ave
Van Wagoner St
2nd St
Carmen Dr
5th St
Lane St
Michigan
Beach
Maple
Elm
Ridge St
Roosevelt
3rd St
Oak
Pine
4th St
6th St
Elm
US Hwy 31
Roosevelt St
Ferry
Hazel
Royal Ln
Willow Dr
Highland Dr
Lake Rd
170th Ave
Cove St
Cove
Leaf St
Virginia
Carlson
168th Ave
Ruehbaur Ave
Reenders Ave
Thornapple Ln
Grand River Ave
Valley City
Bayberry
Peppermill Dr
Doric Dr
Malta Ct
Williams
Lakeview
Jordan Ln
Spring Lake Rd
Suffolk
Harbor Point Dr
Harbor Point Dr
Harbor View
Suffolk
Norfolk Dr
N

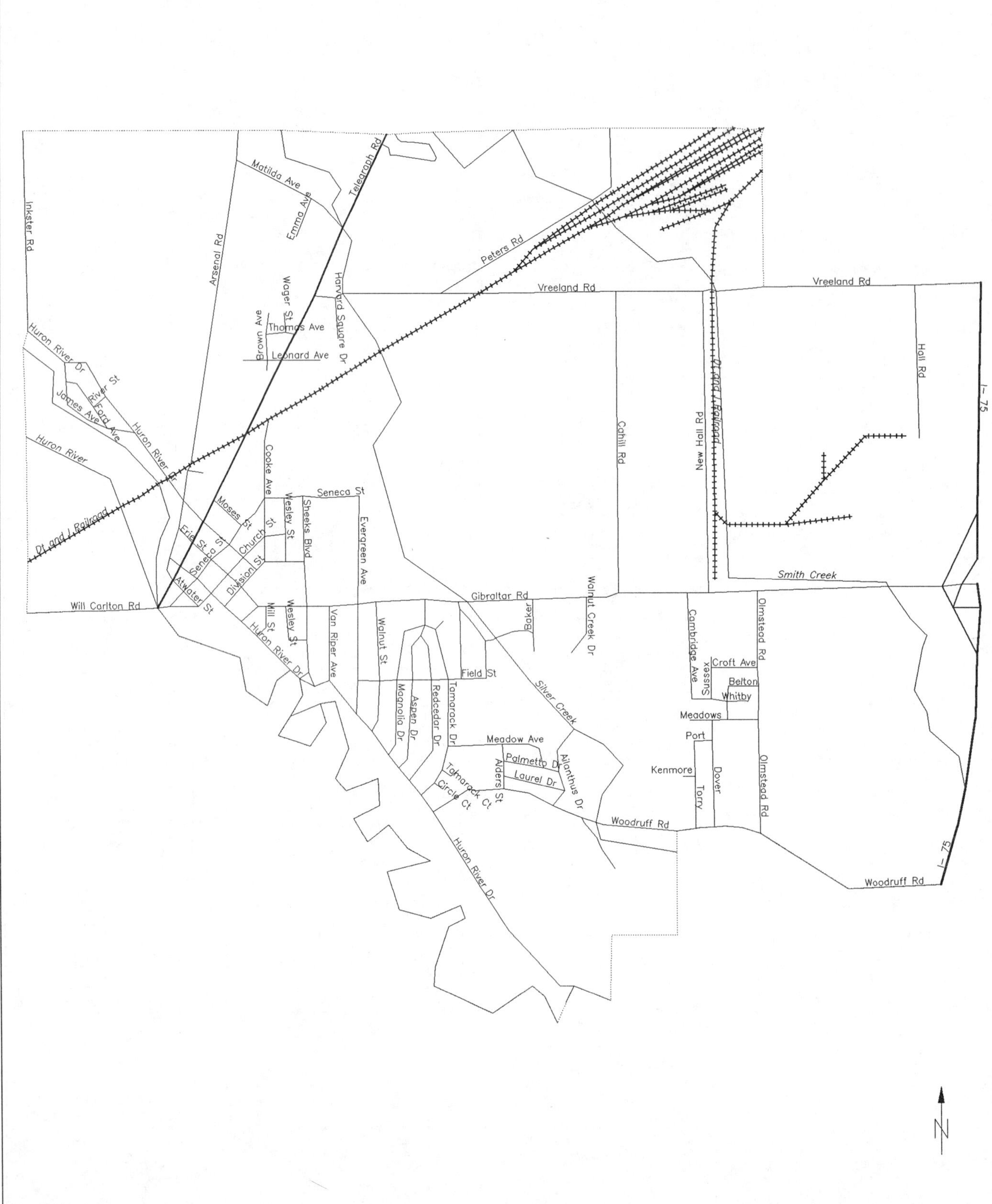
Telegraph Rd
Matilda Ave
Emma Ave
Inkster Rd
Arsenal Rd
Peters Rd
Harvard Square Dr
Wager St
Vreeland Rd
Vreeland Rd
Brown Ave
Thomas Ave
Leonard Ave
Hall Rd
Huron River Dr
River St
James Ave
Ford Ave
Huron River Dr
Huron River
Cooke Ave
Cahill Rd
New Hall Rd
I-75
Dt and I Railroad
Moses St
Seneca St
Wesley St
Sheeks Blvd
Evergreen Ave
Erie St
Church St
Seneca St
Division St
Atwater St
Smith Creek
Will Carlton Rd
Gibraltar Rd
Walnut Creek Dr
Mill St
Wesley St
Van Riper Ave
Walnut St
Baker
Huron River Dr
Cambridge Ave
Olmstead Rd
Croft Ave
Sussex
Belton
Whitby
Field St
Magnolia Dr
Aspen Dr
Redcedar Dr
Tamarack Dr
Silver Creek
Meadows
Meadow Ave
Port
Palmetto Dr
Ailanthus Dr
Kenmore
Dover
Torry
Olmstead Rd
Laurel Dr
Alders St
Tamarack Ct
Circle Ct
Woodruff Rd
Huron River Dr
I-75
Woodruff Rd
N

NOTES

NOTES

NOTES

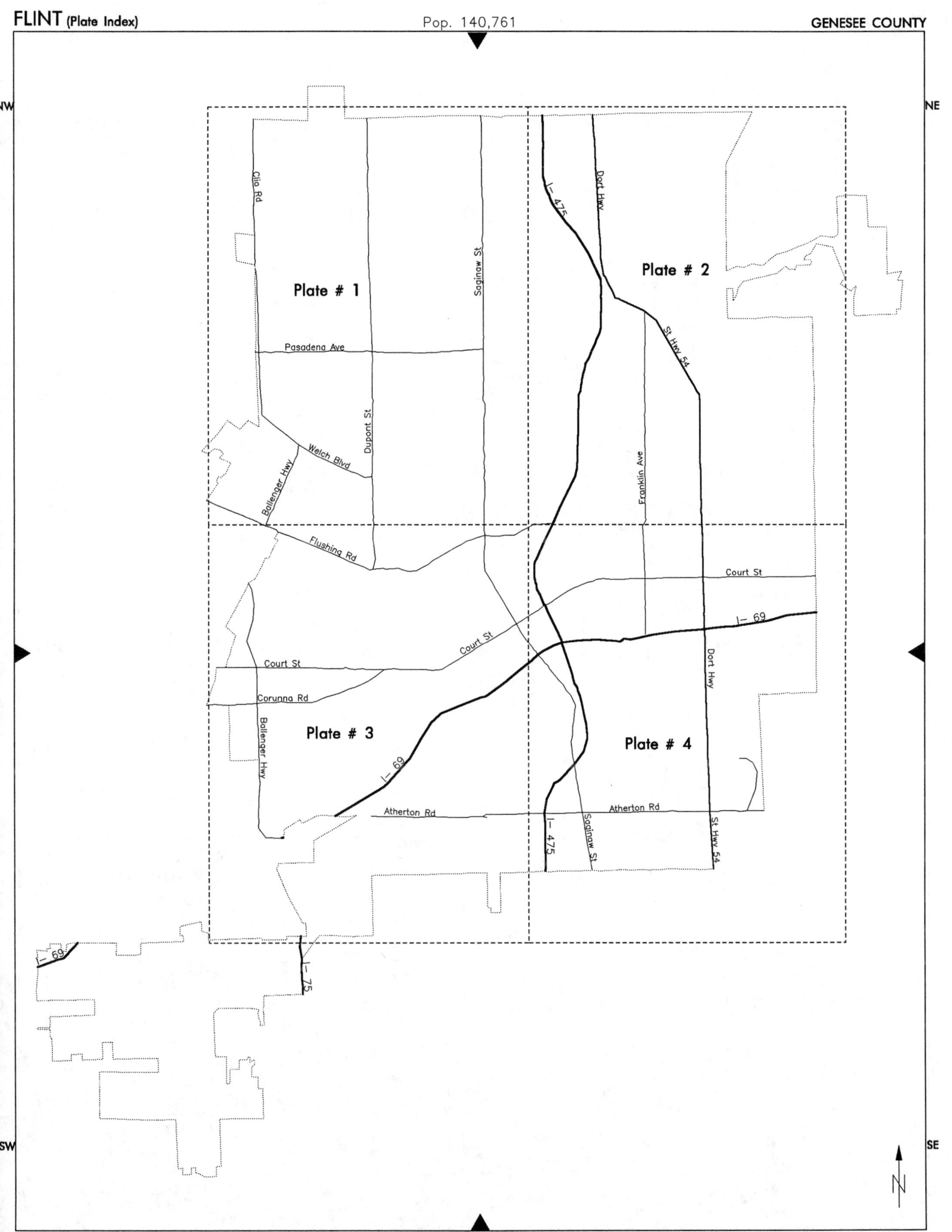
NW
NE
SW
SE
Plate # 1
Plate # 2
Plate # 3
Plate # 4
Clio Rd
Saginaw St
Dupont St
Pasadena Ave
Welch Blvd
Ballenger Hwy
Flushing Rd
I- 475
Dort Hwy
St Hwy 54
Franklin Ave
Court St
I- 69
Corunna Rd
Atherton Rd
I- 75
N

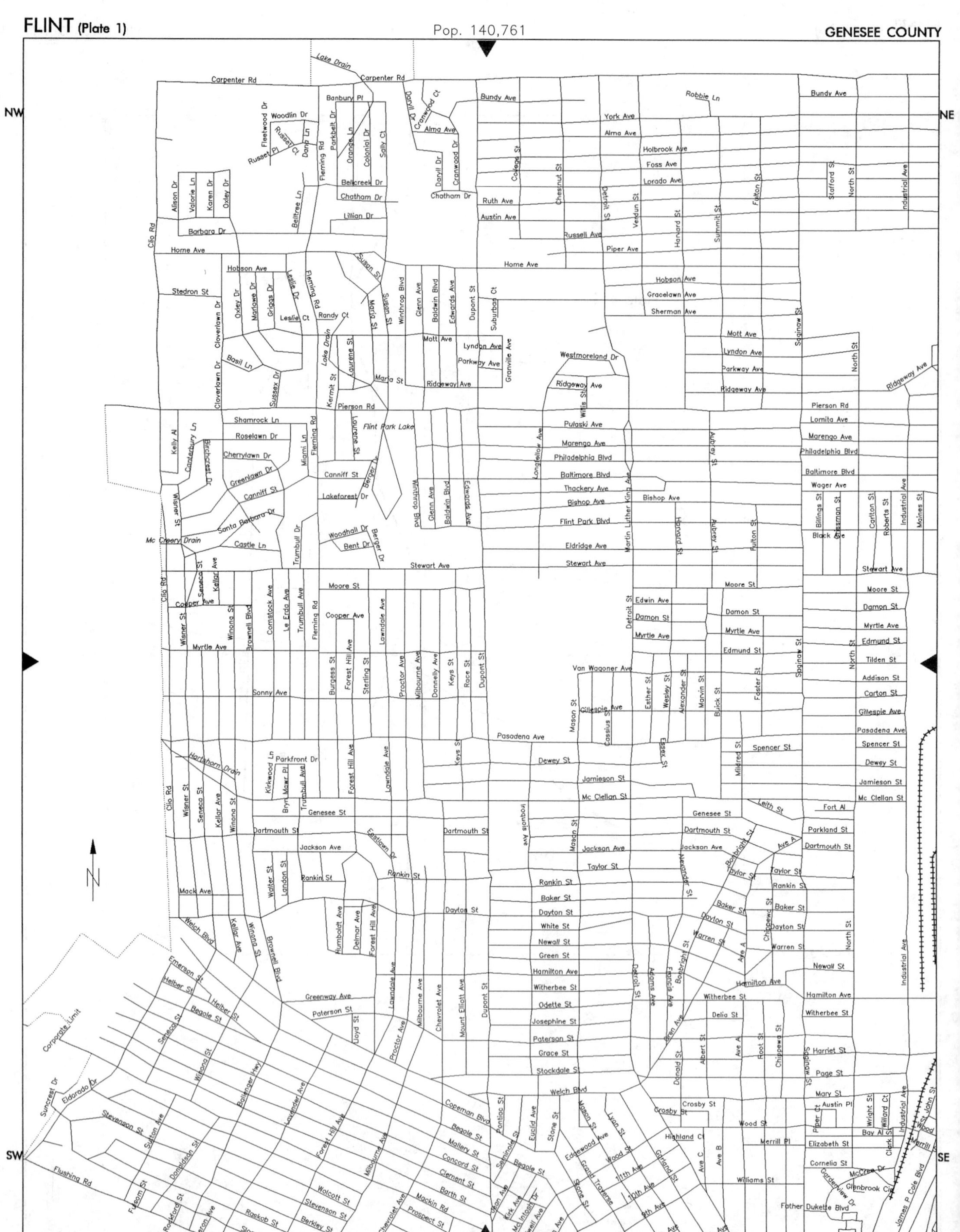

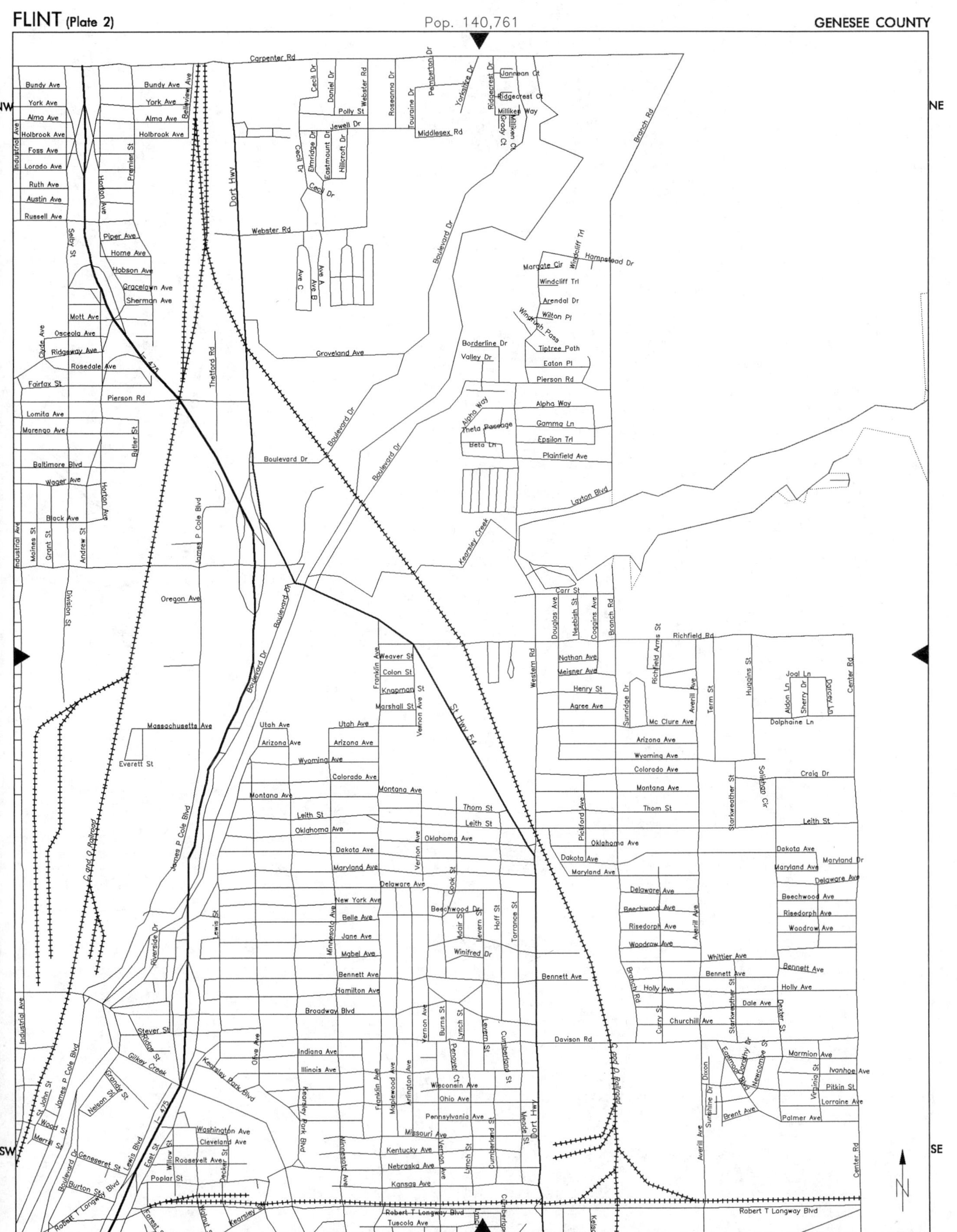
NW
NE
SW
SE
Carpenter Rd
Dort Hwy
Webster Rd
Boulevard Dr
Branch Rd
Groveland Ave
Pierson Rd
Richfield Rd
St Hwy 54
Davison Rd
Robert T Longway Blvd
James P Cole Blvd
C and O Railroad
Kearsley Creek
Gilkey Creek
Layton Blvd
I-475

Pop. 140,761

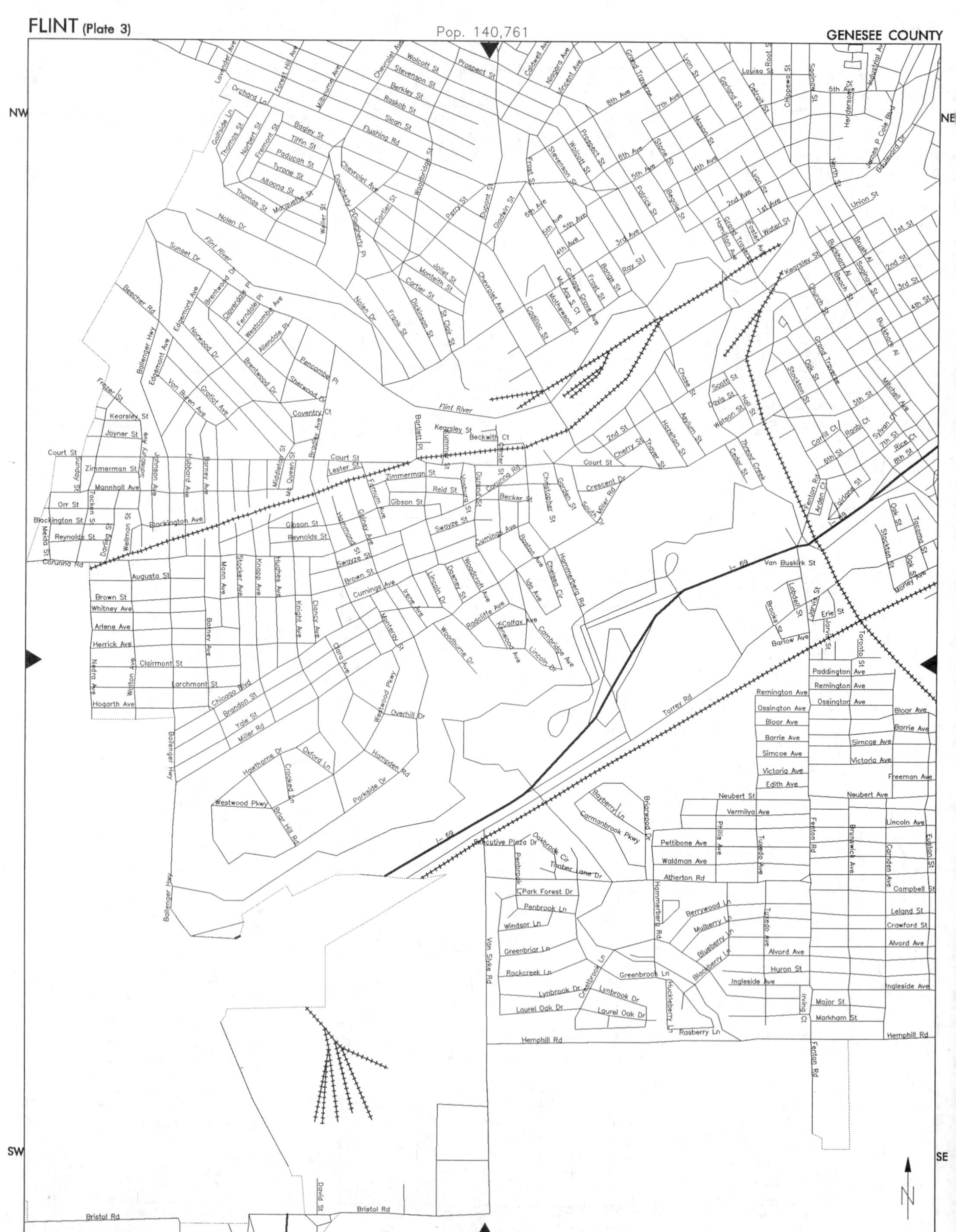
NW
NE
SW
SE
N
Lavender Ave
Forest Hill Ave
Milbourne Ave
Chevrolet Ave
Wolcott St
Stevenson St
Berkley St
Raskob St
Sloan St
Prospect St
Caldwell Ave
Niagara Ave
Vincent Ave
Grand Traverse
Lyon St
Garland St
Detroit St
Louisa St
Root St
Chippewa St
Saginaw St
5th Ave
Henderson St
Industrial Ave
James P Cole Blvd
Boulevard Dr
Orchard Ln
Golfside Ln
Thomas St
Norbert St
Fremont St
Bagley St
Tiffin St
Paducah St
Tyrone St
Altoona St
Marquette St
Flushing Rd
Woodbridge St
8th Ave
7th Ave
6th Ave
5th Ave
4th Ave
3rd Ave
2nd Ave
1st Ave
Mason St
Stone St
Patrick St
Begole St
Union St
North St
Water St
Foster Ave
Hamilton Ave
Weller St
Cartier St
Dougherty Pl
Nolen Dr
Perry St
Dupont St
Gladwin St
Frost St
Ray St
Boggs St
Cottage Grove Ave
Mc Ara S Ct
Mathewson St
Cadillac St
Joliet St
Monteith St
Dickinson St
St Clair St
Frank St
Flint River
Sunset Dr
Beecher Rd
Edgemont Ave
Brentwood Dr
Cloverdale Pl
Ferndale Pl
Westcombe Ave
Allendale Pl
Pencombe Pl
Sherwood Dr
Norwood Dr
Ballenger Hwy
Van Buren Ave
Gratiot Ave
Coventry Ct
Frazer St
Kearsley St
Joyner St
Court St
Zimmerman St
Mannhall Ave
Orr St
Blackington St
Reynolds St
Corunna Rd
Sunday St
Tacken St
Meade St
Darling St
Wellman St
Salisbury Ave
Johnson Ave
Hubbard Ave
Barney Ave
Blackington Ave
Middleton St
Mt Queen St
Bradley Ave
Bartlett Pl
Beckwith Ct
Lester St
Farnum Ave
Gibson St
Swayze St
Hammond St
Gainey Ave
Reid St
Vosburg St
Durand St
Becker St
Christopher St
Garden St
Crescent Dr
Miller Rd
Cumings Ave
Chase St
Asylum St
Hazelton St
Thayer St
Cherry St
Scott St
Davis St
Hall St
Watson St
Thread Creek
Cedar St
Church St
Beach St
Brush Al
Saginaw St
Buckham Al
Kearsley St
1st St
2nd St
3rd St
4th St
5th St
6th St
7th St
8th St
Grand Traverse
Oak St
Stockton St
Mitchell Ave
Carrill Ct
Raab Ct
Sylvan Ct
Rice Ct
Fenton Rd
Arden Ct
Fairland St
Tacoma St
Van Buskirk St
I-69
Augusta St
Brown St
Whitney Ave
Arlene Ave
Herrick Ave
Clairmont St
Larchmont St
Nedra Ave
Walton Ave
Hogarth Ave
Mann Ave
Stocker Ave
Knapp Ave
Hughes Ave
Knight Ave
Clancy Ave
Monteray St
Irene Ave
Lincoln Dr
Downey St
Woodcroft Ave
Radcliffe Ave
Colfax Ave
Kenwood Ave
Boston Ave
Ida Ave
Chelsea Cir
Hammerberg Rd
Cambridge Ave
Lincoln Dr
Woodburne Dr
Clara Ave
Westwood Pkwy
Overhill Dr
Chicago Blvd
Brandon St
Yale St
Hawthorne Dr
Oxford Ln
Crooked Ln
Hampden Rd
Parkside Dr
Briar Hill Rd
Lobdell St
Brooks St
Erie St
Barlow Ave
Toronto St
Paddington Ave
Remington Ave
Ossington Ave
Bloor Ave
Barrie Ave
Simcoe Ave
Victoria Ave
Edith Ave
Freeman Ave
Neubert St
Neubert Ave
Vermilya Ave
Torrey Rd
Bayberry Ln
Briarwood Dr
Carmanbrook Pkwy
Pettibone Ave
Waldman Ave
Atherton Rd
Phillips Ave
Tuxedo Ave
Brunswick Ave
Lincoln Ave
Camden Ave
Euclid St
Executive Plaza Dr
Oakbrook Cir
Timber Lane Dr
Penbrook Ln
Park Forest Dr
Windsor Ln
Greenbriar Ln
Rockcreek Ln
Lynbrook Dr
Laurel Oak Dr
Crestbrook Ln
Greenbrook Ln
Huckleberry Ln
Rasberry Ln
Berrywood Ln
Mulberry Ln
Blueberry Ln
Blackberry Ln
Alvord Ave
Huron St
Ingleside Ave
Irving Ct
Major St
Markham St
Campbell St
Leland St
Crawford St
Hemphill Rd
Van Slyke Rd
David St
Bristol Rd

NW
NE
SW
SE
Robert T Longway Blvd
Tuscola Ave
Gold Ave
Glendale Ave
Commonwealth Ave
Chalmers St
2nd St
Meade St
Commerce St
Kelso St
Gilkey Creek
Averill Ave
Gorey Ave
Ralph St
Klein St
Varty St
Lee St
Virginia St
Dexter St
Center Rd
5th Ave
Avon St
Mathews St
Manning Ct
Kearsley St
Walnut St
Beckwith Dr
I- 475
East St
Crapo St
Thompson St
Young St
Eddy St
Kensington Ave
Lafayette St
Franklin Ave
Vernon Ave
Chandler St
Lynch St
Sherff Pl
Roome Ct
Montclair Ave
Mountain Ave
Court St
Pierce St
Hills St
Calumet Ave
Rangeley Dr
Brimfield Dr
Somerset Ln
Burlington Dr
Barrington Dr
Hampton Dr
Tower St
1st St
2nd St
3rd St
4th St
Pierson St
Stevens St
Clifford St
Woodlawn Park Dr
Woodside Dr
Maxine Ave
Blanchard Ave
6th St
7th St
8th St
9th St
Riverdale Rd
Belmont Ave
Wellington Ave
Kennelworth Ave
Linwood Ave
Brookwood Dr
Ridgelawn Ave
Sunnyside Ave
I- 69
Saginaw St
Beach St
Menlo St
Lapeer St
Seymour Ave
Barks St
Whittlesey St
Chelsea St
Mc Phail St
Owen St
Kent St
Bogardus St
Tower St
Kelso St
Remell St
Gilmartin St
Hosler St
Valley Ln
Worchester St
Evergreen Pkwy
Springfield St
Gloucester St
Lynn St
Eckley Ave
Bagwell St
Tebo St
Averill Ave
Kennelworth Ave
Park St
Liberty St
Jasmine Ave
Magnolia Ave
Floral Park Ave
Wellington Ave
Harrison St
10th St
12th St
13th St
14th St
Howard Ct
Grand Traverse
Cross Ct
Van Lue Ct
Wayne St
Pingree Ave
Warner Ave
Ferris Ave
Dwight Ave
Stanford Ave
Crocker Ave
Rosemary Ave
Channing Cross Dr
Potter Dr
Bra Burn Dr
Tacoma St
Neilson St
Oak St
Lippincott Blvd
Fairbanks Ave
Partridge St
Barton St
Orville St
Wallace St
Linneaus Ave
Church St
Tillinghast Pl
Monroe St
Millett St
Bruce St
Tobias St
Dawson St
Linsey Blvd
Oakley St
Crest Ct
Trout Dr
Forley Dr
Mitchell St
Thread Creek
Elms Dr
Hickory Dr
Birch Dr
Evergreen Dr
Woodslea Dr
Pinetree Dr
Greenhill Ln
Terrace Dr
Crestmore Dr
Arrow Ln
Indian Bow Trl
Mohawk Ave
Shawnee Ave
Cheyenne Ave
Menominee St
Eldon Baker Dr
Circle Dr
Dearborn St
Comanche Ave
Cherokee Ave
Algonquin Ave
Bloor Ave
Barrie Ave
Simcoe Ave
Victoria Ave
Freeman Ave
Neubert Ave
Vermilya Ave
Lincoln Ave
Pettibone Ave
Waldman Ave
Eddington Ave
Belvidere Ave
Madison Ave
Lakeview Ave
Livingston Dr
Collingwood Pkwy
Lakewood Dr
Harold St
Grand Traverse Sb St
Chambers St
Kleinpell St
Atherton Ter
Hillcrest Blvd
Nancy Dr
Deena Dr
Robert Dr
Alan Dr
West St
Atherton Rd
Campbell St
Leland St
Crawford St
Alvord Ave
Clinton St
Huron St
Ingleside Ave
Easton St
Grand Traverse Nb St
Cuthbertson St
Pengelly Rd
Coleridge St
Milton Dr
Poe St
Saginaw St
Bryant Ave
Browning Ave
Bede St
Tennyson Ave
Red Arrow Rd
Custer Ave
Menton Ave
Circle Dr
Buckingham Ave
Burroughs Ave
Leta Ave
Southlawn St
McKinley Ave
Lockhead Ave
Dell Ave
Mc Keighan Ave
Macdonald Ave
Hemphill Rd
Ocemo St
Cheyenne Ave
Shawnee Ave
St Hwy 54
N

NOTES

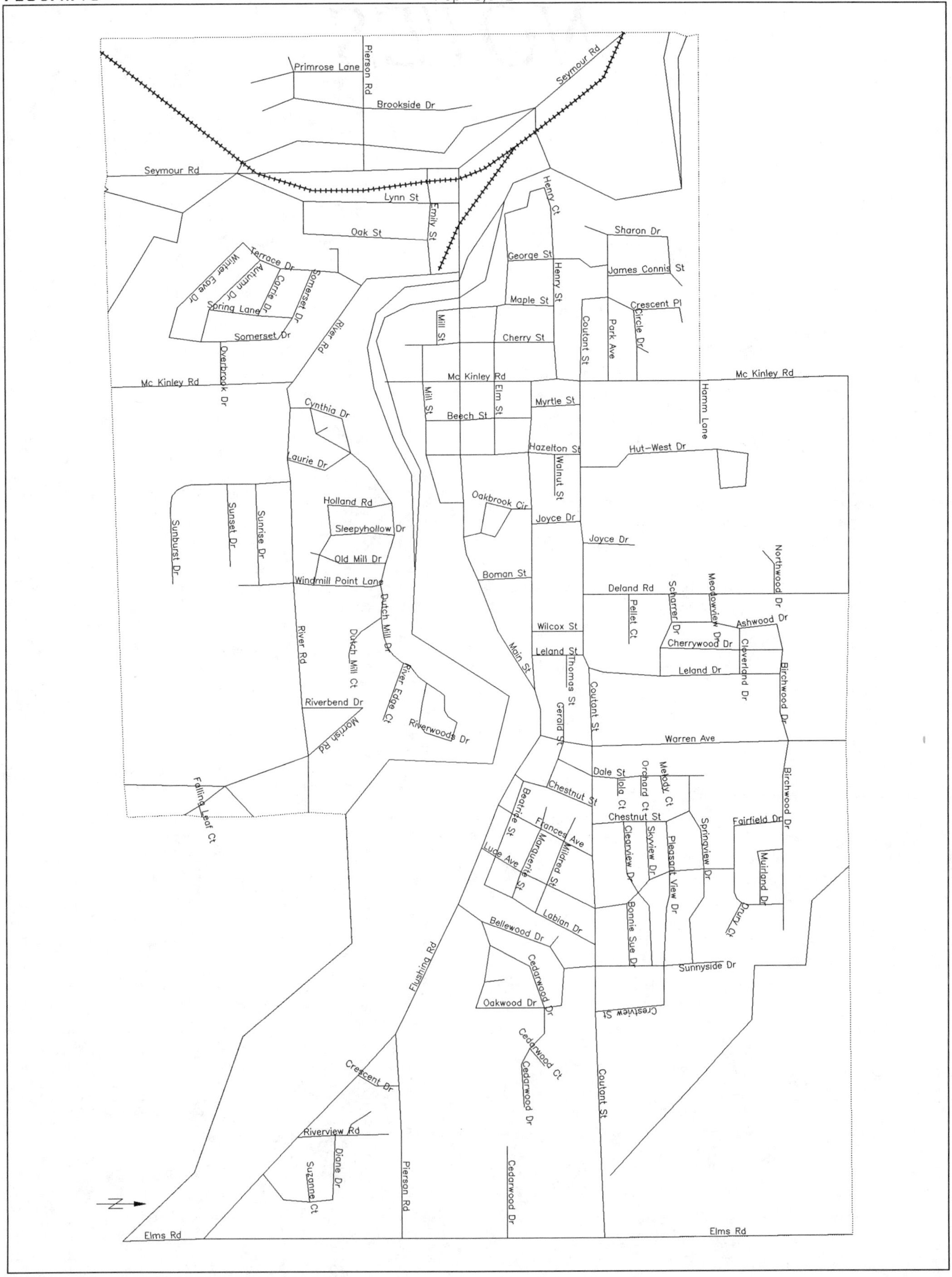

Primrose Lane
Pierson Rd
Brookside Dr
Seymour Rd
Seymour Rd
Lynn St
Oak St
Emily St
Henry Ct
Sharon Dr
George St
Henry St
James Connis St
Terrace Dr
Winter Eave Dr
Autumn Dr
Carrie Dr
Somerset Dr
Spring Lane
Somerset Dr
River Rd
Maple St
Crescent Pl
Mill St
Cherry St
Coutant St
Park Ave
Circle Dr
Mc Kinley Rd
Mc Kinley Rd
Mc Kinley Rd
Overbrook Dr
Mill St
Elm St
Myrtle St
Hamm Lane
Cynthia Dr
Beech St
Hazelton St
Hut-West Dr
Laurie Dr
Walnut St
Oakbrook Cir
Holland Rd
Joyce Dr
Sunset Dr
Sunrise Dr
Sunburst Dr
Sleepyhollow Dr
Joyce Dr
Old Mill Dr
Northwood Dr
Boman St
Windmill Point Lane
Deland Rd
Scharrer Dr
Meadowview Dr
Pellet Ct
Ashwood Dr
Dutch Mill Dr
Wilcox St
River Rd
Dutch Mill Ct
Main St
Cherrywood Dr
Cloverland Dr
Leland St
Leland Dr
Thomas St
Birchwood Dr
River Edge Ct
Coutant St
Riverbend Dr
Gerald St
Morrish Rd
Riverwoods Dr
Warren Ave
Dale St
Orchard Ct
Melody Ct
Birchwood Dr
Falling Leaf Ct
Chestnut St
Iola Ct
Beatrice St
Chestnut St
Springview Dr
Fairfield Dr
Frances Ave
Clearview Dr
Skyview Dr
Pleasant View Dr
Marquerite St
Mildred St
Lude Ave
Muirland Dr
Labian Dr
Bonnie Sue Dr
Drury Ct
Bellewood Dr
Flushing Rd
Cedarwood Dr
Sunnyside Dr
Oakwood Dr
Crestview St
Cedarwood Ct
Cedarwood Dr
Coutant St
Crescent Dr
Riverview Rd
Diane Dr
Suzanne Ct
Pierson Rd
Cedarwood Dr
Elms Rd
Elms Rd
N

NOTES

FOWLERVILLE

Pop. 2,648

LIVINGSTON COUNTY

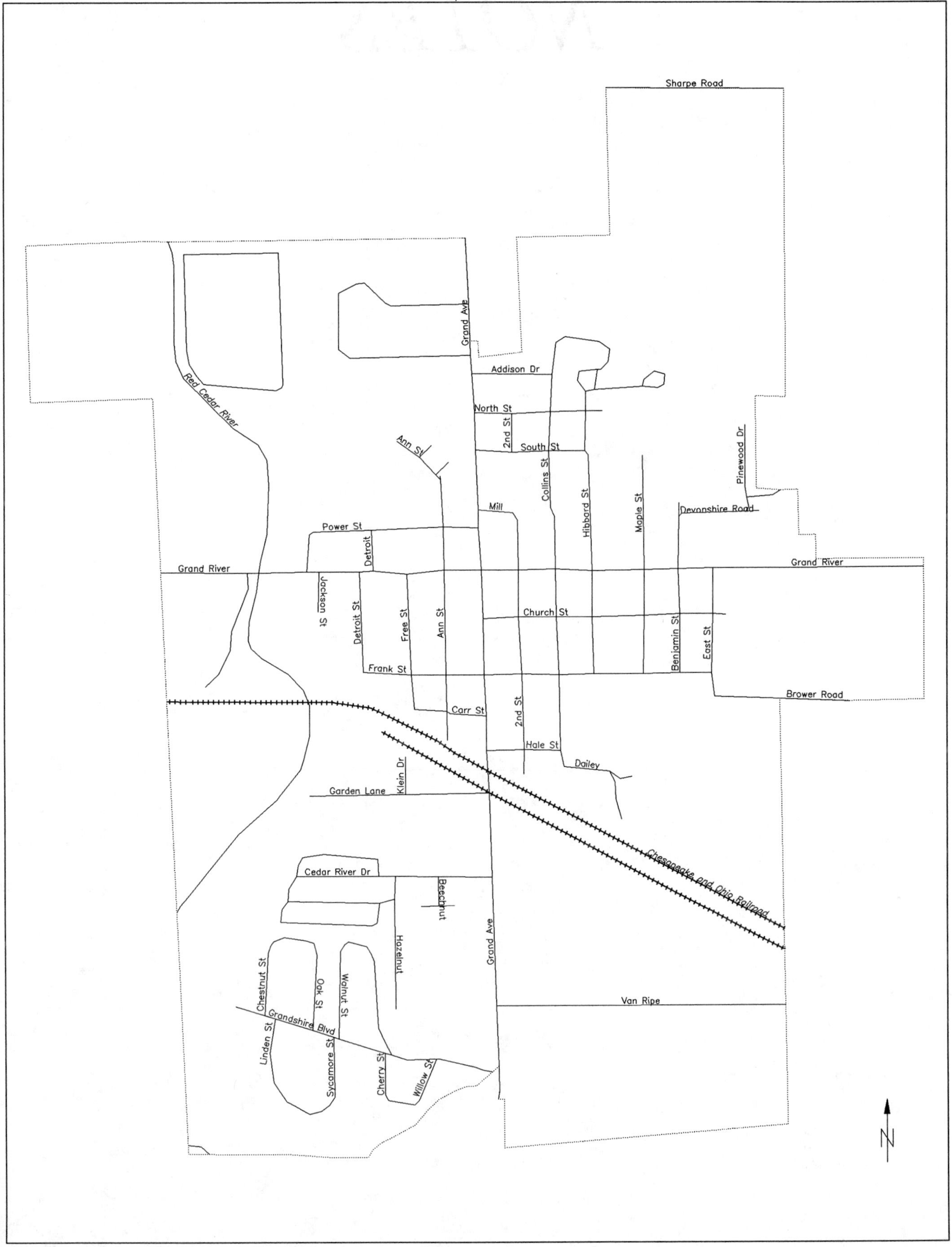

Sharpe Road
Grand Ave
Addison Dr
North St
2nd St
South St
Ann St
Collins St
Hibbard St
Maple St
Pinewood Dr
Devonshire Road
Mill
Power St
Detroit
Red Cedar River
Grand River
Grand River
Jackson St
Detroit St
Free St
Ann St
Church St
Benjamin St
East St
Frank St
Brower Road
Carr St
2nd St
Hale St
Dailey
Klein Dr
Garden Lane
Chesapeake and Ohio Railroad
Cedar River Dr
Beechnut
Hazelnut
Grand Ave
Chestnut St
Oak St
Walnut St
Van Ripe
Grandshire Blvd
Linden St
Sycamore St
Cherry St
Willow St
N

NOTES

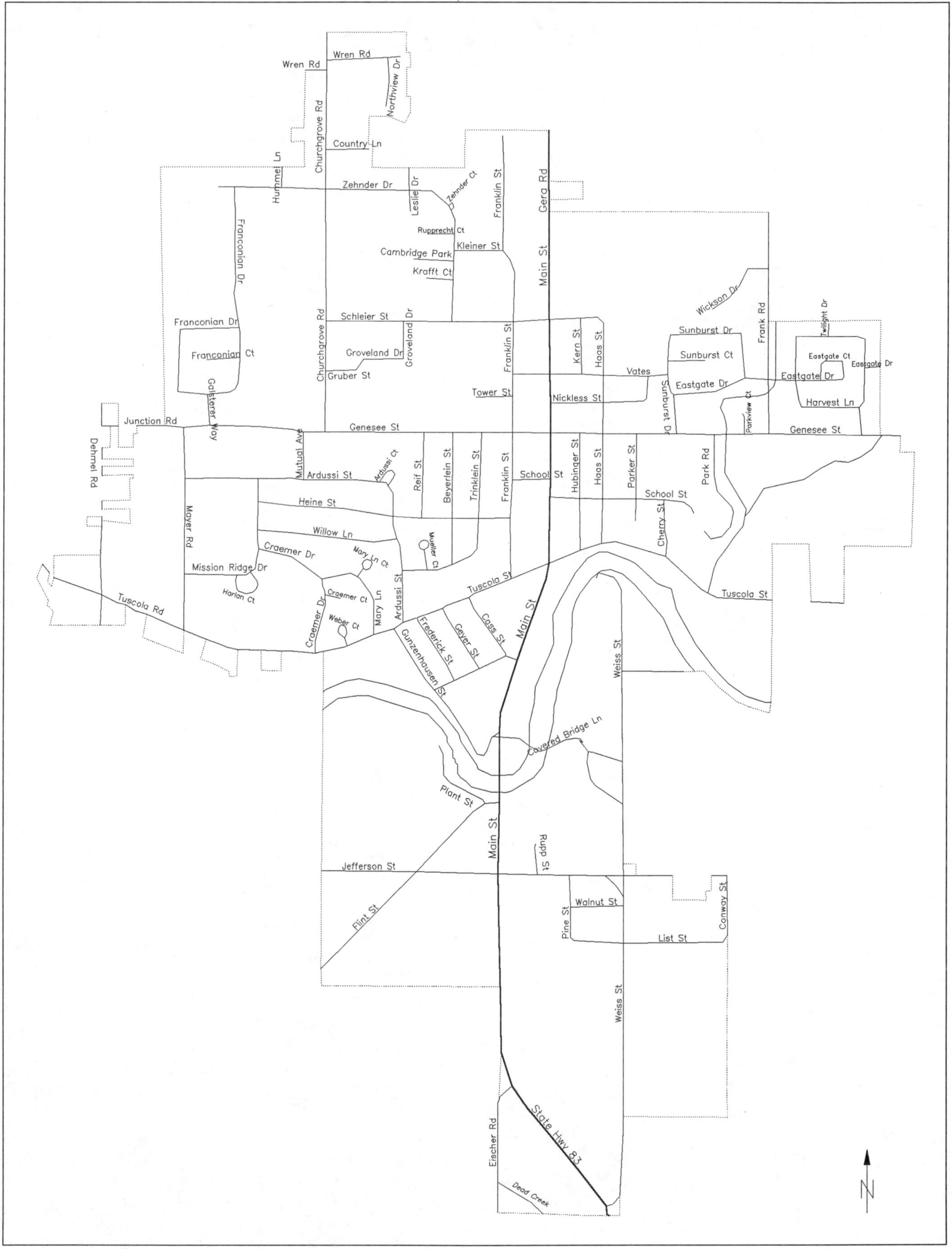

FRANKENMUTH

Pop. 4,408

SAGINAW COUNTY

Wren Rd
Wren Rd
Northview Dr
Churchgrove Rd
Country Ln
Hummel Ln
Zehnder Dr
Leslie Dr
Zehnder Ct
Franklin St
Gera Rd
Franconian Dr
Rupprecht Ct
Cambridge Park
Kleiner St
Krafft Ct
Main St
Wickson Dr
Frank Rd
Twilight Dr
Franconian Dr
Schleier St
Groveland Dr
Churchgrove Rd
Franklin St
Kern St
Haas St
Sunburst Dr
Sunburst Ct
Eastgate Ct
Eastgate Dr
Franconian Ct
Groveland Dr
Gruber St
Vates
Eastgate Dr
Eastgate Dr
Galsterer Way
Tower St
Nickless St
Sunburst Dr
Parkview Ct
Harvest Ln
Junction Rd
Genesee St
Genesee St
Dehmel Rd
Mutual Ave
Reif St
Beyerlein St
Trinklein St
Franklin St
Hubinger St
Haas St
Parker St
Park Rd
Ardussi St
Ardussi Ct
School St
School St
Heine St
Mayer Rd
Willow Ln
Cherry St
Mueller Ct
Craemer Dr
Mary Ln Ct
Mission Ridge Dr
Tuscola St
Tuscola St
Harlan Ct
Craemer Ct
Ardussi St
Mary Ln
Tuscola Rd
Craemer Dr
Weber Ct
Frederick St
Geyer St
Cass St
Main St
Gunzenhausen St
Weiss St
Covered Bridge Ln
Plant St
Main St
Rupp St
Jefferson St
Walnut St
Conway St
Flint St
Pine St
List St
Weiss St
State Hwy 83
Eischer Rd
Dead Creek
N

NOTES

George St
Michigan Ave
Denton Ave
Crystal Ave
7th St
Skinner Rd
Bridge St
Beech St
Cherry Grove Ln
Highland
Corning Ave
Maple Ave
Baldwin Rd
Elm St
Pine Ave
Day Ave
Parkview Ln
9th St
Bellows
Park Ave
6th St
Hall Ave
10th St
Winnebago St
4th St
James St
Nippising St
8th St
Port Pl
11th St
Leelanau Ave
Harbor Pl
Forest Ave
3rd St
5th St
Sag St
Anchor Pl
Main St
Waverly Ct
Grove Pl
2nd St
Lake Michigan
Betsie Lake
Nelson Rd
Lake St
N

Pop. 2,626

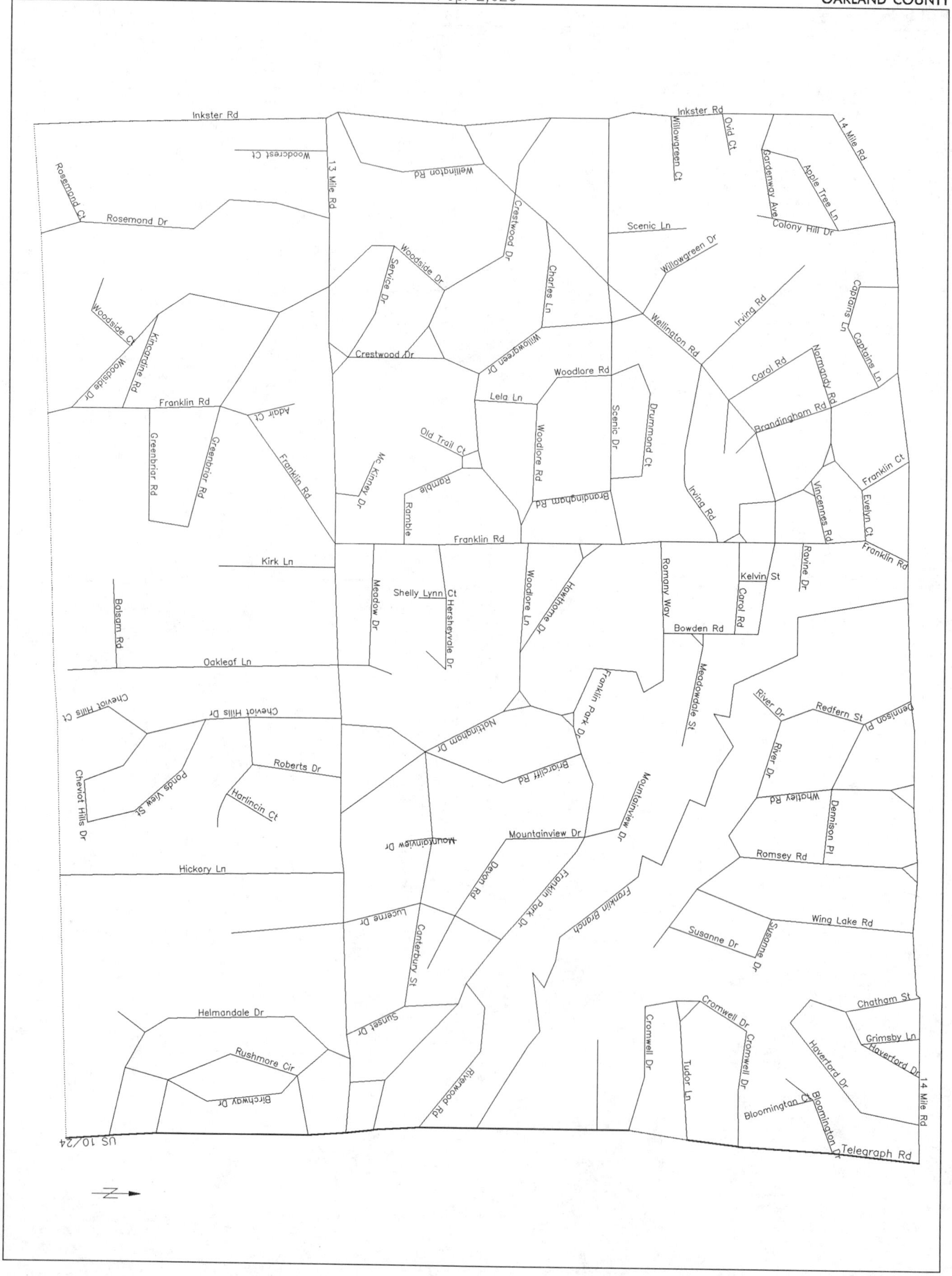

Inkster Rd
Woodcrest Ct
13 Mile Rd
Wellington Rd
Inkster Rd
Willowgreen Ct
Ovid Ct
14 Mile Rd
Gardenway Ave
Apple Tree Ln
Colony Hill Dr
Rosemond Ct
Rosemond Dr
Crestwood Dr
Scenic Ln
Willowgreen Dr
Woodside Dr
Service Dr
Charles Ln
Irving Rd
Captains Ln
Woodside Ct
Woodside Dr
Kincardine Rd
Wellington Rd
Captains Ln
Crestwood Dr
Willowgreen Dr
Normandy Rd
Carol Rd
Woodlore Rd
Lela Ln
Franklin Rd
Adair Ct
Scenic Dr
Drummond Ct
Brandingham Rd
Greenbriar Rd
Greenbriar Rd
Old Trail Ct
Franklin Rd
Mc Kinney Dr
Woodlore Rd
Ramble
Ramble
Brandingham Rd
Irving Rd
Vincennes Rd
Franklin Ct
Evelyn Ct
Franklin Rd
Franklin Rd
Kirk Ln
Meadow Dr
Shelly Lynn Ct
Hersheyvale Dr
Woodlore Ln
Hawthorne Dr
Romany Way
Kelvin St
Carol Rd
Ravine Dr
Bowden Rd
Balsam Rd
Oakleaf Ln
Franklin Park Dr
Meadowdale St
Cheviot Hills Ct
Cheviot Hills Dr
River Dr
Redfern St
Dennison Pl
Nottingham Dr
Briarcliff Rd
River Dr
Roberts Dr
Cheviot Hills Dr
Ponds View St
Harlincin Ct
Mountainview Dr
Whatley Rd
Dennison Pl
Mountainview Dr
Mountainview Dr
Romsey Rd
Hickory Ln
Devon Rd
Franklin Park Dr
Franklin Branch
Lucerne Dr
Canterbury St
Susanne Dr
Susanne Dr
Wing Lake Rd
Helmandale Dr
Sunset Dr
Cromwell Dr
Cromwell Dr
Cromwell Dr
Chatham St
Grimsby Ln
Haverford Dr
Haverford Dr
Rushmore Cir
Birchway Dr
Riverwood Rd
Tudor Ln
Bloomington Ct
Bloomington Dr
14 Mile Rd
US 10/24
Telegraph Rd
N

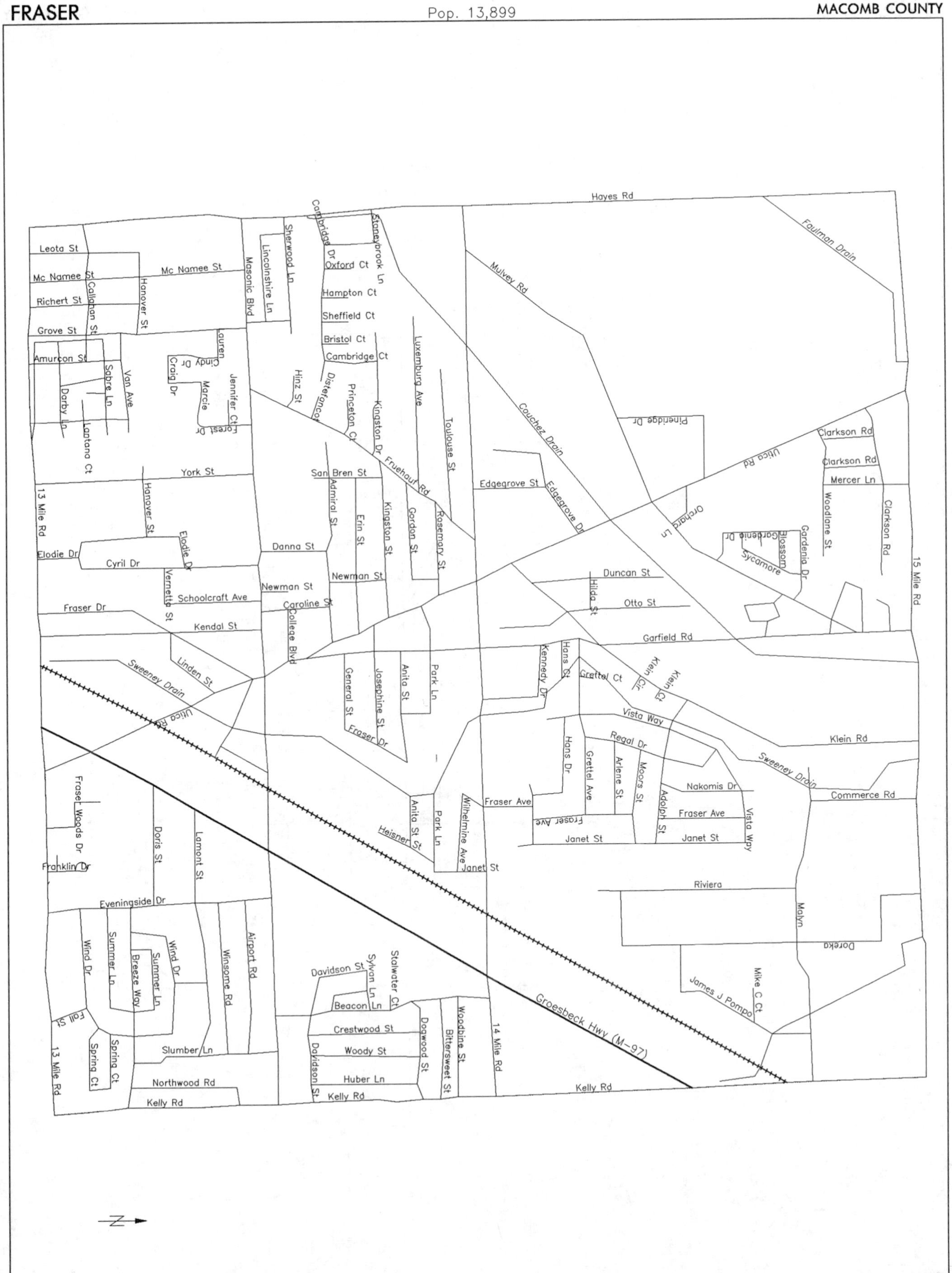

Hayes Rd
Faulman Drain
Mulvey Rd
Couchez Drain
Leota St
Mc Namee St
Richert St
Grove St
Amurcon St
Callahan St
Hanover St
Masonic Blvd
Lincolnshire Ln
Sherwood Ln
Cambridge Dr
Oxford Ct
Hampton Ct
Sheffield Ct
Bristol Ct
Cambridge Ct
Staneybrook Ln
Luxemburg Ave
Toulouse St
Lauren
Cindy Dr
Craig Dr
Marcie
Jennifer Ct
Forest Dr
Sabre Ln
Van Ave
Darby Ln
Lantana Ct
Hinz St
Distefano Ct
Princeton Ct
Kingston Dr
Fruehauf Rd
Pineridge Dr
Clarkson Rd
Utica Rd
Mercer Ln
Woodlane St
York St
San Bren St
Edgegrove St
Edgegrove Dr
13 Mile Rd
Admiral St
Erin St
Kingston St
Gordon St
Rosemary St
Orchard Ln
Gardenia Dr
Blossom
Sycamore
15 Mile Rd
Elodie Dr
Cyril Dr
Elodie Dr
Danna St
Newman St
Duncan St
Hilda St
Vernetta St
Schoolcraft Ave
Newman St
Caroline St
Otto St
Fraser Dr
Kendal St
College Blvd
Garfield Rd
Sweeney Drain
Linden St
Utica Rd
General St
Josephine St
Anita St
Park Ln
Kennedy Dr
Hans Ct
Grettel Ct
Klein Cir
Klein Ct
Vista Way
Fraser Dr
Regal Dr
Klein Rd
Hans Dr
Grettel Ave
Arlene St
Moors St
Sweeney Drain
Nakomis Dr
Commerce Rd
Fraser Woods Dr
Anita St
Park Ln
Wilhelmine Ave
Fraser Ave
Fraser Ave
Adolph St
Fraser Ave
Vista Wpy
Heisner St
Janet St
Janet St
Franklin Dr
Doris St
Lamont St
Janet St
Riviera
Eveningside Dr
Malyn
Doreka
Wind Dr
Summer Ln
Breeze Way
Summer Ln
Wind Dr
Winsome Rd
Airport Rd
Davidson St
Sylvan Ln
Statwater Ct
Beacon Ln
Mike C Ct
James J Pompo
Fall St
Crestwood St
Dogwood St
Woodbine St
Groesbeck Hwy (M-97)
14 Mile Rd
13 Mile Rd
Spring Ct
Spring Ct
Slumber Ln
Woody St
Bittersweet St
Davidson St
Huber Ln
Northwood Rd
Kelly Rd
Kelly Rd
Kelly Rd
N

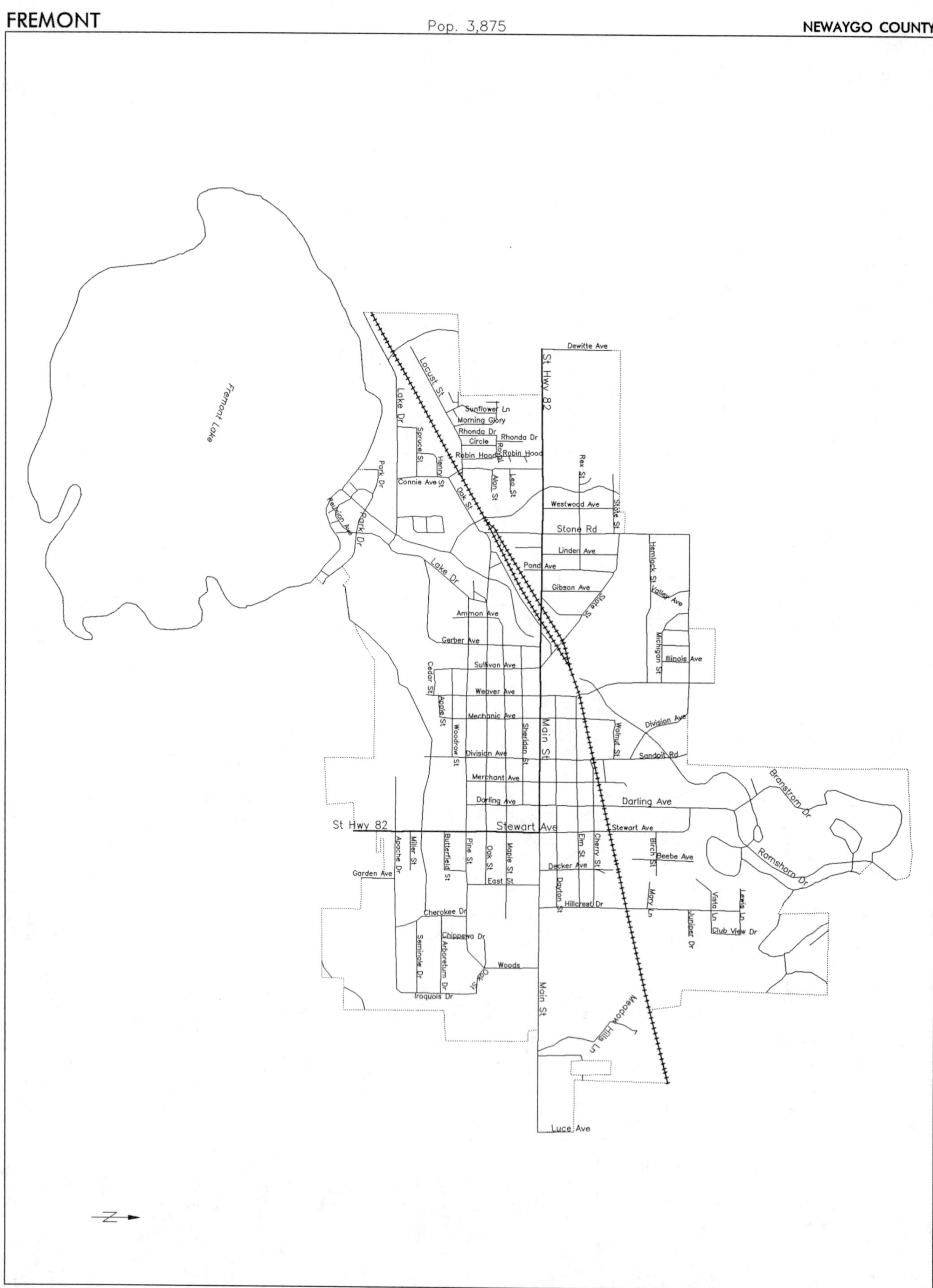
Fremont Lake
Dewitte Ave
St Hwy 82
Locust St
Lake Dr
Sunflower Ln
Morning Glory
Rhonda Dr
Circle
Robin Hood
Spruce St
Henry St
Park Dr
Connie Ave
Oak St
Alan St
Lea St
Rex St
Westwood Ave
State St
Stone Rd
Linden Ave
Pond Ave
Gibson Ave
Hemlock St
Valley Ave
Ammon Ave
Gerber Ave
Michigan St
Illinois Ave
Sullivan Ave
Cedar St
Weaver Ave
Apple St
Mechanic Ave
Woodrow St
Sheridan St
Main St
Walnut St
Division Ave
Sandpit Rd
Merchant Ave
Bronstrom Dr
Darling Ave
Stewart Ave
Apache Dr
Miller St
Butterfield St
Pine St
Maple St
Elm St
Cherry St
Birch St
Beebe Ave
Ramshorn Dr
Garden Ave
Decker Ave
East St
Dayton St
Hillcrest Dr
Mary Ln
Vista Ln
Lewis Ln
Juniper Dr
Club View Dr
Cherokee Dr
Chippewa Dr
Seminole Dr
Arboretum Dr
Woods
Iroquois Dr
Meadow Hills Ln
Luce Ave
N

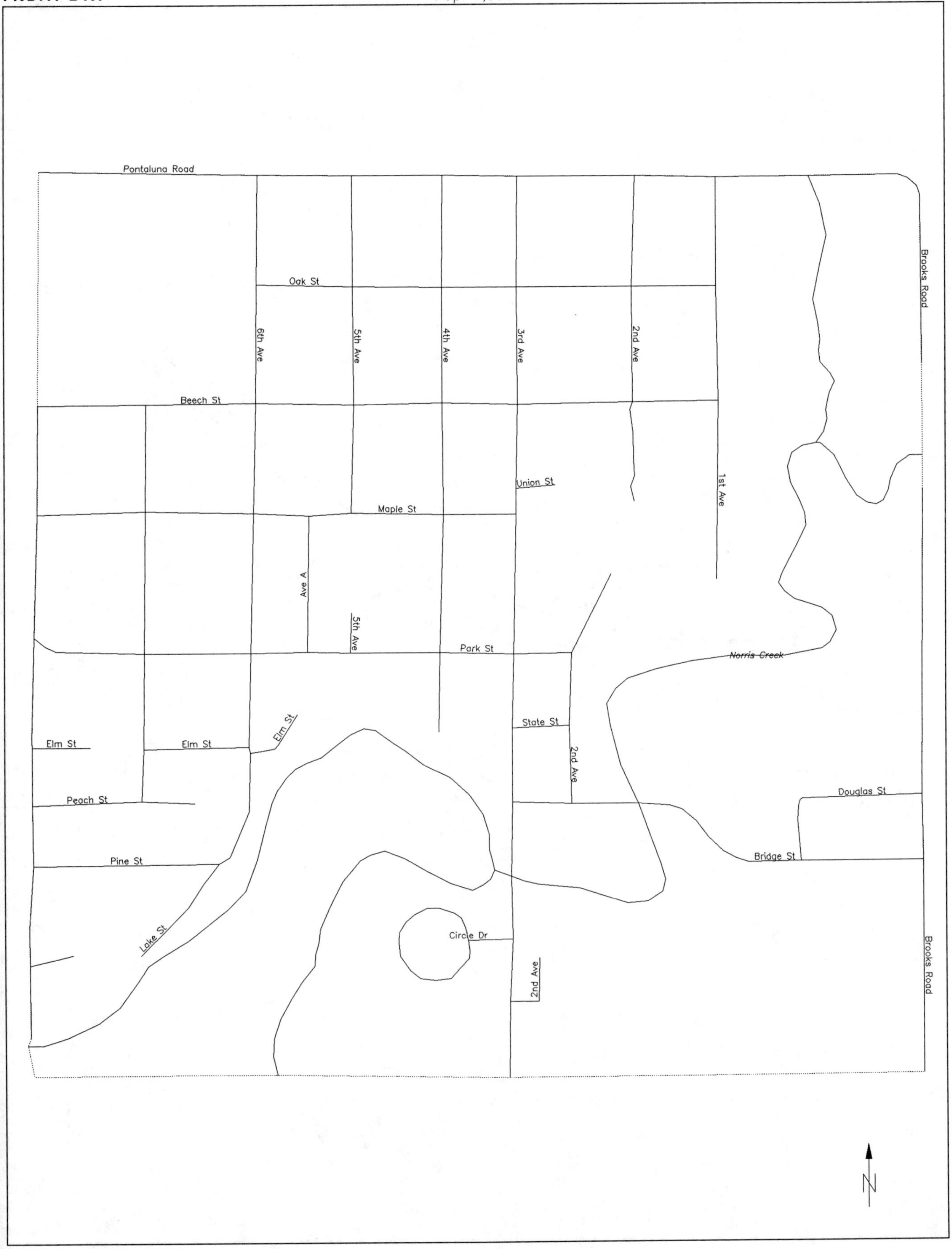

Pontaluna Road
Oak St
6th Ave
5th Ave
4th Ave
3rd Ave
2nd Ave
Brooks Road
Beech St
Union St
1st Ave
Maple St
Ave A
5th Ave
Park St
Norris Creek
State St
Elm St
Elm St
Elm St
2nd Ave
Peach St
Douglas St
Pine St
Bridge St
Lake St
Circle Dr
2nd Ave
Brooks Road
N

GALESBURG

Pop. 1,863

KALAMAZOO COUNTY

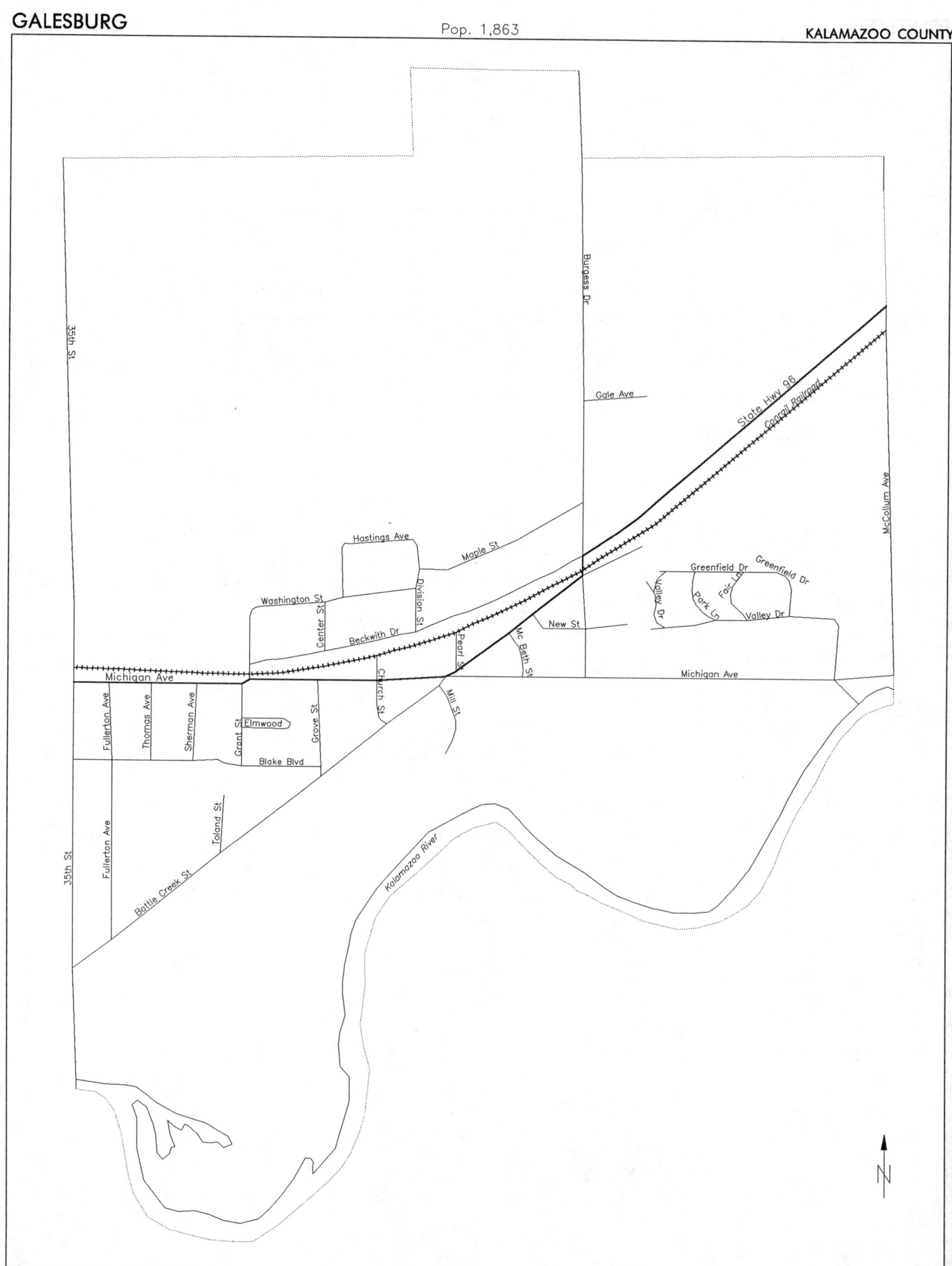

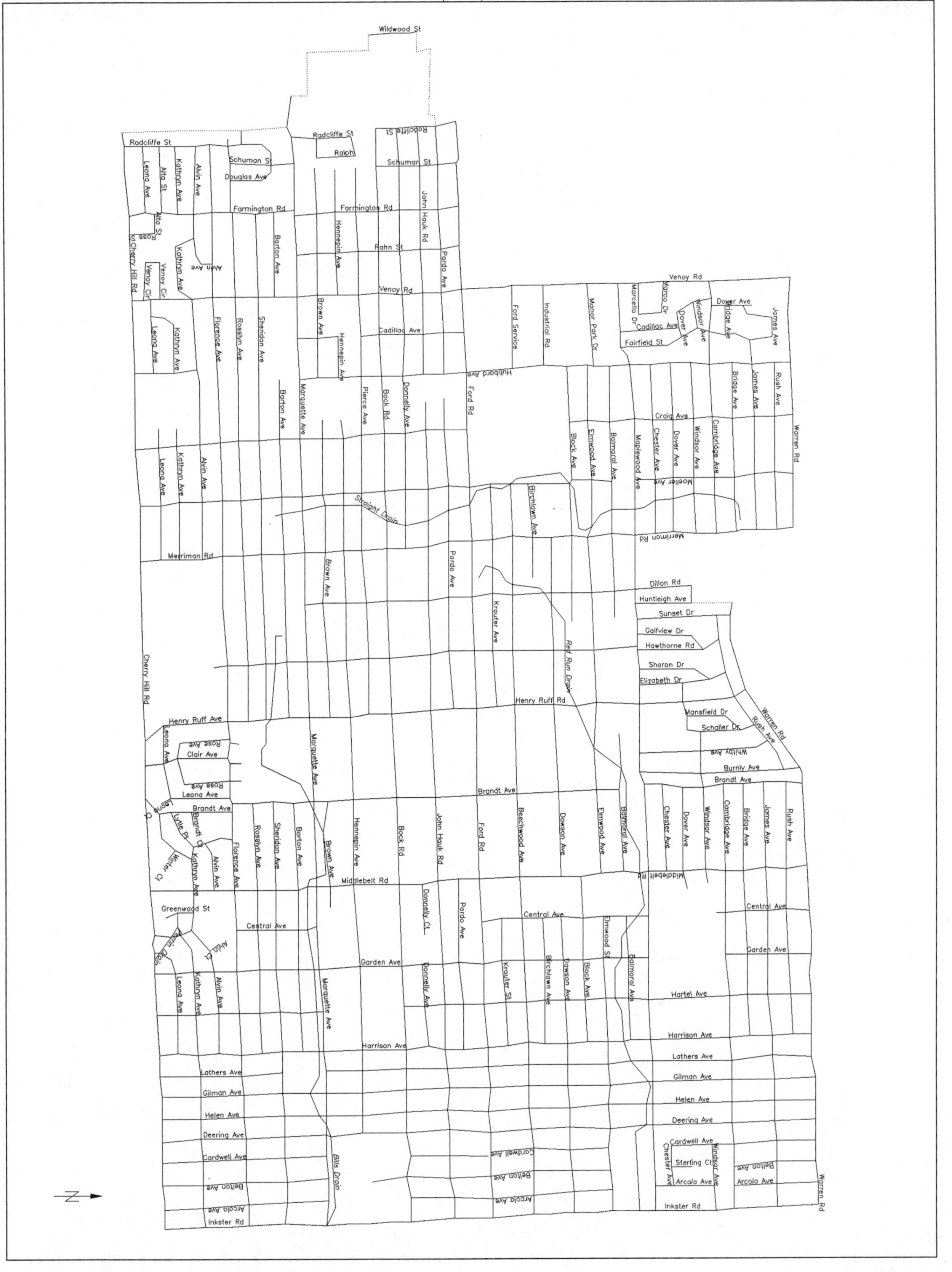
Wildwood St
Radcliffe St
Schuman St
Ralph
Douglas Ave
Leona Ave
Alta St
Kathryn Ave
Alvin Ave
Farmington Rd
John Hauk Rd
Hennepin Ave
Rahn St
Ross
Cherry Hill Rd
Venoy Cir
Barton Ave
Pardo Ave
Venoy Rd
Marcello Dr
Marco Dr
Dover Ave
Windsor Ave
Bridge Ave
James Ave
Ford Service
Industrial Rd
Manor Park Dr
Cadillac Ave
Fairfield St
Brown Ave
Florence Ave
Rosslyn Ave
Sheridan Ave
Hubbard Ave
Marquette Ave
Pierce Ave
Bock Rd
Donnelly Ave
Ford Rd
Rush Ave
Craig Ave
Block Ave
Elmwood Ave
Balmoral Ave
Maplewood Ave
Chester Ave
Cambridge Ave
Warren Rd
Moeller Ave
Straight Drain
Birchlawn Ave
Merriman Rd
Dillon Rd
Huntleigh Ave
Sunset Dr
Krauter Ave
Golfview Dr
Hawthorne Rd
Red Run Drain
Sharon Dr
Elizabeth Dr
Henry Ruff Rd
Henry Ruff Ave
Mansfield Dr
Schaller Dr
Whitby Ave
Rose Ave
Clair Ave
Burnly Ave
Brandt Ave
Lytle Pl
Brandt Ct
Winter Ct
Beechwood Ave
Dawson Ave
Middlebelt Rd
Greenwood St
Central Ave
Donnelly Ct
Elmwood St
Alvin Ct
Garden Ave
Krauter St
Hartel Ave
Harrison Ave
Lathers Ave
Gilman Ave
Helen Ave
Deering Ave
Cardwell Ave
Bills Drain
Sterling Ct
Belton Ave
Arcola Ave
Inkster Rd

GAYLORD

Pop. 3,421

OTSEGO COUNTY

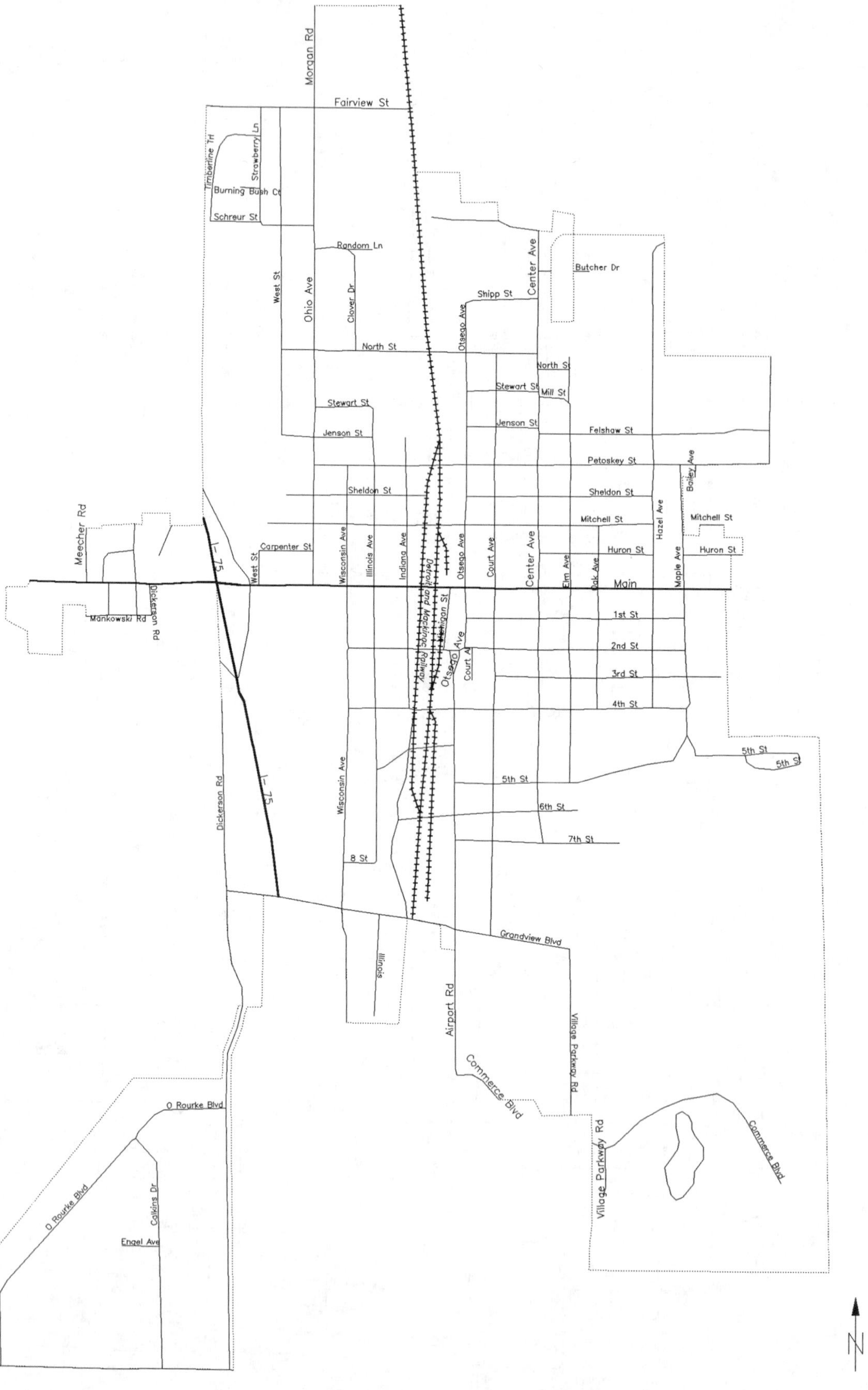

Morgan Rd
Fairview St
Timberline Trl
Strawberry Ln
Burning Bush Ct
Schreur St
Random Ln
West St
Ohio Ave
Clover Dr
Butcher Dr
Center Ave
Shipp St
Otsego Ave
North St
North St
Stewart St
Mill St
Stewart St
Jenson St
Jenson St
Felshaw St
Petoskey St
Bailey Ave
Sheldon St
Sheldon St
Mitchell St
Mitchell St
Hazel Ave
Meecher Rd
I-75
Carpenter St
West St
Wisconsin Ave
Illinois Ave
Indiana Ave
Detroit and Mackinac Railway
Otsego Ave
Court Ave
Center Ave
Elm Ave
Oak Ave
Huron St
Maple Ave
Huron St
Main
Mankowski Rd
Dickerson Rd
Michigan St
1st St
2nd St
Otsego Ave
Court Ave
3rd St
4th St
5th St
5th St
5th St
6th St
7th St
Wisconsin Ave
Dickerson Rd
I-75
8 St
Grandview Blvd
Illinois
Airport Rd
Village Parkway Rd
Commerce Blvd
Village Parkway Rd
Commerce Blvd
O Rourke Blvd
O Rourke Blvd
Calkins Dr
Engel Ave

N

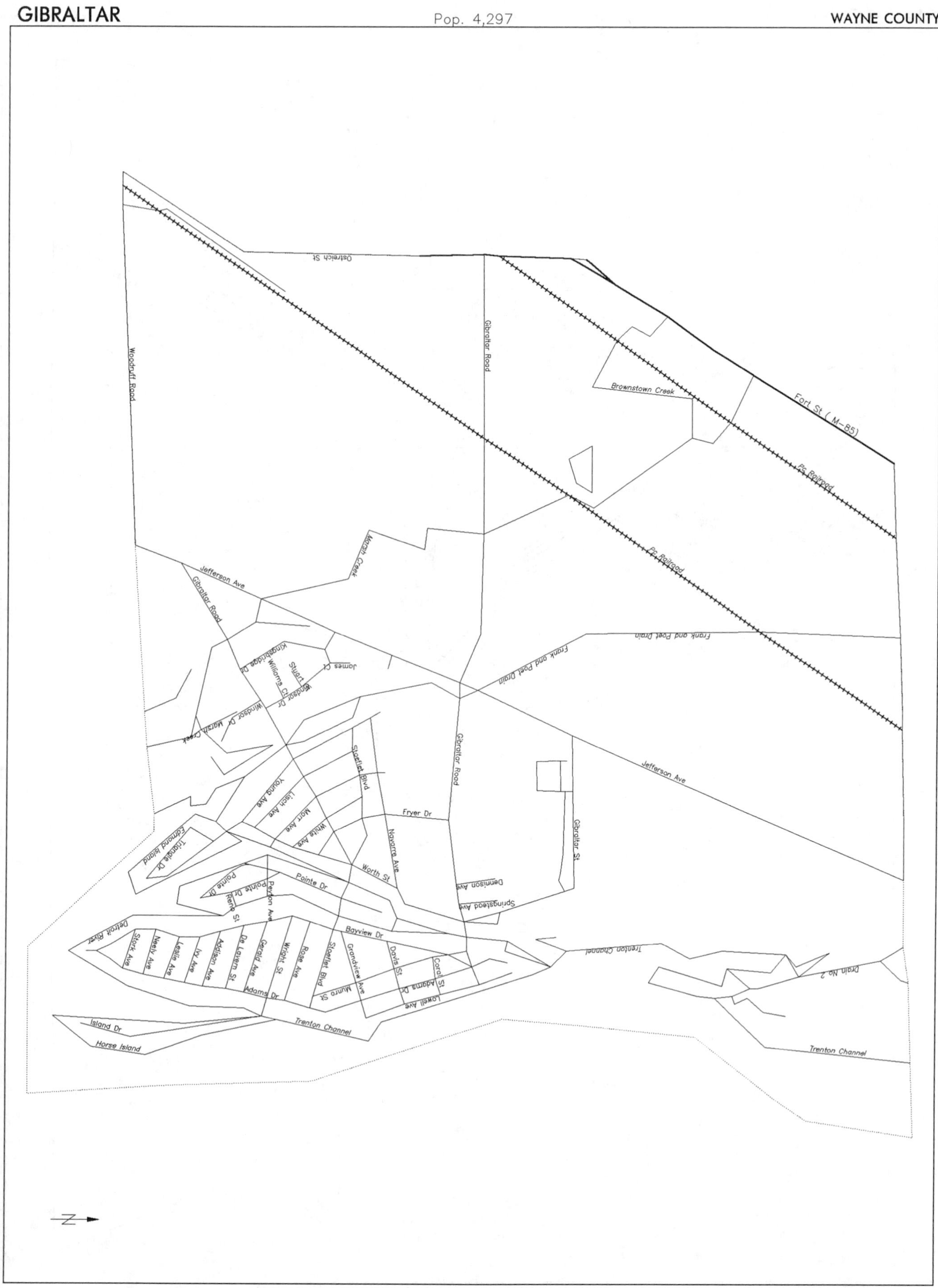
Ostrich St
Woodruff Road
Gibraltar Road
Brownstown Creek
Fort St (M-85)
Pc Railroad
Pc Railroad
Marsh Creek
Jefferson Ave
Gibraltar Road
Frank and Poet Drain
Frank and Poet Drain
Kingsbridge Dr
Williams Ct
Stuart
James Ct
Windsor Dr
Windsor Dr
Marsh Creek
Gibraltar Road
Jefferson Ave
Stoeflet Blvd
Young Ave
Lisch Ave
Mort Ave
White Ave
Fryer Dr
Navarre Ave
Gibraltar St
Edmund Island
Triangle Dr
Worth St
Pointe Dr
Pointe Dr
Pointe Dr
Reno St
Peyton Ave
Dennison Ave
Springstead Ave
Detroit River
Bayview Dr
Trenton Channel
Stork Ave
Neely Ave
Leslie Ave
Ivy Ave
Addison Ave
De Lavern St
Gerald Ave
Wright St
Rose Ave
Stoeflet Blvd
Grandview Ave
Davis St
Coral St
Adams Dr
Adams Dr
Munro St
Lowell Ave
Drain No 2
Island Dr
Trenton Channel
Horse Island
Trenton Channel

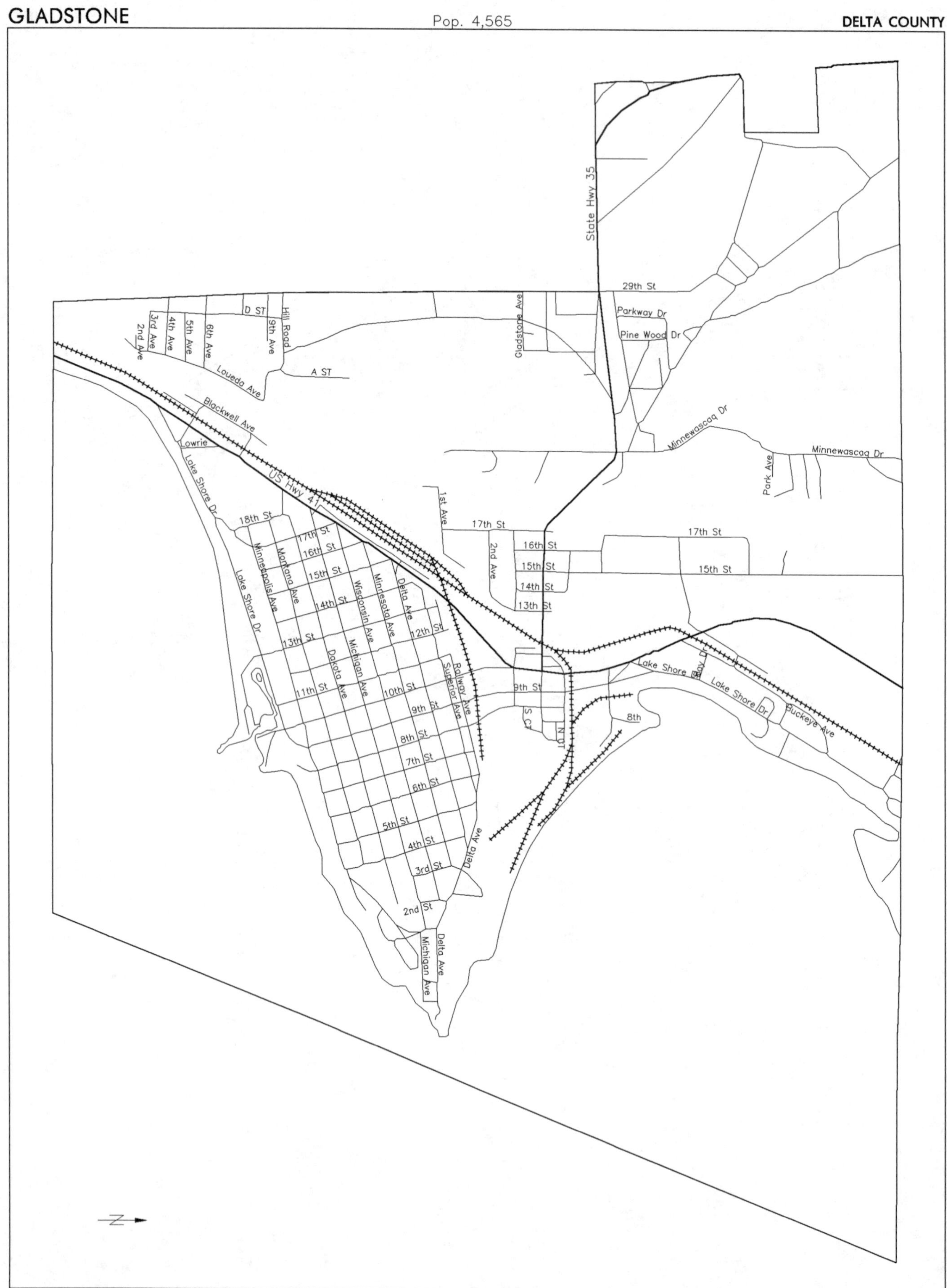
State Hwy 35
29th St
D ST
Hill Road
9th Ave
6th Ave
5th Ave
4th Ave
3rd Ave
2nd Ave
Gladstone Ave
Parkway Dr
Pine Wood Dr
A ST
Loueda Ave
Blackwell Ave
Lowrie
Minnewascaq Dr
Minnewascaq Dr
Park Ave
Lake Shore Dr
US Hwy 41
1st Ave
17th St
17th St
18th St
17th St
16th St
16th St
15th St
15th St
15th St
2nd Ave
14th St
14th St
13th St
Minneapolis Ave
Montana Ave
Wisconsin Ave
Minnesota Ave
Delta Ave
12th St
13th St
Michigan Ave
Dakota Ave
Railway Ave
Superior Ave
Lake Shore
Lake Shore Dr
Buckeye Ave
11th St
10th St
9th St
9th St
8th
8th St
7th St
6th St
5th St
4th St
3rd St
Delta Ave
2nd St
Delta Ave
Michigan Ave

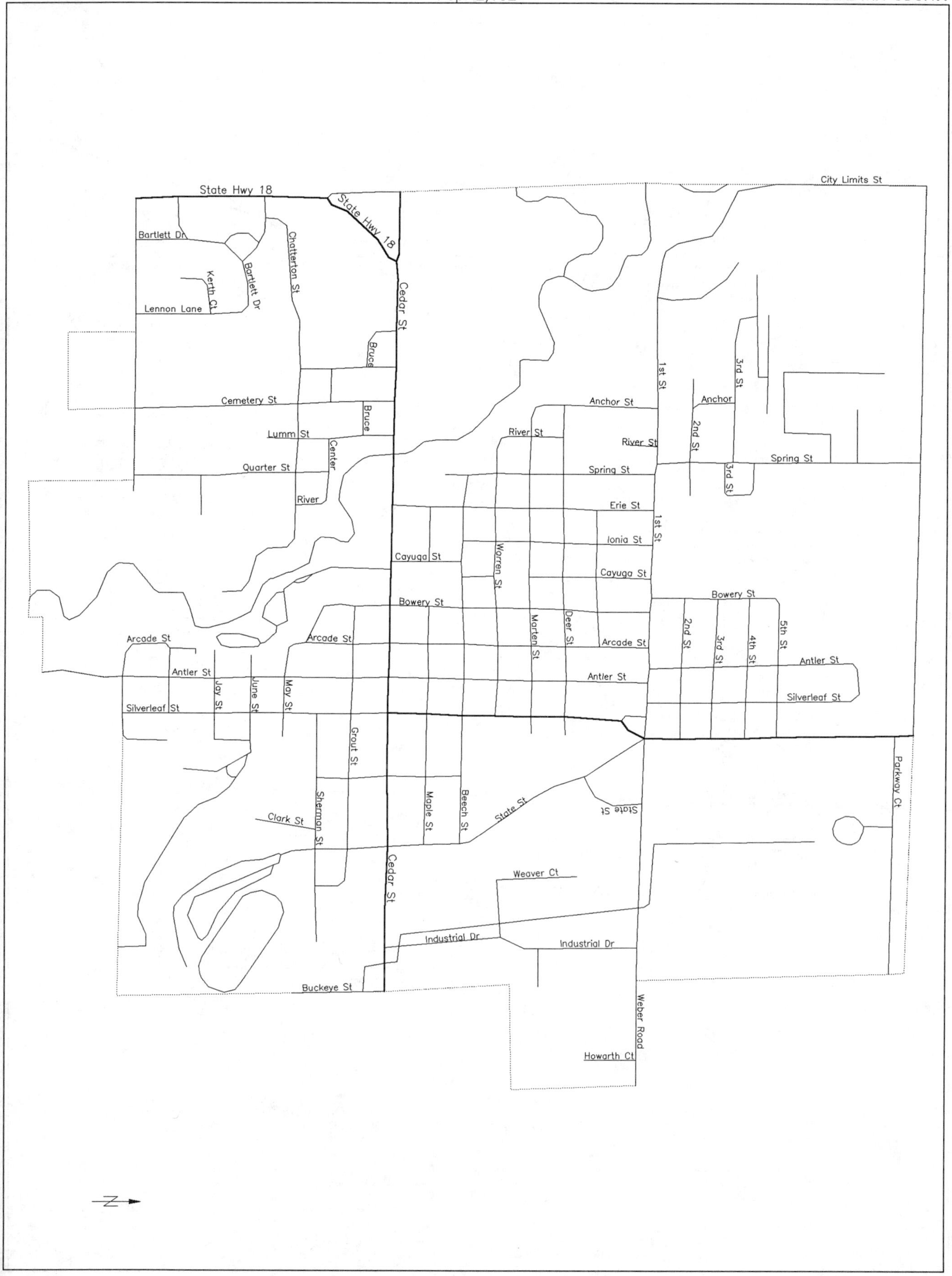

State Hwy 18
State Hwy 18
City Limits St
Bartlett Dr
Bartlett Dr
Chatterton St
Kerth Ct
Lennon Lane
Cedar St
Bruce
Bruce
Cemetery St
Lumm St
Center
Quarter St
River
1st St
3rd St
Anchor St
Anchor
2nd St
River St
River St
Spring St
Spring St
3rd St
Erie St
1st St
Ionia St
Cayuga St
Cayuga St
Warren St
Bowery St
Bowery St
Marten St
Deer St
2nd St
3rd St
4th St
5th St
Arcade St
Arcade St
Arcade St
Antler St
Antler St
Antler St
Jay St
June St
May St
Silverleaf St
Silverleaf St
Grout St
Parkway Ct
Maple St
Beech St
State St
State St
Clark St
Sherman St
Cedar St
Weaver Ct
Industrial Dr
Industrial Dr
Buckeye St
Weber Road
Howarth Ct

Neal St
Grand Oak Dr
Huntington Rd
Grand Blanc Rd
Reid Rd
Grand Oak Dr
Schram St
Kingsley Rd
Case Ave
Saginaw St
Beach St
West St
Union St
Seward St
Walker St
Brainard St
Center Rd
McFarland St
Pleasant View Dr
Fuller St
Rust Park Dr
Riverview Dr
High St
Orchard St
Sawyer St
Bush St
Old Bridge Rd
Woodbridge Dr
Woodbridge Dr
Greenwich Lane
Westover Pass
Brookshire Dr
Stonybrook Dr
Old Bridge Rd
Saginaw St
Stuart St
Grant St
Bush Ave
Terrace Dr
Curwood Dr
Holly Rd
Greenhill Dr
Bella Vista Dr
Perry Rd
Via Catherina Dr
Saginaw St
Joseph Dr
Boutell Dr
Applegate Lane
Genesee Rd
Genesee Rd
Kings Post Rd
Sandhurst Dr
Via Catherina Dr
Francesca Dr
Thomas Lane
Boutell Ct
Ashley Dr
Lockmoor Dr
Bilmar Lane
Kings Pointe Rd
Kings Carriage Rd
Perry Rd
Charing Cross Dr
Old Bilmar Lane
Francesca Dr
Kings Coach Rd
Kings Coach Cir
Charing Cross Dr
Boutell Dr
King Carriage Rd
Kings Bridge Rd
Kings Bridge Trial
Elmwood Dr
Moceri Dr
Moceri Dr
Townline Rd
Old Town Ct
Boutell Dr
Townline Ct
Townline Rd
Woodside Dr
Townline Rd
Pine Row Lane
Riverbend Dr
Belsay Rd
Birchwood Lane
Riverbend Dr
Morninglow Dr
Bluffview Lane
Hilltop Dr
Greenview Dr
Perry Rd
Juniper Way
Riverbend Dr

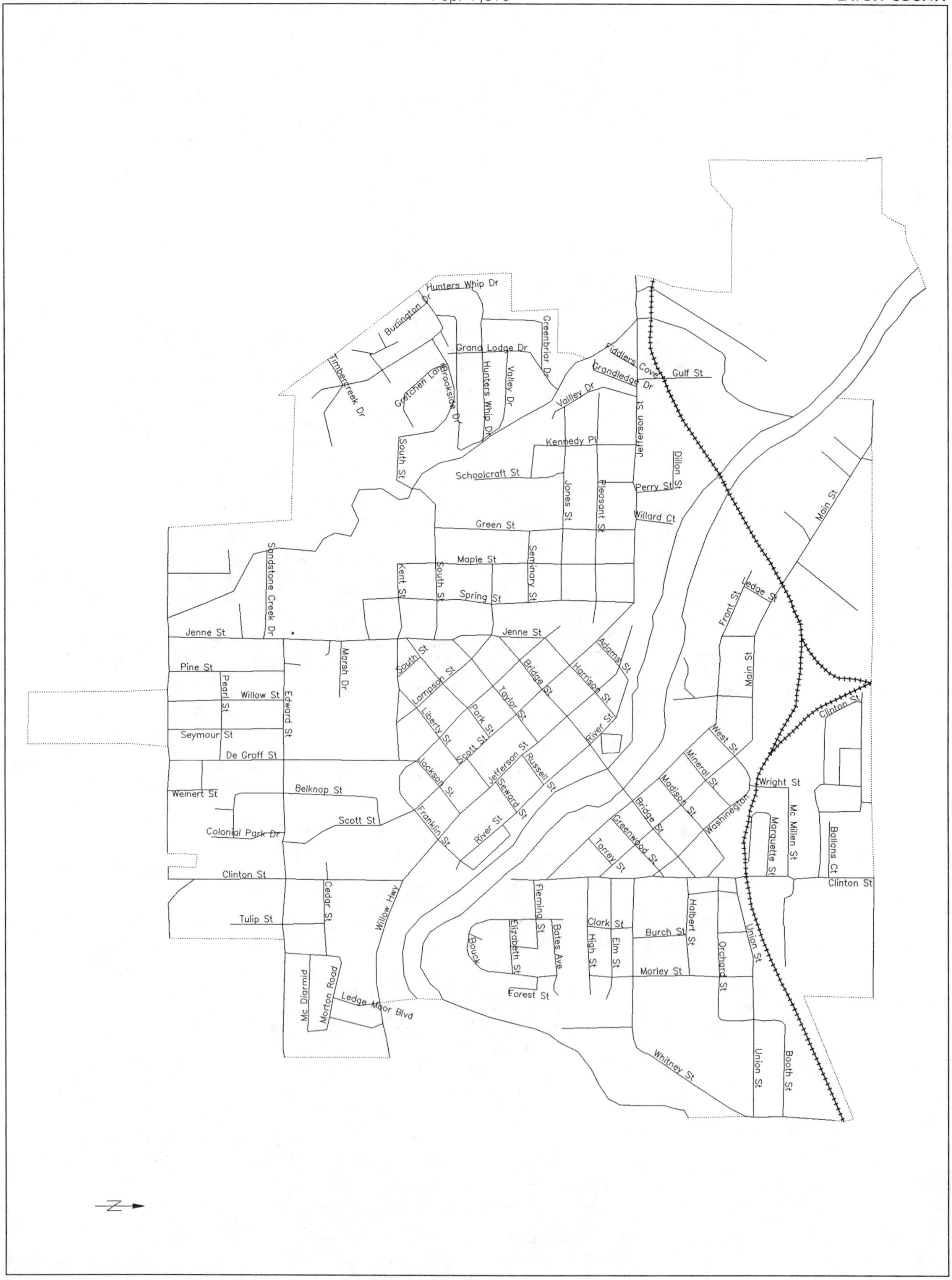

Hunters Whip Dr
Burlington Dr
Greenbriar Dr
Grand Lodge Dr
Timbercreek Dr
Gretchen Lane
Brookside Dr
Hunters Whip Dr
Valley Dr
Fiddlers Cove
Grandledge Dr
Gulf St
Vallley Dr
South St
Kennedy Pl
Jefferson St
Dillon St
Schoolcraft St
Jones St
Pleasant St
Perry St
Willard Ct
Green St
Main St
Sandstone Creek Dr
Seminary St
Maple St
Kent St
South St
Spring St
Ledge St
Front St
Jenne St
Jenne St
Adams St
Main St
South St
Bridge St
Harrison St
Marsh Dr
Pine St
Lampson St
Taylor St
Pearl St
Willow St
Edward St
Liberty St
Park St
River St
Clinton St
Seymour St
Scott St
West St
De Groff St
Jefferson St
Russell St
Mineral St
Jackson St
Weinert St
Belknap St
Seward St
Madison St
Wright St
Bridge St
Scott St
Franklin St
River St
Greenwood St
Washington
Marquette St
Mc Millen St
Ballons Ct
Colonial Park Dr
Torrey St
Clinton St
Clinton St
Fleming St
Cedar St
Willow Hwy
Tulip St
Clark St
Bates Ave
Elizabeth St
High St
Elm St
Burch St
Halbert St
Union St
Orchard St
Bouck
Morley St
Mc Diarmid
Morton Road
Ledge Moor Blvd
Forest St
Whitney St
Union St
Booth St

N

East Grand Rapids

Grand Rapids

Street	Map	Quadrant
Chamberlain	14	NW
Chamberlain	19	NW
Chamberlain Ct	14	SW
Charles Ave	8	SE
Charlotte Ave	7	NW
Charring Cross	16	NW
Chatham St	7	NE
Chatham St	8	NW
Chelsea Dr	4	SW
Cheney Ave	3	NE
Cherry Dr	8	SE
Cherry Hill Dr	4	SW
Cherry St	8	SW
Cherryrun Ct	2	SW
Cherrywood Dr	9	NE
Chesaning Dr	14	NW
Chesapeake Dr	9	NW
Cheshire Dr	3	SW
Chester St	8	SE
Chestnut St	8	SW
Chevy Chase	10	NW
Chippewa Dr	9	SW
Chipwood Ln	7	NW
Chub Ave	8	SW
Church Pl	8	SW
Clancy Ave	8	NW
Claremont Pl	8	NE
Claystone St	14	NE
Claystone St	16	NW
Clearbrook St	14	SW
Clearview St	10	NW
Clifton Pl	8	NE
Clover Crest	2	SE
Clover Ct	8	NW
Clover Dr	2	SW
Coate Ct	13	NW
Cody Ave	8	SW
Coit Ave	3	NE
Coit Ave	8	NW
Coit Rd	7	SE
Coldbrook St	8	NW
Cole Ave	3	SE
Colfax St	3	SW
College Ave	3	NE
College Ave	8	NE
College Ave	13	NE
Collindale Ave	7	NW
Collins Ave	13	NE
Colorado Ave	9	SW
Colorado Ave	14	NW
Colton Dr	14	NE
Columbia Ave	3	SE
Commerce Ave	8	NW
Commons Dr	8	SW
Comstock Blvd	3	NE
Concord Ave	14	NW
Concord St	3	NE
Conger St	3	NE
Congress Ave	8	SE
Conlon Ave	14	NE
Conrad St	3	SW
Cooper Ave	8	SE
Cora St	7	NE
Cordelia St	13	NW
Corinne St	13	NW
Cornelius Ave	14	NW
Cornell Dr	14	NW
Cornwall Ave	8	SW
Corona St	4	NW
Cottage Grove	13	NW
Country Club Dr	2	SW
Country Club Dr	3	SE
Courtney St	2	SE
Courtney St	3	SW
Covell Ave	2	SW
Covell Ave	7	NW
Covington Dr	14	NE
Crahen Ave	10	NE
Cranbrook Dr	9	NW
Cranbrook Ter	9	SW
Cranden Dr	14	NW
Crary St	13	NE
Crawford St	8	SE
Creek Bluff Pl	2	SW
Creekside Dr	14	SW
Crescent Dr	9	NW
Crescent St	8	NW
Creston Plz	8	NE
Crestwood Dr	7	NW
Crofton St	13	NW
Cromwell Ave	8	SE
Crosby St	2	SE
Crosby St	3	SW
Cross Creek Dr	14	SW
Culter St	13	NW
Curtis St	3	SE
Curve St	7	SE
Curve St	8	SW
Curwood	19	NW
Curwood Ave	19	NW
Cusick Pl	3	SW
Cutler St	13	NW
Cutter Pkwy	10	SE
Dale Ct	4	SW
Dale St	3	SW
Dallas Ave	8	SE
Danbury Dr	14	NE
Dartmouth St	2	SE
Darwin Ave	13	NW
Davis Ave	3	SW
Davis Ave	8	NW
Dawes Ave	14	SW
Dawes Ct	19	NW
Dawson Ave	4	SW
Dayton St	7	SE
Dayton St	8	SW
Dean Lake Ave	4	NW
Dean Lake Ave	4	SW
Dean St	3	SW
Dean St	4	SW
Decker Pl	7	NE
Deer Hollow Dr	14	SW
Delange Dr	14	NE
Delaware St	8	SW
Deli Ct	4	NE
Deli Dr	4	NE
Deloney Ave	7	NE
Delray Ave	10	SE
Deming St	13	NE
Dennis Ave	8	SE
Derby Dr	2	SW
Derbyshire St	14	SW
Detroit St	13	NW
Devon Dr	10	NW
Devonshire Dr	4	SW
Dewberry	4	SE
Dewberry Ct	4	SE
Dewberry Dr	4	SW
Dewey Ave	8	NW
Dexter Pl	8	NW
Diamond Ave	3	NE
Diamond Ave	8	NE
Diamond Ct	3	SE
Diamond Pl	8	SE
Dick Ave	7	NE
Dickinson St	13	NW
Dickinson St	14	NW
Division Ave	8	NW
Division Ave	13	NW
Divot Dr	2	SW
Dolbee Ave	8	SE
Donald Pl	8	SE
Donovan Ct	8	SE
Dorais Ct	4	NW
Dorais Dr	4	NW
Dorchester Ave	8	SW
Doremus Pl	13	NW
Doris St	3	NE
Dorothy St	2	SE
Dorrell St	4	SW
Dorrie Ave	8	NE
Dorroll St	3	SE
Dorroll St	4	SW
Douglas St	7	NE
Douglas St	8	NW
Dover Pl	2	SE
Downing St	10	SW
Drexel Ct	4	SW
Drexel Dr	3	SE
Drukker St	13	NW
Ducoma Dr	2	SW
Dudley Ave	8	NE
Duffield Dr	9	NW
Duiker Ave	3	SE
Dunham St	8	SE
Dunham St	9	SW
Dunlap St	2	SE
Dunnigan Ave	6	SW
Durham Ave	4	NW
Dushane St	7	NW
Dutchess Ave	10	SW
Dwight Ave	8	NE
Dykema Ct	8	SE
E AVE	8	SW
Eagle Bluff Dr	6	SW
Eagle Cir	6	SW
Eagle Crest Dr	6	SW
Eagle Crest Dr	10	NW
Eagle Park Dr	6	SW
Eagle Ridge Ct	6	SW
Earldon Ave	8	SE
East Pl	8	NE
Eastern Ave	3	NE
Eastern Ave	8	NE
Eastern Ave	13	NE
Eastern Pl	3	SE
Eastern Pl	8	NE
Eastgate St	14	NW
Eastmont Dr	10	SE
Eastmoor Ave	10	SE
Eastridge Ct	10	NW
Eastridge Dr	10	NW
Eastview Ct	10	NW
Eastview Dr	10	NW
Ebner Ct	8	SW
Ecklund St	3	SE
Ecklund St	4	SW
Edgehill Dr	10	SW
Edgewood Ave	3	NE
Edgewood Ave	14	NE
Edgewood St	14	NE
Edinburgh Dr	10	SW
Edington Ct	14	SE
Edington Dr	14	SE
Edington Ln	14	SE
Edington Ln	19	NE
Edison Ave	7	NW
Edison Park	7	NW
Edith Ave	4	SW
Edith Ave	9	NW
Edmonton St	4	SW
Edmund Ave	8	NE
Edna St	13	NE
Edna St	14	NW
Edward Ave	14	NW
Edwin St	3	SW
Effie Pl	3	NE
Ekhart St	8	NE
El Camino Dr	2	SW
Elder Ct	8	SW
Eleanor St	3	SW
Elizabeth Ave	3	SW
Elizabeth Ave	8	NW
Elliott St	13	NE
Elliott St	14	NW
Ellsmere St	3	NE
Ellsmere St	4	NW
Ellsworth Ave	8	SW
Elm St	13	NW
Elmdale St	3	NE
Elmdale St	4	NW
Elmer Dr	4	NW
Elmgrove Ct	7	NE
Elmherst Ave	9	SE
Elmridge Dr	2	SW
Elmwood St	3	SW
Emerald Ave	3	SE
Emerald Ave	8	NE
Emerald Lake	4	NW
Emerson Ave	2	SE
Emperor St	8	SW
Englewood Ave	14	NW
Englewood Dr	14	SW
Eola St	13	NW
Escott Ave	2	SE
Essex Ave	3	NE
Ethel Ave	9	SW
Eton St	7	SE
Eton St	8	SW
Euclid Ave	13	SW
Eugene St	13	NE
Eureka Ave	8	SE
Evangeline St	9	NW
Evans St	8	SE
Evelyn St	3	SE
Eventide Dr	4	SW
Everest Ave	13	NW
Everglade Dr	13	NE
Evergreen St	13	NE
Evergreen St	14	NW
Evernia Ave	13	NE
Ewing Ave	13	NE
Ext	3	SW
Fair St	13	NW
Fairbanks St	8	NW
Fairfield Ave	7	NW
Fairlane Dr	3	SE
Fairmount St	8	SE
Fairview Ave	8	NW
Farnsworth Ave	10	SE
Fay Ave	2	SE
Feakin Ave	13	NW
Fern Ave	3	SE
Fernando St	3	SE
Ferry St	8	NW
Finney Ave	8	SW
Finsbury Ln	7	NW
Fisk St	8	SE
Fisk St	9	SW
Fitch Pl	8	SE
Fitzhugh Ave	8	SE
Flat St	8	NE
Fletcher Dr	9	NE
Flint Ct	8	SW
Florence St	3	SE
Ford Ave	3	SE
Forest Hills Ct	10	SE
Forest-Hill Ave	10	NE
Forrest Ave	3	SE
Forrester St	14	SW
Foster Ave	3	NE
Foster Ct	3	NE
Fountain Ave	9	NW
Fountain St	8	NW
Fountain St	9	NW
Fox Ridge Dr	4	NW
Fox St	13	NW
Foxboro Ct	2	SW
Francis Ave	13	NW
Frank St	8	NW
Franklin St	8	SW
Franklin St	9	SW
Frans Mtn Pl	7	SE
Frederick Ave	2	NE
Frederick Ave	7	NE
Freeman Ave	7	SE
Fremont Ave	2	SE
Fremont Ave	7	NE
Freyling Pl	8	SE
Front Ave	3	SW
Front Ave	8	NW
Frontage Rd	7	SE
Frontage Rd	8	NE
Fruit St	8	NE
Fruitland Ave	3	NE
Fruitwood Ct	7	NE
Fruitwood Dr	7	NW
Fuller Ave	3	NE
Fuller Ave	4	NW
Fuller Ave	8	NE
Fuller Ave	14	NW
Fuller Ave	19	NW
Fulton St	7	NW
Fulton St	8	NW
Fulton St	9	NW
Fulton St	10	NW
Fulton St	10	NE
Fultonwood Dr	9	NW
Gabrielle Ct	9	NE
Galahad St	4	NW
Garden St	13	NW
Garfield Ave	2	SE
Garfield Ave	7	NE
Garret Dr	4	NW
Gateway Pl	7	NW
Gay Ave	8	SE
Gelock Pl	8	SW
Genecsee St	9	SW
Geneva Ave	8	SE
Georgetown Dr	14	NW
Gerald Ave	3	NE
Gezon Ave	3	SW
Gezon Ave	8	NW
Ghilda Pl	8	NE
Gibson St	8	SE
Giddings Ave	9	SW
Giddings Ave	14	NW
Gilbert St	13	NE
Gill Ave	8	NW
Gilners Ct	8	SW
Gilpin St	3	NW
Gingerwood Dr	14	SW
Gladstone Dr	9	SW
Gladstone Dr	14	NW
Glen Echo Dr	14	NE
Glencairin Dr	2	SW
Glendale St	9	NW
Glengary Ct	14	NE
Glenhaven Ave	7	NE
Glenn Dr	10	SW
Glenview Dr	9	SE
Glenwood Ave	9	SW
Globe St	9	NW
Godfrey Ave	8	SW
Godwin Ave	13	NE
Gold Ave	8	NW
Goldsboro Pl	8	NE
Golf Rd	10	SW
Golfridge Dr	14	NE
Goodrich St	8	SW
Gordon St	7	NW
Gorham Ave	14	NW
Grace St	9	SW
Graceland St	3	SW
Graham Ct	7	NE
Graham Rd	7	NE
Graham St	8	SW
Grand Ave	8	NE
Grandview St	7	NW
Grandville Ave	8	SW
Grandville Ave	13	NW
Grant St	8	SW
Gratiot St	2	SE
Greeleaf Ct	14	SW
Green St	8	SW
Greenbrier Ct	10	SW
Greenbrier Dr	10	SE
Greenfield Cir	9	NW
Greenfield St	13	NW
Greenings St	4	NE
Greentree Dr	14	NE
Greenview Ct	16	NW
Greenwich Rd	9	NE
Grenada Dr	14	NE
Griggs St	13	NW
Griggs St	14	NW
Griswold St	13	NE
Griswold St	14	NW
Grooters St	14	SW
Grove Bluff Ct	14	NE
Grove Bluff Dr	14	NE
Grove Ct	3	SW
Grove Pl	3	SW
Grove St	3	SW
Guild St	3	SW
Gunnison Ave	7	NE
Haifley St	8	SW
Haines Ave	7	NW
Hake Ct	8	NE
Hake Rd	8	NE
Halena St	3	SE
Hall St	7	SE
Hall St	8	SW
Hall St	9	SW
Hall St	10	SW
Hamilton Ave	3	SW
Hamilton Ave	8	NW
Hampshire Blvd	14	NE
Hampton	9	NE
Hampton Ave	9	SW
Hampton Dr	9	NE
Hamstead Dr	7	NW
Hanchett Ave	2	SE
Hanover St	3	SE
Harlan Ave	8	NE
Harvey St	8	NE
Hastings St	8	NW
Hathaway Dr	9	SE
Hawthorne St	8	NE
Hayden St	8	SW
Hazen St	13	NE
Hazen St	14	NW
Heath Dr	14	NE
Heathcliffe Dr	14	NE
Heather Ln	10	SE
Heathfield Dr	4	SE
Helen St	8	NE
Hemlock St	8	SW
Henry Ave	8	SE
Heritage	8	SE
Hermitage St	8	SE
Herrick Ave	3	SE
Herrick Ave	8	NE
Hersman St	10	SE
Hester Pl	8	NW
Hiaeshutter Pl	7	NE
Hiawatha Dr	9	SW
Hickory Ave	14	SW
Hidden Lake Ct	10	SW
Hidden Lake Ln	10	SW
Hidden Spring	6	NW
High St	13	NW
Highbluff Dr	4	SW
Highland St	8	SW
Hill Ave	7	NE
Hillburn Ave	2	SE
Hillcrest Ave	2	SW
Hillmount St	2	SE
Hillview Ave	9	NW
Hoag Ave	6	NW
Hobart St	13	NE
Hoehn St	2	SE
Hogadone Pl	7	SE
Hogan St	13	NW
Holborn Dr	2	SE
Holland Ave	8	NE
Hollis Dr	3	NE
Hollister Ave	8	SE
Hollywood St	3	NE
Hollywood St	4	NW
Holmdene Blvd	9	NW
Holyoke Dr	19	NW
Home St	13	NW
Homer St	3	NE
Honeoye St	13	SW
Hoover St	3	SE
Hope St	8	SE
Hope St	9	SE
Hopson St	8	NE
Horton Ave	13	NW
Houseman Ave	3	SE
Houseman Ave	8	NE
Hovey St	7	NE
Hovey St	8	NW
Howard St	8	SE
Howland St	3	SW
Hoyt St	13	NE
Hoyt St	14	NW
Hubbard St	3	NE
Hubert St	8	NE
Hughart St	8	SW
Humbolt St	8	SE
Hurd St	9	SW
Huron St	8	NW
Hutchinson Ave	14	NW
Hylane Ave	4	NE
Hynes Ave	8	SW
I- 196	7	SE
I- 196	8	NW
I- 196	9	NW
I- 96	3	NE
I- 96	4	NW
I- 96	4	NW
I- 96	9	NE
I- 96	10	NW
I- 96	10	NW
Ida Ave	7	NE
Indian Mounds	7	SW
Indian Ridge Dr	4	NW
Inlet Pl	8	NE
Innes St	8	NE
Innes St	9	NW
Inverness Rd	14	NE
Ionia Ave	8	NW
Ionia Ave	13	NW
Ira Ave	2	SE
Iris Pl	8	NE
Iroquois Dr	9	SW
Isabella Ct	8	SE
Ivanhoe Ave	10	NW
Ives Ave	7	SE
Jackson Pl	7	NE
Jackson St	7	NE
Jackson St	8	NW
Jaglin Dr	4	NW
James Ave	8	SE
Janes Ave	3	SW
Jefferson Ave	8	NW
Jefferson Ave	13	NW
Jennette Ave	2	SE
Jennette Ave	7	NE
Jennings St	14	NW
Jerome Ave	13	NW
Jessie St	3	NE
Joan Ave	4	SW
John Ball Park	7	NE
John St	8	NE
Johnathan Ave	4	NE
Johnathan Ct	4	NE
Johnston St	13	NE
Johnston St	14	NW
Joslin St	13	NE
Julia St	3	SE
Juneberry Ct	14	SW
Kalamazoo Ave	8	SE
Kalamazoo Ave	13	NE
Kalamazoo Ave	14	NW
Kalamazoo Ave	19	NW
Kate Ave	10	SW
Kate St	10	SW
Katherine Dr	3	SW
Kellogg St	8	SE
Kelsey St	3	NE
Kelsey St	4	NW
Ken-O-Par St	19	NW
Ken-O-Sha Blvd	13	NW
Kenan Ave	2	SE
Kendall St	19	NW
Kendalwood Ct	3	NE
Kendalwood St	3	NE
Kenilworth Dr	10	SE
Kenmoor Ave	10	SE
Kenning Dr	7	NW
Kenosha Dr	14	SW
Kensboro Ave	3	NE
Kensington Ave	7	SW
Kensington Ave	8	SW
Kent Blvd	9	NE
Kent Hills Rd	3	SE
Kentridge Dr	19	NW
Kentucky Dr	13	NE
Kentview Dr	3	SE
Kentwood Dr	3	SE
Kenwood St	3	SE
Kimball Ave	19	NW
King Ct	8	SW
Kingstown Dr	19	NW
Kingswood Dr	9	SE
Kirk Dr	10	SE
Kirkshire Dr	19	NW

Grandville

Street	Page	Grid
Woodbine Ave	11	SE
Wyatt St	11	SW
Yellowstone Dr	11	SE

Kentwood

Street	Page	Grid
28th St	14	SE
28th St	16	SW
29th St	14	SE
29th St	16	SW
32nd St	14	SE
32nd St	16	SW
36th St	16	SW
40th St	20	NE
43rd St	18	NE
44th St	18	NE
44th St	19	NE
44th St	20	NW
47th St	18	NE
48th St	18	NE
48th St	19	NE
50th St	19	NW
51st St	18	NE
52nd St	18	NE
52nd St	19	SW
52nd St	20	SW
54th Ave	18	SE
54th St	18	SE
54th St	19	SW
56th St	18	SE
58th St	18	SE
59th St	18	SE
59th St	19	SW
60th St	18	SE
60th St	19	SW
60th St	20	SW
Acquest Dr	16	SE
Airwest Ave	20	NW
Aleda Ave	18	NE
American Ave	18	NE
Andover Ct	18	NE
Andover St	18	NE
Andrew St	19	NW
Appleview Dr	19	SE
Applewood Dr	19	NE
Arbor Ln	18	NE
Artis Dr	16	NW
Ash Ave	19	NW
B ST	16	SW
Barkway Dr	18	SE
Bayham Dr	19	NW
Bellewood Ct	18	SE
Bellewood Dr	18	SE
Bellewood St	18	SE
Beltline Ave	16	NW
Bent Brook Ct	19	SE
Bent Brook St	19	SE
Bentbrook Dr	19	SE
Birchview Dr	18	SE
Blaine Ave	18	NE
Blue Ash Dr	18	NE
Blue Heron Dr	19	NE
Bluegrass Ct	16	NE
Bluegrass Dr	16	NE
Bonnie Ave	19	NW
Bowdoin St	19	SW
Bowen Blvd	19	NW
Bramalea	19	SW
Brattleboro Dr	19	SE
Breton Ct	19	NE
Breton Industrial	14	SE
Breton Rd	14	SE
Breton Rd	19	NE
Briar Creek St	19	NE
Bridgeport Ln	19	NE
Bridle Creek Ct	19	SW
Bridle Creek Dr	19	SW
Brinks St	18	NE
Brinks St	19	SW
Broadmoor Ave	16	SW
Broadmoor Ave	20	NW
Brocton Ct	20	NE
Brocton St	20	NE
Brookcross St	19	SW
Brookfarm Ct	19	SE
Brookfarm Dr	19	SE
Brooklyn Ave	19	NW
Brookmark St	19	SW
Brookridge Ct	19	SW
Brookridge Dr	19	SW
Brookwood Ave	19	SW
Brookwood Ct	19	SW
Brookwood Dr	19	SW
Buddy St	18	NE
Bunker Hill Ct	19	SE
Burgis Ave	19	NW
Burgis Ct	19	NW
Burton St	16	NW
Cambridge St	14	SE
Camille Ct	10	SW
Camille Dr	10	SW
Camille Dr	16	SW
Carriage Hill Dr	19	SW
Carrick Ave	18	NE
Castle Bluff Ct	14	SE
Catamaran Way	14	SE
Cavanagh St	19	SW
Champion Ave	18	NE
Cheryl Ave	19	SW
Christie Ave	19	SW
Circle-Shore Dr	19	NW
Citation Ct	16	NE
Claudia Ave	18	SE
Cloverleaf Dr	16	NE
Coach Ln	14	SE
Collier Ave	16	NW
Common Way	16	NE
Coral Valley Ct	16	SW
Coral Valley Dr	16	SW
Countrywood Ct	19	NE
Countrywood Dr	19	NE
Creek Dr	16	SW
Creekridge Dr	19	SE
Creekview Dr	19	SW
Crestmoor Ct	19	SE
Crestmoor Dr	19	SE
Curvebrook St	18	SE
Curwood Ave	19	NW
Curwood Ct	19	NW
Daniel Ct	18	NE
Daniel Dr	18	NE
Daniel St	18	NE
Danvers Ct	20	NE
Danvers Dr	20	NE
Debarr Dr	18	SE
Deckside Way	14	SE
Diane St	18	SE
Discovery Dr	19	SE
Division Ave	18	NW
Donker Ct	20	NE
Downing St	10	SE
Drummond Blvd	19	NE
Eastern Ave	18	NE
Eastmont Dr	10	SE
Edgelawn Dr	18	SE
Edgelawn Dr	19	SW
Edsel St	18	NE
Edsel St	19	NW
Effingham Dr	19	SW
Eldee Dr	18	SE
Ellora Ct	19	SW
Ellora Dr	19	SW
Embro Dr	19	NE
Engleside Dr	16	NW
Enterprise St	19	NE
Fallingbrook Dr	19	SW
Farmview St	19	NE
Farnham St	18	NE
Fawnwood Ct	19	SE
Fawnwood Dr	19	SE
Fescue Dr	18	SE
Fireside Dr	18	SE
Flying Eagle Dr	18	NE
Forest Creek Ct	16	SE
Forest Creek Ln	16	SE
Forest Creek St	16	SW
Forest Dr	16	NE
Forest Way Dr	16	SE
Forest-Hill Ave	10	SE
Forest-Hill Ave	16	NE
Forest-Lake Ct	16	NE
Forest-Lake Dr	16	NE
Freeton Dr	18	SE
Fuller Ave	19	NW
Fuller Ct	19	NW
Garland St	18	NE
Gatewood Dr	19	SW
Gentian Ct	19	SW
Gentian Dr	19	SW
Gerda St	19	NW
Glenbrook Dr	19	SW
Glenmoor Ct	19	SE
Glenmoor Dr	19	SE
Grand Chateau	18	NE
Grantwood Ave	18	NE
Green Oak Ln	18	NE
Greenacres Dr	18	NE
Greenboro Dr	18	SE
Greenboro Dr	19	SW
Griggs St	16	NW
Hall St	10	SE
Hampton Ct	16	NW
Hampton	14	SE
Harbor Dr	19	NE
Hardwick Dr	19	SW
Hardwick St	18	SE
Harp St	18	NE
Haverhill Blvd	18	SE
Haywood Dr	19	NE
Heathcliffe Dr	19	NW
Heyboer Ave	18	NE
Hickory Way	16	NE
Hidden Lake Dr	19	NE
Hidden Valley	19	SW
Highlander Dr	19	NE
Hillwood Ct	19	NW
Holly Park Ave	18	NE
Hopedale Dr	19	SW
Horton Ave	18	NE
Hunters Ridge	19	NE
I- 96	16	NW
Innwood Dr	19	NW
Ironwood Ln	18	NE
Jamestown Ct	19	SE
Jamestown Dr	19	SE
Janesick Dr	18	SE
Janesick St	18	SW
Jefferson Ave	18	NE
Jeffrey St	19	SW
Jennifer St	18	NE
Jessica St	18	NE
John C Ct	19	NW
Jonfield Ave	18	NE
Jonfield Dr	18	NE
Juanita Dr	19	SW
Julivan Ave	18	NE
Kalamazoo Ave	19	NW
Katrina Dr	19	SW
Kelekent Ave	18	SE
Kellogg Woods	18	SE
Keyhill Ave	16	NW
Kimball Ave	19	NW
Kingbridge Ter	16	NW
Kirk Dr	10	SE
Kirk Dr	16	NE
Kleyla Dr	18	SE
Kropf St	18	NE
La Grange Ct	16	NE
Lake Dr	16	NW
Lake Eastbrook	16	SW
Lamdale Ct	16	NE
Lamplight Ln	16	NE
Lantana Ct	19	NW
Lantana Dr	19	NE
Lark Ln	19	NW
Larkwood Dr	19	NE
Leisure South	18	SE
Lemans Ct	16	SW
Linderwood Dr	20	SW
Little Plaster	16	NE
Lockmere Dr	19	SW
Loftwood Dr	19	SW
Londonderry Dr	19	SW
Lowry Ct	19	NE
Lyles St	18	NE
Madison Ave	18	NE
Majestic St	18	SE
Mall Dr	16	NW
Manorwood Dr	19	SW
Maple Creek	19	SW
Maple Hollow Ct	19	NW
Maple Hollow Dr	19	NW
Maple Hollow St	19	NW
Maplelawn St	18	NE
Maplevalley St	19	NE
Mapleview Ct	19	NE
Mapleview St	19	NW
Mariner Dr	19	NE
Marlette Ave	18	NE
Marlowe Dr	18	NE
Marshall Ave	18	NE
Marwood Ct	19	NW
Marwood Dr	19	NW
Meadowlane Dr	19	NW
Meadows Dr	16	NE
Mick Ave	18	SE
Mick Dr	18	NE
Mildred Ave	18	NE
Miller Pkwy	18	SW
Millhaven Ave	18	NE
Misty Creek Dr	19	NE
Model Ct	20	NW
Monte Carlo Dr	16	SW
Montebello Dr	18	NE
Montebello St	18	NE
Morningside Dr	20	NW
Murphy St	16	NE
Murray St	18	NE
Nancy St	18	SE
Nature Trail Dr	19	NE
New Moon Ave	18	NE
Newcastle Dr	19	NW
Nora St	18	SE
Norway St	16	NW
Oak Forest Ct	16	NE
Oak Forest Ln	16	NE
Observatory	16	NW
Old Kent Rd	14	SE
Old Valley Ct	19	SE
Osborne Ave	18	SE
Outer Dr	14	SE
Outer Dr	16	NW
Oxford Dr	14	SE
Pamela Ave	18	NE
Paris Ave	16	SW
Paris Ave	20	NW
Paris Park Dr	20	SW
Parkway Ave	18	SE
Patterson Ave	16	NE
Patterson Ave	20	NE
Pembroke St	18	SE
Pembroke St	19	SW
Pennwood Ct	19	NW
Penny Ave	18	NE
Pennybrook Ln	19	SW
Pennyfarm Dr	19	SW
Pheasant Ridge	14	SE
Pheasant Run	19	NE
Piccadilly Cir	14	SE
Pickett St	19	NW
Pillar Creek Ave	19	NE
Pine Meadow	16	SW
Pine Needles Ct	18	SE
Pine Pl	18	SE
Pine Place St	18	SE
Pine Vista St	18	SE
Pinebell Ct	18	SE
Pinebluff Dr	19	SW
Pinebrook Ave	18	SE
Pineknoll Ct	19	SW
Pineknoll Dr	19	SW
Pinetree Ave	19	SW
Pinta Ct	16	SE
Plaza Dr	16	SW
Poinsettia Ave	19	NW
Portman Dr	14	SE
Potter Ave	18	NE
Primrose Ave	18	NE
Prince Albert St	18	NE
Promise Dr	19	SE
Queensbury Dr	19	SW
Radcliff Ave	14	SE
Raeboro	19	SW
Ramblewood Ct	19	SE
Ramblewood Dr	19	SE
Raymond Ave	18	NE
Raymond Ave	19	NE
Redwood Ln	18	NE
Regent St	18	SE
Ridgebrook Ct	19	SW
Ridgebrook Dr	19	SW
Ridgecroft Ave	14	NE
Ridgemoor Dr	14	SE
Ridgewood St	18	NE
Rieman Dr	19	NW
Riemen Ct	19	NW
Riviera Ct	16	SW
Riviera Dr	16	SW
Roger B Chafee	18	NE
Rondo St	19	NW
Roseworth Ct	18	SE
Rowland Ave	16	NW
Rum Creek Ct	19	SE
Rum Creek Dr	19	NE
Runido Ct	18	SE
Runido Dr	18	SE
Saladin Dr	16	NW
Sand Piper Dr	19	NE
Sandy Ct	18	SE
Sandy Shore Dr	19	NE
Sandy St	18	SE
Secretariat Dr	16	NE
Shady Pine Ln	16	SE
Shaffer Ave	16	SW
Shaffer Ave	20	NW
Shore Dr	19	NE
Shoreham Pl	19	SW
Silverleaf St	18	SE
Slobey St	18	NE
Sluyter St	18	NE
Sluyter St	19	NW
Southgate Dr	19	NE
Southglow Ct	18	NE
Sparks Dr	16	NW
Springmont Dr	19	NE
Springwood Ct	19	SW
Springwood Dr	18	SE
Springwood Dr	19	SW
Stanford Dr	19	SE
Starbord Ct	19	NE
Stauffer Ave	19	NW
Stone Ave	18	NE
Stonefence Ave	18	NE
Stonyhill Ln	19	SW
Stowehill Dr	19	SE
Stowevalley	19	SE
Stuart Ave	19	NW
Summerfield St	19	SW
Sunny Creek Ct	19	NW
Sunny Ln	19	SW
Sunnycreek St	19	NW
Surrey Pl	19	SW
Sutherland Dr	19	NW
Swan Cave	14	SE
Swank Rd	20	NW
Swansea Dr	14	NE
Tampa St	18	SE
Terry Ct	20	NW
Terry Dr	20	NW
Thorn Creek St	19	SE
Thornberry Ct	16	NE
Thornberry Dr	16	NE
Tierra St	18	SE
Timberwood Dr	19	NE
Trails-End Dr	16	NE
Travelo St	18	NE
Valley Lane Dr	19	SE
Valley-Lane Ct	19	SE
Victoria Ave	18	NE
Viewpond Dr	19	NW
Villa Montee Dr	16	SW
Villa Ridge Dr	16	SW
Vindale St	18	NE
Walma Ave	19	NE
Walnut Hills Dr	19	NE
Walnut Hills Ln	19	NE
Waterbury Dr	19	SW
Waterbury Dr	20	NW
Waterbury Pl	19	SW
Wayside Dr	16	NE
Westminister Dr	14	SE
Whisper Cove	14	SE
Whispering	14	SE
Whispering	14	SE
Wildflower Dr	19	NE
Willow Shores	19	NE
Wilmont Ct	19	SW
Wilmont Dr	19	SE
Wilmont Pl	19	SE
Windy Wood St	19	NE
Windy Wood St	20	NW
Wing Ave	19	SE
Wingate Dr	14	SE
Wingate Dr	16	SW
Wintergreen Dr	19	NE
Wolf Run Ave	18	NE
Wolfboro Dr	19	SE
Wondercrest St	18	NE
Woodbridge Dr	16	SW
Woodland	16	SW
Woodside Oaks	16	NE
Wrightwind Dr	16	NE
York Town Dr	19	SE
la-Casa Dr	18	SE

Walker

Wyoming

NOTES

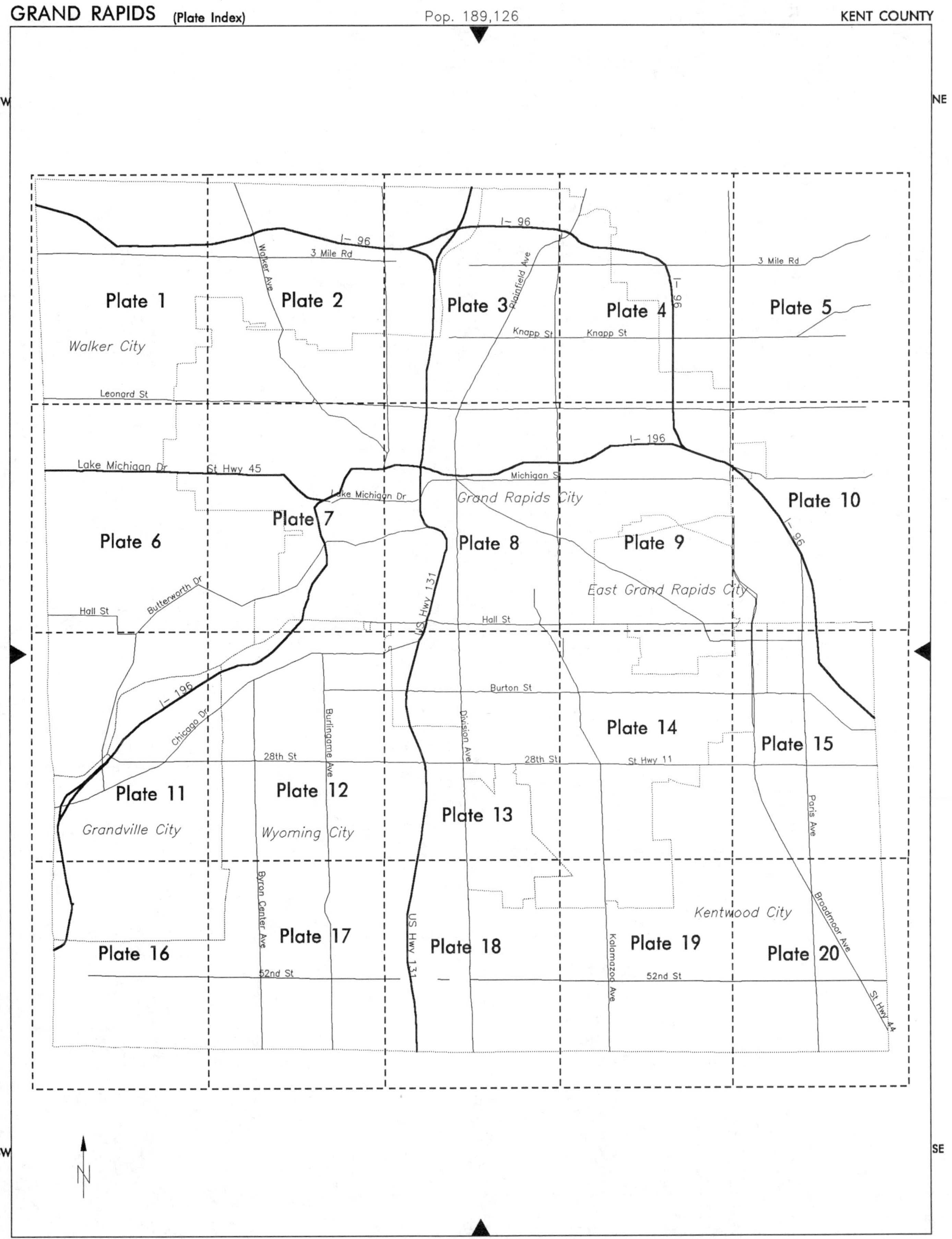
NW
NE
SW
SE
I– 96
3 Mile Rd
Walker Ave
Plainfield Ave
Plate 1
Plate 2
Plate 3
Plate 4
Plate 5
Walker City
Knapp St
Leonard St
I– 196
Lake Michigan Dr
St Hwy 45
Michigan St
Grand Rapids City
Plate 6
Plate 7
Plate 8
Plate 9
Plate 10
East Grand Rapids City
Hall St
Butterworth Dr
US Hwy 131
Burton St
Chicago Dr
Burlingame Ave
Division Ave
28th St
St Hwy 11
Plate 11
Plate 12
Plate 13
Plate 14
Plate 15
Grandville City
Wyoming City
Paris Ave
Byron Center Ave
Kalamazoo Ave
Broadmoor Ave
Kentwood City
Plate 16
Plate 17
Plate 18
Plate 19
Plate 20
52nd St
St Hwy 44
N

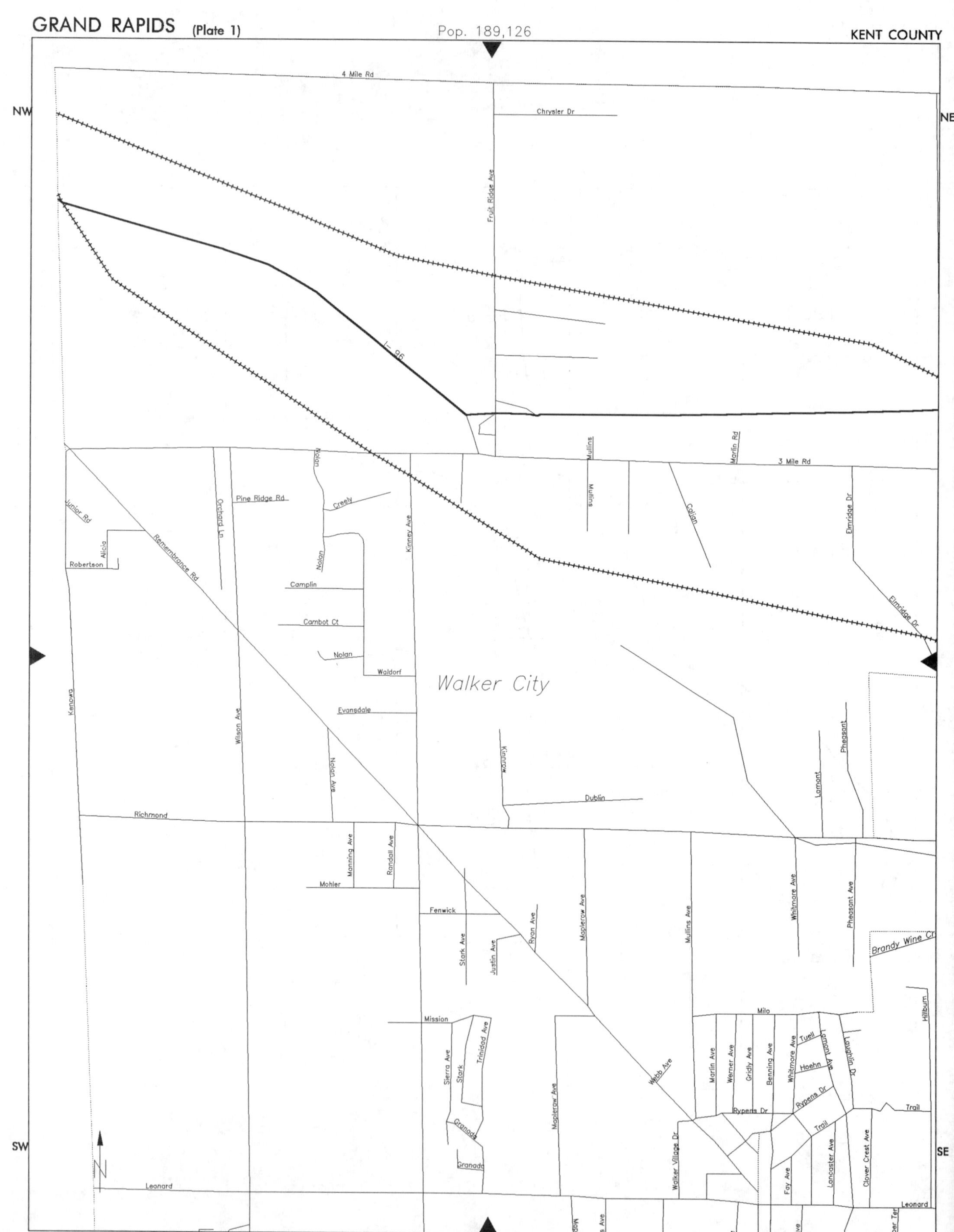
4 Mile Rd
Chrysler Dr
Fruit Ridge Ave
I-96
Mullins
Marlin Rd
3 Mile Rd
Nolan
Pine Ridge Rd
Creely
Orchard Ln
Junior Rd
Alicia
Robertson
Remembrance Rd
Kinney Ave
Callan
Elmridge Dr
Camplin
Cambot Ct
Waldorf
Walker City
Evansdale
Kenowa
Wilson Ave
Nolan Ave
Kinross
Dublin
Lamont
Pheasant
Richmond
Manning Ave
Randall Ave
Mohler
Fenwick
Stark Ave
Justin Ave
Ryan Ave
Maplerow Ave
Mullins Ave
Whitmore Ave
Pheasant Ave
Brandy Wine Cr
Hillburn
Milo
Mission
Trinidad Ave
Sierra Ave
Stark
Webb Ave
Marlin Ave
Werner Ave
Gridly Ave
Benning Ave
Tuell
Lamont Ave
Laughlin Dr
Hoehn
Rypens Dr
Trail
Granada
Walker Village Dr
Fay Ave
Lancaster Ave
Clover Crest Ave
Leonard
NW
NE
SW
SE

4 Mile Rd
3 Mile Rd
I- 96
Walker Ave
Bristol Ave
Indian Creek Ridge Rd
Indian Mill Creek
Brandy Wine Creek
Richmond
Leonard
NW
NE
SW
SE

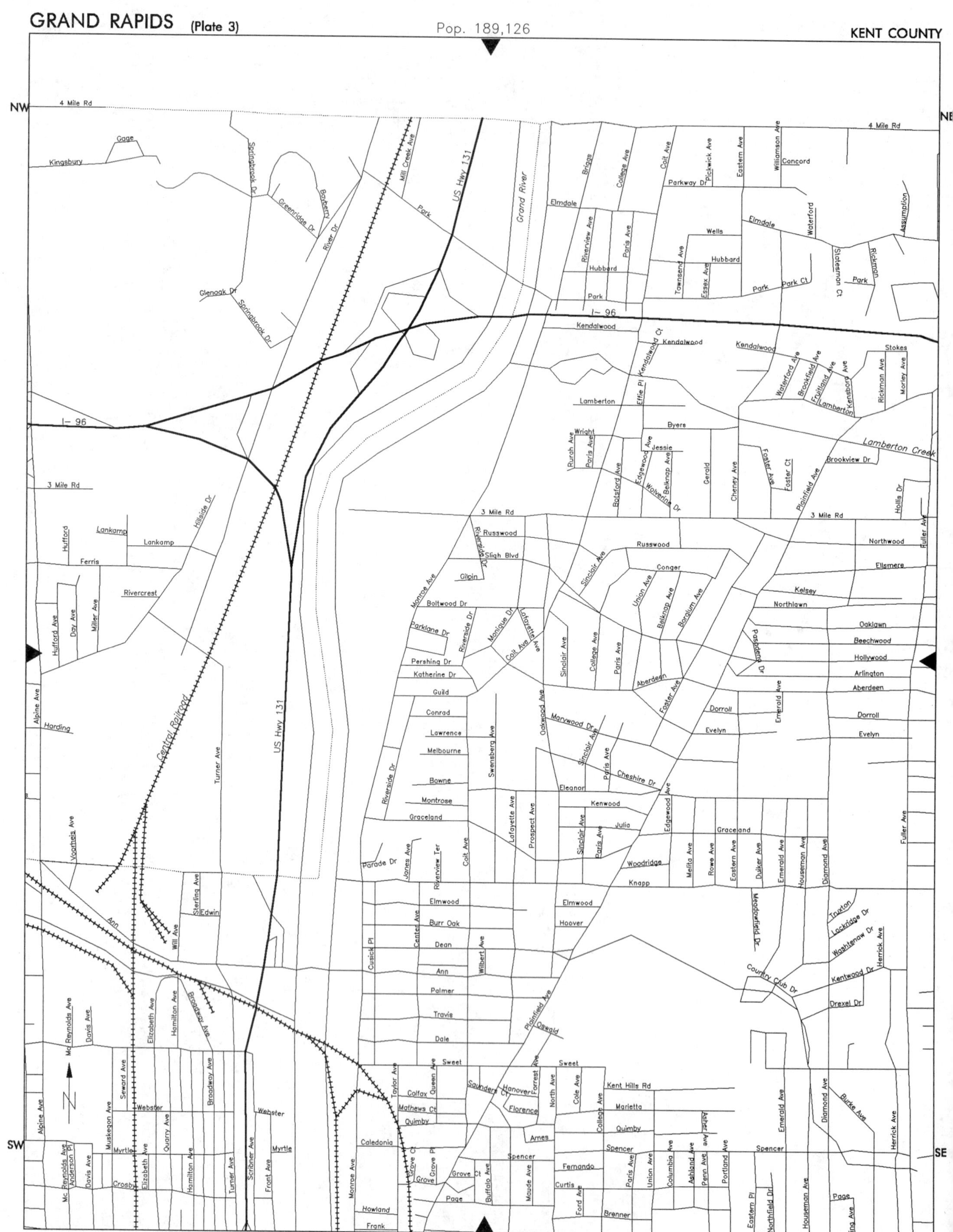
4 Mile Rd
Kingsbury
Gage
Springbrook Dr
Greenridge Dr
Bayberry
River Dr
Mill Creek Ave
US Hwy 131
Park
Grand River
Elmdale
Briggs
College Ave
Coit Ave
Pickwick Ave
Eastern Ave
Williamson Ave
Concord
Parkway Dr
Riverview Ave
Paris Ave
Hubbard
Wells
Townsend Ave
Essex Ave
Waterford
Assumption
Statesman Ct
Rickman
Park Ct
Glenoak Dr
I-96
Kendalwood
Kendalwood Ct
Stokes
Lamberton
Effie Pl
Waterford Ave
Brookfield Ave
Fruitland Ave
Kensboro
Morley Ave
Byers
Wright
Rurah Ave
Jessie
Edgewood Ave
Belknap Ave
Wolverine Dr
Botsford Ave
Gerald
Cheney Ave
Foster Ave
Foster Ct
Plainfield Ave
Lamberton Creek
Brookview Dr
Hollis Dr
3 Mile Rd
Hufford
Lankamp
Hillside Dr
Ferris
Russwood
Riverside Dr
Sligh Blvd
Northwood
Fuller Ave
Ellsmere
Conger
Sinclair Ave
Gilpin
Monroe Ave
Kelsey
Union Ave
Borglum Ave
Northlawn
Rivercrest
Boltwood Dr
Hufford Ave
Day Ave
Miller Ave
Parklane Dr
Monique Dr
Lafayette Ave
Oaklawn
Beechwood
Hollywood
Pasadena Dr
Pershing Dr
Katherine Dr
Aberdeen
Arlington
Alpine Ave
Guild
Oakwood Ave
Marywood Dr
Dorroll
Emerald Ave
Harding
Central Railroad
Conrad
Lawrence
Swensberg Ave
Evelyn
Melbourne
Turner Ave
Cheshire Dr
Bowne
Eleanor
Montrose
Kenwood
Graceland
Julia
Prospect Ave
Voorheis Ave
Parade Dr
James Ave
Riverview Ter
Woodridge
Melita Ave
Rowe Ave
Dukes Ave
Houseman Ave
Diamond Ave
Knapp
Sterling Ave
Edwin
Elmwood
Meadowfield Dr
Truxton
Lockridge Dr
Hoover
Ann
Burr Oak
Washtenaw Dr
Herrick Ave
Will Ave
Dean
Cusick Pl
Wilbert Ave
Center Ave
Kentwood Dr
Country Club Dr
Palmer
Drexel Dr
Mc Reynolds Ave
Davis Ave
Elizabeth Ave
Hamilton Ave
Broadway Ave
Travis
Oswald
Dale
Sweet
Seward Ave
Taylor Ave
Queen Ave
Saunders Ct
Hanover
Forrest
North Ave
Cole Ave
Kent Hills Rd
Burke Ave
Webster
Colfax
Florence
Marietta
Mathews Ct
Quimby
Asher Ave
Muskegon Ave
Quarry Ave
Caledonia
Ames
Myrtle
Anderson Pl
Grove Ct
Grove Pl
Grove
Spencer
Fernando
Columbia Ave
Ashland Ave
Penn Ave
Portland Ave
Crosby
Scribner Ave
Front Ave
Buffalo Ave
Maude Ave
Curtis
Ford Ave
Eastern Pl
Northfield Dr
Page
Howland
Brenner
Frank
NW
NE
SW
SE

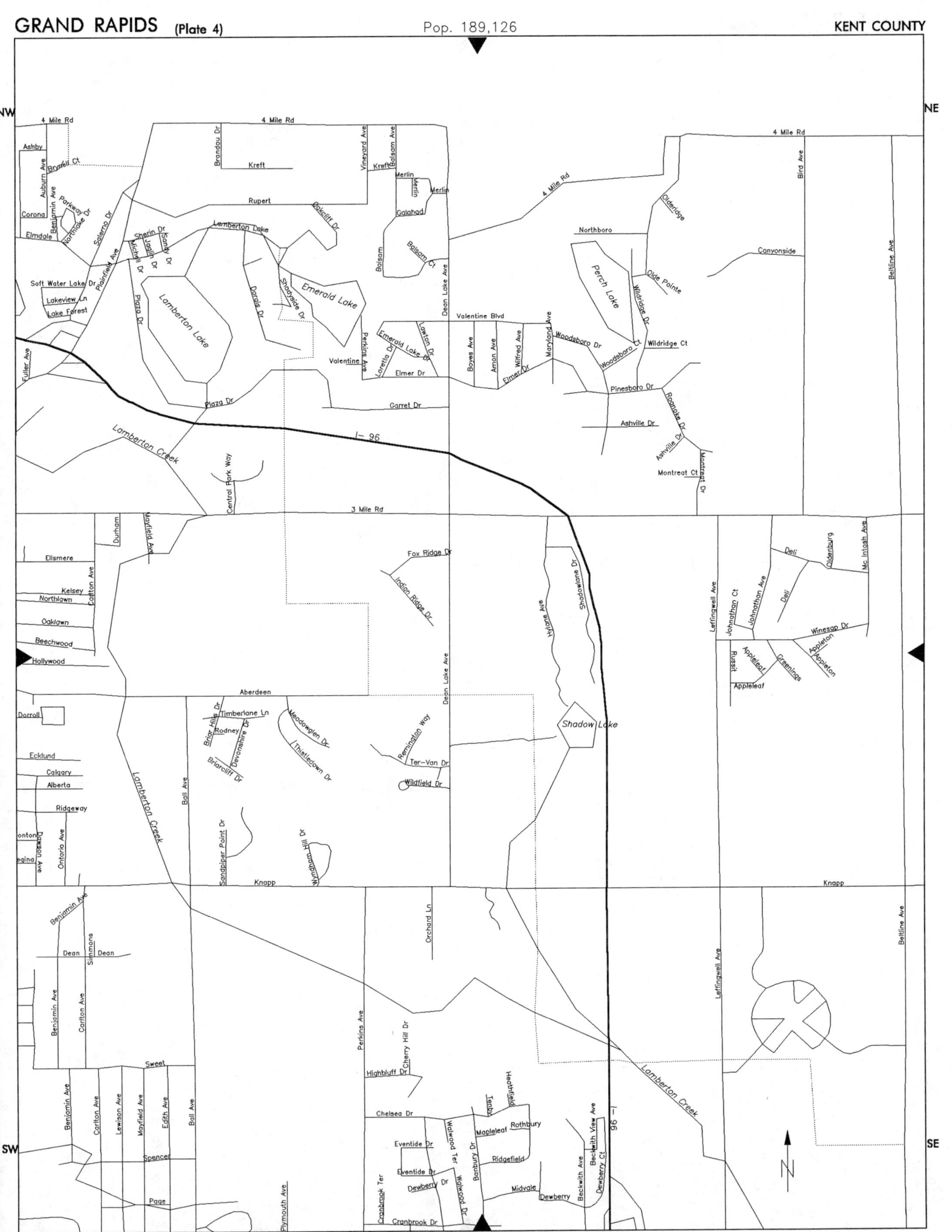
NW
NE
SW
SE
4 Mile Rd
Ashby
Auburn Ave
Brymeli Ct
Benjamin Ave
Parkway
Corona
Northlake Dr
Elmdale
Salerno Dr
Brandau Dr
Kreft
Vineyard Ave
Balsam Ave
Merlin
Galahad
Rupert
Oakcliff Dr
Lamberton Lake
Sherin Dr
Joslin Dr
Sandy Dr
Mitchell Dr
Plainfield Ave
Soft Water Lake Dr
Lakeview Ln
Lake Forest
Plaza Dr
Lamberton Lake
Darais Dr
Shadyside Dr
Emerald Lake
Balsam Ct
Dean Lake Ave
Perkins Ave
Emerald Lake Dr
Lawton Dr
Loretta Dr
Valentine
Elmer Dr
Valentine Blvd
Boyes Ave
Amon Ave
Wilfred Ave
Elmer Dr
Maryland Ave
Woodsboro Dr
Woodsboro Ct
Wildridge Ct
Wildridge Dr
Perch Lake
Olde Pointe
Northboro
Olderidge
Canyonside
Bird Ave
Beltline Ave
Pinesboro Dr
Roanoke Dr
Ashville Dr
Montreat Ct
Montreat Dr
Garret Dr
Fuller Ave
I- 96
Lamberton Creek
Central Park Way
3 Mile Rd
Durham
Mayfield Ave
Ellsmere
Carlton Ave
Kelsey
Northlawn
Oaklawn
Beechwood
Hollywood
Fox Ridge Dr
Indian Ridge Dr
Hylane Ave
Shadowlane Dr
Leffingwell Ave
Johnathan Ct
Johnathan Ave
Deli
Oldenburg
Mc Intosh Ave
Winesap Dr
Appleton
Russit
Appleleaf
Greenings
Aberdeen
Dorroll
Briar Hills Dr
Timberlane Ln
Rodney
Devonshire Dr
Briarcliff Dr
Meadowglen Dr
Thistledown Dr
Remington Way
Ter-Van Dr
Wildfield Dr
Shadow Lake
Ecklund
Calgary
Alberta
Ridgeway
Lamberton Creek
Ball Ave
Ontario Ave
Dawson Ave
Sandpiper Point Dr
Wyndham Hill Dr
Knapp
Benjamin Ave
Dean
Simmons
Orchard Ln
Carlton Ave
Perkins Ave
Cherry Hill Dr
Highbluff Dr
Sweet
Lewison Ave
Mayfield Ave
Edith Ave
Ball Ave
Spencer
Page
Plymouth Ave
Chelsea Dr
Eventide Dr
Walwood Ter
Banbury Dr
Tenby
Heathfield
Rothbury
Mapleleaf
Ridgefield
Midvale
Dewberry
Beckwith Ave
Beckwith View Ave
Dewberry Ct
Cranbrook Ter
Cranbrook Dr
Walwood Dr
Lamberton Creek
N

GRAND RAPIDS (Plate 5) Pop. 189,126 KENT COUNTY

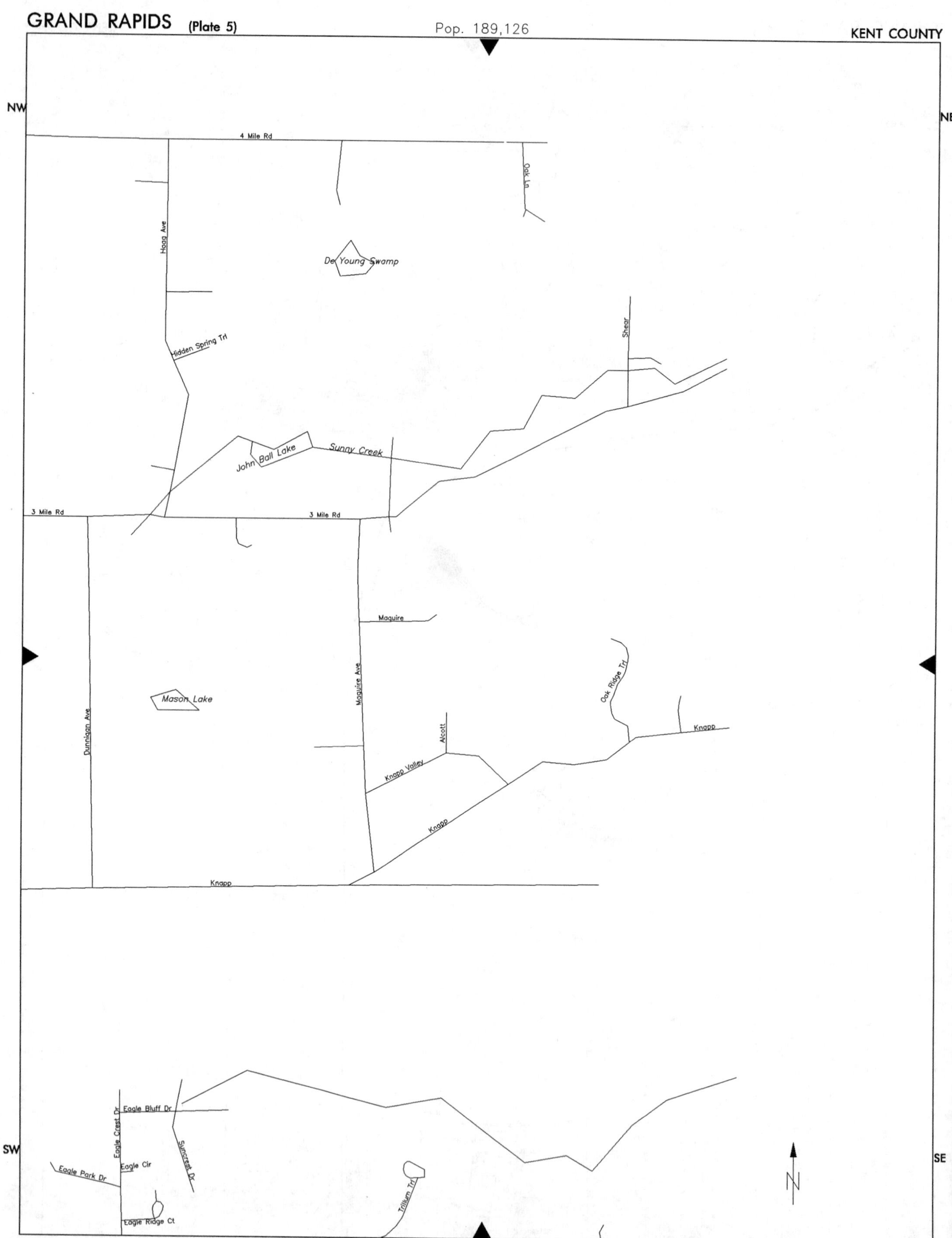

NW
NE
SW
SE
Apple Blossom Dr
River Ct
Mayapple
Pippin Dr
McIntosh Ct
Shiwasse
Winesap Dr
Russett Ct
Green Apple
Jonathan Ct
Red Apple Ct
Old Farm
Crabapple Ct
Apple Hollow Ct
Apple Jack
Appletree Ct
Apple Brook Ct
Appleridge Ct
Kings Row Ct
Imperial Dr
Cummings Ct
Ironwood Ct
Waybury
Kinney Ave
Edenboro
Grand Blvd
Marlboro
Kenowa
Clinton
Lasalle
Macomb
Ferndale Ave
Clayton Ave
Cloverdale Ave
Wilson Ave
Faircrest Ave
St Clair Ave
Parkside Ave
Chesterfield Blvd
Hampton Ln
Barkwood Ct
Service Dr
Standale Pl
Warrington
Lake Michigan Dr
Marlboro Dr
Fairway Dr
Northway Dr
Lincoln Lawns Dr
Westway Dr
Maplerow Ave
Sunset Hills Ave
10th Ave
Kusterer Ave
Allison Ave
Nixon Ave
Brownwood Ave
Rosalie Ave
Van Ess Ave
Barber Ter
Bay Berry Point Dr
Maynard Ave
Manzana
Manzana Ct
Rolling Greene Dr
Ohman Ave
Alewa Dr
Walker City
Sunset Hills
Schoolcraft
Hartford
Lincrest
Athlone
O Brien
Fennessey
Butterworth Dr
Sawyer
Kinney
White Pine
Hall
Su-Lew
N

Pop. 189,126

KENT COUNTY

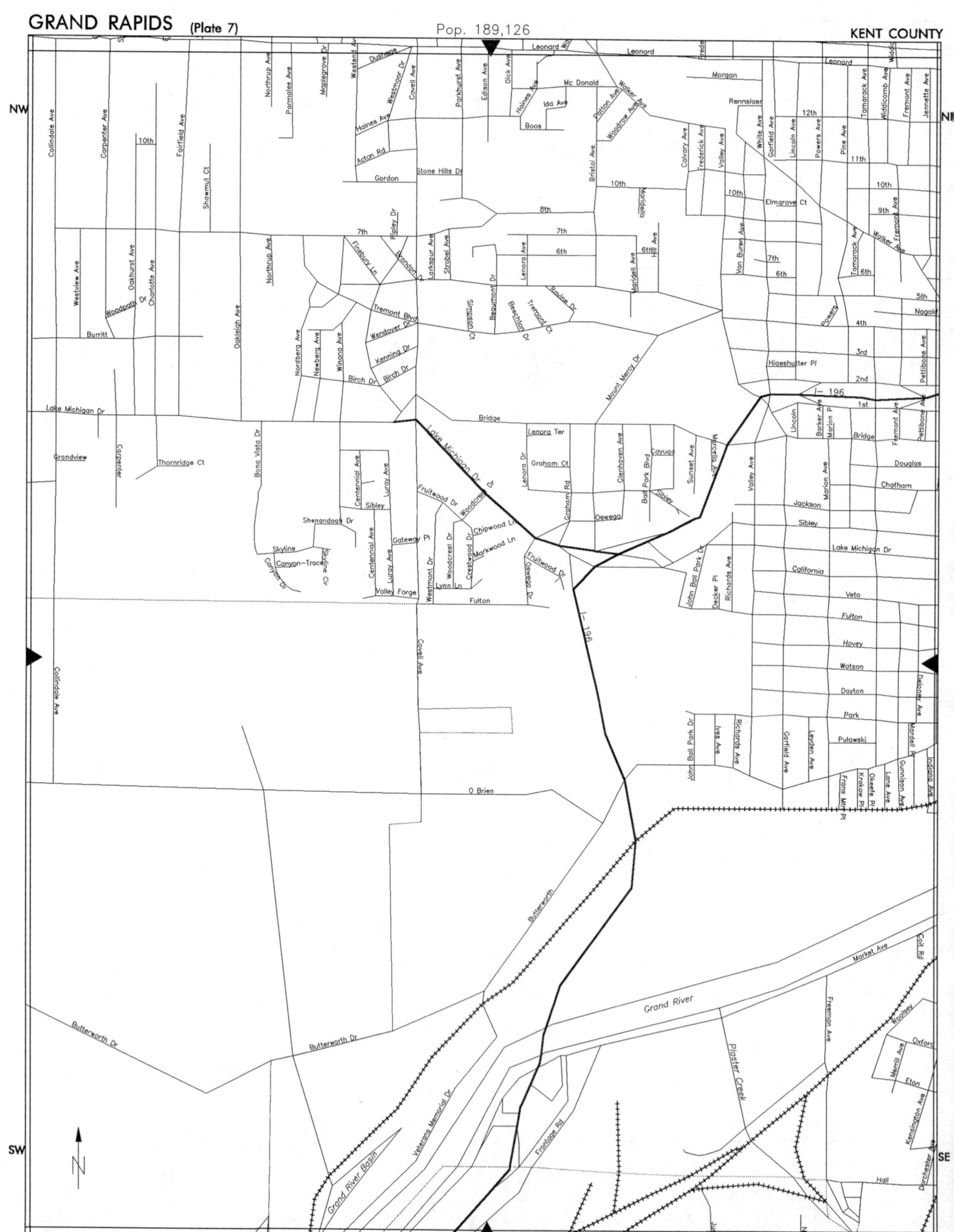

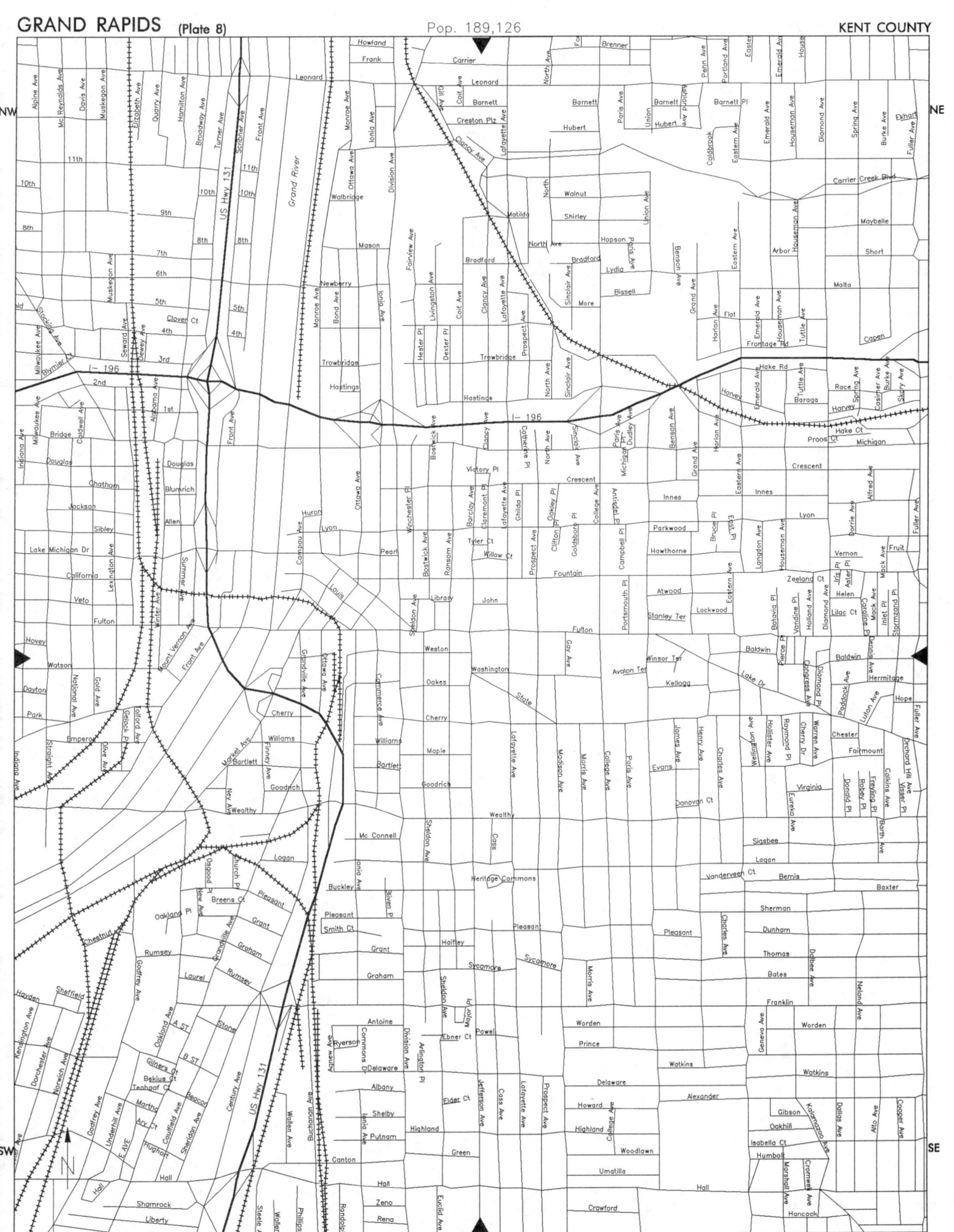
GRAND RAPIDS (Plate 8)
Pop. 189,126
KENT COUNTY
NW
NE
SW
SE
I- 196
US Hwy 131
Grand River
Howland
Frank
Carrier
Leonard
Brenner
Barnett
Barnett Pl
Creston Plz
Hubert
Clancy Ave
Lafayette Ave
North Ave
Paris Ave
Union
Penn Ave
Portland Ave
Emerald Ave
Houseman Ave
Diamond Ave
Spring Ave
Burke Ave
Fuller Ave
Ekhart
Coldbrook
Eastern Ave
Carrier Creek Blvd
Walnut
Shirley
Matilda
Maybelle
Hopson
Bradford
Lydia
Bissell
More
Benson Ave
Grand Ave
Arbor
Short
Malta
Flat
Frontage Rd
Tuttle Ave
Capen
Hake Rd
Race
Baraga
Harvey
Casimer Ave
Skory Ave
Alpine Ave
Mc Reynolds Ave
Davis Ave
Muskegon Ave
Elizabeth Ave
Quarry Ave
Hamilton Ave
Broadway Ave
Turner Ave
Scribner Ave
Front Ave
Monroe Ave
Ionia Ave
Ottawa Ave
Division Ave
Walbridge
Mason
Fairview Ave
Livingston Ave
Coit Ave
Gill Ave
11th
10th
9th
8th
7th
6th
5th
4th
3rd
2nd
1st
Clover Ct
Newberry
Bond Ave
Hester Pl
Dexter Pl
Prospect Ave
Sinclair Ave
Trowbridge
Hastings
Stocking Ave
Milwaukee Ave
Blumrich
Seward Ave
Dewey Ave
Alabama Ave
Indiana Ave
Bridge
Caldwell Ave
Douglas
Chatham
Jackson
Allen
Sibley
Lake Michigan Dr
Lexington Ave
California
Summer Ave
Veto
Fulton
Winter Ave
Hovey
Watson
Dayton
Park
Emperor
National Ave
Gold Ave
Straight Ave
Olive Ave
Tolford Ave
Gelock Pl
Mount Vernon Ave
Huron
Lyon
Campau Ave
Pearl
Louis
Bostwick Ave
Winchester Pl
Barclay Ave
Claremont Pl
Victory Pl
Catherine Pl
Crescent
Ghilda Pl
Oakley Pl
Goldsboro Pl
College Ave
Antisdel Pl
Michigan
Dudley
Campbell Pl
Innes
Parkwood
Bruce Pl
East Pl
Langdon Ave
Alfred Ave
Dorrie Ave
Ransom Ave
Tyler Ct
Willow Ct
Clifton Pl
Hawthorne
Vernon
Fruit
Fountain
Mack Ave
Zeeland Ct
Iris Pl
Aster Pl
Library
John
Sheldon Ave
Portsmouth Pl
Atwood
Lockwood
Stanley Ter
Batavia Pl
Vandine Pl
Holland Ave
Helen
Lilac Ct
Caroline Pl
Inlet Pl
Stormzand Pl
Weston
Washington
State
Gay Ave
Avalon Ter
Winsor Ter
Kellogg
Baldwin
Pierce Pl
Lake Dr
Congress Ave
Diamond Pl
Dennis Ave
Hermitage
Paddock Ave
Luton Ave
Hope
Grandville Ave
Commerce Ave
Oakes
Cherry
Williams
Maple
Bartlett
Market Ave
Finney Ave
Goodrich
Ney Ave
Wealthy
Madison Ave
Morris Ave
James Ave
Henry Ave
Charles Ave
Wellington Ave
Hollister Ave
Raymond Pl
Cherry Dr
Warren Ave
Chester
Fairmount
Orchard Hill Ave
Evans
Donovan Ct
Eureka Ave
Virginia
Donald Pl
Robey Pl
Freyling Pl
Calkins Ave
Visser Pl
Barth Ave
Mc Connell
Cass
Logan
Sigsbee
Osgood Pl
Church Pl
Heritage Commons
Vanderveen Ct
Bemis
Baxter
Buckley
Bliven Pl
New Ave
Breens Ct
Pleasant
Oakland Pl
Grant
Smith Ct
Sherman
Dunham
Chestnut
Rumsey
Graham
Halfley
Sycamore
Thomas
Delbee Ave
Bates
Godfrey Ave
Laurel
Hayden
Sheffield
Franklin
Neland Ave
Oakland Ave
A ST
Stone
Antoine
Powell
Major Pl
Worden
Ebner Ct
Geneva Ave
Kensington Ave
Dorchester Ave
Norwich Ave
Ryerson
Agnew Ave
Commons Dr
Arlington Pl
Prince
Gilners Ct
B ST
Watkins
Bekius Ct
Tenhoaf Ct
Delaware
Albany
Alexander
Century Ave
Elder Ct
Jefferson Ave
Martha
Beacon
Caulfield Ave
Underhill Ave
Ary Ct
Sheridan Ave
Wolfen Ave
Buchanan Ave
Shelby
Howard
Gibson
Kalamazoo Ave
Dallas Ave
Alto Ave
Cooper Ave
Highland
Oakhill
Putnam
Isabella Ct
E AVE
Hughart
Green
Woodlawn
Humbolt
Canton
Umatilla
Marshall Ave
Cromwell Ave
Hall
Zeno
Crawford
Shamrock
Liberty
Steele Ave
Wallen
Phillips
Randolph
Rena
Euclid Ave
Hancock

GRAND RAPIDS (Plate 9)

Pop. 189,126

KENT COUNTY

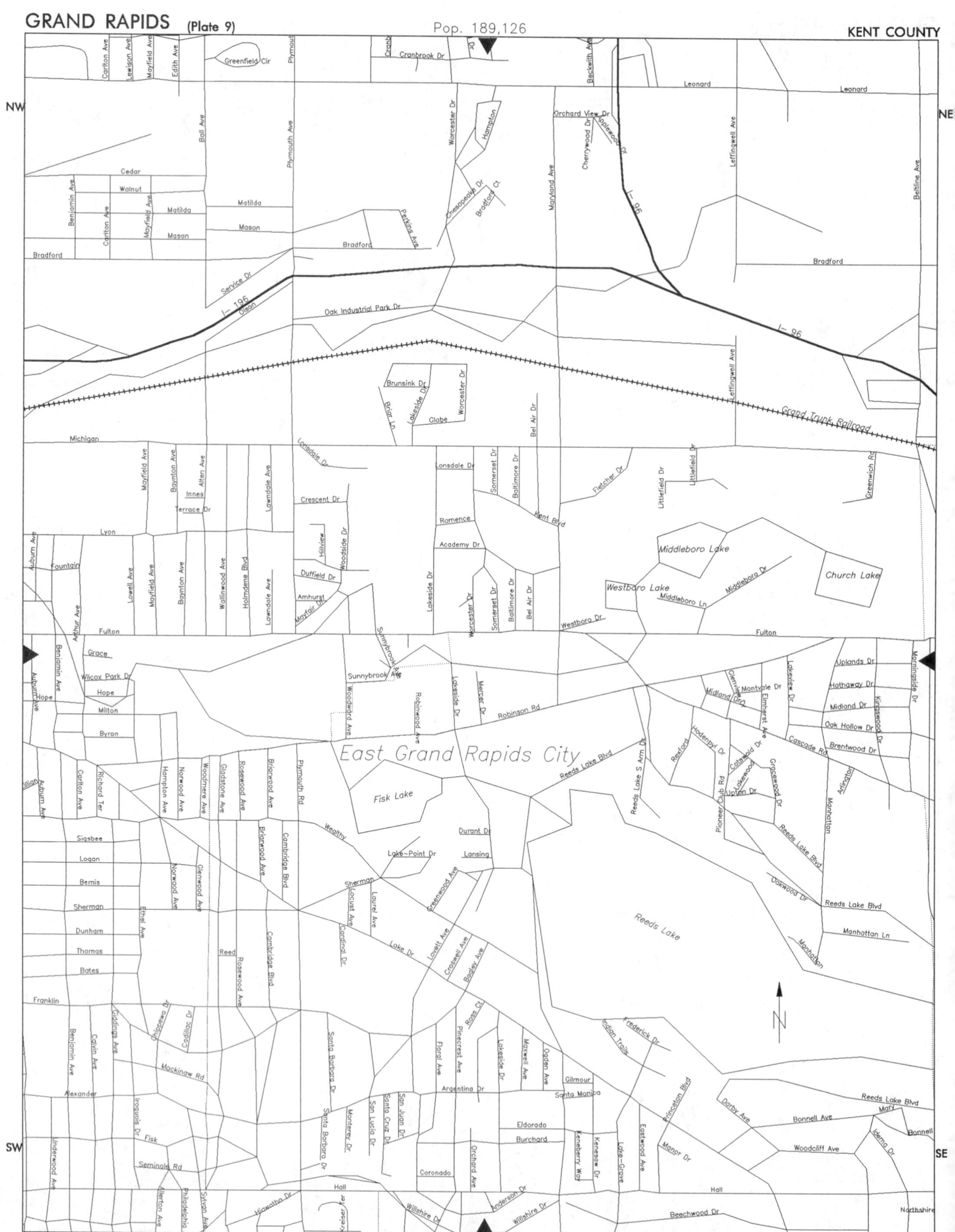

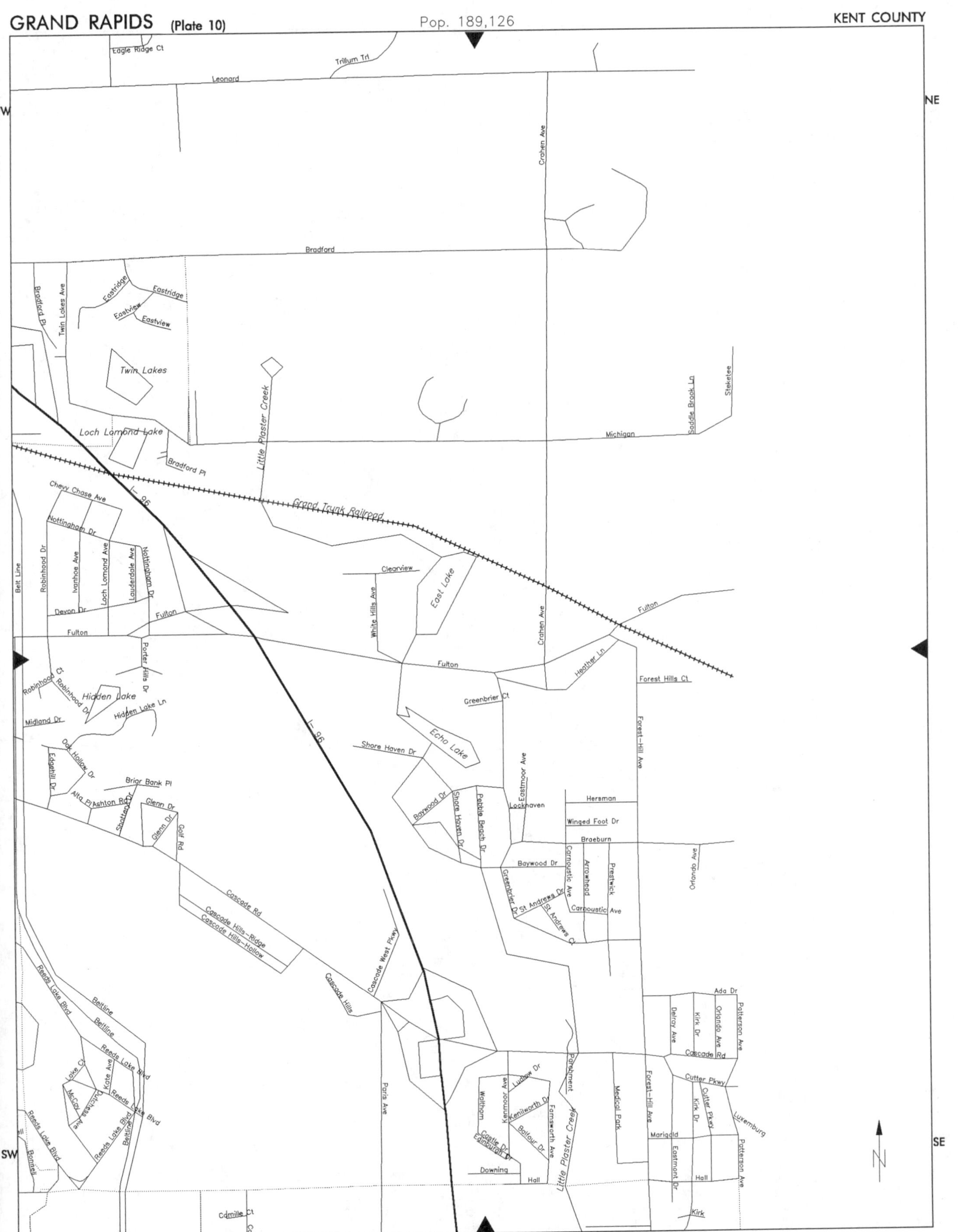

NW
NE
SW
SE
Eagle Ridge Ct
Trillum Trl
Leonard
Crahen Ave
Bradford
Bradford Pl
Twin Lakes Ave
Eastridge
Eastview
Twin Lakes
Little Plaster Creek
Saddle Brook Ln
Steketee
Michigan
Loch Lomond Lake
Bradford Pl
Grand Trunk Railroad
I-96
Chevy Chase Ave
Nottingham Dr
Robinhood Dr
Ivanhoe Ave
Loch Lomond Ave
Lauderdale Ave
Belt Line
Devon Dr
Fulton
Clearview
East Lake
White Hills Ave
Porter Hills Dr
Heather Ln
Forest Hills Ct
Robinhood Ct
Hidden Lake
Hidden Lake Ln
Midland Dr
Greenbrier Ct
Forest-Hill Ave
Echo Lake
Shore Haven Dr
Oak Hollow Dr
Edgehill Dr
Briar Bank Pl
Eastmoor Ave
Alta Pl
Ashton Rd
Glenn Dr
Golf Rd
Baywood Dr
Shore Haven Dr
Pebble Beach Dr
Lockhaven
Hersman
Winged Foot Dr
Braeburn
Greenbrier Dr
Carnoustic Ave
Arrowhead
Prestwick
St Andrews Dr
St Andrews Ct
Orlando Ave
Cascade Rd
Cascade Hills Ridge
Cascade Hills Hollow
Cascade West Pkwy
Cascade Hills
Reeds Lake Blvd
Beltline
Lake Ct
Kate Ave
McCoy
Duchess Ave
Bonnell
Paris Ave
Ada Dr
Delroy Ave
Kirk Dr
Orlando Ave
Patterson Ave
Cutter Pkwy
Luxemburg
Parchment
Medical Park
Waltham
Kenmoor Ave
Ludlow Dr
Kenilworth Dr
Farnsworth Ave
Balfour Dr
Castle Dr
Edinburgh Dr
Downing
Hall
Marigold
Eastmont Dr
Camille Ct
Kirk
N

GRAND RAPIDS (Plate 11)

Pop. 189,126

KENT COUNTY

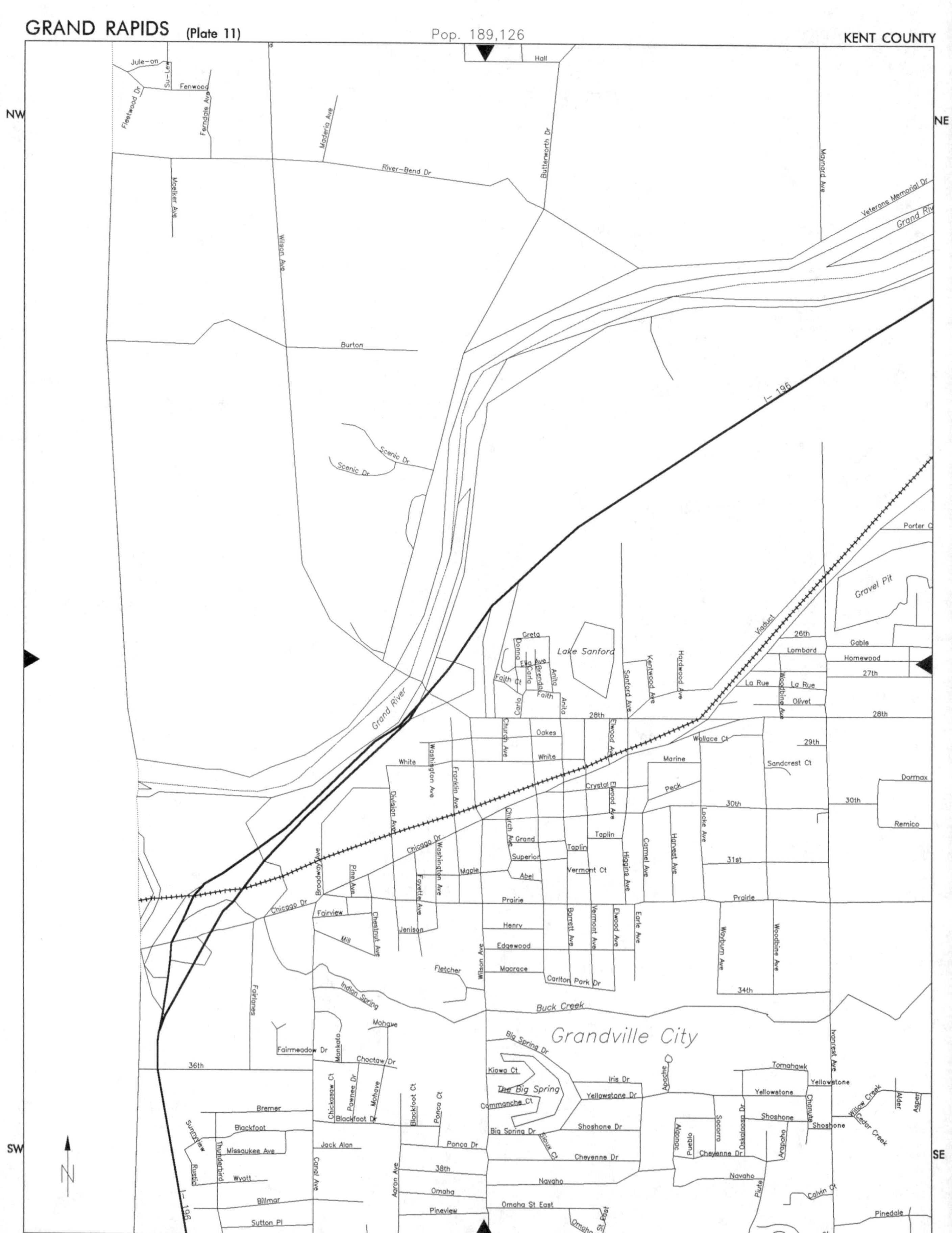

Grand River
Frontage Rd
I-196
Chicago Dr
Batties Lake
Porter Lake
Lamar Lake
Wyoming City
Buck Creek
Porter
28th
36th
Burton
Burlingame Ave
Michael Ave

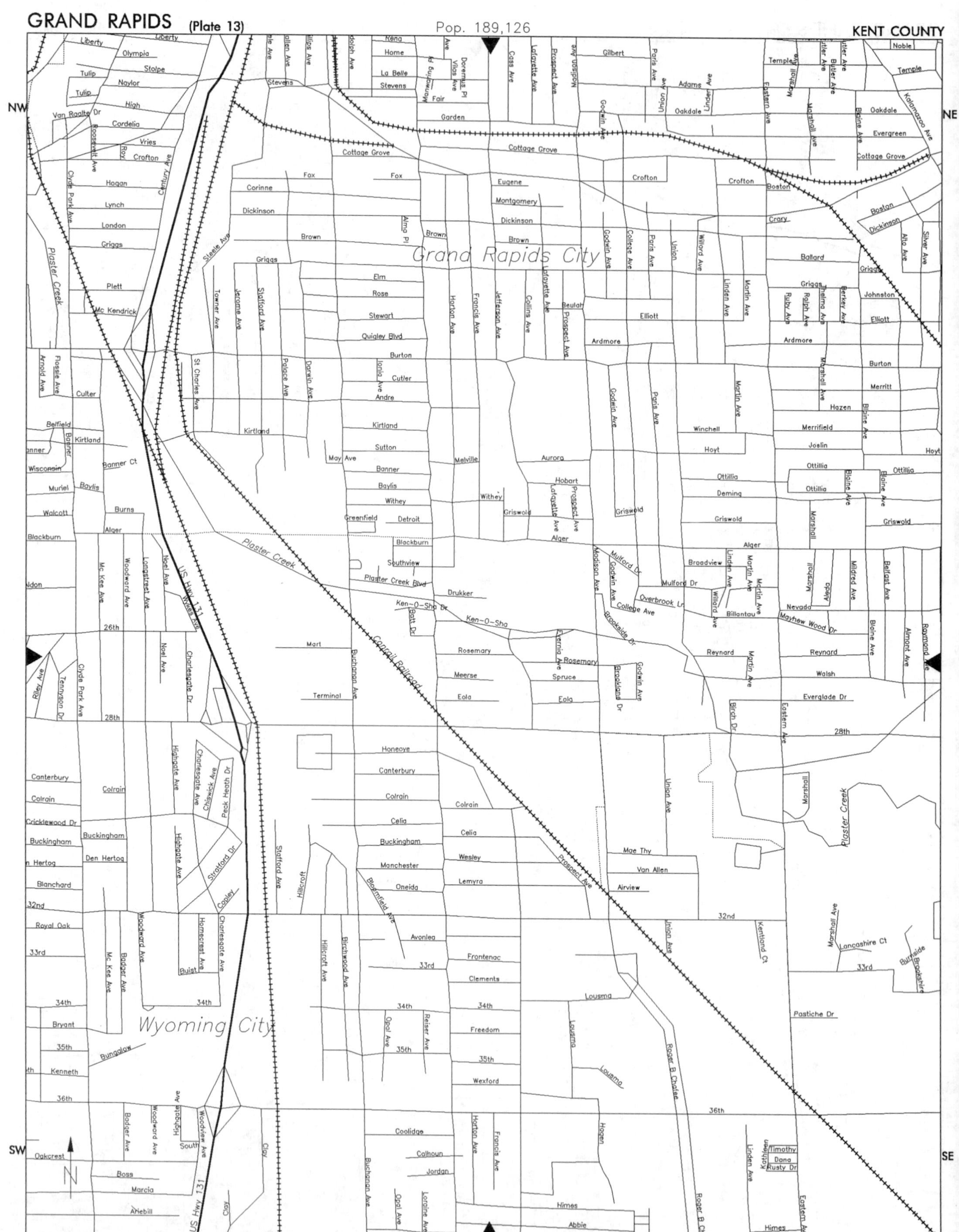
NW
NE
SW
SE
N
Grand Rapids City
Wyoming City
Plaster Creek
Conrail Railroad
U.S. Hwy 131
Liberty
Olympia
Stolpe
Tulip
Naylor
High
Van Raalte Dr
Cordelia
Vries
Crofton
Roosevelt Ave
Century Ave
Hogan
Lynch
London
Griggs
Clyde Park Ave
Plett
Mc Kendrick
Steele Ave
Towner Ave
Jerome Ave
Stafford Ave
Stevens
Home
La Belle
Rena
Fair
Garden
Cottage Grove
Fox
Corinne
Dickinson
Brown
Alma Pl
Elm
Rose
Stewart
Quigley Blvd
Burton
Cutler
Andre
Ionia Ave
Palace Ave
Darwin Ave
St Charles Ave
Kirtland
Sutton
May Ave
Banner
Baylis
Withey
Greenfield
Detroit
Blackburn
Southview
Plaster Creek Blvd
Eugene
Montgomery
Horton Ave
Francis Ave
Jefferson Ave
Collins Ave
Lafayette Ave
Beulah
Prospect Ave
Cass Ave
Madison Ave
Gilbert
Paris Ave
Union Ave
Adams
Oakdale
Godwin Ave
College Ave
Willard Ave
Linden Ave
Martin Ave
Elliott
Ardmore
Winchell
Hoyt
Ottillia
Deming
Griswold
Alger
Broadview
Mulford Dr
Overbrook Ln
Billantau
Eastern Ave
Temple
Noble
Marshall Ave
Blaine Ave
Kalamazoo Ave
Evergreen
Boston
Crary
Ballard
Johnston
Ruby Ave
Ralph Ave
Thelma Ave
Berkey Ave
Alto Ave
Silver Ave
Merritt
Hazen
Merrifield
Joslin
Nevada
Mayhew Wood Dr
Reynard
Walsh
Everglade Dr
Mildred Ave
Belfast Ave
Almont Ave
Raymond Ave
Arnold Ave
Flossie Ave
Culter
Belfield
Banner Ct
Wisconsin
Muriel
Walcott
Burns
Mc Kee Ave
Woodward Ave
Longstreet Ave
Noel Ave
Wykes Ave
26th
Charlesgate Dr
Riley Ave
Tennyson Dr
28th
Melville
Aurora
Hobart
Drukker
Ken-O-Sha Dr
Batt Dr
Ken-O-Sha
Brookside Dr
Rosemary
Meerse
Eola
Spruce
Evernia Ave
Mart
Terminal
Buchanan Ave
Birch Dr
Honeoye
Canterbury
Colrain
Celia
Buckingham
Manchester
Oneida
Wesley
Lemyra
Hillcroft
Bloomfield Ave
Highgate Ave
Chiswick Ave
Peck Heath Dr
Stratford Dr
Copley
Cricklewood Dr
Den Hertog
Blanchard
32nd
Royal Oak
33rd
Badger Ave
Homecrest Ave
Buist
Mae Thy
Van Allen
Airview
Avonlea
Frontenac
Clements
Kentland Ct
Lancashire Ct
Burnside
Brookshire
34th
Lousma
Pastiche Dr
Bryant
35th
Bungalow
Kenneth
36th
Opal Ave
Reiser Ave
Freedom
Wexford
Roger B Chaffee
Hogen
Coolidge
Calhoun
Jordan
Lorraine Ave
Himes
Abbie
Oakcrest
Boss
Marcia
Ariebill
South
Woodview Ave
Clay
Timothy
Dana
Rusty Dr
Kathleen

Pop. 189,126

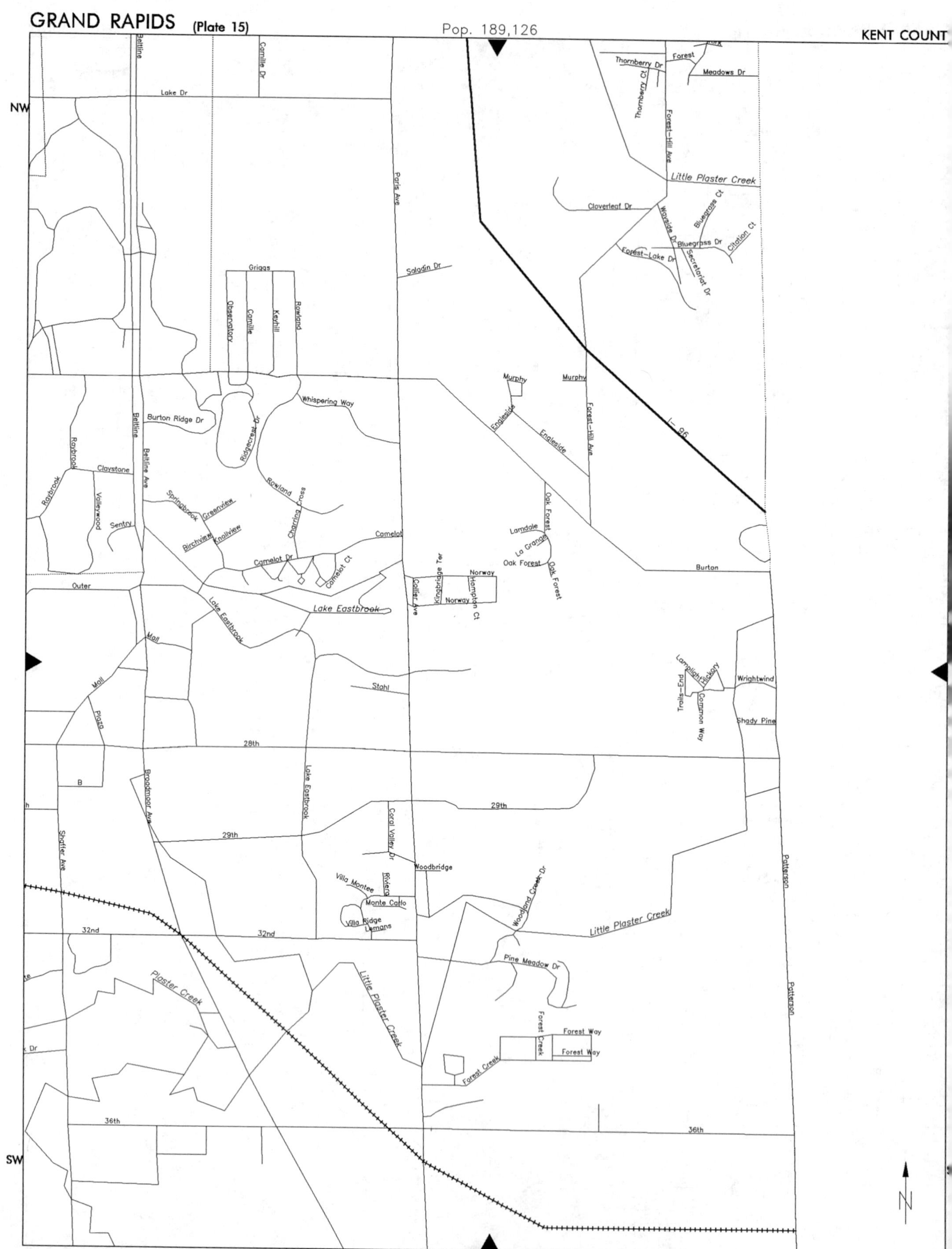

Lake Dr
Camille Dr
Beltline
Thornberry Dr
Forest
Meadows Dr
Thornberry Ct
Forest-Hill Ave
Little Plaster Creek
Cloverleaf Dr
Wayside Dr
Bluegrass Ct
Bluegrass Dr
Citation Ct
Forest-Lake Dr
Secretariat Dr
Paris Ave
Saladin Dr
Griggs
Observatory
Camille
Keyhill
Rowland
Murphy
Whispering Way
Burton Ridge Dr
Ridgecrest Dr
Englesside
Forest-Hill Ave
I-96
Raybrook
Claystone
Beltline Ave
Valleywood
Sentry
Springbrook
Greenview
Birchview
Knollview
Charring Cross
Camelot
Camelot Dr
Camelot Ct
Oak Forest
Lamdale
La Grange
Oak Forest
Burton
Outer
Lake Eastbrook
Collier Ave
Kingsbridge Ter
Norway
Hampton Ct
Mall
Stahl
Plaza
Lamplight
Hickory
Trails-End
Common Way
Wrightwind
Shady Pine
28th
B
Broadmoor Ave
Lake Eastbrook
29th
Coral Valley Dr
Shaffer Ave
Woodbridge
Villa Montee
Riviera
Monte Carlo
Villa Ridge
Lemans
Woodland Creek Dr
32nd
Plaster Creek
Little Plaster Creek
Pine Meadow Dr
Patterson
Forest Creek
Forest Way
36th
NW
SW
N

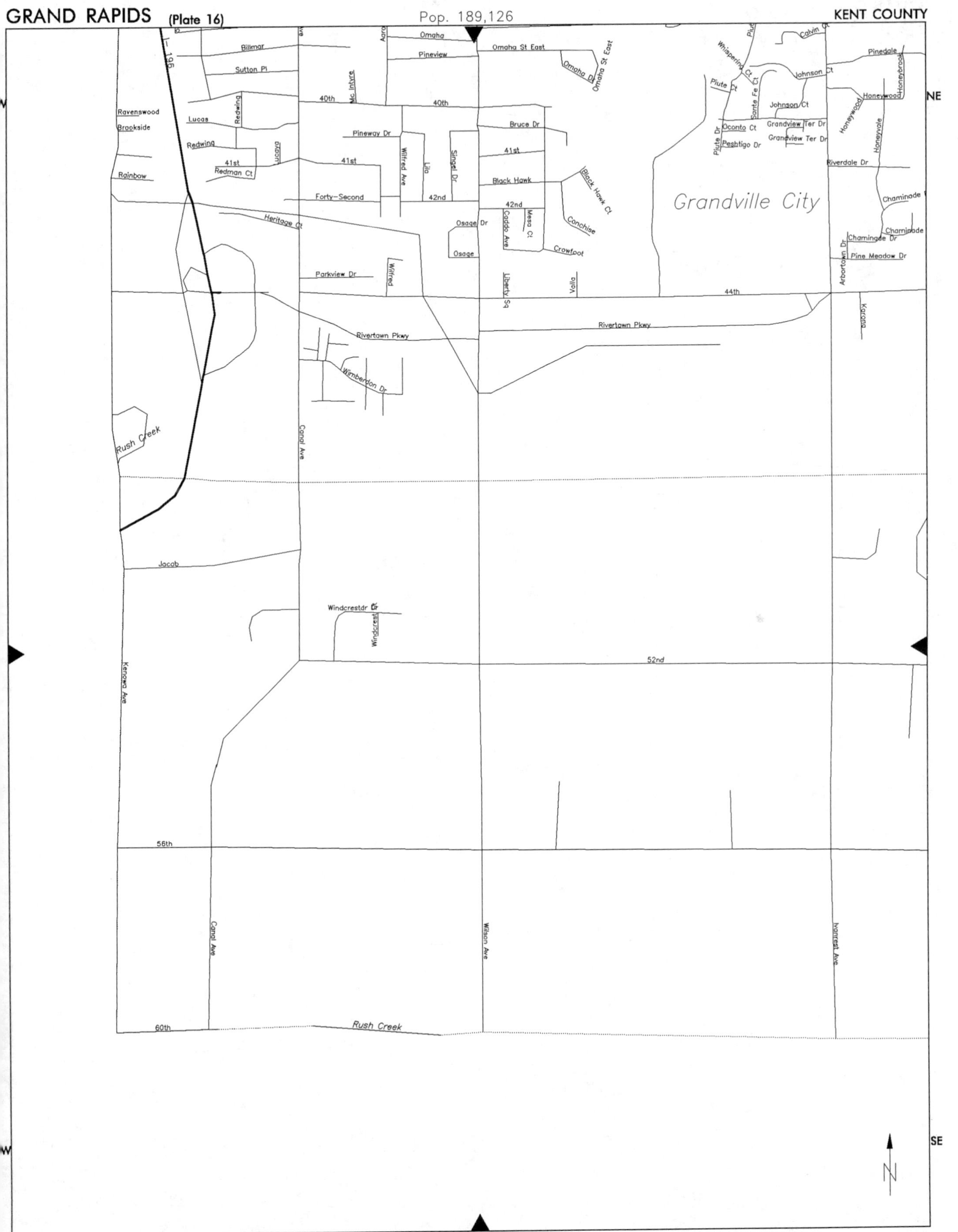
I-196
Billmar
Sutton Pl
Omaha
Pineview
Omaha St East
Omaha Dr
Omaha St East
40th
Mc Intyre
40th
Ravenswood
Brookside
Lucas
Redwing
Redwing
Pineway Dr
Bruce Dr
41st
Redman Ct
41st
Wilfred Ave
Lila
Singel Dr
41st
Rainbow
Black Hawk
Black Hawk Ct
Forty-Second
42nd
42nd
Heritage Ct
Osage Dr
Caddo Ave
Mesa Ct
Conchise
Osage
Crowfoot
Parkview Dr
Wilfred
Liberty Sq
Valla
44th
Rivertown Pkwy
Rivertown Pkwy
Wimberdon Dr
Rush Creek
Canal Ave
Jacob
Windcrestdr Dr
Windcrest
52nd
Kenowa Ave
56th
Canal Ave
Wilson Ave
Ivanrest Ave
60th
Rush Creek
Grandville City
Calvin Ct
Whispering Ct
Piute Ct
Johnson Ct
Johnson Ct
Pinedale
Honeybrook
Honeywood
Honeywood
Honeyvale
Oconto Ct
Grandview Ter Dr
Grandview Ter Dr
Piute Dr
Peshtigo Dr
Sante Fe Ct
Riverdale Dr
Chaminade
Chaminade
Chaminade Dr
Pine Meadow Dr
Arbortown Dr
Karona
NE
SE
N

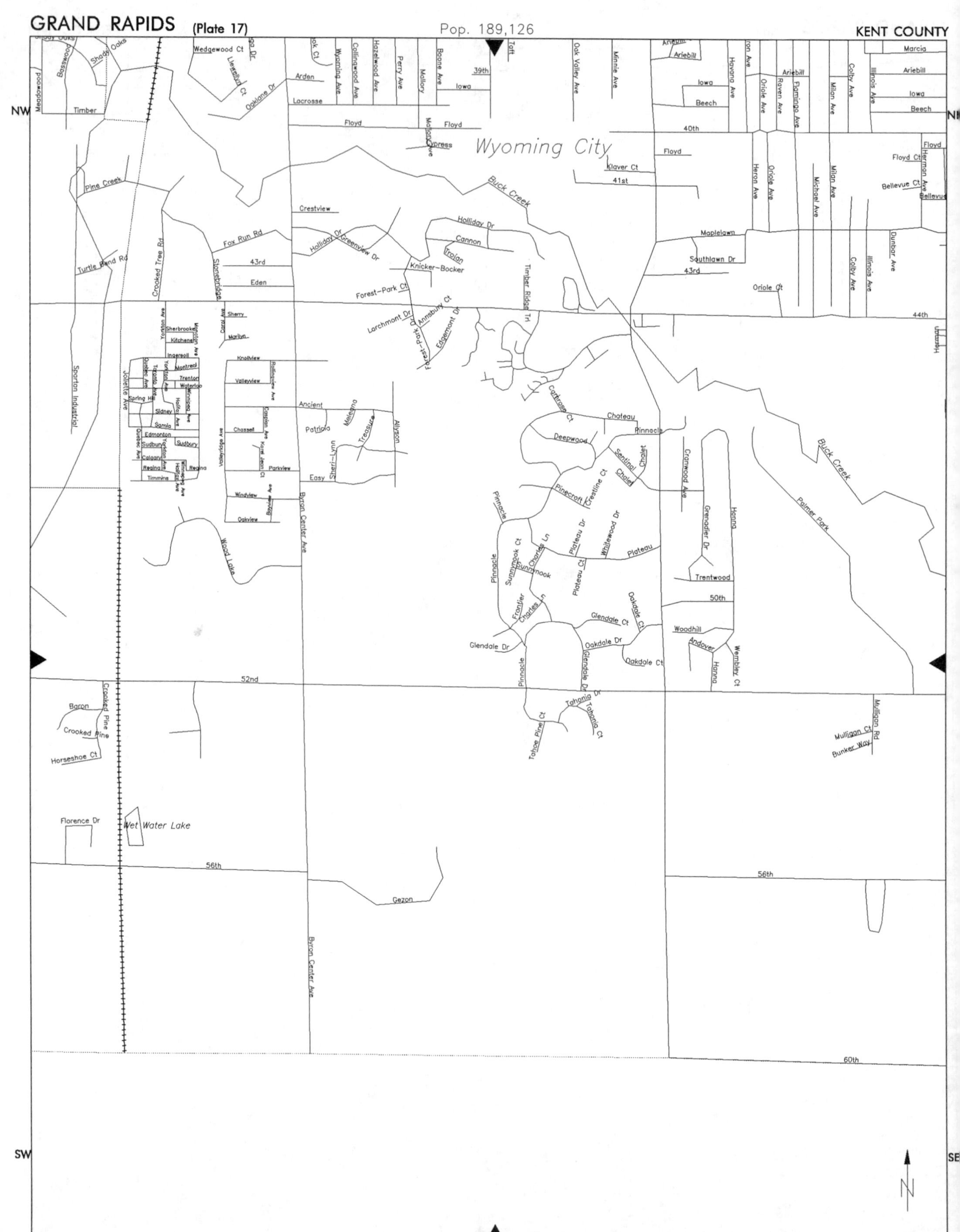
NW
NE
SW
SE
Wyoming City
Buck Creek
Wedgewood Ct
Arden
Lacrosse
Floyd
39th
Iowa
Beech
40th
Cypress
Timber
Pine Creek
Turtle Pond Rd
Crooked Tree Rd
Fox Run Rd
43rd
Eden
Crestview
Holliday Dr
Greenview Dr
Cannon
Trojan
Knicker-Bocker
Forest-Park Ct
Larchmont Dr
Annsbury Ct
Edgemont Dr
Timber Ridge Trl
Oak Valley Ave
Minnie Ave
Klaver Ct
41st
Maplelawn
Southlawn Dr
Oriole Ct
44th
Sportan Industrial
Joliette Ave
Ancient
Patricia
Treasure
Allyson
Sheri-Lynn
Easy
Byron Center Ave
Wood Lake
Chateau
Pinnacle
Deepwood
Sentinel
Chalet
Pinecrest
Crestline Ct
Plateau Dr
Whitewood Dr
Plateau
Sunnybrook Ct
Sunnybrook
Frontier
Glendale Ct
Glendale Dr
Oakdale Dr
Oakdale Ct
Tahoma Dr
Tahoma Ct
Tahoe Pine Ct
Cranwood Ave
Grenadier Dr
Hanna
Trentwood
50th
Woodhill
Andover
Wembley Ct
Palmer Park
52nd
Baron
Crooked Pine
Horseshoe Ct
Florence Dr
Wet Water Lake
56th
Gezon
60th
Mulligan Ct
Bunker Way
Mulligan Rd
Marcia
Ariebill
Floyd Ct
Bellevue Ct
Dunbar Ave
Colby Ave
Illinois Ave
Milan Ave
Michael Ave
Heron Ave
Oriole Ave
N

Wyoming City
Kentwood City
US Hwy 131
Buck Creek
Pine Hill Creek
44th
52nd
54th
56th
60th
Division Ave
Eastern Ave
Madison Ave
Jefferson
Clyde Park Ave
Roger B Chafee
Kalamazoo
NE
SE

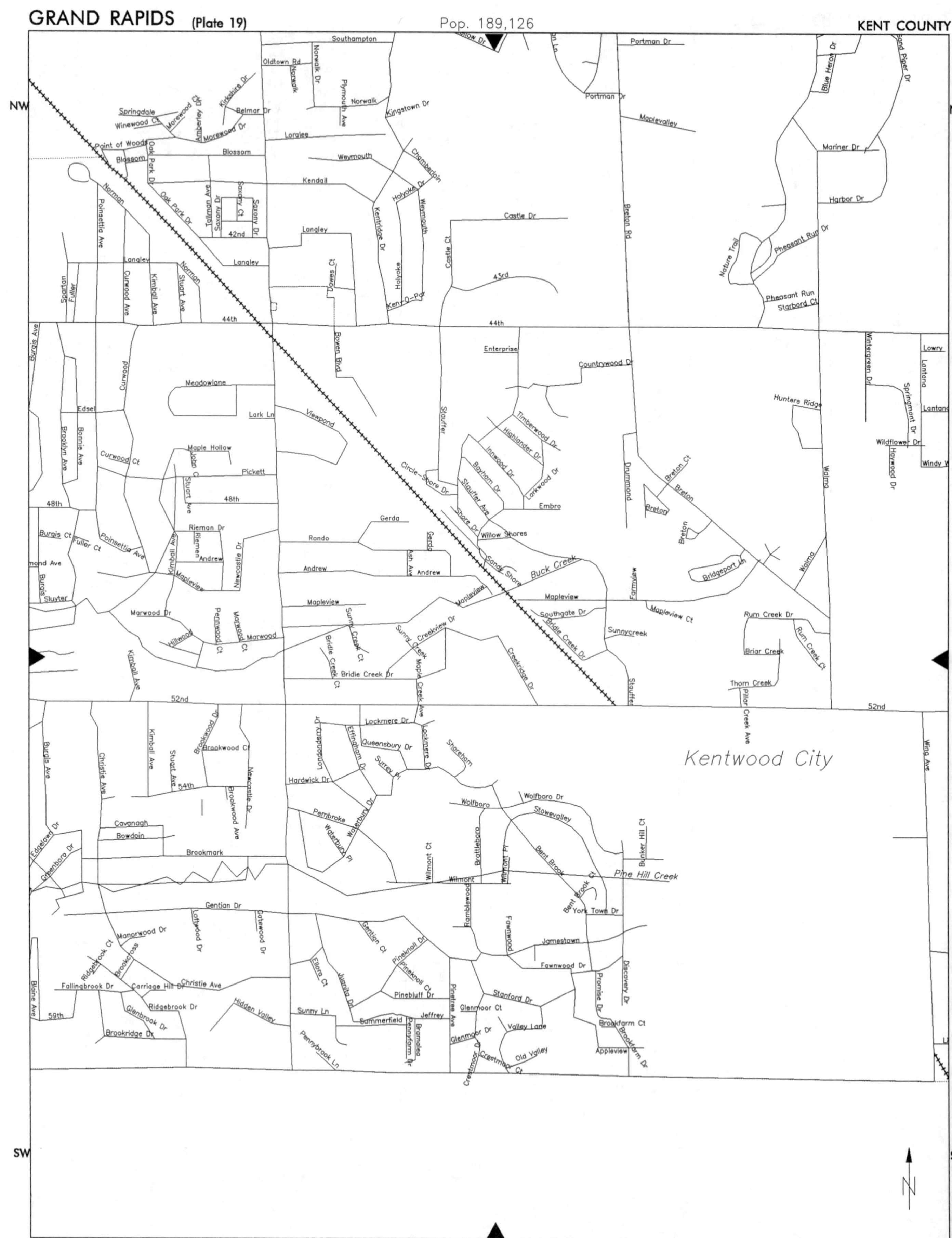
NW
SW
Kentwood City
44th
48th
52nd
Buck Creek
Pine Hill Creek
Breton Rd
Stauffer
Walma
Gentian Dr
Brookmark
Mapleview
Kendall
Langley
Blossom
Southampton
Portman Dr
Castle Dr
43rd
42nd
54th
59th

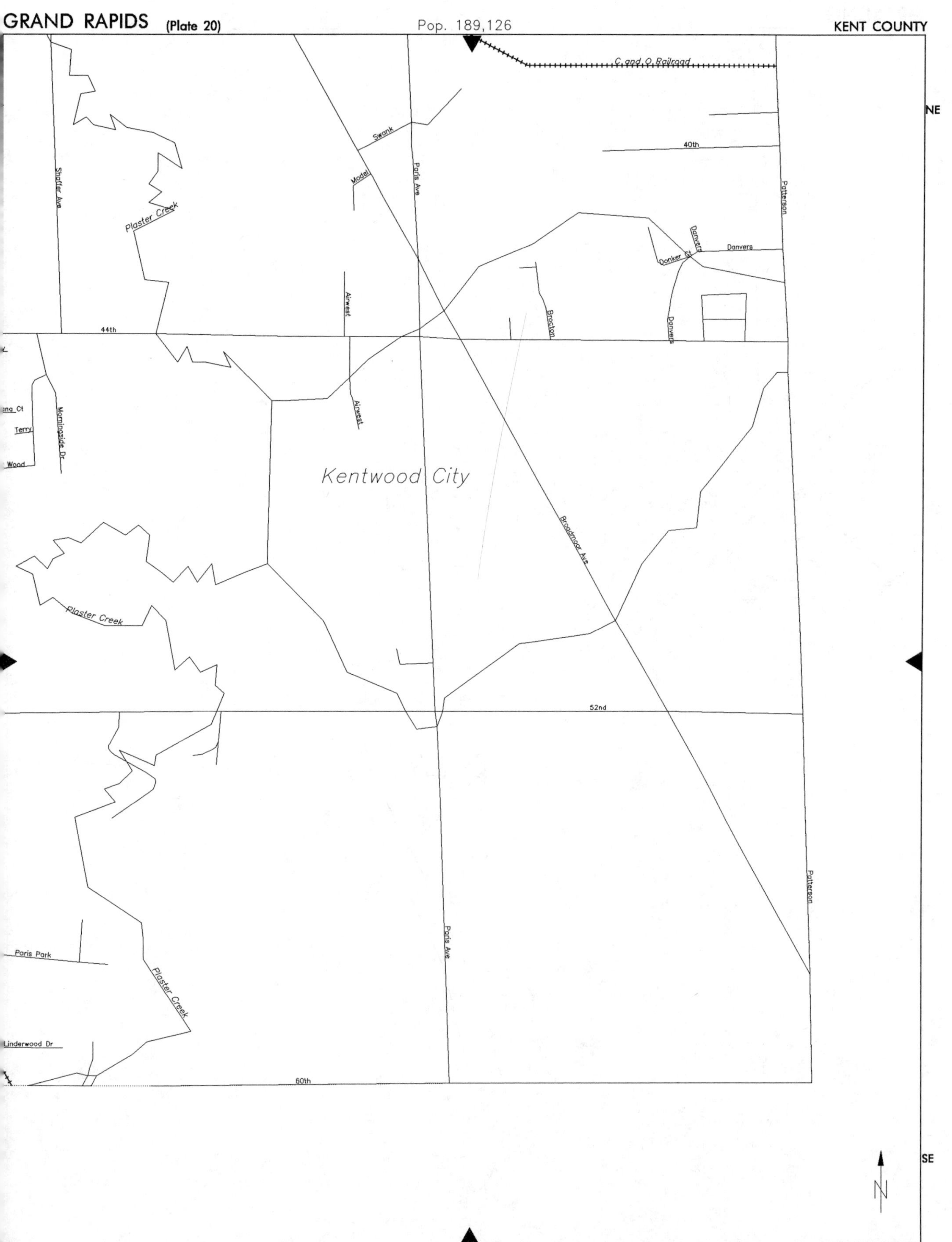
C. and O. Railroad
NE
40th
Swank
Model
Paris Ave
Shaffer Ave
Patterson
Plaster Creek
Danvers
Danvers
Donker Ct
Airwest
Brocton
Danvers
44th
Airwest
ana Ct
Terry
Morningside Dr
Wood
Kentwood City
Broadmoor Ave
Plaster Creek
52nd
Patterson
Paris Ave
Paris Park
Plaster Creek
Linderwood Dr
60th
SE
N

I– 75 Business Loop
County Rd
Down River Rd
Galen St
Smith St
Rose St
Clyde St
Erie St
Vine St
Plum St
Michigan Ave
Elm St
Maple St
Park St
Connine Rd
Ogemaw St
Lake St
Ottawa St
Branch au Sable River
Clare St
Spruce St
Michigan Ave
Vilas St
Chestnut St
Fig St
Peninsular Ave
Ionia St
Ingham St
Vernor Lane
Cedar St
Norway St
Knight St
Walker Dr
State Hwy 93
Fulton St
Mikado St
Gierke Rd
Au Sable Ct
Madsen St
Au Sable River
Alger St
Oliver St
Date St
Lawndale St
Fulton St
Mikado St
Plumb St
Brink St
State Hwy 72
I– 75 HWY
I– 75 HWY
Hanson St
Dupont St
Salling St
I– 75 Business Loop
Game Club Rd
N

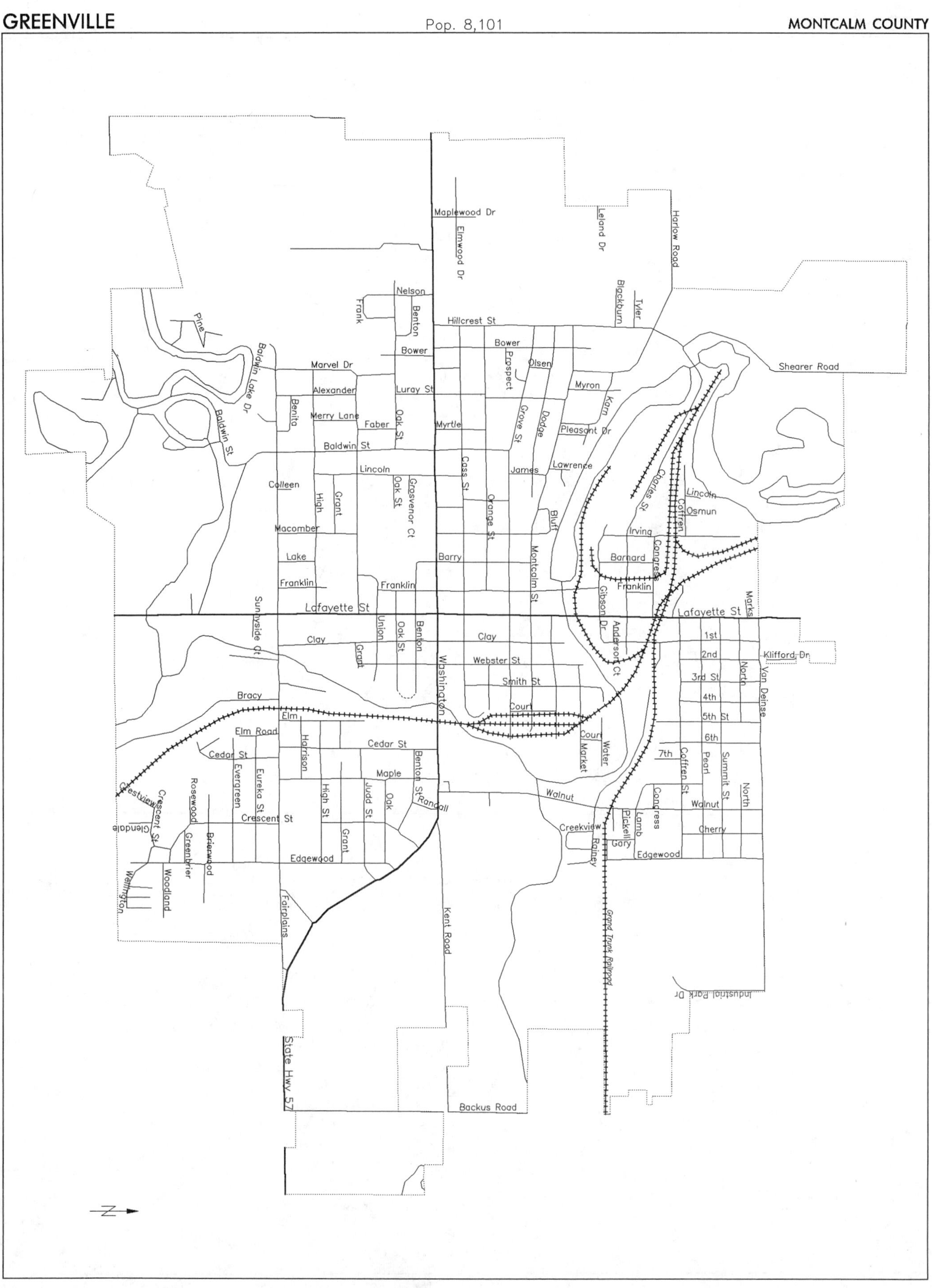
Maplewood Dr
Elmwood Dr
Leland Dr
Harlow Road
Blackburn
Tyler
Nelson
Frank
Benton
Hillcrest St
Shearer Road
Pine
Baldwin Lake Dr
Bower
Marvel Dr
Prospect
Olsen
Alexander
Luray St
Myron
Benita
Merry Lane
Faber
Oak St
Myrtle
Grove St
Dodge
Karn
Pleasant Dr
Baldwin St
Lincoln
Cass St
James
Lawrence
Colleen
High
Grant
Oak St
Grosvenor Ct
Orange St
Bluff
Charles St
Lincoln
Coffren
Osmun
Macomber
Irving
Montcalm St
Congress
Lake
Barry
Barnard
Franklin
Franklin
Franklin
Gibson Dr
Marks
Sunnyside Ct
Lafayette St
Lafayette St
Union
Oak St
Benton
Clay
Clay
Anderson Ct
1st
2nd
Klifford Dr
Grant
Washington
Webster St
North
Van Deinse
3rd St
Smith St
4th
Bracy
Court
5th St
Elm
Elm Road
Harrison
Cedar St
Court
Water
6th
Market
7th
Coffren St
Pearl
Summit St
Cedar St
Evergreen
Eureka St
Benton St
Maple
Crestview
Crescent St
Rosewood
High St
Judd St
Oak
Randall
Walnut
North
Walnut
Congress
Glendale
Crescent St
Briarwood
Greenbrier
Grant
Creekview
Pickell
Lamb
Cherry
Rainey
Gary
Edgewood
Edgewood
Wellington
Woodland
Fairplains
Kent Road
Grand Trunk Railroad
Industrial Park Dr
State Hwy 57
Backus Road

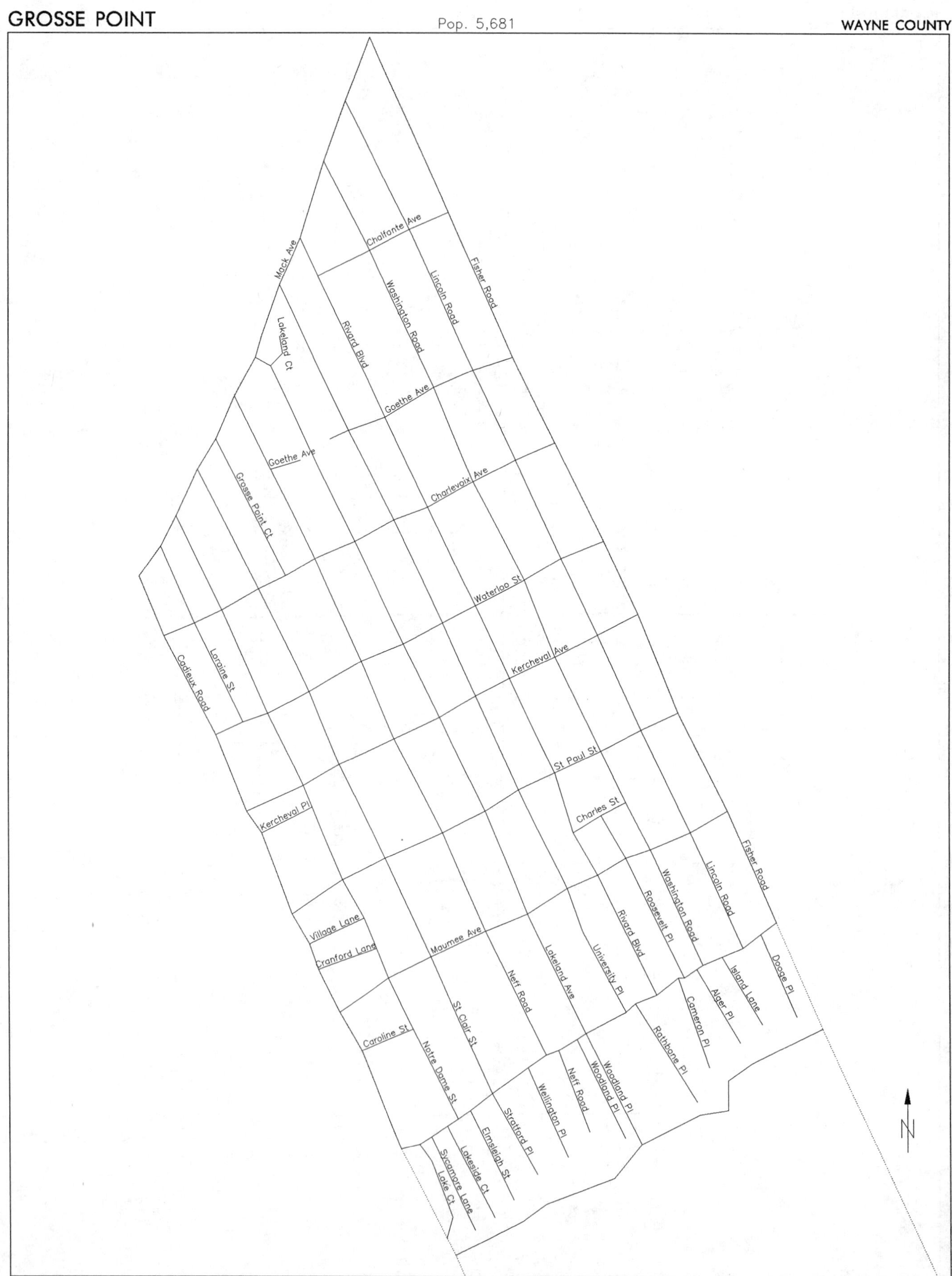
Chalfonte Ave
Mack Ave
Fisher Road
Lincoln Road
Washington Road
Rivard Blvd
Lakeland Ct
Goethe Ave
Goethe Ave
Charlevoix Ave
Grosse Point Ct
Waterloo St
Kercheval Ave
Loraine St
Cadieux Road
St Paul St
Charles St
Kercheval Pl
Fisher Road
Lincoln Road
Washington Road
Roosevelt Pl
Rivard Blvd
University Pl
Lakeland Ave
Neff Road
Maumee Ave
Village Lane
Cranford Lane
St Clair St
Island Lane
Dodge Pl
Alger Pl
Cameron Pl
Rathbone Pl
Caroline St
Notre Dame St
Woodland Pl
Woodland Pl
Neff Road
Wellington Pl
Stratford Pl
Elmsleigh St
Lakeside Ct
Sycamore Lane
Lake Ct
N

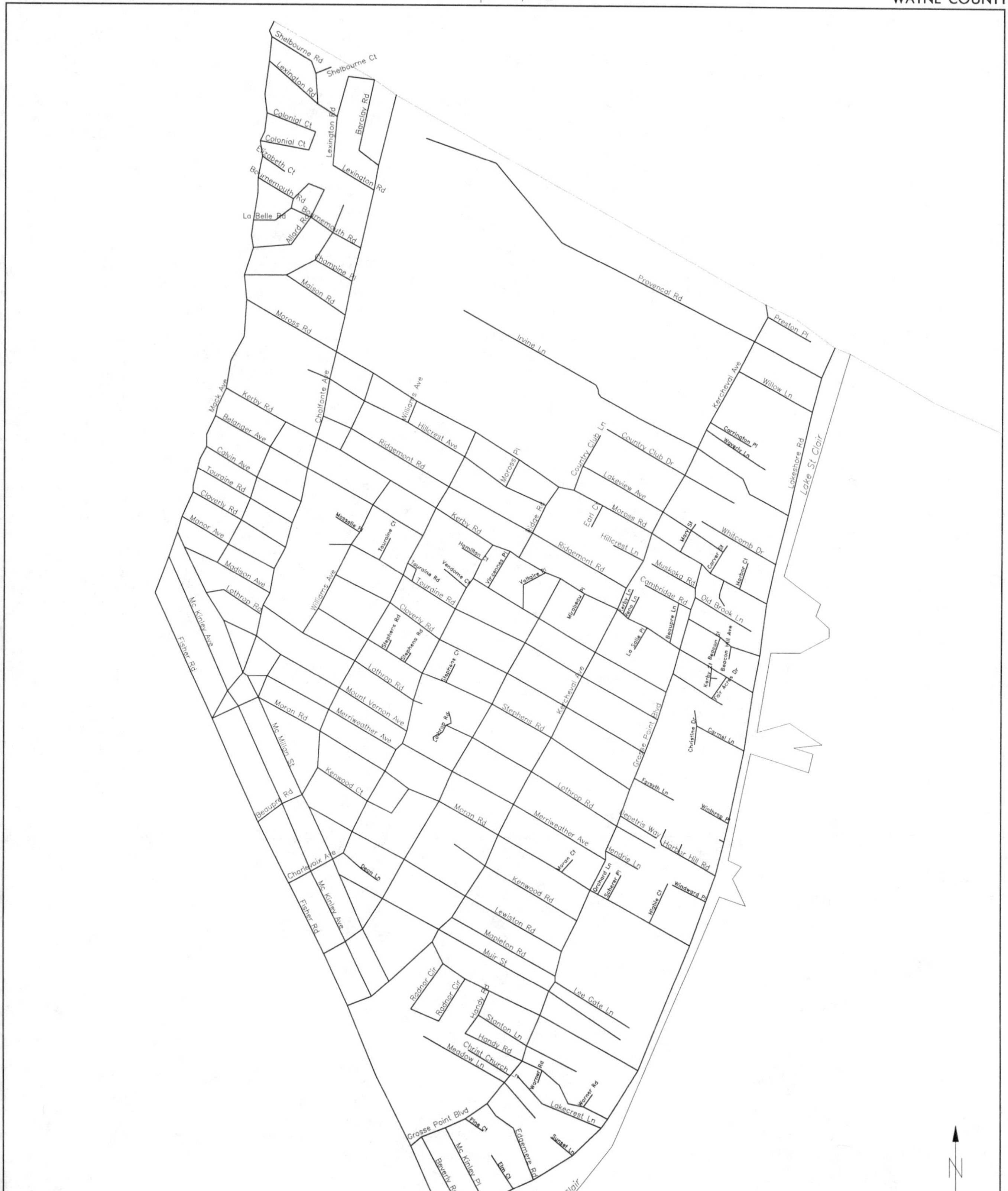

Shelbourne Rd
Shelbourne Ct
Lexington Rd
Barclay Rd
Colonial Ct
Colonial Ct
Elizabeth Ct
Bournemouth Rd
La Belle Rd
Allard Rd
Bournemouth Rd
Champine Pl
Maison Rd
Moross Rd
Provencal Rd
Irvine Ln
Preston Pl
Willow Ln
Kercheval Ave
Lakeshore Rd
Lake St Clair
Mack Ave
Kerby Rd
Belanger Ave
Calvin Ave
Touraine Rd
Cloverly Rd
Manor Ave
Madison Ave
Lothrop Rd
Chalfonte Ave
Williams Ave
Hillcrest Ave
Ridgemont Rd
Moross Pl
Country Club Ln
Country Club Dr
Lakeview Ave
Earl Ct
Moross Rd
Whitcomb Dr
Hillcrest Ln
Ridgemont Rd
Muskoka Rd
Cambridge Rd
Old Brook Ln
Beaupre Ln
La Salle Pl
Mirabeau Pl
Voltaire Pl
Vincennes Pl
Vendome Ct
Hamilton Ct
Touraine Rd
Mosselle Pl
Touraine Ct
Williams Ave
Cloverly Rd
Stephens Rd
Lothrop Rd
Stephens Ct
Mount Vernon Ave
Merriweather Ave
Stephens Rd
Kercheval Ave
Grosse Point Blvd
Christine Dr
Carmel Ln
Forsyth Ln
Winthrop Pl
Depetris Way
Harbor Hill Rd
Lothrop Rd
Merriweather Ave
Hendrie Ln
Moran Rd
Kenwood Ct
Moran Rd
Kenwood Rd
Lewiston Rd
Mapleton Rd
Muir St
Lee Gate Ln
Windward Pl
Highbie Ct
Orchard Ln
Scherer Pl
Moran Ct
Mc Kinley Ave
Fisher Rd
Mc Millan St
Beaupre Rd
Charlevoix Ave
Dean Ln
Mc Kinley Ave
Fisher Rd
Radnor Cir
Radnor Cir
Handy Rd
Stanton Ln
Handy Rd
Christ Church
Meadow Ln
Warner Rd
Warner Rd
Lakecrest Ln
Grosse Point Blvd
Pine Ct
Mc Kinley Pl
Beverly Rd
Elm Ct
Edgemere Rd
Sunset Ln
Lake St Clair
Rose Ter
N

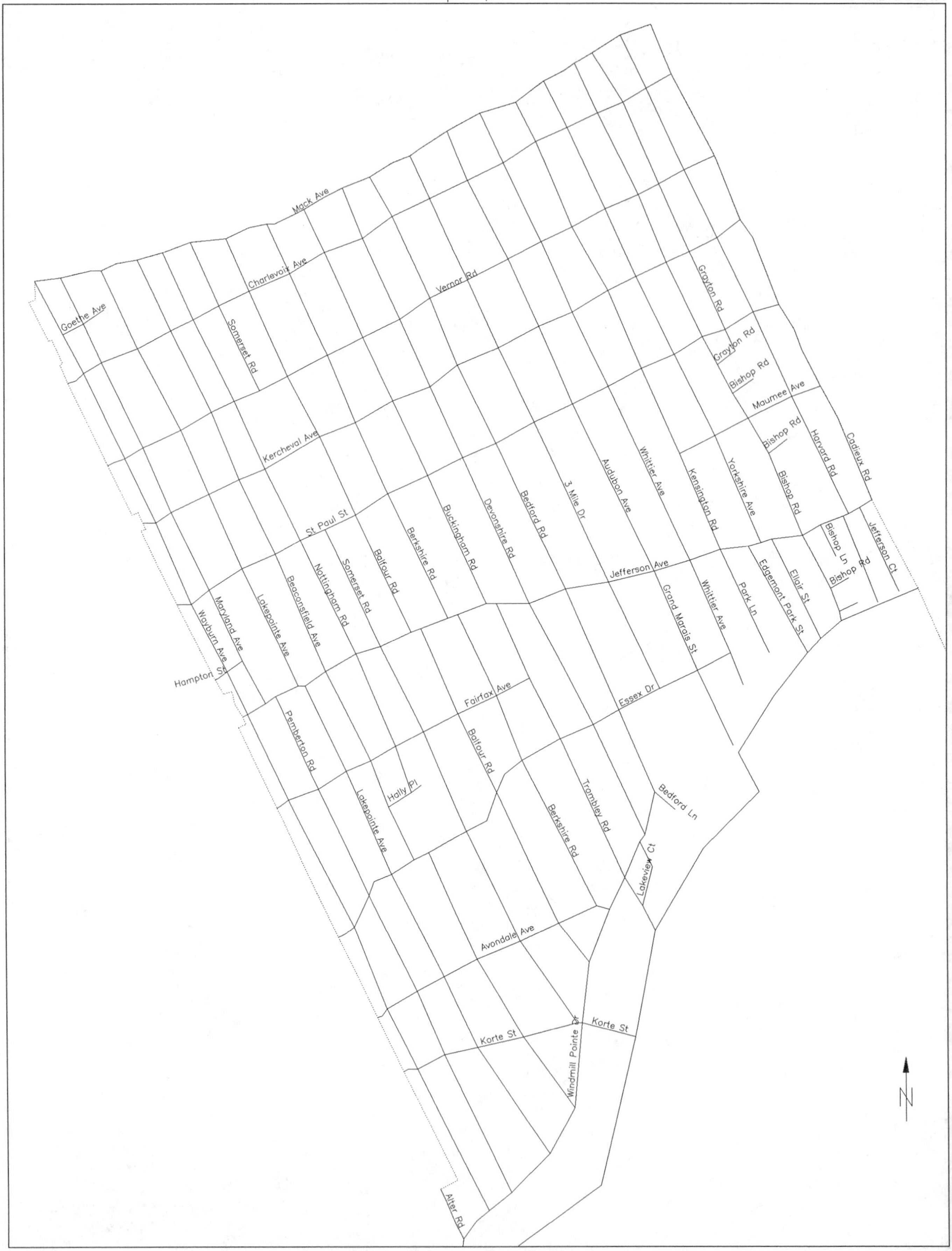

Mack Ave
Charlevoix Ave
Vernor Rd
Goethe Ave
Somerset Rd
Kercheval Ave
St Paul St
Jefferson Ave
Grayton Rd
Grayton Rd
Bishop Rd
Maumee Ave
Bishop Rd
Harvard Rd
Cadieux Rd
Bishop Rd
Yorkshire Ave
Kensington Rd
Whittier Ave
Audubon Ave
3 Mile Dr
Bedford Rd
Devonshire Rd
Buckingham Rd
Berkshire Rd
Balfour Rd
Somerset Rd
Nottingham Rd
Beaconsfield Ave
Lakepointe Ave
Maryland Ave
Wayburn Ave
Hampton St
Bishop Ln
Jefferson Ct
Bishop Rd
Ellair St
Edgemont Park St
Park Ln
Whittier Ave
Grand Marais St
Essex Dr
Fairfax Ave
Pemberton Rd
Balfour Rd
Holly Pl
Lakepointe Ave
Berkshire Rd
Trombley Rd
Bedford Ln
Lakeview Ct
Avondale Ave
Korte St
Korte St
Windmill Pointe Dr
Alter Rd
N

Lake-Shore Rd
Fairlake Lane
Shorecrest Cir
Crestwood Dr
Duval Rd
Duval Rd
Stillmeadow Lane
Briarcliff Pl
Moorland Dr
Putnam Pl
Blairmoor Ct
Edgewood Dr
Edgewood Dr
Roslyn Rd
Hampton Rd
Willowtree Lane
Hawthorne Rd
Regal Pl
Michaux Ct
Vernier Rd
Ballantyne Rd
Willison Rd
Greenbriar Lane
Fontana Lane
Belle Meade
Shelden Rd
Fontana Lane
Sunningdale Dr
Sunningdale Dr
Straton Ct
Lakeshore Rd
Lochmoor Dr
Straton Pl
Colonial Rd
Renaud Rd
Oxford Rd
Lake St Clair
Lake Shore Lane
Shoreham Rd
Webber Lane
Ballantyne Rd
Clairview Rd
Fairford Rd
Stonehurst Rd
Deeplands Rd
Deeplands Rd
Deeplands Rd
Lakeshore Rd
Cook Rd
Deeplands Ct
Shelden Rd
Fordcroft St
Woodland Shore Dr
N

GROSSE POINT WOODS

Pop. 17,715

WAYNE COUNTY

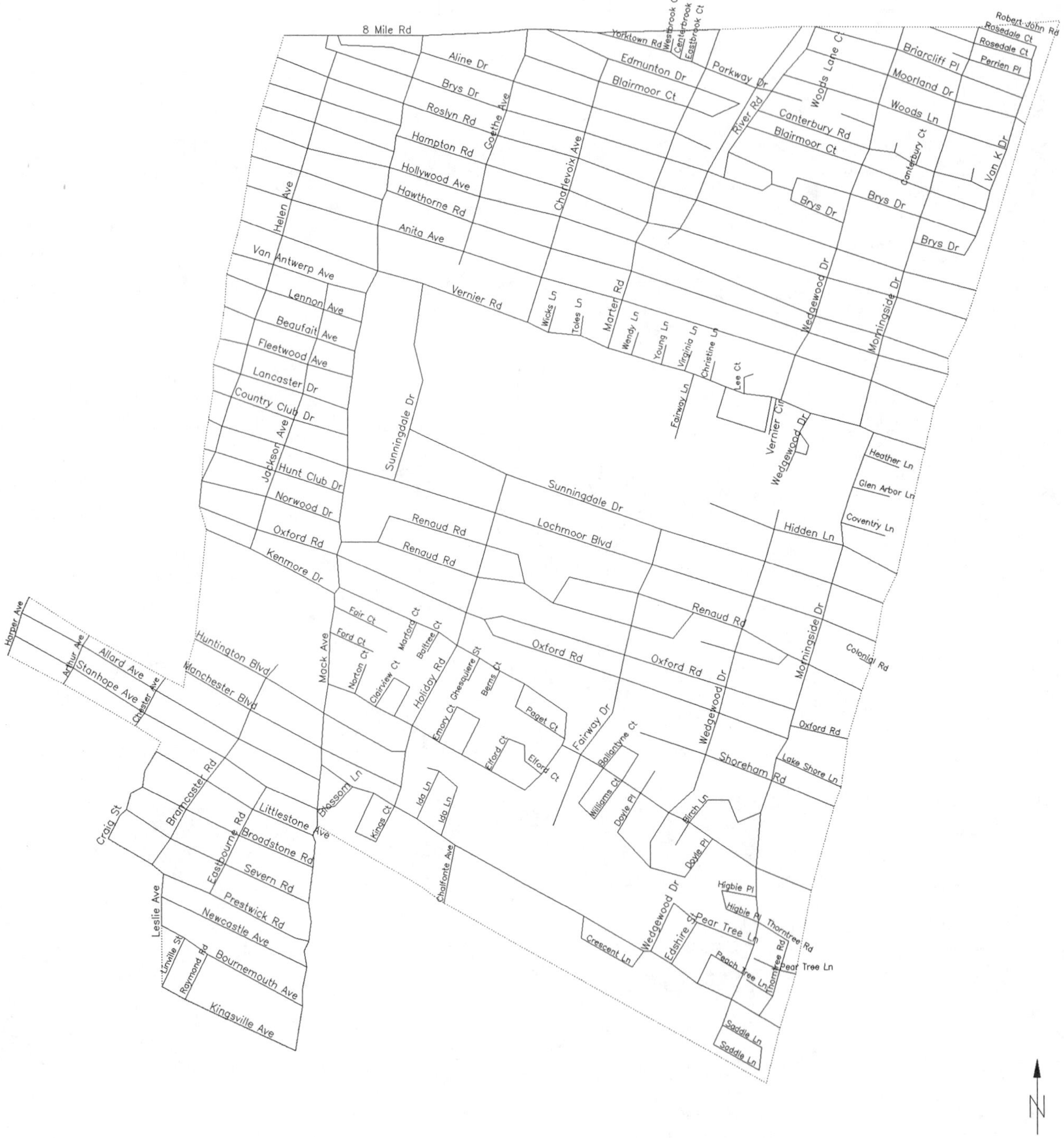

8 Mile Rd
Yorktown Rd
Westbrook Ct
Canterbrook Ct
Eastbrook Ct
Robert John Rd
Rosedale Ct
Rosedale Ct
Perrien Pl
Aline Dr
Edmunton Dr
Parkway Dr
Briarcliff Pl
Woods Lane Ct
Brys Dr
Blairmoor Ct
Moorland Dr
Roslyn Rd
Goethe Ave
River Rd
Canterbury Rd
Woods Ln
Hampton Rd
Blairmoor Ct
Canterbury Ct
Van K Dr
Hollywood Ave
Charlevoix Ave
Hawthorne Rd
Brys Dr
Brys Dr
Helen Ave
Anita Ave
Brys Dr
Van Antwerp Ave
Vernier Rd
Lennon Ave
Wicks Ln
Toles Ln
Marter Rd
Wedgewood Dr
Morningside Dr
Beaufait Ave
Wendy Ln
Young Ln
Virginia Ln
Christine Ln
Fleetwood Ave
Lee Ct
Lancaster Dr
Country Club Dr
Sunningdale Dr
Fairway Ln
Vernier Cir
Wedgewood Dr
Jackson Ave
Heather Ln
Hunt Club Dr
Glen Arbor Ln
Norwood Dr
Sunningdale Dr
Coventry Ln
Renaud Rd
Lochmoor Blvd
Hidden Ln
Oxford Rd
Renaud Rd
Kenmore Dr
Harper Ave
Fair Ct
Renaud Rd
Ford Ct
Marford Ct
Beltree Ct
Arthur Ave
Allard Ave
Huntington Blvd
Mack Ave
Oxford Rd
Morningside Dr
Colonial Rd
Stanhope Ave
Chester Ave
Norton Ct
Oxford Rd
Manchester Blvd
Clairview Ct
Holiday Rd
Chesquiere St
Berns Ct
Wedgewood Dr
Emory Ct
Paget Ct
Fairway Dr
Oxford Rd
Ballantyne Ct
Elford Ct
Elford Ct
Shoreham Rd
Lake Shore Ln
Bramcaster Rd
Williams Ct
Littlestone Ave
Blossom Ln
Ida Ln
Ida Ln
Doyle Pl
Birch Ln
Craig St
Eastbourne Rd
Broadstone Rd
Kings Ct
Doyle Pl
Severn Rd
Chalfonte Ave
Higbie Pl
Prestwick Rd
Higbie Pl
Wedgewood Dr
Thorntree Rd
Leslie Ave
Newcastle Ave
Pear Tree Ln
Crescent Ln
Edshire St
Unville St
Raymond Rd
Bournemouth Ave
Peach Tree Ln
Thorntree Rd
Pear Tree Ln
Kingsville Ave
Saddle Ln
Saddle Ln

N

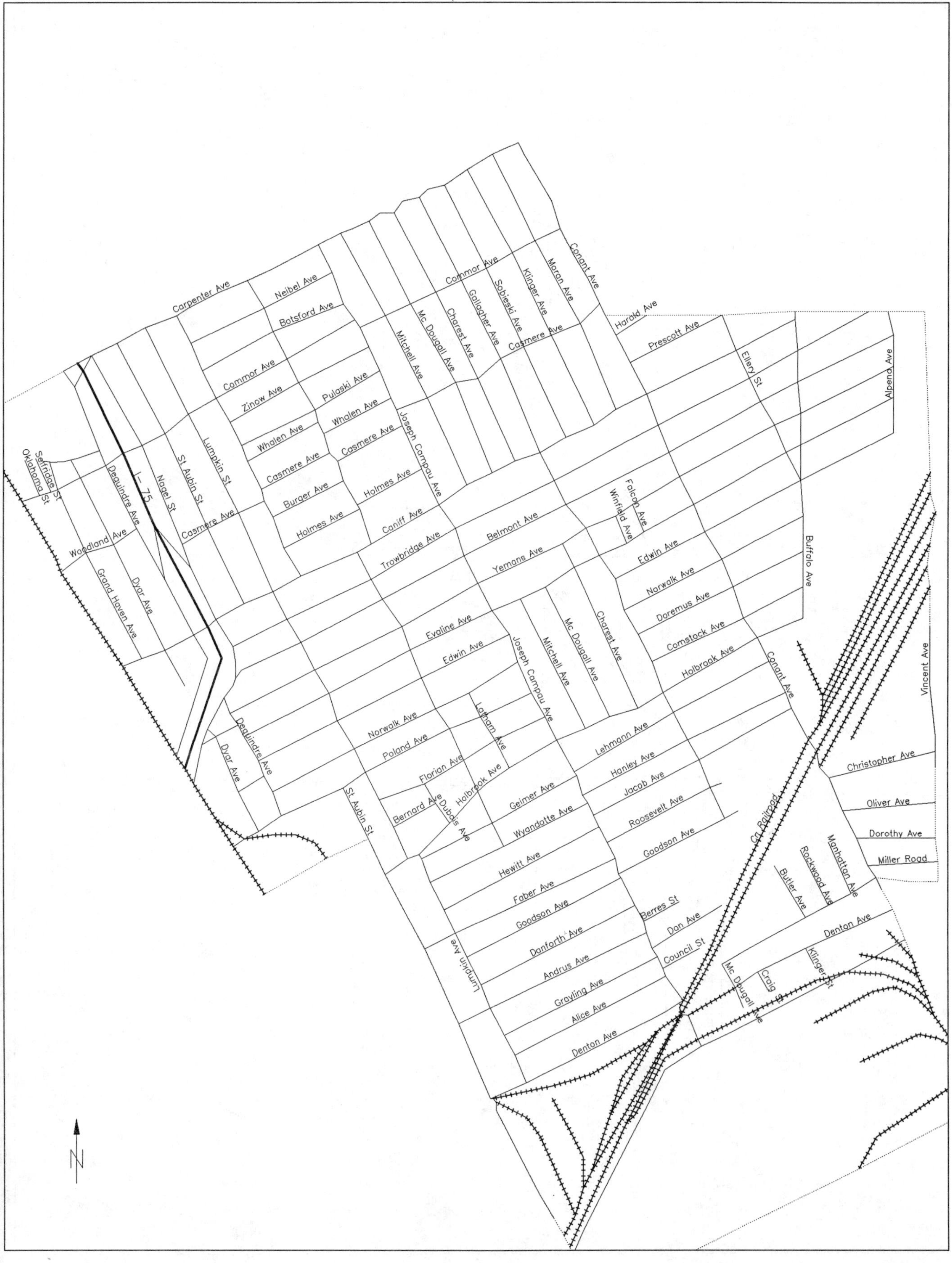

Conant Ave
Commor Ave
Moran Ave
Klinger Ave
Sobieski Ave
Gallagher Ave
Charest Ave
Mc Dougall Ave
Mitchell Ave
Carpenter Ave
Neibel Ave
Botsford Ave
Casmere Ave
Harold Ave
Prescott Ave
Ellery St
Alpena Ave
Commor Ave
Zinow Ave
Pulaski Ave
Whalen Ave
Whalen Ave
Casmere Ave
Casmere Ave
Joseph Campau Ave
Burger Ave
Holmes Ave
Holmes Ave
Caniff Ave
Lumpkin St
St Aubin St
Nagel St
I-75
Dequindre Ave
Selfridge St
Oklahoma St
Casmere Ave
Woodland Ave
Grand Haven Ave
Dyar Ave
Trowbridge Ave
Belmont Ave
Yemans Ave
Falcon Ave
Winfield Ave
Buffalo Ave
Edwin Ave
Norwalk Ave
Daremus Ave
Comstock Ave
Holbrook Ave
Charest Ave
Mc Dougall Ave
Mitchell Ave
Joseph Campau Ave
Evaline Ave
Edwin Ave
Conant Ave
Vincent Ave
Norwalk Ave
Poland Ave
Latham Ave
Florian Ave
Holbrook Ave
Bernard Ave
Dubois Ave
Dequindre Ave
Dyar Ave
St Aubin St
Lehmann Ave
Hanley Ave
Jacob Ave
Roosevelt Ave
Geimer Ave
Wyandotte Ave
Goodson Ave
Christopher Ave
Oliver Ave
Dorothy Ave
Miller Road
Cn Railroad
Hewitt Ave
Faber Ave
Goodson Ave
Danforth Ave
Andrus Ave
Grayling Ave
Alice Ave
Denton Ave
Berres St
Don Ave
Council St
Lumpkin Ave
Manhattan Ave
Rockwood Ave
Butler Ave
Denton Ave
Klinger St
Craig St
Mc Dougall Ave
N

Powder Road
Swedetown Creek
Canal Road
Powder Road
Waterville Ave
Hecla St
Jasberg St
Quincy St
Atlantic St
Anthony St
Cedar St
Roberts St
Calumet St
Driving Park Road
Industrial Dr
Emery St
Garden St
Birch St
Birch St
Minnesota St
Anthony St
North St
Jasberg St
Crestwood Dr
Crestwood Glade
Emma Ave
Sigsbee St
Park St
Ingot St
Quincy St
Ohio St
Summit St
4th St
Michigan St
Prospect St
Poplar St
Ohio St
Hill St
2nd St
Liberty St
Maple St
Fir St
Evergreen St
Willow St
Cypress St
Elevation St
Scallion St
Franklin St
Summit St
Elm St
Pine St
Mill St
US 41 (M-26)
Warren St
Lincoln St (US 41)
Lake Ave
Water St
Ingot St
Mine St
Dakota St
White St
Hancock Ave
Depot St
Olds St
White St
Conrad
Mesnard St
Ryan St
Holland St
Wright St
Montezuma St
White St
Roosevelt St
Water St
Ravine St
Franklin St
Church St
Tezcuco St
White St
Quincy St
Dunstan St
Front Ave
White St
Roosevelt St
Brock St
Center St
Mason Ave
A ST
Harris Ave
Cooper Ave
Vivian St

HARBOR BEACH

Pop. 2,089

HURON COUNTY

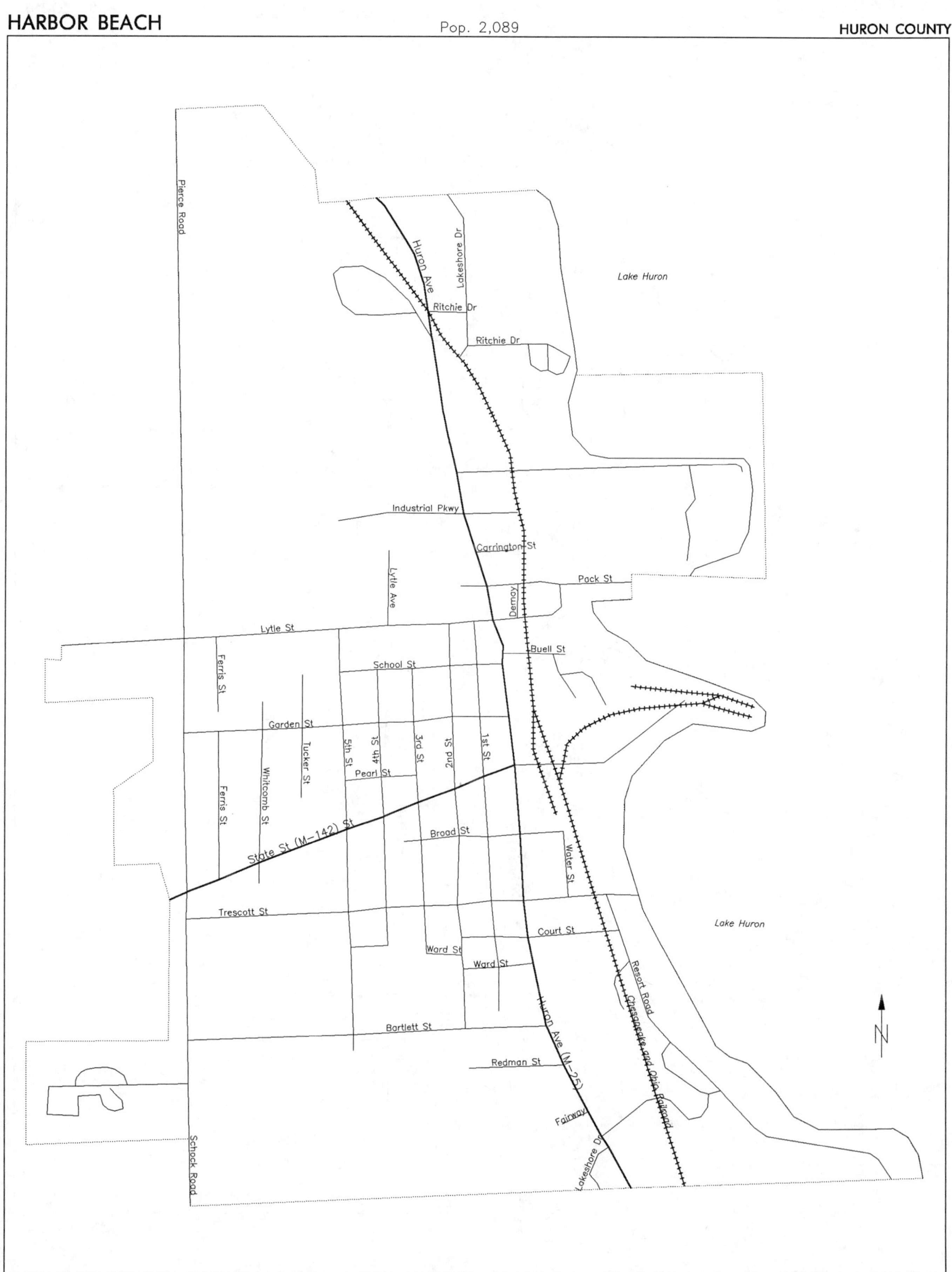

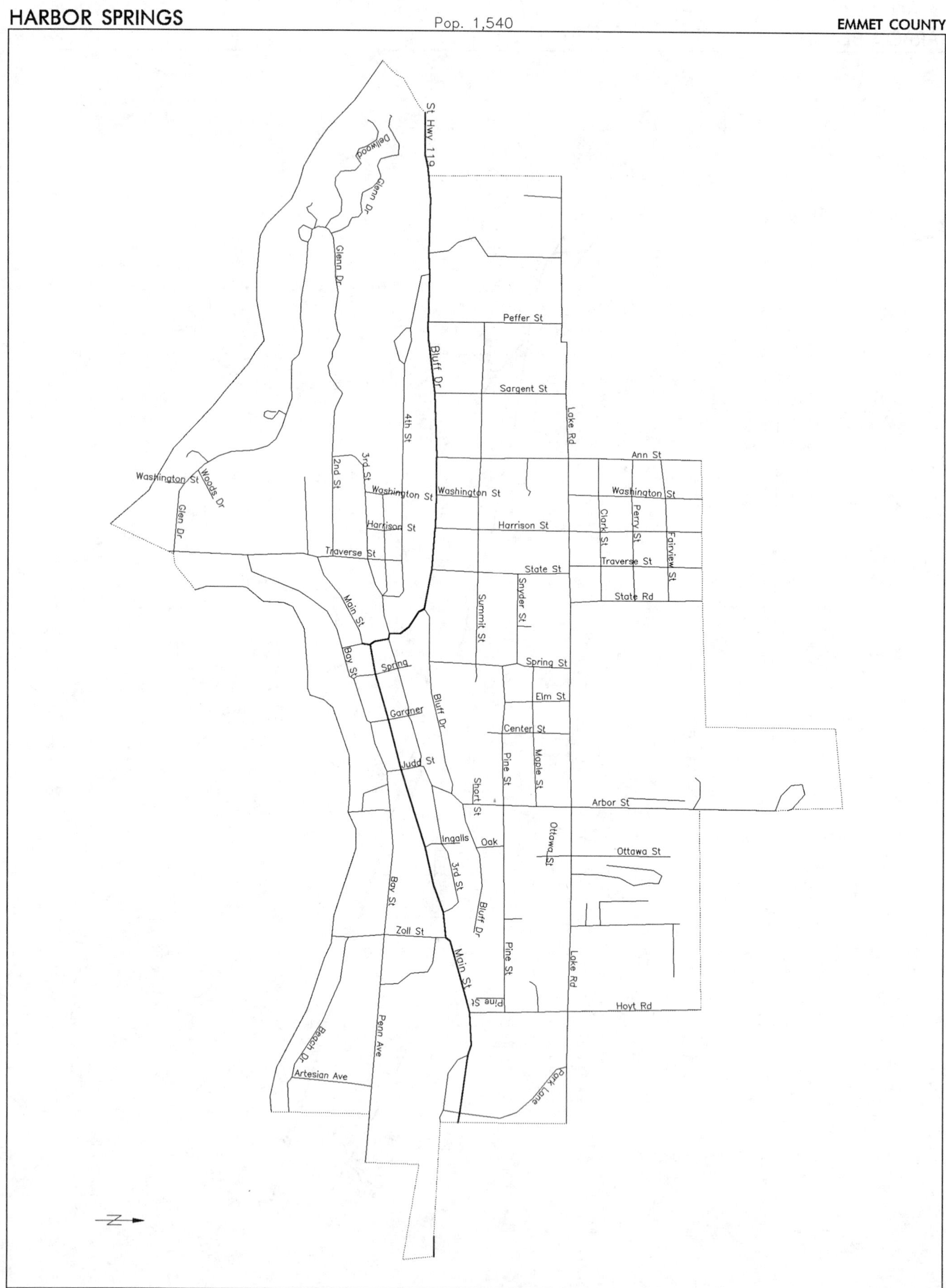
St Hwy 119
Dellwood
Glenn Dr
Glenn Dr
Peffer St
Bluff Dr
Sargent St
Lake Rd
4th St
Ann St
3rd St
2nd St
Washington St
Woods Dr
Washington St
Washington St
Washington St
Glen Dr
Harrison St
Harrison St
Clark St
Perry St
Fairview St
Traverse St
Traverse St
State St
State Rd
Main St
Snyder St
Summit St
Bay St
Spring
Spring St
Elm St
Gardner
Bluff Dr
Center St
Judd St
Pine St
Maple St
Short St
Arbor St
Ottawa St
Ottawa St
Ingalls
Oak
3rd St
Bay St
Bluff Dr
Zoll St
Main St
Pine St
Lake Rd
Pine St
Hoyt Rd
Beach Dr
Penn Ave
Artesian Ave
Park Lane

8 Mile Rd
Vernier Rd
Ridgemont Ave
Hollywood Ave
Danbury Ln
Roslyn Ave
Hampton St
Ridgemont Ave
Harper Ave
Hollywood Ave
Anita Ave
Hawthorne Rd
Webber Dr
Eastland Dr
Eastland Village Dr
Williamsburg Ct
Van Antwerp Ave
Anita St
Vernier Rd
Lennon Ave
Duprey Ave
Peerless Ave
Van Antwerp St
Lennon Ave
Beaufait Ave
Fleetwood Dr
Balfour Ave
Beaconsfield Ave
Lancaster Ave
Beaufait St
Harper Ct
Woodmont Ave
Church Ct
Country Club Dr
Sanilac Ave
Fleetwood Ave
Kelly Rd
Elm Ct
Cedar Ct
Rose Ct
Lochmoor Dr
Duprey Ave
Lancaster St
Country Club Dr
Kenmore Dr
Woodmont Ave
Peerless Ave
Lochmoor Dr
Hunt Club Dr
Woodcrest Dr
Damman Ave
Lansdowne Ave
Huntington Ave
Norwood Dr
Crestland Ave
Eastwood Dr
Kenmore St
Canton Ave
Riad Ave
Laing Ave
Woodside Dr
Old Homestead Dr
Parkcrest Dr
Woodland Ave
Woodmont Ave
Helen Ave
Roscommon Ave
Wildwood Dr
Harper Ave
Rossiter Ave
Elkhart Ave
Arthur Ave
Kenosha Ave
Huntington Ave
Harper Ave
Washtenaw Ave
Peerless Ave
Woodcrest Dr
Manchester St
Kingsville Ave
Balfour Rd
Sanilac Ave
Chester Ave
Littlestone Ct
Arthur Ave
I-94
Littlestone Ave
Duprey Ave
Broadstone Rd
Park Dr
Brierstone Rd
Severn Rd
Prestwick Rd
Newcastle Ave
Rockcastle St
Edgefield St
Bournemouth Ave
Chester Ave
Sloan Dr
Rolandale St
Eastbourne St
N

HARRISON

Pop. 1,835

CLARE COUNTY

State Hwy 61
Byfield Dr
Spruce St
Duggan Dr
Seelinger Dr
Sullivan Dr
Westlawn St
Fairview
Fairlane St
Oaklawn St
Greenlawn St
Eastlawn Dr
1st St
John R St
Cherry St
Harrison St
Lake St
Maple St
Birch St
Norway St
4th St
Broad St
2nd St
Beech St
Main St
Oak St
5th St
Pine St
Short St
Elm St
Bond St
Richard Dr
Diane Circle Dr
Mostetler Rd
Sandy Cir
County Farm Rd
Vass Rd
Harrison Rd
Columbine Dr
Butternut
Hawthorn Ave
Wintergreen Ct
Laura Rd
Hammond St
Hillcrest Ave
Matilda Rd
Mary-Jo Rd
Isabelle Rd
Little Long Lake Dr
Lakeview Dr
Lone Pine Dr
Wilson Ave
Jill St
Green St
Oak Rd
Grant Ave
Saginaw St
Owosso St
Mount Pleasant St
Alma St
Ithaca St
Midland St
Coleman St
Farwell St
N

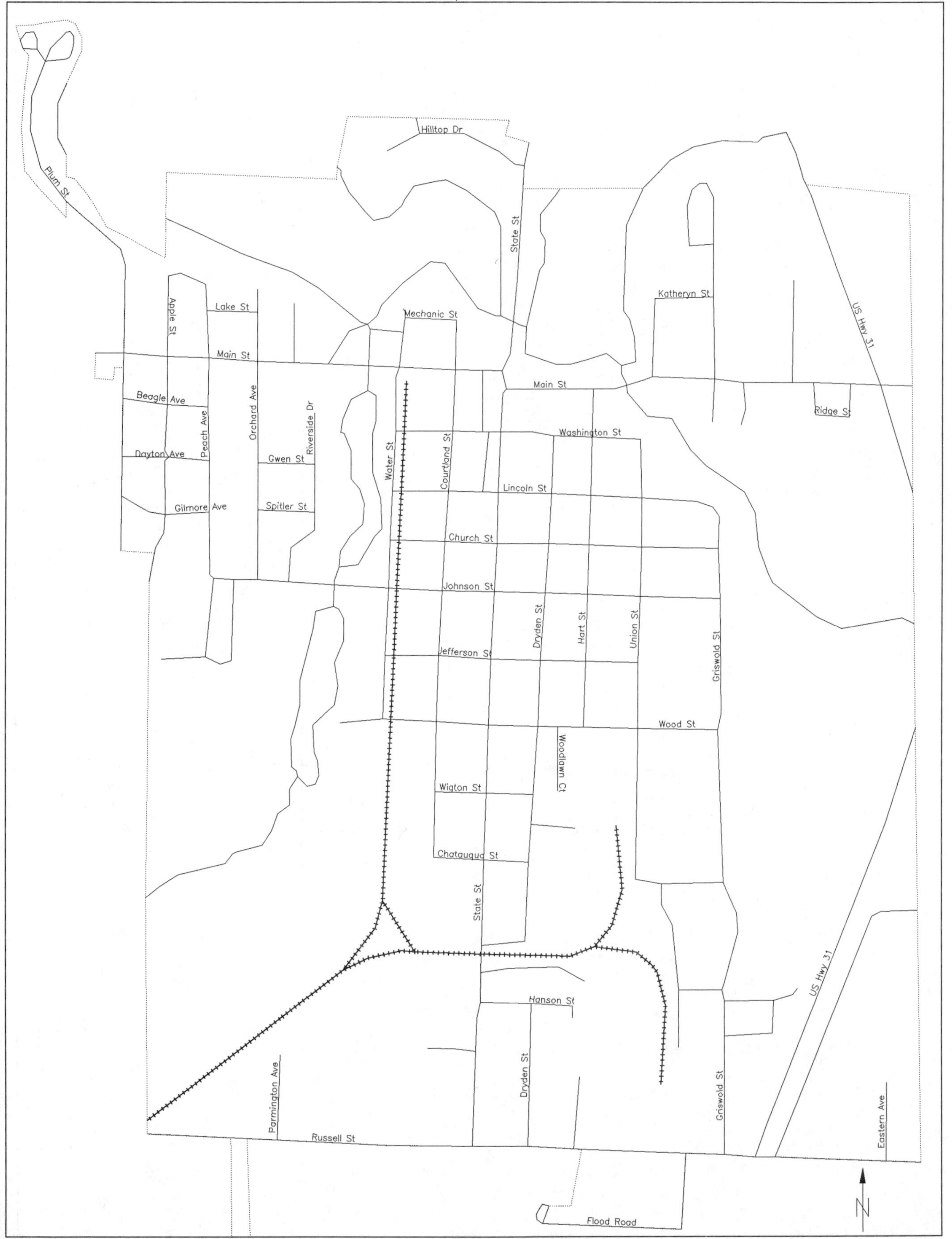
Hilltop Dr
Plum St
State St
Katheryn St
US Hwy 31
Apple St
Lake St
Mechanic St
Main St
Main St
Beagle Ave
Orchard Ave
Peach Ave
Riverside Dr
Ridge St
Washington St
Dayton Ave
Gwen St
Water St
Courtland St
Lincoln St
Gilmore Ave
Spitler St
Church St
Johnson St
Dryden St
Hart St
Union St
Jefferson St
Griswold St
Wood St
Woodlawn Ct
Wigton St
Chatauqua St
State St
US Hwy 31
Hanson St
Dryden St
Parmington Ave
Griswold St
Eastern Ave
Russell St
Flood Road
N

Marion Ave
Pleasant St
Dunbar St
Mechanic St
Bowe St
Heywood St
Drexel St
Railroad St
Mary St
Railroad St
Hillsborough St
Franklin St
Maple St
Beechwood St
Elmwood St
Bernard St
Charles St
Prospect St
Center St
60th Ave
Haver St
East St
Main St
Olds St
Washington St
Hillard St
Church St
Paris Hill Dr
Paris Hill Dr
2nd St
Spaulding St
Oak St
Linden St
Clark
Wendell Ave
Bennett Ave
Hopkins Ct
60th Ave
Austin Ave
Fire Lane
Olds Ave

HASTINGS

Pop. 6,549

BARRY COUNTY

HAZEL PARK

Pop. 20,051

OAKLAND COUNTY

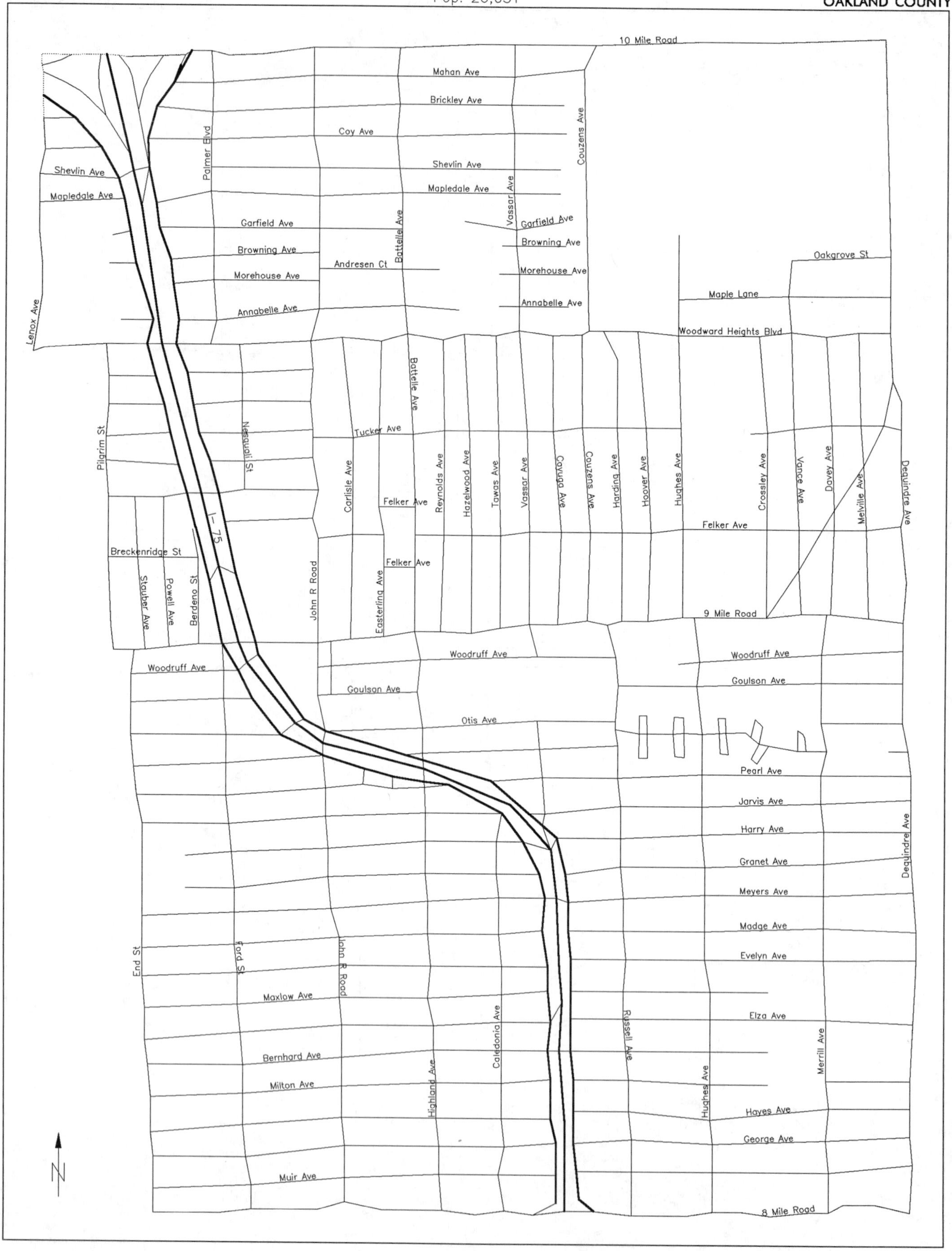

10 Mile Road
Mahan Ave
Brickley Ave
Coy Ave
Couzens Ave
Palmer Blvd
Shevlin Ave
Shevlin Ave
Mapledale Ave
Mapledale Ave
Vassar Ave
Garfield Ave
Battelle Ave
Garfield Ave
Browning Ave
Browning Ave
Andresen Ct
Morehouse Ave
Morehouse Ave
Oakgrove St
Maple Lane
Annabelle Ave
Annabelle Ave
Lenox Ave
Woodward Heights Blvd
Battelle Ave
Tucker Ave
Pilgrim St
Nesquali St
Carlisle Ave
Reynolds Ave
Hazelwood Ave
Tawas Ave
Vassar Ave
Cayuga Ave
Couzens Ave
Harding Ave
Hoover Ave
Hughes Ave
Crossley Ave
Vance Ave
Davey Ave
Melville Ave
Dequindre Ave
Felker Ave
Felker Ave
I-75
Breckenridge St
Felker Ave
Stauber Ave
Powell Ave
Berdeno St
John R Road
Easterling Ave
9 Mile Road
Woodruff Ave
Woodruff Ave
Woodruff Ave
Goulson Ave
Goulson Ave
Otis Ave
Pearl Ave
Jarvis Ave
Harry Ave
Dequindre Ave
Granet Ave
Meyers Ave
Madge Ave
End St
Ford St
John R Road
Evelyn Ave
Maxlow Ave
Elza Ave
Russell Ave
Caledonia Ave
Merrill Ave
Bernhard Ave
Highland Ave
Milton Ave
Hughes Ave
Hayes Ave
George Ave
N
Muir Ave
8 Mile Road

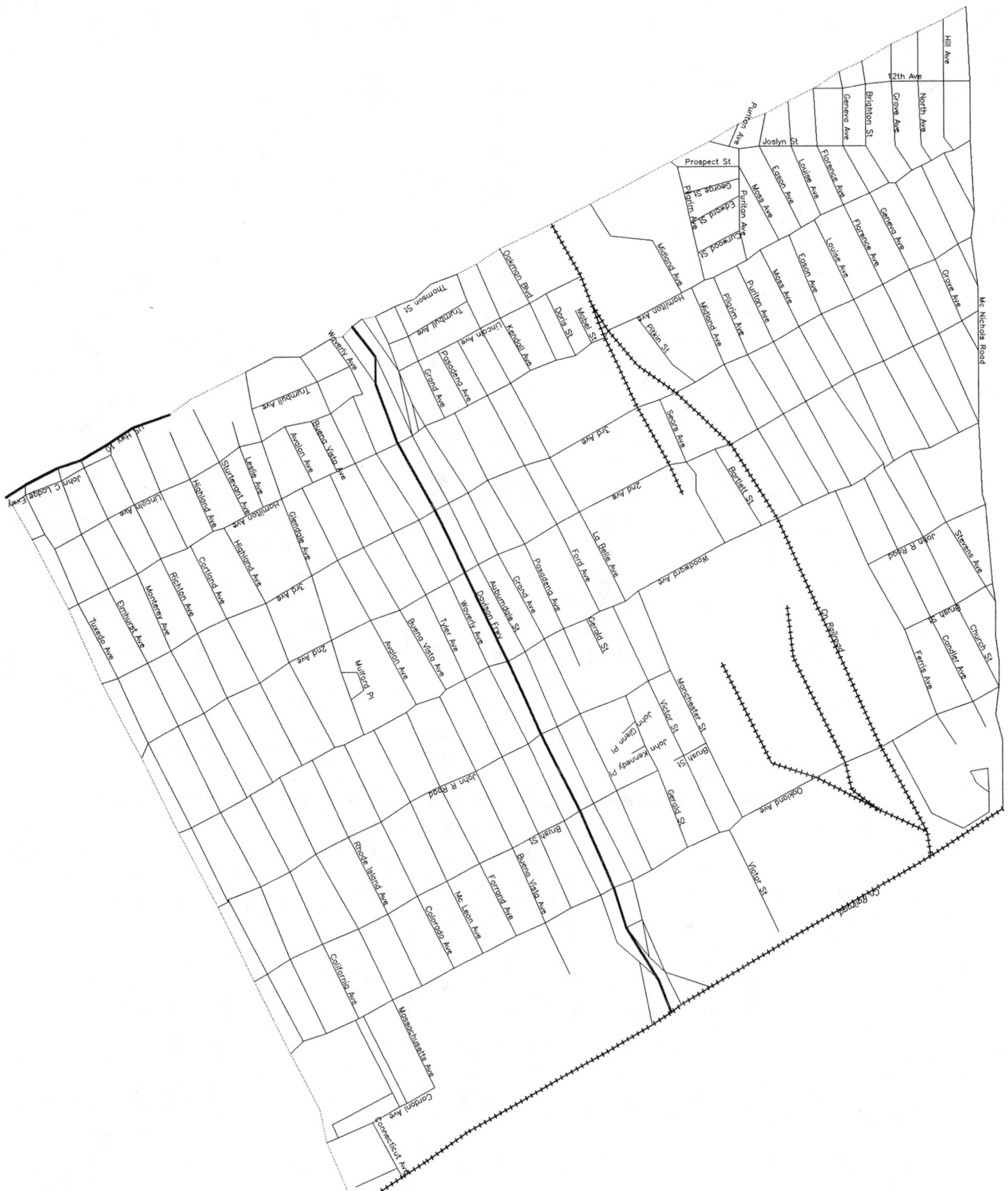

Hill Ave
12th Ave
Geneva Ave
Brighton St
Grove Ave
North Ave
Puritan Ave
Joslyn St
Prospect St
George St
Edward St
Pilgrim Ave
Puritan Ave
Colwood St
Moss Ave
Eason Ave
Louise Ave
Florence Ave
Midland Ave
Genevo Ave
Grove Ave
Mc Nichols Road
Oakman Blvd
Thomson St
Trumbull Ave
Lincoln Ave
Kendall Ave
Doris St
Mabel St
Hamilton Ave
Pitkin St
Waverly Ave
Pasadena Ave
Grand Ave
Trumbull Ave
Buena Vista Ave
Avalon Ave
Leslie Ave
Sturtevant Ave
Highland Ave
Hamilton Ave
Lincoln Ave
John C Lodge Fwy
US Hwy 10
3rd Ave
Seara Ave
Bartlett St
2nd Ave
Glendale Ave
Highland Ave
Cortland Ave
Richton Ave
Monterey Ave
Elmhurst Ave
Tuxedo Ave
3rd Ave
La Belle Ave
Ford Ave
Pasadena Ave
Grand Ave
Auburndale St
Davison Frwy
Waverly Ave
Tyler Ave
Buena Vista Ave
Avalon Ave
Mulford Pl
2nd Ave
Woodward Ave
John R Road
Stevens Ave
Brush St
Church St
Candler Ave
Ferris Ave
Gerald St
CN Railroad
Manchester St
Victor St
John Glenn Pl
John Kennedy Pl
Brush St
Gerald St
Oakland Ave
John R Road
Brush St
Rhode Island Ave
Buena Vista Ave
Farrand Ave
Mc Lean Ave
Colorado Ave
California Ave
Massachusetts Ave
Cardoni Ave
Connecticut Ave
Victor St
CN Railroad
N

HILLSDALE

Pop. 8,170

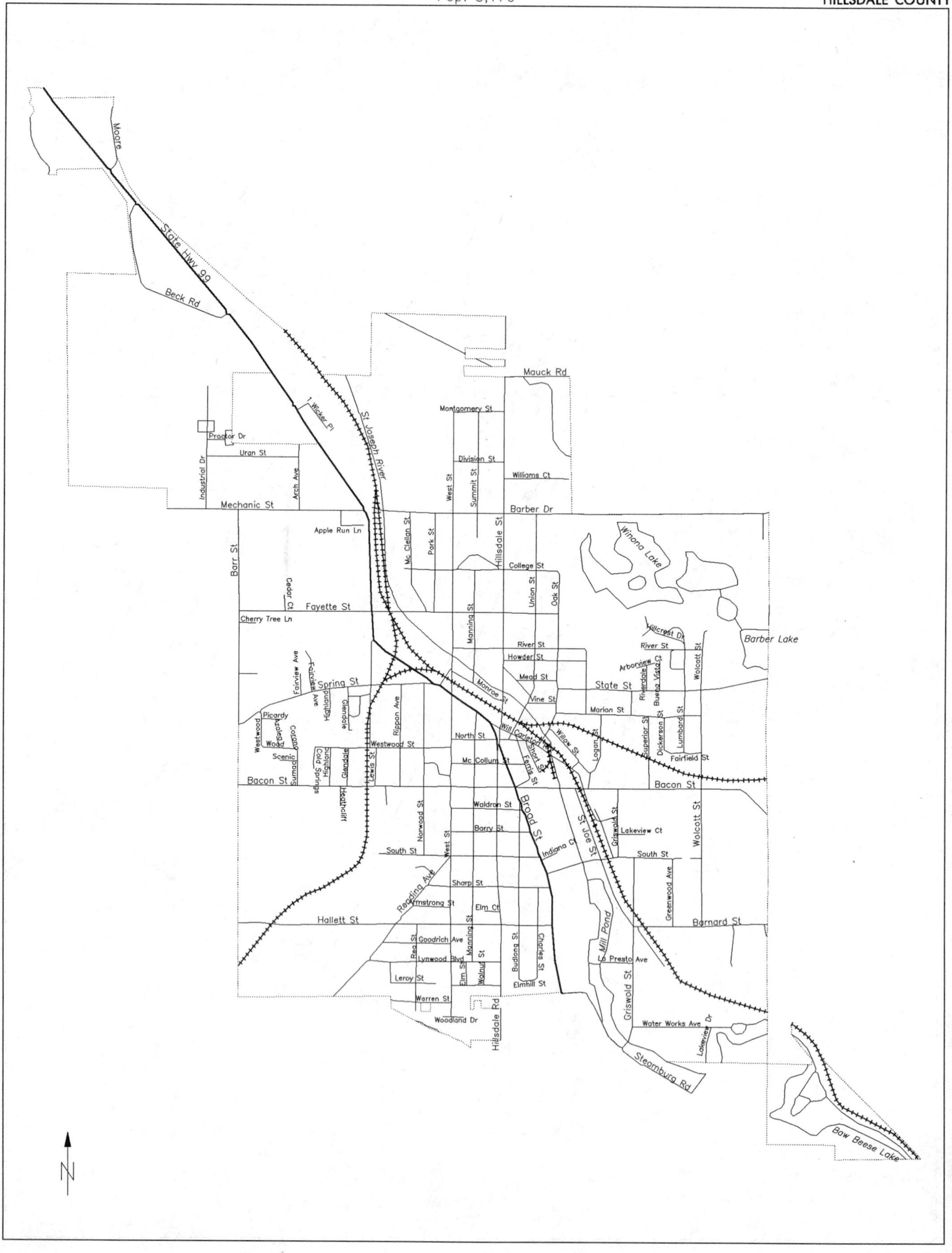

Moore
State Hwy 99
Beck Rd
1 Wicker Pl
St Joseph River
Mauck Rd
Montgomery St
Proctor Dr
Uran St
Division St
Williams Ct
Industrial Dr
Arch Ave
West St
Summit St
Mechanic St
Barber Dr
Apple Run Ln
Mc Clellan St
Park St
Hillsdale St
Winona Lake
Barr St
College St
Union St
Oak St
Cedar Ct
Fayette St
Manning St
Cherry Tree Ln
Hillcrest Dr
River St
Barber Lake
Howder St
Wolcott St
Arborview Ct
Fairview Ave
Spring St
Mead St
Monroe St
State St
Riverdale
Buena Vista Ct
Highland
Glendale
Rippon Ave
Vine St
Marion St
Picardy
Azalea
Westwood
Wood
Coronado
Will Carleton Rd
Superior St
Dickerson St
Lumbard St
Westwood St
North St
Willow St
Logan St
Scenic
Cold Springs
Lewis St
Short St
Fairfield St
Mc Collum St
Ferris St
Bacon St
Sumac
Heathcliff
Waldron St
Broad St
Norwood St
Barry St
St Joe St
Griswold St
Lakeview Ct
South St
Indiana Ct
Reading Ave
Sharp St
Greenwood Ave
Armstrong St
Elm Ct
Hallett St
Mill Pond
Bernard St
Goodrich Ave
Reo St
Budlong St
Charles St
Lynwood Blvd
Walnut St
Lo Presto Ave
Leroy St
Elm St
Elmhill St
Warren St
Woodland Dr
Hillsdale Rd
Water Works Ave
Lakeview Dr
Steamburg Rd
Baw Beese Lake
N

Tulip City Airport
Old Orchard Rd
Central Bay Rd
Midway Ave
Blackbass Ave
Bay Ave
Pleasant Ave
Myrtle Ave
Easy Ct
27th St
Goldenrod Ave
Aster Ave
Ruth Ave
Lugers Rd
Franklin St
Azalea St
Larkwood Dr
Concord Dr
Graafschap Rd
Sandy Ln
Plasman Ave
Diekema Ave
Homestead Ave
Ottawa Ave
Cleveland Ave
Pioneer Ave
Harrison Ave
Van Raalte Ave
Washington Ave
Washington
Maple Ave
Pine Ave
River Ave
Central Ave
College Ave
Columbia Ave
Lincoln Ave
Elmdale Ct
Lawndale Ave
Prospect Ave
Cumberland Ct
Hawthorn Ct
Camelot Pl
Matt Urban Dr
Meadow Ln
Zonne Ct
Standish Ct
Colonial Ct
Alden Ct
Candlelight Dr
Industrial Ave
Royce Ave
Vassar Ave
Apple Ave
Hastings St
Brooks Ave
Windcrest Dr
Waverly Rd
Hunters Run Rd
Fairbanks Ave
Century Ln
Garretson Rd
United States Highway 31 Bus
Settlers Rd
Ferris Ave
Calvin Ave
Dartmouth Ave
Cambridge Ave
Glendale Ave
Cypress Ave
Grandview Ave
Orlando Ave
Farrington Blvd
Ridgeland Ct
Jennifer Ln
Birchwood Ave
Timberwood Ln
Legion Ct
Brook Lane Ave
Country Club Rd
Oxford Ct
Haymarket Rd
Sunset Dr
Quarter Line Rd
Paw Paw Dr
State Hwy 21
State Hwy 40
Mockingbird Dr
64th St
48th St
40th St
32nd St
24th St
16th St
I-196 Business Rte

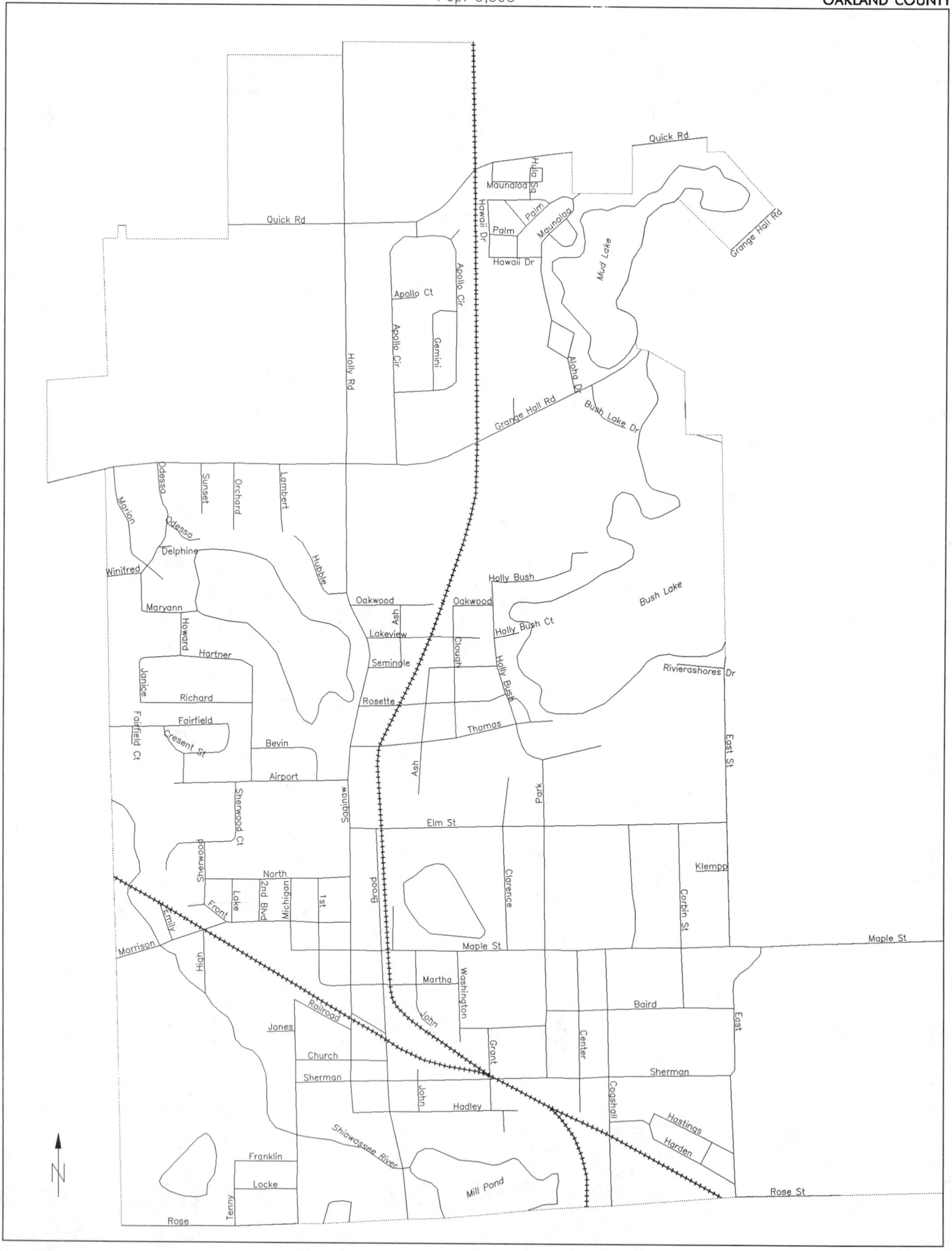

Quick Rd
Hula Sq
Maunaloa
Hawaii Dr
Palm
Maunaloa
Grange Hall Rd
Mud Lake
Quick Rd
Apollo Ct
Apollo Cir
Gemini
Holly Rd
Aloha Dr
Bush Lake Dr
Grange Hall Rd
Odessa
Sunset
Orchard
Lambert
Marion
Odessa
Delphine
Winifred
Hubble
Holly Bush
Maryann
Oakwood
Ash
Oakwood
Bush Lake
Howard
Lakeview
Clough
Holly Bush Ct
Hartner
Seminole
Holly Bush
Rivierashores Dr
Janice
Richard
Rosette
Fairfield
Thomas
Fairfield Ct
Cresent St
Bevin
East St
Airport
Ash
Park
Saginaw
Sherwood Ct
Elm St
Sherwood
Clarence
Klempp
North
Lake
2nd Blvd
Michigan
1st
Broad
Corbin St
Front
Emily
Morrison
Maple St
Maple St
High
Martha
Washington
Baird
Jones
Railroad
John
East
Center
Grant
Church
Sherman
Sherman
John
Hadley
Cogshall
Hastings
Shiowassee River
Harden
Franklin
Locke
Mill Pond
Rose St
Tenny
Rose

N

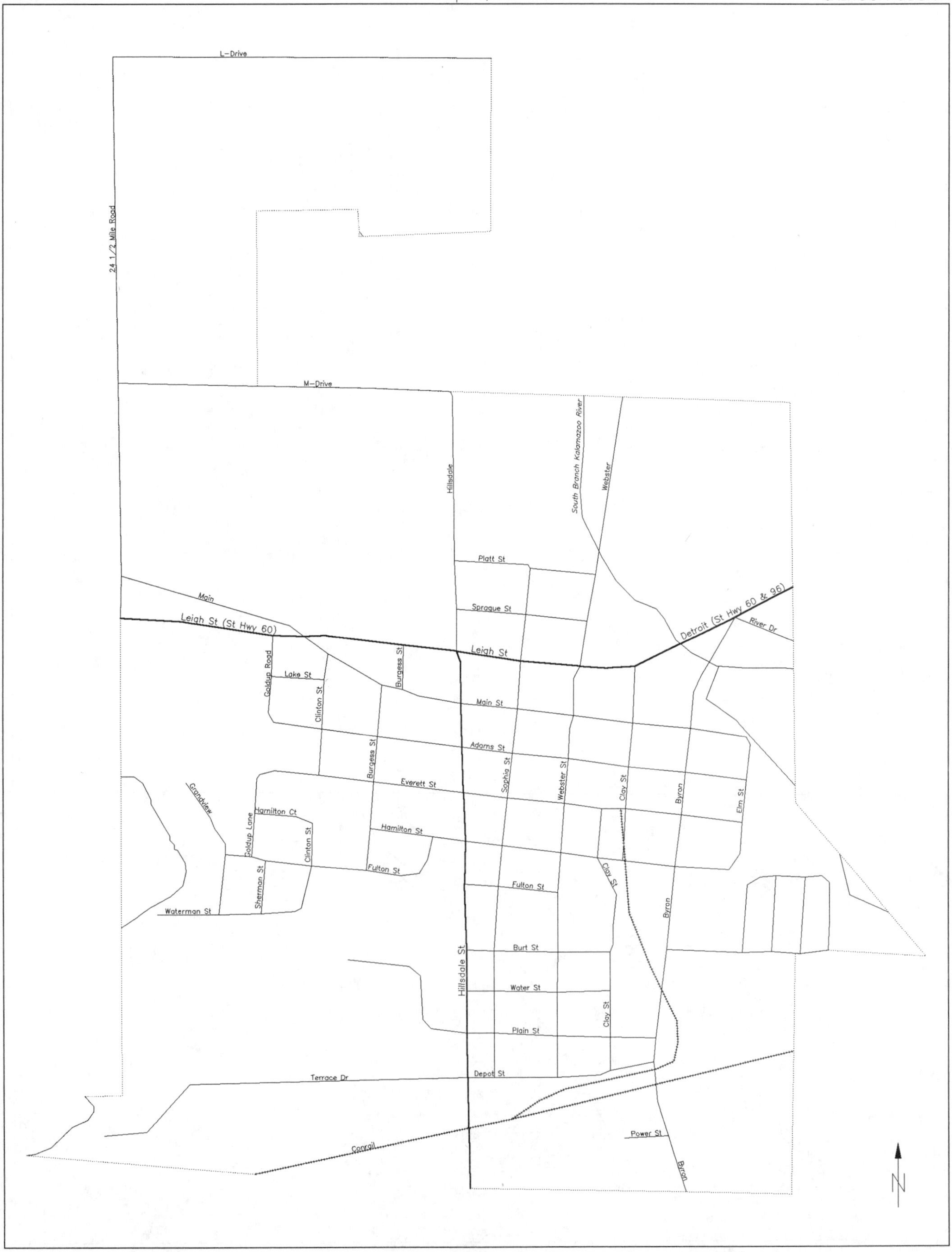

L-Drive
24 1/2 Mile Road
M-Drive
Hillsdale
South Branch Kalamazoo River
Webster
Platt St
Sprague St
Main
Leigh St (St Hwy 60)
Leigh St
Detroit (St Hwy 60 & 96)
River Dr
Goldup Road
Lake St
Clinton St
Burgess St
Main St
Adams St
Everett St
Sophia St
Webster St
Clay St
Byron
Elm St
Grandview
Hamilton Ct
Goldup Lane
Hamilton St
Fulton St
Sherman St
Waterman St
Burt St
Water St
Plain St
Hillsdale St
Terrace Dr
Depot St
Conrail
Power St
N

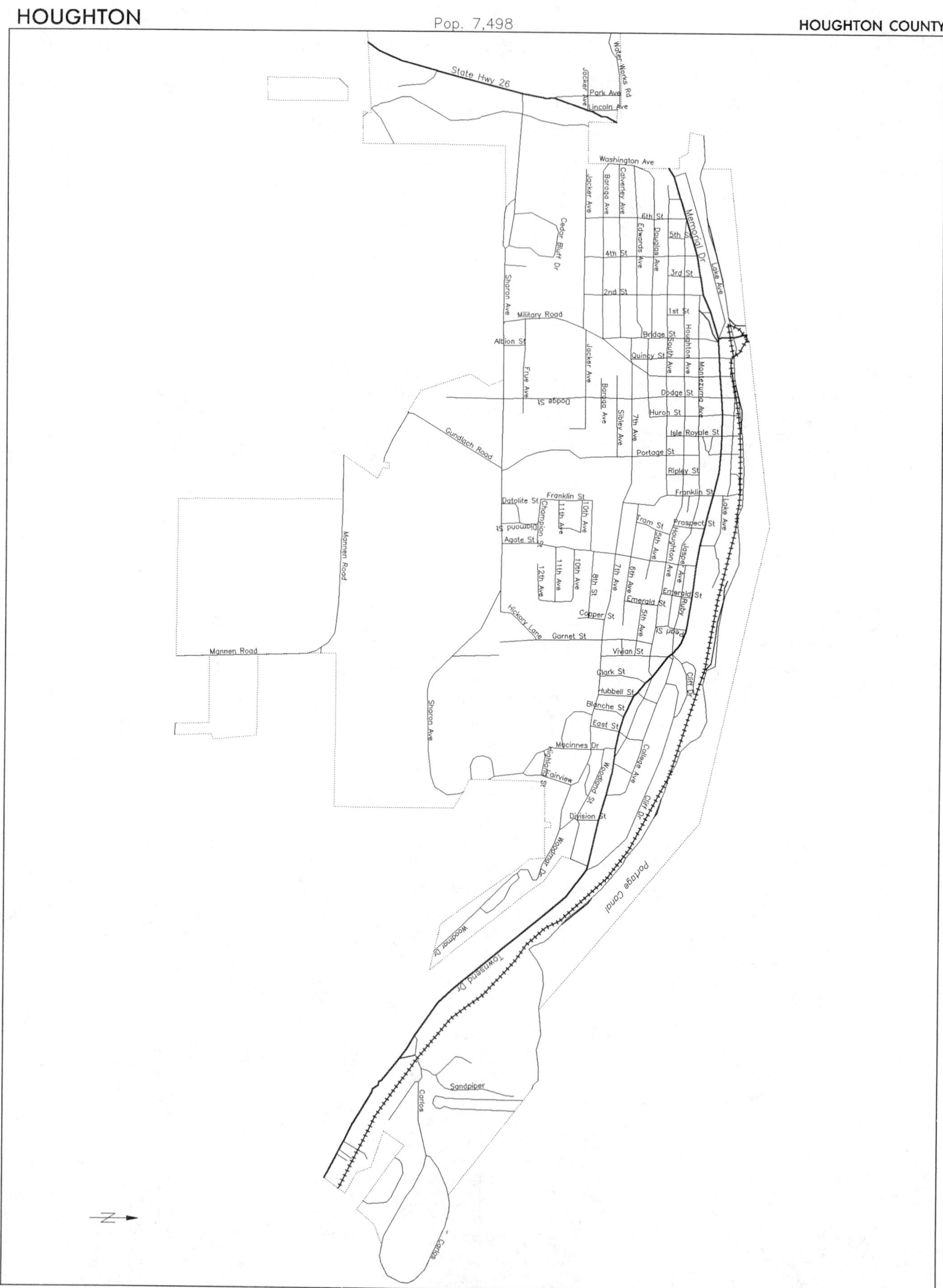
State Hwy 26
Water Works Rd
Park Ave
Lincoln Ave
Jacker Ave
Washington Ave
Calverley Ave
Baraga Ave
6th St
5th St
4th St
3rd St
2nd St
1st St
Edwards Ave
Douglas Ave
Memorial Dr
Lake Ave
Cedar Bluff Dr
Sharon Ave
Military Road
Albion St
Frue Ave
Bridge St
Quincy St
South Ave
Houghton Ave
Montezuma Ave
Dodge St
Huron St
Isle Royale St
Portage St
Ripley St
Franklin St
Sibley Ave
7th Ave
Gundlach Road
Datolite St
Champion St
11th Ave
10th Ave
Diamond St
Agate St
12th Ave
8th St
6th Ave
5th Ave
Tram St
Prospect St
Jasper Ave
Ruby
Emerald St
Copper St
Pearl St
Hickory Lane
Garnet St
Vivian St
Clark St
Hubbell St
Blanche St
East St
Macinnes Dr
Highland St
Fairview
Woodland St
College Ave
Cliff Dr
Division St
Woodmar Dr
Portage Canal
Townsend Dr
Mannen Road
Sharon Ave
Sandpiper
Carlos

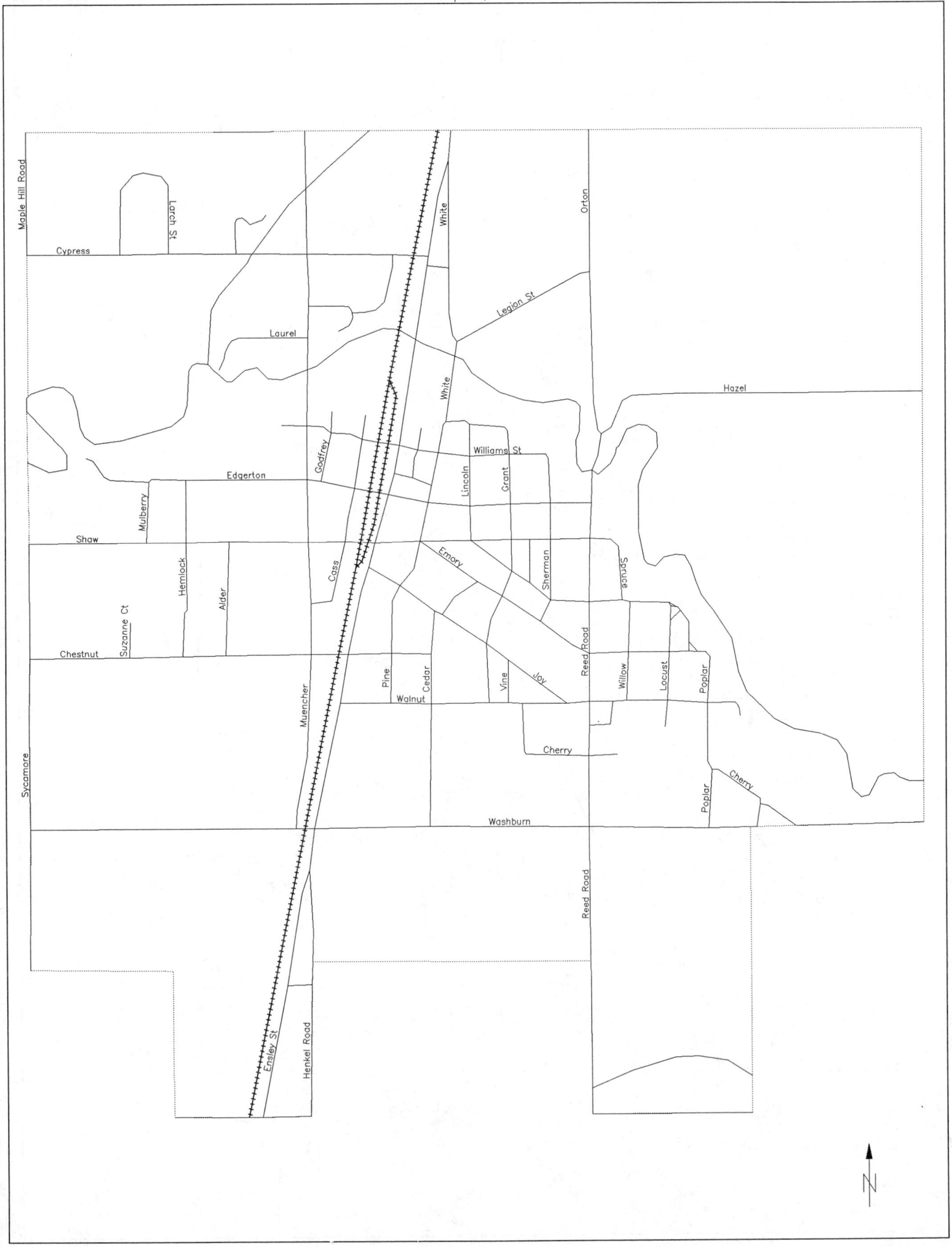

HOWARD CITY

Pop. 1,351

MONTCALM COUNTY

Maple Hill Road
Larch St
White
Orton
Cypress
Legion St
Laurel
White
Hazel
Williams St
Godfrey
Lincoln
Grant
Edgerton
Mulberry
Shaw
Emory
Cass
Hemlock
Sherman
Spruce
Alder
Suzanne Ct
Chestnut
Reed Road
Pine
Cedar
Vine
Joy
Willow
Locust
Poplar
Muencher
Walnut
Cherry
Sycamore
Cherry
Poplar
Washburn
Reed Road
Ensley St
Henkel Road
N

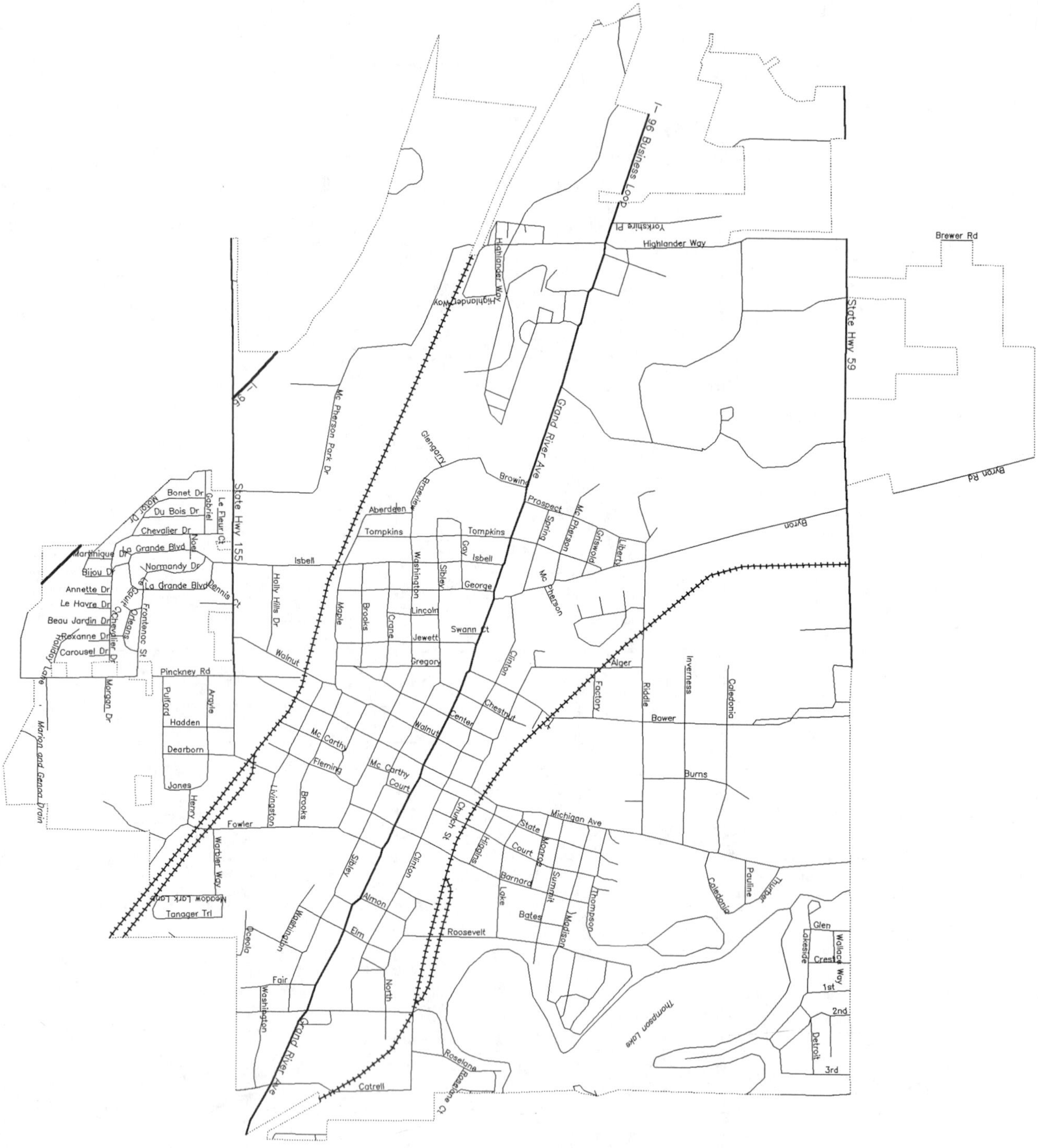

HOWELL

Pop. 8,184

LIVINGSTON COUNTY

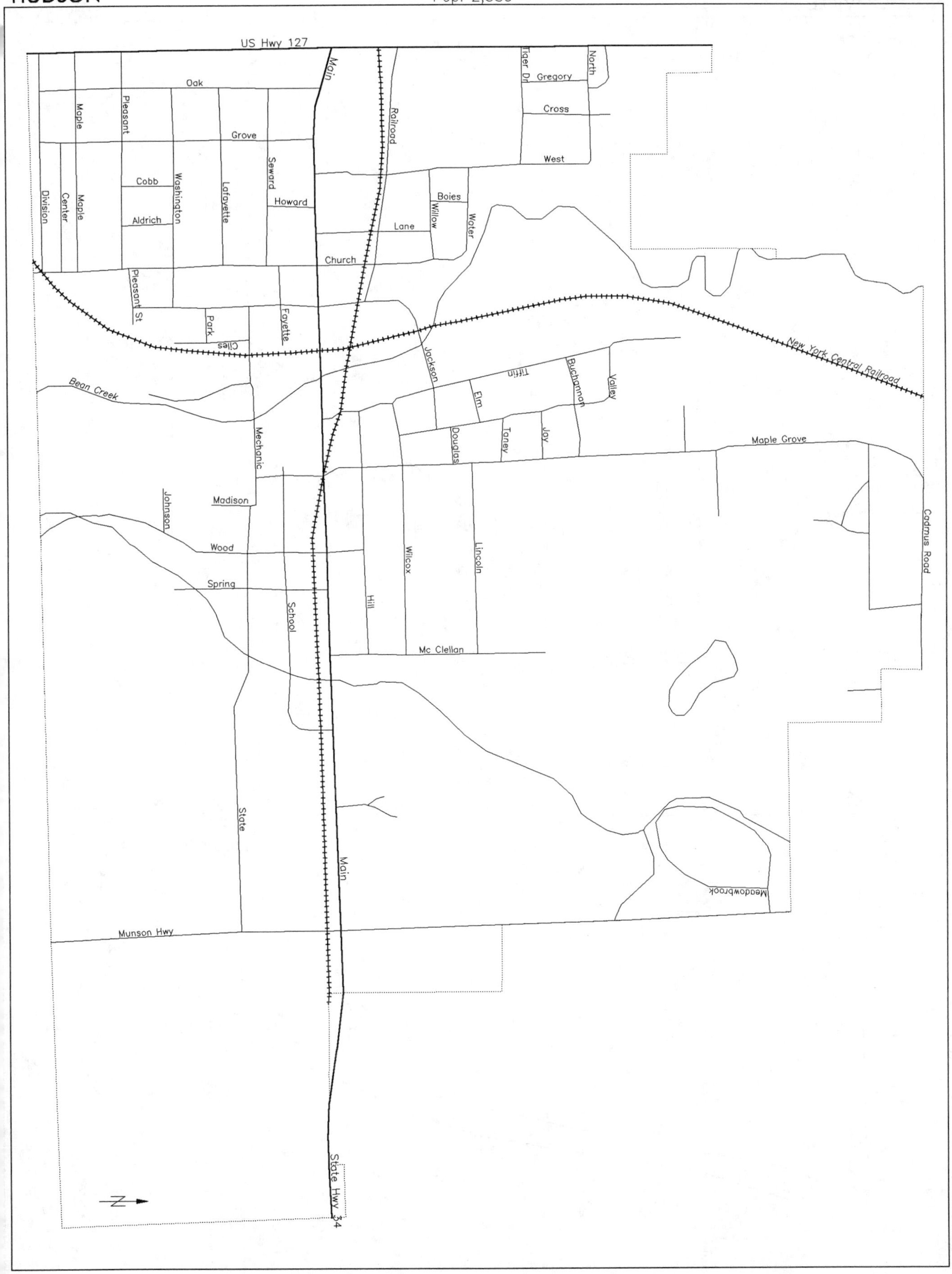

US Hwy 127
Main
Railroad
Tiger Dr
Gregory
North
Oak
Maple
Pleasant
Cross
Grove
West
Seward
Cobb
Washington
Lafayette
Howard
Boies
Willow
Water
Division
Center
Maple
Aldrich
Lane
Church
Pleasant St
Park
Fayette
Giles
New York Central Railroad
Jackson
Tiffin
Buchannan
Valley
Bean Creek
Elm
Douglas
Taney
Jay
Mechanic
Maple Grove
Madison
Johnson
Wood
Wilcox
Lincoln
Cadmus Road
Spring
School
Hill
Mc Clellan
State
Main
Meadowbrook
Munson Hwy
State Hwy 34

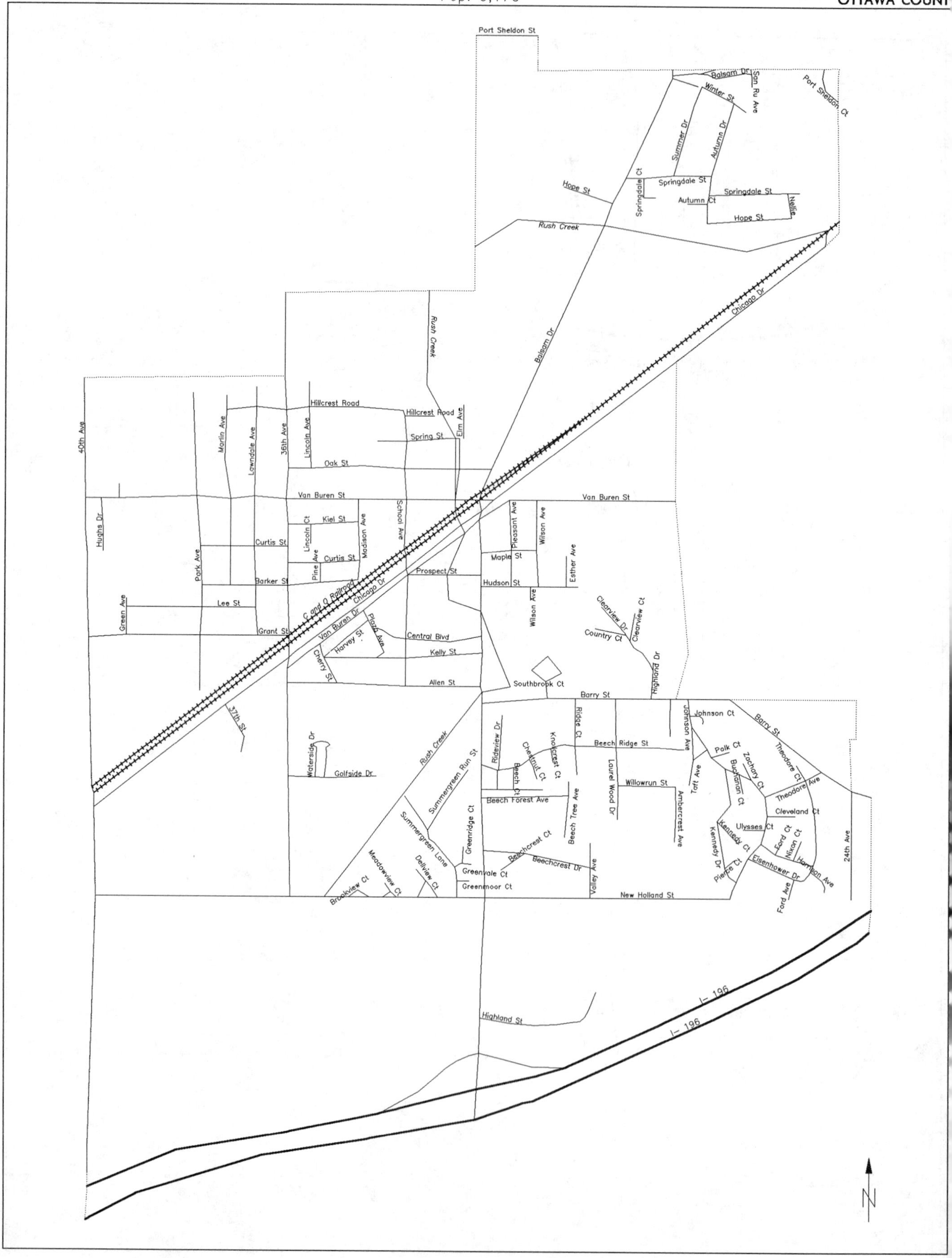
Port Sheldon St
Balsam Dr
San Ru Ave
Port Sheldon Ct
Winter St
Summer Dr
Autumn Dr
Springdale Ct
Springdale St
Autumn Ct
Springdale St
Nellie
Hope St
Hope St
Rush Creek
Chicago Dr
Balsam Dr
Rush Creek
40th Ave
Marlin Ave
Lawndale Ave
36th Ave
Lincoln Ave
Hillcrest Road
Hillcrest Road
Elm Ave
Spring St
Oak St
Van Buren St
Van Buren St
Hughs Dr
School Ave
Kiel St
Lincoln Ct
Madison Ave
Curtis St
Pine Ave
Curtis St
Park Ave
Barker St
Prospect St
Pleasant Ave
Wilson Ave
Maple St
Esther Ave
Hudson St
Wilson Ave
Green Ave
Lee St
C and O Railroad
Chicago Dr
Van Buren Dr
Plaza Ave
Grant St
Harvey St
Central Blvd
Kelly St
Cherry St
Allen St
Clearview Dr
Clearview Ct
Country Ct
Highland Dr
Southbrook Ct
Barry St
37th St
Ridge Ct
Johnson Ave
Johnson Ct
Barry St
Waterside Dr
Golfside Dr
Rush Creek
Summergreen Run St
Rideview Dr
Chestnut Ct
Knollcrest Ct
Beech Ridge St
Beech Ct
Laurel Wood Dr
Willowrun St
Polk Ct
Zachary Ct
Buchanan Ct
Theodore Ct
Theodore Ave
Taft Ave
Beech Forest Ave
Beech Tree Ave
Ambercrest Ave
Cleveland Ct
Greenridge Ct
Summergreen Lane
Beechcrest Ct
Beechcrest Dr
Ulysses Ct
Kennedy Ct
Kennedy Dr
Ford Ct
Nixon Ct
Harrison Ave
Meadowview Ct
Dellview Ct
Greenvale Ct
Valley Ave
Pierce Ct
Eisenhower Dr
24th Ave
Brookview Ct
Greenmoor Ct
New Holland St
Ford Ave
I–196
I–196
Highland St
N

HUNTINGTON WOODS

Pop. 6,419

OAKLAND COUNTY

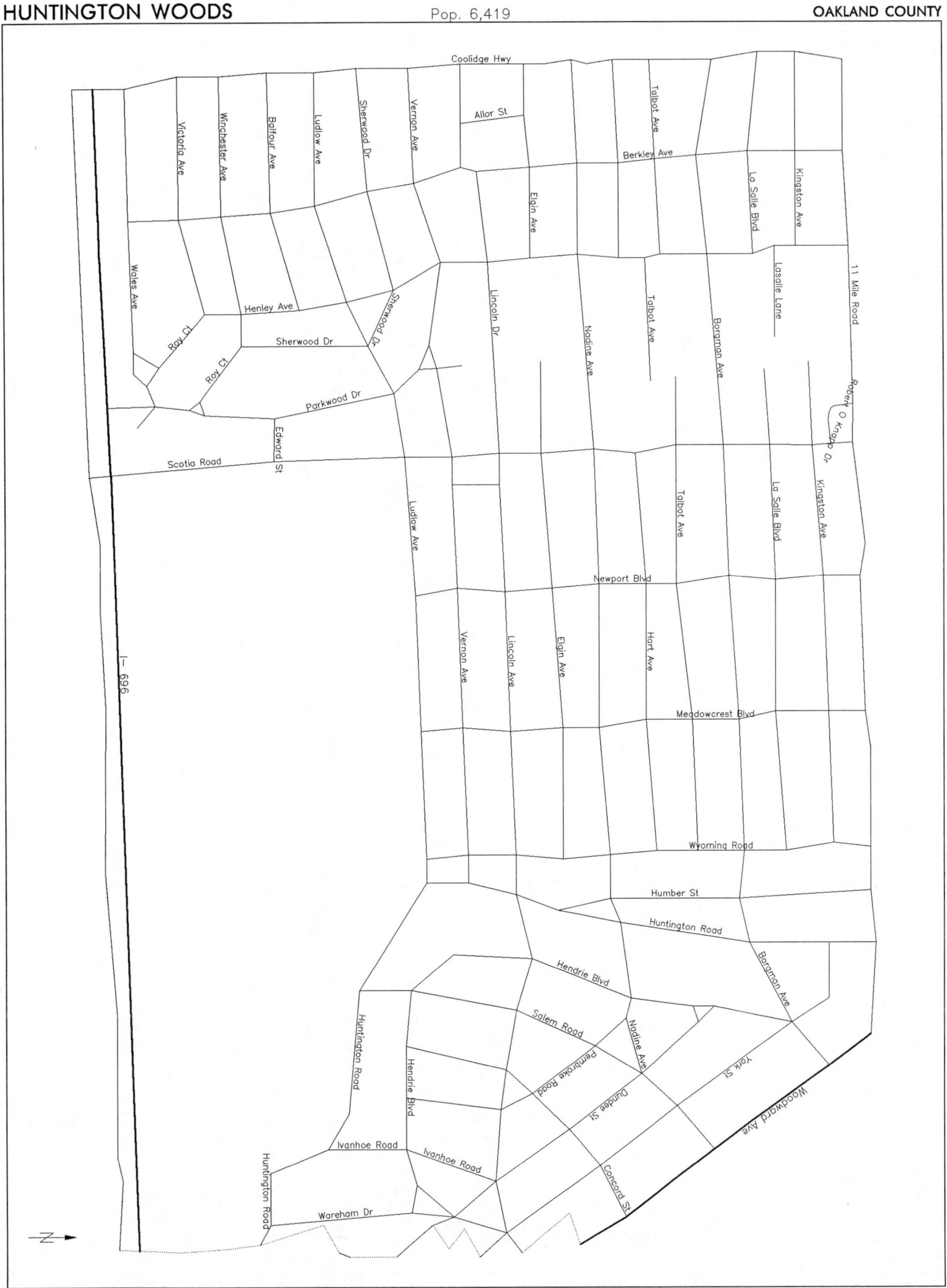

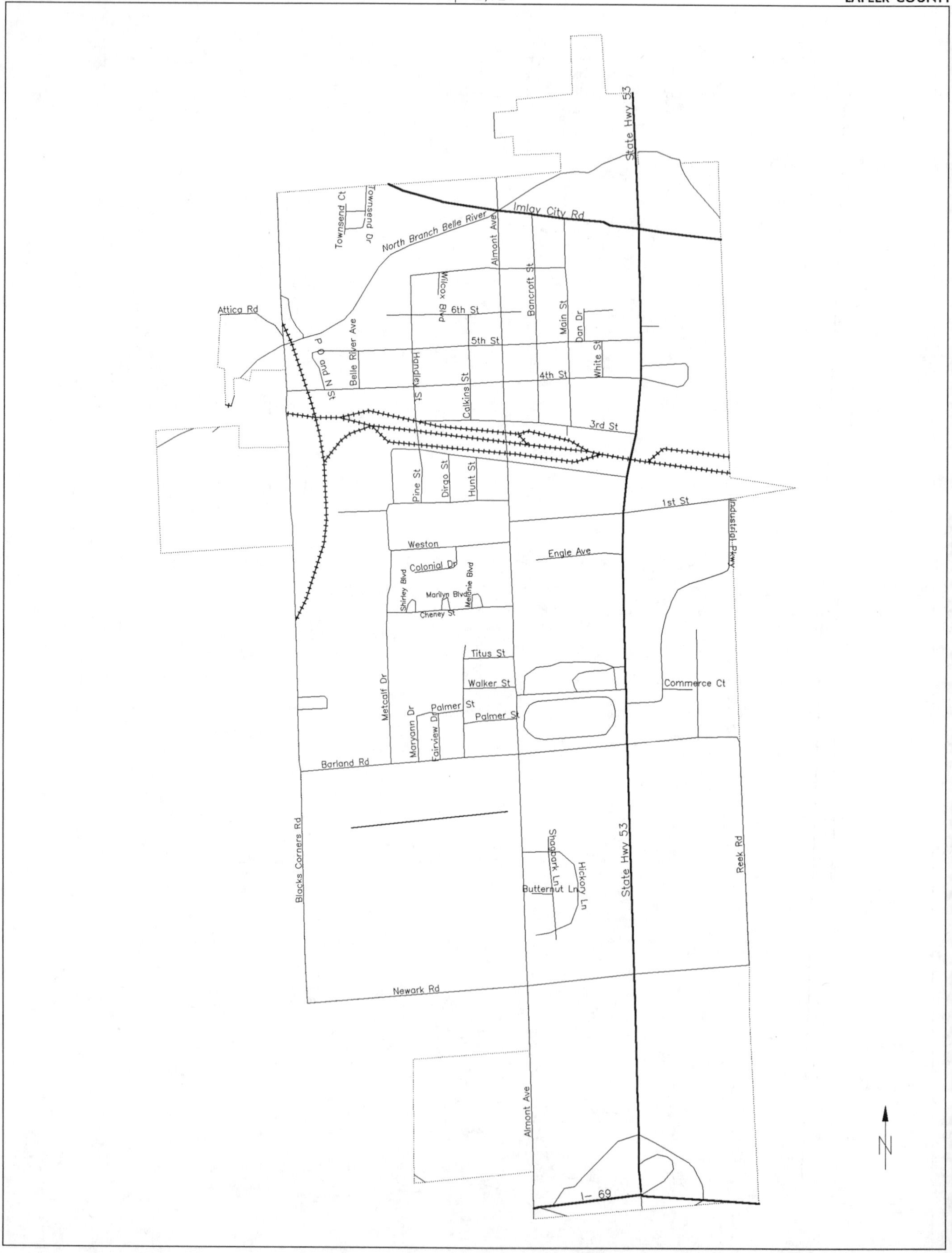

State Hwy 53
Imlay City Rd
Townsend Ct
Townsend Dr
North Branch Belle River
Almont Ave
Wilcox Blvd
Bancroft St
Attica Rd
6th St
Main St
Dan Dr
5th St
P O and N St
Belle River Ave
Handley St
White St
4th St
Calkins St
3rd St
Pine St
Dirgo St
Hunt St
1st St
Industrial Pkwy
Weston
Engle Ave
Colonial Dr
Shirley Blvd
Marilyn Blvd
Melanie Blvd
Cheney St
Titus St
Walker St
Commerce Ct
Metcalf Dr
Palmer St
Palmer St
Maryann Dr
Fairview Dr
Barland Rd
Blacks Corners Rd
Shagbark Ln
Hickory Ln
Butternut Ln
State Hwy 53
Reek Rd
Newark Rd
Almont Ave
I- 69
N

Michigan Ave (US 12)
Henry Ruff Road
Cherry Hill Road
Cherry Hill Trl
Middlebelt Road
Inkster Road
Beech Daly Road
John Daly Road
Rouge River Lower
Pierce Ave
Carlysle Ave
Andover Ave
Kink Ave
Liberty Ct
Annapolis Ct
Annapolis Ter
Annapolis Cir
Liberty Ave
Pine Ct
Lovett Ave
Burton Ave
Meadow Cir
Farnum Ave
Burns Ave
Tegge Ct
Beech Ave
Thomas Cir
Pine Ave
Frazier Ct
Northland Ave
York Ave
Yorkville Ct
Wayland Ct
Vicksburg Ct
Tipton Ct
Bridgeport Ct
Crystal Ct
Durand Ct
Manning St
Ludington Ave
Kewadin Ave
Irene Ave
Springhill Ave
Isabelle Ave
Harriet Ave
Harrison Ave
Walnut Ave
Ash Ave
Hickory Ave
Spruce Ave
Henry Ave
Williams Ave
Moore Ave
Moore Ct
Moore Cir
Lafayette-Allen Ave
Chestnut Ave
Cherry St
Reynolds Ave
Pine St
Robinson Ct
Frederick Ct
Douglas Ct
Wellington Ave
Kitch Ave
Florence Ave
Princeton Ave
Sylvia Ave
Princess Ave
De Soto Ave
New York Ave
Edsel Ave
Hopkins Ave
Ross Ave
Norfolk Road
Dunning Ave
Bayham Ave
Bayhan Drain
Oxford Ave
Plum St
Annapolis Ave
Colgate Ave
Dartmouth Ave
Meadowdale Ave
Carlysle Ave
Penn Ave
Notre Dame Ave
Yale Ave
Lehigh Ave
Stanford Ave
Spring Ct
Spring Arbor Ct
Spring Arbor Dr
Brook Lane
Jeffrey Lane
Wellesley Dr
Meadow Lane
Palmer Ave
Carlton St
Barrington Ave
Hyde Park Dr
Central Ave
Central St
Eastern Ave
Riverview Dr
Isabelle St
Harriet Ave
St Michael
Justine Ave
Algier Ave
Leith Ave
Huck Ct
Phipps Ave
Wietholt Ct
West St
Hill St
Hills Dr
Oakland Dr
River Park Dr
Kean St
Bayhan St
Trowbridge Ave
Fair Bairn Dr
Franklin Dr
Kenwood Dr
Woodbine Dr
Clair Ave
Western Ave
Division Ave
Carver Drain
Grandview St
Steinhauer Ave
Hiveley St
Judith Ave
Edward Dr
Folker Dr
Betty Lane Dr
Bert Ave
Birchwood Ave
Gertrude Ct
Longfellow Ave
Greenwood Ave
Emerson Ave
O Henry Ct
Somerset Ave
Fernwood Ave
Beechnut Ave
Rosewood Dr
Parkwood Ave
Hazelwood Ave
Glenwood Ave
Oakwood Ave
Grandview Ave
Magnolia Dr
Woodland Dr
Helen Dr
Helen Ave
Avondale Ave
Perrin Drain
Cardwell Ave
Trombley Ave
Arcola Ave
Eastwood Ter
Northwood Dr
Colonial Dr
Crescent Dr
Lucerne Dr
Woodsfield Ave
Sherbourne Dr
Sunningdale Dr
Mount Vernon Dr
Fairwood Dr
Arlington Dr
Amherst Dr
Meadowbrook Dr
Monticello Dr
Somerset Dr
Stollman Dr
Marshall St
Vincent St
Joel Ct
Shadowlawn Dr
Grandmont Dr
Patterson Cir
Biltmore Dr
Blackstone Dr
Cherry Valley Dr
Tobin St

Kaiser St
Chapman St
Fargo
M-21
Yeomans St
Rice St
Brooks
King St
Branch St
Hackett St
King St
Yeomans St
State St
State
Grand Trunk Western Railroad
Washington
Marshall Ct
Taylor Ct
Lincoln
Roselawn
Main
Wells
Forest St
Harter St
Kimble St
Hall St
Dexter
Dexter Ct
Dexter St
Dexter (M-66)
Lawton St
Adams St
Baldie St
High St
Stivens St
Louisa
Steele St
Center St
Cyrus St
Yeomans Ct
Depot St
Amphlette Ter
Pleasant St
Tower
Lytle St
Kidd St
Union
Summit St
Fargo
Colby St
Hudson
Library Ct
Davis Ct
Townsend
Weber Ct
Weber Ct
Welton
De Quack Al
Railroad
Rich St
Webber
Terrace Ave
Lovell Ct
Division St
Ellis Al
Grand River
Jackson St
Ridgewood Ct
Bliss
Webber
Jefferson St
Stevenson
Allen St
Lafayette
Wager Pl
Batson St
Mill St
Washington St
Blanchard St
Bagley St
Main
Morse St
Bayard St
Benton Ct
Park St
Johnson St
Johnson St
Robertson Ct
Jones St
Stevenson St
Prospect
Oak St
Lovell St
Crawford
Maple St
Highland Dr
View Dr
Skyview Dr
Prairie View
Chesapeake and Ohio Railroad
Blue Water Hwy (M-21)
Beardsley Road
Prairie Creek
Main St
N

IRON MOUNTAIN

Pop. 8,525

DICKINSON COUNTY

Park Ave
Park View Dr
Park Rd
Harding Ave
Beech St
Birch St
Maple St
Hemlock St
Spruce St
Tamarack St
Pine St
Forest St
Lake St
Foster St
Ludington St
Hughitt St
Fleshiem St
Golfview Dr
Hemlock St
Walker St
Lower Pine Mountain Rd
Upper Pine Mountain Rd
Pinewood Ct
Pine Ct
Evergreen Dr
Hemlock St
D ST
C ST
B ST
A ST
Brown
Wells St
Houghteling St
Fairbanks St
Kent St
Crystal Lake Blvd
Ripley St
Detroit St
Pelham St
Cook St
F ST
E ST
G ST
Kimberly Ave
Stockbridge Ave
Prospect Ave
Woodward Ave
Carpenter Ave
Milwaukee
River Ave
Carollo
Cedar Ave
H ST
Iron Mountain St
Washington St
Madison St
Adams St
Jackson St
Van Buren St
I ST
Alexander Dr
Terminal Ave
Park Ave
Stephenson Ave
Oslo Ave
Ridge Rd
Birch Dr
Oak Dr
Hydraulic Falls Rd
Chicago and Northwestern RR
US Hwy 141
Park Ave
Phill Rahal Dr
2nd St
3rd St
4th St
5th St
6th St
7th
Chapin St
Quinnesec St
Norway St
Ulcan St
Millie St
Margaret St
Smith St
Pewabic St
Aragon St
Blaine St
Stanton St
Grant St
Grand Blvd
Broadway
Crowell St
Devereaux St
Williamson St
Lakeside Dr
Main St
Kennedy
Apollo Dr
Grant
Bayshore Dr
Kimberly Ave
Milwaukee Ave
Iron Mountain St
Iron Mountain
Milliman
Mary Ave
Lehmann Ave
Milwaukee
Railroad St
Railroad
Spring St
Sunset
Pewabic St
Aragon St
Frank Pipp Dr
Quincy St
Industrial Dr
Quinn-Lake Antoine Rd
B ST
E ST
A ST

US Hwy 2
Rosetti Rd
17 Th Ave
Franklin St
Hanson St
Monroe St
Madison St
Buckholz St
Hunter St
County Rd 653
Iron River
14 Th Ave
13 Th Ave
Jackson St
Division St
Adams St
Minkler St
10 Th Ave
Maple St
9 Th Ave
9 Th Ave
8 Th Ave
Genesee St
8 Th
Jackson St
7 Th Ave
7 Th Ave
6 Th Ave
Cayuga St
6 Th
5 Th Ave
Ross St
Minkler St
5 Th
M-189
4 Th
4 Th Ave
3 Rd Ave
2 Nd Ave
2nd Ave
Madison St
1 St Ave
Monroe St
Burns St
1 St Ave
River Ave
River Rd
Allen St
Virgil St
Franklin St
Riverside Ave
Cedar Ave
Minkler St
Hemlock St
Ross St
Boyington St
Maple St
Adams St
Cayuga St
Lay Ave
Lay Ave
Lay Ave
Hunter St
Grant St
Verona Rd
Lincoln Ave
Bushie Dr
US Hwy 2
Lalley Rd
Water Tank Rd
Ice Lake Rd
Hunter St
Joanne Ave
Sturgeon St
Ice Lake Rd
Sunset Lake Rd
Sunset Creek
Keweenaw Ave.
Mc Pherson
Sleeman St
Bowers Ave
Duff St
Homer Rd
Sunset Lake Rd
N

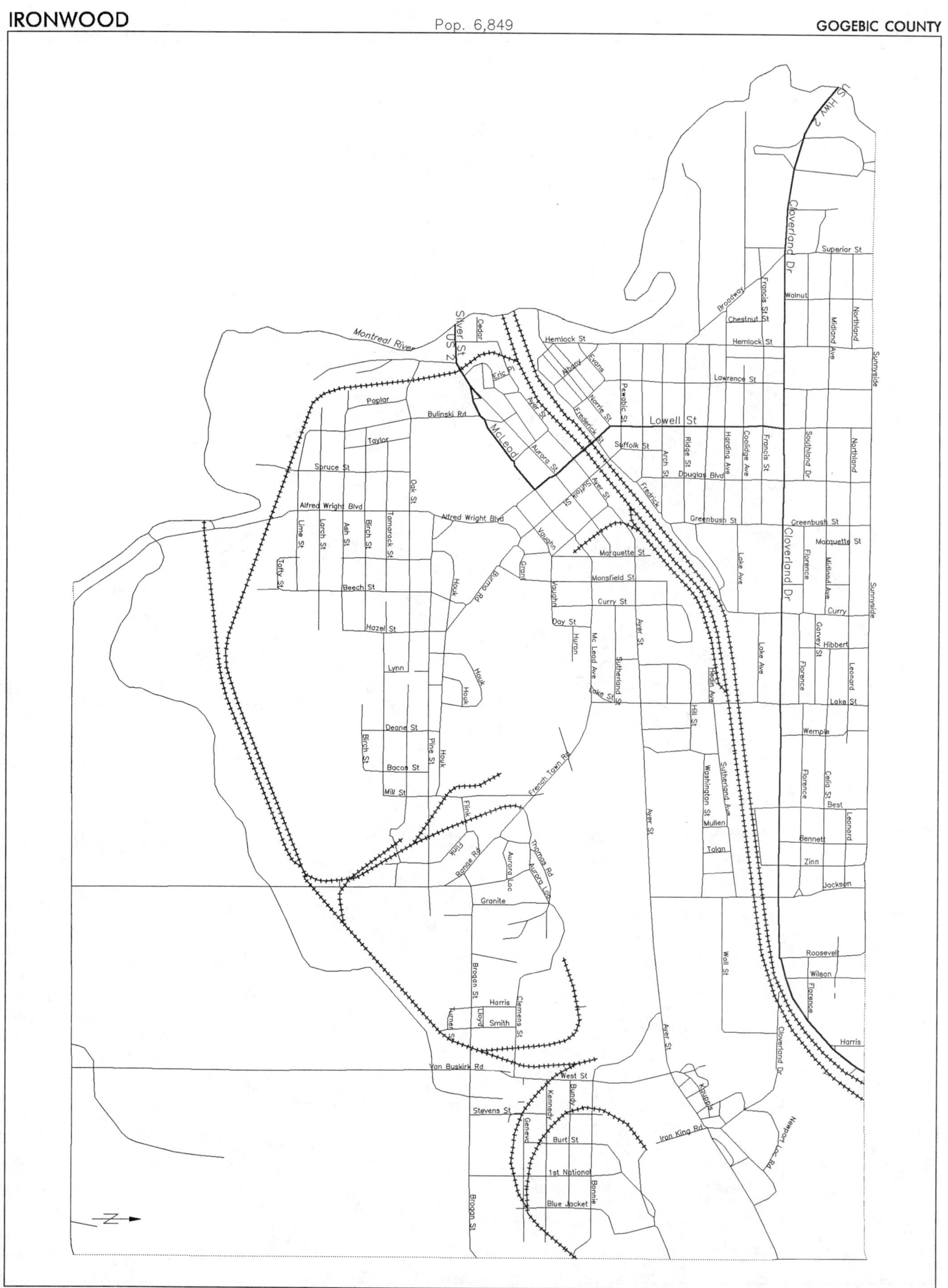

US Hwy 2
Cloverland Dr
Superior St
Walnut
Francis St
Broadway
Chestnut St
Northland
Midland Ave
Sunnyside
Hemlock St
Montreal River
Silver St
US 2
Cedar
Eric Pl
Albany
Evans
Lawrence St
Poplar
Bulinski Rd
Norrie St
Pewabic St
Lowell St
Ayer St
Frederick St
McLeod
Taylor
Suffolk St
Arch St
Ridge St
Harding Ave
Coolidge Ave
Southland Dr
Aurora St
Douglas Blvd
Spruce St
Oak St
Fredrick
Alfred Wright Blvd
Greenbush St
Lime St
Larch St
Ash St
Birch St
Tamarack St
Vaughn
Marquette St
Lake Ave
Florence
Tofty St
Grant
Mansfield St
Beech St
Houk
Burma Rd
Curry St
Curry
Day St
Hazel St
Huron
Mc Lead Ave
Sutherland St
Garvey St
Hibbert
Lynn
Hegan Ave
Leonard
Lake St
Hill St
Deane St
Wemple
Pine St
Bacon St
Washington St
Sutherland Ave
Celia St
French Town Rd
Mill St
Best
Flink
Mullen
Bennett
Tolan
Zinn
Range Rd
Aurora Loc
Thomas Rd
Jackson
Granite
Wall St
Roosevelt
Wilson
Brogan St
Harris
Clemens St
Lloyd
Turner St
Smith
Van Buskirk Rd
West St
Kennedy
Bundy
Knuppis
Stevens St
Geneva
Iron King Rd
Newport Loc Rd
Burt St
1st National
Bonnie
Blue Jacket

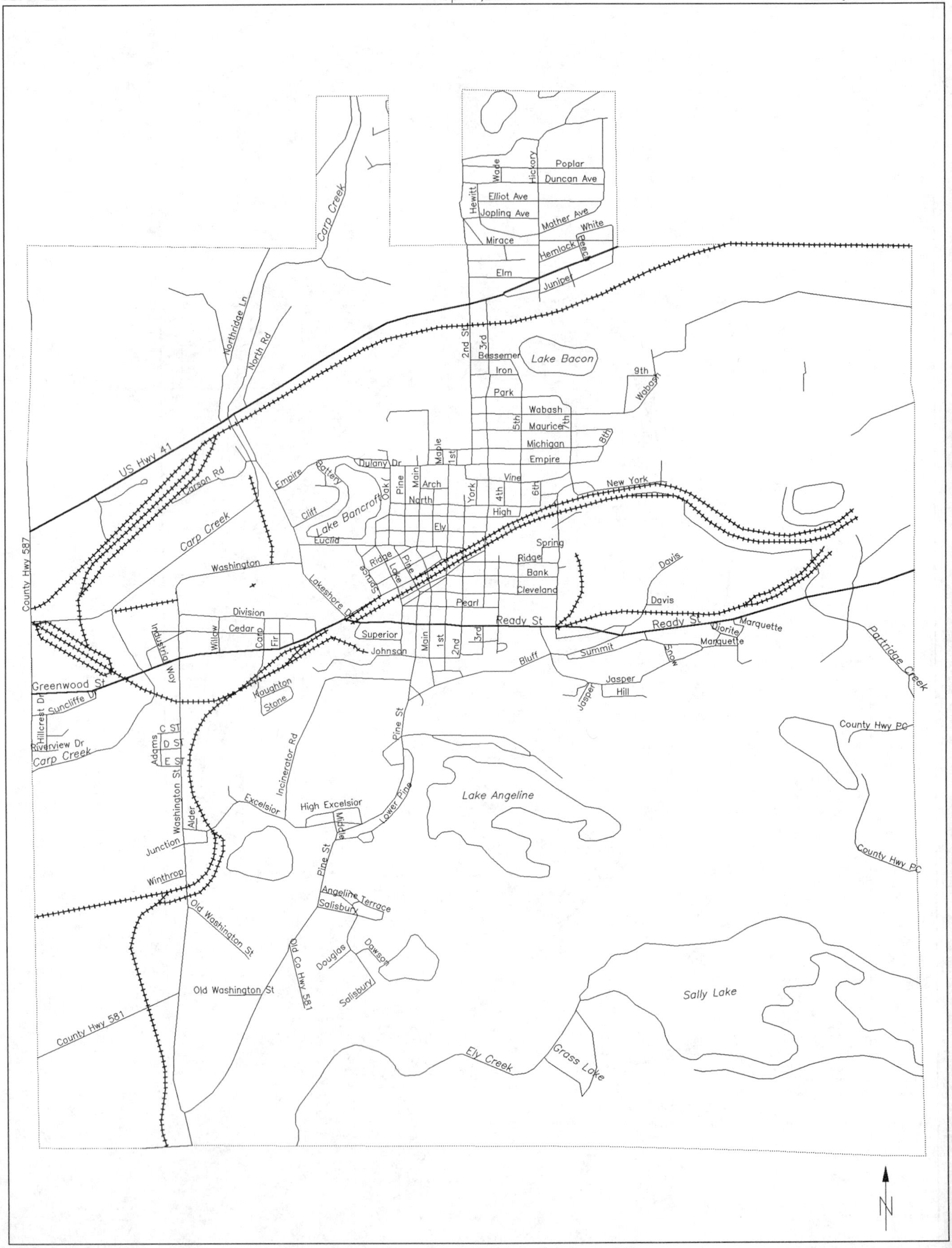
Poplar
Duncan Ave
Wade
Hickory
Hewitt
Elliot Ave
Jopling Ave
Mather Ave
White
Mirace
Hemlock
Beech
Elm
Juniper
Carp Creek
Northridge Ln
North Rd
2nd St
3rd
Bessemer
Lake Bacon
Iron
Park
9th
Wabash
Wabash
5th
7th
Maurice
Michigan
8th
Empire
Maple
1st
Dulany Dr
Battery
Empire
Vine
Pine
Main
Arch
North
York
4th
6th
New York
US Hwy 41
Carson Rd
Oak
Lake Bancroft
Cliff
High
Carp Creek
Ely
Euclid
Spring
Ridge
Ridge
Pine
Lake
Spruce
Bank
Cleveland
Washington
Davis
Davis
County Hwy 587
Lakeshore Dr
Pearl
Division
Cedar
Willow
Carp
Fir
Industrial Way
Superior
Johnson
Main
1st
2nd
3rd
Ready St
Ready St
Diorite
Marquette
Marquette
Summit
Snow
Bluff
Partridge Creek
Jasper
Jasper
Hill
Greenwood St
Suncliffe Dr
Houghton
Stone
Hillcrest Dr
C ST
D ST
E ST
Adams
Riverview Dr
Carp Creek
Pine St
County Hwy PC
Incinerator Rd
Washington St
Lower Pine
Lake Angeline
Excelsior
High Excelsior
Middle
Alder
Junction
Pine St
County Hwy PC
Winthrop
Angeline Terrace
Salisbury
Old Washington St
Old Co Hwy 581
Douglas
Dawson
Salisbury
Old Washington St
Sally Lake
County Hwy 581
Ely Creek
Grass Lake
N

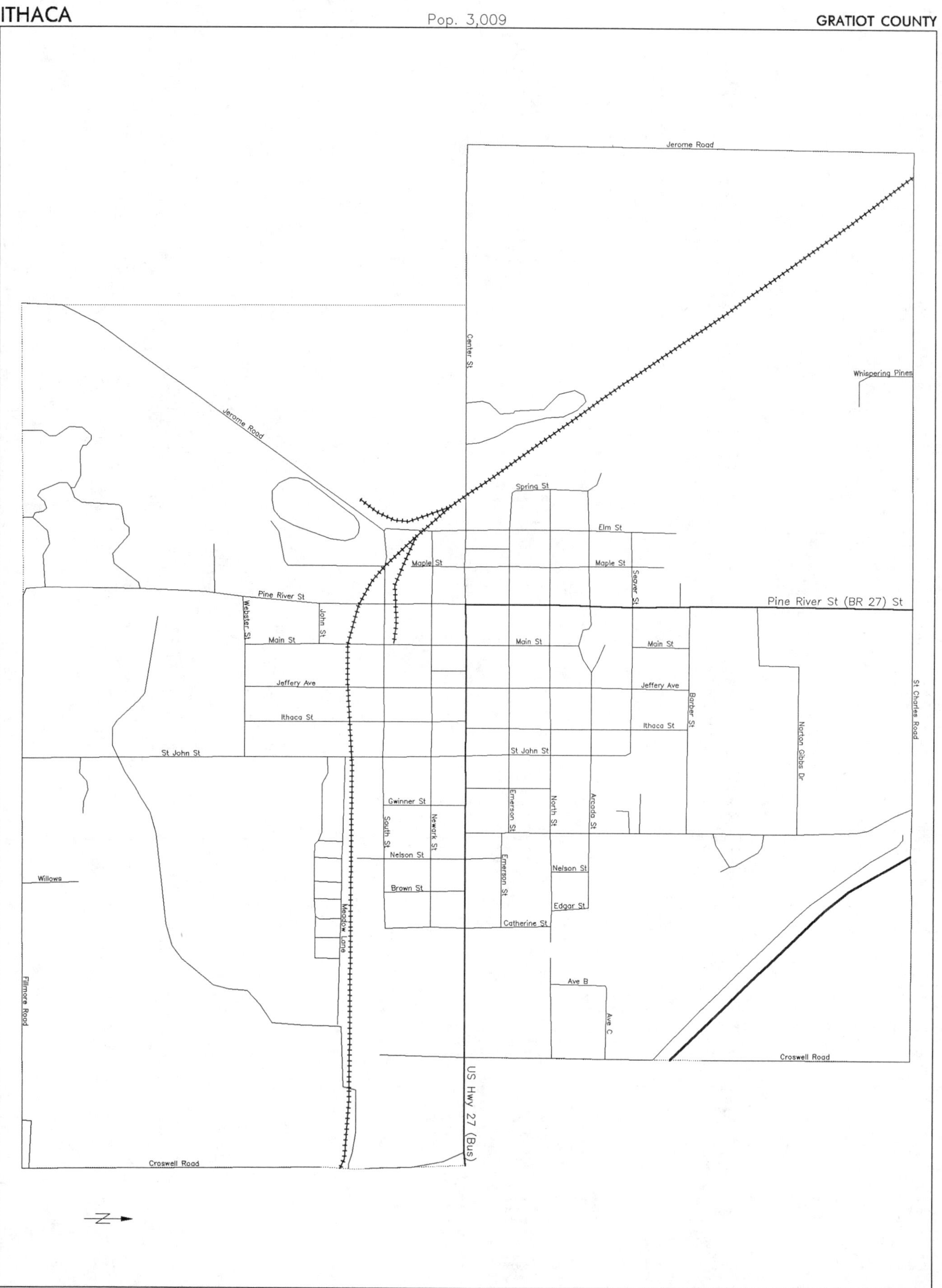
Jerome Road
Center St
Whispering Pines
Jerome Road
Spring St
Elm St
Maple St
Maple St
Seaver St
Pine River St
Pine River St (BR 27) St
Webster St
John St
Main St
Main St
Main St
Jeffery Ave
Jeffery Ave
Ithaca St
Ithaca St
Barber St
St Charles Road
Norton Gibbs Dr
St John St
St John St
Gwinner St
South St
Newark St
Emerson St
North St
Arcada St
Nelson St
Nelson St
Emerson St
Willows
Brown St
Edgar St
Meadow Lane
Catherine St
Ave B
Ave C
Fillmore Road
Croswell Road
US Hwy 27 (Bus)
Croswell Road
N

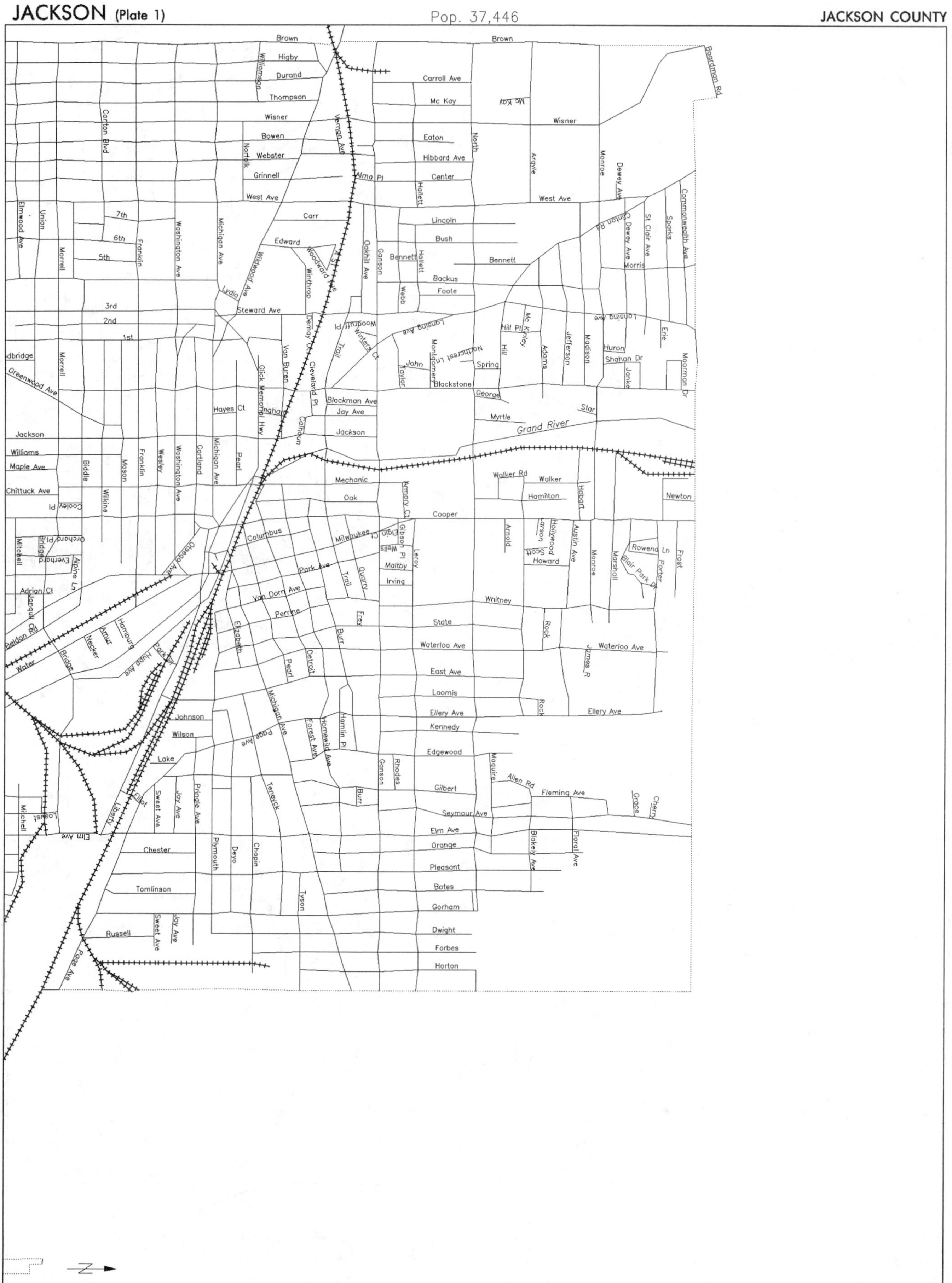
Brown
Higby
Durand
Thompson
Wisner
Bowen
Webster
Grinnell
West Ave
Carroll Ave
Mc Kay
Eaton
Hibbard Ave
Center
North
Argyle
Monroe
Dewey Ave
Boardman Rd
Carlton Blvd
Williamson
Norfolk
Vernon Ave
Alma Pl
Hallett
Elmwood Ave
Union
7th
6th
5th
Franklin
Washington Ave
Michigan Ave
Carr
Edward
Wildwood Ave
Woodward Ave
Winthrop
Oakhill Ave
Ganson
Bennett
Lincoln
Bush
Backus
Foote
Webb
Clinton Rd
St Clair Ave
Sparks
Commonwealth Ave
Morris
Morrell
Lydia
Steward Ave
3rd
2nd
1st
Demoy Ct
Woodruff Pl
Winters Ct
Lansing Ave
Montgomery
Northcrest Ln
John
Taylor
Hill Pl
Mc Kinley
Hill
Spring
Adams
Jefferson
Madison
Huron
Shahan Dr
Janke
Erie
Moorman Dr
Blackstone
George
Star
Myrtle
Grand River
Van Buren
Cleveland Pl
Trail
Blackman Ave
Jay Ave
Jackson
Glick Memorial Hwy
Ingham
Hayes Ct
Calhoun
Woodbridge
Greenwood Ave
Williams
Maple Ave
Chittuck Ave
Cooley Pl
Biddle
Wilkins
Mason
Wesley
Cortland
Pearl
Mechanic
Oak
Armory Ct
Cooper
Walker Rd
Walker
Hamilton
Hobart
Newton
Arnold
Larson
Hollywood
Scott
Howard
Austin Ave
Monroe
Marshall
Rowena Ln
Frost
Porter
Blair Park Dr
Columbus
Milwaukee
Elgin Ct
Gibson Pl
Wells
Maltby
Irving
Leroy
Orchard Pl
Bridges
Everhard
Alpine Ln
Mitchell
Adrian Ct
Janquil
Otsego Ave
Park Ave
Quarry
Van Dorn Ave
Perrine
Whitney
Beldon Ct
Water
Bridge
Necker
Amur
Hamburg
Hupp Ave
Packard
Elizabeth
Frey
Burr
State
Waterloo Ave
Rock
James R
Detroit
East Ave
Loomis
Ellery Ave
Kennedy
Johnson
Wilson
Page Ave
Forest Ave
Homewild Ave
Hamlin Pl
Edgewood
Lake
Rhodes
Maguire
Allen Rd
Fleming Ave
Grace
Cherry
Gilbert
Seymour Ave
Elm Ave
Orange
Pleasant
Bates
Gorham
Dwight
Forbes
Horton
Blakely Ave
Floral Ave
Elliot
Liberty
Sweet Ave
Joy Ave
Pringle Ave
Tenyck
Locust
Chester
Plymouth
Deyo
Chapin
Tomlinson
Tyson
Russell

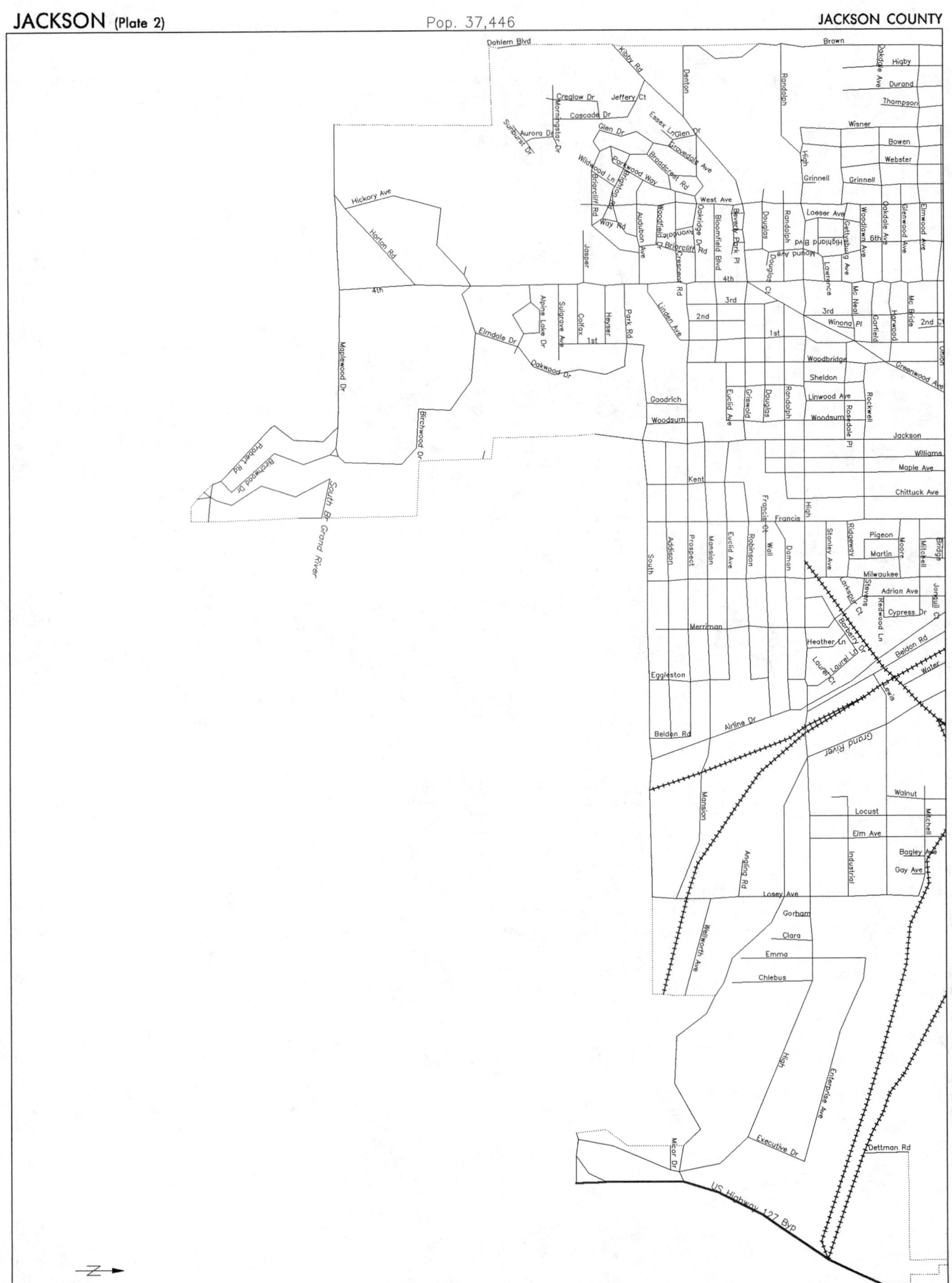

Langs Dr
Ecology Dr
Evans St
Craig St
Parkwood Dr
Greenbrier Pl
Concord Road
Grant St
Salem
Chatam Dr
Strait Ct
Village Lane
Willow St
Chicago St
Jonesville Road
North St
Oak St
Park St
Pinecrest Dr
Church St
Baxter St
Murphy St
Jermain St
South St
Walnut St
Clinton St
Highland St
Baker St
Liberty St
Seneca St
Crest Lane
Franklin St
Drayton
West St
Fayette St
Fayette St
Austin St
Hemlock
Spruce
Juniper
Holly
Fir
Cone
Spruce
Orville
Harley St
Dewitt
Keith
Glendale
Adrian St
Chicago St (US Hwy 12)
Drake St
Olds St
St Joseph River
Maumee St
Gaige St
Reading Ave
Beck Road
Hillsdale County Railway Co.
State Hwy. 99
N

Street	Map	Grid
Lake Forest Dr	4	SE
Lake Forest Ln	4	SE
Lake Hill Dr	4	SW
Lake Ridge Dr	1	SE
Lake St	5	NE
Lake St	6	NW
Lake Terrace Dr	4	SW
Lakesedge Dr	4	NW
Lakeside Dr	5	SW
Lakeview Ave	3	NW
Lakeway Ave	5	SE
Lakeway Ave	6	SW
Lakewood Dr	3	NW
Lama Rd	5	SW
Lamont Ave	6	NW
Lancaster Dr	4	NW
Lane Blvd	5	NE
Lane Blvd	6	NW
Lantern Ln	2	SW
Lark Dr	4	NW
Larkin Ct	3	NW
Larry Ln	4	NE
Lauderdale Dr	1	SE
Laura Ct	2	SW
Law Ave	5	NW
Lawn St	1	SE
Lawrence St	2	SW
Lay Blvd	5	NE
Lay Blvd	6	NW
Leebarton Pl	2	SW
Leighton Ct	3	NW
Leisure Ln	1	SW
Leona Ave	5	SE
Liberty St	5	SW
Lilac Ln	4	NW
Lincoln Ave	3	SW
Lincolnshire	6	SW
Linton St	6	NW
Linwood Dr	4	NW
Little Dr	4	NW
Locust Pl	2	SW
Locust St	2	SW
Logan Ave	4	SE
Lomond Dr	4	NE
Londonderry	1	SW
Long Rd	5	NW
Lookout Ln	6	SW
Lorraine Ave	4	NW
Lovell St	2	SW
Lovers Ln	5	NE
Low Rd	5	NW
Lowden St	4	SE
Lowell St	6	SW
Lucas Ct	2	SW
Luella Ct	5	NE
Luella St	5	NE
Lulu St	2	NW
Lum Ave	3	SW
Lynn Ave	5	SW
Mabel St	2	SW
Madison St	4	SE
Magnolia Cir	4	NW
Main Ct	2	SW
Main St	1	SW
Main St	2	SE
Main St	3	SW
Manchester Rd	6	SE
Manor St	1	NE
Maple Ct	5	NE
Maple St	5	NW
March St	6	NW
Marion Ave	1	SE
Mark Ct	4	NW
Marlane Ave	1	NW
Martin St	2	NE
Marywood St	1	NE
Mason St	2	SW
Mastenbrook Dr	6	SW
Mayfair St	6	SW
Maywood Ave	5	NE
Mc Courtie St	5	NW
Mead St	0	KY
Meadow View	4	NW
Meadowlark Dr	4	SE
Meadowood	3	NW
Melcrest Ave	1	NE
Memory Ln	1	SE
Merrie Ln	5	SW
Merrill St	5	NW
Merriweather	1	SW
Mexicali Ln	4	NW
Meyers St	3	SW
Miami Ave	3	NE
Michael Rd	3	NW
Michigamme	4	NW
Michigan Ave	1	SE
Michigan Ave	2	SW
Michigan Ave	3	SW
Michigan Ave	4	NW
Michigme	4	NW
Michikal St	2	SW
Middlebury Dr	4	NW
Midvale Ter	5	NW
Miles Ave	5	SE
Miles Ave	6	SW
Milham Rd	6	SW
Millard Ct	2	SE
Millcork St	6	SE
Miller Rd	5	NE
Miller Rd	6	NW
Mills St	2	SE
Millview Ave	5	NE
Milwood Ave	6	SW
Minor Ave	2	SW
Mitchell Pl	2	SW
Mockingbird Dr	4	NE
Mohawk St	1	SW
Molhoeks Ct	5	NE
Monarch St	5	NE
Monroe St	2	SW
Monterey Dr	3	NW
Montrose Ave	5	NW
Moonlight Ave	4	SW
Moore Dr	4	NE
Moraine Trl	4	SW
Moreland St	6	SW
Morgan St	6	SW
Mosel Ave	2	NE
Mosel Ave	3	NW
Mount Ct	6	SW
Mount Olivet Rd	0	KY
Mount Olivet Rd	3	NW
Mulhearn Ave	3	NE
Myrtle St	2	SE
Nancy Ln	4	NW
Nassau St	3	NW
Nazareth Rd	0	KY
Nazareth Rd	3	SE
Nazareth Road	3	NE
Nelbert St	6	SW
Nelson Ave	1	SE
Neumaier Ct	2	SE
Newell Pl	5	NW
Newgate Rd	1	SW
Newland Pl	2	SE
Newton Ct	5	NW
Nichols Rd	1	SW
Nola St	2	SW
Nora St	6	NW
Normal Ct	2	SW
Normal View St	2	SW
North St	1	SE
North St	2	SW
Northampton Rd	1	SW
Norton Dr	5	NE
Norway Ave	2	NW
Nottingham Dr	6	SW
Oak Creek Ave	3	NW
Oak Ct	5	NW
Oak Openings	3	SW
Oak St	2	SW
Oak St	5	NW
Oak Tree Dr	3	NE
Oakhurst Ave	5	SE
Oakland Dr	2	SW
Oakland Dr	4	SE
Oakland Dr	5	NW
Oakridge Rd	4	SE
Ogden Ave	2	SW
Ohio Ave	3	NE
Ojibwa Trl	4	NW
Old Colony Rd	5	SW
Old Cork St	6	SE
Old Field Pl	4	SW
Old Orchard Pl	2	SW
Old Riverview	2	NE
Oldfield Trl	4	SW
Olive St	6	NW
Oliver St	1	SE
Oliver St	2	SW
Olmstead Rd	6	NE
Olney St	1	SW
Oneil St	2	SE
Onondaga Ave	0	KY
Onondaga Ave	3	NW
Oonah Pl	3	SW
Orient St	0	KY
Osborne St	2	SW
Ostrander St	5	NE
Ottawa Ave	1	NW
Outlook St	5	NE
Oxford St	3	NW
Paddington Rd	6	SW
Palmer Ave	5	NE
Palmer Ave	6	NW
Pampas Ln	4	NW
Par 4 Cir	5	SW
Par 4 Rd	5	SW
Parchmount St	0	KY
Park Ave	0	KY
Park Pl	5	NE
Park St	2	SW
Park St	5	NW
Parkdale Blvd	0	KY
Parker Ave	5	SW
Parkside Dr	3	NE
Parkview Ave	4	SW
Parkway Ave	2	SE
Parkwood Dr	5	NW
Parkwyn Dr	4	NW
Parsons St	2	NE
Pasadena St	6	SW
Paterson Ct	2	NE
Paterson St	2	NW
Patwood Ct	2	NW
Peake Rd	1	SE
Pearl Ct	2	SW
Pearl St	2	SW
Peekstok Rd	5	SE
Peeler St	5	NW
Pembrook St	5	SW
Pennway St	6	SW
Pesos Pl	4	NW
Phelps St	3	SW
Phillips St	5	NE
Piccadilly Rd	1	SW
Pierce Ave	5	SE
Pine Bluff Ln	4	SW
Pine Cove Cir	1	SW
Pine Ridge Rd	4	NE
Pine Shadow Dr	4	NW
Pine Terrace	4	NW
Pinegrove Ln	4	NW
Pinehurst Blvd	1	SE
Pioneer St	5	NW
Pitcher St	2	SE
Pleasant Ave	5	SW
Pleasant Home	5	SW
Plymouth Ln	5	NW
Pomeroy St	5	NE
Poncho Pl	4	NW
Pond Dr	1	SE
Pontiac St	1	NW
Poplar Pl	6	NW
Portage Ct	5	NE
Portage Rd	6	SW
Portage St	2	SE
Portage St	5	NE
Portage St	6	SW
Porter St	2	SE
Potter St	2	SW
Prairie Ave	1	SE
Prairie Pl	1	SE
Pratt Rd	5	SE
Princeton Ave	2	NW
Prospect Hill St	2	SW
Prospect Pl	2	SW
Prospect St	2	SW
Prouty St	2	NW
Race St	5	NE
Raintree Cir	1	SW
Rambling Rd	4	NE
Random Rd	3	NW
Range St	3	NW
Rankin Ave	1	SE
Ranney St	2	SW
Ransom St	2	SW
Ravine Rd	1	NE
Ravine Rd	2	NW
Ravine Road	1	NW
Ravinia St	5	NE
Ray St	2	SE
Recreation Dr	4	NE
Redmond Ave	5	SE
Redwood Ave	4	NE
Reed Ave	5	NE
Reed Ct	5	NE
Reed St	5	NE
Reed St	6	NW
Reese Pl	2	SW
Regency Sq	5	SW
Regent St	3	NW
Remine St	5	NE
Reycraft Dr	5	NE
Reycraft Dr	6	NW
Richard St	5	NE
Richardson St	2	NE
Richland Ave	1	NE
Ridge Rd	5	NW
Ridgeview Cir	4	NE
Ridgeview Dr	4	NE
Ridgeway Cir	4	NW
Ridgeway Ln	4	NW
Ridgewood St	5	NE
Rio Rd	4	NW
Ritsema Ct	2	NW
River St	2	SE
Riverview Dr	2	SE
Rivington St	5	SW
Roberson	2	NE
Roberson St	2	NE
Robin Ln	5	SW
Rochester Ave	2	SE
Rock Ledge Rd	2	NW
Rockledge Ave	1	NE
Rockwell Ct	3	SW
Roell Rd	4	NE
Rose Ct	2	SE
Rose Pkwy	2	SW
Rose Pl	2	SW
Rose St	2	SE
Rose St	5	NE
Roseland Ave	5	NE
Roseland Ave	6	NW
Roskam Ct	2	SE
Roxbury Ln	4	SE
Royce Ave	5	SE
Royce Ave	6	SW
Rusridge Ave	1	NE
Russell St	2	SE
Russell St	5	NE
Russet Dr	4	NE
Ruthin Rd	4	SE
Ryskamp Ct	5	SE
Sabin St	1	SW
Sage St	1	SW
Sagebrush St	1	NW
Saidla Rd	6	NE
Santos Dr	1	SW
Saxonia Dr	5	NW
Schippers Ln	3	SW
Scholten Ct	2	SE
Schuster Ave	3	SW
Schuster Ave	6	NW
Scudder Ct	2	SE
Seamers St	3	NE
Seemore St	3	NW
Seminole St	1	NW
Seneca Ln	4	NW
Sequoia Ct	1	NW
Shadow Bend	3	NE
Shadyridge Ter	4	SW
Shaffer St	3	NW
Shannon Ct	3	NW
Shaw Ln	4	NE
Sheffield Dr	4	NE
Sheldon Ct	2	SE
Sheldon St	2	SE
Sheridan Dr	5	NE
Sheridan Dr	6	NW
Sherwood Ave	2	SE
Sherwood Ave	3	SW
Short Rd	5	NW
Sierra Ave	3	NW
Siesta St	4	SW
Simpson St	2	SW
Skinner Dr	3	SW
Skirrow Pl	5	NW
Skyler Dr	4	SE
Skyline St	1	NW
Slater Dr	3	NW
Smith Ct	2	SE
Solon St	1	SW
Somerset Ave	6	SW
Songbird Ln	4	SW
Sonora St	3	NW
South St	2	SW
Southern Ave	5	NE
Southern Ave	6	NW
Southworth Ter	3	SW
Sprague Ave	2	SW
Spring Ct	2	SE
Spring St	2	SE
Spring Valley Dr	3	NW
Springhill Dr	5	NW
Springmont Ave	4	SE
Sprinkle Rd	3	SE
Sprinkle Rd	6	SE
Spruce Dr	4	NW
Squires Rd	1	NW
St Albans Way	3	NW
St John Pl	2	SW
St Joseph Ave	5	SE
St Marys St	5	SE
Stadium Dr	1	SE
Stadium Dr	2	SW
Stadium Dr	4	NW
Stamford Ave	3	NW
Standish St	5	SW
Stanwood St	2	SW
Staples Ave	2	SW
Staples Ct	2	NW
Starlite Ave	4	SW
State St	5	NE
Stearns Ave	5	NW
Steers Ave	1	SE
Stetson Ct	5	NE
Stevens Ave	4	SE
Stirling Ct	1	SE
Stockbridge Ave	5	NE
Stockbridge Ave	6	NW
Stone Mill St	1	NW
Stone St	2	SW
Stonebrooke	1	SW
Stonebrooke	1	SW
Stuart Ave	2	SW
Summer St	2	SW
Summit Ave	2	SW
Sun Valley Dr	4	SE
Sunfield St	0	KY
Sunnock Ave	5	SE
Sunnybrook Dr	4	SE
Sunnydale Ave	1	SW
Sunnyside Dr	3	NE
Sunset Dr	5	SW
Sunset Ln	5	NW
Superior Ave	5	NE
Sutherland Ave	4	NE
Sweet Dr	5	SE
Swift Dr	4	NW
Sycamore Ln	4	NW
Sydelle Ave	1	SE
Talbot	3	NW
Taliesin Dr	4	NW
Tampa Ave	3	NE
Tamrack St	1	NW
Tamsin Ave	4	NW
Terrace Ct	5	NE
Texel Dr	3	NW
The Dells St	3	SW
Thompson Ct	2	SW
Thompson St	2	SW
Timber Ridge Dr	1	SE
Timberlane Dr	4	SE
Timberwood Sq	1	SE
Tipperary Rd	4	NE
Todd Ln	4	NW
Torin Dr	2	SE
Town House Ln	6	NW
Trail End	6	NW
Trailswood St	1	NW
Tray Ln	4	NW
Treehaven Dr	4	NE
Tremont St	5	NE
Trimble Ave	3	SW
Troy Ave	3	NW
Turwill Ln	1	SW
US Hwy 131	4	SW
Underwood Ln	6	SW
Union St	2	NE
United States	2	NW
University Ave	5	NW
Upjohn Ave	3	SW
Upjohn Dr	2	SE
Upland Dr	3	NE
Uppingham Rd	1	SW
Valencia Ln	4	NW
Valeview Ave	1	NE
Valley Cir	6	SW
Valley Ridge Ln	1	SW
Valley St	1	SE
Van Bochove Ct	2	SE
Van Vranken Ct	2	SW
Van Zee St	5	NE
Van de Giessen	4	NE
Vandersalm Ct	5	NE
Vanrick Dr	6	SE
Vassar Dr	5	NE
Vassar Dr	6	NW
Verdries Ct	2	SW
Vernon Ct	5	NE
Vernon St	5	NE
Victor Ave	3	SE
Village Ct	2	SW
Village St	2	SW
Vine Pl	2	SW
Vine St	2	SW
Vine St	3	SW
Virginia Ave	0	KY
Virginia Ave	3	NW
Vista St	4	SE
Waite Ave	4	NE
Walbridge St	2	SE
Walden Ct	3	NW
Waldo Ave	1	SW
Wall St	5	NE
Wallace Ave	3	SW
Walnut Ct	2	SW
Walnut St	2	SW
Walter St	2	SE
Walter St	5	SE
Walwood Pl	2	SW
Warren Pl	1	NE
Washburn Ave	3	SW
Washington Ave	5	NE
Washington Ave	6	NW
Washington Ct	5	NE
Water St	2	SW
Waterworth Dr	4	NE
Wattles Pl	2	NE
Waverly Ave	1	SE
Waverly Dr	3	NW
Wayside Rd	3	NW
Wealthy Ave	1	SE
Weaver Ave	1	SW
Weaver Ave	4	NW
Weaver Blvd	4	NE
Weaver Cir	1	SW
Wellington Rd	4	NE
Wells Pl	6	NW
Westbrooke	4	NE
Westbury Ln	1	SW
Westchester Ln	5	NW
Western Dr	1	SE
Western Dr	4	NE
Westfall Ave	1	SE
Westfall Ave	4	NE
Westmoreland	4	NE
Westnedge Ave	2	SW
Westnedge Ave	5	SW
Westnedge Ct	2	SW
Westnedge St	5	SW
Westwood Dr	1	SE
Wheaton Ave	5	NW
Wheeler St	6	NW
Whitcomb St	5	NW
White Oak Dr	5	SW
Whites Rd	4	NE
Whites Rd	5	NW
Whittier Dr	6	SW
Wilbur Ave	1	SE
Wilbur St	1	SE
Wildwood Pl	5	NW
Willard St	2	SW
William St	2	NW
Willow Lake Dr	4	SW
Wilmette St	1	SE
Wilrad Ct	2	SE
Wilshire Blvd	5	NW
Wimbleton Way	1	SW
Winchell Ave	4	NW
Winchell Dr	4	NW
Winchester Pl	1	SW
Winstead St	2	SE
Winton Ave	6	SW
Witwer Ct	5	NE
Wood St	4	SE
Woodbury Ave	2	SW
Woodcliff Dr	4	SW
Woodhaven Dr	4	SE
Woodmont Dr	5	SE
Woodrow Dr	3	NW
Woodside	1	SE
Woodstone Dr	4	SW
Woodward Ave	2	SW
Woodwind Ct	1	SW
Worner Dr	4	NE
Yew Ave	1	NW
Yucca Ave	1	NW
Zuidema Ct	5	SE

NOTES

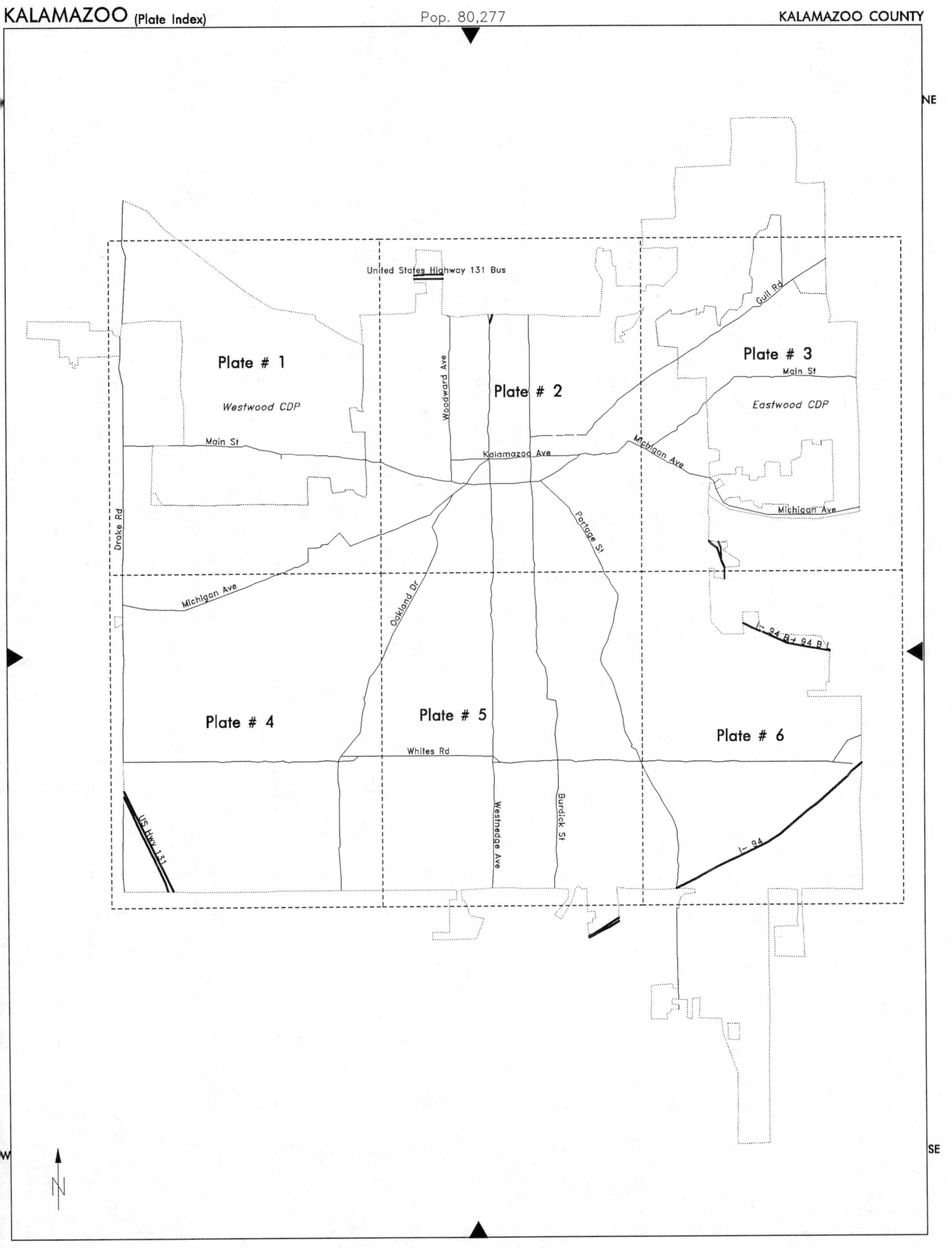

NE
United States Highway 131 Bus
Gull Rd
Plate # 1
Westwood CDP
Woodward Ave
Plate # 2
Plate # 3
Main St
Eastwood CDP
Main St
Kalamazoo Ave
Michigan Ave
Michigan Ave
Drake Rd
Portage St
Oakland Dr
Michigan Ave
I- 94 B.L.
Plate # 4
Plate # 5
Plate # 6
Whites Rd
US Hwy 131
Westnedge Ave
Burdick St
I- 94
W
SE
N

NW
SW
SE
N
Squires Rd
NYC Railroad
Ravine Road
Aspen Dr
Sequoia
Sagebrush
Andora Ave
Cumberland
Chaparral
Skyline
Tamrack
Fir Ave
Yew Ave
Grand Prairie Rd
Ravine Rd
Kingsbrook Dr
Apple Bluff Dr
Trailswood
Stone Mill
Pontiac
Ottawa Ave
Nichols Rd
Junedale Dr
Doncrest Ave
Kaywood Dr
Harvey Ave
Rusridge Ave
Alamo Ave
Alamo Ave
Grand Pre Ave
Iroquois Trl
Beech Ave
Northampton Rd
Highgate Rd
Turwill Ln
Mohawk
Huron Ave
Seminole
Marlane Ave
Calhoun
Bretton Dr
Manor
Coolidge Ave
Ferndale Ave
Climax Ave
Richland Ave
Valeview Ave
Brownell
Croyden Ave
Croyden Ave
Haskell
Haskell
Jenks Blvd
Fletcher Ave
Crown
Pinehurst Blvd
Hilledale Ave
Warren Pl
Prairie Ave
Dunhill Ter
Donnington Ter
Greenway Ter
Piccadilly Rd
Cherokee
Cranbrook Ave
Attlee Ave
Ellamarie Dr
Ellamarie Dr
Crown
Devonshire Ave
Upjingham Rd
Canterbury Ave
Canterbury Ave
Westwood CDP
Althea
Grace Rd
Grace Rd
Sunnydale Ave
Newgate Rd
Wilmette
Campbell Ave
Dartmouth Ave
Londonderry
Olney
Olney
Waverly Ave
Westbury Ln
Darby Ln
Drake Rd
Winchester
Chelten
Gorham Ln
Grand Pre Ave
North
Commonwealth Pl
Crestview Ave
Wealthy Ave
Jennison Ave
Pinehurst Blvd
Jefferson Ave
Main
Main
Commonwealth Ave
Sage
Waldo Ave
Turwill
Sabin
Cherryhill Rd
Lauderdale Dr
Broemer Ln
Lake Forest Blvd
Fletcher Ave
Sydelle Ave
Westwood Dr
Gilkison Ave
Nelson Ave
Clarendon
Berkley
Arlington
Prairie Pl
Meriwether
Cherryhill
Kendall Ave
Greenacre Dr
Pine Cove
Woodwind Ct
Raintree Cir
Sage
Solon
Grove
Kendall Ave
Stonebrooke
Academy
Henderson Ct
Kendall Ave
Pond Dr
Gilkison Ave
Academy
Leisure
Grand Ave
Lawn
Peake Rd
Pond Dr
Greenlawn Ave
Howard
Rankin Ave
Hemingway Dr
Dillingham Ln
Kendall Ave
Gilkison Ave
Weaver Cir
Dormitory Rd
Hays Dr
Michigan Ave
Edinburgh Dr
Duxbury
Hillsboro Cir
Dobbin Dr
Fieldhouse Dr
Barrington Dr
Hylle Ave
Buckhout Ave
Steers Ave
Marion Ave
Wilbur
Dormitory Rd
Western Dr
Hays Dr
Ellendale
Boswell Ln
Eldridge
Berkshire Dr
Dublin Ave
Weaver
Westmoreland Av
Westfall Ave
Farrell Ave
Arcadia Rd
N

NW
NE
SW
SE
N
Mosel Ave
US Hwy 131 Bus
Douglas Ave
Hammond Ave
Ravine Rd
Rock Ledge Rd
Alamo Hills Dr
Dennis Ct
Patwood Ct
Prouty
Lulu
Bosker Ave
Harding Pl
Holland Ave
Cobb Ave
Hopkins
Herbert
Martin
Union
Rose
Burdick
Krom Ave
Edwards
Clay
Bessie
Paterson Ct
Pitcher
Harrison
Kalamazoo River
Riverview Dr
Old Riverview Dr
Paterson
Alamo Ave
Staples Ct
Woodward Ave
William
Elizabeth
Mabel
Norway Ave
Bush
Roberson
Parsons
Porter
Richardson
Wattles Pl
Myrtle
Walbridge
Ampersee Ave
Gull Rd
Ray
Ogden Ave
Mason
Staples Ave
Florence
Princeton Ave
Park
Church
Darden Ct
Verdries Ct
Drexel Pl
Scudder Ct
Bridge
Summit Ave
Cadillac
Stuart Ave
Nola
Simpson
Woodbury Ave
Burrell Ave
Lawrence
Cooley
Judge Ave
North
Hotop Ave
Lantern Ln
Hawley
Butler Ct
Sherwood Ave
Jefferson Ct
Jefferson Pl
Summer
Jefferson Ave
Lucas Ct
Elmwood Ct
Elmwood
Ransom
Westnedge Ave
Harkins Ct
Engleman Ave
Forbes
Willard
Mitchell Pl
Creetwich Pl
Harrison Ct
Mills
Cleveland
Blaine
Oneil
Douglas Ct
Douglas Ter
Kalamazoo Ave
Elm
Ferris Ct
Eleanor
Water
Portage Creek
Parkway Ave
King Hwy
Prospect
Prospect Hill
Main
Grand Ave
Ingleside Ter
Kalamazoo Ct
Michikal
Crosstown
Creek
Elm Pl
Allen Blvd
Old Orchard Pl
Kalamazoo Mall Rd
Bates Al
Thompson Ct
Henderson Dr
Bulkley
Thompson
Carmel
Catherine
Main Ct
Brookside Ct
Michigan Ave
Exchange Pl
Farmers Ave
Devisser Al
South
Spring
Rochester Ave
Torin Dr
Gibson
Academy
College Grove Rd
Health Care Plz
Henrietta
Portage
Fisher
Walnut
Sheldon
South
Lovell
St John Pl
Bellevue Pl
Normal View
Davis
Oakland Dr
Pearl Ct
Reese Pl
Cedar
2nd
Burrows Rd
Crawford Ave
Sprague Ave
Monroe
Stone
Stonwood
Eldred
Arcadia Creek
Normal Ct
Potter
Walnut Ct
Gladys Ct
Den Bleyker Pl
Cedar Ct
Scholten Ct
Edgar
Winstead
Kronduke Ct
Hickory Ct
NYC Railroad
Smith Ct
4th
Campus Dr
Hoffman Pl
Duffield Ct
Pearl
Oak
Dutton
Van Vranken Ct
Dutton Pl
Burnham Dr
Federal Ct
Kook Ct
Dutton Ct
Millard Ct
Pitcher
Walwood Pl
Locust Pl
Wilrad Ct
Van Bochove Ct
Vine
Oliver
Vine Pl
Central Pl
Rose Ct
Rose Pkwy
Crosstown Pkwy
Jackson Ct
Jackson
Neumaier Ct
Cottage Ave
Russell
Grant Ct
Village
Westnedge Ct
Ranney
Heilman Ct
Boerman Ave
Hoek Ct
Walter
Carr
Newland Pl
Garden
Fenwick
Grant
Short Rd
Laura Ct
Minor Ave
Osborne
Burr Oak Ct
Huston Pl
Fellows Ave
Burr Oak
Upjohn Dr

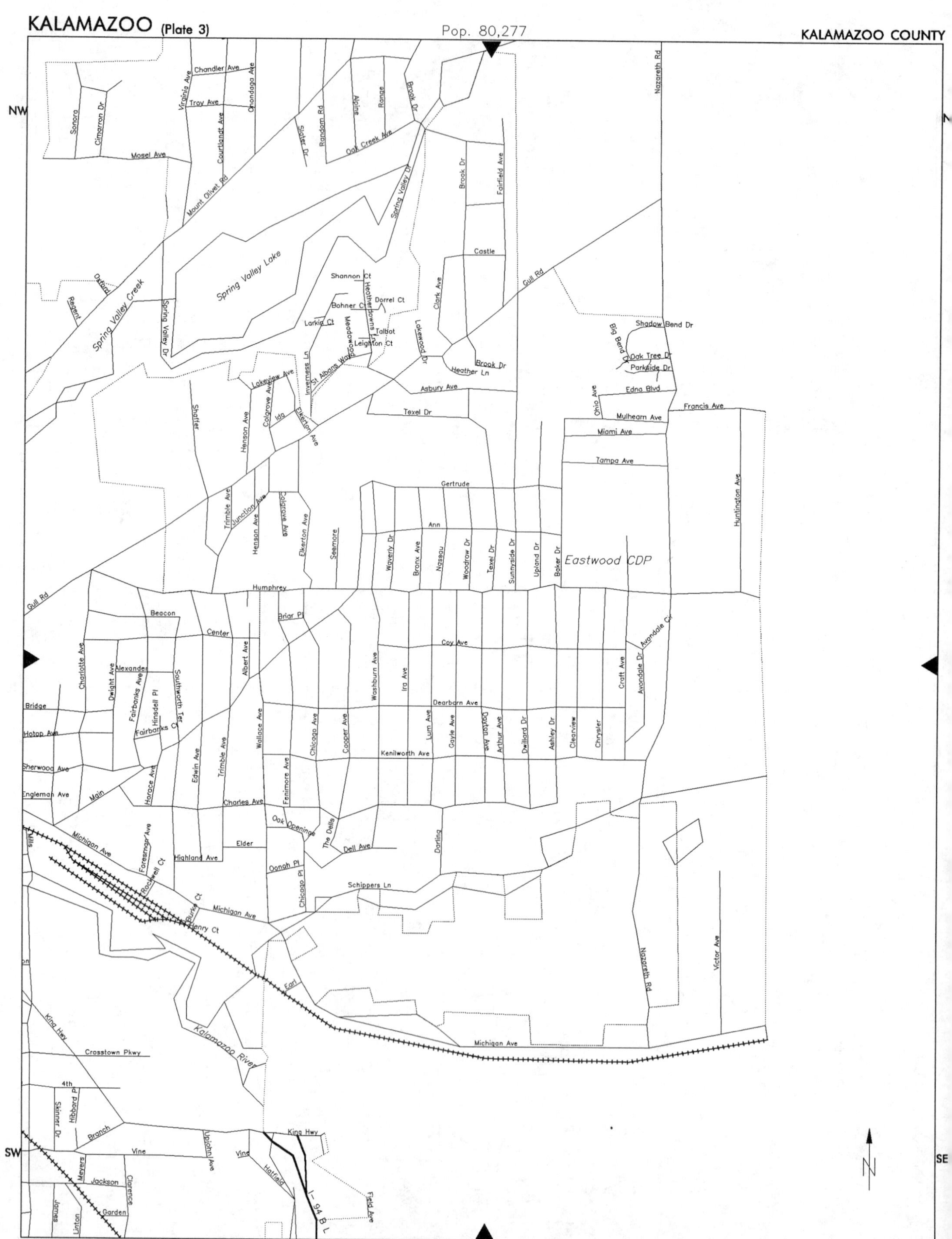
NW
SW
SE
Spring Valley Lake
Spring Valley Creek
Eastwood CDP
Kalamazoo River
Gull Rd
Humphrey
Michigan Ave
King Hwy
Crosstown Pkwy
Nazareth Rd
Victor Ave
Huntington Ave
Francis Ave
Mulhearn Ave
Miami Ave
Tampa Ave
Edna Blvd
Gertrude
Ann
Coy Ave
Dearborn Ave
Kenilworth Ave
Charles Ave
Beacon
Center
Schippers Ln
Chandler Ave
Troy Ave
Mosel Ave
Mount Olivet Rd
Spring Valley Dr
Brook Dr
Fairfield Ave
Castle
Texel Dr
Asbury Ave
I- 94 B L

NW
NE
SW
SE
Clayborne Dr
Middlebury Dr
Eldridge Dr
Berkshire Dr
St Antoine Ave
Donnegal Ave
Boswell Cir
Lancaster Dr
Little Dr
Michigan Ave
Michigan Ave
Pine Terrace Blvd
Kenbrooke Ct
Pine Shadow Dr
Fraternity Village Dr
Michigamme Woods
California Ave
Kimbark Ave
Redwood Ave
Euclid Ave
Greenwood Ave
Laffayette
Westbrooke Ave
Weaver Blvd
Knollwood Ave
Auditorium Dr
Auditorium Dr
Howard
Worner Dr
Recreation Dr
Van de Giessen Rd
Arcadia Rd
Moore Dr
Shaw Ln
Shaw Ln
Western Dr
Gar Ln
Gar Ln
Nyc Railroad
Michigan Ave
Debbie Ln
Mark Ct
Jack Ct
Billy Ct
Debbie Ln
Troy Ln
Nancy Ln
Jody Ln
Kickapoo Ct
Jay Dr
Cardinal Dr
Cardinal Dr
Swift Dr
Lark Dr
Lark Dr
Hawk Dr
Meadow View Rd
El Rancho Dr
Rio Rd
Granada Ln
Valencia Ln
Fiesta Ln
Mexicali Ln
Pompas Ln
Adios Dr
Pancho Pl
Arcadia Creek
Evanston
Ridgeway Ln
Ridgeway Cir
Stadium Dr
Rambling Rd
Bobolink Ln
Mockingbird Dr
Broadway
Aberdeen Dr
Acorn Ln
Crosswind Dr
Waterworth Dr
Sheffield Dr
Benjamin Ave
Dickie Dr
Dickie Dr
Waite Ave
Spruce Dr
Evergreen Dr
Benjamin Ave
Fitch Ave
Linwood Dr
Dover Rd
Embury Rd
Lakeside Dr
Fair Oaks Dr
Pinegrove Ln
Sycamore Ln
Audubon Dr
Treehaven Dr
Frederick Ave
Broadway Ave
Magnolia Cir
Asylum Lake
Winchell Dr
Winchell Ave
Highpointe Dr
Taliesin Dr
Parkway Dr
Larry Ln
Ridgeview Dr
Rambling Rd
Pine Ridge Rd
Ridgeview Cir
Appelane Cir
Applelane Dr
Ferdon Rd
Russet Dr
Lomond Dr
Carlyle Dr
Bruce Dr
Argyle Ave
Sheffield Dr
Hillshire Dr
Chevy Chase
Clovelly Rd
Lake Chevy Chase
Portage Creek
Lorraine Ave
Lorraine Ave
Taliesin Dr
Wellington Rd
Kensington Dr
Crest Dr
Whites Rd
Tamsin Ave
Darmo
Greenleaf Blvd
Parkview Ave
Shadyridge Ter
Pine Bluff Ln
Willow Lake Dr
Greenleaf Blvd
Willow Lake Dr
Knox
Hoover
Adams
Logan Ave
Oakland Dr
Amherst Ave
Wood
Lowden
Madison
Benton Ave
Laird Ave
Kent Ave
Broadway Ave
Springmont Ave
Woodcliff Dr
Greenleaf Cir
Hazel Ave
Stevens Ave
Oakridge Rd
Ruthin Rd
Edgewood Dr
Edgewood Dr
US Hwy 131
US Hwy 131
12th
Old Field Pl
Cricket Ln
Oldfield Tr
Woodstone Dr
Greenleaf Cir
Lake Terrace Dr
Sun Valley Dr
Blackberry Ln
Songbird Ln
Katydid Ln
West Portage Creek
West Portage Creek
Lake Forest Ln
Brandywine Rd
Roxbury Ln
Sunnybrook Dr
Edgecliff Ln
Sunnybrook Dr
Starlite Ave
Eventide Ave
Moonlight Ave
Howard Lake
Lake Hill Dr
Lake Forest Ln
Angling Rd
Oakland Dr
Timberlane Dr
Kilgore Rd
N

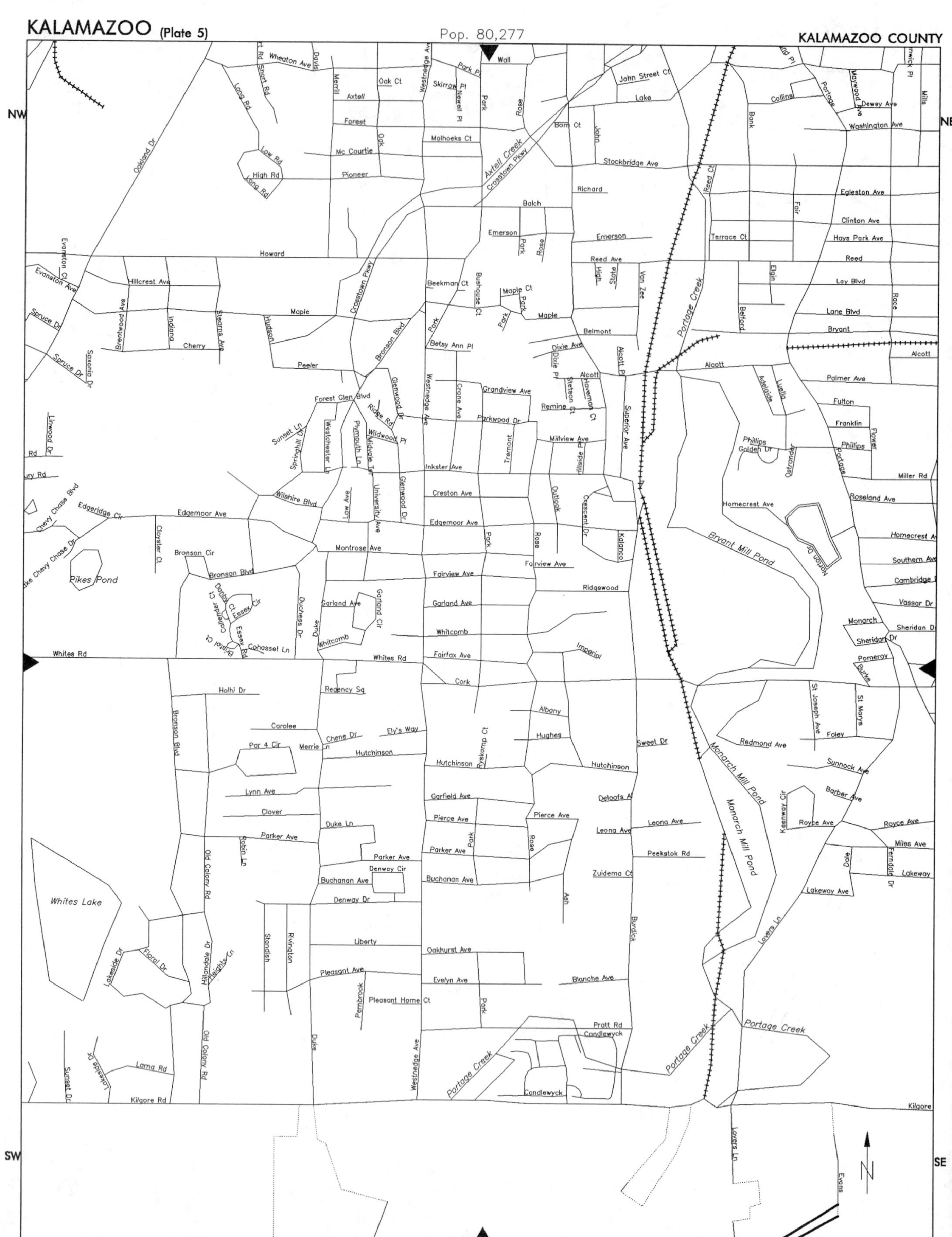

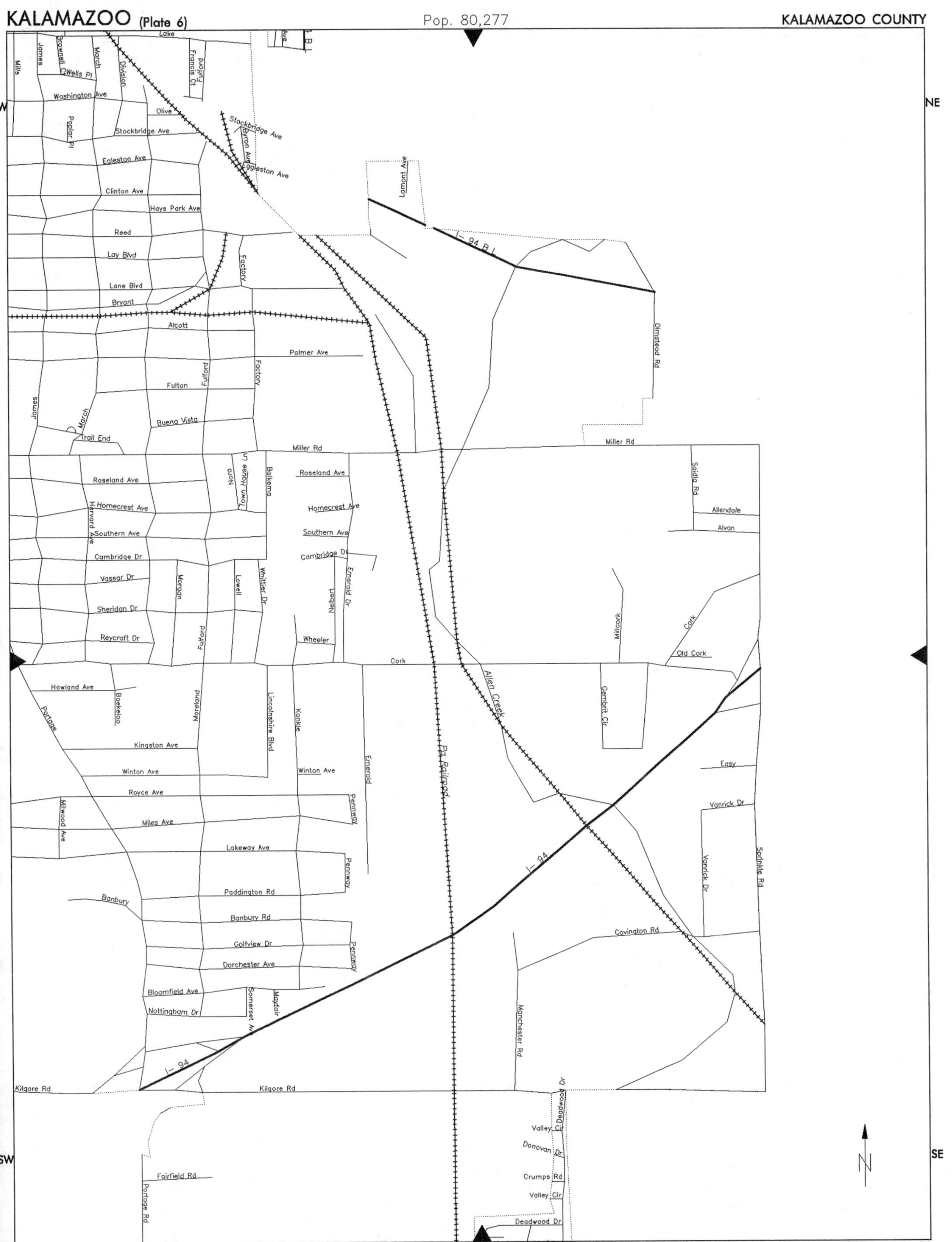
Lake
Mills
James
Brownell
Wells Pl
March
Division
Francis Ct
Fulford
Washington Ave
Olive
Poplar Pl
Stockbridge Ave
Byron Ave
Egleston Ave
Clinton Ave
Hays Park Ave
Lamont Ave
Reed
Lay Blvd
Factory
I-94 B.L.
Lane Blvd
Bryant
Alcott
Olmstead Rd
Palmer Ave
Fulton
Buena Vista
Trail End
Miller Rd
Roseland Ave
Nora
Town Houe Ln
Balkema
Saidla Rd
Allendale
Homecrest Ave
Harvard Ave
Southern Ave
Alvan
Cambridge Dr
Vassar Dr
Morgan
Lowell
Whittier Dr
Nelbert
Emerald Dr
Sheridan Dr
Reycraft Dr
Wheeler
Millcork
Cork
Old Cork
Howland Ave
Boekeloo
Portage
Moreland
Lincolnshire Blvd
Konkle
Allen Creek
Gembrit Cir
Kingston Ave
Winton Ave
Emerald
Pa Railroad
Easy
Royce Ave
Millwood Ave
Pennway
Vanrick Dr
Miles Ave
Lakeway Ave
I-94
Sprinkle Rd
Paddington Rd
Banbury
Banbury Rd
Golfview Dr
Covington Rd
Dorchester Ave
Bloomfield Ave
Nottingham Dr
Somerset Ave
Mayfair
Manchester Rd
Kilgore Rd
Deadwood Dr
Valley Cir
Donovan Dr
Fairfield Rd
Portage Rd
Crumps Rd
NE
SE
SW
W
N

M-72
Nash Road
Birch St
Senior Citizens Dr
US Hwy 131
Norway St
Arbor St
Coral St
Orange St
Cedar St
Evergreen St
Division St
Cherry St
Walnut St
Kalkaska St
Paw Paw St
George St
Lincoln St
Kalkaska Road
Dresden St
Dresden Road
Penncentral Railroad
Park Dr
4th St
Laurel St
3rd St
West St
Oak St
2nd St
Lynn St
Pine St
Maple St
Elm St
Chestnut St
Essex St
Spruce St
Hyde St
North Branch Boardman River
Sandy Pines Dr
Vipond Creek
N

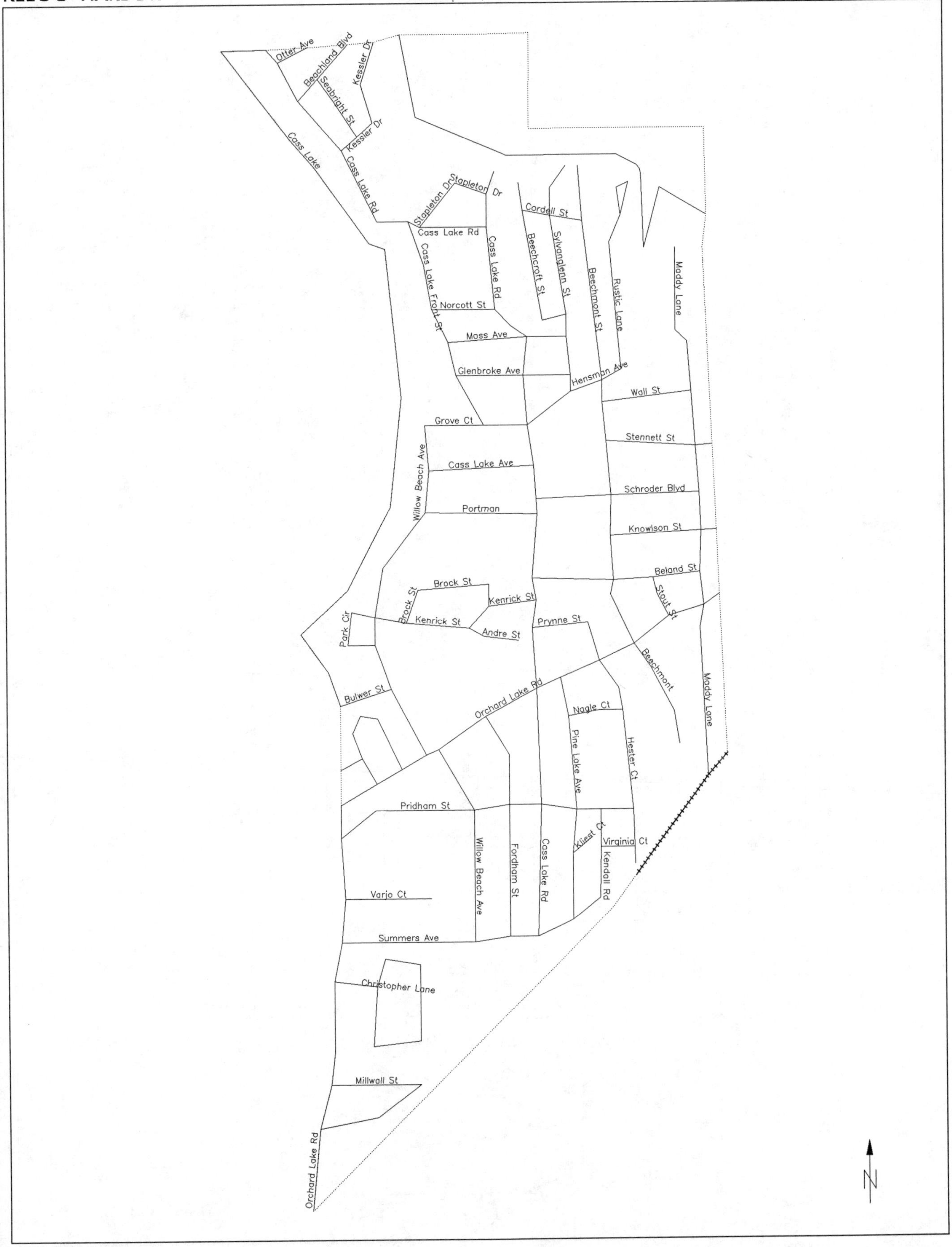

Otter Ave
Beachland Blvd
Kessler Dr
Seabright St
Kessler Dr
Cass Lake
Cass Lake Rd
Stapleton Dr
Stapleton Dr
Cordell St
Cass Lake Rd
Cass Lake Front St
Cass Lake Rd
Beechcroft St
Sylvanglenn St
Beechmont St
Rustic Lane
Maddy Lane
Norcott St
Moss Ave
Glenbroke Ave
Hensman Ave
Wall St
Grove Ct
Stennett St
Willow Beach Ave
Cass Lake Ave
Schroder Blvd
Portman
Knowlson St
Beland St
Brock St
Brock St
Kenrick St
Stout St
Kenrick St
Prynne St
Andre St
Park Cir
Beechmont
Bulwer St
Orchard Lake Rd
Nagle Ct
Maddy Lane
Pine Lake Ave
Hester Ct
Pridham St
Kliest Ct
Virginia Ct
Willow Beach Ave
Fordham St
Cass Lake Rd
Kendall Rd
Varjo Ct
Summers Ave
Christopher Lane
Millwall St
Orchard Lake Rd
N

Pop. 5,480

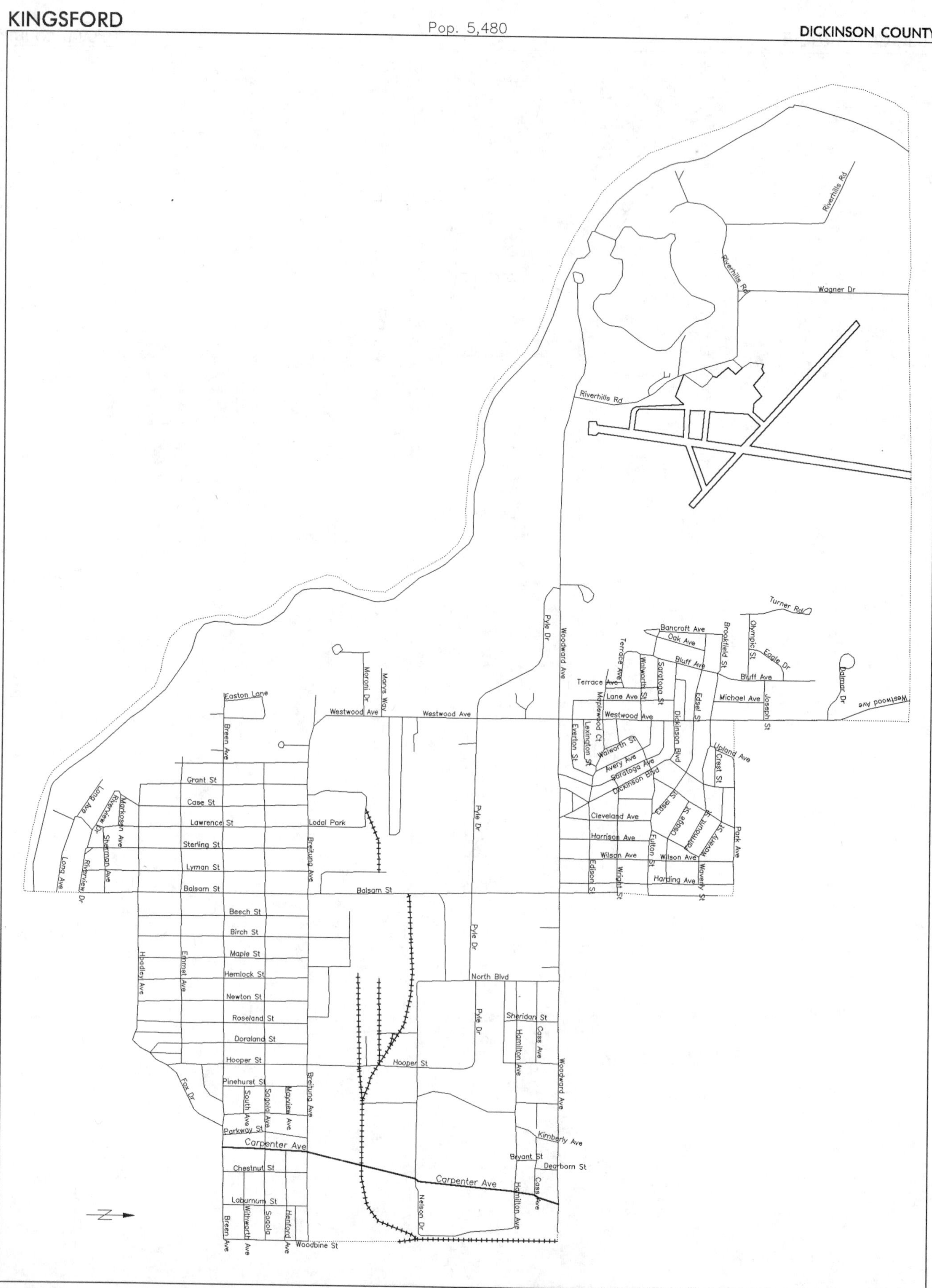
Riverhills Rd
Wagner Dr
Riverhills Rd
Turner Rd
Bancroft Ave
Oak Ave
Brookfield St
Olympic St
Eagle Dr
Bluff Ave
Terrace Ave
Lane Ave
Michael Ave
Westwood Ave
Joseph St
Dalmar Dr
Pyle Dr
Woodward Ave
Easton Lane
Moroni Dr
Marys Way
Westwood Ave
Breen Ave
Grant St
Case St
Lawrence St
Lodal Park
Sterling St
Lyman St
Balsam St
Beech St
Birch St
Maple St
Hemlock St
Newton St
Roseland St
Doraland St
Hooper St
Pinehurst St
Parkway St
Carpenter Ave
Chestnut St
Laburnum St
Woodbine St
Long Ave
Riverview Dr
Markosen Ave
Sherman Ave
Hoadley Ave
Emmet Ave
Breitung Ave
Fox Dr
South Ave
Sagola Ave
Mayview Ave
Withworth Ave
Hanford Ave
North Blvd
Sheridan St
Hamilton Ave
Cass Ave
Kimberly Ave
Bryant St
Dearborn St
Nelson Dr
Cleveland Ave
Harrison Ave
Wilson Ave
Harding Ave
Edison St
Wright St
Fulton St
Everton St
Lexington St
Maplewood Ct
Walworth St
Saratoga St
Dickinson Blvd
Edsel St
Avery Ave
Saratoga Ave
Upland Ave
Crest St
Osage St
Fairmount St
Waverly St
Park Ave

LAINGSBURG

Pop. 1,148

SHIAWASSEE COUNTY

LAKE LINDEN

Pop. 1,203

HOUGHTON COUNTY

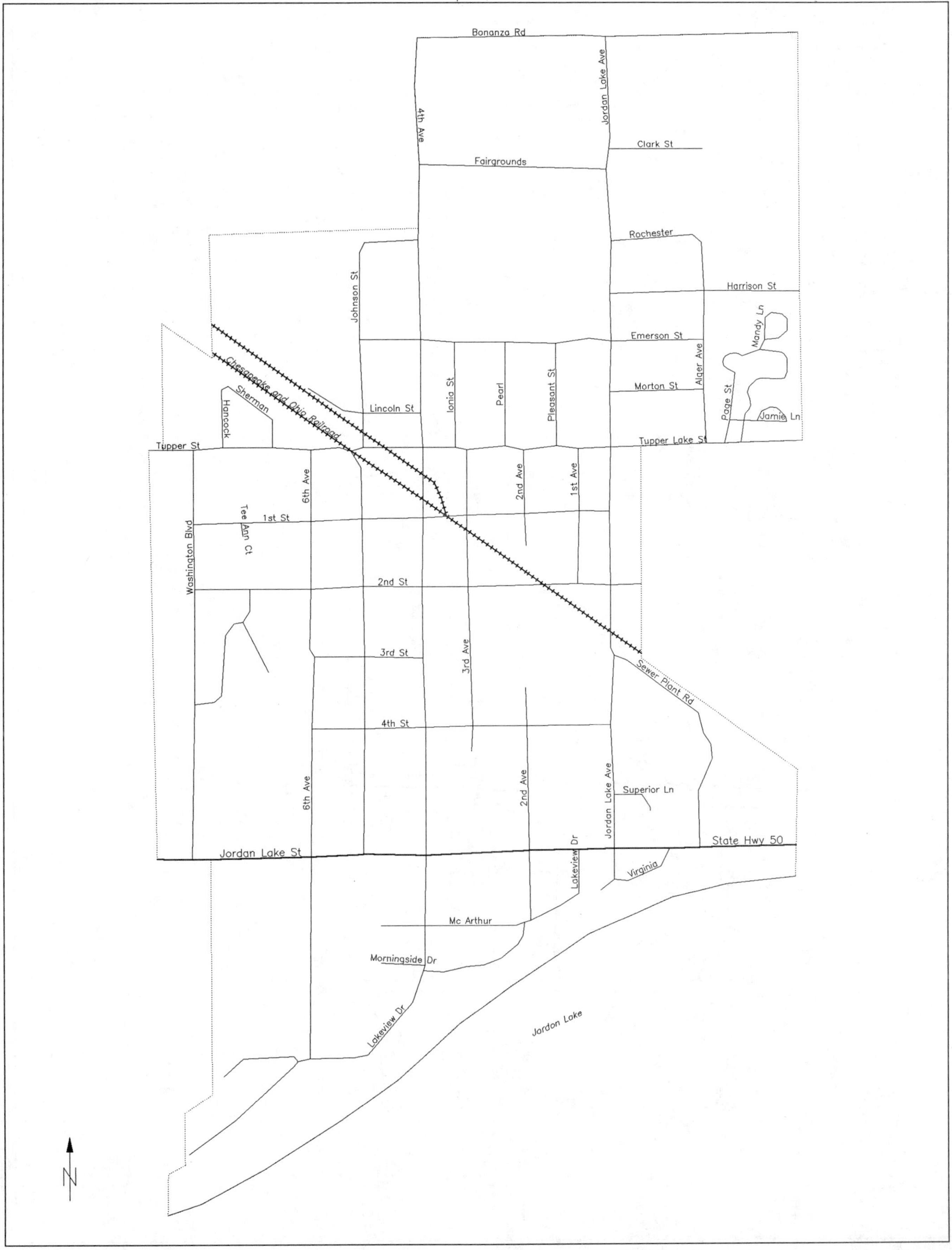

Bonanza Rd
4th Ave
Jordan Lake Ave
Clark St
Fairgrounds
Rochester
Johnson St
Harrison St
Mandy Ln
Emerson St
Alger Ave
Morton St
Page St
Jamie Ln
Chesapeake and Ohio Railroad
Sherman
Hancock
Lincoln St
Ionia St
Pearl
Pleasant St
Tupper St
Tupper Lake St
6th Ave
2nd Ave
1st Ave
Tee Ann Ct
1st St
Washington Blvd
2nd St
3rd St
3rd Ave
Sewer Plant Rd
4th St
6th Ave
2nd Ave
Jordan Lake Ave
Superior Ln
State Hwy 50
Jordan Lake St
Lakeview Dr
Virginia
Mc Arthur
Morningside Dr
Lakeview Dr
Jordon Lake
N

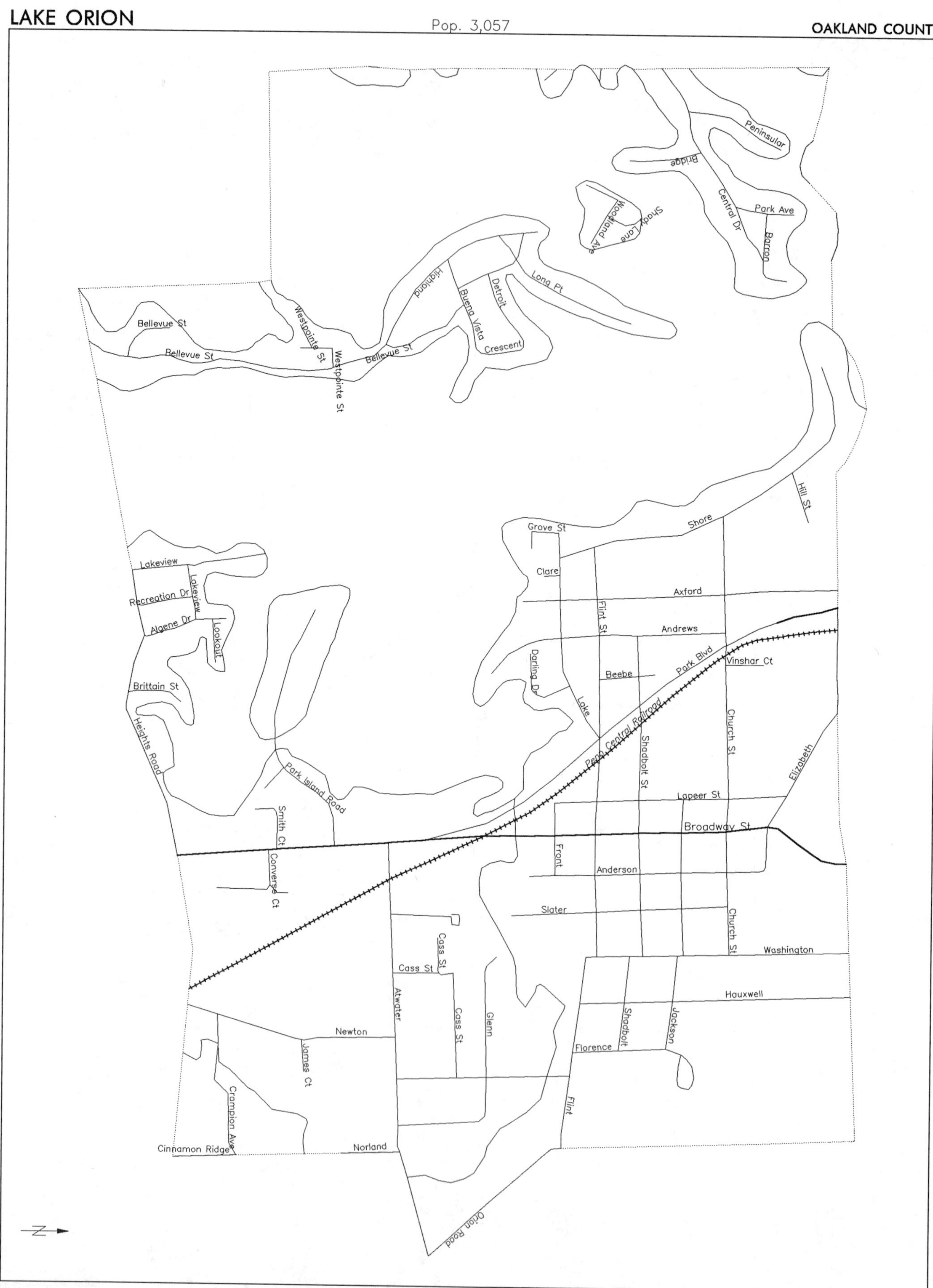
Peninsular
Bridge
Central Dr
Park Ave
Barron
Shady Lane
Woodland Ave
Long Pt
Highland
Buena Vista
Detroit
Crescent
Bellevue St
Bellevue St
Westpointe St
Westpointe St
Bellevue St
Hill St
Shore
Grove St
Clare
Axford
Flint St
Andrews
Lakeview
Lakeview
Recreation Dr
Algene Dr
Lookout
Brittain St
Heights Road
Darling Dr
Beebe
Lake
Park Blvd
Vinshar Ct
Penn Central Railroad
Shadbolt St
Church St
Elizabeth
Park Island Road
Smith Ct
Converse Ct
Lapeer St
Broadway St
Front
Anderson
Slater
Church St
Washington
Cass St
Cass St
Cass St
Atwater
Glenn
Hauxwell
Shadbolt
Jackson
Florence
Newton
James Ct
Crampion Ave
Flint
Cinnamon Ridge
Norland
Orion Road

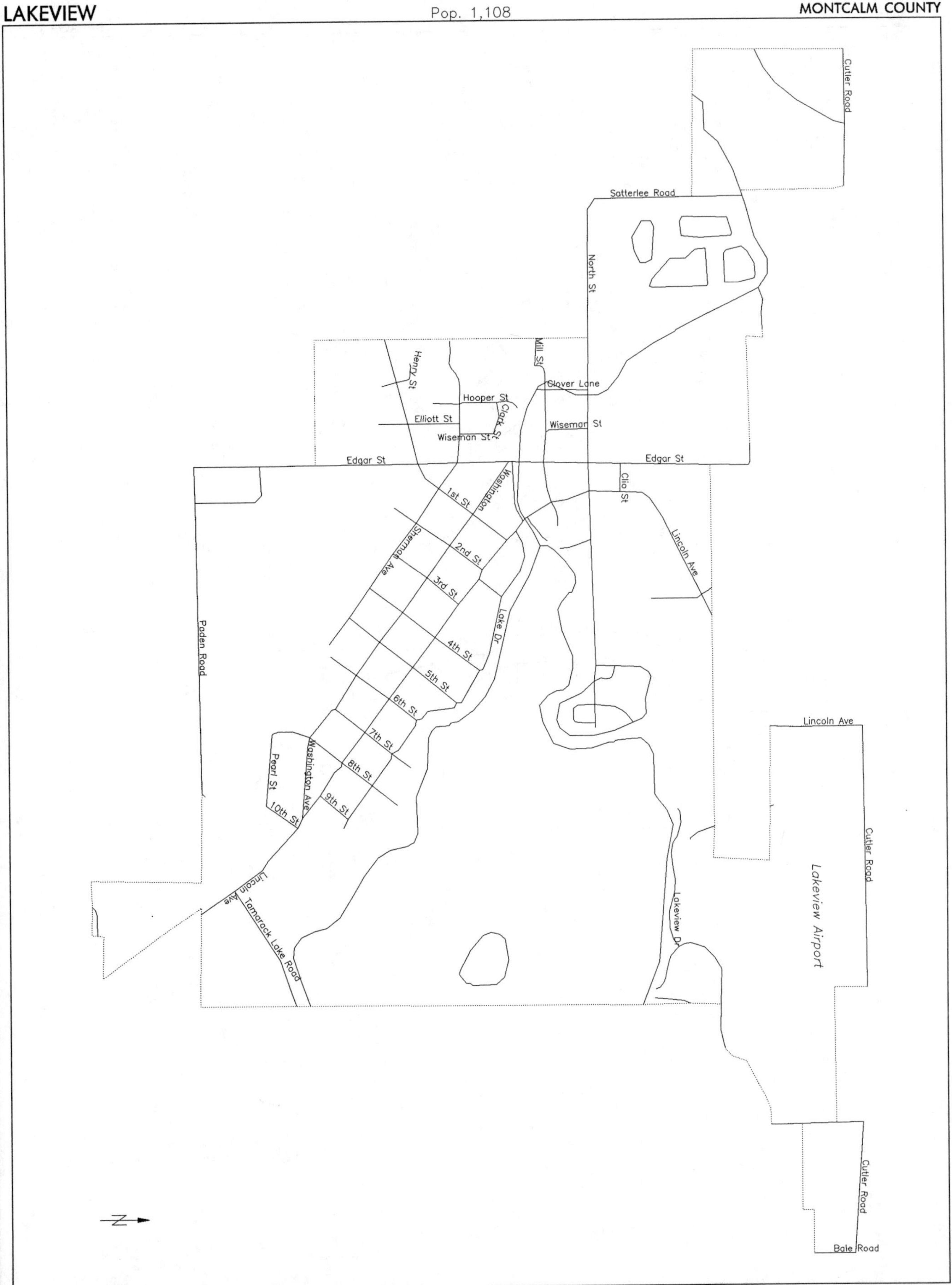
Cutler Road
Satterlee Road
North St
Mill St
Henry St
Clover Lane
Hooper St
Clark St
Elliott St
Wiseman St
Wiseman St
Edgar St
Edgar St
Clio St
Washington
1st St
Sherman Ave
2nd St
Lincoln Ave
3rd St
Lake Dr
4th St
5th St
Paden Road
6th St
7th St
Pearl St
Washington Ave
8th St
9th St
10th St
Lincoln Ave
Lincoln Ave
Tamarack Lake Road
Lakeview Dr
Cutler Road
Lakeview Airport
Cutler Road
Bale Road

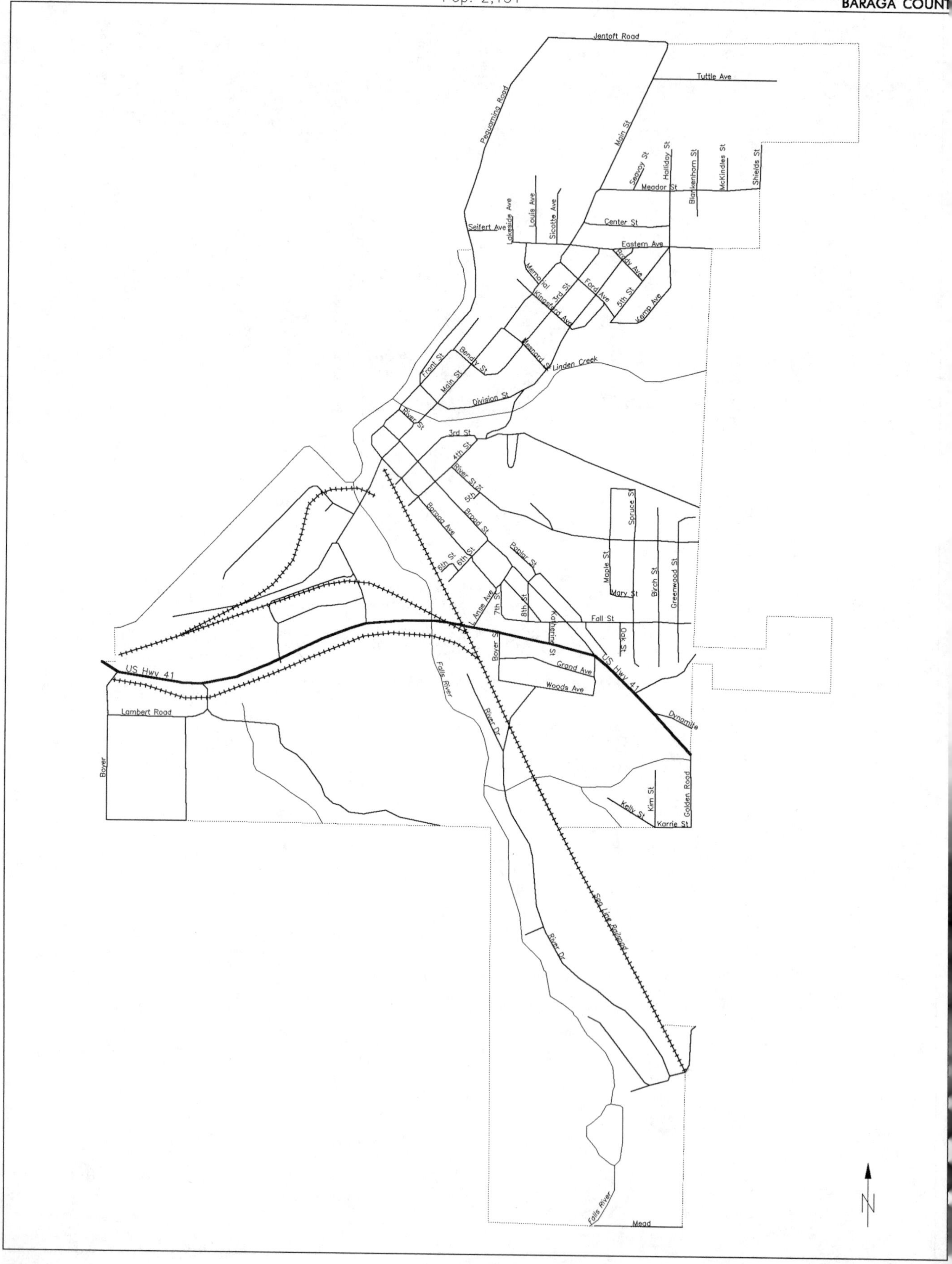

Pop. 2,151

Jentoft Road
Tuttle Ave
Pequaming Road
Main St
Selvay St
Halliday St
Blankenhorn St
McKindles St
Shields St
Meador St
Lakeside Ave
Louis Ave
Sicotte Ave
Center St
Seifert Ave
Eastern Ave
Broady Ave
Memorial
Kingsford Ave
3rd St
Ford Ave
5th St
Kemp Ave
Menard St
Linden Creek
Front St
Bendry St
Main St
Division St
River St
3rd St
4th St
River St
5th
Baraga Ave
Broad St
6th St
6th St
Poplar St
Spruce St
Maple St
Mary St
Birch St
Greenwood St
L'Anse Ave
7th St
8th St
Katherine St
Fall St
Oak St
Bover St
Grand Ave
Woods Ave
US Hwy 41
US Hwy 41
Dynamite
Lambert Road
Bover
Falls River
River Dr
Kim St
Kelly St
Golden Road
Karrie St
Soo Line Railroad
River Dr
Falls River
Mead
N

Street	Map	Quadrant
Kirby Dr	1	SE
Kirkwood Road	2	NE
Knollwood Ave	1	NE
Kuerbitz Dr	1	NW
Kurt Dr	3	SE
Kyes Road	3	SE
La Salle Gdns	2	SE
Labelle Road	3	SW
Lafayette Ave	1	NW
Lafayette Cir	1	NW
Lahoma St	1	SE
Lake Lansing	2	NW
Lama	3	SE
Lamont St	1	NE
Lansing Ave	1	NE
Laparte Dr	3	SE
Lapeer St	1	SE
Larch St	2	SW
Larned St	2	SW
Larrabee	3	SE
Lasalle Blvd	2	SW
Lasalle Ct	2	SW
Latham St	4	SW
Lathrop St	2	SW
Laurie Lane	3	NE
Lawdor Road	3	NW
Lawler Ct	1	NE
Le Grand Dr	3	NE
Leawood Dr	4	NE
Lee Blvd	2	SE
Leitram Ct	1	SE
Lemrock Ct	1	NE
Lenawee St	1	SE
Lenore Ave	3	NE
Lenore St	3	NE
Leon Ave	1	NW
Leonard Ct	1	NE
Lerner Way	4	SW
Lesher Pl	2	SW
Leslie Ave	2	SW
Lewton Pl	3	NW
Leyburn Ct	3	NW
Liberty St	2	NW
Lincoln Ave	3	NE
Lincoln Ave	4	NW
Lindbergh Dr	2	SW
Linden Grove	2	SW
Linlawn St	4	NW
Linval St	2	SW
Linwood Cir	1	NE
Linwood St	1	NE
Little St	2	NW
Livernois Ave	4	NW
Loa St	3	NE
Lochmoor Dr	3	NW
Lockbridge Dr	4	SW
Loder Cir	3	NE
Logan Access	1	NE
Logan St	1	SE
Logan St	3	NE
Londal	4	SW
Londal Cir	4	SW
Londal Ct	4	SW
Long Blvd	4	SW
Loraine Ave	3	NE
Loretta St	4	SW
Louis St	4	NW
Louisa St	4	SW
Lowcroft St	3	NE
Lucie St	3	NW
Lujer Cir	1	NW
Luwanna Dr	4	NW
Lyman Dr	2	NW
Lyncott Dr	4	NW
Lyons Ave	2	SW
Lyons Ave	4	NW
M-99	1	NE
Madison St	1	NE
Magnolia Ave	2	SW
Mahlon St	2	SW
Main St	1	SE
Main St	2	SW
Maisonette	4	SW
Majestic Cir	2	NE
Malibu Dr	3	NW
Mall Ct	2	SE
Maloney St	3	NW
Manchester St	2	NW
Mandell St	4	SW
Manley Dr	4	NW
Manor Dr	3	SE
Maple St	1	NE
Maple St	2	NW
Maplehill Ave	4	NW
Maplewood Ave	1	SE
Maplewood Ave	3	NE
Marcus St	2	SW
Marilyn Plz	3	NW
Marion Ave	3	NE
Mark Ave	2	NW
Mark Twain Dr	3	SE
Markley Pl	3	NE
Marland Dr	3	NE
Marlene Ct	4	SW
Marquette St	1	NE
Marscot Dr	4	SW
Marshall Ave	2	SW
Martin St	1	SE
Mary Ave	3	NW
Maryland Ave	2	NW
Marywood Ave	3	SE
Mason St	3	NE
Massachusetts	2	NW
Max Ave	1	SE
May St	2	NW
Maybel St	3	NW
Mayfair Dr	2	NE
Mc Court St	3	SE
Mc Cullough St	2	SW
Mc Kim Ave	4	NW
Mc Kinley St	2	NW
Mc Pherson	1	SE
McGarry Dr	3	SE
McIntyre Ct	1	SE
Meadowcroft Dr	2	NW
Meadowlane Dr	1	NW
Mechanic St	2	SW
Medburn Ave	3	NW
Meese Dr	3	SE
Mel Ave	3	NE
Melody Lane	2	NE
Melvin Ct	1	NE
Memphis St	1	SE
Mercantile Way	4	SW
Merrill St	2	SE
Mersey Lane	3	NW
Michigan Ave	1	SE
Michigan Ave	2	SE
Middle St	1	SE
Midvale Ave	2	SE
Midwood St	3	NW
Mifflin Ave	2	SW
Mildred St	1	NE
Mill Oak	4	SW
Mill Oak Ave	4	SW
Mill Stone Road	4	SW
Mill Stream	4	SW
Mill Wheel Dr	4	SW
Miller Road	3	SW
Miller Road	4	SW
Mint Road	1	NE
Moffitt St	3	NE
Monroe St	2	NW
Montego Dr	2	NE
Monticello Dr	3	SW
Moores River Dr	1	SW
Moores River Dr	3	NW
Moores River	1	SW
Morgan Lane	2	SE
Morgan St	2	SW
Morningside Dr	1	NW
Mosely Ave	1	NE
Mosher St	2	SW
Motor Ave	2	SW
Mount Hope	1	SW
Mount Hope	2	SW
Mount Hope	2	SE
Muirfield Dr	3	NW
Museum Dr	1	SE
Museum Dr	2	SW
Muskegon Ave	1	NE
Narraganset Dr	4	NE
Neller Ct	1	SE
New York Ave	2	NW
Newark Ave	3	SW
Newcastle Ave	3	NW
Newport Dr	1	NW
Newton St	2	SW
Nipp Ave	1	SE
Nonnette Dr	3	SW
Norburn Way	4	SW
Norman St	1	SE
Norman St	2	SW
North St	2	NW
Northampton	2	NW
Northdale Road	1	NE
Northrup St	3	NE
Northrup St	4	SW
Northwest Ave	1	NW
Norwich Road	3	NW
Nottingham	1	SW
Oak Knoll	3	SE
Oak St	2	NW
Oakbrook Dr	4	NE
Oakland Ave	1	SE
Oakland Ave	2	NW
Oakridge Ave	2	SE
Oban Road	3	NW
Ohio Ave	2	NW
Old Mill Lane	4	SW
Olds Ave	1	SE
Olympia	3	SE
Olympia Dr	3	SE
Ontario St	1	NE
Ora Ave	3	NE
Ora St	3	NE
Orchard Ct	4	SW
Orchard Glen	2	NW
Orchard St	2	SW
Ormond St	2	NW
Osband Ave	1	SE
Osband Ave	3	NE
Osborn Road	1	SE
Ottawa St	1	SE
Ottawa St	2	SW
Otto St	2	NW
Owen Ave	1	NE
Oxford Road	1	SW
Pacific Ave	4	NW
Pacific Pkwy	4	NW
Palmer St	3	NE
Pamela Pl	3	NW
Paris Ave	3	NE
Paris Ave	4	NW
Park Ave	1	SE
Park Blvd	4	NW
Park Pl	2	SW
Park Ter	2	SW
Parkdale Ave	2	SW
Parker St	2	SW
Parkview Ave	4	NW
Parkview St	2	SW
Parkway Dr	4	NW
Patricia St	3	NE
Pattengill Ave	1	SE
Pattengill Ave	3	NE
Paul Ave	1	NW
Paulson St	1	NE
Paulson St	2	NW
Pearl St	2	NW
Peggy Pl	3	NE
Pembroke Road	1	NE
Pennsylvania	2	SW
Pennsylvania	4	SW
Pennsylvania Ct	4	NW
Pennway Dr	4	NW
Penrod Ct	3	SE
Penrose Dr	3	NW
Peony Pl	3	NE
Perkins St	2	SW
Pershing Dr	2	SW
Persons Ct	2	NW
Pettis St	1	SE
Pheasant Ave	3	SW
Picardy St	3	SW
Pickett Blvd	4	SW
Pico Ave	1	SE
Pierce Road	3	NE
Pierpont St	4	SW
Pine St	1	SE
Pinewood St	3	NE
Pingree St	1	SE
Pino Dr	1	NW
Piper Ave	3	SW
Piper Road	3	SW
Platt St	1	SE
Plaza St	1	NW
Pleasant Grove	3	SW
Pleasant St	1	NE
Pleasant View	3	NE
Plymouth Dr	4	NW
Pollard Road	3	SW
Polly Ave	1	NW
Polly Ave	2	NW
Pompton Cir	3	NE
Pontiac St	2	SW
Poplar St	3	NE
Porter St	2	NW
Post Oak Lane	2	NW
Potomac Cir	1	SE
Potter St	3	NE
Poxson Ave	3	NE
Princeton Ave	1	SE
Prospect St	2	SW
Provincial	4	NW
Pulaski St	1	SE
Queen St	1	NE
Quentin Ave	1	SE
Quentin Ave	3	NE
Quincy Lane	3	NE
R G Curtis Ave	3	SE
Race St	1	NE
Radford Dr	3	SW
Radford Road	3	SW
Raider St	2	SW
Ramada Dr	4	SW
Randall St	2	NW
Randolph St	1	NE
Ranger Road	1	NE
Raritan Road	3	SE
Ray St	2	SW
Ray St	4	NW
Rayborn Dr	3	NW
Raymond Dr	1	NE
Raynell Lane	3	NW
Reasoner St	1	NE
Redner St	3	NE
Redwood St	1	NE
Regent St	2	SW
Remy Dr	1	NW
Renee St	3	NW
Rensen St	4	NW
Reo Ave	1	SE
Reo Ct	3	NE
Reo Road	3	NW
Revere Pl	3	NE
Rex St	4	NW
Rheamount Ave	2	NW
Rice Ct	3	NW
Richard Road	3	SE
Richards Road	3	SE
Richmond St	3	NW
Richwood St	4	SW
Ridgefield Road	1	NW
Ridgeline Dr	2	NW
Ridgewood Ave	4	NW
Riley St	3	NE
Riley St	4	NW
Risdale Ave	3	NW
Risdale St	3	NW
Rita St	3	NE
River St	1	SE
River St	2	SE
Riverside Ct	1	NE
Riverview Ave	1	SE
Robert St	4	NW
Roberts Lane	4	NW
Robertson Ave	1	NE
Robinson Road	4	NW
Rock Way	3	NE
Rockford Road	3	NE
Rolfe Road	3	SE
Ronald St	3	NW
Roosevelt Ave	1	NE
Rosadell Ave	3	NE
Rosamond St	2	SW
Rose Ct	1	NE
Rosedale Road	3	SE
Roselawn Ave	1	NE
Rosemont Ave	4	NW
Roseneath Ave	1	NE
Rossiter Pl	3	NW
Roth Dr	4	SW
Rouse St	3	NE
Rulison St	1	SE
Rumsey Ave	2	SW
Rundle Ave	1	SE
Rundle Ave	3	NE
Russell St	1	NE
Ruth Ave	4	NW
Sablain Pkwy	4	NW
Sadie Ct	1	NE
Saginaw Hwy	1	SE
Saginaw Hwy	2	SW
Saginaw St	1	SE
Saginaw St	2	NE
Samantha St	4	NW
Sandhurst Dr	3	NW
Sandlyn Dr	4	NW
Sanford St	2	NW
Savoy Ct	1	SE
Sawyer Road	3	SE
Scarborough	4	NW
Schafer Road	3	SE
Schlee St	3	NE
Schultz St	1	NE
Scotmar Dr	4	SW
Seagar St	1	NE
Selfridge Blvd	3	SE
Sellers Ave	2	SE
Seymour Ave	1	SE
Shady Oak	1	NE
Sharron Ct	3	NE
Sheffer Ave	1	NW
Sheldon St	2	NW
Shelter Lane	2	NE
Shepard St	2	SW
Sheridan Road	1	NE
Sheridan Road	2	NW
Shetland Road	3	NW
Shiawassee St	1	SE
Shiawassee St	2	SW
Shirley St	4	NW
Shreve St	3	SE
Shubel Ave	2	SW
Sidney St	3	NW
Simken Dr	3	NE
Simms Ct	4	NW
Sims Ct	4	NW
Skye Road	3	NW
Smith Ave	1	SE
Solomon	4	NW
Somercroft Dr	2	NW
Sommerset	3	SE
South Park Blvd	4	NW
South St	1	SE
South St	2	SW
Southbrook Ave	3	SE
Southfield Ave	3	SE
Southgate Ave	4	NW
Southland Ave	3	NE
Sparrow Ave	1	SE
Spencer St	1	SE
Spikes St	1	NE
Spokane Ave	4	NW
Springbrook	1	NW
Springdale Dr	1	NW
Sprucewood	3	NE
St Access	2	NW
St Joseph St	1	SW
St Joseph St	2	SW
St Mary Ct	3	NE
Stabler St	3	NE
Stafford Ave	3	NE
Stanley Ct	1	NE
Stanley Ct	2	SW
Stanley St	1	SE
Starlight Lane	3	NW
Starr Ave	3	NE
State Hwy 43	1	SE
State St	1	NE
Staten Ave	4	NE
Stillwell Ave	3	NW
Stirling Ave	1	SE
Stirling Ave	3	NE
Stockman Ct	1	NE
Stoneleigh Dr	4	NW
Stonewood Dr	2	NE
Stratford Ave	3	NW
Strathmore Ave	3	NE
Strathmore	3	NE
Summerville	1	NE
Summit St	2	SW
Sumpter St	3	NW
Sunderland	3	NW
Sunderlin St	3	NW
Sunny Lane	1	NW
Sunnyside Ave	2	SW
Sunnyside Ave	4	NW
Sunrose Ave	3	SE
Sunset Ave	1	NE
Superior St	3	SE
Sussex St	3	NW
Swanee Dr	3	NW
Sycamore St	1	SE
Sylvester Ave	3	NW
Syringa Dr	3	NE
Taffey Pkwy	3	SE
Taft St	2	NW
Tammany Ave	4	NE
Taylor St	1	NE
Tecumseh Ave	1	NE
Tecumseh River	1	NW
Teel Ave	1	SE
Teel Ave	3	NE
Teel Ct	3	SE
Tenny St	3	NE
Tennyson Lane	3	NW
Terminal Road	1	NE
Theodore St	1	NE
Thomas St	1	NE
Thomas St	2	NW
Thompson St	2	NW
Tinley	3	SE
Tisdale Ave	4	NW
Todd Ave	1	SE
Torrence Ct	2	SW
Townsend St	1	SE
Tranter St	4	NW
Trappers Cove	4	NE
Trent St	1	NW
Tressa Dr	3	NE
Trinity Cir	3	NE
Trudy	4	NE
Trudy Lane	4	NE
Truman Cir	4	NE
Tulane Dr	2	NW
Tulip Ave	3	NE
Turner St	1	NE
US 127	2	NE
US Hwy 127	2	SE
Valencia Blvd	3	SE
Vance St	2	NW
Vans Ct	3	NE
Vassar Dr	2	NE
Verlinda Ave	1	NE
Verlinden Ave	1	SE
Vermont Ave	2	NW
Vernon Ave	4	NW
Vernson Dr	3	SE
Vickie Ct	3	NE
Victor Ave	3	NW
Victoria Dr	3	SE
Viking Road	3	NW
Village Dr	3	SE
Vincent Ct	3	NE
Vine St	1	NE
Vine St	2	SW
Viola Dr	3	NW
Violet Ct	3	NE
Virginia St	2	SW
Wabash Road	4	NE
Wadsworth Dr	3	NW
Wainwright Ave	3	NW
Wakefield Ave	3	NE
Walker St	1	NE
Walker St	2	NW
Walnut St	1	SE
Walsh St	2	SW
Walton Dr	3	NE
Warbler Way	4	SW
Warrington St	3	SE
Warwick Dr	3	NE
Washington Ave	1	SE
Washington Ave	3	SE
Washington St	1	SE
Washtenaw St	1	SE
Water St	1	NE
Waverly Road	1	NW
Waverly Road	3	SW
Wayburn Road	3	NE
Waycross Dr	4	SW
Wayfarer Lane	3	SW
Wayne St	4	NW
Weald	4	SW
Webster St	3	SW
Wedgewood Dr	3	NW
Weger Pl	3	NE
Wellesley Dr	3	NW
Wellington Road	1	SE
Wellington Road	3	NE
Wendy Cir	3	SE
Wesley Pl	1	NE
West St	1	SE
Westbury Road	1	NW
Westchester	1	SW
Westgate Road	1	SW
Westmont Ave	1	NW
Westmoreland	1	SE
Westwood Ave	1	NE
Wexford Road	3	SW
Weymouth Ct	3	SE
Whiteley Ct	2	SW
Whyte St	2	NW
Wieland St	2	NW
Wildwood Ave	4	NW
Willard Ave	3	NE
Willard Ave	4	NW
Willemma St	4	NW
William St	1	SE
Willoughby	3	SE
Willoughby	4	SW
Willow St	1	NW
Wilson Ave	1	NW
Wilson St	1	SE
Wilson St	2	SW
Windsor Pl	1	SE
Windsor St	1	NE
Winsford	3	NW
Winston Ave	1	NE
Winterset Dr	3	SE
Wisconsin Ave	1	SE
Wise Road	3	SW
Wood St	2	NW
Woodbine Ave	3	NE
Woodbury Ave	2	NW
Woodgate Dr	3	SE
Woodlawn Ave	1	SE
Woodlyn Dr	4	NW
Woodrow Ave	4	NW
Woodruff Ave	2	NE
Woodview Dr	3	NW
Worden St	4	NW
Wyckham Dr	1	NW
York Road	3	NW
Young Ave	1	NW
Yunker St	3	SE

NOTES

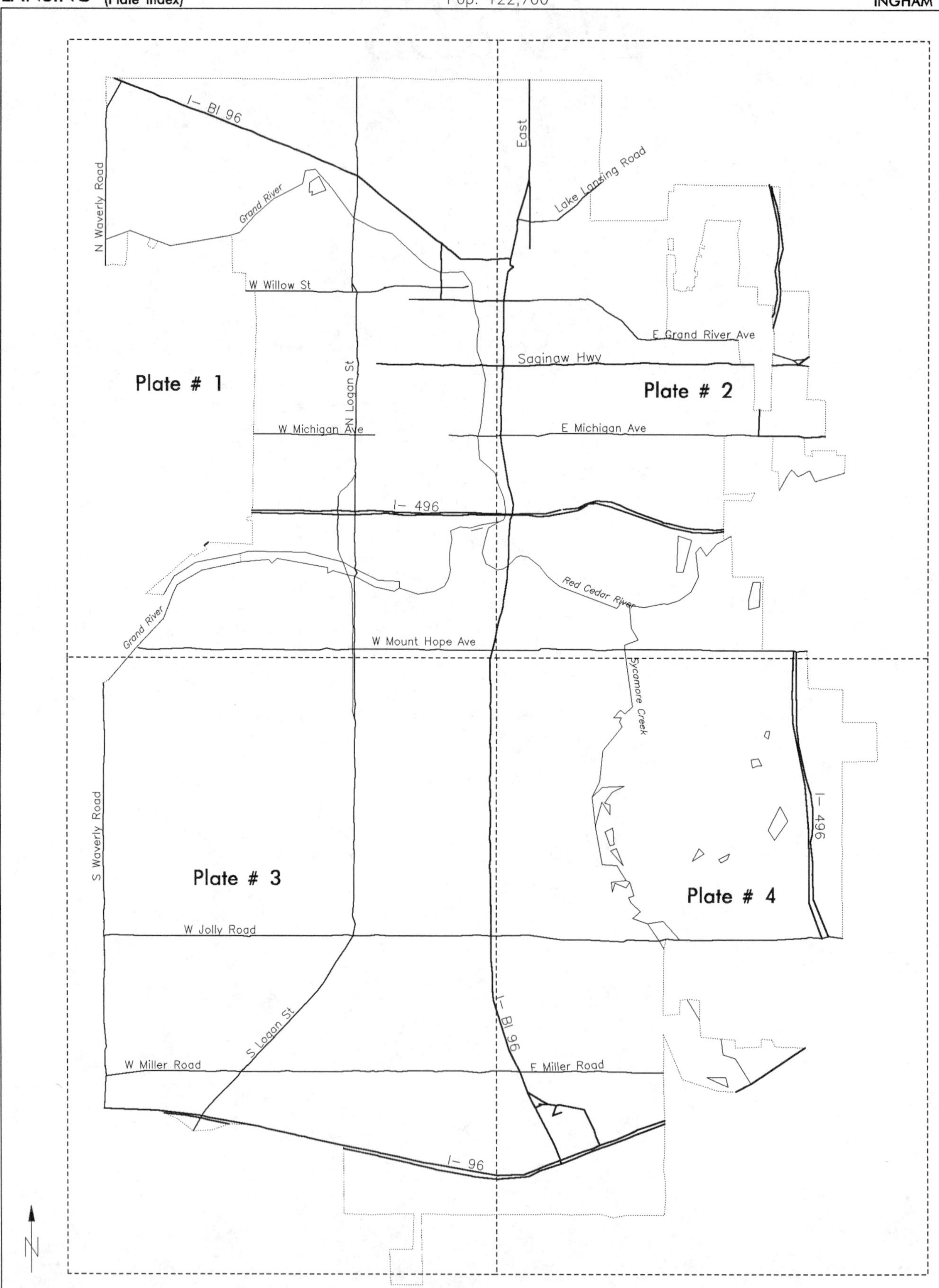
I- BI 96
N Waverly Road
Grand River
East
Lake Lansing Road
W Willow St
E Grand River Ave
Saginaw Hwy
N Logan St
Plate # 1
Plate # 2
W Michigan Ave
E Michigan Ave
I- 496
Red Cedar River
Grand River
W Mount Hope Ave
Sycamore Creek
I- 496
S Waverly Road
Plate # 3
Plate # 4
W Jolly Road
S Logan St
I- BI 96
W Miller Road
E Miller Road
I- 96
N

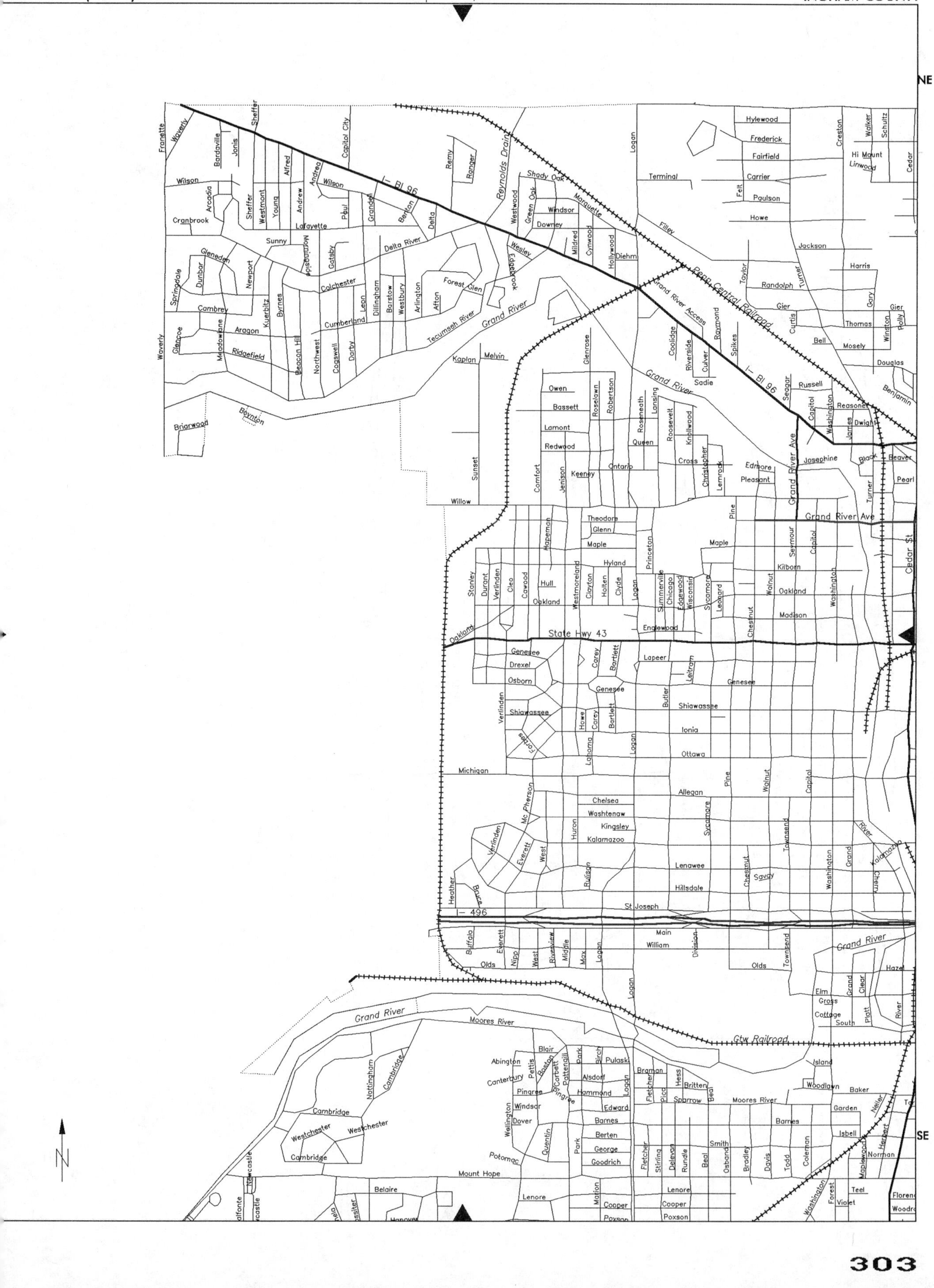

NE
SE
Grand River
Grand River Ave
State Hwy 43
I- 496
I- BI 96
Penn Central Railroad
Gtw Railroad
Reynolds Drain
Moores River
Tecumseh River
Delta River
Michigan
Oakland
Logan
Cedar St
Waverly
Saginaw
Kalamazoo
Washington
Capitol
Mount Hope
Potomac

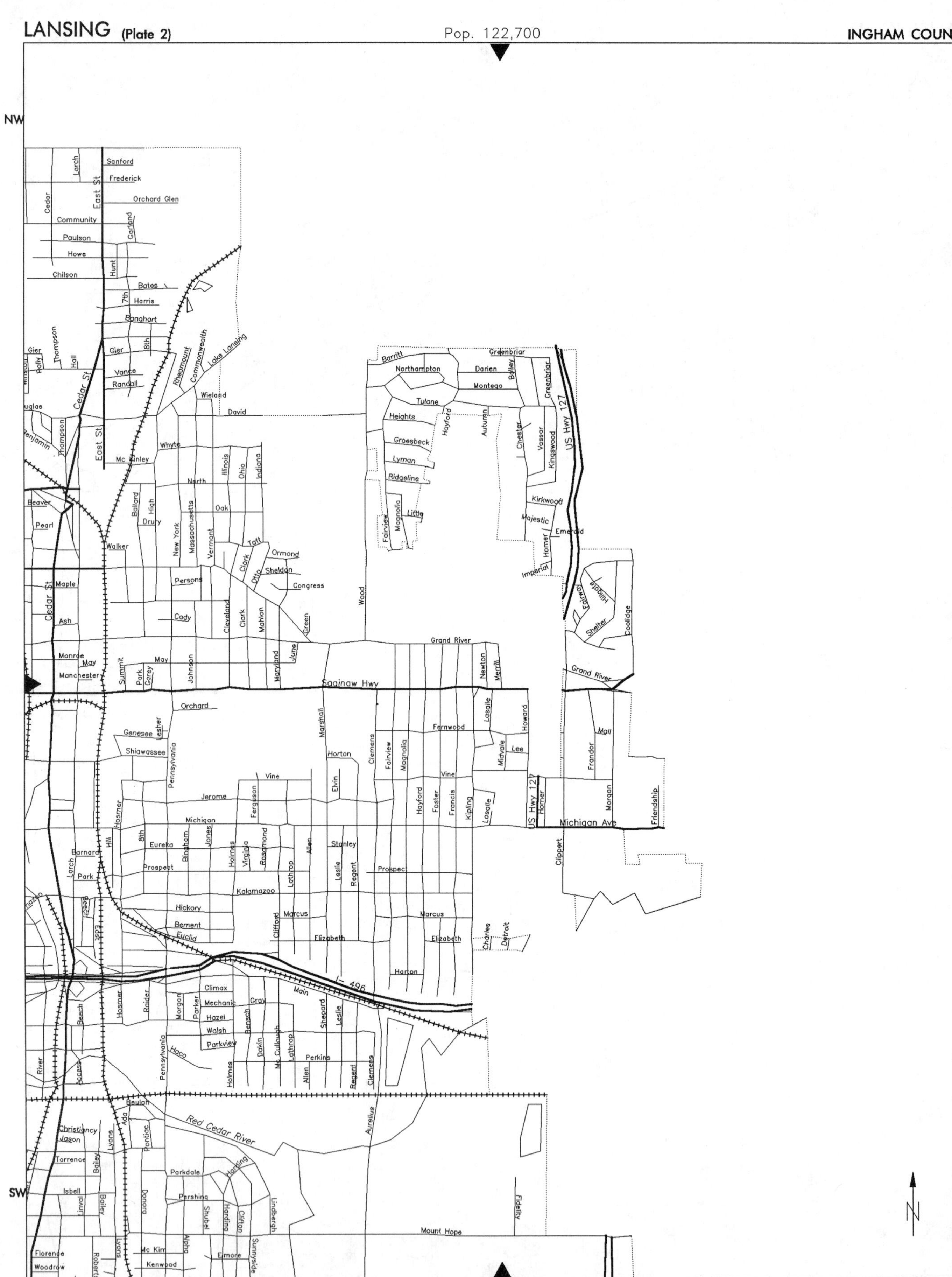
NW
SW
Saginaw Hwy
Michigan Ave
Grand River
US Hwy 127
I - 496
Red Cedar River
Mount Hope
Cedar St
East St

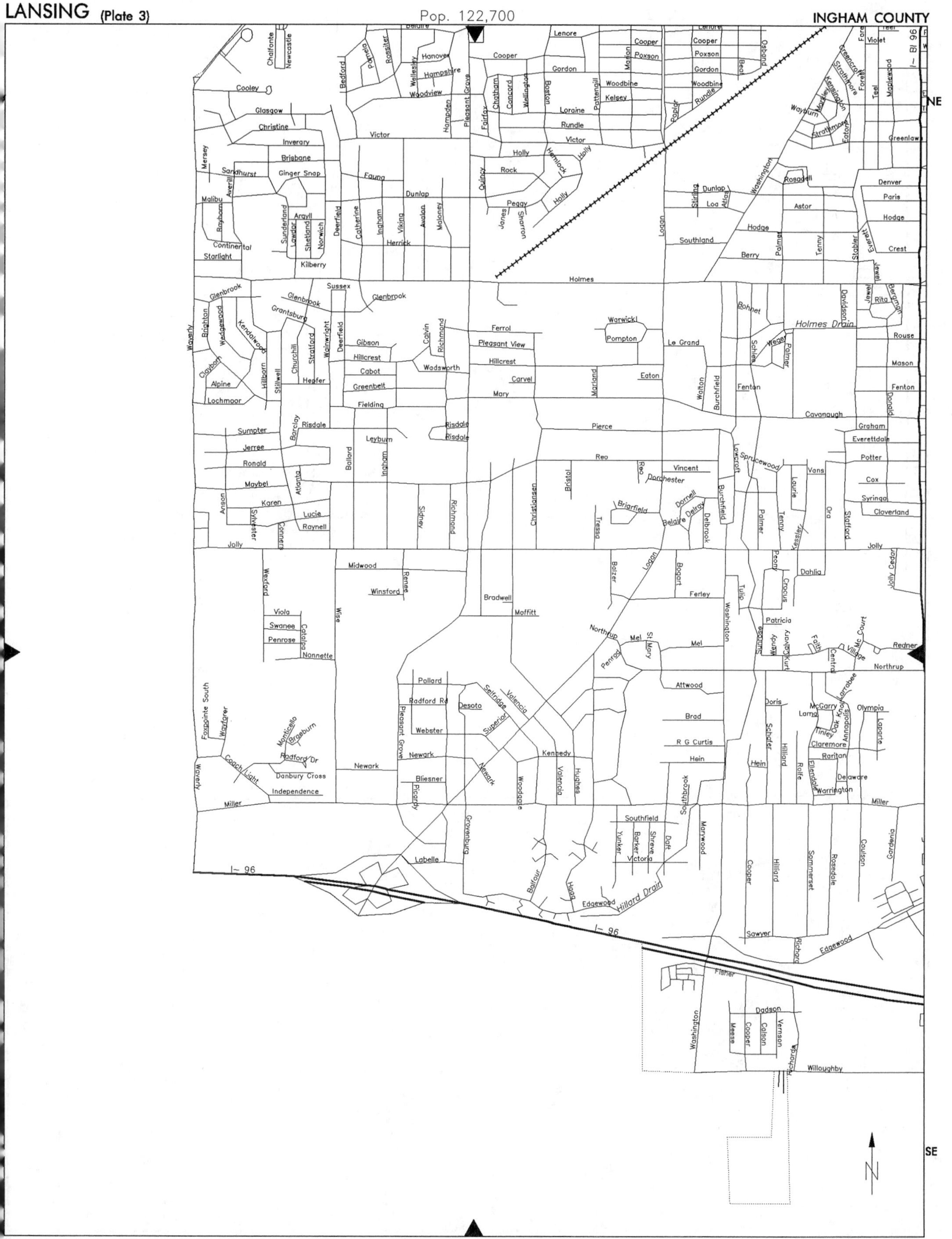

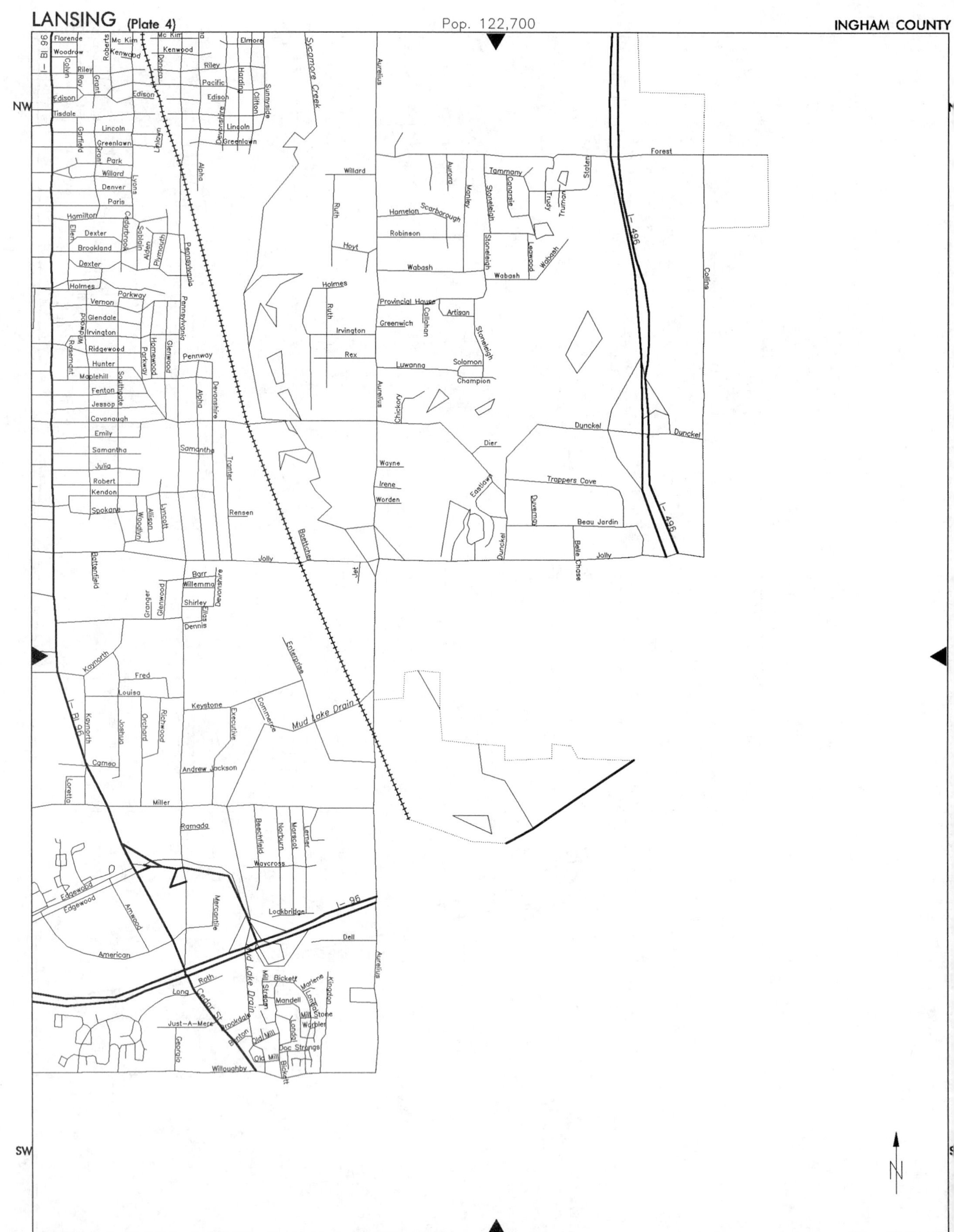

NOTES

Genesee Rd
Gibbons Drain
Mansfield Dr
May and White Drain
Hampshire Dr
Fairway Dr
Circle Dr
Golfview Ln
Oakview Dr
Rolling Hills Ln
Oregon Rd
Millville Rd
Lake Dr
East Ln
Railroad St
De Mill Rd
Village W Dr
Suzanne Dr
Charbridge
Lamoreaux Dr
Lincoln St
Harrison
Gateway Dr
Baldwin Rd
Main St
West
East
Jefferson St
Adams St
Washington St
Madison
Monroe St
Calhoun
Pine
Saginaw Rd
Union
Fair
Industrial Dr
Lyle
Railroad
South Branch
Flint River
Hartley
Pepperdmill Rd
Oriole
Parkway
Raven
Nightingale
Dove Ln
Inlay City Rd (M-21)
Knollwood
Barry Dr
Deer Run Ct
Pheasant Run Dr
Trillium Ct
Killdeer Ct
Gunridge Ln
Partridge Cir
Hunters Creek
Mc Cormick
Higley Rd
Elm St
Turrill
County Ctr
Howard
Bentley
Summit
Oak
Beach St
Liberty St
Park
Jackson
State
Michigan
St Clair
Huron
Church
Court St
Cedar St
Clay
Fox
Horton
Law
North
Mill St
Nepessing Rd
James
Sherman Ct
Grant Ct
A ST
1st St
2nd St
3rd St
4th St
Louis C Cramton St
Mason St
Dewey Dr
Jesse Lee Dr
Decoy Ln
Jacquelyn Dr
Duck Dr
Fern Ct
Hunters Ridge
Mockingbird Ter

LATHRUP VILLAGE

Pop. 4,329

OAKLAND COUNTY

Roseland Blvd
Guy St
Roseland Blvd
Somerset Pl
San Rosa Ave
Santa Barbara St
Alhambra St
Eldorado St
Southfield Road
Avilla Ave
Lathrup Blvd
Sunset Blvd
Lacrosse St
Wiltshire Ave
Wiltshire Ave
Redwood Ave
Dolores Ave
Woodworth Way
Glenwood Ave
Glenwood Ave
Eldorado St
Saratoga St
Catalpa Dr
Goldengate Dr
Monterey St
Evergreen Road
Sunset Dr
San Jose Ave
California Dr N
Rainbow Cir
Rackham St
California Dr N
Eldorado St
Southfield Road
San Quentin St
San Quentin St
Morningside Plz
Sunset Blvd
San Diego Ave
Red River St
Morningside Plz
Bungalow Ave
California Dr S
Rainbow Cir
Meadowbrook Way
Cambridge Ave
Cambridge Ave
Cambridge St
Santa Barbara St
Rainbow Dr
Goldengate St
Bloomfield Dr
Sunnybrook Ave
Sunnybrook Ave
El Dorado Pl
Sunnybrook St
Lathrup Blvd
11 Mile Road
11 Mile Road
Coral Gables St
Coral Gables St
Rainbow Dr
El Dorado Pl
Bloomfield St
Ramsgate St
Southfield Road
Lathrup Blvd
Meadowood St
Meadowood St
Meadowbrook Way
Kilbirnie St
Hampshire St
Rainbow Dr
Margate St
Middlesex St
Sunbright Ave
Rainbow Dr
Arrowhead St
Continental St
Lathrup Blvd
10 1/2 Mile Road

Old Colony Road
Willow Ave
Woodland Ave
Calumet St
Amygdaloid St
Seneca St
Fulton St
Osceola St
Hecla St
Kersarge St
1st St
Tamarack St
Pewabic St
Iroquois St
Florida St
Isle Royale St
3rd St
2nd St
3rd St
4th St
Hecla St
Kearsage St
5th St
Tamarack St
Lake Linden Ave (M-26)
Pewabic St
6th St
Calumet St
7th St
Iroquois St
Florida St
Calumet St
N

32nd St
Ewing Road
White Oak Road
72nd Ave
Walker St
Lawton Drain
4th St
Union St
Harvey St
1st St
St Hwy 40
West St
Main St
Main St
5th St
Railroad St
Franklin St
66th Ave
Liberty St
Adams St
North St
Bitely St
Washington St
Orchard St
1st St
Hamilton St
Morrill St
Durkee St
Fremont
Nursery St
Nursery St
4th St
Concord Dr
Delaware Ct
Cemetary Road
72nd Ave
2nd St
3rd St
29th St
N

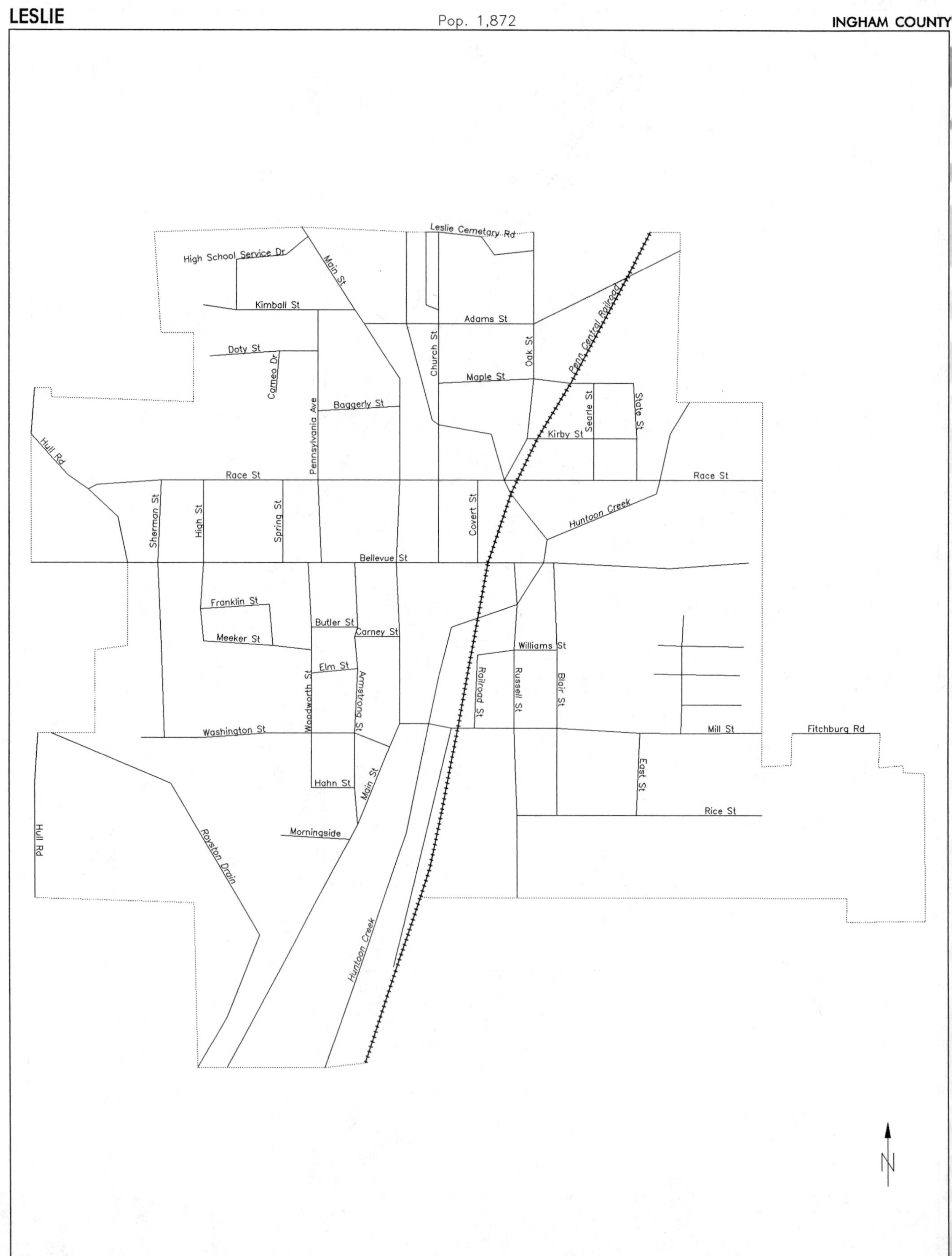
Leslie Cemetary Rd
High School Service Dr
Main St
Kimball St
Adams St
Doty St
Cameo Dr
Church St
Oak St
Penn Central Railroad
Maple St
Baggerly St
Pennsylvania Ave
Searle St
State St
Kirby St
Hull Rd
Race St
Race St
Sherman St
High St
Spring St
Covert St
Huntoon Creek
Bellevue St
Franklin St
Butler St
Carney St
Meeker St
Williams St
Elm St
Woodworth St
Armstrong St
Railroad St
Russell St
Blair St
Washington St
Mill St
Fitchburg Rd
Hahn St
Main St
East St
Rice St
Morningside
Royston Drain
Hull Rd
Huntoon Creek
N

LINCOLN PARK

Pop. 41,832

WAYNE COUNTY

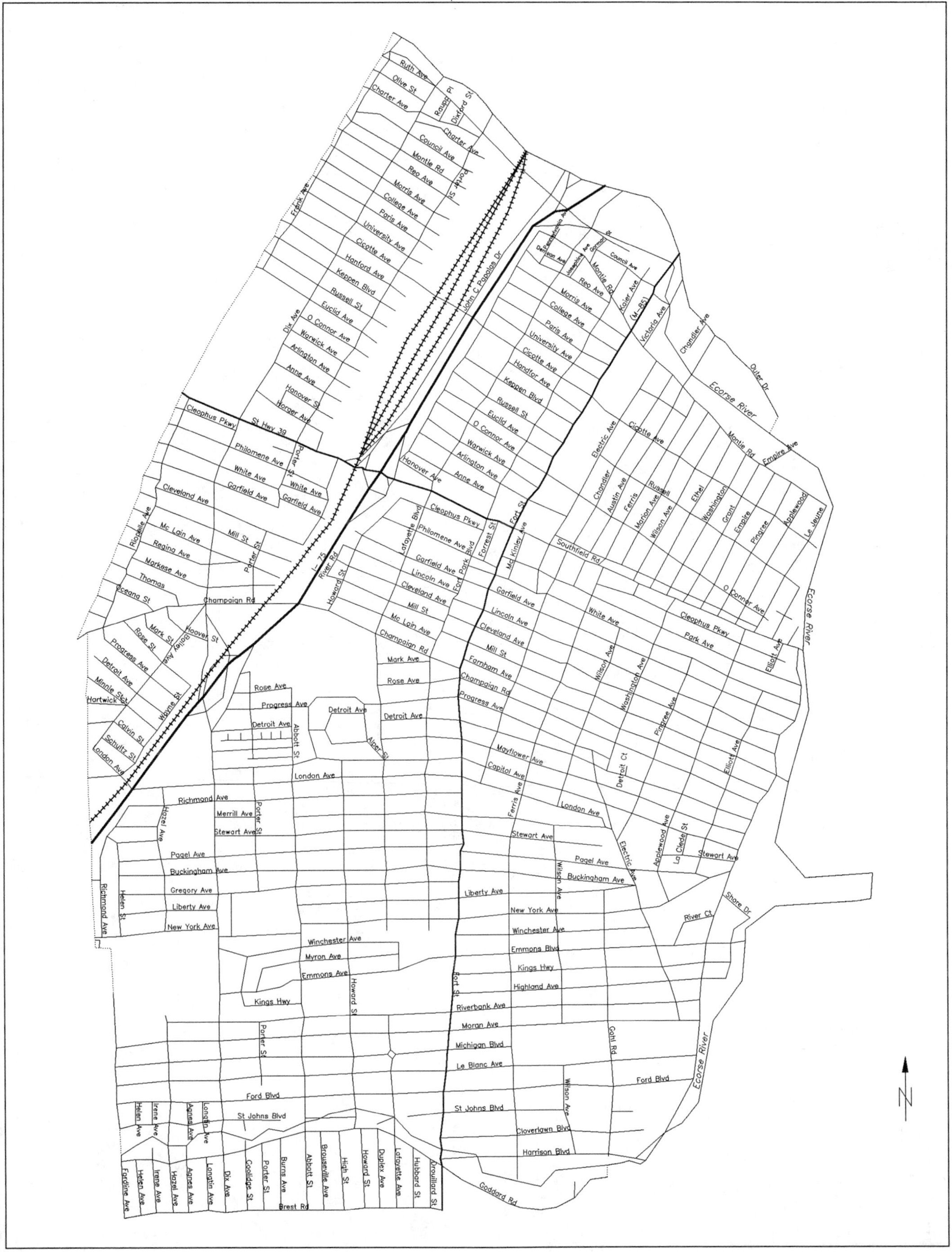

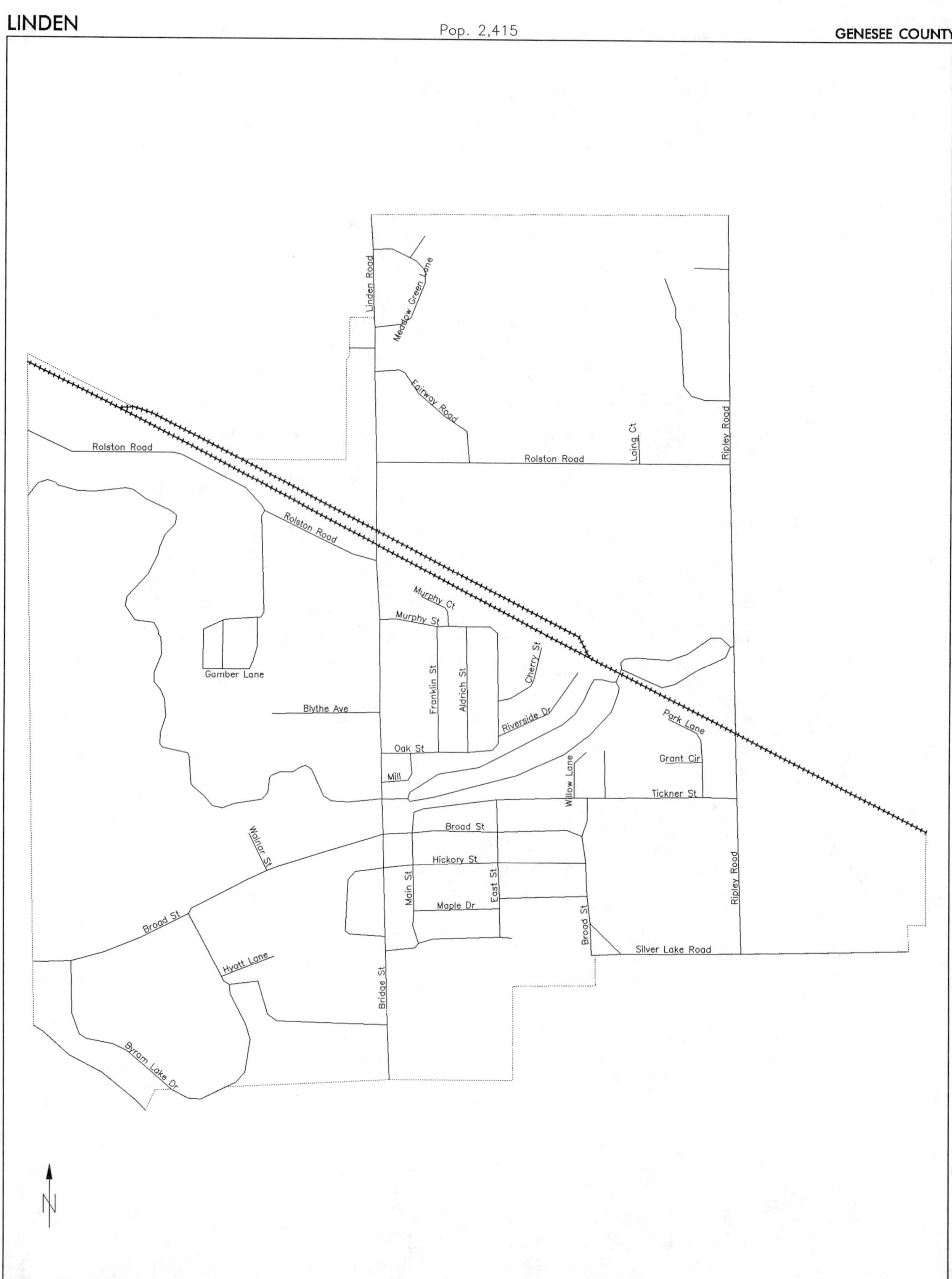
Linden Road
Meadow Green Lane
Fairway Road
Rolston Road
Laing Ct
Ripley Road
Rolston Road
Rolston Road
Murphy Ct
Murphy St
Franklin St
Aldrich St
Cherry St
Gamber Lane
Blythe Ave
Riverside Dr
Park Lane
Oak St
Grant Cir
Mill
Willow Lane
Tickner St
Walnar St
Broad St
Hickory St
Main St
East St
Maple Dr
Ripley Road
Broad St
Broad St
Silver Lake Road
Hyatt Lane
Bridge St
Byram Lake Dr
N

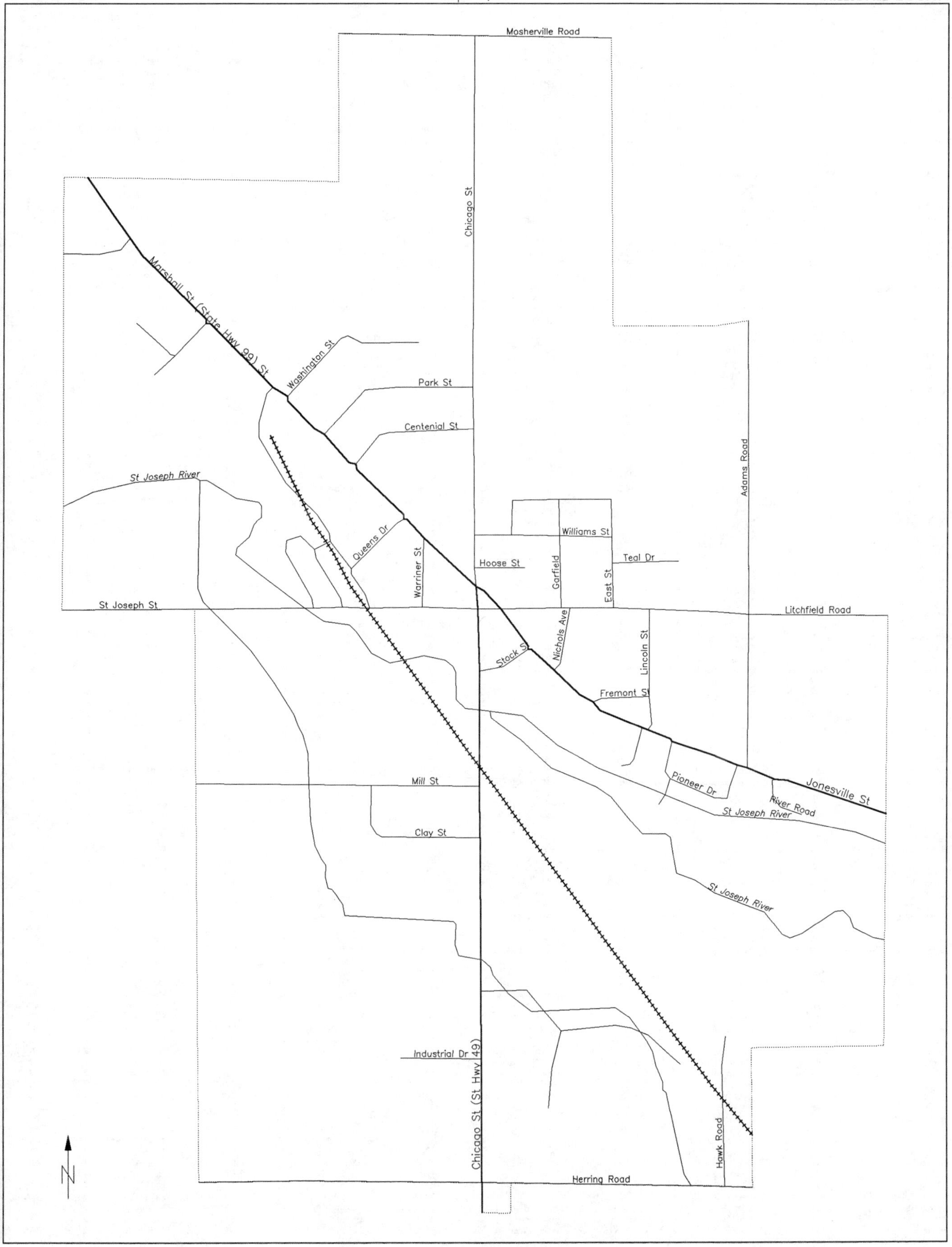

Mosherville Road
Chicago St
Marshall St (State Hwy 99) St
Washington St
Park St
Centenial St
St Joseph River
Adams Road
Williams St
Queens Dr
Warriner St
Hoose St
Garfield
East St
Teal Dr
St Joseph St
Litchfield Road
Nichols Ave
Lincoln St
Stock St
Fremont St
Pioneer Dr
Jonesville St
River Road
St Joseph River
Mill St
Clay St
St Joseph River
Industrial Dr
Chicago St (St Hwy 49)
Hawk Road
Herring Road
N

NOTES

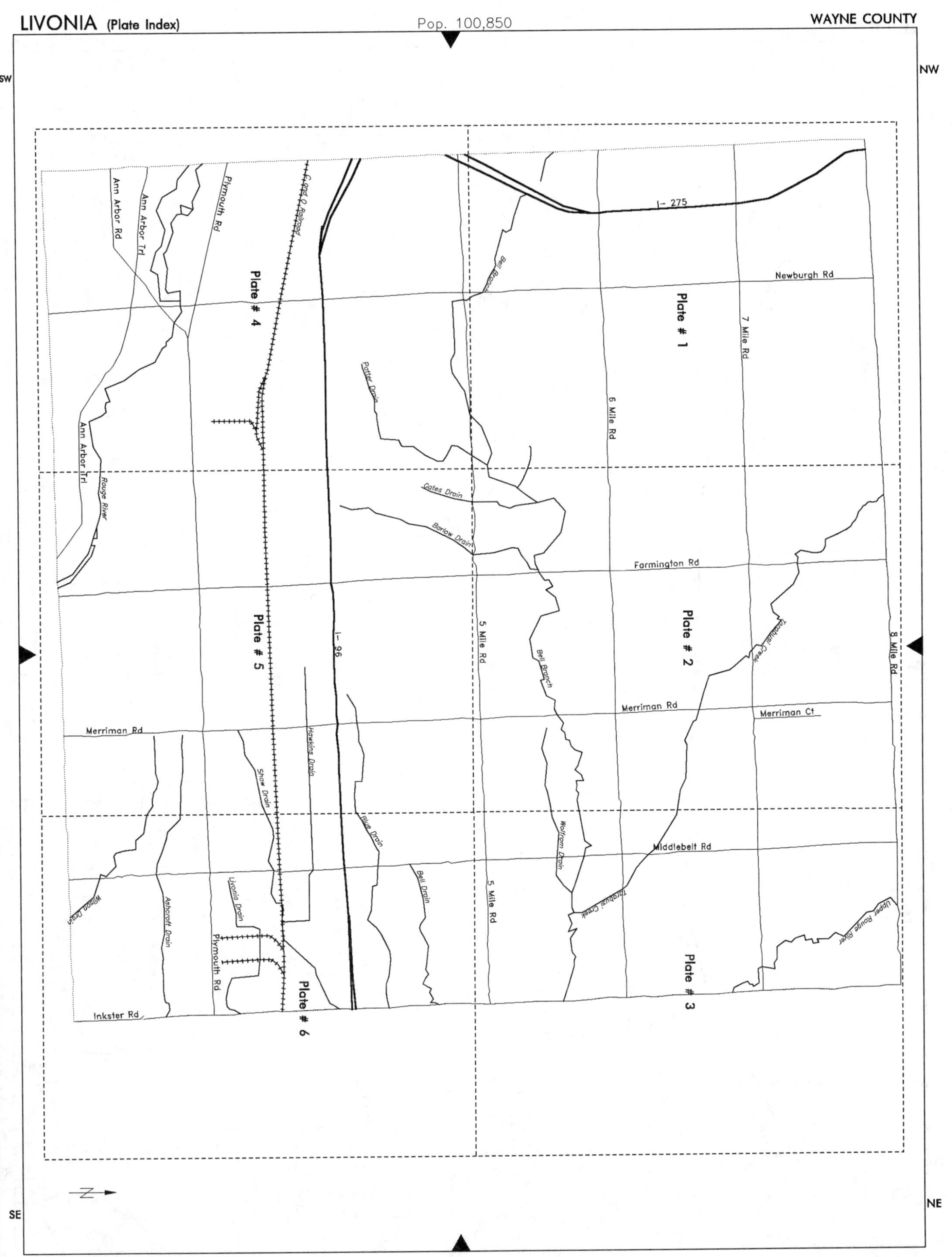
SW
NW
SE
NE
Plate # 1
Plate # 2
Plate # 3
Plate # 4
Plate # 5
Plate # 6
I- 275
I- 96
Newburgh Rd
7 Mile Rd
6 Mile Rd
5 Mile Rd
8 Mile Rd
Farmington Rd
Merriman Rd
Merriman Ct
Middlebelt Rd
Inkster Rd
Plymouth Rd
Ann Arbor Rd
Ann Arbor Trl
C and O Railroad
Rouge River
Upper Rouge River
Bell Branch
Potter Drain
Gates Drain
Barlow Drain
Tarabusi Creek
Wolfrom Drain
Hawkins Drain
Shaw Drain
Blue Drain
Bell Drain
Livonia Drain
Ashcroft Drain
Wilson Drain

8 Mile Rd
7 Mile Rd
6 Mile Rd
I-275
Haggerty Rd
Newburgh Rd
Victor Pkwy
Fitzgerald Ave
Liverpool Ave
St Martins Ave
Northland Dr
Bethany St
Hickory Ln
Meadowview Ln
John Dr
Ellen Dr
Wayne Rd
Norfolk Ave
Fargo Dr
Navin Ave
Edgewood Ave
Pembroke St
Bicentennial Dr
Gary Ln
Fairfax Dr
Dardenella St
Nola St
Susanna
Blue Skies St
Margareta St
Pickford
University Park Dr
Laurel Park Dr
Oval Park
Chippewa Dr
Fox Dr
Menominee Dr
Allegan Dr
Margareta Ave
Comstock Ave
Renwick Ave
Levan St
Westbrook St
Parklane St
Fairway Dr
Van St
Hammer Ln
Curtis Ave
Veri
Banbury St
Banbury Ct
Lancashire Rd
Hampton Ct
Brookview Dr
Northgate Dr
Country Club Dr
Gardner Ave
Bennett Ave
Bennett St
Golfview Dr
Woodside Dr
Vargo Ave
Bobrich Ave
Country Club Ct
Edgewood Dr
Laurel Dr
Quakertown Ln
Meeting House Ln
Lapham
Reo Dr
Reo Ct
Stacey
Stacey Ct
Aldrich Ct
Swathmore Ln
Swathmore Ct
Penn
Bloomfield Dr
Professional Ctr Dr
Laurel Park Dr
Mallory Dr
Munger St
Bristol Ave
Huff
Marsha St
Houghton Dr
Nola Dr
Southampton
Richfield
Sunnydale
Myrna St
Whitcomb
Fitzgerald St
Grove Dr
Bristol St
Wood Dr
Park Ave
Ronnie Ln
Riverside Dr
Munger Ct
Bristol Ct
Ellen Ct
Oakdale Ct
Oakdale Dr
Sunnydale St
Williams Ave
Ladywood Rd
Ladywood Ct
Rayburn Ave
Sherwood St
Sherwood Ct
Marler St
Kingsbury Rd
Roycroft St
Stonehouse Cir
Huff Ave
Bell Branch
Lancaster Ave
Blue Skies Ct
Sweona Cir
Nola Cir
Hix Ct
Hix Rd
Kingsbury Ave Ct
Lancaster Ct
Roycroft Ave
Liverpool St
Sussex St
Comstock St
Westbrook Rd
Parklane Dr
NW
SW
SE

8 Mile Rd
NE
Gill Rd
Pollyanna Dr
Farmington Rd
Westmore St
Shadyside Ave
Mayfield Rd
Hubbard Rd
Parker Ave
Osmus St
Merriwood Park Dr
Morlock Ave
Milburn Ave
Purlingbrook Rd
Louise Ave
Norfolk Ave
Norfolk St
Irving Dr
Myron Dr
Stamford St
Norfolk Rd
Norfolk Rd
Whitby St
Whitby Ct
Fargo Dr
Laurel Ave
Navin Ct
Navin Ave
Fargo Ave
Sunset Blvd
Melvin Ave
Pembroke St
Pembroke St
Fargo
Fargo
Pembroke St
Pembroke St
Doris St
Oporto St
Louise Ave
Bretton Dr
Bretton Dr
Bretton Rd
Bretton Rd
Fairfax Dr
Fairfax St
Fairfax St
Fairfax Dr
Fairfax Ct
Fonville Dr
Fonville Ave
St Martins Ave
Fonville Ct
Carl St
Carl St
Hardy Ave
Parker Ave
Ingram St
St Martins Ave
St Martins Ave
St Martins Ave
St Martins Ave
Northland Dr
Haldane St
Pollyanna Ct
Stamford St
Haldane St
Haldane St
Haldane Ave
Merriman Ct
Bainbridge Ave
Sunset Blvd
Whitby St
Northland Dr
Haldane St
Laurel Rd
Gable St
Gable Ave
Bridge St
Tarabusi Creek
Osmus St
Auburndale St
Merriman Rd
Gable St
Norwich St
Gable Dr
Gary Ln
Service Rd
7 Mile Rd
Bainbridge Ct
Canterbury
Clarita
Whitby Rd
Wooding St
Mayfield Ave
Yorkshire
Shrewsbury
Hillcrest Ave
Bainbridge Ct
Clarita Ave
Purlingbrook Ave
Melvin Ave
Clarita Ave
Bainbridge Ct
Sunset Blvd
Milburn St
Flamingo Blvd
Doris Ln
Gill Rd
Southampton St
Stamford
Irving St
Filmore St
Farmington Rd
Westmore St
Shadyside St
Mayfield Ave
Hillbrook Ave
Bainbridge Ct
Laurel Rd
Loveland Ave
Hillbrook
Pickford Ave
Pickford
Pickford Ave
Pickford Ave
Purlingbrook Ave
Norwich St
Whitby Rd
Curtis Ave
Curtis Ave
Brookview Dr
Vacri Ln
Farmington Rd
Mayfield Ave
Fairfield Ave
Merriman Rd
Hillcrest Ave
Rexwood Dr
Doris Ln
Stanwich Blvd
Bennett Ct
Bennett Ave
Mayville St
Jeanine Ave
Francavilla
Myron Dr
Mc Namara Dr
Vacri Ln
Bell Creek Ln
Loveland Ave
Brier Ct
Bobrich Ave
Sunset Blvd
Myron Ct
Bobrich Ct
Purlingbrook Rd
LaVargo Ave
Burns
Vargo Ave
Ellen Rd
Ellen Dr
6 Mile Rd
Service Rd
6 Mile Rd
Oporto St
Fairlane Dr
Bell Creek Ln
Mayfield Dr
Yorkshire Dr
Shrewsbury Ct
Canterbury Dr
Wood Dr
Wood Dr
Whitby Dr
Fairfield Ave
Munger Ave
Grove Dr
Grove Dr
Grove Ave
Munger St
Bloomfield Dr
Munger Ave
Cambridge Dr
Balmoral Dr
Balmoral Ct
Pollyanna Ct
Burton Ln
Surrey St
Farmington Rd
Bell Creek Ln
Greenland Ave
Buchanan Rd
Greenland Rd
Bristol Dr
Southampton Ct
Bell Branch
Greenland Ct
Puritan Ave
Riverside Dr
Fairlane Dr
Bell Creek Ct
Burton Ct
Camborne Ln
Camborne Ln
Oakdale St
Bell Branch
Hampshire Rd
Hampshire Rd
Wentworth Ave
Southampton St
Whitby Dr
Myrna Ct
Myrna Dr
Myrna Dr
Rayburn St
Myrna Dr
Merriman Rd
Oakhill Ct
Rayburn Ave
Rayburn Ave
Doris Ave
Oporto St
Gary Ln
Riverside Dr
Woodvale Dr
Dorais Ave
Barlow Drain
Edington St
Westmore Ave
Loveland Ave
Ingram Ave
Auburndale Ave
Dorais Ave
SE
SW
Roycroft Ave
Stamford St
Roycroft Ave
Roycroft Ave
Bainbridge Ave
Sunset Ave
Henry Ruff Rd
Fairlane Dr
Alpine Dr
Norwich Rd
Lamoyne St
Surrey St
Wooding Dr
Mayfield Ave
Brookfield Ave
Fairfield Ave
Hubbard Rd
Ashurst St
Coventry Dr
5 Mile Rd
5 Mile Rd
Spanish
Melvin Ave

LIVONIA (Plate 3)

Pop. 1,027,974

WAYNE COUNTY

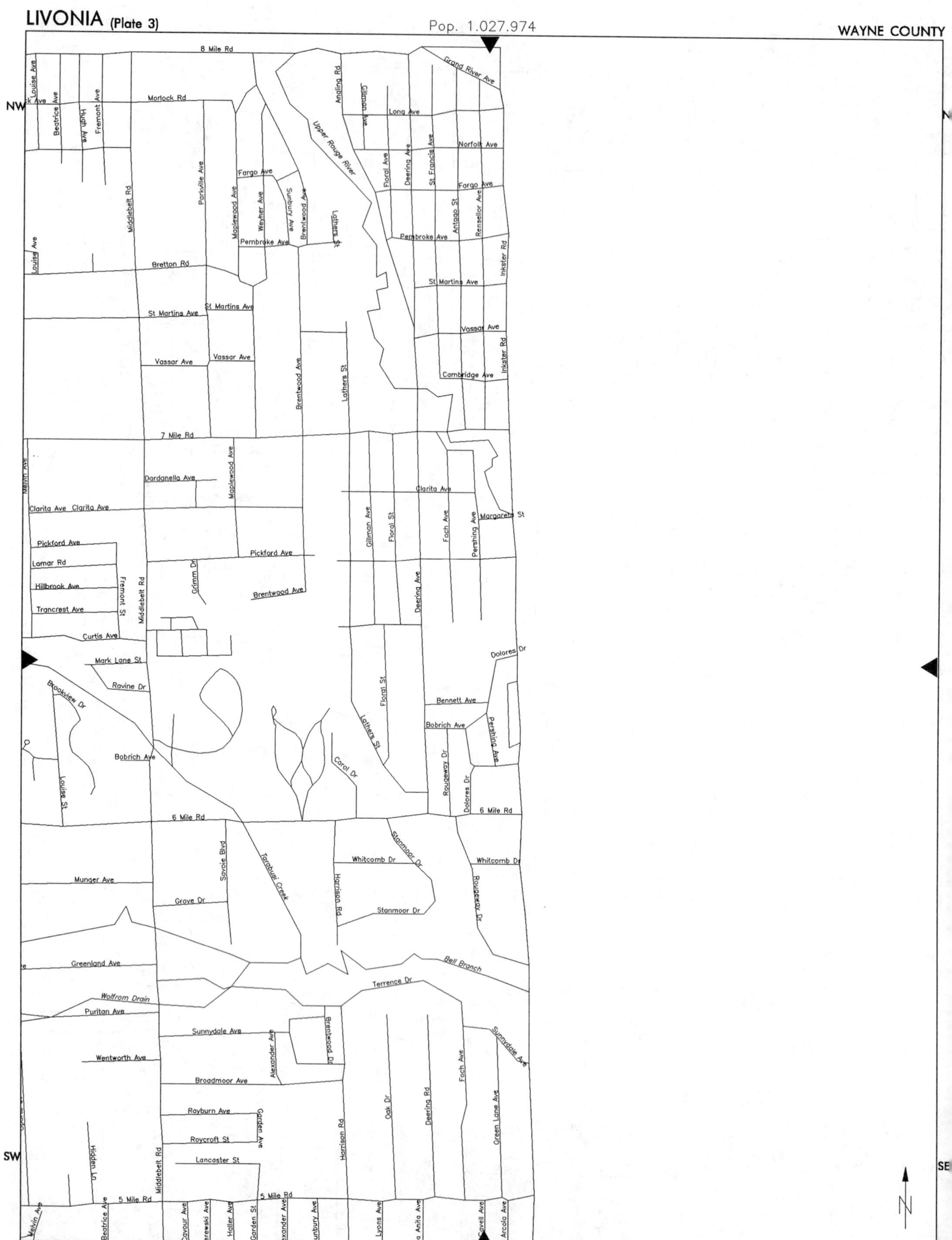

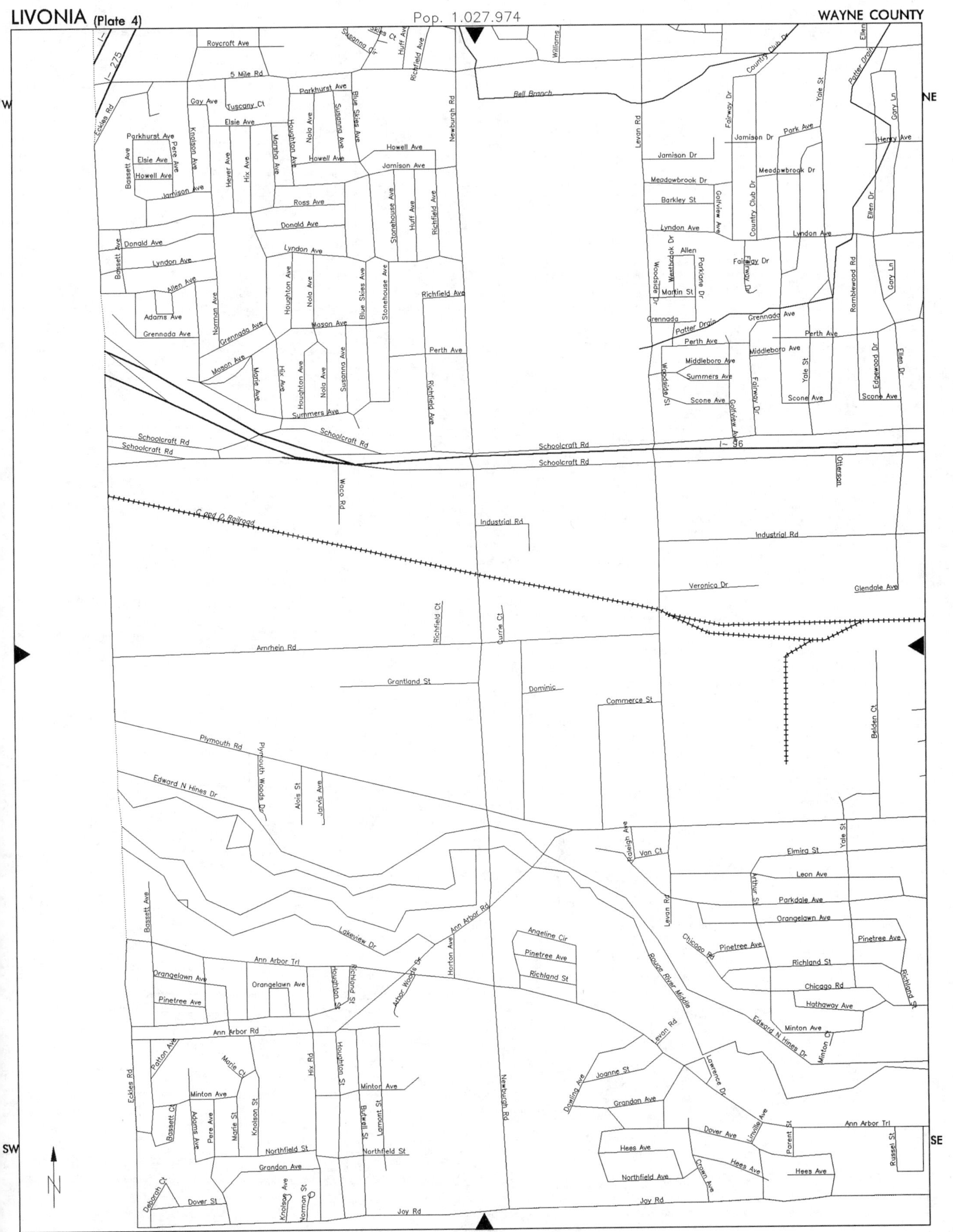

NW
NE
SW
SE
5 Mile Rd
Coventry Dr
Edington St
Westmore Ave
Shadyside St
Brookfield Rd
Fairfield Ave
Hubbard Rd
Berwick Ave
Auburndale Ave
Melrose Ave
Arden Ave
Merriman Rd
Bainbridge Ave
Spanish Ct
Hoy Rd
Riverside Dr
Fairlane Rd
Gates Drain
Barlow Drain
Henry Ave
Jamison St
Meadowbrook Ln
Blackburn Ct
Ingram Ave
Jamison Ave
Nye Ct
Bonnydale Dr
Melvin Ave
Barkley Ave
Oakley St
Bredin Ct
Lyndon Ave
Allen St
Martin Ave
Grennada Ave
Perth Ave
Middleboro Ave
Summers Ave
Scone Ave
Loveland Ave
Auburndale Ct
Cranston Ave
Hubbell Ave
Sunset Ave
Livonia Cres
Hillcrest Ave
Henry Ruff Rd
Mason Ct
Oakview Ave
Bentley Ave
Acacia Ave
Mason Ave
Denne St
Kendal St
Blue Drain
Warner Ct
Schoolcraft Rd
Middleboro St
Summers
Riverside Ct
Ashurst St
Pinehurst Ct
Stark Rd
Stamford Ave
I- 96
Ashurst Ct
Stamford Ct
Surrey
Graytona
Industrial Rd
Autry St
D P W DR
Farmington Rd
Glendale
Hawkins Drain
Pamco Dr
Fairlane
C and O Railroad
Shaw Drain
Capitol Rd
Beacon St
Wadsworth Dr
Boston Post Rd
Standish Rd
Capitol St
Mayfield
Brookfield Ave
Enterprise Dr
Hubbard
Elmira St
Parkdale Ct
Parkdale St
Angeline Cir
Parkdale Ave
Laurel Ave
Wayne Rd
Pinetree Ave
Orangelawn Ave
Richland Ave
Woodring Ave
Mayfield Ave
Hubbard St
Milburn Ave
Ashcroft Drain
Flamingo Ave
Robert Dr
Chicago Ave
Chicago Rd
Hathaway Ave
Minton Ave
Westfield Ave
Grandon Ave
Roseland Ave
Delaware Ave
Vermont Ave
Cindy Ave
Sleepy Hollow Ln
Nancy Ave
Rouge River
Michele Ave
Edward N Hines Dr
Louisiana Ave
Montana Ave
Ohio Ave
Florida Ave
Idaho Ave
Texas Ave
Iowa Ave
Texas Ct
Frederick Dr
Olson St
Danzig Ave
Ann Arbor Trl
Kentucky Ave
Indiana Ave
Washington Ave
Alabama Ave
Denne Dr
Perrin Dr
Hees Ave
Utah Ave
Georgia Ave
Nevada Ave
Nebraska Ave
Joy Rd
Dover Ave
N

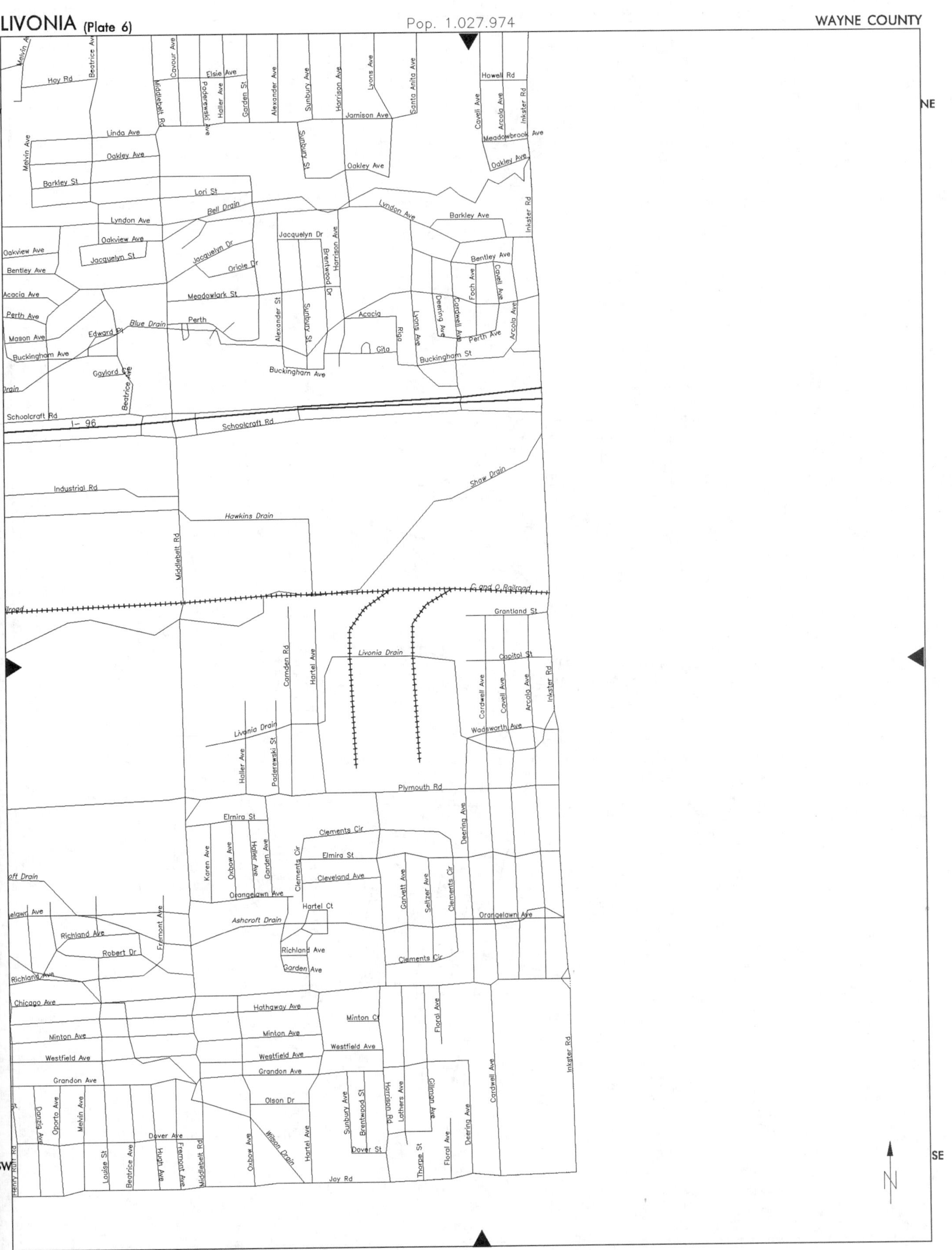
Hay Rd
Beatrice Ave
Cavour Ave
Middlebelt Rd
Elsie Ave
Poderewski Ave
Haller Ave
Garden St
Alexander Ave
Sunbury Ave
Harrison Ave
Lyons Ave
Santa Anita Ave
Jamison Ave
Howell Rd
Cavell Ave
Arcola Ave
Inkster Rd
Meadowbrook Ave
Oakley Ave
Linda Ave
Melvin Ave
Barkley St
Lori St
Bell Drain
Lyndon Ave
Barkley Ave
Oakview Ave
Jacquelyn Dr
Jacquelyn St
Bentley Ave
Oriole Dr
Brentwood Dr
Foch Ave
Acacia Ave
Meadowlark St
Deering Ave
Cardwell Ave
Perth Ave
Blue Drain
Edward Pl
Mason Ave
Buckingham Ave
Gita
Riga
Gaylord Ct
Buckingham St
Schoolcraft Rd
I- 96
Industrial Rd
Hawkins Drain
Shaw Drain
C and O Railroad
Grantland St
Livonia Drain
Capitol St
Camden Rd
Hartel Ave
Wadsworth Ave
Plymouth Rd
Elmira St
Clements Cir
Karen Ave
Oxbow Ave
Cleveland Ave
Orangelawn Ave
Garvett Ave
Seltzer Ave
Hartel Ct
Ashcroft Drain
Fremont Ave
Richland Ave
Robert Dr
Garden Ave
Chicago Ave
Hathaway Ave
Minton Ct
Minton Ave
Floral Ave
Westfield Ave
Grandon Ave
Olson Dr
Danzig Ave
Oporto Ave
Dover Ave
Wilson Drain
Brentwood St
Harrison Rd
Lathers Ave
Gilman Ave
Dover St
Louise St
Hugh Ave
Henry Ruff Rd
Thorpe St
Joy Rd
NE
SE
SW
N

Pop. 3983

Alden Nash Ave
Fulton St
Gee Dr
Bowes St
Allisandra Ave
Helena
Brenda Ave
Clarissa Ave
Glenna St
Donna Ave
Elandra Ave
Francesca Ct
Roberta Jayne Dr
Elizabeth Dean Dr
Faith Dr
Carol Lynne
Jane Ellen Dr
Laurie Gail Dr
Valley Vista Dr
Deborah Dr
Sibley
Church
Jane Ellen Dr
Lee Creek
Foreman St
West Ave
Center Ave
Pleasant Ave
Godfrey St
Hunt St
Birchwood Ct
Beech
Brook St
Maple St
Hudson St
Broadway St
Smith
Elm St
Chatham St
Howard St
Spring St
Amity St
Suffolk St
Elizabeth St
Mercer St
Lincoln Lake Ave
Hunt St
Riverside Dr
Flat River
Water
North St
Monroe St
Lafayette St
Marsac
Pine
Grant
Sherman
Washington St
Jefferson St
King St
Kent St
Avery St
High St
Front St
Jackson St
Shepard Road
Division St
Grand River
Horatio St
Grove St
James St
Hillside Ct
High St
Grindle Dr
Grand River Dr
Main St
N

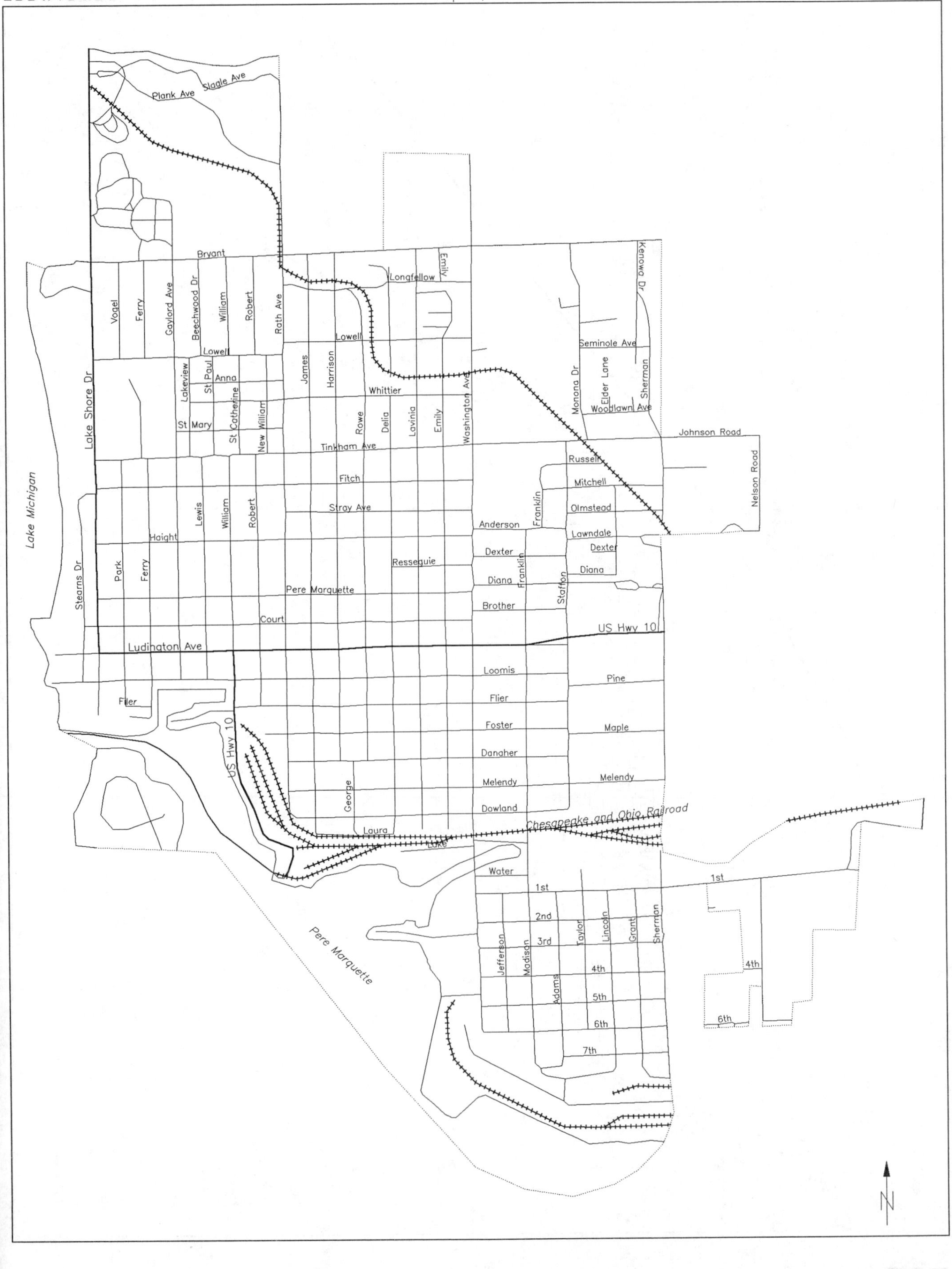

Plank Ave
Slagle Ave
Bryant
Longfellow
Emily
Kenowa Dr
Vogel
Ferry
Gaylord Ave
Beechwood Dr
William
Robert
Rath Ave
Lowell
Seminole Ave
Lakeview
St Paul
Anna
James
Harrison
Whittier
Monona Dr
Elder Lane
Sherman
Woodlawn Ave
Lake Shore Dr
St Mary
St Catherine
New William
Rowe
Delia
Lavinia
Emily
Washington Ave
Johnson Road
Tinkham Ave
Russell
Fitch
Mitchell
Nelson Road
Lake Michigan
Lewis
William
Robert
Stray Ave
Franklin
Olmstead
Anderson
Lawndale
Haight
Dexter
Dexter
Resseguie
Diana
Park
Ferry
Diana
Franklin
Stearns Dr
Pere Marquette
Stafford
Brother
Court
US Hwy 10
Ludington Ave
Loomis
Pine
Filer
Flier
Foster
Maple
US Hwy 10
Dangher
Melendy
Melendy
George
Dowland
Chesapeake and Ohio Railroad
Laura
Lake
Water
1st
1st
2nd
3rd
Jefferson
Madison
Taylor
Lincoln
Grant
Sherman
Pere Marquette
4th
4th
Adams
5th
6th
6th
7th
N

I-75
Allens Cove Rd
Locust St
Allens Cove Rd
Grove
6th St
5th St
Grant
3rd
4th St
3rd St
Harold Dr
2nd St
1st St
Dix St
Ann St
Ann St
Ann St
Center 3rd St
Center 2nd St
Forester Dr
Center 1st St
Elmhurst
Ellen
Spring St
Valleywood Ave
Oak St
Oak St
Buckley St
Elm St
Luna Pier Rd
1st St
2nd St
3rd St
4th St
5th St
6th St
7th St
Eigth St
9th St
10th St
11th St
12th St
13th St
14th St
15th St
Harold Dr
St Marks Dr
Lakewood Ave
Genoa Dr
Grand Blvd
Belvedere Dr
Naples Dr
Amalfi Dr
20th St
20 2nd St
Erie Rd
N

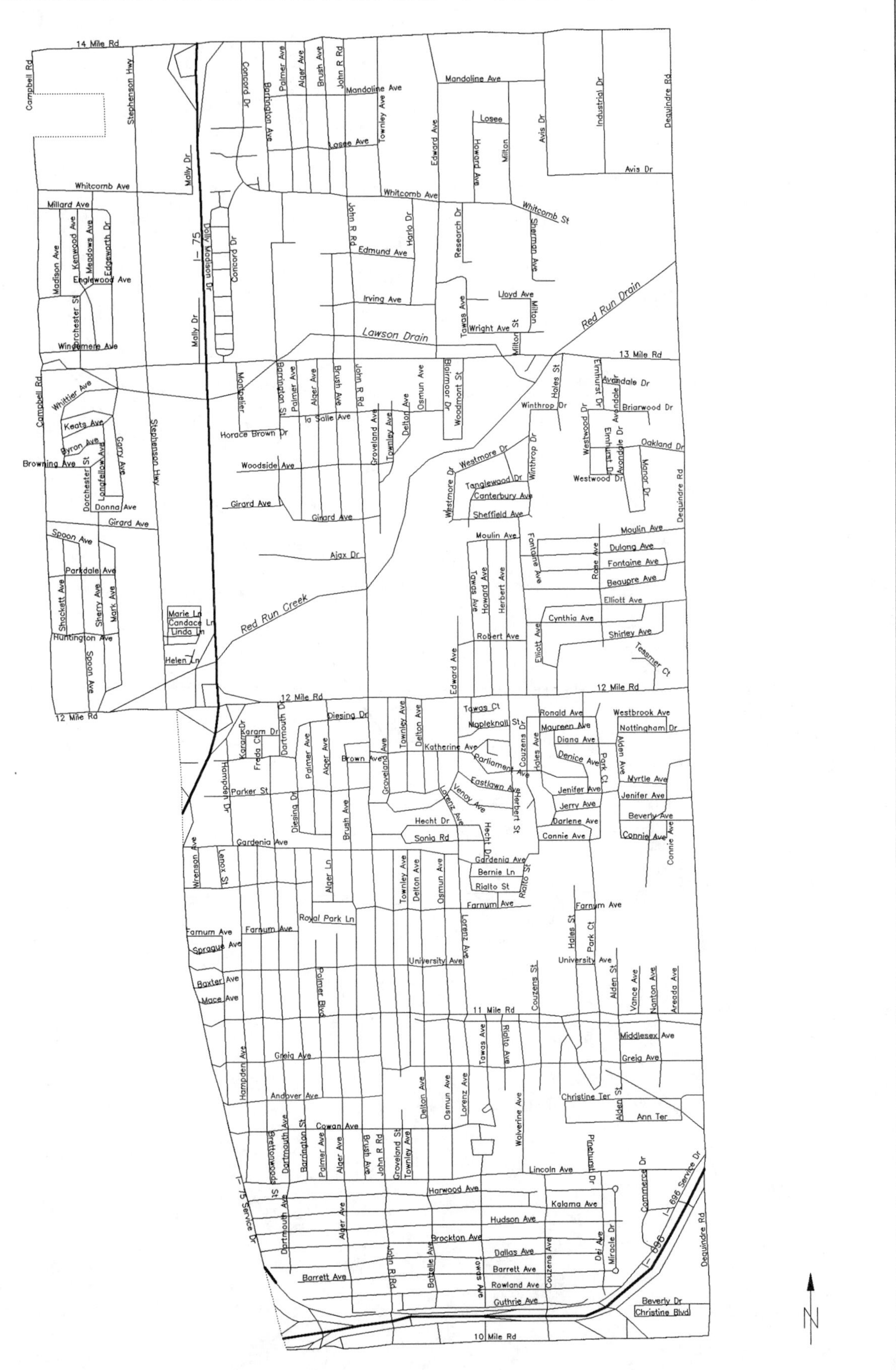
14 Mile Rd
Campbell Rd
Stephenson Hwy
Concord Dr
Barrington Ave
Palmer Ave
Alger Ave
Brush Ave
John R Rd
Mandoline Ave
Townley Ave
Edward Ave
Losee
Losee Ave
Howard Ave
Milton
Avis Dr
Industrial Dr
Dequindre Rd
Whitcomb Ave
Whitcomb St
Mally Dr
Millard Ave
Madison Ave
Kenwood Ave
Meadows Ave
Edgeworth Dr
Englewood Ave
Winchester St
Windemere Ave
I-75
Dolly Madison Dr
Edmund Ave
Harlo Dr
Research Dr
Sherman Ave
Irving Ave
Lloyd Ave
Towas Ave
Wright Ave
Lawson Drain
Red Run Drain
13 Mile Rd
Whittier Ave
Keats Ave
Byron Ave
Browning Ave
Dorchester St
Longfellow Ave
Garry Ave
Donna Ave
Girard Ave
Montpelier
Barrington St
la Salle Ave
Horace Brown Dr
Woodside Ave
Groveland Ave
Delton Ave
Osmun Ave
Blairmoor Dr
Woodmont St
Hales St
Elmhurst Dr
Avondale Dr
Briarwood Dr
Winthrop Dr
Westwood Dr
Oakland Dr
Manor Dr
Westmore Dr
Tanglewood Dr
Canterbury Ave
Sheffield Ave
Spoon Ave
Parkdale Ave
Ajax Dr
Moulin Ave
Fontaine Ave
Dulong Ave
Rose Ave
Beaupre Ave
Shackett Ave
Sherry Ave
Mark Ave
Herbert Ave
Elliott Ave
Cynthia Ave
Shirley Ave
Marie Ln
Candace Ln
Linda Ln
Huntington Ave
Red Run Creek
Robert Ave
Tessmer Ct
Helen Ln
12 Mile Rd
Diesing Dr
Towas Ct
Ronald Ave
Westbrook Ave
Karam Dr
Freda Ct
Dartmouth Dr
Napleknoll St
Maureen Ave
Nottingham Dr
Diana Ave
Katherine Ave
Couzens Dr
Denice Ave
Alden Ave
Brown Ave
Parliament Ave
Park Ct
Hampden Dr
Myrtle Ave
Parker St
Eastlawn Ave
Jenifer Ave
Venoy Ave
Lorenz Ave
Herbert St
Jerry Ave
Beverly Ave
Hecht Dr
Darlene Ave
Connie Ave
Sonia Rd
Gardenia Ave
Wiener Ave
Lenox St
Bernie Ln
Rialto St
Alger Ln
Farnum Ave
Royal Park Ln
Sprague Ave
University Ave
Baxter Ave
Mace Ave
Palmer Blvd
Couzens St
Vance Ave
Alden St
Nanton Ave
Areada Ave
11 Mile Rd
Hampden Ave
Greig Ave
Middlesex Ave
Rialto Ave
Andover Ave
Christine Ter
Ann Ter
Wolverine Ave
Cowan Ave
Brettonwoods St
Dartmouth Ave
Barrington St
Groveland St
Pinehurst Dr
Lincoln Ave
I-75 Service Dr
Harwood Ave
Kalama Ave
Commerce Dr
I-696 Service Dr
Hudson Ave
Brockton Ave
Dallas Ave
Battelle Ave
Dei Ave
Miracle Dr
I-696
Barrett Ave
Rowland Ave
Guthrie Ave
Beverly Dr
Christine Blvd
10 Mile Rd
N

MANCELONA

Pop. 1,370

Limits Road
Ceder River Road
Riverdale St
Hillview St
Sunnyside St
Parkside St
Jefferson Ave
Monroe Ave
Maple St
Elm St
Forest St
William St
Pine St
Lincoln St
Lincoln St
Rose St
Division St
Division St
Franklin St
Division St
Alma St
Danforth St
Calhoun St
Washington St
Hinman St
Goodale Lane
Pierce St
Limit St
State St
Schlund Lane
Main St
Michigan St
Grove St
Washington St
Dale Ave
Ida St
Dale Ave
William St
Maple St
Downey St

Main St
Raisin River
Elton St
Union St
Riverbend Dr
Schaffer St
Territorial St
Auburn St
Lafayette St
Riverbend Dr
Sandborn Rd
Duncan Rd
Madison Rd
Macomb St
Clarkson St
Raisin River
Washington St
Macomb St
Cass St
Wager St
Ann Arbor Rd
Vernon Rd
Clinton St
Washington St
Adrian St
Main St
Grove St
Riverside Dr
Beaufort St
Furnace St
Wolverine St
Adrian St
Duncan Rd
Liberty St
Vernon Rd
Torrey Rd
Raisin River
Granger St
Summit St
Sunset Dr
Division St
Jefferson St
Morgan St
City Rd
Hibbard Rd
Geiske Rd
Spring St
State Hwy 52
State Hwy 52
N

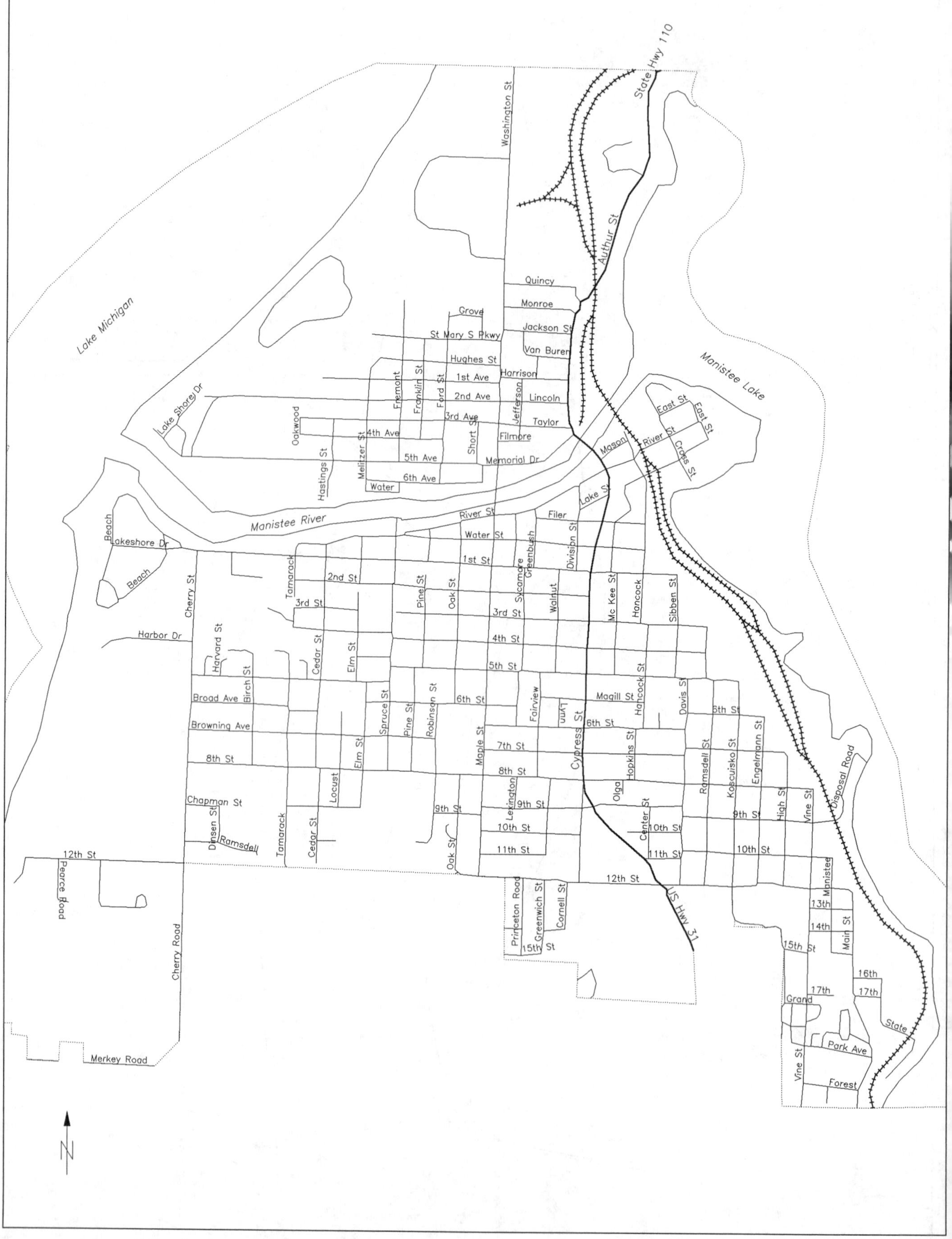
State Hwy 110
Washington St
Authur St
Lake Michigan
Manistee Lake
Quincy
Monroe
Grove
Jackson St
St Mary S Pkwy
Van Buren
Hughes St
Harrison
1st Ave
2nd Ave
Lincoln
Fremont
Franklin St
Ford St
Jefferson
3rd Ave
Taylor
Lake Shore Dr
Oakwood
4th Ave
Filmore
East St
River St
Mason
Cross St
Meilzer St
5th Ave
Short St
Memorial Dr
Hastings St
6th Ave
Water
Lake St
Manistee River
River St
Filer
Beach
Lakeshore Dr
Water St
1st St
Division St
Greenbush
Sycamore
2nd St
Tamarack
Pine St
Oak St
Walnut
Mc Kee St
Hancock
Sibben St
Cherry St
3rd St
4th St
Harbor Dr
Harvard St
Cedar St
Elm St
5th St
Birch St
Broad Ave
Spruce St
Robinson St
6th St
Fairview
Magill St
Davis St
Lynn
Cypress St
Browning Ave
Maple St
Hopkins St
Ramsdell St
Koscuisko St
Engelmann St
7th St
8th St
Locust
Lexington
Olga
High St
Vine St
Disposal Road
Chapman St
9th St
Center St
10th St
Dinsen St
Ramsdell
11th St
12th St
Pearce Road
Manistee
13th
14th
Main St
Princeton Road
Greenwich St
Cornell St
US Hwy 31
15th St
Cherry Road
16th
17th
Grand
State
Park Ave
Vine St
Forest
Merkey Road
N

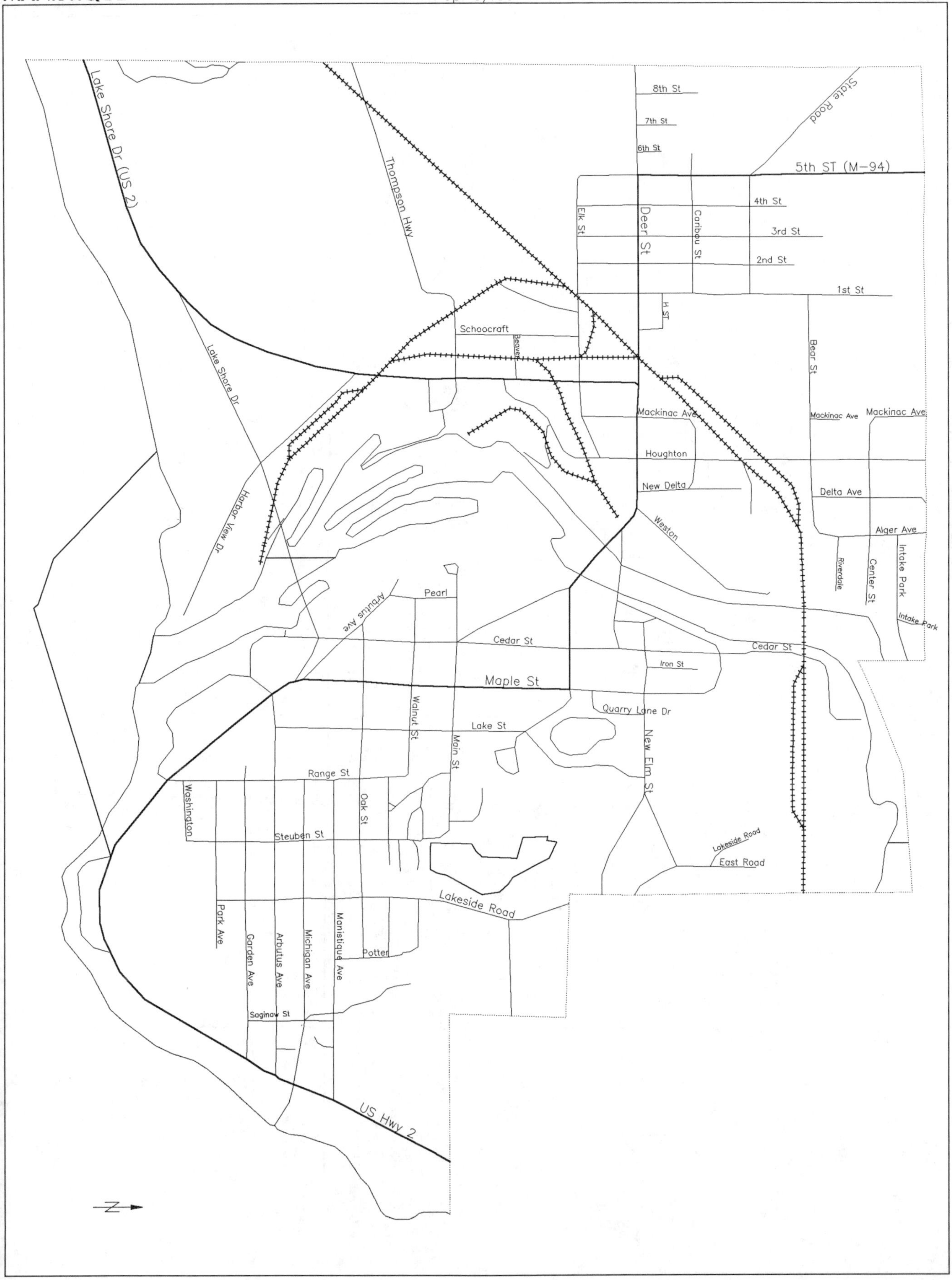

Lake Shore Dr (US 2)
Thompson Hwy
8th St
7th St
6th St
State Road
5th ST (M-94)
4th St
3rd St
2nd St
1st St
Elk St
Deer St
Caribou St
H ST
Schoocraft
Beaver
Lake Shore Dr
Bear St
Mackinac Ave
Mackinac Ave
Mackinac Ave
Houghton
New Delta
Delta Ave
Alger Ave
Harbor View Dr
Weston
Riverdale
Center St
Intake Park
Intake Park
Arbutus Ave
Pearl
Cedar St
Cedar St
Iron St
Maple St
Quarry Lane Dr
Walnut St
Lake St
Main St
New Elm St
Range St
Washington
Oak St
Steuben St
Lakeside Road
East Road
Lakeside Road
Park Ave
Garden Ave
Arbutus Ave
Michigan Ave
Manistique Ave
Potter
Saginaw St
US Hwy 2
N

Michigan Northern Railway Co
14 1/4 Mile Road
R W Harris Industrial Ave
Manton Creek
No 41 Road
Cedar St
Pine St
Holmes St
Roberts St
George St
Griswold St
Griswold St
Lake Billings
Division St
Elm St
West St
Elmore St
Park Dr
Sturtevant Ave
Wiles St
State Hwy 42
Main St
Main St
1st St
Park St
Wall St
2nd St
Indiana Ave
Randolph St
State St
South St
South St
Michigan Ave
4th St
Maple St
Park St
Pearl St
5th St
Harger St
State St
Manton Creek
6th St
7th St
7th St
Michigan Ave

Mable Road
Woodworth St
Main St (M-29)
Pleasant St
De Gurse Ave
Maple St
Charles St
Holland St
Pleasant St
Gladys St
Murray Ct
Pittsburgh St
Harold St
Main St
Katherine St
2nd St
Belle River Ave
Belle River
Minster St
Metropolis St
Mary St
William
Elizabeth St
6th St
5th St
4th St
Butler St
Frederick St
Pearl St
Riverview
West Blvd
Parker St
3rd St
River
Broadway St
Lowell St
Hanover St
Port Huron and Detroit Railroad
Delina St
Hill St
Jefferson St
Market St
Water St
St Clair St
Mary St
Washington St
King Road
Maple St
Parker St
St Clair St
St. Clair River
Ward Ave
Ward St
Union St
Cottrell Blvd
Bell Ave
Marine St
Robertson St
Robertson St
Bridge St
Brown St
Brown St
Main St
4th St
Carroll St
Carroll St
Bruce St
Belle River
Scott St
Water St
Elizabeth St
Catherine St
Chartier Ave
Chartier Road
Parker St
Belle River Ave
Bowery St
Alger St
Thompson Dr
Parker St
Addison Ct
Martindale Ct
River Road
N

Lorraine St
Marlette St
Ayre St
Carpenter St
Sunbold Dr
Mc Gill St
Lilac Dr
Ervin St
Hack Dr
Lamotte St
Little St
Morris St
Doyle St
Ellsworth St
Chard St
Warner St
Angle St
Fenner St
State Hwy 53
Tulane Dr
Locust St
Main St
Main St
Concord St
Sanford
Vail St
Wilson St
Wilson St
Golf Course Dr
Karen
Rogers
Moore St
Church St
Oaks St
Kilgour St
Ervin St
Marlette St
Burke St
Sterling St
Ervin St
Euclid St
Municipal Dr
Boyne Road
N

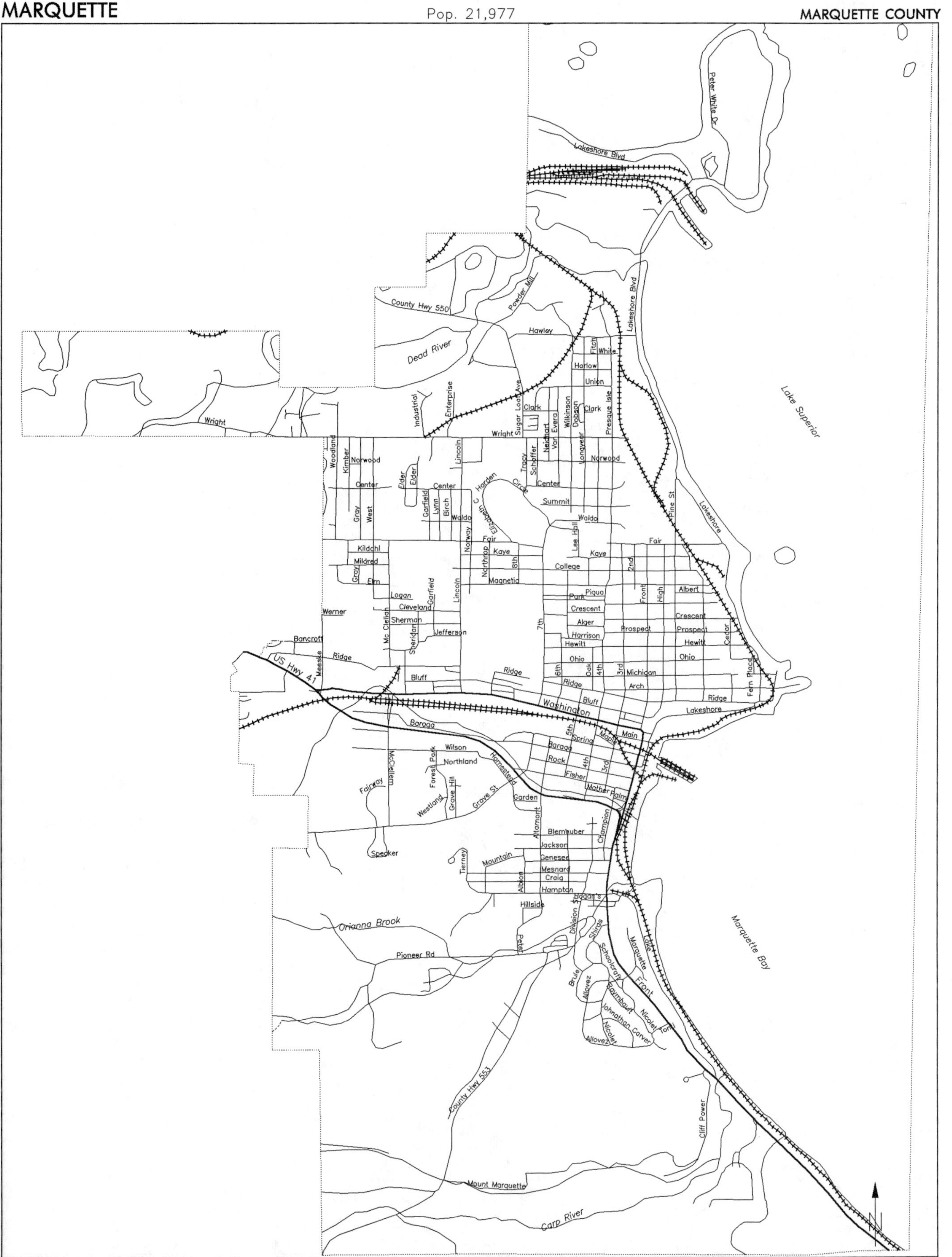
Peter White Dr
Lakeshore Blvd
County Hwy 550
Powder Mill
Dead River
Hawley
Lake Superior
Wright
Industrial
Enterprise
Norwood
Center
Summit
Walda
Fair
Kaye
College
Magnetic
Lakeshore
Pine St
Albert
Crescent
Prospect
Hewitt
Ohio
Michigan
Arch
Ridge
Bluff
Washington
Main
US Hwy 41
Baraga
Wilson
Northland
Homestead
Grove St
Garden
Fairway
Westland
Speaker
Mountain
Jackson
Genesee
Mesnard
Craig
Hampton
Hillside
Orianna Brook
Pioneer Rd
Marquette Bay
Front
County Hwy 553
Cliff Power
Mount Marquette
Carp River

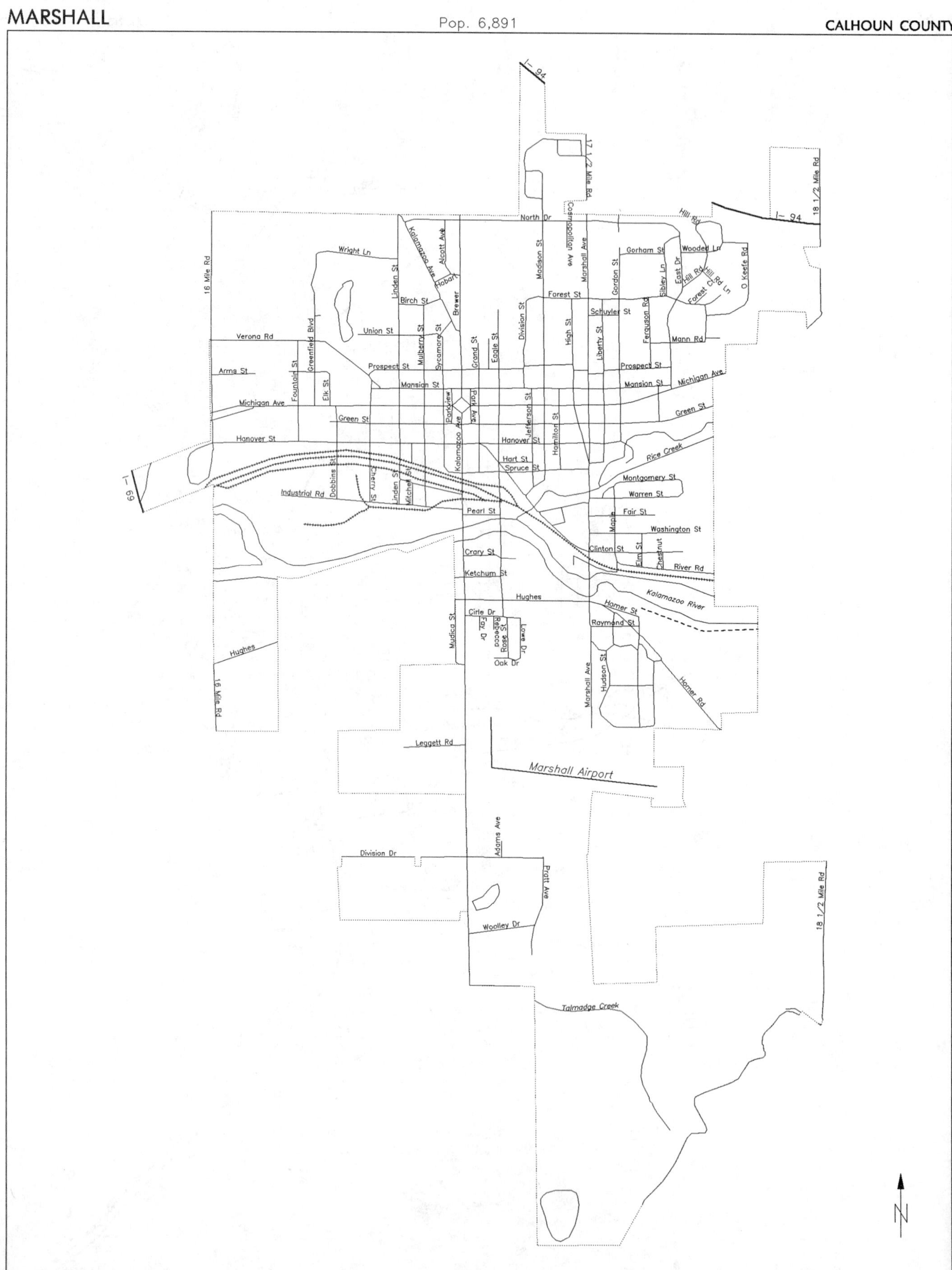
I-94
17 1/2 Mile Rd
18 1/2 Mile Rd
North Dr
Hill Rd
Wright Ln
Kalamazoo Ave
Alcott Ave
Cosmopolitan Ave
Madison St
Marshall Ave
Gorham St
Wooded Ln
O Keefe Rd
Gordon St
Sibley Ln
East Dr
Hill Rd
Forest Ct
16 Mile Rd
Linden St
Hobart
Birch St
Brewer
Forest St
Schuyler St
Ferguson Rd
Division St
High St
Union St
Verona Rd
Greenfield Blvd
Mulberry St
Sycamore St
Grand St
Eagle St
Liberty St
Mann Rd
Fountain St
Prospect St
Arma St
Elk St
Mansion St
Michigan Ave
Parkview
Park Ave
Jefferson St
Green St
Hamilton St
Hanover St
Rice Creek
Hart St
Spruce St
Dobbins St
Cherry St
Mitchell St
Montgomery St
I-69
Industrial Rd
Warren St
Pearl St
Fair St
Maple
Washington St
Crary St
Clinton St
Elm St
Chestnut
Ketchum St
River Rd
Hughes
Kalamazoo River
Homer St
Cirle Dr
Fay Dr
St Rose
Rebecca
Lowe Dr
Raymond St
Mudica St
Oak Dr
Hudson St
Homer Rd
Leggett Rd
Marshall Airport
Adams Ave
Division Dr
Pratt Ave
Woolley Dr
Talmadge Creek
N

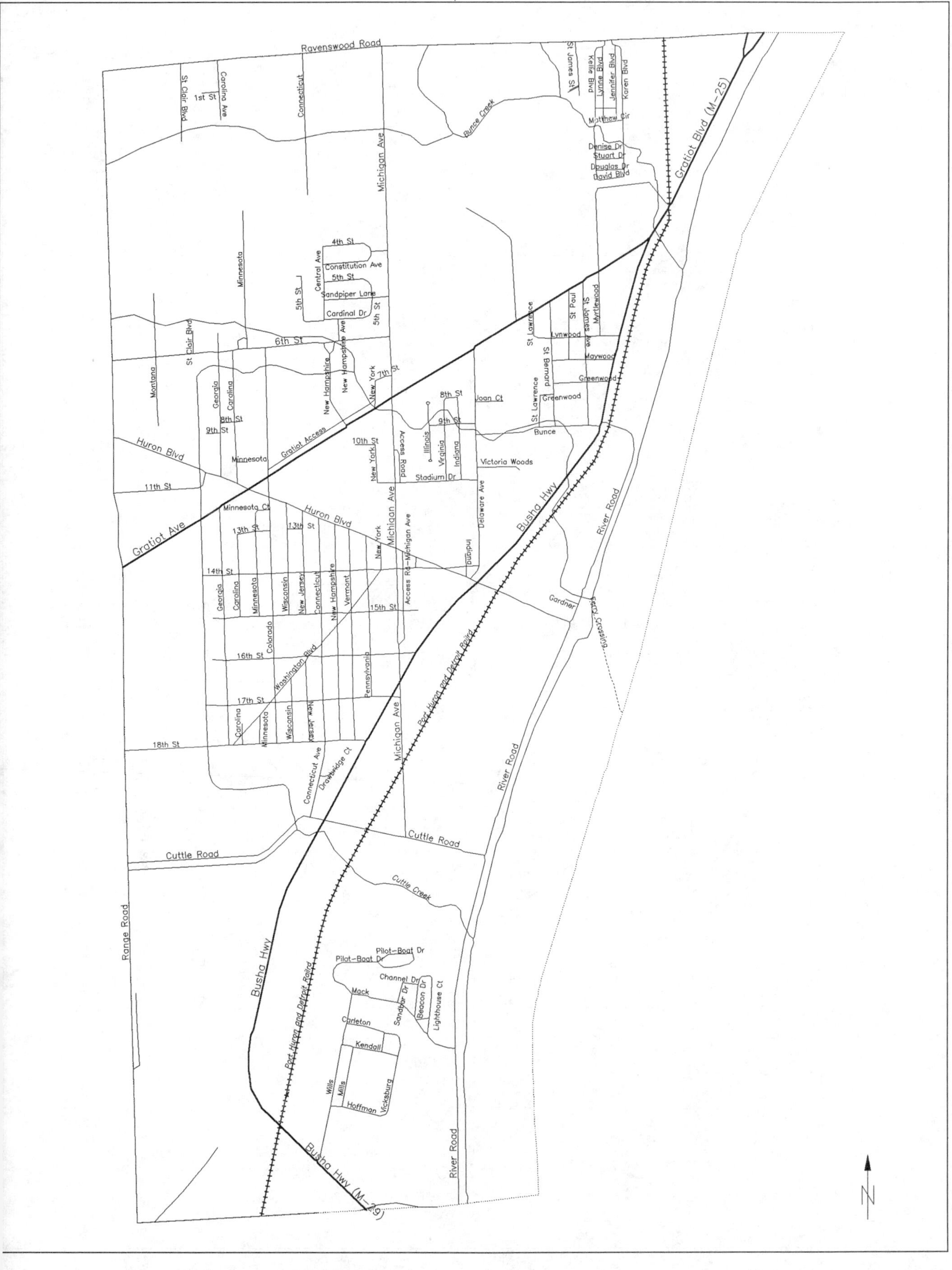
Ravenswood Road
St Clair Blvd
1st St
Carolina Ave
Connecticut
Michigan Ave
Bunce Creek
St James St
Kellie Blvd
Lynne Blvd
Jennifer Blvd
Karen Blvd
Matthew Cir
Denise Dr
Stuart Dr
Douglas Dr
David Blvd
Gratiot Blvd (M-25)
Minnesota
4th St
Central Ave
Constitution Ave
5th St
Sandpiper Lane
Cardinal Dr
5th St
St Lawrence
St Paul
St James Ave
Myrtlewood
Lynwood
Maywood
St Bernard
Greenwood
Greenwood
Joan Ct
Bunce
St Clair Blvd
6th St
New Hampshire Ave
Montana
New Hampshire
New York
7th St
8th St
9th St
Georgia
Carolina
8th St
9th St
Huron Blvd
Gratiot Access
Minnesota
10th St
New York
Access Road
Illinois
Virginia
Indiana
Stadium Dr
Victoria Woods
Delaware Ave
11th St
Gratiot Ave
Minnesota Ct
Huron Blvd
13th St
13th St
New York
Michigan Ave
Access Rd-Michigan Ave
Indiana
Busha Hwy
River Road
14th St
Georgia
Carolina
Minnesota
Wisconsin
New Jersey
Connecticut
New Hampshire
Vermont
15th St
Gardner
Ferry Crossing
Colorado
16th St
Washington Blvd
Pennsylvania
Port Huron and Detroit Railrd
17th St
Carolina
Minnesota
Wisconsin
New Jersey
18th St
Connecticut Ave
Drawbridge Ct
Michigan Ave
River Road
Cuttle Road
Cuttle Road
Cuttle Creek
Range Road
Busha Hwy
Port Huron and Detroit Railrd
Pilot-Boat Dr
Pilot-Boat Dr
Channel Dr
Mack
Sandbar Dr
Beacon Dr
Lighthouse Ct
Carleton
Kendall
Wills
Mills
Hoffman
Vicksburg
Busha Hwy (M-29)
River Road
N

Hogadorn Rd
Howell Rd
Kim Dr
Jerico Dr
Kerns St
Sycamore Creek
Mason St
Okemos Rd
Ingham Jail Service Rd
Cedar St
Royce Ave
Rogers St
Ash Ridge St
Oak Ridge St
Locust Ln
Maple Run St
Lindon Blvd
US Hwy 127
Orchard Ct
North St
Center St
Mechanic St
East St
Ann St
Randolph St
Matthews St
Monroe St
Rayner St
Eaton Dr
Wildemere Dr
Columbia Rd
Columbia St
Columbia St
Columbia St
Corbin St
Katheryn St
Walnut Ct
Peachtree Pl
Kiwanis Dr
Sycamore St
Sycamore St
State St
Jefferson Ave
Lowton St
Steven St
Mark St
Temple St
Maple St
Maine Ct
Maple St
Ash St
Barnes St
Steele St
Roosevelt St
Middlebury Ln
Oak St
Park St
Rogers St
Holt St
Hall Blvd
County Park Rd
County Park Rd
Ash St
Foxview Ln
Cedar St
Cherry St
Henderson St
Cherry St
South St
South St
Northbrook St
Brookdale St
Warner Ave
South St
Holt St
Vanderveen Dr
Gary C St
Eugenia Dr
Alta St
Willow St
High School Srvc Dr
Willow Creek
Lavanne St
US Hwy 127
Kipp Rd
Kipp Rd
Hull Rd
N

County Hwy 364
Western St
26th St
Rumshire Dr
Kingdom Dr
Westpoint Ave
Pershing Ave
Marshall Ave
Pleasant Dr
Cook Drain
Bradley Ct
Cadet Dr
Eisenhower Ave
Macarthur Ave
Patton Ct
25th St
Estates Cir
Estates Cir
Point Dr
Point Dr
Point Dr
Root St
Front Ave
I-94
Murray St
2nd Ave
Scott St
3rd Ave
Pleasant St
Lawernce St
Carpenter
Giddings Ct
Murray St
Pine Grove St
Alvord Ave
Front Ave
Main St
Morrill St
Kinne Ave
Webster St
Concord Ave
Ryan St
Robinson Ave
Mc Gillen Ave
French Ave
Grandeur Ave
Concord Ave

Fulton St
North St
State Hwy 24
Lobdell Road
Main St
Lincoln St
5th St
4th St
Turner St
6th St
5th St
Fox St
Fulton St
Trend St
Pine St
1st St
2nd St
High St
Orchard St
Mill St
N

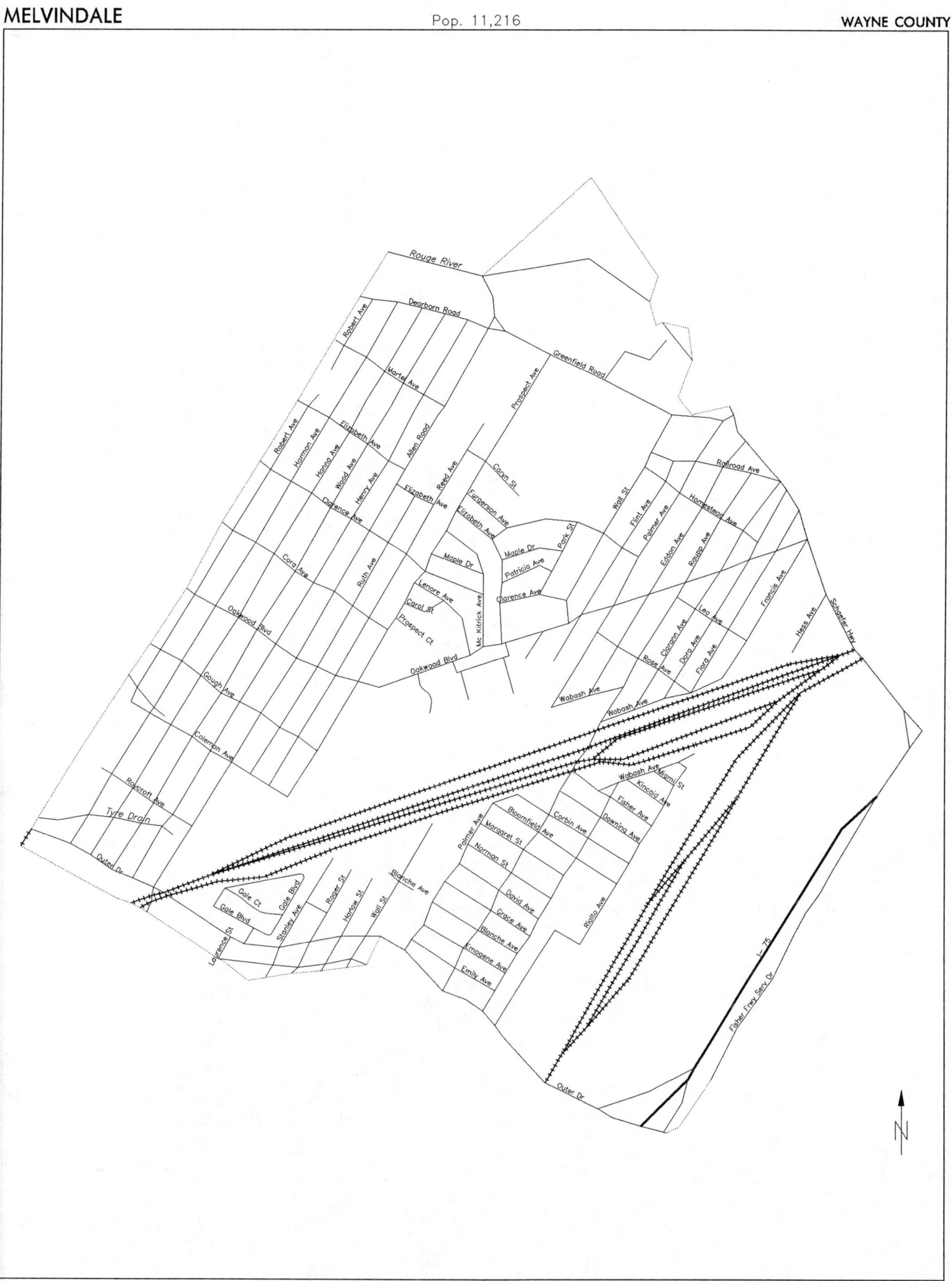
Rouge River
Dearborn Road
Greenfield Road
Robert Ave
Martel Ave
Prospect Ave
Harmon Ave
Hanna Ave
Elizabeth Ave
Wood Ave
Henry Ave
Allen Road
Reed Ave
Caryn St
Clarence Ave
Furgerson Ave
Wall St
Flint Ave
Palmer Ave
Railroad Ave
Homestead Ave
Eddon Ave
Roupp Ave
Park St
Maple Dr
Patricia Ave
Cora Ave
Ruth Ave
Lenore Ave
Carol St
Prospect Ct
Mc Kitrick Ave
Francis Ave
Leo Ave
Clarann Ave
Dora Ave
Flora Ave
Rose Ave
Hess Ave
Schaefer Hwy
Oakwood Blvd
Gough Ave
Wabash Ave
Coleman Ave
Miami St
Kincaid Ave
Fisher Ave
Downing Ave
Corbin Ave
Bloomfield Ave
Margaret St
Norman St
Roycroft Ave
Tyre Drain
Outer Dr
Gale Ct
Gale Blvd
Stanley Ave
Roger St
Harlow St
Blanche Ave
David Ave
Grace Ave
Emogene Ave
Emily Ave
Rialto Ave
Laurence St
I-75
Fisher Frwy Serv Dr
N

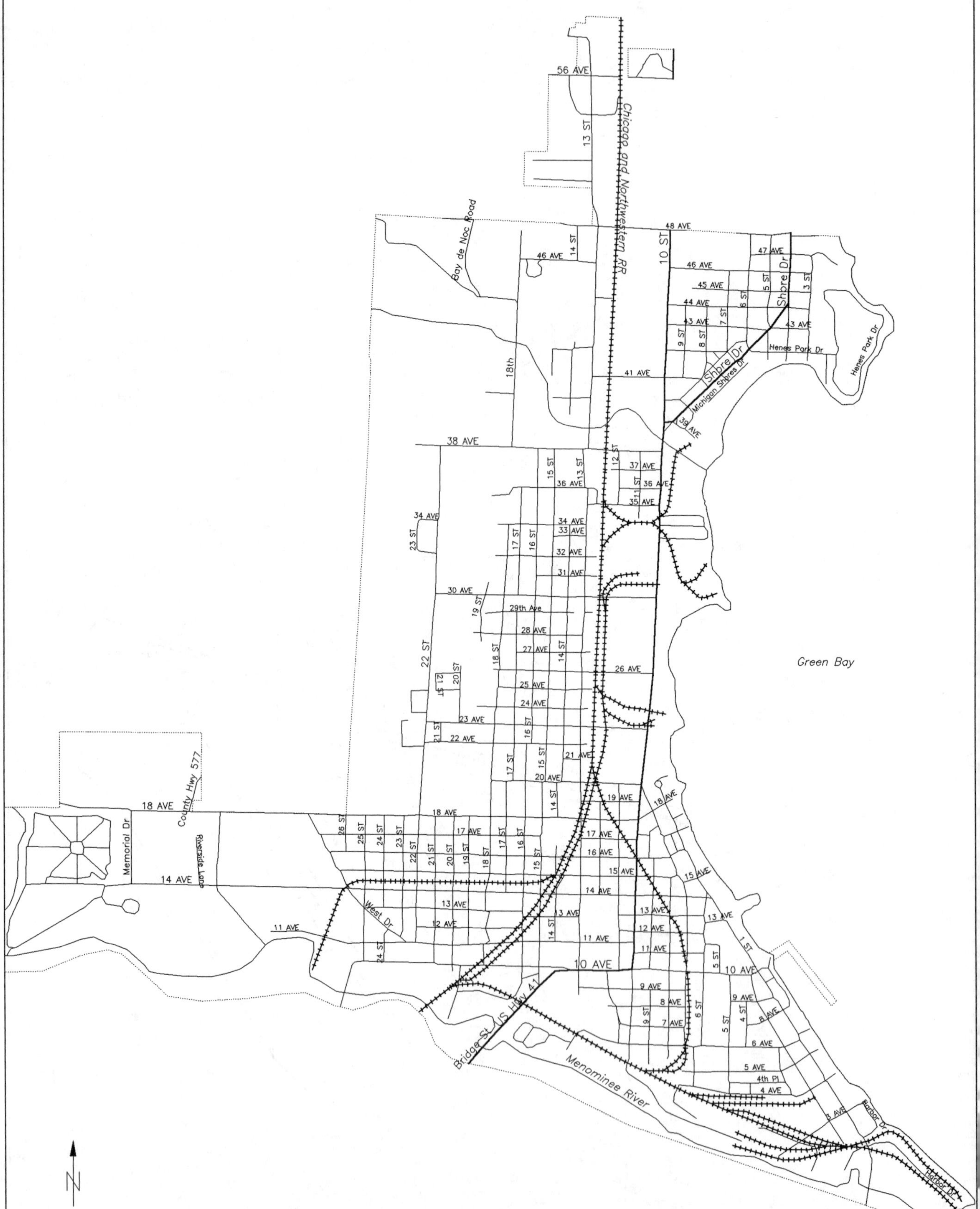

Chicago and Northwestern RR
56 AVE
13 ST
48 AVE
10 ST
Bay de Noc Road
14 ST
46 AVE
47 AVE
45 AVE
44 AVE
43 AVE
Shore Dr
Henes Park Dr
Michigan Shores Dr
41 AVE
18th
39 AVE
38 AVE
37 AVE
36 AVE
35 AVE
34 AVE
33 AVE
32 AVE
31 AVE
30 AVE
29th Ave
28 AVE
27 AVE
26 AVE
25 AVE
24 AVE
23 AVE
22 AVE
21 AVE
20 AVE
19 AVE
18 AVE
17 AVE
16 AVE
15 AVE
14 AVE
13 AVE
12 AVE
11 AVE
10 AVE
9 AVE
8 AVE
7 AVE
6 AVE
5 AVE
4th Pl
4 AVE
3 AVE
22 ST
23 ST
County Hwy 577
Memorial Dr
Riverside Lane
West Dr
Bridge St US Hwy 41
Menominee River
Green Bay
Harbor Dr

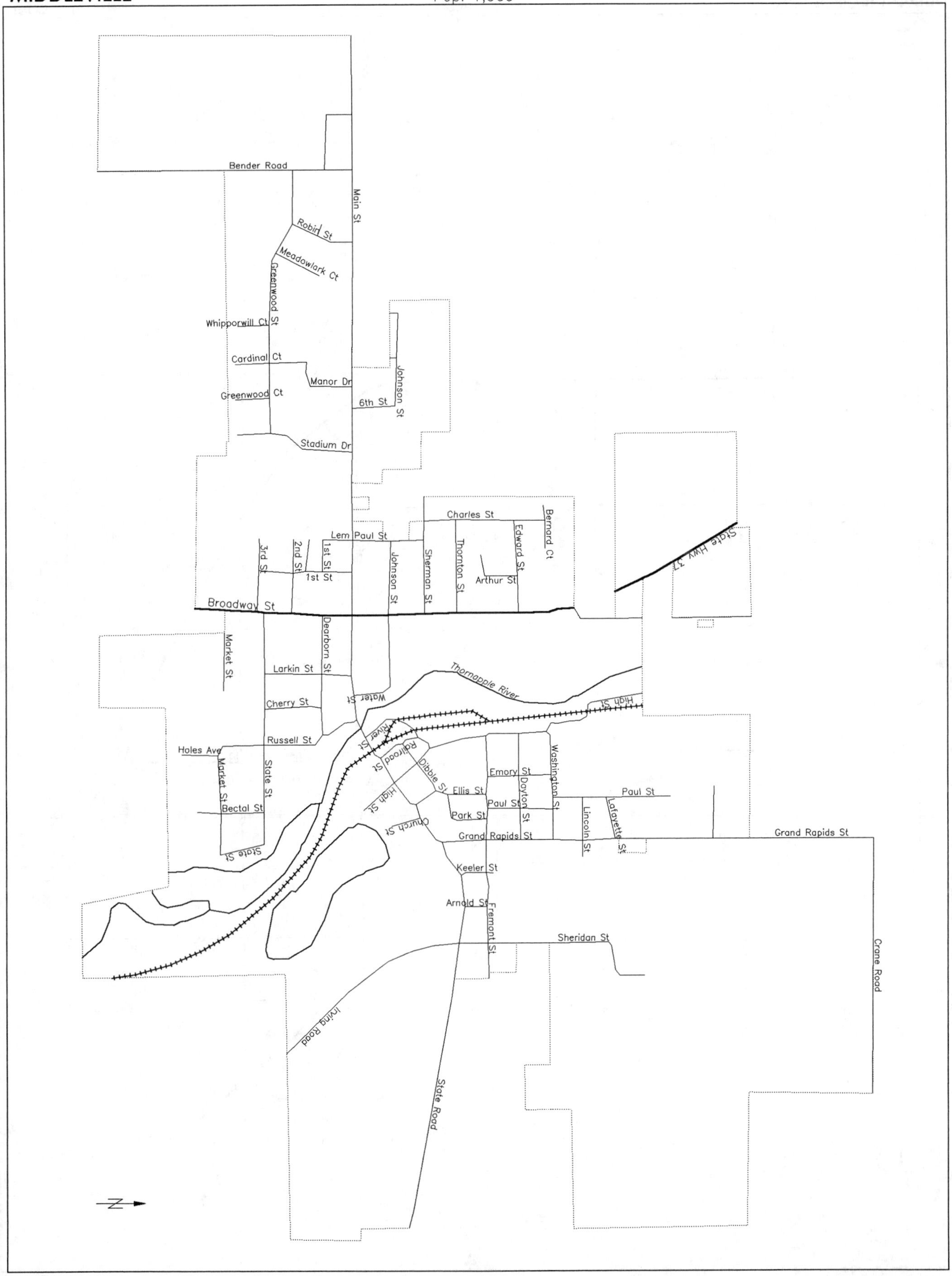

Bender Road
Main St
Robin St
Meadowlark Ct
Greenwood St
Whipporwill Ct
Cardinal Ct
Manor Dr
Greenwood Ct
6th St
Johnson St
Stadium Dr
Charles St
Bernard Ct
Edward St
Lem Paul St
3rd St
2nd St
1st St
1st St
Johnson St
Sherman St
Thornton St
Arthur St
State Hwy 37
Broadway St
Market St
Dearborn St
Larkin St
Thornapple River
Water St
High St
Cherry St
River St
Russell St
Holes Ave
Railroad St
Market St
State St
Dibble St
Emory St
Washington St
Ellis St
Dayton St
Paul St
High St
Bectal St
Paul St
Park St
Lincoln St
Lafayette St
Church St
Grand Rapids St
Grand Rapids St
State St
Keeler St
Arnold St
Fremont St
Sheridan St
Crane Road
Irving Road
State Road

MIDLAND (Plate Index)

Pop. 38,053

MIDLAND COUNTY

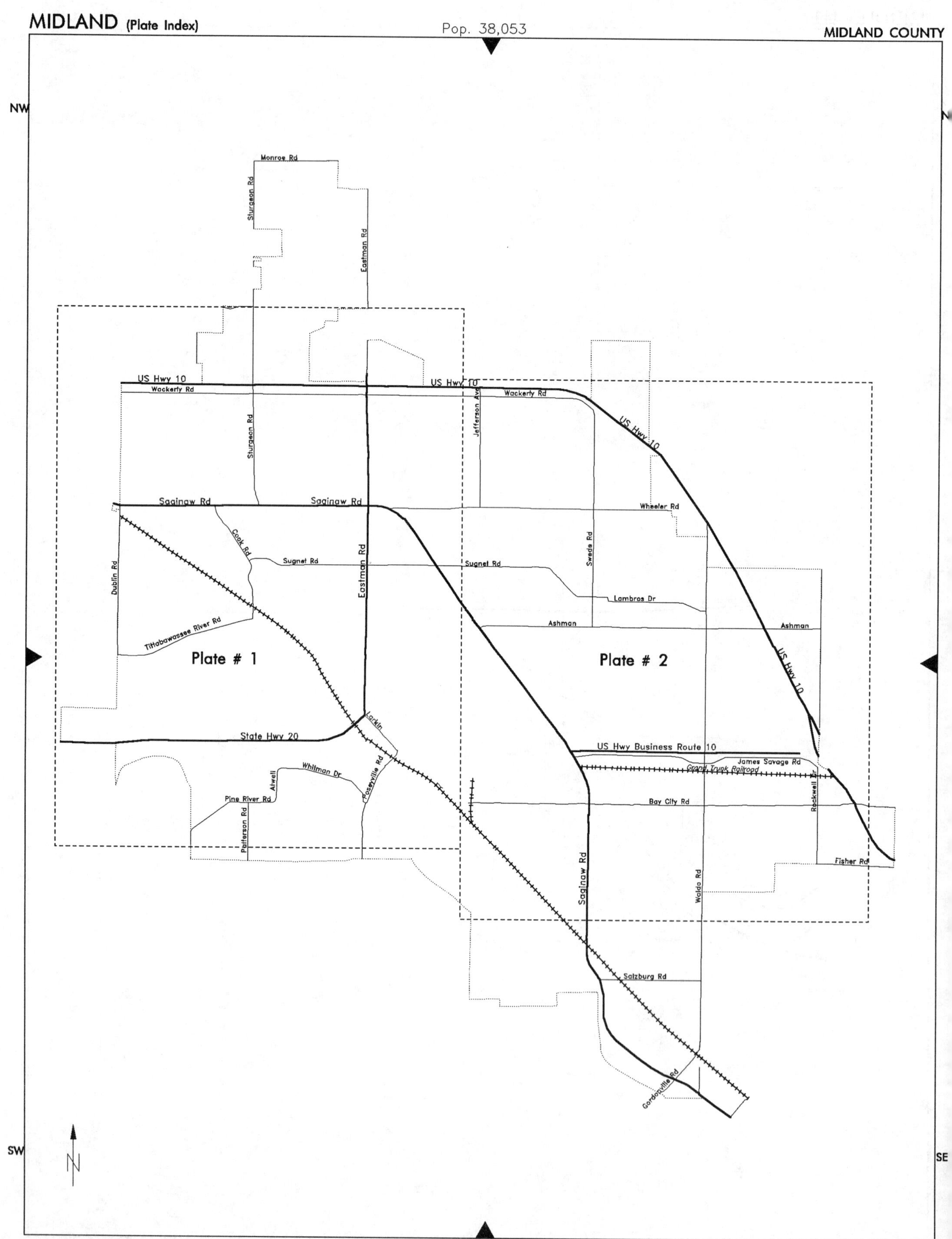

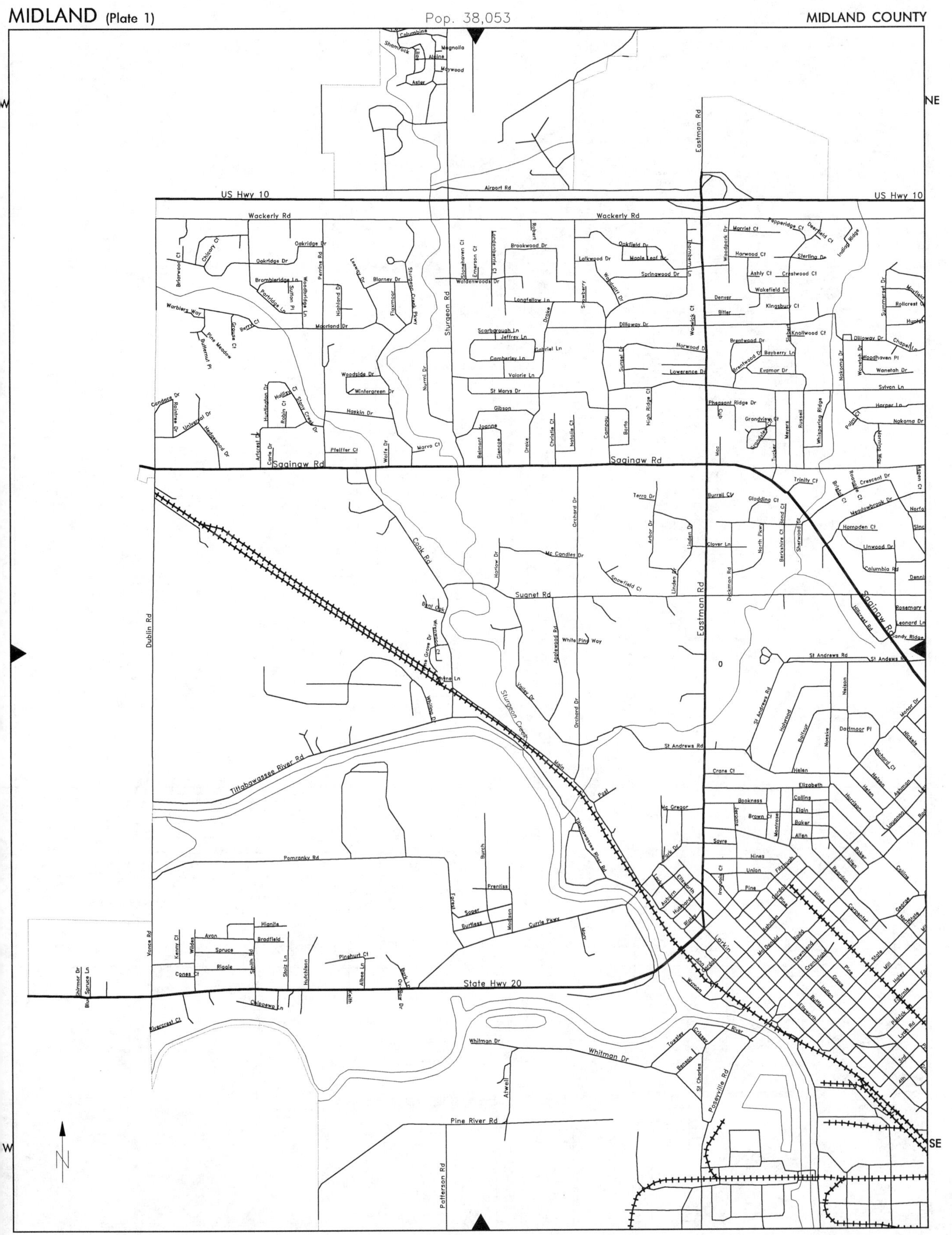
US Hwy 10
Airport Rd
Wackerly Rd
Eastman Rd
Sturgeon Rd
Saginaw Rd
Dublin Rd
Cook Rd
Sugnet Rd
St Andrews Rd
Tittabawassee River Rd
Pomranky Rd
State Hwy 20
Whitman Dr
Pine River Rd
Patterson Rd
Poseyville Rd
Vance Rd
Currie Pkwy
Sturgeon Creek
Larkin
Orchard Dr
Applewood Rd
Harlow Dr
Mc Candles Dr
Arbor Dr
Linden Dr
Dilloway Dr
Moorland Dr
Haskin Dr
Pfeiffer Ct
Oakridge Dr
Brookwood Dr
Springwood Dr
St Marys Dr
Gibson
Nurmi Dr
Wolfe Dr
Marvo Ct
Drake
Christie Ct
Natalie Ct
Campau
Barto
High Ridge Ct
Pheasant Ridge Dr
Whispering Ridge
Russell
Meyers
Tucker
Mac
Dartmoor Pl
Nelson
Helen
Elizabeth
Collins
Elgin
Baker
Allen
Sayre
Hines
Union
Pine
Ellsworth
Auburn
Hubbard
Rodd
Townsend
Gordon
Ashman
Carpenter
George
State
Mill
Cronkright
Grove
Indian
Buttles
Fitzhugh
Benson
Towsley
Crissey
River
St Charles
Atwell
Pinehurst Ct
Chippewa Ln
Rivercrest Ct
Riggle
Spruce
Avon
Bradfield
Hiawatha
Smith Rd
Stolz Ln
Hutchinson
Keith
Burch
Prentiss
Soper
Burtless
Madison
Forest
Main
Post
Mc Gregor
Crane Ct
Bookness
Brown Ct
Montrose
Irvingside Ct
Burrell Ct
Gladding Ct
Clover Ln
Dickman Rd
North Pkwy
Berkshire Ct
Bond Ct
Sherwood Dr
Trinity Ct
Crescent Dr
Meadowbrook Dr
Hampden Ct
Linwood Dr
Columbia Rd
Rosemary Ct
Leonard Ln
Sandy Ridge
Hillcrest Rd
St Andrews Rd
Balfour
Haywood
Noeske
Richard Ct
Harrison
Lauanna
Manor Dr
Nickels
Marriet Ct
Pepperidge Ct
Deerfield Ct
Indian Ridge
Harwood Ct
Sterling Dr
Ashly Ct
Crestwood Ct
Wakefield Dr
Kingsbury Ct
Denver
Bitter
Brentwood Dr
Knollwood Ct
Bayberry Ln
Evamar Dr
Grandview Ct
Summerset Dr
Rollcrest Ct
Dilloway Dr
Woodhaven Pl
Wanetah Dr
Sylvan Ln
Harper Ln
Nakoma Dr
Palm Ct
Morning Way
Wintergreen Dr
Woodside Dr
Flaxmoor
Blarney Dr
Sturgeon Creek Pkwy
Highland Dr
Perrine Rd
Woodbridge Ln
Brambleridge Ln
Sutton Pl
Partridge Ln
Chicory Ct
Briarwood Ct
Warblers Way
Berry Ct
Grouse Ct
Pine Meadow
Butternut Pl
Candace Dr
Raintree Dr
Universal Dr
Hedgewood Dr
Huntington Dr
Hallies Ct
Robin Ct
Stony Creek Dr
Artcrest Dr
Carle Dr
Stonehaven Ct
Emerson Ct
Londonberry Ct
Waldenwoods Dr
Robert
Longfellow Ln
Scarborough Ln
Jeffrey Ln
Camberley Ln
Gabriel Ln
Valorie Ln
Joanne
Belmont
Glencoe
Oakfield Dr
Lakewood Dr
Maple Leaf Dr
Strawberry
Woodcliff Dr
Thornberry Ln
Warwick Ct
Norwood Dr
Lawerence Dr
Sunset Dr
Woodpark Dr
Terra Dr
Snowfield Ct
White Pine Way
Valley Dr
Columbine
Shamrock
Magnolia
Alpine
Maywood
Aster
Cones Ct
Kenny Ct
Wildes
Shirmar Dr
Blue Spruce Ln
Ann
Wyman
N

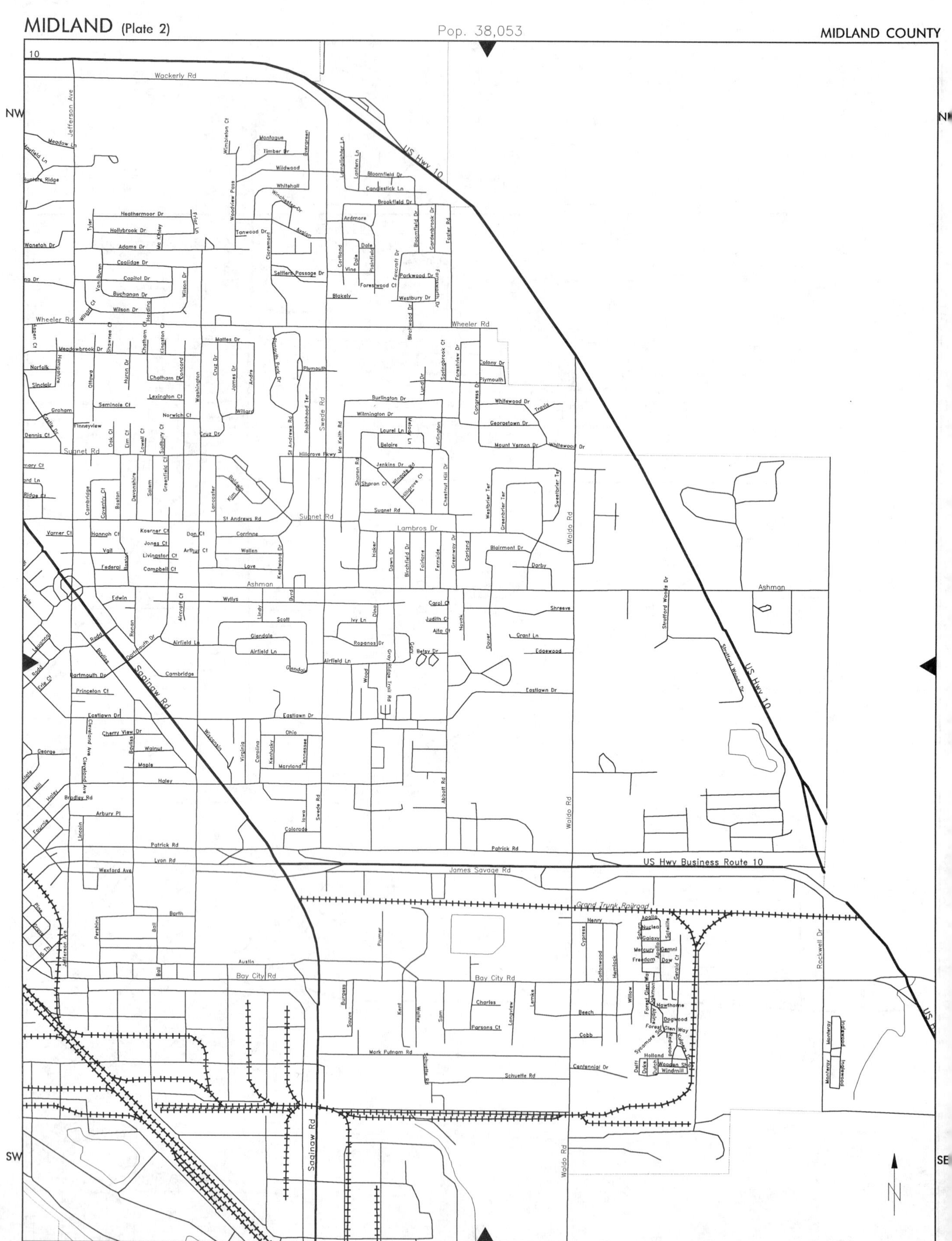

NW
NE
SW
SE
10
Wackerly Rd
Jefferson Ave
Meadow Ln
Hunters Ridge
Wanetah Dr
Wimbleton Ct
Montague
Timber Dr
Evergreen
Wildwood
Whitehall
Lamplighter Ln
Lantern Ln
Bloomfield Dr
Candlestick Ln
Brookfield Dr
US Hwy 10
Heathermoor Dr
Hollybrook Dr
Tyler
Adams Dr
Mc Kinley
Coolidge Dr
Capitol Dr
Buchanan Dr
Wilson Dr
Van Buren
Harding
Woodview Pass
Tanwood Dr
Claremont
Winchester Dr
Avalon
Settlers Passage Dr
Ardmore
Cortland
Vine
Dale
Plainfield
Forestwood Ct
Foxcroft Dr
Bloomfield Dr
Gardenbrook Dr
Foster Rd
Parkwood Dr
Westbury Dr
Blakely
Birchwood Dr
Wheeler Rd
Aspen Ct
Meadowbrook Dr
Shawnee Ct
Chatham Ct
Kingston Ct
Norfolk
Hampshire
Sinclair
Ottawa
Huron Dr
Chatham Dr
Concord
Washington
Mattes Dr
Cruz Dr
James Dr
Andre
Plymouth Park Dr
Plymouth
Lexington Ct
Seminole Ct
Norwich Ct
Willard
Graham
Finneyview
Dennis Ct
Oak Ct
Elm Ct
Lowell Ct
Sudbury Ct
Cruz Dr
St Andrews Rd
Robinhood Ter
Swede Rd
Mc Keith Rd
Burlington Dr
Wilmington Dr
Lund Dr
Springbrook Ct
Forestview Dr
Colony Dr
Plymouth
Congress Dr
Whitewood Dr
Travis
Georgetown Dr
Laurel Ln
Belgaire
Melody Ln
Arlington
Mount Vernon Dr
Whitewood Dr
Sugnet Rd
Hillgrove Pkwy
Jenkins Dr
Sharon Rd
Sharon Ct
Wingate Rd
Hillgrove Ct
Chestnut Hill Dr
Cambridge
Coventry Ct
Boston
Devonshire
Salem
Greenfield Ct
Lancaster
Baldwin
Kim
Sugnet Rd
Westbrier Ter
Greenbrier Ter
Sweetbrier Ter
Waldo Rd
St Andrews Rd
Sugnet Rd
Lambros Dr
Varner Ct
Hannah Ct
Koerner Ct
Dan Ct
Corrinne
Jones Ct
Livingston Ct
Arthur Ct
Wallen
Vail
Federal
Campbell Ct
Love
Kentwood Dr
Haker
Dawn Dr
Birchfield Dr
Fairlane
Fernside
Greenway Dr
Garland
Blairmont Dr
Darby
Ashman
Ashman
Edwin
Wyllys
Aircraft Ct
Byrd
Lindy
Dina
Carol Ct
Novak
Shreeve
Stratford Woods Dr
Scott
Ivy Ln
Judith Ct
Alta Ct
Dauer
Grant Ln
Edgewood
Ronan
Dartmouth Dr
Airfield Ln
Glendale
Airfield Ln
Rapanos Dr
Gail
Betsy Dr
Stratford Woods Dr
Glendale
Airfield Ln
Cambridge
Dartmouth Dr
Saginaw Rd
Princeton Ct
Wood
Grey Ridge Trail Rd
Eastlawn Dr
US Hwy 10
Eastlawn Dr
Eastlawn Dr
Cleveland Ave
Cherry View Dr
Wisconsin
Ohio
Bayliss
Walnut
Virginia
Carolina
Kentucky
Tennessee
Maple
Maryland
George
Haley
Abbott Rd
Bradley Rd
Arbury Pl
Iowa
Swede Rd
Lincoln
Colorado
Waldo Rd
Patrick Rd
Patrick Rd
Lyon Rd
Wexford Ave
US Hwy Business Route 10
James Savage Rd
Grand Trunk Railroad
Barth
Pershing
Ball
Henry
Apollo
Nuclear
Galaxy
Satellite
Saturn
Cypress
Plumer
Mercury
Gemini
Freedom
Dow Ct
Gerald Ct
Austin
Cottonwood
Hemlock
Rockwell Dr
Ball
Bay City Rd
Bay City Rd
Burgess
Charles
Lemke
Willow
Hawthorne
Beech
Sauve
Kent
Walter
Sam
Parsons Ct
Longview
Dogwood
Forest Glen Way
Cobb
Sycamore
Monterey
Inglewood
Mark Putnam Rd
Schuette Rd
Holland
Centennial Dr
Delft
Dyke
Dutch
Wooden Shoe
Windmill
Monterey
Inglewood
Saginaw Rd
Waldo Rd
N

Platt Rd
Redman St
Riverbend Dr
Saline River
Canfield
Argyle Dr
St Louis St
Bodley St
Iva St
Everett St
Yorkshire Sq
Main St
Riverpoint Rd
Greentree Lane
Norfolk and Western Railroad
Anderson St
Penn Ave
Ohio
Wabash St
Division St
Ford Lake
York St
2nd St
Michigan Ave
Elm St
Cherry St
Ash St
Church St
Oak St
Willana St
Phillips Ave
Braman Ave
Lewis Ave
Arkona Rd
1st St
North St
Allen Rd
Stream
Ferman St
2nd St
Ann St
Miller Ave
Marvin St
Hurd St
Ideal Ave
Lafayette Ave
Spink Ave
Smith Ave
Welch St
Wilcox St
Spink Court Walk
Carpenter Rd
Hack St
Federal Ave
Lafayette Ct
US Hwy 23
Case Dr
Ideal Rd
Plank Rd
Oakville
Sanford Rd

Pop. 5,511

Whitlow Dr
Abbey Ln
Liddell Dr
Prince St
Panorama Dr
Sweetbriar Rd
Panorama Dr Ct
Birdsong Dr
Panorama Dr
Panorama
Milford Rd
Pettibone Creek
Main St
Edward St
1st St
Duke Rd
Manordale Ct
Bishop Rd
Queen Ct
Queen St
Manor Dr
Squire Ln
Friar Dr
George St
Union St
Summit St
Summit Ridge Dr
Marjorie St
Commerce Rd
Pleasure St
Milford Rd
East St
Highland St
Detroit St
Aldil Ct
Elizabeth Ave
Hill St
Commerce Rd
Tracy Ln
Granderview
Oak St
Hickory St
Commerce Rd
Center St
Highland St
Cabinet St
Leverett
Bennett St
Noble St
Main St
Liberty St
Liberty St
Liberty St
Noble St
Hill St
Benson St
Canal St
Canal St
Peters St
Atlantic St
Js Brophy Dr
John R St
River Dr
Houghton St
Fairview St
Franklin St
Stephen St
J D Caswell Dr
Clinton St
Dean St
Washington St
Huron River
Mont-Eagle St
General Motors Rd
C and O Railroad
Lafayette St
Mill St
Bellevue St
Hillsdale
Hillsdale Cir
Hillsdale
Garden Rd
Bryon Dr
Bryon Dr
Hillsdale
Dansin Dr
Marlene St
Milford Rd
Cluster A
Cluster C
Cluster D
Gwendolyn
Bryon Dr
Keats Dr
Cluster B
Cluster
Cluster F
Old Plank Rd
Tennyson St
Hubbell St
Eagle Nest Dr
Ravineside Dr
Heritage Dr
Hill Rd
Heritage Dr
N

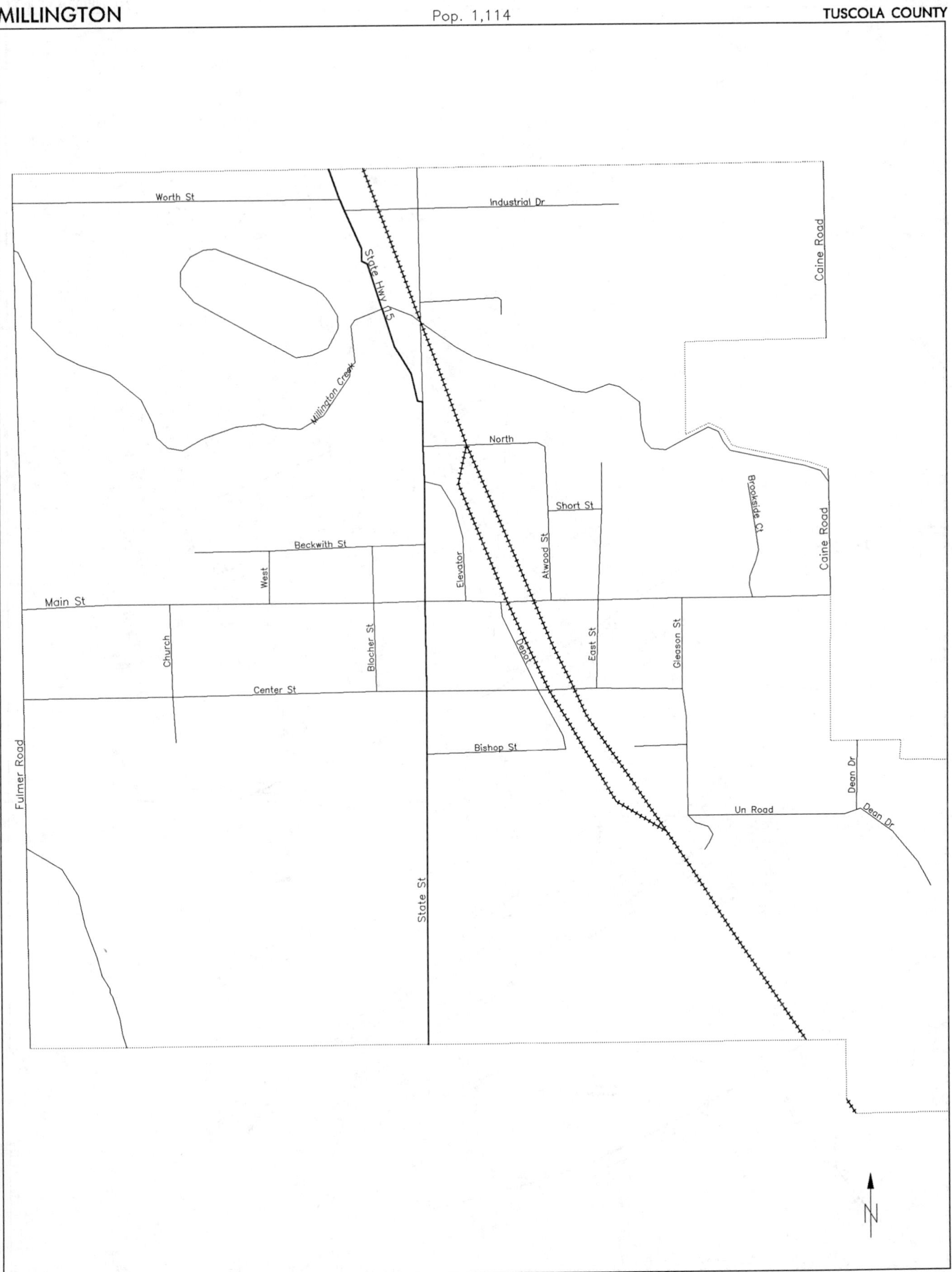
Worth St
Industrial Dr
Caine Road
State Hwy 15
Millington Creek
North
Short St
Brookside Ct
Caine Road
Beckwith St
West
Elevator
Atwood St
Main St
Church
Blocher St
Depot
East St
Gleason St
Center St
Bishop St
Fulmer Road
Dean Dr
Un Road
Dean Dr
State St
N

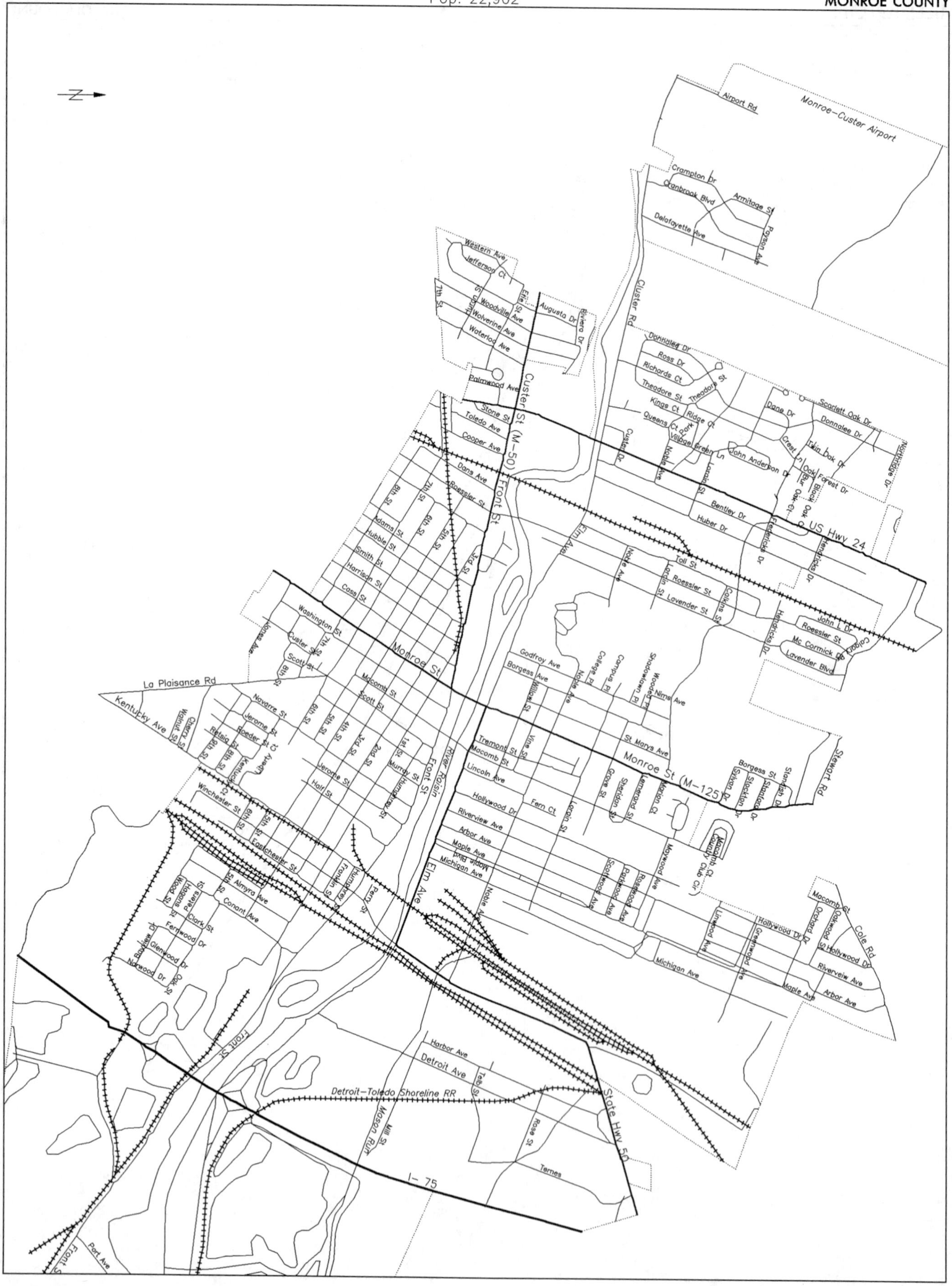

Pop. 22,902

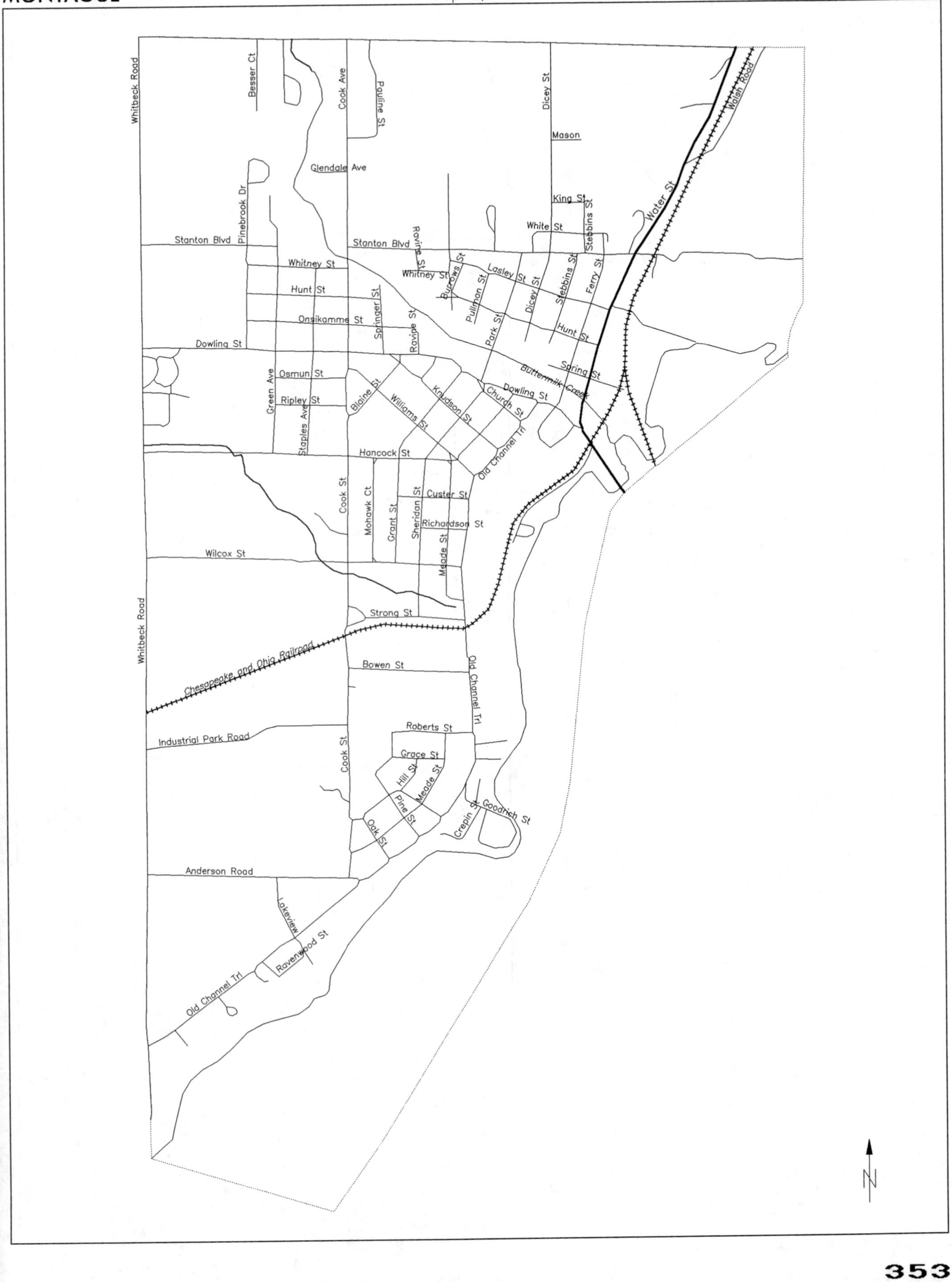
Whitbeck Road
Besser Ct
Cook Ave
Pauline St
Dicey St
Mason
Walsh Road
Glendale Ave
Pinebrook Dr
Water St
King St
Stebbins St
White St
Stanton Blvd
Stanton Blvd
Ravine St
Whitney St
Whitney St
Burrows St
Lasley St
Hunt St
Pullman St
Dicey St
Stebbins St
Ferry St
Onsikamme St
Springer St
Park St
Hunt St
Dowling St
Ravine St
Spring St
Buttermilk Creek
Osmun St
Green Ave
Blaine St
Knudson St
Dowling St
Church St
Ripley St
Williams St
Staples Ave
Old Channel Trl
Hancock St
Custer St
Cook St
Mohawk Ct
Grant St
Sheridan St
Richardson St
Meade St
Wilcox St
Whitbeck Road
Strong St
Chesapeake and Ohio Railroad
Bowen St
Old Channel Trl
Roberts St
Industrial Park Road
Grace St
Cook St
Hill St
Meade St
Pine St
Goodrich St
Crepin St
Oak St
Anderson Road
Lakeview
Ravenwood St
Old Channel Trl
N

MONTROSE

Pop. 1,811

GENESEE COUNTY

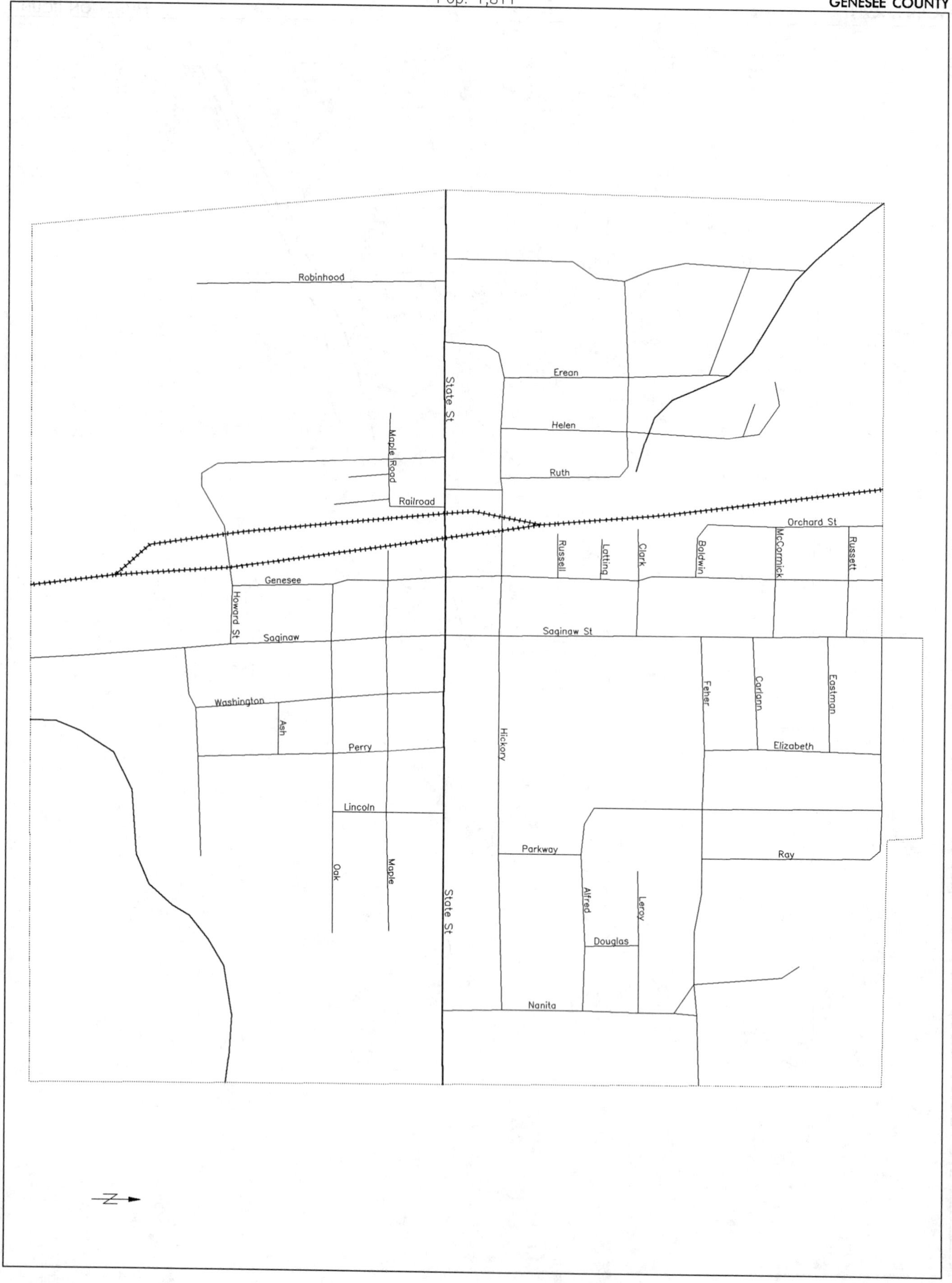

Tiffin River
North St
Park Dr
Smith St
Summit St
Wilson St
Greeley St
Mowry
Baldwin St
Carter Drain
Lenawee County Railroad
Fay Hwy
Page Ct
Simms Hwy
Coomer St
Coomer St
Lincoln St
Clark St
Walnut St
Walnut Ct
Salisbury St
Wakefield Dr
Chestnut St
Clark St
Chestnut St
Main St
Chestnut St
Walnut St
Walnut St
Congress St
Congress St
Maple Dr
Mill St
Cawley Road
Union St
East St
Burley St
Page St
Locust St
Washington St
Baker St
Orchard Dr
La Grange St
Orchard St
Division St
Summit St
Oak St
Whitney Ave
Pearl St
Stephenson St
Owosso St
Buffalo St
Centre St
Elm St
Meadow Dr
Silver Creek
Weston Road
Main St
Gorham St
St Hwy 156
Tiffin River
East St

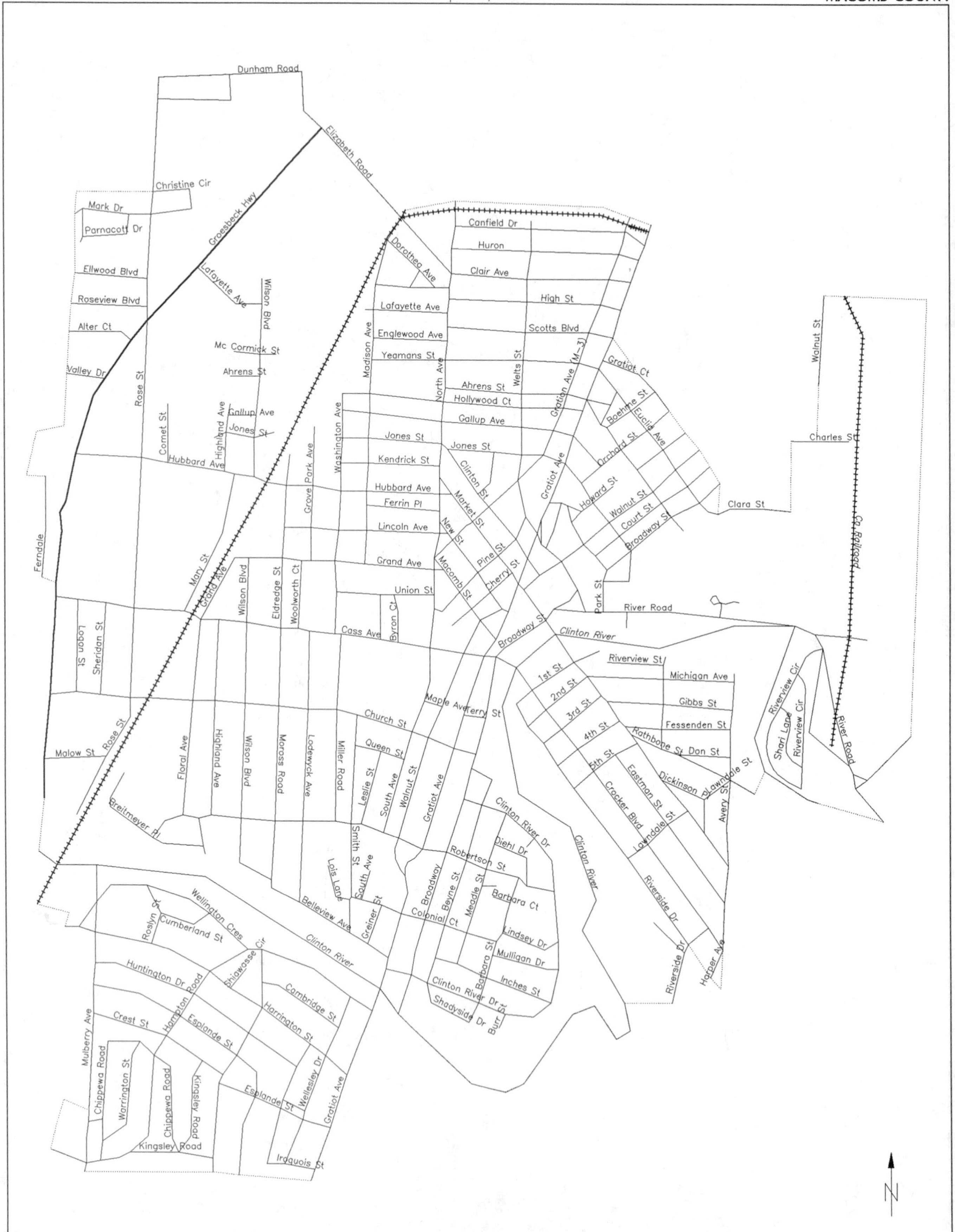

Dunham Road
Elizabeth Road
Christine Cir
Mark Dr
Parnacott Dr
Groesbeck Hwy
Ellwood Blvd
Roseview Blvd
Alter Ct
Valley Dr
Lafayette Ave
Wilson Blvd
Mc Cormick St
Ahrens St
Gallup Ave
Jones St
Rose St
Comet St
Highland Ave
Hubbard Ave
Ferndale
Mary St
Grand Ave
Canfield Dr
Huron
Dorothea Ave
Clair Ave
High St
Lafayette Ave
Englewood Ave
Scotts Blvd
Yeamans St
Madison Ave
North Ave
Welts St
Gratiot Ave (M-3)
Gratiot Ct
Ahrens St
Hollywood Ct
Gallup Ave
Boehme St
Euclid Ave
Washington Ave
Grove Park Ave
Jones St
Jones St
Kendrick St
Clinton St
Gratiot Ave
Orchard St
Hubbard Ave
Ferrin Pl
Market St
Howard St
Walnut St
Court St
Broadway St
Lincoln Ave
New St
Grand Ave
Pine St
Macomb St
Cherry St
Park St
Wilson Blvd
Eldredge St
Woolworth Ct
Union St
Byron Ct
Cass Ave
River Road
Broadway St
Clinton River
Riverview St
Logan St
Sheridan St
1st St
Michigan Ave
2nd St
Gibbs St
Maple Ave
Terry St
3rd St
Fessenden St
Church St
4th St
Rathbone St
Don St
Malow St
Rose St
Floral Ave
Highland Ave
Wilson Blvd
Moross Road
Lodewyck Ave
Miller Road
Queen St
Leslie St
South Ave
Walnut St
Gratiot Ave
5th St
Eastman St
Dickinson Pl
Lawndale St
Avery St
Crocker Blvd
Lawndale St
Breitmeyer Pl
Clinton River Dr
Diehl Dr
Clinton River
Smith St
Robertson St
Lois Lane
South Ave
Broadway
Beyne St
Meadle St
Barbara Ct
Riverside Dr
Wellington Cres
Roslyn St
Cumberland St
Belleview Ave
Greiner St
Colonial Ct
Lindsey Dr
Clinton River
Shiawasse Cir
Barbara St
Mulligan Dr
Huntington Dr
Hampton Road
Cambridge St
Inches St
Riverside Dr
Harper Ave
Clinton River Dr
Shadyside Dr
Burr St
Crest St
Esplande St
Harrington St
Mulberry Ave
Chippewa Road
Warrington St
Chippewa Road
Kingsley Road
Wellesley Dr
Gratiot Ave
Esplande St
Kingsley Road
Irquois St
Walnut St
Charles St
Clara St
Gn Railroad
Riverview Cir
Shari Lane
Riverview Cir
River Road
N

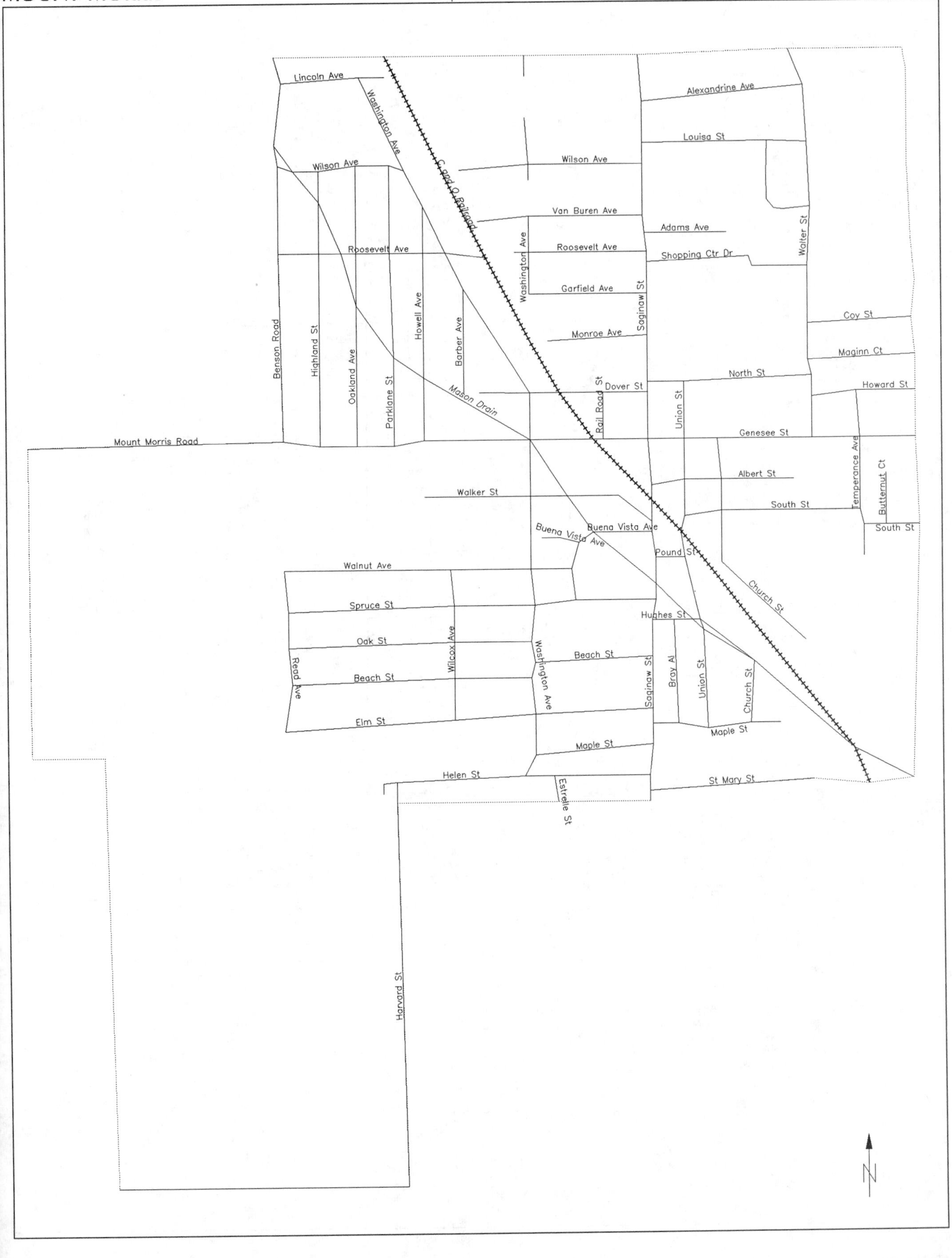

MOUNT MORRIS

Pop. 3,292

GENESEE COUNTY

Lincoln Ave
Washington Ave
C and O Railroad
Alexandrine Ave
Louisa St
Wilson Ave
Wilson Ave
Van Buren Ave
Adams Ave
Roosevelt Ave
Roosevelt Ave
Shopping Ctr Dr
Walter St
Washington Ave
Garfield Ave
Saginaw St
Coy St
Monroe Ave
Maginn Ct
Benson Road
Highland St
Oakland Ave
Parklane St
Howell Ave
Barber Ave
Mason Drain
Rail Road St
Dover St
Union St
North St
Howard St
Mount Morris Road
Genesee St
Temperance Ave
Butternut Ct
Albert St
Walker St
South St
South St
Buena Vista Ave
Buena Vista Ave
Pound St
Walnut Ave
Church St
Spruce St
Hughes St
Oak St
Wilcox Ave
Washington Ave
Beach St
Read Ave
Beach St
Saginaw St
Bray Al
Union St
Church St
Elm St
Maple St
Maple St
Helen St
Estrelle St
St Mary St
Harvard St

N

MOUNT PLEASANT

Pop. 23,285

ISABELLA COUNTY

Lake Superior
South Bay
Munising Ave
Westshore Dr
Pipeline Trl
Jasper Ave
Commercial
Sand Point Rd
City Limits Rd
Becker Rd
Nestor
Center
High
Cleveland Ave
Lake
Bay
St Martin Rd
Walnut
Pine
Hickory
Oak
Fir
Hemlock
Chestnut
Cherry
Spruce
Elm Ave
City Park Dr
Superior
Onota
Chocolay
Maple
Birch
Mill
Lynn
Court
Beech Park
Jewell
Gage Rd
County Hwy 576
Anna River
Brook
Varnum
Cedar
Prospect
Grand
Ishpeming RR
Sheridan Ave
Bell Ave
Lake Superior
State Hwy 28
Cemetery Rd
Connors Rd
N

Street	Page
1st St	2
2nd St	2
3rd St	2
4th St	2
5th St	2
6th St	2
7th St	2
8th St	2
9th St	2
11th St	1
Abbey St	2
Access Rd	2
Ada Ave	2
Adams Ave	2
Adams Ct	2
Addison St	1
Agnes St	2
Airline Rd	2
Albert Ave	2
Alberta St	1
Alberta St	2
Allen Ave	2
Alpha Ave	2
Alva St	2
Ambrosia St	2
Amity Ave	2
Amsterdam Ave	2
Apple Ave	2
Arlington Ave	1
Arthur St	2
Aurora Ave	2
Austin St	2
Baker St	2
Bank St	2
Barclay St	1
Barney Ave	1
Barney Ave	2
Bauer Ave	2
Bayou Ave	2
Beach St	1
Beach Street	1
Beardsley Ave	1
Beidler St	2
Bennett St	2
Benton Ave	2
Black Creek Rd	2
Blodgett St	1
Bluffton Ave	1
Boltwood Dr	1
Bourdon St	1
Boyle St	1
Brighton Ave	1
Broadmoor St	2
Broadway Ave	2
Browne St	1
Brunswick St	2
Brusse Ave	2
Buelah	2
Burton Rd	2
Butler St	2
Calvin Ave	2
Campbell St	2
Campus Ave	2
Carriage Rd	2
Catawba Ave	2
Catherine Ave	2
Cedar St	2
Center St	2
Channel Ave	1
Charles St	2
Cherry St	1
Chestnut St	2
Clay Ave	2
Cleveland Ave	2
Clifford St	1
Clinton St	2
Collins Ave	2
Columbia Ave	2
Commerce St	2
Concord Ave	2
Continental St	2
Corporate Limit	2
Cottage Grove	1
Country Club Dr	1
Creek Dr	1
Crescent Ave	2
Creston St	2
Cross St	2
Crowley St	1
Crozier Ave	1
Cumberland St	1
Cutler Ave	1
Dale Ave	1
Dale Ave	2
Davis St	1
De Baker St	2
Deaner Dr	2
Delano Ave	2
Delaware Ave	2
Denmark St	1
Dewy St	1
Diana Ave	2
Division St	1
Dowd St	1
Dratz St	2
Ducey Ave	2
Dudley Ave	2
Dune St	1
Dyson St	2
Eastern Ave	2
Eastgate St	2
Eastwood Dr	2
Edgewater St	1
Edwin St	2
Elizabeth Ct	2
Ellifson Ave	2
Elm St	1
Elwood St	2
Emerald St	2
Emerson Ave	2
Erickson St	2
Erie St	2
Estes Ct	1
Estes St	1
Evanston Ave	2
Evart St	2
Fair Ave	1
Fairlawn Ct	1
Fairview St	2
Fleming Ave	2
Flower Ave	2
Forest Ave	1
Forest Ave	2
Fork St	2
Fountain St	1
Frances Ave	2
Franklin St	1
Frisbie St	1
Fulton Ave	1
Garden St	2
Getty Ave	2
Getty St	2
Gettysburg St	2
Giddings Ave	2
Glade St	2
Glen Ave	1
Glen Ct	2
Glen Oaks Dr	2
Glendale St	2
Glenmoor Ave	1
Glenside Blvd	1
Grace Ave	2
Grand Ave	1
Grand Ave	2
Greeley St	1
Green Rd	
Green Rd	2
Green St	2
Greenwood St	1
Grove St	1
Gunn St	2
Hackley Ave	1
Hackley Ave	2
Hadden St	1
Hall Ave	2
Hamilton Ave	2
Hancock Ave	1
Hancock Ave	2
Harding Ave	1
Harnau St	2
Harrison Ave	1
Harrison Blvd	2
Harrison Ct	1
Hartford Ave	2
Harvey St	2
Henry St	1
Herrick St	2
High St	1
Highland St	2
Hill St	2
Hillcrest Dr	2
Holbrook Ave	2
Holt St	2
Home St	2
Houston Ave	2
Hovey Ave	2
Howard Ave	2
Howden St	2
Howell Ave	2
Hoyt St	
Hoyt St	2
Hudson St	1
Huizenga St	2
Hume Ave	2
Indiana Ave	1
Industrial Blvd	2
Ireland Ave	1
Irwin Ave	2
Isabella Ave	2
Ivory Ave	2
Ivy St	1
Jackson Ave	2
James Ave	2
Jarman St	2
Jay St	2
Jefferson Ave	2
Jefferson St	2
Jiroch St	2
Kampenga Ave	2
Kanitz St	2
Keating Ave	2
Keaton Ct	1
Kenneth St	2
Kingsley St	2
Kinsey St	1
Knollwood Ct	1
Kraft St	2
La Rue St	1
Lake Shore Blvd	
Lake Shore Dr	1
Lakeshore St	1
Laketon Ave	1
Laketon Ave	2
Langeland Ave	2
Langley St	2
Larch Ave	1
Larch Ave	2
Larkin St	1
Latimer Dr	2
Lawrence Ave	2
Le Boeuf St	1
Leahy St	2
Lemuel St	2
Leon St	1
Leonard Ave	2
Letart Ave	1
Lexington Ave	1
Lighton Dr	2
Lincoln Ave	2
Lincoln Ct	2
Lincoln St	1
Loop Rd	1
Louis Ave	2
Lyman Ave	1
Lyman Ave	2
Madison St	2
Maffett St	2
Manahan Ave	2
Mangin Ave	2
Mann Ave	2
Mann St	1
Manz St	2
Maple St	2
Maplewood Ave	2
Marcoux Ave	2
Margaret St	2
Marlane Ct	2
Marlane Dr	2
Marquette Ave	2
Marsh St	2
Marshall St	2
Mart St	2
Mary St	2
Mason Ave	2
Mason Blvd	2
Mc Cracken St	1
Mc Graft Park	1
Mc Graft St	1
Mc Ilwraith St	2
Mc Laren St	2
Mc Laughlin	2
Meeking St	2
Mercy Dr	2
Merriam St	2
Merrill Ave	2
Messler St	2
Meurer Ct	1
Michigan Ave	1
Millard Ave	1
Miner Ave	1
Mona St	2
Mona View Dr	2
Monroe Ave	2
Montague Ave	1
Montgomery	1
Moon St	1
Moore St	1
Morgan Ave	2
Morris Ave	2
Morton Ave	1
Morton Ave	2
Mulder St	2
Murphy St	2
Muskegon Ave	2
Myrtle Ave	2
Nelson St	1
Nevada St	1
New St	2
Nims St	2
Noland St	1
Norton Ave	2
Oak Ave	2
Oak Grove St	2
Oak Hill Dr	2
Oakwood Ave	2
Octavius St	2
Ohio Ave	1
Ohio St	1
Olthoff Dr	2
Orchard Ave	2
Ottawa St	2
Overbrook Rd	2
Palmer Ave	1
Park Dr	1
Park Pl	1
Park St	2
Parslow Dr	1
Parsons St	1
Peck St	2
Philo Ave	1
Pine St	2
Pinegrove St	1
Plum Ave	1
Plymouth St	2
Poliski Dr	2
Port City Blvd	2
Pulaski Ave	1
Quarterline Rd	2
Randolph Ave	1
Ransom St	2
Rathborne St	2
Ray St	2
Resort Ave	1
Reynolds St	2
Ridge Ave	1
Riordan St	2
Roberts St	2
Robinson St	1
Roblane St	2
Rodgers Ave	1
Roilson St	1
Rosewood Lane	1
Rotterdam Ave	2
Roy Ave	2
Ruddiman St	1
Samburt St	2
Sampson Ave	1
Sand Ave	1
Sanford St	2
Scenic Dr	1
School St	2
Schuyler St	1
Scott Dr	2
Scott St	2
Seaway Dr	
Seaway Dr	2
Shelby St	2
Sheridan Dr	2
Sherin St	1
Sherman Blvd	1
Sherman Blvd	2
Sherwood Ct	1
Shonat St	2
Sicord St	1
Simpson Ave	1
Sisson Ave	1
Smith St	2
Sophia St	2
Southern Ave	1
Southern Ave	2
Spring St	2
State Hwy 120	2
Stebbins Rd	2
Stein St	1
Stevens St	2
Strong Ave	2
Suelane St	2
Summit Ave	2
Sumner Ave	2
Superior St	2
Surfwood Dr	1
Surrey Pl	2
Temple St	2
Terrace St	2
Thayer Ave	2
Thompson Ave	1
Torrent St	1
Turner Ave	2
US Hwy 31	2
Valley St	2
Vanderberg Rd	2
Vanderlinde St	1
Vandinther Dr	1
Vernon Pl	1
Vincent Rd	1
Vulcan St	2
Waalkes St	2
Walnut St	1
Walton Ave	2
Washington Ave	1
Washington Ave	2
Waterworks Rd	1
Watson Ave	1
Webster Ave	2
Wesley Ave	2
Western Ave	1
Western Ave	2
Westwood Dr	1
White Ave	2
Wickham Dr	1
Wilcox Ave	1
Williams Ave	2
Willow Dr	1
Wilson Ave	1
Wilson Ave	2
Winchester Dr	1
Windsor Ave	1
Windward Dr	1
Winters St	2
Wood Rd	2
Wood St	2
Woodcliffe Dr	2
Woodcreek Ave	1
Woodlawn Ct	1
Young Ave	1
Young Ave	2
Yuba St	2

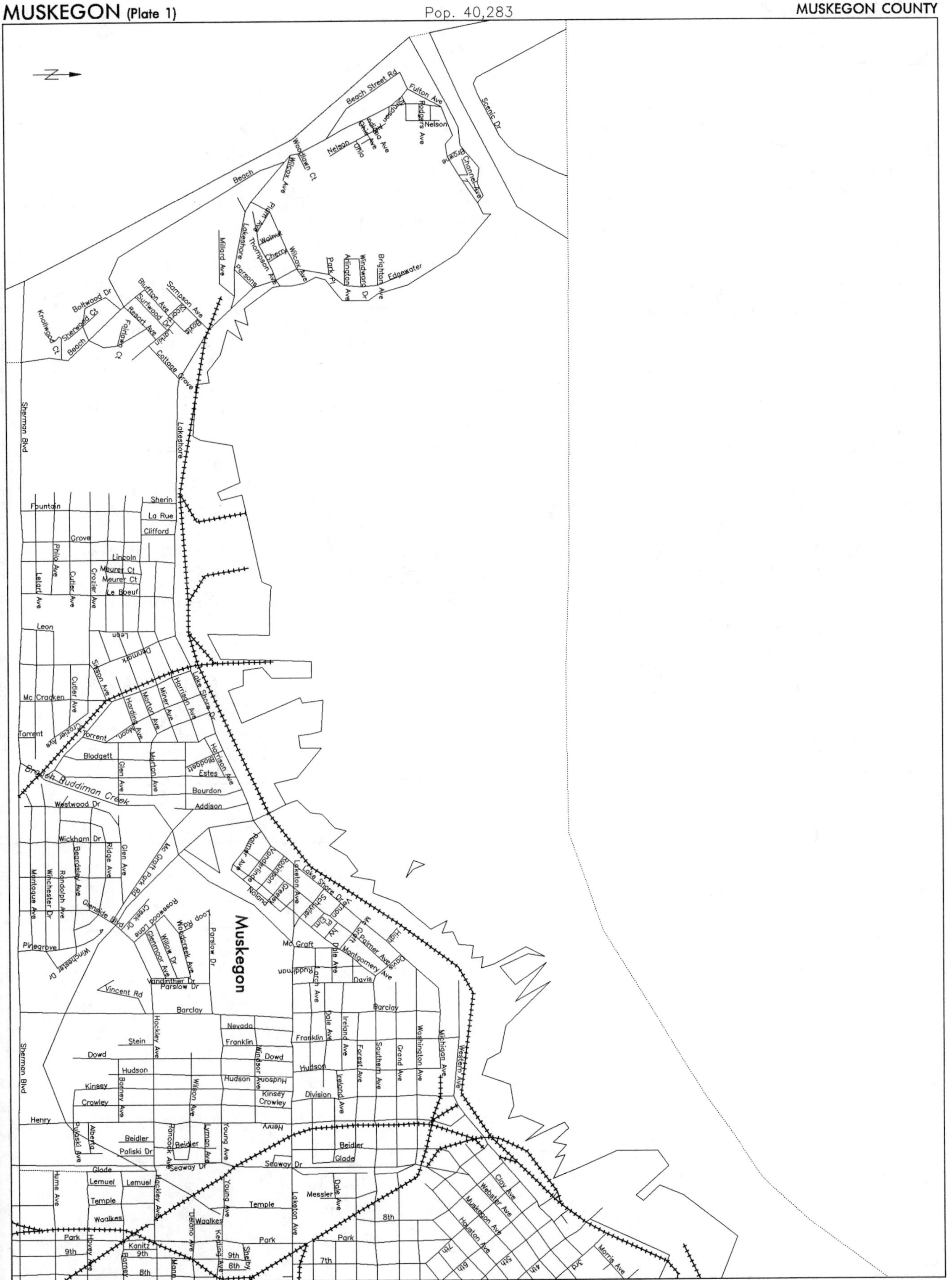

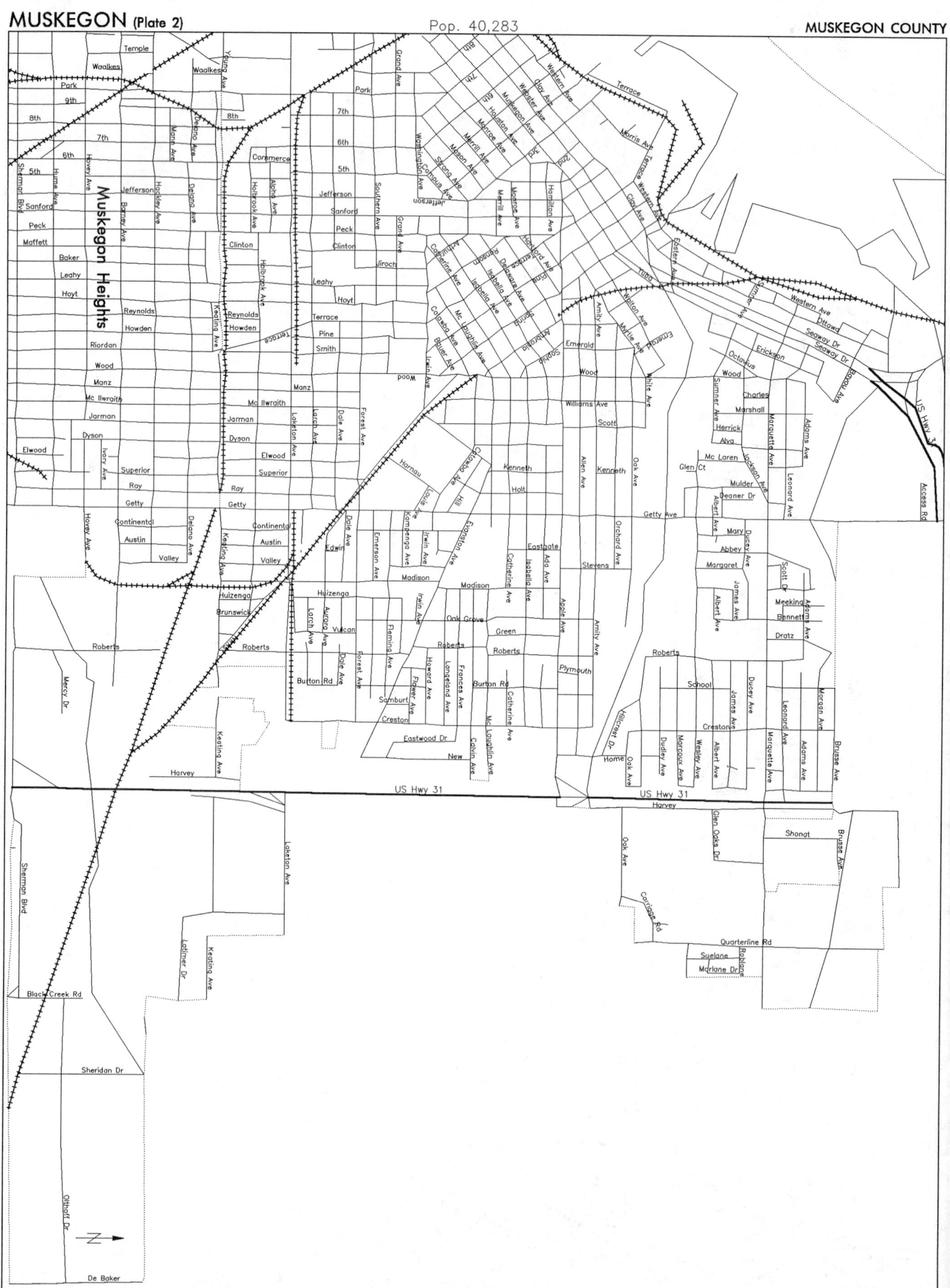
Muskegon Heights
US Hwy 31
Sherman Blvd
Getty Ave
Roberts
Wood
Laketon Ave
Keating Ave
Black Creek Rd
Sheridan Dr
Quarterline Rd
De Baker

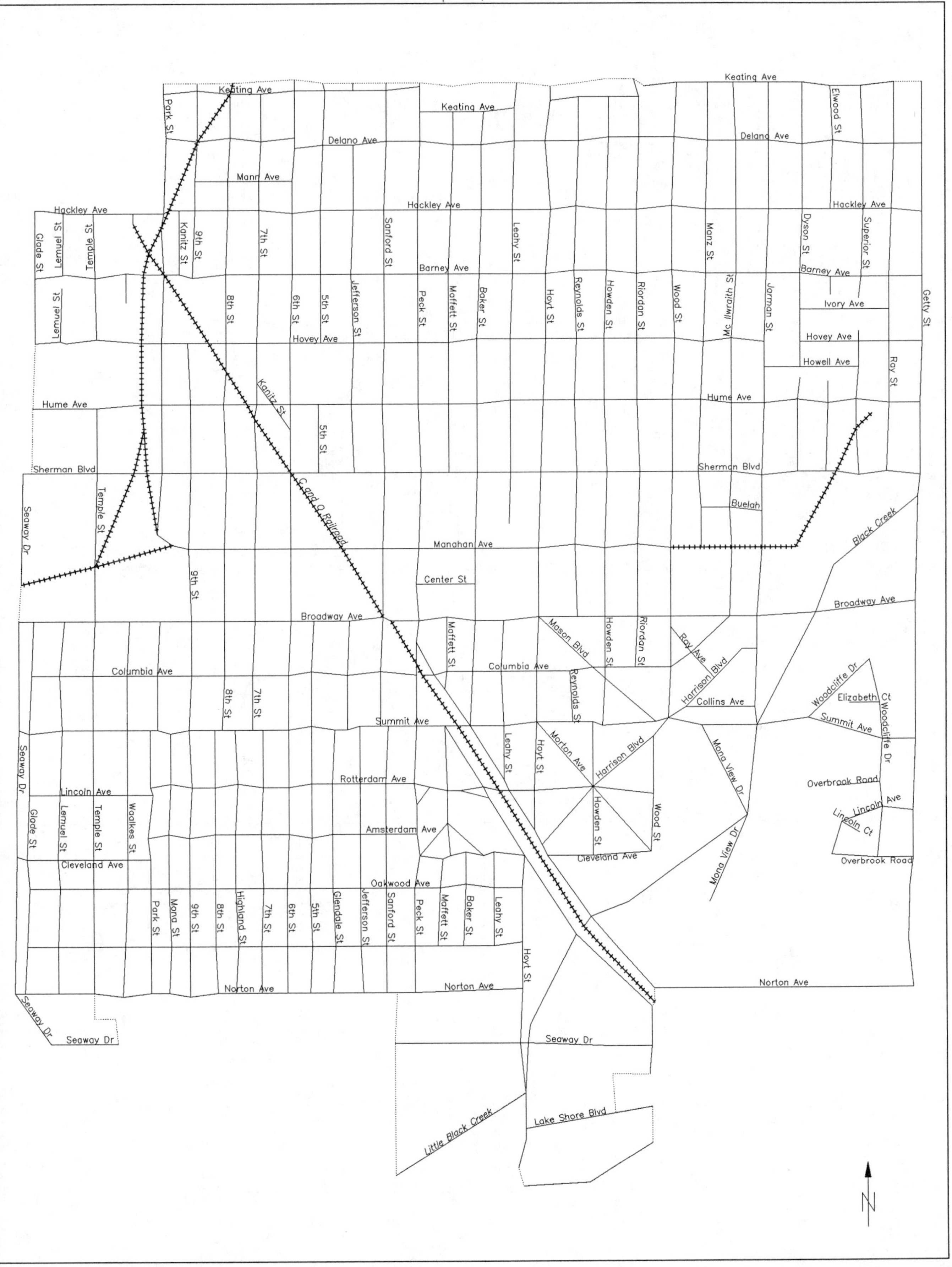
Keating Ave
Keating Ave
Keating Ave
Park St
Delano Ave
Delano Ave
Elwood St
Mann Ave
Hackley Ave
Hackley Ave
Hackley Ave
Glade St
Lemuel St
Temple St
Kanitz St
9th St
7th St
Sanford St
Leahy St
Manz St
Dyson St
Superior St
Barney Ave
Barney Ave
Lemuel St
8th St
6th St
5th St
Jefferson St
Peck St
Maffett St
Baker St
Hoyt St
Reynolds St
Howden St
Riordan St
Wood St
Mc Ilwraith St
Jorman St
Ivory Ave
Getty St
Hovey Ave
Hovey Ave
Howell Ave
Ray St
Hume Ave
Hume Ave
Kanitz St
5th St
Sherman Blvd
Sherman Blvd
Buelah
Seaway Dr
Temple St
C and O Railroad
Manahan Ave
Black Creek
9th St
Center St
Broadway Ave
Broadway Ave
Mason Blvd
Howden St
Riordan St
Maffett St
Ray Ave
Harrison Blvd
Columbia Ave
Columbia Ave
8th St
7th St
Reynolds St
Collins Ave
Woodcliffe Dr
Elizabeth Ct
Summit Ave
Summit Ave
Woodcliffe Dr
Seaway Dr
Leahy St
Hoyt St
Morton Ave
Harrison Blvd
Mona View Dr
Overbrook Road
Rotterdam Ave
Lincoln Ave
Lincoln Ave
Lincoln Ct
Glade St
Lemuel St
Temple St
Waalkes St
Amsterdam Ave
Howden St
Wood St
Mona View Dr
Overbrook Road
Cleveland Ave
Cleveland Ave
Oakwood Ave
Park St
Mona St
9th St
8th St
Highland St
7th St
6th St
5th St
Glendale St
Jefferson St
Sanford St
Peck St
Maffett St
Baker St
Leahy St
Hoyt St
Norton Ave
Norton Ave
Norton Ave
Seaway Dr
Seaway Dr
Seaway Dr
Little Black Creek
Lake Shore Blvd
N

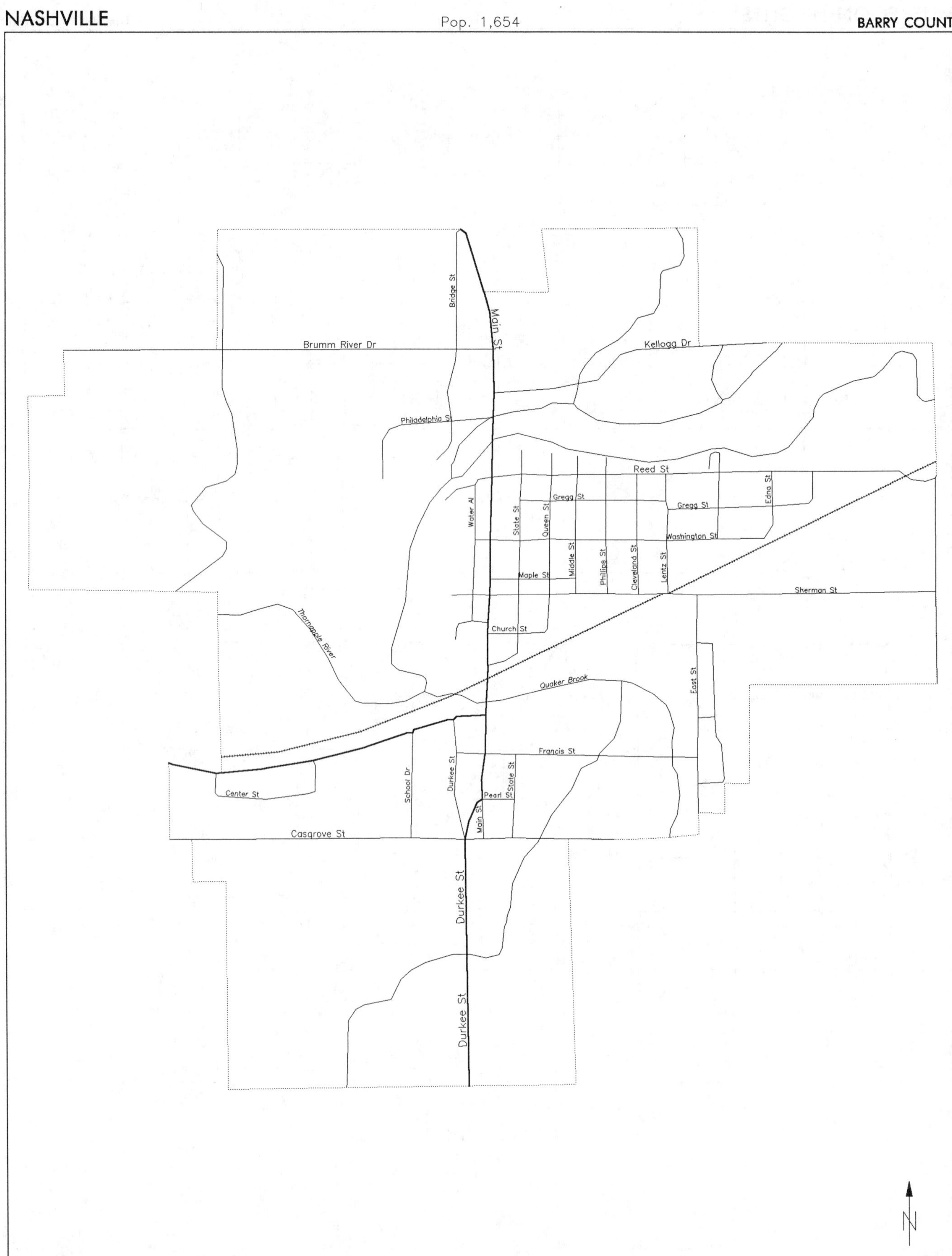
Main St
Bridge St
Brumm River Dr
Kellogg Dr
Philadelphia St
Reed St
Gregg St
Gregg St
Edna St
Water Al
State St
Queen St
Washington St
Middle St
Phillips St
Cleveland St
Lentz St
Maple St
Sherman St
Church St
Thornapple River
East St
Quaker Brook
Francis St
School Dr
Durkee St
State St
Pearl St
Main St
Center St
Casgrove St
Durkee St
Durkee St
N

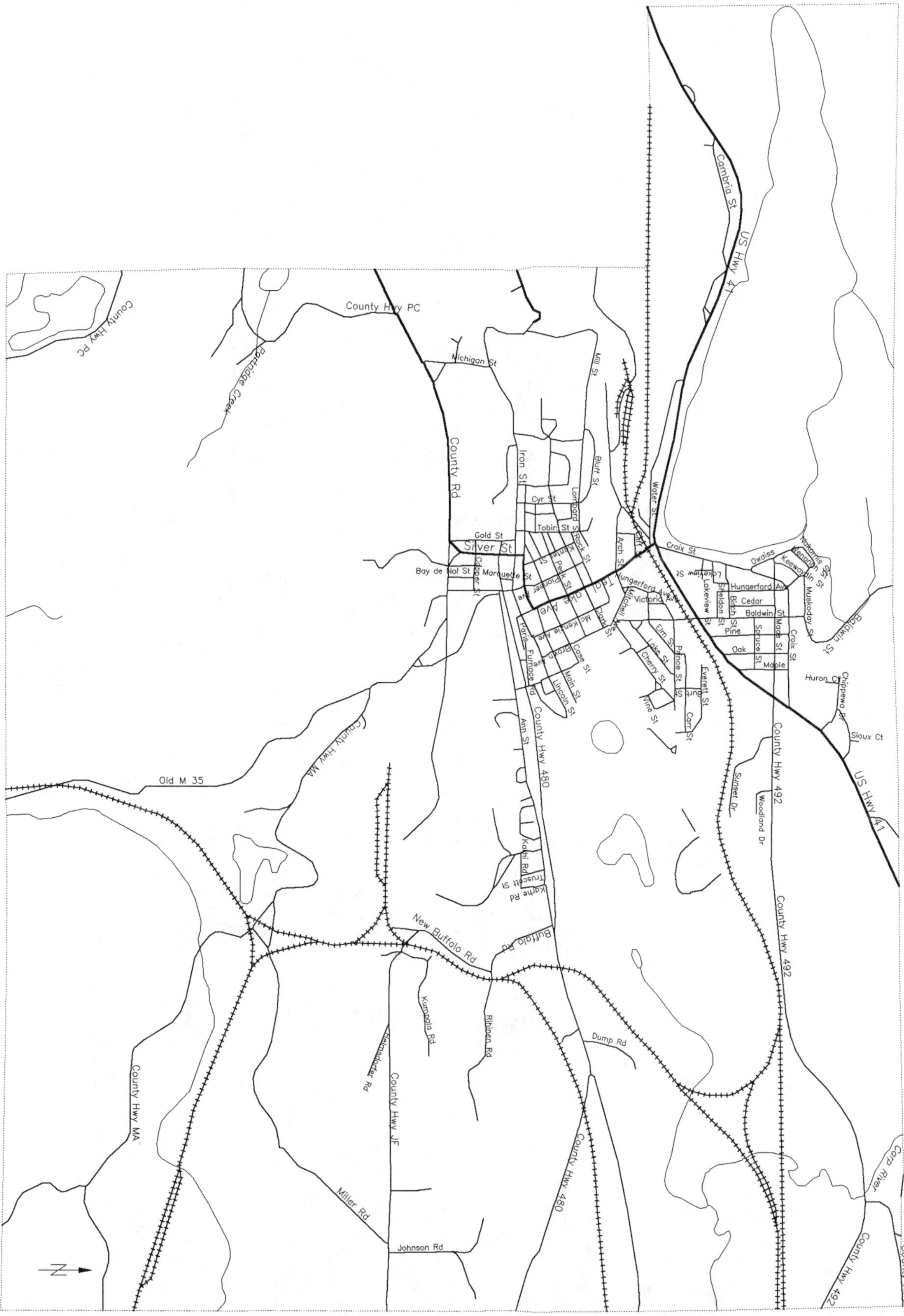

County Hwy PC
Partridge Creek
Michigan St
Mill St
County Rd
Iron St
Butt St
Cyr St
Lombard St
Tobin St
Rock St
Gold St
Silver St
Bay de Noc St
Marquette St
Copper St
Peck St
Pioneer Ave
Oak Ave
Teal Lk Ave
Arch St
Water St
Cambria St
US Hwy 41
Croix St
Hungerford Ave
Victoria Ave
Mitchell Ave
Lakeview St
Owaiss
Nokomis
Kenonah
Keewaydin St
Muskoday St
Hungerford Av
Cedar
Baldwin St
Pine
Oak
Maple
Birch St
Sheldon St
Spruce St
Moss St
Croix St
Elm St
Lake St
Cherry St
Prince St
Vine St
Everett St
Carr St
McKenzie Ave
Case St
Main St
Lincoln St
Furnace Rd
Parris
County Hwy 480
Ann St
Huron Ct
Chippewa Dr
Sioux Ct
County Hwy 492
Sunset Dr
Woodland Dr
Old M 35
County Hwy MA
Kahni Rd
Truscott St
Karhe Rd
New Buffalo Rd
Buffalo Rd
Kumpala Rd
Rihinen Rd
Dump Rd
County Hwy JF
Miller Rd
Johnson Rd
Carp River
County Hwy JQ

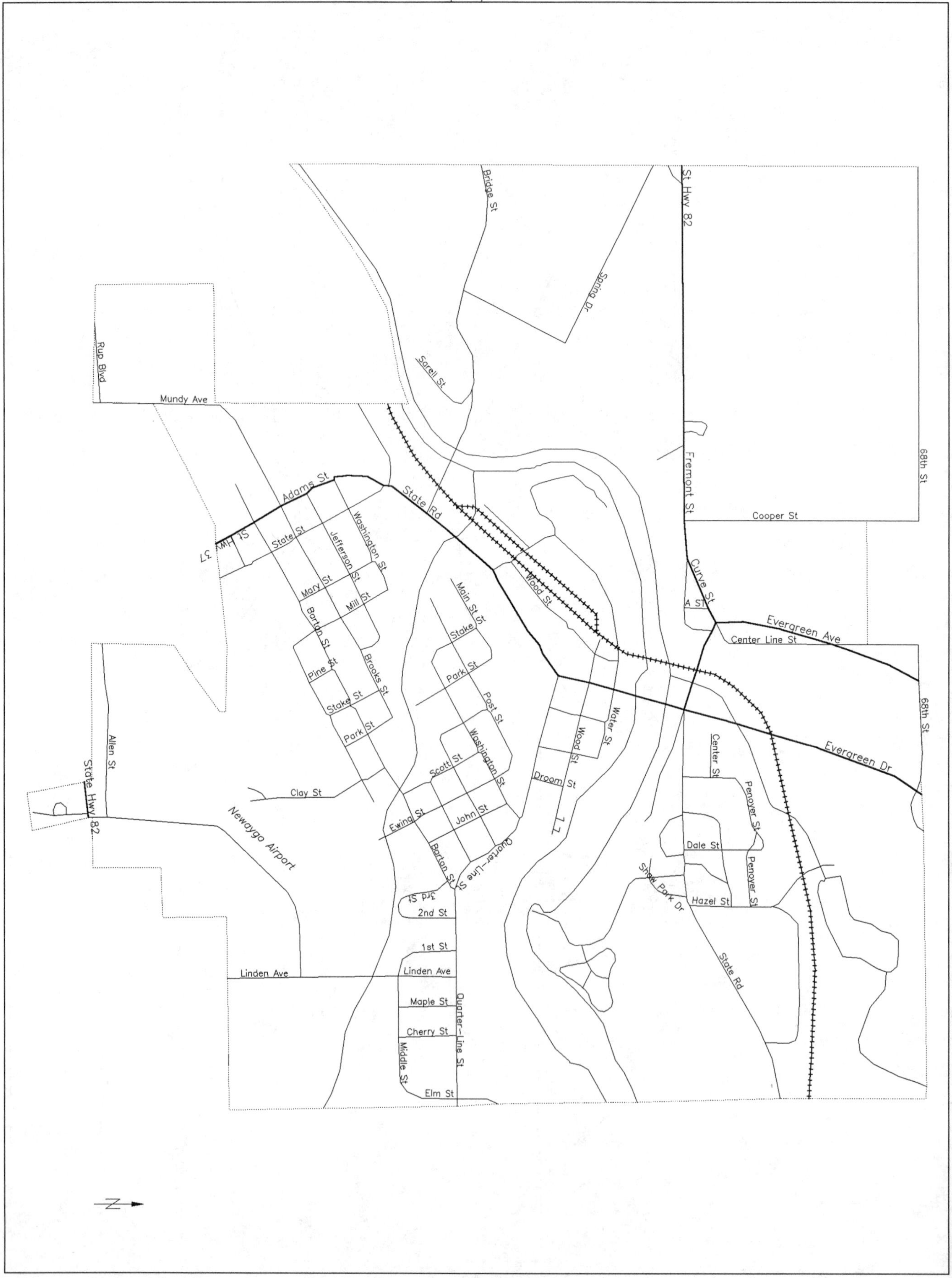

St Hwy 82
Bridge St
Spring Dr
Rup Blvd
Mundy Ave
Sorell St
Fremont St
68th St
Cooper St
Adams St
State Rd
St Hwy 37
State St
Jefferson St
Washington St
Mary St
Mill St
Barton St
Wood St
Main St
Curve St
A ST
Evergreen Ave
Center Line St
Stake St
Pine St
Brooks St
Park St
Post St
Water St
Allen St
State Hwy 82
Clay St
Scott St
Ewing St
John St
Droom St
Center St
Penoyer St
Evergreen Dr
Newaygo Airport
Quarter-Line St
Dale St
Shaw Park Dr
Hazel St
3rd St
2nd St
1st St
Linden Ave
Maple St
Cherry St
Middle St
Elm St

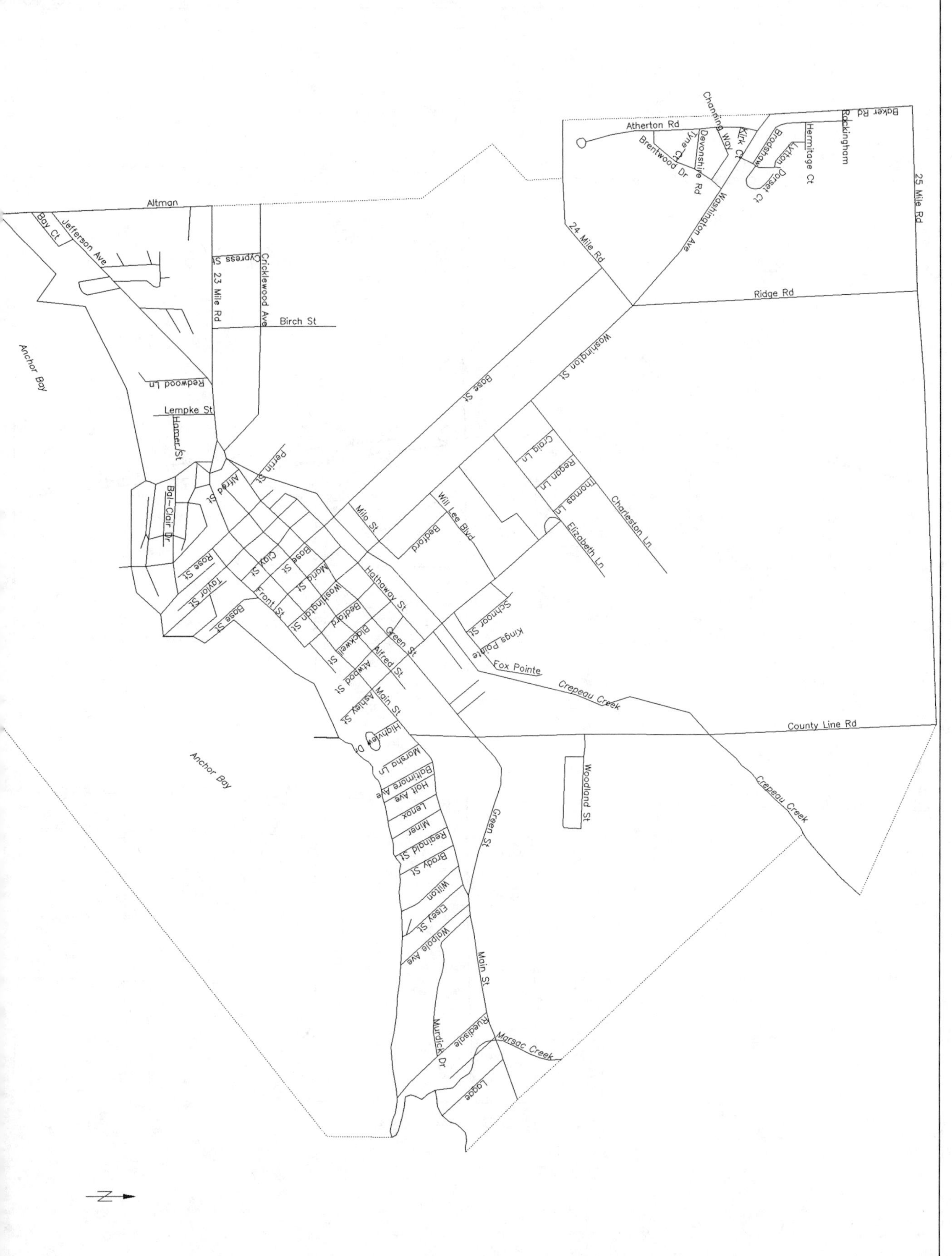
Altman
Baker Rd
Rockingham
Atherton Rd
Channing Way
Kirk Ct
Brentwood Dr
Devonshire Rd
Brodshaw
Lytton
Dorset Ct
Hermitage Ct
25 Mile Rd
Washington Ave
24 Mile Rd
Ridge Rd
Bay Ct
Jefferson Ave
Cypress St
Cricklewood Ave
23 Mile Rd
Birch St
Anchor Bay
Redwood Ln
Lempke St
Hamer St
Perrin St
Alfred St
Bal-Clair Dr
Base St
Washington St
Craig Ln
Regan Ln
Thomas Ln
Charleston Ln
Elizabeth Ln
Milo St
Will Lee Blvd
Bedford
Rose St
Taylor St
Clay St
Front St
Maria St
Hathaway St
Bedford
Blackwell St
Green St
Alfred St
Atwood St
Ashley St
Main St
Highview Dr
Schnoor St
Kings Pointe
Fox Pointe
Crepeau Creek
County Line Rd
Marsha Ln
Baltimore Ave
Holt Ave
Lenox
Miner
Reginald St
Brady St
Wilton
Elsey St
Walpole Ave
Woodland St
Green St
Main St
Murdick Dr
Ruedisale
Marsac Creek
Logge

County Hwy 400
Newberry Ave
County Rd 430
Soo Line Railroad
Railroad St
Helen St
John St
Sherman St
Robinson St
Phelps St
Handy St
Vulcan St
Truman St
Truman St
Harrie St
W CT
E CT
Parmelee St
Charles St
Mc Millan St
Tahquamenon Blvd
Ave A
Ave A
Ave A
Ave B
Ave B
Broad St
Ave C
Ave C
Washington Blvd
Sherman St
Robinson St
Phelps St
Newberry Ave
Ave D
N

Water Ct
Water St
Shore Dr
Creek Dr
Lake Dr
Beach Ct
Eagle St
Chicago St
Berrien St
North Dr
Lake Dr
Michigan St
Clinton
Marshall
Monroe St
Monroe St
Eagle St
Chicago St
Berrien St
Willard St
Mechanic St
Oselka Dr
Buffalo
Indiana St
Willard St
Harrison St
Mayhew St
Michigan St
Detroit St
Barker St
Barton St
Rose City Road
Galien River
Marquette Dr
Madison St
Jefferson
Thompson St
Washington St
Clay St
Townsend St
Merchant
Thompson St
Taylor St
Ramon Ct
Barton St
La Porte Road
Indiana St
Jameson St
Wilson St
Norton St
Norton St
Bronson
Kinzie St
Pulaski Hwy
Griffith
Franklin
Jefferson
Detroit St
Taylor St
Norton
Clay St
Indiana St
US 12
Bell St
Detroit St
11th St
Biddle St
N

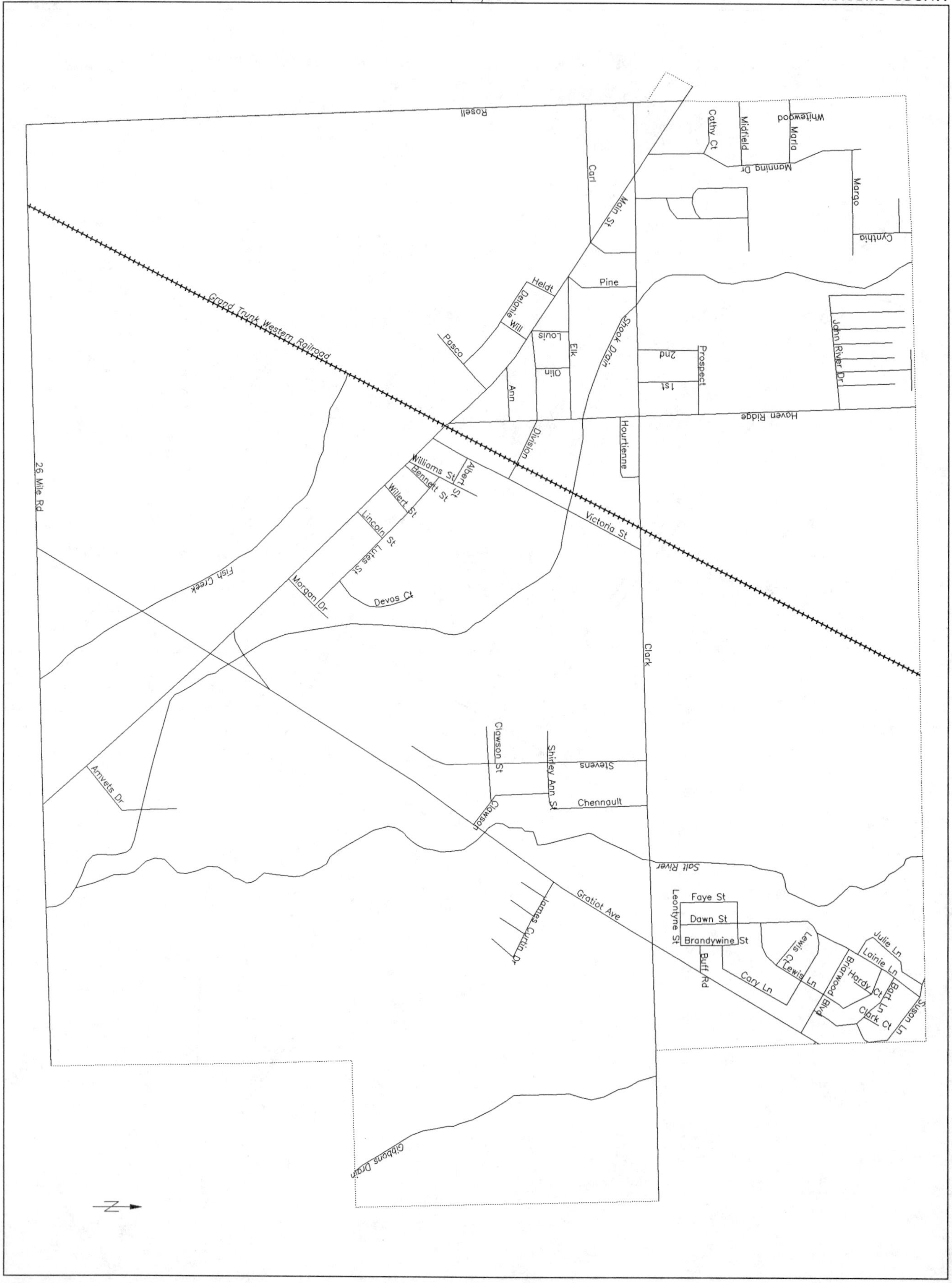

Rosell
Carl
Main St
Cathy Ct
Midfield
Whitewood
Marla
Manning Dr
Margo
Cynthia
Pine
Heldt
Delonie Will
Pasco
Louis
Elk
Olin
Ann
Shook Drain
2nd
1st
Prospect
John River Dr
Haven Ridge
Grand Trunk Western Railroad
Division
Hourtienne
Williams St
Albert St
Bennett St
Willert St
Lincoln St
Lutes St
Victoria St
26 Mile Rd
Fish Creek
Morgan Dr
Devos Ct
Clark
Clawson St
Shirley Ann St
Stevens
Chennault
Clawson
Amvets Dr
Salt River
Gratiot Ave
James Curtin Dr
Faye St
Dawn St
Brandywine St
Leontyne St
Buff Rd
Lewis Ct
Lewis Ln
Cary Ln
Briarwood Blvd
Hardy Ct
Julie Ln
Loinie Ln
Bart Ln
Clark Ct
Susan Ln
Gibbons Drain
N

Michigan Central RR
Terminal Rd
Wurz St
4th St
3rd St
Hill St
Burns St
5th St
12th St
11th St
Dulin St
10th St
Lake St
14th St
Clarendon Ave
Eastlake Ct
Sheridan Ave
Poplar St
8th St
9th St
Vine St
6th St
7th St
Ash St
Sheffield Ave
Merrifield Ave
Marmont St
Phoenix St
Front St
Desair St
Plym Park Rd
River St
Pokagon St
Dey St
Central St
Louis St
Wayne St
17th St
Rolling Hills Dr
Beechwood Dr
Skyline Dr
Wells St
Kensington Dr
Brown St
Christiana Cres
Platt St
Eagle St
Powers St
Howard St
Cass St
Ferry St
Sycamore St
16th St
Regent St
19th St
Lincoln Ave
State St
Water St
1st Ct
Main St
Union St
Fairview Ave
Arbor Dr
St Joseph Ave
St Joseph River
Cedar St
Stowe Ct
15th St
13th St
Broadway
18th St
Oak St
Grant St
Emmons St
Spruce St
Grand Ave
Hickory St
Clay St
Maple St
Nieb St
Elm St
Market
Cherry St
Woodruff St
Michigan St
Pine St
Madison St
Birch St
Brookfield
Parkway
Huron St
Luth Ln
Forest Ave
Venn St
Superior St
Washington
Hillcrest Rd
Chicago Rd
Earl Ct
Taft St
French St
Silverbrook Ave
Federal Ct
Inner Dr
Sioux Trl
Iroquois Trl
Meadow Dr
Old Sauk Trl
Philip Rd
Colony Ct
Tofornee Dr
Springfield Cir
Gettysburg Dr
Sarkin Ln
Ottawa Trl
Miami Rd
Sassafras Ln
Wesaw Rd
Topinabee Rd
Hawthorne Ln
Laurel Dr
Lambert St
Marion St
Decker St
Bond St
Tomahawk Ln
Vernon St
Jerome St
Bybee Ct
Fort St
N

State Hwy 90
Beech St
Huron St
Mill St
West St
Spring St
Monroe St
Orr St
Banker St
Jeffrson Road
Jeffrson Road
Park St
Saginaw St
Pleasant St
Lincoln St
Sherman St
Washington St
Franklin St
John St
North Branch Drain
Brush St
Brush St
Grand Trunk Western Railroad
Baldwin Ave
Country Lane
Huron St
Mill St
Elm Creek Road
N

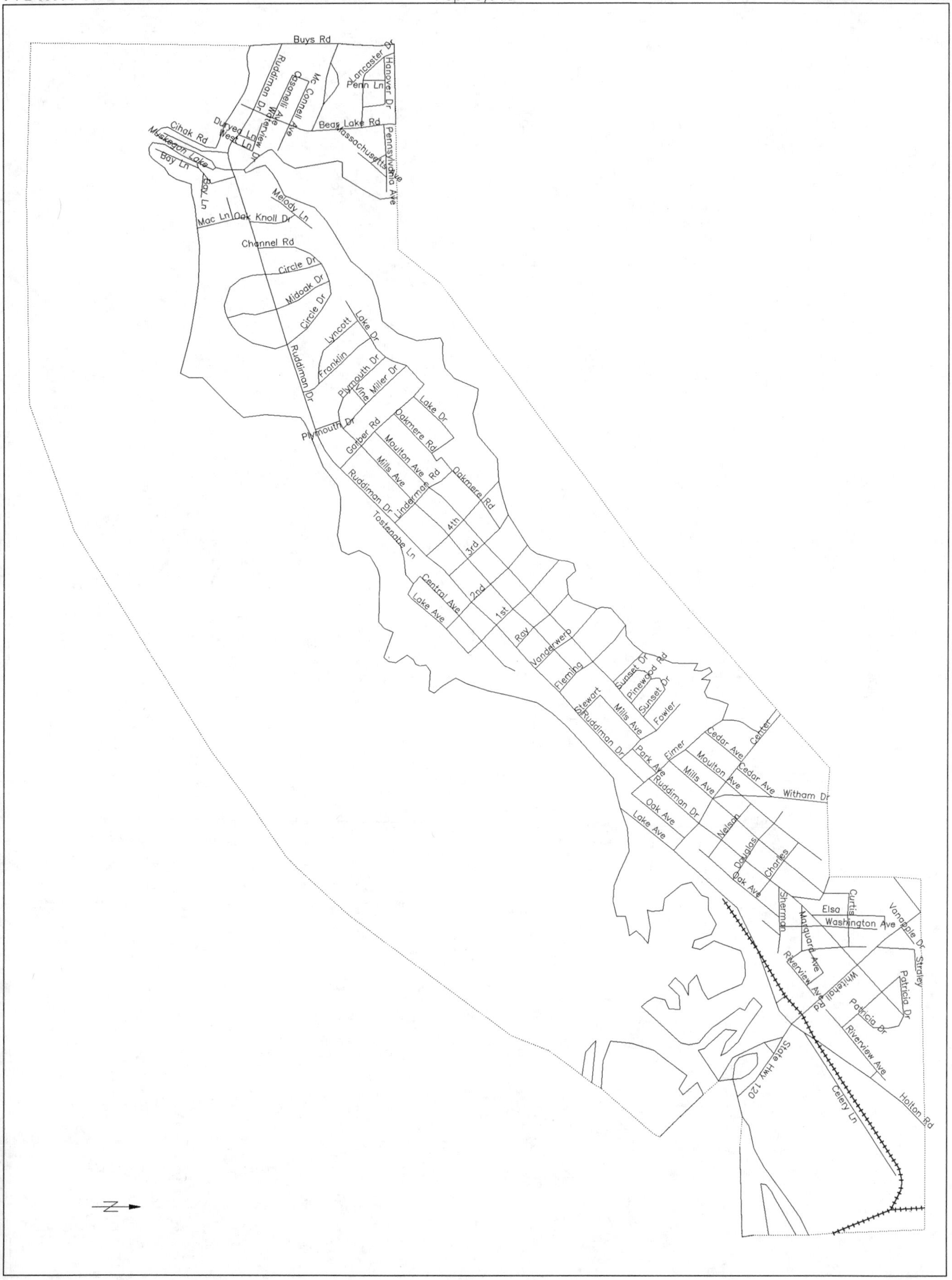

Buys Rd
Lancaster Dr
Hanover Dr
Penn Ln
Mc Connell Ave
Casanelli Ave
Ruddiman Dr
Waterview Dr
Bear Lake Rd
Massachusetts Ave
Pennsylvania Ave
Duryea Ln
West Ln
Cihak Rd
Muskegon Lake
Bay Ln
Melody Ln
Mac Ln
Oak Knoll Dr
Channel Rd
Circle Dr
Midoak Dr
Lyncott
Lake Dr
Franklin
Plymouth Dr
Vine
Miller Dr
Lake Dr
Oakmere Rd
Garber Rd
Moulton Ave
Mills Ave
Linderman Rd
Oakmere Rd
Ruddiman Dr
Tostenabe Ln
4th
3rd
2nd
1st
Central Ave
Lake Ave
Ray
Vanderwerp
Fleming
Sunset Dr
Pinewood Rd
Stewart
Mills Ave
Fowler
Ruddiman Dr
Cedar Ave
Center
Park Ave
Elmer
Moulton Ave
Cedar Ave
Witham Dr
Mills Ave
Ruddiman Dr
Oak Ave
Lake Ave
Nelson
Douglas
Charles
Oak Ave
Sherman
Curtis
Elsa
Washington Ave
Vanapple Dr
Marquard Ave
Staley
Riverview Ave
Whitehall Rd
Patricia Dr
Patricia Dr
Riverview Ave
State Hwy 120
Celery Ln
Holton Rd

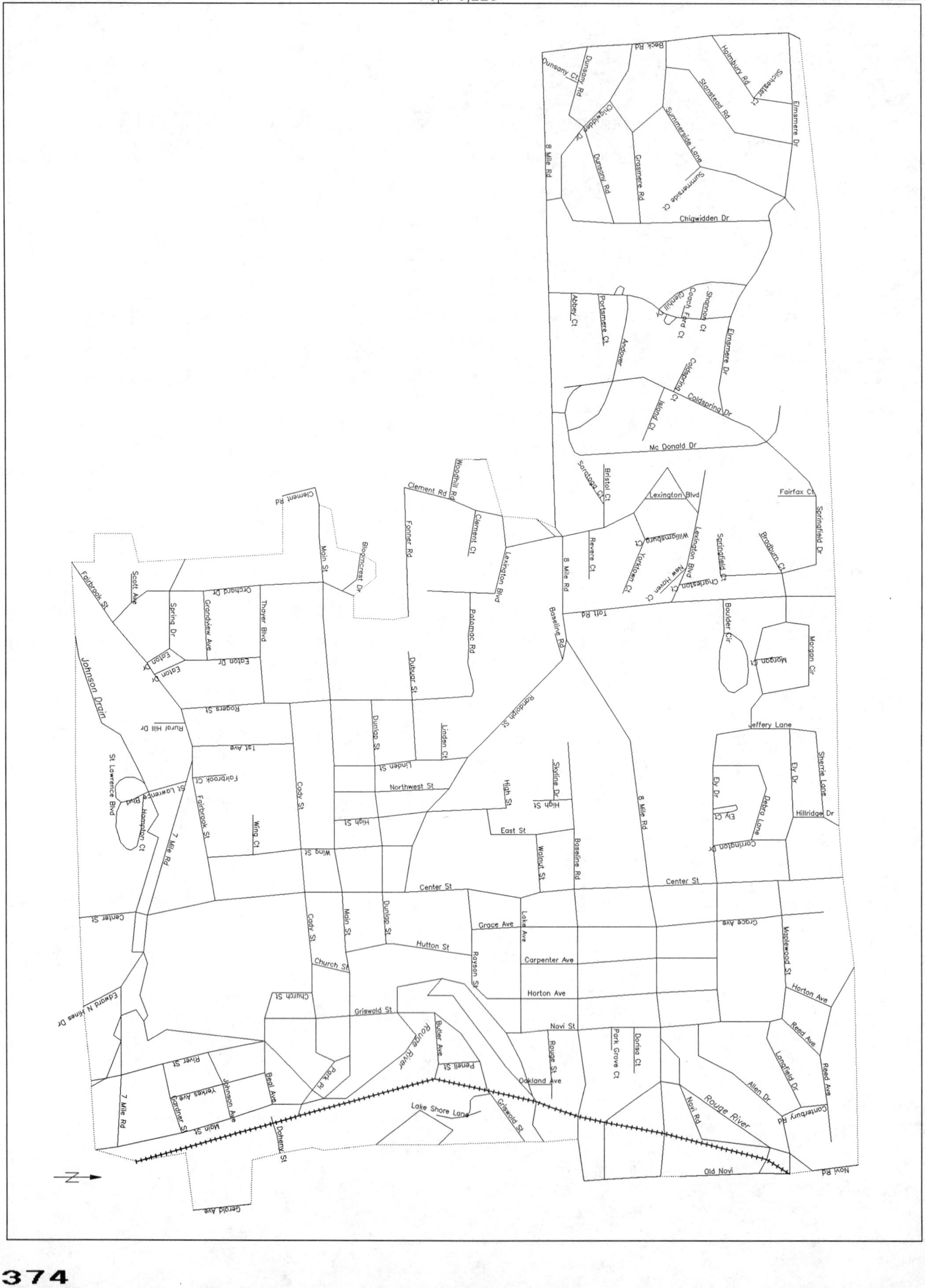

Beck Rd
Dunsany Ct
Dunsany Rd
Holmbury Rd
Sutchester Ct
Stanstead Rd
Elmsmere Dr
Chigwidden Dr
8 Mile Rd
Summerside Lane
Summerside Ct
Grasmere Rd
Abbey Ct
Portsmere Ct
Glenhill Dr
Shannon Ct
Coach Ford Ct
Andover
Coldspring Ct
Coldspring Dr
Island Ct
Mc Donald Dr
Saratoga Ct
Bristol Ct
Lexington Blvd
Fairfax Ct
Springfield Dr
Williamsburg Ct
Revere Ct
Yorktown Ct
New Haven Ct
Springfield Ct
Bradburn Ct
Charleston Ct
Taft Rd
Boulder Cir
Morgan Ct
Morgan Cir
Clement Rd
Woodhill Rd
Clement Ct
Fonner Rd
Bloomcrest Dr
Main St
Orchard Dr
Scott Ave
Fairbrook St
Spring Dr
Grandview Ave
Thayer Blvd
Potomac Rd
Baseline Rd
Eaton Dr
Eaton Ct
Dubuar St
Johnson Drain
Rogers St
Randolph St
Rural Hill Dr
Dunlap St
Linden Ct
Jeffery Lane
1st Ave
Linden St
Skyline Dr
Ely Dr
Ely Ct
Sherrie Lane
Fairbrook Ct
Northwest St
St Lawrence Blvd
Cody St
High St
Debra Lane
Hillridge Dr
Hampton Ct
7 Mile Rd
Wing Ct
Wing St
East St
Walnut St
Carrington Dr
Center St
Grace Ave
Lake Ave
Maplewood St
Church St
Hutton St
Carpenter Ave
Rayson St
Horton Ave
Edward N Hines Dr
Griswold St
Novi St
Reed Ave
Rouge River
Butler Ave
Park Grove Ct
Dorisa Ct
Rouge St
River St
Penell St
Oakland Ave
Longfield Dr
Yerkes Ave
Johnson Ave
Beal Ave
Park Pl
Allen Dr
Gardner St
Lake Shore Lane
Novi Rd
Canterbury Rd
Doheny St
Old Novi
Gerald Ave

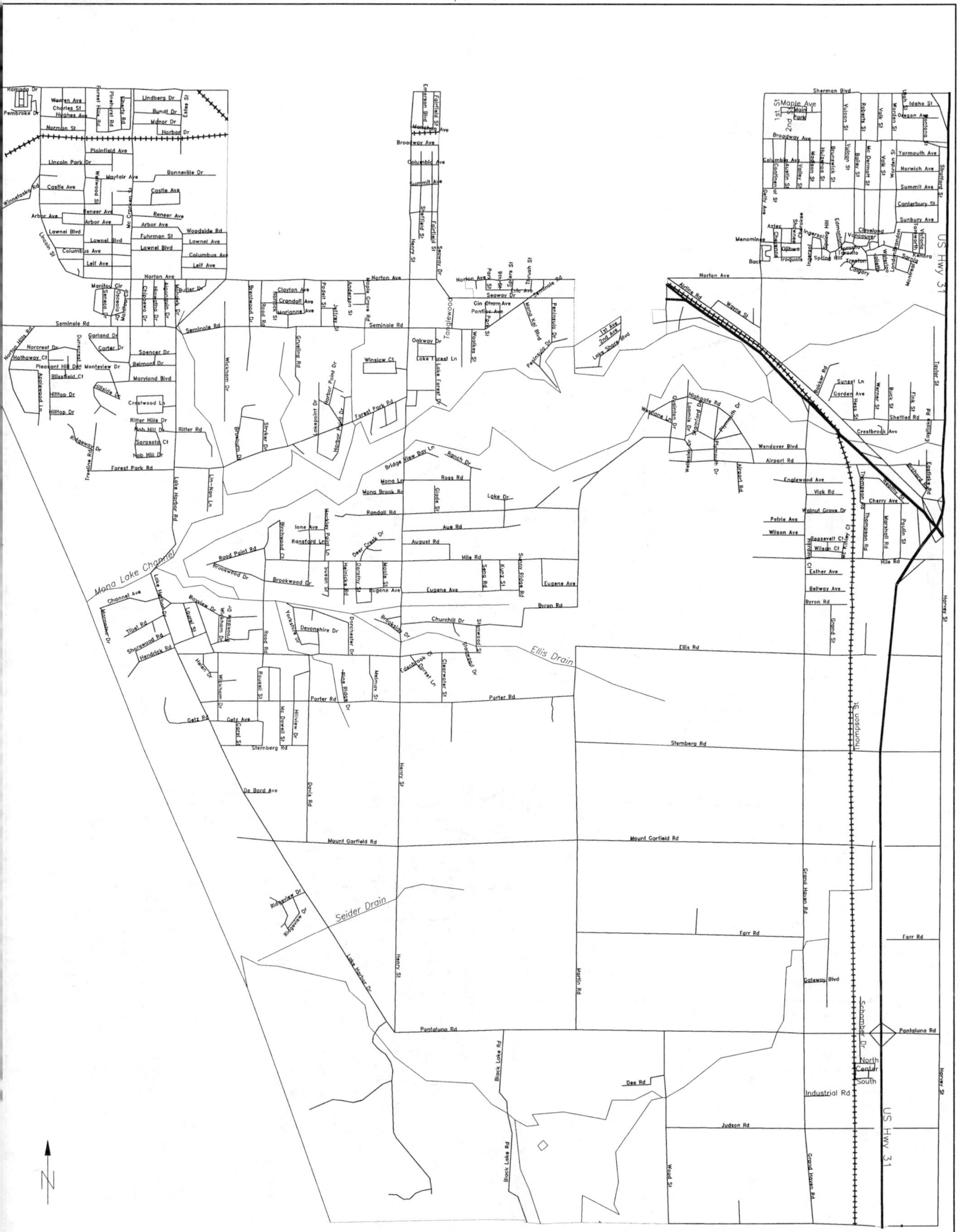

Norton Ave
Seminole Rd
Mona Lake Channel
Ellis Drain
Seider Drain
Lake Harbor Rd
Henry St
Porter Rd
Sternberg Rd
Mount Garfield Rd
Farr Rd
Pontaluna Rd
Martin Rd
Black Lake Rd
Dee Rd
Judson Rd
Wood St
Grand Haven Rd
Industrial Rd
Gateway Blvd
Harvey St
Seaway Dr
Hile Rd
Airport Rd
Wendover Blvd
Sherman Blvd
Broadway Ave
Forest Park Rd
Ritter Rd
Getz Rd
De Bord Ave
Davis Rd
Eugene Ave
Churchill Dr
Byron Rd
Randall Rd
Aue Rd
August Rd
Lake Dr
Ross Rd
Airline Rd
Ellis Rd
Hendrick Rd
Channel Ave
Schamber Dr
North
Center
South
US Hwy 31
N

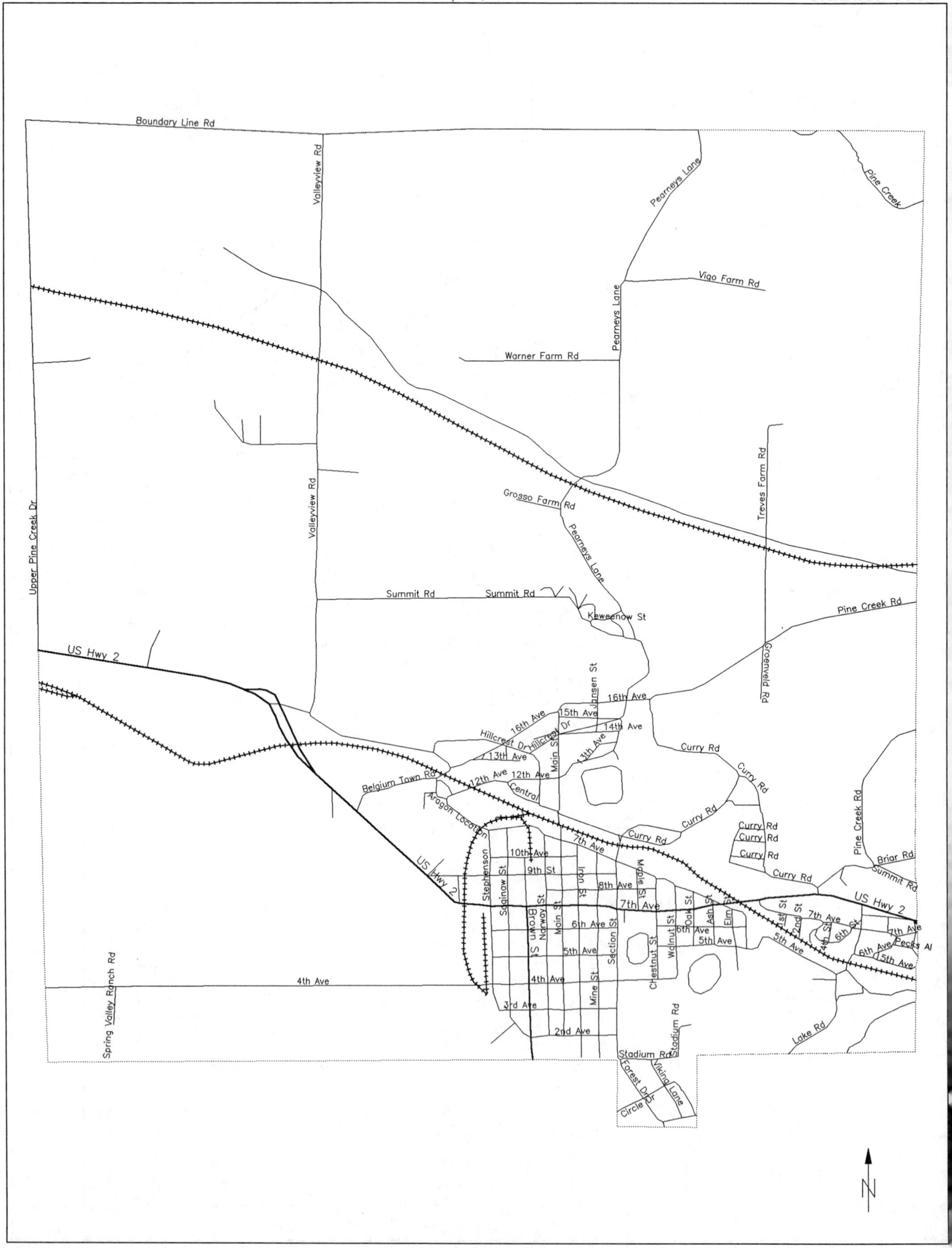
Boundary Line Rd
Valleyview Rd
Pearneys Lane
Pine Creek
Vigo Farm Rd
Warner Farm Rd
Treves Farm Rd
Grosso Farm Rd
Upper Pine Creek Dr
Summit Rd
Keweenow St
Pine Creek Rd
Groenveld Rd
US Hwy 2
Jansen St
16th Ave
15th Ave
14th Ave
Hillcrest Dr
13th Ave
12th Ave
Main St
Curry Rd
Belgium Town Rd
Central
Aragon Location
Pine Creek Rd
Briar Rd
Summit Rd
10th Ave
9th St
8th Ave
7th Ave
6th Ave
5th Ave
4th Ave
3rd Ave
2nd Ave
Stephenson
Saginaw St
Norway St
Brown St
Iron St
Maple St
Mine St
Section St
Chestnut St
Walnut St
Oak St
Ash St
Elm St
1st St
2nd St
4th St
6th St
Pecks Al
Spring Valley Ranch Rd
Stadium Rd
Lake Rd
Forest Dr
Viking Lane
Circle Dr
N

Napier Rd
9 Mile Rd
10 Mile Rd
Garfield Rd
Wixom Rd
Wixom Rd
Plate # 3
8 Mile Rd
Beck Rd
Beck Rd
9 Mile Rd
11 Mile Rd
Grand River Ave
I-96
C and O Railroad
West Rd
West Rd
Taft Rd
Walled Lake Branch
Plate # 2
Dixon Rd
12 1/2 Mile Rd
Walled Lake
Novi Rd
Plate # 1
Decker Rd
Meadowbrook Rd
Meadowbrook Rd
14 Mile Rd
8 Mile Rd
11 Mile Rd
Summit Dr
Seeley Rd
12 Mile Rd
13 Mile Rd
Haggerty Rd
N

Beck Rd
Grand River Ave
I-96
Samuel Linden
C and O Railroad
Pontiac Tr
West Rd
Walled Lake Branch
Walled Lake
Walled Lake
12 1/2 Mile Rd
12 Mile Rd
Shawood Lake
Novi Rd
Donelson
Sheraton
13 Mile Rd
Decker Rd
Meadowbrook Rd
Summit Dr
14 Mile Rd
Haggerty Rd
Delwal Dr
Beachwalk Dr
Montmorency
Rousseau Dr

Beck Rd
9 Mile Rd
10 Mile Rd
11 Mile Rd
Taft Rd
Novi Rd
8 Mile Rd
Meadowbrook Rd
Grand River Ave
Seeley Rd
Haggerty Rd
Haggerty Hwy
I-96

Napier Rd
Napier Rd
Maryland Ave
Virginia Ave
Carolina Ave
Georgia Ave
Louisianna Ave
Ohio Ave
Indiana Ave
Oregon Ave
Arizona Ave
Idaho Ave
Montana Ave
Novi Meadows
Alchebaun
Bauneckschtay
Fleddermouse
Mariga
Nordeer
Nordeer
Ocher
Ocher
Gravel Pit Rd
Davis Creek
12 Mile Rd
10 Mile Rd
Wixom Rd
Jack L
Harold B
Wixom Rd
11 Mile Rd
Grand River Ave
Heartwood
Heartwood
Burnt Wood
Cedarwood Dr
Woodham Rd
Woodham Rd
Rushwood Ln
Lynwood Dr
Lynwood Dr
Forest Park Dr
10 Mile Rd
N
Beck Rd

11 Mile Rd
Kingston Ave
Labelle Ave
Borgman Ave
Talbot Ave
Hart Ave
Nadine Ave
Elgin Ave
Manhattan Ave
Lincoln Dr
Coolidge Hwy
Greenfield Rd
Harding Ave
Raine Ave
Stratford Pl
Loretto Pl
Radclift Pl
Marlow Pl
Gardner Ave
Kipling Ave
Vernon Ave
Sherwood Ct
Sherwood Ave
Colleen Ave
Ludlow Ave
Karren Ave
Ronald Ct
Church St
Balfour Ave
Winchester Ave
Victoria Ave
Wales Ave
I-696
10 Mile Rd
Sussex St
Burton Ave
Radclift Ave
Kenosha Ave
Dartmouth Ave
Sutherland Ave
Kenton Ave
Northfield Ave
Cloverlawn Ave
Parklawn Ave
Westhampton Ave
Ridgedale Ave
Blackstone Ave
Dante Ave
Berkley Ave
Eastwood Ave
Moritz Ave
Jerome Ave
Morton Ave
Rensselaer Ave
Geneva Ave
Oneida Blvd
Manistee Ave
Rosewood Ct
Woodside Park Rd
Woodside Park Blvd
Woodland Ct
Kenberton Dr
Republic Ave
Colgate St
Yale Ave
Roseland Ct
Chapman Ave
Marlow Ave
Joan St
Leslie Ave
Bishop Ave
Church Rd
Allan Ave
Constance Ave
Seneca Ave
Majestic Ave
Ithaca Ave
Rosewood Ave
Norwood Ave
Meadowlark Ave
Roanoke Ave
Beverly Ave
Oak Park Blvd
Coyle Ave
Wildwood Ave
Park Ave
Rosemary Ave
Irvine Blvd
Rosemary Blvd
Forest Ave
Harriet
Avon Ave
Elaine Ct
Geoffrey Ct
Kenwood Ave
Woodvale Ave
Webster St
Mc Clain Dr
Sylvan Ct
Oakcrest Ct
Oakcrest St
Sterling Ct
Breckenridge Ave
9 Mile Rd
Troy Ave
Corning Ave
Saratoga Ave
Albany Ave
Granzon Ave
Elgmon Ave
Condon Ave
Scotia Rd
Vale St
Fern Ave
Sunset Ave
Whitmore Ave
Le Roy Ave
Capital Ave
Wyoming Pl
Wyoming Ct
Wyoming Ave
Stratford Ct
Northend Ave
James St
Miller St
Meyers Rd
Cloverdale Ave
Greenbriar Ave
Pasadena Ave
Hubbell Ave
8 Mile Rd
N

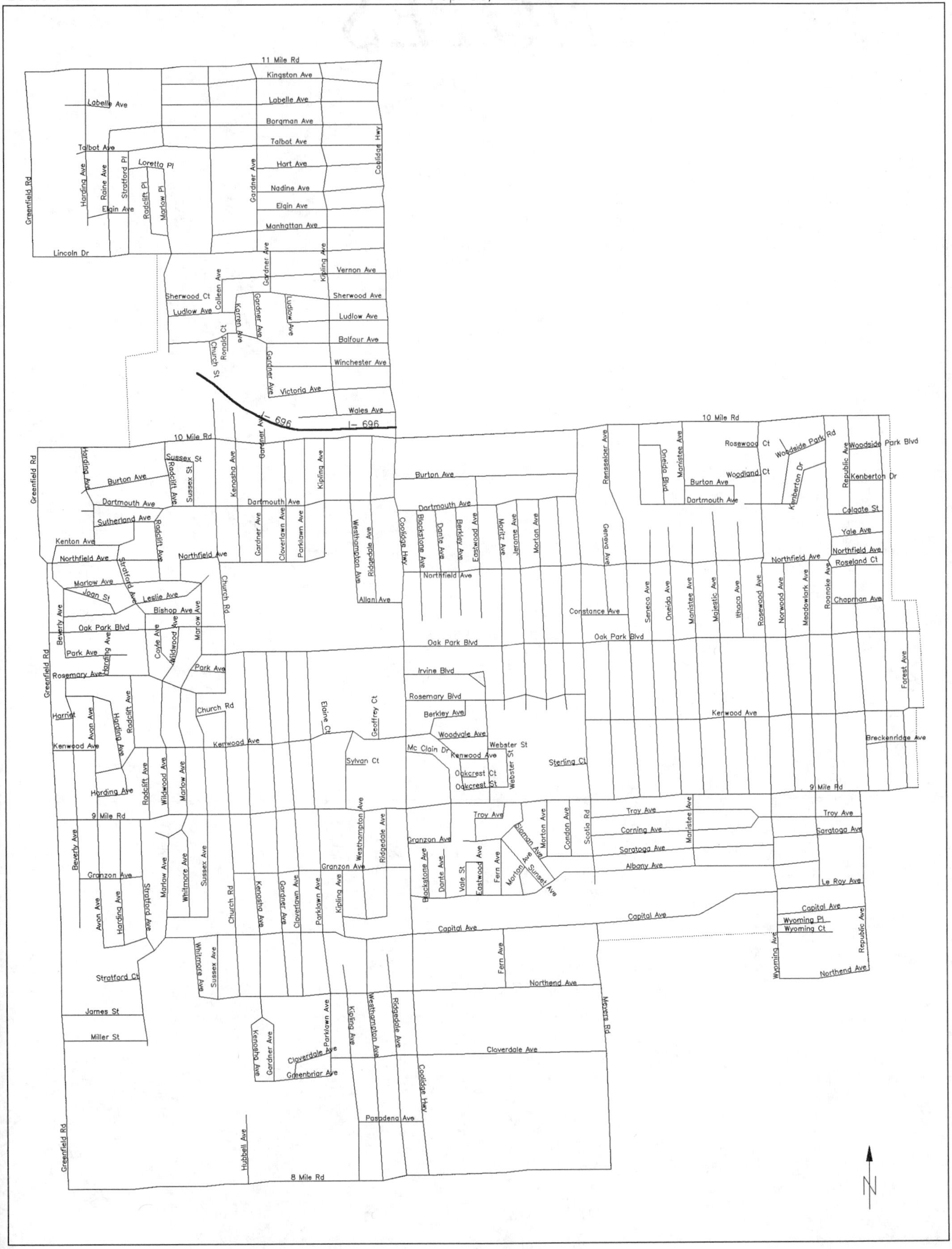

NOTES

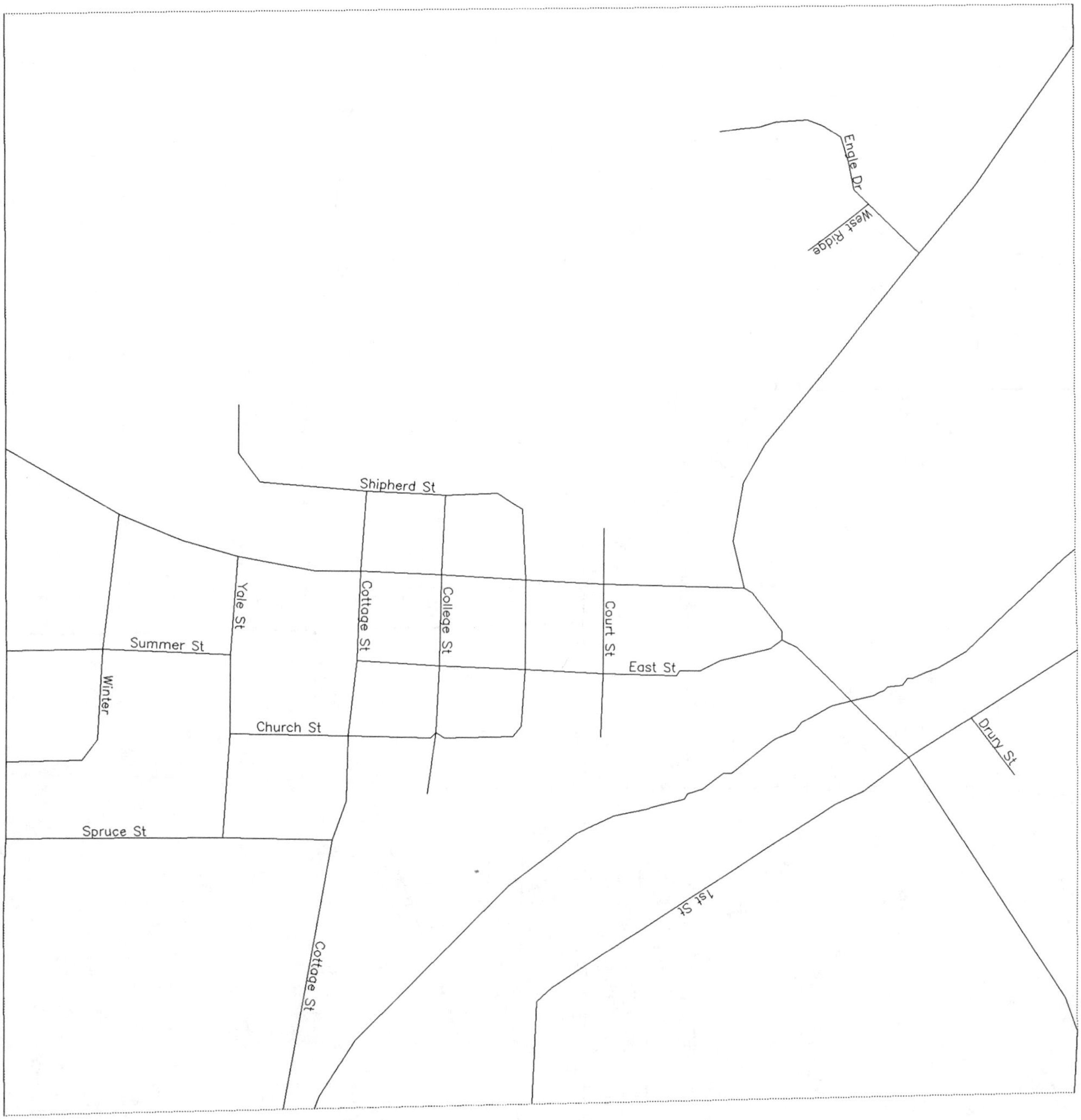

Engle Dr
West Ridge
Shipherd St
Yale St
Cottage St
College St
Court St
Summer St
East St
Winter
Church St
Spruce St
Drury St
1st St
Cottage St

ONAWAY

Pop. 1,039

PRESQUE ISLE COUNTY

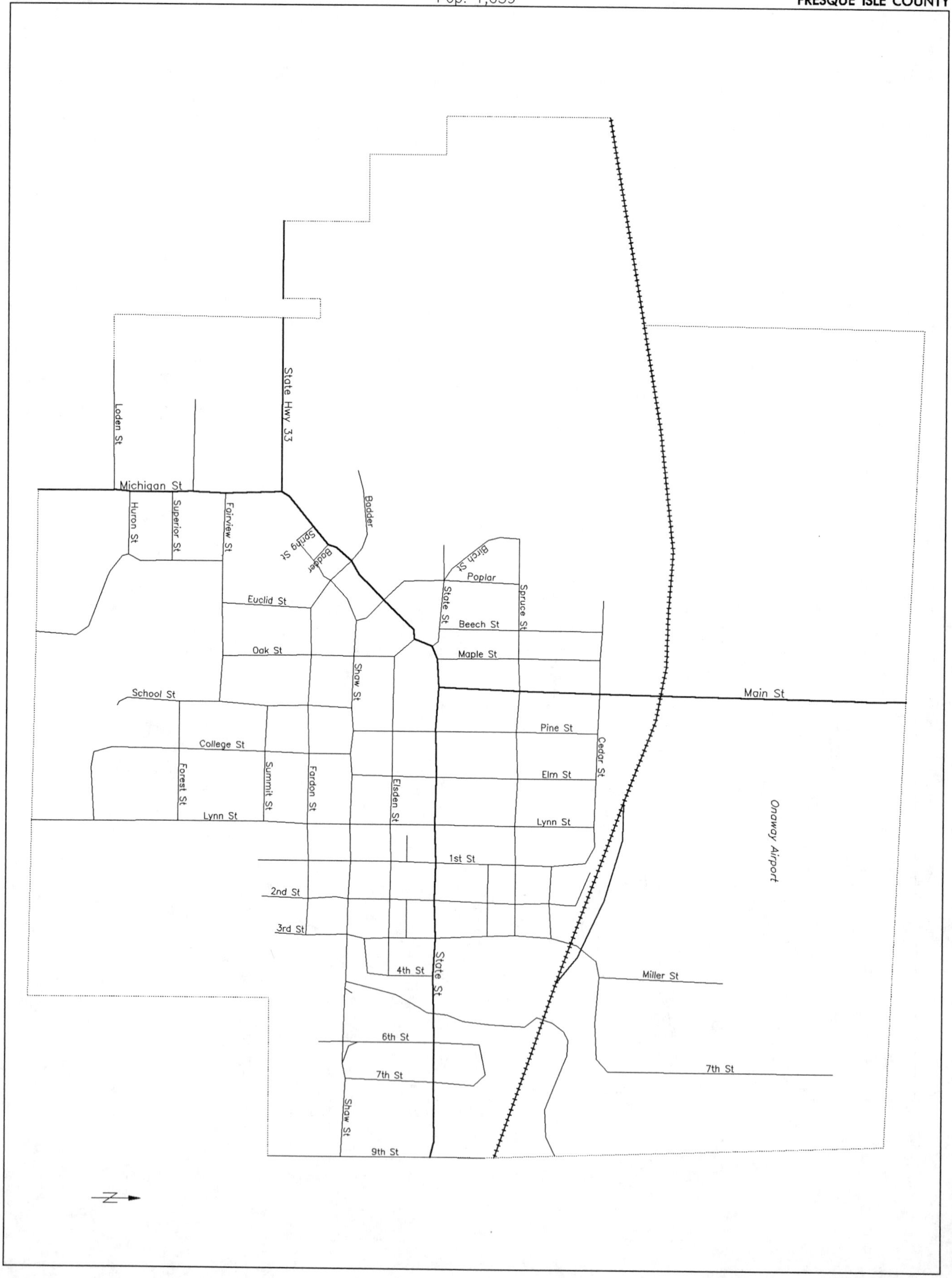
State Hwy 33
Loden St
Michigan St
Huron St
Superior St
Fairview St
Badder
Spring St
Badder
Birch St
Poplar
State St
Spruce St
Euclid St
Beech St
Oak St
Maple St
Shaw St
School St
Main St
Pine St
College St
Cedar St
Forest St
Summit St
Fardon St
Elsden St
Elm St
Lynn St
Lynn St
Onaway Airport
1st St
2nd St
3rd St
4th St
State St
Miller St
6th St
7th St
7th St
Shaw St
9th St

Lake Superior
Lakeshore Dr
Lakeshore Dr
Paul Bunyan Ave
Walnut St
Walnut
Tamarack St
Scovia Ave
Airport Road
Gorman
Hemlock
Pine
7th St
Maple Ct
Glacier
Fred
Spencer Rose Dr
Prehnite
Epidot
Amygdaloid
Conglomerate
Michigan Ave
Pebble Beach Dr
Braceburn Ct
Trap
Michigan
Lake St
Ontonagon St
Chippewa St
Houghton St
Spar
Quartz St
Copper St
Brass St
Pennsylvania Ave
2nd
3rd
4th
5th
6th
Minnesota Ave
Wiscon
Parker Ave
Iron
Lead
Gold
Zinc
Silver
River Greenland Road
7th St
James St
Tamarack
Alsace Ave
Mercury St
Heard
Diamond
Granite
Rockland Road
Mors
4th
Mulock
Payne
Zinc
Rockland Road
Ontonagon River
Mill Road
State Hwy 64
Old Norwich Trl
Old Norwich Trl
(St Hwy 38)
US 45
N

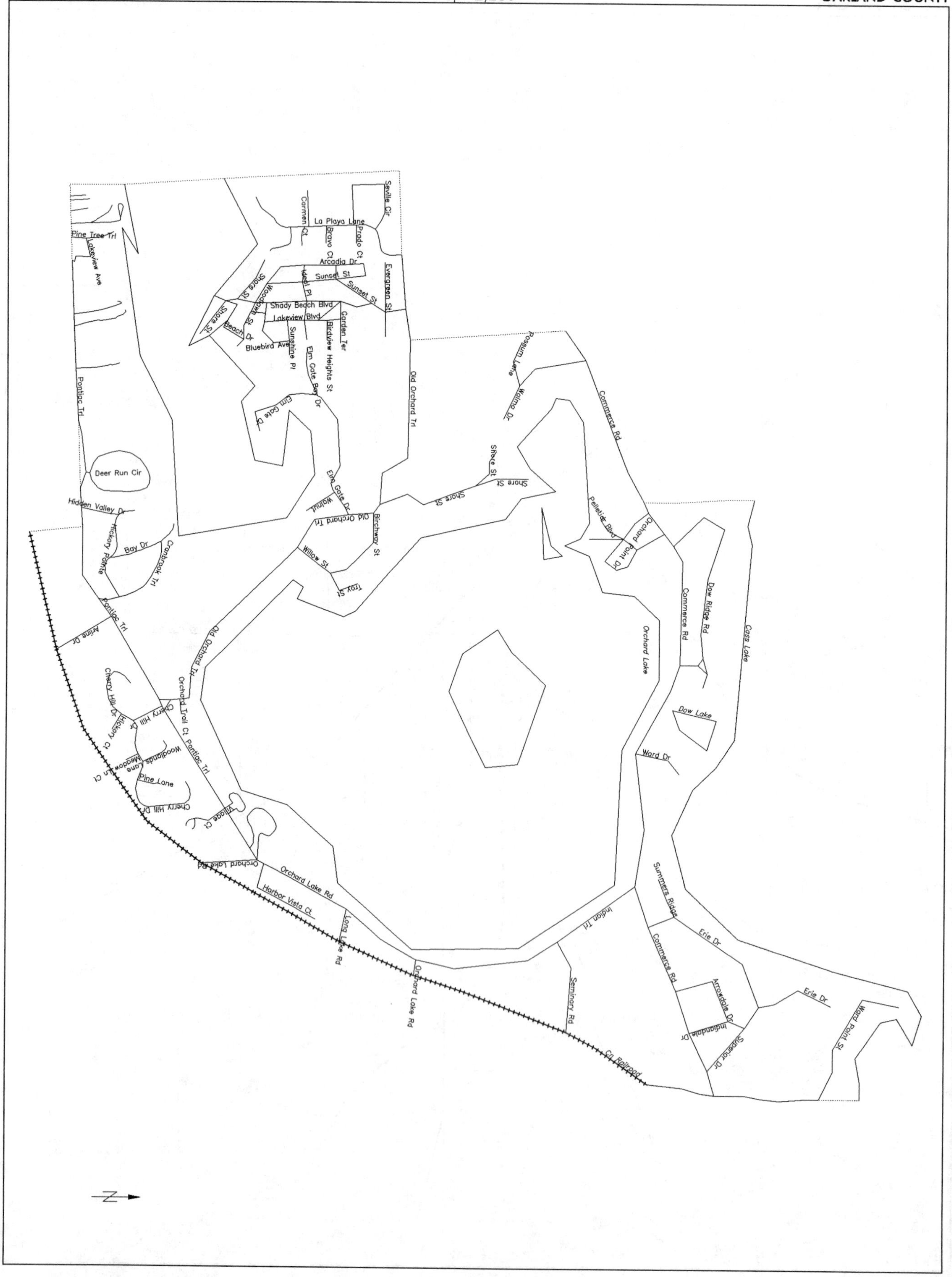

Pine Tree Trl
Lakeview Ave
Pontiac Trl
Deer Run Cir
Hidden Valley Dr
Hickory Pointe
Bay Dr
Cranbrook Trl
Carmen Ct
La Playa Lane
Bravo Ct
Prado Ct
Seville Cir
Arcadia Dr
Evergreen St
Sunset St
Shore St
Woodland St
Ideal Pl
Shady Beach Blvd
Lakeview Blvd
Beach Dr
Bluebird Ave
Sunshine Pl
Birdview Heights St
Garden Ter
Elm Gate Bay Dr
Elm Gate Ct
Old Orchard Trl
Elm Gate Dr
Walnut
Birchway St
Willow St
Troy St
Possum Lane
Walma Dr
Commerce Rd
Shore St
Pelletier Blvd
Orchard Point Dr
Dow Ridge Rd
Cass Lake
Orchard Lake
Dow Lake
Ward Dr
Arline Dr
Cherry Hill Dr
Hickory Ct
Cherry Hill Dr
Orchard Trail Ct
Pontiac Trl
Woodlands Lane
Meadow Ln Ct
Pine Lane
Cherry Hill Dr
Village Ct
Orchard Lake Rd
Harbor Vista Ct
Long Lake Rd
Orchard Lake Rd
Seminary Rd
Indian Trl
Summers Ridge
Erie Dr
Commerce Rd
Arrowdale Dr
Indiandale Dr
Superior Dr
Erie Dr
Ward Point St
Cn Railroad
N

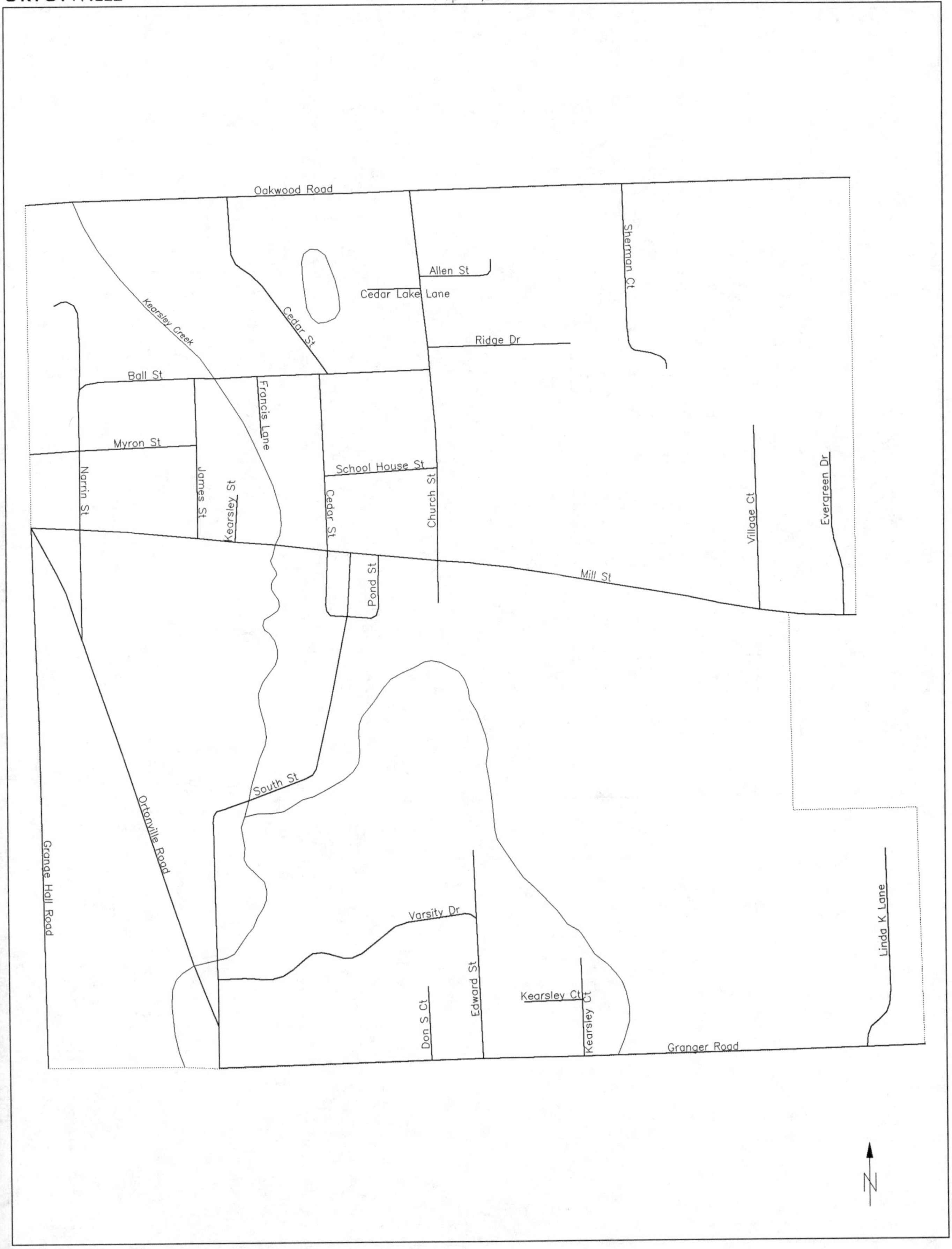

Oakwood Road
Sherman Ct
Allen St
Cedar Lake Lane
Kearsley Creek
Cedar St
Ridge Dr
Ball St
Francis Lane
Myron St
School House St
Narrin St
James St
Kearsley St
Cedar St
Church St
Village Ct
Evergreen Dr
Mill St
Pond St
South St
Ortonville Road
Grange Hall Road
Varsity Dr
Linda K Lane
Edward St
Kearsley Ct
Don S Ct
Kearsley Ct
Granger Road
N

Elizabeth St
Julia St
Catherine St
John St
Clyde St
Penn Central Railroad
Watson Road
Florence St
N Farmer St
Prospect St
Fairview St
E River St
Helen Ave
W River St
Kalamazoo River
Water St
Water St
W Allegan St
Court St
Wilmott St
Jewell St
W Orleans St
North St
Platt St
E Franklin St
Grant St
W Franklin St
Muriel St
Sherwood St
W Orleans St
Mitchell St
W Morrell St
W Franklin St
W Hammond St
Lincoln St
W Morrell St
Garfield St
Kalamazoo St
N Farmer St
Fair St
Walnut St
Mc Kinley St
Charles St
W Hammond St
Washington St
Platt St
Wilmott St
E Allegan St
Grant St
Conference St
Brookside Dr
Temple St
Dix St
Irving St
Allen St
Howard St
Clara St
Kay St
Lawrence Dr
16th St
15th St
Kay St
Sycamore St
Ridge St
Kay St
Windigo Lane
Kay St
N

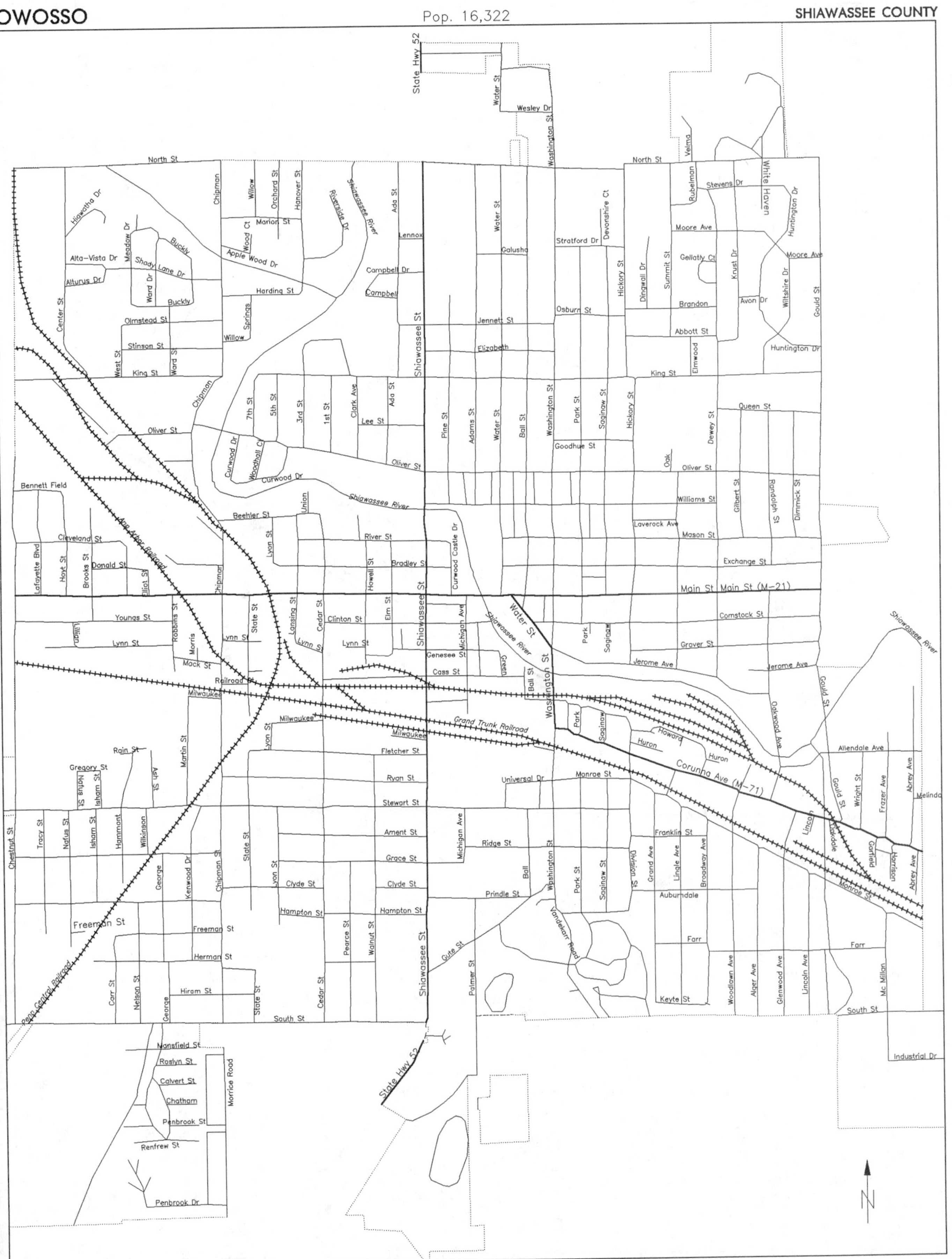

OXFORD

Pop. 2,929

OAKLAND COUNTY

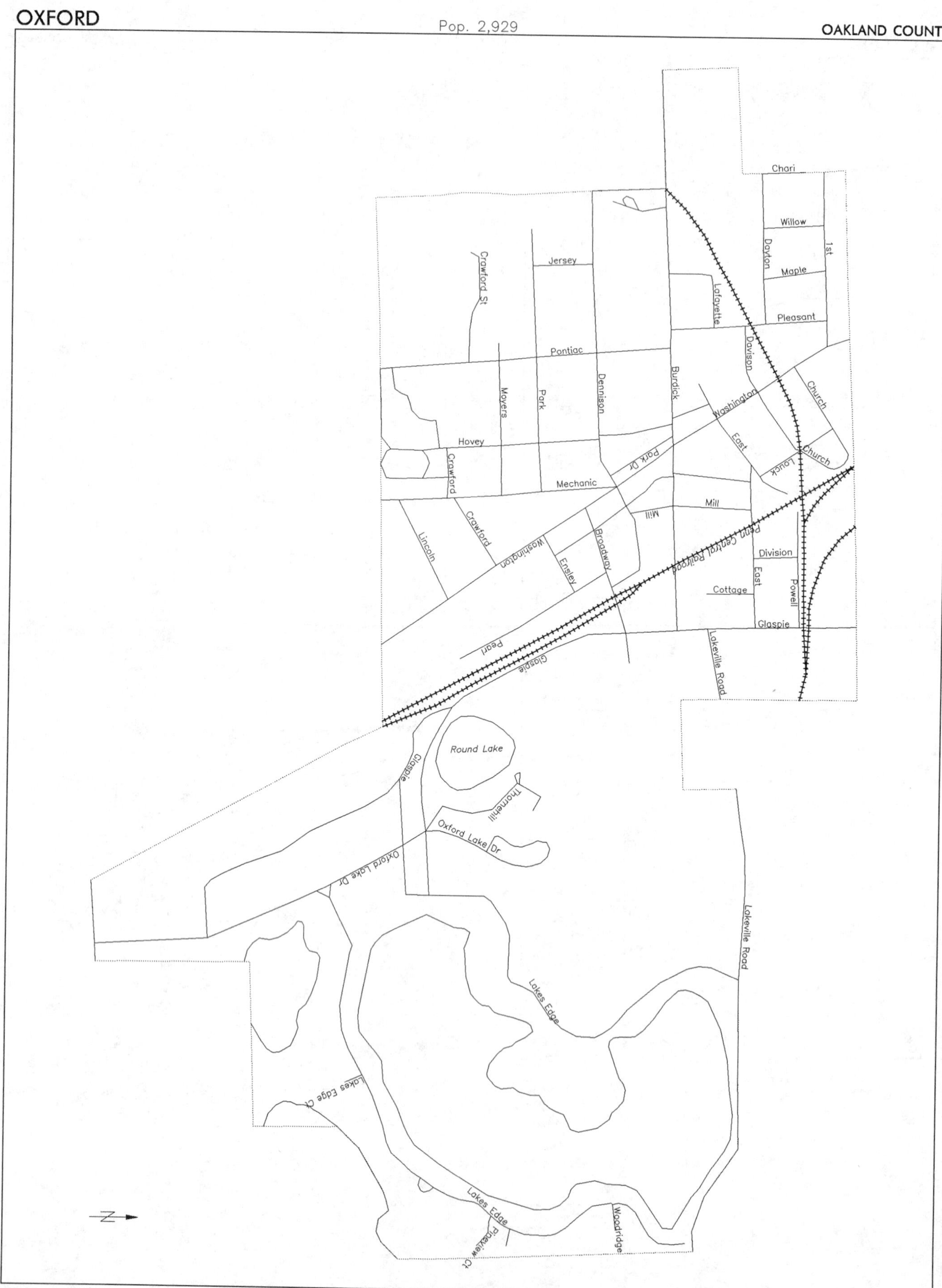

Kalamazoo River
Nyc Railroad
Lottie Ave
Maiden Dr
Eunice Ave
Hercules Ave
Island Ave
Commerce Ln
Link Ln
Mosel Ave
Shoppers Ln
Riverview Dr
Old Riverview Dr
Sanford St
Riverview Dr
Park Dr
Espanola Ave
Devon Ave
Sturgis Rd
Parchmount Ave
Riverview Dr
Keyes Dr
Church St
Elsmere St
Elmhurst Ave
Park Ave
Parchglen Pl
Oak Grove Ave
Hamilton Rd
Parkdale Blvd
Park Dr
Hubbard St
Glenguile Ave
Thomas St
Groveland Ave
Park Ave
Glendale Blvd
Vale Ave
Orient St
Spanish Rd
Orient St
Parchmount St
Haymac Dr
Clarnin St
N

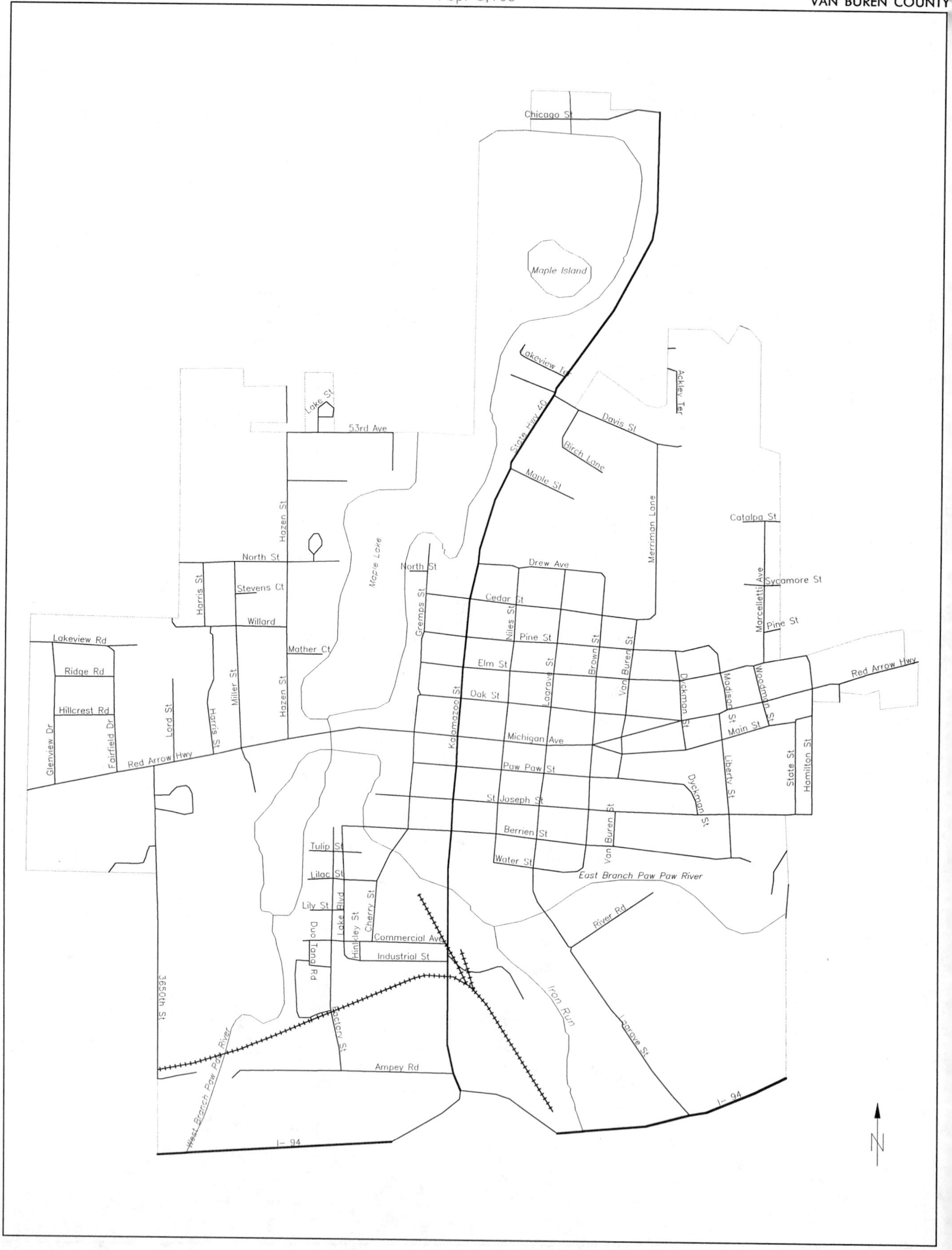

Chicago St
Maple Island
Lakeview Ter
Ackley Ter
Lake St
53rd Ave
State Hwy 40
Davis St
Birch Lane
Maple St
Hazen St
Merriman Lane
Catalpa St
North St
Maple Lake
North St
Drew Ave
Sycamore St
Marcelletti Ave
Stevens Ct
Harris St
Gremps St
Cedar St
Willard
Pine St
Lakeview Rd
Niles St
Pine St
Brown St
Van Buren St
Mather Ct
Ridge Rd
Elm St
Laarove St
Dyckman St
Madison St
Woodman St
Red Arrow Hwy
Miller St
Harris St
Hazen St
Lord St
Hillcrest Rd
Kalamazoo St
Oak St
Main St
Glenview Dr
Fairfield Dr
Red Arrow Hwy
Michigan Ave
Paw Paw St
Dyckman St
Liberty St
State St
Hamilton St
St Joseph St
Berrien St
Van Buren St
Tulip St
Water St
Lilac St
East Branch Paw Paw River
Cherry St
Lily St
Lake Blvd
Hinkley St
River Rd
Duo Tang Rd
Commercial Ave
Industrial St
Iron Run
365th St
Factory St
Laarove St
West Branch Paw Paw River
Ampey Rd
I- 94
I- 94
N

Campbell Park Rd
Sands St
Birch Ln
56th
Wythe St
Rush St
Morris St
3rd Ave
Hanover St
Hancock St
Oceana Dr
Park St
Concord St
Morris St
Mears
Plymouth
Dover St
Carroll St
Lowell St
Channel Ln
Green St
Bridge
Rush St
Washington St
Evergreen St
1st St
Ellery
Division St
2nd St
3rd St
Clymer St
Bay St
Spinaker Dr
4th St
4th St
Morris St
Manchester
Wythe St
Rutledge St
5th St
6th
Bean
Judd
Lake Rd
Russell
Old State Rd
Garrison
Garrison
Suffolk St
Bay St
Tamherst St
Orange
N

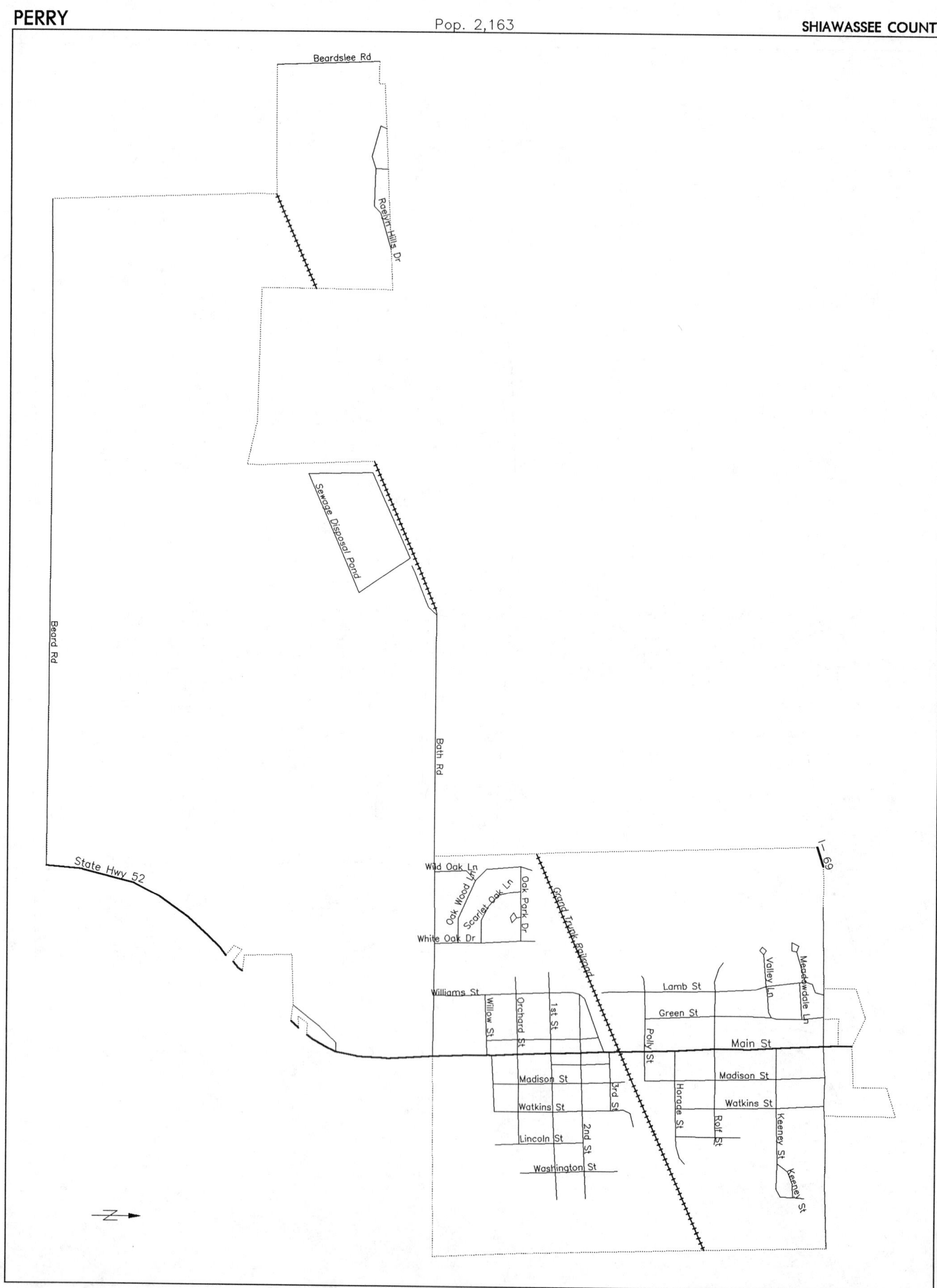
Beardslee Rd
Raelyn Hills Dr
Sewage Disposal Pond
Beard Rd
Bath Rd
State Hwy 52
Wild Oak Ln
Oak Wood Ln
Scarlet Oak Ln
Oak Park Dr
White Oak Dr
Grand Trunk Railroad
I-69
Williams St
Willow St
Orchard St
1st St
Lamb St
Green St
Polly St
Valley Ln
Meadowdale Ln
Main St
Madison St
Watkins St
3rd St
Horace St
Rolf St
Keeney St
Lincoln St
2nd St
Washington St

Petersburg Road
Wittman Dr
Ida West Road
River Raisin
Railroad St
Railroad St
Centre St
Elizabeth St
Division St
Washington St
Wood St
Elm St
Rose Road
Saline St
Walnut St
Forrest St
Chestnut St
Vessey St
Davis St
Division St
Madison St
Madison St
Saline St
Cass St
Albain Road
Saline St
Mc Neil Dr.
N

Pop. 6,056

Rosedale
Stuart
Belle Ave
Arlington Ave
Balsam Ave
McDonald Dr
US Hwy 31
Steuben Ave
Lafayette
Fairview
Sunset
Grand
Winter Park Lane
Lafayette
Rose
Bay
Quinlan
Lake
Jefferson
Lake
US Hwy 31
Lake
Division
Williams
Clinton
Summit
Lake
Kalamazoo
Bay View Ave
Mitchell
Mitchell
Lake
Madison
Madison
Grace
Wachtel Ave
Michigan
Michigan
Madison
Connable Ave
Ingalls Ave
Monroe
Liberty
Elizabeth
Emmet
Jackson
Jackson
Waukazoo
Woodland Ave
Harvey
State
Hill
Grove
Charlevoix Ave
Rush
Hoffman
Beech
Rush
Lockwood Ave
Kalamazoo Ave
Karamol Ave
Branch
Franklin
Mc Dowell
Pleasant
Bridge
Baxter
Petoskey
Lindell Ave
Lindell Ave
Lookout
Pearl
Washington
Sunset Ct
Porter
Cherry
Spencer
Jefferson Ave
Spruce
Selden Ave
Jennings Ave
Campus View
Valley View Ave
Klondike Ave
Curtis Ave
Tall Pine Ct
Sheridan
Petoskey
Myrtle
Hazelton
Mitchell
Spring St
Standish Ave
Wesley
Lawrence
Waukazoo
Ann
Howard
Krusel
Sheridan Road
Sheridan
Atkin
Highland Dr
Adalaide Ave
Regent Dr
C Hayner Dr
C Hayner Dr
Lakeview Ct
Grimes
Winfield Ave
Clarion
Willis Ave
Standish Ave
N

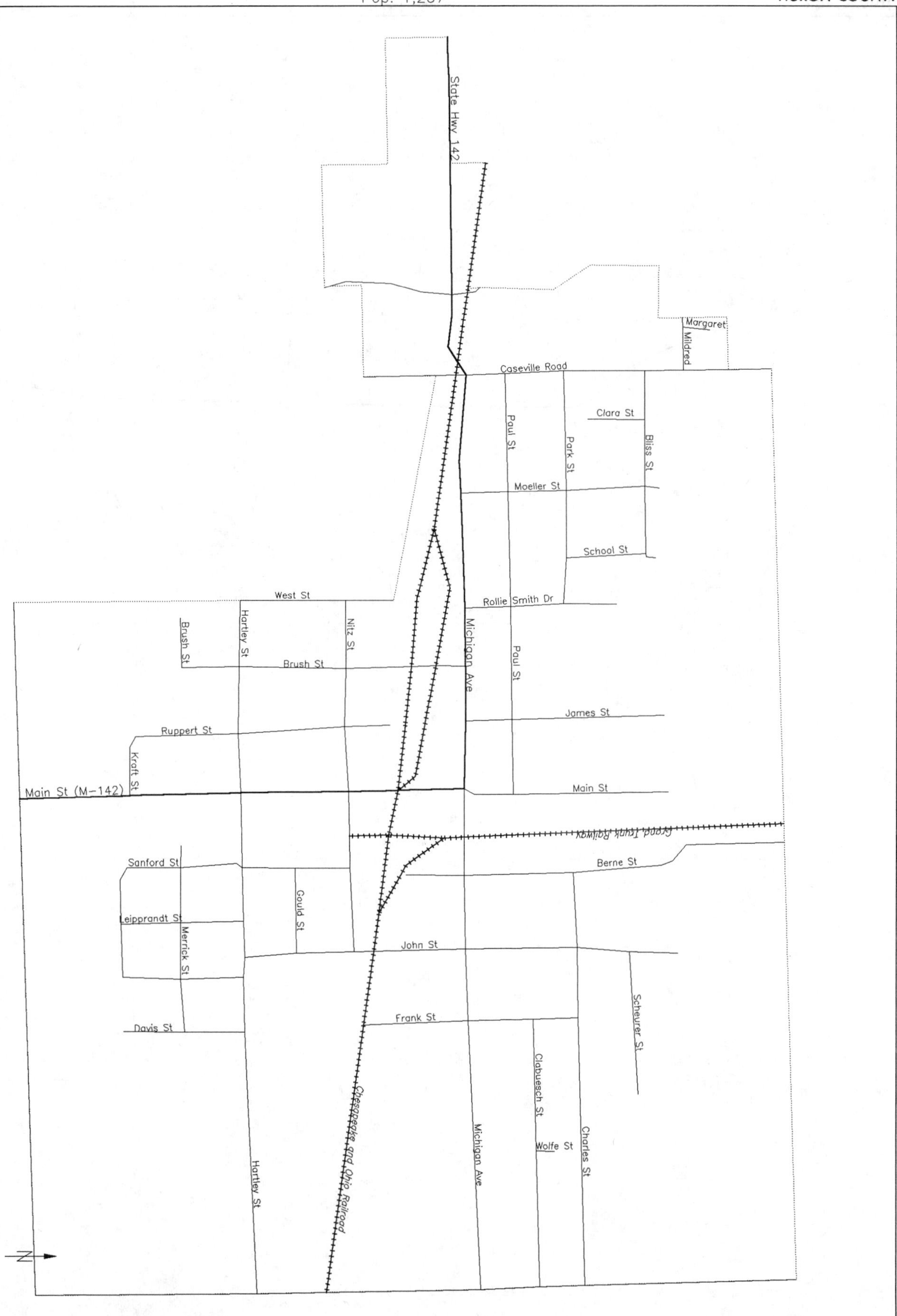
State Hwy 142
Margaret
Mildred
Caseville Road
Clara St
Paul St
Park St
Bliss St
Moeller St
School St
West St
Rollie Smith Dr
Hartley St
Brush St
Nitz St
Michigan Ave
Paul St
Brush St
James St
Ruppert St
Kraft St
Main St (M-142)
Main St
Grand Trunk Railway
Sanford St
Berne St
Gould St
Leipprandt St
Merrick St
John St
Scheurer St
Davis St
Frank St
Clabuesch St
Chesapeake and Ohio Railroad
Michigan Ave
Wolfe St
Charles St
Hartley St
N

Stream
Howell
Pearl
Old-RR-Grade
Old-RR-Grade
Depot St
Depot St
Mill St
Webb
Reeves
Rose St
Haze St
Coleman St
Magic St
Hamburg St
Hamburg St
Hamburg St
Pond
Main St (M-36)
Unadilla St
Unadilla St
Wm Portage St
Haze St
Mill St
Webster
Stuart St
Putnam St
Mann St
Park St
Main St
Marion St
Livingston St
Mill St
Dexter St
Stream
Fairwood Dr
Portage St
Water St
Honey Creek
Mower Road
Brentwood St
Knollwood
Pinckney Road
Vincent Dr
Howell St
Elizabeth Dr
Barbara Dr
Lee St
Lee St
Joan
Toma
Darwin Road
N

Whispering Pines
Mable St
Glenview Ct
Blondin St
Waters St
North St
Lawrence St
Penn Central Railroad
Horn St
Pinconning River
River St
River St
1st St
Manitou St
2nd St
2nd St
3rd St
3rd St
Whyte
Mercer St
Manitou St
Rhodes St
4th St
4th St
Arthur St
Libby St
Van Etten St
Kaiser St
Warren St
Waters St
Jennings St
5th St
6th St
6th St
Mable St
7th St
Bermuda
Oakwood
Rhodes St
8th St
Mary St
N

12th
US Hwy 131
State Hwy 89
Lisa Ave
Robin St
Curt St
Pinecrest Dr
Kim St
River Rd
S Sunset St
Kester St
W Bridge St
Melrose St
Benhoy St
Walnut Woods Ct
Naomi St
Fairlane St
Prince St
Court St
Cottage St
Michigan Ave
Gladys St
Hill St
Gilkey St
Prospect St
Warrant
Brigham St
Plainwell St
Grant St
Chart St
Union St
Cedar St
Kalamazoo River
1st Ave
Penn Central Railroad
Jersey St
Morrel St
2nd Ave
Park St
Brighton St
Wedgewood Dr
Mill Race
Main
Allegan
Water
Bannister
Thomas St
Anderson St
Cushman
Woodhams St
Sherwood Ave
Glenview Cir
Washington Ave
Cherry Wood Dr
Russet Dr
Hicks Ave
Sterling St
Kenwood Ave
Oak St
Marietta St
Floral Ave
Prairie St
Orchard St
Broad St
1st Division St
Forbes St
Roberts St
Pennsylvania Railroad
Acorn
Acorn St
Maple St
Bridge
2nd Division
Industrial Pkwy
Lincoln Pkwy
Locust St
Gray
8th

Maplefield Road
Oakdale Blvd
Cambridge Blvd
Hanover Road
Norwich Road
Kenberton Dr
Woodside Park Dr
Ridge Road
Millington Road
Poplar Park Blvd
Elm Park Blvd
Oakland Park Blvd
Oxford Blvd
Cambridge Blvd
Main St
Woodward Ave
Devonshire Road
Kensington Blvd
10 Mile Road
Indiana Ave
Woodward Heights Blvd
Maywood Ave
Wellesley Dr
Bermuda Ave
Gainsborough Ave
Barber Ave
Bermuda Ave

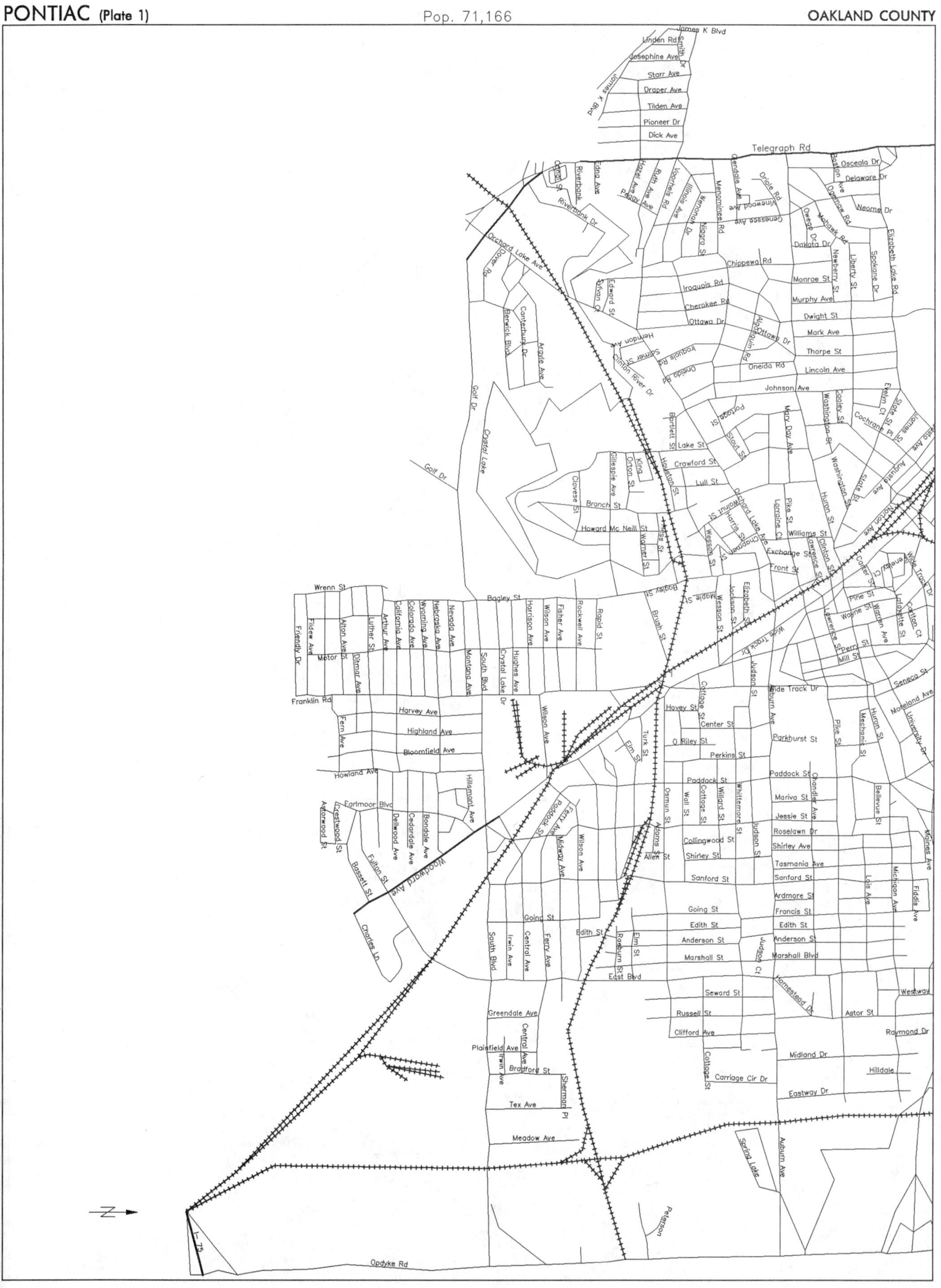

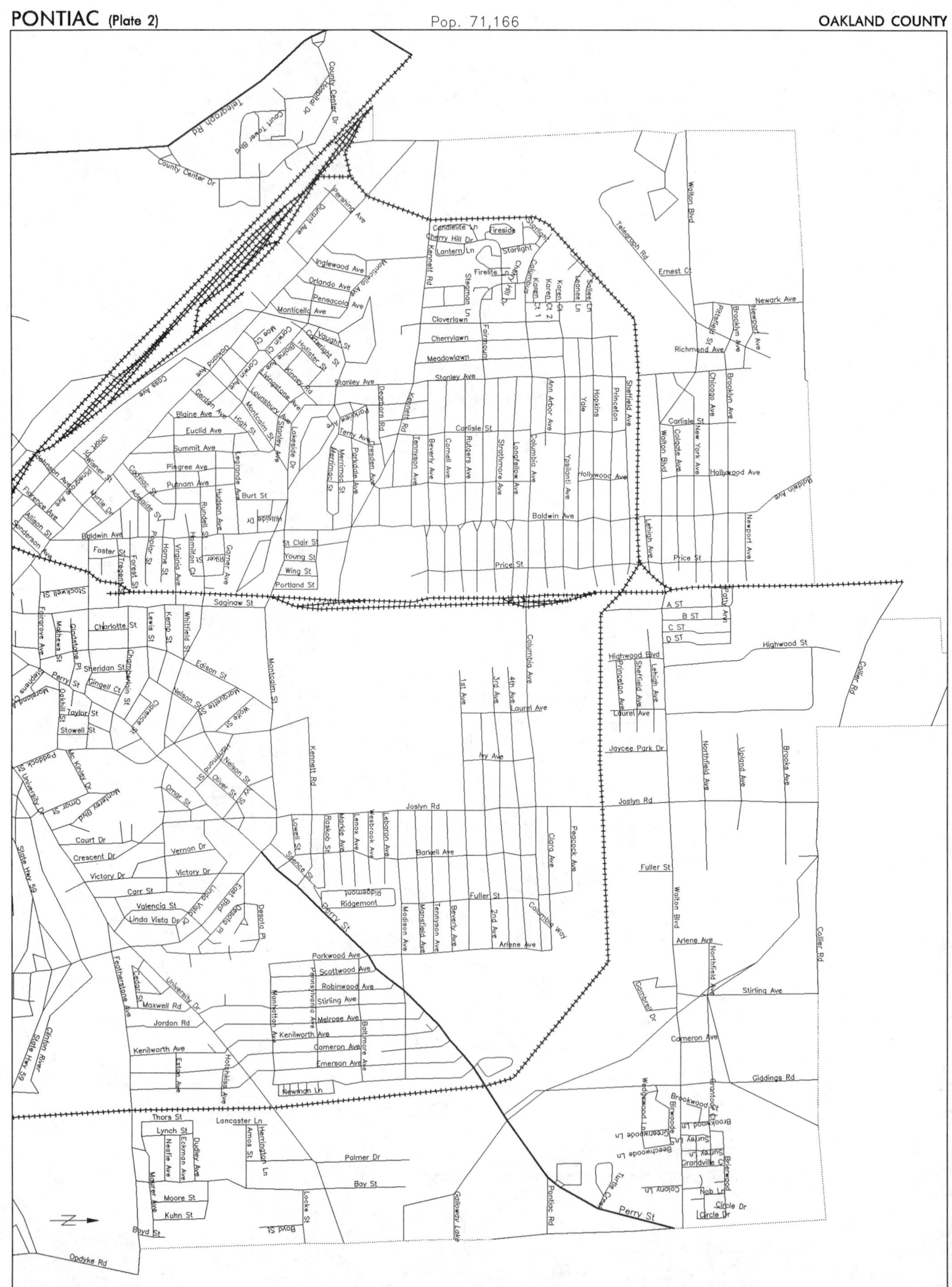

I- 94
Angling Rd
Milham Rd
US Hwy 131
Plate # 1
Constitution Blvd
Westnedge Ave
Portage Rd
Milham Rd
Plate # 3
Plate # 2
Romence Rd
12th
Oakland Dr
Sprinkle Rd
Long Lake
West Lake
Plate # 4
Plate # 5
Plate # 6
Austin Lake
Portage Rd
Westnedge Ave
Osterhout Ave
Osterhout Ave
Shaver Rd
12th
NE
SE
N

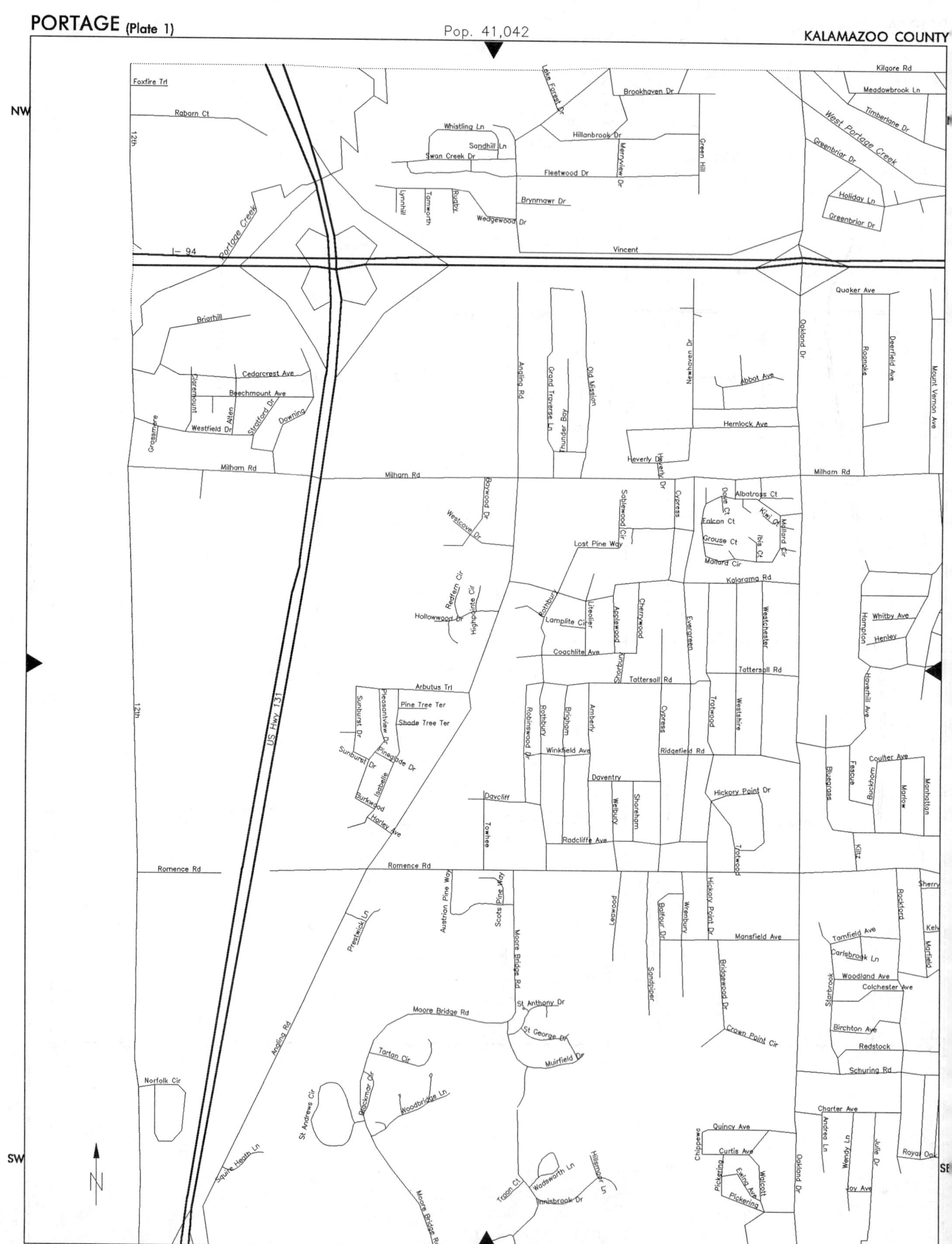
NW
SW
Kilgore Rd
Meadowbrook Ln
Timberlane Dr
West Portage Creek
Greenbriar Dr
Holiday Ln
Foxfire Trl
Raborn Ct
12th
Lake Forest Dr
Brookhaven Dr
Whistling Ln
Hillanbrook Dr
Sandhill Ln
Swan Creek Dr
Merryview Dr
Green Hill
Fleetwood Dr
Lynnhill
Tamworth
Rugby
Brynmawr Dr
Wedgewood Dr
Portage Creek
I-94
Vincent
Quaker Ave
Briarhill
Oakland Dr
Newhaven Dr
Roanoke
Deerfield Ave
Mount Vernon Ave
Cedarcrest Ave
Claremount
Beechmount Ave
Angling Rd
Grand Traverse Ln
Thunder Bay
Old Mission
Abbot Ave
Alten
Stratford Dr
Downing
Westfield Dr
Grassmere
Hemlock Ave
Heverly Dr
Milham Rd
Baywood Dr
Sablewood Cir
Cypress
Albatross Ct
Dove Ct
Kiwi Ct
Mallard Cir
Westcove Dr
Falcon Ct
Grouse Ct
Ibis Ct
Lost Pine Way
Mallard Cir
Kalarama Rd
Redfern Cir
Highpointe Cir
Hollowwood Dr
Rothbury
Lamplite Cir
Litelolier
Applewood
Cherrywood
Evergreen
Westchester
Whitby Ave
Hampton
Henley
Coachlite Ave
Shorebury
Tattersall Rd
Haverhill Ave
Arbutus Trl
Pine Tree Ter
Shade Tree Ter
Sunburst Dr
Pleasantview Dr
Robinswood Dr
Rothbury
Brigham
Amberly
Cypress
Trolwood
Westshire
US Hwy 131
Pineglade Dr
Winkfield Ave
Ridgefield Rd
Bluegrass
Fescue
Coulter Ave
Buckhorn
Marlow
Manhattan
Isabelle
Daventry
Burkwood
Harley Ave
Daycliff
Welbury
Shoreham
Hickory Point Dr
Towhee
Radcliffe Ave
Trolwood
Kiltz
Romence Rd
Austrian Pine Way
Scots Pine Way
Leewood
Balfour Dr
Wrenbury
Hickory Point Dr
Sherry
Rockford
Kelv
Morfield
Prestwick Ln
Moore Bridge Rd
Mansfield Ave
Tamfield Ave
Carlsbrook Ln
Sandpiper
Bridgewood Dr
Woodland Ave
Colchester Ave
Starbrook
St Anthony Dr
Moore Bridge Rd
St George Dr
Birchton Ave
Redstock
Crown Point Cir
Tartan Cir
Muirfield Dr
Schuring Rd
Angling Rd
Norfolk Cir
Brockmar Dr
Woodbridge Ln
Charter Ave
St Andrews Cir
Quincy Ave
Andrea Ln
Wendy Ln
Julie Dr
Chippewa
Curtis Ave
Royal Oak
Oakland Dr
Hillsmoor Ln
Squire Heath Ln
Wadsworth Ln
Troon Ct
Pickering
Ewing Ave
Walcott
Joy Ave
Innisbrook Dr
Pickering
Moore Bridge Rd
N

Kilgore Rd
Meadowbrook Ln
Morningside Dr
Cobble Stone
Stonehenge Dr
Timberlane
Walnut Tree Ter
Mapleridge Dr
Bronson Blvd
Woodheath Ave
Old Colony Rd
Grosse Pointe
Phomcroft Ave
Chalfonte Ave
Grandmarais Ave
Dukeshire Ave
Holiday Ln
West Portage Creek
Dehaan Dr
Clara
Landsdowne Ave
Midfield Dr
Ridgebrook Dr
Brennerton Dr
Windridge Dr
Sunview Ave
Andy Ave
Wisteria
Plateau
Azalea
Woodmont Dr
Garden Rd
Indian Rd
Bender Rd
Evans
Fairfield Rd
I-94
Byrd Dr
Eckener Dr
Ivanhoe Dr
Helen Ave
Winters Dr
NE
Hamelink Dr
Kingsbury Dr
Friendly Ave
Alice
Connecticut Dr
New Hampshire Dr
Burnwood Ave
Dawnlee Ave
Tudor Cir
Westhedge Ave
Idaho Ave
Mount Vernon Ave
Monticello Ave
Utah Ave
Nevada Ave
Dakota Ave
Iowa Ave
Missouri Ave
Ohio Ave
Georgia Ave
Vermont Ave
Boston Ave
Van Hoesen Blvd
Colonial Ave
Oregon Ave
Milham Rd
Bradford
Marlow
Constitution Blvd
Sunbright Ave
Pecan Ave
Flamingo Ave
Southland Ave
Windsor Ln
Alfa Ct
Alfa Ct
Bravo Ct
Delta Ct
Echo Ct
Foxtrot Ct
Newport Rd
Devon
Avon
Surrey
Warwick
Sussex
Regina Ave
Peachtree
Date
Victoria Ct
Lawton Ct
Jason Ct
Thomas Ct
Independence Dr
Mall Dr
Charlie Ct
Portage Creek
Lovers Ln
M L King Dr
C Penny Dr
Crossroads Dr
Della
Ruth
Naomi
Ramona Ave
Crossroads Mall Ring Rd
Rainbow Ave
Jail Hudson Dr
Lansing Ave
Gertrude Dr
Lineman Ave
Kromdyke Ave
Hardwick Ave
Manhattan
Windemere
Cromwell
Arrow Ave
Brotcher
Cornell
Keystone
Sears Dr
Cameo Ave
Dorset
Gernaat Ct
West Rd
Castlewood Ave
Mein Ct
West Rd
Sherry Ave
Winter Forest Dr
Kelvere Ave
Marfield
Woodland Ave
Oakbrook Cir
Bluebrook Dr
Portage Creek
Garden Ln
Garden Ln
Redstock
Gregg Ln
Lamar Ct
Quail
Schuring Rd
Sandy Ridge
Arborcrest
Hampton Oaks Dr
Ravenswood Dr
Curry Ln
Timbercreek Ct
Whispering Brook Cir
Portage Creek
Kingston Dr
Lakewood Dr
Garden Ln
Ludgate Ln
Lasalle
Vaucelles
Drury Ln
Drury Ln
Garden Ln
Portage Creek
Royal Oak Ave
SE
N
Kenmur Dr
Portage Creek
Shaver Rd
NYC Railroad
Library Ln
Brown Ave
Currier Dr
Cent
Engel Ct

PORTAGE (Plate 3)

Pop. 41,042

KALAMAZOO COUNTY

PORTAGE (Plate 4) Pop. 41,042 KALAMAZOO COUNTY

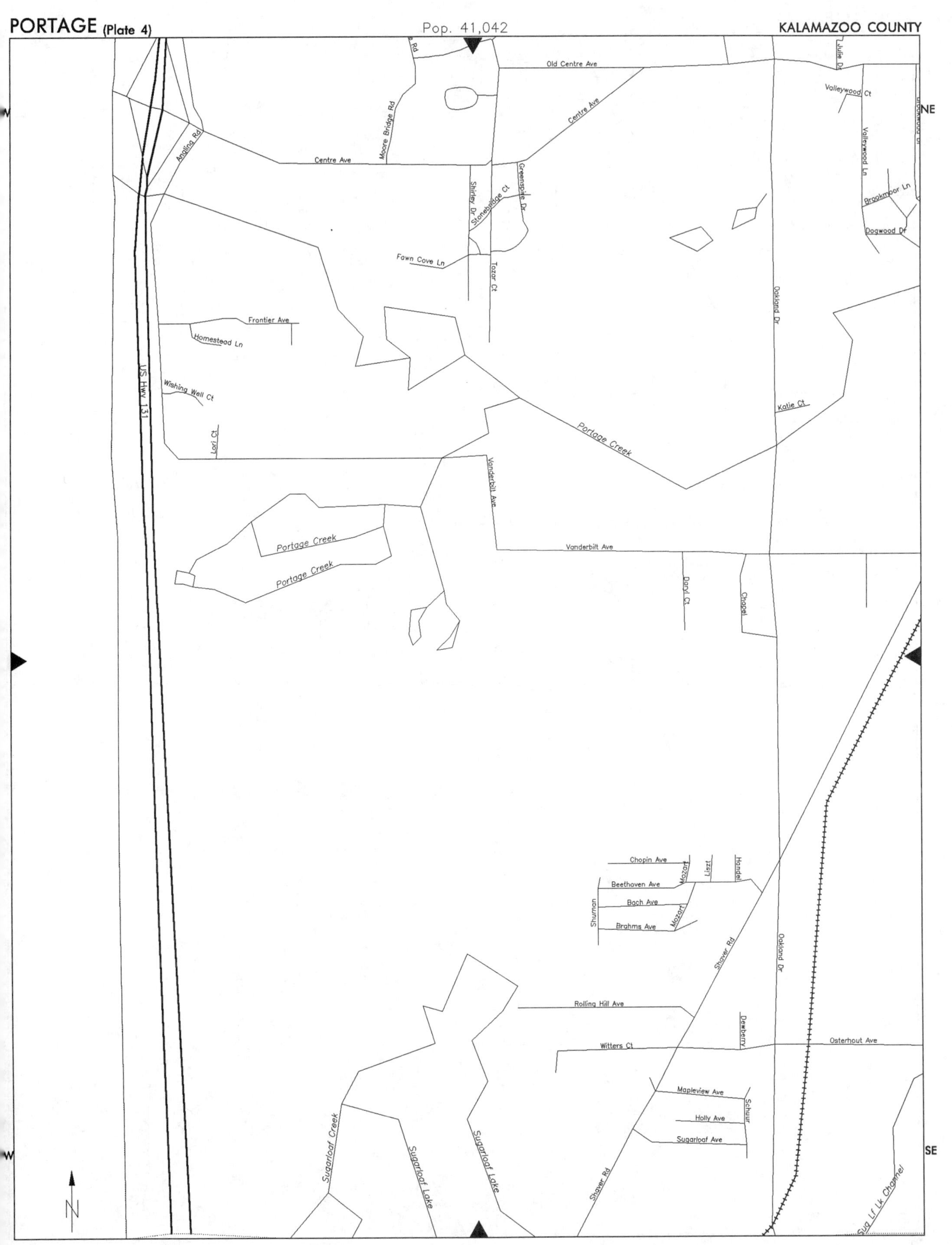

PORTAGE (Plate 5)

Pop. 41,042

KALAMAZOO COUNT

Centre Ave
Pleasant Dr
Prosperity Dr
Coxs Dr
Fireside Ave
Zylman Ave
Zylman Ave
Sylvan Ct
Edgewater Dr
Constance Rd
Carrie Ln
Coxs Dr
Highland Dr
Florinda
Woodedge Ln
Austin Lake
Balmoral
Biscayne Ave
Windwood
Gray
Shore Dr
Mahoney
Long Lake
Pompano Ave
Lum
Portage Rd
Ward Ave
Austin Dr
Hayes
Mc Clish Ct
Wells
Ames Dr
Long Lake Rd
Austin Dr
Long Lake Rd
Emily Ave
Clarence Dr
Sprinkle Rd
Burt Dr
Dixie Dr
Branch Ave
Barry Ct
Woodbine Ave
Sprinkle Rd
Stanley Ave
Woodlawn Dr
Kenneth Ct
Nash Ave
Woodlawn Dr
Woodhams Ave
Austin Lake Drain
Woody Knoll Dr
Shore Dr
Andrews
N
NE
SE
W

NOTES

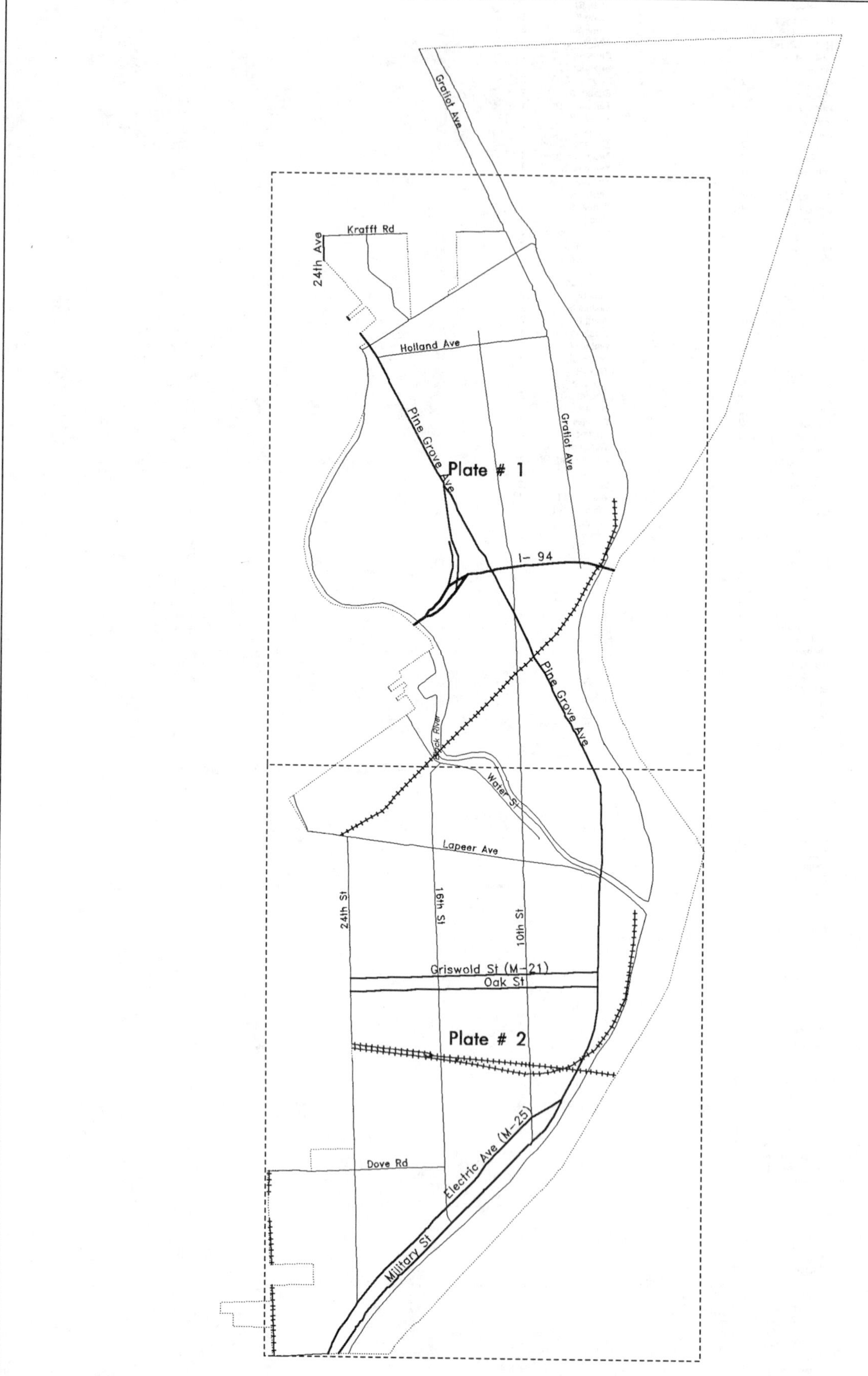
Gratiot Ave
Krafft Rd
24th Ave
Holland Ave
Pine Grove Ave
Plate # 1
Gratiot Ave
I- 94
Pine Grove Ave
Black River
Water St
Lapeer Ave
24th St
16th St
10th St
Griswold St (M-21)
Oak St
Plate # 2
Electric Ave (M-25)
Dove Rd
Military St
N

Gratiot Ave
Krafft Rd
24th Ave
Glenview Ct
Tamarack Dr
Birch
Jackpine Ln
Butternut Dr
Butternut Ct
Oak Hills Ct
Black River Canal
Ramblewood Dr
Holland Park Ln
Continental Ct
Williamsburg Dr
Shenandoah Ave
Devonshire
Appomattox Ave
Coventry
Old Squire
Briarwood Dr
Holland Ave
Walnut St
Lasalle Blvd
Maple St
Cherry St
Armour St
Conger St
Sherman Ct
10th Ave
Edison Blvd
San Born St
Jones Pl
Poplar St
Elk St
Florida Ave
Hollis St
Bonhomme Ct
Ballentine St
Lakeview Ave
Wright St
Omar St
Woodland Dr
Hickory Ln
Concord
Colonial
Pine Grove Ave
Joann Ct
Palmer Ct
Stone St
Alden Ct
Village
Brandywine Ln
15th Ave
12th Ave
Copper
11th
Homer Pl
Monticello Dr
Village Ln
Wilbur St
17th Ave
16th Ave
Schumaker
Garfield St
Riverside Dr
20th Ave
19th Ave
18th Ave
Riverview St
13th
Myrtle St
Forest St
Hancock St
Russell Ct
Church St
Elmwood St
Woodstock Dr
22nd Ave
21st Ave
Church
Canal Dr
Riverwood Dr
I- 94
State St
Harker St
Scenic Ct
Riverwood Ct
Mansfield St
St Clair St
Scott Ave
Thomas Edison Pkwy
Lyon St
Riverside Ave
Willow
Mc Pherson St
Mc Brady
Whipple St
Thomas St
Sedgwick St
Washington Ave
Michigan
Richardson St
Kearney St
Lincoln Ave
Rawlins St
Erie St
Ontario St
Superior St
Huron Ave
Taylor St
Water St
Kern St
Rural St
N

Stanton St
Sherman St
Runnels St
Taylor St
Nelson St
Glenwood Ave
Locust
Carleton St
Beers St
Gordon St
Young
Spruce St
Botsford St
Rural St
17th St
10th Ave
Stone St
Ontario St
Bard St
Francis St
Ward St
John L St
Varney Ave
River St
Erie St
Andrew Murphy Ave
Wells St
Wells St
Mc Morran Blvd
Miller St
Crescent
Grand River Ave
Lapeer Ave
Farrand St
Pearl St
Lapeer Ct
Quay St
22nd St
Martin
Katherine St
Jenks St
Cross Pointe Dr
Fort St
Merchant
Farley St
18th St
Gillett St
9 1/2 St
Howard St
20th St
Pine St
3rd St
19th St
24th St
Wall St
Military St
Court St
18th St
17th St
16th St
15th St
14th St
13th St
12th St
11th St
10th St
9th St
8th St
7th St
6th St
4th St
Union St
Chestnut St
23rd St
22nd St
21st St
White St
Griswold St
Oak St
Way St
Division St
Minnie St
Bancroft St
Cypress St
Cypress St
Tunnel St
Cedar St
Jenkinson St
Johnstone St
Petit St
15th St
14th St
13th St
22nd St
Beard St
8th St
11th St
9th St
Columbus St
Vanderburg Pl
Chadwick Ave
12th St
20th St
16th St
Susan Ct
11th St
Westrick Dr
Center Rd
Dove Rd
Mason Ave
26th St
24th St
23rd St
16th St
30th St
Cleveland Ave
Belmar Pl
28th St
27th St
25th St
22nd St
Nern St
Manuel St
Thornhill
Grant Pl
Vanness St
Vanness St
Parkdale
Lakewood
Little St
Parkdale
29th St
Electric Ave
Moak St
Buena Vista
Goulden St
30th St
Conner St
31st St
North Blvd
Military St
South Blvd
Peavey St
30th St
29th St
Sturges St
Barlow St
Ravenswood Rd
N

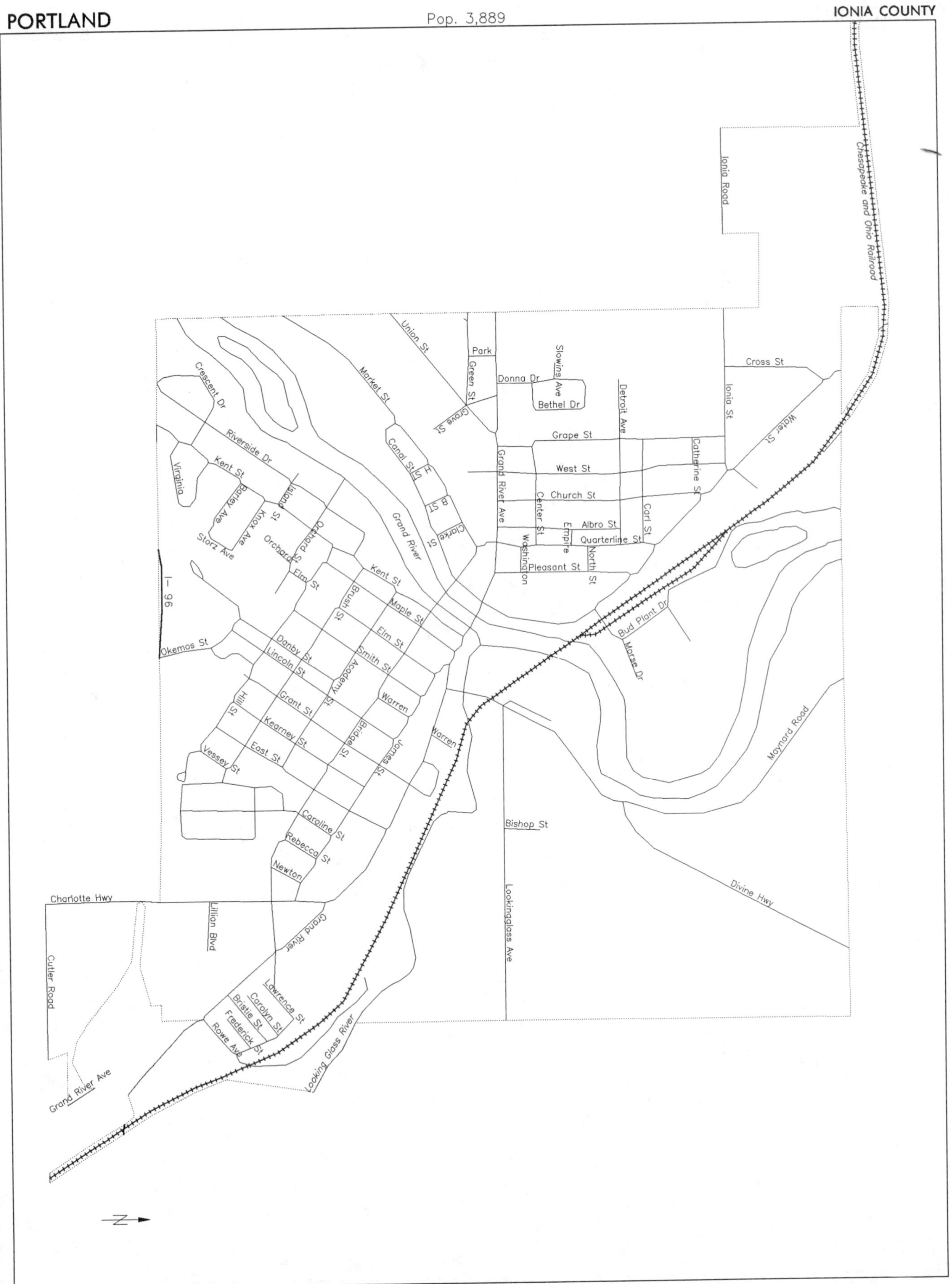
Chesapeake and Ohio Railroad
Ionia Road
Union St
Park
Green St
Slowins Ave
Donna Dr
Bethel Dr
Cross St
Ionia St
Detroit Ave
Market St
Grove St
Crescent Dr
Grape St
Water St
Riverside Dr
Canal St
Kent St
Virginia
West St
Catherine St
Grand River Ave
Church St
Island St
Barley Ave
Knox Ave
Grand River
Center St
Albro St
Carl St
Empire
Quarterline St
Clarke
Orchard St
Storz Ave
Orchard St
Washington
Pleasant St
North St
Elm St
Kent St
I–96
Brush St
Maple St
Bud Plant Dr
Elm St
Morse Dr
Okemos St
Danby St
Lincoln St
Smith St
Academy St
Hill St
Grant St
Warren
Kearney St
Bridge St
Warren
Maynard Road
East St
Vessey St
James St
Caroline St
Bishop St
Rebecca St
Newton
Divine Hwy
Charlotte Hwy
Lillian Blvd
Grand River
Lookingglass Ave
Cutler Road
Lawrence St
Carolyn St
Bristie St
Frederick St
Rowe Ave
Looking Glass River
Grand River Ave
N

POTTERVILLE

Pop. 1,523

EATON COUNTY

Belle St
Grand Blvd
Lake Blvd
West St
US Hwy 12
Taylor St
Berry St
Bond St
Bennett St
Arnold St
Church St
Pleasant St
Jefferson St
Liberty St
Maiden Ln
Park St
Cole St
Hewitt St
Broughton
Ray Quincy Road
Main St
Wood Ave
Orange St
Depot St
Park St
Hawley St
Jackson St
Glenn Ave
Fulton St
Colfax St
Bagley Creek
Daley
Hillsdale County Railway Co.
Hawley St
Grove St
Brown St
Chicago St

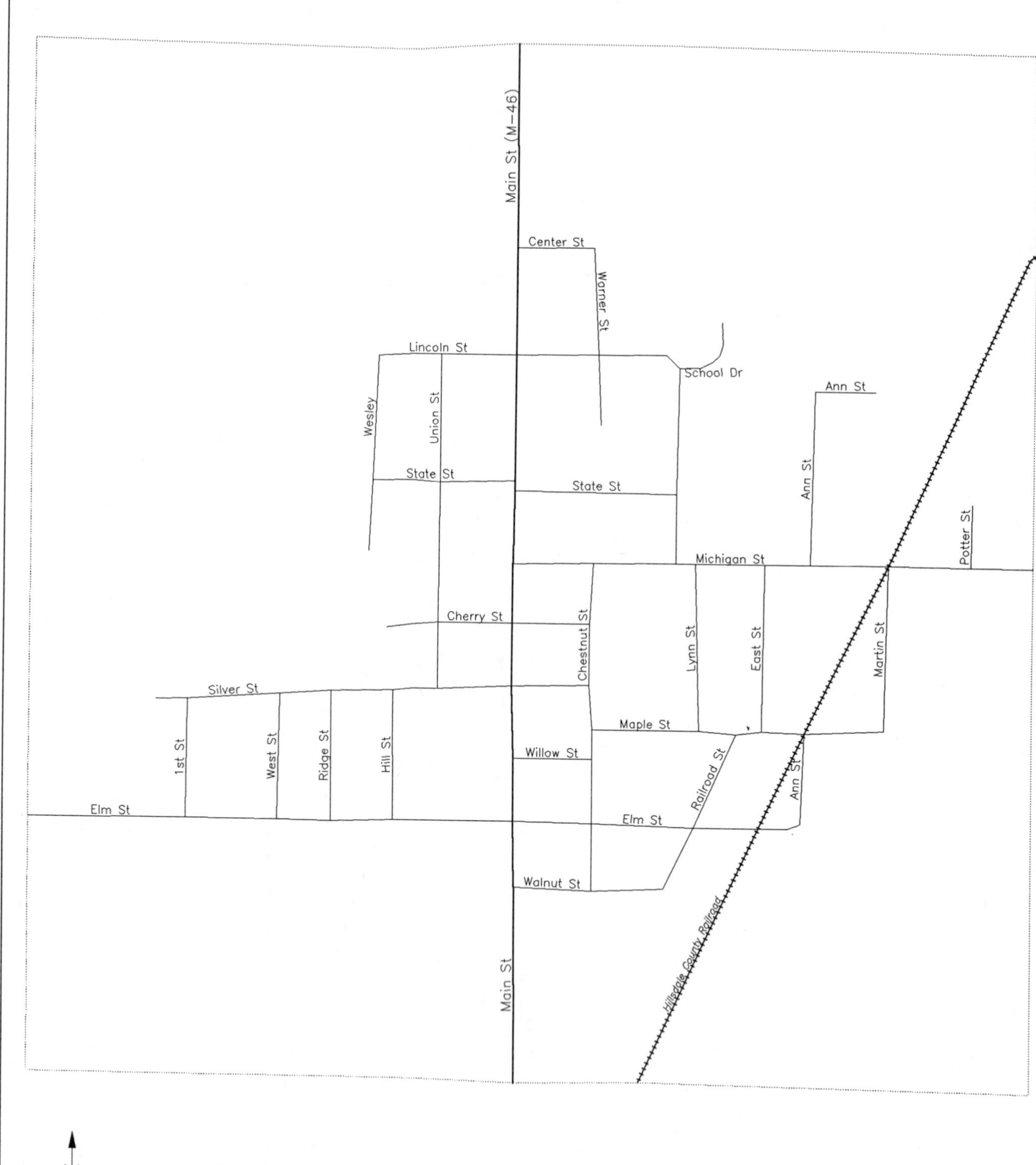
Main St (M-46)
Center St
Warner St
Lincoln St
School Dr
Ann St
Wesley
Union St
State St
State St
Ann St
Potter St
Michigan St
Cherry St
Chestnut St
Lynn St
East St
Martin St
Silver St
Maple St
1st St
West St
Ridge St
Hill St
Willow St
Railroad St
Ann St
Elm St
Elm St
Walnut St
Main St
Hillsdale County Railroad
N

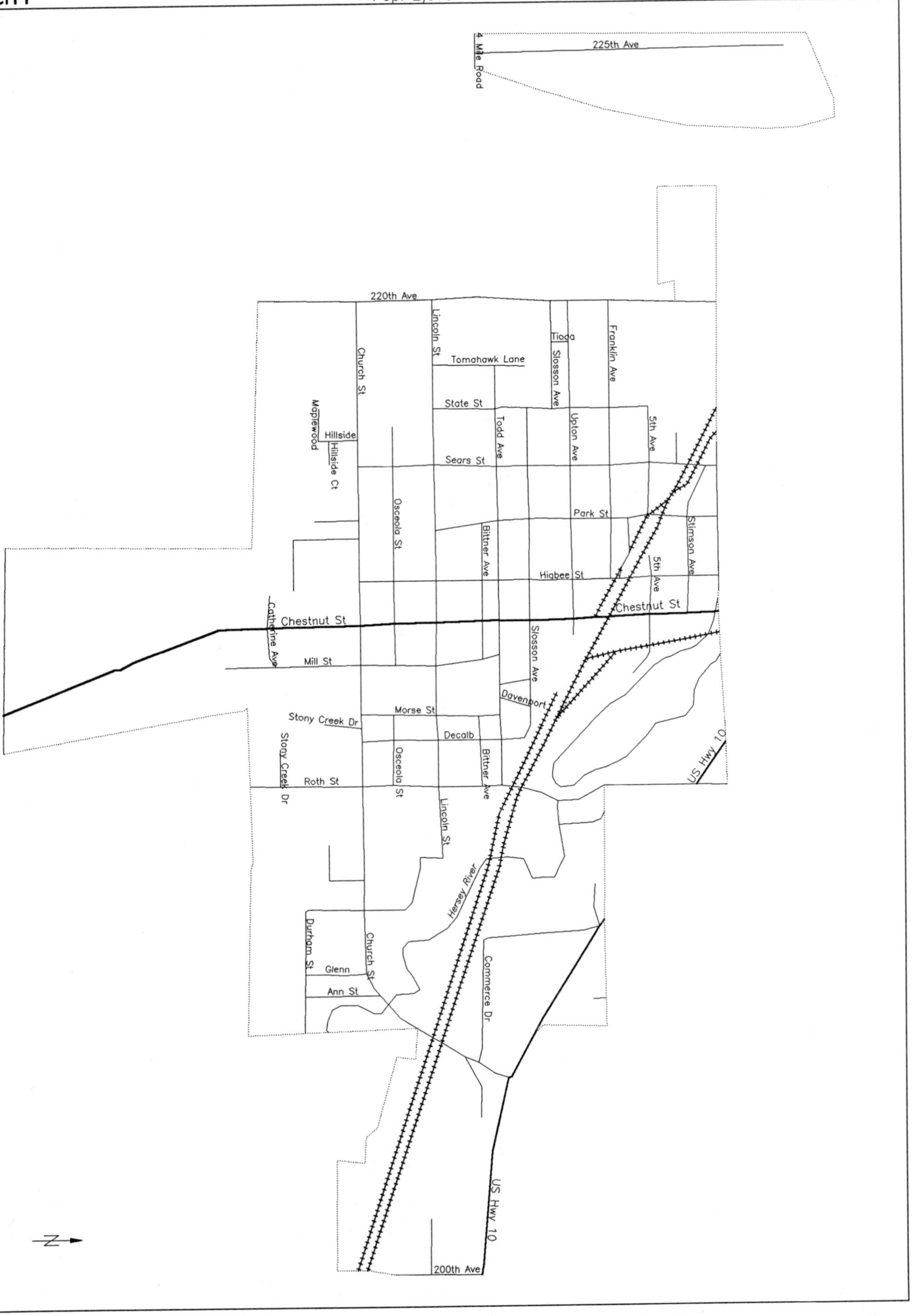

225th Ave
4 Mile Road
220th Ave
Lincoln St
Church St
Tioga
Franklin Ave
Tomahawk Lane
Slosson Ave
State St
Maplewood
Hillside
Hillside Ct
Todd Ave
Upton Ave
5th Ave
Sears St
Osceola St
Park St
Bittner Ave
Stimson Ave
Higbee St
5th Ave
Chestnut St
Catherine Ave
Chestnut St
Slosson Ave
Mill St
Davenport
Morse St
Stony Creek Dr
Decalb
Stony Creek Dr
Osceola St
Bittner Ave
US Hwy 10
Roth St
Lincoln St
Hersey River
Durham St
Church St
Glenn
Commerce Dr
Ann St
US Hwy 10
200th Ave
N

Pop. 1,414

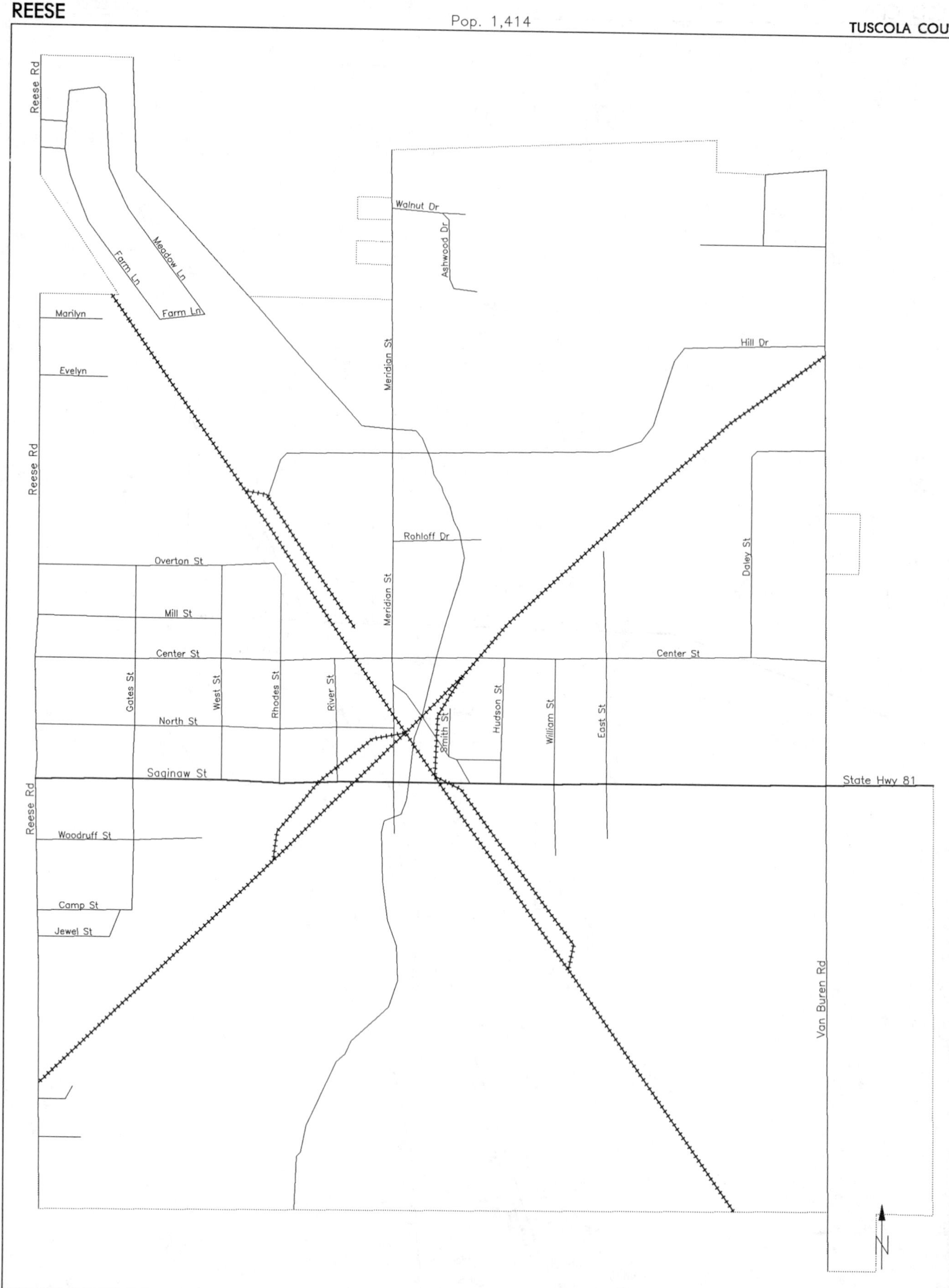
Reese Rd
Meadow Ln
Farm Ln
Farm Ln
Walnut Dr
Ashwood Dr
Marilyn
Evelyn
Meridian St
Hill Dr
Reese Rd
Rohloff Dr
Overton St
Daley St
Mill St
Meridian St
Center St
Center St
Gates St
West St
Rhodes St
River St
Hudson St
William St
East St
Smith St
North St
Saginaw St
State Hwy 81
Reese Rd
Woodruff St
Camp St
Jewel St
Van Buren Rd
N

33 Mile Rd
Willow Ln
Pound Rd
Pound Rd
Gillette Drain
Chaucer Dr
Canterbury Dr
Pierce Dr
Pierce Dr
Karen St
Main St
Canterbury Dr
Madison St
Ferguson
Jefferson St
Circle Dr
Washington St
Ridge St
Churchill St
Bernard
Park St
Monroe St
Walnut St
Parker St
Water St
Emma Dr
Florence
Skinner Dr
Beebe St
Stone St
Forest Ave
Burke Dr
Grove St
Division St
32 Mile Rd
Howard St
Bartell St
Priestap St
Dow St
Seymour Ln
Rosewood Ln
Stoecker Ln
Mary St
Beier St
Beech St
Oakwood Ln
Friday
Lenon
Howard St
Lakeview Ln
Clarkston Ln
Fitzgerald
Mert
Ow
Howard St
Main St
Gleason Ln
Richwood Ln
Gierk St
Diane Ln
Chaskey Ave
31 Mile Rd
State Hwy 19
N

Campbell Ave
Hall Road
Morrow Ave
Lenoir Ave
Superior Ave
Visger Road
Eaton Ave
Coriston Ave
Palmerston Dr
Kleinow Ave
Polk Ave
Holford Ave
Melvin Ave
Campbell Ave
Frazier Ave
Beechwood Ave
Bromley Ave
Hart Ave
Kleinow Ave
Pleasant Ave
Florence Ave
Le Blanc Ave
Elizabeth Ave
Fairmont Ave
Ermine St
Summit Ave
Cora Ave
Nieman Ave
Great Lakes Ave
Louis Ave
Burke Ave
Rulof St
Haltiner Ave
Coolidge Hwy
Charles St
Dwight Ave
Henry St
Linden St
Orchard Ave
Genessee St
Chestnut St
Myrtle Ave
Furgason St
Forest Ave
Hill Ave
Stoner Ave
Perrin Ave
Abbott Ave
Catherine St
Great Lakes Ave
Richter Ave
Walnut St
Elm St
Maple St
Pine St
Oak St
Byron Ave
Coolidge Hwy
Batavia St
Henry St
Leroy Ave
Pleasant Ave
James St
Cicotte St
Anchor St
Marion Industrial Hwy
Jefferson Ave
Rouge River
Goodell Ave
Harris St
Marion Industrial Hwy
Marion Industrial Hwy
Dt. and I. Railroad
Berlanger Park Dr
N

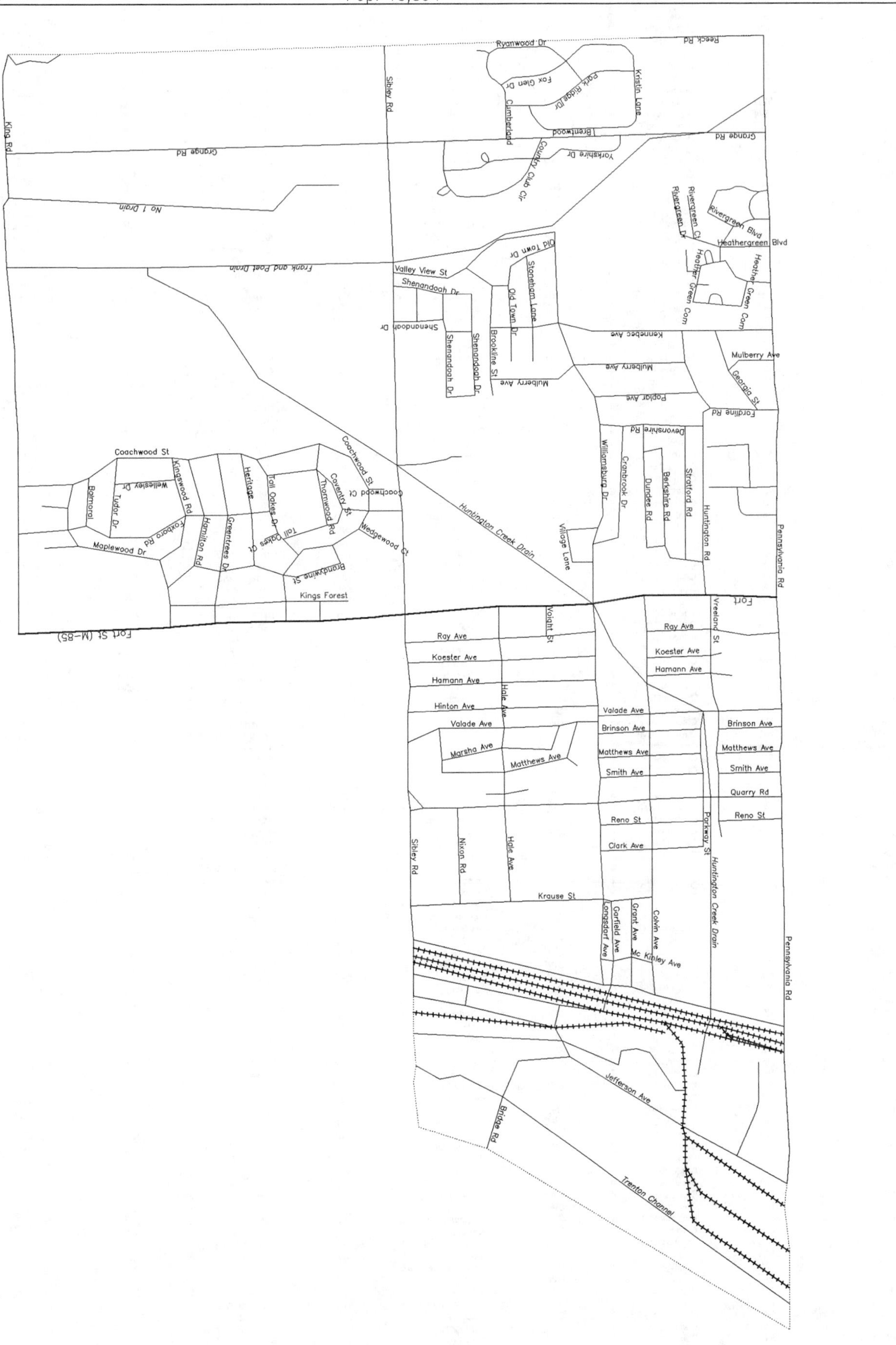

Street	Page	Grid
10 Point Dr	3	NW
1st St	4	NW
2nd St	4	NW
3rd St	4	NW
4th St	4	NW
6Greenleaf Dr	1	SE
6th St	2	SW
7th St	2	SW
Abbey Ct	6	NW
Abington Ct	2	NW
Acre Dr	1	NE
Adams Rd	1	SW
Adams Rd	3	SW
Adams Rd	5	NW
Albany Dr	2	NW
Albertson St	2	SW
Alexander St	5	NE
Alice Ave	4	NW
Alida Ave	5	SE
Allen Way	3	SE
Allenway Ct	3	SE
Allston Dr	1	SE
Alpine Ct	3	NW
Alsdorf Ave	5	NE
Angara St	5	NE
Ann Maria Dr	2	SW
Annchester	2	NW
Ansal Dr	3	NW
Antler Ct	3	NW
Antoinette Dr	2	SW
Apple Hill Ln	2	NW
Apple Orchard	2	NW
Aquinas Dr	1	SW
Aquinas St	2	SW
Arbor Creek Dr	2	SW
Arbor Ln	4	NW
Arizona Ave	1	SE
Arizona Ave	3	NW
Arizona Ct	1	SE
Arizona St	1	SE
Arlington	4	NW
Arlington Dr	4	NW
Arrowood Ct	2	SW
Ashley Cir	6	NW
Ashton Dr	3	NW
Aspen Dr	2	SW
Auburn Rd	5	NE
Auburn Rd	6	NW
Audubon Blvd	5	NW
Augusta Ct	1	SE
Augusta Ct	2	SE
Augusta Dr	1	SE
Augusta Dr	2	SE
Austin	5	NE
Autumn	2	NW
Autumn Ct	4	SW
Avalanche	2	SW
Avalon Rd	5	NW
Avon Cir	3	SE
Avon Crest Ct	3	NW
Avon Crest Dr	3	NW
Avon Industrial	3	SE
Avon Industrial	5	NE
Avon Manor Rd	6	NE
Avon Rd	3	SW
Avon Rd	4	NW
Avonstoke	4	SW
Avonwood Blvd	3	NW
Axford Pl	2	SW
Aynsley	2	SW
Bagley St	5	NE
Bagley St	6	NE
Baker St	6	NE
Baldwin Ave	4	NW
Barclay Cir	6	NW
Barneswood Ct	1	SE
Barneswood Ln	1	SE
Barneswood Ln	2	SE
Baroque Ct	2	SW
Basswood Dr	1	SE
Bathurst St	5	NW
Bay Pt	2	SW
Baylor Rd	3	NW
Beacon Hill Ct	2	SW
Beacon Hill Dr	1	SW
Beacon Hill Dr	2	SE
Bedford Sq	2	SW
Bellarmine Dr	1	SW
Bellarmine Dr	2	SW
Bellarmine Dr	3	NE
Belle Vernon Dr	3	NW
Bendelow Rd	6	SE
Berry-Nook Ln	4	NE
Beryl Ct	4	SE
Bevington Rd	3	SW
Biggers Ct	1	SE
Biggers Dr	1	SE
Biggers Rd	1	SE
Birch Leaf	5	NE
Birch Tree Ct	2	NW
Birch Tree Ln	2	NW
Black Maple Dr	3	NW
Blake Dr	4	NW
Blockton Rd	1	SW
Bloomer St	4	NE
Blue Beech Ct	2	NW
Blue Beech St	2	NW
Bluegrass Dr	1	NE
Bobolink	5	NW
Bolinger	4	NW
Bond St	5	NW
Bonnie Brae	3	SE
Bourbon Ct	6	NW
Bowdoinhill Dr	3	NE
Box Canyon Ct	3	NE
Boyken Rd	4	SW
Braeburn Rd	3	NE
Brandon Ct	2	SW
Bretton Dr	3	SE
Brewster Rd	1	SW
Brewster Rd	3	NE
Brians Way	4	SW
Briar Ct	3	NW
Bridgestone Dr	1	SE
Bridgett St	6	NE
Briston Dr	6	NE
Brittany Ct	3	NW
Broadmoor Ct	2	SW
Broadmoor Dr	2	SW
Bromley Ln	2	NW
Brook	2	NW
Brookfield	2	NE
Brookside	2	SW
Brookway Ct	4	SW
Brookwood Ct	2	SE
Brookwood Ln	1	SE
Brookwood Ln	2	SE
Bucknell Ct	3	NW
Bunker Hill Rd	3	SW
Burgoyne Blvd	3	NW
Burgoyne Blvd	4	NW
Burhaven Dr	1	SW
Burlington Ct	2	NW
Burlington Dr	2	NW
Burning Bush	3	SE
Burning Bush Ct	3	SE
Butler Rd	3	SW
Buttercup Dr	6	NW
Byron Ct	4	SE
Byron Ct	6	NE
Cal Ave	6	NE
Cambridge Dr	3	NE
Campbell St	4	NW
Campus Ct	3	NW
Campus Rd	3	NW
Candlestick	2	SW
Canterbury Trl	3	NE
Carlo Ct	3	NW
Carondelet Ct	4	NE
Carondelet Dr	4	NE
Carriage	2	NW
Carter Rd	2	NE
Castell Ave	4	NW
Castlebar Dr	3	NW
Catalpa Dr	2	SW
Cedaredge	1	NE
Chaffer	2	SW
Chalet Dr	3	NE
Chalmers Ct	1	SE
Chalmers Dr	1	SE
Chalmers Dr	2	SE
Chancery Ct	2	NW
Charles Rd	2	SW
Charlwood Dr	1	NW
Charm Ct	2	NW
Charter Oak Dr	3	SW
Chelsea Ct	2	NW
Cherry	6	NW
Cherry Blossom	2	NW
Cherry Tree Ln	2	NW
Chestnut Cir	1	SE
Chestnut Ln	1	SE
Chevy Circuit	2	NE
Chickadee	5	NW
Childress Ave	4	NW
Chippenham	1	SE
Christian Hills	3	SW
Christy Ct	3	SE
Clair Hill Dr	3	NW
Clairwood	6	NE
Clear Point Ct	2	NE
Clemens Cir	6	SE
Cliff View Dr	2	SW
Clinton River	5	SE
Clinton River	6	SW
Clinton View Cir	3	SE
Clopton Brdg	1	SE
Clovelly Ave	6	NE
Cloverport Ave	4	NW
Cobblestone Ct	1	SE
Cobblestone Dr	1	SE
Cobridge	2	SW
Cobridge Ct	2	SW
Coldiron	4	SW
Coldiron	6	NW
Collingwood Dr	6	NE
Colonial Dr	5	NE
Colony Dr	4	SW
Colorado Ave	1	SW
Commerce	5	NE
Concord Rd	3	SW
Cone Ave	5	SE
Coolidge Hwy	5	NW
Copperstone	5	NE
Corbin	6	NW
Corinthia St	5	NE
Country Club Dr	3	NE
Courtland Blvd	2	SW
Cove	2	SW
Crescent	2	NW
Crestline	4	SW
Crestline Ct	4	SW
Crestline Ln	4	SW
Crestline St	4	SW
Crestwater Ct	3	SW
Crimson Ct	4	SW
Cripple Creek	1	NE
Crooks Rd	3	SE
Crooks Rd	5	SE
Croyden Rd	3	NW
Croydon Rd	3	NW
Crystal Ct	5	NE
Culbertson Ave	6	SE
Cumberland	4	SW
Cumberland	6	NW
Current Dr	3	SW
Curzon St	4	NW
Cypress Ct	3	NW
Cypress Rd	3	NW
Dahlia Ln	4	SW
Dalton Dr	4	NW
Danbury Ln	4	SW
Dancer Dr	4	SW
Dartford Pl	4	SW
Darthmouth	6	NE
Darwin Pl	4	SW
Dawes Ave	6	NE
Dawson	4	SW
Daylily Dr	6	NW
Dearborn Ave	5	SE
Dearborn Dr	5	SE
Deerfield Ct	3	NW
Deerhurst Ln	4	SW
Deerview Ct	4	SW
Deguise Ct	2	NW
Demar	6	NE
Denham Ln	4	SW
Dennet Ln	4	SW
Dequindre Rd	1	SE
Dequindre Rd	2	NE
Dequindre Rd	4	SE
Dequindre Rd	6	NE
Devondale St	5	NE
Devonshire Dr	4	SW
Devonwood	2	NE
Dickson Ln	4	SW
Diversion St	4	NW
Dolliver Dr	1	SE
Donaldson Ave	6	SW
Donegal	2	SW
Donegal Dr	1	SW
Donley Ave	5	SE
Doral	2	SW
Doral Ct	2	SW
Dorfield Dr	6	NE
Dorset St	4	SW
Dove	5	NW
Downhill Ln	4	SW
Drace St	2	SW
Dressler Ln	4	SW
Drexelgate Dr	4	SW
Drexelgate	3	SE
Drexelgate	4	SW
Driftwood Ln	4	NE
Ducks Cross	2	SW
Dumont Pl	4	SW
Dunedin	2	SW
Dunedin Ct	2	SW
Dunning Rd	5	NW
Dutton Rd	1	NW
Dutton Rd	2	NW
Eagle Ct	3	SW
Eagle Dr	3	SW
East Al	4	NW
East St	4	NW
Eastern Ave	6	SE
Eastlawn St	6	SW
Eastwood Dr	5	NW
Eddington Blvd	4	SW
Edgewood Ct	4	SW
Edinborough Dr	2	NW
Edmunton	2	NW
Elizabeth St	2	SW
Elizabeth St	4	NW
Elkhorn	4	SW
Elm St	4	NW
Elmhill Rd	2	NW
Elton Ct	2	SE
Emerson Cir	6	SE
Emmons Ave	6	SE
Enfield St	6	SE
Englewood Dr	2	SW
Enid St	4	NW
Enterprise Dr	5	NE
Ernest Rd	5	SE
Essex Dr	4	SW
Evelyn Ln	4	SW
Evergreen Ct	3	NE
Fair Oak Ct	3	NW
Fair Oak Dr	3	NW
Fairview Ave	4	NW
Fairview Ct	1	SE
Fairview Ln	1	SE
Fairview Ln	2	NE
Fallen Oaks Ct	3	SW
Farmridge Ct	4	SW
Fauteux Ct	4	NE
Fawn Ct	3	NW
Ferndale Ave	2	SW
Fernhill Ct	4	SW
Fieldcrest Ct	4	SW
Fielding Dr	4	SW
Fieldstone Ct	1	SE
Fieldstone Dr	1	SE
Firewood Dr	1	SW
Firewood Dr	2	SW
Firewood Dr	3	NE
Flamingo	5	NW
Flanders	6	NW
Flicker	5	NW
Fontainbleau Ct	4	NE
Fontainbleau Dr	4	NE
Fordcroft	2	SW
Foxboro	1	SW
Foxboro	3	NE
Francis St	6	SW
Frankson Ave	6	NE
Fraser St	4	NW
Gabrielle Dr	4	NE
Gallaland St	4	NE
Galloway Ct	3	SW
Gas Light	2	NW
Gerald Ave	4	SE
Gerald Ave	6	NE
Gettysburg Ct	1	SW
Gilsam St	5	NE
Glen Cir	4	NW
Glen Meadow	4	SW
Glen Point Ct	4	SW
Glenbrooke Ct	4	SW
Glendale Ct	2	SW
Glengrove Dr	3	SW
Glouchester Rd	3	SW
Goldenrod Dr	6	NW
Goldfinch Ln	5	NW
Golfview Ct	1	SE
Grace Ave	5	SE
Grace Ave	6	SW
Gracedale Dr	3	NW
Grandview	2	SE
Grant Rd	5	SE
Gravel Ridge Dr	4	SE
Gravel Ridge St	6	NE
Great Oaks	2	SW
Great Oaks	4	NW
Green Ridge Rd	3	SE
Green Spring Ln	3	SW
Green View	1	SE
Green View	2	SW
Greenbriar	1	NW
Greenwood Dr	5	SW
Gregory St	4	NW
Griggs St	2	SW
Grosse Pines	2	SE
Grosse Pines	3	NW
Grosse Pines Ct	2	SE
Grosse Pines	1	SE
Grosse Pines	2	SE
Gunder	2	SW
Gunder Ct	3	NE
Gunder Dr	1	SW
Hackberry Cir	1	SE
Hackberry Ct	1	SE
Hacker St	4	NW
Hadley Dr	4	NW
Hamlin Ct	4	SW
Hamlin Rd	3	SW
Hamlin Rd	4	SW
Hamlin Rd	5	NW
Hampstead Ln	3	SE
Hampton Blvd	6	NW
Hampton Cir	4	SW
Hampton Cir	6	NW
Harding Ave	3	NW
Harding Ave	4	NW
Harrington Rd	6	NW
Harrison Ave	4	NW
Harrison Ave	6	SE
Harrod St	6	SE
Hartford	2	NW
Hartline St	5	NE
Harvey St	5	NE
Hathaway	1	SE
Hathaway	2	NE
Hattie Fox Ln	1	NE
Hayfield Rd	1	SE
Hazelton	6	NW
Hazelton Ave	6	SW
Heatherwood Ct	2	SW
Heidelberg Dr	3	NE
Helen Allen Ln	6	SW
Helen Ave	4	NW
Helen St	2	SW
Helen St	4	NW
Helmond	4	NW
Hemlock Ct	2	SW
Hemlock Dr	2	SW
Heritage Hills Ct	2	NW
Heritage Ln	1	SE
Heritage Ln	2	SE
Hessel Ave	6	NE
Hickory Hill Ct	1	SE
Hickory Hill Dr	1	SE
Hickory Lawn St	6	NW
Hickory Leaf	3	SE
Hickory Leaf	5	NE
Hickory Leaf Ct	5	NE
Hickory Trl	3	SW
Hidden Creek	2	SW
Hidden Ln	3	NW
Hidden Valley	2	SW
Hiel St	4	NW
High St	2	SW
Highland Ave	2	SW
Highplint Dr	4	SW
Highplint Dr	6	NW
Highpoint Cir	4	SW
Hill Cir	2	SW
Hill St	2	SW
Hillendale Dr	3	NE
Hillside Ct	4	SW
Hillside Ln	4	SW
Hillview Ln	2	NW
Holiday Ct	2	NW
Hollen Shade Dr	1	SW
Homestead	2	SW
Horseshoe	1	SE
Horseshoe Ct	1	NE
Huntington Ct	4	SW
Huntington Park	3	NW
Hutchins Dr	3	SE
Independence	2	NW
Independence	2	NW
Industrial Dr	5	NW
Inglewood Ave	2	SW
Innsbrook	2	SW
Innsbrook Ct	2	SW
Ironstone Dr	1	SE
Ironwood Ct	2	SW
Ironwood Dr	2	SW
Ivy Glen Ct	4	SW
Ivy Wood Ct	4	NW
Jason Cir	2	NW
Jenny Ln	3	SE
John R Rd	4	SE
John R Rd	6	SE
Jones St	2	SE
Juengel St	4	SW
Juengel St	6	NW
June St	5	NE
Kalhaven Rd	4	SW
Keats Dr	6	NE
Kennedy Dr	3	SE
Kensington Dr	4	SW
Kentucky	6	NW
Kenwood Dr	3	SW
Keystone	2	SW
Kilburn Ct	2	NW
Kilburn Rd	2	NW
Kimberly Fair	3	NW
Kinglet St	5	NW
Kings Cove	2	NW
Kings Cove Ct	2	SW
Kings Cove Dr	2	SW
Kings Path Dr	1	SW
Kingsford Rd	3	SW
Kingsmere Cir	3	SE
Kingstree Ct	3	NW
Kingsview	3	NW
Kingsview St	3	NW
Kingview Ct	3	NW
Kirk S Ct	3	NE
Kirkton Ct	4	NW
Knights Ridge	2	NW
Knollcrest	3	NW
La Porte Ct	4	NE
Labadie Ct	4	NE
Labrosse Ct	4	NE
Lafayette Ct	4	SW
Lafferty Ct	4	NE
Lafferty Dr	4	NE
Lake Forest Ct	3	NW
Lake Forest Rd	3	NW
Lalonde Ct	4	NE
Lambeth Park	2	NW
Lamplighter	2	NW
Langdon Ct	4	SW
Langley Ct	2	SE
Langley Dr	1	SE
Langley Dr	2	SE
Lantern	2	NW
Larchwood Dr	4	NW
Largo	4	SW
Larned Ave	6	NE
Larson Ct	4	SW
Lassiter	2	SW
Laurel	4	SW
Laurel Ave	1	SE
Laurence Dr	4	NE
Lawnview	4	SW
Lawton	4	SW
Le Grand Blvd	4	NE
Le Grande	4	NE
Le Grande Blvd	4	NE
Leach Rd	5	NW
Leaf	4	SW
Lear	4	SW
Legault Ct	4	NE
Lehigh Ave	5	NE
Lehigh Ave	6	NW
Leinster Rd	3	NW
Lenomar	2	SE
Lesperance Ct	4	NE
Lesperance Dr	4	NE
Letour Ct	4	NE
Leupp	4	SW
Lexington Dr	4	SE
Leyton Ct	2	NW
Liberty Bell Ct	4	SW
Linwood Ave	2	SW
Lion	6	NE
Little Creek St	2	NW
Little Hill Ct	4	SW
Live Oak	3	NE
Livernois Rd	1	SE
Livernois Rd	3	NW
Livernois Rd	5	NE
Livernois Rd	6	SW
Lockmoore	6	NE
Lockport	4	SW
Lodge Pole Ln	3	SE
Lomas Verdes	1	NW
Lomas Verdes	2	NW
Lomond Ln	1	SE
London Ridge	4	SE
London Ridge	6	NE
Lonedale Rd	3	NE
Loneford Dr	3	NW
Longfellow	4	SW
Longford Dr	3	NW
Longview Ave	6	SE
Lounsbury Ave	2	SW
Lower Ridge Dr	6	NW
Ludgate Ln	3	SE
Ludlow Ave	2	SW
Ludlow Ave	4	NW
Lynhaven Ct	4	SW
Lynndale Ct	3	NW
Lynndale Dr	3	NW
Lyric	4	SW
Lysander St	2	SW
Machette Ct	4	NE
Mackwood St	4	SE
Madison Ave	2	SW
Madison Ave	4	NW
Magnolia Ct	4	SW
Mahaffy Ave	2	SW
Main St	2	SW
Main St	4	NW
Mallard St	5	NW

NOTES

NW
NE
Plate # 1
Plate # 2
Plate # 3
Plate # 4
Plate # 5
Plate # 6
Rochester Hills City
Rochester City
Adams Rd
Brewster Rd
Crooks Rd
Livernois Rd
Rochester Rd
Orion Rd
Dequindre Rd
Tienken Rd
Walton Blvd
Hamlin Rd
Avon Rd
Avon Cir
State Hwy 59
Auburn Rd
Runyon Rd

NW
NE
Great Oaks Blvd
Hemlock Dr
Aspen Dr
Oakwood Dr
Ironwood Dr
Ludlow Ave
Wilcox St
Ducks Cross
Wilcox Ave
Oak St
Pine St
Main St
High St
Mahaffy Ave
Inglewood Ave
Elizabeth St
Lounsbury Ave
Plate St
Miller Ave
Sycamore Dr
Catalpa Dr
Maple Dr
Red Oak Ln
Romeo Rd
Parkdale Ave
Stony Creek
Tienken Rd
Runyon Rd
Washington Rd
Mill Race
Winkler Mill St
Carter Rd
Winkler Pond
Dequindre Rd
Rochester Rd
Sheldon Rd
Mead Rd
Blue Beech St
Blue Beech Ct
Little Creek St
Wimberly Dr
Tree Top Ln
Perridale Rd
Hillview Ln
Oaklane Dr
Oaklane Dr
Ronnoco Rd
Deguise Ct
Orion Rd
Birch Tree Ln
Birch Tree Ct
Peach Tree Ln
Apple Hill Ln
Apple Orchard Ln
Cherry Tree Ln
Willowtree Ln
Cherry Blossom Ln
Willowtree Ln
Elmhill Rd
Maplehill Rd
Bedford Sq
Cliff View Dr
Oakbrook
Oakbrook Ridge Dr
Thalia St
Reitman Ct
Winry Dr
Hill Cir
Albertson St
Griggs St
Drace St
Woodward Ave
Ferndale Ave
Glendale Ct
Terry Ave
Highland Ave
Linwood Ave
Northwood Ave
Lysander St
Charles Rd
William Rd
Reweld Dr
Hill St
Meadow Ln
Whispering Heights Ct
Surrey
Carriage
Lantern
Gas Light
Paddle Wheel
Wagon Wheel
Autumn
Hidden Valley
Crescent
Lamplighter
Kings Cove
Pine Ridge
Brookside
Kings Cove Dr
Windmill
Brook
Oakwood Ct
Helen St
7th St
6th St
Railroad

Adams Rd
Butler Rd
Hamlin Rd
Crooks Rd
Avon Rd
Christian Hills Dr
Old Perch Rd
Livernois Rd
Walton Blvd
Clinton River
Rochester Industrial Dr
Clair Hill Dr
Lake Forest Rd
Avon Cir
Seville Rd
Maryknoll Rd
Stanford Cir
Castlebar Dr
Longford Dr

SW
SE
Adams Rd
Nelda Hill Ln
Woodcrest Rd
Dunning Rd
Avalon Rd
St Clair Dr
York Rd
Greenwood Dr
Eastwood Dr
Auburn Rd
Industrial Dr
Cn Railroad
Waterview Dr
Leach Rd
Martell St
Willet Ave
Coolidge Hwy
Technology Dr
South Blvd
State Hwy 59
Research Dr
Kinglet St
Mallard St
Bond St
Bathurst St
Vendome St
Rockhaven St
Quail
Bobolink
Whippoorwill
Audubon Blvd
Dove
Sandpiper
Nightingale Rd
Goldfinch Ln
Skylark
Chickadee
Flicker
Flamingo
Toucan
Tanager
Warbler
Angara St
Harvey St
Devondale St
Midvale St
Star Ct
Ernest Rd
Grant Rd
Colonial Dr
Austin
Donley Ave
Nearing Rd
Grace Ave
Crooks Rd
Ruby Ave
Alsdorf Ave
Gilsam St
Tamm St
June St
Northfield
Enterprise Dr
Alexander St
Commerce
Product Dr
Alida Ave
Samuel Ave
Mildred Ave
Cone Ave
Dearborn Ave
Production Square Dr
Crystal Ct
Sidney Ct
Rochelle Park Dr
Hickory Leaf
Dearborn Dr
Hartline St
Simpson Dr
Woodelm St
Walsh St
Bagley St
Corinthia St
Copperstone
Livernois Rd

NW
NE
Livernois Rd
Grace Ave
Francis St
Hazelton
Donaldson Ave
Shortridge
Overlook Dr
Harrington Rd
Sarsfield Dr
Walbridge Rd
Lehigh Ave
Kentucky
Highpoint Dr
Cumberland
Norton Rd
Norton Lawn St
Walnut Ave
Hazelton Ave
Orchardview Ave
State Hwy 59
Shadywood St
Cherry
Hickory Lawn St
Wabash St
Coldron
Bourbon Ct
Stark Rd
Montmorency Rd
Rochester Rd
Barclay Cir
Timberview Dr
Village Circle Dr
Hampton Cir
Auburn Rd
Michelson Rd
Eastlawn St
South Blvd
Winter Creek Dr
Old Creek Rd
Primrose Dr
Daylily Dr
Goldenrod Dr
Buttercup Dr
Vardon St
Ashley Cir
Oxford Ct
Plymouth Ct
Darthmouth
Abbey Ct
Baker St
Lockmoore
Shelley
Lion
Gibson Drain
Bendelow Rd
Stonebury Dr
Stonebury Ct
Briston Dr
Dorfield Dr
Wortham Dr
Woodlane St
John R Rd
Larned Ave
Enfield St
Avon Manor Rd
Collingwood Dr
Truwood Dr
Clairwood
Gravel Ridge St
Demar
Frankson Ave
Weaverton St
Bridgett St
Clovelly Ave
Morley Ave
Culbertson Ave
Porter Cir
Emmons Ave
O'Neil Cir
Longview Ave
Emerson Cir
Southern Ave
Harrod St
Milton Ave
Harrison Ave
Marlowe Ave
Sibley Ave
Eastern Ave
Dawes Ave
Clemens Cir
Gerald Ave
Cal Ave
Melvin Ave
Hessel Ave
Mayville Dr
Dequindre Rd

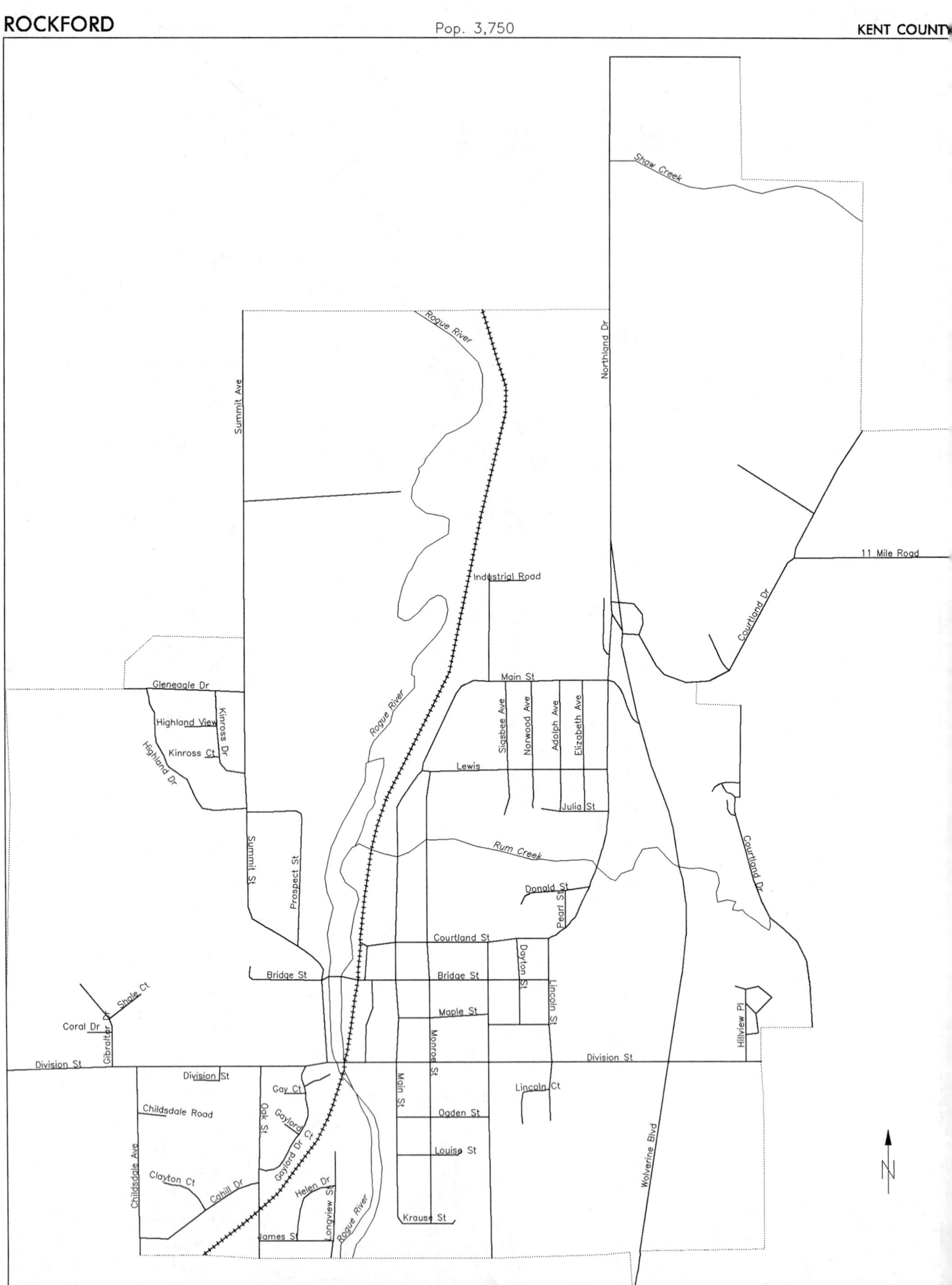

Shaw Creek
Northland Dr
Rogue River
Summit Ave
11 Mile Road
Industrial Road
Courtland Dr
Main St
Gleneagle Dr
Highland View
Kinross Dr
Kinross Ct
Highland Dr
Sigsbee Ave
Norwood Ave
Adolph Ave
Elizabeth Ave
Lewis
Julia St
Rum Creek
Summit St
Prospect St
Donald St
Pearl St
Courtland St
Bridge St
Dayton St
Lincoln St
Shale Ct
Coral Dr
Gibraltar Dr
Maple St
Monroe St
Hillview Pl
Division St
Division St
Division St
Gay Ct
Lincoln Ct
Childsdale Road
Oak St
Gaylord Ct
Main St
Ogden St
Louise St
Wolverine Blvd
Childsdale Ave
Clayton Ct
Gaylord Dr
Cahill Dr
Helen Dr
Longview St
Krause St
James St
N

ROCKWOOD

Pop. 3,141

WAYNE COUNTY

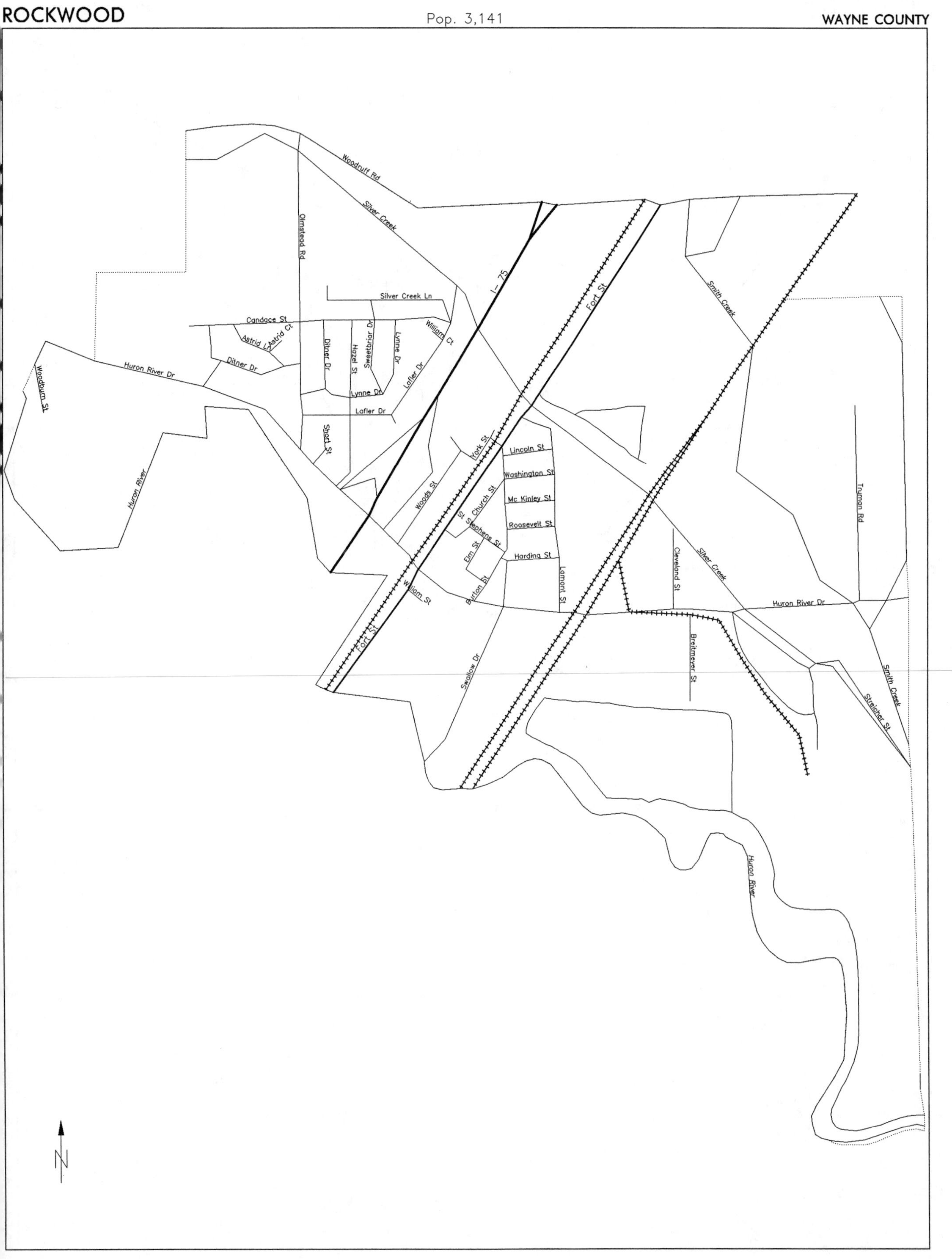

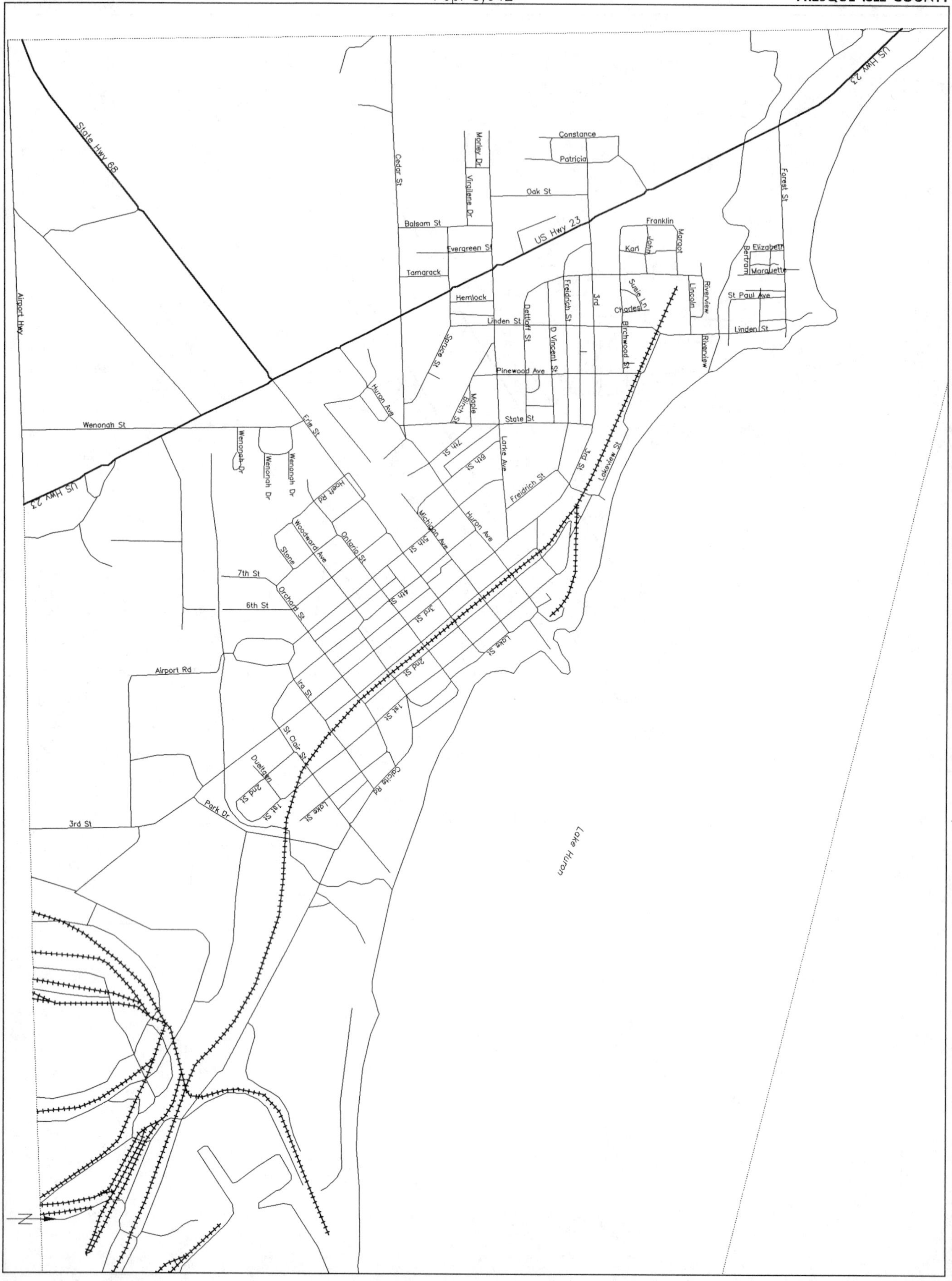

State Hwy 68
US Hwy 23
Airport Hwy
Wenonah St
Wenonah Dr
Cedar St
Morley Dr
Virgiliene Dr
Constance
Patricia
Oak St
Balsam St
Evergreen St
Tamarack
Hemlock
Linden St
Spruce St
Franklin
Karl
John
Margot
Elizabeth
Bertram
Marquette
Forest St
St Paul Ave
Linden St
Riverview
Lincoln
Susie Ln
Charles
3rd
Friedrich St
Dettloff St
D Vincent St
Birchwood St
Pinewood Ave
Huron Ave
Maple
Birch St
State St
Larke Ave
Erie St
7th St
6th St
Friedrich St
3rd St
Lakeview St
Hoeft Rd
Michigan Ave
Woodward Ave
Ontario St
Stone
5th St
Huron Ave
Orchard St
4th St
3rd St
Lake St
Airport Rd
2nd St
Ira St
1st St
St Clair St
Duetigan
2nd St
Calcite Rd
1st St
Lake St
Park Dr
3rd St
Lake Huron
N

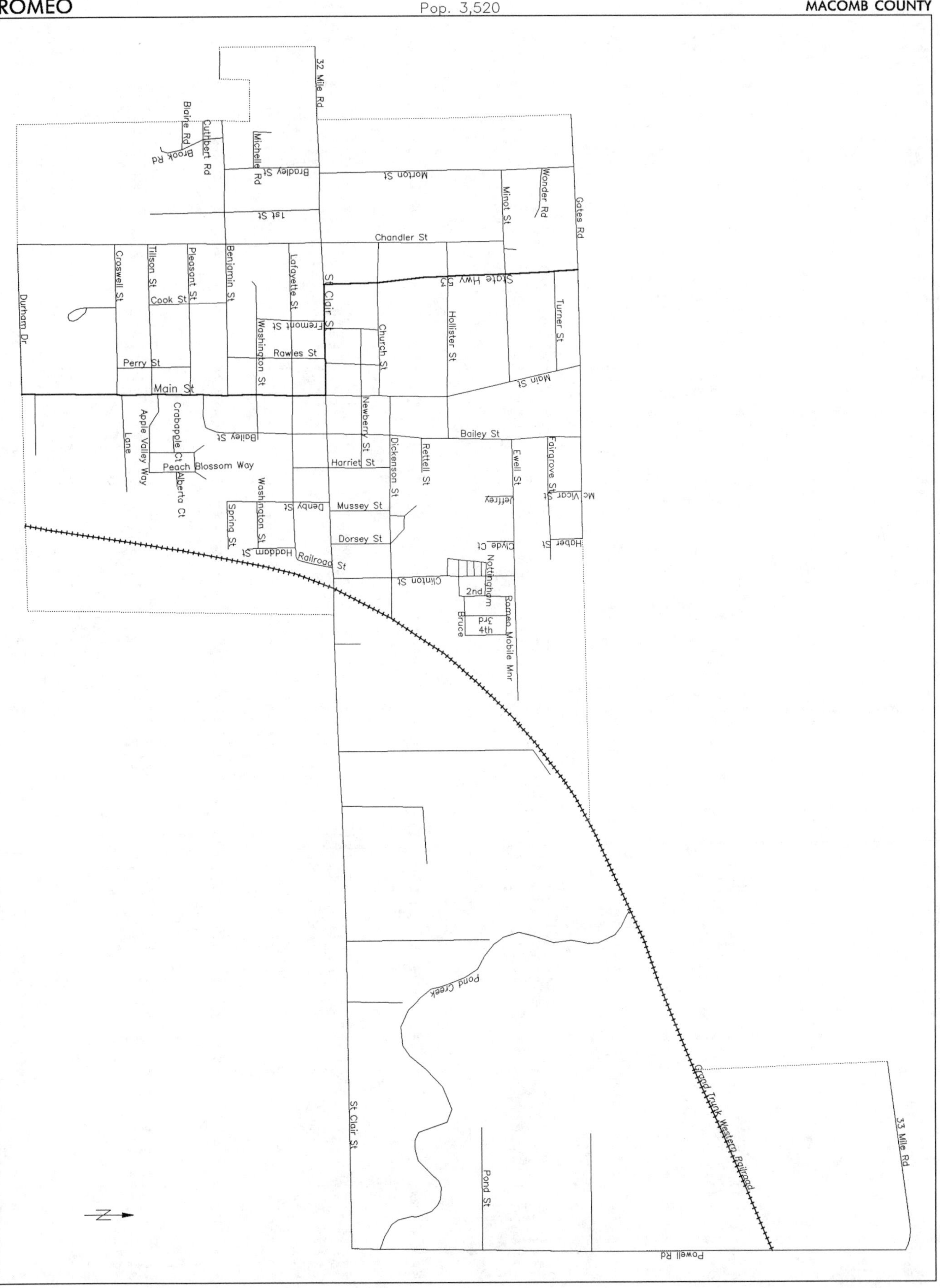
32 Mile Rd
Blarie Rd
Brook Rd
Cuthbert Rd
Michelle Rd
Bradley St
Morton St
Wonder Rd
Minot St
Gates Rd
1st St
Chandler St
Croswell St
Tillson St
Pleasant St
Benjamin St
Lafayette St
St Clair St
State Hwy 53
Turner St
Durham Dr.
Cook St
Fremont St
Church St
Hollister St
Washington St
Rawles St
Perry St
Main St
Apple Valley Way
Lane
Crabapple Ct
Bailey St
Newberry St
Dickenson St
Rettell St
Ewell St
Fairgrove St
Peach Blossom Way
Alberta Ct
Harriet St
Mc Vicar St
Jeffrey
Spring St
Denby St
Mussey St
Dorsey St
Hober St
Clyde Ct
Haddam St
Railroad St
Nottingham
Clinton St
2nd
3rd
4th
Bruce
Romeo Mobile Mnr
Pond Creek
Grand Trunk Western Railroad
33 Mile Rd
Pond St
Powell Rd

10 Mile Rd 3 NW
10 Mile Rd 4 NW
11 Mile Rd 1 SE
11 Mile Rd 2 SW
11 Mile Rd 3 NE
11 Mile Rd 4 NW
12 Mile Rd 1 SW
12 Mile Rd 2 SW
13 Mile Rd 1 NE
13 Mile Rd 2 NW
14 Mile Rd 1 NW
14 Mile Rd 2 NW
1st St 3 SW
7th St 1 NE
8 Mile Rd 3 SW
8 Mile Rd 4 SW
9 Mile Rd 3 SW
9 Mile Rd 4 SW
A ST 4 NW
Abe Dr 2 NW
Achyl Ave 4 NE
Acton Dr 1 NW
Ada Ave 3 NW
Ada Dr 3 NW
Adair St 4 NW
Adams Ave 1 NE
Adams Dr 2 NE
Addelia Dr 2 SW
Adler Dr 2 SE
Afton Dr 4 NW
Albany 3 NE
Albany Ave 3 SE
Albert J Dr 3 NE
Alberta St 4 NE
Aleta Cir 2 SW
Alex 4 NW
Alex St 4 NW
Alger Ave 2 NE
Alger Dr 1 NW
Alger Dr 2 NW
Alger St 2 NE
Aline Dr 2 SW
Allyn Ave 4 SE
Alvin Ave 4 NE
Alvina Ave 3 SW
Amber Ave 4 SE
Amber Le Dr 2 NW
Amel Dr 2 NW
Andrith St 3 NE
Angela Dr 2 SE
Anita Dr 2 NW
Anna St 1 SW
Anna St 2 SW
Antoinette Ave 4 NW
Antonia Dr 3 NW
Apolonia Dr 1 SW
Applewood Dr 2 SW
April Lane 2 NE
Arden Ave 1 NW
Arden Ave 2 NE
Arden Dr 1 NW
Arden Dr 2 NW
Armanda Dr 2 SE
Arnold Dr 2 SE
Arsenal Ave 2 SW
Arsenal Ave 4 NW
Artesian Dr 1 NE
Ascension Ave 4 SW
Aspen Dr 2 SW
Atlantic Ave 3 SE
Audrey Ave 3 SE
Audrey Dr 1 SE
Audrey Dr 3 NE
Audubon Dr 1 NW
Augustina Dr 3 NW
Austin Dr 1 SW
Automobile Blvd 4 SW
Autumn Lane 2 SE
Avondale Ave 4 NW
B ST 4 NW
Bach St 3 SW
Bade Dr 2 SE
Baird Dr 2 SE
Baird St 2 SW
Baldwin Ave 1 SE
Balfour Dr 2 SE
Barbary Ct 2 NW
Barber 2 SE
Barclay Square 2 NW
Barcroft Way 2 SE
Barfield 2 NE
Bart St 3 SW
Bartholomaei St 3 SW
Bates Ct 1 NE
Bates Dr 1 NW
Bayliss Ave 3 NW
Bear Creek 2 NW
Bear Creek Dr 2 NW
Becker Ave 4 SW
Beebe Ave 1 NE
Beechwood Dr 2 NE
Behrendt Ave 3 SW
Beierman Ave 3 SE
Belleau Dr 1 NW
Belmont Ave 4 SW
Bennington Ave 2 NW
Berkshire Ave 3 SW
Bernice Ave 3 NE
Bernice Ave 4 NE
Bernice Rd 3 NW
Berry Ave 4 NE
Berwyn Dr 1 NW
Besmore Dr 2 SW
Beth Dr 2 SE
Betty Dr 1 NE
Bicsak Dr 1 SW
Billette Dr 3 NW
Binney Dr 2 NW
Birch Tree Dr 2 NW
Birchcrest Dr 2 SW
Blackett Ave 4 SE
Blackmar 3 NE
Blackmar Ave 3 SE
Blackstone Ave 4 SE
Blair Dr 1 NW
Blanck Ave 1 SE
Blancke Ave 2 NW
Bloomfield Ave 4 NW
Blossom Lane 2 SE
Boewe Dr 1 SW
Bolam Ave 4 SE
Bon Brae Dr 2 SE
Bon Mar Dr 2 SE
Bonnie Ave 1 SE
Bonnie Ave 2 SW
Bonnie Ave 4 NW
Bonnie Dr 2 SW
Bonnie Rd 2 SW
Bonning Ave 3 NW
Bradford Ct 3 NW
Bradner Ave 2 SE
Bradner Dr 2 SE
Brainbridge Ave 4 NE
Brainwood Ave 4 NE
Brandner Dr 2 NE
Braun Ave 3 NE
Bretz Dr 2 NW
Briarcliff Dr 2 SW
Bristol Dr 1 SW
Brixham Dr 2 NE
Broadmoor Dr 2 SE
Brockington Dr 2 SE
Brohl Dr 2 NE
Brown Dr 1 NW
Bruce St 3 SW
Bruggeman 2 NE
Buchanan Dr 1 NW
Buckingham Dr 1 SW
Bunert Dr 2 NE
Bunert Rd 2 SE
Bunert Rd 4 NE
Burg Rd 4 NW
Burgundy Ave 4 NE
Burr St 4 SE
Burssens Dr 1 SW
Burt St 4 NW
Busch Ave 4 NW
Busch St 3 NE
Busko Cir 2 SW
Busko Ct 2 SW
Busko St 2 SW
Buster Dr 3 NW
Butte Ave 4 SE
C ST 4 NW
Cadillac Ave 3 SW
Cadillac Ave 4 SW
Callahan Dr 2 NE
Cambridge Ct 2 NW
Cambridge Dr 2 NW
Campbell Ave 4 SW
Campbell Dr 2 SW
Campbell St 4 NW
Canterbury Dr 2 NW
Canterbury 1 NE
Capri Dr 2 NW
Caradonna St 2 SW
Cardigan Ct 3 NW
Carion Dr 1 NW
Carmody Dr 1 NW
Carney St 4 NW
Carol Ave 2 SW
Carrier Ave 4 NW
Casmere Ave 1 NE
Castle Ave 2 NE
Cedar Ridge Ct 2 NW
Cedars Dr 2 NW
Center Dr 1 SW
Central Ave 4 NW
Chalfonte Dr 1 NW
Chalk Farm Rd 3 NW
Chalmers Ave 3 SE
Chalmers Ave 4 SW
Champaign Ave 4 NW
Chapp Ave 4 NW
Chard Ave 1 SW
Charles Dr 2 NW
Charlotte Ave 4 SE
Chase Ave 3 NW
Check Dr 2 NW
Cheshire Ct 3 NW
Chesterfield Ave 4 NE
Chestnut Lane 3 SW
Chicago Rd 1 NW
Chicago Rd 2 NW
Chippewa Dr 2 NW
Christi Dr 3 NE
Christine St 2 SW
Christopher Ave 3 SW
City Ctr 2 SW
Civic Ctr Blvd 1 SE
Civic Ctr Blvd 2 SW
Claeys Dr 2 NW
Clairpointe Dr 2 SE
Cline St 3 SW
Cloie Dr 4 NE
Cloverly Ct 1 NE
Cole Dr 2 SW
Coleen Ave 4 SE
Colendale St 3 SW
Colin Kelly St 4 NW
Collins Dr 2 NE
Colman Dr 3 NW
Colpaert Dr 2 NW
Columbus Ave 4 SE
Columbus Dr 2 NE
Comfort St 4 NW
Commerce Ave 4 NW
Common Rd 1 SW
Common Rd 2 SW
Community Blvd 2 SW
Concord Ave 2 SW
Conner Ave 3 SE
Conner St 4 NW
Continental Ave 3 SE
Continental Ave 4 SW
Coolidge 4 NW
Coolidge Ave 3 NE
Coolidge Ave 4 NW
Cosgrove Dr 1 SW
Cottage Lane 4 NE
Cour Louis 3 SW
Cour Marie 3 SW
Cour Renee 3 SW
Cour Retta 3 SW
Cour Ville 3 SW
Cousino Dr 1 NW
Couwlier Ave 4 SE
Coventry Pl 2 NW
Crabapple Lane 2 NW
Craig Ct 2 NE
Creekside Cir 2 NW
Creekside Dr 2 NW
Crestwood Dr 2 SE
Cromie Ct 1 SW
Cromie Dr 2 SE
Cromie St 1 SW
Crystal Ave 3 NE
Cunningham 3 SW
Cunningham Dr 1 SW
Curie Ave 3 SE
Curie Ct 3 NE
Cyman Ave 3 SE
Dale Ave 3 NE
Dale Ave 4 NW
Dallas Ave 3 SW
Darla Ct 4 NW
Darlene St 2 SW
Darmouth Dr 2 SW
Darryl Dr 2 NE
David Givens St 1 SW
David Givens St 3 NW
Davy St 1 NE
Dawn Dr 1 NW
Dawson Ave 1 NW
Dawson Dr 1 NW
De Mott Ct 2 SE
Dean St 3 SW
Dearden Dr 2 NW
Decatur Ave 4 NW
Dell Lane 1 SW
Denmar Dr 2 SW
Dennis Lane 1 NW
Denton Dr 1 NE
Dequindre Ave 3 SW
Dequindre Rd 1 SW
Dequindre Rd 3 NW
Desmond Dr 2 SW
Dewey St 4 NW
Dexter Blvd 4 SE
Dexter Ct 4 SE
Diegel Rd 2 NW
Diena Dr 2 SE
Dimas Dr 1 NE
Dodge Ave 3 SE
Dodge Ave 4 SW
Doepfer Rd 3 SE
Dogwood Lane 2 NW
Dohran Dr 2 SE
Dolores Ave 3 NW
Dominic Dr 2 NE
Don Ct 1 NW
Doncea Dr 3 NW
Doncea St 3 NW
Donna Ave 3 NW
Dormont Ave 3 SW
Dover Ave 2 SE
Dover Ave 4 NE
Dover Ct 4 NE
Dover Dr 2 SE
Dowland Dr 1 NW
Dowland St 1 SW
Dowland St 3 NW
Doyle Ave 4 SE
Dundee Dr 1 NW
Dunn Dr 1 SW
Durham Dr 2 NE
Dwight Dr 1 SW
Dwyer Ave 3 NE
Earl Dr 1 NW
Eastwood Ave 4 SE
Eastwood Ct 4 SE
Easy St 4 NE
Eckstein St 1 NE
Edgemont Ave 4 NW
Edgeton Dr 2 SW
Edgewater Lane 2 NW
Edison St 2 SE
Edna Ct 2 NW
Edna Dr 2 NW
Edna St 2 NW
Edom Ave 4 SW
Edward Griggs 1 SW
Edward St 3 NE
Edward St 4 NW
Edwin Ct 2 SE
Edwin Dr 1 SW
Edwin Dr 2 SW
Edwood Ave 2 NE
Eelcoo Ave 4 SE
Ehlert Ave 4 SE
Eiffel Ave 2 SE
Eiffel Ct 2 NE
Eiffel Dr 2 NE
El Capitan Dr 1 SW
El Capitan Dr 3 NW
Elaine Ct 3 NE
Elderwood Dr 2 NE
Eldorado Plz 2 SE
Eldorado Ter 2 SE
Eleanor Ave 4 NE
Elly Ct 2 NW
Elm Tree Lane 1 SE
Elmer Ave 1 SE
Elmgrove Ave 1 SE
Elroy Ave 4 SE
Elza St 3 SW
Emmons St 3 SW
Engleman Ave 3 NE
Engleman Ave 4 NW
Engleman Rd 4 NW
Enterprise Ct 1 SE
Esch Ave 3 NW
Essex Ave 4 SW
Estate Plaza Dr 2 SW
Eureka Ave 3 SW
Eureka Dr 3 NW
Evelyn Ave 2 SW
Evelyn Ave 4 NW
Evelyn Ct 2 SW
Exeter Ct 1 NW
Exeter Dr 1 NW
Fairfield Ave 2 SE
Fairfield Ave 4 SE
Fairfield Dr 2 SE
Falmouth Dr 4 NW
Farnum Ave 1 SE
Farnum Ave 2 SW
Farnum Cir 2 SW
Farnum Ct 2 SW
Farnum Rd 2 SW
Farro Ct 4 NW
Fayette Dr 2 SE
Federal Ave 4 SW
Fenwick Dr 1 SW
Fillmore Ave 1 NE
Fina Dr 2 NE
Firwood Ave 4 NE
Firwood Dr 2 NE
Fisher Ave 3 SE
Fisher Ave 4 SW
Fisk Ave 4 SE
Flanders Ave 2 NE
Flanders Dr 2 SE
Flanders St 4 NE
Flo St 3 SW
Flynn Ave 1 NE
Fora Ct 3 NE
Ford Ave 3 SE
Ford Ave 4 SW
Forest Ct 2 NW
Forest Lane 2 NW
Forterra Dr 4 NE
Fox Ct 3 NW
Francesca Dr 3 NW
Francine St 1 SE
Francine St 2 SW
Frank Dr 2 NW
Frazho Rd 3 NE
Frazho Rd 4 NW
Fred St 1 NW
Freda Dr 2 NW
Freeman St 4 SE
Ft Lauderdale 2 SW
Gail Ave 2 SW
Gail Dr 2 SW
Gainsborough 2 NE
Gander Ave 2 SE
Garbor Ave 2 SW
Garbor St 1 SW
Garbor St 2 SW
Garden Ct 3 NE
Gardendale Dr 2 NE
Garrick Ave 3 SW
Garson Ave 4 SE
Gentner St 4 SE
Geoffry Dr 1 SW
Geoffry Dr 2 SW
George Dr 1 NW
George St 4 NW
Georgiana Ave 4 SE
Gerald Dr 1 SE
Gerald Dr 2 SW
Gerald St 1 SW
Gerald St 2 SW
Geraldine Ct 2 SW
Geraldine Dr 2 SW
Gibson Ave 4 SW
Gilbert Dr 2 SW
Girard Dr 1 NW
Glen Dr 2 SE
Glenita St 3 SW
Glenwood Cir 2 NE
Globe Ave 4 SW
Gloede Dr 2 SE
Gloede St 2 SE
Gloria Ct 2 NW
Godin St 3 NE
Gorbe 3 NE
Goulson Ave 3 SW
Grabar Sq 4 SE
Grace Dr 3 NW
Granada Plz 2 SE
Granado Plz 2 SE
Grand Oaks Dr 1 SE
Green Ct 4 NW
Green Meadow 2 NW
Greenbriar Lane 1 NE
Greenhill Rd 3 NW
Greentree Dr 2 NW
Grey Ave 4 NE
Griffin Ave 4 SW
Grinsell Dr 1 NE
Grobbel 3 NE
Grobbel Ave 3 NE
Grobbel Dr 1 SE
Grobbel Dr 3 NE
Groesbeck Hwy 2 SE
Groesbeck Hwy 4 SW
Gronow Ave 3 NE
Gronow Ave 4 NW
Gruenberg Dr 1 SW
Grunalt Ave 3 NW
Gunston Ave 4 NW
Guy Ct 2 NW
Haff Ave 2 NW
Halmich Dr 1 NE
Hanford Ct 2 SE
Hanford Dr 2 SW
Hanley St 2 NW
Hanover Dr 2 NW
Harder Dr 2 SW
Harding Ave 4 NW
Harold St 4 NW
Harrington Dr 2 SE
Harrison Dr 2 SE
Hartford Dr 2 NE
Hartill Ave 4 NE
Hartlein Dr 1 NE
Hartlein Dr 2 NE
Hartsig Ave 1 SE
Hartwick Dr 2 NE
Haupt Dr 2 NE
Haverhill Dr 1 SW
Haverhill Dr 3 NW
Hawaii Dr 2 SW
Hawthorne Dr 1 NW
Hayden St 3 SW
Hayes Rd 2 SE
Hayes Rd 4 NE
Hayman Dr 1 SW
Heathdale Ave 1 SW
Hebe St 3 NW
Helen Ave 3 NE
Helen Ave 4 NW
Helen Dr 2 NW
Helle Ave 4 SW
Hendricks Ave 4 SE
Henry St 3 NE
Henry St 4 NW
Herbert Ave 4 NW
Hesse Ave 4 NW
Hettenberger 2 SW
Heussner Ave 4 SE
Hickory Lane 2 NW
Highland Dr 4 NW
Hill Ave 3 NE
Hill St 3 SE
Hillcrest Ave 1 NW
Hillcrest Ct 1 NW
Hillcrest Dr 1 NW
Hillock Ave 4 SE
Hobart Ave 4 SE
Hoerning Ave 2 SE
Holden Dr 1 NE
Holly Ct 1 SW
Hollywood Dr 2 SW
Holmes Dr 1 NW
Hoover Rd 2 SW
Hoover Rd 4 SW
Hoverford Ct 3 NW
Hovey Ave 4 NE
Hovey St 4 NW
Hudson Ave 3 SW
Hudson Ave 4 SW
Huff Dr 2 SE
Hughes Ct 1 SW
Hughes Dr 1 SW
Huntington Dr 2 SE
Hupp Ave 3 SE
Hupp Ave 4 SW
I- 696 2 SE
I- 696 3 NE
I- 696 4 NW
I- 696 Service 3 NW
Ida Ave 4 SE
Imperial Dr 2 SW
Industrial Hwy 4 NE
Iowa Dr 1 NE
Iowa Dr 2 SW
Ira Blvd 3 SE
Irene Ave 2 SW
Irene Ct 2 SE
Irene Dr 2 SW
Irma St 1 NW
Ironwood Dr 2 SW
Iroquois Dr 2 NE
Irvington Ct 2 SE
Irvington Dr 2 SE
Ivanhoe Dr 2 SE
Ivy Lane 2 NW
Jackson Ave 3 SE
Jackson Ave 4 SW
Jacobs Dr 2 SE
Jade Ct 3 SE
James Dr 1 SW
James Dr 3 NW
James St 1 SW
Jan Dr 2 SE
Jane Ct 2 SE
Janet Dr 1 SW
Jarvis Ave 3 SW
Jay Dr 2 NW
Jean Rd 2 SW
Jeannie Ct 3 SW
Jenerous St 3 NE
Jenny Ave 1 NE
Jenny Ave 2 NW
Jenny Dr 2 NW
Jewett Ave 4 NW
Jim Pl 4 NW

NOTES

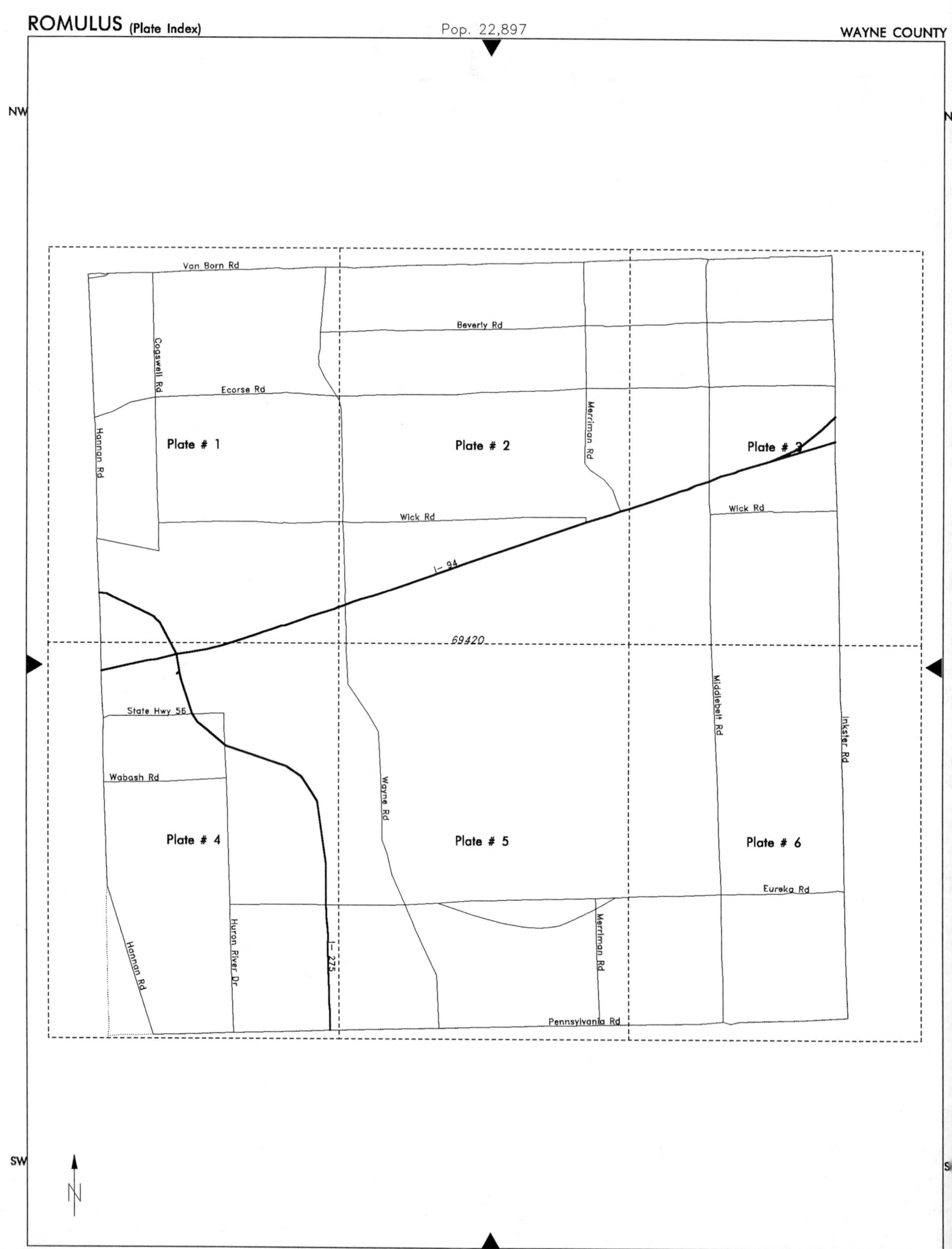
NW
NE
SW
S
Van Born Rd
Beverly Rd
Ecorse Rd
Cogswell Rd
Hannan Rd
Merriman Rd
Plate # 1
Plate # 2
Plate # 3
Wick Rd
Wick Rd
I- 94
69420
State Hwy 56
Wabash Rd
Wayne Rd
Middlebelt Rd
Inkster Rd
Plate # 4
Plate # 5
Plate # 6
Eureka Rd
Hannan Rd
Huron River Dr
I- 275
Merriman Rd
Pennsylvania Rd
N

Van Born Rd
Moore St
Avalon St
Newberry St
Wayne Rd
Ecorse River
Boice Drain
Alexander Dr
Tyndall Cir
Golden Blvd
Joan St
Irma St
Hunt St
Heyer St
Edmund Creek
Mc Claughrey Drain
Wilbur Drain
Beverly Rd
Park Pl
Vinewood St
Cypress St
Border St
Arlene Ct
Ecorse River
C and O Railroad
Coggswell Rd
Ecorse Rd
Ozga Rd
Delano St
Wahrman St
Hannan Rd
Grover St
Smith
Whitehorn St
Garner St
Haskell
Mary St
Gabriel St
Post Drain
Wick Rd
Shook St
Ronald St
Tyler Rd
Tobine St
Delaney Drain
Leek and Bower Drain
Mc Bride Rd
Romaine St
Miriam St
Sterling St
Stephanie
Herman Ave
Margaret
Diane
Filmore St
Herman St
Crossman St
Menton St
I-275
I-94
Chase Rd
and W Railroad
NE
SE
N

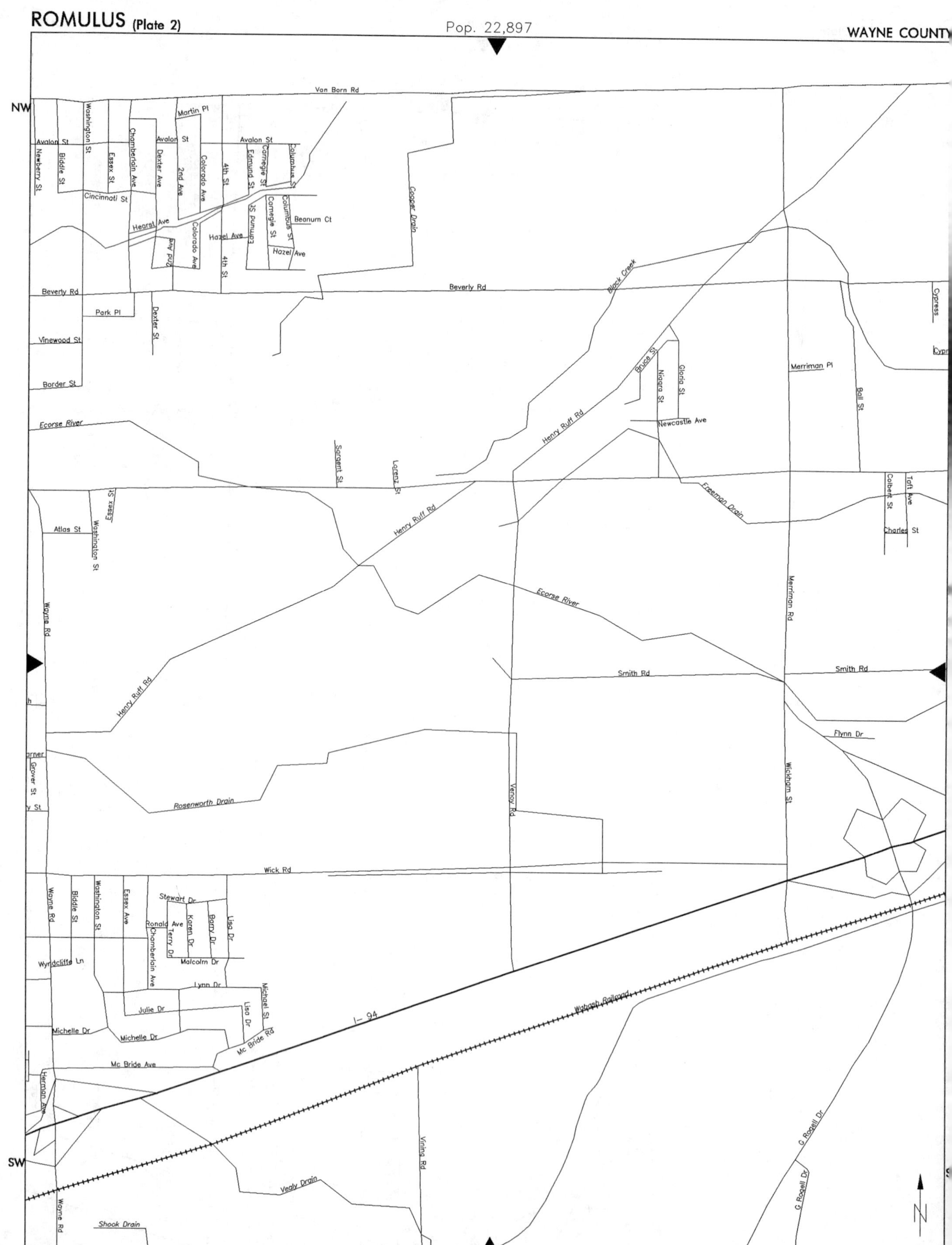
NW
SW
Van Born Rd
Martin Pl
Avalon St
Avalon St
Avalon St
Newberry St
Biddle St
Washington St
Essex St
Chamberlain Ave
Dexter Ave
2nd Ave
Colorado Ave
4th St
Edmund St
Carnegie St
Columbus St
Cincinnati St
Hearst Ave
Hazel Ave
Hazel Ave
Edmund St
Carnegie St
Columbus St
Beanum Ct
2nd Ave
Colorado Ave
4th St
Cooper Drain
Beverly Rd
Beverly Rd
Park Pl
Dexter St
Vinewood St
Border St
Black Creek
Cypress
Cypr
Merriman Pl
Bruce St
Niagra St
Gloria St
Ball St
Henry Ruff Rd
Newcastle Ave
Ecorse River
Sargent St
Lorenz St
Freeman Drain
Colbert St
Taft Ave
Charles St
Essex St
Atlas St
Washington St
Henry Ruff Rd
Wayne Rd
Ecorse River
Merriman Rd
Smith Rd
Smith Rd
Henry Ruff Rd
Flynn Dr
Grover St
Rosenworth Drain
Venoy Rd
Wickham St
Wick Rd
Wayne Rd
Biddle St
Washington St
Essex Ave
Stewart Dr
Ronald Ave
Terry Dr
Karen Dr
Barry Dr
Lisa Dr
Chamberlain Ave
Wyndcliffe Ln
Malcolm Dr
Lynn Dr
Michael St
Julie Dr
Lisa Dr
Michelle Dr
Michelle Dr
Mc Bride Rd
Mc Bride Ave
I- 94
Wabash Railroad
Herman Ave
Vining Rd
Vealy Drain
G Rogell Dr
G Rogell Dr
Wayne Rd
Shook Drain
N

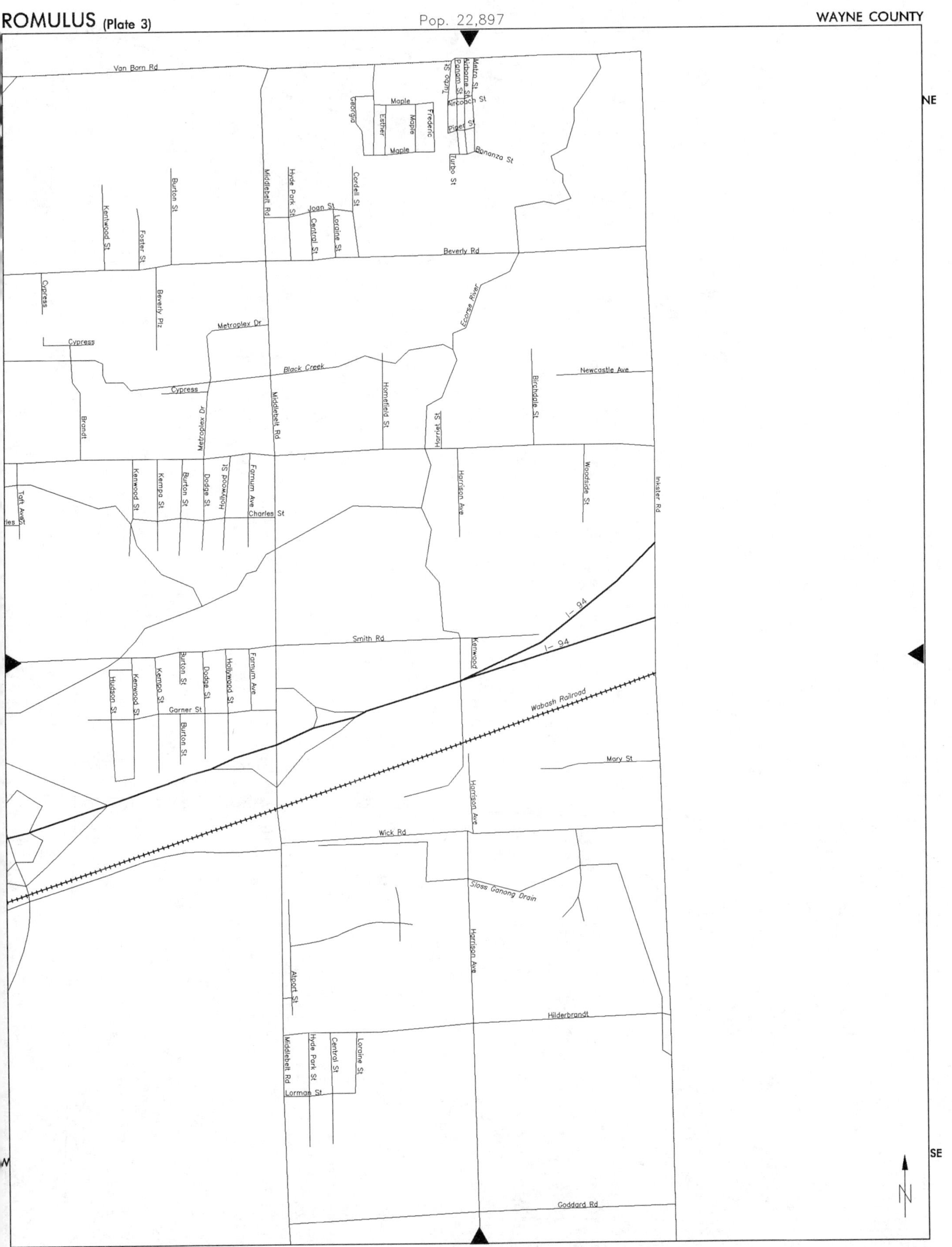
Van Born Rd
Metro St
Airborne St
Panam St
Turbo St
Aircoach St
Maple
Georgia
Esther
Maple
Frederic
Piper St
Maple
Bonanza St
Turbo St
Cordell St
Hyde Park St
Middlebelt Rd
Burton St
Joan St
Central St
Loraine St
Kentwood St
Foster St
Beverly Rd
Cypress
Beverly Plz
Ecorse River
Metroplex Dr
Cypress
Black Creek
Cypress
Newcastle Ave
Homefield St
Birchdale St
Brandt
Metroplex Dr
Middlebelt Rd
Harriet St
Kenwood St
Kempa St
Burton St
Dodge St
Hollywood St
Farnum Ave
Harrison Ave
Woodside St
Inkster Rd
Taft Ave
Charles St
I- 94
I- 94
Smith Rd
Kenwood
Burton St
Dodge St
Hollywood St
Farnum Ave
Hudson St
Kenwood St
Kempa St
Garner St
Burton St
Wabash Railroad
Mary St
Harrison Ave
Wick Rd
Sloss Ganong Drain
Harrison Ave
Alport St
Hilderbrandt
Middlebelt Rd
Hyde Park St
Central St
Loraine St
Lorman St
Goddard Rd
NE
SE
N

Pop. 22,897

WAYNE COUNTY

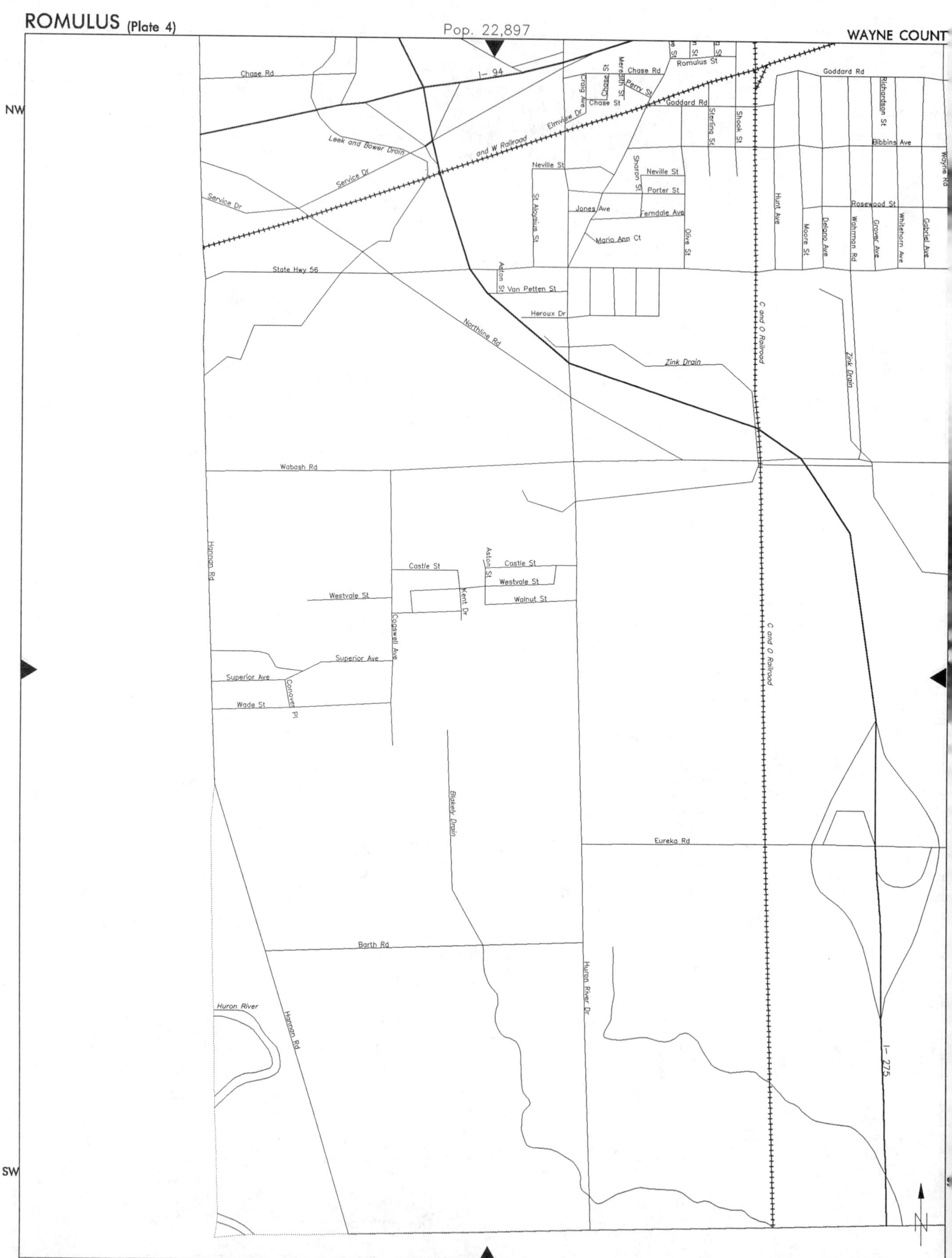

Goddard Rd
Shook Drain
Gabriel Ave
Bibbins Ave
Rosewood St
Gabriel Ave
Sidney St
Vining Rd
G Rogell Dr
NE
Grant Rd
Wayne Rd
Crane Rd
Vealy Drain
Wayne Rd
Zink Drain
Superior Rd
Wahrman Rd
Wayne Rd
Eureka Rd
Redwood
Cherry
Dorset Av
Eureka Rd
Carter Drain
Colbert Ave
Taft Ave
Merriman Rd
Vining Rd
W
SE
Pennsylvania Rd
N

Pop. 22,897

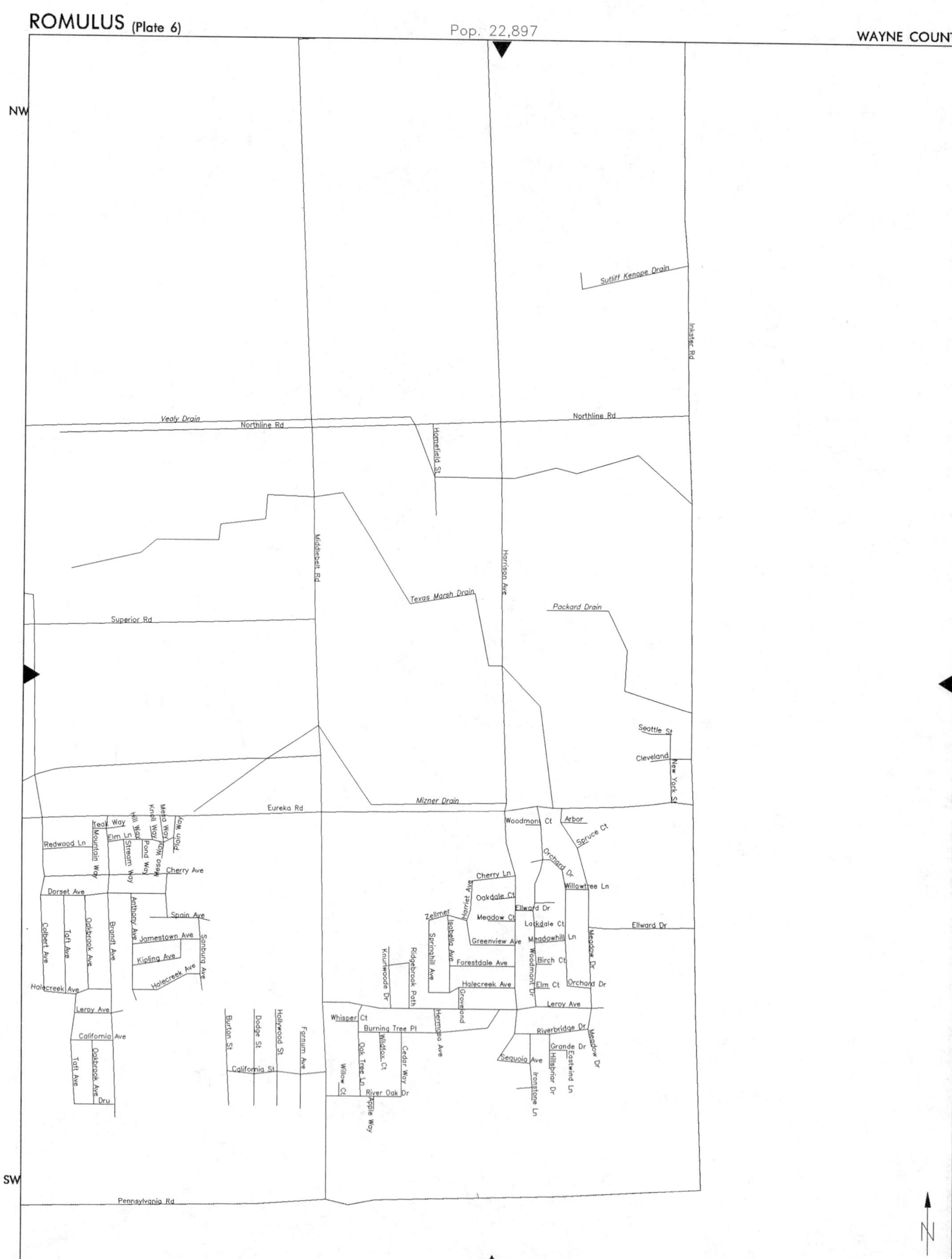
NW
SW
Sutliff Kenope Drain
Inkster Rd
Vealy Drain
Northline Rd
Northline Rd
Homefield St
Middlebelt Rd
Harrison Ave
Texas Marsh Drain
Packard Drain
Superior Rd
Seattle St
Cleveland
New York St
Mizner Drain
Eureka Rd
Woodmont Ct
Arbor
Spruce Ct
Orchard Dr
Willowtree Ln
Cherry Ln
Oakdale Ct
Ellward Dr
Ellward Dr
Meadow Ct
Lakdale Ct
Greenview Ave
Meadowhill Ln
Meadow Dr
Birch Ct
Forestdale Ave
Halecreek Ave
Elm Ct
Orchard Dr
Leroy Ave
Riverbridge Dr
Grande Dr
Meadow Dr
Sequoia Ave
Hillsbriar Dr
Eastwind Ln
Ironstone Ln
Woodmont Dr
Zellmer
Harriet Ave
Isabella Ave
Springhill Ave
Groveland
Hermosa Ave
Knurlwoode Dr
Ridgebrook Path
Whisper Ct
Burning Tree Pl
Wildfox Ct
Cedar Way
Oak Tree Ln
Willow Ct
River Oak Dr
Apple Way
Burton St
Dodge St
Hollywood St
Farnum Ave
California St
Teak Way
Elm Ln
Mountain Way
Hill Way
Stream Way
Pond Way
Knoll Way
Mesa Way
Redwood Ln
Cherry Ave
Dorset Ave
Spain Ave
Anthony Ave
Jamestown Ave
Kipling Ave
Halecreek Ave
Sanburg Ave
Colbert Ave
Taft Ave
Oakbrook Ave
Brandt Ave
Halecreek Ave
Leroy Ave
California Ave
Taft Ave
Oakbrook Ave
Dru
Pennsylvania Rd
N

Sherman Blvd
Wickham Dr
Glenside Blvd
Pa Railroad
Broadway Ave
Cornell Rd
Cornell Ct
Summit Ave
Dawes Rd
Ashland Rd
Henry St
Princeton Rd
Princeton Ct
Greenwich Rd
Eastland Rd
Coolidge Rd
Westland Rd
Roosevelt Rd
Summit Ave
Colonial Rd
Greenwich Rd
Amherst Rd
Chapel Ct
Chapel Rd
Glenside Blvd
Eastland Rd
Drexel Rd
Haverhill Ct
Haverhill Rd
Lambert Dr
Sherwood Rd
Marlboro Rd
Hampden Rd
Roosevelt Rd
Lindland Rd
Woodside Rd
Eastland Rd
Woodside Rd
Hanley Rd
Germaine Rd
Maple Grove Rd
Davis Rd
Fordham Ct
Glenside Blvd
Rockland Rd
Durham Rd
Coventry Rd
Royal Oak Rd
Brookfield Rd
Fordham Rd
Roosevelt Rd
Le Roux Rd
Kloap Rd
Norton Ave
Norton Ave

N

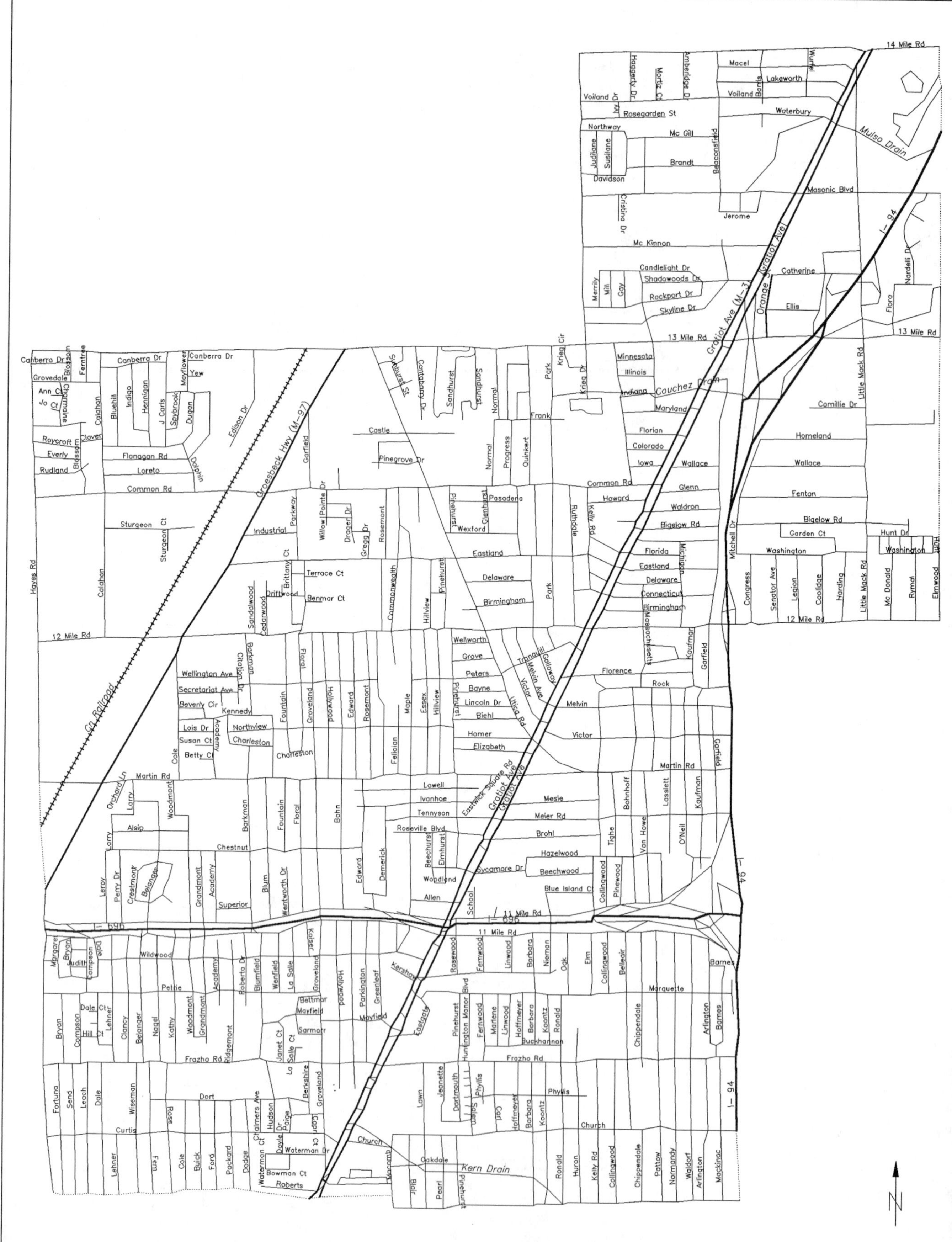
14 Mile Rd
Macel
Lakeworth
Voiland Dr
Voiland
Haggerty Dr
Mortiz Ct
Amberidge Dr
Rosegarden St
Waterbury
Northway
Mc Gill
Judiliane
Susilane
Brandt
Beaconsfield
Davidson
Mulso Drain
Masonic Blvd
Cristina Dr
Jerome
Mc Kinnon
I-94
Candlelight Dr
Shadowoods Dr
Catherine
Nardelli
Merrily
Mill
Gay
Rockport Dr
Skyline Dr
Ellis
Flora
Orange St
Gratiot Ave (M-3)
13 Mile Rd
Krieg Cir
Krieg Ct
Minnesota
Illinois
Indiana
Couchez Drain
Maryland
Comillie Dr
Little Mack Rd
Florian
Colorado
Iowa
Wallace
Homeland
Common Rd
Howard
Glenn
Fenton
Waldron
Bigelow Rd
Garden Ct
Hunt Dr
Washington
Florida
Michigan
Mitchell Dr
Eastland
Delaware
Connecticut
Birmingham
Congress
Senator Ave
Legion
Coolidge
Harding
Mc Donald
Rymal
Elmwood
12 Mile Rd
Canberra Dr
Blossom
Ferntree
Grovedale
Ann Ct
Jo Ct
Charmaine
Calahan
Bluehill
Indigo
Hennigan
J Carls
Spybrook
Mayflower
Yew
Dugan
Edison Dr
Roycroft
Clover
Everly
Flanagan Rd
Rudland
Bidsson
Loreto
Dolphin
Groesbeck Hwy (M-97)
Garfield
Sunburst St
Cottonbury Dr
Sandhurst
Normal
Park
Frank
Castle
Pinegrove Dr
Progress
Quinkert
Pasadena
Pinehurst
Glenhurst
Wexford
Ruthdale
Kelly Rd
Sturgeon Ct
Industrial
Parkway
Willow Pointe Dr
Drager Dr
Gregg Dr
Rosemont
Hayes Rd
Terrace Ct
Benmar Ct
Brittany Ct
Driftwood
Sandalwood
Cedarwood
Commonwealth
Hillview
Massachusetts
Kaufman
Wellworth
Grove
Peters
Bayne
Lincoln Dr
Biehl
Homer
Elizabeth
Tronquill
Galloway
Melvin Ave
Victor
Utica Rd
Florence
Rock
Melvin
Wellington Ave
Secretariat Ave
Beverly Cir
Kennedy
Citation Dr
Barkman
Fountain
Floral
Groveland
Hollywood
Edward
Maple
Essex
Felician
Lois Dr
Susan Ct
Betty Ct
Academy
Northview
Charleston
Cole
Cn Railroad
Martin Rd
Orchard Ln
Larry
Woodmont
Lowell
Ivanhoe
Tennyson
Roseville Blvd
Eastwick Square Rd
Mesle
Meier Rd
Brohl
Bohnhoff
Lasslett
Alsip
Chestnut
Bohn
Beechurst
Elmhurst
Tighe
Van Howe
O'Neil
Hazelwood
Sycamore Dr
Beechwood
Woodland
Allen
School
Blue Island Ct
Collingwood
Pinewood
Leroy
Perry Dr
Crestmont
Belanger
Grandmont
Superior
Blum
Wentworth Dr
Demerick
11 Mile Rd
I-696
Margaret
Bryan
Judith
Dale
Compson
Wildwood
Kaiser
Kershaw
Rosewood
Fernwood
Linwood
Barbara
Nieman
Oak
Elm
Bellair
Barnes
Petrie
Roberta Dr
Blumfield
Wenfield
La Salle
Parkington
Greenleaf
Marquette
Dale Ctr
Lehner
Hill Ct
Clancy
Nagel
Kathy
Ridgemont
Bettmar
Mayfield
Sarmour
Janet Ct
Eastgate
Pinehurst
Huntington Manor Blvd
Marlene
Hoffmeyer
Koontz
Ronald
Buckhannon
Chippendale
Arlington
Frazho Rd
Berkshire
Fortuna
Send
Leach
Wiseman
Rose
Dort
Chalmers Ave
Hudson
Paige
Capri Ct
Lawn
Jeanette
Dartmouth
Salem
Phyllis
Carl
Curtis
Church
Waterman Dr
Waterman Ct
Doyle Dr
Bowman Ct
Roberts
Buick
Ford
Packard
Dodge
Fern
Macomb
Oakdale
Kern Drain
Blair
Pearl
Huron
Pattow
Normandy
Waldorf
Mackinac
N

NOTES

Woodsboro Dr
Greenleaf Dr
Vinton Rd
Bassett Rd
Vinsetta Blvd
Fairlawn Rd
Catalpa Dr
Lawndale Dr
Mayfield Dr
Farnum Ave
Oakridge Ave
Maplegrove Ave
Forestdale Rd
Fernwood Rd
Cambridge Rd
Alfred Ave
Hendrie Blvd
Josephine Ave
Lockwood Rd
Crane Ave
Austin Ave
Hilldale Dr
Woodcrest Dr
Cloverdale Dr
Baker St
Sherman Dr
Maxwell Ave
Oak St
Oakdale St
Maple Ave
Maple Ct
3rd St
Pleasant St
Laurel St
West St
Louis Ave
Oakland Ave
Florence Ave
Park Ave
Derby Ave
Marywood Dr
Lafayette Ave
Washington Ave
Center St
University Ave
Rochester Rd
Pingree Blvd
Troy St
Rosedale Ave
Hawthorne Ave
Gardenia Ave
Virginia Ave
Fairgrove Ave
Curry Ave
Simon Ct
Oakmont St
Baldwin Ave
Frederick St
St Charles Ct
Chambers St
Stanley Ct
Potter Ave
Mason Ct
Phillips Pl
Hamilton Ct
11 Mile Rd
Knowles Ave
2nd St
4th St
5th St
6th St
7th St
Williams St
Lincoln Ave
Lawson St
Kayser St
Irving Ave
Batavia Ave
Longfellow Ave
Alexander Ave
Alladena Ave
Gainsborough Ave
Rembrandt Ave
Blair Ave
Vermont Ave
Connecticut Ave
Grove Ave
Bellaire Ave
Wilson Ave
Mc Lean Ave
Edison Ave
Dorchester Ave
Kenwood Ave
Edgeworth Ave
Symes Ave
Symes Ct
Stephenson Hwy
Baxter Ave
Mace Ave
Sprague Ave
Taylor Ave
Rossell Ave
Minerva Ave
Helena Ave
Middlesex St
Wellesley Ave
Yale Ave
Tufts Ave
Brinkey Ave
Hudson Ave
Katona Ave
Harwood Ave
Barrett Ave
Guthrie Ave
Kenneth Ave
Rowland Ave
Dallas Ave
Brockton Ave
Lenox Ave
I-75 Service Dr
Campbell Rd
Hoffman Ave
Owana Ave
Elowah Ave
Cherokee Ave
Wyandotte Ave
Mohawk Ave
Dondero Ave
Parent Ave
Harrison Ave
Morse Ave
Williams Ct
Delaware Ave
Kenilworth Ave
California Ave
Rhode Island Ave
Maryland Ave
Allenhurst Ave
10 Mile Rd
Woodward Ave
Hudson Ave
9th St
York Rd
Huntington Rd
Dundee Rd
Hereford Dr
Elm Ct
Willits Ave
Ashton Ave
Forest Ave
Farnum Ave

Wadsworth St	2	SW
Walcott St	4	NE
Waller St	3	NW
Wallgren Ct	1	SW
Walnut St	2	SE
Ward St	4	NW
Warner Rd	1	SW
Warren Ave	2	SW
Warren Ave	4	NW
Warwick St	1	SW
Washburn Pl	1	SW
Washington Ave	2	SW
Washington Ave	3	SE
Washington Ave	4	NW
Washington Rd	4	SW
Water St	2	SW
Water St	4	NW
Wayne St	3	NW
Weadock Ave	2	SW
Weadock Ave	4	NW
Webber St	3	NE
Webber St	4	NW
Weber St	3	NE
Webster St	1	SE
Webster St	3	NW
Weiss St	1	NW
Weiss St	2	NW
Welch St	2	NE
Wells St	3	NW
Wesley Dr	4	SW
Westchester Ln	3	SW
Westfield St	3	NW
Westview Ct	1	NW
Westview Dr	1	NW
Wheeler St	3	NW
White St	4	NE
Whitemore Pl	1	SW
Whittier St	4	NE
Wickespark Dr	3	NE
Wilkins St	3	SE
Willard St	1	SW
Williams St	3	NE
Williamson Rd	4	SW
Williamson St	3	NE
Williamson St	4	SW
Willowside Ct	3	SE
Winfred Pl	1	NW
Wisner St	3	NE
Wisner St	4	NW
Witters St	1	NW
Wood St	3	NW
Woodbridge St	1	SW
Woodbridge St	3	NW
Woodward Dr	4	SE
Wright St	1	SW
Wylie Ct	1	SW
Wylie St	1	SW
Wynes Pl	1	SW
Yale St	3	NW
Yawkey St	3	NE
York Dr	4	SW
Youmans St	3	SE
Zauel St	3	SW

NOTES

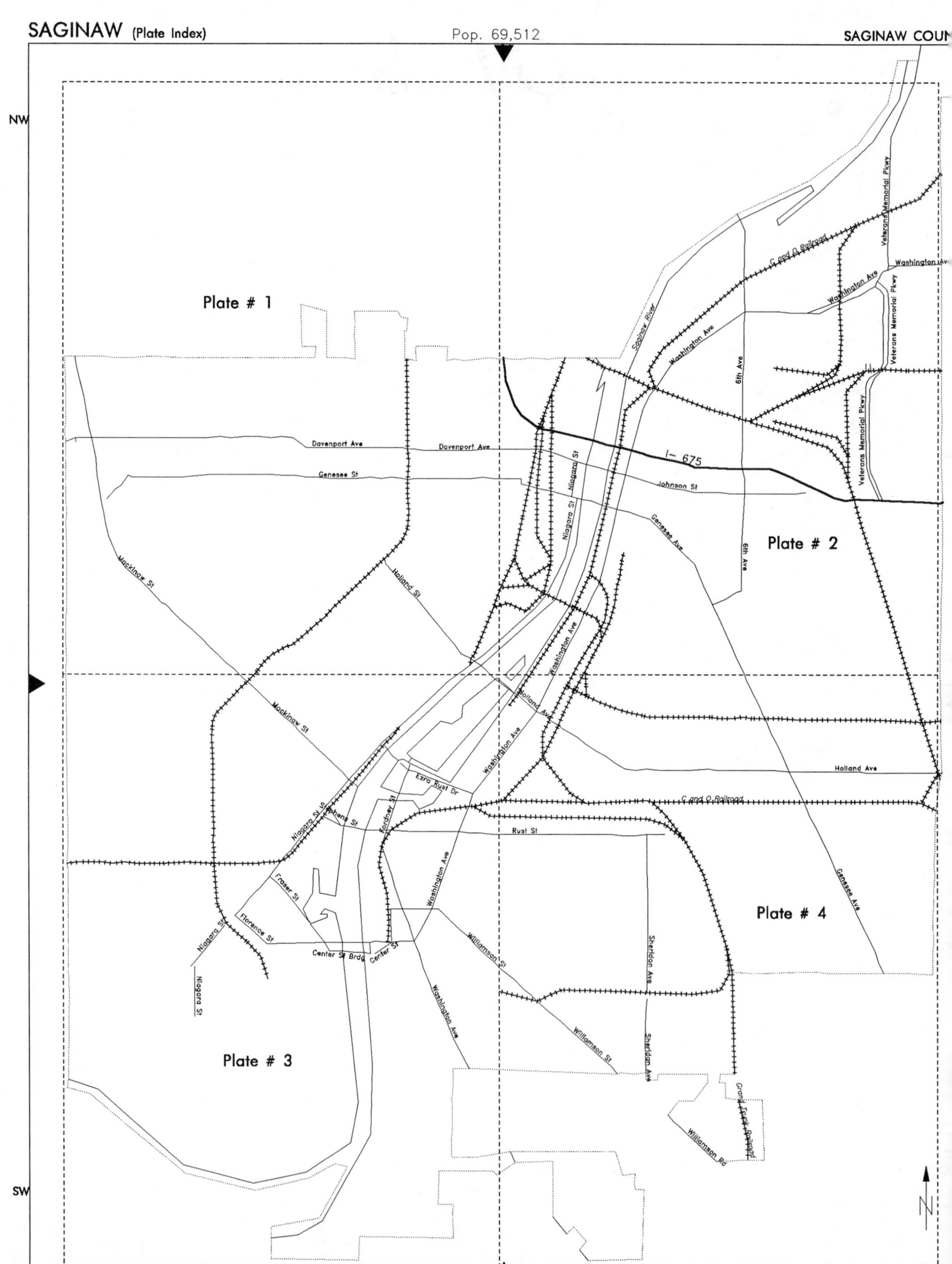
NW
SW
Plate # 1
Plate # 2
Plate # 3
Plate # 4
Davenport Ave
Genesee St
Johnson St
Genesee Ave
I- 675
Mackinaw St
Holland St
Holland Ave
Niagara St
Washington Ave
Saginaw River
6th Ave
C and O Railroad
Veterans Memorial Pkwy
Ezra Rust Dr
Rust St
Fordney St
Fraser St
Florence St
Center St Brdg
Center St
Williamson St
Sheridan Ave
Williamson Rd
Grand Trunk Railroad
N

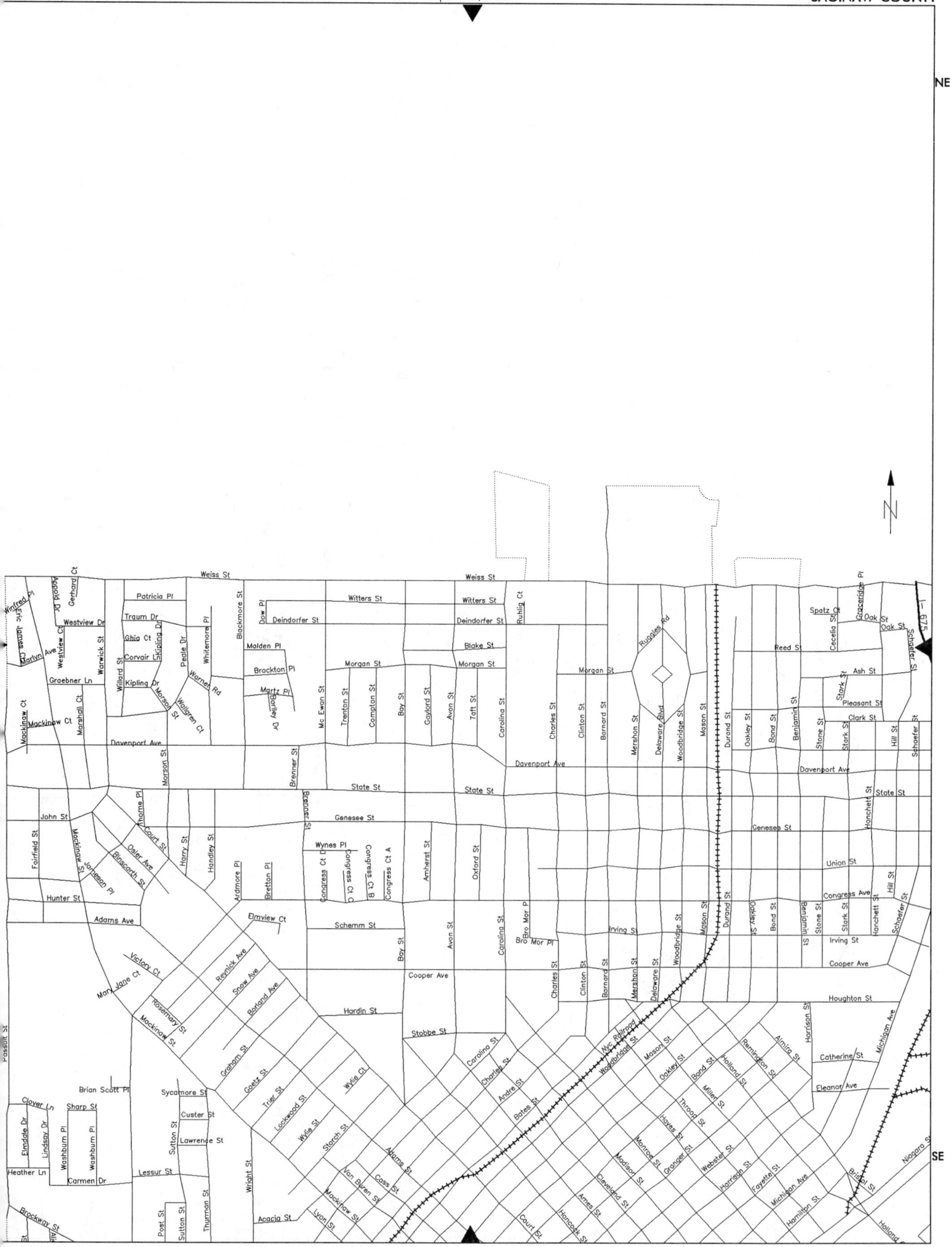

Pop. 69,512

NE

SE

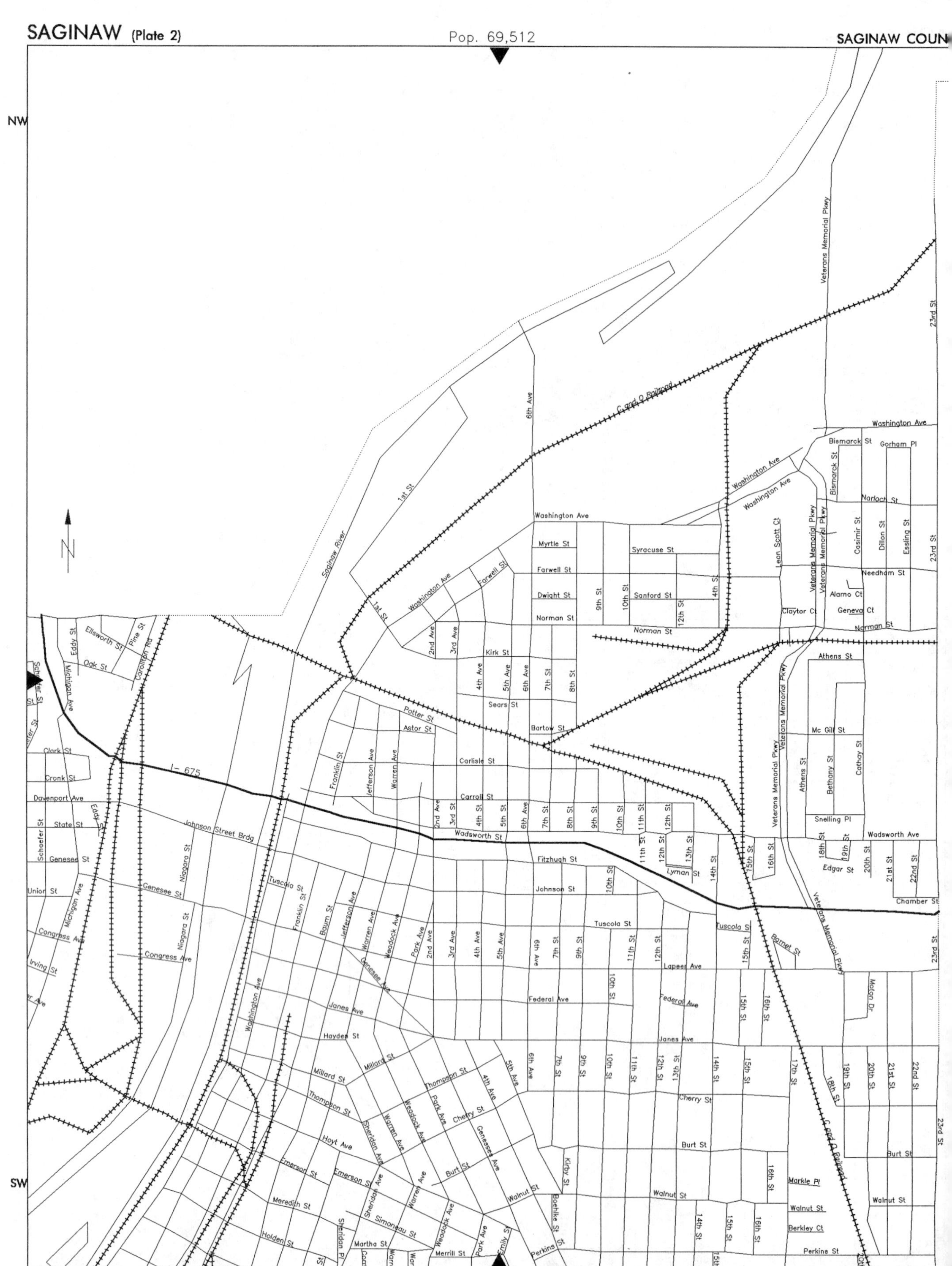
NW
SW
Saginaw River
C and O Railroad
I-675
Veterans Memorial Pkwy
Washington Ave
6th Ave
1st St
Johnson Street Brdg
Wadsworth St
Fitzhugh St
Johnson St
Tuscola St
Genesee Ave
Lapeer Ave
Federal Ave
Janes Ave
Cherry St
Burt St
Walnut St
Perkins St
Michigan Ave
Niagara St
Genesee St
Congress Ave
Carlisle St
Carroll St
Potter St
Astor St
Norman St
Kirk St
Sears St
Bartow St
Myrtle St
Farwell St
Dwight St
Sanford St
Syracuse St
Bismarck St
Gorham Pl
Needham St
Athens St
Mc Gill St
Snelling Pl
Edgar St
Chamber St
Hoyt Ave
Emerson St
Meredith St
Holden St
Martha St
Merrill St
Thompson St
Millard St
Hayden St
Markle Pl
Berkley Ct
Kirby St
Boehike St
Emily St

Brockway St
Kollen St
Wheeler St
Eymer St
Holcomb St
Newberry St
Ottawa St
Birney St
Beech St
Osborn St
Cypress St
Laurel St
Ottawa Blvd
Allegan St
Bliss St
Gratiot Ave
Roethke Ct
Northlawn Ct
Roselawn Ct
Southlawn Ct
Vernon St
Chestnut St
Greenwich St
Vine St
Division St
Marquette St
Vermont St
Maine St
Green St
Jordan St
Emerick St
Kendrick St
Ring St
Burnham St
Wood St
Joslin St
Michigan Ave
Stanley St
Gilbert St
Arthur St
Beacon Dr
Riverside Blvd
Tittabwassee River
Saginaw River
Ezra Rust Access
Ezra Rust Dr
Rust St
Birch St
Eaton St
Webber St
Ketcham St
Linton St
Cambrey St
Williamson St
Rellis St
Randolph St
Gallagher St
Wisner St
Hess St
Ortman St
Gilmore St
Nimons St
Brianfield Ct
Youmans St
Pinemeadow Ct
Bradley St
Willowside Ct
Southview St
Naval Reserve Dr
Mc Lean St
Tarrant St
Parkside Ct
Wickespark Dr
Center St Brdg
Washington Ave
East St
NE
SE

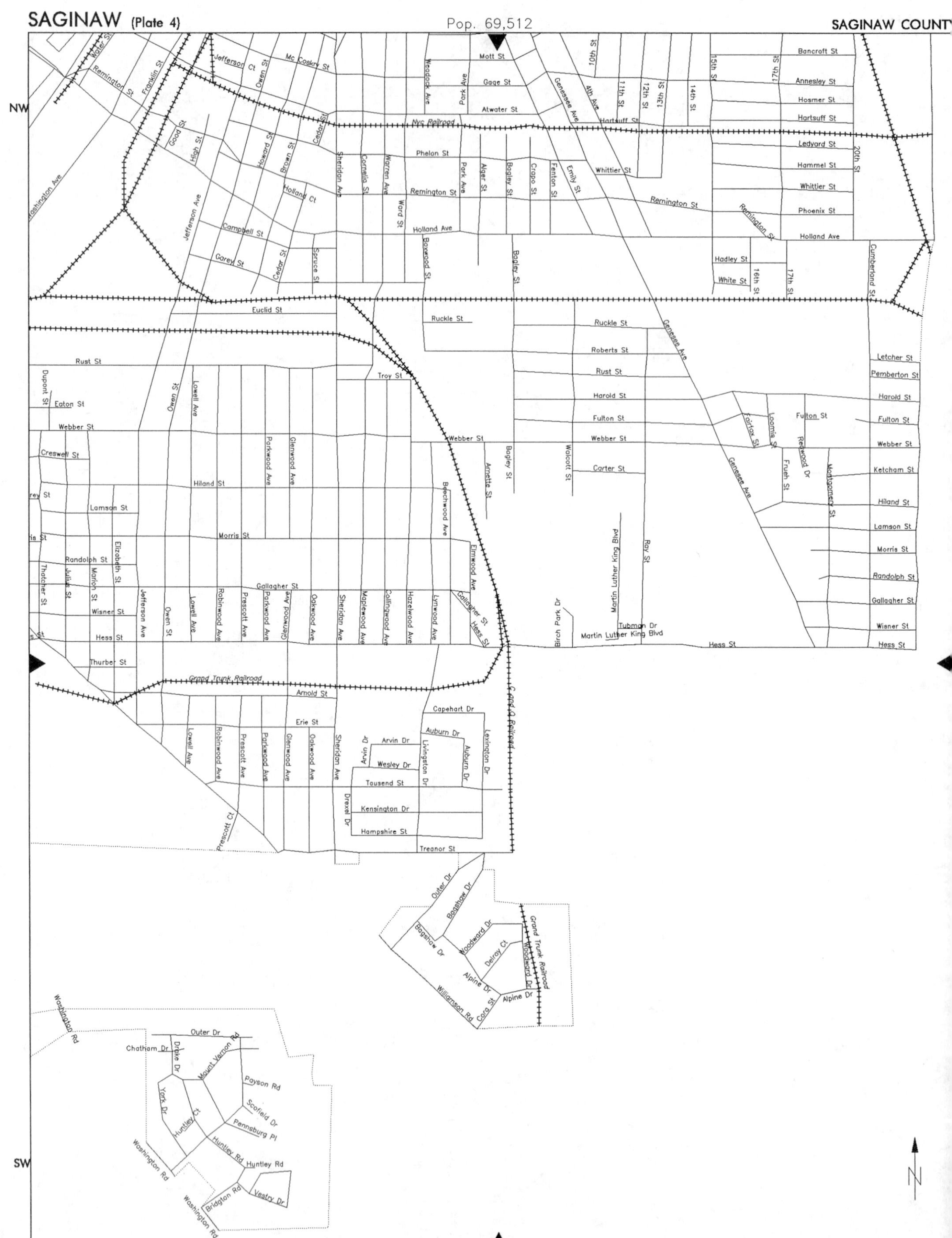
NW
Water St
Remington St
Franklin St
Jefferson Ct
Owen St
Mc Coskry St
Mott St
Gage St
Atwater St
Weadock Ave
Park Ave
10th St
11th St
12th St
13th St
14th St
15th St
17th St
Bancroft St
Annesley St
Hosmer St
Hartsuff St
Genesee Ave
4th Ave
Nyc Railroad
Good St
High St
Howard St
Brown St
Cedar St
Washington Ave
Ledyard St
Hammel St
Whittier St
Phoenix St
20th St
Phelon St
Sheridan Ave
Cornelia St
Warren Ave
Park Ave
Alger St
Bagley St
Crapo St
Fenton St
Emily St
Holland Ct
Remington St
Ward St
Jefferson Ave
Campbell St
Holland Ave
Garey St
Cedar St
Spruce St
Boxwood St
Hadley St
White St
16th St
17th St
Cumberland St
Euclid St
Ruckle St
Roberts St
Rust St
Harold St
Fulton St
Webber St
Carter St
Letcher St
Pemberton St
Dupont St
Eaton St
Troy St
Owen St
Lowell Ave
Creswell St
Parkwood Ave
Glenwood Ave
Arnette St
Walcott St
Fairfax St
Loomis St
Redwood Dr
Frueh St
Montgomery St
Ketcham St
Hiland St
Lamson St
Beechwood Ave
Morris St
Randolph St
Elizabeth St
Elmwood Ave
Martin Luther King Blvd
Ray St
Thatcher St
Julius St
Marion St
Gallagher St
Robinwood Ave
Prescott Ave
Oakwood Ave
Maplewood Ave
Collingwood Ave
Hazelwood Ave
Lynwood Ave
Wisner St
Hess St
Birch Park Dr
Tubman Dr
Thurber St
Grand Trunk Railroad
Arnold St
Capehart Dr
Erie St
Auburn Dr
Lexington Dr
Arvin Dr
Livingston Dr
Wesley Dr
Tausend St
Drexel Dr
Kensington Dr
Hampshire St
Treanor St
Prescott Ct
Outer Dr
Bagshaw Dr
Woodward Dr
Delray Ct
Alpine Dr
Williamson Rd
Cora St
Washington Rd
Chatham Dr
Drake Dr
Mount Vernon Rd
Payson Rd
York Dr
Huntley Ct
Scofield Dr
Penneburg Pl
Huntley Rd
Vestry Dr
Bridgton Rd
SW
N

Woodlawn Dr
Bristol Dr
Sunview Dr
Beaver Road
Parkway Dr
Main St
Saginaw Ave
Park Ct
North St
Oak St
Walnut St
Maple St
Christy Dr
Chestnut St
Locust St
Cherry St
Saginaw Ave
Miami St
Belle Ave
Randolph St
Vine St
Pine St
Spruce St
Water St
Marcy St
Clinton St
Hosmer St
Charles St
Fort St
Lake St
Flint St
Fulton St
Jay St
Clifford St
Sanderson St
Belle Ave
Hosmer St
Florence
Baltic
Coal St
Benton St
Hanchett St
Flint St
N

Range Rd
State Hwy 29
Turnberry
Highland Dr
Meldrum Cir
Hawthorne
Stratford
6th St
2nd St
Benedict Ave
Brown St
9th St
Langley Cir
3rd St
Royal St
10th St
Waterloo
Royal St
Robinson
Vine St
5th St
4th St
2nd St
Orchard St
Cox Rd
Carney Dr
8th
Thornapple
Adams
6th St
5th St
Jay St
4th St
3rd St
7th St
10th St
9th St
Jay St
Trumbull
2nd St
Cass St
Clinton Ave
Witherall St
Jackson St
Oakwood Lane
Hugo St
Whiting St
Pine
Sinclair St
Cedar
11th St
5th St
Hugo St
Fort
15th St
6th St
Henry St
Whiting St
12th St
10th St
9th St
Juliet
Fort
Frances
Fred W Moore
Mary St
Laura St
Harriet
Palmer Rd
St Clair Hwy
Edison St
Glendale St
Goffe
Riverside Ave
Elmdale Rd
Oak Rd
M-29
N

NOTES

14 Mile Rd
I-94
Freeway Dr
Mulso Drain
Robeson Ave
Country Club Dr
Masonic Blvd
Harper Ave
Larkmoor Ct
Larkmoor Ave
New York Ave
Allor Ave
Heathwood Dr
Tanglewood
Timberidge Rd
Briarcliff
Thorncrest Rd
Parkway Ave
Brookwood Rd
Sunset Ln
Share Ave
Fairway Ln
St Margaret
Lakebreeze Dr
Willow Wisp
Arrowhead Rd
Vandover Ct
Rhode Island Ct
Edgewater Ave
Masonic Blvd
Port Ave
Shoreview Dr
Detour Ave
Euclid Ave
Socia Ave
13 Mile Rd
Greater Mack Ave
Lac Ste Claire Dr
Jefferson Ave
Recreation Dr
Playview Dr
Glenbrook Ave
Joy Ave
Beverly Ave
Deziel Ave
Elmira Blvd
Tebo Drain
Talbot Ave
Lakewood Blvd
Harvard Shore Dr
Deanhurst
Donaldson Ave
Love Ave
Burton Ave
Angeline Ct
Waterloo Ave
Dorian
Dorian Ave
Hoffman Ave
Manhattan Ave
Violet Ave
Evergreen Ave
Evergreen
Elmgrove
Champine Dr
Manton Ave
Francis
Raymond Ave
Raymond Ct
Jewell Ave
Grossedale Lake Ave
Lake Blvd
Lincoln Ave
Taylor Ave
Maison Ave
6th
5th
1st
Garfield Ave
Furton Ave
Arcadia Ave
Lake Dr
Oakgrove Ave
Maplegrove Ave
Elmgrove Ave
Gloria Ave
Roosevelt Ave
Rosebriar Ave
Elmwood
12 Mile Rd
Visnaw
Winsholl St
Elmwood Ct
Millenbach Ave
Corteville Ave
Barton Ave
Mylls Ave
Lanse Ave
French Drain
St Gertrude Ave
Roy Ave
Hughes Ave
Beste Ave
Grant Ave
Ursuline Ave
Gaffke Ave
Sussex Dr
Scarsdale Dr
Sherry Ave
Joan
Boston Blvd
Jane Ave
Rockwood Blvd
Little Mack Rd
Michael Ct
Winkel Dr
Thiele Dr
Martin Rd
Gordon Rd
Crane Ct
Briar Ct
Stanley Ave
Larchmont Ave
Hazelwood Ave
Elmdale Ave
Shock Ave
Jay Ct
Robin Ct
Lark Ct
Glenwood Ave
Gladstone Ave
Florence Ave
Nieman Ave
Vogt Ave
Elba Ave
Worthington Ct
Poplar Beach Dr
Gordon Switch
Grove Pointe Dr
11 Mile Rd
Cedar
Milner Rd
N

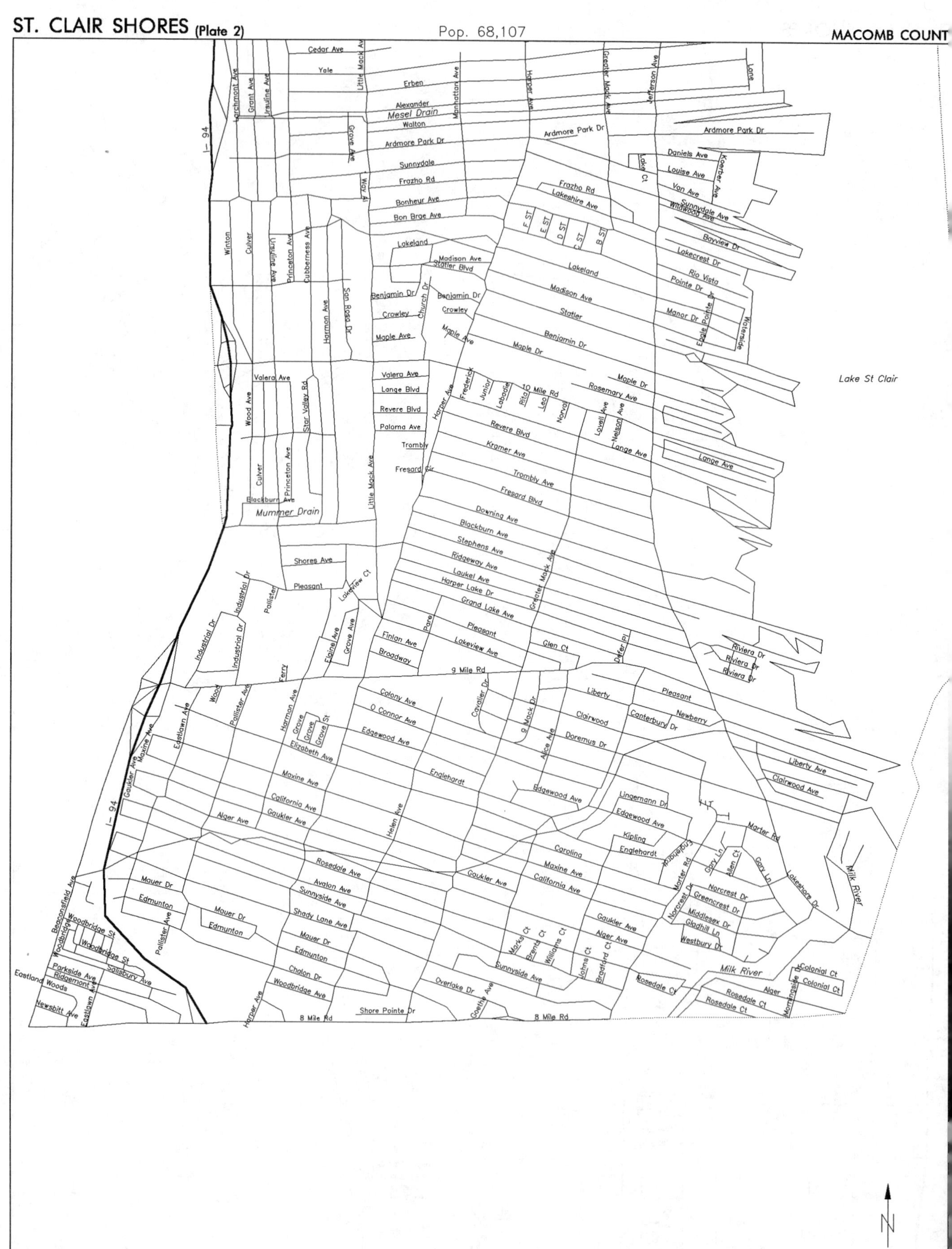
Cedar Ave
Yale
Little Mack Ave
Larchmont Ave
Grant Ave
Ursuline Ave
Erben
Manhattan Ave
Harper Ave
Greater Mack Ave
Jefferson Ave
Lane
Alexander
Mesel Drain
Walton
I- 94
Grove Ave
Ardmore Park Dr
Sunnydale
Frazho Rd
Way Al
Bonheur Ave
Bon Brae Ave
Daniels Ave
Louise Ave
Van Ave
Lake Ct
Koerber Ave
Sunnydale Ave
Wildwood Ave
Lakeshire Ave
F ST
E ST
D ST
C ST
B ST
Bayview Dr
Lakecrest Dr
Rio Vista
Pointe Dr
Winton
Culver
Ursuline Ave
Princeton Ave
Cubberness Ave
Lakeland
Madison Ave
Statler Blvd
Benjamin Dr
Church Dr
San Rosa Dr
Harmon Ave
Crowley
Maple Ave
Statler
Manor Dr
Eagle Pointe Dr
Waterside
Maple Dr
Lake St Clair
Valera Ave
Wood Ave
Star Valley Rd
Lange Blvd
Revere Blvd
Paloma Ave
Frederick
Junior
Labadie
Rita
Leo
Norval
10 Mile Rd
Rosemary Ave
Lovell Ave
Nelson Ave
Revere Blvd
Lange Ave
Kramer Ave
Trombly
Trombly Ave
Fresard Cir
Fresard Blvd
Blackburn Ave
Mummer Drain
Downing Ave
Blackburn Ave
Stephens Ave
Ridgeway Ave
Shores Ave
Pleasant
Lakeview Ct
Industrial Dr
Pallister
Laukel Ave
Harper Lake Dr
Grand Lake Ave
Elaine Ave
Pare
Pleasant
Finlan Ave
Broadway
Lakeview Ave
Glen Ct
Defer Pl
Riviera Dr
Ferry
9 Mile Rd
Wood
Pallister Ave
Eastlawn Ave
Maxine Ave
Harmon Ave
Grove
Grove St
Colony Ave
O Connor Ave
Edgewood Ave
Elizabeth Ave
Cavalier Dr
9 Mack Dr
Liberty
Clairwood
Canterbury Dr
Newberry
Doremus Dr
Alice Ave
Liberty Ave
Clairwood Ave
Englehardt
Gaukler Ave
California Ave
Alger Ave
Helen Ave
Lingemann Dr
Kipling
Marter Rd
Gary Ln
Allen Ct
Carolina
Rosedale Ave
Avalon Ave
Sunnyside Ave
Shady Lane Ave
Mauer Dr
Edmunton
Chalon Dr
Woodbridge Ave
Norcrest Dr
Greencrest Dr
Middlesex Dr
Gladhill Ln
Westbury Dr
Lakeshore Dr
Milk River
Beaconsfield Ave
Woodbridge St
Salisbury Ave
Parkside Ave
Ridgemont
Eastland Woods
Newsbitt Ave
Marks Ct
Brents Ct
Williams Ct
Johns Ct
Bradford Ct
Sunnyside Ave
Overlake Dr
Goethe Ave
Shore Pointe Dr
8 Mile Rd
Rosedale Ct
Colonial Ct
Morningside
N

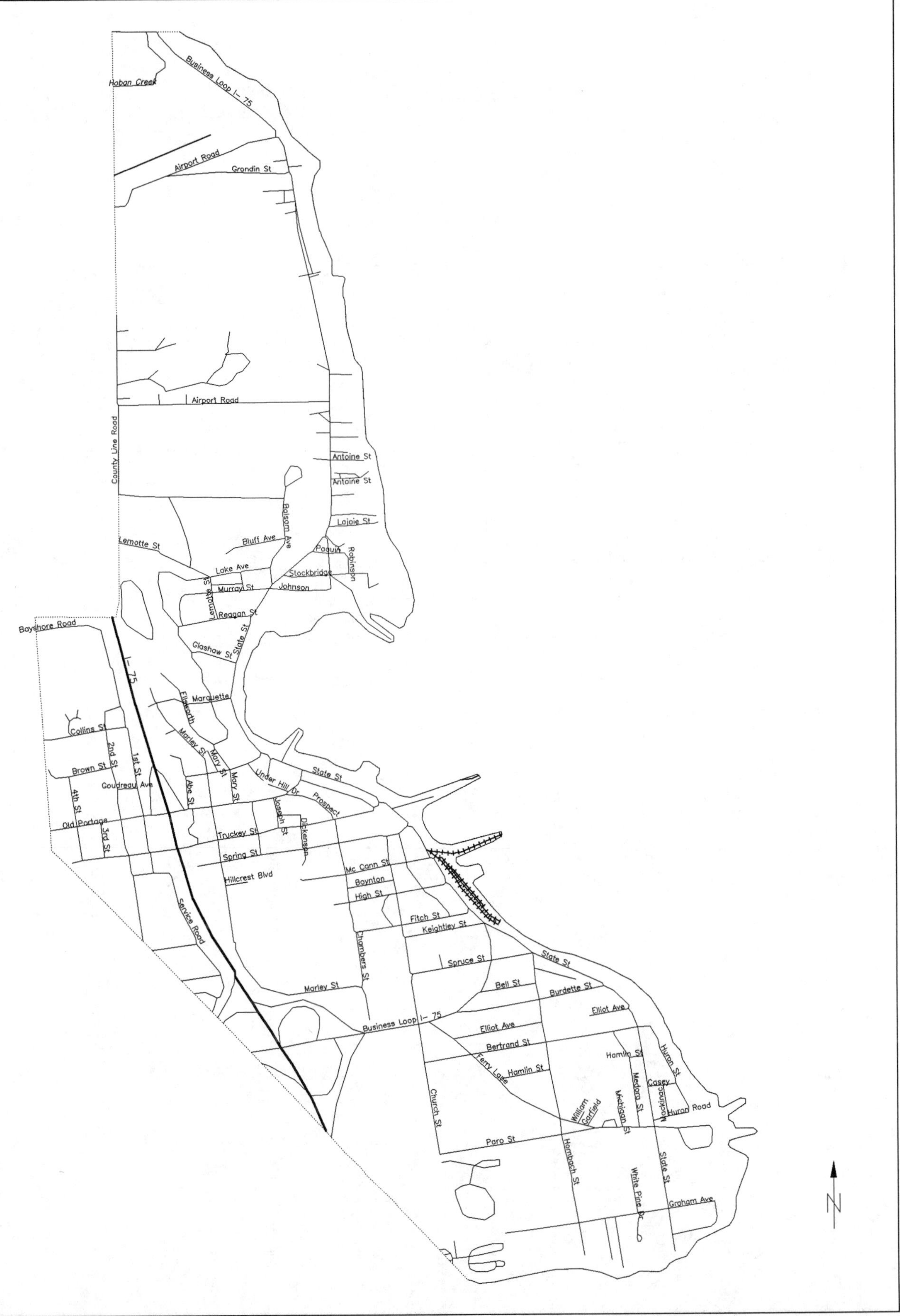

Hoban Creek
Business Loop I-75
Airport Road
Grondin St
Airport Road
County Line Road
Antoine St
Antoine St
Lajoie St
Balsam Ave
Bluff Ave
Lemotte St
Paquin
Robinson
Lake Ave
Stockbridge
Murray St
Johnson
Lemotte St
Reagan St
Bayshore Road
Glashaw St
State St
I-75
Marquette
Ellsworth
Collins St
Marley St
Mary St
2nd St
1st St
Brown St
Goudreau Ave
Mary St
Under Hill Dr
State St
Abe St
4th St
Old Portage
3rd St
Joseph St
Prospect
Dickenson
Truckey St
Spring St
Hillcrest Blvd
Mc Cann St
Boynton
High St
Fitch St
Keightley St
Service Road
Chambers St
Spruce St
State St
Bell St
Burdette St
Marley St
Elliot Ave
Business Loop I-75
Elliot Ave
Bertrand St
Hamlin St
Ferry Lane
Hamlin St
Huron St
Church St
Medora St
Casey
William Corfield
Michigan St
Huron Road
Paro St
Hornbach St
State St
White Pine Dr
Graham Ave
N

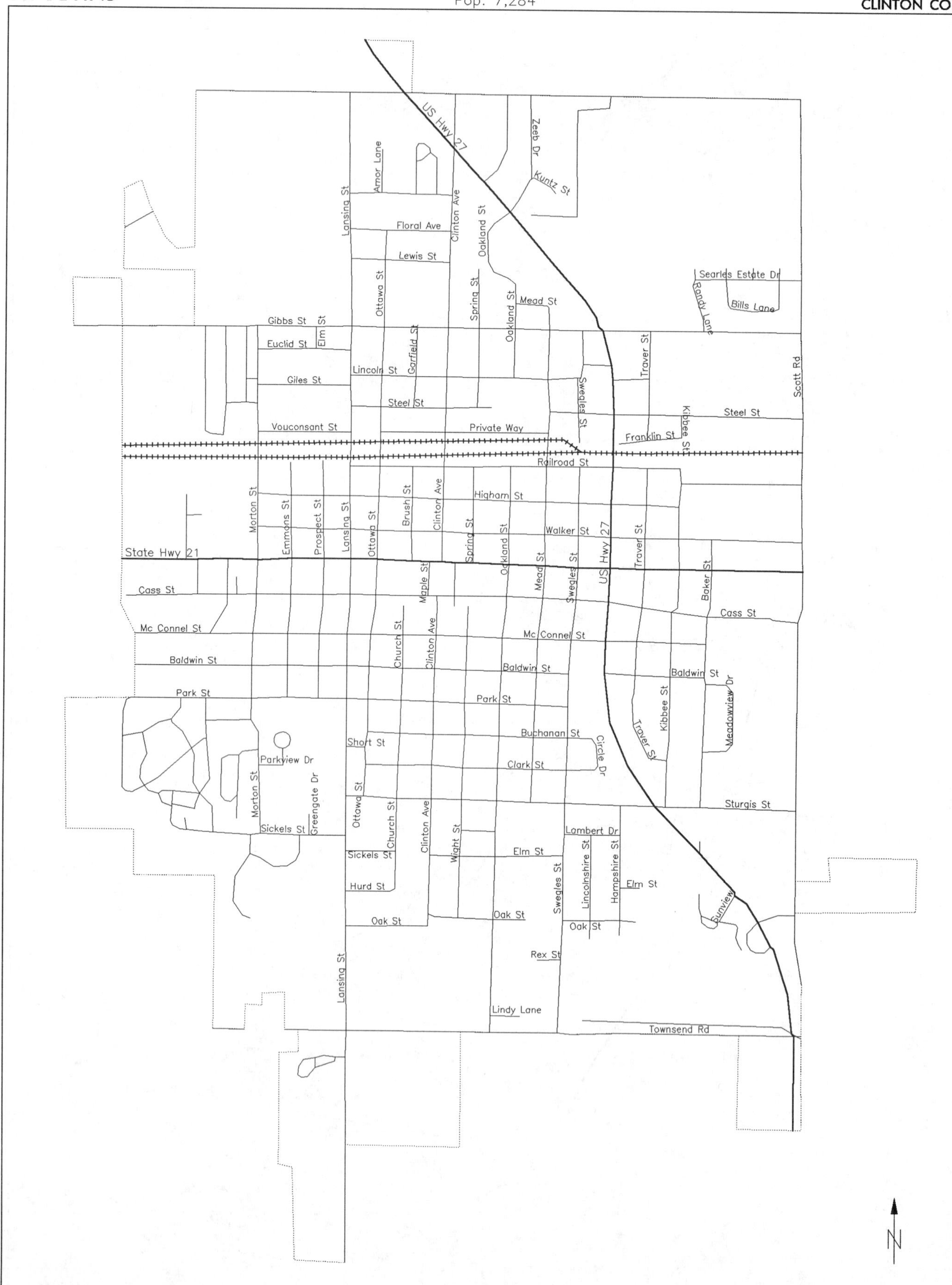
US Hwy 27
Zeeb Dr
Kuntz St
Amor Lane
Lansing St
Clinton Ave
Oakland St
Floral Ave
Lewis St
Searles Estate Dr
Randy Lane
Bills Lane
Ottawa St
Spring St
Oakland St
Mead St
Gibbs St
Elm St
Euclid St
Garfield St
Lincoln St
Giles St
Traver St
Scott Rd
Swegles St
Steel St
Steel St
Kibbee St
Vouconsant St
Private Way
Franklin St
Railroad St
Morton St
Higham St
Emmons St
Prospect St
Lansing St
Ottawa St
Brush St
Clinton Ave
Spring St
Oakland St
Walker St
US Hwy 27
Traver St
State Hwy 21
Maple St
Mead St
Swegles St
Baker St
Cass St
Cass St
Mc Connel St
Church St
Clinton Ave
Mc Connel St
Baldwin St
Baldwin St
Baldwin St
Park St
Park St
Meadowview Dr
Kibbee St
Buchanan St
Short St
Traver St
Circle Dr
Parkview Dr
Clark St
Morton St
Greengate Dr
Ottawa St
Church St
Sturgis St
Sickels St
Clinton Ave
Wight St
Lambert Dr
Elm St
Lincolnshire St
Hampshire St
Sickels St
Swegles St
Elm St
Hurd St
Sunview
Oak St
Oak St
Oak St
Rex St
Lansing St
Lindy Lane
Townsend Rd
N

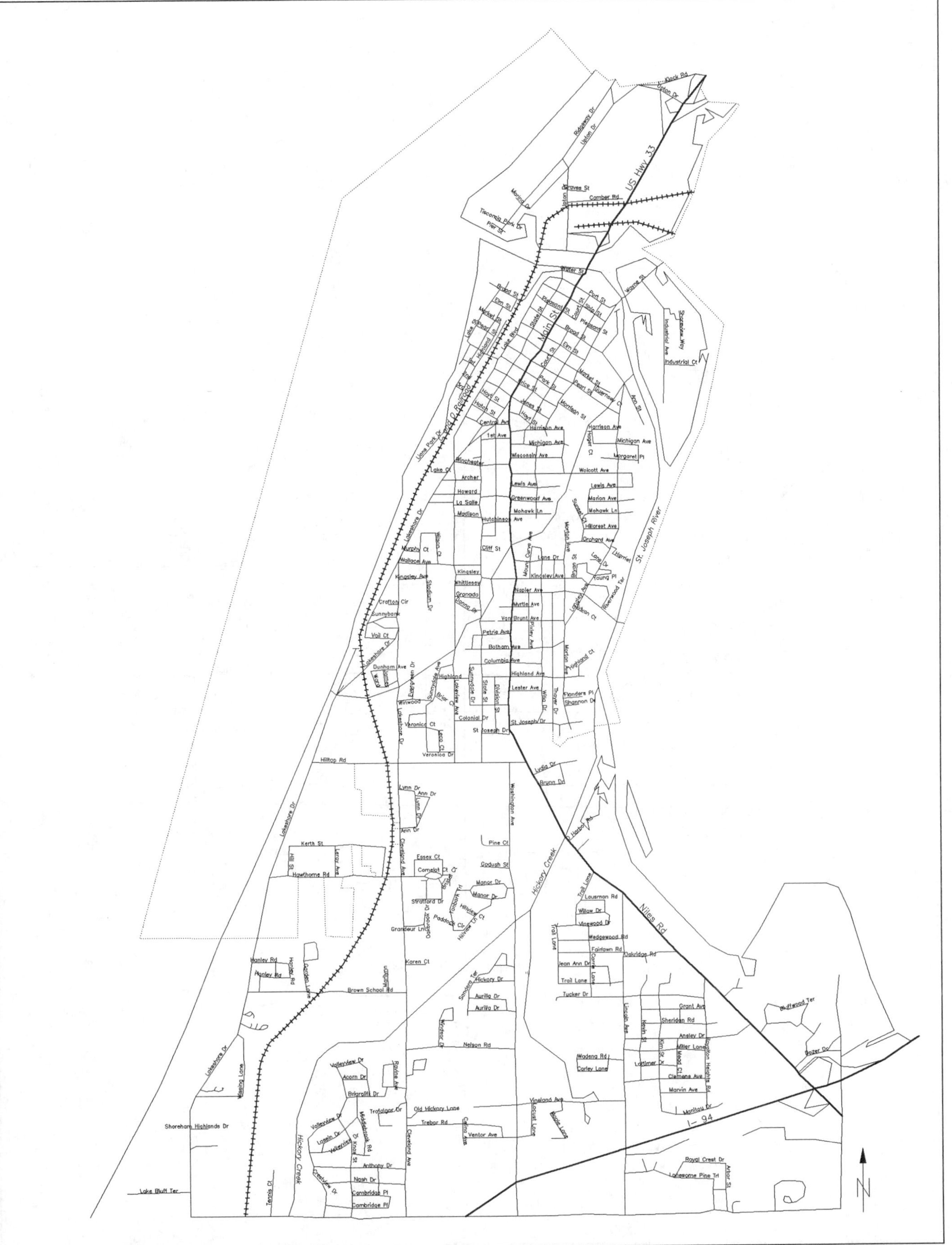

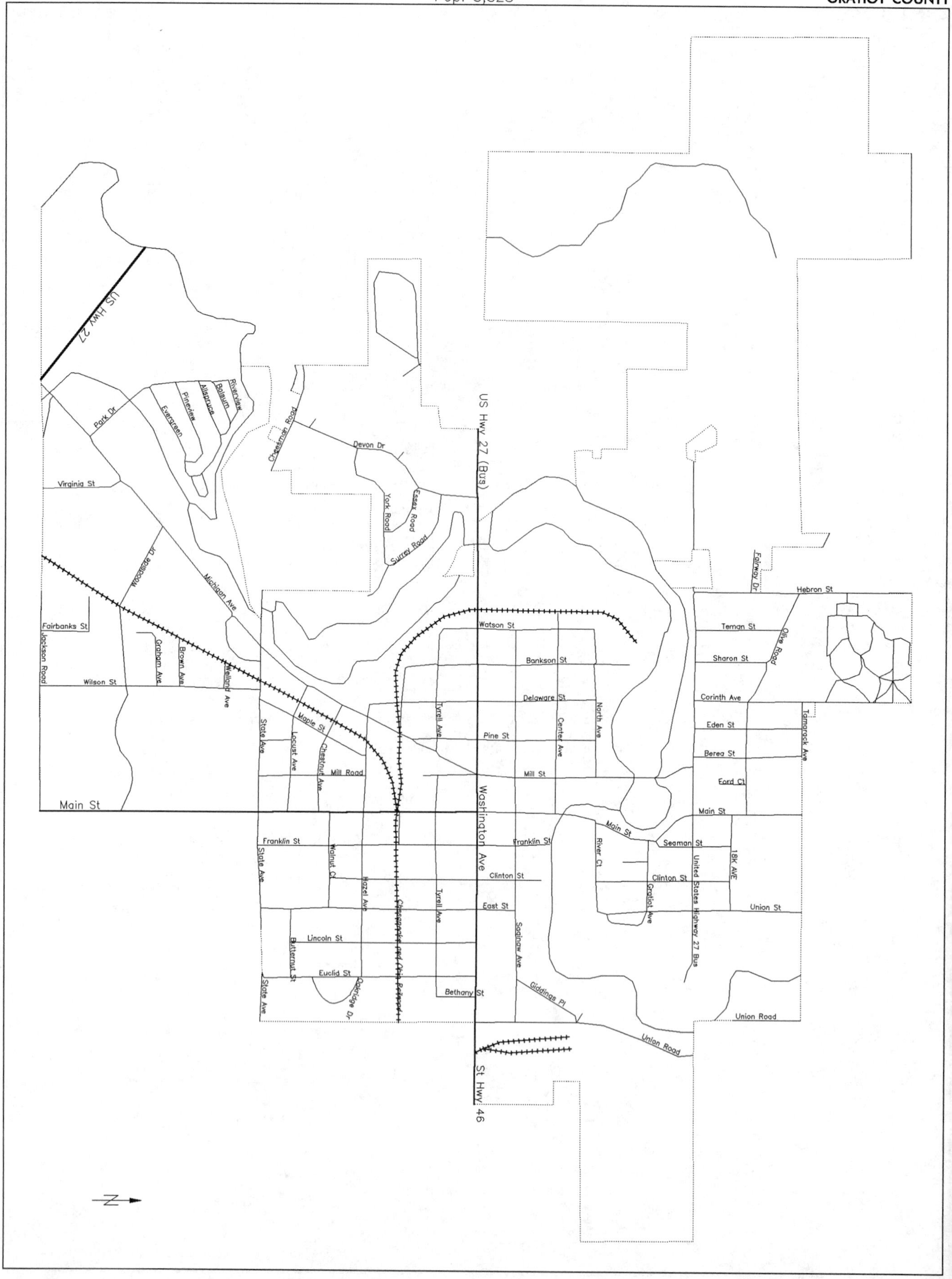
US Hwy 27
Riverview
Balsam
Allspruce
Pineview
Evergreen
Park Dr
Cheesman Road
Devon Dr
US Hwy 27 (Bus)
Virginia St
York Road
Essex Road
Surrey Road
Woodside Dr
Michigan Ave
Fairway Dr
Hebron St
Fairbanks St
Jackson Road
Graham Ave
Brown Ave
Welland Ave
Wilson St
Watson St
Teman St
Olive Road
Bankson St
Sharon St
Delaware St
Corinth Ave
Tyrell Ave
North Ave
Maple St
State Ave
Locust Ave
Chestnut Ave
Pine St
Center Ave
Eden St
Tamarack Ave
Berea St
Mill Road
Mill St
Ford Ct
Main St
Washington Ave
Main St
Main St
Franklin St
Walnut Ct
Franklin St
Seaman St
River Ct
18K AVE
State Ave
Clinton St
Clinton St
United States Highway 27 Bus
Hazel Ave
Tyrell Ave
Gratiot Ave
East St
Union St
Chesapeake and Ohio Railroad
Lincoln St
Butternut St
Saginaw Ave
Euclid St
Oakridge Dr
State Ave
Giddings Pl
Bethany St
Union Road
Union Road
St Hwy 46

Tefft Ct
Maplewood Dr
Maplewood Ct
Maplewood Dr
Industrial Dr
Colony Dr
Wiltshire
Woodland Ct
Woodland Dr
Steiner Ct
Berkshire Dr
Berkshire Dr
Ann Arbor Saline Rd
Maple St
Pc Railroad
Industrial Dr
Barnes Ct
Bennington Ct
Woodbridge Ct
Tower Dr
Nichols Dr
Nichols Dr
Watson St
Colony Ct
Wallace St
Lambkins Rd
Harris St
Heritage Dr
Lexington Dr
Saline Waterworks Rd
Harper St
Bossett St
Calder Ct
Wittier Ct
Echo Ct
Wood Outlet Drain
Park Pl
Hartman Lane
Leuthueser Dr
US Hwy 12
Hickory Lane
Clark St
Bennett St
Highland St
Spring St
Keveling Dr
Lewis St
Detroit St
Bemis Rd
Linden Ct
Hollywood Dr
Marion Ct
Wheeler Ct
Owen Pl
Michigan Ave
Maple Rd
Mc Kay St
Davenport St
Williams St
Hall St
Russell St
Saline River
Old Creek Dr
Pondview
Mc Kay St
Lewis St
Henry St
Risdon Dr
Harris St
Saline River Dr
Mark Hannah Ct
Glenbrook Ct
Whitlock St
Washington St
Pleasant Ridge Dr
Forestbrook Ct
Forestbrook Dr
Austin Rd
Circle Ct
Canterberry Dr
Rosemont Ave
Old Creek Ct
Marpool Dr
Woodhill Dr
Valley Blvd
Annwood Ct
Crestwood Ave
Eastlook Dr
Elmwood Ct
Monroe St
Springbrook Cres
Springbrook Ct
Valley Cir
Woodingham Ct
Willis Rd
Knollwood Ct
Koch Warner Drain
N

Gates Road
Sunset
Westbrook
Woodland Dr
Stoney Creek Dr
Green Acres Dr
Dawson St
Dawson St
Maplevalley St
Lamotte St
Sanilac Ave
Loraine St
Marion Ave
Worth St
Hart St
Marlette St
Bridgehampton Road
Mills St
Custer St
Minden St
Marion Ave
Colonial Dr
Flynn St
Bennett Dr
Washington St
Washington St
Delaware St
Morgan St
Redmond St
Austin St
Lexington St
Elk St
Elk St
Elk St (M-19)
Morse St
Morse St
Morse St
Moore St
Moore St
Gaige St
Mills St
Truman St
Jefferson St
Speaker Ave
Lincoln St
Marion Ave
Argyle Ave
Moffatt
Fulton St
Fulton St
Fulton St
Jackson St
Jackson St
Jackson St
Roberts St
Margaret St
Stoutenberg Road
Stoutenberg Road
Industrial Dr
Thelma Dr
Sanilac Ave
Orval St

Summit
Summit St
Parsonage St
Parsonage St
Liberty St
Washington St
Union St
Dewitt St
Shawnee Dr
Jackson St
Wyandotte
Washington St
Bridge St
Bridge St
Lake Creek
Main St
Grand River
Center St
Depot
Clover Lane
Vosper St
Orchard St
Church St
Weeks Road
Pleasant St
Mill St
Ada-Lyons Road
Grand Trunk Western Railroad

SAULT STE. MARIE (Plate 1)

Pop. 14,689

CHIPPEWA COUNTY

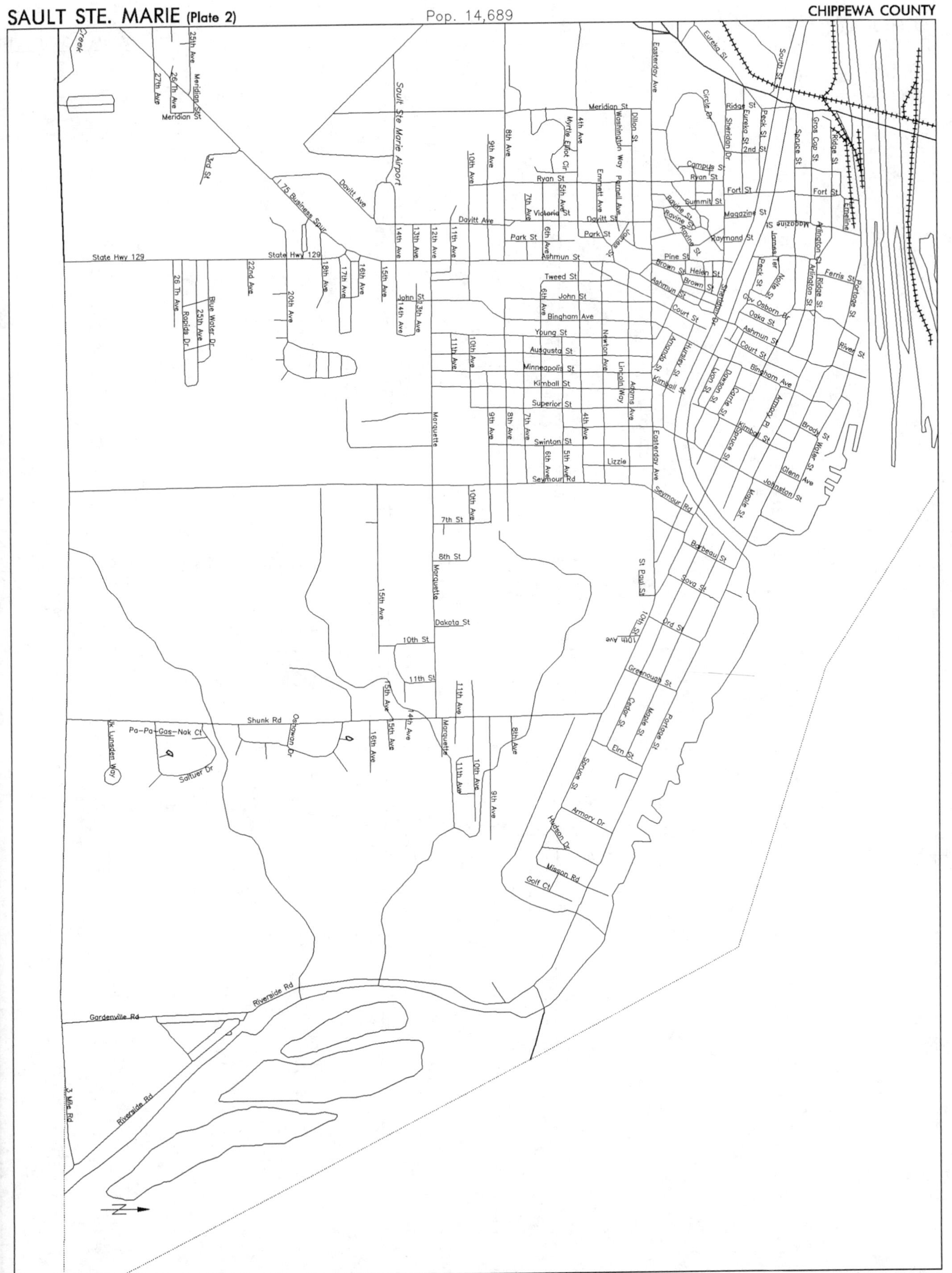
Creek
25th Ave
Meridian St
26 Th Ave
27th Ave
Meridian St
3rd St
I 75 Business Spur
Davitt Ave
Sault Ste Marie Airport
State Hwy 129
State Hwy 129
26 Th Ave
Rapids Dr
25th Ave
Blue Water Dr
22nd Ave
20th Ave
18th Ave
17th Ave
16th Ave
15th Ave
14th Ave
13th Ave
12th Ave
11th Ave
10th Ave
9th Ave
8th Ave
John St
13th Ave
14th Ave
Easterday Ave
Meridian St
Dillon St
Washington Way
4th Ave
Myrtle Elliot Cir
Parnell Ave
Emmett Ave
Ryan St
5th Ave
7th Ave
Victoria St
Davitt Ave
Davitt St
Park St
Park St
6th Ave
Ashmun St
Tweed St
John St
6th Ave
Bingham Ave
Young St
11th Ave
10th Ave
Ausgusta St
Minneapolis St
Kimball St
Superior St
Newton Ave
Lincoln Way
Adams Ave
Marquette
9th Ave
8th Ave
7th Ave
4th Ave
Swinton St
6th Ave
5th Ave
Lizzie
Seymour Rd
Easterday Ave
Eureka St
South St
Circle Dr
Ridge St
Eureka St
Sheridan Dr
Peck St
2nd St
Spruce St
Gros Cap St
Ridge St
Campus St
Ryan St
Fort St
Fort St
Summit St
Ravine St
Magazine St
Magazine St
Raymond St
Arlington St
Pine St
Brown St
Helen St
Brown St
Ashmun St
James Ter
Peck St
Nolte St
Ridge St
Ferris St
Portage St
Court St
Gov Osborn Dr
Oaka St
Ashmun St
Court St
River St
Armando St
Huralley St
Kimball St
Lyon St
Dawson St
Carrie St
Bingham Ave
Armory Pl
Kimball St
Spruce St
Brady St
Water St
Glenn Ave
Johnston St
Maple St
Seymour Rd
10th Ave
7th St
8th St
Marquette
Barbeau St
St Paul St
Sova St
15th Ave
Dakota St
Ord St
10th St
10th Ave
10th St
11th St
Greenough St
Cedar St
Maple St
Portage St
Elm St
Shunk Rd
Ostowan Dr
Pa-Pa-Gas-Nak Ct
Lunsden Way
Saltuer Dr
15th Ave
14th Ave
15th Ave
16th Ave
Marquette
11th Ave
8th Ave
10th Ave
11th Ave
9th Ave
Spruce St
Armory Dr
Hudson Dr
Mission Rd
Golf Ct
Riverside Rd
Gardenville Rd
Riverside Rd
3 Mile Rd

SCHOOLCRAFT

Pop. 1,517

US Hwy 131
Angell Dr
Lyon St
Lincoln St
Centre St
Tulip Dr
Poplar Lane
Vienna St
Bernard St
14th St
Birch Dr
Willow Ct
Maple Dr
Clay St
B and L Dr
Cass St
Centre St
Hayward St
Robinson St
Cedar St
Osterhout St
Earl St
W AVE
Eliza St
Ashery Dr
Duncan St
Holmes St
Lee Ave
Pine St
Cherry St
Lovell St
Elm St
Grand Trunk Western Railroad
South St
US Hwy 131
N

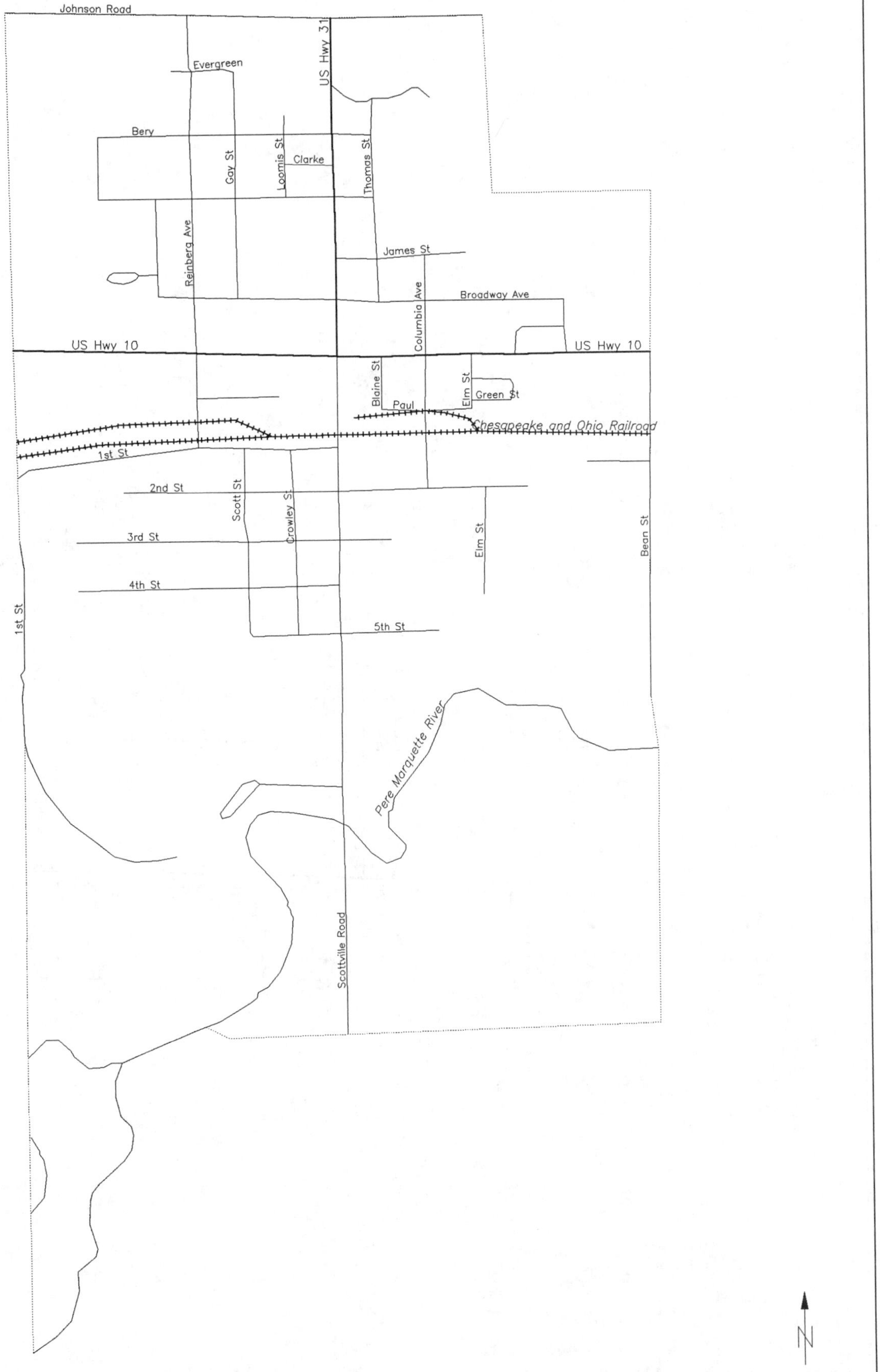

Johnson Road
Evergreen
US Hwy 31
Bery
Gay St
Loomis St
Clarke
Thomas St
Reinberg Ave
James St
Columbia Ave
Broadway Ave
US Hwy 10
US Hwy 10
Blaine St
Elm St
Green St
Paul
Chesapeake and Ohio Railroad
1st St
2nd St
Scott St
Crowley St
3rd St
Elm St
Bean St
4th St
1st St
5th St
Pere Marquette River
Scottville Road
N

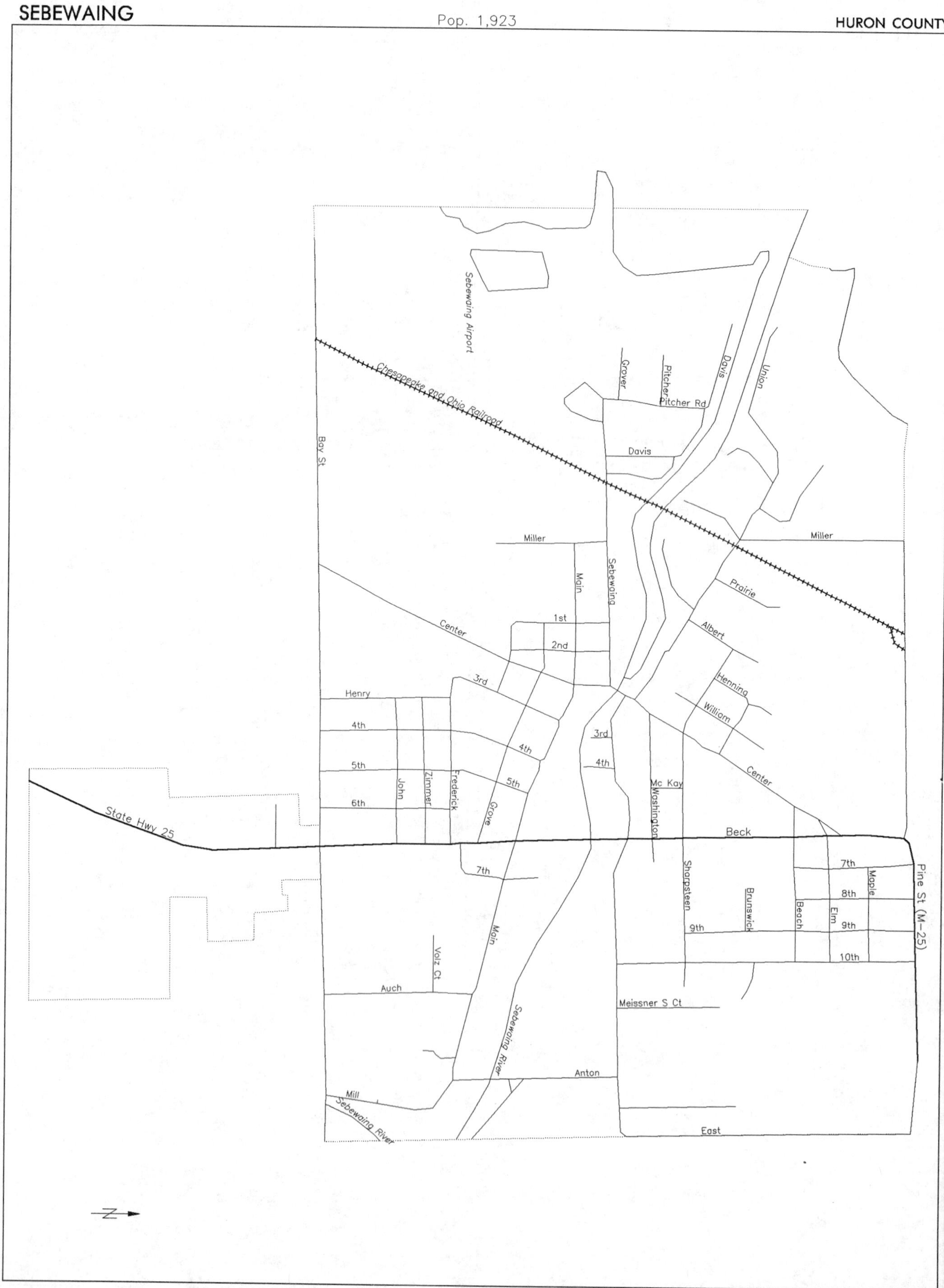
Sebewaing Airport
Chesapeake and Ohio Railroad
Grover
Pitcher
Pitcher Rd
Davis
Union
Davis
Bay St
Miller
Miller
Main
Sebewaing
Prairie
Albert
Center
1st
2nd
3rd
Henning
William
Henry
4th
4th
3rd
4th
5th
5th
6th
John
Zimmer
Frederick
Grove
Mc Kay
Washington
Center
State Hwy 25
Beck
7th
7th
8th
9th
10th
Maple
Elm
Beach
Brunswick
Sharpsteen
9th
Pine St (M-25)
Main
Volz Ct
Auch
Meissner S Ct
Sebewaing River
Anton
Mill
Sebewaing River
East

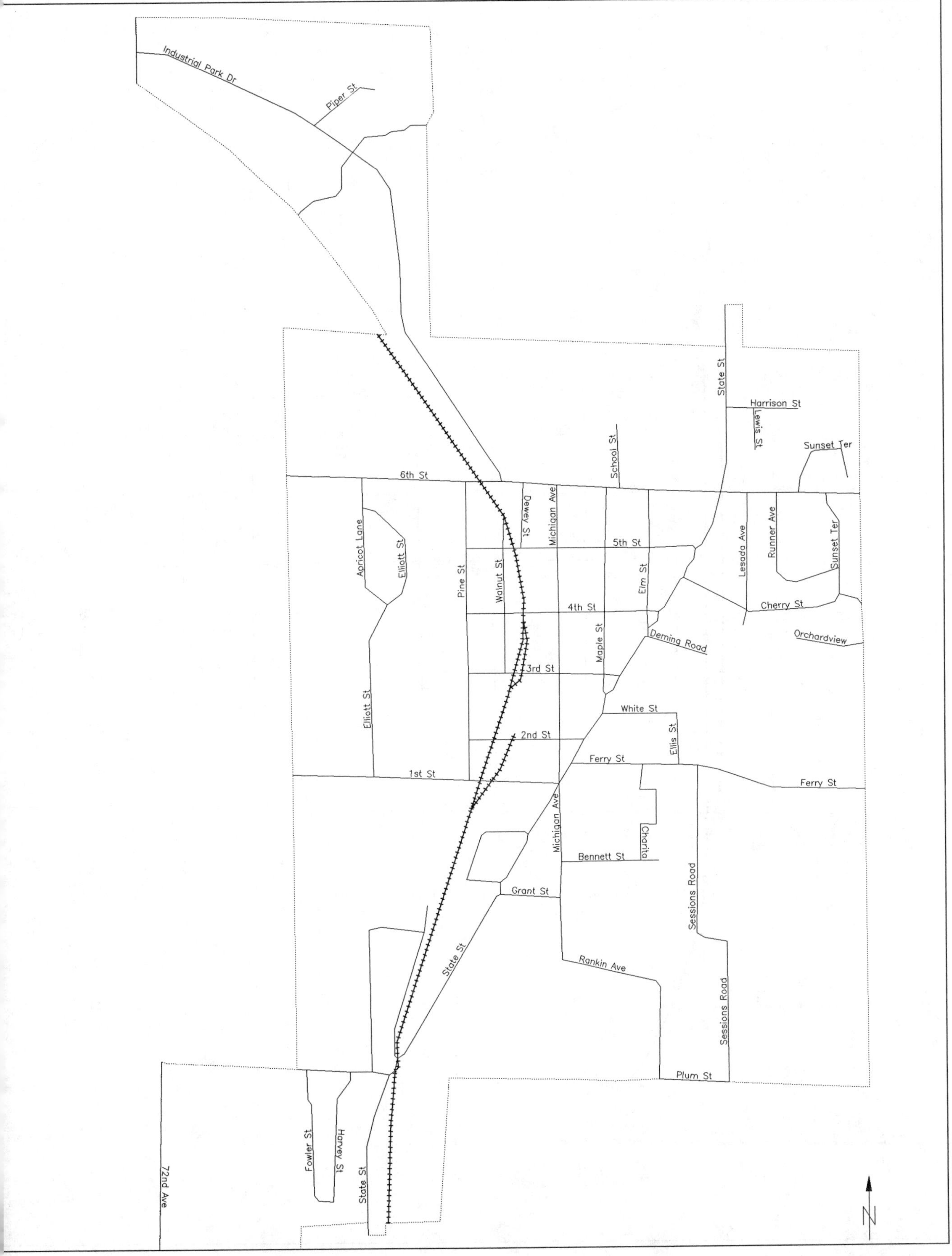

Industrial Park Dr
Piper St
State St
Harrison St
Lewis St
Sunset Ter
School St
6th St
Dewey St
Michigan Ave
Apricot Lane
Elliott St
5th St
Lesada Ave
Runner Ave
Sunset Ter
Pine St
Walnut St
Elm St
4th St
Cherry St
Orchardview
Maple St
Deming Road
3rd St
Elliott St
White St
2nd St
Ellis St
Ferry St
1st St
Ferry St
Michigan Ave
Charita
Bennett St
Grant St
Sessions Road
State St
Rankin Ave
Sessions Road
Plum St
Fowler St
Harvey St
State St
72nd Ave
N

Ann Arbor Railroad
Boulevard
Central Ave
Central Ave
Central Ave
Clark
Miller
5th St
Cottage
Tara Ct
Cottage Ave
Orchard Ave
1st St
2nd St
3rd St
4th St
Chippewa Ave
Union Ave
Wright Ave
Dearing
5th St
Little Salt River
Lynn Ave
Maple Ave
Maple Ave
Michael Ave
Hall Ave
Hall Ave
Upton Ct
Upton Dr
Cambell St
North Dr
East Dr
N

NOTES

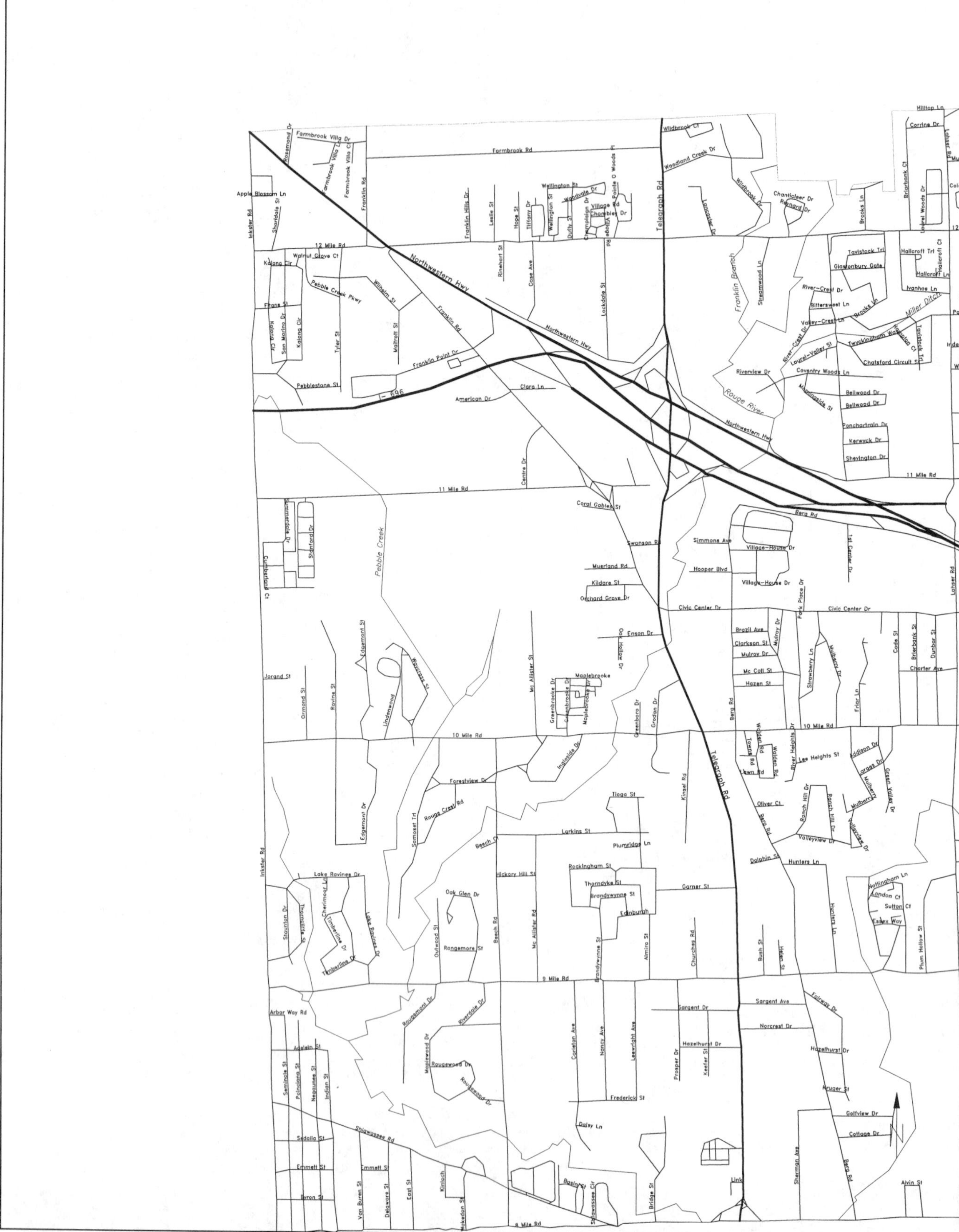
Farmbrook Rd
Telegraph Rd
Wildbrook Ct
Woodland Creek Dr
Apple Blossom Ln
Inkster Rd
Franklin Rd
Franklin Hills Dr
Wellington Ct
Village Rd
Chanticleer Dr
Brooks Ln
Hilltop Ln
Corrine Dr
Lahser Rd
12 Mile Rd
Walnut Grove Ct
Pebble Creek Pkwy
Northwestern Hwy
Franklin Branch
Streamwood Ln
Tavistock Trl
Glastonbury Gate
Hallcroft Trl
Ivanhoe Ln
River-Crest Dr
Bittersweet Ln
Miller Ditch
Tyler St
Maltrott St
Lockdale St
Franklin Point Dr
Riverview Dr
Coventry Woods Ln
Chatsford Circuit St
Pebblestone St
I-696
American Dr
Clara Ln
Rouge River
Bellwood Dr
Ponchartrain Dr
Kerwyck Dr
Shevington Dr
11 Mile Rd
Centre Dr
Coral Gables St
Berg Rd
Swanson Rd
Simmons Ave
Village-House Dr
Pebble Creek
Muerland Rd
Hooper Blvd
Kildare St
Orchard Grove Dr
Civic Center Dr
Enson Dr
Brazil Ave
Clarkson St
Mulroy Dr
Mc Coll St
Hazen St
Park Place Dr
Code St
Briarbank St
Dunbar St
Charter Ave
Jorand St
Edgemont St
Ormond St
Ravine St
Lindenwood
Mc Allister St
Maplebrooke
Greenbrooke Dr
Greenboro Dr
Gradan Dr
Strawberry Ln
Mulberry Dr
Friar Ln
10 Mile Rd
Ingleside Dr
Lee Heights St
Forestview Dr
Tioga St
Kinsel Rd
Oliver Ct
Ranch Hill Dr
Green Valley Dr
Edgemont Dr
Somoset Trl
Rouge Crest Rd
Larkins St
Beech Ct
Plumridge Ln
Valleyview Dr
Dolphin St
Hunters Ln
Lake Ravines Dr
Hickory Hill St
Rockingham St
Thorndyke St
Brandywynne St
Garner St
Edinburgh
Nottingham Ln
London Ct
Sutton Ct
Essex Way
Staunton Dr
Oak Glen Dr
Outwood St
Rangemore St
Beech Rd
Almira St
Churches Rd
Bush St
Helen St
Plum Hollow St
9 Mile Rd
Arbor Way Rd
Rougemont Dr
Riverdale Dr
Sargent Dr
Sargent Ave
Fairway Dr
Norcrest Dr
Carleton Ave
Nancy Ave
Hazelhurst Dr
Seminole St
Indian St
Maplewood Dr
Rougewood Dr
Prosper Dr
Keefer St
Kruger St
Frederick St
Golfview Dr
Cottage Dr
Shiawassee Rd
Daisy Ln
Sedalia St
Emmett St
Sherman Ave
Van Buren St
Delaware St
East St
Kinloch
Bridge St
Alvin St
Byron St
8 Mile Rd

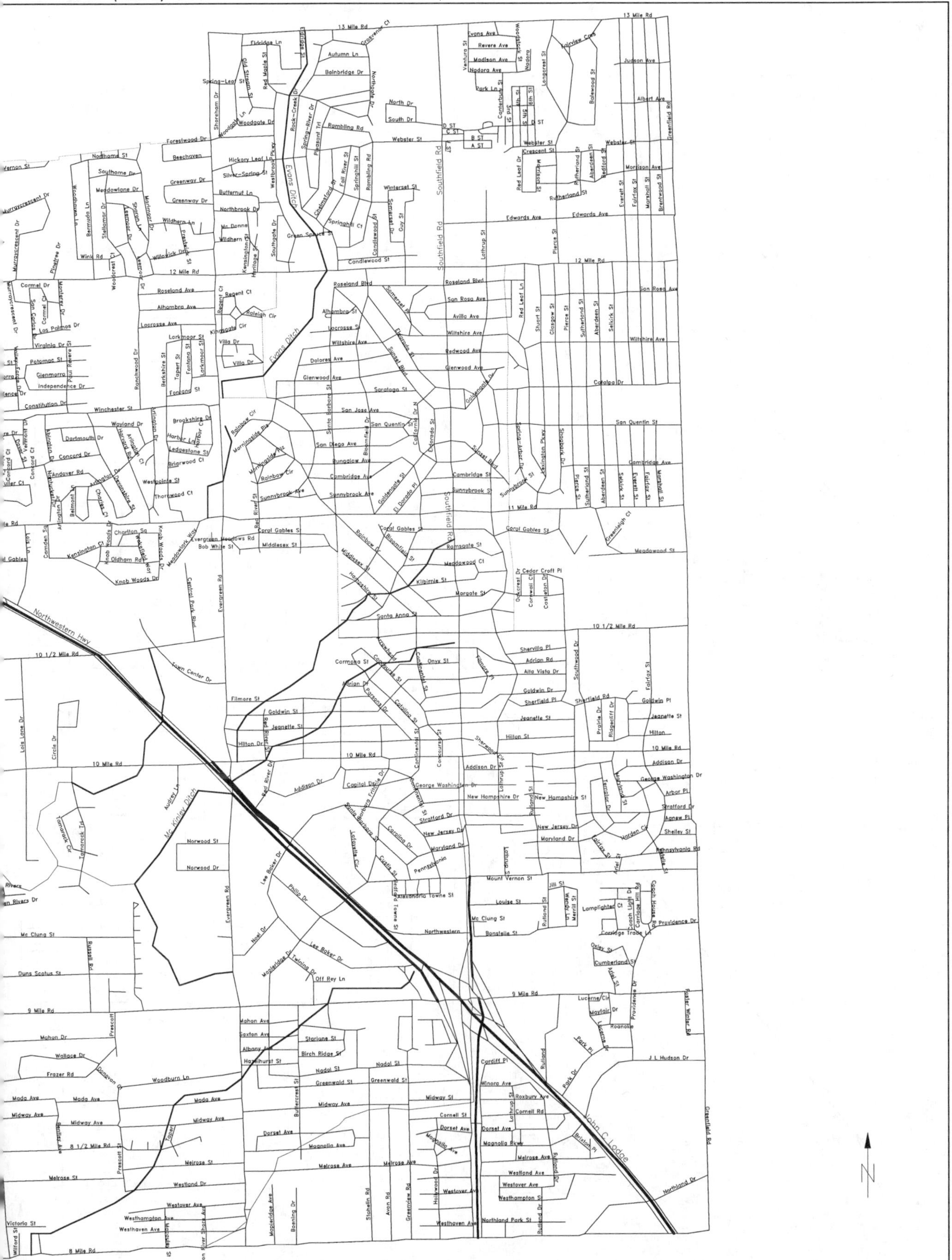

13 Mile Rd
Eldridge Ln
Grosvenor Ct
Autumn Ln
Bainbridge Dr
Northgate Dr
Evans Ave
Revere Ave
Madison Ave
Nadora Ave
Park Ln
Ventura St
Woodstock St
Nadora
Fairview Cres
Judson Ave
Lenacrest St
Balewood St
Albert Ave
Greenfield Rd
Spring-Leaf St
Red Maple St
Old Stream St
Shoreham Dr
Woodgate Ln
Woodgate Dr
Rock-Creek Dr
Spring-River Dr
Pleasant Trl
Rambling Rd
North Dr
South Dr
D ST
C ST
B ST
A ST
Webster St
Canterbury St
3rd St
4th St
5th St
6th St
Forestwood Dr
Beechaven
Hickory Leaf Ln
Silver-Spring St
Westbrook Pkwy
Evans Ditch
Greenway Dr
Butternut Ln
Northbrook Dr
Northome St
Southome Dr
Meadowlane Dr
Woodhaven Ln
Bermuda Ln
Stellamar Dr
Marimoor Dr
Fall River St
Springhill St
Rambling Rd
Chelmsford St
Winterset St
Guy St
Somerset Dr
Springhill Ct
Candlewood St
Green Spruce St
Southgate Dr
Southfield Rd
Lathrup St
Crescent St
Red Leaf Dr
Sutherland St
Aberdeen St
Bedford St
Rutherland St
Morrison Ave
Everett St
Fairfax St
Marshall St
Brentwood St
Edwards Ave
Pierce St
Wildhern Ln
Wildhern
Mc Donnel
Kensington St
Heritage St
Willowick Dr
Wink Rd
Woodcrest Ct
Plumtree Dr
Murraycrescent Dr
12 Mile Rd
Candlewood St
Vernon St
Cormel Dr
Monterey Dr
San Carlos Dr
Los Palmos Dr
Virginia Dr
Potomac St
Glenmorra
Independence Dr
Paul Revere
Constitution Dr
Roseland Ave
Alhambra Ave
Lacrosse Ave
Regent Ct
Raleigh Cir
Kingsgate Cir
Villa Dr
Larkmoor St
Berkshire St
Tapert St
Fontana St
Larkmoor Blvd
Ranchwood Dr
Fontana St
Roseland Blvd
Roseland Blvd
Somerset Pl
San Rosa Ave
Avilla Ave
Wiltshire Ave
Redwood Ave
Glenwood Ave
Alhambra St
Lacrosse St
Wiltshire Ave
Dolores Ave
Glenwood Ave
Saratoga St
Eldorado St
Sunset Blvd
Goldengate Dr
Stuart St
Glasgow St
Pierce St
Sutherland St
Aberdeen St
Selkirk St
San Rosa Ave
Wiltshire Ave
Catalpa Dr
Winchester St
Wayland Dr
Dartmouth Dr
Concord Dr
Andover Rd
Belmont Ln
Arlington Dr
Brookshire Dr
Harbor Ln
Ledgestone St
Briarwood Ct
Westpointe St
Thornwood Ct
Rainbow Cir
Morningside Plz
Rainbow Cir
Sunnybrook Ave
Santa Barbara Dr
San Jose Ave
San Quentin St
San Diego Ave
Bungalow Ave
Cambridge Ave
Sunnybrook Ave
Goldengate Pl
El Dorado Pl
Cambridge St
Sunnybrook St
Sunset Blvd
Lexington Pkwy
Shagbark Dr
San Quentin St
Cambridge Ave
Pierce St
Sutherland St
Aberdeen St
Selkirk St
Everett St
Fairfax St
Marshall St
11 Mile Rd
Coral Gables St
Middlesex St
Evergreen Meadows Rd
Bob White St
Charlton Sq
Kensington Ct
Oldham Rd
Knob Woods Dr
Camden Sq
Lois Ln
Coral Gables St
Rainbow Cir
Bloomfield St
Ramsgate St
Middlesex St
Meadowood Ct
Kilbirnie St
Margate St
Santa Anna St
Coral Gables St
Greenleigh Ct
Meadowood St
Oakcrest Dr
Cornwall Ct
Castleton Dr
Cedar Croft Pl
Northwestern Hwy
Central Park Blvd
Evergreen Rd
10 1/2 Mile Rd
Town Center Dr
Carmona St
Onyx St
Continental St
Fillmore Pl
Shervilla Pl
Adrian Rd
Alta Vista Dr
Goldwin Dr
Sherfield Pl
Southwood Dr
Fairfax St
Goldwin Pl
Jeanette St
Hilton
10 Mile Rd
Addison Dr
Filmore St
Goldwin St
Jeanette St
Hilton Dr
Red River Dr
Lois Lane Dr
Circle Dr
10 Mile Rd
Prairie Dr
Ridgecliff Dr
Jeanette St
Hilton St
Sherwood Dr
Concourse St
Addison Dr
Capitol Dr
George Washington Dr
New Hampshire Dr
New Hampshire St
Rutland St
George Washington Dr
Arbor Pl
Stratford Dr
Agnew Pl
Shelley St
Pennsylvania Rd
Stratford Dr
New Jersey Dr
Maryland Dr
Carolina Dr
Lafayette Cir
Pennsylvania
New Jersey Dr
Maryland Dr
Harden Cir
Audrey Ln
Mc Kinley Ditch
Tamarack Cir
Norwood St
Norwood Dr
Lee Baker Dr
Philip Dr
Mount Vernon St
Jill St
Louise St
Mc Clung St
Bonstelle St
Northwestern
Alexandria Towne St
Lamplighter Ct
Coach Light Dr
Carriage Hill Rd
Coach House Rd
Providence Dr
Carriage Trade Ln
Oxley St
Cumberland St
Rivers
Rivers Dr
Mc Clung St
Russell Rd
Duns Scotus St
Noel Dr
Lee Baker Dr
Twining Dr
Off Rey Ln
9 Mile Rd
9 Mile Rd
Lucerne Cir
Maytair Dr
Roanoke
Foster Winter Rd
Mahon Dr
Prescott
Mahon Ave
Saxton Ave
Albany
Starlane St
Birch Ridge St
Hazelhurst St
Nadol St
Nadol St
Greenwald St
Greenwald St
Park Pl
Cardiff Pl
J L Hudson Dr
Wallace Dr
Frazer Rd
Donovan Ct
Woodburn Ln
Mada Ave
Mada Ave
Mada Ave
Midway Ave
Midway Ave
Midway Ave
Midway Ave
Midway St
Winora Ave
Roxbury Ave
Cornell St
Cornell Rd
Dorset Ave
Dorset Ave
Dorset Ave
Magnolia Ave
Magnolia Ave
Magnolia Pkwy
Buttercrest St
8 1/2 Mile Rd
Melrose St
Melrose Ave
Melrose Ave
Melrose Ave
Westland Dr
Westland Ave
Westover Ave
Westover Ave
Westover Ave
Westhampton St
Westhampton Ave
Westhaven Ave
Westhaven Ave
Northland Park St
Northland Dr
John C Lodge
Bristol Pl
Rutland Dr
Greenfield Rd
Victoria St
Wilford St
8 Mile Rd
Clinton River Shore Ave
Mapleridge Ave
Boening Dr
Stahelin Rd
Avon Rd
Greenview Rd
Hollywood Dr
Lathrup St
N

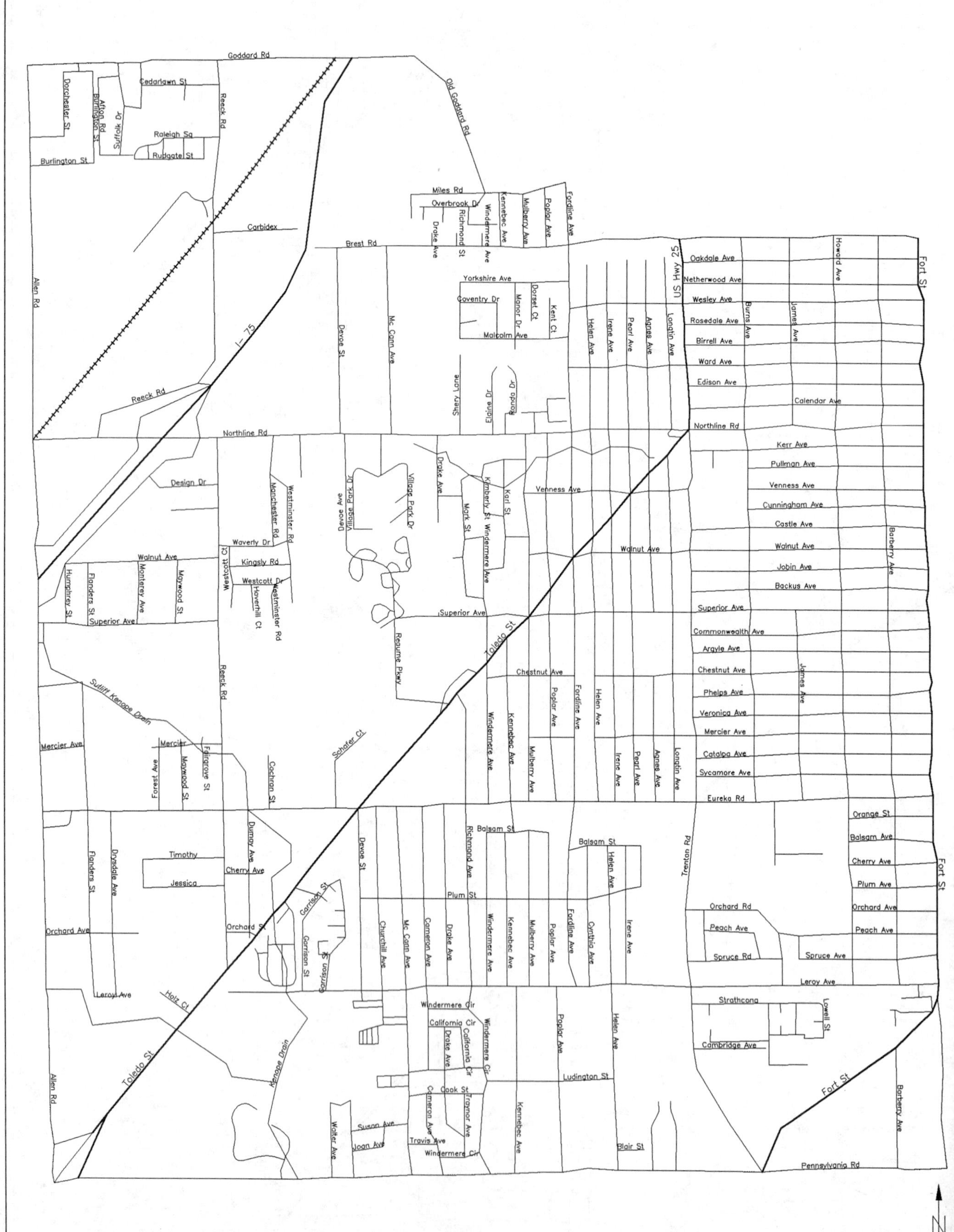
Goddard Rd
Old Goddard Rd
Cedarlawn St
Dorchester St
Afton Rd
Burlington St
Suffolk Dr
Raleigh Sq
Rudgate St
Reeck Rd
Miles Rd
Overbrook Dr
Kennebec Ave
Mulberry Ave
Poplar Ave
Fordline Ave
Carbidex
Brest Rd
Drake Ave
Richmond St
Windermere Ave
US Hwy 25
Oakdale Ave
Netherwood Ave
Wesley Ave
Rosedale Ave
Birrell Ave
Ward Ave
Edison Ave
Howard Ave
Burns Ave
James Ave
Calendar Ave
Fort St
Allen Rd
Yorkshire Ave
Coventry Dr
Manor Dr
Dorset Ct
Kent Ct
Malcolm Ave
Helen Ave
Irene Ave
Pearl Ave
Agnes Ave
Longtin Ave
Devoe St
Mc Cann Ave
I-75
Reeck Rd
Shea Lane
Elaine Dr
Rhonda Dr
Northline Rd
Kerr Ave
Pullman Ave
Venness Ave
Cunningham Ave
Castle Ave
Walnut Ave
Jobin Ave
Backus Ave
Barberry Ave
Design Dr
Manchester Rd
Westminster Rd
Devoe Ave
Village Park Dr
Drake Ave
Kimberly St
Mark St
Karl St
Windermere Ave
Waverly Dr
Kingsly Rd
Westcott Dr
Westcott Ct
Haverhill Ct
Humphrey St
Flanders St
Monterey Ave
Maywood St
Superior Ave
Commonwealth Ave
Argyle Ave
Chestnut Ave
Phelps Ave
Veronica Ave
Mercier Ave
Catalpa Ave
Sycamore Ave
Eureka Rd
Reaume Pkwy
Toledo St
Sutliff Kenope Drain
Mercier Ave
Mercier
Forest Ave
Fairgrove St
Cochran St
Schafer Ct
Kennebec Ave
Trenton Rd
Orange St
Balsam Ave
Cherry Ave
Plum Ave
Orchard Ave
Peach Ave
Spruce Ave
Leroy Ave
Balsam St
Richmond Ave
Dumay Ave
Cherry Ave
Timothy
Jessica
Drysdale Ave
Garrison St
Orchard St
Plum St
Churchill Ave
Cameron Ave
Cynthia Ave
Orchard Rd
Peach Ave
Spruce Rd
Orchard Ave
Holz Ct
Strathcona
Lowell St
Cambridge Ave
Windermere Cir
California Cir
Kenope Drain
Ludington St
Cook St
Traynor Ave
Susan Ave
Joan Ave
Walter Ave
Travis Ave
Blair St
Pennsylvania Rd
N

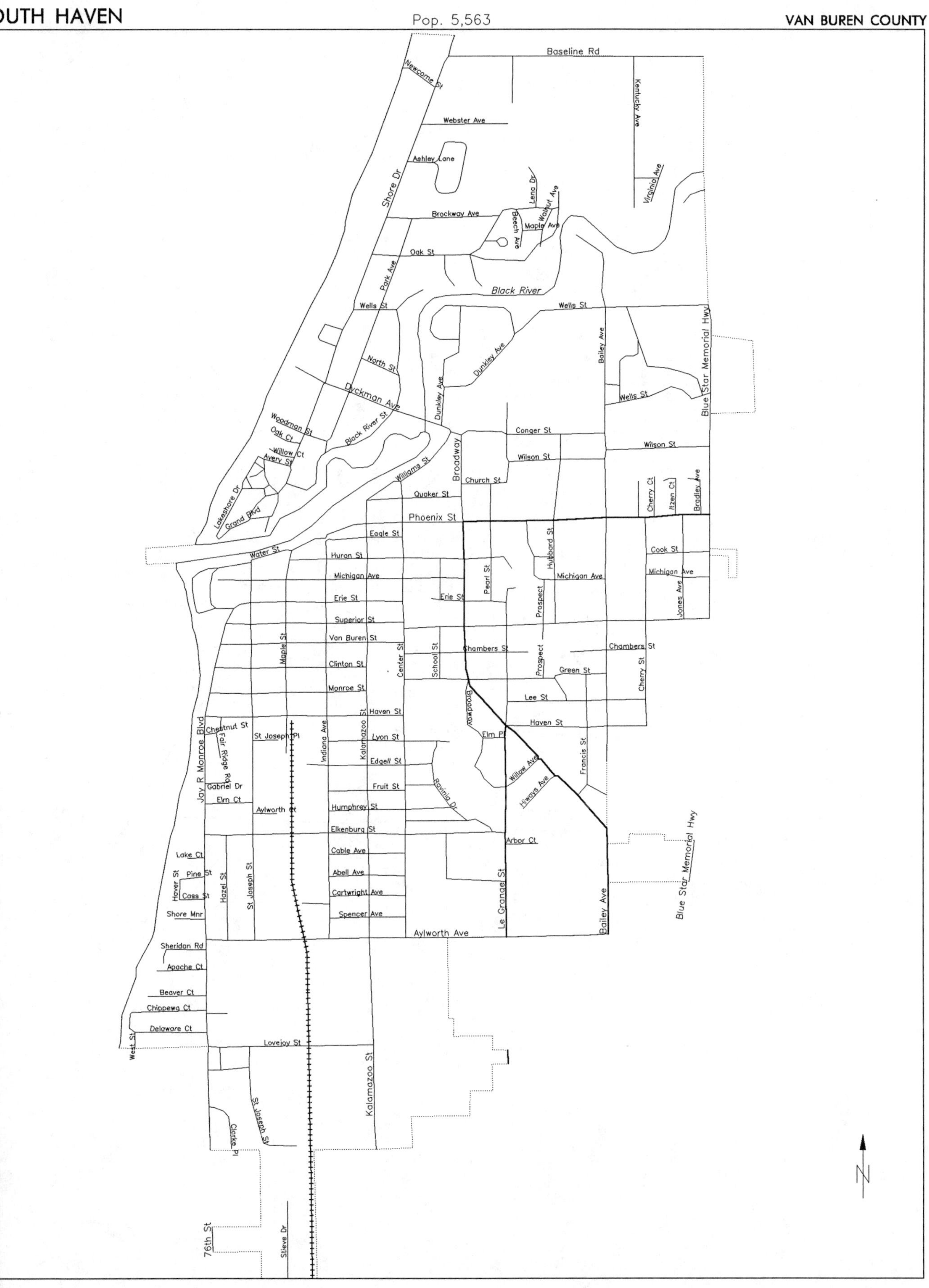
Baseline Rd
Newcome St
Kentucky Ave
Webster Ave
Ashley Lane
Shore Dr
Virginia Ave
Lena Dr
Walnut Ave
Brockway Ave
Beech Ave
Maple Ave
Oak St
Park Ave
Black River
Wells St
Wells St
Bailey Ave
Blue Star Memorial Hwy
Dunkley Ave
North St
Dunkley Ave
Dyckman Ave
Wells St
Woodman St
Oak Ct
Black River St
Conger St
Willow Ct
Avery St
Broadway
Wilson St
Wilson St
Williams St
Church St
Lakeshore Dr
Cherry Ct
Itzen Ct
Bradley Ave
Quaker St
Grand Blvd
Phoenix St
Eagle St
Water St
Huron St
Cook St
Hubbard St
Michigan Ave
Michigan Ave
Michigan Ave
Pearl St
Erie St
Erie St
Prospect
Jones Ave
Superior St
Van Buren St
Maple St
Chambers St
Chambers St
Center St
School St
Clinton St
Prospect
Green St
Cherry St
Monroe St
Broadway
Lee St
Haven St
Jay R Monroe Blvd
Chestnut St
St Joseph Pl
Haven St
Lyon St
Indiana Ave
Kalamazoo St
Elm Pl
Fair Ridge Rd
Edgell St
Francis St
Willow Ave
Gabriel Dr
Fruit St
Ravinia Dr
Hiways Ave
Elm Ct
Aylworth Ct
Humphrey St
Elkenburg St
Arbor Ct
Blue Star Memorial Hwy
Cable Ave
Lake Ct
Abell Ave
Pine St
Haver St
Hazel St
St Joseph St
Cass St
Cartwright Ave
Le Grange St
Bailey Ave
Shore Mnr
Spencer Ave
Aylworth Ave
Sheridan Rd
Apache Ct
Beaver Ct
Chippewa Ct
Delaware Ct
West St
Lovejoy St
Kalamazoo St
St Joseph St
Clarke Pl
76th St
Steve Dr
N

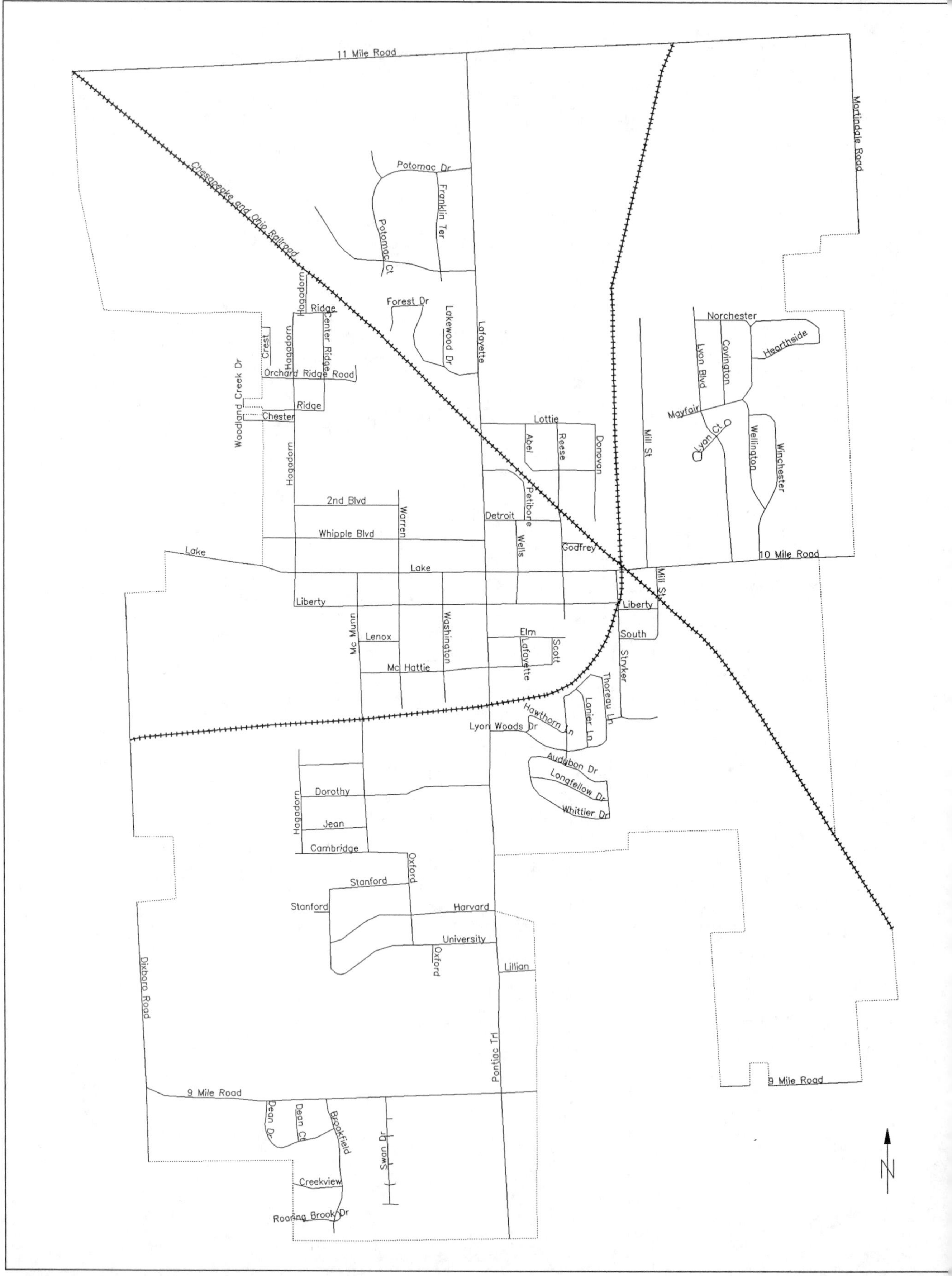

11 Mile Road
Chesapeake and Ohio Railroad
Martindale Road
Potomac Dr
Franklin Ter
Potomac Ct
Forest Dr
Lakewood Dr
Lafayette
Hagadorn
Ridge
Center Ridge
Crest
Orchard Ridge Road
Woodland Creek Dr
Chester
Norchester
Hearthside
Lyon Blvd
Covington
Mayfair
Lyon Ct
Wellington
Winchester
Mill St
Lottie
Abel
Reese
Donovan
Petibone
Detroit
Wells
Godfrey
2nd Blvd
Whipple Blvd
Warren
Lake
10 Mile Road
Liberty
Mill St
South
Mc Munn
Lenox
Washington
Elm
Lafayette
Scott
Mc Hattie
Stryker
Thoreau Ln
Lanier Ln
Hawthorn Ln
Lyon Woods Dr
Audubon Dr
Longfellow Dr
Whittier Dr
Dorothy
Jean
Cambridge
Oxford
Stanford
Harvard
University
Lillian
Dixboro Road
Pontiac Trl
9 Mile Road
Dean Dr
Dean Ct
Brookfield
Swan Dr
Creekview
Roaring Brook Dr
N

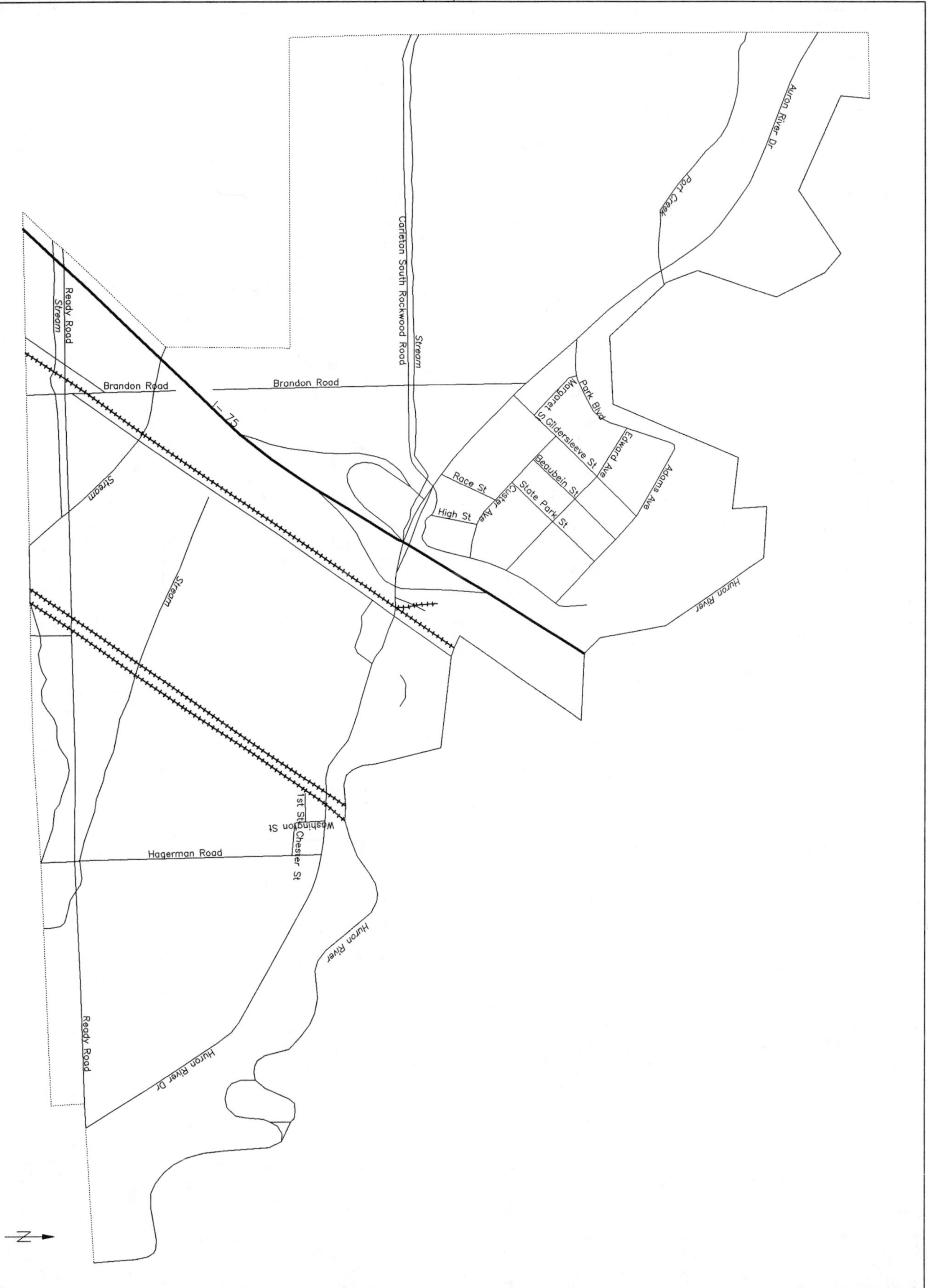
Huron River Dr
Port Creek
Carleton South Rockwood Road
Stream
Ready Road
Stream
Brandon Road
Brandon Road
I-75
Park Blvd
Margaret St
Gildersleeve St
Edward Ave
Adams Ave
Beaubein St
Race St
Custer Ave
State Park St
High St
Stream
Stream
Huron River
1st St
Washington St
Chester St
Hagerman Road
Huron River
Ready Road
Huron River Dr
N

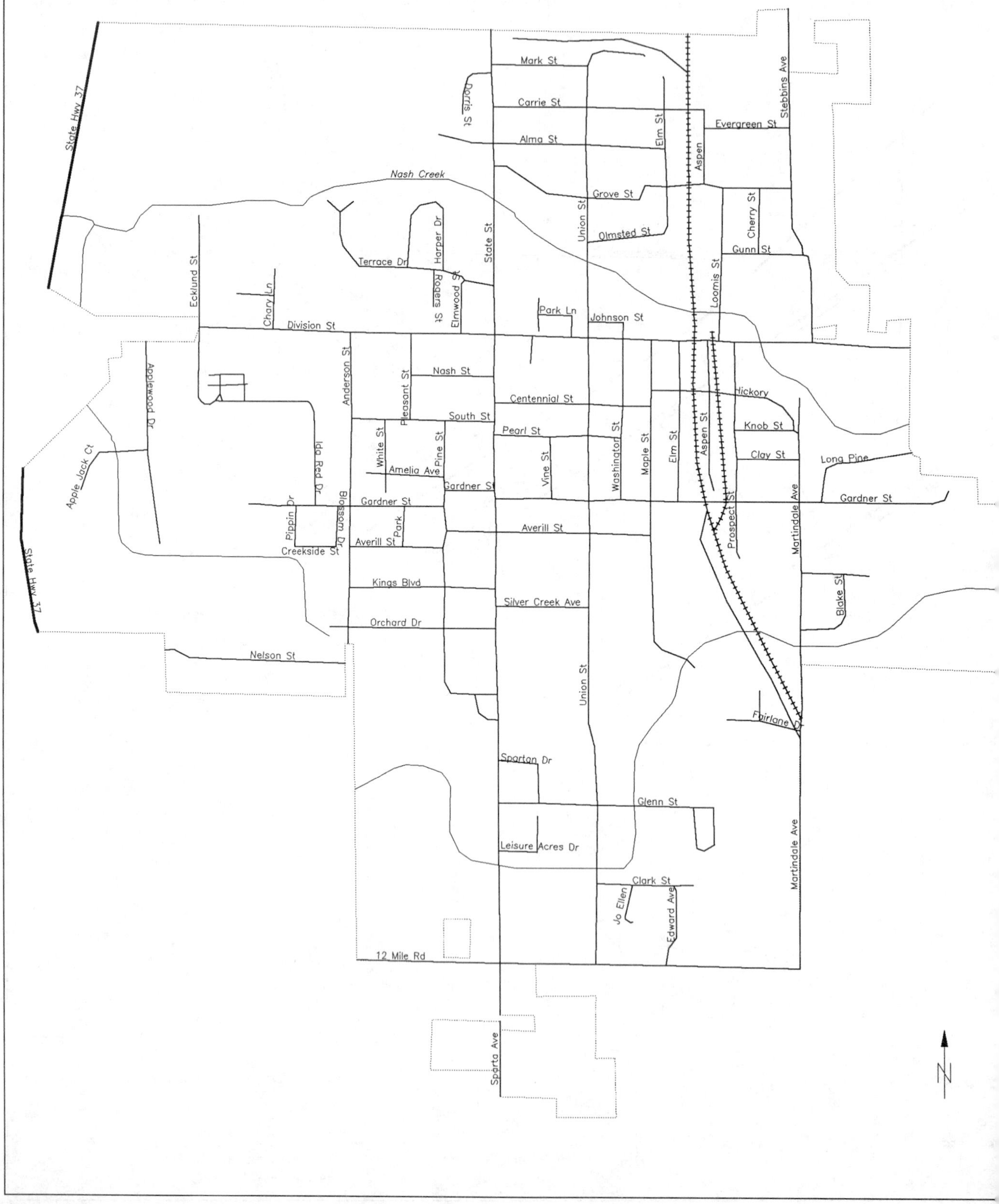

State Hwy 37
Mark St
Carrie St
Dorris St
Alma St
Elm St
Aspen
Evergreen St
Stebbins Ave
Nash Creek
Grove St
Cherry St
Union St
Harper Dr
State St
Olmsted St
Gunn St
Terrace Dr
Loomis St
Ecklund St
Chary Ln
Rogers St
Elmwood St
Park Ln
Johnson St
Division St
Applewood Dr
Anderson St
Nash St
Pleasant St
Centennial St
Hickory
South St
Knob St
Pearl St
Washington St
Apple Jack Ct
White St
Pine St
Maple St
Elm St
Aspen St
Clay St
Long Pine
Ida Red Dr
Amelia Ave
Vine St
Gardner St
Pippin Dr
Blossom Dr
Gardner St
Gardner St
Prospect St
Martindale Ave
Park
Averill St
Averill St
Creekside St
Kings Blvd
Silver Creek Ave
Blake St
Orchard Dr
Nelson St
Union St
Fairlane Dr
Sparton Dr
Glenn St
Martindale Ave
Leisure Acres Dr
Clark St
Jo Ellen
Edward Ave
12 Mile Rd
Sparta Ave
N

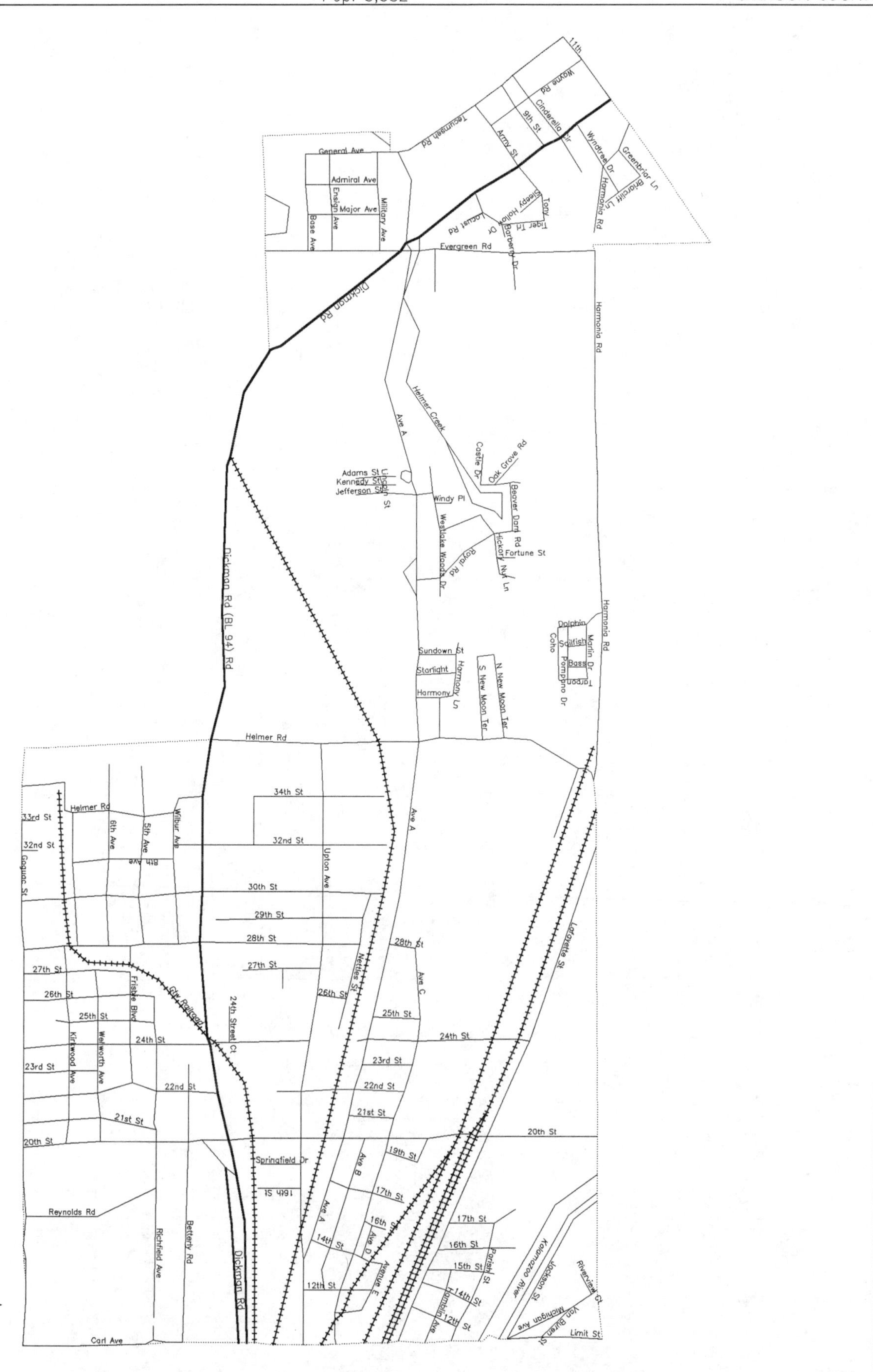

Dickman Rd (BL 94) Rd
Helmer Rd
Harmonia Rd
Ave A
Helmer Creek
20th St
24th St
Lafayette St
Kalamazoo River
Carl Ave
Limit St
Evergreen Rd
Tecumseh Rd
General Ave
Admiral Ave
Major Ave
Military Ave
Upton Ave
Reynolds Rd
Richfield Ave
Betterly Rd
Springfield Dr
Wilbur Ave
30th St
32nd St
34th St

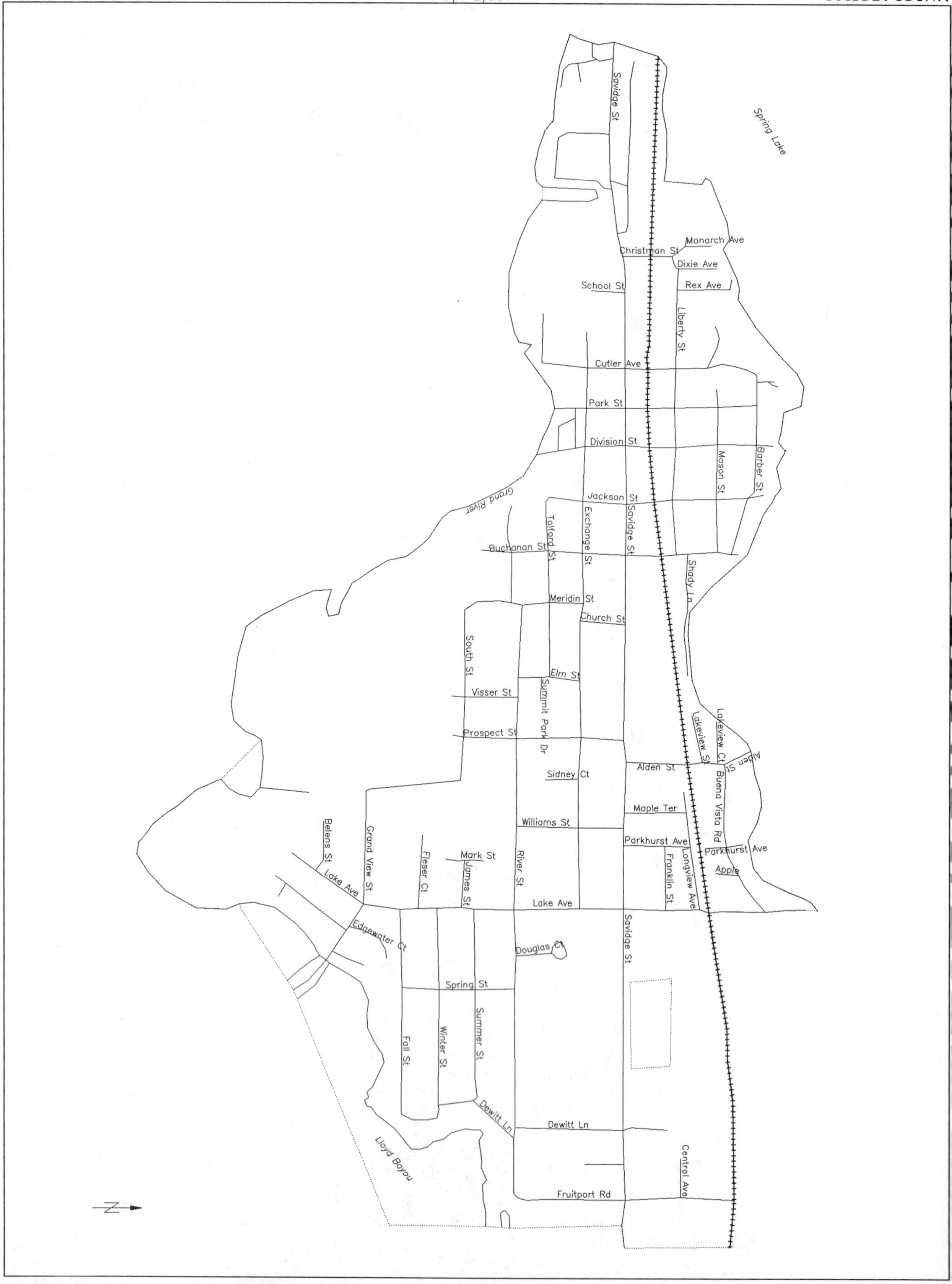
Spring Lake
Savidge St
Monarch Ave
Christman St
Dixie Ave
School St
Rex Ave
Liberty St
Cutler Ave
Park St
Division St
Mason St
Barber St
Grand River
Jackson St
Talford St
Exchange St
Savidge St
Buchanan St
Shady Ln
Meridin St
Church St
South St
Elm St
Summit Park Dr
Visser St
Lakeview St
Lakeview Ct
Alden St
Prospect St
Alden St
Sidney Ct
Buena Vista Rd
Maple Ter
Williams St
Parkhurst Ave
Parkhurst Ave
Belens St
Grand View St
Fleser Ct
Mark St
James St
River St
Franklin St
Longview Ave
Apple
Lake Ave
Lake Ave
Edgewater Ct
Douglas Ct
Savidge St
Spring St
Fall St
Winter St
Summer St
Dewitt Ln
Dewitt Ln
Lloyd Bayou
Central Ave
Fruitport Rd
N

Hiawatha Road
Division St
Selden Rd
Selden Rd (M-189)
7th St
Iron River
Chicago and Northwestern RR
Madison Ave
Garfield Ave
Washington Ave
8th St
19th St
2nd St
7th St
Adams Ave
18th St
14th St
13th St
10th St
5th St
1st St
Lenox St
Jefferson Ave
18th St
16th St
15th St
10th St
9th St
8th St
7th St
4th St
3rd St
19th St
Lincoln Ave
Lincoln Ave
2nd St
Roosevelt Ave
Wilson Ave
6th St
Harding Ave
Coolidge Ave
Kofmehl Road

Johnsfield Road
State Hwy 61
Deep River Road
Limits Road
Airpark Dr
Franklin Road
Cedar St
Airpark Dr
Standish City Airport
Airport Road
Industrial Road
Limits Road
Airpark Dr
Pine River
Middle Branch
Wheeler Road
Mill St
Court St
Court St
Washington
Church St
Pine St
Beaver St
Front St
Bulk Station
Old M-10
Front St
US Hwy 23
Old M-76
Elm
Forest St
Forest St
Pine St
Grove St
Mill St
Downer
Beaver St
Orchard Ave
North St
James St
Cass St
Almont St
Diane St
Lapeer St
Lapeer St
Cherry St
Cedar St
Lindenwood St
City Limits Road
N

State St
New St
Sherman St
Quarter Line St
North St
Cedar St
Ridge St
Summit St
Crawford St
Bellevue St
Peoples Road
Pine St
Court St
Camburn St
Lincoln St
Mills St
Chesapeake and Ohio Railroad
Mc Pherson St
New St
Bradford St
2nd St
1st St
Day St
Day St
3rd St
Cemetery St
Main St
Main St
Walnut St
Nelson St
Vine St
Court St
Lincoln St
Mills St
Grove St
Hill St
Lake St
Lake St
Brown Road
Oak St
State Hwy 66
N

Street	Map	Quadrant
14 Mile Rd	4	SW
14 Mile Rd	5	SW
14 Mile Rd	6	SW
15 Mile Rd	4	SW
15 Mile Rd	5	SW
15 Mile Rd	6	SW
16 1/2 Mile Rd	5	NW
16 Mile Rd	4	NW
16 Mile Rd	5	NW
16 Mile Rd	6	NW
17 Mile Rd	2	SE
17 Mile Rd	4	NW
17 Mile Rd	5	NW
18 1/2 Mile Rd	1	SE
18 1/2 Mile Rd	2	SW
18 Mile Rd	1	SW
18 Mile Rd	2	SW
19 1/2 Mile Rd	1	NE
19 1/2 Mile Rd	2	NW
19 Mile Rd	1	NW
19 Mile Rd	2	NW
19 Mile Rd	3	NW
4 Lakes Dr	3	NW
Aaron Ct	5	NE
Abbey Ct	6	NW
Aberdien	6	NW
Academy Dr	1	SW
Ackley Dr	5	SE
Adair St	1	SE
Adams Dr	2	SE
Adele Dr	5	NE
Admiral Dr	4	NE
Adrian Dr	4	NE
Afton Dr	4	NE
Agar Dr	4	NW
Agatha Dr	5	NE
Albany Dr	4	NW
Alcoy Dr	5	NE
Alden Dr	4	SW
Alderdale Dr	1	SW
Aldine Dr	3	SW
Alexandria Dr	3	SW
Alexis Ct	5	NE
Algonquin Dr	4	NE
Alice Ct	2	NW
Allar Dr	5	SW
Allison Dr	4	NE
Alma Dr	3	SW
Almont Ct	4	NE
Almont Dr	4	NE
Almore St	5	SW
Alpena Dr	3	SW
Alper Dr	5	NE
Alspice Dr	1	SE
Alta Vista Dr	6	SW
Alwardt Dr	2	SW
Amanda Dr	3	SW
Amber Ct	5	NE
Amherst Dr	4	NE
Amsterdam Dr	5	SE
Andrew Dr	5	NW
Angeline Dr	4	SE
Angus Cir	5	NE
Anna Lisa Dr	5	NE
Annapolis Dr	3	SW
Annette Dr	4	SE
Anson St	2	SW
Anthon St	2	SW
Anthony Dr	4	SE
Antwerp St	2	SW
Applegrove Ln	2	NE
Aquarias Dr	4	SE
Aragona Blvd	2	SE
Arathorn Dr	3	SW
Arcaida Dr	2	NE
Arcaida Dr	3	NW
Arcola Dr	5	NW
Ardel Dr	2	NE
Ardmore Dr	4	NE
Argyle Ct	1	SE
Arlene Dr	4	NW
Arlingdale Dr	4	NW
Armonk Dr	4	NE
Arrow Dr	2	NW
Arvil St	2	SW
Ascot Ct	6	SW
Ash Grove Dr	3	SW
Ashburton Pl	4	SE
Ashby Dr	5	NE
Ashford Dr	5	SW
Ashland Dr	3	SW
Ashley Ct	4	NW
Ashton Dr	5	SW
Aspen Dr	3	NW
Astor St	2	SW
Atkinson Dr	2	SE
Atwater	3	NW
Auburndale Dr	2	SE
Augusta Ave	3	SW
Augustine Dr	4	SE
Aurora Dr	3	NW
Autumn Ridge	4	NW
Averill Dr	2	NE
Avinger Dr	3	SW
Avis Dr	4	SW
Avon Ct	2	NE
Awdey Dr	6	SW
Badger Dr	5	NE
Bagdad Dr	5	NE
Bahama Dr	6	NW
Bainbridge Dr	4	NW
Baker Dr	1	SE
Balboa Dr	2	SW
Balfour Dr	3	SW
Bangor Dr	3	SW
Barbara Ct	4	SW
Barbara Dr	4	SW
Barcroft Way	4	SE
Barg Dr	1	SW
Barkway Dr	1	SW
Barnum Dr	5	SE
Barrett Dr	5	SE
Barrington Dr	5	NE
Barton Dr	4	NW
Bates Dr	1	SW
Bathgate Dr	6	SW
Bay Ct	3	NW
Bayleaf Dr	1	SE
Baylor Dr	4	NE
Baypointe Dr	4	SE
Bayview Dr	3	NW
Beacon Ct	1	SE
Beacon Rd	1	SE
Beattie Dr	5	SW
Beaver Dr	5	SE
Bedell Rd	4	NE
Bedford Dr	2	SW
Beech Dr	5	SW
Beecher Dr	5	NE
Belcher Dr	4	NW
Belcrest Dr	5	NE
Belinda Dr	4	NW
Bella Vista Dr	2	SE
Belle Ct	6	NW
Belmont Dr	1	SW
Bender Dr	2	SE
Benjamin Dr	1	SE
Bennington Dr	4	NE
Beresford Dr	2	SE
Berg Dr	6	NW
Bernadette Ct	3	SW
Bernard Dr	3	SW
Berwick Dr	4	NE
Beth Ann Dr	4	SE
Betley Dr	2	NE
Beverly Dr	4	NE
Beyer Ln	1	SW
Bieber Dr	4	SE
Billette Dr	3	NW
Bimini Ct	6	NW
Bingham	6	NW
Birch Tree Dr	3	SW
Birchgrove Dr	5	SW
Birkhill Dr	2	NE
Biscayne Dr	3	NW
Blackstone Dr	2	SE
Blairmoor Ct	3	NW
Blairmoor Dr	3	NW
Bliss	5	NE
Bloomfield Dr	4	NE
Bobjean St	1	NE
Boca Grande	6	NW
Bockley Dr	2	NE
Bonaparte Ave	2	NW
Bonaparte Ct	2	NW
Bond Ct	2	NE
Bonington	6	NW
Bonnett Dr	2	SW
Bonneville Dr	5	SE
Bora Ct	5	NE
Bordeaux Ave	2	NW
Boston Dr	2	SE
Boswell Ct	1	SE
Botsford Ave	4	SE
Boulder Dr	4	NE
Bowling Green	3	SW
Bradford	6	NW
Braebury Ct	1	SE
Branch St	1	SE
Brandi Dr	4	NW
Brandon Ct	1	SE
Brandywine Rd	6	SW
Bratly Ct	1	SE
Breckenridge Dr	4	SW
Breezy Dr	3	NW
Brentwood Dr	1	SE
Briarcliff St	5	NW
Bridal Ln	2	NE
Bridgeview Dr	3	NW
Bridgewood Dr	1	SE
Brierstone Dr	5	NE
Brierstone Dr	6	NW
Briggs Dr	5	NW
Brightmore	6	NW
Brighton Dr	4	SE
Brightside Ct	1	SW
Brisbane Dr	5	NW
Bristor Dr	4	NE
Brittany Ct	1	SE
Brixham Ct	1	SE
Broad St	5	SE
Brockham Way	4	SE
Brockton Ave	2	NW
Bromley Ct	1	SE
Bromwell Ct	1	SE
Bronson Dr	4	NW
Brookfield Blvd	4	SE
Brookings Dr	3	SW
Brookshire Dr	6	SW
Brookside Dr	3	NW
Brookwood Dr	5	NW
Brougham Dr	5	SW
Brougham Dr	6	NW
Brown Dr	3	SW
Brownlea Ct	6	SW
Brownlea Dr	6	SW
Bruce Collins Ct	2	NW
Bruner Dr	1	SE
Brunswick Dr	6	NW
Bryan Dr	4	SE
Bubar Ct	5	NE
Buckingham Dr	2	NE
Bucknell Dr	3	SW
Burke Ct	4	SE
Burns Dr	2	SE
Burr Ct	1	SW
Burroughs Ave	1	NE
Burroughs Ave	2	NW
Burtley Dr	2	NE
Butler Dr	3	SW
Buttercup Ln	2	NE
Byers Dr	1	SE
Byers Dr	4	NE
Byrd Dr	4	SW
Cabot St	5	NE
Calais Ave	2	NW
Calenderar Ct	4	SE
Calka Dr	4	NW
Calvert Dr	5	NW
Calvin Ct	1	SE
Cambridge Dr	2	NE
Camel	4	SW
Camel Dr	4	SW
Camelot	6	NW
Cameron Dr	4	NW
Campus St	5	SE
Canal Rd	2	NW
Canal Rd	3	NW
Candlewood	6	NW
Cannon Dr	2	NE
Canterbury Dr	5	NE
Canterbury Dr	6	NW
Canvey Ct	1	SE
Cape Dr	3	NW
Capitol Dr	3	SW
Caraway Dr	1	SE
Carbon St	5	SE
Cardamon Dr	1	SE
Cardoni Dr	6	NW
Cardova Ct	5	NE
Carlisle	6	SW
Carlisle Dr	6	SW
Carlton Rd	1	SE
Carmel Dr	6	SW
Carnaby Ct	2	SE
Carol Dr	4	NE
Carpathia Blvd	4	NE
Carriage Dr	4	NW
Carrie St	2	SE
Carnation Dr	2	NE
Cascade Dr	3	SW
Casimira Ave	3	SW
Castle Ct	4	SW
Castleton Dr	5	NE
Catalpa St	1	NE
Cathedral Dr	6	SW
Catherine Marie	5	NE
Cavalier Dr	2	SE
Cavant Dr	4	SE
Cayenne Dr	1	SE
Cedar Ct	4	NW
Centennial Ct	5	SW
Central Dr	3	SW
Century Dr	4	NW
Cero Dr	4	SW
Chadbourne Ct	4	SE
Chadbourne Dr	4	SE
Chadwick Ct	1	SE
Chalon Ave	2	NW
Champagne	6	NW
Chantilly Dr	2	SE
Chapel Dr	4	NW
Chapman Dr	1	SW
Chardon Dr	3	SW
Charity Dr	4	NW
Charlemagne	2	NW
Charlemagne Ct	2	NW
Charles Ct	5	NW
Charrington Dr	3	SW
Charwood Dr	5	NE
Chateau Rouge	2	SW
Chatham Ct	4	NE
Chatsworth Dr	5	SW
Chattman Dr	2	NE
Chaucer Ct	2	NE
Chaucer Dr	2	NE
Chene Dr	4	NE
Cherrylawn Dr	2	SW
Cheryl Ct	1	SE
Chesley Rd	4	SW
Chesterfield Dr	2	NE
Chestnut Dr	4	NE
Chevelle Dr	5	SE
Cheviot Dr	4	NE
Chippendale Dr	4	NW
Chippewa Ct	1	SE
Chris Dr	4	NE
Churchill Dr	2	NE
Ciara Dr	4	SE
Cilantro Dr	1	SE
Claremont Ct	4	NE
Claremont Dr	4	NE
Clauoia Ct	4	SE
Clay Ct	2	SW
Clemson Dr	3	NW
Clifford Dr	5	NE
Clifton Dr	4	SW
Clinton River Rd	2	NW
Clinton River Rd	3	SW
Cloverlawn Dr	5	NE
Cloverlawn Dr	6	NW
Clubhouse Dr	5	NE
Coach Making	3	NW
Coachwood Dr	6	SW
Coastal Dr	4	SE
Cobb Dr	5	SW
Cobden Dr	1	SW
Cocoa Ct	5	NE
Coldwater Dr	3	NW
Colfax Dr	4	SW
Colgate Ct	4	NE
Collingwood Dr	6	SW
Cologne Dr	2	NW
Colonial Ct	5	SW
Colony Dr	2	SW
Columbia Ct	3	NW
Commerce Dr	5	NW
Compton Ct	1	SE
Comstock Dr	4	SE
Concord Dr	2	NE
Concord Dr	3	NW
Congress Dr	3	SW
Connecticut Dr	4	SW
Connie Dr	4	NE
Constitution	2	SW
Cooper Dr	5	NE
Coplin Dr	4	NE
Copperstone Dr	5	NW
Corbin Dr	2	SE
Corey Ct	4	SE
Cornelissen St	6	SW
Cornell Dr	3	NW
Cornwall Cir	1	SE
Coronation Dr	4	NW
Corriander Dr	1	SE
Corvair Dr	5	SE
Cotter Ave	1	NE
Cotter Ave	2	NW
Cottonwood Ct	4	NE
Cottonwood Dr	4	NE
Coulee Dr	3	SW
Count Ct	1	SE
Cove Ct	3	NW
Covington Dr	5	NE
Cranbrook Rd	6	SW
Creek Dr	1	NE
Crescendo Dr	2	NW
Crestview Dr	5	SW
Crestwell Dr	4	SW
Cromwell Ct	1	SE
Cromwell Rd	1	SE
Crossman Dr	5	NW
Croton Dr	4	NE
Crown Dr	2	NE
Crystal Dr	1	SW
Crystal St	1	SW
Curcio Ct	4	SE
Curcio Dr	4	SE
Curry Dr	1	SE
Curwood Dr	4	NW
Cypress Ct	4	SE
Daily Dr	2	SE
Daisy Ct	2	NE
Dale Ct	2	SE
Dame	2	NW
Danbury Ct	5	SE
Dane Ct	6	SW
Danforth Dr	5	NE
Daniel Dr	5	SE
Darcy	5	NE
Darlene Dr	5	NW
Dart Dr	2	SE
Dartmouth Dr	4	NE
Dasher St	5	SE
Daventry Ct	5	SW
Davison St	4	SE
Dawn St	2	NW
Daytona Dr	6	NW
De Cook Dr	2	SE
Dearing Dr	5	SE
Debbie Dr	3	SW
Deborah Dr	2	NE
Declerck Dr	2	SE
Deepwood Ct	6	SW
Defour St	4	SE
Degrove Dr	5	NE
Del Ray Dr	4	NE
Delco Blvd	2	NE
Delia Dr	4	SW
Della Rosa Dr	2	SE
Delmonte Dr	4	NW
Delvin Dr	2	NE
Deming Dr	5	NE
Denbigh Dr	1	SW
Denise Dr	4	NW
Deno Dr	2	NE
Denoter Dr	2	SE
Denson Dr	4	NW
Denver Cir	6	NW
Denwood Dr	5	SW
Dequindre Rd	1	NW
Dequindre Rd	4	NW
Derby Dr	5	NE
Deville Dr	5	SE
Devonshire Dr	4	NW
Dewbury Ct	1	SE
Diamond Dr	2	NE
Diane Dr	2	SE
Dickson Dr	4	NE
Diehl Dr	2	NE
Dill Ct	5	NE
Dill Dr	5	NW
Diplomat Dr	2	NW
Diversion Dr	3	SW
Dobbin Dr	4	NW
Dobry Dr	1	NW
Dobry Dr	2	NW
Docksin St	2	SE
Dodge Park Rd	2	SE
Dodge Park Rd	5	NE
Dog Wood Dr	3	SW
Doncaster Dr	5	NW
Donley St	2	NE
Donna Dr	4	NW
Dor-Sal Dr	6	NW
Dorian Dr	1	SW
Dotson Ct	3	NW
Douglas Ct	4	NW
Douglas Dr	4	NW
Dover Ct	1	SE
Doyle	4	SE
Dray Dr	4	NW
Dreon Ct	4	NE
Dresden Dr	6	SW
Driftwood Dr	3	NW
Drumright Dr	3	SW
Drury Rd	1	SE
Dryden Dr	5	SE
Du Pon Dr	1	SW
Dublin Way	2	NW
Duchess	4	SE
Duffield Ave	2	NW
Duke	4	SE
Duncan Ct	1	SE
Dundee St	4	NW
Dunhill Ct	1	SE
Dunhill Rd	1	SE
Dunkirk Ct	1	SE
Dunston Dr	4	SW
Durand Ct	4	NW
Durand Dr	1	SW
Durham Dr	5	NW
Durussel Dr	3	NW
Dyar Ct	4	SW
Eagle Dr	1	SE
Eason Dr	5	SE
Eastbrook Dr	3	NW
Eastmont Dr	5	SW
Eastport Dr	3	SW
Ebony Ct	5	NE
Echo Dr	4	NE
Eclipse Ct	1	SW
Eden Park Dr	5	SE
Edgemont Dr	1	SW
Edgevale Dr	2	SE
Edith Ct	1	SE
Edmanton	6	NW
Edshire Dr	6	SW
El Camino Dr	5	SE
Eldorado Dr	5	SE
Electra Dr	5	SE
Elford Dr	5	SW
Elgin Ct	4	SW
Elizabeth Dr	5	SE
Elk Ct	1	SW
Ellicot Dr	5	NE
Ellsworth Dr	5	SE
Elmcrest Rd	4	SW
Elmridge Dr	1	SE
Elphin Dr	1	SW
Elrond Dr	3	SW
Embassy Dr	2	SW
Emmons Ct	1	SE
Engleside Dr	4	NE
English Dr	4	NW
Ensign	6	SW
Epsom Ct	1	SE
Erdmann Rd	2	NW
Erin Dr	4	NW
Erna Dr	6	NW
Esper Dr	5	SE
Essen Dr	2	NW
Essex Ct	1	SE
Estate Dr	2	SW
Eton Ct	4	NW
Eunice Dr	4	SW
Eva Ct	3	SW
Evanston St	5	SE
Evergreen Dr	4	NE
Ewald	5	NE
Executive Dr	3	SW
Ext	3	SW
Fable Dr	1	SW
Fairfax Dr	5	SW
Fairfield Dr	4	NE
Fairmount Ct	4	SE
Fairview Dr	5	NE
Fairview St	5	NE
Fairway Dr	5	SE
Faith Dr	1	SW
Faith Dr	4	NW
Falcon Dr	2	SE
Fanning Rd	5	NW
Fargo St	5	SE
Farm Ln	2	SE
Farmbrook Ct	5	SW
Farmhill Dr	2	SE
Farnsworth Dr	6	SW
Farnum Ct	1	SE
Farr Dr	6	NW
Farthing Dr	2	NE
Felstone Dr	2	NE
Fenmore Ct	2	SE
Fern Rd	6	SW
Ferris Dr	4	NE
Fieldcrest Ln	6	NW
Fieldview Dr	3	SW
Filer St	5	SE
Filly Dr	4	NW
Finchley Ct	1	SE
Firesteel Dr	3	SW
Firestone Dr	4	SW
Fisher Dr	4	NW
Flagstaff Dr	2	SW
Fleet Ct	5	NE
Fleming Ct	4	SE
Foothill Dr	6	NW
Forbes Dr	1	SW
Forbes Dr	4	NW
Forburg Ct	1	SE
Ford Country Ln	2	SW
Fordham Dr	3	NW
Fordwich Dr	1	SW
Forester St	6	NW
Forman Dr	4	SW
Forrer Ct	5	SE
Forrer Dr	5	SE
Forsdale Dr	4	NW
Fortner Dr	2	NE
Foss St	4	SE

Street	Map	Grid
Rosebush St	4	NE
Roslyn Dr	2	SE
Rotunda Dr	3	SW
Rowe Ct	6	NW
Rowe Dr	6	NW
Roxanne Rd	6	SW
Roxbury Dr	5	NE
Roxbury Dr	6	NW
Royal Dr	6	SW
Royce St	2	SW
Rudgate Blvd	1	SE
Rudgate Cir	1	SE
Runton Ct	1	SE
Russel Ct	5	NE
Rutgers Dr	3	NW
Ruth Dr	5	NW
Rutland Dr	6	NW
Ryan Rd	1	NW
Ryan Rd	4	NW
Ryer Ct	2	NE
Saal Rd	3	NW
Saar Dr	2	NE
Sage Dr	1	SE
Salem	4	NE
Salisbury Dr	3	NW
Salvatore Dr	2	SE
Samantha Dr	4	NW
Sambra Dr	5	NE
San Marco Blvd	2	SW
Sandpebble Dr	4	SE
Sandwood Dr	4	SW
Sanford Dr	4	SE
Sano Ct	4	SW
Santa Rose St	6	NW
Sarafina Dr	5	NE
Savage Dr	5	NE
Savory Ct	1	SE
Sawyer Dr	1	SW
Saxony Dr	4	SE
Scarsdale Dr	4	NE
Schoenherr Rd	3	NW
Schoenherr Rd	6	NW
Schoenherr St	6	NW
School Creek Dr	4	SE
Scotia Dr	5	SW
Sea Oats Dr	4	SE
Seagull Dr	3	NW
Seaton Dr	5	SE
Sebastian Lane	5	SW
Sebring Dr	3	SW
Seminole Ct	4	NE
Serra Dr	4	SW
Sesame Dr	1	SE
Shakespeare Dr	2	SE
Shannon Dr	2	NE
Sharron Dr	3	SW
Shaver Ct	3	SW
Shawn Dr	5	SW
Shearing	5	SE
Sheffield Ct	1	SE
Shell Dr	4	SW
Shelley Lynne	5	SW
Sheri Dr	4	NE
Sherwood	4	SE
Shetland Ct	2	NE
Shilling Dr	2	NE
Shire Ct	6	NW
Sholitz St	2	SE
Shoreline Dr	3	NW
Shrewsbury Dr	4	SE
Shruboak Dr	4	NE
Silver Dr	2	NE
Sims Dr		SW
Sims St	2	SW
Singh Dr	4	SE
Skylark Ct	5	SE
Sleigh Dr	4	NW
Smethwick Rd	5	NW
Smith Ct	4	SW
Snowden Dr	5	SE
Sobsom Dr	4	SW
Somerset Dr	5	SW
Sorrento Blvd	5	NE
South Blvd	1	NW
Southcove Dr	3	NW
Southgate St	3	SW
Southlawn Dr	4	SE
Southpointe Dr	3	NW
Southshore Dr	6	SW
Spalding Dr	2	SW
Spicemill Dr	1	SE
Spitz Dr	2	SE
Spring Dr	1	SW
St Joan Ct	2	NW
St Joseph Dr	4	NE
Stacy St	1	NE
Stadler Rd	3	SW
Stanberry Dr	2	NE
Stanley Dr	5	SW
Starlite	5	NE
State Highway	2	SW
State Hwy 53	2	SW
State Hwy 59	1	NW
State Hwy 59	2	NW
State Hwy 59	3	NW
Steede Dr	4	NW
Steel Ct	1	SE
Steel Dr	1	SE
Stephanie Dr	4	SE
Sterling Dr	4	SE
Sterling Dr	5	SW
Sterling Oaks	3	SW
Sterritt St	2	NE
Steven Dr	5	NE
Stimpson Dr	1	SE
Stober St	4	SE
Stonegate Dr	6	SW
Stoner Dr	6	SW
Stonewood Dr	6	SW
Stratford Dr	2	NE
Strawberry Ln	2	NE
Streamview Dr	6	NW
Strom Dr	2	NW
Sturbridge Dr	4	NW
Suffield Ln	6	NW
Summerset St	5	NW
Sumpter Dr	4	NW
Suncrest St	2	NW
Sunnypoint Dr	3	NW
Sunnyside Dr	3	NW
Sunrise Dr	5	SE
Sunset Dr	6	SW
Supreme Ct	3	SW
Surf Dr	4	SE
Surrey Dr	4	SE
Susan St	4	NE
Sutton Dr	4	NW
Swan Dr	6	SW
Sycamore Dr	3	NW
Sylvan Dr	4	NW
Taconite Dr	3	SW
Taffy Dr	5	SW
Tahiti Dr	5	NE
Takoma Dr	2	SE
Tall Oaks Dr	5	SW
Tamarack Dr	4	NE
Tanglewood Dr	5	SW
Tarpon Dr	5	NE
Tarragon Dr	1	SE
Tarry Dr	4	SW
Teak Ct	6	NW
Temple Dr	4	NE
Tericrest Dr	4	NE
Terra Santa Dr	6	SW
Terrybrook Dr	5	SW
Tessmer Dr	1	NE
Tetley Dr	2	SE
Thames Ct	5	NW
Theresa Ct	2	SE
Thomas Dr	5	NE
Thornton Dr	4	SE
Thornwood Ct	5	SW
Tiffany Dr	5	SW
Timberlane Dr	1	SW
Timmy Dr	4	SW
Tina Dr	4	SE
Tindell Dr	6	NW
Tinkler Rd	5	NW
Tipton Dr	2	NE
Tiverton Dr	1	SW
Tonabee Ct	2	SE
Tonabee Dr	2	SE
Torrington Dr	4	SE
Tothill Cir	1	SE
Tottenham St	5	NW
Townley Dr	5	SW
Tracy Dr	1	SW
Trafalgar Way	5	NW
Travis Dr	5	NE
Travistock Ct	4	NW
Trawick Ct	4	NW
Triangle Dr	2	NW
Tricia Dr	4	NW
Trinity Ct	3	NW
Tristram Dr	4	NW
Tudor Ct	6	SW
Tufts Dr	3	NW
Tulane Dr	5	NE
Tumeric Dr	1	SE
Turner Dr	5	SE
Twickingham	4	SE
Twickingham Dr	4	SE
Twin Ct	5	NE
Twining Dr	3	SW
Tyler Dr	4	SE
Ulman Dr	3	NW
University Dr	1	SE
University Dr	4	NE
Updale Dr	4	NE
Urbana Dr	3	SW
Utah Dr	3	NW
Utica Rd	2	NW
Utica Rd	3	SW
Utica Rd	6	NW
Uxton Ct	1	SE
Vachon Dr	3	SW
Vale Ct	6	NW
Valiant Dr	2	SE
Valley Dr	4	SW
Valleyview Dr	5	SE
Valusek Dr	6	SW
Van Dyke Ave	2	NW
Van Dyke Rd	2	NW
Van Dyke Rd	5	NW
Vanderbilt Dr	3	SW
Vanessa Dr	2	SE
Vega Dr	1	SE
Venetian Dr	4	SE
Vernon Dr	4	NE
Veronica Dr	4	NW
Versaille Ave	2	NW
Viceroy Dr	4	SW
Viceroy St	4	SW
Village Dr	5	NE
Villanova Dr	3	NW
Vine Dr	5	NE
Vinsetta Dr	3	NW
Viola Dr	6	SW
Virginia Dr	4	NE
Vista	4	SE
Vito Dr	4	SE
Vivian Dr	2	NE
Volpe Dr	5	SE
Waiteley Dr	2	NE
Wakefield Ct	6	NW
Walden Dr	2	SE
Waldo St	1	NE
Wales Ct	6	SW
Wall St	4	NE
Wall St	5	NW
Walnut Ln	2	SW
Walter Dr	1	SE
Waltham Dr	4	NE
Wanda Ave	3	SW
Warren Dr	6	NW
Warrington Dr	4	NW
Warsaw St	5	SE
Warwickshire Dr	5	NW
Waterbury Dr	3	NW
Watkins Dr	6	NW
Waverly Ct	1	SE
Wayne Dr	5	NE
Weber Dr	4	NE
Wedgewood St	6	SW
Wellston Dr	5	SE
Wembly Ct	1	SE
Wessel Ct	3	SW
Wessel Dr	3	SW
Westbrook Dr	3	NW
Westchester Rd	4	NE
Westlake Dr	6	SW
Westminster Dr	2	NE
Westview Dr	3	NW
Wheaton Dr	2	NE
White Cap Dr	3	NW
Whitehall Dr	2	SE
Whitfield Dr	5	NE
Whitfield Dr	6	NW
Whithorn Dr	2	NE
Whitson Ct	1	SE
Wickes Ln	5	SE
Wildwood Dr	3	SW
Wilke St	4	SW
Willesdon Sq	5	NW
William Dr	2	SE
Williamsburg Ct	5	SW
Willow Ct	3	NW
Willsharon St	1	NE
Wilmette Dr	3	SW
Wilmington Ct	2	NE
Wilmington Dr	2	NE
Wilseck Ct	2	NE
Wilshire Ct	2	NW
Winchester Dr	2	SW
Windham Dr	1	SE
Windsor Ct	2	SE
Windwood Dr	3	NW
Windy Cove Ct	2	SE
Wingate Dr	1	SE
Winona Dr	5	NE
Winona Dr	6	NW
Winslow Ct	1	SE
Winston Dr	4	SW
Witt Ct	5	SE
Woodchase Ct	4	SW
Woodford Dr	1	SW
Woodmont Dr	4	NE
Woodridge Dr	3	NW
Woodvilla Dr	6	SW
Woolwich Ct	1	SE
Wright Cir	4	SE
Xavier Dr	3	NW
Yale Ct	3	NW
Yeargo Dr	2	SW
Yonkers Dr	4	NE
York Dr	2	NE
Yorkshire	6	NW
Zimmer Dr	4	SW

NOTES

NW
SW
State Hwy 59
State Hwy 59
State Hwy 53
Clinton River Rd
Clinton River Rd
Utica Rd
Dequindre Rd
Ryan Rd
Mound Rd
Schoenherr Rd
Schoenherr St
Saal Rd
Pc Railroad
19 Mile Rd
18 Mile Rd
17 Mile Rd
16 Mile Rd
15 Mile Rd
14 Mile Rd
Plate # 1
Plate # 2
Plate # 3
Plate # 4
Plate # 5
Plate # 6
N

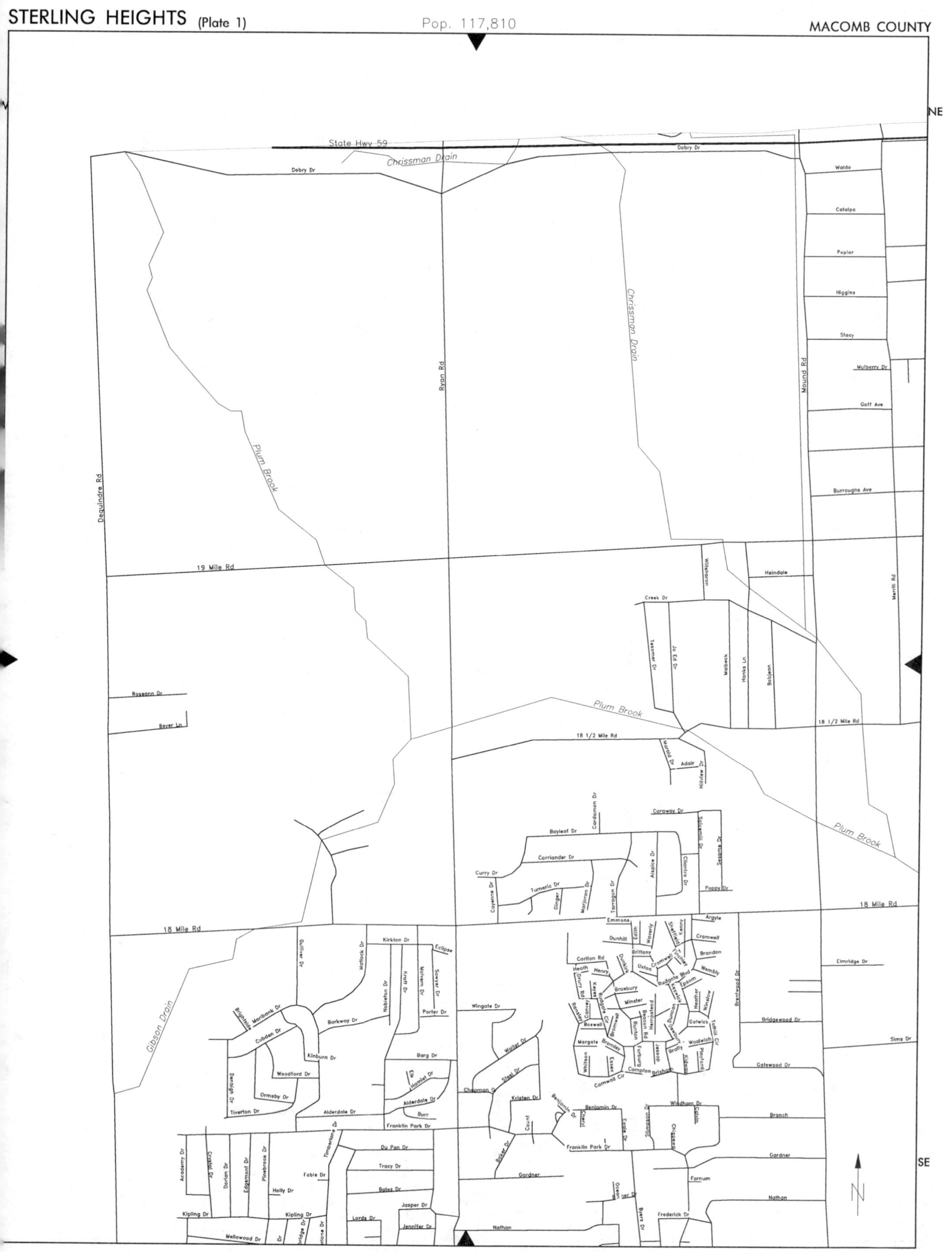
State Hwy 59
Chrissman Drain
Debry Dr
Debry Dr
Waldo
Catalpa
Poplar
Higgins
Stacy
Mulberry Dr
Goff Ave
Burroughs Ave
Ryan Rd
Mound Rd
Plum Brook
Deguindre Rd
Chrissman Drain
19 Mile Rd
Heindale
Merrill Rd
Creek Dr
Roseann Dr
Beyer Ln
Plum Brook
18 1/2 Mile Rd
18 1/2 Mile Rd
Adair
Caraway Dr
Bayleaf Dr
Corriander Dr
Curry Dr
Tumeric Dr
Poppy Dr
Plum Brook
18 Mile Rd
18 Mile Rd
Emmons
Argyle
Dunhill
Cromwell
Brandon
Carlton Rd
Elmridge Dr
Kirkton Dr
Eclipse
Wingate Dr
Barkway Dr
Porter Dr
Braebury
Minster
Bridgewood Dr
Sims Dr
Gibson Drain
Cubden Dr
Kinburn Dr
Barg Dr
Margate
Gatewood Dr
Woodford Dr
Chapman Dr
Kristen Dr
Ormsby Dr
Tiverton Dr
Alderdale Dr
Franklin Park Dr
Benjamin Dr
Windham Dr
Branch
Du Pon Dr
Franklin Park Dr
Tracy Dr
Gardner
Gardner
Foble Dr
Holly Dr
Bates Dr
Farnum
Nathan
Jasper Dr
Kipling Dr
Kipling Dr
Lords Dr
Jennifer Dr
Nathan
Frederick Dr
Mellowood Dr
NE
SE

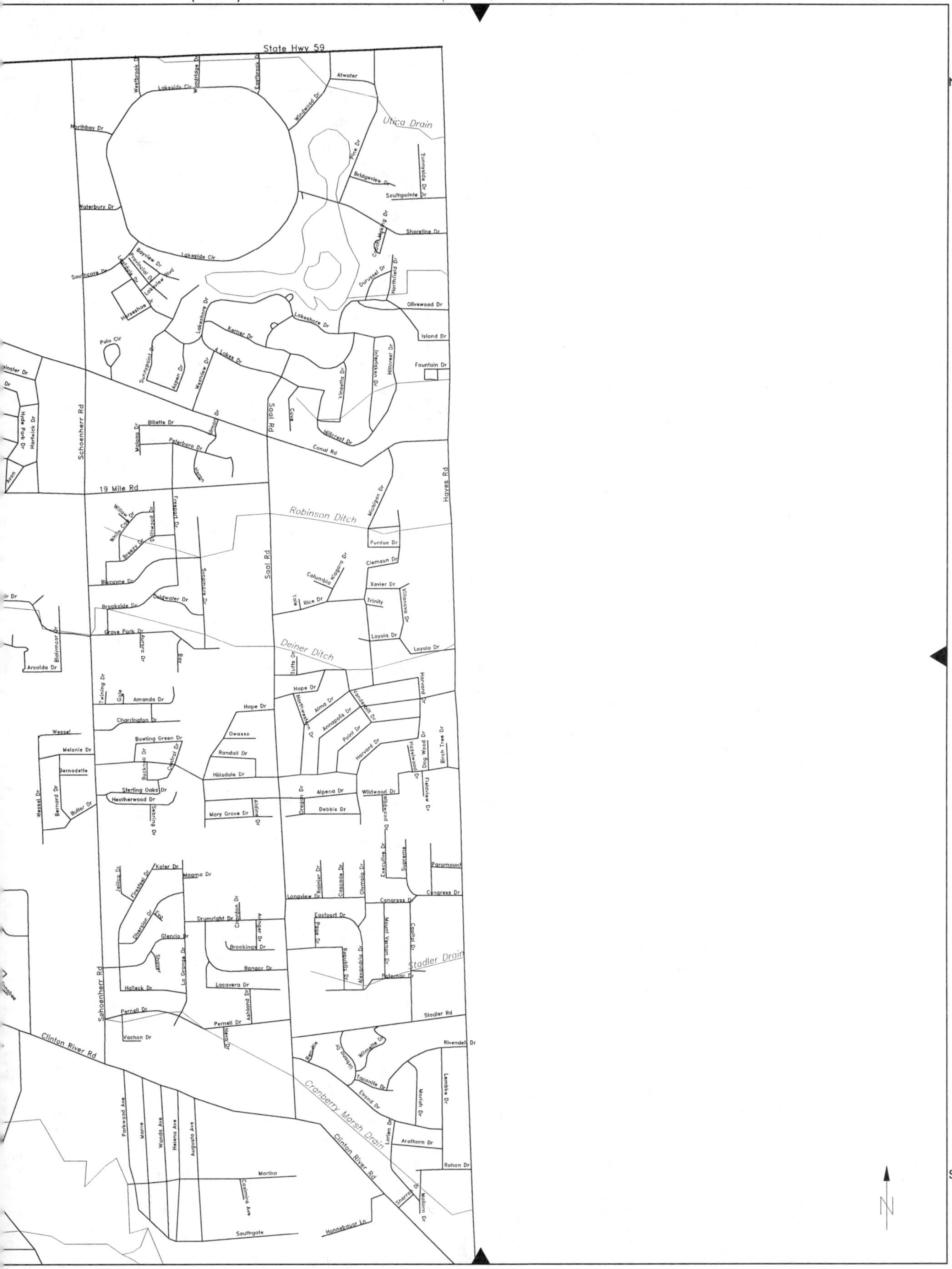
State Hwy 59
Atwater
Utica Drain
Lakeside Clr
Northbay Dr
Waterbury Dr
Southpointe Dr
Shoreline Dr
Bridgeview Dr
Sunnyside Dr
Olivewood Dr
Island Dr
Fountain Dr
Lakeshore Dr
Kerner Dr
Polo Cir
Schoenherr Rd
Saal Rd
Hayes Rd
Canal Rd
Hillcrest Dr
Interlaken Dr
Billette Dr
Peterboro Dr
Malaga Dr
19 Mile Rd
Robinson Ditch
Purdue Dr
Clemson Dr
Xavier Dr
Trinity
Villanova Dr
Loyola Dr
Columbia
Niagara Dr
Rice Dr
Yale
Biscayne Dr
Brookside Dr
Coldwater Dr
Sycamore Dr
Grove Park Dr
Aurora Dr
Blairmoor Dr
Arcadia Dr
Deiner Ditch
Tufts Dr
Hope Dr
Harvard Dr
Vanderbilt Dr
Annapolis Dr
Alma Dr
Northwestern Dr
Birch Tree Dr
Dog Wood Dr
Hazelwood Dr
Fieldview Dr
Twining Dr
Amanda Dr
Charrington Dr
Bowling Green Dr
Owasso
Randall Dr
Hillsdale Dr
Wessel
Melanie Dr
Bernadette
Wessel Dr
Bernard Dr
Butler Dr
Sterling Oaks Dr
Heatherwood Dr
Sebring Dr
Mary Grove Dr
Aldine Dr
Alpena Dr
Debbie Dr
Oregon Dr
Wildwood Dr
Kaler Dr
Magma Dr
Drumright Dr
Brookings Dr
Bangor Dr
Lacavera Dr
Halleck Dr
Pernell Dr
Vachon Dr
Longview Dr
Rainier Dr
Cascade Dr
Olympia Dr
Executive Dr
Supreme
Paramount
Congress Dr
Eastport Dr
Mount Vernon Dr
Capitol Dr
Republic Dr
Alexandria Dr
Potomac Dr
Stadler Drain
Stadler Rd
Clinton River Rd
Rivendell Dr
Lembke Dr
Taconite Dr
Elrond Dr
Moriah Dr
Lorien Dr
Arathorn Dr
Rohan Dr
Cranberry Marsh Drain
Parkwood Ave
Marnie
Wanda Ave
Helena Ave
Augusta Ave
Martha
Casimira Ave
Southgate
Hannebauer Ln
Sharron Dr
Mallorn Dr
NE
SE
N

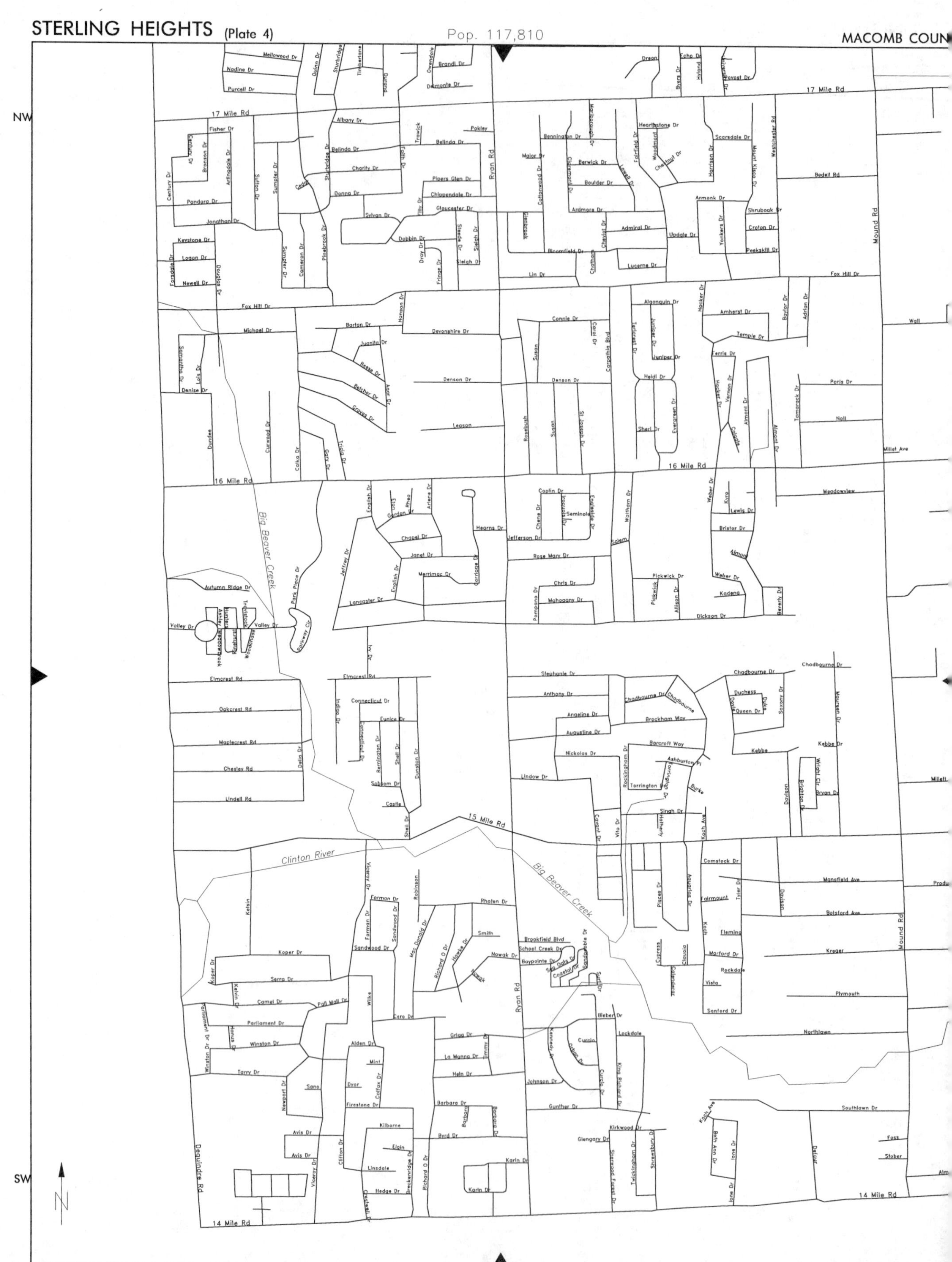
17 Mile Rd
16 Mile Rd
15 Mile Rd
14 Mile Rd
Ryan Rd
Mound Rd
Dequindre Rd
Fox Hill Dr
Big Beaver Creek
Clinton River
NW
SW
N

STERLING HEIGHTS (Plate 5)

Pop. 117,810

MACOMB COUNTY

Utica Rd
Schoenherr Rd
Clinton River
Plum Brook
Plumbrook Rd
16 Mile Rd
Metropolitan Beach Pkwy
Red Run River
15 Mile Rd
14 Mile Rd
Hayes Rd
Red Run Rd
NW
SW

Puetz Rd
Red Arrow Hwy
Wildwood Lane
St Joseph Ave
Ridge Rd
I- 94
Notre Dame Ave
Red Arrow Hwy
Pine St
Karen Ct
Karen Ct
Hickory Creek
Oak St
Phillips Dr
Bluff St
Fairview St
John Beers Rd
Kimmel St
Center St
Demorrow Rd
Grand Mere Rd
George St
Lawrence St
Lawrence St
Ridge Rd
Yasdick Dr
Grand Mere Rd
Legion Ave
Johnson Rd
Demorrow Cir
Red Arrow Hwy
N

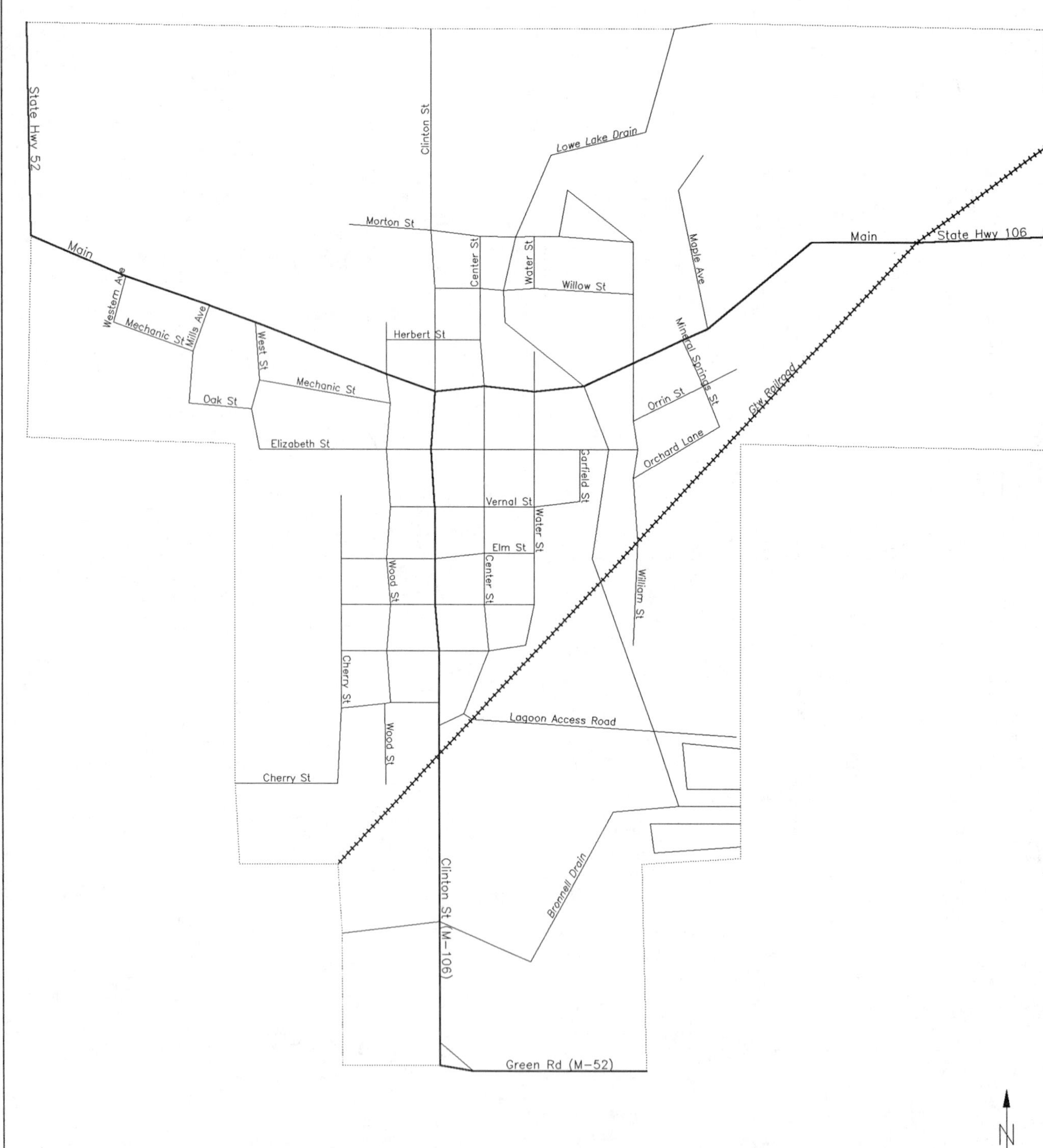
State Hwy 52
Clinton St
Lowe Lake Drain
Morton St
Main
Center St
Water St
Willow St
Maple Ave
Main
State Hwy 106
Western Ave
Mechanic St
Mills Ave
West St
Herbert St
Mineral Springs St
Mechanic St
Oak St
Orrin St
Glw Railroad
Elizabeth St
Orchard Lane
Garfield St
Vernal St
Water St
Elm St
Wood St
Center St
William St
Cherry St
Lagoon Access Road
Wood St
Cherry St
Clinton St (M-106)
Bronnell Drain
Green Rd (M-52)
N

Kirsch Municipal Airport
Lafayette St
Industrial Dr
Broadus St
Centerville St
Mc Kee St
Grobhiser St
Clay St
Nottawa ST (M-66)
Wren Rd
Meadowlane Dr
Merryview
Dove Rd
Timothy
Lauri Ln
Nottingham Rd
Cheshire
Hempshire
Buckingham Dr
Lancashire Dr
Wilshire Park Dr
Devonshire Dr
Wall School Ln
Canterbury
Sherwood
Robin Hood Trl
Robin Hood St
Friar Tuck Dr
Marion St
Lakeview Ave
Elizabeth St
Jerolene St
Beverly St
Ellerman St
Langrick St
Washington St
Main St
Sturgis Ave
George St
4th St
Prospect St
Jean Ave
Center Ave
Susan Ave
Ulm St
Hatch St
Oakwood Dr
Tulip Dr
Griffith St
Laura Dr
Pine
Spruce St
US 12
St Joseph St
West St
3rd St
2nd St
1st St
Orange St
Park St
John St
Chicago Rd
Franklin
Ivanhoe St
Trojan St
Hazel Ave
Maplecrest Ave
Pioneer Ave
Forwell Ave
Maple St
William St
Cornelia St
Electric Ct
Congress St
Grove St
Walker Ave
Mechanic
Rose Ct
Enterprise Ave
Wenzel Ave
Myrtle Ave
Parkside Dr
Parkside Cir
Clinton
Independence Ave
Ohio Ave
Ohio Ct
Albert St
Prairie Ave
Forest Ave
Jefferson St
Cottage St
Cherry Ave
Grand Ave
Edna Ave
Magnolia Ave
Mortimer Ave
Elm St
South St
Chelia
Wilson Ave
Liberty St
Galyn St
Merribe St
Rolling Ridge Ln
Hawthorne
Sunnyfield Rd
Nottawa St
Fawn River Rd
Commerce Rd
Clark St
Wade St
Treatment Plant Rd
State Hwy 66
N

Cordigan Dr
Chesterfield Dr
Young Dr
Hill Rd
Birchcrest Dr
Seymour Rd
Valleyview Dr
Seymour Rd
Greenleaf Dr
Durwood Dr
Chelmsford Dr
Chesterfield Dr
Narbury Dr
Durwood Dr
Whitney Ct
Worchester Dr
Oakview Dr
Helmsley Dr
Daval Dr
Don Shenk Dr
Oxford Ct
Winshall Dr
Seymour Rd
Winston Dr
Cappy Lane
Miller Rd
Dargon St
Fairchild St
Crapo St
Mc Lain St
School St
Ingalls St
Ita Ct
Brady St
Ford St
Maple St
Fortino Dr
Morrish Rd
Ingalls St
Wade St
1st St
Church St
Mason St
Mary St
Roundhouse
Grove St
3rd St
Fredrick St
Roundhouse
Depot St
Miller Rd
Raubinger Rd
Bristol Rd
I- 69
Miller Rd
Jenny Lane
Jenny Lane
Yarmy Dr
Abbey Lane
Elms Rd
Bristol Rd
Miller Rd
Clw and Co Railroad
Dye Rd
N

Telegraph
Dick Ave
Pioneer Dr
James K Blvd
Sylvan Lake
Pontiac Ave
Ferndale Ave
Avondale St
Glenwood Ave
Rosedale Ave
Oakwood Ave
Garland Ave
Pontiac Ave
Lakeview Ave
Benvenue Ave
Maplewood Ave
Benvenue Ave
Maplewood Ave
Cheltingham Ave
Avondale St
Garland Ave
Renfrew Ave
Briarcliff St
Beverly Ave
Warwick Ave
Woodland Ave
Lakeland Ave
Sherwood Rd
Stratford Ln
Avondale
Inverness Ave
Orchard Lake Rd
Pleasant St
Knowlson St
Orchard Lake Rd
Greer St
Woodrow Wilson Blvd
Littletell St
Square Lake Rd
N

Nunn Rd
Victoria Lane
Tim Ct
Manor Dr
Sunset Dr
Roberta Dr
Roberta Dr
Anna Dr
Tawas River
Riverview
Spring
River St
Murphy
Hemlock St
German St
Ottawa
Cedar St
Beech
Maple St
Oak St
Spruce
US Hwy 23
Birch Rd
Murphy
North St
Harris Ave
10th Ave
9th Ave
8th Ave
7th Ave
1st Ave
Wheeler
1st St
12th Ave
6th Ave
5th
4th Ave
3rd Ave
2nd Ave
2nd St
Meadowview
Whittimore St
8th Ave
12th
11th Ave
10th Ave
9th Ave
7th Ave
Tawas River
6th St
Margo St
Michigan
Woodward
Nannette
Grove Rd
Elms Ave
US Hwy 23
Bay Dr
Elms Ave
Crocker
N

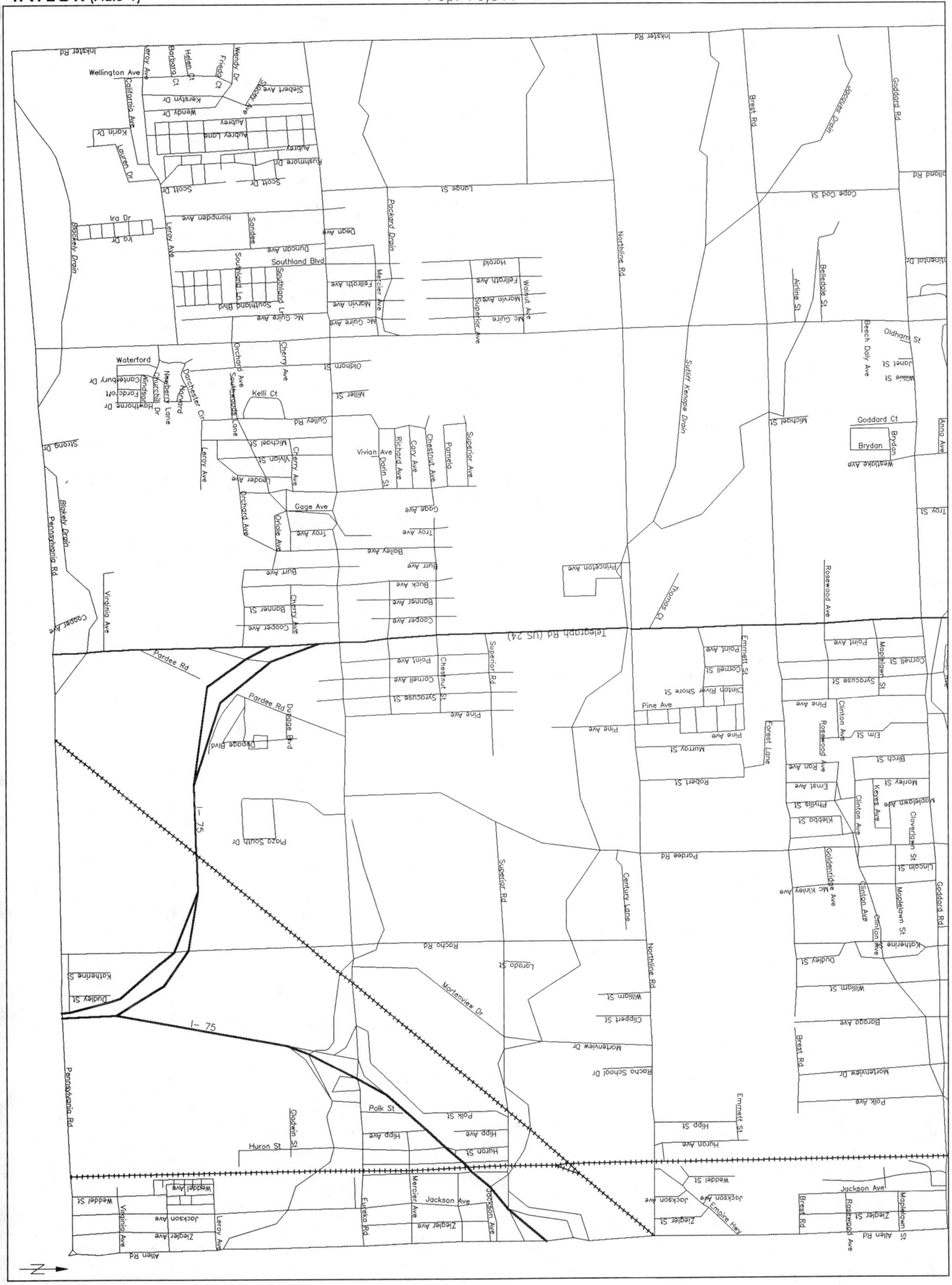

Inkster Rd
Wellington Ave
Leroy Ave
Barbara Ct
Helen Ct
Frieda Ct
Wendy Dr
Siebert Ave
California Ave
Kerstyn Dr
Aubrey Lane
Karin Dr
Lauren Dr
Rushmore Dr
Scott Dr
Ira Dr
Hampden Ave
Blakely Drain
Sandee
Dean Ave
Duncan Ave
Southland Blvd
Southland Ln
Mc Guire Ave
Packard Drain
Mercier Ave
Fellrath Ave
Marvin Ave
Harold
Walnut Ave
Superior Ave
Lange St
Northline Rd
Brest Rd
Jacques Drain
Goddard Rd
Cape Cod St
Airline St
Belledale St
Sutliff Kenope Drain
Beech Daly Ave
Oldham St
Waterford
Canterbury Dr
Fordcroft
Hawthorne Dr
Windsor
Churchill Dr
Newberry Lane
Harvard
Dorchester Cir
Orchard Ave
Southwoods Lane
Cherry Ave
Kelli Ct
Miller St
Gulley Rd
Strong Dr
Michael St
Vivian St
Vivian Ave
Richard Ave
Darin St
Cory Ave
Chestnut Ave
Pamela
Goddard Ct
Brydan
Westlake Ave
Anna Ave
Leader Ave
Gage Ave
Troy Ave
Troy St
Oriole Ave
Bailey Ave
Burt Ave
Buck Ave
Banner Ave
Banner St
Cooper Ave
Virginia Ave
Pennsylvania Rd
Princeton Ave
Thomas Ct
Rosewood Ave
Telegraph Rd (US 24)
Pardee Rd
Dupage Blvd
Point Ave
Cornell Ave
Syracuse St
Pine Ave
Superior Rd
Emmett St
Clinton River Shore St
Maplelawn St
Murray St
Robert St
Forest Lane
Clinton Ave
Elm St
Birch St
Ran Ave
Ernst Ave
Morley St
Keyes Ave
Phyllis St
Klebba St
Cloverlawn St
I-75
Plaza South Dr
Century Lane
Goldenridge Ave
Mc Kinley Ave
Lincoln St
Racho Rd
Larado St
Mortenview Dr
Katherine St
Dudley St
William St
Clippert St
Baraga Ave
Racho School Dr
Polk St
Polk Ave
Hipp St
Hipp Ave
Huron St
Huron Ave
Gladwin St
Weddel St
Jackson Ave
Ziegler Ave
Ziegler St
Eureka Rd
Empire Hwy
Allen Rd

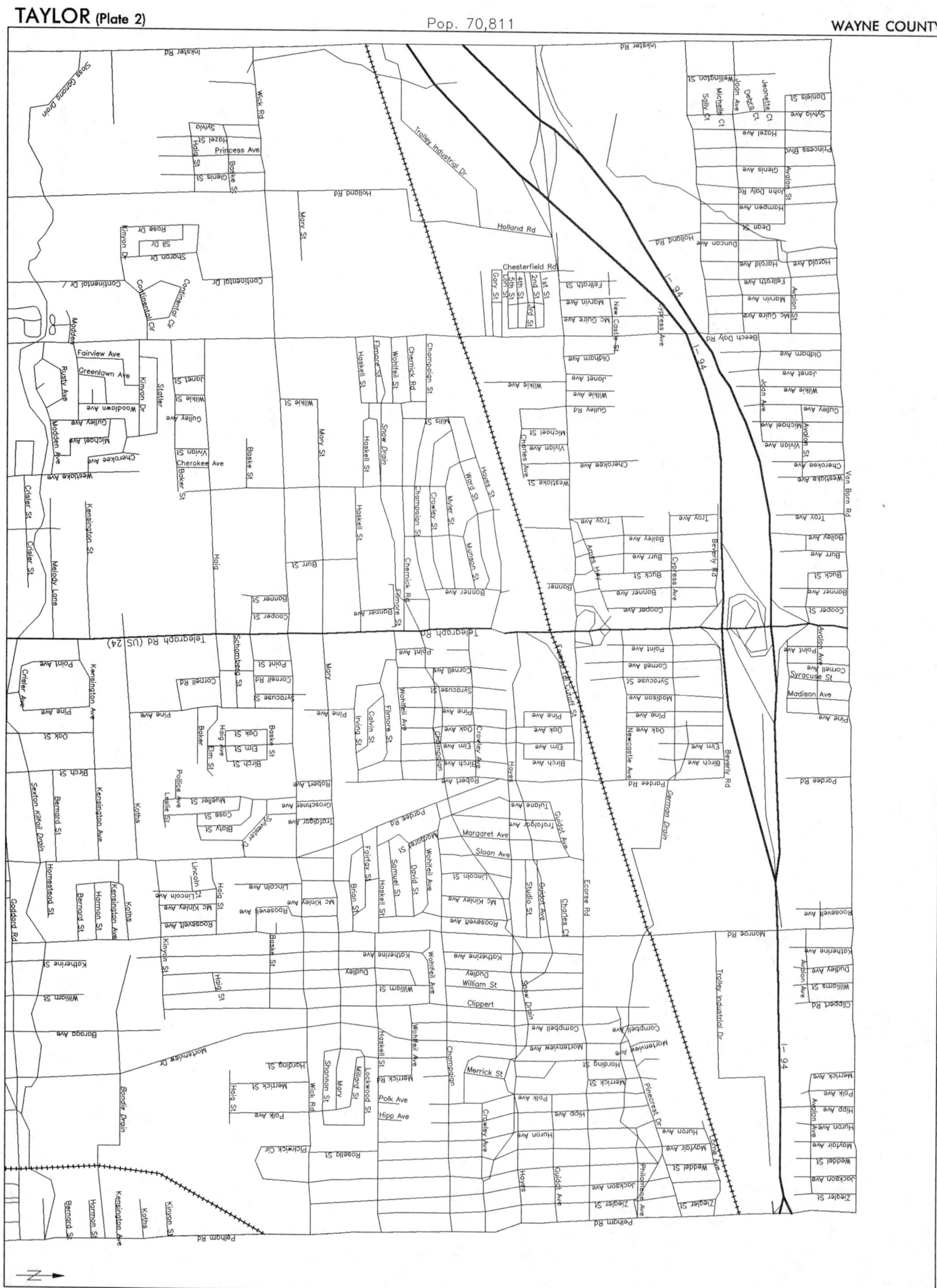

Inkster Rd
Sloss Gannon Drain
Wick Rd
Trolley Industrial Dr
Holland Rd
Chesterfield Rd
Continental Dr
Continental Cir
Fairview Ave
Greenlawn Ave
Rusty Ave
Modden Ave
Kinyon Dr
Statler
Beech Daly Rd
I-94
Cypress Ave
Mary St
Haskell St
Filmore St
Wohlfeil St
Chermick Rd
Champaign St
Snow Drain
Hayes St
Ward St
Crowley St
Myler St
Munson St
Baske St
Baker St
Kensington St
Melody Lane
Crisler St
Haig
Troy Ave
Beverly Rd
Van Born Rd
Telegraph Rd (US 24)
Avalon Ave
Cooper St
Point Ave
Cornell Ave
Syracuse St
Madison Ave
Pine Ave
Oak Ave
Elm Ave
Birch Ave
Pardee Rd
Newcastle Ave
German Drain
Sexton Kilfoil Drain
Bernard St
Kensington Ave
Koths
Margaret Ave
Sloan Ave
Goddard Rd
Homestead St
Harmon St
Lincoln St
Studio St
Charles Ct
Ecorse Rd
Monroe Rd
Trolley Industrial Dr
Katherine Ave
William St
Clippert
Campbell Ave
Mortenview Dr
Bondie Drain
Merrick St
Champaign
Polk Ave
Hipp Ave
Pinecrest Dr
Huron Ave
Crowley Ave
Mayfair Ave
Weddel St
Jackson Ave
Ziegler St
Philomene Ave
Coyle Ave
Hayes
Guidot Ave
Pelham Rd
Kinyon St

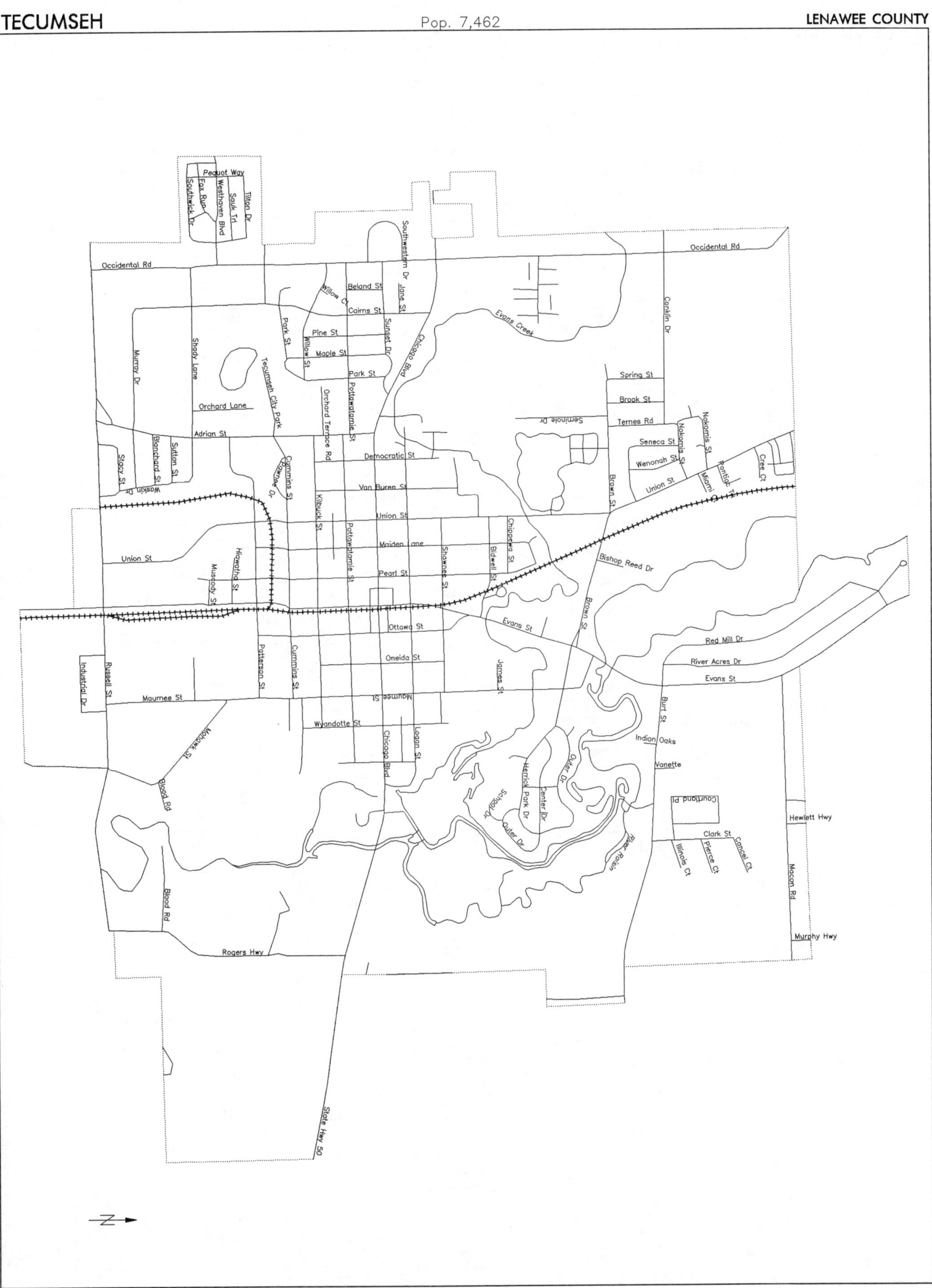
Pequot Way
Fox Run
Westhaven Blvd
Sauk Trl
Tilton Dr
Southwick Dr
Occidental Rd
Southwestern Dr
Willow Ct
Beland St
Jane St
Cairns St
Evans Creek
Conklin Dr
Park St
Pine St
Sunset Dr
Chicago Blvd
Maple St
Willow St
Murray Dr
Shady Lane
Park St
Tecumseh City Park
Orchard Terrace Rd
Pottawatamie St
Spring St
Brook St
Orchard Lane
Seminole Dr
Ternes Rd
Nokomis St
Adrian St
Seneca St
Democratic St
Wenonah St
Cree Ct
Stacy St
Blanchard St
Sutton St
Waskin Dr
Cummins St
Bowen Dr
Brown St
Union St
Miami Ct
Pontiac Tr
Van Buren St
Kilbuck St
Union St
Chippewa St
Maiden Lane
Union St
Hiawatha St
Bishop Reed Dr
Bidwell St
Shawnee St
Pearl St
Mussody St
Brown St
Ottawa St
Evans St
Red Mill Dr
Oneida St
River Acres Dr
Industrial Dr
Russell St
Patterson St
Cummins St
James St
Evans St
Maumee St
Maumee St
Burt St
Wyandotte St
Mohawk St
Logan St
Chicago Blvd
Indian Oaks
Vanette
Blood Rd
Herrick Park Dr
Outer Dr
Center Dr
Seneca Dr
Outer Dr
Courtland Pl
Hewlett Hwy
Clark St
Illinois Ct
Pierce Ct
Cancel Ct
River Raisin
Macon Rd
Blood Rd
Murphy Hwy
Rogers Hwy
State Hwy 50
N

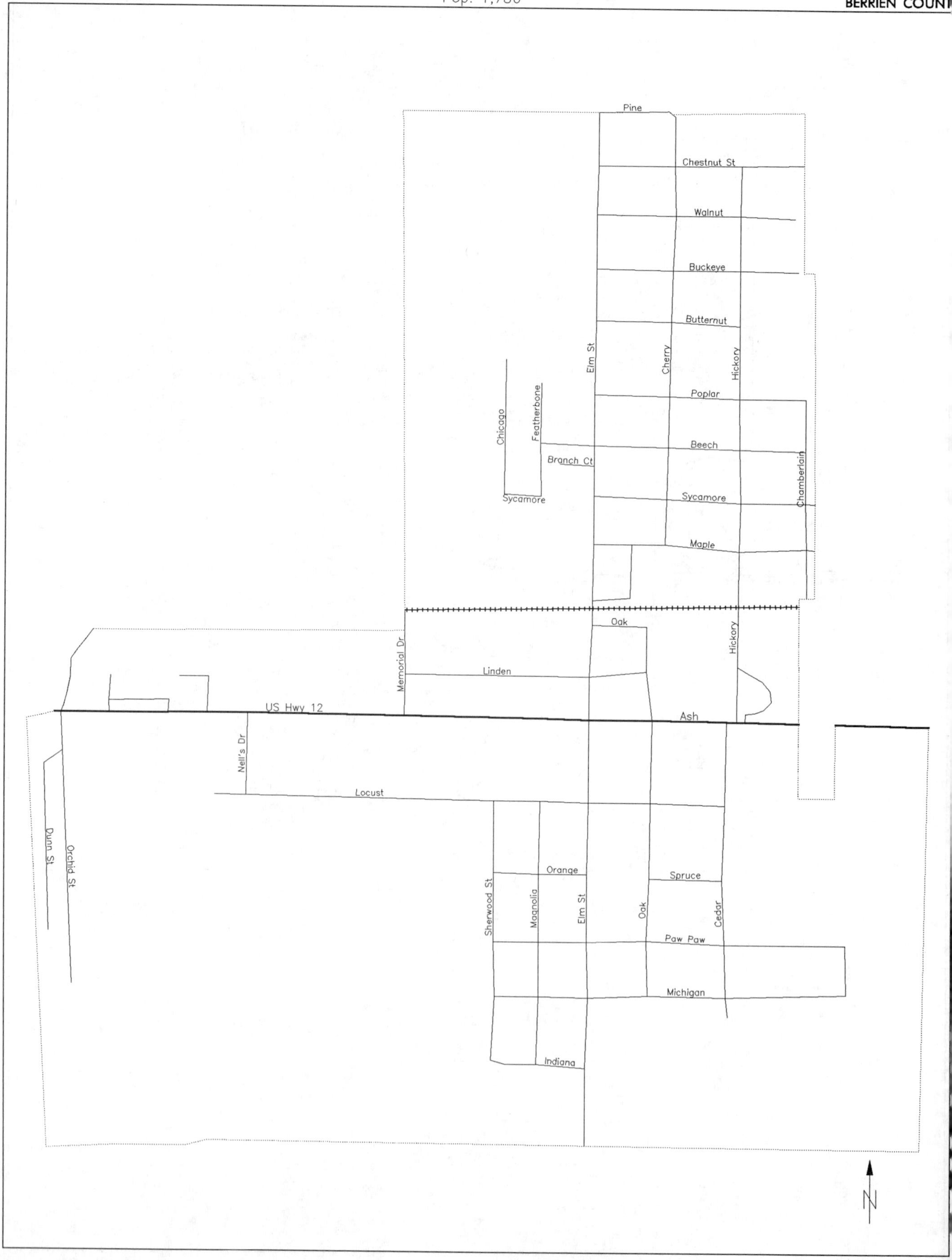

Pine
Chestnut St
Walnut
Buckeye
Butternut
Elm St
Cherry
Hickory
Poplar
Chicago
Featherbone
Beech
Branch Ct
Chamberlain
Sycamore
Sycamore
Maple
Oak
Hickory
Memorial Dr
Linden
US Hwy 12
Ash
Nell's Dr
Locust
Dunn St
Orchid St
Orange
Spruce
Sherwood St
Magnolia
Elm St
Oak
Cedar
Paw Paw
Michigan
Indiana
N

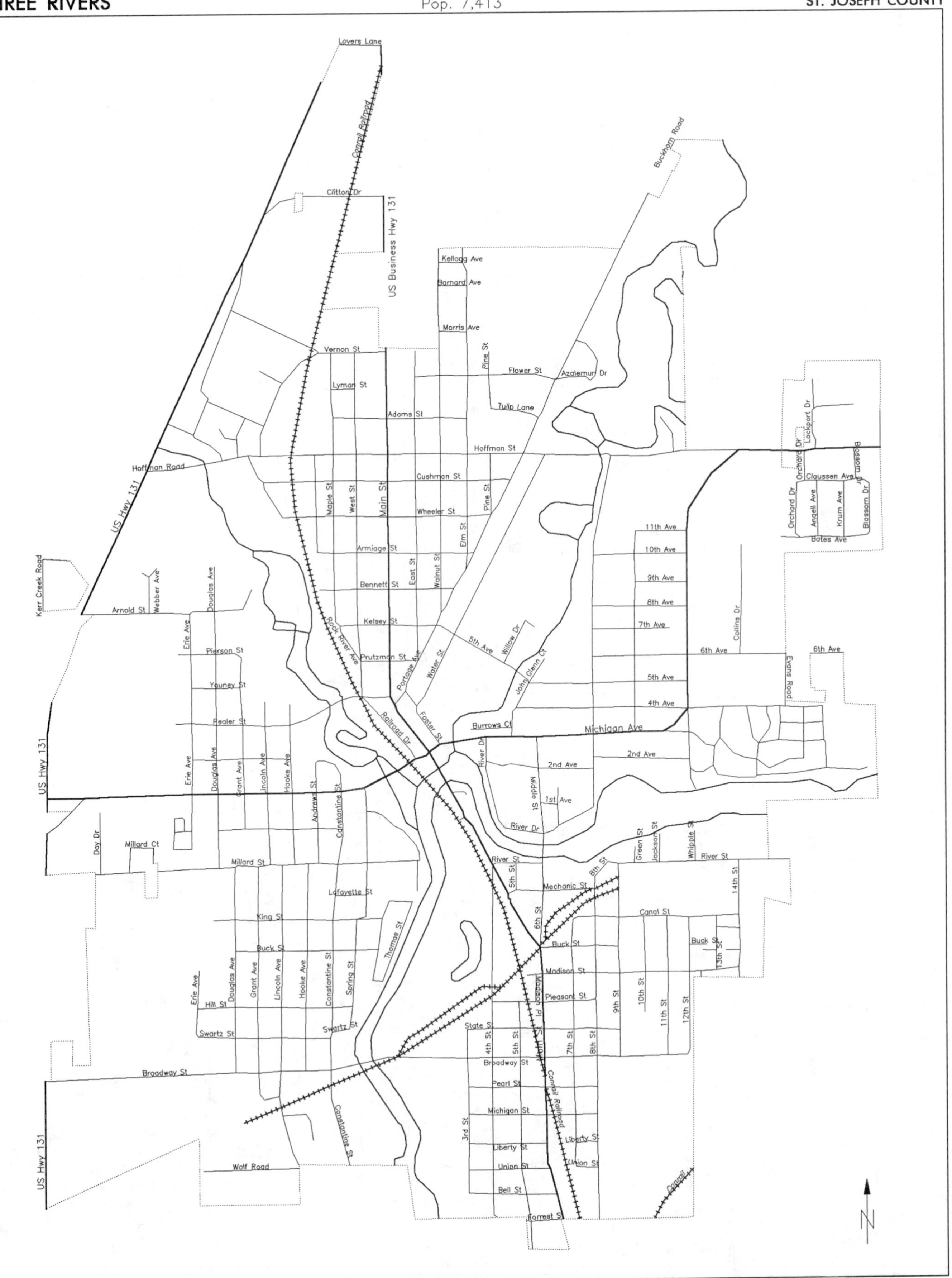
Lovers Lane
Conrail Railroad
Buckhorn Road
Clifton Dr
US Business Hwy 131
Kellogg Ave
Barnard Ave
Morris Ave
Vernon St
Pine St
Flower St
Azalemun Dr
Lyman St
Tulip Lane
Adams St
Hoffman St
Hoffman Road
Cushman St
Maple St
West St
Main St
Wheeler St
Pine St
US Hwy 131
Elm St
11th Ave
Armiage St
10th Ave
East St
Walnut St
Kerr Creek Road
Webber Ave
Douglas Ave
9th Ave
Bennett St
8th Ave
Arnold St
Kelsey St
7th Ave
Collins Dr
Erie Ave
Rock River Ave
5th Ave
Willow Dr
Pierson St
Prutzman St
Portage Ave
Water St
John Glenn Ct
6th Ave
6th Ave
Evans Road
Youney St
5th Ave
4th Ave
Fealer St
Railroad Dr
Foster St
Burrows Ct
Michigan Ave
River Dr
2nd Ave
2nd Ave
Hooke Ave
Lincoln Ave
Grant Ave
Andrews St
Constantine St
Middle St
1st Ave
River Dr
Day Dr
Millard Ct
Millard St
River St
Green St
Jackson St
Whipple St
River St
8th St
5th St
Mechanic St
14th St
Lafayette St
Canal St
King St
6th St
Thomas St
Buck St
Buck St
Buck St
13th St
Madison St
Madison Pl
Pleasant St
Hill St
Spring St
9th St
10th St
11th St
12th St
Swartz St
Swartz St
State St
4th St
5th St
7th St
8th St
Broadway St
Broadway St
Pearl St
Michigan St
Conrail Railroad
3rd St
Liberty St
Liberty St
Union St
Union St
Wolf Road
Bell St
Forrest St
Conrail
Orchard Dr
Lockport Dr
Blossom Dr
Claussen Ave
Angell Ave
Krum Ave
Bates Ave
N

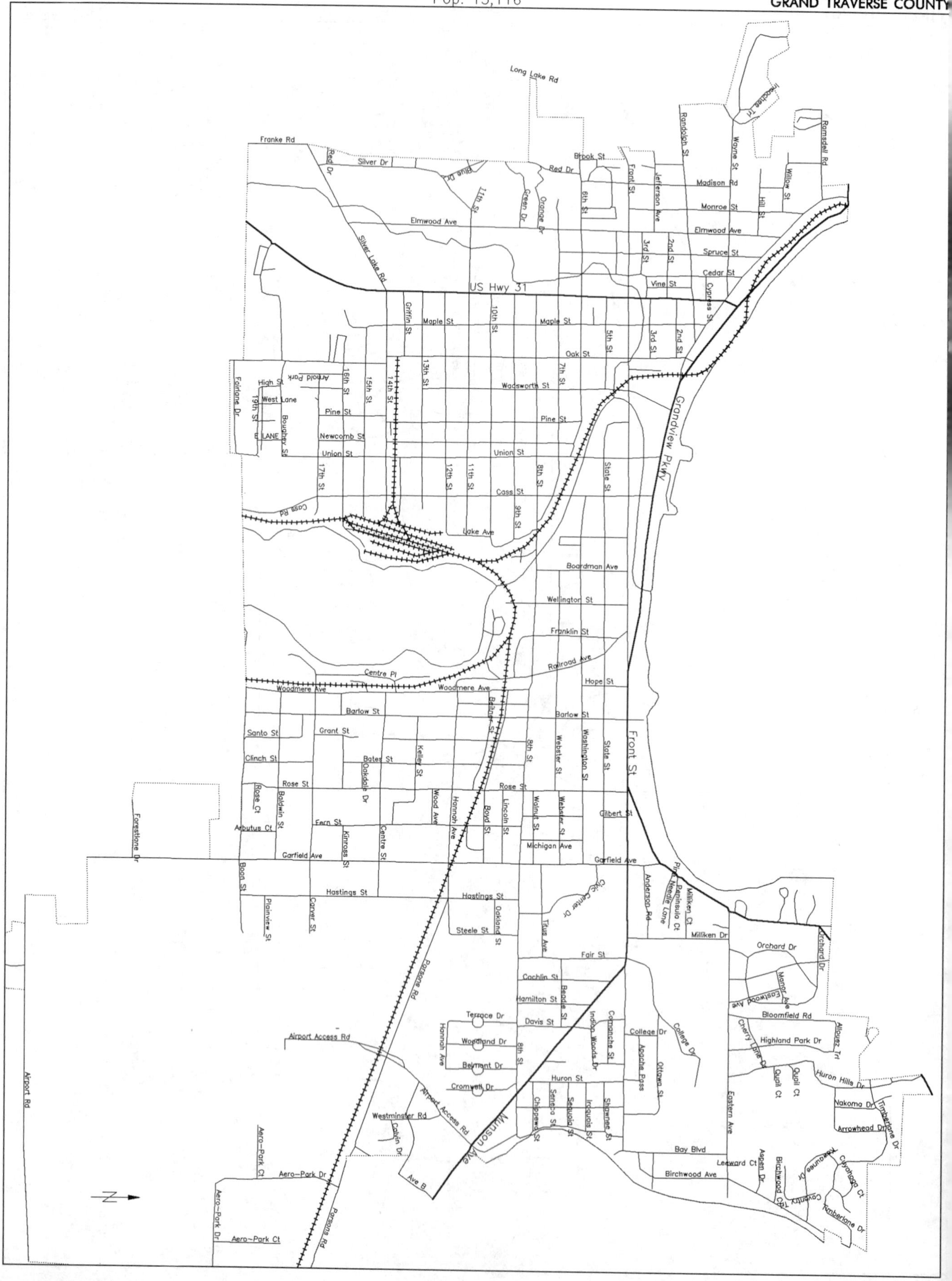

Pop. 15,116

14 Mile Rd	4	SW
3 Lakes Dr	2	NE
3 Oaks Blvd	1	SE
Abbey Dr	2	SE
Abbotsford St	2	NE
Aberdeen Dr	1	SE
Aberdeen Dr	2	SW
Abington	2	SW
Academy Dr	4	NE
Adams Ave	3	NW
Adams Rd	1	SW
Adams Rd	3	NW
Adams School	2	SE
Adonis St	4	NE
Adrienne Dr	2	NE
Afton St	4	NE
Alexander Dr	4	NE
Alfred St	2	NE
Algansee St	4	NW
Alger	4	NE
Alger St	4	NE
Allegheny St	2	SE
Allen Dr	4	SW
Allison	2	SE
Almond Dr	1	NE
Alpine St	3	NE
Alton Ct	2	SE
Alton Dr	2	SE
American	4	SE
Andover Ct	1	NW
Andover Rd	1	NW
Andrew	1	NE
Anslow Ln	1	NW
Anvil Dr	2	SE
Anvil Dr	4	NE
Apple	1	NW
Ardmore Dr	4	NW
Argyle	2	SE
Argyle Dr	2	SE
Arlund Way	1	NW
Arlundway	1	NW
Arrowhead	4	NE
Arthur St	4	NW
Ashley	2	SW
Aspinwall St	1	NE
Aster Dr	2	NE
Athena Dr	4	NE
Athena St	4	NE
Atkins Rd	2	NW
Atlas Ct	4	NE
Atlas St	4	NE
Auburn Dr	4	NE
Augusta Dr	2	NW
Aurora Dr	1	NE
Austin St	4	NE
Avalon Dr	4	NE
Avery Dr	2	SE
Avonhurst Dr	1	SW
Avonhurst Dr	3	NW
Axtell St	3	NW
Babbit	2	SW
Babcock Dr	3	NW
Badder St	4	SW
Baldwin Rd	1	NE
Balfour Dr	3	NW
Bankle Dr	2	SE
Banmoor St	3	NE
Barabeau St	2	NW
Barbara	1	SE
Barclay Ct	2	SW
Barclay Dr	2	SW
Barilaine St	1	SE
Barnes	1	SW
Barrett St	3	NE
Barton Way	1	NE
Basewood Dr	1	NE
Bayside	1	SW
Beach Rd	1	SW
Beach Rd	3	NW
Beacon Hill Dr	4	NW
Beattie Dr	2	NW
Beech Ln	4	NW
Beldale St	2	SW
Belhaven St	2	SW
Bellingham	4	NE
Bellows Ct	4	NE
Bellows Dr	4	NE
Belzair St	2	SW
Bender	1	SE
Bentley Dr	1	SE
Berkshire St	4	NE
Berwyck	2	SW
Bev Ct	2	SW
Big Beaver Rd	3	NW
Big Beaver Rd	4	NW
Big Oak Trl	1	SW
Biltmore St	4	NW
Binbrooke St	1	SW
Binbrooke St	3	NW
Bingham Dr	2	NE
Birch Run Dr	1	SW
Birchwood St	4	NW
Bishop Dr	4	NW
Black Pine Trl	1	SW
Blackwall St	1	NE
Blair Dr	2	SE
Blanche St	1	NE
Blaney St	3	NE
Bloomingdale	2	SE
Bluff Ct	1	SW
Bolingbroke St	3	NW
Bonito Dr	2	NE
Bonniebrook Ln	2	SW
Booth St	2	NW
Borden St	4	NE
Boros Ct	2	SW
Boros Dr	2	NW
Boulan St	3	NE

Boulder Dr	1	SW
Boulder Dr	3	NW
Boyd St	4	NW
Bradbury	1	SE
Bradley St	2	SW
Braemar	1	SE
Braemar	2	SW
Bramford Dr	2	SE
Brandywine St	1	SW
Breeze Hill Pl	1	SW
Brentwood	1	SW
Bretby Dr	1	NW
Briargrove St	1	SW
Bridge Park Dr	1	NE
Brinston	4	NE
Brinston St	4	NE
Bristol Dr	2	SW
Bristol Dr	4	NW
Brittany Tree	2	NE
Bronson Dr	1	SW
Brookings Dr	1	NE
Brooklawn Ct	3	NW
Brooklawn St	3	NW
Buckingham Pl	1	SW
Burdic St	2	NE
Burkoff	1	SW
Burkoff	3	NW
Burns Dr	2	SW
Burtman Dr	4	SW
Butler Dr	2	SE
Butterfield Rd	3	NE
Butternut Hill Dr	1	SW
Byron	1	SE
Cadmus St	2	NW
Cahill	1	SE
Caitlin Ct	1	NE
Caliper	1	SW
Calvert Ct	2	SE
Calvert Dr	2	SE
Cambria St	2	NW
Cambridge	2	SE
Cameo	1	SW
Cameron Ct	1	SW
Cameron Dr	1	SW
Camilla	4	NE
Canary Ct	3	NW
Canham St	1	NE
Canmoor	1	NE
Canmoor St	1	NE
Capri	1	SW
Cardinal Ct	1	SW
Cardinal Dr	1	SW
Carmel Dr	2	SE
Carmel Dr	4	NE
Carnaby	2	SW
Carol Dr	2	SE
Carpenter Dr	1	SW
Carr Dr	2	SE
Carson	1	SE
Carter St	1	SE
Carter St	2	SW
Casper Dr	2	NW
Castleton St	4	NE
Caswell St	3	NE
Catalpa Ct	1	NW
Cattermole St	4	NW
Cecil St	4	NE
Cedar Ridge Dr	3	NW
Century	4	NW
Century Dr	4	NW
Chalgrove St	1	NW
Champlain	1	SW
Chancery Ave	2	NE
Chancery St	2	NE
Chapel Dr	2	SE
Charlevios	2	SE
Charnwood St	1	NW
Charrington Dr	4	NW
Charter	4	NW
Charter Blvd	4	NW
Chatham Dr	1	SW
Chatham Dr	3	NW
Chaucer Dr	4	NW
Chelsea Ct	3	NW
Chelsea Ln	3	NW
Cheltenham	1	SW
Cherokee	1	SW
Cherry St	4	NW
Cherrywood St	1	SW
Chesapeake	1	SW
Chesterfield St	4	NE
Chestnut Hill Dr	1	SW
Cheswick Dr	3	NW
Chicago St	4	SE
Chopin St	4	NE
Church Hill	2	SW
Cinder Mill	1	NW
Civic Ctr	3	NE
Clarke Dr	2	SW
Claymont	1	SW
Clayton Dr	4	NE
Clearview	1	SW
Cleveland Dr	4	NE
Cliffside Dr	2	NE
Clinton River	1	NE
Clinton River	2	NE
Clock Gate Cir	1	NW
Cloister Ct	2	SE
Cloister Dr	2	SE
Cloveridge St	4	NW
Club Dr	1	SW
Coachman	4	NW
Coachman Dr	4	NW
Cobbs Dr	1	SE
Colebrook St	4	NW
Colleen	2	NE
Colling	2	SW
Collington	1	SW

Colonial St	2	SE
Colony	4	NW
Columbia Dr	4	NE
Colwell Dr	4	NE
Combermere St	4	SW
Condor Dr	3	NW
Congress	2	NW
Congress Ct	2	NW
Connolly	1	SW
Continental Dr	4	NE
Cook Ct	4	NW
Coolidge Hwy	1	SW
Coolidge Hwy	3	NW
Coral Dr	2	NE
Corbin	1	SW
Corporate Dr	1	SE
Costswold	2	NW
Country Dr	1	NE
Country Ridge	1	NW
Coventry St	4	NE
Cranapple	1	NW
Cranbrook	1	SE
Creek Bend	1	SW
Creekside Dr	2	NW
Crescent Way	2	NE
Crestline Dr	4	NE
Crestmont	1	SW
Creston St	2	SW
Crestview	2	SW
Crestview Dr	1	NE
Crimson Dr	4	NE
Crooks Rd	1	SE
Crooks Rd	3	NE
Crowfoot	2	SE
Cumberland Dr	2	SE
Cunningham	3	NW
Curran Dr	1	SW
Cutting St	2	NW
Cynthia	2	SE
Cypress Dr	2	SW
Dalesford Dr	1	NW
Daley St	4	NW
Danbury	2	SE
Daniels St	1	SE
Darlene Ct	1	SE
Darlene Ct	3	NE
Dartmoor St	3	NW
Dashwood St	4	SE
Davis Ct	2	SW
Dayton Dr	2	SE
De Etta St	2	NW
De Wulf	2	SE
Deepwood	1	SW
Deer Path Ct	1	SW
Deinmore Ave	1	SE
Delaware Dr	3	NE
Deloy	2	SE
Delta	2	NE
Demaret	2	NW
Denise Dr	2	NE
Denton	1	NE
Denton Ct	1	NE
Denton Dr	1	NE
Dequindre Rd	2	SE
Derby St	3	NW
Devonshire Dr	1	SW
Devonwood St	1	SW
Dewey	1	NE
Dexter Rd	2	SE
Diamond Dr	2	NE
Diane	2	NW
Dickens Dr	4	NW
Doenges St	2	NE
Donaldson	2	NW
Donaldson St	2	NW
Donegal St	1	NW
Doral Ct	2	NW
Doral Dr	2	NW
Dorchester Rd	3	NW
Dorothea Ct	3	NW
Dorre St	4	NW
Dorset Dr	2	SW
Dorshire St	2	SW
Dover St	4	NE
Downey Dr	4	NE
Drew Dr	1	NE
Drexel Dr	1	SW
Dublin Fair St	1	NW
Duchess Ct	1	NW
Duke Dr	2	SE
Duncan Dr	2	SW
Durand	1	SE
Durham Ct	3	NE
Eagle Dr	4	NE
Eastbourne St	1	SW
Eastbourne St	3	NW
Eastport St	4	NW
Eckerman St	2	NW
Eckford Ct	2	SW
Eckford St	2	SW
Edenborough St	3	NW
Edgemont Dr	1	SW
Edgemont Dr	3	NW
Edith St	2	NE
Elaine St	4	NW
Elbow Ln	3	NE
Eldridge Dr	4	NE
Eleanor St	2	SE
Elgin Rd	1	SE
Elizabeth Dr	1	SE
Ellenboro St	4	NW
Ellery Dr	2	SE
Elliott St	4	SE
Ellis	2	NE
Elm	1	NW
Elm	4	SE
Elmoor St	1	NE
Elmsford St	4	SW

Elmwood Ave	4	SW
Elsey	1	NE
Emerald Lake	2	NE
Emerald Shores	2	NE
Emerson St	3	NE
Endicott Dr	2	NE
Engle Ct	3	NW
English Dr	2	SE
Enterprise St	4	NW
Erickson Ave	2	SE
Erin Way	1	NW
Essex Ave	3	NW
Essex St	3	NW
Estates Ct	1	SW
Estates Dr	1	SW
Estates Dr	3	NW
Eton St	3	NW
Euclid	4	NE
Eva St	4	NE
Evaline Ct	2	SW
Evaline St	2	SW
Evanston	2	SE
Evanswood	2	NE
Evanswood St	2	NE
Executive Dr	4	SE
Fabius St	1	SE
Fabius St	2	SW
Faircastle Dr	1	NW
Fairfax St	2	SE
Fairfield St	2	SE
Fairmont Dr	2	SE
Fairway Blvd	2	NW
Falcon	1	NE
Falmouth Rd	2	SW
Farmbrook Dr	1	NW
Fawn Ct	1	SW
Fedora Dr	2	SE
Fenwicke Blvd	1	SW
Fernleigh St	2	SE
Fernleigh St	4	NE
Finch Rd	1	SE
Finch Rd	3	NE
Finch St	1	SE
Firwood Dr	1	SW
Fleetwood Dr	1	NW
Flemington Dr	1	NW
Flint	1	NW
Flora	2	NE
Florence St	1	NE
Flower Hill Dr	1	SW
Floyd	4	NE
Folkstone Ct	2	SW
Folkstone Dr	2	NW
Fordham Dr	1	NW
Forest Park	1	NW
Forest Trl	2	SE
Forge Dr	2	SE
Forge Dr	4	NE
Forsythe Ave	2	SE
Forthton St	4	NW
Fountain	1	SE
Fox Ct	1	SW
Fox Dr	1	SW
Foxchase Rd	1	SW
Foxcroft	2	SE
Frankton St	4	NW
Fredmoor St	1	NE
Freemont Dr	1	SW
French Creek	1	SW
Frostwood Ct	1	SW
Fulton	1	NE
Galloway Bay	1	NW
Gamber Dr	2	SE
Garden	1	NE
Garrige Trl	1	NW
Garry Dr	4	NE
Gate Dr	2	SE
Gatesford Cir	2	SE
Gaylord	1	SE
Genick	2	SE
Georgian Ct	1	NE
Glaser St	2	SW
Glasglow Ct	2	NW
Glasgow	2	NW
Glen Dr	1	SW
Glencastle	1	SE
Glendale	1	NE
Glenshire Dr	2	SW
Glenwood Dr	2	SW
Gloucester Ave	3	NW
Glyndebourne	1	NW
Golfview Dr	3	NW
Gordon Dr	1	SE
Graefield St	3	NW
Grand Haven	4	SE
Granger	1	NE
Grant Ave	4	SW
Greendale	2	SE
Greenhill	1	NW
Greensboro St	2	SE
Greenwich Dr	1	SW
Grenadier	1	NW
Grove	4	NE
Gulason	4	SE
Gulliver St	2	NE
Habrand St	1	NE
Haldane St	1	NE
Hale Dr	2	SW
Hallmark	1	SW
Hamman Dr	2	SE
Hampshire	2	SW
Hampton Ln	3	NW
Hannah St	2	NW
Hanover	2	SW
Harbor	2	NE
Harmony Dr	4	NE
Harned St	2	NE
Harold Dr	2	SW

Harris St	4	NW
Hart St	1	SE
Hart St	2	SW
Hartland St	4	NW
Hartshorn St	4	NW
Hartwig St	2	NW
Harwich Dr	2	SW
Haverford Rd	1	NW
Hawthorne Dr	2	SW
Hearthside	1	NW
Heatherbrook	1	SE
Heatherwood	1	SW
Heatherwood Dr	1	SW
Heide St	3	NE
Helena St	4	NW
Hempstead St	4	NE
Hendrickson	4	SW
Henhawk St	3	NW
Henrietta St	4	NW
Herbmoor St	1	NE
Heritage	4	NE
Hertford	2	SW
Hickory St	4	NW
Hidden Forest	1	NW
Hidden Pine	1	SW
Hidden Ridge	4	NW
High Oaks Dr	1	NE
Highbury Dr	2	NE
Highland Dr	2	SE
Highmount	1	SW
Hill Ct	2	SE
Hill Dr	2	SE
Hillcrescent	2	SE
Hillcrescent Dr	2	SE
Hilltop Dr	1	NE
Hilmore St	2	NW
Hinge	4	NE
Historic	2	SE
Historic	4	NE
Holly Dr	2	SW
Holm St	2	NE
Homestead	1	NE
Homewood Dr	1	SW
Hopedale St	2	SE
Horseshoe	2	SE
Houghton St	1	NE
Hounds Chase	1	NW
Hubbard Dr	2	SE
Hunters Gate	1	NW
Huntsford Ct	3	NE
Huntsford Dr	3	NE
Huntsford Rd	3	NE
Hurst	1	NE
Hurst St	1	NE
Hurst St	2	NW
Hyde Park Dr	2	SE
Hylane Dr	1	SW
I- 75	1	SE
I- 75	3	NE
I- 75	4	NE
Ida	4	NW
Indusco Ct	4	SE
Iowa St	4	NE
Irene St	4	NW
Isabell St	4	NE
Ivanhoe Dr	2	NE
Jack Dr	3	NW
Jackson Dr	4	NE
Jade Dr	2	NE
Jamaica Dr	4	SW
Jandale	2	NE
Jarman St	2	NE
Jason Dr	2	SE
Jasper Ct	4	NE
Jeffrey Dr	2	NE
Jennings St	2	SW
Jennings St	4	NW
Jill	3	NW
Joanne St	1	SW
Joanne St	3	NW
John R Rd	2	SE
John R Rd	4	NE
Johnathon	1	NW
Jordan St	1	NE
Joshua Dr	1	NE
Judy	2	SW
Julian St	2	SE
Juniper Ct	1	SW
Justine	1	NE
Keaton	1	NE
Keats	2	SW
Kelley St	4	NW
Kelly St	4	NE
Kent Dr	3	NW
Kenwyck	2	SE
Kenyon St	4	SW
Kerry St	3	NW
Kettle	2	SE
Kevin Dr	4	NE
Key West Dr	4	SW
Killarney Ln	1	NW
Kilmer St	4	NW
Kimberly	1	NE
King	2	SE
Kingsbury	1	SW
Kingsley St	3	NW
Kingspoint Dr	2	SE
Kingspoint Dr	4	NE
Kingston St	3	NW
Kingsway	1	SW
Kinlock	1	NE
Kipling Ct	2	SW
Kirk Ln	3	NE
Kirk Ln	4	NW
Kirkton St	4	NW
Kirts Blvd	3	NE
Kirts Blvd	4	NW
Knight Dr	2	SE

NOTES

Plate # 1
Plate # 2
Plate # 3
Plate # 4
Square Lake Rd
Long Lake Rd
Wattles Rd
Big Beaver Rd
Maple Rd
14 Mile Rd
Livernois Ave
Rochester Rd
Adams Rd
Beach Rd
Coolidge Hwy
Crooks Rd
I- 75
Dequindre Rd
State Hwy 150
NE
SE
N

TROY (Plate 1)

Pop. 72,884

OAKLAND COUN

NW

SW

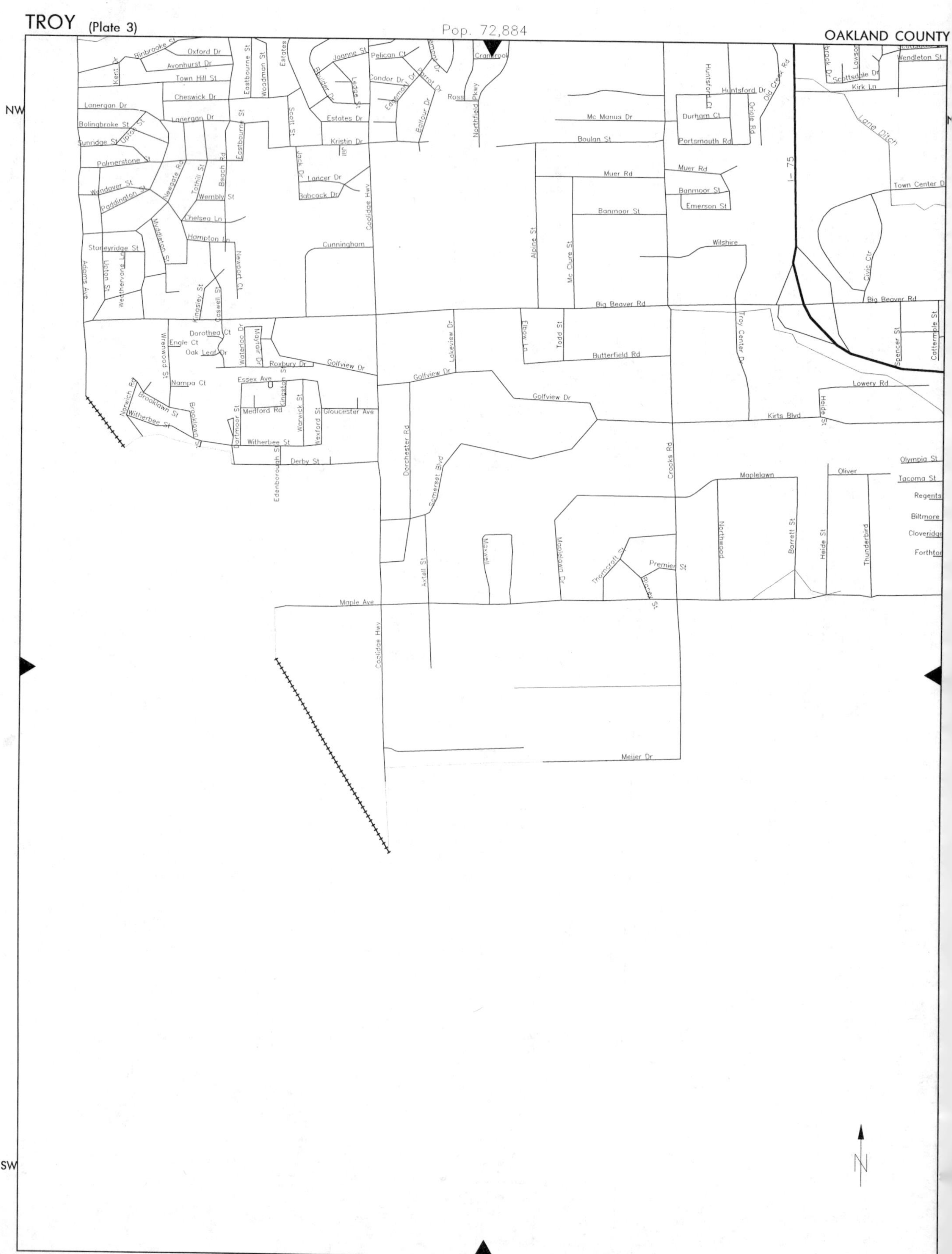
Oxford Dr
Avonhurst Dr
Town Hill St
Cheswick Dr
Lanergan Dr
Bolingbroke St
Sunridge St
Palmerstone St
Wendover St
Paddington St
Newgate Rd
Tothill St
Beach Rd
Wembly St
Chelsea Ln
Hampton Ln
Middleton St
Stoneyridge St
Adams Ave
Upton St
Weathervane Ln
Kingsley St
Caswell St
Newport Ct
Eastbourne St
Woodman St
Estates
Scott St
Joanna St
Pelican Ct
Condor Dr
Estates Dr
Kristin Dr
Jack Dr
Jill
Lancer Dr
Babcock Dr
Coolidge Hwy
Cunningham
Balfour Dr
Ross
Northfield Pkwy
Cranbrook
Mc Manus Dr
Boulan St
Muer Rd
Banmoor St
Alpine St
Mc Clure St
Big Beaver Rd
Huntsford Ct
Huntsford Dr
Old Creek Rd
Durham Ct
Oriole Rd
Portsmouth Rd
Muer Rd
Banmoor St
Emerson St
Wilshire
I-75
Wendleton St
Scottsdale Dr
Kirk Ln
Lane Ditch
Town Center Dr
Civic Ctr
Big Beaver Rd
Spencer St
Cattermole St
Wrenwood St
Dorothea Ct
Engle Ct
Oak Leaf Dr
Waterloo Dr
Mayfair Dr
Roxbury Dr
Golfview Dr
Essex Ave
Kingston St
Nampa Ct
Norwich Rd
Brooklawn St
Witherbee St
Dartmoor St
Medford Rd
Warwick St
Wexford St
Gloucester Ave
Witherbee St
Derby St
Edenborough St
Lakeview Dr
Golfview Dr
Elbow Ln
Todd St
Butterfield Rd
Golfview Dr
Dorchester Rd
Somerset Blvd
Crooks Rd
Troy Center Dr
Lowery Rd
Kirts Blvd
Heide St
Olympia St
Oliver
Tacoma St
Regents
Biltmore
Cloveridge
Forthton
Maplelawn
Northwood
Barrett St
Heide St
Thunderbird
Maxwell
Maplelawn Dr
Thorncroft St
Premier St
Axtell St
Maple Ave
Coolidge Hwy
Meijer Dr
NW
SW
N

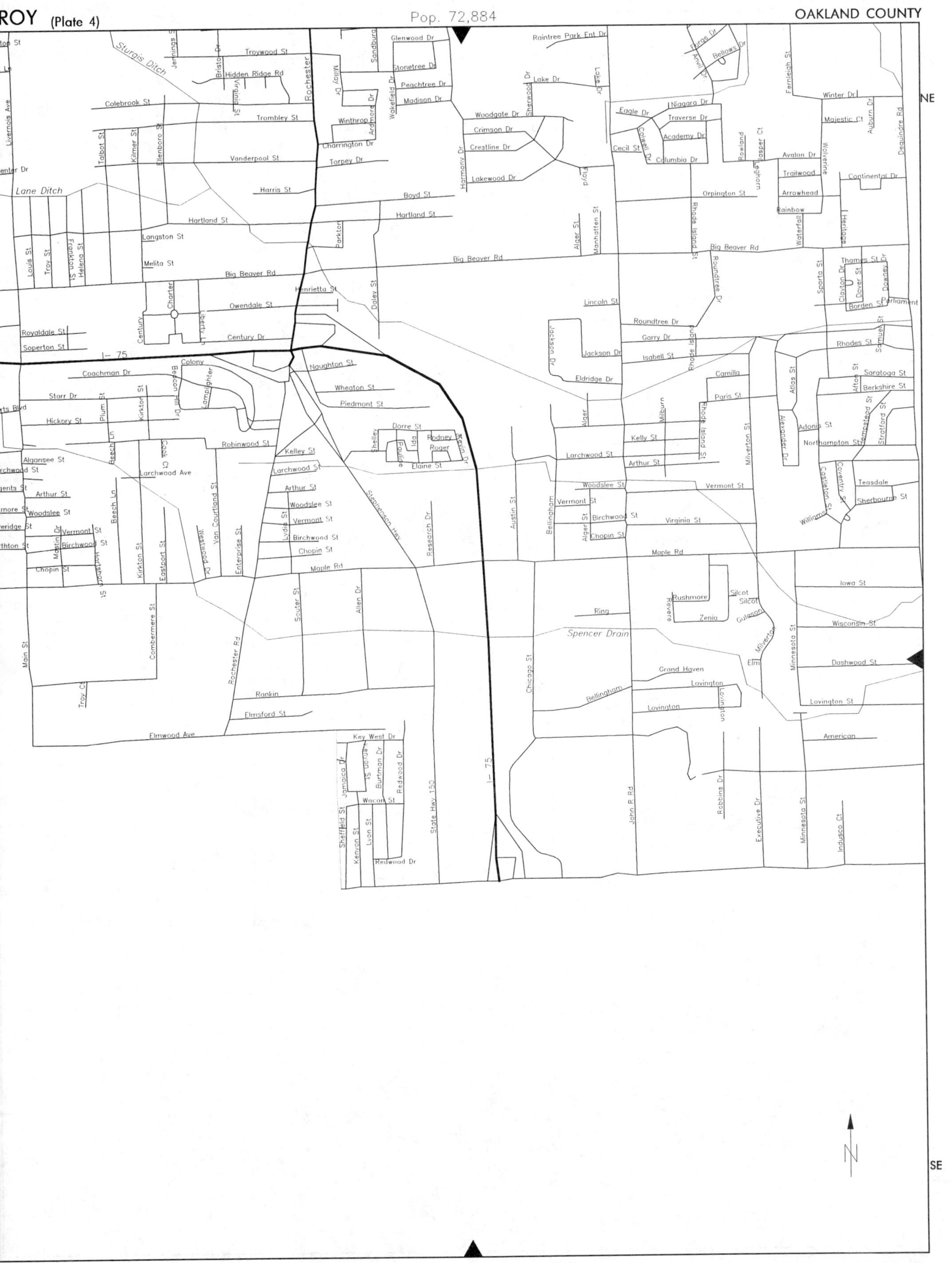
Sturgis Ditch
Troywood St
Hidden Ridge Rd
Jennings
Bristol Dr
Virginia St
Rochester
Colebrook St
Trombley St
Livernois Ave
Vanderpool St
Talbot St
Kilmer St
Ellenboro St
Lane Ditch
Harris St
Hartland St
Langston St
Melita St
Louis St
Troy St
Frankton St
Helena St
Big Beaver Rd
Charter
Owendale St
Century
Liberty Ln
Century Dr
Royaldale St
Soperton St
I– 75
Colony
Coachman Dr
Beacon Hill Dr
Lamplighter
Starr Dr
Plum St
Kirkton St
Hickory St
Robinwood St
Beech Ln
Cook Ct
Algansee St
Larchwood Ave
Arthur St
Woodslee St
Vermont St
Birchwood St
Martin Dr
Chopin St
Hartshorn St
Westwood Dr
Van Courtland St
Enterprise St
Eastport St
Main St
Combermere St
Troy Ct
Rochester Rd
Rankin
Elmsford St
Elmwood Ave
Glenwood Dr
Sandburg
Stonetree Dr
Peachtree Dr
Madison Dr
Milly Dr
Wakefield Dr
Ardmore Dr
Winthrop
Charrington Dr
Torpey Dr
Boyd St
Hartland St
Parkton
Daley St
Henrietta St
Naughton St
Wheaton St
Piedmont St
Dorre St
Shelley
Ida
Rodney
Roger
Pauline
Elaine St
Kelley St
Larchwood St
Lydia St
Chopin St
Maple Rd
Stephenson Hwy
Research Dr
Souter St
Allen Dr
Key West Dr
Jamaica Dr
Burtman Dr
Redwood Dr
Wacon St
Sheffield St
Kenyon St
Lyon St
State Hwy 150
Raintree Park Ent Dr
Lake Dr
Sherwood Dr
Woodgate Dr
Crimson Dr
Crestline Dr
Harmony Dr
Lakewood Dr
Floyd
Alger St
Manhatten St
Lincoln St
Jackson Dr
Eldridge Dr
Austin St
Bellingham
Chicago St
Spencer Drain
Ring
Forge Dr
Anvil Dr
Bellows Dr
Eagle Dr
Niagara Dr
Traverse Dr
Academy Dr
Cecil St
Columbia Dr
Rowland
Jasper Ct
Leghorn
Orpington St
Rhode Island St
Roundtree Dr
Roundtree Dr
Garry Dr
Isabell St
Camilla
Paris St
Milburn
Kelly St
Arthur St
Vermont St
Virginia St
Milverton St
Maple Rd
Rushmore
Revere
Silcot
Zenia
Gulasoni
Milverton
Elm
Grand Haven
Lovington
Bellingham
John R Rd
Robbins Dr
Executive Dr
Fernleigh St
Winter Dr
Majestic Ct
Auburn Dr
Dequindre Rd
Wolverine
Avalon Dr
Trailwood
Arrowhead
Rainbow
Waterfall
Continental Dr
Heritage
Sparta St
Thames St
Clayton Dr
Dover St
Downey Dr
Borden St
Parliament
Rhodes St
Samuel St
Atlas St
Afton St
Saratoga St
Berkshire St
Adonis St
Hempstead St
Stratford St
Northampton St
Alexander Dr
Castleton St
Coventry St
Teasdale
Sherbourne St
Williams
Iowa St
Wisconsin St
Minnesota St
Dashwood St
Lovington St
American
Minnesota St
Indusco Ct
NE
SE
N

Arbogast Road
State Hwy 60
County Line Dr
Dirks Road
Goodwin Dr
Sycamore
Goodwin Dr
North Dr
St Joseph St
Division St
State Hwy 60
County Line Dr
Poly Ann Ct
Summit St
Walnut Lake
St Joseph River
Thomas St
Ellen St
Charlotte St
Park St
South St
Railroad St
Lee St
Fenton St
Barry St
Lincoln St
Ann St
Mary St
Broadway St
8 Mile Road
Railroad St
Coldwater River
Woodruff St
Allen St
John St
High St
St Joseph River
Conrail Railroad
Broadway St
Fenton St
Spruce St
Crane St
Clark St
Pine St
Cedar St

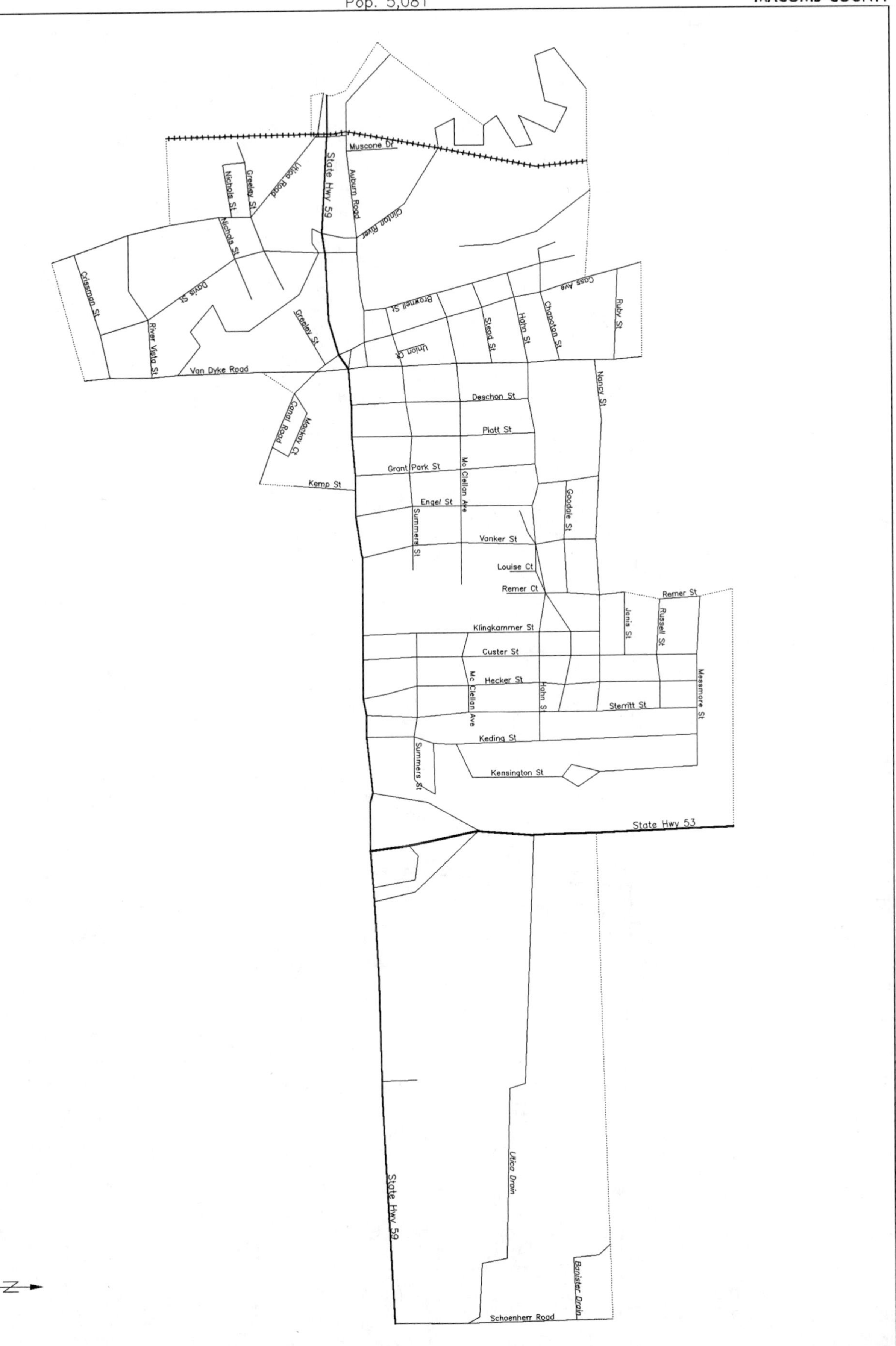
Muscone Dr
State Hwy 59
Auburn Road
Clinton River
Utica Road
Greeley St
Nichols St
Nichols St
Crissman St
Davis St
River Vista St
Van Dyke Road
Greeley St
Brownell St
Union Ct
Stead St
Hahn St
Chapaton St
Cass Ave
Ruby St
Nancy St
Canal Road
Mackay Ct
Kemp St
Deschon St
Platt St
Grant Park St
Mc Clellan Ave
Engel St
Summers St
Goodale St
Vanker St
Louise Ct
Remer Ct
Remer St
Janis St
Russell St
Klingkammer St
Custer St
Hecker St
Mc Clellan Ave
Hahn St
Sterritt St
Messmore St
Keding St
Summers St
Kensington St
State Hwy 53
State Hwy 59
Utica Drain
Banister Drain
Schoenherr Road

Jay Road
Margery
Shirley
Cork Pine
Cork Pine
Richards
Saginaw
Brady
Adams
Athletic
Brady
Emerson
Harrington
Oak
Lee
West
Spruce
Prospect
Jefferson
Huron
Madison
Main
Saginaw
Athletic
Oak
Washington
Spring
Division
Water
Proctor
Oak
Cherry
Cass
Main
Water
State Hwy 15
Park
East
Cedar
Arch
Butler
Hoxie
Sheridan
Blurn
Grant
Birch
Sherman
Chestnut
Briarwood
Water
Lynn St
Andy
Hazel
North
Walnut
Norman
Lane
Huron
Cass
Enterprise Dr
Commerce
Scotch Road

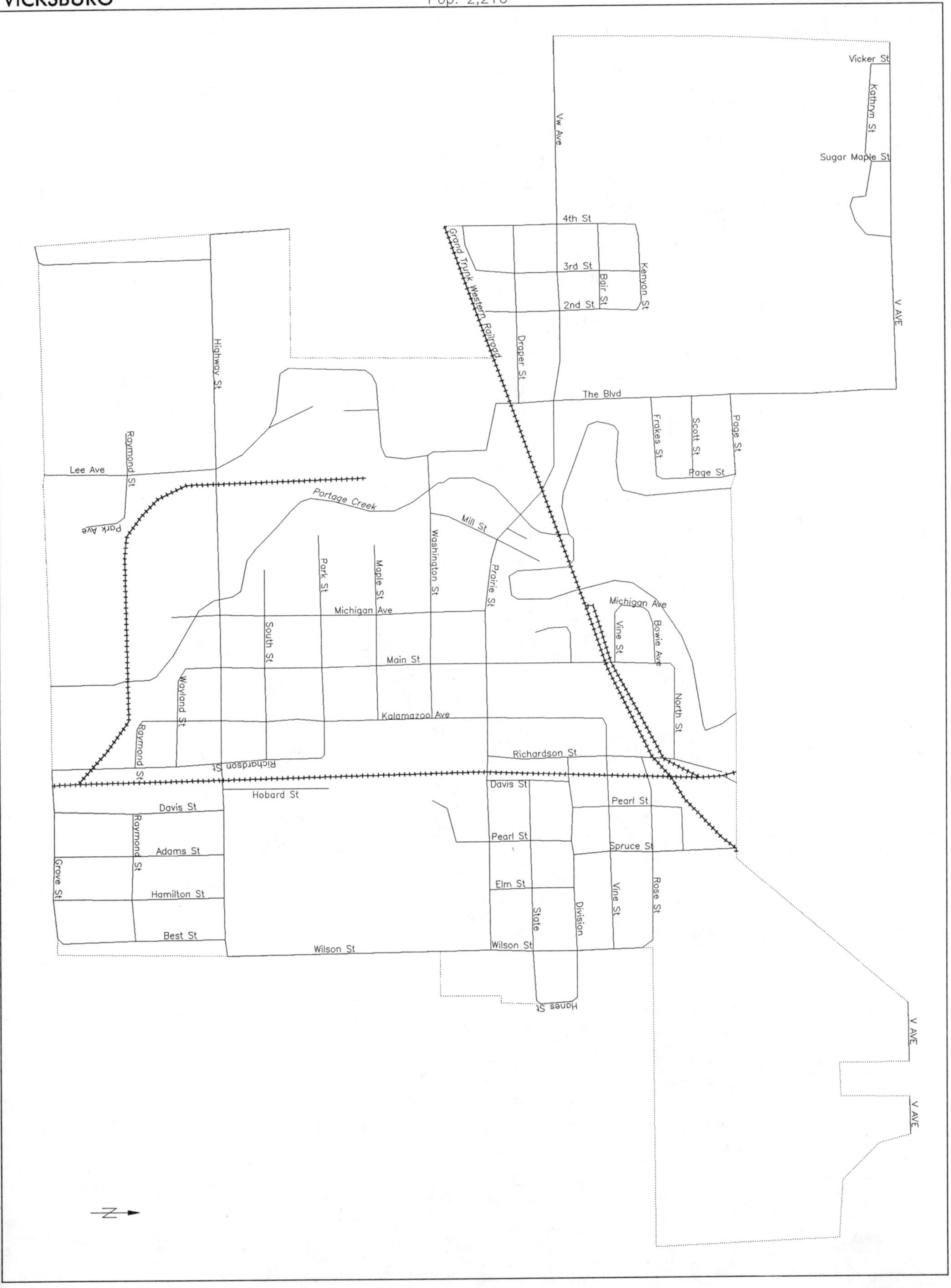

Vicker St
Kathryn St
Sugar Maple St
Vw Ave
4th St
3rd St
2nd St
Bair St
Kenyon St
V AVE
Grand Trunk Western Railroad
Draper St
Highway St
The Blvd
Frakes St
Scott St
Page St
Page St
Raymond St
Lee Ave
Portage Creek
Park Ave
Mill St
Washington St
Park St
Maple St
Prairie St
Michigan Ave
Michigan Ave
Vine St
Bowie Ave
South St
Main St
Wayland St
North St
Kalamazoo Ave
Raymond St
Richardson St
Richardson St
Davis St
Hobard St
Davis St
Pearl St
Raymond St
Adams St
Pearl St
Spruce St
Grove St
Hamilton St
Elm St
Vine St
Rose St
State
Division
Best St
Wilson St
Wilson St
Hanes St
V AVE
V AVE
N

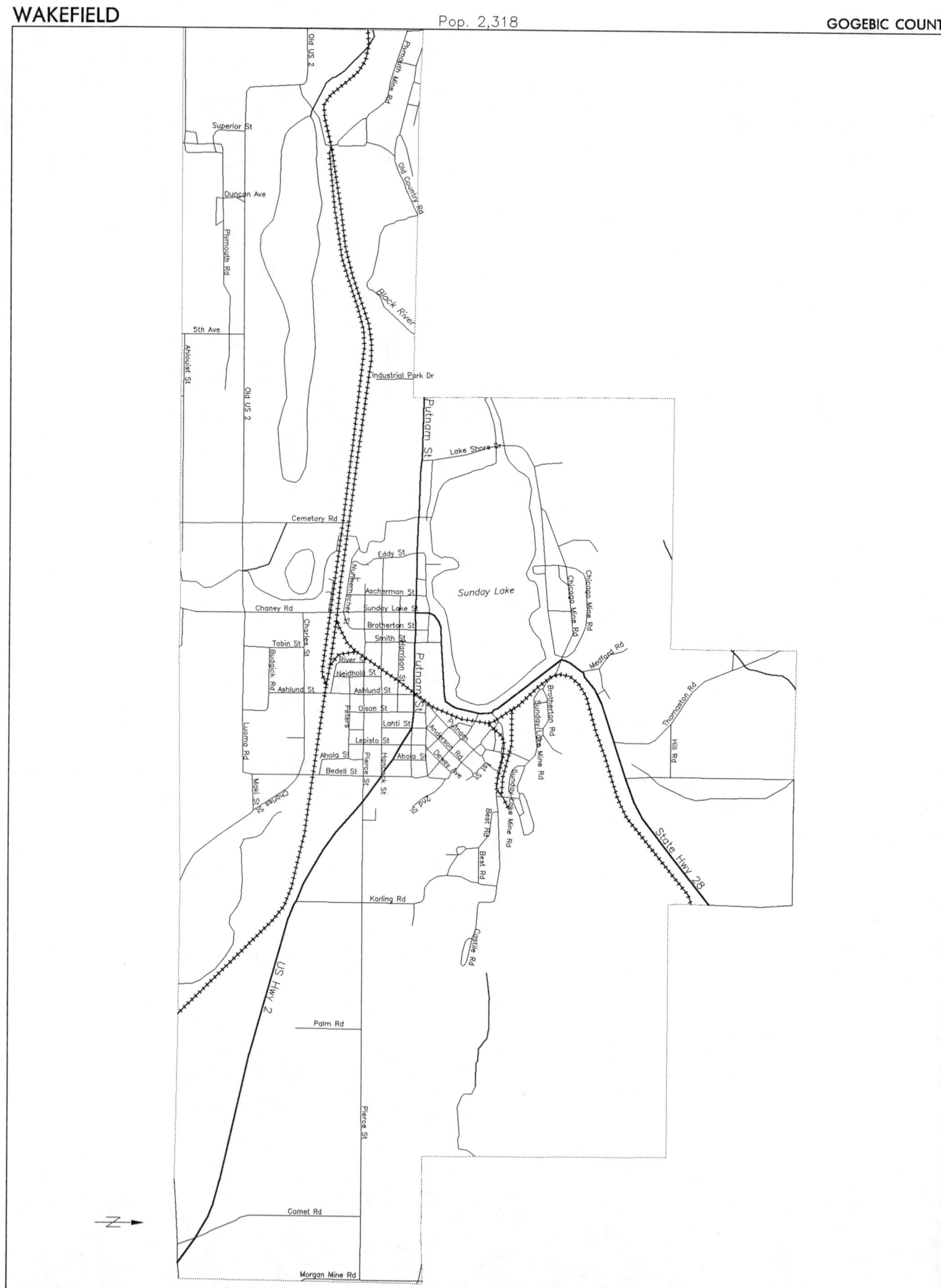
Old US 2
Plymouth Mine Rd
Superior St
Old Country Rd
Duncan Ave
Plymouth Rd
Black River
5th Ave
Ahlquist St
Old US 2
Industrial Park Dr
Putnam St
Lake Shore Dr
Cemetery Rd
Eddy St
Sunday Lake
Ascherman St
Sunday Lake St
Chaney Rd
Brotherton St
Charles St
Tobin St
Smith St
Harrison St
Chicago Mine Rd
Chicago Mine Rd
Medford Rd
River St
Budgick Rd
Neidhold St
Ashlund St
Ashlund St
Putnam St
Olson St
Peters
Lahti St
Brotherton Rd
Sunday Lake Mine Rd
Thomaston Rd
Hill Rd
Anderson Rd
Putnam
Lepisto St
Luoma Rd
Ahola St
Pierce St
Ahola St
Dewey Ave
Bedell St
Hancock St
Maki St
Charles St
2nd St
Best Rd
Sunday Lake Mine Rd
State Hwy 28
Best Rd
Karling Rd
Castile Rd
US Hwy 2
Palm Rd
Pierce St
Comet Rd
Morgan Mine Rd

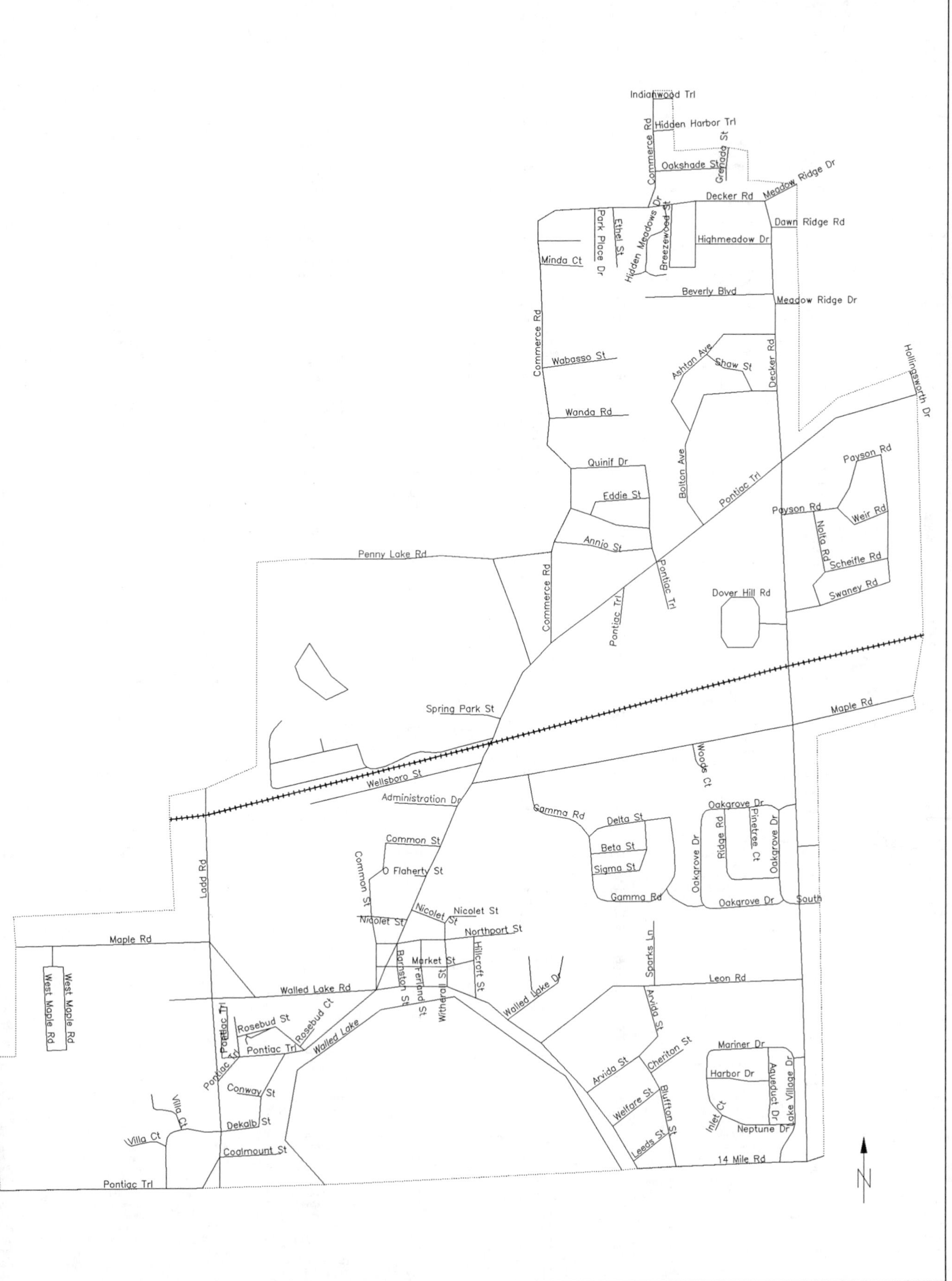
Indianwood Trl
Hidden Harbor Trl
Commerce Rd
Grenada St
Oakshade St
Meadow Ridge Dr
Decker Rd
Dawn Ridge Rd
Park Place Dr
Ethel St
Hidden Meadows Dr
Breezewood St
Highmeadow Dr
Minda Ct
Beverly Blvd
Meadow Ridge Dr
Commerce Rd
Decker Rd
Hollingsworth Dr
Ashtan Ave
Shaw St
Wabasso St
Wanda Rd
Payson Rd
Quinif Dr
Bolton Ave
Pontiac Trl
Eddie St
Payson Rd
Weir Rd
Nolta Rd
Annio St
Scheifle Rd
Penny Lake Rd
Pontiac Trl
Commerce Rd
Pontiac Trl
Dover Hill Rd
Swaney Rd
Spring Park St
Maple Rd
Woods Ct
Wellsboro St
Administration Dr
Oakgrove Dr
Gamma Rd
Delta St
Ridge Rd
Pinetree Ct
Oakgrove Dr
Common St
Beta St
Oakgrove Dr
Common St
O Flaherty St
Sigma St
Ladd Rd
Gamma Rd
Oakgrove Dr
South
Nicolet St
Nicolet St
Nicolet St
Northport St
Maple Rd
Market St
Sparks Ln
Barnston St
Ferland St
Withera St
Hillcroft St
West Maple Rd
West Maple Rd
Walled Lake Rd
Walled Lake Dr
Leon Rd
Arvida St
Pontiac Trl
Rosebud St
Rosebud Ct
Walled Lake
Pontiac Trl
Pontiac Trl
Cheriton St
Mariner Dr
Arvida St
Harbor Dr
Aqueduct Dr
Lake Village Dr
Conway St
Welfare St
Bluffton St
Inlet Ct
Villa Ct
Dekalb St
Neptune Dr
Villa Ct
Leeds St
Coalmount St
14 Mile Rd
Pontiac Trl
N

NOTES

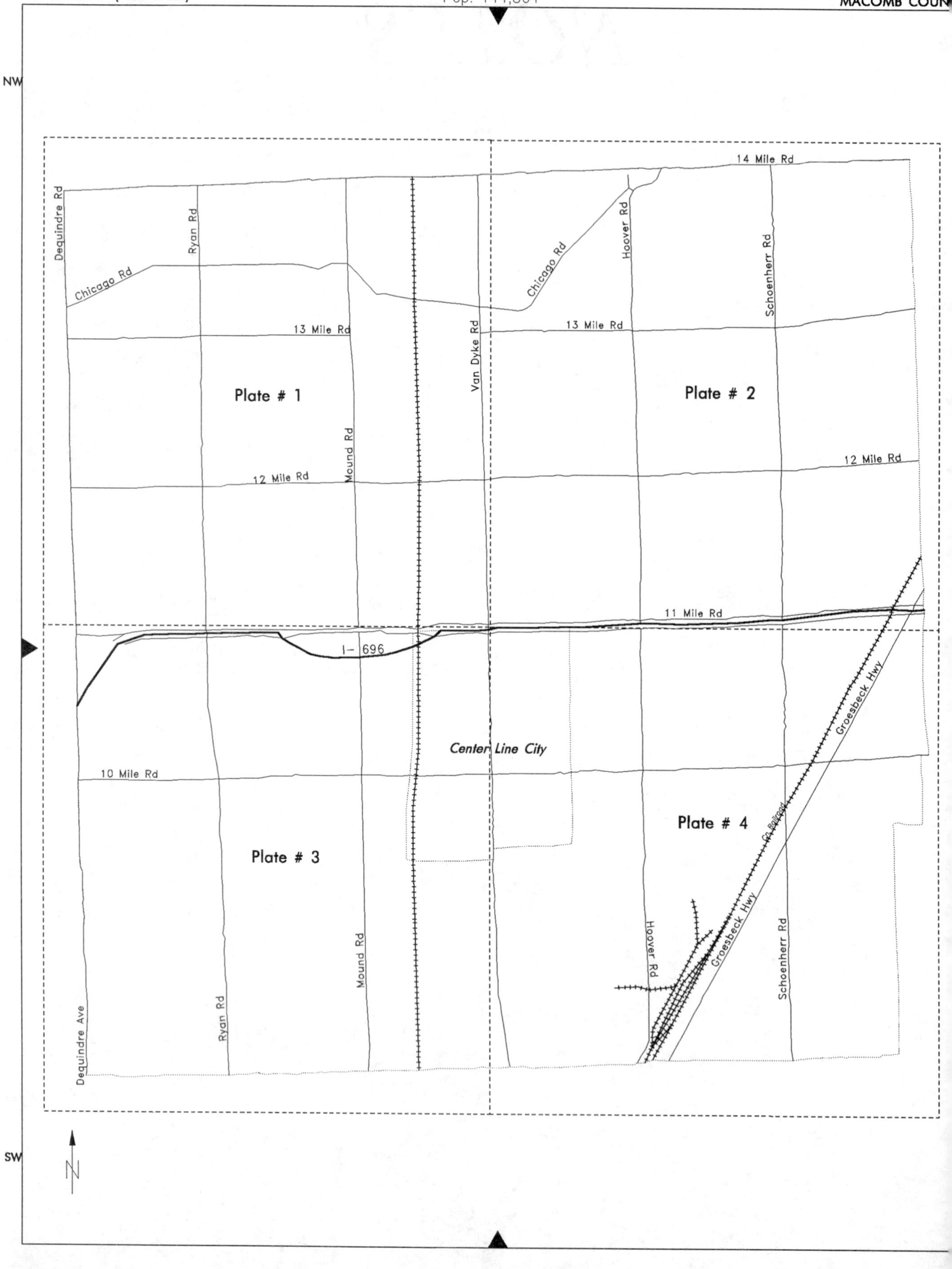
NW
SW
14 Mile Rd
Dequindre Rd
Ryan Rd
Chicago Rd
Chicago Rd
Hoover Rd
Schoenherr Rd
13 Mile Rd
13 Mile Rd
Van Dyke Rd
Plate # 1
Plate # 2
Mound Rd
12 Mile Rd
12 Mile Rd
11 Mile Rd
I- 696
Center Line City
Groesbeck Hwy
10 Mile Rd
Plate # 4
Plate # 3
Hoover Rd
Groesbeck Hwy
Schoenherr Rd
Mound Rd
Ryan Rd
Dequindre Ave
N

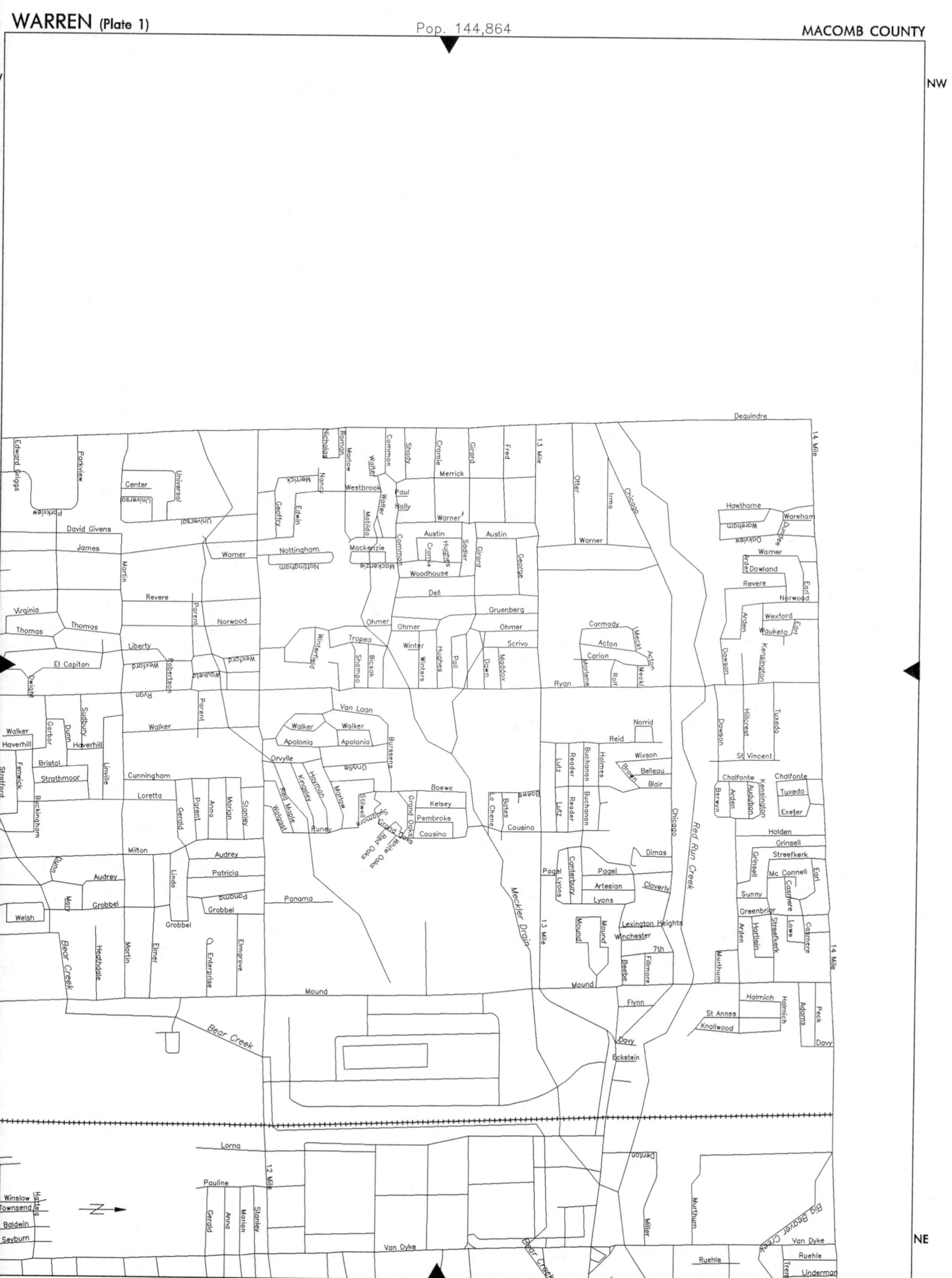
NW
NE
Dequindre
14 Mile
13 Mile
12 Mile
Edward Griggs
Parkview
Center
Universal
Merrick
Nancy
Nicholas
Roman
Marlow
Walter
Common
Shady
Cromie
Girard
Fred
Otter
Irma
Chicago
Westbrook
Paul
Holly
Geoffry
Edwin
Matilda
Warner
Austin
David Givens
James
Nottingham
Mackenzie
Hughes
Sadler
George
Woodhouse
Martin
Revere
Dell
Gruenberg
Virginia
Thomas
Parent
Norwood
Ohmer
Tropea
Winterfield
Winter
Carmody
Acton
Mecki
Scrivo
Carlon
Marlene
Rolf
Liberty
Wexford
Waukelo
Robertson
El Capitan
Dwight
Shampo
Bicsak
Winters
Poll
Dawn
Maddox
Ryan
Van Loan
Walker
Apolonia
Burssens
Norrid
Reid
Wixson
Belleau
Blair
Braun
Holmes
Buchanan
Reeder
Lutz
Sudbury
Garbor
Dunn
Haverhill
Bristol
Strathmoor
Fenwick
Stratford
Linville
Cunningham
Loretta
Gerald
Anna
Marion
Stanley
Orvylle
Kingsley
Hayman
Marlow
Red Maple
Wolgast
Runey
Stilwell
Sycamore
Grand Oaks
Red Oaks
White Oaks
Boewe
Kelsey
Pembroke
Cousino
La Chene
Bates
Buckingham
Milton
Audrey
Patricia
Panama
Grobbel
Linda
Welsh
Mary
Bear Creek
Heatherdale
Elmer
Enterprise
Elmgrove
Meckler Drain
Red Run Creek
Dimas
Pagel
Artesian
Lyons
Canterbury
Cloverly
Lexington Heights
Winchester
7th
Mound
Beebe
Fillmore
Hawthorne
Wareham
Oakview
Dundee
Dowland
Earl
Arden
Wauketa
Dawson
Kensington
Hillcrest
Tuxedo
St Vincent
Chalfonte
Berwyn
Audubon
Exeter
Holden
Grinsell
Streefkerk
Mc Connell
Cashmere
Sunny
Greenbriar
Hartlein
Lowe
Catmere
Murthum
Flynn
Halmich
Adams
Peck
St Annes
Knollwood
Davy
Eckstein
Lorna
Denton
Pauline
Winslow
Townsend
Baldwin
Seyburn
Hatala
Miller
Van Dyke
Big Beaver Creek
Ruehle
Trembath
Underman

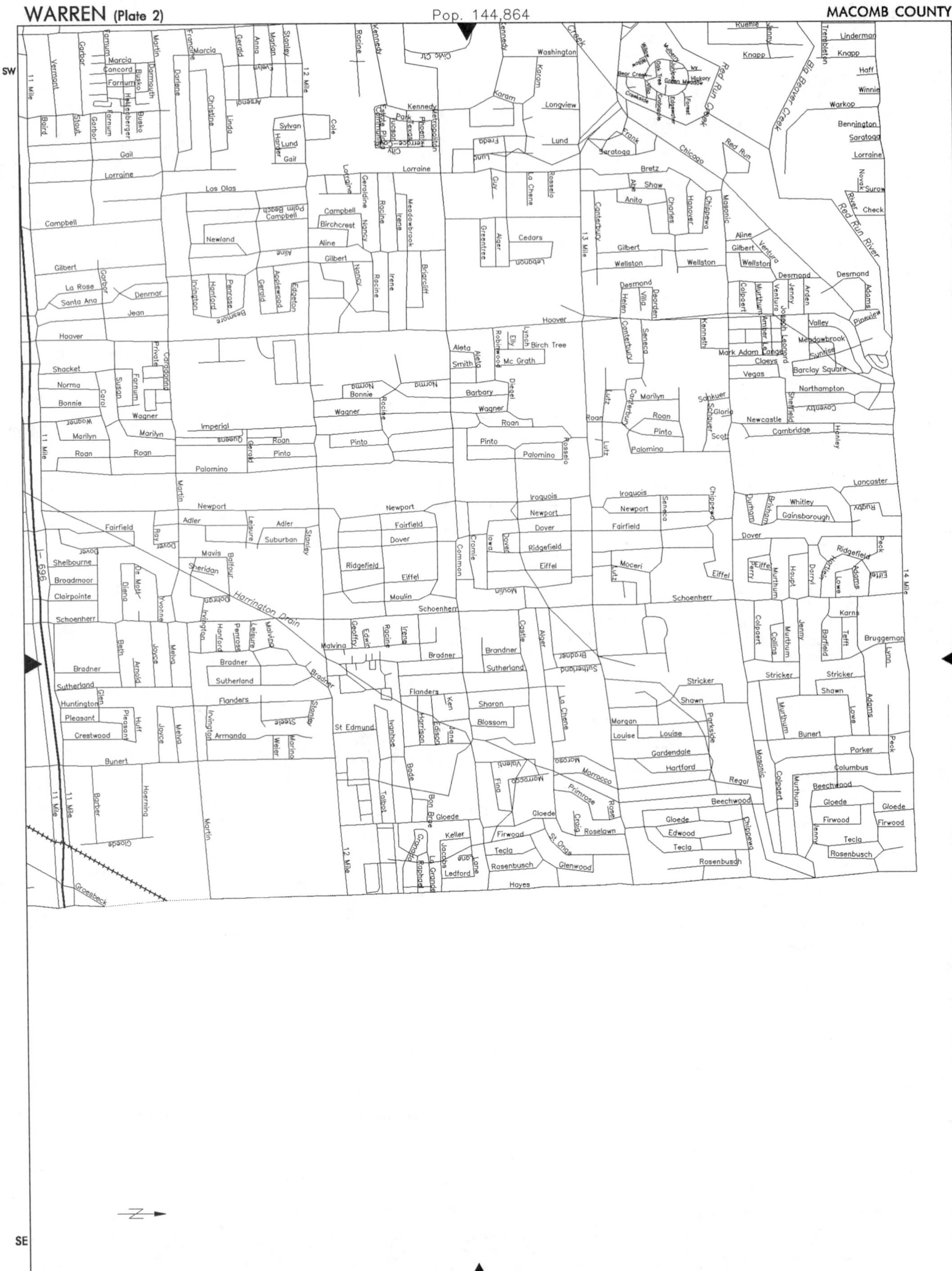

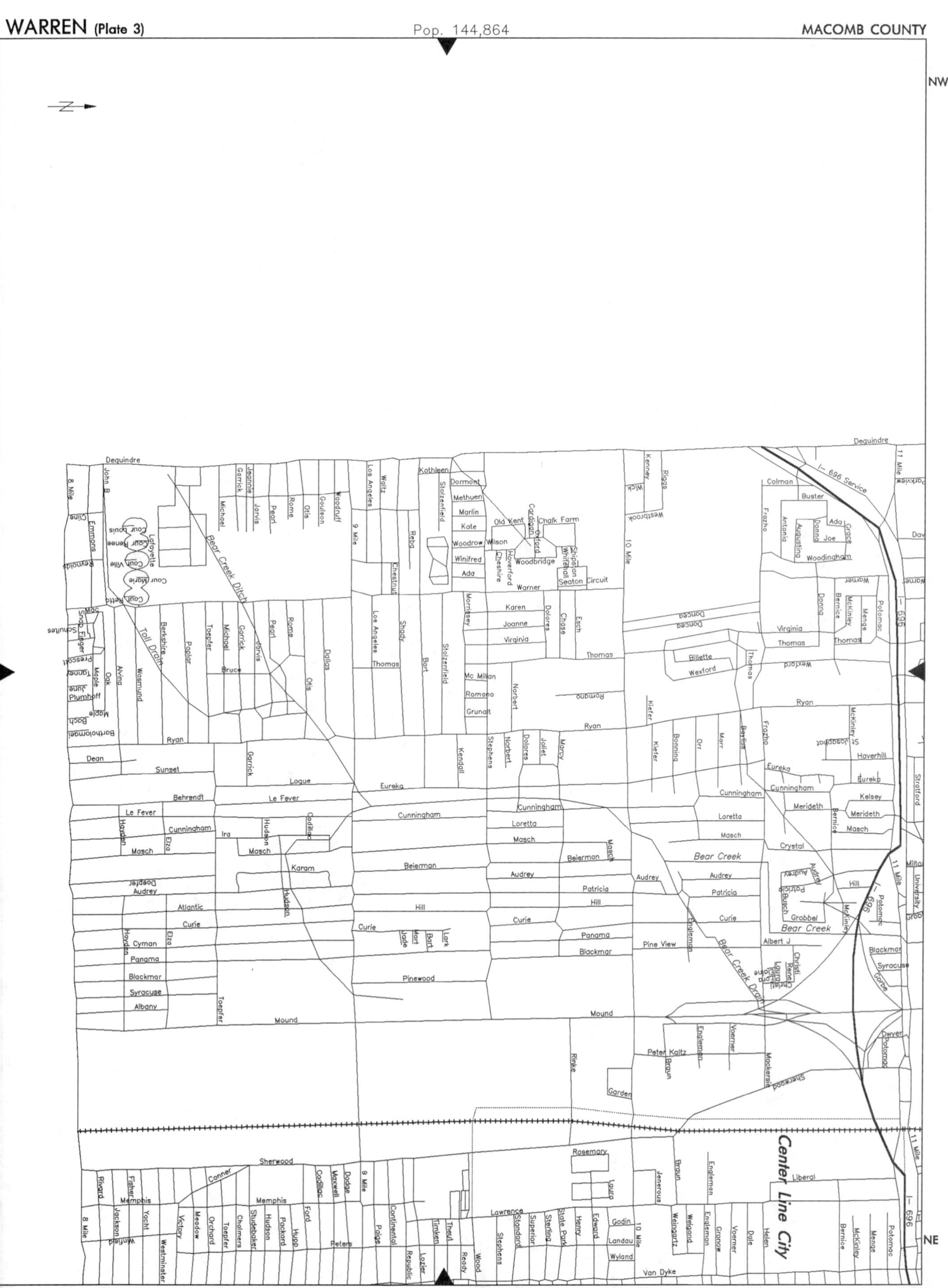
NW
NE
Dequindre
8 Mile
9 Mile
10 Mile
11 Mile
I-696
I-696 Service
Bear Creek Ditch
Toll Drain
Bear Creek
Bear Creek Drain
Center Line City
Ryan
Eureka
Cunningham
Masch
Mound
Sherwood
Memphis
Van Dyke
Stephens
Beierman
Audrey
Hill
Curie
Blackmar
Pinewood
Thomas
Warner
Lawrence
Liberal
Rosemary
Peters

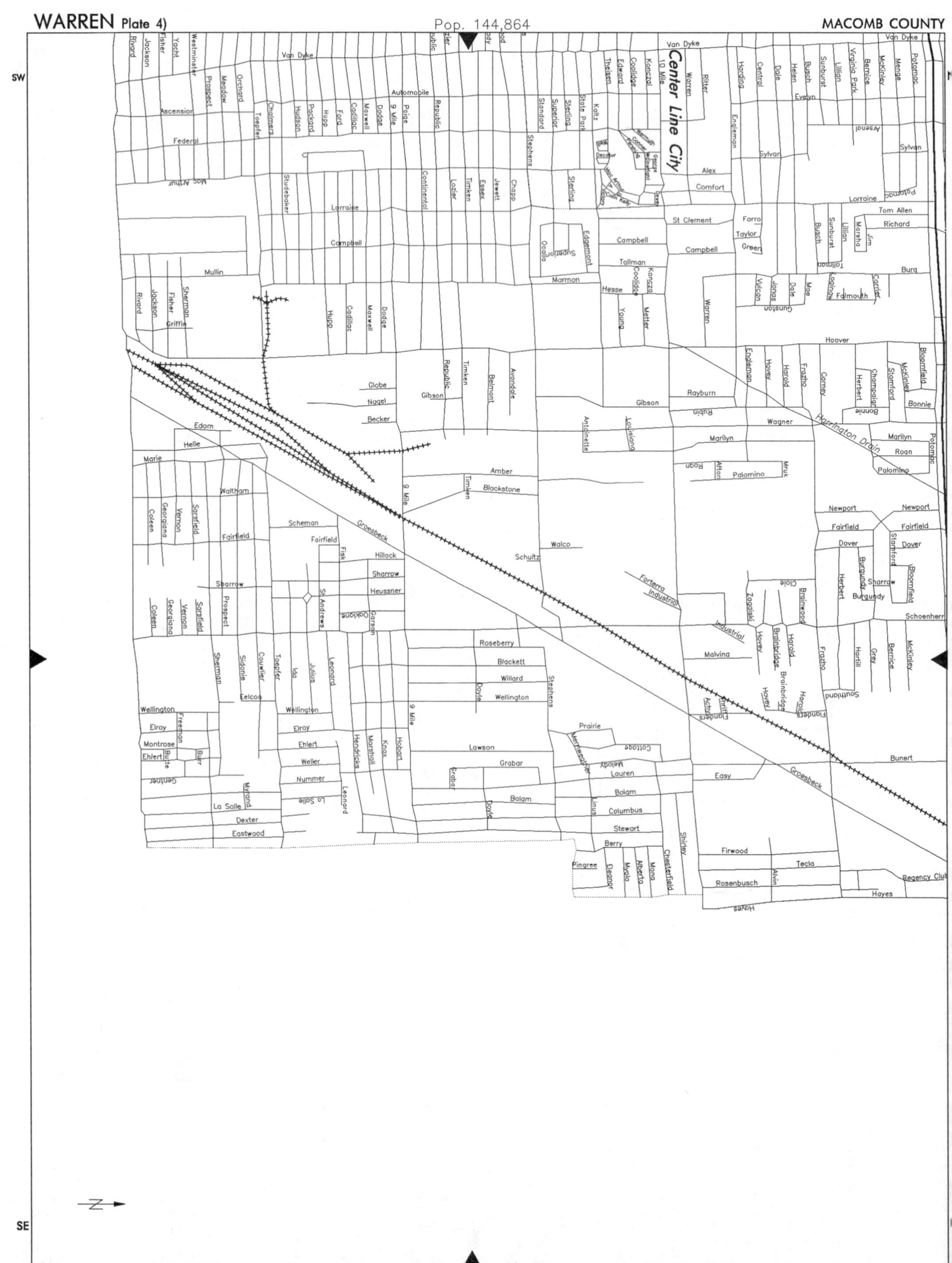
Center Line City
Van Dyke
Groesbeck
Harrington Drain
9 Mile
10 Mile
Hoover
Schoenherr
Stephens
Campbell
Lorraine
Gibson
Industrial
Forterra Industrial
Regency Club
Hayes
SW
SE

Western Ave
Twin Hills Dr
Baldwin Ave
Baldwin Ave
Shepard Pl
Parsons Ave
Richard Ave
Peach Tree Pl
Prospect Ct
Forest Park Ave
Main St
Baldwin Dr
Vannatter Ct
Lewiston Ave
Riverside Dr
Riverside Dr
Paw Paw Ave
Paw Paw River
Mill Creek
North Ct
Butternut St
1st St
Walnut St
High View St
1st St
Chesapeake and Ohio Railroad
Lewis St
Harper Ave
Pleasant St
St Joseph St
Medical Park Dr
Elm St
Maple St
Mill St
Allen Ct
Sutherland
Brown
Congress St
Park St
Crescent St
Myrtle St
Allen Ct
Medical Park Dr
Sutherland
Bluff View St
Division St
Division St
Lucinda Lane
Silver Ter
Mill Creek
Pleasant St
Summit St
Main St
N

US Hwy 131
US Hwy 131
Edmonton Trl
Edmonton Trl
Calgary Lane
Toronto Trl
Regina
Manitoba Trl
Halifax Pl
Alberta Pl
Vancouver Pl
Saskatoon Trl
Dahlia Ave
Quebec Trl
Quebec Trl
Windsor Woods
Windsor Woods Dr
Mill St
Clark St
Pennsylvania Railroad
Railroad St
Commerce St
Pine St
Alpine St
133rd Ave
Superior St
Maple St
Cherry St
Elm St
Sycamore St
Vine St
Penn Central Railroad
Park St
Pearl St
Church St
School St
Cedar St
Pine St
Main St
Main St
Plum St
Hanlon Ct
Forrest St
Locust St
Locust St
Sib Rumery St
Frank Ct
Norman Ct
Elm St
Lorene St
Hickory Dr
Falcon Way
Standish Dr
Plum St
Anderson Dr
Rabbit River
135th Ave
Geneva Dr
Marlo Lane
8th St

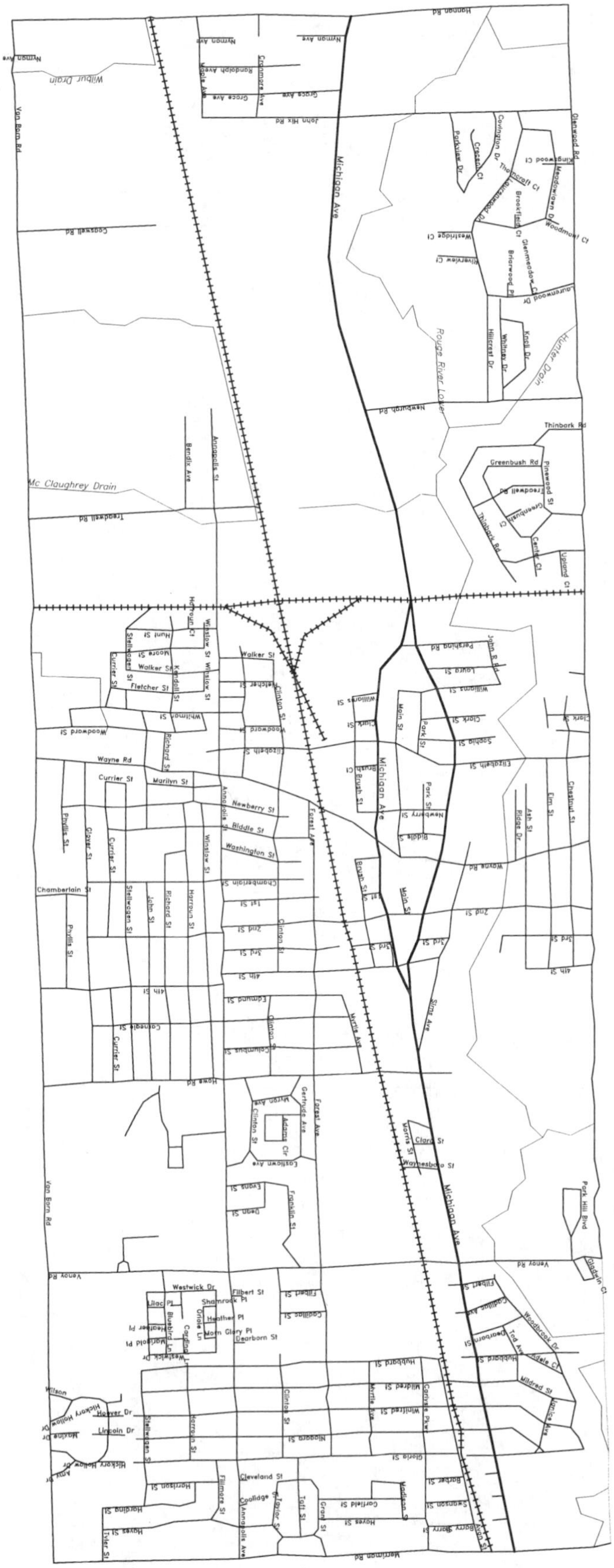
Hannan Rd
Michigan Ave
Van Born Rd
Wilbur Drain
Rouge River Lower
Hunter Drain
Mc Claughrey Drain
Newburgh Rd
Tredwell Rd
Wayne Rd
Venoy Rd
Merriman Rd

Stockbridge Rd
Chesapeake Ohio Railroad
Grand River Ave
Webberville Rd
Outer Ln
Kalamink Creek
Elm St
Outer Ln
Lagoon Access Rd
Howard St
Howard St
Beech St
Pine St
Summit St
Oak St
Main St
Main St
Walnut St
Clark St
Chestnut St
Maple St
Oak St
Monroe St
Franklin St
Pardee Rd
Detroit St
Jackson St
Grand River Ave
Epley Ct
Gramer Rd
N

Willow St
Dow Road
3rd St
2nd St
1st St
Thomas St
Annie St
Spruce St
Fairview Road
Keith Ct
6th St
5th St
4th St
Lindsay St
7th St
State Road
Burgess St
Fremont St
Alto Ct
Carpenter St
8th St
7th St
Valley St
Houghton Ave
Houghton Ave
I 75-Business Rte
Livingston St
Mac Gregor
Page St
Brookside Dr
Wright Ave
Wright Ave
Meid St
Court St
6th St
5th St
2nd St
Ripley Ave
Ripley Ave
3rd St
Victory St
Morrison St
Shrigley Dr
Columbus St
4th St
Valley Road
1st St
Griffin Road
Griffin Road
Parkway Dr
Progress St
Refinery Road
Cook Road
Hansen Road
N

NOTES

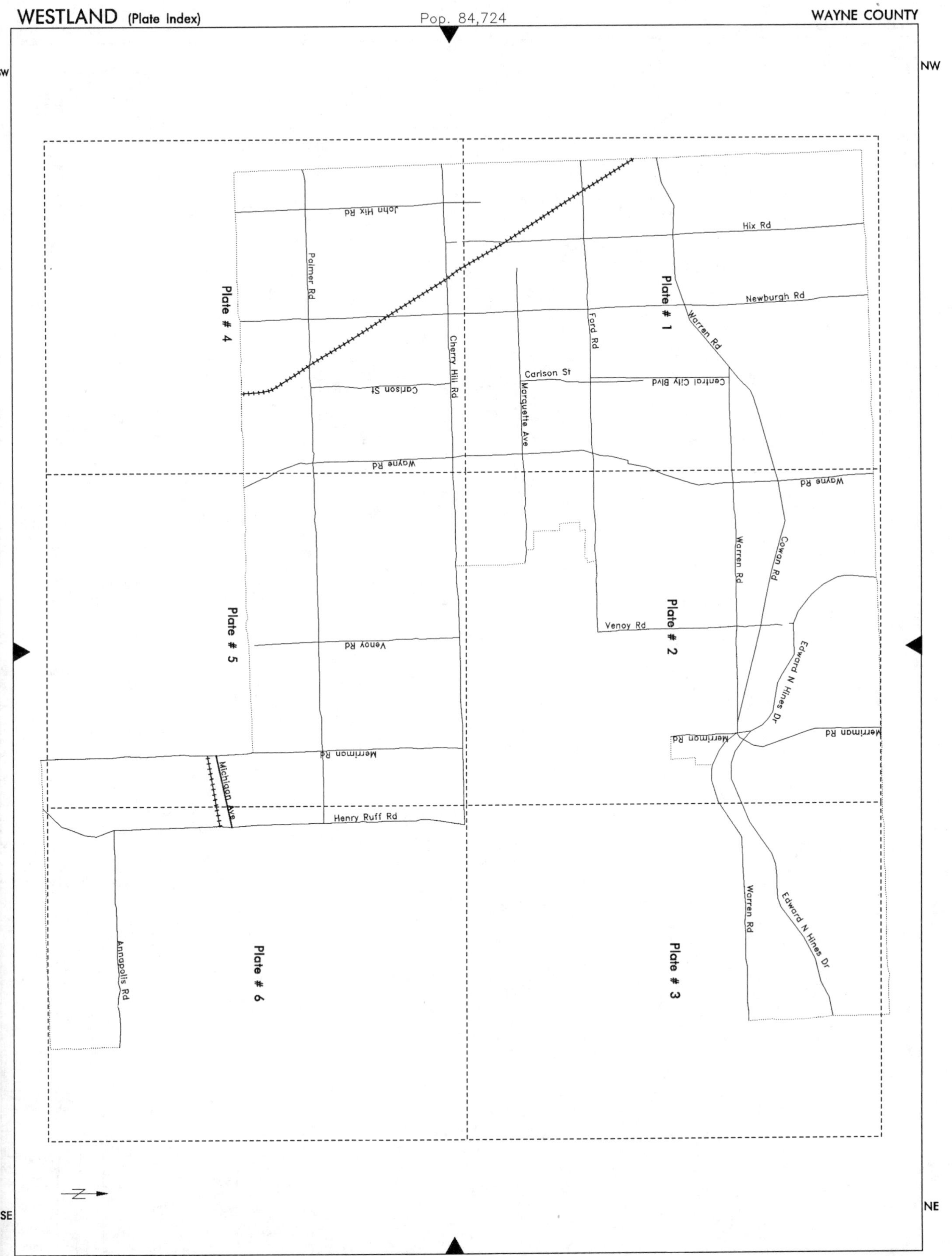
SW
NW
SE
NE
Plate # 1
Plate # 2
Plate # 3
Plate # 4
Plate # 5
Plate # 6
John Hix Rd
Hix Rd
Newburgh Rd
Palmer Rd
Ford Rd
Warren Rd
Cherry Hill Rd
Carlson St
Central City Blvd
Marquette Ave
Wayne Rd
Cowan Rd
Venoy Rd
Edward N Hines Dr
Merriman Rd
Michigan Ave
Henry Ruff Rd
Annapolis Rd

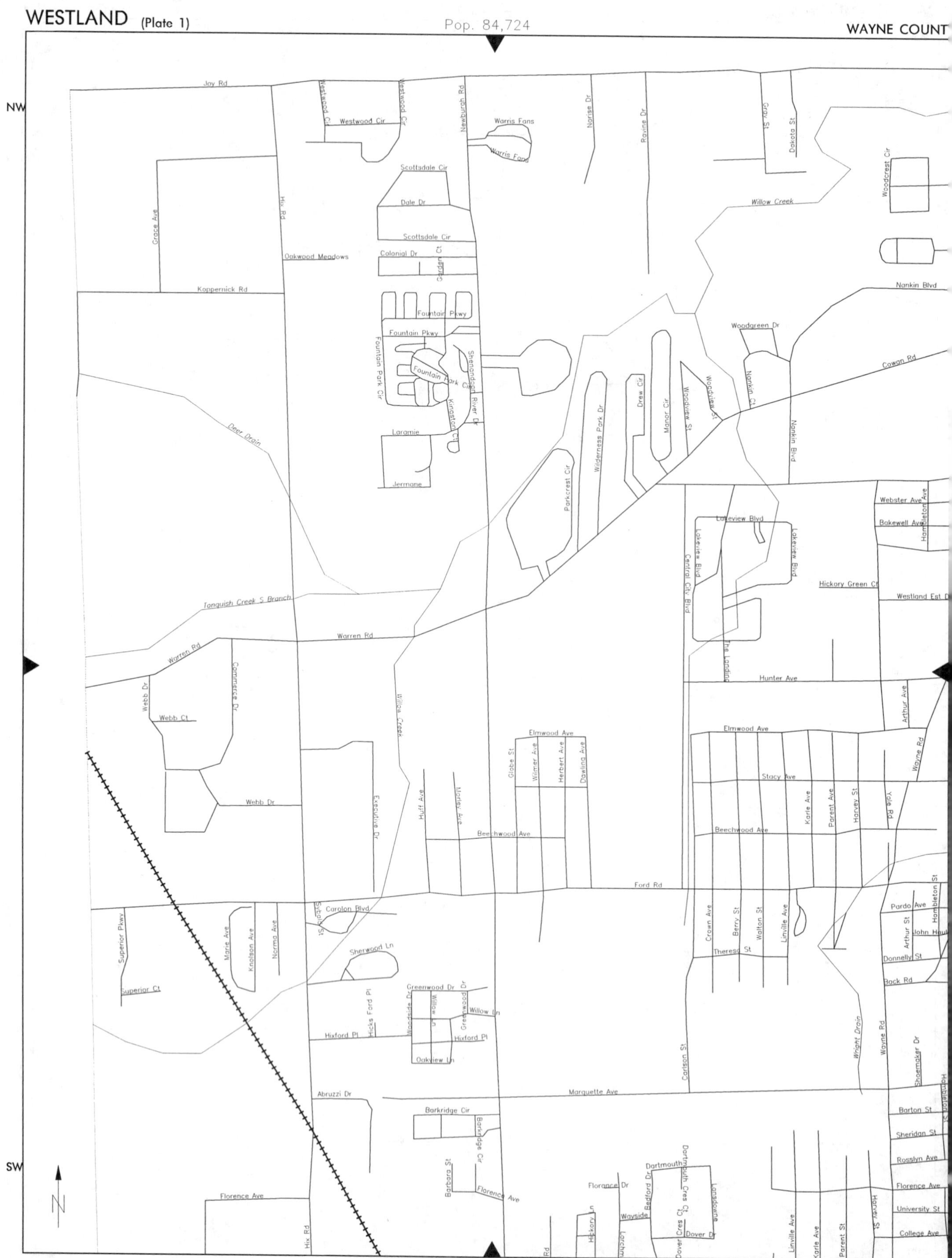
NW
SW
Joy Rd
Westwood Ct
Westwood Cir
Newburgh Rd
Warris Fans
Norise Dr
Ravine Dr
Gary St
Dakota St
Woodcrest Cir
Scottsdale Cir
Dale Dr
Willow Creek
Hix Rd
Grace Ave
Scottsdale Cir
Oakwood Meadows
Colonial Dr
Garden Ct
Koppernick Rd
Nankin Blvd
Fountain Pkwy
Fountain Park Cir
Shenandoah River Dr
Fountain Park Cir
Kingston Ct
Woodgreen Dr
Cowan Rd
Laramie
Jermane
Deer Drain
Wilderness Park Dr
Drew Cir
Manor Cir
Woodview St
Nankin Ct
Parkcrest Cir
Webster Ave
Bakewell Ave
Hambleton
Lakeview Blvd
Central City Blvd
Hickory Green Ct
Westland Est Dr
Tonquish Creek S Branch
Warren Rd
The Landing
Hunter Ave
Commerce Dr
Webb Dr
Webb Ct
Willow Creek
Arthur Ave
Elmwood Ave
Wayne Rd
Globe St
Wimer Ave
Herbert Ave
Dowling Ave
Stacy Ave
Webb Dr
Executive Dr
Huff Ave
Morley Ave
Beechwood Ave
Karle Ave
Parent Ave
Harvey St
Yale Rd
Ford Rd
Carolon Blvd
Superior Pkwy
Marie Ave
Knolson Ave
Norma Ave
Crown Ave
Berry St
Walton St
Linville Ave
Pardo Ave
John Hauk
Theresa St
Sherwood Ln
Donnelly St
Back Rd
Superior Ct
Greenwood Dr
Hicks Ford Pl
Willow Ln
Hixford Pl
Oakview Ln
Wright Drain
Shoemaker Dr
Carlson St
Abruzzi Dr
Marquette Ave
Barton St
Barkridge Cir
Sheridan St
Rosslyn Ave
Barbara St
Dartmouth
Dartmouth Cres Ct
Lansdowne
Florence Dr
Florence Ave
Florence Ave
University St
Bedford Dr
Wayside
Hickory Ln
Dover Dr
Dover Cres Ct
Linville Ave
Karle Ave
Parent St
Harvey St
College Ave
Hix Rd
N

Joy Rd
Willow Creek
Spring Valley Dr
Fountain Blvd
Parkgrove Dr
Marina Ct
Claudia Ct
Deborah Ct
Shellye Ct
Wayne Rd
Nankin Mills Rd
Nankin Mill St
Millwood Dr
Cowan Rd
Farmington Rd
Anita Dr
Benson Dr
Merritt Dr
Sandra Ln
Sanford Dr
Ann Arbor Trl
Edward N Hines Dr
Rouge River Middle
Judy Dr
Hubbard St
Bertram Dr
Cranston Dr
Blackburn Dr
Ingram Dr
Berwick Dr
Mackenzie Dr
Diane Ct
Shari Dr
Merriman Rd
Cooley St
Liberty St
Mackenzie Dr
Geraldine St
Stephen Ave
Flamingo St
Mountain Ct
Gladys St
Donna St
Carousel Blvd
Milburn St
Hillcrest St
Henry Ruff Rd
Terri Dr
Rickie Dr
Roselawn Dr
Lonnie Dr
Conway Dr
Huntington St
Perrin Rd
Karen St
Merritt Dr
Ritz St
Capri Trl
Lynx St
Winona Ct
Cochise Dr
Chief Ln
Iroquois Ave
Lone Pine Dr
Kennedy St
Lacrosse Dr
Tawas Trl
Standish St
Majestic St
Wildwood St
Hawthorn St
Mohawk Dr
Yuma Dr
Bison St
Warren Rd
Avon Ct
Ledgecliff St
Webster Ave
Bakewell Ave
Lewis Ave
Arrowhead Trl
Blackfoot Ln
Pawnee St
Sequoia Rd
Redman Dr
Shawnee Trl
Algonquin Ln
Aztec Dr
Tomahawk Rd
Tonquish Trl
Geronimo St
Caribou St
Bordeaux Ct
Fran Ct
Yorkdale Ct
Emily Ct
Yorkdale Dr
Bonnie Cir
Alexander Drain
Wexford Dr
Forest Ct
Windsor Ave
Dillon Rd
Maplewood Ave
Est Dr
Hunter Ave
Winchester Dr
Radcliffe St
Westland Dr
Hunter Ct
Harmon Ct
Balmoral Ct
Glastonbury St
Canterbury Ct
Hampshire Ct
Hampshire Dr
Farmington Ct
Lancashire Dr
Oak Point Dr
Venoy Rd
Elmwood Ave
Stacy St
Birchlawn St
Hampton Ct
Christine
Wright Drain
Beechwood Ave
Krauter Ave
Ford Rd
Pardo Ave
Imperial Hwy
John Hauk Rd
Donnelly St
Bock Rd
Hambleton St
Hanlon St
Marquette Rd
Barton St
Sheridan St
Rosslyn Ave
Frances Ave
Florence Ave
University St
College Ave
Dobson St
Byfield St
School St
Hawthorne St
Hawthorne Ave
Insull Ave
NE
SE
N

Joy Rd
Wilson Drain
Mackenzie Dr
Cardwell St
Inkster Rd
Brooke Cir
Cavell St
Merritt Dr
Gilman St
Ann Arbor Trl
Valley View Cir
Gladys St
August St
Beatrice St
Hugh St
Fremont St
Middlebelt Rd
Lonewood St
Oxbow St
Haller St
Hempstead St
Bristol St
Manchester St
Coventry St
Donna St
Randy Dr
Gary St
Melvin Ave
Lonnie Dr
Shackett St
Louise Ct
Louise St
Brody St
Lear Ct
Badelt St
Edward N Hines Dr
Rouge River Middle
Avon Pl
Avon Ct
Ledgecliff St
Malvern St
Frumin Ct
Warren Rd
Central St
Garden St
Kubis Ave
Hartel Ave
Affeldt Ave
Harrison Ave
Lathers Ave
Standish St
Floral St
Deering Ave
Arcola Ave
NW
SW

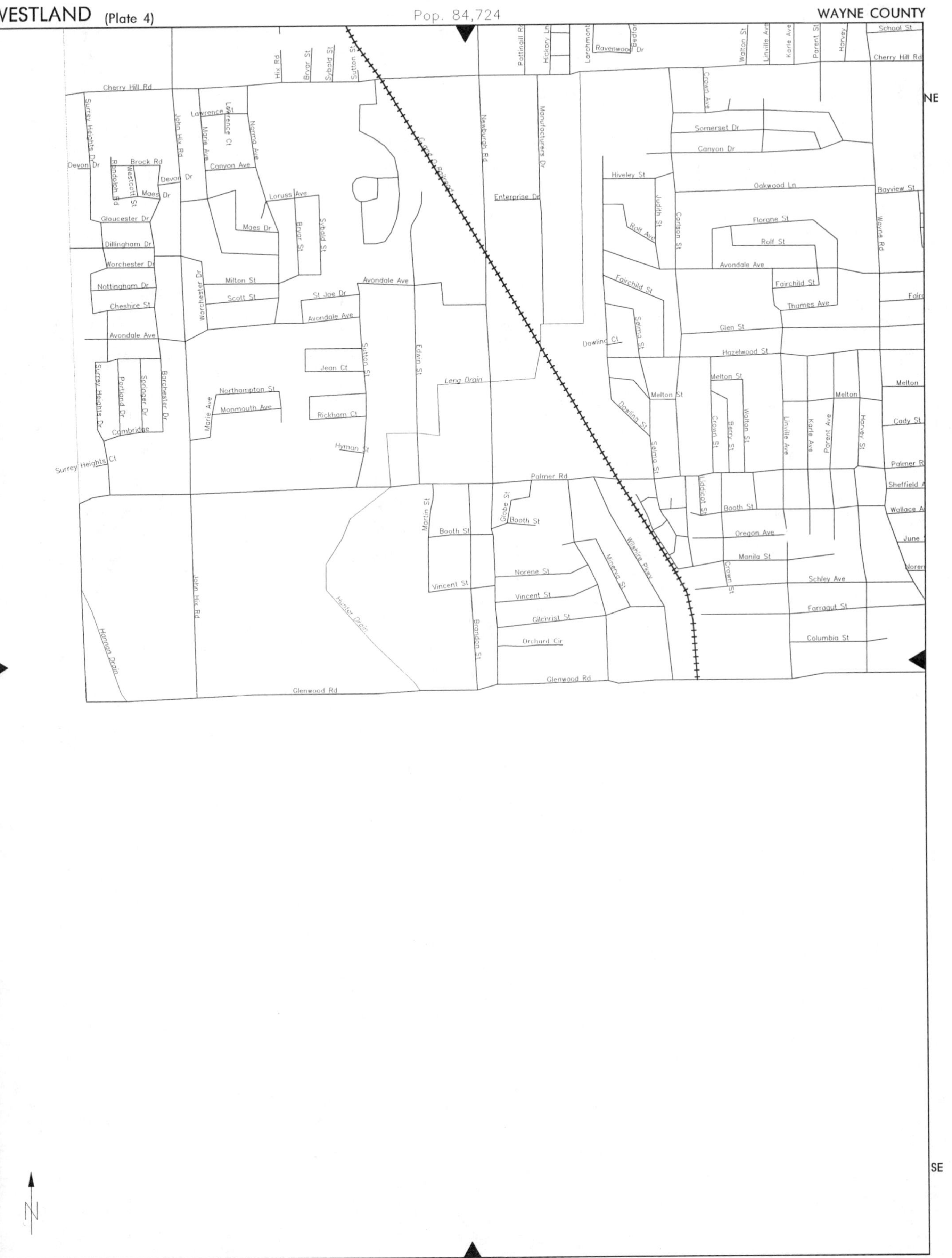
Cherry Hill Rd
Hix Rd
Bryar St
Sybald St
Sutton St
Pattingill Rd
Hickory Ln
Larchmont
Ravenwood Dr
Bedford
Walton St
Linville Ave
Karle Ave
Parent St
Harvey
School St
NE
Surrey Heights Dr
Lawrence
Lawrence Ct
John Hix Rd
Marie Ave
Norma Ave
Canyon Ave
Devon Dr
Brock Rd
Randolph Rd
Westcott St
Maes Dr
Loruss Ave
Gloucester Dr
Dillingham Dr
Worchester Dr
Nottingham Dr
Cheshire St
Avondale Ave
Milton St
Scott St
St Joe Dr
Jean Ct
Sutton St
Edwin St
Newburgh Rd
Manufacturers Dr
Enterprise Dr
Leng Drain
Crown Ave
Somerset Dr
Canyon Dr
Hiveley St
Judith St
Carlson St
Oakwood Ln
Bayview St
Wayne Rd
Rolf Ave
Florane St
Rolf St
Fairchild St
Thames Ave
Glen St
Hazelwood St
Dowling Ct
Selma St
Melton St
Fair
Portland Dr
Springer Dr
Barchester Dr
Northampton St
Monmouth Ave
Cambridge
Surrey Heights Ct
Rickham Ct
Hyman St
Dowling St
Crown St
Berry St
Walton St
Linville Ave
Karle Ave
Parent Ave
Harvey St
Melton
Cady St
Palmer Rd
Sheffield A
Wallace A
June
Noren
Martin St
Booth St
Globe St
Liddicot St
Oregon Ave
Manila St
Wilshire Pkwy
Minerva St
Norene St
Vincent St
Schley Ave
Farragut St
Gilchrist St
Orchard Cir
Columbia St
Brandon St
Hunter Drain
Hannan Drain
Glenwood Rd
SE
N

WESTLAND (Plate 5)

Pop. 84,724

WAYNE COUNT

Tami Cir
Hiveley Ave
Birchwood St
Grandview St
Avondale Ave
Mar Ann Dr
Henry Ruff Rd
Michigan Ave
Annapolis Rd
Mc Donald St
Eton St
Richard St
Powers St
Currier Ave
Hanover St
Hanover Blvd
Matthew Dr
Julius Blvd
Middlebelt Rd
Farnum
Harrison St
Admiral St
Inkster Rd
Van Born Rd
NE
SE
N

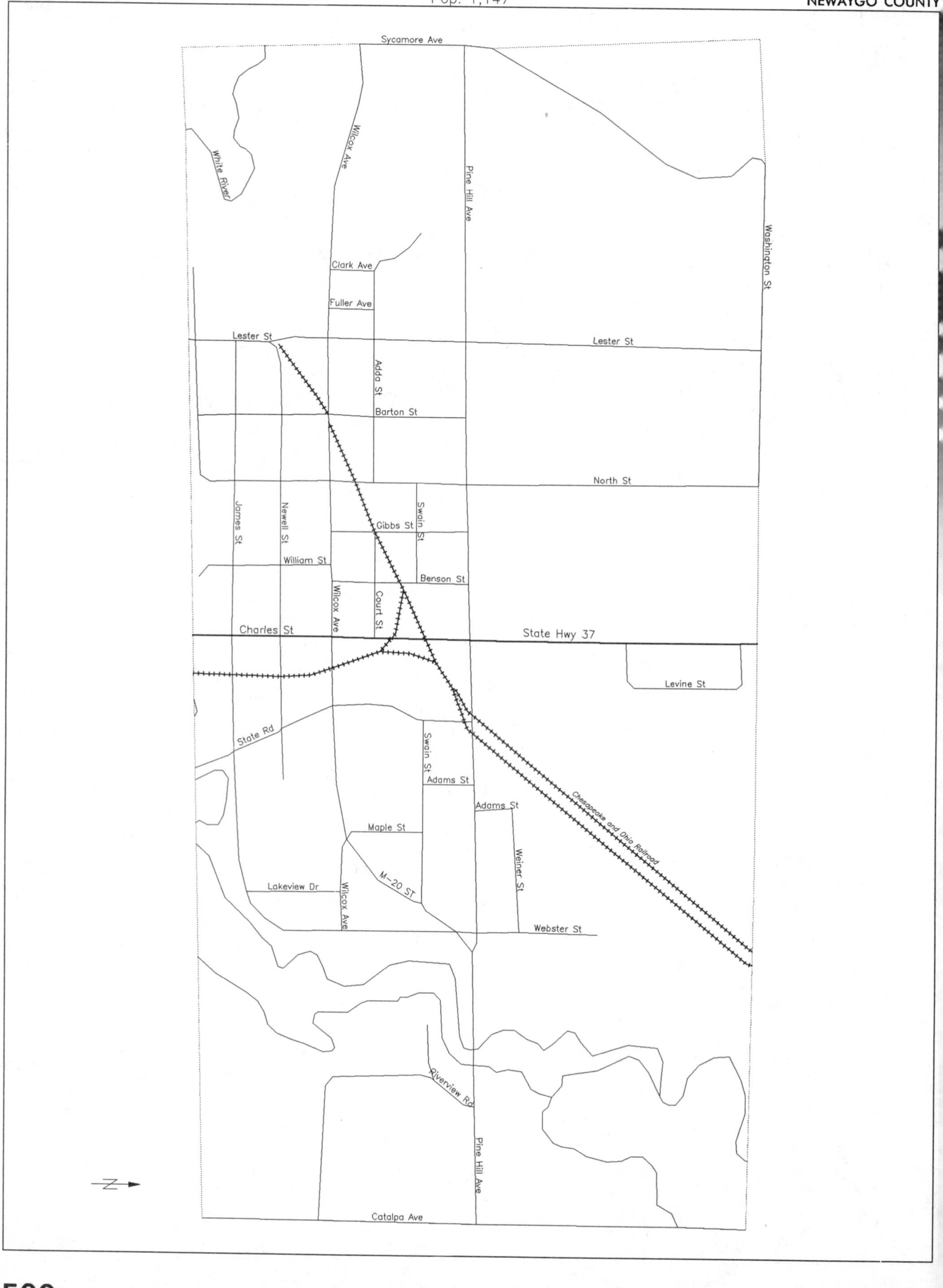

Pop. 1,147

Sycamore Ave
White River
Wilcox Ave
Pine Hill Ave
Washington St
Clark Ave
Fuller Ave
Lester St
Lester St
Adda St
Barton St
North St
James St
Newell St
Swain St
Gibbs St
William St
Benson St
Wilcox Ave
Court St
Charles St
State Hwy 37
Levine St
State Rd
Swain St
Adams St
Adams St
Chesapeake and Ohio Railroad
Maple St
Weiner St
M-20 ST
Lakeview Dr
Wilcox Ave
Webster St
Riverview Rd
Pine Hill Ave
Catalpa Ave
N

Peterson Road
River St
River St
Hanson St
Franklin St
Warner St
Colby
Lake St
Division St
Livingston St
Baldwin St
1st St
Spring St
Covell St
Hall St
Slocum St
Iowa St
Wilshire Dr
Mears Ave
Franklin St
Sophia St
Elizabeth St
Eliott St
Baldwin St
Warner St
Peach St
Alice St
Lincoln Ave
Lincoln Ave
Lake St
Spring Valley Lane
Muskegon Ave
Lewis St
Lakeview St
Gibbs St
Mears Ave
Division St
Livingston St
Warner St
Market St
King St
Johnson St
Johanna St
Main St
Obell St
Benston Road
Fairlawn Ct
Carleton St
Gee St
Moody St
Nelson St
Collier Dr
Lier Road
Southgate Dr
Sunset Dr
Tulgey Wood Lane
Pinecrest Road
Lake St
Mill Pond Road
White Lake Dr
Zeller Road
N

Pop. 1,458

Chicago Rd (US 12)
Miller Dr
Elkhart St
State St
Saint Joseph St
Washington St
Kalamazoo St
Company St
Lincoln St
Lincoln St
Laird St
Laird St
Laird St
Athletic St
Elm St
Hickory St
Peck Ave
Peck Ave
Murray Ave
Hotchin Ave
Heath Ave
Michigan Ave
Michigan Ave
Vermont Ave
Vermont Ave
Broadway
Prairie St
Conrail Railroad
Mill Road

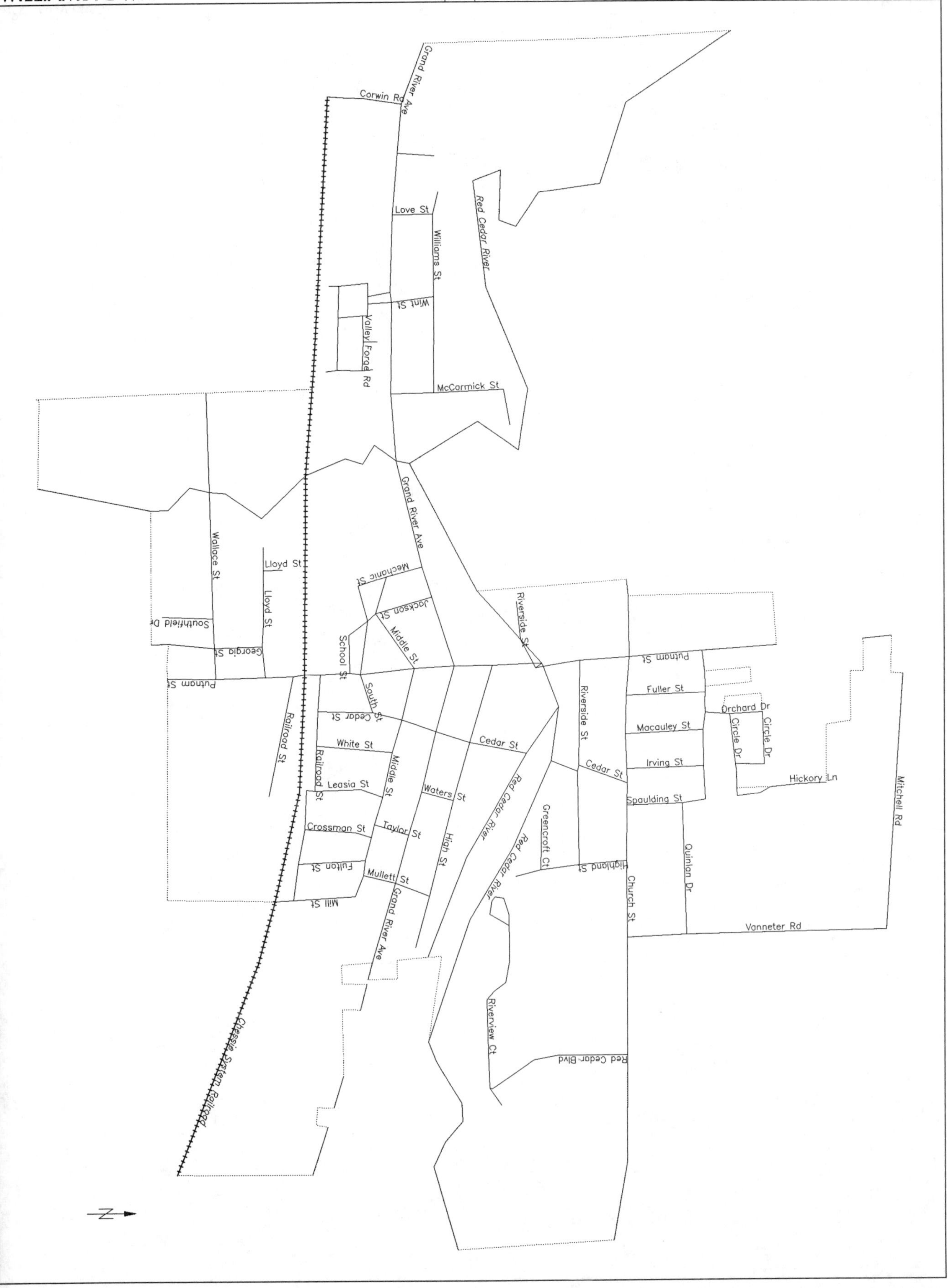

Grand River Ave
Corwin Rd
Red Cedar River
Love St
Williams St
Wint St
Valley Forge Rd
McCormick St
Grand River Ave
Wallace St
Lloyd St
Lloyd St
Mechanic St
Jackson St
Riverside St
Southfield Dr
Georgia St
School St
Middle St
Putnam St
Putnam St
South St
Riverside St
Fuller St
Orchard Dr
Circle Dr
Circle Dr
Cedar St
Railroad St
White St
Cedar St
Macauley St
Railroad St
Middle St
Cedar St
Irving St
Leasia St
Waters St
Red Cedar River
Hickory Ln
Spaulding St
Mitchell Rd
Crossman St
Taylor St
High St
Greencroft Ct
Red Cedar River
Fulton St
Mullett St
Highland St
Quinlan Dr
Church St
Mill St
Grand River Ave
Vanneter Rd
Riverview Ct
Red Cedar Blvd
Chessie System Railroad
N

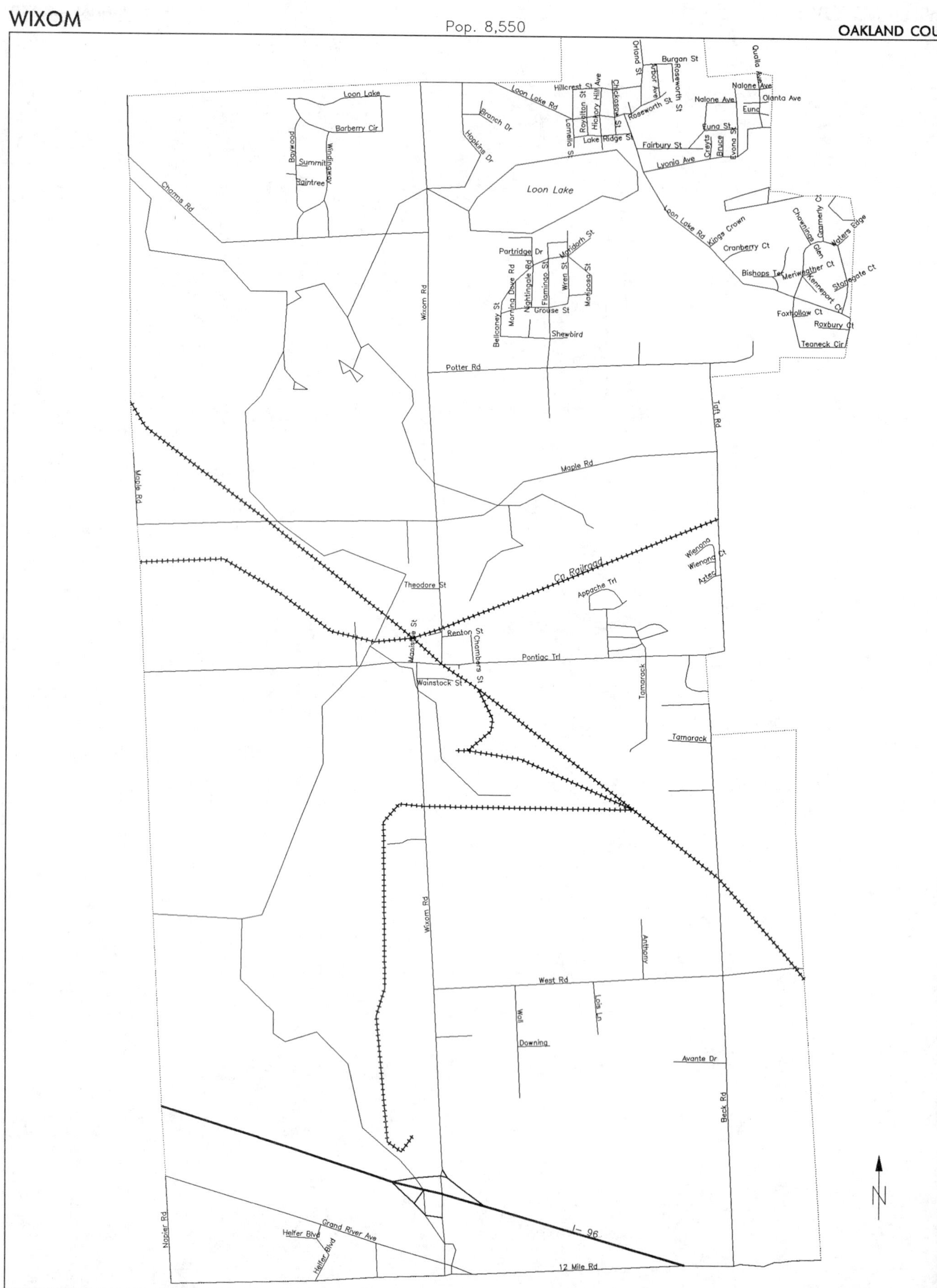
Loon Lake
Barberry Cir
Baywood
Summit
Windingway
Raintree
Charms Rd
Branch Dr
Hopkins Dr
Loon Lake Rd
Hillcrest St
Orland St
Burgan St
Arbor Ave
Roseworth St
Chickasaw St
Hickory Hill Ave
Royalton St
Lamella St
Lake Ridge St
Fairbury St
Lyonia Ave
Creyts
Bruce
Evona St
Euna St
Euna
Nalone Ave
Qualla Ave
Olanta Ave
Loon Lake
Kings Crown
Cranberry Ct
Bishops Ter
Chownings Glen
Cramerly Ct
Waters Edge
Meriwether Ct
Kenneport Ct
Stonegate Ct
Foxhollow Ct
Roxbury Ct
Teaneck Cir
Partridge Dr
Morning Dove Rd
Nightingale Rd
Flamingo St
Wren St
Mariposa St
Bellconey St
Grouse St
Shewbird
Wixom Rd
Potter Rd
Taft Rd
Maple Rd
Maple Rd
Wienona
Wienona Ct
Aztec
Appache Trl
Co. Railroad
Theodore St
Manistee St
Renton St
Chambers St
Pontiac Trl
Wainstock St
Tamarack
Tamarack
Wixom Rd
Anthony
West Rd
Wolf
Lois Ln
Downing
Avante Dr
Beck Rd
Napier Rd
Helfer Blvd
Helfer Blvd
Grand River Ave
I-96
12 Mile Rd
N

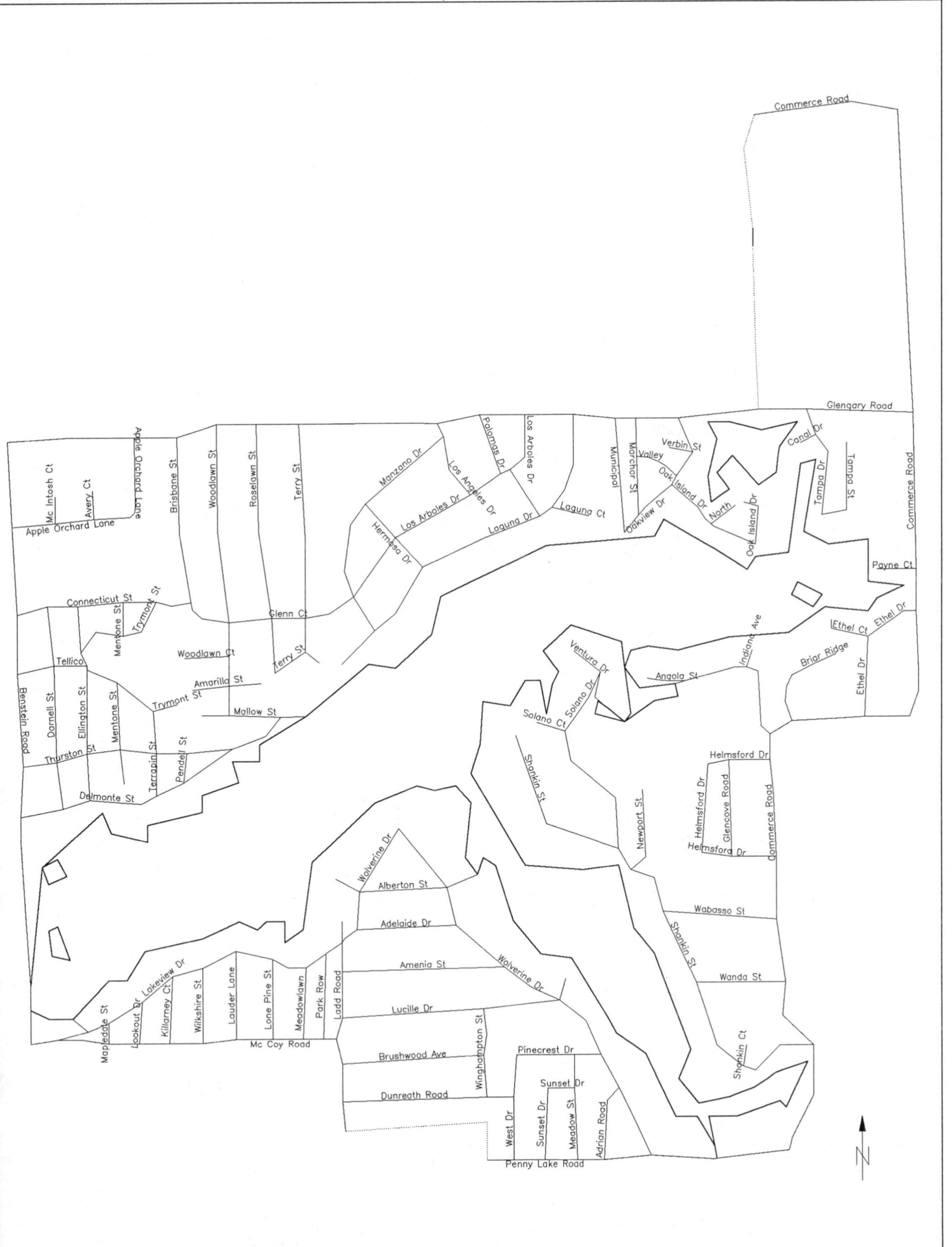
Commerce Road
Glengary Road
Apple Orchard Lane
Mc Intosh Ct
Avery Ct
Brisbane St
Woodlawn St
Roselawn St
Terry St
Manzano Dr
Palomas Dr
Los Arboles Dr
Los Angeles Dr
Hermosa Dr
Laguna Dr
Laguna Ct
Municipal
Marchar St
Valley
Verbin St
Oak Island Dr
Oakview Dr
North
Canal Dr
Tampa Dr
Tampa St
Payne Ct
Connecticut St
Mentone St
Trymont St
Glenn Ct
Woodlawn Ct
Terry St
Tellico
Amarillo St
Mallow St
Benstein Road
Darnell St
Ellington St
Thurston St
Terrapin St
Pendell St
Delmonte St
Ventura Dr
Solano Dr
Solano Ct
Angola St
Indiana Ave
Ethel Ct
Ethel Dr
Briar Ridge
Shankin St
Newport St
Helmsford Dr
Glencove Road
Wolverine Dr
Alberton St
Adelaide Dr
Wabasso St
Amenia St
Wanda St
Lakeview Dr
Mapledale St
Lookout Dr
Killarney Ct
Wilkshire St
Lauder Lane
Lone Pine St
Meadowlawn
Park Row
Ladd Road
Mc Coy Road
Lucille Dr
Winghampton St
Brushwood Ave
Pinecrest Dr
Sunset Dr
Shankin Ct
Dunreath Road
West Dr
Meadow St
Adrian Road
Penny Lake Road
N

King Road
Toledo Road
Colette Dr
Camille Dr
Colette Ct
Camille Ct
Judith Road
Larch Dr
Birch Dr
Lilac Dr
Tulipwood Ave
Bellwood Dr
Nottingham Ct
Quail Hollow Dr
Crosswick Ct
Chipmunk Trl
Carter Road
Willow Ct
Hillcrest Ct
Orchard
Canterbury Dr
Loretta Dr
Hillcrest Dr
Reinhardt Dr
Oak St
Nelson Dr
Brunswick Dr
Cranbrook Dr
Foxcroft Road
Devonshire Dr
Canterbury Dr
Southpoint
Huntington Ct
Old Mill Ct
Foxcroft Road
Williamsburg
Dt and I Railroad
Clee Drain
Camden Road
Wellington Dr
Millbury Dr
Tiffany Dr
Woodland Dr
Sherwood Lane
Danbury Dr
Mayfair Road
Pine Cone Dr
Gatehouse
Pinehurst Ct
Sunningdale Ct
Woodview
Gatehouse Dr
Mayfair Road
Truwood Road
Trufant Ct
Brimley Ct
Tiffany Ct
Carter Ave
Monterey Ave
West Road
Williamsburg Ct
Longmeadow Dr
Fairway Dr
Heritage Sq
Heritage Sq
Mel Plz
Westwood St
Woodstock Ct
Old Forge Ct
Kingston Ct
Chestnut Lane
Kings Ct
Beechwood Ct
Grix Road
I-75
Allen Road
Brownstown Creek
Provincial Road
Ryegate Road
Colonial Dr
Independence St
Hanover Ct
Colonial Dr
Cabot Ct
Heritage Dr
Crescent Road
Cambridge Dr
Hamilton Ct
Hampton Ct
Cabot Dr
Chapel Dr
Iron Gate Dr
Clee Drain
Derby Road
Village Dr
Village Ct
Cabot Dr
Colonial Ct
Windsor Ct
Sussex Ct
Van Horn Road
Van Horn Road
Oxford
Oxford
Saxony
Middlesex
Carmel
Balfour
Oxford
Peters Road
Orleans Dr
Castlewood Dr
Albert St
Castlewood Dr
Reeck Road
Arlington Dr
Salem Dr
Bradford Dr
Montebello Ct
Forrest Hill Dr
Alice St
Lancaster Dr
Hyde Park Dr
Hyde Park Dr
Brownstown Creek
Martin Pl
Marsh Creek
Blakley Dr
Dover Dr
Angela Ct
Reeck Road
Laurie Ct
Bodsford Dr
Bodsford Dr
Willow Cove
Maywood Ave
Sandra Ct
Mayfair Ave
Reaume St
Cass Drain

N

North Dr
Emmons Blvd
Kings Hwy
Highland Ave
Riverbank Ave
Clinton St
Bondie St
St Johns St
Perry Pl
Hazel Ave
Goddard Rd
Baumey Ave
Antoine St
Hudson St
Clark St
Alkali Ave
Davis St
Ford Ave
Spruce St
Cedar St
Oxford Ct
Glenn Ct
Mulberry St
Molling Ave
Walnut St
Poplar St
Vinewood Ave
Superior Blvd
Ash St
Chestnut St
Oak St
Elm St
Maple St
Dee St
Sycamore St
Eureka Ave
Orange St
Pine St
Adelaide Ave
Lee Ave
Cherry St
Plum St
Arch St
Orchard St
Forest St
Grove St
Hillsdale Ave
Albion Ave
Marshall Ave
Ludington Ave
St Ignace St
St Ignace Ave
Pennsylvania Rd
Quarry Rd
Fort St
Central Ave
Pc Railroad
Dt and I Railroad
Electric Ave
Cora Ave
Lincoln Ave
Lindbergh Ave
Garfield Ave
Alfred St
James St
Parklane St
Edcliff Ct
Emmons Ct
Bennett St
Labadie St
Clifford St
Stoll Ave
Felice St
Miller St
Sullivan St
Mc Kinley Ave
Biddle Ave
Regent Dr
Virginia Ave
Van Alstyne Blvd
Wye St
Trenton Channel
Ecorse River
Grassy Island
1st St
2nd St
3rd St
4th St
5th St
6th St
7th St
8th St
9th St
10th St
11th St
12th St
13th St
14th St
15th St
16th St
17th St
18th St
19th St
20th St
21st St
22nd St
23rd St
N

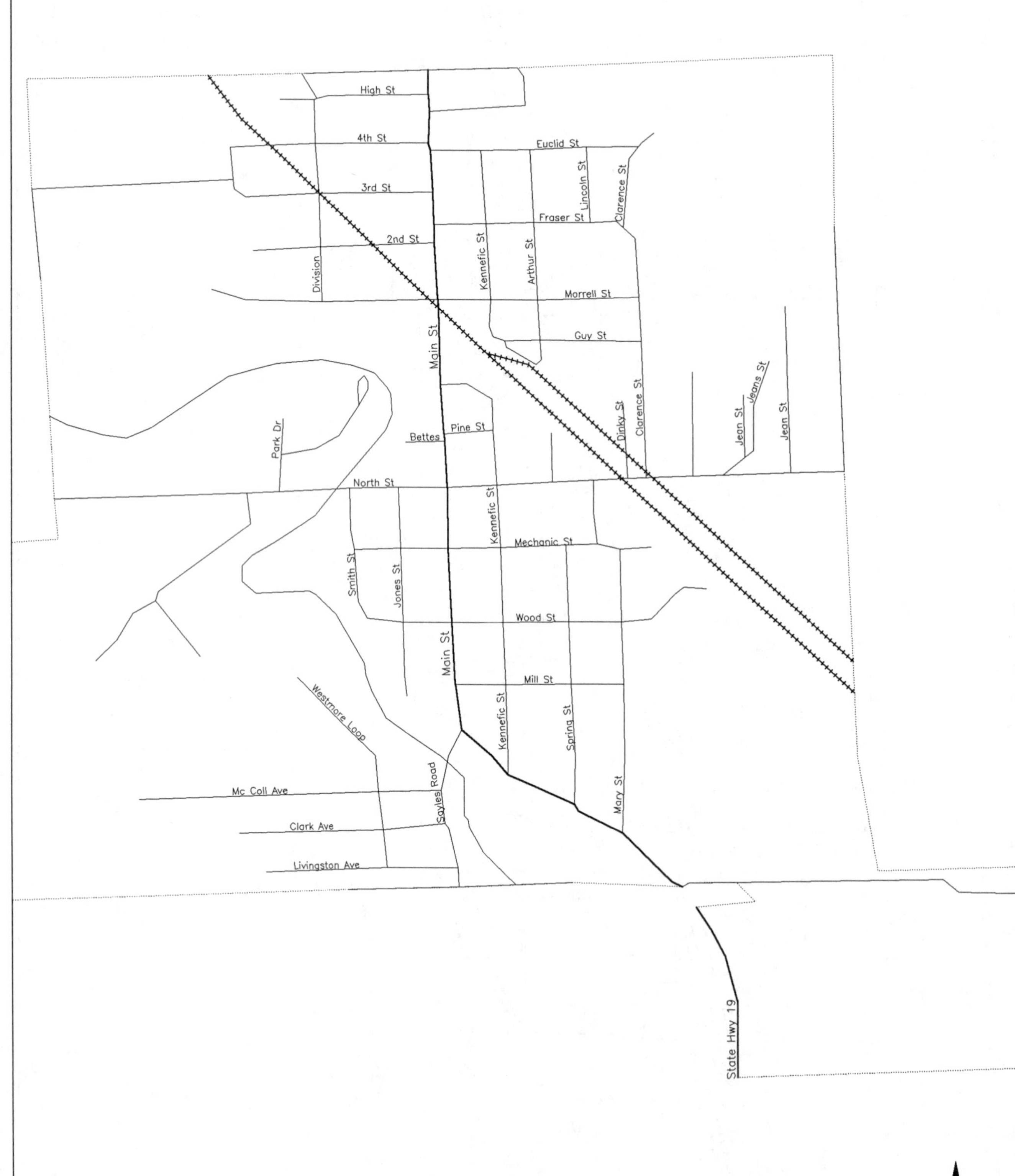
High St
4th St
Euclid St
3rd St
Lincoln St
Clarence St
Fraser St
2nd St
Kennefic St
Arthur St
Division
Morrell St
Main St
Guy St
Jeans St
Jean St
Jean St
Dinky St
Clarence St
Park Dr
Bettes
Pine St
North St
Kennefic St
Mechanic St
Smith St
Jones St
Wood St
Main St
Mill St
Westmore Loop
Kennefic St
Spring St
Sayles Road
Mary St
Mc Coll Ave
Clark Ave
Livingston Ave
State Hwy 19
N

Hewitt Rd
Huron River Dr
Access
Bellevue Ave
University Ct
Washtenaw Ave
Whittier Rd
Wilmire Ave
Courtland St
Marion St
Douglas St
Roosevelt St
Mark St
Louise St
Superior Rd
Gregory Ave
Ainsley Ave
Lansing St
Lyman St
Mansfield St
Owendale St
Westmoreland Rd
Sherman Ave
Kingwood Ave
Collegewood Dr
Cornell Rd
Anna Ave
Cambridge Rd
Oxford Rd
Congress St
Wallace Blvd
Pearl Ave
Grant Ave
Cross Ave
Fairview Cir
Oakwood Ave
Oakwood St
Pine Grove
Pray St
Boardman St
Huron River
Clark Rd
Green Rd
Leer Ct
Arbor Dr
Timberlane St
Crossland St
Hart Pl
Small Pl
2nd Ave
Michigan Ave
Woods Ave
Pleasant Dr
Elm St
Sheridan Ave
Forest Ave
Walton St
Smith St
Pittman
Linden Pl
1st Ave
1st Ct
Armstrong Dr
Short St
Frederick Ave
Orchard St
Summit St
Watling Blvd
Jefferson Ave
Madison Blvd
Brooks St
Monroe Ave
Armstrong Ct
Harriet Ave
Worden St
Hawkins St
Hill St
Normal St
Burton Ct
Ann St Loop
Ford Ave
Newton St
Mayhew
Green Rd
Le Forge Rd
Ainsworth St
Ainsworth Blvd
College St
Bowman
Perrin St
Blount
Hawkins St
Perry St
Ainsworth Cir
Middle Dr
Ferris St
Congress Ave
Washtenaw Ave
Goodman St
Driscoll Ct
Florence St
Lowell St
Jenness St
St Johns
Hamilton St
Buffalo Ave
Woodward Ave
Pearson St
Olive St
Adams St
Arcade Ave
Huron St
Emmet St
Washington St
Kramer
Bell St
Cosler St
Chidister St
River St
Catherine St
Ninde St
Photo St
Furnace St
Norris St
Clark Rd
River St
Huron River
Lincoln St
Ferris
North St
Cherry Ct
Dwight St
Hemphill St
Maple Ct
Maple Ave
Oak St
Gordon Ave
Stanley St
I-94
Factory Ave
Stewart Ave
Farmer St
Parsons
Smith Ave
Grove St
Babbitt St
High Ave
Prospect Ct
Locust St
Prospect Rd
Carver Ave
Holmes Rd
Prospect St
Martin Pl
Miles St
Cross Ave
Vought St
Thomas Ave
Tyler Rd
Mouse Ave
Davis Ave
Arnet St
Mildred St
Ford St
Center St
Vinewood
Charles St
Helen St
Virginia Pl
Forest Ave
Youngs St
Garland Ave
Osband St
Grove Rd
I-94
N

Paw Paw Dr
Huizenga Ave
Alice St
William St
Sycamore Ln
Washington Ave
Lee St
Lawrence Ave
Winterhalder Dr
100th Ave
Franklin St
Gordon
Westenbroek
Hillview Dr
Lindy St
Jefferson St
Parkside Dr
Valley Ave
Taft St
Alpine Ave
Woodward St
Colonial St
Michigan St
Zeeland Pkwy
State Hwy 21
Central Ave
Cherry Ave
Main Ave
Ottawa St
Perry St
Royal Ct
Garfield Ave
Madison Ave
Oak Ave
State St
Mc Kinley Ave
Madison Ct
Roosevelt Ave
Elm St
Cherry St
Riley Ave
Church St
Centennial St
Peck St
Lincoln Ave
Rich Ave
Maple St
Wall St
Carlton St
Park St
Division St
Sanford St
Woodlawn St
Goodrich
Fairview Rd
Plainfield Ct
Riley St
84th Ave

I-75
Wacker Rd
Commonwealth Ave
Edison Rd
Westervelt Rd
Doro Ln
Lindberg St
Waukee Ln
Stout St
Venoy Rd
Dana Dr
Jones St
Oscoda St
Purdue St
Shepard St
Knox St
Tittabawasee Rd
Tittabawasee Rd
Johnson St
Sherman Rd
Cornell St
Moran St
Adams Ave
Fisher St
Fisher St
Franklin Ave
Jefferson Ave
Westervelt Ave
Bush St
Capitol St
Bradington Rd
Bittersweet Ln
Schust St
Schust St
Adams Ave
Wellington St
Wellington St
Ash St
N

Automobile Mileage Between Michigan Cities

TO \ FROM	Alpena	Ann Arbor	Bay City	Cadillac	Charlevoix	Clare	Detroit	Flint	Grand Rapids	Lansing	Ludington	Mackinaw City	Marquette	Muskegon	Sault Ste. Marie	Traverse City
Adrian	264	40	136	199	279	153	68	95	133	73	227	297	463	172	354	244
Albion	251	53	123	165	245	121	91	90	86	40	171	264	431	123	322	209
Alma	89	110	52	80	159	33	132	73	80	49	123	177	344	95	235	124
Alpena	—	225	129	150	114	151	233	173	247	211	220	94	261	257	152	137
Ann Arbor	225	—	96	188	257	142	38	54	127	63	220	272	439	166	330	233
Bad Axe	188	140	59	155	223	109	108	86	181	134	199	238	405	196	296	200
Battle Creek	260	76	132	146	226	130	114	99	61	49	153	266	433	98	324	191
Bay City	129	96	—	96	164	50	104	44	128	82	140	179	346	143	237	141
Benton Harbor	327	145	202	178	262	181	183	170	83	120	145	302	469	90	360	220
Big Rapids	190	169	89	40	124	51	189	130	57	107	64	164	331	67	222	85
Brighton	207	18	78	170	240	124	40	36	109	45	203	254	421	148	312	215
Cadillac	150	188	96	—	84	46	197	137	97	127	73	124	291	107	182	49
Charlevoix	114	257	164	84	—	126	267	207	180	206	142	52	219	184	110	50
Cheboygan	79	262	169	126	59	135	272	212	223	216	197	16	183	233	74	109
Clare	151	142	50	46	126	—	151	91	99	80	90	143	310	114	201	91
Coldwater	279	81	151	181	261	149	109	119	99	69	190	292	459	135	350	226
Copper Harbor	408	585	492	437	365	457	595	535	534	537	507	313	147	544	311	415
Crystal Falls	324	502	409	353	282	373	511	451	450	453	424	230	72	460	237	332
Detour	156	334	241	186	114	205	343	284	282	286	256	62	207	293	59	164
Detroit	233	38	104	197	267	151	—	60	149	85	241	281	448	188	339	242
Escanaba	242	420	327	272	200	291	429	369	368	372	342	148	65	378	175	250
Flint	173	54	44	137	207	91	60	—	104	50	184	222	388	144	279	182
Frankfort	175	238	147	55	88	97	248	188	142	177	64	140	307	118	198	38
Gaylord	72	216	123	79	42	87	225	166	175	168	149	57	224	185	115	65
Grand Haven	266	158	152	116	194	123	180	136	32	96	67	240	407	13	298	144
Grand Rapids	247	127	128	97	180	99	149	104	—	65	95	221	387	40	278	139
Grayling	93	190	96	60	69	61	199	139	156	141	131	84	250	167	141	52
Hillsdale	278	69	149	194	274	150	96	117	116	70	207	294	460	152	352	239
Holland	274	140	155	124	207	126	172	132	29	88	90	247	414	35	305	165
Houghton	361	538	445	390	318	410	548	488	487	490	460	266	100	497	264	368
Imlay City	203	87	73	170	238	124	51	34	139	84	213	252	419	178	310	214
Ionia	226	100	99	97	177	80	122	71	33	38	127	217	384	72	275	141
Iron Mountain	294	472	378	323	252	343	481	421	420	423	394	200	79	430	227	302
Iron River	340	518	424	369	298	389	527	467	466	469	440	246	88	476	253	348
Ironwood	406	583	490	435	363	455	593	533	532	535	505	311	145	542	309	413
Ishpeming	273	451	358	302	231	322	460	400	399	402	378	179	12	409	177	281

Automobile Mileage Between Michigan Cities

TO \ FROM	Alpena	Ann Arbor	Bay City	Cadillac	Charlevoix	Clare	Detroit	Flint	Grand Rapids	Lansing	Ludington	Mackinaw City	Marquette	Muskegon	Sault Ste. Marie	Traverse City
Jackson	241	35	113	164	244	118	73	80	98	38	192	261	428	137	319	209
Kalamazoo	283	98	155	147	230	148	136	123	50	73	138	270	437	84	328	188
L'Anse	328	506	413	357	286	377	515	455	454	457	428	234	67	464	232	336
Lansing	211	63	82	127	206	80	85	50	65	—	158	224	391	104	282	171
Lapeer	189	75	60	156	224	110	56	21	126	71	200	239	406	165	297	201
Ludington	220	220	140	73	142	90	241	181	95	158	—	194	361	58	252	92
Mackinaw City	94	272	179	124	52	143	281	222	221	224	194	—	167	231	58	102
Manistee	196	232	141	49	112	91	242	182	119	171	31	164	331	85	222	62
Manistique	188	366	273	218	146	238	375	316	315	318	288	94	87	325	121	196
Marquette	261	439	346	291	219	310	448	388	387	391	361	167	—	397	165	269
Marshall	256	65	127	157	237	125	102	95	75	45	166	269	436	112	327	202
Menominee	296	474	381	326	254	345	483	424	423	426	396	202	120	433	229	304
Midland	145	110	19	79	159	33	120	60	111	86	122	174	341	126	232	124
Monroe	260	39	131	224	294	178	37	87	161	101	255	308	475	200	366	269
Mt. Clemens	234	57	104	197	267	151	21	60	158	94	241	282	448	197	339	242
Mt. Pleasant	167	127	46	62	142	16	147	87	84	65	106	159	326	99	217	107
Munising	218	396	303	248	176	267	405	345	344	348	318	124	43	354	122	226
Muskegon	257	166	143	107	84	114	188	144	40	104	58	231	397	—	289	134
Newberry	169	346	253	198	127	218	356	296	295	298	268	74	105	305	67	177
New Buffalo	354	171	231	204	287	207	206	198	109	148	170	328	494	116	387	247
Niles	338	144	210	194	277	196	181	178	98	128	160	317	484	106	377	237
Northport	164	260	168	76	77	118	269	210	166	199	120	130	295	162	187	27
Ontonagon	375	553	460	405	333	424	562	503	501	505	475	281	115	512	279	383
Owosso	180	69	53	127	207	81	83	25	79	31	170	224	391	119	282	172
Petoskey	101	251	158	88	16	122	260	200	185	202	158	36	203	195	94	67
Pontiac	209	48	79	173	242	126	25	35	133	69	216	257	423	172	315	217
Port Austin	196	157	67	163	231	117	124	103	195	149	207	246	413	210	304	208
Port Huron	237	96	108	204	272	158	59	69	174	119	248	287	454	213	345	249
Port Sanilac	204	127	75	172	239	125	90	85	186	134	215	254	421	200	312	216
Roscommon	91	177	83	59	84	60	186	126	156	141	132	98	265	166	156	67
Saginaw	141	86	13	102	173	55	96	36	116	70	145	188	355	131	246	146
St. Ignace	101	279	186	131	59	150	288	228	227	231	201	7	162	237	52	109
Sault Ste. Marie	152	330	237	182	110	201	339	279	278	282	252	58	165	289	—	160
Sturgis	302	107	174	189	269	172	134	141	93	91	181	309	476	126	367	231
Tawas City	64	161	65	105	147	89	169	109	189	146	178	159	325	204	216	131
Traverse City	137	233	141	49	50	91	242	182	139	171	92	102	269	134	160	—

To Order Additional City Map Books:

(Please photocopy orderblank and send in with payment)

Please Mail Check To:

CitMap
8951 Trezwood Tr.
Traverse City, Michigan 49684

Shipping Information

Name____
Address____
City__________________________ State________ Zip__________

Other states interested in______________________________
____
____

1 book at the regular rate of $19.95 ea.

Quantity	**Discount**	**Price**	
2 books	10%off	$17.95 ea.	($35.90)
3 books	20%off	$15.95 ea.	($47.85)
5 books	25%off	$14.95 ea.	($74.75)
10 books	30%off	$13.95 ea.	($139.50)

Please add: $3.50 postage and handling. $.50 for postage and handling for each additional book.

TOTAL # BOOKS__________ **AMOUNT $__________**
Payment Enclosed $__________

Toll Free Telephone service:
1-800-507-2665
Visa and MasterCard Accepted